CRIMINOLOGY
A Global Perspective

ROBERT W. WINSLOW, PH.D.
San Diego State University

SHELDON X. ZHANG, PH.D.
San Diego State University

Upper Saddle River, New Jersey 07458

Library of Congress Cataloging-in-Publication Data

Winslow, Robert Wallace
　Criminology : a global perspective / Robert W. Winslow, Sheldon Zhang.
　　　p. cm.
　Includes bibliographical references and index.
　ISBN 0–13–183902–0
1. Criminology—Cross-cultural studies.　I. Zhang, Sheldon.　II. Title.
HV6025.W55 2007
　364—dc22

2006035526

Editor-in-Chief: Vernon R. Anthony
Senior Acquisitions Editor: Tim Peyton
Associate Editor: Sarah Holle
Editorial Assistant: Jillian Allison
Marketing Manager: Adam Kloza
Production Editor: Bruce Hobart, Pine Tree Composition
Production Liaison: Barbara Marttine Cappuccio
Managing Editor: Mary Carnis
Manufacturing Manager: Ilene Sanford
Manufacturing Buyer: Cathleen Petersen
Senior Design Coordinator: Christopher Weigand
Cover Design: Jill Little
Cover Image: Getty Images (Royalty Free)
Composition: Laserwords Pvt. Ltd.
Printer/Binding: Hamilton Printing

Pearson Education LTD.
Pearson Education Australia PTY, Limited
Pearson Education Singapore, Pte. Ltd.
Pearson Education North Asia Ltd.
Pearson Education Canada, Ltd.
Pearson Educación de Mexico, S.A. de C.V.
Pearson Education—Japan
Pearson Education Malaysia, Pte. Ltd.
Pearson Education, Upper Saddle River, New Jersey

PEARSON
Prentice
Hall

10 9 8 7 6 5 4 3 2 1
ISBN 0-13-183902-0

DEDICATION

To my mother, Josephine; my daughters, Cindy and Cheryl, and their husbands, Andreas and Mike . . . world travelers all. And to Julia and Caroline, who regularly make the commute from America to Sweden. With this family, how could I *not* take a global approach?

R.W.W.

To my parents, who allowed me to travel afar and pursue my own dreams.

S.X.Z.

BRIEF CONTENTS

CONTENTS

3 Historical Theories of Crime   75

4 Sociological Theories of Crime   102

8 Robbery   263

9 Assault   299

10 Sneak Thieves: Burglary, Larceny, and Motor Vehicle Theft   353

15 Terrorism 615

PREFACE

Because of recent changes in communication, transportation, and commerce, crime has become a global phenomenon. Given that assumption, criminology itself must become global in its scope. This means that *comparative criminology*, the international study of crime, should no longer be treated as a separate subject. Instead, criminology at all levels should be comparative in nature. Based upon this assumption, we have designed a text for introductory criminology that is inherently comparative.

To create such a text, it was our goal to compile crime and criminal justice information about all of the countries of the world. We found such information scattered in textbooks, anthologies, journal articles, government reports, and in reports by nongovernment organizations. We have gathered this information and placed it on a Website that is referred to as the Comparative Criminology Website (CCW). This Website can be viewed at the following URL:
http://www.rohan.sdsu.edu/faculty/rwinslow/index.html

The Website contains qualitative and quantitative information on 200 countries, including international and domestic databases from the Federal Bureau of Investigation (FBI), the National Crime Victimization Survey (NCVS), INTERPOL, and the United Nations. The CCW is a compilation drawn from government publications that are public domain. The Website is not copyrighted, and will not be, because the purpose of it is to create a research tool that can be drawn upon freely to facilitate the development of research papers, texts, and other media. Permissions are not required for materials quoted from the CCW. We welcome the submission of research papers, which we will publish on the Website if desired.

Many of the country comparisons we make in *Criminology: A Global Perspective* are drawn from this Website. Others are drawn from textbooks, journal articles, anthologies, and news stories. Some comparisons appear in text boxes accompanying topics that are covered in the text. In addition, country profiles on countries high or low in a given crime and international data analyses are done in chapters pertaining to particular crimes. These are drawn from the CCW and data sets contained within the CCW. We term these data sets collectively the Comparative Criminology Database.

Thus, our goal has been to develop an introductory criminology text that is not only thorough in its coverage of the usual topics, but, in addition, includes international comparisons throughout the text. By "usual topics," we refer to definitions, extent and trend statistics, typologies, etiological studies, theories, and policy recommendations.

In addition to the international comparisons, what is noteworthy about this text is our approach to theory. We provide three introductory chapters (Chapters 3–5). These chapters are comparative and historical in showing how various theories of crime developed. We include a discussion of the social context or "climate of the times" in which a given theory was developed. For instance, Lombroso's "born criminal" theory was developed during a time when Social Darwinism was popular. In the early 20th century, the Chicago School of Criminology was a product of the Progressive Movement that flourished during the Great Depression. We also provide biographical information on the major theorists. The biographies are interesting and helpful in understanding the personal and social circumstances that helped shaped the theorists' perspectives.

Our theoretical analysis, however, does not end with these three chapters. Instead, we continue with the theoretical analysis in each of the subsequent chapters dealing with particular crimes. In many cases, theories have been developed to explain a particular type of crime, such as the "subculture of violence theory" for criminal homicide. In many ways, most of the chapters in this book are devoted to criminological theory. However, once students are exposed to general criminological theories in Chapters 3–5, the remainder of the text is devoted to applying theories to various crimes or forms of crime. We have found that applying theories as explanations for crimes or sets of crime is what makes the theories interesting to students. We have also found that when searching for theories to explain individual crimes, we have located theories that are not included in many criminological texts. For example, we found a theory that seems to provide an empirically valid explanation of "stealthy theft" crime, such as burglary, larceny, and motor vehicle theft. That theory is called the "Easterlin Hypothesis," named for an economist, Richard Easterlin, who linked economic crime with the "baby boom" and its "aftershocks." We found Easterlin's theory to be very useful in explaining the property crimes of young people in "affluent societies" when viewed internationally.

The introductory theory chapters are followed by five chapters on the FBI's "seven major crimes," the Index crimes of the FBI's Uniform Crime Reports. These crimes were selected for analysis for two reasons. The first is that all seven of these crimes are judged to be "serious crimes" or "real crimes," not only by the police, but also in public opinion surveys. The second reason is that data are available for all seven of these crimes in international databases published by the United Nations and INTERPOL. In these "crime chapters," the various theories are "tested," using international crime data and through an examination of qualitative information on the countries that exhibit high rates of the crime. Through this process, we have been challenged by anomalous findings to seek out explanatory theories not usually covered in criminology textbooks. In addition to Easterlin's hypothesis, Thio's "power-control theory" is also introduced as a useful explanation for "simple assault." This theory seems to fit the country profiles of several countries that registered high rates of assault.

The following is a brief overview and synopsis of the chapters that shows, where applicable, how the comparative method is used to enhance the subject matter of each chapter.

Chapter 1 (Criminology in a Fast-Changing World) contains an analysis of how crime is defined in the United States. Some historical analysis is done to show how a "common law legal system" developed in the United States. The major legal systems of the world (common law, civil law, indigenous/customary, Islamic, and socialist) are identified and described. The impact of America's common law system upon the definition of crime is explained. We discuss how America's history and its legal system led to the emphasis upon the seriousness of certain crimes, such as drug offenses and crimes against morality. The United States is compared with countries that have "civil law" legal systems. Civil law countries, such as France, Italy, and Spain, tend to be more responsive to "white-collar crimes" than the United States, and they tend to downplay drug and sex offenses. The emphasis upon contemporary white-collar crimes in these countries is related to the fact that civil law legal systems adapt more quickly to conditions of the modern world because they are based upon codified law rather than legal precedent. A brief introduction to the comparative approach used in this text is also given in this chapter.

Chapter 2 (Extent and Trends in Crime) begins with a discussion of the scientific method. This section contains a primer on how surveys are conducted and the meaning of correlation coefficients (which are used throughout the text). The chapter provides estimates of the extent and trends in crime in the United States, comparing FBI and NCVS data. Also included are incidence and trend data from self-report surveys of high school seniors conducted nationally, since 1975, by the Michigan Institute for Social Research. These national data are compared with incidence and trend data compiled by the United Nations, INTERPOL, and the United Nations victim survey, the International Crime Victim Surveys. Definitions of crime from these sources and criticisms of each of these sources are given in the chapter.

Chapter 3 (Historical Theories of Crime) covers theories of crime that predate sociological theories. Discussion includes the Classical School and Utilitarianism in France, Italy, and England. Next, attention is turned to the rise of positivism in the form of the "born criminal theory" of biological determinism. Special emphasis is given to religious beliefs about crime—including Christian, Islamic, and Buddhist beliefs. The rise of fundamentalism worldwide has brought these beliefs into the public consciousness. Christian and Islamic beliefs are being used today as a basis for explanations of crime and/or its prevention.

Chapter 4 (Sociological Theories of Crime) focuses upon the theories of crime that dominated criminology during most of the 20th century. A product of Progressivism, the sociological approach was pioneered by Robert Park and his followers at the University of Chicago. Although the Chicago School focused upon local community organization, direction was shifted to the macrosociological (societal) emphasis in the writings of Robert K. Merton and his associates, whose opportunity theory was well received by the Kennedy/Johnson administrations during the 1960s. During the 1970s and 1980s, when politics shifted away from "big government" and "entitlement" programs during the Nixon and Reagan administrations, the labeling theory of Howard S. Becker called for "diversion" of criminals and the mentally ill from government programs. As the 20th century ended, it became evident that the diversion approach had "widened the net." While more and more people were being sentenced to "do time in community-based organizations," the prison population also grew exponentially. This led to an attack by sociologists of the "conflict school" upon the criminal justice system itself as a source of crime. This school, also called "critical criminology," was prominent during the 1990s, at a time when nonsociological approaches started to emerge in criminological literature.

Chapter 5 (Contemporary Theories of Crime) calls attention to alternative approaches to sociological theories of crime that have emerged to challenge sociological theories. These theories developed a following based upon a variety of reasons—the public fear of crime, the development of the "nothing works" doctrine, and a trend toward conservatism. Many of these new theories are actually revisions of historical theories, such as the Classical School and biological theories. Another new approach is "self-control theory," which stems from the Chicago School. This chapter also covers sociological theories that have withstood the test of time. An example is Akers' "social learning theory," an expanded version of Sutherland's differential association theory. Social learning theory continues to be respected because of its relationship to the therapeutic community programs that have been successful in treating drug addiction. The chapter contains a description of attempts to reformulate sociological theories to overcome flaws thought to have characterized earlier efforts. "New and improved" sociological theories include the "restorative justice approach," which arises from the "labeling theory" of the 20th century. In addition, "peacemaking criminology" is a surviving nonviolent version of "conflict theory."

We propose another approach to theory that entails the use of the comparative method. Briefly, the comparative method leads to the discovery of different theories for different crimes. Thus, deterrence theory might be appropriate for crimes (such as auto theft and larceny) that are leniently treated by the criminal justice system. Conflict theory seems to provide a viable explanation for criminal homicide when this crime is viewed cross-nationally. The comparative method is not new. The comparative method, in fact, was used by the pioneers of criminology—Quetelet, Tarde, Verkko, and Durkheim—soon after national police statistics were developed in Europe, beginning with the French *Compte general* in 1827. These pioneers maximized what data existed in Europe at the time in developing theories that were cross-nationally valid. One can hardly imagine how they would feel if they were able to awaken today and see what fantastic statistical and electronic resources are available—international crime databases for most countries of the world published by INTERPOL and the United Nations—and the Internet, where everything published everywhere is or will soon be available at the click of a hand-operated-device (mouse).

Chapter 6 (Criminal Homicide) begins the sequence of chapters examining individual crimes. Each chapter begins with a case study (i.e., biographies of various criminals). Many of these were derived from actual interviews done in the classroom. Following the case study, each chapter contains a discussion of definitions, extent and trends, typologies, etiological factors, and theories pertaining to the subject. In Chapter 6, it is found that income inequality seems to be a key factor in murder, as manifested in the black/white income gap within the United States. The racial difference in murder in the United States may simply be a manifestation of income inequality.

Chapter 7 (Forcible Rape) provides a discussion of how rape is defined in the United States and why some countries (e.g., Canada and Australia) don't report data on this crime, but instead prefer the term "sexual assault." In this chapter, "deterrence theory" seems to emerge as a relevant approach. The deterrence of Islamic law, and the enforcement of American laws pertaining to domestic violence, both seem to have produced lower rates of rape during the 1990s.

Chapter 8 (Robbery) emphasizes the changing nature of robbery, from a crime that was once done by professional criminals, to a crime today typically committed by drug addicts with little in the way of criminal skills. Robbery today is a crime shown to be linked with the drug trade (especially heroin), as well as with the black/white income gap.

Chapter 9 (Assault) describes assault as the "common cold" of crime. It is noted that there is no extant "theory of assault," apart from homicide theories. Because assault is far more prevalent than homicide, it is argued that a separate theory of assault is needed. In the absence of theories of assault, this chapter draws even more extensively upon country profiles to isolate variables that might lead to a rudimentary "theory of assault." Based upon this analysis, the "power-control theory," suggested by Thio, seems to provide a promising approach to the crime of assault.

Chapter 10 (Sneak Thieves: Burglary, Larceny, and Motor Vehicle theft) identifies "stealthy theft"—burglary, larceny, and vehicle theft—as a crime that is different in many ways from robbery. Robbery is often a desperate act of violence and confrontation, whereas stealthy theft is done secretly, quietly, and (often) successfully. Cross-nationally, the acts of stealthy theft are the opposite of robbery in that they correlate negatively with inequality. They are most prevalent in the most equalitarian countries. In common with robbery, however, stealthy theft seems to correlate well with alcohol consumption. It is done most in wealthy countries and is inversely related to poverty and unemployment. Australia is shown by various indices to be high in its rate of burglary. In Australia, burglary seems to be associated with participation in a "surfer subculture" of youth who have adapted to unemployment with a "life-as-party" orientation in which burglary is a major source of financial support. Larceny as a crime in which females and young people contribute a larger share of the perpetrators than is the case with other Index crimes. Sweden has the highest larceny rate in the world, a fact thought to be accounted for by the role of youth and immigrants. Sweden is an egalitarian "welfare state" where there is very little difference in salary between occupational groups. Analysis indicates that two groups, youth and immigrants, share similar financial stress, as well as the highest rates of unemployment in Sweden. In an egalitarian nation like Sweden, the young and immigrants who are unemployed are the *lumpenproletariat* (lowest class) of society. Their high aspirations (travel, home ownership, family) can be attained either through the slow process of assimilation or aging or, as an alternative, through crime. Motor vehicle theft is a crime of youth, and it is a crime done almost exclusively by male offenders. In terms of volume, motor vehicle theft comes close to being primarily an act of "juvenile delinquents." Great Britain is profiled as a country that, by a variety of measures, seems to be a "hot spot" for auto theft. One factor in the British profile is that the crime seems to be "trivialized" in the criminal justice system. Sanctions for auto theft typically include a "caution" by the police or a "summary judgment" (fine) by the magistrate's court. Thus, there is little or no deterrence of motor vehicle theft through law in Britain. At the same time, there are plenty of "motivated offenders" in that country—not just young British citizens, but migrants coming from other parts of Europe as result of its "open borders" policy as a member of the European Union. In addition, there are growing numbers of migrants from the Commonwealth countries who enjoy free trade and freedom of movement within the Commonwealth. Many of these Commonwealth countries are former British Empire colonies that are now sovereign developing nations with high crime rates.

Chapter 11 (Organized Crime) seems a likely sequel to the previous chapter on motor vehicle theft. In England, auto theft has become a form of transnational organized crime (OC). Auto thieves may "barter trade" their vehicles for drugs or other contraband in other European countries. They may then return to England with undocumented aliens, drugs, or other contraband. In this chapter, trafficking in heroin is proposed as an imperfect "marker" for organized crime, imperfect because OC is actually a cluster of crimes. We cannot perform comparative statistical analysis on OC, because the FBI keeps no offense reports on such crimes. Countries that seem to have a large number of OC groups typically also have a history of military rule. Several countries, including the United States, are profiled in terms of this observation, and OC groups that are prevalent in the United States are discussed in terms of their country of origin.

Chapter 12 (The Drug Trade) covers the social definition of drugs that are defined as "dangerous" in the United States. The War on Drugs is traced to the earlier Prohibition movement, as well as to intergroup conflict with various ethnic groups—black, Asian, and Latino. Trafficking in drugs as a form of OC has a strong link with past wars, when soldiers made connections with international drug markets. Based upon its ranking (in Chapter 11) of Kg of heroin seized, Pakistan is second only to China (profiled in Chapter 11). "History of military rule" clearly characterized Pakistan both before and after independence from Great Britain, due to partitioning more or less imposed by the British Parliament. Pakistan has been accused of harboring a major Indian OC boss, Dawood Ibraham, who has also been accused of subsidizing acts of terrorism and terrorist organizations. A growing number of terrorist cells in that country (highest of any country in the world) are increasingly trafficking in heroin as a means of funding their activities. Pakistan is also number one in the world in its rate of trafficking in heroin.

Chapter 13 (The Sex Trade) includes a discussion of prostitution and pornography Both, when involving consenting adults, are considered "victimless crimes" that are subject to "moral panics" from time to time in America. Cross-nationally, these two offenses are defined as problems in the United States. However, many other countries, including Japan, Denmark, Sweden, and the Netherlands, do not criminalize these offenses. The sex trade has a military connection because soldiers are often clients for prostitutes in foreign countries. They also sometimes marry the prostitutes and require them to engage in prostitution when they return to the United States. The sex trade is also linked to transnational OC, and major corporations are participating in the profits from the pornography industry. The sex trade is difficult to quantify for international study, because neither Interpol nor the United Nations publish statistics on prostitution or pornography. However, trafficking in women may prove to be a good indicator, since it is almost always for purposes of sexual exploitation. With limited data available, Germany was profiled as a country in Europe noted for its recent increase in the sex trade, including trafficking in women, prostitution, and pornography. Factors such as former military rule, the country's affluent economy, the consequences of reunification, and the dissolution of the Soviet Union are discussed as relevant to the growing sex trade in Germany.

Chapter 14 (White-Collar Crime) covers a number of "paper crimes" that are not severely punished in the United States. These include crimes that range from check forgery to electronic crimes, such as "identity theft," to "big business crime," such as false advertising, fraud, and money laundering. The officers of corporations that commit such crimes, when caught, are given fines rather than jail time. Incorporation provides not only protection from liability lawsuits, but it can also shield criminal acts because it is difficult to prove who in a corporation was responsible for corporate misdeeds. Thus, the unprecedented growth of corporations in the United States provides a fertile ground for white-collar crime. White-collar crime can cause not only financial loss to victims, but also disease and even death from toxic dumping and similar crimes against the environment. Corporate crime, such as the Enron scandal, can also cause increasing inequality—the rich get richer and the the poor get poorer.

Chapter 15 (Terrorism) is the concluding chapter. There is evidence that large corporations have engaged in white-collar crimes not only in the United States, but also in foreign countries. The expansion of U.S. corporations to other countries has been, indirectly, supported by the U.S. government. It has been alleged that the CIA has deliberately installed repressive regimes abroad to provide a "business-friendly" climate for American corporations. In some instances, the CIA is alleged to have provided a favorable climate for drug traffickers in conducting its foreign campaigns. When activities such as these occur, white-collar crime becomes a basis for "political crime." Such activities can lead to retaliatory terrorist acts against U.S. citizens abroad, and more recently in the homeland with the terrorist attacks of September 11, 2001, covered in Chapter 15.

It seems clear that much of the terrorism that has taken place over the last 30 years has targeted U.S. business interests abroad. A major finding in this chapter is that terrorists differ from common criminals demographically. Data produced for the chapter show that the usual variables that correlate with common crime (unemployment, poverty, inequality, etc.) do not correlate with the index of terrorism developed for the chapter (the estimated number of terrorist organizations per country). Instead, this index seems to correlate best with adherence to Islamic faith and, even more strongly, with the heroin drug trade (as a possible funding source). Turkey is discussed as an example of this linkage, because Turkey is an active transit country for South Asian heroin, as well as being a country with a legacy of Kurdish terrorism. Discussion in the chapter also includes the USA PATRIOT Act and the dungeon torture scenario that developed at the "Abu Graib" correctional facility in Iraq.

In sum, *Criminology: A Global Perspective* is intended as an introductory text in criminology that addresses the problem of "provincialism" that seems inherent in many, if not most, U.S. criminology studies and texts. Global comparisons are necessary to develop improved theories about crime based upon the fact that the theories hold true anywhere (i.e., they are "universal generalizations"). These are also theories that take into consideration the fact that "crime comes from everywhere, and goes everywhere."

We hope that the foregoing text will be helpful in expanding the horizons of criminology. We believe that criminology must keep pace with the international world of commerce, the World Wide Web of information available on the Internet, and, most of all, the global nature of crime.

ACKNOWLEDGMENTS

We want to extend our thanks first to Virginia L. Winslow for her careful and thorough job of copyediting this text. Ginny is an award-winning journalist who has worked as a newspaper editor, reporter, columnist, and magazine journalist in San Diego for a number of years. It has been our goal to make the text interesting and readable, an objective that could not have been attained without the thousands of hours Ginny spent copyediting, rewriting, and shaping the text.

Great appreciation must also be extended to Sarah Holle, Editor at Pearson/Prentice-Hall, without whose guidance an introductory criminology text that is global in nature would not have become a reality.

We would like to thank the following reviewers: Holly Dersham-Bruce, Dawson Community College, Glendive MT; Katie Culotta, Indiana State University, Indianapolis, IN; Julia Glover-Hall, Drexel University, Philadelphia, PA; Xin Ren, California State University, Sacramento, CA; Sudipto Roy, Indiana State University, Terre Haute, IN; Susan Brinkly, University of Tampa, Tampa, FL; Ronald Thrasher, Oklahoma State University, Stillwater, OK; and Paul Becken, University of Dayton, Dayton, OH.

We would also like to thank Artie Pajak, who, as administrator of San Diego State University's Instructional Technology Services, provided the assistance and staff needed in developing the Website linked with this text.

http://www.rohan.sdsu.edu/faculty/rwinslow/index.html

In addition, we would like to thank the hundreds of students who participated in the development of text for over 200 countries on the Website. Their names are listed at the end of each country profile.

1

CRIMINOLOGY IN A FAST-CHANGING WORLD

KEY TERMS

adversarial system
case law
civil law systems
common law systems
crime
criminal
criminal behavior
criminology
customary law systems

factual guilt
felony
international crimes
Islamic law systems
legal guilt
socialist law systems
torts
transnational crime

OUTLINE

Introduction
The Need for a Global Approach
Legal Systems of the World
History of Crime and Punishment in the United States

Development of Criminal Law in America
Definitions of Crime in Civil Law Systems
Global Approach Taken in this Text

LEARNING OBJECTIVES

After reading this chapter, students should be able to:

1. Understand what criminology as a discipline attempts to do (as compared with the legal profession in the United States) and how the global perspective can enhance the study of criminology.

2. Distinguish between the major legal systems in the world today and understand the nature of the U.S. criminal justice system as a common law system.

3. Understand the history of the U.S. common law system and the development of the concepts of crime and punishment from the colonial period until today.

4. Gain insight into the nature of the U.S. criminal justice system as a common law adversarial system as compared with European civil law systems.

5. Identify the three basic global theories that are intended to explain crime cross-culturally and compare the approach taken in this text with these theories.

INTRODUCTION

Criminology: A Global Perspective is a text about crime, criminals, and criminal behavior; hence, it is a text in criminology. In this text, we attempt to explain crime and criminal motivation from a global point of view. We describe the criminal justice system's role (either in the United States or other countries) in deterring crime or, at the other extreme, in contributing to it. The primary focus of this text is to explain crime and criminal behavior.

There are a number of terms that must be defined before moving on to specific subjects within criminology. Terms to be defined include crime, criminal, criminal behavior, and criminology, as well as criminal justice. **Criminology** can be defined simply as the study of the causes of crime and criminal behavior. Criminology includes study of the criminal justice system insofar as it can deter crime or, in some cases, cause crime. Criminal justice as a discipline within criminology focuses upon the agencies of the criminal justice system—police, courts, and corrections—in and of themselves without regard to causation of crime. **Criminal behavior** refers to the commission of crime or violation of criminal law, whether or not the perpetrator was caught, convicted, or punished. A **criminal** is a person who has committed a crime and been caught and convicted of that crime. What then is crime? **Crime** refers to a violation of criminal law.

These are short and to the point definitions; however, the situation is more complicated that it first appears. That is because the United States has a **common law system.** If the United States had a **civil law system,** like most countries in Europe, the situation would be simpler. In civil law systems, laws are passed by legislatures, and the courts simply judge whether or not a law has been violated and whether or not the accused intentionally did the crime. In our common law system, there are a host of complications that have to do with **common law** and **case law.** Both of these determine what is a crime and procedures that must be followed to convict a person of a crime, thus making him or her a criminal. Common law refers to the history of English unwritten law while case law refers to court decisions of the past. In a common law system like ours, students of law must know more about the history of common law and case law than do law students in civil law systems, who primarily have to know the law as passed by the legislature. The study of law usually requires approximately three years of postgraduate training in our common law system. Not only is the study of law more complicated in our system than in the civil law system, but the basic definitions of crime and criminal are also more complicated. To prove that a crime has been committed and that the person accused of the crime is guilty, the prosecution must surmount all kinds of legal technicalities pertaining to the "elements of the crime" to prove **legal guilt,** which refers to a person being found guilty in a court of law. If a defense attorney can prove that his or her client lacked criminal intent (for reasons of insanity, infancy, or numerous other defenses), then the accused will be found not guilty and will not be deemed a "criminal." These considerations are just a taste of what goes on in a court of law in our system. In criminology, when we are studying criminal behavior, there is less concern about the legal technicalities (or legal guilt) because we are only concerned about getting at **factual guilt,** rather than **legal guilt.** Factual guilt in criminology refers to a person's admitted commission of crime in an interview or on a questionnaire, regardless of whether or not a capable attorney can obtain an acquittal in court. Thus, what we try to determine in criminology (factual guilt) is more akin to what is found in courts of law in civil law countries, such as many European countries, which focus more upon fact-finding than our courts do. Courts in civil law countries, for that reason, have relatively low acquittal rates, such as 6%, whereas our common law courts have relatively high acquittal rates of 25% or higher, based upon our **adversarial system**.[1]

In any event, the United States has developed a criminal justice system known as the common law system. We need to study the history of that system to understand how crime is conceptualized in our legal system. However, it is important to know that our legal system is quite different from civil law systems that characterize many other countries. Students often experience culture shock when they visit a foreign country, such as Mexico, and encounter a different justice system. Thus, it is important at the outset to discuss other legal systems that exist in the world. Our justice system is not the only one that exists, and it is not the only one used in "modern" countries, or developed nations, or democratic countries. Comparison of our common law system with others will be helpful in understanding how our system differs in its approach to crime. Our system is different in its emphasis upon tradition—upon precedent—in the definition of crime. As a result, those that are considered to be serious crimes in our legal system differ from crimes that are the focus in other legal systems of the world. We will trace the development of the definition of serious crime in America, but first, a brief coverage of other legal systems will be helpful in viewing our legal system comparatively.

THE NEED FOR A GLOBAL APPROACH

The observation that crime has "gone global" has been prompted by two outstanding texts. The first is *Criminology and the Criminal Justice System,* by Adler, Mueller, and Laufer. The second is *Criminal Justice Today,* by Schmalleger. Both texts have chapters on *comparative criminology* and both texts urge the promotion of this approach. Adler, et al. indicate the need for global criminology in the introduction to their text, as well as in the chapter on comparative criminology.

> Crime, like life itself, has become globalized, and responses to law-breaking have inevitably extended beyond local and national boarders . . . the countries of the world gradually became more interdependent. Commercial relations among countries increased. The jet age brought a huge increase in international travel and transport. Satellite communications facilitated intense and continuous public and private relationships. The Internet added the final touch to globalization. . . . These developments, which turned the world into what has been called a "global village," have also had considerable negative consequences. As everything else in life became globalized, so did crime. Transnational crimes . . . suddenly boomed. Then there are the truly **international crimes**—those that are proscribed by international law—such as crimes against the peace and security of mankind, genocide, and war crimes. But even many apparently purely local crimes, whether local drug crime or handgun violence, now have international dimensions. . . . Consequently, national criminology had to become international criminology. *Criminology has in fact been*

globalized. . . . Economic globalization, as much as it promotes useful commerce, also aids organized crime and fosters the global spread of frauds. . . . Consider that drugs produced abroad and distributed locally create a vast problem of crime: Not only is drug dealing illegal, but a considerable portion of street crime is associated with narcotics.[2]

In both of the previously mentioned texts, students are introduced to comparative criminology through features on various international topics. We are inspired to carry the analysis one additional step—to the inclusion of comparative quantitative and qualitative analysis throughout this introductory text. This is because we are finding out more and more that *crime goes everywhere and comes from everywhere.*

Adler et al. point out that the reach of comparative criminology includes not only "internationally induced local crime problems," but also transnational crime and international crime. "Local problems" refers to common law crimes such as murder, robbery, larceny, and other offenses. **Transnational crimes** involve activities that violate the laws of more than one country (e.g., money laundering, terrorist activities, illicit traffic in arms, environmental crimes, illicit drug trafficking, and trafficking in persons). *International crimes* refer to activities that are contrary to the interests of humankind. International crimes include genocide, apartheid (suppression of a racial or ethnic group), war crimes, and international terrorism. Although Adler et al. introduce these topics in their text, a complete coverage of all of these topics would result in a volume of encyclopedic proportions. Thus, it is necessary to limit analysis to selected crimes to produce a text of reasonable size.

As discussed later, we have chosen to focus our analysis upon crimes that are considered to be serious crimes in the United States. Most particularly, these are the seven major crimes that constitute the Federal Bureau of Investigation (FBI) Index crimes: murder, forcible rape, robbery, aggravated assault, burglary, larceny, and motor vehicle theft. In addition to the consideration of "seriousness," a very practical consideration enters into the selection of these crimes for analysis—these are crimes that are included in international crime databases, such as those gathered by INTERPOL and the United Nations. Thus, data exist for the purpose of international comparisons. The fact that such data are gathered by international organizations is a partial indication of the worldwide perception that these are serious crimes.

Focusing upon the "seven major crimes" does not mean that transnational and international crimes are ignored in our analysis. Throughout the text, reference is paid to numerous transnational and international crimes in the analysis of the Index crimes. For instance, a relationship is drawn between drug trafficking, a transnational crime, and the prevalence of murder, a "local crime," in Colombia. Similarly, a discussion of forcible rape pays reference to an international crime, "genocidal rape," in Bosnia.

Although the Index crimes constitute the bulk of comparative analysis in this text, other topics are also addressed, including organized crime, the drug trade, the sex trade, and white-collar crime. These topics involve transnational crimes and the discussion of these topics is comparative in nature.

This text emphasizes the Index crimes for comparative analysis. One benefit of this approach is that international data are available on each of these crimes. In addition, these are crimes that are considered to be "serious crime," both in terms of theoretical classifications and in public opinion. The question of what is a serious crime is addressed later in this chapter. However, first the questions of what is a crime, what is a criminal, and what is criminal behavior in the United States must be answered. The answers to these questions have very much to do with the legal system that has been developed in the United States. As will be shown, what is considered a crime varies considerably with the legal system that is in place in a particular country. For instance, prostitution is a crime in most jurisdictions throughout the United States, but it is not a crime in many European countries, such as the Netherlands and Sweden. Adultery is not a crime in America, but it is considered to be a major crime in many Islamic countries. So, before discussing the definition of crime and the subject of "serious crime," it is important to understand more about the legal system we have in America compared with other legal systems of the world. This topic is also important in the sense that the terms for different legal systems (civil law system, common law system, etc.) are used repeatedly throughout this text in describing various countries.

LEGAL SYSTEMS OF THE WORLD

There are essentially five legal systems that are referred to in discussions of countries of the world. Descriptions of these countries are given on the Website linked to this text, to be referred to as the Comparative Criminology Website. The Website can be located at: *http://www.rohan.sdsu.edu/faculty/rwinslow/index.html*. On the Website, countries are described as having one of the following legal systems: (a) civil law, (b) common law, (c) Islamic law, (d) socialist law, or (e) customary law. A good number of countries have a mixture of different legal systems. Many of these mixtures were the result of conquest and colonization, whereas some countries may have developed blended systems as result of choice.

Civil Law Systems

Civil law systems (not to be confused with American civil vs. criminal courts) resulted from the Roman legal tradition of codifying law done originally by the sixth century Roman emperor Justinian. Subsequently, Napoleon developed a similar written law known as *Code Civil* or Code Napoleon, proclaimed in 1804. What characterizes a *civil law system* is that it is written law and is revolutionary in nature, because when a new code is developed in civil law countries, all prior law is repealed. Of course, the new code may incorporate the old code; however, the validation of the old code comes from being incorporated in the new code, rather than the other way around, as in common law systems. Civil law systems characterize most European countries and are generally associated with parliamentary forms of government in which the legislative branch of the government is the most powerful branch. Civil law systems have an obvious advantage of being able to quickly adapt to newly emerging crimes, such as terrorism or computer crimes, because laws to control such crimes can be quickly passed and enforced with less possibility of judicial nullification. Courts in civil law countries typically do not use juries to decide innocence or guilt, and focus upon determining the facts of the case rather than whether or not due process has been followed.[3]

Common Law Systems

Common law systems are sometimes referred to as being based upon a tradition of unwritten law. *Common law* developed in Britain to resolve conflicts between landlords and vassals (tenants) during feudalism. Essentially, common law courts, with the aid of a jury of peers, settled disputes on the basis of what was customary. Common law was passed on through word of mouth initially. However, it developed into written case law. Citing precedent, based upon what was done in prior cases, reference to common law became a method for defense or prosecution for winning or losing cases. What evolved was the principle of *stare decisis,* which meant that the court was expected to abide by previously decided cases. The distinction between crimes that are *mala in se* (bad in themselves) and *mala prohibita* (bad because they are prohibited) derives from common law. Crimes that are *mala in se* are derived from customs, whereas crimes that are *mala prohibita* derive from government legislation. Based upon the principle of *stare decisis,* it is difficult to overturn existing laws and prior court decisions. Thus, in common law countries, laws supporting traditional morality are more likely to continue, while new laws pertaining to new social problems are less likely to be developed than in civil law countries. Although legislated law is given priority in civil law countries, the judiciary is given much more power in common law countries.

Islamic Law Systems

Islamic law systems are, in a sense, entirely based upon *mala in se*. Islamic law, called Sharia, is based in part upon the Koran and is said to be of divine origin. Although religious beliefs helped shape civil and common legal systems, with Islamic law, religion and law are one and the same. Judges in Islamic countries are trained primarily in religious law. While crimes against morality are downplayed in civil and common law systems, they are considered to be the most serious of all offenses in Islamic law. Thus, in Islamic countries, an offender may face the death penalty for moral crimes such as adultery and severe punishment for consumption of alcohol. In a sense, countries that practice Islamic Law are theocracies in which there is no separation between religion and government. It should be noted that, during colonial America in the 1600s, the Puritans developed a theocracy similar in many respects to that of Islamic countries today. Puritan theocratic jurisprudence was similar to Islamic law in its emphasis upon moral crimes and harsh punishments for these crimes. (Islamic law is discussed more fully in Chapter 3.)

Socialist Law Systems

Socialist law systems, as developed in the former Soviet Union and in Communist China, were an expression of distrust of law and the courts. Historically, law in Russia reflected both the will of the czars and customary law. Customary law came into play because the princes and czars felt no need to develop rules for everyone in all situations. The English and Europeans came to appreciate the rule of law as a natural compliment to morality and a fundamental base for society. However, the Russians never did so. Law was considered to be the arbitrary work of an autocratic sovereign and a privilege of the bourgeoisie. It was thus considered to be of no import to the common person. The negative view of law was compatible, ultimately, with the basic tenets of Marxist–Leninism. This philosophy held that the need for law under communism would ultimately wither away. After the Bolshevik Revolution, courts loyal to the working class were instructed to apply the old imperial codes as interpreted by judges who were in touch with revolutionary ideals. However, subsequent Soviet law became a tool for the leaders to achieve socially desirable ends. Law did not serve as a check on the leader's conduct, as it did in the West. Thus, law became subordinate to policy as a means of social engineering as well as a means of educating the people to the goals of socialism. Although there was systematic denial of even the existence of crime such as murder, rape and robbery during the Soviet era, the policy emphasis enforced through the courts was upon crimes that would be considered white-collar crimes in the West. One prominent text classified criminals as "money-grubbers and loafers, the litigious persons, the slanderers, the anonymous letter writers, the formalists and bureaucrats, the careerists, time servers and traitors, the dodgers and self-seekers."[4] Public policy education through judicial sanction was not always benign in the Soviet Union, but sometimes amounted to "public education through execution." The Soviet Union executed about 800 people each year for various offenses, including bribery and misuse of official position.[5] It should be noted that since the dissolution of the Soviet Union in 1991, the socialist legal system has largely been abandoned in the former Soviet countries (including Russia) in favor of the European civil legal model.

Customary Law Systems

As previously pointed out, the English system of common law developed as an outgrowth of custom and tradition. Customary law usually refers to rules for conduct that are passed from generation to generation in tribal cultures and is typically unwritten law. Few countries or political entities in the world today operate under a legal system that could be characterized as wholly customary. Yet **customary law systems** still play a sometimes significant role, particularly in regard to matters of personal conduct, in a large number of countries, especially in Africa, South America, and Asia.[6] For instance, customary or tribal courts are frequently charged with the task of dealing with problems pertaining to family or neighborhood disputes, whereas common law or civil law courts deal with violations of criminal codes. Thus, the numerous countries that utilize customary law may be more accurately characterized as "mixed systems." In many of these countries, the problem arises that many "serious" crimes, such as rape and assault, may be dealt with by tribal counsels or customary courts. As such, they do not come to the attention of the police and are underreported in international data.

HISTORY OF CRIME AND PUNISHMENT IN THE UNITED STATES

If we were criminologists from another country who decided to use the comparative method to study the United States, how would we proceed? Adler et al. recommend several steps: (a) determining the legal system to which the country belongs, (b) understanding the foreign criminal justice system, (c) learning about the foreign culture, and (d) collecting data. We are going to gather data and test theories about the United States compared to other countries of the world, but first, we must pause and reflect upon the first three steps.

As discussed earlier, America has a common law system; like many other former colonies of England, including Australia, Canada, and India, as well as countless Commonwealth countries, many of which have recently obtained sovereignty. This one fact alone—the type of legal system—explains much about the definition of crime in the United States. Being a common law country, America is to some extent bound by tradition. Thus, much of what was defined as crime during and before colonial days became a basis for case law precedent for modern America. A brief history of crime and its treatment in America should provide an important and interesting background related to the development of contemporary law in America.

Convict Colony   Compared to the Spanish, Portuguese, and French, the English settlers were actually late in their arrival to the New World. A less known fact about American history was that a good number of them were convicted criminals, exiled from England. In the early years, the colonies served as havens for religious heretics, the Puritans. The colonies also served as an important outlet for England for disposing of its unwanted criminals. According to one estimate, one fourth of British immigrants to colonial America during the 18th century were criminal exiles.[7] England used both Australia and America as a destination point for its convicted criminals. This was particularly true after the invention of gin in 1720, which precipitated binges of drinking and rioting by working class people in the urban industrial ghettos of England.[8] However, the exporting of convicted criminals to America was not the only connection between British foreign policy and crime. Had it not been for piracy, the English might not have successfully colonized the New World. Quite possibly, the United States would have been a Spanish-speaking nation, instead of an English-speaking nation.

As every school child has been taught, it was Christopher Columbus, an Italian from Genoa sailing for the monarchs of Spain, who in 1492 "discovered America." In reality, he landed in the Caribbean on an island in the Bahamas, thinking he had reached the East Indies. Subsequently, the Italian navigator Amerigo Vespucci sailed to the north coast of South America in 1499, and European mapmakers named it America in his honor. Spaniard Hernan Cortez invaded Mexico in 1519, and Francisco Pizarro conquered Peru in 1532. Later, in 1534, Jacques Cartier, sailing for France, explored nearly the whole Atlantic coast of the present United States. All of this occurred a full century before English colonization began.[9]

The Spaniards and Portuguese proceeded to denude the newly found lands of their wealth in gold and silver, and wealth enhanced the military might of both countries in competition with other European nation states. According to Chambliss, England devised a plan to offset the increasing power of Spain and Portugal through seeking an alliance with pirates—an alliance Chambliss termed "state organized crime."[10] Many of the pirates and crews of pirate ships had come to the New World as convicts or indentured servants, and the lure of the pirate's life served as an alternative that was more appealing than the conditions of serfdom and indentured slavery.

Subsequently, Sir Richard Hawkins and his apprentice, Sir Francis Drake, were issued "letters of marque" from the English admiralty directing governors of British colonies and captains of British warships to give safe passage, as well as assistance, to Hawkins and Drake who were "under orders of the Crown."[11] In the United States, Charleston, South Carolina, several New England towns, and New York provided safe harbors for pirates in exchange for sharing the booty. John Paul Jones became an American hero as a result of his success as a pirate. Later Jean and Pierre Lafitte organized and aided pirates and smugglers at the mouth of the Mississippi River. They were later enlisted by the U.S. government in the war against England. Thus, Chambliss concludes, "nations enlisted pirates to serve in their navy. In times of peace, they shared in the profits."[12]

The Bahamas, a country composed of an archipelago of over 100 islands, and which once served as hideouts for pirates, received its first Royal Governor in 1717. He was a former pirate named Woodes Rogers. After the American Revolution, Loyalists from the United States settled in the Bahamas, bringing with them black slaves to provide labor for cotton plantations. The Bahamas prospered during the Civil War as a center of Confederate blockade-running, and after World War I, The Bahamas also served as a base for American rum-runners during Prohibition.[13]

The aforementioned analysis demonstrates that crime and criminals played an important part in the early development of America. Criminals served as indentured servants, but then served the British Crown as pirates to offset the Spanish power at sea, and then later served the United States in combating British sea power.

Although crime and criminals formed the "dark underbelly" that served as a foundation for English settlement in America, the colonies were the forerunners of the definition of "sin" as crime. This definition (sin as crime) has continued through precedent until today. Puritans were among the first English colonists in America. They were advocates of the Protestant Reformation in

The Puritan Ethos

BOX 1–1

The Pillory and Post

The *pillory* consisted of hinged wooden boards with holes in which the head and arms were inserted while the offender remained standing, usually for two to four hours. Being placed in the pillory was considered a more severe punishment than confinement in the *stocks*, which held the offender while seated. In the absence of detention facilities in the New England colonies, the pillory and stocks served as gaols (jails) with the purpose of inflicting public humiliation for minor offenses. The pillory and stocks usually were placed in town squares or next to public meeting houses.

Source: Colonial Williamsburg Foundation. Abby Aldrich Rockefeller Folk Art Museum, Williamsburg, VA.

The *pillory* and *post* from 17th-century Colonies held an offender by the neck and hands. On several occasion, onlookers pelted the pilloried prisoner with such heavy missiles that death resulted. Thomas Granger of Plymouth, a boy of 17, was indicted in 1642 for buggery "with a mare, a cow, two goats, five sheep, two calves and a turkey." Granger was hanged. The animals, for their part in the affair, were

BOX 1–1 (*continued*)

executed according to the law. . . . The pillory, or "stretch-neck," . . . stood in the main squares of towns up and down the colonies. An upright board, hinged or divided in half with a hole in which the head was set fast, it usually also had two openings for the hands. Often the ears of the subject were nailed to the wood on either side of the head hole. . . . The *pillory* was employed for lying and idleness, general lewdness, masturbation, fornication, adultery, sodomy, buggery, treason, sedition, arson, blasphemy, witchcraft, perjury, wife-beating, cheating, forgery, coin-clipping, dice-cogging, slandering, conjuring, fortune-telling, and drunkenness. . . . Burglary was punished in all the colonies by branding with a capital B in the right hand for the first offense, in the left hand for the second, "and if either be committed on the Lord's Daye his Brand shall bee set on his Forehead as a mark of infamy.". . . M stood for manslaughter, T for thief, R for rogue or vagabond, F for forgery.[14]

England, persecuted by English royals, such as Queen Mary I, because the royals wanted to retain much of Catholic liturgy and ritual forms, whereas the Puritans wanted to suppress the remaining Catholic forms. The Puritans developed an extreme form of Protestantism when they formed their independent colony at Massachusetts Bay in 1630. The Puritans criminalized moral offenses such as fornication, adultery, misbehavior on the Sabbath, consumption of alcohol, and idleness, and sanctioned violation of the moral code with extreme penalties.

Heresy for the Puritans was *antinomianism,* the doctrine that the Gospel frees Christians from required obedience to any law, and that salvation is attained solely through faith and the gift of divine grace. Ann Hutchinson, who advocated antinomianism, was tried and banished from the Puritan colony for this belief. Later, as a result of the Salem witch trials, some 22 persons were brought to death either through execution or through death in prison.[15]

The Puritan experiment in Massachusetts ended in 1700 after England took actions to regularize the legal systems of the colonies, which were found to be divergent from those of English common law. Succeeding generations of Puritans adopted a conventionalism that saw no conflict between English common law and Biblical law.[16] Nevertheless, the early Puritan experiment left an indelible stamp upon American culture, and the return to fundamentalism in the form of harsh punishments for moral offenses has, from time to time, occurred in the form of evangelical moral enterprise, as will be discussed below.

The Protestant Ethic and Crime

Max Weber was one of the founders of sociology who wrote about the development of capitalism in the West. Weber believed that rational action was the heart of modern society, as manifested in modern day bureaucracy.[17] However, such rational organization is often opposed by tradition. Thus, Weber attempted to discover what forces in the West caused people to abandon traditional religions and encouraged them to develop a desire to acquire goods and wealth. Through empirical study, Weber concluded that the Protestant ethic, which was linked with Calvinism, enabled people to break the hold of tradition. It also urged followers to apply themselves rationally to work. This "work ethic" ironically stemmed from the Calvinist doctrine of predestination—ironic because predestination meant that good works or acts of faith would not assure the person's place in heaven.

To be admitted to heaven, one had to be among the "elect." Although good works did not assure membership in this elite group, wealth was taken

Max Weber (1864–1920)
Source: Library of Congress.

as a sign that a person was one of God's elect. Thus, followers were encouraged to work to acquire wealth to show that they were among the elect, fostering a work ethic called the Protestant Ethic.[18] The Protestant Work Ethic became very much a part of the American value system. Sociologist Robin Williams, Jr. developed a text in which he summarized the American value system. The list of central themes summarized by Williams heavily emphasized values related to the Protestant Ethic. These included achievement and success, activity and work, efficiency and practicality, progress, science and rationality, moral orientation, and individual personality. Values Williams listed that were not related to the Protestant Ethic included humanitarianism, equality, freedom, external conformity, nationalism/patriotism, and democracy.[19] One may observe that there may be some incompatibility between the achievement and success theme in the Protestant Ethic and other values such as humanitarianism and equality, because achievement often involves exploiting the services of others and the "doctrine of the elect" precludes equality. In the 20th century, the Protestant Ethic came to be called *the American Dream*, as it was described by historian James Truslow Adams in 1931.[20] However, as Robert Merton later pointed out, the American Dream was at once a cardinal American virtue that subsequently promoted a cardinal American vice—that of deviant behavior.[21] "The cultural emphasis on achievement, which promotes productivity and innovation, also generates pressures to succeed at any cost."[22]

The Penitentiary Movement

The Quakers, like the antinomians, came into conflict with the Puritans, based upon a claim that they, like the antinomians, need not submit their religious experiences to the review of any church official. For this belief, Quakers were persecuted by the Puritans, and some were put to death. However, long after the Puritan experiment had ended, Quakers were well represented in the United States. The Quakers believed that errant sinners could be redeemed if they were given time alone to wrestle with the evils they harbored. Along with this, the study of the Bible was strongly encouraged. Thus, the first penitentiary was developed in 1790 through remodeling Philadelphia's Walnut Street Jail by the Pennsylvania Quakers to provide solitary confinement, with minimum contact between inmates and between inmates and staff. The penitentiary approach became known as the Pennsylvania system, and it was advocated by both Benjamin Franklin and Benjamin Rush as a humane measure whereby the inmate had an opportunity for penance.[23] Although the penitentiary is today thought of as one of the harshest of confinement settings, in its early days it served as an alternative to the cruel methods used by the Puritans, which included not only the gallows, but burning at the stake, branding, whipping, and other methods of punishment that are considered inhumane today in Western society.

It may be observed that the development of the first Penitentiary occurred after the American Revolution (1775–76), both of which were influenced by the Enlightenment movement that was taking place in Europe. The Enlightenment movement was spurred by liberal thinkers such as Voltaire, Rousseau, Hume, and Locke. Enlightenment concepts such as separation of church and state, natural law, inherent freedoms, equality, and self-determinism, as referenced in the Declaration of Independence, were derived from the authors of the Enlightenment, especially John Locke.[24] It may be added that the doctrines of the Enlightenment could be seen as in conflict with those Protestant religious groups, such as the Congregationalists (formerly Puritans) who had burned people at the stake for exercising "freedom of speech." It should be pointed out that the founding fathers weren't, for the most part, Puritans. A good share of the major leaders of the American Revolution were, in fact, Deists. Deist founders included John Quincy Adams, Ethan Allen, Benjamin Franklin, James Madison, Thomas Paine, and George Washington.[25] Deism was essentially a nondenominational religion that supported the Protestant belief in a direct link between the individual and God, without the intervention of organized religion, and it was compatible with the doctrines of the Enlightenment.

The Temperance Movement

Although the American Revolution may have been influenced by the Enlightenment and spearheaded by leaders of the Deist faith, it was supported, perhaps with some reluctance, by other religious groups who "agreed to disagree" on the question of which faith was to prevail in America and accepted the doctrine of separation of church and state.

Protestant evangelical groups were quite opposed to the principles of the Deists. Evangelical groups, such as the Wesleyans and later Baptists and Congregationalists, believed that loyal parishioners could "be saved from sin and made holy through church attendance." They supported the notion of proselytizing through encouraging people to become lay preachers. They also strongly supported temperance and encouraged members to abstain from consumption of alcohol.[26]

Starting in the 1820s, evangelical members of the Northern Whig Party began a campaign against the use of alcohol. They argued that various social problems that were developing—poverty, crime, family violence, poor child rearing, and so forth—were traceable to heavy drinking. Beginning with Maine in 1851, 13 states adopted legislation that outlawed alcohol by 1855. All but Delaware were Northern states. The Temperance Movement continued,

BOX 1–2

Characteristics of Deists

Deists

- Do not accept the belief of most religions that God revealed himself to humanity through the writings of the Bible, the Qur'an, or other religious texts.
- Disagree with strong Atheists who assert that there is no evidence of the existence of God.
- Believe that God created the universe, "wound it up," and then disassociated himself from his creation.
- Do not view God as an entity in human form.
- Believe that one cannot access God through any organized religion, set of beliefs, rituals, sacraments, or other practice.
- Believe that God has not selected a chosen people (e.g., Jews or Christians) to be the recipients of any special revelation or gifts.

- Deny the existence of the Trinity as conceived by Christians. They often view Jesus as a philosopher, rabbi, teacher, and healer, but not as the Son of God.
- Believe that miracles do not happen. The "world operates by natural and self-sustaining laws of the creator."
- Believe that a practical morality can be derived from reason without the need to appeal to religious revelation and church dogma."
- Pray, but only to express their appreciation to God for his works. They generally do not ask for special privileges, or try to assess the will of God through prayer, or ask God to perform miracles.
- Do not actively evangelize the public.[27]

basing its case against alcohol upon various quotations from the Bible. As a result of their efforts, the 18th Amendment, supported by the Volstead Act, was passed, outlawing the manufacture, transportation, import, export, and sale of alcoholic beverages. Prohibition was in effect from 1920 to 1933.[28]

The Harrison Narcotics Tax Act of 1914

Originally represented merely as a tax act, the Harrison Narcotics Tax Act of 1914 was the work of then Secretary of State William Jennings Bryan, who was described as a man of deep prohibitionist and missionary convictions. Although the Harrison Act appeared on the surface to be an innocuous tax act, the provision protecting physicians contained the phrase, "in the course of his professional practice only." The law was interpreted by law enforcement officers to mean that a doctor was prohibited from prescribing opiates to an addict to maintain his addiction.[29] This law opened the door for a series of laws that ultimately made it illegal to possess and/or sell an ever-increasing list of substances.[30]

Bryan was the Democratic Party nominee for President three times. Largely based upon his famous 1896 Democratic Convention "Cross of Gold" speech, Bryan was known for his brilliant oratory. In his speech to the Democratic Convention in 1920 in support of Prohibition, Bryan said: "Are you afraid that we shall lose some votes? Oh my countrymen, have more faith in the virtue of the people! If there be any here who would seek the support of those who desire to carry us back into bondage to alcohol, let them remember that it is better to have the gratitude of one soul saved from drink than the applause of a drunken world." Bryan's lecture "Is the Bible True?" was distributed in printed form all over the country and furnished the impetus for the passage of Tennessee's Butler Act, which prohibited teaching evolution in public schools. The prosecution of teacher John Scopes for violation of this act was the basis for the famous "Scopes Monkey Trial" (see text box).[31]

BOX 1–3

State v. John Scopes ("The Monkey Trial")

During the 1920s, traditionalists, the older Victorians came into conflict with modernists who danced to the sound of the Jazz Age, showed their contempt for prohibitions and debated abstract art and Freudian theories. A showdown between these two groups occurred in a Dayton, Tennessee courtroom in the summer of 1925. The trial of John Scopes, a high school teacher who was charged with illegally teaching the theory of evolution, caught nationwide attention. The trial pitted the defense skills of noted agnostic Clarence Darrow against prosecution by William Jennings Bryan. In a surprise move, Darrow put Bryan on the stand and grilled Bryan with questions about the Bible. Bryan was forced to admit that various portions of the Bible, such as the seven-day creation of the world, were not to be taken literally. Although the jury voted to convict (on Darrow's instructions, hoping for an appeal), the case was overturned on a technicality by the Tennessee Supreme Court. Thus, Darrow never got the constitutional test he had hoped for.[32]

Religion and the Death Penalty

Evangelicalism has deep roots both in English Puritanism and in the Wesleyan revival of the 18th century.[33] Protestant evangelicals today have carried forth the Puritan legacy of physical punishment in their support for the death penalty. During the 1970s, the National Association of Evangelicals (NAE), representing over 10 million conservative Christians and 47 denominations, and the Moral Majority were among the Christian groups that supported the

"Wayward Puritan" Dennis Rader, the BTK Killer, carried on a campaign of Puritan style executions as a serial killer who gave himself the nickname BTK for "bind, torture, and kill." BTK has claimed responsibility for at least eight deaths in the Wichita area since 1974. Rader was president of the 400-member congregation at Christ Evangelical Lutheran Church where he was a member for 30 years.[34]

Source: AP World Wide Photos.

death penalty. NAE's successor, the Christian Coalition, continues to support the death penalty. In addition, Fundamentalist and Pentecostal churches, as well as the Church of Jesus Christ of Latter-day Saints (Mormons), also support the death penalty. However, mainline Protestant denominations, including Baptists, Episcopalians, Lutherans, Methodists, Presbyterians, and the United Church of Christ, oppose the death penalty, as does the Roman Catholic Church.[35]

DEVELOPMENT OF CRIMINAL LAW IN AMERICA

Law is one of the oldest professions to deal with the subject of crime and classifications of crime. The legal profession in the United States was a transplant from England, and early lawyers were trained in England. Accordingly, they were viewed as agents of the crown, which made them unpopular. In fact, lawyers during the 17th century in colonial North America were despised, and the legal profession was prohibited in many courts. Most English colonists were uneducated, unemployed men who felt they had been oppressed and cheated by the upper-class elite of England, and lawyers were part of this elite. The Puritans especially hated lawyers. The Puritans believed in Divine Providence and Predestination and wanted to start a new Utopia where everyone got along under the grace of God. Because there would be no disputes in this new Utopia, there would be no use for the legal profession, which, they reasoned, would facilitate the corruption of money-hungry robber barons. However, the Puritans decided that it was necessary to develop laws pertaining to morality. These laws were administered by the clergy. The Massachusetts Code of 1648 defined moral offenses and stated them for the public to read. Moral offenses included drunkenness, fornication, blasphemy, bastardy, swearing, rape, slander, and adultery. Under the Massachusetts Code, adultery was punishable by death.

In most of the colonies, it was against the law to swear, to not attend church services, to exhibit inappropriate conduct on the Sabbath, and to engage in premarital sex and/or postmarital adultery. *Blasphemy* involved denying the existence of God or the Holy Trinity, declaring that there was more than one God, or worshipping another god or goddess. Although prisons were not in use (due to cost), jails were used to hold the accused, who, if convicted, were given a fine or some physical penalty. Physical punishments included the *stock* and *pillory*, whipping, and *ducking*. The *stock* was a wooden framework in which the convicted would be locked while sitting, and the *pillory* locked the convict while standing. It was permissible for onlookers to throw rotten fruit or even rocks at the convict, in some case resulting in death. The *ducking stool* was a chair to which criminals were tied and dunked into water as a punishment.[36]

In the 18th century, lawyers became more prevalent in colonial America as a result of massive immigration and a population explosion due to a high birth rate. As property disputes occurred, the law became a useful and well-paid profession. Although initially most lawyers were educated in England, legal training was subsequently obtained at Harvard College (Harvard University today) and the College of New Jersey

(Princeton University today). Many of the lawyers educated in America, such as Thomas Jefferson, began to speak out in the English Parliament against increased taxes and ultimately participated in the American Revolution of 1776.

During colonial times, the only real law that was established was that of English common law, which was based on one principle—*stare decisis*—that which has been decided stands. The term *common law* referred to the law arising from tradition, and judicial decision, rather than laws passed by legislatures. Revolutionary lawyers initially tried to find a way to overthrow English rule through common law. However, this attempt failed because the English judges were corrupt, would not rule against each other, and were free to determine any punishment they deemed necessary.[37] Ultimately, the documents that led to and followed the American Revolution (Declaration of Independence, Articles of Confederacy, and the Constitution) pertained as much to the arbitrary and dictatorial nature of the English judiciary as they did to English policing practices. However, much of what became law in America was a codification of English common law. American law that was not codified accepted the English common law, by default. Thus, a brief review of common law principles is appropriate in understanding how the concept of crime and of the criminal was (and is) defined under law in America.

Common Law Definitions

An excellent source of definitions and classifications drawn from common law is a website developed by Pennsylvania's Unified Judicial System.[38] A crime is a type of behavior defined by law as deserving punishment (upon conviction), including imprisonment, fine, or both. It should be noted that the punishment component helps to distinguish between crimes and **torts**. Torts are civil wrongs for which the law does not prescribe punishment but does grant the injured party the right to recover damages.[39] However, it should be noted that this distinction between torts and crimes was less clear historically (see text box on the Golden Age of the Victim).

Crimes are classified as either misdemeanors or felonies. A **misdemeanor** is a criminal offense generally punishable by fine or limited local jail term, but not by imprisonment in prison or penitentiary. A **felony** is a serious crime punishable by imprisonment for more than a year or by death, and/or substantial fines. By contrast, an **infraction** is a violation of law not punishable by imprisonment, but usually by a fine.

Although the term felony designates a "serious offense," there are major inconsistencies between states in regard to particular acts so designated. For instance, "animal abuse" is a felony in 35 states, but a misdemeanor in the remaining 15.[40] Up until a recent Supreme Court ruling, sodomy laws made homosexual acts felonies in 13 states. As recently as 1969, every state had an antisodomy law, but in November 2003 a six to three decision by the Supreme Court struck down a Texas state law banning private consensual sex between adults of the same sex.[41] Before the court decision, sodomy was a felony in 13 states and a misdemeanor in 10 additional states.[42] Simple possession of less than one ounce of marijuana is an infraction in 10 states,

BOX 1–4

Golden Age of the Victim

In ancient times, wrongs done to a person or his property included what we would call crimes today. However, they were regarded as private matters, subject to remedial action by a victim and his family against the offender and his family. Norms of permissible retaliation arose in tribal cultures for what are now regarded as criminal offenses, and are referenced in the Torah, the Code of Hammurabi, and other ancient codes. The codes require offenders' repayment for victim suffering in addition to retributive sanctions. The goal was to make the victim whole again and to minimize private revenge. This system continued in England and in colonial America up to the formation of the first Metropolitan Police in England and until the Revolution and formation of the confederation of states in America. In colonial America, criminal justice was conducted by individual victims often with the assistance of public officials who charged fees for their services. The victim was responsible for arresting the offender—either alone or with the assistance of the local watchman, justice of the peace, or constable who was paid by the victim. The victim also investigated the crime, filed the formal charges, and prosecuted the offender. If successful in prosecution, the victim could receive damages from offenders who could pay or victims could keep or sell the offender's services for a period corresponding to the damages owed. Today in Austria, Norway, and Sweden, victims still retain a right to prosecute if the public prosecutor declines to initiate criminal proceedings.[43] This early historical period has been called the *Golden Age of the Victim* because victims had considerable influence in the imposition of punishments upon apprehended offenders.[44]

---

but a misdemeanor or felony in the remaining 40 states and a felony in the United States Code.[45]

In common law, the prosecution must prove three things to obtain a conviction, termed "elements of a crime." These are the specific factors that define a crime, which the prosecution must prove beyond reasonable doubt to obtain a conviction. Elements that must be proven are: (a) that a crime actually occurred (*actus reus);* (b) that the accused intended the crime to happen (*mens rea*); and (c) that a timely relationship exists between the first two factors (concurrence). The term *corpus delicti,* which literally means "the body of the crime," refers to the facts that show that a crime has occurred.[46]

The trial method used in the United States and other countries that have a common law system is termed the adversarial system. It is a system of determining truth by giving opposing parties full opportunity to present and establish evidence. In addition, opposing parties are allowed to test by cross-examination evidence presented by adversaries under established rules or procedure before an impartial judge and/or jury. It should be pointed out that the adversarial system that developed in England lacked the Constitutional guarantees, such as the exclusionary rule (evidence unlawfully seized must be excluded), which American defendants have today. It should also be noted that the English court system is considered to be a unitary system, with the Magistrate Courts at the bottom and the House of Lords at the top—one court system. The system of courts that developed in America was quite the opposite. The United States was founded not as one nation, but as a union of 13 colonies, each claiming independence from the British Crown. The Declaration of Independence referred to the colonies as "free and independent states." As a result, court systems developed independently in the various colonies. Criminal trials today typically take place in state courts of various jurisdictions. Today, there are well over 50 court systems in the United States, including the 50 states, the District of Colombia, and the federal judiciary, as well as territories and possessions. Moreover, many specialized state courts have been created with very narrow jurisdictions to take care of high caseloads in the trial courts. As a result, the court system that developed in the United States, consisting of over 1,000 jurisdictions, is the polar opposite of England's unified system and has been characterized as "fragmented."[47] The result of this peculiar mixture of codified law and decentralized common law justice is a situation in which those who can afford legal representation often receive lenient treatment because they can exploit constitutional protections. Those who cannot afford private attorneys must wait in detention, often for years, or file a guilty plea for a crime for which they may be innocent.

"Guilty Till Proven Affluent"

In the common law courts that have been passed on to us from colonial days and before, the seriousness of a crime is not based solely on the distinction between felonies and misdemeanors. There is also one unspoken criterion that can determine whether the defendant goes to prison or is set free—provability. Thus, people with good legal representation who are guilty of heinous crimes can be set free. Yet others, whose offense is often a trivial one against public morality, may spend many years in jail or prison. Both situations are the result of the legal approach to seriousness that emphasizes provability, combined with the common law traditional focus upon "crimes against morality," which remain on the books because of *stare decisis* or because of the crusading work of moralists of the recent past.

Criminology, the study of the causes of crime and criminal behavior, differs from the discipline of criminal law in a common law system such as our

O.J. Simpson, shown in a booking photo taken June 17, 1994, achieved fame and fortune as a Heisman Trophy-winning running back in the National Football League and through his post-football career as a TV and movie actor, commentator on ABC's Monday Night Football, and star of a series of TV ads. Simpson was accused of murdering his ex-wife, Nicole Brown Simpson and her acquaintance, Ronald Goldman, in 1994. He avoided a conviction (described by UCLA law professor Peter Arenella as a "slam dunk") through the efforts of his "dream team" of lawyers, who were described as "the best lawyers money could buy," including Robert Shapiro, Johnnie Cochran, F. Lee Bailey, and Alan Dershowitz.

Source: AP World Wide Photos.

own. As discussed earlier, criminologists are more concerned with factual guilt than legal guilt. Law focuses upon the determination of who is a criminal, or those convicted of a crime. Criminology, on the other hand, is the scientific pursuit of the causes of criminal behavior—violations of criminal law—regardless of whether the offender has been convicted or not. For instance, one study of burglars done by criminologists utilized the "snowball technique," locating informants through word-of-mouth referrals by other burglar informants. The study found that relatively few admitted burglars in the sample had been arrested or convicted of the crime.[48] Despite the fact that few had been charged in court, the study expanded scientific knowledge of burglars beyond that which could be obtained through the study of those convicted of the offense.

In addition to focusing upon factual guilt, criminology includes attempts to determine which crimes are considered to be serious and which are considered minor in current public opinion. Criminologists recognize that there may be offenses that are violations of criminal law that may be considered felonies in a court of law, but are not considered to be serious crimes in public opinion. This is in part because of a "carry over" on the books of offenses that were considered serious in the past, but are not considered serious today, a byproduct of our common law system of justice.

Victimization

There is a body of research that was done by Sellin and Wolfgang expressly on the subject of the seriousness of crime. In their research, they began with the goal of measuring the seriousness of juvenile delinquency (defined as crime committed by youth under age 18 in most jurisdictions). Their goal was to develop an index that would, as accurately as possible, measure the real or actual incidence of delinquency during a given period or in a given area.[49] To develop this index, it was necessary to narrow down a list of offenses that could be included to those that, based upon public opinion, constituted serious delinquency. Toward this goal, Sellin and Wolfgang developed a list of 141 offense descriptions, drawing from a list of offenses committed by juveniles in Philadelphia in 1960. They then had the list of offenses ranked in terms of seriousness by four subsamples of respondents. These included (a) university students, (b) police line officers, (c) police assigned to the Juvenile Aid Division, and (d) juvenile court judges. Their finding was that offenses rated in the most serious category had at least one of three components of seriousness: *bodily harm, property damage*, and *theft*.[50]

Index Crimes

There may be many problems with data-gathering techniques done by law enforcement bodies, as discussed in Chapter 2. However, there is much wisdom in the categories of crime used by the FBI to develop a Crime Index used for incidence and trend analysis. The Index crimes, listed in rank order according to seriousness, are: (a) murder and nonnegligent manslaughter, (b) forcible rape, (c) robbery, (d) aggravated assault, (e) burglary, (f) larceny-theft, and (g) motor vehicle theft. These crimes have the virtue of including two of Sellin and Wolfgang's criteria of seriousness—bodily harm and theft.

Another advantage of accepting this typology of offenses is that they are represented in the international databases assembled by both the United Nations and INTERPOL. Because the FBI's Index Crimes are considered to be serious both in domestic public opinion research and internationally by the United Nations and INTERPOL surveys, they will serve as a framework for the organization of this text.

DEFINITIONS OF CRIME IN CIVIL LAW SYSTEMS

Much of this chapter has been devoted to the development of definitions of crime in the United States, which has a common law system. Though civil law systems were briefly discussed, we would be remiss if we completed this chapter without discussing how crimes are defined in civil law systems. Civil law as a legal tradition is the basis of law in the majority of countries in the world. Civil law legal systems characterize most of continental Europe, Quebec (Canada), Japan, Latin America, and most former colonies of continental European countries in Asia and Africa (see Table 1–1).

Also, civil law is formally the basis of the law of one of the states in the United States—Louisiana.[51] Just as the adoption of a common law system had implications for the development of law in America, the choice of a civil law system had a significant influence upon law in countries like France, Italy, and Spain, who developed civil legal systems. The major impact of the choice of a civil law system stems from the fact that the codification of laws is revolutionary and changes with the times. Thus, the civil law countries tend to be ahead of common law countries in developing laws to cope with emerging threats, such as terrorism, computer crime, white-collar crime, and organized crime. For this reason, civil law attorneys tend to view themselves as superior to common law attorneys. They also are said to find the common law to be crude, unorganized, and culturally inferior to civil law and common law lawyers as relatively uncultured people.[52]

France France is a good place to start with an analysis of laws in a civil law system. France was one of the earliest countries to progress from feudalism to a nation-state. The French essentially pioneered the civil legal approach with the Civil Code (Code Napoleon of 1804). Napoleon cannot be credited with creating civil law, but, instead, with reviving it. The original civil law code was the *Corpus Juris Civilis (*Body of Civil Law), also called the Justinian Code, which itself was an update and compendium of Roman law done in the 6th century A.D. by Emperor Justianian.[53] The *French Penal Code of 1994* divides criminal offenses into three categories: *crimes* (serious felonies), *delits* (less serious felonies and misdemeanors), and *contraventions* (violations). *Crimes* are heard before the highest level court (Assize Court) and they are punishable by imprisonment for life or a specific number of years. A Correctional Court hears *delits,* which are punishable by a prison term between six months and 10 years; a fine; or a noncustodial sentence, such as probation. *Contraventions* can result in a fine or noncustodial sentence, such as probation and community service, and hearings for these offenses are held before a Police Tribunal.[54] The Penal Code of 1994 addresses some new issues, such as corporate crime, and includes definitions of new *crimes,* such as offenses wherein persons are placed in dangerous situations by others, ecological terrorism, sexual

Table 1–1 Legal Systems of the World's Countries.[55]

Civil Law Systems			Common Law Systems	Common/ Customary
Andorra	Martinique	Gabon	Anguilla	Bhutan
Angola	Moldova	Guinea	Australia	Ghana
Antigua & Barbuda	Monaco	Indonesia	Bahamas, The	Israel
Armenia	Namibia	Laos*	Bangladesh	Kenya*
Austria	Netherlands	Madagascar	Barbados	Liberia
Azerbaijan	Nicaragua	Mali	Belize	Malawi
Belarus	Panama	Mozambigue	Bermuda	Micronesia
Belgium	Paraguay	Niger	Bolivia	Nepal
Bosnia &	Peru	Norway*	Canada	Samoa
Herzegovina	Portugal	Rwanda	Central African	Sierra Leone
Brazil	Romania	Sao Tome & Principe	Republic	Uganda
Bulgaria	Russia	Swaziland	Dominica	Zambia
Cape Verde	Senegal	**Civil/Socialist**	El Salvador	**Islamic Law**
Chile	Serbia & Montenegro	Cuba*	Fuji	**Systems**
China	Slovenia	Korea, North	Gibraltar	Afghanistan
Colombia	Spain	Poland	Grenada	Iran
Costa Rica	Suriname	Uzbekistan	Hong Kong	Maldives
Croatia	Taiwan	Vietnam	India	Saudi Arabia
Czech Republic	Tajikistan	**Civil/Common**	Ireland	Somalia
Denmark	Thailand	Argentina	Jamaica	**Islamic/Civil**
Dominican Republic	Togo	Aruba	Malaysia	Comoros
Ecuador	Turkey	Cameroon	Montserrat	Djibouti
Estonia	Turkmenistan	Cyprus	Nauru	Iraq
Finland	Ukraine	Honduras	New Zealand	Jordan
France	Uruguay	Japan	Papau New Guinea	Kuwait
Georgia	**Civil Law Mixed**	Korea, South	Saint Kitts & Nevis	Lebanon
Germany	**Civil/Customary**	Lesothro	Saint Lucia	Libya
Greece	Angola	Malta	Singapore	Mauritania
Greenland	Belize	Mauritius	Slovakia	Morocco
Guatemala	Botswana	Mexico	Tanzania	Qatar
Haiti	Burkina Faso	Mongolia*	Tonga	Syria
Hungary	Burundi	Philippines	Trinidad & Tobago	Tunisia
Iceland	Cambodia*	Seychelles*	Turks & Caicos	United Arab Emirates
Italy	Chad	South Africa	United States	Yemen
Kazakhstan	Congo, Democratic	Sri Lanka*	Venezuela	**Islamic/Common**
Latvia	Republic	United Kingdom		Bahrain
Liechtenstein	Congo, Republic	Vanatu		Brunei
Lithuania	Cote díIvoire	Zimbabwe		Egypt*
Luxembourg	Equatorial Guinea			Gambia, The
Macau	Eritrea*			Nigeria*
Macedonia	Ethiopia			Oman
				Pakistan
				Sudan

harassment, crimes against humanity, and genocide.[56] Under the 1994 Code, *crimes* also includes attacks against property that include, in addition to theft, fraud and breach of trust.[57]

It was noted earlier that *contraventions* can be tried before a Police Tribunal, a practice often shocking to American tourists. However, the French system essentially replaces American "plea bargaining," whereby the caseload of courts is reduced through defendants being allowed to plead guilty (often to a lesser offense). In France, suspects are not allowed to plead guilty, but the caseload volume is dealt with through assignment to lower courts (Police Courts or Correctional Courts), thus freeing the Assize courts to deal with serious crimes.

Spain   Spain has a civil law system similar to France, but with its own approach to the definitions of crime. There is a distinction between serious (*delitos)* and less serious (*faltas)* offenses. Serious offenses are indictable and less serious offenses are nonindictable. Serious offenses include a cross-section of crimes that would be considered white-collar crimes in American. The Penal Code in Spain includes as indictable crimes: (a) offenses against state security, (b) fakes and falsifications, (c) offenses against the administration of justice, (d) offenses against sanitation and health (including drug offenses), (e) offenses by public officers, (f) offenses against reputation (libel and slander), and (g) offenses against freedom and personal security. These offenses are considered to be serious, in addition to offenses against individuals (murder, homicide, illegal abortions, assault, and sexual offenses). Although growing, processing, trafficking, promoting, and facilitating the consumption of illicit drugs is punishable by two to eight years in prison, individual consumption of illegal drugs is not subject to penalty. An average of three days drug supply for individual consumption by drug-addicted individuals does not constitute illegal possession as ruled by the Spanish supreme court.[58]

Italy   In Italy, criminal offenses (*reati*) are divided by the Penal Code (*Codice Penale*) into two broad categories: *delitti,* which are serious offenses, and *contravvenzioni,* which are less serious offenses. For *delitti* crimes, the penalty is 15 days to life imprisonment, whereas for *contravvenzioni* crimes, the penalty is 5 days to 3 years imprisonment. *Delitti* crimes include a wide range of crimes, old and new: (a) crimes against the Nation (e.g., espionage, assassination of the President, armed bands, terrorism); (b) crimes against public authority (e.g., corruption, bribery, embezzlement of public property by an officer); (c) crimes against judicial authority (e.g., perjury, to suborn a witness); (d) crimes against public safety (poisoning food, water, or drugs; provoking a railway or air disaster); (e) crimes against public faithfulness (forgery and counterfeiting); (f) crimes against public economy, industry, and commerce (commercial fraud); and (g) crimes against property (theft, money laundering, robbery, extortion, ransom, kidnapping). The Penal Code considers the violent crimes of robbery, extortion, and ransom kidnapping as property crimes because their main intent is to gain property.[59] The personal use of drugs in Italy has recently been decriminalized, following a national referendum. The law does not permit imprisonment for drug-related activities involving personal use only. Only administrative sanctions, such as revoking a driving license, can be imposed. However, producing, selling, or trafficking drugs are considered very serious crimes.[60]

Although these three countries—France, Spain, and Italy—are only three examples of civil legal systems, they are certainly good examples. Italy was the country of origin for the Justinian Code that later was reshaped in France by Napoleon into the Code Napoleon, the first of the modern civil legal systems. Spain is also an important country in that it emulated the Code Napoleon and brought that codified law to the New World in its conquest of South and Central America. American settlers encountered civil law courts in the American West when they occupied California and the Southwest.

It is sometimes pointed out that civil law systems and common law systems are tending to become more like each other. For instance, common law systems often develop codified laws, and civil law systems often adopt features of common law systems, such as adversarial proceedings. However, it is still true that common law systems tend to be "judge-made law" in the sense that the judiciary can overturn laws passed by Congress and state legislatures. On the other hand, in civil law countries, judicial review of laws is rare. Thus, legislative bodies in civil law countries can pass laws to deal with current-day social problems and threats without as much concern about judicial reversal. The laws in these three countries have kept up with the times, as well as with public opinion. In Italy and Spain, it was noted that possession of illicit drugs for personal use has recently been legalized or decriminalized. In addition, these countries have been proactive in treating white-collar, corporate, and political crimes as serious as street crimes.

Civil Law Definitions versus Common Law Definitions

GLOBAL APPROACH TAKEN IN THIS TEXT

It should be pointed out that comparative criminology itself is an old, not a new, discipline. The founders of both sociology (the parent discipline of much criminological theory) and the founders of criminology were comparativists. They studied the cultures of the world, both historically and cross-nationally, and developed "grand theories" to explain the relationship between crime and social development, as well as other sociological variables. Their analyses were based upon the reading of historical documents and a variety of texts in various languages. However, these analyses were too lacking in access to cross-national data to be used for comparison. In addition, the authors were often not trained in the methodology of science, whereas criminologists today are typically trained and adept in the use of statistics and the scientific method. However, despite this training in scientific analysis, it is probably more accurate to say that criminologists are *striving* to be scientific, rather than to say that criminology is a science. This is because criminology is lacking in the development of the universal generalizations that characterize the "hard sciences." The cross-national data that are available today provide criminologists with the opportunity for the development of such generalizations. There are a number of contemporary theories that are attempts at the development of universal generalizations. These theories are different from earlier attempts to arrive at a global theory in that they are based upon international data (available through the United Nations, INTERPOL, and the World Health Organization). Examples include *modernization theory, world system theory,* and *opportunity theory.* According to Barak:

First, there are the *modernization explanations* that have argued that social changes, such as urbanization and industrialization, are associated with changes in crime and victimization patterns. According to these models, the changes in crime and crime control are primarily the products of the internal influences of development, regardless of time and place. Second, there are the *world system explanations* that have argued that contemporary developing nations are dependent on—and to varying degrees, exploited by—already developed nations. Hence, the changes in crime and crime control in any country, regardless of its developmental status, are primarily the product of external influences, in relationship to a changing political economy. Third, there are the *opportunity explanations* that have argued that both crime and crime control reflect a mixture of developing material resources and social environments. Thus, changes in the patterns of crime and victimization, over time, are primarily the products of interacting internal and external factors.[61]

These theories are derived from general sociological theories, as discussed in later chapters. However, also to be discussed is the point that all of these theories fall short of being satisfactory explanations in regard to the data that are at hand. This indicates either that the theories or the data are inadequate. It is fair to state that probably both are true. It is also fair to state that there is some truth to all of the theories that have been developed, and that new theories will be developed that account for aspects missed by the existing theories.

Existing theories are often derived from the experience of their authors and may be correct in analysis within the cultural context in which they were developed. However, we believe that it is too early in the game to develop a "grand theory" that explains all crime. Instead, it seems more fruitful to examine crimes, one at a time, to determine which of these theories (or other theories) seems to fit the crime best. Thus, in terms of correlations, in Chapter 6, on criminal homicide, we find that *world systems theory* might be most suitable for explaining murder cross-nationally (i.e., murder stems from conflict traced to social inequality that exists in society). On the other hand, we will show in Chapter 10 that burglary, larceny, and auto theft may be crimes best explained by *opportunity theory*—people steal because "they can." Thus, the approach to "grand theory" taken in this text is exploratory and eclectic.

We have found that the FBI's Index Crimes are recognized as serious crimes both in public opinion and by their inclusion in the two major international databases on crime compiled by INTERPOL and the United Nations.

SUMMARY AND CONCLUSION

We believe that students should be exposed to comparative criminology, the international study of crime, as part of their introduction to criminology.

In this first chapter, five of the world's "great legal systems" were described. These include the civil law, common law, Islamic, socialist, and customary legal systems. The United States, as a former English colony, has a common law system inherited from England. However, in many ways America has deviated from the common law system in its purest form of "judge made law." The early Puritan colonists rejected lawyers and the common law system of England in favor of church law. America, before and after the Revolution, was, in fact, in a state of conflict over religious doctrine. The Quakers and Deists, who favored the principles of the Enlightenment, were in conflict with the many denominations of Puritans, who favored various measures of punishment whose purpose was to exorcise the devil from sinning criminals. The American Revolution had not settled these religious differences, but, instead, the various Protestant denominations "agreed to disagree" through the Constitutional principle of separation of church and state.

The Puritan Ethos, with its harsh punishments, did not disappear completely after the Salem witch trials. It has reappeared, from time to time, in various movements favored by evangelical Protestants. One movement sponsored by evangelicals and spearheaded by evangelist William Jennings Bryan was the Temperance Movement to ban alcohol, which reached its fruition during the Prohibition era. Bryan's crusade for Temperance resulted not only in the passage of the 18th Amendment banning alcohol, but also in the passage of the Harrison Act of 1914, which for all practical purposes rendered opium and cocaine illegal in the United States, as well.

Thus, all of these forces together led to America's unique form of common law system. Fear of the devil led to an emphasis upon law that punished immorality, including drug and alcohol consumption. Fear of tyranny by central government led to an extremely decentralized and fragmented judiciary and a tradition of distrusting lawyers. An abundance of laws pertaining to individual morality led to prolonged detention and harsh punishment for the multitude of offenders who are without adequate legal representation. These various forces have led to crowded jails, crowded courts, and crowded prisons in today's America. We note that the majority of countries in the world do not have common law legal systems. Most have civil law legal systems. Such systems seem amenable to the increasing pace of change that characterizes the modern world.

Scientific criminology has recently been challenged by evangelical Christians and by neoclassicists who want to revive deterrence theory. However, the real reason scientific criminology has fallen from favor, we believe, is that it has essentially "run out of gas," attempting to confine scientific study to the continental United States, despite the fact that, with the global economy, countries of the world are growing more interconnected.

In Chapter 2, we review basic methods of data gathering using both national and international databases. We then give a historical overview of the development of criminological theory in Chapters 3, 4, and 5. Subsequently, we present one chapter each on the FBI's crimes against persons—criminal homicide, forcible rape, robbery, and aggravated assault. One additional chapter will be devoted to crimes against property: burglary, larceny, and motor vehicle theft. In addition, we have included chapters that pertain to "sets of crimes"—organized crime, drug trafficking, the sex trade, white-collar crime, and terrorism. Studying these crimes using the comparative perspective will help us to further understand how *crime goes everywhere and comes from everywhere.*

DISCUSSION QUESTIONS

1. Do you accept the premise introduced in this chapter that "crime goes everywhere and comes from everywhere"? What are some examples of crimes that illustrate this premise? Can you think of any crimes that are exclusively local?

2. Do you think that the U.S. common law system is less effective in combating crime than the civil law systems of many European countries?

3. What role did crime and criminals play in the early development of the United States?

4. Do you think there is a link between today's evangelical movement in the United States and early colonial Puritanism? What bearing do you think the evangelical movement has upon criminal justice today?

5. Do you believe that "money buys justice" in America? On the other hand, do you think that many ordinary criminals "get off on a technicality"?

6. Do you think that cross-national analysis can be helpful in understanding crime in America or that we should confine our analysis to the territorial United States?

SUGGESTED WEBSITES

http://www.rohan.sdsu.edu/faculty/rwinslow/index-.html   Website linked to this textbook providing text profiles on over 200 countries of the world, data used in this text, and links to numerous national and international websites.

http://www.talkjustice.com/cybrary.asp   Prentice Hall's criminal justice Website presenting links to Websites organized by topic ranging from community corrections to violence against women.

http://www.odci.gov/cia/publications/factbook/fields/2100.html   The CIA's Website, which provides a complete list of the legal systems of the countries of the world.

http://www.courts.state.pa.us/Index/Aopc/Glossary/a.htm   Complete glossary of legal terms.

http://www.droitcivil.uottawa.ca/world-legalsystems/eng-presentation.html   Description of the world's legal systems.

http://www.historicaldocuments.com/index.htm   Compilation of American history documents and speeches.

http://teacher.deathpenaltyinfo.msu.edu/c/about/history/history.PDF   Document revealing the history of the use of the death penalty in America from colonial times until today.

ENDNOTES

1. Adler, Mueller, & Laufer, 2004, p. 497.
2. Adler, et al, 2004, pp. 18–19, 386.
3. Reichel, 2005, pp. 109–123.
4. Avanesov, 1982, p. 102, as cited in Schmalleger, 1991, p. 589.
5. Schmalleger, 1991, p. 591.
6. University of Ottawa, 2003.
7. Ekirch, 1991.
8. Schmalleger, 2003, p. 185.
9. Woloch, Johnson, & Turque, 2003, p. 3.
10. Chambliss, 1989, p. 2.
11. British Museum, 1977, as quoted in Chambliss, 1989.
12. Chambliss, 1989, p. 3.
13. Winslow, 2003, hereinafter refered to as Comparative Criminology Website: (The Bahamas.)
14. Cox, 2003.
15. Erikson, 1966, p. 149.
16. McClendon, 1990.
17. Weber, 1947.
18. Weber, 1958.
19. Williams, Jr., 1960.
20. Messner & Rosenfeld, 1994, p. 6.
21. Merton, 1968.
22. Messner & Rosenfeld, 1994, p. 8.
23. Schmalleger, 2003, p. 485.
24. Brians, 1998.
25. Robinson, 1999.
26. Spartacus Educational, 2002.
27. Robinson, 1999.
28. Woloch, Johnson, & Turque, 2003.
29. Brecher, 1972.
30. Americans.net, 2005.
31. Sword of the Lord Publishers, 2002.
32. Linder, 2000.
33. The Blinne Blogg, 2004.
34. Gruver, 2005, Feb. 28.
35. Michigan State University and Death Penalty Information Center, 2000.
36. Langley, Munger, Litteral, & Camper, 2001.
37. Langler, et al., 2001.
38. Administrative Office of Pennsylvania Courts, 2004.
39. Adler et al., p. 27.
40. Lisaviolet, 2004.
41. *CNN.com*, 2003, November 18.
42. Alliance of Sodomy Supporters, 1998.
43. Tobolowsky, 1999.
44. Schmalleger, 2002, p. 467.
45. Suellentrop, 2001.

46. Schmalleger, 2003, p. 152.
47. U.S. Department of State's Bureau of International Information Programs, 2005.
48. Wright & Decker, 1994.
49. Sellin & Wolfgang, 1964, p. 300.
50. Sellin & Wolfgang, 1964, pp. 62–70.
51. Wikipedia, 2006a; Reichel, 2005, p. 122.
52. Merryman, 1985, as quoted in Reichel, 2005, p. 156.
53. Levene, 2005.
54. Reichel, 2005, p. 157.
55. Central Intelligence Agency, 2005. Countries with more than two legal systems are indicated by an asterisk (*).
56. Borricand, 1995, p. 1.
57. Borricand, 1995, p. 2.
58. Canivell, 1993.
59. Marongiu, & Biddau, 1993, p. 6.
60. Marongiu, & Biddau, 1993, p. 7.
61. Barak, 2000, p. xv.

2

EXTENT
AND TRENDS
IN CRIME

KEY TERMS

clearance rates
comparative criminology
dark figure of crime
ethnocentric viewpoint
Index crimes
operational definitions
Part I offenses
Part II offenses

positivist criminology
primary data
provincial theories
scientific method
secondary data
trend analysis
universal generalizations

OUTLINE

Introduction
United States versus the World
The Historical Development of Criminology
Statistics

Scientific Method
United States National Crime Databases
International Crime Databases

LEARNING OBJECTIVES

After reading this chapter, students should be able to:

1. Understand the need for comparative studies in criminology and the relationship of these studies to science.

2. Characterize the United States as compared to other countries of the world in its rate of Index crime, violent crime, and property crime.

3. Appreciate how comparative criminology related to the early 19th century development of crime statistics in France.

4. Draw a relationship between the various kinds of statistical studies that are or were done by criminologists in relation to the scientific method.

5. Analyze the various U.S. national crime databases, as well as international crime databases, that are used in this text.

INTRODUCTION

Criminology is the scientific study of crime, criminals, and criminal behavior. As discussed in the first chapter, crime has "gone global"; thus, the study of **comparative criminology** now is not merely an option, but a necessity. We have argued that, given the global nature of crime, the treatment of crime as a global phenomenon should not be confined to advanced courses in criminology, but should also be part of introductory courses in criminology.

Besides the imperative of tracking crime internationally, there is another reason for the cross-cultural study of criminology—science. The goal of criminology is to test theories using available data. If theories are tested using data drawn from the United States, then they are limited in their generalizibility to the United States. Heiner argued strongly that we must test theories outside of the geographical boundaries of the United States:

> (Cross-cultural criminology) is essential in evaluating current criminological theory. In testing these theories, other countries can serve as our laboratories. The social sciences, as all other sciences, are engaged in the search for universal laws, and if a relationship between two or more variables is asserted in a theory, then it should be observable in other countries as well as our own. If the relationship is not observable, then the reason for this inconsistency needs to be identified or the theory needs to be reworked.[1]

The various chapters of this text show that crime in the United States is very much connected with race and racial differences in economic equality. For instance, Chapter 6 demonstrates that (using FBI and Census data) a strong correlate of murder within the United States is race. Blacks have a much higher murder rate than whites. Such a finding might be used by racists to argue for suppression of African Americans within the United States. However, in that same chapter we find that an even stronger correlation than race is the black/white differential in income within the United States. This finding suggests that it is not race, per se, that leads to higher murder rates, but the income difference between blacks and whites in the United States that is the underlying variable. These findings on race and crime are so strong that we might be inclined to believe that we have found the answer to the issue of murder—it is a race issue. However, is this true in other countries? Is murder always high in countries with a high percentage of blacks in the population? Do blacks who are at the bottom of the income ladder always account for high rates of homicide in other countries? If the answer to either question is negative, then it is possible that our findings about the "black subculture of violence" may be limited to the United States, or perhaps a few countries, such as countries with a history of slavery. If that is so, then these generalizations are, in a sense, provincial and possibly even ethnocentric. The term *provincial* refers to being confined to a province or region—in this case the United States. *Ethnocentric* means that a viewpoint is characterized by, or based on, the attitude that one's own group is superior. **Provincial theories** are those that have been tested only in the United States. Such theories may lead to the **ethnocentric viewpoint** that whites are superior to blacks because of the apparent higher crime rate (in this case of murder) of blacks within the United States. When we study crime in other parts of the world, it is apparent that blacks are not always the underclass. For instance, in Peru it is the Indians (called campesinos) who are the underclass and who have been recruited by terrorist organizations, such as *Sendero Luminoso,* to participate in violent acts against the government, which is controlled by white descendents of the Spanish conquerors. In Hungary, the underclass consists of gypsies who are stigmatized as the criminal class, said to be responsible for much property and violent crime. In India, Muslims constitute an underclass, working in service to the more affluent Hindus. Muslims in India are often credited with terrorist acts of violence. In Germany, Turkish immigrants are considered to be a criminal underclass and the object of neo-Nazi skinhead violence. When we study Africa, it is evident that perhaps the majority of African nations report very low crime rates. The African countries with high crime rates are typically those with a large white ruling class (or former white ruling class), a product of colonialism. Examples of this include South Africa and Zimbabwe.

The purpose for the rather extensive discussion of murder, race, and income within the United States is to call attention to the importance of testing theories cross-nationally, because provincial theories may very well lead to ethnocentrism. To test theories cross-nationally, it is necessary to obtain crime data, not just from agencies of the United States, but also from international crime agencies. In addition, we will apply the **scientific method** in utilizing this cross-national data. As we analyze the data in various chapters, we assume that users of this text are familiar both with the scientific method and the various databases that are being used. One purpose of this chapter is to familiarize the reader with both—the numerous databases and the principles of the scientific method. In this chapter we also deal with issues having to do with the extent and trends of crime in the United States and how the United States compares with other countries in its overall crime rate. We analyze individual crimes in the United States, including the FBI's Index crimes—murder, forcible rape, robbery, aggravated assault, burglary, larceny, and auto theft. We also discuss the overall crime rate, which is the sum of the individual crime rates, as measured by the Index.

UNITED STATES VERSUS THE WORLD

Does the United States have the highest crime rate in the world? Before addressing that subject, it should be pointed out that, compared to many if not most countries of the world, the United States is quite advanced in terms of its crime statistics gathering. We have two major national indices of crime— three if you count the 30 years of national self-report studies that have been done by the Institute for Social Research at the University of Michigan. Thus, the United States is quite advanced when it comes to self-analysis. However, are we at the top of the world in terms of the Crime Index? Where do we stand in terms of violent crime? What about property crime—theft? The answer is NO to all three questions. It certainly can be said that, in terms of the database developed for this text (drawn from United Nations and INTERPOL data—discussed later), the United States is at or just below the top 10% in all three respects. However, the United States is typically near the bottom of this top 10%. First, take a look at the United States compared to other countries of the world in terms of its Crime Index in Table 2–1.

Although the United States ranks 12th out of 165 countries in the world in its overall Crime Index, there are quite a few developed countries that rank

Table 2–1 **Rank of the United States among 165 Countries of the World by Crime Index[2]**

Country	Rank	Rate per 100,000
Sweden	1	9604.57
Denmark	2	6971.16
Australia	3	6666.07
Great Britain	4	5955.05
New Zealand	5	5773.43
Netherlands	6	5765.97
Turks & Caicos	7	5138.73
Finland	8	4789.92
France	9	4434.51
South Africa	10	4399.53
Gibraltar	11	4256.68
United States	**12**	**4160.51**

higher. In fact, all of the countries except Turks & Caicos could be considered developed countries.

Alarmists complain that the United States is a violent society, often implying that it is the most violent country in the world. Now look at Table 2–2, which is based upon a comparison of the United States with 164 other countries of the world in terms of its rate of violence. Here the United States is *not* in the top 10% of countries in its rate of violent crime (murder, rape, robbery, and aggravated assault). Although many of the countries ranked higher than the United States in violent crime are developing nations, quite a few are developed countries—Australia, Sweden, Belgium, and South Africa.

Finally, what about property crime? Adding the three property crimes (burglary, larceny-theft, and motor vehicle theft) together, we obtain a "theft" index. Comparing the United States with other countries in the world, the United States ranks 13th out of 160 countries in its rate of theft, as seen in Table 2–3.

Once again, the United States is near the bottom of the top 10 percent of countries. All of the countries with higher theft rates are developed countries, except Turks & Caicos. Why is the United States 12th in its Crime Index when it is lower in both components (violence and theft)? It is probably true that the rate of violence in America is high for a developed country, so that raises the Crime Index compared to other countries of the world. Again, one should bear in mind that what almost all of these countries have in common is good statistical record keeping. They also have professionalized police agencies that not only keep good statistical records, but also manage to affect crime rates through their efforts to catch criminals and encourage the public to report crimes to the police when such crimes occur. Another factor that should be kept in mind is that these are not "tribal" countries, like many in Asia and Africa. In tribal countries, crimes such as theft are dealt with by community courts or councils and may never attain the recognition of official record. Thus, we are not comparing "apples with apples" in these international data comparisons.

Table 2–2 **United States Ranked from High to Low among 164 Countries of the World in Rate of Violent Crime[3]**

Country	Rank	Rate per 100,000
St. Vincent and the Grenadines	1	1468.72
Grenada	2	1449.48
South Africa	3	1302.58
Turks & Caicos	4	875.55
Australia	5	862.13
Sweden	6	796.65
Dominica	7	790.20
Swaziland	8	773.63
Namibia	9	687.64
Antigua & Barbuda	10	649.45
Puerto Rico	11	623.61
Saint Kitts & Nevis	12	604.00
Bahamas, The	13	601.67
Belgium	14	586.51
Latvia	15	570.97
Costa Rica	16	542.94
Botswana	17	523.51
Jamaica	18	511.89
United States	**19**	**504.43**

Table 2–3 **United States Ranked from High to Low with 160 Countries of the World in Property Crime Rate[4]**

Country	Rank	Rate per 100,000
Sweden	1	8808.92
Denmark	2	7402.53
Australia	3	6533.13
Great Britain	4	5724.16
New Zealand	5	5601.72
Netherlands	6	5394.52
Finland	7	4686.91
Turks & Caicos	8	4263.18
Gibraltar	9	3986.67
France	10	3977.20
Germany	11	3748.36
Canada	12	3677.33
United States	**13**	**3656.08**

THE HISTORICAL DEVELOPMENT OF CRIMINOLOGY STATISTICS

The term *statistics* derives from the 17th-century English term "state-istics," which referred to data gathered by the state about births, marriages, and deaths.[5] One of the earliest uses of statistics was the official counts by national governments of their countries' populations. The ancient Greeks conducted censuses to be used as bases for taxation as early as 594 B.C.[6] The publication of national crime statistics dates back to the publication of the *Compte general* (General Account) by the French government in 1827. The *Compte* included data on the annual number of known and prosecuted crimes against persons and property. It indicated whether the accused (if prosecuted) were acquitted or convicted and included the punishment pronounced. Additional data provided in this first crime census included the time of year when the offenses were committed, as well as the age, sex, occupation, and educational status of both the accused and convicted. This first crime report was a response, in part, to public concern about the rising crime rate of the "dangerous classes"—members of the working classes, the unemployed, and the unemployable, who seemed to provide a threat to law and order. It was this publication that enabled the Belgian statistician Adolphe Quetelet to pioneer **positivist criminology.** *Positivism* involved the collection of data to uncover, explain, and predict the ways in which observable facts followed uniform patterns. Quetelet found that there was astonishing uniformity to the rate of crime between 1826–1829, despite the imprisonment of offenders. He also found that certain groups—young males, the poor, and those without employment—had the highest crime rates.[7] In the early 1800s through 1900s, early European criminologists such as Quetelet, Tarde, Verkko, and Durkheim also used government statistics to do *comparative* studies of crime.

Quetelet published a report in 1831 in which he analyzed reported crime data from France and southern European countries. Using these crime data,

Lambert Adolphe Jacques Quetelet (1796–1874)
Source: North Wind Picture Archives.

he examined the effects of education, climate, seasons, sex, and age upon crime. This research produced a surprising finding: that increased education did not produce decreasing crime rates.[8]

Veli Verkko was a Finish criminologist who developed the Finish system of criminal statistics in the early 1900s. He theorized that the Finns' poor tolerance for alcohol, which he believed to be a biological trait, was responsible for the high level of Finnish violent crime. Verkko used very broad international statistical comparisons to test his theory pertaining to "national character."[9]

Even biological criminologist Raffaele Garofalo ventured into comparative study when he described a group of non-Scandinavian people living in Sweden that he felt could support the doctrine of inborn criminality.[10]

Thus, attempts at comparative analysis go back to the very beginnings of criminology as a scientific discipline. In fact, attempts to collect data on crime at the international level date back to 1853 at the General Statistical Congress in Brussels. This attempt was followed by a discussion of international crime data at the International Congress on the Prevention and Repression of Crime in London. At both meetings, the issue of how to define certain crimes proved to be a stumbling block in the collection of crime data.[11] This early interest in comparative databases no doubt reflected the geographical proximity of European nations. The European efforts to develop "international databases" were at that point analogous to U.S. government efforts to develop national statistics for the states. Ultimately, these early efforts culminated in the international crime data gathering by the United Nations and INTERPOL.

SCIENTIFIC METHOD

A goal of science is the development of scientific laws. These are also referred to as **universal generalizations.** There are no scientific laws in the realm of criminology, although ideologues may act as if one or another theory is, in fact, a scientific law. Before generalizations were scientific laws, they were at one time theories. Theories are empirically based explanations and systems of concepts and knowledge explaining facts and phenomena.[12] A theory is evaluated by testing hypotheses, or testable propositions that describe how two or more variables are related, that are drawn from the theory. For a theory to become a scientific law, its hypotheses must be found true universally—throughout the world. For example, one theory discussed in Chapter 4 is ecological theory. This theory states that crime is more prevalent in the inner city and is related to deterioration of inner-city neighborhoods and other factors. A hypothesis drawn from this theory would be something like "the rate of crime varies inversely with geographical location in relation to the center of the city—the further one is from the center of the city, the less the crime." Normally in science, the theory is stated first, then hypotheses are derived from the theory, then a method is derived to test the theory. Terms are "operationalized," or given an **operational definition,** which means the experimenter indicates what data will be used to measure the variables. In the aforementioned hypothesis, distance from the center of the city would probably refer to miles or kilometers from a particular location deemed to be the center of the city.

The operational definition of crime is a more complex manner. Crime rates can be measured by police data, which is referred to as *official data*. Police departments can provide information to researchers on arrest rates in given census areas, as well as offenses that have been reported to the police. Either of these could be used to operationalize the variable, "crime." However, the researcher may be aware that the police do not arrest all criminals. In fact, only about 20% of **Index crimes** in the United States lead to an arrest. Furthermore, not all crimes are reported to the police. Knowing this, the researcher may prefer to obtain victimization data through doing a household survey asking a random sample of residents if they have been victims of crime. Another possibility is that the researcher may measure crime by doing a self-report survey, asking a random sample of residents if they have committed various crimes. Let us suppose that the researcher had the financial resources to do research using all forms of data in a given city such as Chicago—official, victimization, and self-report, and having done such research, the hypothesis being tested was found to be correct in all cases. Would we then have a scientific law? Not yet. The hypothesis (and all other hypotheses drawn from the theory) would have to be tested throughout the world for the theory to be considered a universal generalization or scientific law. The researcher might find cities like Lima, Peru, where the deteriorated housing surrounds the city, while the city itself contains the upscale housing and businesses. Now you are probably beginning to see why social science has yet to discover any universal generalizations.

The Goal of Social Science

The development of one or two scientific laws in social science would probably result in social science becoming accepted as a true science rather than a pseudo-science. However, although this would elevate the prestige of social science, it would not constitute the "end game." This is because of the concern in social science with the development of general theories of causation. General theories invariably involve more than one universal generalization. For instance, ecological theory would predict not just that crime varies inversely with distance from the center of the city. It also holds that living in the inner city makes residents more likely to commit crime or become criminals. In the literature on ecological theory the question has been asked, "does living in the inner city cause a person to become a criminal, or do people who are criminally inclined migrate to the inner city?" In the first instance, the deterioration (or some other aspect) of the inner city would cause the crime (consistent with ecological theory), but in the second instance the criminals cause or are attracted by the deterioration of the inner city (sometimes called the "drift hypothesis," or more recently, "broken windows theory"). To find out about causation, it is necessary to gather data in such a way that the question of which comes first can be answered. There are various methods of data analysis that can be used to answer this question.

Methods of Data Analysis

Two major methods of testing hypotheses are controlled experiments and surveys. Often social scientists, such as sociologists, are found doing surveys, whereas psychologists and biologists may be thought of as running controlled experiments.

Controlled Experiments

The ideal method of data analysis used in science is the controlled experiment. In a controlled experiment, the investigator can manipulate one variable at a time and then observe the outcome of that change on a stimulus group as compared with a control group. Variables are easier to control in a laboratory setting. However, some famous controlled experiments have taken the form of field studies and have been done in law enforcement. In one such study, the effectiveness of one- versus two-police-officer patrols was tested in San Diego, California. The findings were that one-person patrols were just as productive and safe as two-person patrols.[13] Experiments regarding general crime theories, such as the ecological theory, are rare, due to the difficulty of controlling all variables. Ecological theory might be tested in a controlled study of a new housing development or planned community. However, such an experiment would be enormous in its magnitude and costs. Thus, other methods are generally resorted to in order to test theories. It is considered preferable in science that the facts and observations are gathered by the researcher expressly to test the hypotheses of the study. These kinds of data are termed **primary data,** as opposed to accessing information that was previously collected for a different, and often government-related, purpose. These are termed **secondary data**—data that are collected for different reasons than to test an investigator's hypotheses or theory. For instance, the police may collect arrest data to determine where to deploy the most police patrols. If social scientists subsequently use these data to test hypotheses about the relationship between police arrest rates and demographic data such as the location of the crime or offenders within a city, then the social scientists are employing the police data as secondary data.

Surveys

The usual alternative to experiments in social science is to conduct a survey. Examples of surveys that are based on primary data gathered by the investigator are self-report surveys. Surveys that are based on secondary data are those that rely upon data developed by government agencies. These include the FBI's *Uniform Crime Reports* (UCR), which, in a sense, is a survey of police departments' reporting crime arrest rates and offense reports. Also included would be the Department of Justice's *National Crime Victimization Survey* (NCVS), which is based upon interviews with residents of a random sample of households in the United States.

Although we don't have the opportunity to do controlled experiments with whole populations of cities or nations to refute or validate criminological theories, researchers have found ways to simulate controlled experiments using multivariate analysis and longitudinal surveys. *Multivariate analysis* involves using statistical techniques to determine which variables that are involved in a survey are the strongest predictors of a particular variable. *Longitudinal surveys* attempt to measure a given phenomenon over time to determine the effect of a certain variable or variables. For instance, observation of a group of subjects at various intervals in their life might be a fairly good way of determining the effect of age upon the subjects' crime rates. Multivariate analysis might be used along with longitudinal surveys to hold other variables constant (e.g., employment, marriage, education) to determine the significance of age, by itself, as a factor in crime.

Correlation Analysis

Although the development of "planned communities" for the purpose of testing scientific hypotheses is unheard of, another approach may be just as insightful—cross-cultural analysis. In one sense, as suggested earlier by Heiner, the countries of the world are, themselves, conducting one giant experiment. For instance, the former Soviet Block of countries conducted an experiment regarding the effects of a socialist form of government over the better part of the 20th century. We can now see the effects of the socialist experiment upon crime. Thus, comparative analysis can allow us to empirically observe experiments going on all the time in different countries throughout the world. To benefit from this analysis, it is necessary to do **trend analysis,** as well as correlation analysis. Trend analysis consists of observing the increase or decrease in crime in various countries before and after the introduction of a given variable. For instance, for the past 10 years, Switzerland has been experimenting with the administration of "prescription heroin" for registered drug addicts. Trend analysis can indicate whether or not crime in general, or specific crimes such as robbery, have increased or decreased as a result of this experiment. Although multivariate analysis is beyond the domain of this text, some preliminary analyses will be conducted, through the use of correlations, in the chapters pertaining to the Index crimes (Chapters 6–10).

Correlation analysis can also be useful in evaluating the results of various social policy experiments that have been conducted throughout the world. If a particular crime (e.g., automobile theft) seems to correlate strongly with another variable, such as international trade, then we may be observing the results of a national policy experiment. If increasing international trade is followed by an increase in automobile theft, then a causal link *may* be suggested, though by no means proven. We hope that the correlations that are presented in this text will provide a stimulus to further research by researchers who have an interest in the topic.

Because correlation analysis is referred to frequently in this text, the nature of correlation analysis should be discussed before proceeding further. The statistical test we use to measure the degree and direction of association between two variables is Pearson's coefficient of correlation, or *Pearson's r.* The term *correlation* refers to an interrelation between two conditions or events. These events are called *variables* because we are studying the way in which the two conditions or events vary together. Correlations can be negative, positive, or zero. If families with many children tend to have higher rates of crime than families with few children, we say that there is a *positive correlation* between the size of the family and crime rates. On the other hand, if we find that families with a lower income have a higher rate of crime, then a *negative correlation* exists between income and the rate of crime. A third possibility is that the rate of crime is the same regardless of the family income or number of children in the family. This would lead us to say that there is a *zero correlation* between the rate of crime and family income or number of children. The Pearson correlation coefficient is named in honor of Karl Pearson, one of the pioneers of statistics. Pearson's *r* is also known as Pearson's correlation, or zero-order correlation, or linear correlation, or often simply as the coefficient of correlation. Pearson's *r* describes the degree and direction of linear association between two variables, each of which is expressed on an interval scale. Interval scales are the most exacting among scales and are illustrated by variables like height, weight, and temperature. In this text, we typically deal with crime rates and demographic variables that qualify as interval variables. Thus, Pearson's *r* is an appropriate measurement. Pearson's *r* is a function in the Microsoft Excel spreadsheet program, so that those who wish to may check the accuracy of computations given in this text, or do additional analysis using the databases provided with this text. It should be added that a specific correlation value is a measure of the linear relationship between a specific set of paired X and Y scores and nothing more or nothing less. Pearson's *r* does not tell us anything about cause. It is possible that X causes Y or that Y causes X, or that a third variable causes both X and Y.

In various tables throughout the text, different sized correlations will appear. The correlations will usually be between X and Y variables for the states of the United States or the countries of the world. A significance test can also tell us whether or not a correlation could be arrived at "by chance." Using the 1% level of significance, correlations in excess of .372 for the United States and .254 for the world would be statistically significant. We are assuming in this observation a sample size (*N*) of 50 states and 100 or more countries.[14]

Both the United Nations and INTERPOL have warned users against making country comparisons, because of the different definitions used for crimes by different countries, different rates of reporting, and other factors. In fact, at this time INTERPOL no longer offers its data for public view, primarily because such comparisons were being made. The reporting of data by various countries is a sensitive issue. If rates of one or another crime are high compared to other countries, this may lead to a decline in tourism or even of international business trade with the country. However, to do a comparative criminological study, it is, nevertheless, necessary to do country comparisons. We rank order countries in this text to locate countries that are high or low in a particular crime. As a compromise to help meet United Nations and INTERPOL concerns about stigmatizing various countries, we do not present tables that compare all countries for public viewing in the text. However, the tables can be accessed on our website so that investigators who wish to check the accuracy of our computations or do further research can view the data. We also make every effort to validate country rankings with several measures, including United Nations data, INTERPOL data, the *International Crime Victim Surveys* (ICVS), other published surveys, and journalistic accounts.

UNITED STATES NATIONAL CRIME DATABASES

Given these preliminary and historical considerations, a brief review of the different kinds of crime data that we consult in this text is appropriate. In this text, we utilize numerous databases to assess various theories of crime. These include both national and international crime databases, such as the UCR, the NCVS, self-report surveys, United Nations Surveys, INTERPOL crime data, and the ICVS. This overview includes some findings on the extent and trends in crime for the United States in various databases. The extent and trend data for the UCR, the NCVS, and some national self-report surveys are compared. These data are found in most introductory criminology texts. Unique to this text, however, is a comparison of crime rates for the United States with those of the other countries of the world, such as the comparisons that were made at the beginning of this chapter. These comparisons are made using the Comparative Criminology Database (CCDB), which is described along with the other databases that follow.

The FBI's UCR was a product of a committee of the International Association of Chiefs of Police:

> The International Association of Chiefs of Police, recognizing a need for national crime statistics, formed the Committee on Uniform Crime Records in the 1920s to develop a system of uniform police statistics. Establishing offenses known to law enforcement as the appropriate measure, the committee evaluated various crimes on the basis of their seriousness, frequency of occurrence, pervasiveness in all geographic areas of the country, and likelihood of being reported to law enforcement. After studying state criminal codes and evaluating the record keeping practices in use, in 1929 the committee completed a plan for crime reporting that became the foundation of the UCR Program.
>
> Seven offenses were chosen to serve as an index for gauging fluctuations in the overall volume and rate of crime. Known collectively as the Crime Index, these offenses included the violent crimes of murder and nonnegligent manslaughter, forcible rape, robbery and aggravated assault and the property crimes of burglary, larceny-theft, and motor vehicle theft. By congressional mandate, arson was added as the eighth index offense in 1979.
>
> In January 1930, 400 cities collectively representing 20 million inhabitants in 43 states began participating in the UCR Program. Congress enacted Title 28, Section 534, of the United States Code authorizing the attorney general to gather crime information that same year. The attorney general, in turn, designated the FBI to serve as the national clearinghouse for the data collected. Since that time, data based on uniform classifications and procedures for reporting have been obtained from the nation's law enforcement agencies.[15]

J. Edgar Hoover and the Development of the UCR

No discussion of the history of the UCR would be complete without some reference to the role played by J. Edgar Hoover in the development and use of the UCR statistics.

J. Edgar Hoover (1895–1972)

Source: Getty Images, Inc.–Hulton Archive Photos.

In 1924, Hoover was named Director of the Bureau of Investigation, later to be called the Federal Bureau of Investigation (FBI), and held the post for nearly 49 years until his death in 1972.[16] Because Hoover presided over the FBI during nine presidential administrations, his personality undoubtedly had an impact upon the development of the UCR and its use.

Hoover was the son of a low-level federal bureaucrat. His father was an engraver for the U.S. Coast and Geodetic Survey.[17] Hoover was a Christian conservative, a product of a segregated, turn-of-the-century Washington, DC. Hoover graduated from George Washington University with a master of laws degree in 1917. He served as an assistant in the alien registration section of the Department of Justice during World War I, where he monitored "alien radicals," a prelude to a lifetime antiradical crusade.[18] His job involved targeting aliens, pacifists, socialists, and communists who were considered a threat to the nation. In this early employment, Hoover began a practice of accumulating files on the "ultra-radical movement," a procedure that would serve as the bedrock of the FBI's secret security apparatus for nearly 50 years.[19] In keeping with his Southern conservative past, Hoover exhibited attitudes that today would be considered "racist" in regard to African Americans:

> He lectured the cabinet that the law of master and slave in the South was "still the rule." He talked of intelligence, stating that "the claim is made that Southern Negroes are usually below the intellectual level of white children. The further claim is made that it would take a generation to bring the races to parity." He added that southern whites were frightened to share bathrooms and gymnasiums for "colored parents are not as careful in looking after the health and cleanliness of their children." As for the Court-mandated "mixed education," Hoover stated that it "stalks the specter of racial intermarriage."[20]

Thus, Hoover's orientation, a result of his childhood upbringing and his occupational affiliation, could be characterized as antiradical, anticommunist, and prosegregation. One other facet of his biography is relevant—his view of organized crime. During the 1950s, while the FBI was devoting much attention to pursuing communists and alleged communist front organizations, there was little attention given to organized crime. In fact, J. Edgar Hoover was quoted, on the eve of the Kefauver hearings on organized crime in 1950, as announcing that there was no such thing as a "national crime syndicate." "At the time of that statement, Hoover had met socially with Frank Costello, Meyer Lansky, Sam Giancana, and Santos Trafficante, representing the heads of the New York, Las Vegas, Chicago, and Miami Mafia families."[21]

It is shown next that many of the weaknesses of the FBI statistics could be seen as a manifestation of Hoover's personal biases in data gathering. The picture of crime that is drawn using FBI statistics is that crime is committed disproportionately by young black men in urban inner-city areas. Little or no data are available from FBI statistics on organized crime, professional crime, or white-collar crime. Nor are any data included on socioeconomic variables that could be used to interpret a possible relationship between race and crime.

The development of national crime statistics had been an agenda item debated by the International Association of Chiefs of Police (IACP) since it was founded in 1892, and the discussions of crime statistics became a fixed agenda item within the Association of Chiefs of Police after 1898. Efforts to get a bill before Congress were unsuccessful. Starting in 1923, the Association initiated negotiations with the Department of Justice through J. Edgar Hoover, who was enthusiastic about having the Bureau of Investigation assume responsibility for crime reporting, and Hoover was rewarded with his nomination by August Vollmer as an honorary member of the Association in 1924. August Vollmer was Chief of the Berkeley, California Police Department from 1905 to 1932 and 1921 president of the Association. With the monetary support of the Laura Spelman Rockefeller Memorial, the Association published the first edition of *Uniform Crime Reporting: A Complete Manual for Police*, in November, 1929. This document was the result of work by the IACP Committee on Uniform Crime Records. The committee accomplished several objectives. It provided definitions for collecting uniform police data, definitions that were standardized to overcome regional differences in the definitions of criminal offenses. The committee chose to obtain data on offenses that came to the attention of law enforcement agencies because they were more readily available than other crime data. As mentioned earlier, seven offenses, because of their seriousness, frequency of occurrence, and likelihood of being reported to law enforcement, were initially selected to serve as an index for evaluating fluctuations in the volume of crime. These crimes, which became known as the Crime Index, included (a) murder and nonnegligent manslaughter, (b) forcible rape, (c) robbery, (d) aggravated assault, (e) burglary, (f) larceny/theft, and (g) motor vehicle theft. The FBI's definitions of these crimes are given in the text box.

BOX 2–1

Definitions—Part I Offenses in Uniform Crime Reporting[22]

Criminal homicide—a.) Murder and nonnegligent manslaughter: the willful (nonnegligent) killing of one human being by another. Deaths caused by negligence, attempts to kill, assaults to kill, suicides, and accidental deaths are excluded. The Program classifies justifiable homicides separately and limits the definition to: (1) the killing of a felon by a law enforcement officer in the line of duty; or (2) the killing of a felon, during the commission of a felony, by a private citizen. b.) Manslaughter by negligence: the killing of another person through gross negligence. Traffic fatalities are excluded. Although manslaughter by negligence is a Part I crime, it is not included in the Crime Index.

Forcible rape—The carnal knowledge of a female forcibly and against her will. Rapes by force and attempts or assaults to rape regardless of the age of the victim are included. Statutory offenses (no force used—victim under age of consent) are excluded.

Robbery—The taking or attempting to take anything of value from the care, custody, or control of a person or persons by force or threat of force or violence and/or by putting the victim in fear.

Aggravated assault—An unlawful attack by one person upon another for the purpose of inflicting severe or aggravated bodily injury. This type of assault is usually accompanied by the use of a weapon or by means likely to produce death or great bodily harm. Simple assaults are excluded.

Burglary (breaking or entering)—The unlawful entry of a structure to commit a felony or a theft. Attempted forcible entry is included.

Larceny-theft (except motor vehicle theft)—The unlawful taking, carrying, leading, or riding away of property from the possession or constructive possession of another. Examples are thefts of bicycles or automobile accessories, shoplifting, pocket-picking, or the stealing of any property or article that is not taken by force and violence or by fraud. Attempted larcenies are included. Embezzlement, confidence games, forgery, worthless checks, and so forth are excluded.

Motor vehicle theft—The theft or attempted theft of a motor vehicle. A motor vehicle is self-propelled and runs on the surface and not on rails. Motorboats, construction equipment, airplanes, and farming equipment are specifically excluded from this category.

In 1930, Congress enacted legislation authorizing the U.S. Attorney General to gather crime data, and the Attorney General designated the FBI as the national clearinghouse for data collected by the program. Two purposes were initially indicated for the gathering of data: (a) to determine the nature and distribution of crime and (b) to combat the perception of "crime waves" created by the media.[23] On September 1, 1930, the Bureau of Investigation assumed responsibility for collecting, tabulating, and disseminating the UCR.[24]

The FBI gathers both offense data (crimes reported to the police) and arrest data on the Index Crimes. In 1979, arson was added to the list of Part I crimes, but has not been included in the total for Crime Index purposes. UCR offenses are divided into **Part I offenses** and **Part II offenses.** Part I offenses consist of "major crimes known to the police," whereas Part II crimes are measured by the number of arrests for these acts.

Table 2–4 shows the number of offenses, rate of offenses, and clearance rates for the FBI Index crimes.

The FBI does not provide estimates for the crime of arson. Because arson does not form a basis for the Crime Index and is not even estimated by the FBI, it will not be subject to further analysis in this text. (See text box for further discussion of the crime of arson.)

Methodology of the UCR

How can the methodology of the UCR be described in terms of the norms of science, as described previously in this chapter? The FBI provides a lot of data, but one might wonder "for what purpose?" In science, data are usually gathered to test a hypothesis or hypotheses drawn from a theory. The stated purpose of the UCR is to describe the extent and trends in crime, not to test a hypothesis or hypotheses.

The Program's primary objective is to generate a reliable set of criminal statistics for use in law enforcement administration, operation, and management; however, its data have over the years become one of the country's leading social indicators. The American public looks to the UCR for information on

BOX 2–2

Arson

Arson in the UCR is defined as "any willful or malicious burning or attempting to burn, with or without intent to defraud, a dwelling house, public building, motor vehicle or aircraft, personal property of another, etc."[25] Arson was not considered to be a Part I offense in the UCR before 1978. However, it has been estimated that the number of incidents of arson increased by over 3,100 percent, from 5,600 incidents to over 177,000, from 1951 to 1977.[26] Possibly for this reason, arson was designated as a Part I offense by congressional mandate in October 1978, and subsequently added to the FBI Crime Index in 1979.[27] However, it would seem that the reporting of arson by the FBI as an Index Crime has always been problematic. The UCR Program staff does not include arson data in the national offense rates. Rates are computed separately based upon arson data received from all law enforcement agencies that provide data for 12 complete months. Also, arson offenses are excluded from Tables 1–7 of the UCR. The stated reason for this exclusion is the fluctuations in law enforcement agencies' reporting of arson offenses.[28] Because the approach taken in this text is to focus upon serious crimes that are reported internationally, arson must be excluded from our analysis. This is because data are reported for this crime neither to INTERPOL nor the United Nations.

Table 2–4 Offenses in the UCR, 2004[29]

Offense	Number	Rate per 100,000	Arrests	Clearance Rate*
Part I Offenses				
Murder	16,137	5.5	14,004	62.6
Forcible rape	94,635	32.2	26,173	41.8
Robbery	401,326	136.7	109,528	26.2
Aggravated assault	854,911	291.1	440,553	55.6
Burglary	2,143,456	729.9	294,591	12.9
Larceny-theft	6,947,685	2,365.9	1,191,945	18.3
Motor vehicle theft	1,237,114	421.3	147,732	13.0
Crime Index total	11,695,264	3,982.6	2,224,526	20.0
Part II Offenses				
Other assaults			1,285,501	
Forgery/counterfeiting			119.41	
Fraud			282,884	
Embezzlement			17,386	
Stolen property			129,280	
Vandalism			276,543	
Weapons			177,330	
Prostitution			90,231	
Sex offenses			91,395	
Drug abuse violations			1,745,712	
Gambling			10,916	
Offenses against family			125,955	
Driving under influence			1,432,524	
Liquor laws			613,922	
Drunkenness			550,795	
Disorderly conduct			683,850	
Vagrancy			36,082	
All other offenses			3,836,887	
Suspicion			3,554	
Curfew and loitering			138,685	
Runaways			118,966	

*The clearance rate for the Index total is from the 2002 UCR. The FBI ceased reporting the Index and its clearance rate after that report.

fluctuations in the level of crime, and criminologists, sociologists, legislators, municipal planners, the media, and other students of criminal justice use the statistics for varied research and planning purposes.[30] If one is willing to accept the assumption that there is no theory underlying the FBI's quest for data, then the next question is, how is the data gathered? What if a social scientist wanted to find out the extent and trends of crime in America? A single researcher, with limited financial means, could not do a survey of crime victimization or of crime participation by the populace. Let us say that the researcher has received a grant that provides the financial means to send a questionnaire to all of the 20,000 police agencies in the country and ask them to give an estimate of various crimes. The returned questionnaires would serve as a basis for estimating crimes. The returned questionnaires would constitute a **census** of police departments on the issue of crime (as opposed to a **sample**). Police departments, however, don't actually know how many crimes have been committed within their jurisdictions. Instead, they rely upon citizens to report crimes to them. The police do not call all residents within their jurisdiction to ask if they have been victims of crime. Instead, they rely upon people (on their own initiative) to call to report crimes they have observed or have been victimized by. Thus, what the researcher finally ends up with is a sample of all crimes, and it is not even a random sample. Such sampling is referred to as "accidental, haphazard, or convenience sampling." This is similar to using mental patients to estimate the extent of mental illness, disregarding the fact that the mental illness may be highly prevalent among untreated persons in the community.[31]

The method described earlier is what the FBI does in its data gathering on crime—it develops an accidental, haphazard, or convenience sample. Thus, police data are not scientific and probably have to be taken "with a grain of salt." Sutherland and Cressey referred to such statistics as "probably the most unreliable and most difficult of all social statistics," adding that "a large proportion of all law violations goes undetected. Other crimes are detected but not reported, and still others are reported but not officially recorded" and that "in crime statistics the rate as indicated by any set of figures cannot be a sample, for the whole cannot be specified. Both the true rate and the relationship between the true rate and any 'index' of this rate are capricious 'dark figures' which vary with changes in police policies, court policies, and public opinion."[32]

Although Sutherland and Cressey considered the FBI crime statistics to be an inadequate index of the true crime rate, they acknowledged that "the decision to use this rate is probably the best way out of a bad situation."[33] They based their analysis upon Thorsten Sellin's assertion that "The value of criminal statistics as a basis for measurement of criminality decreases as the procedures take us farther away from the offense itself." Thus, Sutherland and Cressey concluded that "these police records are a more reliable index than arrest statistics; arrest statistics are more reliable than court statistics; and court statistics are more reliable than prison statistics."[34]

What exactly is the method used by the FBI in gathering crime statistics? The method used by the FBI is very similar to that hypothetically described

BOX 2–3

Use of Police-Based Data in This Text

Throughout this text, reference will be made to police statistics, not only for the United States, but for countries throughout the world. We are fully aware of the limitations of police-based crime statistics pointed out earlier and discussed more fully later. Thus, we treat them only as a starting point for research. In the comparisons we make, we will be looking primarily at countries at the extreme high end or low end of the nations of the world in terms of one or another crime. However, we recognize that even with these high- or low-end comparisons, it is entirely possible that we are wrong about the country, based upon such data. So in all cases we seek to draw upon other data, such as self-reports or victim surveys, to corroborate our ranking of countries.

earlier. The FBI receives data through state UCR Programs in 46 states and Washington, DC. For the remaining states, data are received by the FBI directly from local law enforcement agencies. State UCR Programs serve as liaisons between local contributors and the FBI. Many of the state Programs have mandatory reporting requirements. For states with state UCR Programs, the national UCR Program does not collect data from individual law enforcement agencies within those states.

The FBI has criteria for the state Programs to ensure consistency and comparability of the data submitted to the national Program, as well as regular and timely reporting. The criteria are as follows:

1. The state Program must conform to national UCR Program standards, definitions, and information requirements.

2. The state criminal justice agency must have a proven, effective, statewide Program and demonstrate acceptable quality control procedures.

3. Coverage within the state by a state agency must be, at least, equal to that attained by the national UCR Program.

4. The state agency must have adequate field staff assigned to conduct audits and to assist contributing agencies in record keeping practices and crime-reporting procedures.

5. The state agency must furnish the FBI with all of the detailed data regularly collected by the FBI in the form of duplicate returns, computer printouts, and/or magnetic tapes.

6. The state agency must have the proven capability (tested over a period of time) to supply all the statistical data required in time to meet deadlines established for publication of the national UCR.[35]

Agencies across the country tabulate the number of Crime Index (Part I) offenses each month, based upon records of all reports of crime received from victims, officers who discover offenses, or other sources. Agencies report to the FBI the number of actual offenses known regardless of whether anyone is arrested for the crime, stolen property is recovered, or prosecution is undertaken. In addition to the account of Index crimes reported, the monthly submission also includes the total number of actual Crime Index offenses cleared. Crimes are cleared in one of two ways: (a) by arrest of at least one person, who is charged and turned over to the court for prosecution, or (b) by "exceptional means" when some element beyond law enforcement control precludes the arrest of a known offender (e.g., the offender is in another country and cannot be extradited). In addition to data on Index offenses, the monthly report includes data on persons arrested for all crimes except traffic violations. The age, sex, and race of arrestees are reported by crime category, both Part I and Part II. Part II offenses include all crimes not classified as Part I. Monthly data are also collected on law enforcement officers killed or assaulted, and at the end of each quarter, summary information is collected on hate crimes. Hate crimes are offenses motivated by an offender's bias against the race, religion, ethnic origin, sexual orientation, or physical or mental disability of the victim.

Throughout the country, the national UCR Program provides training sessions for police departments and provides copies of the *Uniform Crime Reporting Handbook,* which details procedures for classifying and scoring offenses. In

BOX 2–4

How to Compute Crime Rates

$$\text{Crime Rate} = \frac{\text{Number of Reported Crimes}}{\text{Total Population}} \times 100{,}000$$

addition, the FBI provides the *Manual of Law Enforcement Records* to instruct departments in the basics of building a good recordkeeping system. The UCR Program is a nationwide, cooperative statistical effort of more than 17,000 city, county, and state law enforcement agencies. During 2004, law enforcement agencies active in the UCR Program represented 95.4% of the total population as established by the Bureau of the Census.[36] The total population estimate for the United States in 2004 was 293,655,404.[37] Because the population varies by year, the FBI reports not just the number of offenses, but also the rate of offenses. The rate of offenses is a means of standardizing the data to make them comparable on a year-by-year basis (or cross-nationally). The formula for computation of rates is provided in the text box.

For instance, in 2004 there were 16,137 reported instances of "murder and nonnegligent manslaughter." This figure (16,137) divided by the population (293,655,404) times 100,000 equals a crime rate of 5.5 for the year 2004.

Extent and Trends in Crime

How extensive is crime in America and what are the trends? We consider the questions of extent and trends together because the issue of how extensive crime is can only be dealt with comparatively. If we say that the Crime Index rate (all seven major crimes combined) in 2004 was 3,982.6 per 100,000 inhabitants, the rate quoted is meaningless except when compared to something. It is helpful to compare this rate with historical rates. The study of history is intrinsically comparative in nature. However, it is also insightful to compare this rate with that of other countries of the world, as was done earlier in this chapter.

For now we need to know if a rate of 3,982.6 per 100,000 inhabitants is high or low historically. Table 2–5 shows the Crime Index rates for years 1960–2004.

It can be seen that the 2004 Index rate of 3,982.6 is low compared to 1980 (5,950), when the Crime Index rate peaked in the United States. However, the crime rate of 3,982.6 is high compared to the rate for 1960, which was 1,887.2. The 2004 rate of 3,982.6 is a steep drop compared to the 1991 rate of 5,897.8, which was a more recent high rate, very close to that of 1980.

It should be noted that the Crime Index combines seven different crimes that, we believe, should be examined individually. The variation in trends for different Index crimes is shown in the trend analysis. In 2004, the murder rate for the United States was 5.5 per 100,000 inhabitants. This was down from a high of 9.8 in 1991 and a 44-year high of 10.2 in 1980, but up from 4.6 in 1962 and 1963. The rate of aggravated assault was 291.1 per 100,000 inhabitants in 2004. Aggravated assault is often grouped with murder as a crime of violence, but it can be seen that its trend analysis is more like rape than like murder. The rate of forcible rape was 32.2 in 2004. Both forcible

Table 2–5 **Crime Index Rates by Year**[38]

Year	Index	Year	Index
1960	1,887.2	1983	5,175.0
1961	1,906.1	1984	5,031.3
1962	2,019.8	1985	5,207.1
1963	2,180.3	1986	5,480.4
1964	2,388.1	1987	5,550.0
1965	2,449.0	1988	5,664.2
1966	2,670.8	1989	5,741.0
1967	2,989.7	1990	5,820.3
1968	3,370.2	1991	5,897.8
1969	3,680.0	1992	5,660.2
1970	3,984.5	1993	5,484.4
1971	4,164.7	1994	5,373.5
1972	3,961.4	1995	5,274.9
1973	4,154.4	1996	5,087.6
1974	4,850.4	1997	4,927.3
1975	5,298.5	1998	4,615.5
1976	5,287.3	1999	4,266.5
1977	5,077.6	2000	4,124.0
1978	5,140.4	2001	4,162.6
1979	5,565.5	2002	4,125.0
1980	5,950.0	2003	4,067.0
1981	5,858.2	2004	3982.6
1982	5,603.7		

rape and aggravated assault increased steadily from 1960 up to a peak year of 1992, when the rate of forcible rape was 42.8 per 100,000 inhabitants and the rate of aggravated assault was 441.8 per 100,000 inhabitants. Rape was lowest in 1961–1963 at 9.4 per 100,000 inhabitants, whereas aggravated assault was lowest in 1961. The rate of robbery in 2004 was 136.7 per 100,000 inhabitants. Robbery peaked in 1991 with a rate of 272.7 and had its lowest rate of 58.3 in 1961.

In the UCR, property crimes include burglary, larceny-theft, and motor vehicle theft. In 2004, the rate of burglary per 100,000 inhabitants was 729.9, whereas the rate of larceny-theft was 2,365.9 and the rate of motor vehicle theft was 421.3 per 100,000 inhabitants. A 41-year analysis shows larceny-theft and motor vehicle theft to be following the same trend. Both peaked in 1991, larceny-theft with a rate of 3,228.8 and motor vehicle theft with a rate of 658.9. Both were at their lowest in 1960, larceny theft with a rate of 1,034.7 and motor vehicle theft with a rate of 183.0. By contrast, burglary peaked in 1980 with a rate of 1,684.1, and has declined almost every year since that peak. Today's rate of burglary is slightly lower than half that of the peak rate in 1980, and not much higher than the lowest year, which was 1960, with a burglary rate of 508.6. Of the seven major crimes, murder and burglary today are pretty close to their 1960 rate, whereas the remaining crimes of rape, robbery, assault, larceny, and vehicle theft are multiples of two to four times their 1960 rate.

The basis for these changes has been the subject of speculation regarding the underlying causes. The term "speculation" is used here because, as will be noted, a number of variables can account for the rise and fall of crime rates besides actual changes in crime. Nevertheless, the explanations that have been given for these trends are interesting to note. Schmalleger has provided an excellent analysis of long-term trends shown by the FBI data:

Since the UCR began, there have been two major shifts in crime rates—and we are in the middle of what is now a third. The first occurred during the early 1940s, when crime decreased sharply due to the large number of young men who entered military service during World War II. . . . From 1933 to 1941, the Crime Index declined from 770 to 508 offenses per 100,000. . . . The second noteworthy shift in offense statistics—a dramatic increase in most forms of crime between 1960 and the early 1990s—also had a link to World War II. . . . Birthrates skyrocketed between 1945 and 1955, creating a postwar baby boom. By 1960, baby boomers were entering their teenage years . . . the baby boom generation swelled the proportion of the American population in the crime-prone age range. . . . The 1960s were tumultuous years. . . . The "normless" quality of American society in the 1960s contributed greatly to the rise in crime. From 1960 to 1980, crime rates rose from 1,887 to 5,590 offenses per every 100,000 U.S. residents. Crime rates continued their upward swing, with a brief respite in the early 1980s when postwar boomers began to age out of the crime-prone years. . . . About the same time, however, an increase in drug-related criminal activity led crime rates to soar once again. . . . Crime rates peaked during the early 1990s. We have since undergone a third major shift, with significant declines in the rate of most major crimes being reported.[39]

Numerous reasons for the apparent decline in crime in the 1990s were described in a Department of Justice report.

Essentially, the report credited a national initiative that led to a more coordinated national law enforcement effort; collaboration between government agencies; stronger criminal justice agencies, including improved technology; an emphasis upon community policing; gun control legislation; "get tough on crime" sentencing reform; a national effort to assist victims of crime; and increasing incarceration of offenders. Especially noteworthy, as discussed in Chapter 9, is the Violence against Women Act, passed in 1994. In the chapter on assault, we characterize assault as the "common cold of crime." What seems to be the case is that crime is very much a product of domestic violence. There seems to be a "ripple effect" of this form of assault upon the children being raised in families affected by domestic violence. A movement to assist victims of domestic violence that occurred in the 1990s may have had an indirect effect upon many forms of crime, because children from such families often come to live on the street as runaways and to pursue a life of crime themselves.

Criticisms of the UCR

Debate regarding the adequacy of the statistics presented in the UCR occurred both during its development and after the publication of the first volume in

BOX 2-5

Reversing the Upward Trend of Crime [40]

- A more coordinated national effort—In 1968, Congress passed the Safe Streets Act.
- Stronger, better prepared criminal justice agencies—Criminal justice capabilities of all levels of government have been significantly strengthened over the past three decades.
- Community policing—Beginning in the 1980s more and more agencies shifted to a community policing model.
- Combating gun violence—In the 1990s, the Federal Government, as well as many states, adopted a more aggressive approach to gun control.
- Involving victims—A movement to focus on the needs of crime victims began to gather strength in the late 1970s. In 1984, the federal Victims of Crime Act established an Office for Victims of Crime in the Department. In addition, the Violence Against Women Act, enacted in 1994, improved the response of the nation's criminal and civil justice systems to victims of domestic violence, sexual assault, and stalking.
- Sentencing reform—Faced with demands to "get tough on crime" in some quarters and to eliminate what was thought to be unequal justice in others, legislatures began curtailing judicial discretion and prescribing mandatory prison sentences for particular classes of offenses and for particular types of offenders. At the federal level, the Sentencing Reform Act of 1984 established federal sentencing guidelines requiring mandatory prison terms for certain offenses. It also abolished federal parole.
- Incarceration of offenders—By 1999, about 1.8 million persons were incarcerated—an all-time high.

1930. In 1930, the UCR was questioned by, among others, the U.S. Census Bureau, on the basis of UCR statistical deficiencies.[41] In 1931, despite the existence of the UCR, the Wickersham Commission recommended development of a "comprehensive plan for a complete body of statistics covering crime, criminals, criminal justice, and penal treatment" at the Federal, State, and local levels.[42] Over the years, numerous criticisms of the UCR by social scientists have been generated.

> Uniform Crime Reports attempt to satisfy ". . . the need of the police, the demands of the general public, and the concerns of scholars seeking to understand social deviance." They possess limited utility as a tool for scholars. They are marred by the failure of victims to report crimes and the failure of officers to record crimes accurately. The reporting system itself—categorizing police reports into typologies (Part I, Part II offenses)—invites further statistical error. Donald Black has described the complexity of producing official crime reports: Whether or not a complaint, if it ever reaches the police, enters into the official process of reporting is dependent upon its legal seriousness, the complainant's preference for police action, the distance of the relationship between the complainant and the suspect, the complainant's degree of deference toward the officer, and the complainant's social status. There is ample evidence to suggest that organizational imperatives also impinge upon the collection of data for the Uniform Crime Reports. David Seedman and Michael Conzens have argued persuasively that police departments show evidence of rising or falling crime rates based upon the political pressures they are experiencing. The Uniform Crime Reports, being merely the summation of a series of

local responses to partisan issues, are ". . . highly misleading for what they are said to measure . . ." The UCR system, then, is ". . . useless as a tool for evaluation of social policy."[43]

Despite the avalanche of social science criticism, the UCR showed little change in the data reported and the methodology behind the data reporting since 1930. However, the pressure for reform became evident at the national level with the publication of the 1967 *President's Commission Report on Law Enforcement and The Administration of Justice*. That commission, through focusing upon the crime data needed at the national level, produced a harsh critique of the UCR:

> Given the importance of sound data to both crime control and public understanding, it is hard to believe that such basic facts as the trend of juvenile delinquency, the percent of crimes committed by professionals, or the likelihood of recidivism are beyond the capacity of our present statistical resources. In some respects the present system is not as good as that used in some European countries 100 years ago. There are no national and almost no State or local statistics at all in a number of important areas: the courts, probation, sentencing, and the jails. There are important deficiencies in those statistics which are collected. There is no reliable measure of the extent of organized crime and no satisfactory test for police performance. In short, the United States is today, in the era of the high speed computer, trying to keep track of crime and criminals with a system that was less than adequate in the days of the horse and buggy.[44]

In regard to the previous comment that the "present system is not as good as that used in some European countries 100 years ago," it may be recalled that the French *Compte* of 1827 contained the following data:

> The *Compte* included data on the annual number of known and prosecuted crimes against persons and property. It indicated whether the *accused (if prosecuted) were acquitted or convicted, and included the punishment pronounced.* Additional data included in this first census included the time of year when the offenses were committed, as well as the age, sex, *occupation, and educational status of both accused and convicted.* (Italics added for emphasis.)

The previous paragraph contains in italics the data obtained from that first French survey that are not contained in the current UCR. Further, we see that, insofar as occupation and educational status of both the accused and convicted, such data is left out of all U.S. government national surveys of crime. Although the UCR contains information on the race of offenders, no data are given in that publication having to do with the economic circumstances of the offender or victim (occupation, income, education). Thus, potential findings concerning a link between race and crime cannot be controlled for possible socioeconomic variables underlying this relationship.

The 1967 President's Commission argued for the development of an autonomous National Criminal Justice Statistics Center (separate from the FBI) to be located within the Department of Justice. The commission also pointed out the need for victim surveys to be conducted by the federal government. Furthermore, in 1966 the commission conducted, with the help of the National Opinion Research Corporation, the first such wide-scale survey of crime victimization ever undertaken. The federal government has responded to these suggestions through establishing the National Criminal Justice Reference Service (NCJRS) within the Department of Justice. The NCJRS has performed the function of coordinating the data-gathering efforts of numerous government agencies and provides online access to data and publications.[45] In addition, a national crime victimization survey conducted by the Bureau of Census in cooperation with the Bureau of Justice Statistics, within the Department of Justice, began in 1972.

Besides criticisms by the Census Bureau and the 1967 President's Commission, numerous other criticisms have been advanced in regard to the UCR. It is shown later that very different trends in crime have been shown by the NCVS (the Nation's "other" major database), notably that the crime rate has not been increasing, but instead has been declining. Are there any reasons to distrust the UCR as a source of data? Could the trends discussed earlier be a product of factors other than actual increases or decreases in crime?

1. **Improved data tabulation**—There is evidence that as police departments become more professional, they tend to become more efficient in reporting crime, so that increasing police professionalism rather than increasing crime may be what is being measured. Sometimes tremendous apparent increases of crime can occur because of improvements in police data tabulation techniques. For instance, Daniel Bell found that in New York in 1948 reports of crime were made to precinct stations. Reportedly:

> Detectives receiving slips regarding burglaries would "paste them in their hats" and wait, usually, until a burglar might be nabbed who would confess to other "unsolved" burglaries. Following a survey by police expert Bruce Smith, a new system of central recording was installed. All precinct numbers, for example, were taken out of the New York telephone book, and any person wishing to report a crime had to call the central station. . . . In the one year following the change, assaults rose 200 percent, robberies 400 percent, and burglaries 1,300 percent over 1948 figures. As Smith concluded, "such startling rises . . . do not themselves represent an increase in crime, but rather a vast improvement in crime reporting."[46]

The computerization of data tabulation improved significantly in the mid-1980s and could have accounted for some of the rise in crime rates that peaked in 1991 and 1992.

2. **Padding of clearance rates**—Some departments may be touting a new program, such as community policing, and may pad **clearance rates** in a practice known as "slate cleaning" to demonstrate the effectiveness of their

new program. For instance, a burglar may confess to a hundred burglaries (in exchange for a generous plea bargain) thus "clearing" the crimes and upping the burglary clearance rate.[47]

3. **Clearance rate effect upon reporting**—Clearance rates themselves can have an effect upon "crimes known to the police" in the sense that if clearance rates are high, crime victims may be more likely to report the crime because of victims' perceptions of law enforcement effectiveness. In 1960, 75.8% of aggravated assaults were cleared compared to only 55.6% in 2004. If the odds are not good that the police will arrest an assaulter, victims are less likely to report the crime, fearing possible revenge by the perpetrator if the police fail to make an arrest. Similarly, victims of burglary are probably less likely to report a burglary if the police catch only 12.9% of burglars in 2004 compared to almost one third of burglars (29.5%) for 1960.

4. **Police misclassification of crime**—Police have discretion in classifying crimes that may result in a change in the rate of crime and the clearance rate. For instance, as shown in Chapter 8, reports of rape increased tremendously between 1995 and 2001, yet the rate of forcible rape went down during that time. It is possible that the police responded to this wave of rape reporting by recording the rapes as "sex offenses" or "other assaults (simple)" that are Part II offenses. During the late 1990s, police departments were striving to get a cut of the grants that emanated from President Bill Clinton's Cops on the Beat program, which was signed into law by the President in 1994. This bill provided $8.8 billion in competitive grants for state and local law enforcement agencies to hire community policing officers and to implement community policing, with a goal of putting 100,000 police officers on America's streets.[48] Because clearance rates are a major way that police departments demonstrate their efficiency, departments had an interest in improving these rates either through a campaign of "slate cleaning" (described earlier) or through classifying solvable cases of rape as forcible rapes, and unsolvable cases as "sex offenses" or "simple assaults."

BOX 2–6

Clearance Rates

The term "clearance rate" refers to the proportion of reported crimes that have been "solved."[49] Crimes can be cleared by arrest or by exceptional means. The usual way that offenses are cleared is that the perpetrator is arrested, charged with the commission of an offense, and turned over to the court for prosecution. The arrest of a single person may result in the clearance of any number of crimes, if the person confesses to those crimes or can be linked to them by eye witness testimony, forensic evidence, or other evidence. Examples of this would be serial killers and serial rapists. If law enforcement authorities are unable to make an arrest but have gathered enough evidence to support an arrest, make a charge, and turn the offender over to the court for prosecution, the crime can be cleared by exceptional means. Examples of exceptional clearances include the death of the offender, denial of extradition by a foreign country, or refusal of the victim to cooperate with the prosecution after the identification of the offender.[50]

In 2004, the clearance rates for offenses cleared by arrest were murder 62.6, forcible rape 41.8, robbery 26.2, aggravated assault 55.6, burglary 12.9, larceny-theft 18.3, and motor vehicle theft 13.[51] By way of comparison, the clearance rates in 1960 for those same crimes were murder 92.7, forcible rape 72.5, robbery 38.5, aggravated assault 75.8, burglary 29.5, larceny-theft 20.1, and motor vehicle theft 25.7.[52]

5. **The "dark figure" of crime**—The reporting of crimes to the police may be variable. In fact, there is an unknown, but possibly considerable, amount of crime that goes unreported to the police and therefore never shows up in the UCR. This component is often referred to as the **dark figure of crime.** As mentioned previously, victims may fear reprisals from offenders, and/or may not trust the police. It is possible that an influx of Asian and Latino immigrants that occurred in the 1990s may have affected reporting rates, because members of the immigrant community may be disinclined to report crimes. Their reason for not reporting crime may have to do with their undocumented status or a distrust of police that may stem from experience with police in their country of origin.

6. **Omission of serious crimes**—A major criticism of the UCR (that may or may not have to do with trends) is the fact that some serious crimes are not included in Part I offenses. No federal crimes are recorded by the FBI. Some Part II offenses, such as forgery and counterfeiting, fraud, embezzlement, and drug-law violations may be treated by both federal and state law as serious felonies, yet they are omitted from Part I. In addition, the emphasis in the UCR upon conventional street crimes is said to deflect attention from such illegal acts as corporate violence, political crime, and organized crime.[53]

7. **Lack of police department participation**—Not all police departments send crime reports to the FBI, causing the FBI to estimate the crime rates in such jurisdictions.

8. **The hierarchy rule**—In the UCR's traditional reporting system, if multiple crimes are committed in a single incident of crime, only the most serious crime is reported. For instance, if a family is victimized by a carjacking in which the husband is murdered, the wife is raped, and the children are abducted, only the murder would be reported to the FBI. The kidnapping would not be reported at all, since it is neither a Part I nor Part II offense. In this incident, the rape and the robbery (carjacking) would be underreported as Index crimes.

9. **Bias in the crime rate total**—The Crime Index total actually misrepresents the crime rate in a given year, because there is no weighting for seriousness of the component crimes. In some years, high larceny rates may inflate the Crime Index, even though crimes of violence may be relatively low. For instance, in 1980 the Crime Index rate was 5,950.0, highest for the 41 years from 1960 to 2004. However, this rate was inflated by the burglary rate of 1,684.1, which was highest that year, as well. How ever, in 1991, violent crimes were considerably higher than 1980, with a combined total rate for violent crimes of 758.1 in 1991, compared to only 596.6 for 1980.

The FBI has continued with its annual UCR but has moved toward developing a "new UCR," termed the National Incident-Based Reporting System (NIBRS), which will capture detailed information on not seven but 22 crime categories and 46 separate offenses (see text box). Despite its advantages, only 29 states were certified for NIBRS participation by 2004. Thus, we cannot use the NIBRS as a basis for estimating the extent or trends in crime for the United States. It may be noted that even with the massive amount of new data provided by the NIBRS, there are no socioeconomic data

BOX 2–7

The National Incident-Based Reporting System (NIBRS)[54]

The NIBRS is a part of the UCR Program, administered by the FBI. In the late 1970s, the law enforcement community called for a thorough evaluative study of the UCR with the objective of recommending an expanded and enhanced UCR program to meet law enforcement needs into the 21st century. The FBI fully concurred with the need for an updated program to meet contemporary needs and provided its support, formulating a comprehensive redesign effort. Following a multiyear study, a "Blueprint for the Future of the UCR Program" was developed. Using the "Blueprint" and in consultation with local and state law enforcement executives, the FBI formulated new guidelines for the Uniform Crime Reports. The NIBRS is being implemented to meet these guidelines. The data focus on a variety of aspects of a crime incident, including data on the incident itself (date and time). Also provided are offense characteristics (offense type, location, weapon use, and bias motivation), type and value of property stolen and recovered, characteristics of the victim(s) (age, sex, race, ethnicity, and injuries), characteristics of the offender(s) (age, sex, and race), and characteristics of

persons arrested (arrest date, age, sex, race, and weapon use). This extensive data is provided for 22 general Group A offenses which, with subtypes, include 46 actual offenses. These include the eight Index crimes, plus some crimes that may fall into the categories of political, organized, or white-collar crime, such as bribery, counterfeiting, drug offenses, embezzlement, extortion, fraud, gambling offenses, and kidnapping. In addition to these and the Index crimes, Group A also includes vandalism, pornography, prostitution, sex offenses, stolen property offenses, and weapon law violations. Some Part I offenses that might have been diverted to Part II previously are covered as Group A offenses in the NIBRS. These include simple assault, forcible sodomy, sexual assault with an object, forcible fondling, incest, and statutory rape. Group B offenses includes only arrestee data for crimes that include bad checks, curfew violations, disorderly conduct, and other minor offenses. As with UCR, participation in NIBRS is voluntary on the part of law enforcement agencies. The data are not a representative sample of crime in the United States. For 2002, 23 states, fully or partially participating in NIBRS, were included in the dataset.

(occupation, education, income) pertaining either to offenders or victims in this new 21st century program.

In this volume, one study using the NIBRS is described in detail. However, because the NIBRS is not yet a national database, most discussion will continue to draw from the UCR and one other national publication—the NCVS. Because the NCVS, recommended by the 1967 President's Crime Commission, was second to develop as a national measure of crime, we turn our attention to that survey next.

NCVS The NCVS is a "scientific survey" in the sense that it is a survey based upon the scientific methodology of random sampling. The survey consists of interviews with persons aged 12 and older in a random sample of U.S. households. The interviews pertain to the respondent's experiences as victims of crime. By contrast, the UCR is an unscientific survey based upon an "accidental" sample of crime cases that are encountered by the police. A large number of studies have been done by criminologists using both of these surveys (the NCVS and the UCR) as sources of data; however, studies derived from both sources should be considered to be the product of *secondary data analysis*. Frequently, researchers have tested hypotheses using these secondary data sources. Unfortunately, the hypotheses are often limited by the lack of variables that are provided by the UCR or the NCVS.

Development of the NCVS

The pilot study for today's NCVS was conducted by the President's Commission on Law Enforcement and Administration of Justice during the 1960s. Findings and recommendations of that study were published by the 1967 President's Commission on Law Enforcement and Administration of Justice. A product of the recommendations of this report was federal funding for the Law Enforcement Assistance Administration (LEAA), which conducted the first few national victimization surveys in 1972, 1973, and 1974 (published in 1973–1975).[55] The findings of these surveys were published in a report entitled the *National Crime Survey*. These first few reports proved to be controversial. On the one hand, these reports showed the incidence of crime to be far greater than estimated by the FBI. On the other hand, the reports suggested that crime victimization was declining. After 1975, the *National Crime Survey* continued as an effort of the Bureau of Justice Statistics in cooperation with the Census Bureau.[56] Starting in 1989, the survey was redesigned and a new methodology was field-tested. The redesign was based upon criticism of the earlier survey's capacity to gather information about certain crimes, including sexual assaults and domestic violence. The improved survey methodology was said to enhance the ability of people being interviewed to recall events.[57] More direct questioning about sexual assaults was permitted in the survey. In fact, the revised method of questioning may be described as "relentless":

> Perhaps the single most pronounced change to the survey was the total revision of the screener. A number of different screening strategies were tested during the research and development phase of the redesign project, with the aim of improving the respondent's ability to define, search for, recall, and report victimizations suffered during the reference period. *The most effective approach was to pepper respondents with a number of short cues to evoke the context in which victimizations might occur,* including types of places where an attack could take place, possible relationships to the offender, type of property that might have been stolen, and types of weapons that might have been used in an attack. (Italics added for emphasis.) . . . This screener revision resulted in an increase of 48% in rates of personal crimes, 54% in violent crime, and 23% in property crime.[58]

The first annual results from the redesigned survey were published for 1993. Before the redesign in 1988, the survey was termed the *National Crime Survey,* whereas during and after the redesign (starting in 1989), the survey was termed the NCVS. Kappeler, Blumberg, and Potter argued that the "redesign" was done with a political agenda in mind:

> This redesign may have simply been part of the ongoing methodological review of the NCVS, which attempts annually to increase the reliability and validity of the data. On the other hand, this redesign may have had more sinister and diabolical implications. As we have seen, the NCVS has demonstrated clearly that contrary to politicians' proclamations and public impressions, serious crime has been declining precipitously in America for the past two decades. Those are hardly data which justify new expenditures on law enforcement and prisons; expansion of the criminal law; the extension of the death penalty to a plethora of new offenses; and a "crime crisis" mentality in policy making. The reclassification of criminal

acts in the redesigned survey makes it inevitable that the victimization rates and frequencies will be higher than in the surveys of the previous twenty years. Perhaps the survey redesign was a bit of methodological legerdemain intended to give the appearance that the incidence of victimizations was increasing. Perhaps the intent was simpler. By changing the survey and the classification of crimes in that survey the Justice Department has made it impossible to continue a longitudinal comparison of data into the future. . . . The Department of Justice has, intentionally or otherwise, made continuing analysis of a trend which negates the official position impossible.[59]

The "precipitous decline" talked about by Kappeler, Blumberg, and Potter referred to the decline in crime from 1973 to 1991. They found that, during this period, personal crimes (rape, robbery, assault, and personal larceny) decreased by 25.3%. Also, household crimes (burglary, household larceny, and motor vehicle theft) decreased 25.2%. Only simple assault and motor vehicle theft (among these crimes) showed increases.

We have found that, regardless of the fears of a diabolical plot by politicians and statisticians, the NCVS rates have continued to decline, as shown in Table 2–6, drawn in part from data compiled by Kappeler, Blumberg, and Potter.

It would seem from Table 2–6 that the new improved "methodological legerdemain" did not result, in the long run, in an explosion in crimes reported by the NCVS, nor did it make future comparisons impossible. However, there is evidence that the methodological changes may have produced *short-run* apparent increases in some crime categories. When the NCVS became available online in 1995, there were reported increases in various categories over the 1991 data given earlier. During the period from 1991 to 1995, rape increased from 0.8 per 1,000 households to 1.1 per 1,000. Robbery actually declined slightly from 5.6 per 1,000 in 1991 to 5.3 per 1,000 in 1995. Reported aggravated assault increased from 7.8 per 1,000 in 1991 to 8.7 per 1,000 in 1995. Simple assault increased significantly from a rate of 17.0 in 1991 to 28.9 in 1995. Larceny with contact decreased from a rate of 2.3 in 1991 to

Table 2–6 **Victimization Rates per 1,000 Households in 1973, 1991, 1995, and 2004**[60]

Crime	Victimization Rates				Percentage Change		
	1973	1991	1995	2004	1973–1991	1991–2004	1973–2004
Rape	1.0	0.8	1.1	0.4	− 20.0	− 100.0	− 60.0
Robbery	6.7	5.6	5.3	2.1	− 16.4	− 166.7	− 68.7
Aggravated assault	10.1	7.8	8.7	4.3	− 22.8	− 81.4	− 57.4
Simple assault	14.8	17.0	28.9	14.2	14.9	− 19.7	− 4.0
Larceny with contact	3.1	2.3	1.7	0.9	− 25.8	− 155.6	− 71.0
Larceny without contact	195.0	146.7	216.0	122.8	− 24.8	− 19.5	− 37.0
Household burglary	91.7	53.1	47.3	29.6	− 42.1	− 79.4	− 67.7
Motor vehicle theft	19.1	21.8	16.2	8.8	14.1	− 147.7	− 53.9
Total	341.5	255.1	325.0	183.1	− 25.3	− 39.3	− 46.4

1.7 in 1995. Larceny without contact increased from 146.7 to 216.0 over the two time periods, while motor vehicle theft declined from 21.8 to 16.2 from 1991 to 1995. Thus, the new methodology of the NCVS may have affected short-term trends in the positive direction, particularly for simple assault and larceny without contact. However, the long-run impetus of the downward trend in reported crime was not altered by the improved methodology. Were the changes in the NCVS necessary, or were they just a means of "jacking up" the crime rate as a means of promoting a conservative political agenda? Frankly, there were some serious concerns about the validity of the victimization survey data that will be discussed later. It would seem that the NCVS has benefited appreciably from the improved methodology.

Methodology of the NCVS

Today's NCVS is a survey of victimization based upon a stratified, multistage cluster sample. In 2004, the survey included 84,360 households and 149,000 persons interviewed. Each person 12 years or older in the household is interviewed. Each housing unit remains in the sample for three years, with each of seven interviews taking place at six-month intervals. An NCVS interviewer's first contact with a housing unit selected for the survey is in person. The interviewer may then conduct subsequent interviews by telephone. Some interviews are conducted using Computer-Assisted Telephone Interviewing, a data collection mode that involves interviewing from centralized facilities and using a computerized survey instrument. To conduct field interviews, the sample is divided into six groups, or rotations, and each group of households is interviewed once every six months over a period of three years. The first interview is used to "bound" the interviews (bounding establishes a time frame to avoid duplication of crimes on subsequent interviews), but is not used to compute the annual estimates. Each rotation group is further divided into six panels. A different panel of households, corresponding to one sixth of each rotation group, is interviewed each month during the 6-month period.[61]

The original purpose of the National Crime Survey was to provide data pertaining to the FBI's Index crimes. Only six Index crimes were included: rape, robbery, aggravated assault, burglary, larceny, and motor vehicle theft. Criminal homicide was excluded because the victim could not be interviewed. Arson was added to the Index as a crime by Act of Congress in 1979, since the inception of the National Crime Survey. It was decided not to include arson as a survey crime because it is not used by the FBI for trend analysis, among other reasons.

Since the revision of the NCVS, the survey coverage has expanded to include a more general category of sexual assault and simple assault, neither of which are part of the FBI's Index. In addition, purse snatching and pocket picking are separated from other forms of theft because they involve personal contact. Thus, today's NCVS includes essentially nine crime categories (although still covering six of the seven Index crimes). These categories include rape, sexual assault, robbery, aggravated assault, simple assault, purse snatching/pocket-picking, burglary, motor vehicle theft, and theft. Our following trend analysis will include all of those categories. Definitions that are given for these offenses in the NCVS are shown in the text box.

BOX 2-8

Definitions of Crimes Included in NCVS Report[62]

Rape—Forced sexual intercourse including both psychological coercion as well as physical force. Forced sexual intercourse means vaginal, anal, or oral penetration by the offender(s). This category also includes incidents where the penetration is from a foreign object such as a bottle. Includes attempted rapes, male as well as female victims, and both heterosexual and homosexual rape. Attempted rape includes verbal threats of rape.

Sexual Assault—A wide range of victimizations, separate from rape or attempted rape. These crimes include attacks or attempted attacks generally involving unwanted sexual contact between victim and offender. Sexual assaults may or may not involve force and include such things as grabbing or fondling. Sexual assault also includes verbal threats.

Robbery—Completed or attempted theft, directly from a person, of property or cash by force or threat of force, with or without a weapon, and with or without injury.

Aggravated Assault—Attack or attempted attack with a weapon, regardless of whether or not an injury occurred and attack without a weapon when serious injury results.

Simple Assault—Attack without a weapon resulting either in no injury, minor injury (e.g., bruises, black eyes, cuts, scratches, or swelling) or in undetermined injury requiring less than 2 days of hospitalization. Also includes attempted assault without a weapon.

Personal Theft (Purse Snatching/Pocket Picking)—Theft or attempted theft of property or cash directly from the victim by stealth, without force, or threat of force.

Household Burglary—Unlawful or forcible entry or attempted entry of a residence. This crime usually, but not always, involves theft. The illegal entry may be by force, such as breaking a window or slashing a screen, or may be without force by entering through an unlocked door or an open window. As long as the person entering has no legal right to be present in the structure a burglary has occurred. Furthermore, the structure need not be the house itself for a burglary to take place; illegal entry of a garage, shed, or any other structure on the premises also constitutes household burglary. If breaking and entering occurs in a hotel or vacation residence, it is still classified as a burglary for the household whose member or members were staying there at the time the entry occurred.

Motor Vehicle Theft—Stealing or unauthorized taking of a motor vehicle, including attempted thefts. A motor vehicle is an automobile, truck, motorcycle, or any other motorized vehicle legally allowed on public roads and highways.

Theft—Completed or attempted theft of property or cash without personal contact. Incident involving theft of property from with the sample household would classify as theft if the offender has a legal right to be in the house (e.g., a maid, delivery person, or guest). If the offender has no legal right to be in the house, the incident would classify as a burglary.

Extent and Trends in the NCVS

Although long-range trends have already been discussed, it is useful to provide a comparison of rates over the years 1995–2004, since the NCVS and UCR became available online. This will enable a presentation of information on all nine of the crimes covered in the new NCVS and will serve as a benchmark for future editions of this text.

The rates of crime per 1,000 households or persons for all nine of the NCVS crimes for 1995 and 2004 are shown in Table 2-7.

Although some categories of crime increased right after the change in methodology from 1989–1991, the crime total continued its historical downward trend. The trend is downward in all categories of crime since 1995,

Table 2–7 **Victimization Rates per 1,000 Households in 1995 and 2004**[63]

	Victimization Rate		Percentage Change
Crime	1995	2004	1995–2004
Rape/attempted rape	1.1	0.4	−63.6
Sexual assault	0.5	0.5	0.0
Robbery	5.3	2.1	−60.4
Aggravated assault	8.7	4.3	−50.6
Simple assault	28.9	14.2	−50.9
Personal theft*	1.7	0.9	−47.1
Household burglary	47.3	29.6	−37.4
Motor vehicle theft	16.2	8.8	−45.7
Theft	216.0	122.8	−43.1
Total	326.0	183.6	−43.7

*Purse snatching/Pocket-picking

although simple assault and motor vehicle theft are slightly higher than the rates given for 1973. Total victimization is down 69% since 1995 and 43.7% since 1973.

Social scientists may be inclined to accept these finding as valid. However, public opinion polls indicate that the public fear of crime is high. Although public fear of crime may be irrational and based upon mass media sensationalism, the NCVS results should not be taken at face value. Many criticisms have been raised about the validity of the NCVS findings, some of which led to methodological improvements of the NCVS in the early 1990s. It should be noted that the NCVS today is predominantly a *telephone survey*. It is entirely possible that the apparent downward trend indicated in these data may simply indicate an increasing reluctance of respondents to give out personal information over the telephone, rather than an actual decline in the incidence of crime.

Criticisms of the NCVS

In addition to the possible increasing reluctance of survey informants to provide sensitive information over the telephone, other criticisms have been made with regard to the NCVS.

- Informants may forget about a crime that actually happened within the period called for either because of memory problems or because the crime was judged to be insignificant (e.g., the theft of an inexpensive item).
- Underreporting is greater for less educated than more educated persons, greater for blacks than whites, and greater for lower class than middle class persons.
- Respondents are interviewed every six months for a total of seven interviews, but tend to report less victimization with each successive interview, either because the victims take precautions against victimization or because of respondent fatigue, which results in respondents being less cooperative in the interview process.[64]

- Victims may overreport crimes due to misinterpretation of events. For instance, a lost wallet may be reported as stolen, or an open door may be reported as a burglary attempt.

- Victims may underreport crime to interviewers due to embarrassment or fear of getting in trouble (particularly if they themselves were perpetrators of the crime).

- Sampling error may produce a group of respondents who are not representative of the nation as a whole.[65]

- Respondents may actually try to please the interviewer by fabricating incidents of crime.

- Respondents may "telescope" events, which refers to moving events that took place in an earlier time period to that referred to in the study.

- Data may be lost because, like the UCR, the NCVS includes only the most serious offense committed during an event in which several crimes were committed.[66]

- Because interviews are conducted in various locations throughout the country, recording styles may differ significantly.[67]

- Victims may not inform on a violent abusive perpetrator within their family, either because of fear of the perpetrator or because of a desire to protect the perpetrator from prosecution.[68]

Problems with Studies Using NCVS Data

Since the inception of the NCVS in 1972, there have been countless studies using Survey data to test hypotheses or simply to explore factors connected with crime victimization. It should be stated again that these studies are using NCVS data as secondary data rather than primary data. The NCVS was designed to measure the incidence of crime victimization. The availability of hard national data on crime victimization has been enticing to researchers, and the NCVS data have been particularly inviting because of the expanded list of demographic data that accompany the surveys (as compared with databases produced by the FBI). The demographic data include the age, sex, race, ethnicity, marital status, and annual household income of victims. Offender characteristics include age, race, sex, and drug and alcohol use, as well as the victim-offender relationship. Although annual income of the victim can be used to do limited socioeconomic analysis, there is no data on the occupation or educational level on either the victim or offender in NCVS data.

A plethora of literature on theories that are testable using the NCVS data has been developed. In a sense, the available data are driving the theories, rather than the data being developed to test the theories, which is the intended direction of scientific analysis. Curiously, some of these theories have recently been popular, such as the econometric theories, situational theories, and neoclassical theories, coincidental with their major variables being measurable using the NCVS data. A prime example of this phenomenon of "data-driving theories" is a situational crime theory called *routine activities theory,* the "lifestyle" theory of victimization. The development of this theory was enhanced greatly by the victimization data on age, race, income, major activity, and other data in the NCVS.[69] Similarly, numerous studies stressing economic factors have utilized the NCVS data.[70] Several studies using NCVS data have emphasized the significance of race as an etiological variable;[71] however, one study that controlled for income found that race was no longer of significance in intimate partner violence.[72]

Self-Report Surveys

Perhaps because no such data were available from government sources, social scientists have been doing self-report surveys of offenders in America since the 1940s. Such studies were developed, in part, in response to the need for more information on offenders, especially socioeconomic data. Numerous surveys have been conducted using "convenience samples" of students in sociology or psychology classes; however, some recent efforts have sought more wide-based samples of subjects. A brief history of these studies, including some of their findings on the extent of crime, as well as trends shown in such research, is discussed later.

Development of Self-Report Surveys

Austin Porterfield was the first to use self-report offending (SRO) questionnaires in a study published in 1943. The research compared criminal behavior among male and female college students with that of a group of youth who had been processed by the juvenile court.[73] Porterfield found no significant difference between the delinquent involvement, as measured by the self-report questionnaires, of the college students and the court-processed delinquents. However, Porterfield argued that there was a difference between the two groups in socioeconomic status and family disorganization. The court youth were overwhelmingly from a lower socioeconomic background and from families that were socially disrupted.

The second attempt to survey SRO behavior was that of James Wallerstein and Clement Wyle in 1947. They obtained responses from 1,698 adults in New York by distributing a 49-item questionnaire by mail. Their main finding was that 99% of adults admitted to at least one offense. They also found that 91% of the sample admitted to imprisonable offenses. Even church ministers admitted to an average of 8.2 offenses since the age of 18. Over 80% of the men admitted committing malicious mischief, disorderly conduct, and larceny, and 50% admitted a history of crimes such as reckless driving, driving while intoxicated, indecency, gambling, fraud, and tax evasion. Although Wallerstein and Wyle's study admittedly was neither based upon a representative nor a random sample, the findings did call attention to the extent of unreported crime.[74] Wallerstein and Wyle concluded "the solid truth remains that there is a large chance element in our administration of justice and it's the unlucky ones who are caught."[75]

After these groundbreaking studies, the major influence of SRO research began in the 1950s with the research of Short and Nye.[76] Whereas Porterfield had administered SRO questionnaires to college students and court youth, Short and Nye administered their 19-item questionnaires to both high school students in a classroom setting and institutionalized youth. The high school sample consisted of 9th through 12th grade students in three schools in the state of Washington. No samples were taken from large cities or from large non-Caucasian groups. They found no relationship between socioeconomic status and self-reported delinquency among the public school youth. They also found that quality of family life was not related to self-reported delinquency.

Like Porterfield, however, they found few differences in self-reported delinquency between institutionalized delinquents and public school youth and that institutionalized delinquents came from much lower socioeconomic backgrounds.

Although Short and Nye's efforts were an improvement upon the earlier work, the SRO questionnaire used had two major flaws. First, the questions were posed in a "have you ever" format. Respondents were asked to check any regulations they had broken since grade school. Second, the emphasis was upon relatively trivial offenses. Of the FBI seven major crimes, only auto theft and larceny theft were included, while murder, rape, robbery, aggravated assault, and burglary were not included.

A major pitfall of the self-report studies covered so far was that they were based upon accidental or convenience samples (college students, public school students, incarcerated youth, and willing respondents in a mailed questionnaire). Another consideration is that, with the exception of the study done by Wallerstein and Wyle, all the SRO studies were of young people or juveniles, a limitation that had not yet been overcome.

While attempts to estimate SRO criminality in the nation had not yet been made, such efforts did begin for youth in the 1960s. Starting in 1967, the Institute for Social Research at the University of Michigan conducted an interview survey of SRO delinquency on a national probability sample of 13- to 16-year-old boys and girls, a study termed the National Survey of Youth (NSY). Interviews were conducted in community centers, libraries, or churches, in such a way that parents could not overhear the questions or responses.[77] The interviews, lasting an average of nearly two hours, culminated in a 16-item SRO delinquency scale that included serious as well as trivial offenses. The serious offenses included drug use, gang fighting, auto theft, and carrying a concealed weapon. The time frame for the self-reports was limited to the previous three years. All respondents admitted at least one chargeable offense within the three years prior to their interviews,[78] and the relationship between social status and delinquency was not strong. However, only a minority of the respondents admitted involvement in more than one serious offense. Black youths admitted to more serious offenses than white youths.[79]

Although the NSY was an improvement upon previous attempts through providing some indices of serious delinquency, a subsequent study by Delbert Elliott and his colleagues at the University of Colorado was geared to approximate 40 UCR crime categories, including all but one Part I offenses (homicide) and 60% of Part II offenses. The study, termed the National Youth Survey (NYS), began in 1977 and was based upon a probability sample of youth in the continental United States.[80] The cohort sample consisted of 1,726 male and female adolescents between the ages of 11 and 17 that were subsequently interviewed again in 1984, 1987, 1990, and 1993. The last wave provided data about a national sample of young adults from 27 to 33 years of age. Respondents were interviewed during January and February of each of these years and instructed to indicate how many times during the past year they had committed each specified offense, with a follow-up question if respondents indicated 10 or more times. The follow-up question required further details of the frequency of offenses ranging from once a month to two to three times a day. At the low end of the frequency scale, no differences were found between subgroups in social class, age, and race. However, at the high end of the frequency of delinquency scale, differences by race and social class were discovered. Lower class and African American respondents appeared more frequently in the high-frequency offender group than middle-class youths and whites.[81] Subsequent analysis using data from the first five years of the NYS (1977–1981) showed that once social class was controlled, differences by race disappeared.[82]

Extent and Trends in Self-Report Surveys

Since 1975, researchers at the University of Michigan's Institute for Social Research (ISR) have been conducting an annual survey of a representative sample of self-reported delinquency and other attributes of about 16,000 high school seniors at 133 public and private high schools nationwide. Since 1991, the surveys included 8th graders and 10th graders. The surveys, like those done by Elliott and colleagues, have included items to measure UCR Index offenses (except murder and forcible rape) and have shown high rates of such offenses. The ISR surveys between 1991 and 2003 typically found around 12% admitting to aggravated assault, 42% larceny, and 24% burglary. Roughly 3–4% admitted to robbery and 5–6% admitted to vehicle theft.[83] Since 1975, the ISR data indicated as shown in Table 2–8, a fairly stable trend in most delinquent offenses, except larceny in general, and shoplifting in particular, which showed a decrease.[84]

Criticisms of Self-Report Surveys

The obvious limitation of self-report surveys described here is that they have been largely limited to surveys of school or institutionalized populations. The high school samples have been nationwide, but studies done with older age groups have been, at best, convenience samples or follow-up surveys of high school students who are now adults. The ISR questionnaires are administered in classrooms during normal class periods. Teachers are not asked to do anything more than introduce the survey staff members and to remain in the classroom to help guarantee an orderly atmosphere for the survey.[85]

There are numerous criticisms that have been made of this way of gathering data.

- As mentioned earlier, self-report studies have been done primarily with adolescent populations in a classroom setting, yielding little information about the adult population.

Table 2–8 **Percentage of High School Seniors Reporting Involvement in Selected Delinquent Activities in the Last 12 Months[86]**

Delinquent Act	Year of Survey												
Delinquency	1991	1992	1993	1994	1995	1996	1997	1998	1999	2000	2001	2002	2003
Robbery	3.4	4.3	4.6	4.8	3.5	3.7	4.5	4.3	3.8	2.8	2.8	3.2	3.9
Aggravated assault	12.9	12.8	13.4	13.4	12.3	14.3	14.6	14.4	13.4	11.9	13.1	11.7	12.0
Burglary	24.3	26.0	26.3	24.8	23.5	24.0	24.7	24.6	23.6	22.7	24.3	22.6	23.0
Larceny	42.0	43.1	43.4	41.7	40.7	44.7	47.0	42.8	41.6	43.0	43.0	38.9	37.3
Shoplifting	31.1	30.4	30.7	30.3	29.9	32.2	33.4	29.7	27.7	28.7	30.6	27.9	26.8
Vehicle theft	6.2	6.0	6.4	5.9	4.8	5.2	6.1	4.8	6.9	5.2	6.7	4.9	5.3

- Emphasis upon trivial offenses makes it difficult to compare the data with official crime rates (although this problem is largely corrected in recent SRO surveys, such as the ISR survey).

- Respondents may have difficulty recalling offenses they have committed as recently as one year ago, not to mention the time span of 10 years in earlier studies.

- Many, if not most, self-report studies have been based upon convenience samples, such as college students, or inmates, so that generalizibility is "in the eye of the beholder."

- Some prospective respondents may refuse to participate or be absent at the time of a questionnaire administration. Absentees, especially, may be offenders that have a high rate of crime, such as gang members, alcohol or drug consumers, mentally ill persons, homeless youth, runaways, and even incarcerated delinquents. In both the NSY and NYS studies, the minimal loss was 25%.[87]

- In addition to memory error, it is entirely possible that informants may falsify their self-reported offenses, although studies using validity testing measures such as polygraphs, community informants, police records, and benchmark questions to identify those who are lying have indicated the validity of self-reports.[88]

Although there are numerous reasons to doubt the validity of self-reports, as we have seen, the same can be said of victimization surveys and official reports. The UCR is in the stage of developing into the "new UCR," the NIBRS, and the NCR became the NCVS as a result of methodological improvement. The same is true of self-report studies, which have improved over time. While more improvement is needed, the self-report studies are valuable in providing a cross-check on findings from other sources of data. Self-reports also constitute (unfortunately) the only way that many theories can be tested because of the absence of socioeconomic variables from FBI and NCVS data. Although it may be true that these two major databases can be correlated or controlled using Census data, the result is an "ecological correlation" that may be doubtful.

Whereas our analysis so far has been confined to databases that are developed for studies done within the United States, there are still numerous international databases that must be discussed, because it will be necessary to use these to do a comparative analysis. These databases for offenses include United Nations Surveys and INTERPOL data, as well as International Crime Victim Surveys and international self-report surveys. Finally, it seems appropriate to discuss some of the demographic indices that are used in this text.

INTERNATIONAL CRIME DATABASES

The collection of statistics on crime on an international level was first considered at the General Statistical Congress held in Brussels in 1853 and subsequently at the International Congress on the Prevention and Repression of Crime, held in London in 1872. At both meetings, the issue of comparability of definitions proved to be a stumbling block. In 1946, the question of definitions was still of concern in the conclusions of the International Penal and Penitentiary Foundation in 1946. Soon thereafter, the IPPF handed over most of its functions to the newly formed United Nations Organization. With the exception of one limited cross-national crime survey conducted over the period 1937–1946, little seems to have been done until the early 1970s, when the present series of surveys was initiated by a Resolution at the United Nations General Assembly.

The Surveys, referred to as "sweeps" (surveys of many nations that are part of a series) were published first in 1977, covering five-year intervals starting in 1970. A succession of institutions in the United States hosted expert group meetings to consider the results of one sweep and plan an improved version of the next. The hosts were: the School of Criminal Justice, Rutgers University, New Jersey, 1981; the Criminal Justice Center, Sam Houston State University, Texas, 1983; and the Bureau of Justice Statistics, U.S. Department of Justice, Washington, DC, 1986.[89]

The United Nations Surveys of Crime

Since its first survey covering the years 1970–1975, the United Nations Center for International Crime Prevention has conducted the survey every five years. The data gathered has broadened beyond statistical information on crime to include data on various aspects of the criminal justice systems for United Nations member countries. The United Nations surveys standardized crime definitions and, over the years, more and more countries have adapted their own statistical definitions to coincide with the standard United Nations categories. These standardized crime definitions may be seen in Table 2–9, along with their definition and equivalent UCR crimes.

The crimes that are measured in the United Nations Surveys of Crime and Trends and operation of Criminal Justice Systems (UNCJS) include the FBI Index crimes of murder, rape, robbery, assault, and theft. Data are also included on fraud, embezzlement, drug offenses, and bribery. Regrettably,

Table 2–9 **United Nations Crimes Equivalent to UCR Index Offenses**[90]

UCR Index Offense	United Nations Equivalent
Murder and nonnegligent manslaughter	**Intentional homicide:** death deliberately inflicted on another person by another person, including infanticide.
Forcible rape	**Rape:** sexual intercourse without valid consent.
Robbery	**Robbery:** theft of property from a person, overcoming resistance by force or threat of force.
Aggravated assault	**Major assault:** physical attack against the body of another person resulting in serious injury, including battery by excluding indecent assault.
Burglary	**Burglary:** unlawful entry into someone else's premises with the intention to commit a crime.
Larceny-theft	**Total recorded theft:** the removal of property without the property owner's consent excluding burglary and housebreaking as well as theft of a motor vehicle.
Motor vehicle theft	**Automobile theft:** the removal of a motor vehicle without the consent of the owner of the vehicle.

the UCR can provide no comparable data for fraud, embezzlement, drug offenses, and bribery, because the FBI only provides arrest statistics for these crimes. However, in the future, the NIBRS should be able to provide such information.

INTERPOL Crime Data

Although the UNCJS has provided data on around 90 nations, INTERPOL has developed a database that includes all of its member states, which numbered 182 as of the time of this writing (2005). Thus, in terms of the total number of countries included, the INTERPOL database is superior to the UNCJS by a factor of two times. In preparing this text, a database was developed that combined INTERPOL data with data from the UNCJS in cases of countries where no INTERPOL data were available. The result is a database of 165 countries. INTERPOL data were available online from 2000 through the end of 2003; however, the site has been made available only to official police agencies since then. In terms of definitions, the INTERPOL categories are similar to the FBI UCR Index crimes, as seen in Table 2–10.

INTERPOL data are published annually in electronic form, providing statistics by country on the FBI seven major crimes, as well as on three additional crimes—fraud, counterfeiting, and drug offenses.

INTERPOL, it should be noted, is not an operational international police force, as it may have been portrayed in the mass media. Instead, INTERPOL acts as a clearing house for information on offenses and subjects believed to be operating across national borders. The incentive for nations to apply for membership in INTERPOL, pay dues, send delegates, and follow organizational rules

Secretary General of INTERPOL Robert Noble speaks during the opening ceremony of an ICAC (Independent Commission against Corruption)/INTERPOL conference in Hong Kong on January 22, 2003.

Source: CORBIS/Reuters America, LLC.

Table 2–10 INTERPOL Crimes Equivalent to UCR Index Offenses[91]

UCR Index Offense	INTERPOL Equivalent
Murder and nonnegligent manslaughter	Murder
Forcible rape	Rape
Robbery	Robbery and violent theft
Aggravated assault	Serious assault
Burglary	Breaking and entering
Larceny-theft	Other thefts
Motor vehicle theft	Theft of motor cars

is that INTERPOL can provide massive amounts of information through its computer database, called the Lyon Criminal Information System. Member countries can perform searches on INTERPOL's records regarding international criminals and can obtain fingerprints and photos of criminals, as well as search for stolen property.[92] The recent rapid growth in INTERPOL member states seems to attest to the importance of the international study of crime.

Comparative Criminology Database

To maximize the amount of data that can be examined in this text, we combined the INTERPOL and United Nations data sets into one data set called the Comparative Criminology Database (CCDB). For purposes of judging the extent of crime in a country, we searched for the most recent data available on a given country. If INTERPOL had the most recent data available, then we used that data. If the UNCJS data was the most recent, we used that. The CCDB is available for view on the website linked with this text (see suggested Websites at the end of this chapter).

Some may argue that these two different data sets should not be merged. However, it has been demonstrated that the two different data sets (United Nations and INTERPOL) are essentially equivalent for analytic or explanatory cross-sectional purposes.[93] We feel that in light of the global basis of crime today, the two major international data sets should be used to their full advantage to help understand the rapidly growing international world of crime.

Criticisms of International Police Statistics

Official data reported to the United Nations and INTERPOL reflect many of the same problems as data reported to the FBI in regard to definitions, reporting of crime, and recording of crime statistics. It is generally agreed that these problems are even greater in regard to international data than FBI data. Although the United Nations has published definitions that responding countries are supposed to use in gathering data, INTERPOL has no such definitions and reports data based upon general categories. Countries reporting to both agencies may actively suppress crime data for political or economic reasons. For instance, it was not uncommon during the Cold War for the former Soviet Union and other Soviet Block countries to underreport crime to provide a favorable image for their system, as compared with capitalism.[94] Similarly, Islamic countries may underreport crime to promote the view that Sharia law is conducive to low rates of crime. Other countries may deliberately underreport crimes, or not report crime statistics at all, because reports of high crime rates might reduce tourism or international trade. Gerhard Mueller found that all countries do collect some form of crime data, but many do not participate in international crime surveys for the following reasons:

- Countries are so small that administrative staffs may not be able to handle the requests.
- Some countries are too involved in civil war to keep track of crime problems.
- "New" countries have not developed a system of collection and dissemination of crime data.
- Some countries lack the technical resources and knowledge necessary to report crime data.
- Some countries have the resources but still refuse because they are concerned that crime will negatively affect the nation's world standing or its tourist trade.[95]

Underreporting

In addition to these country-based reasons for not reporting and/or underreporting crime to the United Nations and INTERPOL, there are a variety of reasons why individual citizens may not report crimes to the police, which might vary by country, and also affect the international reporting of crime. People who live in underdeveloped countries may lack phone communication and/or transportation that would enable them to report crimes to the police. Countries where household insurance is more developed may report a higher proportion of crime. In some countries, the police may directly or indirectly support perpetrators of crime, such as vigilante groups. Citizens are likely to avoid reporting crimes to the police in those countries, possibly fearing reprisals. There is a considerable variation between countries on the extent to which citizens report crimes to the police. For instance, the 2000 International Crime Victims Survey found that fewer than one third of robbery offenses were reported to the police in Japan and France, but more than 70% of robberies in Northern Ireland were reported.[96]

Nonstandard Definitions

Even though member countries may have been given definitions by the United Nations, they may take reports of crime and make arrests based upon their own definitions of crime. Thus, it is difficult if not impossible to provide data fitting the United Nations standardized definitions. For instance, Italy counts as rapes events involving sexual intercourse with a minor without force or other forms of sexual assault, whereas Croatia's figures on rape exclude violent intramarital intercourse, as well as sexual intercourse with force with a minor.[97]

Crime Recording Problems

Many countries, especially those in developing or war-torn nations, may lack the manpower and technical capability to collect crime statistics on a national level. The numbers and structure of police personnel varies among countries. Low rates of recorded crimes may simply reflect system inefficiency. Some countries may lack computers or have access only to antiquated computer

BOX 2–9

Official Statistics in China— Misleading Measures of Crime

Crime statistics in China are gathered in much the same way as they are in the United States in the form of successive crime reports by local police stations from one level of government agency to the next. Official crime statistics in China also share the same problem of underreporting as occurs in most other countries.[98] For instance, in an internal police report on "Policing in China: 1995" (China's version of the UCR), there were only 1.69 million criminal cases recorded by the police and 2.96 million minor offenses in 1995.[99] In the world's most populous country, with more than 1.3 billion people, these figures seem almost too good to be true. There are two major explanations for these low reporting rates— official and cultural.

Changes in crime definitions due to political and social concerns can contribute to the underreporting problem. China's Criminal Law contains two categories of offenses—*criminal offenses* (serious offenses), for which formalized procedures and penalties are applied, and *administrative offenses* (minor offenses), for which administrative penalties are applied. Although specific criteria are established, the same theft behavior can often be interpreted and recorded into either of the two categories. For instance, stealing goods worth less than 500 *yuan* (about $60) is considered an administrative offense and therefore handled informally. If the value surpasses 500 yuan, formal court proceedings will be invoked. In all cases, police decide how much the stolen goods are worth. Because crime statistics are a major indicator of social health, they inevitably reflect the behavior and concerns of those who generate them (i.e., the police).[100]

Official crime statistics are also a product of the cultural milieu unique to Chinese society. Many crimes go unreported because they are handled through informal social control channels. In situations where perpetrators and victims know one another (such as domestic violence, child abuse, assaults, and even rape), crime often goes unreported due to shame and embarrassment. Neighborhood committees, community leaders, and village elders also play a role in the maintenance of social order. As a result of these "filtering" mechanisms, many crimes do not show up in official records, thus giving a distorted picture about crime and victimization in China.

technology, whereas others may possess state-of-the art computer systems, with network hook-ups to laptop computers in patrol cars. The odds are that the technologically more sophisticated countries would record more crime of all kinds, simply because of the ease and efficiency with which crime can be recorded. Also, in some countries, crimes that elsewhere would typically be handled and recorded by the police, are handled through informal social control channels.

Comparative Analysis with International Police Data

With all of these limitations, many researchers are reluctant to make comparisons using international police data. However, there are ways to improve comparability of data. One way is to limit comparisons to a few or a single crime. Of course, it is appropriate to make comparisons using rates of crime rather than absolute numbers. In addition, rates can be compared for countries at the same level of development and/or technical efficiency of police data gathering. Probably the most important tool in making a valid comparison is the use of triangulation—multiple measures of the incidence of a particular crime.[101] In this text, designations of countries high or low in crime will be made, typically using different indices as a means of cross-validating. For instance, triangulation will typically involve consulting INTERPOL data, United Nations data, World Health Organization data (on homicide), and ICVS data.

International Crime Victim Surveys

Just as within the United States (maybe even more so), internationally there is a "dark figure" of crimes that are not reported to the police. The United Nations has been aware of this and has undertaken a series of International Crime Victim Surveys (ICVS), somewhat similar to the NCVS that is done within the United States. After the first victimization survey was done by the Johnson President's Commission in 1966, similar national studies were carried out in Finland in 1970, followed by surveys in Denmark, Sweden, Norway, England, and Wales.[102] International comparative victimization surveys were developed and carried out in 1988 by three European criminologists: Jan van Dijk, Pat Mahew, and Martin Killias. Their efforts resulted in the first sweep in 1989 of what is today known as the ICVS. Three additional sweeps were conducted, culminating in the 1992, 1996, and 2000 surveys, sponsored by the United Nations Interregional Crime and Justice Research Institute. The sweeps have been conducted in approximately 55 countries.

Like the NCVS, the primary method of data collection used in the ICVS is computer-assisted telephone interviewing, which randomly selects a sample of at least 1,000 individuals in each country. Where telephone ownership is limited, in-person interviews are conducted with a smaller sample. Respondents are asked about selected offenses they have experienced over a five-year period. Although extensive results from the four survey sweeps are available, we do not provide a detailed analysis of them here because they will be referred to throughout this book, primarily as ways of cross-checking findings pertaining to high reported rates of INTERPOL or United Nations–based crime data.

A summary of ICVS results for the first three sweeps indicated that the United States is at the median (23rd) of all 55 countries surveyed in terms of "any crime." This is also true for "contact crimes" (such as robbery) and assaults. Although the United States ranks high in "car crimes" and burglary, it ranks low in terms of "other thefts"[103]

Criticisms of the ICVS

Although the ICVS data serve as a good cross-check, they are probably not satisfactory as a basis for ranking of countries high or low in a particular crime. Samples as small as 1,000 for countries with populations of 300 million (for the United States) or one billion (for India) are obviously bound by sampling error. Also, the telephone interviews had a relatively low (64%) response rate.[104] In addition, the ICVS has methodological problems similar to the NCVS in the United States. Certain population groups like the homeless, children, and the very poor may be excluded because they are difficult to locate. Commercial property is also excluded. Memory and objectivity of respondents may vary. However, when ICVS data are available they may be helpful in confirming the designation of a country as high or low in a particular form of crime, as will be the starting point for the comparative analysis of various crimes throughout this text.

The International Self-Report Survey

Although most self-report research has been conducted in the United States, a project sponsored by the North Atlantic Treaty Organization (NATO) led to data collection efforts in 13 countries, including Belgium, Canada, France, Germany, Greece, Italy, the Netherlands, Northern Ireland, Spain, Sweden, Switzerland, the United Kingdom, as well as the United States.[105] The study found that between 80 and 90% of juveniles in all of the countries had committed either one or a combination of property, violent, and drug crimes.[106]

Although these studies may provide interesting insights, the international self-report studies have not been developed to the extent of the SRO studies conducted by the University of Michigan ISR survey. Nevertheless, some self-report surveys done in some of the Nordic countries will be cited in the course of exploring the high rates of theft in those countries.

In addition to various indices of crime, numerous demographic variables are used in the comparative criminology database from a variety of sources including the *CIA World Factbook,* the *United Nations Human Development Reports,* the *World Health Organization* online database, the United Nations Office on Drugs and Crime database, and other sources (see suggested Websites at the end of this chapter).

Other Databases Used in this Text

SUMMARY AND CONCLUSION

Criminologists strive to engage in the scientific study of crime, criminals, and criminal behavior. To realize the goal of scientific study, we must study crime, not just within our nation, but globally, to derive universal generalizations. Comparative criminology, the international study of crime, dates back to the gathering of the first crime statistics in France in 1827.

Because scientific study is a goal, this chapter reviewed some of the procedures of the scientific method. Universal generalizations are easiest to derive through controlled experiments. Such experiments are simulated in social science by surveys, typically using government-based statistics, which are termed secondary data because they were developed for some other purpose than to test a theory or hypothesis. Cross-national study furthers this analysis by using nations as laboratories where grand experiments—such as socialism or free trade—are carried out.

Discussed in this chapter are various databases or data sets that are often used to study crime, starting with the UCR. Looking at FBI data, the total of Index crimes, the Crime Index, was 3,982.6 for the year 2004. Is this a high or low rate of crime? This question cannot be answered except when *compared* with something—compared with historical rates or rates for other countries. Both tasks were done in this chapter. Since 1960 in the United States, the Crime Index was at its highest in 1980 (5,950). However, the United States ranks 12th of 165 countries in the world in its crime rate. In this chapter, a long-term analysis of the FBI statistical trends was attempted, including an analysis of periods when the crime rate was high and when it was low. However, there are many reasons to doubt the veracity of these trends, because of the multitude of "uncontrolled variables" that can also account for highs and lows.

Coexisting with the UCR is a yearly survey of individuals in a random sample of U.S. households, a victim survey termed the NCVS. The NCVS focuses upon Index crimes, but excludes murder and arson. Controversy over the NCVS springs from the fact that it has reported progressively lower crime rates since its inception in 1973. Many theories that have proved very popular in criminal justice studies—routine activities, econometric, and neo-classical theories—have been nourished by the NCVS data.

Perhaps in part to fulfill the need for socioeconomic data, sociologists have, since 1940, been conducting SRO studies. Since 1975, the ISR at the University of Michigan has conducted annual SRO surveys of high school seniors. These surveys have contradicted FBI survey results by finding delinquency to be stable over time. The SRO studies have provided a useful function by opening up another avenue to explore the "dark figures" of crime not accessible via police-based data surveys.

In this text, additional databases are used for the analysis of crime in the United States—international databases. We have developed a database that combines the police data from two data sets—the United Nations database and the IN-TERPOL report—into one database that we term the CCDB. That database enables the assessment of the U.S. Crime Index as compared with other countries in the world.

The purpose of this text is exploratory and the destination of that exploration is the world. As countries of the world become interconnected through international commerce, international communications, and, most particularly, the Internet, we cannot really understand crime without following it wherever it goes. That will be the interesting and challenging task of this text.

DISCUSSION QUESTIONS

1. Do you agree that criminology should strive to be a science and that cross-national studies can help in that pursuit? Why or why not?

2. Do you believe that the United States has the highest crime rate in the world? Why or why not?

3. In a quote from a President's Commission study, it was stated that the U.S. is 100 years behind Europe in its present system of gathering criminal statistics. What information in the 1827 *Compte general* is not included in the present day UCR? Why do you think this information is left out?

4. Do you think that the FBI's UCR can be trusted in its analysis of the extent of crime and crime trends? Why or why not?

5. Do you believe that crime has been declining in the United States in recent years? Why or why not?

6. The NCVS has indicated that crime has declined significantly since 1973 until today. Do you trust this finding? Why or why not?

7. Do you think that international crime statistics, such as those gathered by the United Nations and INTERPOL, have any validity as a starting point for comparative study? Why or why not?

SUGGESTED WEBSITES

http://www.fbi.gov/ucr/ucr.htm Web page containing the FBI's UCR, downloadable, from 1995 until the most recent year published.

http://www.ojp.usdoj.gov/bjs/cvictgen.htm#publications Web page containing the Bureau of Justice Statistic's publication *Criminal Victimization in the United States: A National Crime Victimization Survey Report* (NCVS), downloadable, from 1992 until the most recent year published.

http://www.albany.edu/sourcebook/pdf/section3.pdf Web page containing data from the national self-report survey of high school seniors from 1991 to the most recent year published (Table 3–43) in Johnston, Bachman, and O'Malley's *Monitoring the Future*. Data on numerous other criminal justice topics are also included on this Website.

www.unodc.org/unodc/crime_cicp_surveys.html The Website for the United Nations Office on Drugs and Crime containing United Nations surveys, referred to as the UNCJS.

http://www.unodc.org/pdf/crime/seventh_survey/567pvr.pdf Website that includes the Fifth, Sixth, and Seventh Surveys combined into one data set.

http://www.rohan.sdsu.edu/faculty/rwinslow/links/CCDBONLINE.html Website containing United Nations, INTERPOL, and World Health Organization data on crime. A separate "read me" file is also accessible on that same Website. It describes exactly what data were used with each country.

http://www.unicri.it/wwd/analysis/icvs/index.php Website containing survey data from ICVS from 1988 until the most recent year published.

http://www.rohan.sdsu.edu/faculty/rwinslow/links/stateindices.html describes Web locations for census, Drug Enforcement Administration, and FBI data state-by-state for the United States.

ENDNOTES

1. Heiner, 1996, p. xi.
2. Comparative Criminology Database (CCDB), which may be accessed at the Website: *http://www.rohan.sdsu.edu/faculty/rwinslow/links/CCDBONLINE.htm*l. Crime data on Index crimes are drawn from United Nations or INTERPOL data, the most recent available as of December 26, 2003. For the United States, this was data for the year 2001. For specific details on the source of data for Index crimes, go to the Website: *http://www.rohan.sdsu.edu/faculty/rwinslow/links/CCDBIndexCrimesSources.htm*
3. CCDB as described in endnote 2.
4. CCDB as described in endnote 2.
5. Beirne & Messerschmidt, 1991, p. 30.
6. Singer, 2005.
7. Beirne & Messerschmidt, 1991, pp. 296–303.
8. Quetelet, 1984.
9. Risto, 1986.
10. Lithner, 1986.
11. Fairchild & Dammer, 2001, p. 16.
12. Falcone, 2005, p. 252.
13. Wilson, 1990.
14. Underwood, Duncan, Taylor, Cotton, 1954, pp. 135–151, 231.
15. Phoenix Police Department, 2005.
16. Who2, 2004.
17. Hack, 2004, p. 29.
18. Theoharis & Cox, 2001.
19. Powers, 1987.
20. Hack, 2004, p. 294.
21. Hack, 2004, p. 285.
22. FBI, UCR, 2004, Appendix II, p. 505.
23. Maguire & Uchida, 2000, p. 500.
24. Banas & Trojanowicz, 1985.
25. FBI, UCR, 2004, p. 61.
26. Beirne & Messerschmidt, 1995, p. 163.
27. Yablonsky, 1990, p. 79.
28. FBI, 2004, p. 61.
29. FBI, UCR, 2004, Tables 1, 25, 29, pp. 72, 266, 280.
30. FBI, 2004, p. 3.
31. Trochim, 2002.
32. Sutherland & Cressey, 1970, p. 25.
33. Sutherland & Cressey, 1970, p. 25.
34. Sutherland & Cressey, 1970, pp. 25–26.
35. FBI, 2004, Appendix I, p. 488.
36. FBI, 2004, p. 3.
37. FBI, 2004, Table 1, p. 72.
38. Source: The Disaster Center, 2005.
39. Schmalleger, 2005, pp. 41–42.
40. U.S. Department of Justice, 2000.
41. Banas & Trojanowicz, 1985.
42. U.S. National Commission on Law Observance and Enforcement, 1931.
43. Banas & Trojanowicz, 1985 p. 1–2.
44. Winslow, 1969, p. 73.
45. The National Criminal Justice Reference Service may be accessed online at: *http://www.ncjrs.org/*
46. Bell, 1965, pp. 152–153.
47. Sutherland & Cressey, p. 26.
48. U.S. Department of Justice, 1994.
49. Schmalleger, 2005, p. 43.
50. FBI, 2004, p. 263.
51. FBI, UCR, 2004, Table 25, p. 266.
52. Winslow, 1969, p. 67.
53. Brown, Esbensen, & Geis, 2001, p. 95.
54. U.S. Department of Justice. FBI, 2002.
55. Eck & Riccio, 1979.
56. Schmalleger, 1991, p. 53.
57. Maxwell, 1996.
58. Taylor & Rand, 1995, p. 2.
59. Kappeler, Blumberg, & Potter, 1996, pp. 43–44.
60. Kappeler, Blumberg, & Potter, 1996, p. 40; Catalano, 2005, p. 5. In this table, "Larceny without Contact" includes both "Larceny without Contact" and "Household Larceny" from the table developed by Kappeler, Blumberg, and Potter, since the 2004 NCVS did not make such a distinction. Larceny with Contact is equated with "Personal Theft" in the NCVS 2004 report, whereas Larceny without Contact is equated with "Theft" in the NCVS 2004 report.
61. BJS, 2003b, 2004c.
62. BJS, 2003b, pp. 138–143.
63. BJS, 1995, Table 1, and BJS, 2004c, Table 3.
64. Bierne & Messerschmidt, 1995, p. 47.

65. Siegel, 2003, pp. 52–53.

66. Adler, Mueller, & Laufer, 2004, pp. 37–38.

67. Fairchild & Dammer, 2001, p. 18.

68. A 1994 survey estimating the number of persons treated in hospital emergency departments for nonfatal injuries estimated the estimated number of those treated for injuries inflicted by intimates was four times higher than estimates from the U.S. NCVS. See Rand, 1997. Another study comparing the NCVS with two other national data sets, the NYS and the Monitoring the Future survey, found the victimization rates for general violence were four times larger than the corresponding rates from the NCVS. See Wells & Rankin, 1995.

69. See, e.g., Cohen & Cantor, 1980, and Madriz, 1996.

70. See, e.g., Levitt, 1999.

71. Studies on race and violence include the following: Dugan & Apel, 2003; Finkelhor & Ormrod, 2000a; and Cook & Laub, 1998.

72. Rennison & Planty, 2003.

73. Porterfield, 1943.

74. Wallerstein & Wyle, 1947.

75. Wallerstein & Wyle, 1947, pp. 111–112.

76. Short & Nye, 1957; Short & Nye, 1958.

77. Gold & Reimer, 1975.

78. Williams & Gold, 1972, p. 213.

79. Williams & Gold, 1972, p. 217.

80. Elliott, Huizinga, & Ageton, 1985.

81. Elliott & Ageton, 1980.

82. Huizinga & Elliott, 1987.

83. Johnston, Bachman, & O'Malley, 2003.

84. Osgood, O'Malley, Bachman, & Johnston, 1989.

85. Johnston, Bachman, & O'Malley, 2003.

86. Johnston, Bachman, & O'Malley, 2003; These are approximations for the UCR index offenses based upon the content of the questions. For instance, robbery is "Used a knife or gun or some other thing (like a club) to get something from a person."

87. Brown, Esbensen, & Geis, 2001, p. 107.

88. Brown, Esbensen, & Geis, 2001, p. 108; Siegel & Senna, 2000, p. 49.

89. Burnham, 1997.

90. Center for International Crime Prevention Office for Drug Control and Crime Prevention and Statistics Division Department of Economic and Social Affairs, United Nations, 1995.

91. Cross-references are based upon location of data entry. For instance, for year 2001, the UCR rates for the United States were murder 5.6, forcible rape 31.8, robbery 148.5, aggravated assault 318.5, burglary 740.8, larceny-theft 2,484.6, and motor vehicle theft 430.6. Compare with INTERPOL rates for 2001 for murder 5.61, rape 31.77, robbery and violent theft 148.50, serious assault 318.55, breaking and entering 740.8, other thefts 2,484.64, and theft of motor cars 430.64.

92. Fairchild & Dammer, p. 20–21.

93. Bennett & Lynch, 1990.

94. Fairchild & Dammer, 2001, p. 27.

95. As quoted in Fairchild & Dammer, 2001, p. 25.

96. Reichel, 2005, p. 37.

97. Reichel, 2005, p. 37.

98. He & Marshall, 1997; Yu & Zhang, 1999; Liu, 2005.

99. Li, 1998.

100. Yu & Zhang, 1999.

101. Fairchild & Dammer, 2001, p. 29.

102. Fairchild & Dammer, 2001, p. 21.

103. Fairchild & Dammer, 2001, pp. 22–23.

104. Van Kesteren, Mayhew, & Nieuwbeerta, 2000.

105. Junger-Tas, & Klein, 1994.

106. Junger-Tas, Terlouw, & Klein, 1994.

3

HISTORICAL THEORIES OF CRIME

KEY TERMS

atavism
born criminal
Classical School of Criminology
constitutional theory
criminology
diyya
eugenics movement
Five Pillars of Islam
hedonistic calculus

Hudud crimes
mesomorphy
psychoanalytic theory
psychological trait theory
Social Darwinism
somatotyping
stigmata of degeneracy
utilitarianism

OUTLINE

Religious Theories of Crime Causation
The Classical School of Criminology
Biological Determinism

Mind, Self, and Crime
"Born Criminal" Revisited: IQ and Delinquency
Psychological Trait Theory

LEARNING OBJECTIVES

After reading this chapter, students should be able to:

1. Describe the historical role of Christian beliefs in the development of the current American criminal justice system

2. Understand the relationship between Buddhism and the Chinese rehabilitation program of "reform through labor"

3. Describe the link between the worldwide growth of Islamic fundamentalism and the desire for the control of crime in developing nations

4. Derive insight as to the Classical School of Criminology and the development of the American criminal justice system

5. Show awareness of the born criminal theory and its relationship to English colonization and, more recently, to the eugenics movement in the United States

6. Derive a relationship between the born criminal theory and constitutional theory, psychological trait theory, and IQ studies

7. Appreciate the significance of Freudian theory in introducing the relevance of socialization as a factor in the development of criminality

INTRODUCTION

An offense does not become a crime until it is defined as such by law, and legal codes date back to the Babylonian Code of Hammurabi of around 1700 B.C.[1] Given that a "theory" is "a belief not yet tested in practice,"[2] theories about crime may date back to the early legal codes that defined crimes. Such theories may have formed the basis for punishments as prescribed by law. Volumes could be written on the subject of theories about crime throughout history. However, this chapter focuses on historical theories that are related to the United States common law system, as well as related to the other legal systems of the world—civil law, Islamic law, and socialist law. It should be noted that many of these theories about crime are widely supported today. For instance, evangelical Christian beliefs are popular in the United States today and are influential in forming public policy regarding crime. Similarly, there has been a growth in Islamic fundamentalism during the last half of the 20th century and continuing into the 21st century. Concurrently, the growth of the use of Islamic Shari'a law influences the treatment of those defined as criminals in many countries today.[3] Also, the neoclassical movement is currently seeking to revive the utilitarianism approach to crime that dates back to the Enlightenment of the late 18th century in Europe. A review of these historical theories can be helpful in understanding the full range of theories about crime that are prevalent in the United States today. In addition, early positivism in the form of the "born criminal" theory is discussed in this chapter as "historical" in the sense that it emerged in the 19th century. Finally, the 19th-century Freudian theory that came to challenge the "born criminal" concept is discussed in this chapter.

RELIGIOUS THEORIES OF CRIME CAUSATION

Religious beliefs regarding the origin of crime and criminal behavior are often ignored in discussions of criminological theory. Many texts suggest that such views were prevalent in the past, but are not widely held today. Others reject religious theories because they cannot be tested scientifically. As one text put it, "Because the cause of crime according to this theory is other-worldly, it cannot be verified empirically. It is primarily for this reason that modern theories of crime and social order rely on explanations that are based on this world."[4]

Although it is probably true that religious beliefs were more influential in Western societies in the past than in the present, it is by no means true that they have no relevance today. In fact, there is evidence that religious fundamentalism is becoming a worldwide movement.[5] In the United States, conservative Christian religious groups have gained a foothold and have exerted a growing influence upon both national and state government, particularly in the South. In Southeast Asia, Buddhism has had an impact upon crime and criminal justice policy. In Central Asia, the Mideast, and North Africa, a large number of countries have recently "gone Islamic," especially since the fall of the Soviet Union and the decline of Western colonial rule. Islamic countries recently freed from Soviet rule include Afghanistan, Azerbaijan, Kazakstan, Kyrgyzstan, Tajikistan, and Uzbekistan, while Islamic countries freed from colonial domination by France and England include Algeria, Bahrain,

Bangladesh, Egypt, Iran, Iraq, Kuwait, Lebanon, Oman, Pakistan, Qatar, Somalia, Sudan, Syria, and the United Arab Emirates. Of the remaining Islamic countries, Indonesia became independent of Dutch rule, Turkey was "liberated" by the Allies from Ottoman rule after WWI, and Saudi Arabia has always been independent of colonial domination. Although colonial and Soviet rule imposed secular states in these countries, liberation resulted in Islam being endorsed as the state religion, with the consequence that the influence of Islam has re-emerged.[6]

Christian Beliefs

Historically, Christian religious beliefs were very influential in determining criminal justice policy in the Western hemisphere. In the middle ages in Europe, criminal justice policy evolved from the belief that God would punish transgressors. As a means of counteracting blood feuds that would continue indefinitely, feudal lords instituted *trial by battle* in which the victim or family member would fight the offender or member of his or her family. It was assumed that the winner was ordained by God, so that the loser had no basis for exacting vengeance. However, "might did not always make right" in the sense that great warriors would engage in criminal behavior to win, knowing that winning would support their claim of innocence. To avoid this problem, *trial by ordeal* was instituted. The accused was subjected to some painful test, and it was assumed that an innocent person would emerge unharmed, whereas a guilty person would die a painful death. These tests included being thrown into water, running the gauntlet, walking on fire, and being buried by stones. After the practice of trial by ordeal was condemned by the Pope in 1215, it was replaced by *compurgation*. In this procedure, the accused gathered together 12 reputable people who would swear under oath that the accused was innocent. It was assumed that nobody would lie for fear of being punished by God. This practice ultimately evolved into testimony under oath and trial by jury.[7]

Closely related to the belief that God would protect the innocent was the belief that persons who commit "evil deeds" (such as crimes) are possessed by demons. During the Middle Ages and during the colonial period of America, it was strongly believed that persons could be possessed by the devil and this belief was linked with the Christian concept of original sin.[8] During the first 60 years of its existence, the Puritan colony on Massachusetts Bay experienced three "crime waves" believed to be caused by the devil, related to a belief that the colony had been invaded by witches. Witches were tested by professional witch finders by pricking various parts of the body. Witches were said to have some spot that was insensitive to pain, and if such a spot was found, this would be evidence of witchcraft. Another test was to throw the suspected person into a body of water. If she sunk, it was assumed she was innocent, but if she stayed afloat, she was found guilty. In 1692, 20 people were executed in Massachusetts after the Salem witch trials, when a group of young girls became hysterical after playing at magic, and it was assumed that they were bewitched.[9]

As discussed in Chapter 1, the prison system that we have today owes its origin to spiritual beliefs. The first prison system originated partly as a reaction to some of the barbaric punishments done in Europe and in the Colonies. In 1790, some Pennsylvania Quakers conceived the idea of isolating criminals in cells and giving them a Bible to read and some manual labor to perform. It was assumed that the criminals would think about their wrongdoings and

BOX 3–1

Animism and Voodoo in Benin

Several religions are practiced in Benin. *Animism* is widespread (50%), and its practices vary from one ethnic group to the other. Animism involves a belief in a multitude of localized and limited spiritual forces, some friendly and some hostile. Arab merchants introduced Islam in the north and among the Yoruba. European missionaries brought Christianity to the south and central areas of Benin. Moslems account for 20% of the population and Christians for 30%.

Many nominal Moslems and Christians continue to practice animistic traditions. It is believed that voodoo originated in Benin and was introduced to Brazil and the Caribbean Islands by slaves taken from this particular area of the Slave Coast. Voodoo is a blend of Roman Catholicism and tribal religions of western Africa, particularly Benin. Voodoo cults worship a supreme being, the dead, twins, and spirits called *loa*, usually identified with Roman Catholic saints. Dancing, drumming, and the worship of ancestors and twins are African practices linked with Voodooism.[10]

repent. Thus, the term *penitentiary* was used to describe a place for such persons, the first of which was the Walnut Street Jail in Philadelphia.[11]

Demonology influenced the legal codes and practices of the courts in England and the United States during the 19th century. In England, during the 19th century, a formal indictment accused the criminal of "being prompted and instigated by the devil." In the United States, a state supreme court in 1862 stated that "to know the right, and still the wrong pursue, proceeds from a perverse will brought about by the seduction of the evil one."[12]

Religious leaders have often attributed crime to the influence of the devil. In 1972, Pope Paul VI was quoted as saying that the devil is dominating "communities and entire societies through sex, narcotics, and doctrinal errors." He added that "We are all under obscure domination. It is by Satan, the prince of this world, the number one enemy."[13] More recently, in January 1999 the Vatican issued a new exorcism ritual, while blaming Satan for many of today's ills. The actual formula for the ritual remains unchanged and has two parts:

> The first is the "imploring formula," in which the evils of the devil are listed and God is entreated to free the possessed. The second, more intense formula, is the "imperative formula" in which the devil is ordered to leave the possessed. The imperative formula begins: "I order you, Satan . . ." It then goes on to denounce Satan as "prince of the world" and "enemy of human salvation." It ends: "Therefore, Go Back, Satan."[14]

Today in America there is evidence of a rising influence of fundamentalist individuals and groups such as Pat Robertson, Jerry Falwell, Benny Hinn, Jim Bakker, and the Christian Coalition, seeking to reverse the tide of what they see as the secularization of institutions in the country. The devil is typically blamed for criminality and wrongdoing in public statements. In 1987, Jim Bakker of the PTL Club (Praise the Lord and People That Love) admitted to an adulterous affair with a former church secretary, and some of his followers said it was the result of the "devil's work." When the Internal Revenue Service found several million dollars unaccounted for by the PTL organization, Tammy Faye Bakker maintained that the devil must have gotten into the computer.[15] Another public figure who attributed crime to his "sinful human nature" was Charles Colson, special counsel to President Nixon, who spent several months in prison and then began taking the Christian message to prisoners as a solution to their problems.[16]

BOX 3-2

The Ten Commandment Controversy

Stone Tablets Wield "Magical Powers" Say Town Leaders (Story dated Tuesday August 5, 2003)

BEARDSTOWN, ILLINOIS—On Friday, the city council voted 6 to 1 in favor of placing a pair of mysterious stone tablets in the courthouse square. According to legend, this fused pair of quarter ton granite slabs is covered in strange writing, presumably some sort of spell, that grants it the power to protect the town from common evils such as "street crime, homosexuality, and dancing."

At first many in the town were skeptical that these "Ten Commandments" carried such powers, but Rev. Shaw Moore convinced them all during last week's public hearing on the issue. Moore presented a full-color chart illustrating social trends since the tablets were removed in 1959 to make way for an indoor restroom. Beginning in 1960, the line representing the "Society Going to Hell Index" rose sharply, going off the edge of the chart by the beginning of the Clinton administration in 1993.

Supporters say the tablets will defend the town from immorality and crime. Yet voodoo practitioners argue that their proposal for a 10-foot high display of bloody rags and chicken bones would similarly protect the town from evil spirits but was summarily rejected by the city council last year on the grounds that it would be unsanitary.[17]

The Beardstown, Illinois, story quoted here relates to a controversy that is occurring elsewhere in the nation concerning the display of Christian symbols on public property (such as Christian cross and Ten Commandments monuments). In 2005, the United States Supreme Court ruled unconstitutional a display of the Ten Commandments that had been posted in a Kentucky county courthouse. Pictured above is a Ten Commandments Monument at the Texas State Capitol.

Source: Getty Images, Inc.

Buddhist Beliefs

The incidence of common crime is reported to be low in Laos, Sri Lanka, Thailand, and Cambodia, where the dominant religion is Buddhism.

Buddhism has been the state religion of the Kingdom of Laos, and the organization of the Buddhist community of monks and novices, the clergy (*sangha*), paralleled the political hierarchy.

Virtually all lowland Lao were Buddhists in the early 1990s, as well as some Lao Theung who have assimilated into lowland culture. Since 1975 the communist government has not opposed Buddhism but rather has attempted to manipulate it to support political goals, and with some success. Increased prosperity and a relaxation of political control stimulated a revival of popular Buddhist practices in the early 1990s.

Lao Buddhists belong to the Theravada tradition, based on the earliest teachings of the Buddha. Theravada Buddhism is neither prescriptive, authoritative, nor exclusive in its attitude toward its followers and is tolerant of other religions. It is based on three concepts: *dharma*, the doctrine of the Buddha, a guide to right action and belief; *karma*, the retribution of actions, the responsibility of a person for all his or her actions in all past and present incarnations; and *sangha*, within which a man can improve the sum of his actions. There is no promise of heaven or life after death but rather salvation in the form of a final extinction of one's being and release from the cycle of births and deaths and the inevitable suffering while part of that cycle. This state of extinction, *nirvana*, comes after having achieved enlightenment regarding the illusory nature of existence.

The essence of Buddhism is contained in the Four Noble Truths taught by the Buddha: suffering exists; suffering has a cause, which is the thirst or craving for existence; this craving can be stopped; and there is an Eightfold Path by which a permanent state of peace can be attained. Simply stated, the Eightfold Path consists of right understanding, right purpose, right speech, right conduct, right vocation, right effort, right thinking, and right meditation. The average person cannot hope for nirvana at the end of this life, but by complying with the basic rules of moral conduct, can improve karma and thereby better his or her condition in the next incarnation. The doctrine of karma holds that, through the working of a just and impersonal cosmic law, actions in this life and in all previous incarnations determine which position along the hierarchy of living beings a person will occupy in the next incarnation. Karma can be favorably affected by avoiding these five prohibitions: killing, stealing, forbidden sexual pleasures, lying, and taking intoxicants. The most effective way to improve karma is to earn merit (*het boun*—literally, to do good—in Lao). Although any act of benevolence or generosity can earn merit, Laotians believe the best opportunities for merit come from support for the *sangha* and participation in its activities.[18]

BOX 3–3

Buddhism and Prison Reform in China

China adopted a Western practice of imprisonment during the Qing dynasty in the early 20th century, partly to show that it was a modern country. Prior to the 20th century, punishment for crime included ritualized beatings, banishments, and executions in which the prisoner was beheaded and his head was publicly displayed. Central to the early prisons was the concept of *ganhua*, or reformation, which was a concept influenced by Confucian and Buddhist teachings. Although western countries largely abandoned the doctrine of rehabilitation in the late 20th century, Chinese authorities have continued to believe that prison can reform. After the development of a communist state in China, doctrine of *ganhua* has been largely replaced by *laogai*, which means "reform through labor." Chinese prisons manufacture products that include everything from green tea to industrial engines to coal dug from mines.[19]

BOX 3–4

Islam in Former Soviet Countries

Although 87% of the population was Muslim in 1989, as in the other former Soviet Muslim republics, religious observances in Azerbaijan do not follow all the traditional precepts of Islam. For example, drinking wine is permitted, and women are not veiled or segregated.[20]

Islamic Beliefs

No discussion of the influence of the rise of fundamentalism should be concluded without some discussion of Islamic law and beliefs. As mentioned earlier, Islam has risen to prominence in some 24 countries in the Mideast and North Africa, endorsed as the state religion. Some of the punishments under Shari'a law (the law of Islam) in these countries are reminiscent of those practiced during the Middle Ages in Western society (whipping, mutilation, capital punishment, etc.).

However, proponents of Islamic law argue that such methods result in a very low crime rate, as well as low rates of recidivism and a minimal use of imprisonment. The spread of Islam in countries that are emerging from colonial rule may be partly explained by the reduction from crime that it brings in developing nations that otherwise would be beset by civil and tribal warfare, along with concomitant rising rates of property crime and crimes against persons. A brief review of the "Islamic theory of crime" seems appropriate here.

Islamic law serves, not so much as a theory of the cause of crime, but as a theory as to the prevention or deterrence of crime.[21] Devotion to Islam is thus a remedy for crime. Devotion to Islam means following the precepts of the Prophet Mohammad. Muslims believe that Mohammad received the Islamic religion from God in Mecca in the year 622 A.D. Believers adhere to the **Five Pillars of Islam,** which are: (a) *shahada:* belief in one God; (b) *al-Salat:* prayer five times per day at dawn, noon, afternoon, sunset, and night; (c) *al-Sayam:* fasting during the month of Ramadan; (d) *al-Hajj:* pilgrimage to Mecca once in a lifetime; and (e) *al-Zakat:* or charity—taking from the rich and giving to the poor. The believer is to pray in a prescribed manner after purification through ritual ablutions at dawn, midday, midafternoon, sunset, and nightfall. Prescribed genuflections and prostrations are to accompany the prayers, which the worshiper recites while facing Mecca.[22]

Compared to Judaism and Christianity, Islam is not a new religion—just the most recent. It is believed that God sent his messengers successively: Moses, Jesus, and Muhammad. Thus, Christians and Jewish people, known as Zimmi, have the right to practice their religious rituals and are equal to Muslim people in terms of their personal rights in Muslim countries.

What distinguishes Islamic criminal justice from Western justice is an emphasis upon crimes against religion and morality and the use of harsh physical punishments for crimes that would be considered minor offenses in the West. There are three categories of offenses in Islamic penal law: *Hudud* crimes, *Qisas* crimes, and *Ta'zir* crimes. **Hudud crimes** are those described in the Koran (Holy Book) and the Sunna of the Prophet, and include adultery, theft, banditry (robbery), and defamation. Three additional crimes—transgression, drinking alcohol, and apostasy—are considered by the majority of Muslim scholars to be *Hudud* crimes as well. Adultery carries a maximum penalty of death by stoning. Theft is punishable by amputation of the hands.

BOX 3-5

Death Penalty for Converts from Islam in Sudan

In Sudan, under the 1991 Criminal Act, non-Muslims may convert to Islam; however, conversion by a Muslim was punishable by death. In practice, converts were usually subjected to intense scrutiny, ostracization, intimidation, torture by authorities, and were encouraged to leave the country. Popular Defense Force (militia) trainees, including non-Muslims, were indoctrinated in the Islamic faith. In prisons and juvenile detention facilities, government officials and government-supported Islamic non-governmental organizations, or NGOs, pressured and offered inducements to non-Muslim inmates to convert. Some persons in the government-controlled camps for displaced persons reportedly at times were pressured to convert to Islam. Children, including non-Muslim children, in camps for vagrant minors were required to study the Koran, and there was pressure on non-Muslim children to convert to Islam.[23]

Banditry can result in death by crucifixion, and defamation (false accusation of unchastity) may be punished by whipping. Lesser punishments are specified for the remaining *Hudud* crimes. The two less serious crimes are *Qisas* and *Ta'zir* crimes. *Qisas* crimes are crimes against person, such as murder, manslaughter, and assault. Punishments are either *Qisas* or *diyya*.

Qisas penalties, reserved for intentional crimes against the body, are of the order of "The life for the life, the eye for the eye, the nose for the nose, the ear for the ear, the tooth for the tooth, and for wounds, retaliation."[24] This means equivalent infliction of bodily harm against the person who committed the act by the victim or his family. **Diyya** involves money to be paid in compensation, in cases where the harm was unintentional or the evidence is inconclusive. *Ta'zir* crimes include all inappropriate behaviors that do not fall either in the *Hudud* category or in the *Qisas* one. Such acts include petty theft, attempted adultery, homosexuality, lesbianism, rape, eating pork, providing false testimony, usury, fraud, embezzlement, and so forth. Penalties are discretionary on the part of the judge and include death, flagellation, imprisonment, and monetary fine.

It has been argued that these penalties, particularly those for *Hudud* crimes, have been instrumental in providing a very low rate of crime in Saudi Arabia (see text box below).[25] It is further argued that corporal punishments are of short duration, that the offender is deterred by them, that he can return to earn a living for himself and his family, and that the use of corporal punishment lowers the cost of imprisonment, which only inducts first-time criminals into a life of crime.[26]

BOX 3-6

Does Shari'a Law Curb Crime?

A study compared the 1970–1979 crime rates in the Kingdom of Saudi Arabia, which applies Shari'a law, with those of six adjacent Moslem countries that do not. Crime was measured by official crime statistics and data derived from three panels made up of judges, police officials, and laymen. Saudi Arabia's crime rate stood at about one ninth the median rate among the other nations. The rate of property crime in the kingdom was about one half the median rate among the other nations, and the rate of sex offenses was one fourth the median rate compared with the other nations. The author of the study concluded that the continuing application of Shari'a law in Saudi Arabia has a cleansing influence, promotes collective morality, and helps to foster a noncriminogenic environment.[27]

Religious beliefs about crime derive from religious teachings that are thought to be divinely inspired rather than derived from rational thought. During the middle ages in the West, and today in some Islamic countries, harsh physical punishments have been used as sanctions for crime. A reaction to this during the 18th century was the development of the **Classical School of Criminology.** The school of criminology we now call the Classical School was developed by Cesare Beccaria.

Born in Milan as the eldest son in an aristocratic family, Cesare Beccaria studied with Jesuits and later graduated in law from the University of Pavia in 1760. He became "nauseated" with the environment of the nobility and became close friends with Pietro and Alessandro Verri, two brothers who sought to reform the criminal justice system through their intellectual group called "the academy of fists." Through this group, Beccaria became aware of various French and British social contract philosophers of the Age of Enlightenment. These included Hobbes, Hume, Diderot, Helvetius, and Montesquieu, who emphasized hedonism, rationality, and free will as the bases of human action. It was as a result of encouragement by Pietro that Beccaria wrote *On Crimes and Punishments*.[28]

The French Revolution (1789–1799) and the American Revolution (1775–1783) were influenced considerably by the essay, *On Crimes and Punishments,* published anonymously by Cesare Beccaria in 1764. At the time of publication, social life in Europe could be described as chaotic and tyrannical. The middle class "bourgeoisie" was attempting to rise against opposition from a corrupt and repressive union of Church leaders and the landed aristocracy. To enforce this order, the criminal justice systems in most European countries were marred by arbitrary, biased, and capricious judicial decisions. Confessions were often coerced through the use of torture, and, once an offender was convicted, cruel punishments were exacted,

Cesare Beccaria (1738–1794)
Source: Getty Images, Inc.

BOX 3–7

Beccaria's argument can be summarized in 11 propositions.[29]

1. Individuals give up their liberty and establish society through a social contract, to escape war and chaos, establishing national sovereignty and the ability of the nation to create criminal law and punish offenders.

2. Criminal laws should be restricted in scope and not be used to enforce moral virtue, because to do so would increase rather than decrease crime.

3. The guiding principle of the administration of justice is the presumption of innocence.

4. A complete criminal law code should be written, with all offenses and punishments defined in advance, permitting public oversight of judicial proceedings.

5. Retributive reasoning should serve as a basis for punishment because one person's individual rights were attacked by another person.

6. The severity of the punishment should not exceed that which is necessary for crime prevention and deterrence.

7. The punishment should fit the severity of the crime.

8. Punishment should be swiftly administered and certain.

9. Punishment should not be administered to set an example; neither should it have to do with reforming the offender.

10. The offender is viewed as a reasoning and independent person.

11. Prevention of crime is the goal of every good system of legislation.

including whipping, public hanging, burning alive, breaking on the wheel, working as an oarsman on galleys, branding, the pillory, and mutilation. Beccaria, an Italian mathematician and economist, who was incensed by these conditions, distilled many of the most powerful 18th century ideas of democratic liberalism and applied these ideas to criminal justice. He published his essay anonymously because he feared reprisals from the monarchy.[30]

Although Beccaria's 11 principles have probably had the greatest impact on public policy over time, Jeremy Bentham (1748–1832), a British philosopher and contemporary of Beccaria, is considered to be cofounder of the Classical School of Criminology. Bentham provided a theory of human nature known as **utilitarianism**, which served as the philosophical basis for the Classical School of Criminology.[31] Utilitarianism was a system of ethics based upon the hedonistic premise that good can be judged by whatever brings the greatest happiness to the greatest number of people. It is the business of government to promote happiness for the greatest number by rewarding and punishing. Bentham argued that all human action is motivated by the pursuit of pleasure and avoidance of pain. Punishment is a necessary evil that government must engage in to prevent the rampant criminality that would naturally occur due to hedonistic human nature. However, the purpose of punishment is deterrence and not vengeance, and the pain inflicted by the punishment should just exceed the pleasure of the crime. Bentham proposed that a **hedonistic calculus** could be developed for this purpose for all forms of crime.

Probably no other works in history have influenced the American criminal justice system, as well as that of much of Europe, than the writings of Beccaria and Bentham. Their ideas not only inspired the French and American Revolutions, but also provided a basis for the famous French Code of 1791 and the United States Constitution, which serves as the ultimate basis for law in the United States.

BOX 3–8

Theory vs. Practice in France

A study of the French criminal justice system from 1871 to 1940 found that the egalitarian and libertarian principles espoused in the French Revolution were conspicuously absent from France's actual criminal justice system.[32]

Although the Classical School of Criminology has provided a more or less continuous basis for law in the United States, explanations of criminal motivation departed in varying degrees from the assumption inherent in the classical school that criminal behavior is the product of a rational mind. That is particularly true of the early positivist school. However, recently there has been a return to classical theories, perhaps brought about by disenchantment with criminological theory in general. The neoclassical theories are reviewed in Chapter 5.

BIOLOGICAL DETERMINISM

The most significant early contribution to the school of criminology we now call biological determinism was the work of Cesare Lombroso. Lombroso's theories would be today viewed by contemporary criminologists as a manifestation of racism.[33] Yet his work is tremendously important in two senses—one having to do with his methodology and the other having to do with public policy. Most significant in terms of the history of criminology was Lombroso's use of the scientific method to study criminals. The latter achievement led to Lombroso being proclaimed "the father of modern criminology."[34] The word "theories" rather than "theory" is used because Lombroso's theory changed over time in response to criticism and alternative intellectual views.

Cesare Lombroso (1835–1909)
Source: © Bettmann/CORBIS.

Although Lombroso's inauguration of the use of the scientific method to the study of criminology constituted a positive contribution, there was a dark side to his theorizing, having to do with public policy implications. Lombroso's work led to the concept of the **born criminal,** which had a role in the development of fascism in Europe, as well as the British conquest of India. The born criminal theory was tremendously influential both then and today among groups of neo-Nazis who still accept the doctrine.

Cesare Lombroso was born in Verona, Italy. He was educated by the Jesuits and received a degree in medicine in 1858 from the University of Pavia and in surgery in 1859 from the University of Genoa. After serving as an army physician, he held positions at the University of Turin. These included professor of legal medicine and public hygiene (1876), professor of psychiatry and clinical psychiatry (1896), and professor of criminal anthropology (1906).[35]

Curiously, Cesare Beccaria graduated from that same university exactly one century before, in 1758. What had occurred in that century (1758–1858) was a movement toward secular, rational-scientific thinking and experimentation, as opposed to the "pure reason" of the Age of Enlightenment. Along with the scientific thinking came the doctrine of human evolution developed by Charles Darwin (1809–1882) in his major works, including *Origins of the Species,* published in 1859 and *Descent of Man,* published in 1871.[36] Lombroso developed an interest in biological influences on criminal behavior while he was serving as an army physician between 1859 and 1863. During this period, Lombroso conducted autopsies on 66 executed offenders, including a well-known criminal named Vilella. While examining Vilella's brain, Lombroso found features that he identified as similar to those found in lower primates, findings supported by the study of another offender named Misdea. Lombroso also examined 832 living prison inmates and compared body part measurements with those of 390 soldiers.[37] From this research, Lombroso identified body features that he considered to be **stigmata of degeneracy** indicative of **atavism** or reversion to earlier forms of the human species. In a perspective viewed as racism today, Lombroso observed that those traits could be observed in the "savages" or aborigines of Africa and the Americas. Lombroso said "many of the characteristics presented by savage races are very often found among born criminals."[38] Such traits, Lombroso said, included sloping foreheads; ears of unusual size; excessively long arms; receding chins; excessive cheek bones; twisted noses; fleshy, swollen, and protruding lips; premature and abundant wrinkling of the skin; inability to blush; anomalies of the hair; extra fingers, toes, or nipples; ambidexterity; insensitivity to pain; and excessive tattooing.[39] Summarizing the results of a study of 383 Italian men convicted of various crimes, Lombroso found that 21% had just one of these traits, but 43% had five or more.[40] Lombroso published his findings in *The Criminal Man* in 1876.

Further evidence that Lombroso felt that indigenous peoples were "throwbacks to primitive man" is found in the following quote:

> To those who . . . object that there are savage peoples who are honorable and chaste, we must reply that a certain degree of density of population and of association among men is necessary for crime. It is not possible for example, to steal when property does not exist, or to swindle when there is no trade. But the proof that these tendencies exist in germ in the savage, is that when they begin to pass from their stage of savagery and take on a little civilization they always develop the characteristics of criminality in an exaggerated form.[41]

BOX 3-9

The Thugs of India

Sir William Henry Sleeman (1788–1856) was a British soldier and administrator in India who was known for his suppression of the Thugs or religious murderers in India. He became superintendent of the operations against them in 1835 and commissioner for the suppression of *Thuggi* and *Dacoity* in 1839. Over 1,400 Thugs were hanged or transported for life, one of whom confessed to having committed over 700 murders. Informers were used as a means of detection; however, informers were protected from the vengeance of their associates through incarceration in a special prison at Jubbulpore. Sleeman implemented the "born criminal theory" by incarcerating both husbands and wives separately to prevent additional offspring.[42]

In response to criticism by scientists, including Lombroso's student Enrico Ferri, who argued that Lombroso had ignored social and economic causes of crime, Lombroso revised his approach in subsequent editions of *The Criminal Man* and in another book, *Crime: Its Causes and Remedies,* published in 1912. He developed an expanded typology of criminals that included (a) the born criminal; (b) the insane—those who were criminals because of insanity and epilepsy; (c) the passionate—criminals of passion; and occasional criminals. Occasional criminals included three subtypes, including (d) pseudocriminals, who are forced to commit crime in self-defense or to defend family honor; (e) criminaloids, who are enticed into crime by environmental circumstances or opportunities; and (f) habitual criminals, who have encountered poor socialization in school and by parents.

Lombroso ultimately revised his first estimate of atavists down from two thirds to one third of the criminal population. Yet he remained committed to his original thesis that criminal behavior has biological roots.[43]

Lombroso's theory of atavistic criminals may have had a profound impact internationally. In India, some 126 tribes/castes were designated criminal tribes under the *Criminal Tribes and Castes Act of 1871.* The police, during their training, were instructed to treat these tribes and castes as "born criminals." The application of the born criminal theory, largely a byproduct of Lombroso's work, turned out to be a very potent tool for English colonial domination in India. During the late 19th century, Britain developed a criminal justice system devoted to rooting out the "criminal tribes," particularly those who practiced thuggery. The notion of genetically inferior criminal tribes, promulgated by the British, was compatible with the ruling Hindu concept of caste.[44]

BOX 3-10

Raffaele Garofalo's Typology

Raffaele Garofalo, one of Lombroso's most important followers, was an Italian law professor who was also a practicing lawyer, prosecutor, and magistrate.[45] Garofalo is best known for having coined the term **criminology**.[46] Garofalo developed a fourfold typology of criminals that placed greater importance upon psychological degeneracy than physical abnormalities. The typology included (a) typical criminals, or murderers who kill for enjoyment; (b) violent criminals; (c) lascivious criminals; and (d) criminals deficient in *pity* and *probity*. *Pity* referred to the sentiment of revulsion against the voluntary infliction of suffering on others, whereas *probity* referred to respect for the property of others.[47]

After Lombroso's death in 1909, his legacy of biological determinism was carried on by his students, Enrico Ferri and Raffaele Garofalo. Ultimately they become politically involved with the fascist movement in Italy. Both Ferri and Garofalo were willing to sacrifice individual rights to the opinion of "scientific experts." Their ideas were accepted by Mussolini's regime in Italy because they lent "the mantle of scientific credence to the ideas of racial purity, national strength, and authoritarian leadership."[48] In fact, after Mussolini came to power in the 1920s, Ferri was invited to write a new penal code in Italy (which was later rejected by the regime because it was too much of a departure from classical legal reasoning).[49]

Lombroso's Legacy

Many if not most criminology texts dismiss Lombroso's findings as "bad science." For instance, one popular text argues that "Lombroso's version of strict biological determinism is no longer taken seriously."[50] Lombroso is criticized for his methodological errors. Akers indicated that Lombroso was attacked for engaging in tautological reasoning, that is, including traits of criminals in his definition of the "criminal type."[51] Also, Lombroso used Italian soldiers as a control group, which might not represent the general "non-criminal" population. Lombroso has also been assailed for drawing unwarranted conclusions about the significance of differences between samples that would not be considered significant using today's rigorous statistical tests.[52] Further evidence against Lombroso's findings has been drawn from Charles Goring's study, described in his book, *The English Convict*, in which he replicated Lombroso's study comparing 3,000 English convicts with a large group of noncriminal (meaning without criminal convictions) Englishmen. Goring used more sophisticated statistical techniques and found no significant differences between the two groups in terms of physical measurements or the presence of physical anomalies. Even assuming that Lombroso had found true differences in his Italian samples, the possibility always remains that the convicted criminals in Lombroso's samples were prejudicially selected by agents of the criminal justice system because of their distinctive physical appearance.

The question remains as to whether Lombroso's findings have indeed been truly discredited by contemporary science, or if there is an undercurrent of controversy that prevails. Clearly it can be said that biological determinism is not entirely dead, because there are periodic efforts to resurrect this point of view. In 1939, Harvard anthropologist Ernest A. Hooton published a study critical of Goring's research methods that contained measurement of more than 17,000 criminals and noncriminals from eight different states.[53] In a comparison between 3,203 "civilians" and 14,000 male prisoners, he claimed that in 19 out of 33 measurements, there were significant differences between the two samples, nearly all indicating inmate inferiority. Criminals had more straight hair, mixed patterns of eye color, sloping foreheads, pointed chins, and so forth.[54] He also maintained that low foreheads indicated inferiority and that "a depressed physical and social environment determines Negro and Negroid delinquency to a much greater extent than it does the case of Whites."[55]

Once again, just as followers of Lombroso had provided support for fascist Italy, Hooton did not limit his efforts to merely reporting his findings. He made public policy statements "calling for biological purges and compulsory sterilization of inferiors."[56] In a conclusion to his book, *The American Criminal*, he asserted:

> Criminals are organically inferior. Crime is the resultant of the impact of environment upon low grade human organisms. It follows that the elimination of crime can be effected only by the extirpation of the physically, mentally, and morally unfit, or by their complete segregation in a socially aseptic environment.[57]

As with Lombroso's findings, critics have attacked Hooton's findings as being based upon a biased sample of incarcerated inmates. Merton and Montague re-analyzed Hooton's findings, asserting that Hooton had made an *ex post factum* interpretation of the inferiority of the inmate traits in his sample. In Merton and Montague's secondary analysis of Hooting's findings, they deemed traits that were "apelike" rather than human as more primitive, and found that the criminals were superior to the civilian group in a higher percentage of advanced (non-apelike) characteristics.[58]

After Merton and Montague's research, as well as other criticisms of Hooton's methodology, many criminologists rejected his findings. However, the idea of biological determinism was very much in play during the 1920s through the 1940s. The **eugenics movement** was institutionalized in 1927 in the U.S. Supreme Court case of *Buck v. Bell*. In that case, Justice Oliver Wendell Holmes, Jr. made a statement suggesting support for biological determinism: "It is better for all the world, if instead of waiting to execute degenerate offspring for crime, or to let them starve for their imbecility, society can prevent those persons who are manifestly unfit from continuing their kind."[59] Thus, by 1949 there was a hospitable atmosphere in the United States for the findings of William Sheldon, whose **somatotyping** gave biological determinism a new twist.

Constitutional Theory

The term **constitutional theory** refers to the "constitutional psychology" of William H. Sheldon that involved the study of how physical attributes are related to personality traits. Raised on a farm in Rhode Island, William Sheldon obtained a Ph.D. in Psychology from the University of Chicago in 1925 and in 1933 earned his M.D. degree from the University of Chicago.

In 1946, he became Director of the Constitution Clinic and Laboratory at Columbia University where he pursued his work on the human constitution.[60] Following earlier work by the German psychiatrist Ernst Kretschmer, Sheldon identified three components of the human body including: (1) *endomorphy*—soft roundness; (2) **mesomorphy**—square masculinity and skeletal massiveness; and (3) *ectomorphy*—linearity and frailty. Individuals being studied are typed on all three components, such that an extreme endomorph would have a rating of 7-1-1 (7 for endomorphy, 1 for mesomorphy, and 1 for ectomorphy).

Next, Sheldon developed a schedule of temperament or personality type for each of the body types. According to Sheldon, *endomorphs* are relaxed, sociable, and love physical comfort and the company of others. *Mesomorphs* are active, assertive, aggressive, and noisy, with a lust for power and love of dominating others. *Ectomorphs* are private, restrained, and inhibited.[61] In his

William H. Sheldon (1898–1977)
Source: Brown Brothers.

work, *Varieties of Delinquent Youth,* Sheldon reported the results of his research at the Hayden Goodwill Inn, a small private home for boys in Massachusetts.[62] He found that when he compared the somatotypes of 200 youths residing at the Inn with 4,000 male college students he had examined previously, the Inn youth were high in mesomorphy and low in ectomorphy, with no significant difference in endomorphy. Further, he compared the "delinquency scores" of his subjects with those of their parents, and concluded that the tendency to become delinquent is hereditary.[63] Like Hooton and other biological determinists before him, Sheldon then made the cognitive jump to the public policy arena, once again recommending "selective breeding" or eugenics.

> In the present situation, which is purely a human arrangement . . . reproduction has been made so easy and so safe that even the weakest and least gifted of the species can spawn. The consequence is that those (least gifted) not only participate in but tend to monopolize the spawning business. . . . This is merely to say that bad reproduction drives out good. In consequence, under conditions soft and unregulated, our best stock tends to be out bred by stock that is inferior to it in every respect.[64]

Sheldon's findings met with criticism by Edwin Sutherland who, like Merton and Montague, re-analyzed Sheldon's data.[65] Sutherland correlated a measure of seriousness of delinquency with the subjects' somatotype scores, finding no significant correlation. However, Sheldon gained some support with the publication of Sheldon and Eleanor Glueck's controlled study of 500 delinquent boys, *Unraveling Juvenile Delinquency.*[66] They found that 60% of the delinquents were mesomorphs, compared with only 30.7% of the controls. In turn, the Gluecks were criticized for their methodology, namely the fact that they used photographs of the boys rather than measuring them. Also, an alternative explanation to biological determinism was given by Gibbons. Gibbons argued that muscular boys are more likely to be selected for participation in delinquent groups, rather than being motivated in some way to delinquency solely by virtue of their tendency toward mesomorphy.[67]

Sheldon's findings were not favorably received by the academic community. Nor were they acted upon by public policy makers. However, many laws had already been passed, influenced by the eugenics movement with which Sheldon's recommendations were compatible. During this time, many states passed laws against interracial marriage. Between 1911 and 1930, more than 30 states established laws requiring sterilization for behavior such as criminality, alcoholism, sodomy, bestiality, feeblemindedness, and the tendency to commit rape. Some 64,000 people were sterilized under these laws, and an unknown number of others were subjected to psychosurgeries, such as frontal lobotomies, under similar laws in the same states.[68]

MIND, SELF, AND CRIME

Many criminology texts dichotomize theories as either psychological or sociological theories of crime. The reality is that many sociological theories are tied to an underlying psychological or even psychiatric approach to crime. Although sociological variables may be the focus of sociological theories, there are often assumptions in those theories about how the mind and self interface with the sociological variables.

These assumptions are drawn, directly or indirectly, from psychological or psychiatric theories. Some examples of links between sociological and psychological theories can be drawn from theories yet to be discussed. Probably the most obvious example of a link between sociological and psychological theory would be the link between Ronald Akers' *social learning theory* and the behaviorist school of psychology. Less obvious would be the underlying use of the frustration-aggression theory, drawn ultimately from Freudian psychiatric theory, in the theories of Robert Merton, Albert Cohen, and David Matza. Merton's theory of *anomie* posits that individuals who are frustrated with their place in an unfair socioeconomic system would be drawn to "innovation" as an adaptation, meaning they would turn to illicit means to achieve their goals. Cohen borrows the concept of "reaction formation" from the Freudian concept of defense mechanisms to explain how delinquent boys reverse middle class values. David Matza borrowed from the theory of defense mechanisms when he argued that delinquents may use "techniques of neutralization" (another name for rationalizations) to neutralize the guilt they feel regarding their delinquent acts. Thus, psychological variables mediate between sociological processes and criminal and delinquent behavior. For this reason, a discussion of psychological theories should precede a full exposition of sociological theories, which are the major theories in the field of criminology today.

Sigmund Freud, though he did not write specifically on crime, may have had a profound influence in directing scientific opinion away from the born criminal theory that was so widely believed in Europe during the latter part of the 19th century. Freud could very well be credited with introducing the notion of "socialization" that is commonly accepted in sociology today.

Sigmund Freud (1856–1939)
Source: Getty Images, Inc.—Hulton Archive Photos.

Freud's background may have given him the detachment that led to his indirect challenge to the Social Darwinism of the time. He was born in Frieberg, Moravia in 1856, moving at the age of four to Vienna, where he lived and worked until the last year of his life. After the Nazis annexed Austria, Freud, who was Jewish, was allowed to leave for England. In Vienna, Freud founded the "first Viennese school" of psychoanalysis, from which all subsequent developments in the field of psychoanalysis flowed up until today.[69]

Psychoanalytic theory as applied to crime and delinquency is essentially a theory of childhood development, or "socialization." There are three components to the personality—the id, the ego, and the superego—and they develop in the same sequential order. The *id* is composed of instinctual impulses, typically of a sexual nature, developing through five stages, in which id impulses seek gratification. The *oral phase* occurs during infancy, from birth until approximately six months of age. Gratification during this stage is attained through the mouth, tongue, and lips, but frustration and conflict occurs if food is not available upon demand, and acutely so during the process of weaning. The *anal phase* continues until about age three. During this phase the bowel movement is a source of pleasure for the child, but conflict occurs during potty training and the child may even experience trauma through the loss of and disposal of the feces down the toilet. Yet this conflict leads to the development of the *ego* or differentiation between self and others. The *phallic stage* extends until age five. During this stage boys and girls develop gender identification, boys identifying with their fathers and girls with their mothers. Boys develop a sexual love for their mothers (Oedipus complex) but develop a fear of castration after a glimpse of the female genitalia, which the boy assumes to be the product of castration (castration anxiety). To avoid castration by the more powerful father, the boy identifies with and emulates the father and stops seeking sexual gratification from the mother. The *superego* develops when the child identifies with the same-sex parent, represses the id impulses, and internalizes parental control. The girl, on the other hand, develops, at the same time as her identification with her mother, a sense of inferiority after seeing the male genitals, which she perceives to be superior to her own. She then shifts her love from her mother to her father (Electra complex) and then seeks to obtain a penis in two ways. First, she can temporarily possess a penis during the act of intercourse, but secondly, she seeks to symbolically obtain a penis through giving birth to a baby boy. The *latency phase*, from 5 to 12 years of age, runs up to the time of puberty. During this phase, sexual impulses become somewhat dormant. After this, the mature *genital phase* begins and continues throughout adulthood. Delinquency, and later criminality, results from fixation at one of these stages, owed to a conflict or trauma occurring in childhood.[70]

Typically, the delinquent or criminal is unaware of the conflicts or traumas that led to the arrested development. Earlier childhood problems can result in an underdeveloped superego and ego. An underdeveloped superego

BOX 3–11

Freudian Typologies Used in Corrections

A number of psychological typologies of crime and delinquency have been developed primarily by psychiatrists using a Freudian framework of ego-id-superego. The id represents unconscious impulses, usually of a sexual nature. The ego represents the conscious self that refines the demands of the id and reconciles the impulses with social convention. The superego refers to standards of morality usually taught by parents and is commonly known as the conscience. Freudian typologies of criminals were developed by, among others, Sanford and Weinberg. Sanford describes a similar typology, but because his typology focuses upon prison inmates, it neglects the accidental or momentary offender described in the aforementioned typologies. Sanford sees essentially three types of chronic offenders, based upon variations of ego and superego. They are: *presocial criminals*, characterized by a weak superego and weak ego; the *asocial criminal*, with a strong ego but weak superego; and the *antisocial criminal*, with a strong superego and strong ego. Antisocial offenders have rebelled against their superegos and must neutralize their guilt by rationalization and through constant reassurance from compatriots.[71] Weinberg suggested a psychological typology that pertains to the presence or absence of affectionate ties in childhood, a typology that is less Freudian in its origination. Weinberg identified four criminal types, on the basis of childhood ties: (a) the *true psychopath*, who is egocentric,

irresponsible, and impulsive and has few if any childhood attachments; (b) the *acting-out neurotic*, who is capable of forming attachments, but due to inner hostility becomes alienated and isolated from relationships; (c) the *self-centered overindulged person*, who is exploitative and unscrupulous, and has experienced emotional ties with one parent, usually the mother; and (d) the *cultural delinquent*, who has had affectional relations with parents or other family members who have encultured him with a deviant value system.[72]

The psychological typologies, it may be noted, have generally fallen from favor in corrections. A typology, termed *I-level typology* or interpersonal maturity level typology, similar to Sanford's Freudian typology, was developed for use by probation and parole officers, as well as correctional personnel who work in institutions. The typology was used in several facilities for youthful offenders in California, and became the official classification system of the California Youth Authority.[73] Based upon a two-hour interview with the Jesness Inventory, an I-level was determined. *Infancy* was represented by immaturity level one (I1). The delinquent subjects tended to range from I2 to I4, with I2 representing *cultural conformers*, I3 representing *antisocial manipulators*, and I4 representing *neurotic acting out* individuals. However, I-level typology failed to be useful in lowering recidivism. Also, the overcrowding that occurred in correctional settings made individual treatment unfeasible, and thus may have discouraged interest the use of psychological typologies.[74]

involves inadequately internalized societal norms, with resulting nonconformity and unregulated id impulses.[75] Crime may also relate to an overdeveloped superego that is harsh and rigid. Persons with an overdeveloped superego experience intense feelings of guilt, and consequently, they unconsciously wish to be caught and punished to relieve guilt feelings, often leaving clues that lead to their capture. An underdeveloped ego might entail fixation at a particular stage, such as the phallic stage. An example of this would be a female who, fixated at the phallic stage, is egregiously rebellious, as an expression of her desire to be a man resulting from her "penis envy." The ego may utilize a number of defense mechanisms that may result in crime. For instance, a man who has a seductive but rejecting mother may displace his aggression by raping and murdering a woman he met at a party who spurned his advances.[76]

Although Sigmund Freud did not actually apply psychoanalytic theory directly to crime and delinquency, as mentioned previously, Freud's theory was applied to crime by followers of Freud, including Alexander and Healy,[77] Aichorn,[78] and Friedlander.[79] Psychoanalytic theory contends that delinquency and crime can only be treated via treatment of the underlying emotional disturbances through psychoanalytic treatment. Deviant behavior is, according to this approach, only a symptom of underlying deep-seated problems. Attempts at suppression of the criminal behavior will only result in manifestation of deviance in some other way.

It will be shown that psychoanalysis, along with other psychological approaches, resulted in the application of a medical model in treatment of delinquent and criminal behavior that was particularly influential during the post-WWII era. However, it subsequently fell from favor due to the failure of treatment methods (derived from this theory) to reduce delinquency and crime.[80] Also, criticism led to an awareness of inherent flaws in the theory. The main criticism of the theory is that it is untestable. Unconscious motivations imputed to offenders are unmeasurable, because they are unknown even to the offender. A statement regarding what these motivations are can only be derived from the interpretation of the therapist, and these interpretations are after the fact, tautological, and untestable.[81]

"BORN CRIMINAL" REVISITED: IQ AND DELINQUENCY

Lombroso's findings were congruent with a social philosophy of **Social Darwinism** that was popular during the late 19th and early 20th century. Just as Lombroso believed that criminals were biologically inferior throwbacks to primitive man, the Social Darwinists believed that people occupy their place in the socioeconomic system due to their superiority or inferiority. Wealthy people are so because of their genetic superiority, whereas the contrary is true of people in the underclass of society. Race typically emerges in this discussion, because African Americans, Latinos, and other people of color constitute a disproportion of people of low income in the United States. This doctrine of Social Darwinism has surfaced from time to time throughout the history of criminology.

In regard to IQ and delinquency, Social Darwinism took the form of favoring "nature" in the nature-nurture controversy. Namely, the argument was that IQ is determined primarily by the genetic makeup of the individual, rather than by environmental influences. If IQ is primarily determined by genetic makeup, and if lower IQs are found among minorities and the poor, then it follows that minorities and the poor are genetically inferior. The early findings on delinquency and IQ tended to take this orientation.

People who were brought up in the early part of the 20th century typically became aware of the story of the "Jukes and the Kallikak's" that worked its way into popular culture. Along with this story were two popular assumptions: (a) that crime and delinquency are passed on genetically through a "bad seed" running in families and (b) that crime and delinquency are linked with "feeblemindedness" or low intelligence. The story of the Jukes and Kallikaks was not merely a fable, but was an outgrowth of studies done by Richard Dugdale and Henry Goddard. Dugdale[82] explored the idea that mental degeneration is an inherited contributor to crime in a study of a family he called the Jukes. Dugdale studied some 1,200 descendents of Ada Juke, finding that most of her 1,200 heirs were "social degenerates." Henry Goddard published a similar study of the Kallikak family in 1912. Martin Kallikak was a Revolutionary War soldier who had mated with two women. The first was a "feebleminded" barmaid, who bore an illegitimate son. Her son's heirs contained some 480 descendents, half of whom were "feebleminded" or deviant progeny. The second was a "virtuous" Quaker woman whom Kallikak married. The legitimate line produced 496 offspring by 1912. Of these, only three were abnormal and none were criminal. Though these studies were highly influential and compatible with then-popular views on genetic inheritance, they were unscientific. Statistical tests for probabilities were not done and there were no controls regarding environmental influences that could have served as alternative explanations for the outcomes. Goddard continued his research on intelligence and criminality through research on prison inmates. Goddard is credited with being the first person to test the IQs of prison inmates, using an intelligence test originally developed by the French psychologist Alfred Binet. He concluded that most inmates were feebleminded.[83] However, when an IQ test similar to the one used by Goddard was subsequently used to determine who was fit for military service in World War I, it was determined that nearly one third of the army draftees were found to be "feebleminded." Nevertheless, faith in lack of intelligence as an explanation for crime continued well past World War I into the 1920s and 1930s.[84] Subsequently, the nurture theory has tended to be assumed by social scientists on the subject of delinquency and IQ. This view holds that intelligence is partly biological but primarily environmental. Also, this view holds that lack of environmental stimulation encourages both low IQ and delinquency.[85] Along with this, studies have challenged that there is a relationship between IQ and delinquency at all.[86]

More recently, the IQ and delinquency debate was revived by Hirschi and Hindelang. Hirschi and Hindelang[87] argued that low IQ increases the chance of delinquent behavior by virtue of its effect on school performance and that it is more important than race and social class in predicting delinquency involvement. This view was supported in Wilson and Herrnstein's widely read book, *Crime and Human Nature.*[88] Low IQ has been linked with delinquency for various reasons, including its role in school failure and underachievement,[89] as well as its relationship to lack of future orientation and lack of empathy for victims.[90] The publication that sparked the most controversy (including some 11,000 links on the web search engine Google) has probably been the best-selling book *The Bell Curve,*[91] by Richard J. Herrnstein and Charles Murray, originally published in 1994 (see text box). Much of the academic criticism of

BOX 3–12

The Bell Curve

In their book, *The Bell Curve,* Herrnstein and Murray make certain assumptions—that there is such a thing as a general factor of cognitive ability on which human beings differ (g); that IQ tests measure this factor accurately; that this is equivalent to what most people refer to as *intelligent* or *smart;* that IQ scores are stable over a person's life; that IQ tests are not biased against social, economic, or racial groups; and (most important) that cognitive ability is heritable (inherited) no less than 40% and no more than 80%. Based upon these assumptions, they argue that society is increasingly being stratified socioeconomically by IQ—the smart are getting richer. Correlations with IQ constitute the remainder of the book, many of which are based on the National Longitudinal Survey of Labor Market Experience of Youth (NLSY), which began in 1979 with 12,686 participants aged 14 to 22. Herrnstein and Murray argue that IQ is a stronger precursor to poverty than low socioeconomic status; that IQ is a stronger determinant of dropping out of school than poverty; that low IQ rather than socioeconomic background is the strongest risk factor for criminality; that low IQ accounts for a host of other social problems, such as unemployment, the decline of rates of marriage, welfare dependency, and illegitimacy; and that African Americans have an average IQ deficit of 15 points when compared with Caucasians. This last finding is probably what sparked the most controversy, especially because Herrnstein and Murray asserted that the IQ racial differential is primarily genetic and unresponsive to social programs. Policy implications of these findings, according to Herrnstein and Murray, are an end to programs that attempt to raise IQs of inferior children and a reallocation of educational funds to "gifted" students; an end to affirmative action in education and employment; and for a movement toward "letting people find their valued place in society," along with simplification of rules for the populace.

The Bell Curve has been an attack upon the basic methodological assumptions, as well as the right wing, or even fascist or racist implications of the book.

However, we note that for "validity testing" of variables related to IQ, Herrnstein and Murray rely strictly upon demographic data available from the Census Bureau (education, income, unemployment, etc.) and that they neglect some "microsociological" variables that are important in the criminological literature. First, there was no discussion of the influence of peers or gang membership and its impact upon school achievement and/or IQ in Herrnstein and Murray's analysis. Second, Herrnstein and Murray did not discuss the impact of school quality and/or segregation of children into different "tracks" (e.g., vocational vs. college bound) in its impact upon achievement and IQ. In fact, the major study cited (NLSY) at its beginning included youth aged 14 to 22, who may have already suffered the effects of discriminatory treatment in school upon their cognitive ability or IQ.

Yet to be introduced in the discussion about IQ and crime is the concept of *spurious correlation.* A correlation between one variable and another is no indication of causation, because a third variable could be causing both. Using somewhat the same logic of those who blame low intelligence for delinquency, if one observes overweight people drinking diet drinks 100% of the time, one could arrive at the conclusion that diet drinks cause obesity.

There is yet another twist to the IQ and delinquency controversy that was introduced in an insightful study of school and delinquency by Kenneth Polk and Walter Schafer.[92] Children in their study were placed into school tracks (college bound vs. non-college bound) based in part upon prejudicial criteria (race, parents' occupation), in addition to IQ. The result of this segregation was that the lower track children (noncollege bound) had a lowered achievement level, as measured by grade point average, as compared with the upper track (college bound). At the same time, lower track children accumulated a record for increasing delinquency, both official and self-reported. If this lowered achievement is indicative of lowered performance on IQ tests, then Polk and Schafer's study is the strongest evidence yet of lowered intelligence, as well as delinquency, being an outcome of environmental influences (in this case, discretionary treatment in school) rather than lowered intelligence causing the higher rates of delinquency.

PSYCHOLOGICAL TRAIT THEORY

Closely akin to the born criminal approaches of Lombroso, Sheldon, and others have been the countless attempts by psychologists to identify a "criminal type" in psychological terms. The focus is upon the presence of a negative or abnormal core personality that is conducive to criminality.[93] Many of these theories, because they do not attempt to trace the environmental or sociological origins of such types, seem to be assuming that such traits are genetic, in-born, or at least intrafamily in origin. Although intrafamily origins of a behavior may seem environmental, at face value, if inquiry stops at the family level we are left with a "bad seed" explanation reminiscent of the "Jukes and Kallikaks." Sutherland and Cressey expressed a similar view when they stated:

> A widely held belief is that criminal behavior is due to some characteristic or trait of the personality and that this trait is in the nature of a pathological condition which exists prior to the criminal behavior and is the cause of it. The Lombrosian notion that criminals constitute a distinct physical type has continued as a neo-Lombrosian notion that maintains the same logic but substitutes psychopathological type for physical type.[94]

The list of personality attributes that are said to be conducive to criminality include mental illness (psychosis or neurosis), psychopathy, retardation, and other character disorders. The heyday of **psychological trait theory** coincided with the period during which the biological determinist theories were prevalent in America, from the turn of the 20th century through the 1940s. One stated objective of these theories was to obtain knowledge of the causes of delinquency and crime to predict and control the behavior. Great optimism was being expressed that "science could save us" and that through the application of the scientific method to the social sciences, we could prevent crime through judicious intervention.[95] For the trait theorists, the goal was to determine a personality profile that could predict delinquency and then crime in later life. Individuals with a crime-prone personality could be singled out early in life for treatment. It was based upon this faith that the juvenile court began a campaign of preventive detention of juvenile status offenders in the 1920s. Status offenders were "predelinquent" youth who had not committed an adult crime but who had committed offenses that it was assumed were predictive of delinquency, such as running away from home, truancy, incorrigibility, drinking, associating with "immoral persons," and the like. The imprisonment of noncriminal youth continued through the late 1960s, based upon the faith that the juvenile court could provide a cure for the underlying emotional problems of such youth. This violation of juvenile civil rights was predicated upon the outcome of studies, such as those done by Healy and Bronner,[96] as well as Sheldon and Eleanor Glueck.[97]

One of the best and earliest scientific studies of personal traits in relation to delinquency was done by Healy and Bronner. It may be recalled that William Healy was a disciple of Sigmund Freud, and he sought to apply Freudian theory to the prediction of delinquency, whereas August Bronner was a psychologist. Healy and Bronner did a controlled analysis of 105 delinquents who were treated over a three-year period in three clinics, comparing them with 105 nondelinquent siblings. The siblings lived in the same homes and neighborhoods and were matched with the delinquents by age and gender. Ninety-one percent of the delinquents compared to only 13% of their nondelinquent siblings were found to have "deep emotional disturbances." This finding was cited as final proof that delinquency is due largely to emotional disturbances. However, these results were questioned by Sutherland and Cressey on several grounds.[98] One problem was the lack of objectivity in the measurement of emotional disturbance. Diagnosis was done by the staff of the clinics who were psychiatrists and psychiatric social workers, trained to interpret delinquency in terms of emotional disturbance. Another problem was the interpretation of cause and effect. Even if the delinquents were more emotionally disturbed than the nondelinquents, their disturbance might have resulted from the delinquency, or both delinquency and/or emotional disturbance might have been the product of a third cause (treatment by parents, teachers, etc.). In fact, the only way in which the delinquent differed from his nondelinquent sibling in the study was in the nature of the relationship to his parents. "In 91 percent of the cases, the delinquent child felt thwarted and rejected, even though in many instances the parent or parents were unaware either of their own role in the delinquent's concept of himself or of his feeling toward his family."[99] Also, emotional disturbance might have led to association with delinquent peers, which in turn could be the true cause of delinquency.

Eleanor and Sheldon Glueck conducted a more ambitious experimental study, the results from which were published in 1950. Although Healy and Bronner's study raised hopes that psychiatric treatment might "cure" juvenile delinquency, the Gluecks reported additional encouraging results from a study of children referred to the Judge Baker Foundation Clinic attached to the Boston Juvenile Court.[100] They then conducted a controlled study of 500 delinquents committed by the Boston juvenile court to the Lyman School for Delinquents, compared to 500 nondelinquent controls who were matched for age, ethnicity, IQ, and area of residence. The Gluecks' study included one psychiatric interview, and psychological tests, including the Bellevue-Wechsler IQ Test and Rorschach (ink blot) Test. Physical examinations were done, and school records were analyzed. Results were in agreement with Sheldon's findings, as well as those of Healy and Bronner. The delinquents were characterized as being physically mesomorphic in constitution, and restlessly energetic, impulsive, extroverted, aggressive, and destructive in temperament. In attitude, they were described as hostile, defiant, resentful, suspicious, stubborn, socially assertive, adventurous, unconventional, and nonsubmissive to authority. The delinquents were further described as intellectually concrete rather than abstract in their intellectual expression and less methodical in their approach to problems, and disproportionately came from homes of little understanding, affection, stability, and "moral fiber."

After the Gluecks study, efforts turned to more objective measurement of personality traits in studies using the Minnesota Multiphasic Personality

Inventory and the California Psychological Intentory, based upon the assumption that delinquency is symptomatic of mental illness. Research showed that institutionalized delinquents scored higher on scales that measured asocial, amoral, and psychopathic behavior, whereas nondelinquents tended to be more introverted than delinquents. However, these studies contained the methodological problem of tautology, being "true by definition" and involving "circular reasoning." These studies are tautological because they include questions like "trouble with the law" in the scale measuring "psychopathic tendencies" (the independent variable) contaminating the independent variable (psychopathy) with the dependent variable (delinquency) in the study. These scales also failed to predict future delinquency. Other research using personality inventories and other measures of personality characteristics have not been able to produce findings to support personality variables as major causes of delinquent behavior.[101]

SUMMARY AND CONCLUSION

Religious beliefs historically and today play an important role in shaping public opinion about crime and criminal justice policy. Historically, the Quaker belief that criminals can be reformed through "repenting" led to the development of the first penitentiaries in America, and references to "good" versus "evil" and the influence of the devil are evident in the Western media today. Harsh punishments, at one time a product of the Christian belief in demons, have been revived as a remedy for crime in a growing number of Islamic developing nations today. Historically, the Classical School of Beccaria and Bentham opposed such punishments that were common during the middle ages in Europe. The Classical School was a factor contributing to the French and American Revolution, the French Code of 1791, and the United States Constitution. The appeal to "pure reason" of the Classical School was opposed a century later by the work of Cesare Lombroso, who because of his use of the scientific method was credited as being the "father of modern criminology." Lombroso maintained that his observations proved that criminals were "atavists" or throwbacks to earlier stages of evolution. Although Lombroso's early use of the scientific method was refuted by Goring and others as "bad science," Lombroso's concept of the "born criminal" was influential in leading to such diverse Social Darwinist movements as the conquest of "criminal tribes" in India, fascist genocide in Europe, and the eugenics movement in the United States. The work of Sigmund Freud, a contemporary of Lombroso, was antithetical to Social Darwinism in its emphasis upon early childhood environment in shaping personality. However, the "born criminal" doctrine, popularized by Lombroso, continued (and continues) to be influential in studies of "feeblemindedness," IQ, and personality traits in relation to crime and criminal justice policy.

DISCUSSION QUESTIONS

1. Do you think religious theories and beliefs about crime have any relevance in understanding crime in today's world? Why or why not?

2. How important were Christian beliefs in the development of the U.S. criminal justice system?

3. Do you think that the Chinese doctrine of "reform through labor" could work in U.S. corrections? Why or why not?

4. How do you account for the recent growth of Islamic fundamentalism in the world today? What foreign policy do you think that the United States should adopt in regard to this movement?

5. How much influence did the Classical School have on the development of the U.S. criminal justice system? How does the U.S. criminal justice system depart from Beccaria's 11 principles?

6. Do you think that some people are "born criminals"? If so, what should be done about it? If not, why not?

7. A "medical model" based upon Freudian theory was applied in corrections after World War II, but subsequently lost influence. Why do you think the medical model lost favor in corrections? Do you think that remnants of the medical model are still in use in corrections today? Do you think we should return to the medical model? Why or why not?

SUGGESTED WEBSITES

http://www.islamic-world.net/ Website listing 55 countries of the world in which Islam is a major influence today.

http://mb-soft.com/believe/text/fundamen.htm Website describing the rise of Christian fundamentalism in the United States today.

http://www.utm.edu/research/iep/b/beccaria.htm Website for the *Internet Encyclopedia of Philosophy* providing profiles of the world's great philosophers.

http://www.rohan.sdsu.edu/faculty/rwinslow/index.html Website providing criminal justice country profiles for over 200 nations, as well as quantitative information and links to other Websites.

http://www.findarticles.com/cf_dls/g2699/0006/26990 00622/p2/article.jhtml Website for the *Gale Encyclopedia of Psychology* providing biographies for well-known psychologists.

ENDNOTES

1. Schmalleger, 2006, p. 111.
2. Webster, 1984, p. 328.
3. See *Islamic-world.net*. (2000), a Website that shows some 55 countries in which Islam is a major influence today.
4. Lilly, Cullin, & Ball, 1995, p. 14.
5. Basset, n.d.; Jones, 2001.
6. *About.com*, 2003; while today "oaths" in western jurisprudence are often quaint rituals, oaths in Islamic courts (oral statements given by devout Muslims) are taken very seriously. By themselves, they can be sufficient enough to result in a conviction—Reichel, 2005, pp. 133–134.
7. Vold & Snipes, 1998, pp. 4–5.
8. Yablonsky, 1990, p. 425.
9. Ellwood, 2003.
10. Retrieved on May 4, 2004 from a country profile on Benin; Website linked with this text at: <*http://www.rohan.sdsu.edu/faculty/rwinslow/index.html*> (hereinafter referred to as Comparative Criminology Website).
11. Vold & Snipes, 1998, p. 5.
12. Yablonsky, 1990, p. 425.
13. Yablonsky, 1990, p. 425.
14. *CNN.com*, 1999.
15. Lilly et al., 1995, p. 13.
16. Vold & Snipes, 1998, p. 5.
17. Arenz, 2003.
18. Comparative Criminology Website, Laos.
19. Kiely, 2001.
20. Comparative Criminology Website, Azerbaijan.
21. Sanad, 1991.
22. Comparative Criminology Website, Iraq.
23. Comparative Criminology Website, Sudan.
24. Sanad, 1991, p. 61.
25. Sanad, 1991, p. 57.
26. Sanad, 1991, p. 57.
27. Souryal, 1987.
28. Internet Encyclopedia of Philosophy, 2001.
29. Lilly et al., 1995, pp. 16–17.
30. Lilly et al., 1995, p. 16.
31. Bentham, 1969.
32. Martin, 1990.
33. Henderson, 1995.
34. Wolfgang, 1973, p. 232.
35. Williams & McShane, 1998, p. 40.
36. Darwin, 1999a, 1999b.
37. Schmalleger, 2002, p. 143.
38. Williams & McShane, 1998, p. 41.
39. Akers & Sellers, 2004, p. 46; Curran & Renzetti, 2001, p. 30; Lilly, 1995, p. 20.
40. Curran & Renzetti, 2001, p. 30.

41. Williams & McShane, 1998, p. 42.

42. Encyclopedia Britannica, 1911.

43. Curran & Renzetti, 1994, p. 43.

44. Hobson, n.d.

45. Lilly et al., 1995, p. 24.

46. Adler, Mueller, & Laufer, 2004, p. 12.

47. Garofalo, 1885.

48. Vold, 1958, as cited in Lilly et al., 1995, p. 26.

49. Lilly, 1995, p. 22.

50. Siegel, 2000, p. 7.

51. Akers & Sellers, 2004, p. 49.

52. Curran & Renzetti, 1994, p. 44.

53. Hooton, 1939b.

54. Curran & Renzetti, 1994, p. 46.

55. Hooton, 1939a, p. 388, as cited in Lilly et al., 1995, p. 27.

56. Henderson, 1995, p. 3.

57. Hooton, 1939a, p. 309, as cited in Curran & Renzetti, 1994, p. 47.

58. Merton & Montague, 1940, p. 400, as cited in Curran & Renzetti, 1994, p. 48.

59. Schmalleger, 2003, p. 101.

60. Alic, M., 1995.

61. Curran & Renzetti, 1994, p. 50.

62. Sheldon, 1949.

63. Curran & Renzetti, 1994, p. 51.

64. Sheldon, 1949, p. 836, as cited in Curran & Renzetti, 1994, p. 51.

65. Sutherland, 1951.

66. Glueck & Glueck, 1950.

67. Gibbons, 1970, pp. 75–76.

68. Lilly et al., 1995, p. 34.

69. Thornton, 2001.

70. Curran & Renzetti, 2001, pp. 75–77.

71. Sanford, 1943.

72. Weinberg, 1952, pp. 264–69.

73. Wedge, White, & Palmer, 1980.

74. Jesness, 1971.

75. Akers, 2000, pp. 59–60.

76. Curran & Renzetti, 2001, p. 77.

77. Alexander & Healy, 1935.

78. Aichorn, 1936.

79. Friedlander, 1949.

80. Winslow, 1976, p. 142.

81. Akers, 1997, p. 53.

82. Dugdale, 1877.

83. Goddard, 1912, 1914, 1921.

84. Lilly et al., 1995, p. 31.

85. Eels, 1951.

86. Slawson, 1926; Sutherland, 1973.

87. Hirschi & Hindelang, 1977.

88. Wilson & Herrnstein, 1985.

89. Moffitt & Silva, 1988.

90. Siegel & Senna, 2000, p. 114.

91. Herrnstein & Murray, 1996.

92. Polk & Schafer, 1972.

93. Shoemaker, 2000, p. 60.

94. Sutherland & Cressey, 1970, p. 151.

95. Lundberg, 1961.

96. Healy & Bronner, 1936.

97. Glueck & Glueck, 1934.

98. Sutherland & Cressey, 1970, pp. 161–162.

99. Robison, 1960, p. 77.

100. Glueck & Glueck, 1934.

101. Akers & Sellers, 2004, pp. 62–63.

SOCIOLOGICAL THEORIES OF CRIME

KEY TERMS

anomie theory
Chicago School of Criminology
conflict theory
containment/control theories
differential association theory
labeling theory
opportunity theory

paradigm shift
Progressivism
social disorganization
social ecology theory
social reaction theory
strain theory
symbolic interactionism

OUTLINE

The Chicago School of Criminology
Opportunity Theory

Labeling Theory
Conflict Theory

LEARNING OBJECTIVES

After reading this chapter, students should be able to:

1. Understand how the sociological approach to crime developed in America as a product of the Progressive movement

2. Name the founders of the sociological approach to crime and describe the Chicago School of Criminology

3. Describe the "paradigm shifts" in criminological thought:

   a. during the 1960s from ecological theory to opportunity theory

   b. during the 1970s from opportunity theory to labeling theory

   c. during the 1980s from labeling theory to conflict theory

4. Identify the "greats" in 20th century sociological thought about crime and know something about their biographies, the social context in which their theories developed, and the basic propositions of their theories

5. Show a relationship between these major sociological theories and the important public policy outcomes that resulted from acceptance of these theories

INTRODUCTION

Sociological explanations of crime were dominant in the 20th century and, until the 1990s, were not challenged by the rekindling of individualistic biological and psychological explanations. It is important to review why individualistic explanations were rejected in the first place and how they were replaced by sociological explanations.

Positivists of the 19th century and the first quarter of the 20th century placed the causes of all crime with in individual offenders. This orientation of positivists was partly a result of disciplinary bias. Early positivitists, such as Lombroso, Ferri, and Garofalo in Italy; Freud, Aichorn, and Kretchmer in Austria and Germany; and Alexander and Healy in the United States, were typically educated in medicine, law, or both fields. These disciplines place considerable emphasis upon factors located in the individual as an explanation of crime. However, the explanations were also influenced by the general temper of the times, the social context. The temper of the times was "Darwinism strongly flavored by Victorianism."[1] This position was inherently conservative. It was believed that government programs that provided equal treatment or social welfare would interfere with the "survival of the fittest." Such programs would prolong the survival of "inferior" people who were negligent, shiftless, incompetent, immoral, lazy, and so forth. Instead, what was advocated were "scientifically justified" forms of control combining genetics with Victorian concerns for morality and purity. Along with sterilization surgery and abortion came policies to exterminate, exclude, and imprison "unfit" and immoral individuals.

Against the backdrop of the largely European view that the causes of crime resided in the aberrant individual was a contrasting point of view emerging in the United States. During the 19th century, America witnessed industrialization and urbanization that had a more observable effect upon the United States than it may have had upon older, more established parts of the world. A major product of urbanization and industrialization was social problems linked with those trends. A major social movement called **Progressivism** began in the 1890s in response to these social problems. Progressives rejected the Social Darwinist argument that criminality was traced to the biological inferiority of the poor. Instead, they believed that the poor were driven by their environment into a criminal way of life. The Progressives pushed for government programs to save the poor by providing social services, including schools, clinics, recreational outlets, settlement homes, foster care, and reformatories. Progressives were also concerned about the excesses of industry, and muckraking authors of the Progressive tradition, including Lincoln Steffens, Theodore Dreiser, and Upton Sinclair, exposed corruption in city government, the corporate abuses of oil companies, fraud in patent medicine, railroad practices, and improper processing of food. Progressives campaigned to control the greed of industry, but also to provide assistance to the poor. In the field of criminal justice, Progressives supported practices to treat the needs of offenders, to include the juvenile court, and to expand community treatment through probation and parole and the use of the indeterminate sentence.[2] It was in this social context that sociology emerged as a discipline in America, starting first at the University of Chicago. The nation's oldest sociology program began in 1892.

THE CHICAGO SCHOOL OF CRIMINOLOGY

Although the University of Chicago's Department of Sociology was founded in 1892 by Albion Small, it was Robert Ezra Park, who joined the department in 1913, who founded the department's school of criminology.

Robert E. Park　Later to be known for his eclectic approach to sociology, Park's background was similarly diverse. He lived in various cities and towns in the Midwest during his childhood. Park was born in 1864, in Harveyville, Pennsylvania, and grew up in Talk Wing, Minnesota. His father was a grain wholesaler, and his mother was a teacher.

Park studied engineering at the State University of Minnesota from 1882 to 1883, then studied history and philosophy at the University of Michigan from 1883 to 1887. There he enrolled in several of Progressive educator John Dewey's courses. After graduating from the University of Michigan in 1887, Park worked as a muckraking journalist with daily papers in Minneapolis, Detroit, Denver, New York, and Chicago. During this time, he roamed the streets of urban areas looking for human interest stories. He studied psychology and philosophy at Harvard from 1898 to 1899 and obtained a M.A. in Philosophy in 1899. He then studied in Germany in philosophy and sociology with George Simmel and obtained his Ph.D. from the University of Heidelberg in 1903. He subsequently became a press agent and ghostwriter for Booker T. Washington, head of the Tuskegee Institute of Alabama. While working in this capacity, he met W. I. Thomas, who recruited him to a position as guest lecturer at the University of Chicago. He became a Full Professor there in 1923 and played a major role in the development of Chicago School sociology from 1920 until World War II.

Much of Park's contribution to the **Chicago School of Criminology** derived from Park's background in journalism. He said, "I expect I have actually covered more ground tramping about in cities in different parts of the world, than any living man."[3] From these journeys Park made two important conclusions. First, he observed that like any ecological system, urban development was patterned and could be understood in terms of social processes such as *invasion, conflict, accommodation,* and *assimilation.* Second, he added that the nature of these social processes in relation to human behaviors could be determined only through a careful first hand study of city life. Park felt that principles of animal and plant ecology could be applied to the distribution of human population in a city and, along with his colleagues Ernest Burgess and Louis Wirth, identified several concentric zones that expanded out from the center of the city.[4] These included the "Loop" (commercial district in inner city), the Zone in Transition (deteriorating tenements amidst aging factories), the Zone of Workingmen's Homes, the Residential Zone, and the Commuters' Zone (Zones I–V, respectively). Although residents of the Residential and Commuters' Zones were typically established white, middle- and upper-class homeowners, those living in The Loop and Zone in Transition experienced constant displacement as the business district moved outward and they faced competition from waves of immigrants and other migrants who could not yet afford to live elsewhere in the city. Such patterns, Burgess theorized, lead to weakening of family and communal ties, as well as social disorganization. These areas were characterized by normative conflicts between cultures and between the young and old, resulting in various forms of pathology, including crime.

The test of this theory was subsequently done by Shaw and McKay.[5] Curiously, Clifford Shaw and Henry McKay, whose works would come to be identified with the Chicago School of Criminology, were not faculty members at the University of Chicago. Instead, they were researchers at a state-supported child guidance clinic. But they were profoundly influenced by the theorizing of the Chicago School, most particularly with the work of Ernest Burgess, W. I. Thomas, and Louis Wirth. Shaw and McKay sought, through examining juvenile court statistics, to map the spatial distribution of delinquency throughout Chicago. They sought to determine if rates of delinquency were, as predicted by Burgess' model, directly related to residing close to the center of the city (Zones 1 and 2), declining progressively with residence toward the periphery of the city (Zones 3, 4, and 5). Their findings confirmed that prediction. They also found that in terms of personality, intelligence, and physical condition, delinquents were not significantly different from nondelinquents. They continued to study Chicago's court records over several decades and found that this pattern of delinquency, being highest in the slum neighborhoods and lowest in the affluent suburbs, prevailed, regardless of which racial or ethnic group resided in the slum. They also found that as racial and ethnic groups moved out of the slum to other zones, their delinquency rates decreased commensurately. Furthermore, as the racial and ethnic composition of neighborhoods changed over the years, the rates of delinquency remained relatively constant in these neighborhoods. Thus, Shaw and McKay provided fairly convincing empirical data directly contradicting the individual trait theories that were prevalent at the time.

The inner-city slum was termed the "Zone in Transition," referring to its likelihood of redevelopment, by the Chicago School of Criminology. Such real estate is often left to deteriorate by absentee landlords who speculate that their property will be sold at a high price to business interests who will replace it with expensive high-rise commercial buildings. Pictured here is an inner-city black teen girl walking next to a trash-laden chain-link fence surrounding land that has been cleared for development.

Source: Peter Byron, Photo Edit, Inc.

BOX 4–1

Urbanization and Crime in Korea and India

Critics of the Chicago School have argued that urbanization may work as an explanation of crime in the United States, but might not work in foreign countries. However, a study of urbanization from 1966–1975 in Korea found that levels of crime differ according to degree of urbanization and that the level of urbanization (measured by population size) was found to be the major factor affecting the rates of two crimes—theft and aggravated assault.[6] In a similar study done in India, density of population and work force was found to be highly correlated with murder for the years 1961–1980.[7]

Policy Consequences of the Chicago School

Following the theoretical paradigm of the Chicago School, Shaw and McKay viewed delinquency to be a product of the **social disorganization** of the slum neighborhoods. These findings were swiftly translated into policy applications. The solution to the crime problem lay not in treatment of individuals, which previously had ranged from sterilization to psychotherapy. Instead, the approach taken by Shaw and McKay was to encourage enhanced community organization. Toward this goal, Clifford Shaw developed the Chicago Area Project (CAP), in 1932, in three high-delinquency neighborhoods. CAP encouraged the development of neighborhood councils of local residents who would originate social programs, such as sports and recreation, as well as summer camps. CAP also encouraged residents to take pride in their community through neighborhood cleanup projects. In addition, CAP staff members advocated for juveniles in trouble with the law and at school, and staff members indigenous to the community provided street counseling to encourage prosocial activities. CAP was never evaluated using a randomized control group; however, in a 50-year evaluation of CAP, Schlossman and associates concluded that the data justify "a strong hypothesis that CAP has long been effective in reducing rates of reported juvenile delinquency."[8]

Although the success or failure of CAP has not been decided, the work of Shaw and McKay has been assailed on methodological grounds, most specifically for the reliance of Shaw and McKay upon official statistics for identifying offenders and offense rates. For instance, in 1936 Robison found that data on juvenile delinquents reported by social welfare agencies revealed a more even distribution of delinquency among the neighborhoods than was reported by Shaw and McKay.[9] Self-report studies, starting with the work of Austin Porterfield in the 1940s, Short and Nye in the 1950s, and countless others up until today, have also challenged the assumption that delinquency is associated with area or social class.[10] However, these studies are far from a refutation of Shaw and McKay, or for that matter the **social ecology theory** pioneered by Park and Burgess, because most of the questionnaire studies have been done in schools, leaving open the possibility that delinquent gang members, homeless youth, drug and alcohol abusers, and others who are notoriously absent from school, are omitted from such studies.

While social ecological studies perhaps first come to mind when one thinks of the Chicago School of Criminology, contributions to criminological theory do not end there. The Chicago School also provided a fertile ground for the development of such theories as differential association/social learning theory; symbolic interactionism/labeling theory; and containment/control theory.

106   CRIMINOLOGY: A GLOBAL PERSPECTIVE

Like many others of the Chicago School, Edwin Sutherland was born in the Midwest (Gibbon, Nebraska). He was the son of a Baptist minister. In 1906, he left Nebraska and enrolled in several courses in the divinity school at the University of Chicago. However, after taking a course from Charles R. Henderson on the "Social Treatment of Crime," Sutherland decided to enter the sociology program and devoted the remainder of his career to criminology.[11] After obtaining his Ph.D. in Sociology and Political Economy in 1913, Sutherland held a series of positions at Midwestern institutions, including the University of Illinois (1919–1925) and University of Minnesota (1925–1929). From 1930 to 1935 he held a Professorship at the University of Chicago, but went to Indiana University where he served as professor and chair of the department of sociology until his death in 1950.

Edwin Sutherland

In Sutherland's work one can find what is probably the most extreme opposition to biological and psychological trait theory in all of criminological theory. Sutherland's text, *Principles of Criminology,* which became the most influential textbook in the history of criminology, became a forum for the development of his **differential association theory.** The first of nine principles Sutherland developed declares "Criminal behavior is learned," denying the relevance of theories of biological inheritance and psychological trait theories in one simple statement. During the years 1934–1951, Sutherland, through book reviews, harshly attacked scholars who linked criminal behavior with the physical inferiority of offenders, to "mesomorphy," or to "constitutional" elements. These include E. A. Hooton, William H. Sheldon, and Sheldon and Eleanor Glueck.

The story of how Sutherland's theory came into existence is interesting in itself. Sutherland's differential association theory was a byproduct of his text and the theory developed progressively with each edition of the text. Sutherland was first asked to write a criminology textbook by Edward C. Hayes in 1921. Hayes was chair of the department of sociology at the University of Illinois and also was editor of sociology books for J. B. Lippincott. The first edition of Sutherland's text, entitled *Criminology,* was published in 1924. It was retitled *Principles of Criminology* in 1934. In the first edition, Sutherland rejected existing literature that explained criminal behavior as a product of "feeble-mindedness," but endorsed the "multifactor" approach, that was also prevalent. Three events, however, shaped Sutherland's movement toward the development of a general theory of criminology. One was taking a position as professor at the University of Chicago where he was influenced by an article, published by Louis Wirth in 1931, that attributed criminal behavior to "culture conflict" in his *culture conflict theory.* Wirth argued that the rules followed by some groups (especially immigrants) clash with those of the dominant culture, and Sutherland deduced that criminals may actually be conforming to some subcultural standards. Another event that influenced Sutherland was the publication in 1932 of the Michael-Adler Report by the Bureau of Social Hygiene in New York (where Sutherland had worked as a researcher). This report was highly critical of multiple factor approaches and urged criminologists to develop general theories to explain all forms of criminal behavior. The last event in the development of Sutherland's theory was almost comedic. In 1932, Sutherland came to know a fast-talking, boastful, and articulate Chicago area con man known as Broadway Jones. Jones relayed many stories to Sutherland about his own criminal exploits and about the various specialties of professional crime. Together Sutherland and Jones published *The Professional Thief.*[12] Jones was identified in the book by the alias "Chic Conwell," and

BOX 4–2

Test of Differential Association Theory in Iran

A participant observation study related to 27 official delinquents in Tehran, Iran provided a refinement of Sutherland's differential association theory. It was found that most of the people in southern Iran expressed a variety of definitions that were not favorable to the law or the judicial system. Yet only a few of the children of these people turned to delinquency. Thus acquaintance with or belief in the definitions was not the sole cause of juvenile delinquency. However, it was concluded that 19 of the 27 subjects had become delinquent as a result of differential association based upon other assumptions of that theory.[13]

curiously this book was later to be celebrated by Hollywood filmmakers who borrowed freely from it in writing the screenplay for the movie, *The Sting* (1973). From his conversations with Broadway Jones, Sutherland became convinced that criminality is learned through close relationships between experienced criminals and their "apprentices." Subsequently, in the 1934 edition of *Principles of Criminology,* Sutherland referred to the learning that takes place within different cultures and as a product of group conflict. Sutherland didn't even think of this as an explanation for criminality until Henry McKay, in a conversation with Sutherland, referred to this passage as "your theory." From that point on, Sutherland began developing his differential association theory.

As discussed earlier, Shaw and McKay used the term *social disorganization* to describe why inner city slums had higher rates of delinquency than areas farther out toward the periphery of the city. It was at the suggestion of Albert Cohen that Sutherland substituted the term *differential social organization* for *social disorganization.* Sutherland felt that the term social disorganization was value laden and did not accurately describe the actual criminal organization that existed in these neighborhoods. Closely related to the term "differential social organization" was the term "differential association," a term that Sutherland coined to describe the process by which people in high-crime neighborhoods learn or "culturally transmit" criminal values, attitudes, techniques, and motivations. It was in the fourth edition of *Principles of Criminology*[14] that Sutherland clearly articulated his differential association theory in a set of nine principles.

To summarize Sutherlands nine principles, he stated that criminal behavior is learned in interaction in intimate personal groups, and such learning involves all the mechanisms involved in other learning. The learning includes techniques of crime, motives, drives, rationalizations, and attitudes favorable or unfavorable to the violation of law, an excess of which, if favorable to the violation of law, will result in delinquency. Such associations vary in frequency, duration, priority, and intensity. Finally, criminality cannot be explained by general needs and values, since noncriminal behavior is an expression of those same needs and values.

Sutherland's graduate students became influential criminologists, including Donald Cressey, Lloyd Ohlin, Mary Owen Cameron, Albert Cohen, and Karl Schuessler. Sutherland had a major impact in developing "the sociological approach" to crime and in diminishing the role of biological and psychological trait theories. By the time of his death in 1950, he became known as the "Dean of American Criminology."[15]

BOX 4–3

Typology of Crime Based Upon Differential Association Theory

Marshal B. Clinard and Richard Quinney developed a typology that was an application of Sutherland's theory of differential association. Clinard and Quinney proposed a classification of crimes on a continuum from *career* to *noncareer crimes*, based upon the criteria of role crystallization (specialization), identification with crime, and progression in crime. Accordingly, Clinard and Quinney rank criminal offenses from least to most serious in the following order:

1. Violent personal criminal behavior
2. Occasional property criminal behavior
3. Public order criminal behavior
4. Conventional criminal behavior
5. Political criminal behavior
6. Occupational criminal behavior
7. Corporate criminal behavior
8. Organized criminal behavior
9. Professional criminal behavior[16]

Other Theories Rooted in the Chicago School

To some extent the roots of **symbolic interactionism/labeling theory** may also lie in the Chicago School with George Herbert Mead's studies in social psychology. W. I. Thomas developed the symbolic interactionist term "definition of the situation" in his book, *The Unadjusted Girl.*[17] Also, Frederick Thrasher's book, *The Gang,*[18] resulting from a study of 1,313 juvenile gangs in Chicago, was one of the first publications in which the negative consequences of official labels of delinquency were recognized.[19] Also, as mentioned earlier, containment/control theory has its roots in the Chicago School. Chicago School students Walter Reckless and Albert J. Reiss developed **containment/control theories** that became relevant in the post-WWII period. Because these theories are related to "self-control theory," a contemporary theory, they are discussed in Chapter 5.

OPPORTUNITY THEORY

Opportunity theory, sometimes termed **strain theory** and **anomie theory,** became very popular during the 1960s in large part due to the politics of the times. During the 1960s, America witnessed an economic boom. At the same time, it was recognized that not everybody enjoyed affluence during this time. A prevailing government view in Washington, DC was that crime was primarily a product of slums and poverty. This view was a theme of President John Kennedy's "New Frontier" program and President Lyndon Johnson's "War on Poverty." Social programs were developed whose goal was to increase economic opportunity for the poor, in part, as a remedy for crime. Many of these programs owe their origin to the work of Robert Merton who articulated such views in academic journals over 20 years before the opportunity programs of the 1960s.

Robert King Merton

Robert King Merton was born Meyer R. Schkolnick on July 4, 1910 in Philadelphia, Pennsylvania. His parents were Jewish immigrants from Eastern Europe. His father became a carpenter's assistant after the family's dairy product shop burned down with no insurance. However, Merton insisted that

Robert K. Merton (1910–2003)
Source: The Estate of Robert Merton.

his childhood did not lack opportunity. He attended what he characterized as a very decent public school, where he was taught four years of Latin, and had access to a local library donated by Andrew Carnegie. Merton characterized his seemingly deprived South Philadelphia slum as providing "a youngster with every sort of capital—social capital, cultural capital, human capital, and, above all, what we may call public capital—that is, with every sort of capital except the personally financial."[20]

The assumed name, Robert King Merton, developed as a result of his teenage career as an amateur magician. The last name Merton was related to the magician's name, "Merlin" and his first name, Robert, was borrowed from the magician Robert Houdin, the French magician whose name Harry Houdini (himself originally Erich Weiss) had adopted. When Merton won a scholarship to Temple College, he was content to let his new name become permanent. Temple College, though fully accredited, was founded for "the poor boys and girls of Philadelphia." While attending Temple College, Merton became an assistant to the sociologist George E. Simpson in a project on race and the media. Through this project Merton met Ralph Bunche and Franklin Frazier and later was introduced to Pitirim Sorokin, founding chair of the Harvard sociology department. Subsequently, Merton attended Harvard and obtained his Ph.D. there in 1936. Although Merton attended a theory course offered at Harvard by Talcott Parsons, he later came to depart from Parson's "grand theory" style in favor of clearly written "theories of the middle range." Merton characterized his own such theory as "structural functionalism." Grand theories, as exemplified by Parson's work, purported to explain all human behavior, while Merton felt that it was better to scale down theorizing to a limited set of variables and hypotheses that could be measured and tested—hence, theories of the middle range (between individual trait theory and grand theory).

As discussed earlier, the Chicago School had produced a view that crime was rooted in the slums of America. However, because Merton had in fact been the product of, on the one hand, a childhood of being raised in a slum, but, on the other hand, of a superb educational opportunity system all the way through Harvard University, he viewed the origins of crime differently. Perhaps through his Harvard experience with grand theory and Talcott Parsons, Merton shifted the focus to an analysis of the whole American culture. Merton's concern in this analysis was that there was a universal mandate in American culture to achieve the "American dream" of economic success. He observed that children of all social classes in America were enjoined to pursue economic success, and were imbued with the "Horatio Alger myth" that even the lowliest of us can rise from rags to riches. However, though Merton was fortunate enough to rise from a lowly background to the top level of society, he was aware that such opportunity is atypical. As was noted by Stephen Pfohl, "most of Merton's slum neighbors did not fare so well . . . a lesson of slum life which Merton never forgot."[21] Merton also witnessed the Great Depression and the consequences of large numbers of people being deprived of the opportunity to reach the goals they had been taught to desire. He believed that there was a disjunction between what the culture encourages (economic success) and the means available to make economic success possible. The means to economic success pertained to access to legitimate opportunity through education, employment, and family connections. Thus, large segments of the American population suffer from structured strain in the sense that they desire a goal that they cannot reach through conventional means. The result is a pressure for deviation.[22] Merton realized that there were different ways that people could deviate, and he proposed a relatively simple typology that he put in table form, which he said was for heuristic purposes (see Table 4–1).

Merton viewed two variables as central in characterizing deviance and conformity. The first was acceptance or rejection of the cultural goal of financial success. The second had to do with acceptance or rejection of the culturally approved rules or institutionalized means for attaining those goals (working hard, going to school, saving, investing, etc.). Merton believed that regardless of the fact that many people are subject to strain, the social order would break down unless most people conformed, meaning that they would strive for the cultural goal of success while playing by the rules (*conformity*). However others would, while adhering to the goal of success, utilize illegal means (theft, embezzlement, etc.) to attain those goals (*innovation*). Others would scale

Table 4–1 **Merton's Paradigm of Deviancy**[23]

Modes of Adaptation	Cultural Goals	Institutional Means
I. Conformity	+	+
II. Innovation	+	−
III. Ritualism	−	+
IV. Retreatism	−	−
V. Rebellion	±	±

+ signifies acceptance; − signifies rejection; ± signifies rejection of prevailing values and substitution of new values

BOX 4–4

Anomie and Synnomie

The French sociologist Emile Durkheim[24] may be credited as the historical source of Merton's "anomie theory." Durkheim's *anomie* refers to a state of society in which the various functional parts of society are poorly regulated, a state of society that results in conflict. Freda Adler[25] did a study of a selected group of 10 countries that were known for being low in crime in United Nations data. She found that all 10 countries appeared to have a social structure that was the opposite of Durkheim's anomie—a condition she termed *synnomie*. One study done by Helal and Coston[26] explained the low crime rate in Bahrain using Adler's synnomie concept. He said that Islamic religion had provided the vehicle of continuous integration of society in the wake of rapid industrialization from the traditional village society whose economy was based upon pearl diving. Bahrainis encourage men to marry early and place a high value on the family, as a product of this religious orientation.

down their aspirations and/or give up on the goal of financial success so that they could continue to adhere to institutional means (*ritualism*). Such individuals, for instance, might consider themselves "poor, but honest." An even more extreme reaction, however, is to reject both the goals and the means advocated by society (*retreatism*). This adaptation could result in alcoholism, drug addiction, psychosis, vagrancy, and even suicide. Finally, there are those who not only reject the accepted means and success goals, but wish to substitute new goals and means (*rebellion*). Followers of a cult, for instance, may renounce worldly possessions and follow the edicts of the cult leader to find what they consider a better life.

Merton's theory was distinctive when it was developed in its rejection of individualistic theories by placing the blame for crime on the culture and inequality of contemporary capitalist society. It also presented a viewpoint different from the social disorganization approach of the Chicago school of criminology. Merton maintained that crime was a product of the frustration of people at the bottom rung of society in attaining the "American dream" of economic success, rather than a product of lack of social control in the slum. Like Sutherland, as discussed earlier, Merton was a vocal critic of the individualist theories that were popular in the 1930s.[27]

Though Merton's article (published in 1938) did not bring him instant recognition, it did, over time, become one of the most cited articles in all of sociology. His theory was one that received the most attempts at empirical testing. Merton's contribution of 1938 had to await a change in the social climate of America, a change that took some 20 years in the making, before Merton's essay became a "must read" for graduate and undergraduate students of sociology alike. Merton's theory came into the limelight in part through two important books by students of Merton. One was Albert K. Cohen's *Delinquent Boys*, published in 1955, and the other was Richard A. Cloward and Lloyd E. Ohlin's *Delinquency and Opportunity*, published in 1960. It was perhaps a "harmonic convergence" of such influences as the civil rights movement, President John F. Kennedy's "New Frontier," and later President Lyndon Johnson's "War on Poverty" that thrust Merton's theory into an elevated state of relevance. Merton's theory ultimately came to result in major changes in the nation's approach to criminality and delinquency. It is because of the convergence of all of these events and those that followed that Merton's theory "opportunity theory" came to prominence.

Albert K. Cohen studied first with Robert K. Merton at Harvard University and, a year later, with Edwin H. Sutherland, at Indiana University. Although Cohen became convinced of the importance of differential association and cultural transmission through his instruction by Sutherland, he wondered about the origin of the criminal cultures in the first place. He also wondered about the slum location of the delinquent subcultures and the origin of the norms held by such subcultures. After returning to Harvard, Cohen dealt with these questions in his Ph.D. dissertation, later to be published in 1955 entitled, *Delinquent Boys: The Culture of the Gang.* In his dissertation, Cohen merged points from the Chicago School with Merton's theory and threw in a bit of frustration-aggression theory (focusing upon status frustration in school). He argued that lower class youth can't compete with their middle and upper class classmates, so they engage in a process of reaction formation, rejecting the middle class goals and norms. In so doing they become "nonutilitarian, malicious, and negativistic" and manifest their values in behavior such as being truant, flouting authority, fighting, and vandalizing property for "kicks," a process similar to Merton's "rebellion" adaptation to anomie. In keeping with the Chicago School, Cohen argued that the norms come to take on a reality of their own, being passed on from generation to generation. These norms can also be transmitted to youth who are not status frustrated but who are attracted to the lure of the gang and its offer of friendship, excitement, and protection.[28]

Albert K. Cohen

Like Cohen, Cloward and Ohlin attempted to combine Merton's theory with the Chicago school. However, they went beyond Cohen in bringing opportunity theory within the realm of public policy, bringing notoriety to Merton's theory, and perhaps even to Cohen's work. Like Cohen, Cloward and Ohlin had prior contact with both Merton and Sutherland. Ohlin had studied under Sutherland and then received a doctorate from the University of Chicago, while Cloward had been Merton's student at Columbia University (where Merton taught after Harvard). Cloward and Ohlin subsequently became colleagues on Columbia University's social work faculty, where they collaborated to create their important work, *Delinquency and Opportunity.*[29] While they agreed with Merton that lower class youth lack access to legitimate means to attain the highly valued cultural goal of financial success, they suggested that Merton had ignored access to *illegitimate means* in explaining what form of deviancy might be adopted. Some slum areas are heavily involved with professional or organized criminal activity, whereas other slum areas lack such structures. In slum areas dominated by organized crime, *criminal subcultures* develop among the youth, but in slum areas without such illegitimate opportunities, youth turn to violence and enter into *conflict subcultures.* Youths who fail to achieve access to legitimate means and who fail to enter either of these subcultures become "double-failures" who may enter *retreatist subcultures,* such as drug-using gangs.

Cloward and Ohlin

The importance of Cloward and Ohlin's theory, as mentioned earlier, lay in its impact on public policy during the 1960s. Just as the CAP was a policy outgrowth of the Chicago School, New Yorks Mobilization for Youth Project (MFY) was based directly upon Cloward and Ohlin's opportunity theory. Moreover, Cloward and Ohlin developed a 617-page report providing an action program in *A Proposal for the Prevention and Control of Delinquency by*

Policy Consequences of Opportunity Theory

Expanding Opportunities.[30] Cloward and Ohlin's work was "in the right place at the right time." In 1961, the Kennedy administration pledged to provide a "New Frontier of equal opportunity" and created the President's Committee on Juvenile Delinquency and Youth Crime, with David Hackett as head. Hackett learned of Cloward and Ohlin's work and invited Lloyd Ohlin to Washington, DC to assume a Health, Education, and Welfare post to assist in formulating delinquency policy. MFY, then directed by Richard Cloward, received a $12.5 million grant, half of which came from the federal government. Ohlin was subsequently appointed to head the Task Force on Juvenile Delinquency for the *President's Commission on Law Enforcement and Administration of Justice.* That report, whose impact is still being felt, was heavily influenced by the opportunity theory approach of Cloward, Ohlin, Merton, and Cohen. Although criticisms of opportunity theory will be discussed later, this approach began to be discredited with the administration of Richard Nixon with cutbacks in various opportunity programs, such as Headstart. However, the redirection of social policy was probably due more to the growing negative political backlash against civil rights activism than to failure of opportunity theory. Programs such as MFY resulted in protest activity as part of attempts to obtain equality of opportunity. However, the resulting civil turmoil frightened the voting public, and the election of Richard Nixon in 1968 was a signal that such activity, along with programs related to the political activism, should be curtailed.

While programs based upon opportunity theory began to fall from favor with the Nixon Administration, a **paradigm shift** away from opportunity theory occurred in the 1970s in the direction of labeling theory, which will be discussed next.[31] Various criticisms of opportunity theory were stated. Some scholars questioned Merton's assumption that all in society share the same high economic aspirations. Others argued that a sense of relative deprivation may actually cause strain to be just as great within the upper social classes, resulting in "white-collar crimes." Similarly, Cohen was assailed for excluding middle class forms of delinquency. Cloward and Ohlin were questioned regarding the exclusivity and integrity of their three delinquent subcultures—criminal, conflict, and retreatist. Probably the most important criticism, however, arose from numerous studies, starting in the early 1960s, showing that self-reported delinquency was not significantly associated with social class. Along with these studies were those that indicated a disproportionate amount of police attention to slum areas, suggesting that police bias is the major reason in differential rates of delinquency and crime between social classes. If, as these studies implied, there were no true differences between social classes in delinquency, then both the opportunity theories and the Chicago School would be essentially defunct, because they would be based upon a fallacious premise that delinquency is a lower class phenomenon. Labeling theories described next start with that assumption.

LABELING THEORY

During the 1970s there was a "paradigm shift" that owed its origin to several trends. One trend was the anti-Vietnam war movement, which led to widespread disenchantment with the "military industrial complex" which was said to be responsible for U.S. participation in the war in Southeast Asia. Another trend was the movement to legalize drugs, particularly marijuana, along with a general disenchantment with traditional morality. Coinciding with these trends was a rejection of traditional theories that viewed crime as a product of poverty or low socioeconomic status. One manifestation of this view was the abandonment of efforts to explain the causes of crime, instead shifting emphasis to discussing the societal reaction to crime. This new approach became known as **labeling theory** or **social reaction theory.** As will be shown, this was not merely an academic approach but one that had a profound influence on policy, leading to a vast movement of deinstitutionalization and diversion in the criminal justice system.

Labeling theory was developed by Howard S. Becker in his 1963 book *Outsiders: Studies in the Sociology of Deviance.* Becker's theory was rooted in the tradition of the Chicago School of Criminology in the symbolic interaction foundation of Cooley and Mead, as well as the labeling influences of Frank Tannenbaum and Edwin Lemert.[32] Becker considers his "sociological heroes" to be Everett C. Hughes, Herbert Blumer, and Alfred Lindesmith.[33] From Cooley,[34] Becker derived the idea that through the "looking glass self" people define themselves according to society's perception of them, and from George Herbert Mead,[35] the idea that the self is the product of the mind's perception of social symbols and interactions.

Howard S. Becker

Tannenbaum[36] developed the idea that as juveniles go through the justice system they experience a *dramatization of evil* and are "tagged" as juvenile delinquents and the associated stigma causes them to fall into deeper nonconformity. *Tagging* involved defining, identifying, segregating, and singling out individuals for special treatment. A consequence of tagging is the stimulation, suggestion, and evoking of the very traits that the person is accused of. The person becomes the thing they are accused of being.

Lemert[37] described the process of going from *primary deviance* to *secondary deviance,* the first of which is rationalized by the offender as part of a socially acceptable role. When the behavior is reacted to by agents of society, especially when reacted to repeatedly, the individual changes his or her self concept to that of a deviant and organizes identity around this deviant self concept. Lemert is thought of as the founder of the *social reaction theory* of deviancy. He said that primary deviance can develop for a wide variety of reasons—biological, psychological, and/or sociological. However, secondary deviance is more important because it is intensified deviance. Secondary deviance develops as a means of defense, attack, or adaptation to the problems caused by society's reaction to the primary deviance. As an instance of this process, in Chapter 8 we examine a case study of Ray Johnson, who progressed from being a minor juvenile offender to a professional bank robber as a result of his brutal treatment in institutions for juvenile delinquents.

BOX 4–5

Official Labeling and Self-Esteem in China

A study of data gathered in 1989 from 443 nondelinquents and 369 delinquents from Tianjjin, a large Chinese city, confirmed the hypothesis that official labeling reduces self-esteem of delinquents. The study also showed that friend deviance also lowers self-esteem.[38]

Becker's statement of labeling theory is (like Sutherland's exposition of differential association theory) a more radical approach to symbolic interactionism than that of any of his predecessors. In *Outsiders: Studies in the Sociology of Deviance,* he argued that *deviance* is the creation of social groups rather than the quality of some act or behavior. He argued against studying criminal behavior itself, because such behavior is simply deviance that has been labeled as such by people in positions of power who may benefit by the labeling and enforcement of rules against such behavior. Also (in keeping with the self-report studies described earlier), the rule-breaking behavior is constant, but the labeling of the behavior varies. Those who are labeled as deviant by those in power are morally at odds with members of the rule-abiding society, and thus they are *outsiders.*

Following Lemert's earlier analysis, Becker charts the pathway from primary to secondary deviance. Although many people think or fantasize in a deviant manner, Becker postulated that rule-breaking is constant in society. However, it is the process of being caught and labeled by an authority figure that leads to the second step, which involves the acceptance of the deviant label as one's *master status.* Once a person has accepted the deviant label as his master status, he becomes an outsider and is denied the means of carrying on everyday life. Once this happens, the outsider turns to illegitimate means to make a living. Finally, the person becomes involved in a *deviant subculture* that provides moral support and a self-justifying rationale, and through such association the person may learn new forms of deviance through differential association.

Becker argued that rules are created by *moral entrepreneurs,* crusaders for a rule that would right evil in society. Along with this, the enforcement of society's rules is an enterprising act by people who may have a moral crusade to stop crime, although most engage in the process simply as part of their occupation. Such enforcers have a great deal of discretion and may use their power to label innocent persons to gain respect. Thus, Becker developed a four-fold typology of "citizens" based upon two variables—behavior and the deviant label: (a) *conforming citizens* are those who are rule abiding and free of labels, whereas (b) *falsely accused* are those who are labeled without breaking a rule; (c) *pure deviants* are those who exhibit rule breaking behavior, whereas (d) *secret deviants* are those who break rules yet avoid labeling.

Becker used two cases to illustrate labeling theory—the history of marijuana legislation in the United States and the process of becoming a marijuana user.

The history of the Marijuana Tax Act of 1937 involved the crusading activities of Harry Anslinger, who headed the Federal Bureau of Narcotics. Anslinger used the mass media to promote this legislation using stories of marijuana-crazed Mexican immigrants, children engaging in acts of violence and suicide under the influence of marijuana, and marijuana-induced gang rapes.[39]

Becker described three stages of marijuana use and three types of users—beginners, occasional users, and regular users. Peer associations mediated the transition from beginner to regular users. Peers provide the drug, describe how to use it, and help the user define the effects of the drug as pleasurable.[40]

Policy Consequences of Labeling Theory

As opportunity theory was curtailed in the late 1960s during the Nixon administration, labeling theory provided a welcome alternative, not only by liberals rallying against state intervention, but also by tax-cutting conservatives whose inclination was to cut social programs.

As Empey[41] put it, labeling theorists championed four policies—the Four "Ds" of decriminalization, diversion, due process, and deinstitutionalization. Labeling theorists sought *decriminalization* to reduce or eliminate criminal penalties against "victimless crimes" (e.g., public drunkenness, homosexuality, prostitution, drug use, and gambling) as well as juvenile status offenses, such as truancy and premarital sex. They sought *diversion* programs that would lead to release from institutional care, or treatment in the community in lieu of imprisonment. In hopes of shorter and more equitable sentences, labeling theorists advocated extending *due process* rights to juveniles and to adults in the form of determinate sentences. Finally, labeling theorists promoted *deinstitutionalization* in the form of a moratorium on prison construction and even the closing of a state's major juvenile facilities, as in the case of the action taken by Department of Youth Services Commissioner Jerome Miller in Massachusetts in 1972. Although the 1960s could be characterized as the era of opportunity theory, the 1970s were the heyday of the Four Ds of labeling theory. Many of the community-based programs and approaches created during this period are still active today and are a frequent part of many court-sentencing practices. However, with the arrival of the conservative Reagan administration in Washington came another policy shift, away from the Four Ds and in the opposite direction of "getting tough on crime," and tougher than ever before.

The policy shift was accompanied by some considerable criticism of labeling theory from within the discipline of criminology. Conflict theorists argued that labeling theorists did not go far enough in exposing how the origins of criminal labels were rooted in inequities caused by capitalism. Moreover, conflict theorists and others held that labeling theory had inadvertently "widened the net," by creating community-sentencing alternatives that became an "add on" to the criminal justice system, rather than a means of deinstitutionalization. The product of this net widening was an increasing number of people involved in the criminal justice system, along with a simultaneous increase of those in prison and jail. Critics argued that labeling theory wasn't actually a theory of criminality at all, because it directed inquiry away from studying underlying causes. Also, labeling theorists had not made any attempt to test the prime thesis that state intervention increased criminality.[42]

CONFLICT THEORY

Given the growing skepticism regarding labeling theory in the late 1970s, the time was right for yet another paradigm shift. As mentioned earlier, the "reincarceration movement" of the Reagan administration led to increasing imprisonment. At the same time, within criminology, conflict or radical theory became popular. While labeling theory seemed compatible with budget-cutting conservative policy makers, conflict theory was directly at odds with the policies of the conservative think tanks of the 1980s and beyond. Few sociologists who supported these theories would be going to Washington and fewer would be getting government grants to apply their programs.

Conflict theory owes its origin to the writings of Karl Marx and Frederick Engels whose revolutionary theory of scientific socialism had a significant impact upon the history of Russia, China, Cuba, and many other countries, including recently nearly half of the countries of the world.

Marx and Engels

Karl Marx (1818–1883)
Source: CORBIS/Bettmann.

Friedrich Engels (1820–1895)
Source: Lebrecht Music & Arts Photo Library.

Both Marx and Engels were born in Germany. Marx was born into a comfortable middle class home in Trier, Germany. He came from a long line of rabbis on both sides of his family, although his father converted to Protestantism so that he would not lose his job as a respected attorney. Marx was educated at the universities of Bonn, Berlin, and Jena and became a political philosopher. Engels came from a wealthy Protestant family and was influenced by the poet Heinrich Hein and the German philosopher Georg Hegel. Engels became a political economist. Engels was converted to communist

BOX 4–6

Marxist-Leninism in Vietnam

In the years 1999–2000, Vietnam (North and South Vietnam combined as one nation) reported extremely low rates of crime to INTERPOL—1.08 per 100,000 for murder, 1.64 for rape, 1.48 for robbery, and 7.15 for aggravated assault. (No data were reported for burglary, larceny, or auto theft.) Vietnamese legal thought with regard to the treatment of criminals is the result of three major influences: classic Confucianism, the Napoleonic Code, and Marxist-Leninism. Marxist-Leninism added the perspective that crime is a reflection of environmental factors that victimize the individual by turning him into a criminal. The proper remedy for this condition is to eliminate the causal factors while rehabilitating the criminal. The combination of the three legacies has produced in Vietnamese society a legal philosophy that is inquisitional rather than adversarial, seeking reform rather than punishment. In contrast to the West, where law is the guarantee of rights that all may claim, in Vietnam the law concerns duties that all must fulfill. Vietnamese law seeks to give the prisoner the right to reformation. In theory, at least, there are very few incorrigibles. It also permits a relativist approach in fixing sentences, much more so than do the precedent-based systems of the West. Mitigating circumstances, such as whether the accused acted out of passion or premeditation, loom large as a factor in sentencing. Murder by stabbing is treated more leniently than murder by poison, for example, because the latter is perceived to require a greater degree of premeditation than the former. The personal circumstances of the accused are also a factor in determining punishment . . . the notion of permanent or extended incarceration is rejected in favor of an effort to determine whether or not and, if so, how the criminal can be rehabilitated and restored to society.[43]

beliefs by the German Socialist Moses Hess in 1844 and met Karl Marx the same year in Paris. Both Marx and Engels had worked as journalists—Marx as editor of the newspaper *Rheinische Zeitung* in Cologne and Engels as a contributor to the *Northern Star* newspaper in Manchester, England. The meeting occurred after Marx was forced to resign from *Rheinische Zeitung* because of controversy that resulted from articles he wrote critical of contemporary political and social conditions. After that, Marx went to Paris, where he engaged in further studies of philosophy, history, and political science, and adopted communist beliefs in 1844. That year, when Engels visited Marx in Paris, both discovered that they had independently arrived at identical views on the nature of societal problems. In 1847, Marx was forced to leave Paris and moved to Brussels. There, Marx and Engels were commissioned by the Communist League in 1848 to write a statement of principles, which resulted in *The Communist Manifesto*. This document contained the basic statement of the theory of historical materialism. This theory held that in every era of history, the prevailing economic system determines the form of social organization, as well as the political and intellectual history of the times. History is characterized by a struggle between the ruling and oppressed social classes; however, the most recent epoch of capitalism, according to the *Manifesto,* would result in the overthrow of the bourgeoisie ruling class by the proletariat, who would then replace capitalism with a classless society.

Marx and Engels did not directly address the issues of crime or criminal justice either in their writings or political activities. It wasn't until the 20th century that the Dutch criminologist Willem Bonger[44] applied the conflict perspective of Marx and Engels to criminological theory. Bonger argued that under capitalism, (generally good) human nature was distorted by intense

Willem Bonger

"egoism" and greed that provided the basis for crime. Crimes are committed among the subordinate class as a means of survival and motivated by resentment. However, crimes are also committed by the more powerful bourgeoisie because of the opportunities they have to commit crime with impunity, as well as the decline of morality that accompanied capitalism. Bonger stated that actions become defined as crimes when they threaten the interests of the bourgeoisie, yet the legal system does not comparably punish the egoistic actions of the ruling class. Thus, to Bonger, the crime problem can be resolved only through the abolition of capitalism.[45]

Today there are a growing number of theorists who are considered to be conflict theorists. Many follow the tradition of Durkheim and Simmel in considering conflict to be pluralistic in nature, not just between the "ruling class" and "labor," but between a wide variety of competing interest groups, subcultures, and the like. Authors in this camp include Thorsten Sellin, George B. Vold, Ralf Dahrendorf, Austin Turk, and William Chambliss. Although these approaches are interesting, they depart from the Marxist approach that has been so important internationally. For this reason, reviewed here is the work of one contemporary theorist whose work is most truly neo-Marxian in nature—Richard Quinney.

Richard Quinney

Richard Quinney is to the Marxist approach what Howard Becker is to labeling theory. Quinney's books, especially his early works, developed a criminological theory that grew increasingly more Marxist in its orientation. In his third published book, *The Social Reality of Crime*,[46] Quinney developed a six-proposition conflict theory that focused on interest and power, but would today be viewed as more pluralist than materialist. Fours years later, Quinney published *Critique of Legal Order: Crime Control in Capitalist Society*,[47] providing an unabashed true Marxian approach to criminology. In this book, Quinney criticized criminologists for "legitimating the legal order" in their scholarship. He further charged that criminological research provides information used by the governing elites to manipulate and control those who threaten the system. He argued that the legal order was constructed by the capitalist ruling class, and law exists for the promotion of the capitalist system. Quinney studied the composition of various criminal justice policymaking bodies in the United States and documented that they were overwhelmingly dominated by members of the financial and political elite. He maintained that this elite was a small, cohesive group of persons who were interconnected by power, wealth, and corporate ties. It is this class that makes decisions affecting the lives of the vast majority of citizens who are subordinate to it. The purpose of such policy making, he said, was to assure the social and economic hegemony of the capitalist system.

Quinney analyzed the repressive criminal justice measures taken against Vietnam War and civil rights protesters during the mid-1960s, including labeling the actions of protesters as crimes. These actions were motivated by a desire to suppress activities that might pose a threat to the status quo and to make sure that public opinion about crime and crime control conformed to official ideology. The solution to this problem of repressive domination by the ruling class, Quinney concluded, was the development of *democratic socialism*, in which private ownership of capital is abolished, providing equality of opportunity for all in society. Such a society would bring an end to state law, and behavior would be regulated by community custom, breaches to which would be resolved by the popular tribunal.

As a summary statement in *Critique of the Legal Order,* Quinney provided six Marxist propositions, which read as follows:

> (1) American society is based on an advanced capitalist economy; (2) the state is organized to serve the interests of the dominant economic class, the capitalist ruling class; (3) criminal law is an instrument of the state and ruling class to maintain and perpetuate the existing social and economic order; (4) crime control in capitalist society is accomplished through a variety of institutions and agencies established and administered by a governmental elite, representing ruling class interests, for the purpose of establishing domestic order; (5) the contradictions of advanced capitalism . . . require that the subordinate classes remain oppressed by whatever means necessary, especially through the coercion of violence of the legal system; and (6) only with the collapse of the capitalist society and the creation of a new society based on socialist principles will there be a solution to the crime problem.[48]

Although Quinney's belief was that the positivist approach to criminology was merely a means by which criminologists ingratiate themselves to the capitalist rulers, providing the rulers the means to "predict and control" crime, he did address the issue of causation in his next major book, *Class, State, and Crime.* He maintained that capitalism creates crime through generating a surplus population made up of unemployed laborers who must turn to crime to survive. He provided a typology of crime that included crimes of domination, crimes of accommodation, and crimes of resistance. *Crimes of domination* included such forms as police brutality, Watergate-style offenses, as well as white-collar and organized crime. *Crimes of accommodation* included predatory crimes, such as theft, and personal crimes, such as homicide, provoked by the conditions of capitalism. *Crimes of resistance,* such as terrorism, involved the political struggle against the state.[49]

Policy Consequences of Conflict Theory

Conflict theory, especially as expressed by Marx, Engels, and Quinney, implied the need for a revolution against capitalism. Though a communist revolution took place in Russia, China, Cuba, and Vietnam, the U.S. government during the 1980s was advancing policies quite opposed to communism. In fact, the policies of the Reagan-Bush administration were said to have led to the demise of the Soviet Union, which was indicated by the tearing down of the Berlin Wall in 1991. However, not all conflict theorists advocated revolution. Some advocated programs to overhaul the criminal justice system or to change the criminal justice system to reduce the class bias inherent in the justice process under capitalism. These conflict theorists might be termed "reformist" as opposed to "revolutionaries." Reformists have advocated changes within the criminal justice system. Examples of such changes include the use of "peacemaking" criminology, as well as "demystification" and debunking of capitalism in the form of postmodernist approaches to criminology. These approaches are discussed in Chapter 5.

SUMMARY AND CONCLUSION

In the late 19th century and early 20th century, the Progressive Movement in the United States rejected the Social Darwinist views of Lombroso and other biological determinists that criminality could be traced to the biological inferiority of the poor. The Chicago School of Criminology was founded by Robert Park in 1913 in America's first sociology department at the University of Chicago as a manifestation of Progressive doctrines. Park and colleagues theorized that crime and other social problems were traceable to natural ecological processes in the development of cities. Researchers Shaw and McKay later confirmed Park's hypothesis using juvenile court statistics. Shaw and McKay subsequently founded the CAP, which attempted to institute neighborhood organization in high-crime areas, as an application of Park's theory and their findings. The Chicago School served as a foundation for a number of derivative theories including differential association theory, symbolic interactionism, labeling theory, and containment/control theory.

Whereas the Chicago School explored the consequences of urbanism upon crime, a more macrosociological approach to crime was developed at Columbia University by Robert K. Merton, who had been a student of Talcott Parsons at Harvard. Merton developed a crime "theory of the middle range" termed opportunity theory or anomie theory. In contrast to the ecological theory of the Chicago school, Merton's theory was not just about urban development, but pertained to American society and culture as a whole. Merton attributed crime in America to lack of access to opportunity to attain cultural goals of monetary success on the part of the urban poor. Merton assumed these aspirations for financial success to be universal in American society among all social classes. Although Merton's theory was originally published in 1938, it became popular during the 1960s as a result of its application to the subject of gang delinquency by students of Merton—Albert Cohen, as well as Lloyd Ohlin and Richard Cloward. Cloward and Ohlin worked their adaptation of Merton's theory into a social program, New York's MFY project, which won government support from the Kennedy and later Johnson administrations. However, the antiwar and civil rights disturbances of the late 1960s led to a conservative backlash and the election of Richard Nixon in 1968. Nixon dismantled many of the social programs of the 1960s and the social atmosphere changed in a direction unfavorable to opportunity theory.

While opportunity theory was favored during the 1960s, it was replaced by a significantly different approach during the 1970s—labeling theory. Labeling theory, whose major author was Howard S. Becker, produced a sea change in the approach to crime. Labeling theory de-emphasized the quest for underlying causes of crime, such as poverty or inner-city life. Becker, in a sense, blamed the stigmatizing of deviants by the criminal justice system, itself, as the major "cause of crime." Because it emphasized the "Four Ds" of *decriminalization, diversion, due process,* and *deinstitutionalization,* labeling theory was widely supported by academic criminologists, civil libertarians, and conservative politicians (who wanted to cut government costs). Diversion became the catch-phrase of the 1970s in the criminal justice system. However, as time passed it became evident that diversion was not working. The population of the criminal justice system, both in and out of prison, was increasing regardless of the labeling theory rhetoric of diversion and deinstitutionalization. Within criminology, conflict theorists accused labeling theorists of "net widening" (i.e., of increasing the size of the criminal justice system by adding an additional layer of community-based agencies that were used by judges, along with prison, as added sanctions). Subsequently, during the 1980s, conflict theory became a popular view among academic criminologists. However, the link between conflict theory and the ideological doctrines of Marx and Engels has not provided a favorable relationship between criminologists of the conflict school and the national government in the United States, a capitalist country. As discussed in Chapter 5, this impasse may have led to the development of more conservative "alternative theories" in criminology in recent years by authors from fields outside of sociology, including biology, psychology, economics, political science, and the medical profession.

DISCUSSION QUESTIONS

1. Do you think that juvenile delinquency is most prevalent in the inner city slums and less prevalent in the suburbs (Chicago School)? Why or why not? What studies cast doubt on the findings of the Chicago School? What counter-arguments have been made against critics of the Chicago School?

2. How important are friends and/or family in influencing a person's decision to commit delinquent or criminal acts (differential association theory)? If you accept differential association theory, what does this say about the "free will doctrine" that crime is mostly a matter of individual choice?

3. Do you think that lack of economic opportunity is the major cause of criminal behavior in American society? Do you think (as Merton said) that most everybody in the United States shares the same goal of economic success?

4. Howard S. Becker believed that deviant behavior is, more or less, equally prevalent at all economic levels of society. Do you agree with this assumption? Do you believe that labeling by the justice system drives people to commit more serious and more frequent crimes? If so, how and when, if ever, should official labels be applied to deviant conduct?

5. Do you agree with Willem Bonger that most crimes of the working class are motivated by survival needs and/or resentment? Do you think that most crime of the upper class is motivated by greed?

6. What do you think about Quinney's assertion that the crime problem can be resolved only through the collapse of the capitalist society and creation of democratic socialism? (Consider in your answer what we now know about crime in the former Soviet Union countries.)

SUGGESTED WEBSITES

http://www.criminology.fsu.edu/crimtheory/criminology_theory_link2.htm A page that lists links to numerous criminology theory Websites.

http://www.mdx.ac.uk/www/study/crimtim.htm A Website published in the United Kingdom giving a criminology and deviancy timeline from the year 1154 and the development of common law in England up to recent publications by "new criminology" authors Ian Taylor and Jock Young.

http://www.uwec.edu/patchinj/crmj301/theorysummaries.pdf A Website giving quick summaries of the key propositions of 16 major criminological theories, listing major authors of the theories.

http://faculty.ncwc.edu/toconnor/111/111lect03.htm A Website listing in table form the major criminological theories, along with causes associated with these theories and policy outcomes.

ENDNOTES

1. Lilly, Cullin, & Ball, 1995, pp. 31–32.
2. Rothman, 1980.
3. Madge, 1962, p. 89, as quoted in Lilly, 1995, p. 40.
4. Park, Burgess, & McKenzie, 1967.
5. Shaw & McKay, 1972.
6. Kim, 1980.
7. Kamalakara & Ramesh, 1984.
8. Schlossman, Zellman, Shavelson, Sedlak, & Cobb, 1984, p. 47.
9. Robison, 1936.
10. Porterfield, 1946; Short & Nye, 1958; Lawrence & Shireman, 1980.
11. Lilly et al., 1995, p. 45.
12. Sutherland, 1937.
13. Nakhshab, 1979.

14. Sutherland, 1947.
15. Wright, 2003.
16. Clinard & Quinney, 1973.
17. Thomas, 1923.
18. Thrasher, 1927.
19. Schmalleger, 2002.
20. Calhoun, 2003.
21. Pfohl, 1985, p. 211.
22. Merton, 1938, 1968.
23. Merton, 1968, p. 140.
24. Merton & Montagu, 1940.
25. Durkheim, 1947.
26. Adler, 1983.
27. Helal & Coston, 1991.
28. Cohen, 1955.
29. Cloward & Ohlin, 1960.
30. Empey, 1982, p. 241.
31. A *paradigm* is a school of thought within a discipline that provides scientists with a model for choosing problems to be analyzed, methods for analyzing them, and the theoretical framework to explain them (Curran & Renzitti, 2001, p. 25). Curran & Renzitti discuss paradigm revolutions such as those resulting from the change from the classical school to the positivist school and, finally, the Marxist/radical school. However, we will use the term *paradigm shift* to refer to major changes that took place within sociological thought during the 20th century—from the Chicago School, to opportunity theory, to labeling theory, and finally to Marxist/conflict theory.
32. Telfer, 1998.
33. Becker, 2003.
34. Cooley, 1902.
35. Mead, 1934.
36. Tannenbaum, 1938.
37. Lemert, 1951.
38. Zhang, 2003.
39. Becker, 1963.
40. Becker, 1953.
41. Empey, 1982.
42. Lilly et al., 1995, p. 121.
43. Comparative Criminology Website: Vietnam.
44. Bonger, 1916.
45. Lilly et al., 1995, p. 136.
46. Quinney, 1970.
47. Quinney, 1974.
48. Quinney, 1974, p. 16.
49. Quinney, 1977.

CONTEMPORARY THEORIES OF CRIME

KEY TERMS

chronic offender
conflict theory
critical criminology
econometric theory
feminist theory
integrated theory
peacemaking criminology
power-control theory

rational choice theory
reintegrative shaming
situational choice theory
restorative justice theory
routine activities theory
self-control theory
social learning theory

OUTLINE

Neoclassical Approaches

Feminist Theory

Biological Theories

Self-Control Theory

Social Learning Theory

Restorative Justice Theory

Postmodern Criminology

Integrating Criminolgical Theories

Comparative View of Crime

LEARNING OBJECTIVES

After reading this chapter, students should be able to:

1. Identify and characterize various "new" theories that are actually updates of the historical theories discussed in Chapter 3

2. Trace the history of feminist theory and be able to list the various types of feminist theories that are represented in criminology today

3. Characterize various containment and control theories and show how these have culminated in Gottfredson and Hirschi's recent self-control theory

4. Show how some 20th century sociological theories have been reborn as contemporary theories, such as social learning theory and restorative justice theory

5. Indicate a familiarity with additional movements in criminology such as postmodern criminology, integrating criminological theory, and the comparative approach taken in this text

INTRODUCTION

Chapter 4 was devoted to sociological theories that were dominant in criminology during the 20th century. That dominance was partly due to the "goodness-of-fit" of those theories to the social climate of the times during which they prevailed. The Chicago School of the early 20th century fit the Progressive thinking of the times. The opportunity theory of R.K. Merton came into vogue during the 1960s when there was a strong movement for civil rights and equality of opportunity in Washington, DC. The "diversion movement," spearheaded by Becker's labeling theory, moved in to fill the void when disenchantment was rising about the efficacy of social programs, and conservative politicians embraced it as a way to "cut the budget." Within the discipline of criminology, conflict theory started to replace labeling theory in the 1980s. However, conflict theory, originating in the writings of Marx and Engels, put the discipline at odds with mainstream thinking, which then tended to be conservative in regard to politics and punitive in regard to treatment of criminals. As Schmalleger put it, in the last decade of the 20th century, the prevailing orientation in public opinion in regard to treatment of criminals was "just deserts."[1]

Possibly as a result of this disconnect between academic criminology, with its interest in conflict theory, and public opinion, there has been a tendency for alternative theories to traditional sociological theories to develop in criminology. Many of these alternative theories have challenged the hegemony of traditional sociological theory as the dominant mode of orientation in regard to crime. An example was already given in Herrnstein and Murrays' treatise on IQ (*The Bell Curve*), which challenged the use of social programs to remedy IQ disparities between social classes and racial groups. In this chapter, a sizable group of studies of the human brain, hormones, and other biological factors are explored that potentially can challenge sociological explanations in a similar way as *The Bell Curve*. Another alternative theory approach has been an attempt to reinstate Classical School thinking about deterrence of crime through legal sanction. Closely related to deterrence theories are "situational theories of crime," which are also a form of neoclassical thinking in the sense that they seek to deter crime. The situational theories do not attempt to determine underlying causes of criminality, but, instead, focus upon the victim and seek the prevention of crime through the manipulation of the victim's environment or situation. Also in the alternative to sociological theories camp are the feminist theories, which have taken the view that sociological theories have been male dominated and do not incorporate the point of view of women. Feminist theories share with the situational theories a concern for the victim, particularly for the female victim, as a key element in crime. It should be mentioned that fundamentalist religious theories, discussed extensively in Chapter 3, also serve as alternative theories about crime that are held by a growing number of people today.

Although these alternative theories represent, to some extent, nostalgia for theories that existed prior to the 20th century (demonology, utilitarianism, Social Darwinism), there has also been some effort to update sociological theories of criminality. These new versions of the earlier theories expand upon the narrow versions of their theories that were popularized during the 20th century. Gottfredson and Hirschi's recent **self-control theory** is an extension of containment/control theory, and both the self-control theory and containment/control theories are discussed in this chapter. Ronald Akers'

social learning theory is a broadened version of Sutherland's differential association theory, incorporating variables from learning theory and social control theory. There has also been an attempt to revive labeling theory in the form of **restorative justice theory.** Restorative justice theory, in providing remedial measures for crime, departs from Becker's version of labeling theory, which seemingly rejected "cause and cure" approaches altogether. Closely related are versions of **conflict theory** (also known as **critical criminology**), which are reformist rather than Marxist-Leninist revolutionary in nature. Reformist conflict theorists have sought to provide viable programs of reform, such as those proposed by **peacemaking criminologists.** Criminologists of the conflict school have also sought to reform the social construction of criminality by the mass media in the work of postmodernist theorists, critical criminologists, and constitutive criminologists. Another attempt to revive sociological theory is **integrated theory** approaches, which combine different causative sociological theories with the hope of developing theories that have better explanatory potential than the general theories of crime, such as those formulated by Sutherland and Merton.

Finally, a comparative approach used in this text is explored. This approach is to use the comparative method, looking at crime as it occurs, not just in the United States, but throughout the world. The comparative approach is to seek explanations of crime that "work" cross-nationally. As a theme that will be developed in this text, the different types of crime cannot be explained by one general theory when crime is looked at cross-nationally. Instead, different types of crime are explained by different theories. Future chapters show that social inequality is a strong correlate of murder, whereas increased penalties for violence against women seems to reduce rates of rape. Also, "target hardening" seems to be a successful intervention for theft-related crimes. Thus, Merton's theory might work best with murder, deterrence theory with rape, situational theories with theft, and so forth. The advantage of the comparative approach is that it is flexible rather than dogmatic. It has the potential of providing a means of understanding the basis for different types of crime. It may also be helpful in developing policy that reduces crime. Thus, it can provide a way out of the impasse whereby criminology no longer plays an active role in public policy. More will be said about the comparative method near the end of this chapter.

NEOCLASSICAL APPROACHES

As discussed in Chapter 3, the Classical School of crime of Beccaria and Bentham was popular during the 18th century prior to the early development of Positivism in the form of Lombroso's biological approach, sometimes called the "born criminal" theory. Both schools (the Classical and Positivist) may have served as a catalyst for major political changes. The Classical School was instrumental in the French and American revolutions, as well as in the drafting of the French Code of 1791 and the United States Constitution. The "born criminal theory" was used as a justification for the conquest of whole continents, mainly Asia and Africa, by Great Britain and other European countries, insofar as the theory justified a "White man's burden" approach to colonialism.

Recent trends have been to reject scientific theories in favor of theories that existed before criminology. One trend has been to return to religious fundamentalism as an explanation of crime, and "backward" thinking groups have arisen both within the United States and in Islamic countries. That trend was discussed at length at the beginning of Chapter 3. However, the neoclassical approaches that are becoming increasingly popular today have not yet been discussed. These approaches owe their origins to Beccaria and Bentham and bear an implicit rejection of scientific criminology. They carry the assumption that crime is the product of a rational or calculative mind and must be managed based upon that assumption. If crime is the product of a rational mind, the criminal cannot be dissuaded from resorting to crime through therapy, but primarily through punishment, whether the punishment be a fine, imprisonment, or even the death penalty. Surely it cannot be denied that many crimes are, indeed, the product of a rational mind, so it may be worthwhile to revisit these theories and to have them as part of a "tool kit" in dealing with crime.

However, punishment is only one way to cope with persistent offenders. Another way is to prevent offenders from committing crimes through crime prevention techniques, such as illuminating targets, installing automobile burglary alarms, and so forth. Thus, the perception that the causes of crime cannot be remedied has led not only to the return of *deterrence theory,* but also to a new group of *situational theories,* whose aim is to prevent crime. It should be noted that these are not theories of crime but of victimization, and how to prevent it, because these theories do not address the causes of crime.

The re-emergence of classical theory today constitutes a radical break with the positivist approach taken by criminology during most of the 20th century. Why would criminologists make such a change, calling into question all that was believed for a century? Several factors led to disenchantment of many criminologists with positivism. From within the discipline came some findings that criminal motivation was intractable. During the 1970s, Robert Martinson published a comprehensive survey of the literature on rehabilitation programs that were done in and outside of prison. He found that there was no evidence that any rehabilitation program lowered rates of recidivism.[2] The phrase "nothing works" resonated both within the profession and among some politicians. Another related finding published about the same time (1972) was the discovery by Wolfgang and his associates of the **chronic offender.** Through the study of a cohort of children arrested for delinquency in Philadelphia, they discovered that 54% of the sample of delinquent youths were repeat offenders. They also found that 6% of the sample, who had been arrested five or more times, were responsible for 51.9% of all offenses. These same delinquents were also responsible for 71% of the homicides, 73% of the rapes, 82% of the robberies, and 69% of the aggravated assaults committed by the cohort. Follow-up study revealed that the chronic offenders had an 80% chance of becoming adult offenders.[3]

What did these findings have to do with **rational choice theory?** For some criminologists, it looked as though crime was a steadfast, rational choice made by criminals. No matter what was done to rehabilitate criminals, they would choose crime. From an early age, they would find that they could not make it in school or succeed in legitimate employment, and after a succession of arrests, they would become confirmed criminals.

For some criminologists who subscribe to rational choice theory, the answer to such a deliberate choice was lengthy incarceration and even a life sentence if the person continued to commit offenses.

For other criminologists of the rational choice school, the "best defense is a good offense." They argued that we should refocus our efforts towards preventing criminals from committing their crimes. The new school of rational choice theory was manifested in various forms, including deterrence theory (discussed in Chapter 3), **econometric theory, routine activities theory,** and **situational choice theory.**

One type of neoclassical theorizing is that done by economists who have essentially tried to operationalize Bentham's "hedonistic calculus." These include Gary Becker[4] as well as Peter Schmidt and Ann Witte.[5] Gary Becker suggested that three variables be used to minimize the loss for society from crime. The first is the probability (p) that an offense will be discovered and the offender apprehended and convicted. The second is the size of the punishment for convicted offenders and the form of punishment (f). The third is damages caused by a given number of illegal actions or offenses (O). Becker then developed theorems relating the three variables. He suggested through this approach that entry into illegal activities can be explained by the same economic model of choice used to explain legal activities.

Similarly, Schmidt and Witte provided a formula for calculation based on a time-allocation model (i.e. determining the amount of time in a 24-hour period that an individual will spend in legal as opposed to illegal activities). Factors the individual would take into consideration would be the amount of income that can be gained through legal activities as opposed to illegal activities; the probability of being arrested, convicted, and/or imprisoned for the crime; or the cost of a fine if convicted. Also taken into consideration are personal tastes, convenience, shame or guilt, and psychic benefits. The course of action will be made once all of these computations are done, though the decision may, of course, be an incorrect one, and the offender may be caught.

In theory, one should be able to precisely calculate the likelihood of a crime taking place, once all the variables are known. However, it seems unlikely that all variables (including personal tastes, guilt, and psychic benefits) can be known. Thus, the econometric model has not received much empirical corroboration.

Econometric Theories

Another theory often considered to be a form of neoclassical theorizing is Lawrence Cohen and Marcus Felson's routine activities theory.[6] This theory postulates that crime will occur if three elements are present: (a) *motivated offenders,* (b) *suitable targets* of criminal victimization, and (c) *an absence of capable guardians* of persons and property. This theory is sometimes called *lifestyle theory,* because it focuses upon the relationship between a victim's daily activities and vulnerability to crime. The link to classical criminality is the assumption that the only variables of concern in a crime are those that pertain to rational choice of the offender. The offender rationally studies the targets to see if they are vulnerable and checks to see if the targets are or are not guarded.[7]

The theory also became known as the lifestyle theory because Cohen and Felson's analysis pertained to the changes in lifestyle that took place after World War II, from 1947 to 1974. During this period of prosperity, the fact that crime increased was puzzling to criminologists who had associated crime with poverty. However, Cohen and Felson noted that changes had taken place in the form of increased female participation in the workforce,

Routine Activities Theory

BOX 5-1

Elderly Murdered in Homes in Canada

Routine activities theory would hold that elderly persons are vulnerable to crime if they venture outside their homes. One study of official Canadian data on all homicide cases committed between 1961 and 1983 found that a large proportion of elderly victims were murdered during theft-based attacks in their own homes. The findings point to a need for revisions in the routine activities approach.[8]

out-of-town travel, and automobile usage that could contribute to a situation whereby people could become victims of crime, particularly theft. In addition, people participating in the new lifestyle are simultaneously enjoying a new affluence, and carry not only money, but jewelry, expensive watches, and other electronic devices that make them likely victims of theft.

In an important application of routine activities theory, Felson developed a model of child sexual predatory crime focusing upon offender characteristics and routines, victim characteristics and behavior, and how guardians can be made more "capable" and accountable.[9] In agreement with Felson's model, a study of sex offenders ($n = 252$) in Arkansas found that there is a definite convergence of potentially motivated child sex offenders living in close proximity to concentrations of potential child victims.[10]

So the offender is constantly engaging in the "utilitarian calculus" of whether or not the victim/target is "easy" and whether or not the crime can be committed without law enforcement intervention. This theory can also be viewed as a variant of the Chicago School in its emphasis upon neighborhood social control (available guardians) as a deterrent to crime. As mentioned in Chapter 2, routine activities theory has been the subject of much publication, using data from the NCVS that are amenable to this theory. The virtue of this theory is that it seems to lend itself to ex post facto interpretations of statistics, such as the finding that crime increases as temperature rises.[11] However, that virtue may also be indicative of the vice—the theory is rarely, if ever, tested with primary data collected for purposes of testing the theory, as is the intended practice in scientific studies.

Situational Choice Theory

Given the routine opportunity theory assumption that offenders are motivated, targets are suitable, and guardians are absent, what is one to do to prevent crime? The answer given by situational theories is target hardening and measures of informal social control. Cornish and Clarke[12] developed an approach that has been termed *situational choice theory*.[13] Cornish and Clarke's rational choice perspective involves a view of criminal behavior as the outcome of decisions and choices by the offender.[14] This theory features environmental contingencies that can serve as a deterrent to crime. These are choice structuring properties that provide opportunities, costs, and benefits attached to specific crimes. For instance, a person who has decided to engage in a theft is likely to consider the following choices:

- The number of targets and their accessibility
- Familiarity with the chosen method (e.g., a purse-snatching)
- The monetary yield per crime
- The expertise needed

- The time required to commit the act
- The physical danger involved
- The risk of apprehension[15]

Cornish and Clarke suggest a list of 12 situational strategies that can lead to lowering the likelihood of criminal victimization. These include:

1. Target hardening, (making objects of crime less vulnerable)
2. Access control (e.g., deadbolt locks)
3. Deflecting offenders (e.g., through physical barriers)
4. Controlling crime facilitators (e.g., gun control)
5. Entry/exit screening (e.g., metal detectors)
6. Formal surveillance (e.g., security guards, television monitoring)
7. Surveillance by employees (e.g., doormen, clerks)
8. Natural surveillance (e.g., sufficient lighting)
9. Target removal (e.g., removal of cash from registers after hours)
10. Identifying property (e.g., etching identification numbers on property)
11. Removing inducements (e.g., prompt repair of vehicle left by roadside)
12. Rule setting (e.g., "No one allowed beyond this point")[16]

Ronald Clarke listed additional measures that involve the management, design, or manipulation of the immediate environment to reduce the opportunities for crime and increase its risk as perceived by offenders, including:

- Defensible space architecture
- Community crime prevention initiatives (e.g., neighborhood watch and citizen patrols)
- Improving coordination of public transport with pub (bar) closing times
- Public housing policies that avoid the concentration of children in particular housing developments[17]

Marcus Feldman argued that simple and inexpensive changes in the physical environment and patterns of everyday activity can often produce substantial decreases in crime rates.[18]

Looking at the list of 12 situational crime prevention strategies and additional ideas suggested by Ronald Clarke, it may be true that some can be achieved inexpensively (etching, posting signs). However, other techniques such as erecting barriers, employing security guards, television monitoring, gun control, metal detectors, installing suitable lighting, neighborhood watch programs, controlling public transport, and affecting public housing policies can be expensive items. Furthermore, they usually require the coordination and participation of a good number of individuals—a whole neighborhood or a business organization. Not surprisingly, attempts to apply this theory have typically been done, not by individuals, but by organizations. For instance, a local estate housing authority in Dudley, West Midlands (United Kingdom) tested the efficacy of improved street lighting on crime as a means of evaluating situational crime prevention and found (not surprisingly) a reduction in after-dark crime.[19] Similarly, another study of Crime Prevention through Environmental Design (CPTED) at Ohio State University found that improved

A "sign of the times," this crime watch sign indicates the presence of a Neighborhood Watch program in a community, an application of situational choice theory. Local police departments offer instructional meetings for neighbors who want to start a Neighborhood Watch program. Neighbors are chosen to be block captains, phone and email information is exchanged, and arrangements are made to put up a Crime Watch sign. Fear of crime is said to be reduced and crime reporting to the police enhanced by such programs.

Source: ©Bob Daemmrich/The Image Works

lighting in campus parking garages resulted in a significant reduction in crime in those garages.[20] In fact, a housing project intending to implement situational prevention efforts in Spokane, Washington—the Reclaiming Our Area Residences (ROAR) project—developed a neighborhood organization on the level of the CAP done years ago. The project involved:

- Collaborative problem-solving meetings among all key stakeholders in the targeted neighborhood
- The development of a neighborhood improvement committee comprised of public housing tenants, social service agency staff, local business owners, and so forth
- Hiring a residence resource coordinator to act as a liaison between public housing residents and other program participants
- Coordinating crime prevention education programs with the city's Crime Prevention Center
- Initiating physical target hardening and neighborhood physical improvements
- Opening a community-oriented policing substation within the public housing area, and assigning a neighborhood resource officer to the target area[21]

Although the outcome of the program was favorable in terms of neighborhood perception of crime and the incidence of crime, it can be seen that this program involved a lot more than "etching and posting signs." In fact, the success of such programs could result more from the neighborhood organization they entail than from the physical changes that are made. Also, it cannot be said that all CPTED projects are successful. The shear magnitude of such projects may result in failure. For instance, an attempt to implement situational crime prevention to reduce vandalism in 11 schools in Manchester, England, resulted in no improvement in vandalism. This was after two years, during which only 15 of the 30 project recommendations were implemented.[22] In addition to the costliness of situational crime prevention programs, other criticisms have been made of this approach: they may result in the displacement of crime to other sites, they contribute to the prospect of a "fortress society" and the "big brother" forms of state control, and they have little lasting effect upon urban decay and divert attention from the root causes of crime.[23]

It should be noted, however, that situational crime prevention may be successfully implemented at the level of urban planning and community-oriented policing. For instance, as one study suggested, it is conceivable that crime can be "designed out" of new subway systems.[24] It also seems logical that situational crime control can be achieved by the police if they target crime "hotspots" for purposes of directed patrol, a practice made possible by a new computer mapping technology known as Geographic Information System.[25]

Policy Implications

In terms of policy implications, neoclassical theories, like classical theories before them, emphasize a deterrence doctrine that underlies our entire criminal justice system, as well as recent "get tough" reforms emphasizing prosecution and imprisonment and programs such as juvenile "boot camps."

As far as empirical support for neoclassical theories, there is probably not enough empirical study to determine their effectiveness. Akers and Sellers maintain that rational choice theory does not stand up well to empirical evidence in its pure form of deterrence theory. Deterrence theory, they said, states that if legal penalties are certain, severe, and swift, crime will be deterred. However, severity is seldom found to have a deterrent effect on crime. For instance, Akers and Sellers argued, neither the existence of capital punishment nor the certainty of the death penalty has had a deterrent effect on the rate of homicides. However, research studies do find a negative correlation between perceived certainty of punishment and illegal behavior, but it is a weak correlation. However, Akers and Sellers argued, deterrence theory does well when low levels of rationality are assumed and explanatory variables are brought in from other theories. Thus, when deterrence concepts are expanded to include informal social control (reward or punishment by peers, family, etc.), then the theory works better to reduce criminality. However, when deterrence and rational choice theories are so modified, they resemble social bonding or social learning theories, as opposed to pure classical deterrence or rational choice models.[26]

The trend toward imprisonment may be seen as a negative outcome of rational choice theory in terms of the costs of imprisonment and other factors. Situational prevention can lead to an ever-increasing trend toward "do it yourself justice," ranging from vigilantism to gate guarded communities, and the omnipresence of closed circuit television observation of citizens. It can also lead to neighborhood efforts to close off streets and lead to "garrison communities," such as those that have developed in countries like Jamaica, as described in Chapter 8. Such outcomes may be construed as negative in terms of a decline of civil liberties as well as a decline in civility.

FEMINIST THEORY

Another new line of theorizing, essentially rejective of traditional causation theory, has been a number of writings by feminists who have rejected much of criminological theory as gender based and male dominated. Some of these theorists argue that the major sociological theories are "for men only"—they apply only to males and have little or no relevance for explaining female criminality or delinquency. Some **feminist theory** is closely allied with the situational theories discussed earlier, shareing a concern with the victim, and in particular, the female victim of crime, as well as the unequal way that women are treated in relation to crime.

Although the feminist movement has historical roots in antiquity, the first wave of the feminist perspective in the United States was akin to the movement to emancipate slaves. The culmination of this effort was the first women's rights convention held at Seneca Falls, New York, in 1848. The convention issued a "Declaration of Sentiments and Resolutions," which held that women have historically been tyrannized by men.[27] However, it was not until 1920, with the 19th Amendment to the Constitution, that women achieved the right to vote. It was not until 1975 in the case of *Taylor v. Louisiana* that the Supreme Court reversed itself and held that excluding women from jury duty was unconstitutional.[28]

Early Criminological Views of the Female Criminal

It is not entirely true that women have been excluded from consideration in previous criminological theory, although such theories were written by men and could be classified clearly as male chauvinistic in nature. Actually, many of these early theories were degrading and contemptuous of women, and they may have actually contributed to the perpetuation of female subjugation. These theories of female criminality were developed by Cesare Lombroso, W. I. Thomas, Sigmund Freud, and Otto Pollack.

Women as "Atavists"

Lombroso considered men to be more advanced in evolution than women, and he considered criminal women as biologically less evolved than noncriminal women.[29] The normal atavist primitive traits of women include being naturally vengeful and jealous, being deficient in moral sensibilities, and being insensitive to pain. These traits, according to Lombroso, are normally neutralized by other traits of females that include passivity, physical weakness, low intelligence, and a maternal "instinct." However, if these traits are absent, then women become born criminals more terrible than any man—"monsters." The physical traits of such women include cranial and facial features such as moles, unusually tall height, dark hair, masculine cranial and facial features, and dark skin. Although male atavists could be identified in Lombroso's theory by five or more anomalies, female atavists could be identified by as few as three anomalies. Lombroso later advocated continued subjugation of women in his book, *Crime: Its Causes and Remedies*. He opposed giving women the same education and occupational access as men because these only provided them the means and opportunities to commit additional crimes.[30]

Women as "Plants"

W. I. Thomas, as discussed earlier, was a scholar of the Chicago School, and though his early discussion of females and their criminality resembled Lombroso's, his later work and recommendations were drastically different from Lombroso's. *Sex and Society*[31] was a product of Thomas' doctoral dissertation, *On a Difference in the Metabolism of the Sexes,* developed at the University of Chicago. He maintained that women differed from men in being more like plants in storing energy, and thus were more motionless and conservative than men. This absence of motor fitness causes a decline of women's status in civilized societies, confining their sexual behavior to monogamous procreation. In *The Unadjusted Girl,*[32] Thomas argued that, although middle class women submit to monogamy, lower class women have not been sufficiently socialized to suppress their desire for excitement and new experiences, and they pursue sexual behavior as a means of realizing their wishes. Unlike Lombroso's born criminal recommendations that such women should be locked away and/or sterilized, Thomas kept with the Chicago school approach that criminal women could be resocialized to bring them in line with middle class role expectations.

Penis Envy

For Sigmund Freud, the inferiority of women is indicated by their lack of a penis, resulting in a life-long pattern of "penis envy" and jealousy of men. Women develop an inferiority complex, compensating for their inadequacy by being exhibitionistic, narcissistic, and well-dressed. Because of their obsession with personal concerns, women are unable to sublimate their individual needs, and so they are irrational and contribute little or nothing to building civilization, compared to men who are rational builders of civilization. As an expression of this longing for a penis, deviant women are those who strive to be like a man, engaging in various crimes as part of that orientation. Treatment for this "neurosis" has to do with helping criminal women to become "normal" and adjusted to the duties of wife and mother without regard to gender equity.[33]

Chivalry Hypothesis

Otto Pollack[34] developed a biocriminological theory of female crime. First, he viewed women as deceitful and covert in their criminality, traced to their ability to conceal their presence or absence of sexual arousal (unlike males who must achieve an erection to perform a sex act, making their sexual arousal obvious). Second, he linked the onset of female criminality to physiological changes resulting from the advent of menstruation, pregnancy, and menopause. According to Pollack, menstruation is correlated with such crimes as shoplifting, arson, and homicide. He believed that pregnancy increases the possibility of feticide or attempted feticide, whereas menopause might bring on such crimes as arson, breaches of the peace, and perjury.[35] Pollack argued that women actually have the same rate of crime as men, but men are treated less favorably by the criminal justice system, a theory that has been termed the "chivalry hypothesis." Females, he said, are the instigators of many crimes carried out by men, and when females are, in fact, charged with a crime, they use their sexual charms to induce police, judges, probation officers, and others in the justice system to obtain more lenient treatment for their crimes.

Feminist Views of the Female Criminal

These early theories of female criminality were written by men and were the antithesis of feminist theories. Feminist theories in criminology were not a product of the earlier emancipation movement, nor were they related to the women's movement for suffrage. Instead, they developed as an outgrowth of the civil rights movement of the 1960s. It may have been President John F. Kennedy's 1961 appointment of a federal commission to study the problem of sex discrimination, or it may have been Betty Friedan's 1963 book, *The Feminine Mystique,* that sparked the feminist movement. However, for many women, feminism became a key issue during the 1960s; they joined organizations such as the National Organization of Women and embraced the idea that gender discrimination is the central issue that must be addressed. Many branches of feminism emerged during this time including liberal, radical, Marxist, socialist, lesbian, postmodern, and others. Such views have been criticized in the mass media as "femi-Nazi" viewpoints that must be curtailed; however, feminist concerns seem to be paving the way to a valid new way of explaining crime. As discussed later, feminist views have been nullified when tested by provincial data drawn from within the United States (in fact, even more narrowly pertaining to treatment of women by the justice system). However, feminist concerns and theories hold more promise when tested cross-culturally and help to explain differentials in a variety of crimes of violence, and perhaps even property crimes. Because the feminist theories are likely to increase in prominence in the future, a brief review of existing feminist theories by liberal feminists, radical feminists, Marxist feminists, and socialist feminists is presented here.

Liberal Feminism

Liberal feminism seeks to redress inequality in the workplace as well as to change socialization practices so that women are taught to be just as aggressive and competitive as men, rather than passive and dependent. Within criminology, the *emancipation theory* has been termed as an example of liberal feminism.[36] As exemplified by studies done by Freda Adler[37] and Rita James Simon,[38] this theory is, it would seem, neither liberal nor feminist. This is because in emancipation theory the increase in female offending is viewed as being an outgrowth of the women's liberation movement. Because an increase in crime would be a negative outcome of the women's liberation movement, this theory is in reality critical of feminism and could be more properly termed "conservative anti-feminism." Also, the liberation hypothesis has not received much support by empirical studies. Although there has been an increase in female crime relative to male crime, the crimes that have increased have typically been non-white-collar crimes, such as shoplifting and drug offenses.[39]

Another variant of liberal feminist theory is a **power-control theory** developed by Hagan, Simpson, and Gillis.[40] They argue that in the family, boys are trained to be risk-takers and girls to be risk-averse in traditional "patriarchal" families, but to a lesser extent within "equalitarian families." The structure of the family is linked with parental occupational status. If the father's job has superior status to the mother's, or if the mother is not employed outside the house, then the family will be patriarchal, whereas if the father is absent or both parents have an equal status job, then the family will be equalitarian.

Females will be more equal to males in their delinquency (as a form of risk-taking) in equalitarian families and less delinquent relative to male siblings in patriarchal families. Thus, another theory dubbed "liberal feminist" in nature postulates that emancipation (in the form of an equalitarian family) yields a negative consequence—delinquency. Once again, for reasons stated before about Adler and Simon's theory, power-control theory seems to be neither liberal nor feminist. Also, there is mixed empirical support for the power-control theory.[41]

Radical Feminism

Radical feminists Kathleen Daly and Meda Chesney-Lind,[42] rejected the liberal feminism of Adler and Simon, as well as Hagan et al., saying that their theories are flawed and in fact not feminist theories. They are among the feminists termed *radical feminists*. *Radical feminism* holds that gender inequality is the most significant form of oppression and women are the most oppressed social group in the world, in all social groups—races, ethnic groups, and social classes. The maintenance of male dominance in patriarchal society is the result of various crimes against women relating to pornography, rape, sexual harassment, battering, and other forms of abuse. What is needed, according to Daly and Chesney-Lind, is not the elimination of capitalism, but to end male dominance. Radical feminists have focused their research not on offenders but on victims of crime, including rape and violence victims, and their findings have indeed revealed gender inequities in these crimes. However, because this theory pertains to a phenomenon that would characterize a whole society or nation, the most appropriate data to test this theory would be cross-national in nature. One such study was attempted by Steffensmeier, Allan, and Streifel,[43] with a somewhat dubious outcome, owed perhaps to the inadequacy of international data. Later in this text, some international information will be drawn from the Comparative Criminology Website developed for this text that will pertain to the radical feminist hypothesis. However, analysis will rely upon "case studies" of countries that appear to have trustworthy data, rather than correlational studies using data of dubious reliability and validity.

Marxist Feminists

Although radical feminist criminologists argue that gender inequality has priority over social class inequality as a form of oppression, *Marxist feminists,* such as Julia and Herman Schwendinger,[44] argue that modern capitalist societies have exceptionally high rape rates because the male dominance is produced by the exploitative class relations involved in capitalism. They argue further that gender inequity would be eliminated if capitalism were to be overthrown.

A balanced position on the relative importance of class and gender is offered by socialist feminists such as James Messerschmidt.[45] *Socialist feminists* indicate that we must examine both class inequality and gender inequality together to have a complete analysis of crime and victimization. Socialist feminists also challenge the traditional assumption that victims and offenders are distinct groups, that the home is a safe place and public places are dangerous, and that the legal system is a value-neutral place acting in the best interests of females.

Policy Implications of Feminist Criminology

Although feminist criminology is still in its infancy, it has already had a significant impact upon public policy in the adoption of such practices as mandatory arrests for domestic violence, changes in rape laws providing for the possibility of spousal rape, and the development of rape shield laws to protect victims from the "double victimization" of character assassination by defense attorneys in a public court of law. Laws against sexual harassment, as well as public support for shelters for battered domestic partners, have also been an outcome of feminist criminology.

The general thrust of feminist criminology has been to point out that male dominance results in violence toward women in various forms. The violence manifests itself in harassment of women in the workplace and school. It results in domestic battering, as well as sexual violence. A major achievement of feminists was the passage of the Violence Against Women Act of 1994 and 1998 (VAWA II). Both acts provided funding for criminal justice programs targeting violence against women. In Chapter 9, which deals with assault, the impact of VAWA is discussed. The emphasis upon empowering women to deal with various forms of violence may have been instrumental in the considerable drop in the overall crime rate from 1994 to 2000.

BIOLOGICAL THEORIES

Just as there has been a recent movement toward fundamentalism in religion, as well as the rekindled interest in deterrence theories, there has been a recent revival of focus upon biological explanations of crime. The reasons for the development of these new perspectives are varied. One reason may be the rising tide of conservatism that may in fact be allied with religious fundamentalism in its principled defense of individual responsibility and respect for tradition.[46] Another factor in this trend might be technological improvements in the biological sciences leading to some provocative findings related to the biosocial approaches to crime. All of these reasons point to a growing trend toward individual explanations for crime that began in the 1990s and continues today.

Biological theories, like the rational choice perspectives discussed previously, may have commanded recent interest in explaining the "nothing works" and "chronic offender" phenomena described earlier. The reason for the persistence of chronic career offenders, biological theorists might maintain, is that there are deep-seated biological causes that, when left untreated, drive the criminal.

The battle to revive an interest in biological and psychological trait theories has occurred on a number of fronts. Following the "Jukes and Kallikaks" tradition of family pedigree studies are twin studies, adoption studies, and faulty chromosome studies. In keeping with earlier studies of phrenology, atavisms, and temperament are various studies of hormones, neurotransmitters, and brain functioning. Noble may be the motivations for the development of such theories, perhaps in hopes of developing a "magic bullet" cure for crime through the administration of an injection by hypodermic needle or even genetic engineering. However, the policy implications of this reversion to "blaming the individual" can be, as discussed next, less noble.

Sociological theories that dominated criminology during the 20th century were typically developed by theorists who rejected individual explanations for criminal behavior. Sociologists Edwin Sutherland, Robert Merton, and Alfred Lindesmith steadfastly opposed explanations of crime that traced it to biological traits. The reason sociologists reject biological explanations stems from their methodological training, particularly in the sociological methodology of Emile Durkheim. Durkheim, one of the founders of sociology, argued convincingly that *social facts* (such as criminal behavior) can best be explained by other social facts.[47] Thus, sociologists are skeptical with regard to biological links with crime, ruling such findings as not deserving further examination, because biological traits are not "social facts." However, discussion below may explore the possibility that biological findings, such as those about the poor diet of juvenile delinquents, may indeed pertain to social facts. Poor diet may be a product of one's environment and may be linked with social class, race, gender, and other sociodemographic variables. Underlying social causes of biological problems might also include prenatal environment, child abuse, and hazardous living conditions.

Sociological Perspective

Twin studies have compared the concordance (similarity) of behavior of identical twins (monozygotic) with fraternal twins (dizygotic). These studies have invariably found greater concordance in terms of indices of criminality among the identical twins than among the fraternal twins.[48] Although such studies are often cited as clear proof of the heritability of criminality, there are limitations of such studies. In addition to methodological issues such as sampling errors, one variable that cannot be factored out of these studies is the environmental variable of social reaction to the twins. For instance, identical twins tend to be treated more alike by others and to spend more time together than fraternal twins. Even if identical twins are separated at birth, they may be treated similarly because of their physical appearance. Because these environmental variables can, perhaps, never be excluded, twin studies do not serve as a definitive test of hereditary component in criminality.

Twin Studies

Studies of adoptees have indicated some evidence of the independent influence of biology upon crime. One study done in Denmark is worth noting. Hutchings and Mednick studied 1,145 male adoptees born in Copenhagen, Denmark during the years 1927 through 1941, and found that the criminality of the biological father was the strongest predictor of the child's criminal behavior.[49] This and other studies seem to indicate that individuals are more likely to become criminals even when raised by noncriminal adoptive parents if their biological parents were criminals than if they were not criminals.[50] However, all such studies fail to rule out such contaminating variables as early experience with the criminal parents prior to adoption; early foster home or institutional experience prior to adoption; and even neonatal experiences, such as the drug ingestion of one's birth mother. So, once again, as with the twin studies, the adoption studies must be taken on faith as proof of the influence of heredity.

Adoptee Studies

Chromosome Studies

Chromosome studies of criminality began in 1965 when Patricia Jacobs and her colleagues reported that 7 of 197 inmates studied at a maximum-security hospital in Edinburgh Scotland had an extra Y chromosome, described as the XYY syndrome.[51] The interpretation given at the time was that XYY males were "supermales" whose extra Y chromosome triggered the secretion of testosterone, the male sex hormone, which in turn triggered aggressive behavior. However, further study revealed that XYY males were actually less likely than the general inmate population to commit violent crimes, typically committing petty property offenses. Given the tiny proportion of XYY offenders in the inmate population in Jacob's study (7 in 197), the XYY chromosome cannot account for much of crime or the criminal population. Possible bias in the criminal justice system against features such as excessive height linked with the XYY chromosome may account for the overrepresentation of this tiny proportion. Also, the "supermale" explanation is somewhat nullified by the finding that studies also found higher rates of criminality among XXY (extra X) males compared with normal XY males.[52]

Hormones

Probably one of the most enticing areas of biocriminology has to do with the role of hormones, especially the male hormone testosterone, in producing aggressive criminal behavior. The common sense observation that testosterone evokes aggressive behavior derives from "barnyard psychology" that leads farmers to have their male cattle castrated to prevent later aggressive behavior usually related to male domination of the herd and competition for mating privileges. Rats, mice, and monkeys injected with testosterone in the laboratory show an increase in aggressive behavior such as rough play and fighting. It also stands to reason that differentials in testosterone may account for male/female differences in humans in rates of violent crimes. Studies of prisoners have shown a fairly consistent finding of high levels of testosterone among violent offenders.[53] Observations such as these are persuasive in leading to the belief that we are close to a remedy in treating the most problematic of all behavior, violent criminality, with a quick cure in the form of the injection of a testosterone reducing drug such as Depo-Provera, or through castration. However, with human beings, there are complicating considerations. Studies have found that drugs that lower testosterone levels seem to be successful in treating sexual problems such as pedophilia, but are unsuccessful in treating nonsexual violent behavior.[54] Also, studies suggest that elevated testosterone may be a *product* of competitive activity in males, as well as a precursor to those activities, suggesting that thought processes may be an important variable in producing the elevated levels of the chemical in the body.

BOX 5-2

Castration of Sex Offenders in West Germany

A study of the surgical castration of sex offenders in the Federal Republic of (West) Germany was done on 104 voluntary castrates compared with a control group of 53 individuals who had applied for castration but did not have the surgery during the years 1970 through 1980. The castrates were 70% pedophiles, 25% aggressive sex offenders, 3% exhibitionists, and 2% homosexuals. Sexual interest, libido, erection, and ejaculation decreased in 75% of the subjects within 6 months. Furthermore, the postoperative recidivism rate for sex crimes was 3%, compared to 46% for the noncastrated subjects. Among the castrates, approximately 70% were satisfied with the intervention, 20% were ambivalent, and 10% were not satisfied.[55]

BOX 5–3

Female Hormone Implants Cut Sex Offenses

In a study done in Great Britain, male sex offenders were treated with subcutaneous implants of female hormone. A two-year follow-up after release indicated the effect of the hormone was to nearly eliminate further sexual offenses. Only one of the 25 treated sex offenders was reconvicted for a sex crime within two years of release, whereas the reconviction rate for the control group was considerably higher.[56]

To complicate the matter still further, there is evidence that *female* sex hormones—estrone, estradial, estriol, and progesterone—are also implicated in violent crimes for women. In this regard, both *premenstrual syndrome* and *postpartum depression syndrome* have been implicated in violent behavior in women and have been used in court as legal defenses. In regard to postpartum depression, cross-cultural studies indicate the cultural and environmental factors contribute to or mitigate the disorder.

One cannot deny that hormones are powerful forces working in both males and females; however, sociocultural factors are likely determinants of whether the aggressive outcome is crime, athletic achievement, artistic creativity, scientific discovery, exploration, or others of the myriad of possible forms of aggression in human experience. To quote Curran and Renzetti:

> In sum, our review of studies of the relationship between various hormones and crime indicates that considerably more research is needed before we can confidently link hormonal levels or changes with either male or female criminality. However, these studies do point to a strong interaction between biological processes and socio-environmental conditions that may help produce criminality.[57]

The Criminal Brain

Related to the aforementioned attempts to find something wrong with the body of criminals have been the battery of attempts to find something wrong with the brain itself, attempts that might be termed "neo-phrenology," although the original study of phrenology by Franz Joseph Gall (1758–1828) was not scientific (see text box). Some of these attempts are a byproduct of contemporary technologies to assess brain functioning such as the electroencephalograph (EEG), computed tomography or CT scans, magnetic resonance imaging (MRI), positron emission tomography, brain electrical activity mapping, super-conducting interference device (SQUID), and single photon emission computed tomography (SPECT) scans. Emerging as a product of these new technologies are a plethora of new diagnostic classifications with which many parents of school children have become familiar, including minimal brain dysfunction (MBD) and attention deficit/hyperactivity disorder (ADD). Studies of violent criminals have found them to have impairment in the prefrontal lobes, thalamus, medial temporal lobe, as well as superior parietal and left angular gyrus areas of the brain. In fact, Pallone and Hennessy[58] found that the incidence of brain pathology in murderers is 32 times higher than in the general population. One form of MBD results in episodes of explosive rage in an otherwise warm and pleasant personality. Researchers have predicted with 95% accuracy the recidivism of violent criminals, using brain wave data.[59]

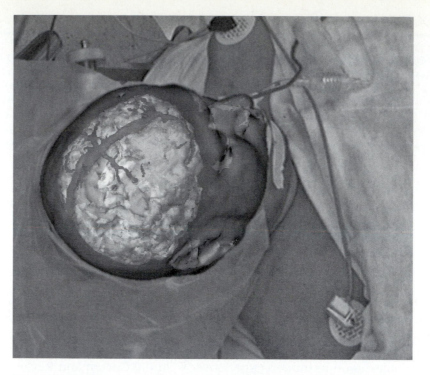

Recent technology shows potential for more accurately identifying brain pathology that can lead to murder and other violent crime. This 3-D image of a brain, showing a tumor, is created from a series of MRI scans of slices through the brain. With the help of contour mapping, a virtual reality image of the brain is superimposed onto an image of the patient's head to locate abnormalities.

Source: MIT AI Lab/Surg. Planning Lab, BWH. Photo Researchers, Inc.

BOX 5–4

Phrenology

The expression "you ought to have your head examined" probably derives from the work of criminal anthropologist and Viennese physician Franz Joseph Gall. Gall theorized that the shape of the human skull and bumps on the head could be used to predict criminal behavior and personality traits. The basic tenets of Gall's system were:

1. The brain is the organ of the mind.
2. The mind is composed of multiple distinct, innate faculties.
3. Because they are distinct, each faculty must have a separate seat or "organ" in the brain.
4. The size of an organ, other things being equal, is a measure of its power.
5. The shape of the brain is determined by the development of the various organs.
6. As the skull takes its shape from the brain, the surface of the skull can be read as an accurate index of psychological aptitudes and tendencies.

Gall divided the skull into 27 different functions. The first seven of the 27 functions were related to criminality, as follows:

1. Impulse to propagation
2. Tenderness for the offspring, or parental love
3. Friendly attachment or fidelity
4. Valor, self-defense
5. Murder, carnivorousness
6. Sense of cunning
7. Larceny, sense of property

By checking the size of the bumps in the various parts of the skull, Gall felt he could predict criminality as well as other propensities.[60]

Although Gall never tested his theory, it was widely accepted by his contemporaries. One of Gall's students, Johan Spurzheim (1776–1853), brought phrenology to America, where it continued to be used to classify new prisoners until the turn of the 20th century.[61]

According to Anne Moir and David Jessel, between 89% and 95% of all crime is committed by men because the male brain has a lower level of the neurotransmitter *serotonin* responsible for controlling impulsivity and because they have higher levels of testosterone.[62] Closely related to brain structure and brain damage is the effect of neurotransmitters or chemicals that influence or activate brain functions. Of the some 50 neurotransmitters that have been studied, three are of greatest interests to criminologists—*norepinephrine*, a chemical that pertains to perceived threats or danger; *dopamine*, a chemical that participates in feelings of pleasure, reinforcement, or reward; and *serotonin*, a chemical that regulates impulsiveness and sensory reactions.[63] Although high levels of norepinephrine and dopamine have been linked to violence, low levels of serotonin have been linked to impulsive crimes such as arson and unpremeditated murders.[64]

As provocative as these findings on brain and brain chemicals are, it should be remembered that such studies only produce evidence of links or correlations between criminal behavior and the biological variable at hand (damaged frontal lobe, low serotonin, etc.). It is possible that the observed differences are not a cause of the criminal behavior, but in fact may be an effect. For instance, there is evidence that trauma experienced by *victims* of crime results in structural brain defects, such as a reduction in short-term memory. Thus, the brain dysfunction and criminality may both have been the product of an earlier childhood trauma, such as child abuse.[65]

Neurotransmitters

Diet is a biological factor that sociologists might find of valid interest, because diet has a strong environmental component. Of interest, too, is the possibility that American diets have changed, especially since World War II, along with the growth in packaged foods, TV dinners, and fast-food takeout. Foods on the mass market are highly responsive to sales, and foods that taste good produce high sales. Unfortunately these high selling foods are typically high in sugar, fat, and chemicals. The home cooked meal, prepared from scratch, is often a thing of the past in an age of double-income parents and single-parent homes. There are a number of studies showing that antisocial youth who are given a balanced diet (typically involving reduced sugar) participate in reduced incidents of antisocial behavior and/or institutional rule infractions.[66]

Diet

The following scenario, although imaginary, is one that could happen quite frequently. Although the scenario is based upon a variety of studies, its purpose is to show how biological outcomes can result from environmental sources. One such environmental source is the use of drugs by the mother during pregnancy. A frequently cited nationwide survey of 36 hospitals done in 1988 found that 11% of all newborns had been exposed perinatally to illegal drugs.[67]

A single mother who is a polydrug user (heroin, crack, alcohol) gives birth to a premature male baby by caesarian section. The mother is administered various drugs during the delivery, to stimulate uterine contractions, to control the mother's blood pressure, and then to control pain during the surgery. The infant's brain was damaged during the delivery as result of inadequate obstetric intervention procedures. The baby's shoulder was caught behind the pelvic bone of the mother, resulting in inability of the infant to breath. After some time, medical personnel pushed the infant's head back inside the mother's body so that a caesarian section could be performed.[68]

Sociobiological Scenario

Prior to birth, poor nutrition and substance abuse on the part of the mother resulted in the infant's low birth weight, premature birth, and possible abnormal brain development upon delivery.[69] The child has to be withdrawn from the drugs that it shared with the mother via the placenta prior to birth.

The infant was a "fussy baby," crying continuously, which resulted in numerous incidents of child abuse in which the infant was shaken by the mother, increasing its brain damage. The infant suffers from malnutrition in its home environment, where fast-food, sugary snacks, and soft drinks are the main menu. The infant, by now, has received significant brain damage. The mother works as a prostitute and in occasional part-time legitimate employment. The child is left with friends and sometimes left alone while the mother works.

When the child begins regular school, it has an ADD and is combative with the other children. Subsequently, the child is placed in a class for slow learners, which results in teasing and name-calling by other children. The child fights with the other children and the teachers, and by fifth grade is constantly absent from school. Ultimately, the child drops out of school altogether and joins a teenage violent gang and, subsequently, becomes a chronic offender.[70]

This scenario, although fictionalized, shows how environmental factors (drugs, poor health care, poverty, premature birth, and single parenthood) can work hand and glove to contribute to biological factors that can predispose a child to a life of violent crime.

Problems with Biological Studies

Besides the problem of possible "spurious correlations," discussed earlier, biological research on crime suffers from such additional methodological difficulties as the measurement of criminality, sample size, sampling bias, statistical procedures, and generalizibility. Akers and Sellers concluded:

> Thus far, newer biological explanations have garnered mixed and generally weak empirical support. Biological theories that posit crime specific genetic or physiological defects have not been, and are not likely to be, accepted as sound explanations in criminology.[71]

Policy Implications

Perhaps because of the climate of fear of crime that currently prevails, these explanations have provided the basis for many touted "cures" for crime. "It is not uncommon for violence-prone people to be treated with antipsychotic drugs, such as Haldol, Stelazine, Prolixin, and Risperdal, which help control levels of neurotransmitters (such as serotonin or dopamine)." Such drugs are referred to as *chemical restraints* or *chemical straitjackets*.[72] Similarly, De-Provera has been prescribed for child molesters and other sex offenders to provide a form of chemical castration. A weekly injection of this drug was required in 1997 for twice-convicted child molesters in California.[73] Ritalin and other antidepressive drugs have been administered to school children, without concern with long term side-effects, as a treatment for ADD throughout the United States. The effect of this drug upon children has been characterized as a *chemical lobotomy*.[74] As discussed previously, invasive criminal justice policies, including drug treatment, segregation, surgery, forced sterilization, and even death for those who could not be cured, characterized early biological theorists, some even part of the Nazi movement in Germany and Fascist movement in Italy. However, intrusive policies have also been proposed recently by biocriminologists. Lawrence Taylor in his 1984 book, *Born to Crime: The Genetic Causes of Criminal Behavior*,[75] suggested that persons diagnosed as genetically predisposed to crime, whether or not they had actually committed criminal acts, should be dealt with through isolation, ingestion of chemicals, lobotomies, gene splicing, sterilization, and abortion to prevent transmission of criminal genes. From the late 1950s to the late 1970s, various medical procedures were performed on a small number of violent offenders, including brain surgery and implantation of electrodes that provide remote-controlled brain stimulation, as well as physical and chemical castration.

It would seem that studies that link a physical characteristic to criminality often lead their authors to follow the "slippery slope" of generalizing beyond their correlational studies to social policy recommendations going far beyond the scope of the findings that have been made. Therein lies the danger of such studies. What may be needed is the development of strict scientific guidelines for such studies in regard to making policy generalizations beyond the scope of limited scientific findings. The danger now, as in the past, is that such incorrect generalizations may carry the "halo prestige" of science and may be used by unscrupulous politicians and other policy makers to support draconian programs that can border on "crimes against humanity," as illustrated by the eugenics movement of the early part of the 20th century.

The promise of biological theories is to deliver a "magic bullet" for the treatment of crime in the form of drugs, surgery, psychosurgery, plastic surgery, and genetic counseling. Although today's biological theories factor in the influence of both heredity and environment, there is always the potential of misuse of "scientific findings" for purposes of social control. Eugenics, defined as the use of science applied to improvement of the human genome, was initiated by Francis Galton with considerable support from Charles Darwin in the latter half of the 19th century. Most people believe that eugenics has been put aside, recognizing the gross abuse in the United States between 1931 and 1945, when compulsory sterilization was practiced, and in Nazi Germany between 1933 and 1945, when mass extermination and compulsory sterilization were performed. However, the prospects for a revival of eugenics as a practice have increased since the recent revolution in molecular genetics that make possible such practices as somatic gene therapy and the possibility of human gene manipulation.[76]

SELF-CONTROL THEORY

We have seen that neoclassical theorists in the 1970s viewed the criminal as making a rational choice based upon something like Bentham's "utilitarian calculus" to engage in crime and/or pursue a career in crime. Gottfredson and Hirschi developed a theory in the 1990s that focuses upon the other side of Bentham's theory—universal hedonism. In a sense, Gottfredson and Hirschi's criminal doesn't deliberately pursue a career in crime—he just can't stop! This theory makes some degree of sense in light of the high recidivism rate of career criminals. If they were truly rational, they might take steps to avoid being caught, over and over again.

This relatively recent theory is (like the rational choice theories) essentially rejecting of prior sociological theories of motivation, as well as rehabilitation programs, and thus may play into the conservative theme of "anti-rehabilitation" and perhaps even "pro-prison." As discussed next, Gottfredson and Hirschi argue that self-control must be learned through early childhood socialization. However, if it is not taught, by implication, one is destined to a life of crime. If individuals have not learned self-control in childhood, and if they pursue a life of crime because of this, they are "set in their ways" and they cannot be rehabilitated as adults. Thus, such socialization failures, by implication, can only be dealt with by imprisonment, and/or rigorous monitoring through probation or parole. *Social control theory* is preceded historically by a long list of theories, termed *containment/control theories,* which were rooted in Freudian theory, on the one hand, and the Chicago School, on the other. Before discussing the Gottfredson and Hirschi formulation, a brief review of containment and control theories is appropriate.

Containment/ Control Theories

Prior to Gottfredson and Hirschi's recent social control approach, there were several contributions by authors, influenced by the Chicago School of Criminology, who developed social control theory. These included Albert J. Reiss,[77] F. Ivan Nye,[78] Walter C. Reckless,[79] Sykes and Matza,[80] and Travis Hirschi.[81]

Albert J. Reiss: Personal and Social Controls

Reiss published an article that developed from his doctoral dissertation at the University of Chicago. In it he viewed delinquency as a failure of personal and social controls. He conceptualized personal control to be the result of internalized norms and rules and social control to be the ability of social groups to make norms effective. He viewed the delinquent group as an outgrowth of the failure of personal and social controls, and he viewed the primary groups of family, neighborhood, and school as the basic institutions for the development of personal and social controls.[82]

F. Ivan Nye: Family Controls

Although Reiss did not produce any empirical data in regard to his theory, the other control theorists made attempts in that direction. F. Ivan Nye obtained his doctorate at Michigan State University, which was itself influenced by the Chicago school.[83] Like the classical theorists, Nye, followed the Hobbsian concept of universal hedonism and wondered why delinquent behavior was *not* more common (again rejecting the pursuit of a causal explanation). Nye believed that the family was the most important buffer against delinquency, providing a variety of controls—direct control, internalized control, indirect control, and control through alternative means of need satisfaction. In his research on self-reported delinquency, Nye found weak relationships between delinquency and various family variables such as broken homes, marital adjustment, employed mothers, family disorganization, absence of parental discipline, parent-child value disagreements, and rejection.[84]

Walter Reckless: Containment Theory

A more extensive control theory was proposed by Walter Reckless in the late 1950s and early 1960s.[85] Reckless, like Reiss, obtained his doctorate at the University of Chicago. The theory he developed was called *containment theory*.[86] Although Reckless acknowledged that a variety of factors, such as biophysical forces, psychological pressures, and social conditions such as poverty, might "push" a person toward delinquency, and other factors, such as the temptation of illegitimate opportunities, might "pull" a person toward deviance, most people engage in conforming behavior. It is only when these pushes and pulls can break through *outer containment* and *inner containment* (which insulates a person against illegal behavior) that a person engages in criminal behavior. *Outer containment* refers to such things as reasonable limits, meaningful roles and activities, and supportive relationships, whereas *inner containment* refers to self-concept, goal orientation, frustration tolerance, and norm retention. Inner containment was the more significant of the two, because through inner containment, the person is insulated against delinquency regardless of circumstances and even in the absence of outer containment. It should be noted that the "goal orientation" component of inner containment suggests a hypothesis contrary to the strain theory assumption that high aspirations lead to increased delinquency. Reckless obtained some research findings on his theory; however, his measurement was later criticized for being tautological.[87]

Sykes and Matza: Drift Theory

Sykes and Matza provided a theory that at one time appeared rejective of traditional theory and leaned toward the "free will" doctrine of utilitarian theory. First, they argued that in order for delinquency to occur, the delinquent must employ one or more "techniques of neutralization" or, in Freudian terms, "rationalizations," to justify delinquent behavior (and neutralize guilt).[88] Such theorizing contradicts the cultural transmission view, because it is assumed that delinquents have internalized society's norms regarding crime. The techniques of neutralization include denial of responsibility, denial of injury, and denial of victim, as well as condemnation of condemners, and appeal to higher loyalties. *Denial of responsibility* may involve citing social or personal problems that pushed the delinquent to delinquency. *Denial of injury* might involve such excuses as "the victim will be compensated by the insurance company." *Denial of victim* might be involved in "jack rolling" or "gay bashing," whereby the victim is construed as "deserving it." *Condemning of condemners* might involve referring to illegitimate activities of control agents, such as parents who use alcohol, judges who consort with prostitutes, and so forth. *Appeal to higher loyalties* is exemplified by gang members defending "turf" or fellow "homeboys." It should be pointed out that the first of these, "denial of responsibility," actually carries an implied criticism of causal theory, because the offenders may refer to them in excusing their own behavior ("I came from a broken home," "My dad beat me," "I was born in poverty," etc.). In his subsequent theoretical book, *Delinquency and Drift*, Matza argued for a "soft determinism" for placing some of the onus back onto the delinquents through undermining the rationalizations they use.[89] Once again, as with control theorists, Matza is rejecting traditional causation theories and moving in the direction of support for the earlier classical theory.

Hirschi's Social Bonding Theory

Despite the significant contributions of the students of the Chicago School described earlier, it is probably Travis Hirschi's *social bonding theory* that is most often cited as the definitive social control theory.

Ironically, Hirschi was not of the Chicago school. In fact, working on his doctorate at the University of California at Berkeley during the late 1960s student revolt there, Hirschi had to work quietly on a theory that was the very antithesis of the student movement to "tune in, turn on, and drop out." Aware of methodological flaws in earlier scientific efforts, Hirschi developed a testable theory of social control, and then tested it in a self-report study of a sample of the general adolescent population in Contra Costa County, California. Hirschi argued that there are four principle elements that make up the social bond. They are: attachment, commitment, involvement, and belief.[90] *Attachment* to others was proposed by Hirschi as a substitute for the inner control variables that were used by earlier theorists, because such variables had been measured in a tautological way. Tautological measurement involved using an index related to the "dependent variable" (e.g., truancy) as an index of the "independent variable" (in this case, "lack of inner control").

Hirschi argued that attachment to family and friends could control delinquency. *Commitment* referred to a "stake in conformity." *Involvement* had to do with engrossment or preoccupation with conventional activities, whereas *belief* is the endorsement of conventional values and norms. In his self-report study of adolescents, Hirschi developed and tested measures of all of these variables and found them correlated with measures of delinquency, (with the exception of involvement), the weaker the bond, the higher the probability of delinquency. Hirschi also found that delinquency was most strongly related to association with delinquent friends, a finding contrary to his thinking on attachment.[91] In regard to the evidence in favor of Hirschi's

Travis Hirschi, 2001

Source: Courtesy of Travis Hirschi, Steve Agan Photography

BOX 5–5

Hirschi's Bonding Theory Tested in Jordan and Saudi Arabia

A study of self-reported juvenile delinquency using a sample of 147 juvenile male 11th graders from seven public high schools in the Tafielah Governate in Jordan revealed that the Jordanian youth did indeed maintain strong ties to the conventional order. However, the sample reported significant involvement in delinquent activities since 76.2% of the sample fell into the nondelinquent category, with 23.8% falling into the delinquent category. Thus, the ties that Jordanian youth had to the social order were not sufficient to constrain their delinquency involvement,

casting serious doubt on the adequacy of Hirschi's theory when applied in a cross-cultural context. Another test of Hirschi's theory was done in Saudi Arabi with a sample comprised of 140 high school students, 205 youth institutionalized for serious offenses, and 71 youth institutionalized for status offenses. Neither social class nor family structure were found to be related to delinquency; however, both religious practice and religious belief were significantly negatively related to delinquency, as were parental attachment and involvement in school. Religious practice was more strongly negatively related to delinquency than religious belief. Association with delinquent friends was positively related to delinquency.[92]

theory, Akers and Sellers commented upon the strength of the relationships or correlations in Hirschi's own data. The strength of the relationships in Hirschi's findings, as well as replications of Hirschi's findings, has ranged from moderate to low.[93]

As an outgrowth of containment and control theory, in Hirschi's 1990 publication with Michael Gottfredson, a General Theory of Crime (GTC) was proposed that is based upon one type of control only—self-control.[94] Gottfredson and Hirschi argue that crime provides short-term gratification and is committed by people who lack the self-control to resist this mode of gratification because they have lacked effective parenting during their formative years. In addition to not being able to resist crime, such persons will fail in school, in employment, and in intimate relations. Although the results of studies testing Gottfredson and Hirschi's theory are generally favorable,[95] the policy implications of this theory have not been made clear by its authors. It is fairly clear that programs that affect long-term prospects by reducing social or economic inequality would be opposed by the theory, because criminals are viewed as short-term in their thinking.[96] Although Gottfredson and Hirschi would advocate policies that take effect early in life, they leave open the questions of what to do with people whose families have failed to provide them impulse control. Politicians who are so disposed might take such pessimism about the possibilities for change later in life to be conducive to a position that supports incarceration for such intractable criminals. So Gottfredson and Hirschi, with their self-control theory, along with their findings on IQ and delinquency, seem to have brought criminology back to, once again, a neo-Lombrosian way of thinking about crime.

Gottfredson and Hirschi's Self-Control Theory

BOX 5–6

"Danwei" and Criminality in China

A survey done in 1988 of 369 incarcerated youths compared with 443 nonoffending youths confirmed

the hypothesis that individuals with bonds to their work units ("danwei") are at lesser risk of becoming official criminals (inmates) than those whose bonds were weaker.[97]

Self-control theory has received much acclaim. Scales have been developed to measure the variable of self-control, and numerous studies have been done testing hypotheses based upon the assumptions of the theory. However, there have also been numerous criticisms of the theory. First, it has been suggested that the theory is tautological in the sense that impulsiveness (lack of self-control) is indicated by the commission of crimes. Second, self-control is said to be nothing more than a personality defect, reminiscent of the personality trait theories of the 1940s. Third, the theory does not account for statistical differences between cities, racial groups, and gender differences. Fourth, there is evidence that people do age out of crime and become less impulsive as time goes on (contrary to one of the assumptions of the theory). Most important (for our purposes), there is evidence that criminals in other countries do not lack self-control, suggesting that the GTC is culturally bound, which negates it as far as cross-cultural comparisons are concerned.[98]

Policy Consequences of Control Theory   The early control theory of the Chicago School emphasized the restoration of neighborhood organization as a means of establishing control over deviant behavior. Hirschi's bonding theory has been applied in various ways. School-based parent training programs have been offered in many states to increase parenting skills and restore the family bond. Another program called Positive Action Through Holistic Education or PATHE attempts to increase students' commitment to school and attachment to conforming members. Other programs have employed teenagers to create new activities for children tempted to join gangs or sell drugs.[99] Although Gottfredson and Hirschi's more recent self-control theory would probably keep such childhood programs intact, it would probably support punitive deterrence approaches for chronic offenders, whose unchanging loss of self-control has been revealed by their pattern of chronic recidivist offending.

SOCIAL LEARNING THEORY

Sutherland's theory of differential association, discussed in Chapter 4, continues today in the form of Ronald Akers' social learning theory. Social learning theory is a spin-off of differential association theory, with details of the learning process added. Akers indicates that his social learning theory expands upon differential association theory by relying on four major concepts: *differential association, definitions, differential reinforcement,* and *imitation.* Akers has tested his new theory as compared with other theories, using self-report questionnaires in a variety of settings and has concluded that social learning theory is the best predictor of delinquent behavior.[100]

Differential association theory has also maintained its vitality in another sense—an applied sense. Paul Gendreau, who realized the damaging effect of Robert Martinson's "nothing works" doctrine, has tried to mitigate the damage through pointing to programs that do work. In 1983, Gendreau declared that the "nothing works" credo is invalid. He praised, in particular, therapeutic community programs based upon social learning theory and the theory of differential association.[101]

Donald Cressey essentially explained the link between differential association and 12-step programs like Alcoholic Anonymous, as well as therapeutic communities, such as Synanon, a residential self-help program for drug addicts.

Cressey proposed that the process involved in these programs was *retroflexive reformation,* which is actually the reverse process of differential association.[102] In *retroflexive reformation,* ex-offenders are used as correctional paraprofessionals. The ex-offender is transformed from a help recipient to a help giver and, in a role reversal, finds that he is incorporating into his life-style the same patterns that he seeks to have his clients adopt.[103] Sociologist Lewis Yablonsky was one of the first to recognize the potential of an experiment that was beginning during the 1960s in California. He had learned about Synanon from Donald Cressey:

> I first learned about Synanon at a United Nations conference on crime and delinquency in London in the summer of 1960. One evening, at an informal gathering, this new experiment for treating criminal addicts was described to me by noted criminologist Dr. Donald Cressey. According to Dr. Cressey, Synanon involved a small group of criminal addicts living together in an old beach house then located in Santa Monica, California. Synanon was a residential counterpart of the community-based AA.[104]

Yablonsky subsequently became, for all practical purposes, the "resident sociologist" for Synanon, and wrote two books on the subject of the organization. Yablonsky explained the principles that make a therapeutic community (TC), such as Synanon, a success:

> On the basis of my extensive research into TCs around the world since 1961, I have concluded that there are several basic factors that must exist in order for an organization to be defined as a true TC: (1) voluntary entrance; (2) the use of various methods, especially the encounter group process; (3) the proper use of former offenders in combination with college-trained psychotherapists as co-therapists in the program; and (4) an open-ended social structure that allows the residents to move up the status ladder of the organization into an increasingly responsible therapeutic position in the TC.[105]

Synanon was started by a member of Alcoholics Anonymous (AA) named Charles E. Dederich. Dederich believed that the methodology of AA should be extended into a residential setting where alcoholics and drug addicts could live together and help each other reclaim their lives. The new community was called Synanon after Dederich overheard a recovering addict mangle the words symposium and anonymous. Synanon began in 1958 and existed for approximately 35 years. As a result of Synanon's success in training former criminal addicts to become effective therapists, the concept and methodology of the original Synanon TC has been replicated in thousands of spin-off organizations in the United States and around the world.[106]

RESTORATIVE JUSTICE THEORY

Labeling theory lost its following after it became evident that it apparently led to "net widening." Although the implication of labeling theory was that stigma should be removed through deinstitutionalization and diversion, the practical effect of the theory was the opposite. The diversion movement that was derived from labeling theory led to the development of a plethora of community-based organizations that simply added an additional layer to the criminal justice system. Judges continued to send convicted offenders to prison or put them on probation. However, sentencing options now included requiring the offenders to spend time in a community-based organization. Offenders who might have otherwise been released or put on straight probation were now sent to community-based organizations. Some of these organizations became, in essence, "community jails" where the offenders were required to "do time." A large number of residential treatment programs served the purpose of community jails because offenders were required to stay at such programs or face violation of the terms of probation that would result in incarceration in an actual prison or jail. Even attendance at meetings of Alcoholics Anonymous and various spin-off organizations, such as Cocaine Anonymous and Gamblers Anonymous, became a required part of sentences.

So it was broadly recognized that the effect of labeling theory was to increase rather than decrease the number of people in the criminal justice system. Assignment of offenders to a community-based organization did not necessarily remove stigma. In fact, they were required to go to a place that served as a sentence for criminals, a place where a person would encounter and fraternize with other criminals.

An attempt to revise labeling theory to correct these problems was made in the late 1980s by Australian criminologist John Braithwaite.[107] Braithwaite argued that not all labeling leads to increased criminality. He argued that beneficial labeling can take place in the form of *shaming*. Braithwaite defined *shaming* as social disapproval that invokes remorse or condemnation by others who become aware of the shaming, and he argued that societies with low crime rates are those that shame potently and judiciously. Braithwaite, it would seem, is contradicting the labeling theory assumption that shaming pushes offenders into deviant subcultures and launches deviant careers.

However, his answer is that labeling theorists fail to distinguish between *disintegrative shaming* and **reintegrative shaming.** *Disintegrative shaming* is stigmatizing and involves separating the offenders from the community and treating them as outcasts. As a result, the offenders are more likely to become members of criminal subcultures, because they receive social support from these groups. As members of criminal subcultures, the offenders are more likely to recidivate. *Reintegrative shaming,* by contrast, is that done by members of the community as an expression of disappointment in the individual who has done wrong. The offender is not treated as a "bad person," but a "good person" who has done wrong, reaffirming the offender's morality. Community disapproval may range from a mild rebuke to degradation ceremonies. These are followed by gestures of reacceptance of the offender into the community of law-abiding citizens.

BOX 5–7

Reintegrative Shaming in China

Braithwaite's reintegrative shaming theory is perhaps more appropriate in its application to China than it is in the West. This is because the concept of shaming is consistent with the cultural ethos of Chinese collectivism rather than Western individualism. In China, the collectivist nature, strong social bonds, effective informal social control, and emphasis on social education all make shaming a positive rather than negative tool of social control.[108] In China, the practice of *bang-jiao* whereby an offender on parole is reintegrated back to the community confirms the theory of reintegrative shaming.[109] Another Chinese practice, *tiao-jie*, the use of community groups to resolve disputes among neighbors and family members, is also compatible with Braithwaite's theory.[110]

Restorative justice (RJ) programs advocated by Braithwaite[111] include offenders performing community service, apologizing to victims, participating in conflict management training, making reparations to the victims, and *victim-offender mediation* (VOM). "Faith-based" prison and community programs are also considered to reflect principles of restorative justice and reintegrative shaming.[112] In 1999, Braitwaite indicated that RJ has an extensive history and takes a variety of forms cross-nationally. Although it is viewed in the West as a major innovation in criminological thinking, it is grounded in traditions of justice from the ancient Arab, Greek, and Roman civilizations; the Germanic peoples after the Fall of Rome; Indian Hindus; and ancient Buddhist, Taoist, and Confusion traditions. RJ, according to Braithwaite, includes VOM, healing circles, family group conferences, restorative probation, reparation boards, whole-school anti-bullying programs, Chinese "Bang Jiao" programs, and exit conferences in business.[113]

Very similar to Braithwaite's reintegrative theory is the new approach of conflict criminologists Hal Pepinsky and Richard Quinney called **peacemaking criminology**.[114] They argue that crime is a form of violence and suffering, but to respond to crime with violence in the form of punishment is counterproductive, as violence begets violence. Instead, they advocate peacemaking in the form of bringing offenders and victims together for mediation, conflict resolution, and reconciliation. They also favor nonpunitive approaches including having the offender apologize to the victim, make restitution by paying the victim and/or community back through fee or service, and requiring the offender to make charitable contributions.

BOX 5–8

Peacemaking Circle Process[115]

Peacemaking circles provide a process for bringing people together as equals to talk about very difficult issues and painful experiences in an atmosphere of respect and concern for everyone. Peacemaking circles create a space in which all people, regardless of their role, can reach out to one another as equals and recognize their mutual interdependence in the struggle to live in a good way and to help one another through the difficult spots in life.

Peacemaking circles are built on the tradition of talking circles, common among indigenous people of North America, in which a talking piece, passed from person to person consecutively around the circle, regulates the dialog. The person holding the talking piece has the undivided attention of everyone else in the circle and can speak without interruption. The use of the talking piece allows for full expression of emotions, deeper listening, thoughtful reflection, and an unrushed pace. Additionally, the talking piece creates space for people who find it difficult to speak in a group. Drawing on both traditional wisdom and contemporary knowledge, the circle process also incorporates elements of modern peacemaking and consensus building processes. Participants are seated in a circle of chairs with no tables. Sometimes objects with meaning to the group are placed in the center as a focal point to remind participants of shared values and common ground. The physical format of the circle symbolizes shared leadership, equality, connection and inclusion. It also promotes focus, accountability, and participation from all. The circle process typically involves four stages:

1. Acceptance: The community and the immediately affected parties determine whether the circle process is appropriate for the situation.

2. Preparation: Separate circles for various interests (family, social workers) are held to explore issues and concerns and prepare all parties to participate effectively. Thorough preparation is critical to the overall effectiveness of the circle process. Preparation includes identifying possible supporters in the natural network of the family to participate in the process.

3. Gathering: All parties are brought together to express feelings and concerns and to develop mutually acceptable solutions to issues identified.

4. Follow-up: Regular communication and check-ins are used to assess progress and adjust agreements as conditions change.

At any stage, multiple circles may be held to complete the tasks of that stage.

BOX 5–9

Tribal Punishments in Recent East African History

Tribal justice in recent African history has not always been benign, but contains a variety of options not typically used in Western justice. The various sanctions used to punish and control deviance in recent history in East African societies included reconciliation between offender and victim and between their respective families; restitution of property stolen or destroyed; compensation of the victim and his family by the victim and his reference group; compensation to the tribal community as a whole (comparable to a fine); corporal punishment sometimes including mutilation, beating, and torture for serious offenses; capital punishment for offenses of extreme gravity (e.g., witchcraft, but not usually homicide); social ostracism and public ridicule; religious sanctions such as repudiation by elders through issuance of a formal curse; and expulsion of the offender from the community.[116]

A recent review of the impact of restorative justice programs evaluated 46 studies of VOM, 13 of family group conferencing, and four of peace-making circles (see text box). The studies were done in the United States, England, Scotland, Canada, and New Zealand. Overall, the research reflected remarkably consistent levels of victim and offender satisfaction with conferencing strategies. They also found the method increases the likelihood that restitution contracts will be paid and that recidivism levels will be decreased for a significant number of offenders.[117] Another study revealed that VOM is a widely used method of restorative justice, with more than 1,300 programs in 18 countries worldwide.[118]

RJ programs are, like TCs, a worldwide movement.[119] However, RJ programs also have a major following within the United States. They have been used with date rape victims and offenders.[120] Police-based RJ programs are being used in Pennsylvania.[121] A "Resolve to Stop the Violence" program is underway in San Francisco, with the goal of reintegrating violent offenders back into the community while simultaneously addressing the needs of victims.[122] VOM today has advanced far beyond the "pilot" stage. VOM currently has received statutory authority in the codes of 29 states.[123] As of year 2000, there were 289 VOM programs established in the United States.[124]

POSTMODERN CRIMINOLOGY

The ultimate challenge to traditional causative theory in criminology has been done by a group of criminologists who follow the philosophical foundations laid down by the French philosopher Michel Foucault. These postmodernists reject the whole idea of objectivity and doubt that it is possible to discover truth using the scientific method. They argue that truth is socially constructed through everyday social interaction, and what is accepted as truth changes from time to time and place to place. Although Marxist criminologists might like to overthrow capitalism, postmodernists are concerned with "deconstructing" the meanings and social processes that are attached to crime and justice in a capitalist society. Within criminology, postmodernists are represented by authors referred to as *constitutive criminologists,*

Michel Foucault (1926–1984)
Source: CORBIS/Bettmann

most notable of whom are Stuart Henry and Dragan Milovanovic. A major theme in their writing has been the redefinition of crime itself. Denying that crime is what criminal law says it is, they argue that crime is the ability or the power to impose one's will upon others. They further argue for the abolition of all taken-for-granted assumptions about the "causes" of crime (i.e., the abolition of criminology itself).[125] More specifically, postmodern penology abandons the idea of reducing crime through broad social programs and rehabilitative efforts and aims to reduce the harm that crime inflicts.[126] Even restorative justice programs, such as VOM, are rejected by postmodernists as a "discourse that marginalizes juveniles."[127]

Although such armchair philosophizing has been attacked as being anarchistic, apolitical, and/or politically neutral, postmodernists argue that through deconstruction, they can actively resist the negative, harmful, and hierarchical group identities that have been constructed by both the powerful and oppressed.[128] However, because postmodernism rejects all causal theory, it has been attacked as "theoretical poverty." Because it attacks all social programs, it is critiqued as failing to foster fundamental social change, and it has been termed a detour or obstacle to the development of a truly critical criminology.[129]

BOX 5–10

Critical Criminology

Critical criminology refers to a theory known variously as Marxist, conflict, or radical criminology. It includes peacemaking, radical feminism, left realism, and postmodernism. Conflict theorists see crime as a result of class struggles and the inequitable distribution of limited resources within society. Key concepts include the role of government, capitalism, and political power in relation to crime rates.[130]

INTEGRATING CRIMINOLOGICAL THEORIES

Although restorative justice, peacemaking criminology, and postmodernism have attempted to revive interest in labeling theory and conflict theories, some criminologists have attempted to renew interest in extant criminological theories by providing composite theories, combining different theories into one sequential model. The idea is to provide theories with greater explanatory value through use of multiple variables that are said to be causative. This approach departs from the "general theory" orientation of Sutherland and Merton, tending toward the eclecticism that Sutherland and Merton tried to avoid. Integrating theories are also called integrative, integrated, mixed, synthetic, and convergent theories.[131] Instead of viewing various theories, such as control theory, differential association, and strain theory, as competing theories, the integrating theories are attempts to combine the theories into a single, usually sequential, developmental theory. The theory can then be tested, often using multivariate statistical analysis (regression, path analysis, factor analysis) to determine which variables account for the greatest percentage of variance.

Probably the best example of integrating theory is Elliott's integrative model, which combines strain, control, and social learning theories. Elliott and associates' postulated that strain (discrepancy in aspirations/achievements) in family and school leads to a weakening of conventional bonds (attachment, involvement, commitment, belief), and this leads to the development of strong bonds to delinquent peers (differential association), which, in turn, leads to delinquent behavior.[132] This model, it should be pointed out, ignores Hirschi's bonding theory assumption that there is a natural motivation to crime. Using multivariate analysis with data from their National Youth Survey, Elliott and associates found that strain and conventional bonding had no direct effect upon delinquency, but bonding to delinquent peers had a strong, direct effect.

Similar attempts to combine strain, control, and social learning theories have appeared in Krohn's network analysis, Thornberry's interactional theory, Kaplan's self-derogation theory, and Sampson and Laub's life-course theories.[133] However, the attempts at theoretical integration have met with mixed success and acceptance. Although there has been a favorable climate of opinion in criminology toward theoretical integration, there continues to be a considerable indifference in regard to integration efforts, as well as skepticism toward integration as a theory-building strategy.[134] As pointed out earlier with Elliott's approach, the integrating theories tend to blur actual differences between theories that are blended in their integrating theory. They usually limit their integrating to a limited selection of "factors" from the theories that are blended, thus providing an "eclectic" rather than truly integrating theory.

Policy Implications of Integrated Theory

Because the integrated theories blend several general theories of crime, policy implications are ambiguous and depend upon which theories are included. For instance, Elliott and associates' theory combines strain, control, and differential association theory—in that order. Thus, the theory might address equality of opportunity in early childhood through improved access to education, followed by attempts to improve ties to family and school. Subsequently, the focus might be upon directing at-risk students to conventional peer associations, as opposed to gang membership.

Unfortunately, funding is usually not available for such comprehensive programs, but more likely available to test the efficacy of one theory or another. Because the integrating theories lack decisiveness as to priorities, these approaches have received little recognition by criminologists, the public, or policy makers.

Our analysis of different crimes cross-nationally has led to another alternative to the integrating theory approach. This new orientation, which emphasizes different theories for different crimes, is discussed next.

COMPARATIVE VIEW OF CRIME

It is the position taken in this text that the traditional pursuit of causal explanations of crime in criminology is the very essence of that discipline, and that pursuit should not be abandoned. Crime is a phenomenon that can be explained, and efforts to explain crime must be continued. However, past efforts to find causes and cures may have failed because they have been too limited in scope. The majority of these theories have been either reductionistic biological or psychological individual trait theories or microsociological theories that are provincial in the sense that they are developed to explain crime in the United States and principally tested only within the United States. As has been shown through biographical sketches of various theorist's, more often than not, the theories have been a product of the theorist's own limited experience and the social context of his or her time and, if any empirical testing was done at all, based upon observations within a limited geographical area.

Most of the failed theories (or theories that have been disregarded) discussed earlier have neglected a very important point—that crime today is global in its nature and causes. To understand crime, we must trace it to its global origins. Explaining crime by looking at crime only within the United States is like trying to explain a disease, such as SARS, HIV/AIDS, or West Nile Virus, or even Mad Cow disease, by simply looking at such diseases as though they originated within the United States. The reality is that such diseases began in other countries. To deal with these diseases we must find out where they are coming from and deal with them at their source as well as in the United States.

The goal of this text is *not* to develop a full comparative *theory* of crime, but rather to use the comparative *method* to explore the roots of various crimes. One theory, such as Merton's anomie theory, may work with one form of crime, such as murder. However, to explain other crimes, it may be necessary to utilize other theories, such as deterrence theory with rape, or routine-activities theory with burglary.

Studies will be done of countries that have very high rates of certain crimes to determine why they are high in these crimes. Studies will be done of countries that are (or claim to be) low in crime with the goal of understanding why that might be, or if the claims are actual or spurious. Many former Soviet-era countries were said to be low in crime, as illustrations of the success of Communism; however, since the breakup of the USSR, many countries are now starting to show rising crime rates (or at least reporting the crime rates more truthfully). Similarly, many Islamic countries report very low crime rates. These countries will be investigated to see if there is any basis for the claim of low crime rates, and/or if the data are being suppressed or poorly gathered in these countries. Lastly, capitalist countries similar to the

BOX 5–11

Crime Booms

The goal of this text is eclectic—to look at individual crimes and determine which theory or theories best explain the crime. However, some authors have attempted to develop global theories to explain crime generally. Among the extant global theories are social constructionism (labeling), modernization (anomie), and globalization (Marxist) theories. LaFree and Drass[135] tested these theories using INTERPOL, United Nations, and World Health Organization data. They studied "crime booms," rates of crime the increase rapidly, in relation to the aforementioned theories. They postulated that constructionism would predict that crime booms are rare or nonexistent, whereas globalization predicts widespread crime booms throughout most nations. Modernization theory would predict crime booms to be most common among industralizing rather than developed nations. Out of 34 nations studied, they said that 12 nations were exhibiting crime booms. These were too many to support the constructionist explanation and too few to support globalization. Further, they found that 70% of the industrializing nations exhibited crime booms versus only 21% of industrialized nations. The evidence, they concluded, most supported modernization theory.

United States will be analyzed to see if they have lower crime rates than the United States and, if so, to try to explain why this might be the case.

The approach taken in this text is new for an introductory text in criminology. It differs from the "general theory" approach taken by Sutherland and Merton in that no one theory is endorsed as explaining all crime. Rather, different theories are brought into play to explain different crimes or types of crime.

The comparative approach differs from the "eclectic" approach, which employs a variety of factors to completely explain a crime or crime in general within the United States. Instead, a variable or group of variables are located that appear to explain a particular crime cross-nationally. The search for universal explanations or explanations that account for crime throughout the world can yield fresh insights on how to view crime within the United States.

The comparative approach also differs from that taken by integrating theories of crime that have been developed for the United States. These theories are provincial in the sense that they are combinations of theories that have been developed to explain crime within the United States. Also, as was pointed out earlier, these theories typically incorrectly blend theories that are conflicting theories, ignoring the inconsistencies. The approach taken in this text is, essentially, to avoid the development of either a general theory or integrating theory, because it seems presumptuous to develop such theories without first exploring the data cross-nationally.

The decline of sociological theories in the field of criminology, from our perspective, stems from a lack of comparative analysis in these theories. In a sense, sociological theories in the field of criminology have not been sociological enough. In the words of Emile Durkheim, one of the founders of sociology (who was himself a comparativist):

> One cannot explain a social fact of any complexity except by following its complete development through all social species. Comparative sociology is not a particular branch of sociology; it is sociology itself, in so far as it ceases to be purely descriptive and aspires to account for facts.[136]

Sociological theories, such as those discussed in Chapter 4, contain propositions that are stated as if they apply to all mankind, not just residents of the

United States. In that sense, the testing of such propositions only within the United States is incomplete in terms of the logic of scientific analysis. As Robert Marsh wrote in his book *Comparative Sociology:*

> The major shortcoming of all types of intra-societal comparative analysis is that they minimize the range of variation found in all human societies. . . . The close link between cross-societal analysis and studies limited to a single society can also be seen in terms of the logic of scientific method. A science strives to formulate universal propositions. Once a proposition has been tentatively formulated, the task of research is to replicate it, attempt to state limiting conditions and intervening variables, and analyze "exceptional" cases. In this process, inter-societal comparative analysis is but a necessary extension of intra-societal comparative analysis. It is a necessary step, but one that many sociologists and anthropologists fail to take.[137]

It is fortunate that, as a result of the development of the Internet, a wide variety of data are now available for study from a growing number of databases that are posted on Websites all over the world. The pursuit in this text is exploratory, not to develop either a general theory or global framework. It seems too early to attempt to provide such outcomes—and to attempt to do so would be likely to result in the production of provincial explanations.

SUMMARY AND CONCLUSION

The 20th century witnessed the rise and fall of sociological explanations of crime as the dominant approach to criminology. From the 1990s up until the present day, alternative theories, competitive with sociological explanations, have been developing. Some of these new theories are a revival of the historical theories described in Chapter 3. They assume that offenders, from an early age, cannot be dissuaded from a criminal way of life. Such theories include religious beliefs, neo-Classical models, some feminist perspectives, biological explanations, and social control theories. Neoclassical thinking has recently been explored by economists and in the form of routine activities theory and situational choice theory. Feminists have also opposed traditional sociological theories as "male dominated" and have, like the situational theorists, focused upon helping victims, particularly females as victims of crime. Also, a host of new biological studies have surfaced to serve as an alternative to sociological thought. Biological studies raise, once again, the "neo-Lombrosian" specter of draconian programs such as sterilization. Yet another trend, and one that stands opposed to most sociological theory, comes from within sociology itself with the development of Gottfredson and Hirschi's self-control theory called the GTC. The GTC, arising from containment/control theory, maintains that the criminal personality is fixed for life after the offender has been improperly socialized in early childhood, suggesting the irrelevancy of many remedial social programs.

The aforementioned alternative theories are based upon the assumption that the sociological approaches of the 20th century are obsolete. One response to this assault upon sociological theory has been to question Martinson's "nothing works" assumption. Gendreau has done this by pointing to the success of therapeutic community programs that are based upon the theory of differential association and social learning theory.

There have also been attempts to revise sociological theories to remedy mistakes of the past. For instance, Braithwaite suggested the use of "reintegrative shaming," in the form of restorative justice, as an improvement upon labeling theory. Also, "peacemaking criminology" has suggested programs like VOM as a means of reform as well as an application of conflict theory. These approaches utilize examples drawn from countries and cultures outside of the United States, and are thus comparative in nature.

To carry this comparative approach one step further, it is the goal of this text to make even better use of comparisons. Namely, it is our intention to use the "comparative method" continuously throughout the text. Comparisons will be made regarding crime and criminal justice between United States and other countries of the world. Also, comparisons will be made, of both a qualitative and quantitative nature, between the nations of the world. In that way, we hope to present a new orientation to American criminology as an inherently comparative discipline, utilizing all the information that can be obtained from studies of other nations. In light of the seemingly unlimited information available on the World Wide Web, this is a realistic objective.

DISCUSSION QUESTIONS

1. Do you think that the sociological criminological theories of the 20th century are essentially obsolete and will be replaced by new theories?

2. Why do you suppose that historical theories, such as the Classical School and biological theories, have become popular today?

3. Has the feminist movement resulted in an increase in female criminality? Do you think that being a woman is more important than a woman's social class in determining the probability of her criminal victimization?

4. Do you think that biological theories are completely incompatible with sociological approaches? Explain your reasoning.

5. Do you think that Gottfredson and Hirschi's "self-control theory" is as good as or better than the containment and control theories that preceded it? If so, why so? If not, why not?

6. Do you think that differential association theory continues to be a vital theory today? Why or why not?

7. How are the RJ programs both similar and different from the labeling and conflict theories that preceded the RJ programs?

8. What do you feel, if any, are the limitations of theories that have been developed and tested only in the United States?

SUGGESTED WEBSITES

http://faculty.ncwc.edu/toconnor/301/301lect02.htm
A historical account of the classical and positive schools, with a discussion of the emergence of the "neoclassical school" of criminology.

http://web.mala.bc.ca/crim/Student/Erin%20VZBakker.pdf A 22-page paper on "nature versus nurture" with pages of references to recent and historical literature.

http://faculty.ncwc.edu/toconnor/301/301lect14.htm
Website giving history of feminist criminology, statistics on female criminals, a list of feminist criminologists, and links.

http://www.umsl.edu/~rkeel/200/socdisor.html
Website showing the development of Gottfredson and Hirschi's self-control theory from the Chicago School until today, with links to original documents.

http://teachnet.edb.utexas.edu/~lynda_abbott/Social.html Website giving the social learning theory in detail.

ENDNOTES

1. Schmalleger, 2003.
2. Martinson, 1974.
3. Wolfgang, Figlio, & Sellin, 1972.
4. Becker, 1968.
5. Schmidt & Witte, 1984.
6. Cohen & Felson, 1979.
7. Cohen & Felson, 1979.
8. Kennedy & Silverman, 1988.

9. Mannon, 1997.
10. Walker, Golden, & VanHouten, 2001.
11. Cohn & Rotton, 2000.
12. Cornish & Clarke, 1986.
13. Curran & Renzetti, 2001, p. 11.
14. Cornish & Clarke, 1987.
15. Cornish & Clarke, 1985.
16. Clarke, 1992.
17. Clarke, 1983.
18. Felson, 1998.
19. Painter & Farrington, 2001.
20. Tseng, Duane, & Hadipriono, 2004.
21. Giacomazzi, 1995.
22. Hope & Murphy, 1983.
23. Trasler, 1986; MacKay, 1988.
24. Smith & Clarke, 2000.
25. Rengert, Mattson, & Henderson, 2001.
26. Akers & Sellers, 2004, p. 41.
27. Daly & Chesney-Lind, 1988, p. 221.
28. Herlihy, 1997.
29. Lombroso, 1895.
30. Lombroso, 1912, p. 54.
31. Thomas, 1907
32. Thomas, 1923.
33. Klein, 1973, pp. 16–18.
34. Pollack, 1950.
35. Pollack, 1950, p. 158.
36. Curran & Renzetti, 2001, p. 212.
37. Adler, 1975.
38. Simon, 1975.
39. Akers & Sellers, 2004, p. 254.
40. Hagan, Simpson, & Gillis, 1987.
41. Akers & Sellers, 2004, p. 256.
42. Daly & Chesney-Lind, 1988; Chesney-Lind, Daly, 1989.
43. Steffensmeier, Allan, & Streifel, 1989.
44. Schwendinger & Schwendinger, 1983.
45. Messerschmidt, 1986.
46. Lilly Cullin, & Ball,1995, p. 207.
47. Durkheim, 1938.
48. Christianson, 1974; Rowe, 1986.
49. Hutchings & Mednick, 1977.
50. Mednick, Gabrielli, & Hutchings, 1987; Crowe, 1972.
51. Ellis, 1982.

52. Curran & Renzetti, 2001, pp. 48–49.
53. Rubin, 1987.
54. Dirks-Linhorst & Laster, 1998; Rubin, 1987.
55. Wille & Beier, 1989.
56. Field & Williams, 1970.
57. Curran & Renzetti, 2001, p. 53.
58. Pallone & Hennessy, 1988.
59. Siegel, 2000, p. 155.
60. van Wyhe, 2002.
61. Schmalleger, 2002, pp. 142–143.
62. Moir & Jessel, 1995.
63. Niehoff, 1999.
64. Curran & Renzetti, 2001, p. 59.
65. Curran & Renzetti, 2001, p. 55.
66. Schoenthaler & Doraz, 1983; Schoenthaler, 1985.
67. Gittler, 2004.
68. Kegel Exercise.com, 2003.
69. Thornton, Clune, Maguire, Griffin, & O'Connor, 1990.
70. The scenario was drawn in part from a study by the California Crime Control and Violence Prevention Commission, 1981.
71. Akers & Sellers, 2004, p. 63.
72. Siegel, 2000, p. 157.
73. Schmalleger, 2003, p. 729.
74. Jura, 2005.
75. Taylor, 1984.
76. Galton & Galton, 1998.
77. Reiss, 1951.
78. Nye, 1958.
79. Reckless, 1961.
80. Sykes & Matza, 1957.
81. Hirschi, 1969.
82. Reiss, 1951.
83. Lilly et al., 1995, p. 83.
84. Nye, 1958.
85. Reckless, Dinitz, & Murray, 1956; Reckless, 1961.
86. Reckless, 1961.
87. Akers, 2000, p. 104.
88. Sykes & Matza, 1957.
89. Matza, 1964.
90. Hirschi, 1969.
91. Akers & Sellers, 2004, p. 120.
92. Irfaifeh,1990; AlRomaih, 1993.
93. Akers & Sellers, 2004, p. 122.

94. Gottfredson & Hirschi, 1990.
95. Lilly et al., 1995, p. 103.
96. Akers & Sellers, 2004, p. 131.
97. Zhang & Messner, 1999.
98. Siegel, 2003, pp. 288–289.
99. Adler, Mueller, & Laufer, 2004, pp. 183–185.
100. Akers & Sellers, 2004, pp. 83–98.
101. Gendreau & Ross, 1983.
102. Seaberg, 1981.
103. Priestino & Allen, 1975.
104. Yablonsky, 1990, p. 561.
105. Yablonsky, 1990, p. 562.
106. Yablonsky, 2002.
107. Braithwaite, 1989.
108. Chen, 2002.
109. Lu, 1999.
110. Zhang, Zho, & Messner, 1996.
111. Braithwaite, 1995.
112. Akers & Sellers, 2004.
113. Braithwaite, 1999.
114. Pepinsky & Quinney, 1991.
115. Minnesota Department of Corrections, 2005.
116. Kercher, 1981.
117. Umbreit, Coates, & Vos, 2002.
118. Umbreit, Coates, & Vos, 2001.
119. Zehr & Toews, 2004.
120. Koss, Bachar, & Hopkins, 2004.
121. McCold, 2003.
122. Schwartz, Hennessey, & Levitas, 2003.
123. Lightfoot & Umbreit, 2004.
124. Umbreit & Greenwood, 2000.
125. Beirne & Messerschmidt, 1995, pp. 534–535.
126. Miller, 2001.
127. Bruce & Schehr, 1998.
128. Curran & Renzetti, 2001, p. 204.
129. Arrigo & Bernard, 1997.
130. Falcone, 2005, p. 65.
131. Shoemaker, 2000, p. 260.
132. Elliott, Huizinga, & Ageton, 1985.
133. Akers & Sellers, 2004, pp. 278–285.
134. Akers & Sellers, 2004, p. 286.
135. LaFree & Drass, 2002.
136. Durkheim, 1938, p. 139.
137. Marsh, 1967, p. 7, 11.

CRIMINAL HOMICIDE

KEY TERMS

criminal homicide
deinstitutionalization movement
dowry murders
enforcement terrorism
external restraint theory
felony murder
homicide design theory
honor killings

manslaughter
mass murderers
moral insanity
murder
serial killers
subculture of violence theory
violentization theory

OUTLINE

Definition
Extent and Trends
Types of Murder

Theory
Country Profiles

LEARNING OBJECTIVES

After reading this chapter, students should be able to:

1. Define murder in its various degrees and distinguish it from manslaughter, both in terms of its legal definition, and in terms of its social definition

2. Characterize "typical murders" and factors usually associated with them

3. Identify various types of murder, both domestic and foreign

4. Describe recent studies of brain pathology in relation to murder

5. Understand how deinstitutionalization of the mentally ill may have resulted in an increase in certain types of murder

6. Show the relationship between paranoid schizophrenia and mass murder

7. Show how psychopaths become serial killers

8. Explain and critique the subculture of violence theory and the associated victim precipitation theory

9. Understand the cross-cultural association between inequality and murder and the relevance of external restraint theory to this relationship

10. Discuss both sides of the question "Do drugs cause crime?" or "Does the War on Drugs cause crime?"

INTRODUCTION

After a year of estrangement from my wife—in a moment of madness—I took the lives of my three small children and almost destroyed my wife and myself. My wife and children were my little world. When my wife withdrew her love and affection, when she rejected me again and again, my mind and energy over the months, night and day, were bent on getting her back. When, after attempting to please her, waiting, arguing with her, when my wife said things to me I could not stand to hear, and struck me—when this happened, I felt cut off with terrible finality, violated, betrayed, almost inundated with terror. I could no longer contain myself. It was as though something burst deep inside me. I felt impelled to destroy and did. While I was attacking my wife, the children came screaming out of their bedroom, and my violence was transferred from her to them. It was all over in a few seconds. The explosion into violence, the manner and means of it, what I did to myself afterwards (cut both wrists to the bone and severed my esophagus with a razor blade)—these were not the actions of a sane man. Emotional upheaval had transported me beyond a focus of awareness that included rational decision. If the ambulance had arrived a few minutes later, I would not be here. At the county hospital, a team of surgeons worked hours to save my life and repair the damage.

For five days I was given private nursing care around the clock. I could do nothing for myself. My hands and forearms were bound on boards to protect my wounded wrists. A tracheotomy had been done to permit me to breathe. Only my mother was permitted to visit me. I felt strange and frightened. Every time I opened my eyes, a nurse was there looking at me, waiting to care for me. I began to mend, to want to live. After five days I was arraigned in municipal court and taken by the sheriff and two of his deputies to prison for safekeeping. The authorities there, I was told, would be able to provide medical care and protection not available in the county jail.

After five months at the prison I went to trial. There, after a month-long trial, the jury found me guilty of three counts of murder in the second degree and one count of assault with intent to commit murder. The judge sentenced me to prison for the maximum sentence he could hand down: three 5 to life sentences and one 1 to 14 to run consecutively.

This meant 16 years to life. Later these sentences were aggregated by state law to 10 to life, which meant I became eligible for parole in three years and four months.

In my first two years at prison, I just put one foot in front of the other. The betting on the Big Yard was that I would commit suicide in the first year. Nights—after a hard workout in the gym on the top floor of an old building down in the alley—when I came out on the fire escape and looked five floors down to the pavement, it would have been very easy to have stepped off. It was not until I was transferred to a medical facility that I began to find myself. There I had five years of individual and group therapy. Therapy there was much like that at Synanon—hard-driving, uncovering. For months I had diarrhea and difficulty in sleeping. But I learned some things. I learned that quite early my mother communicated to me an unstated proposal that had far-reaching effects upon my life: "If you love me, you will do everything I want you to do because everything I want you to do is right and good and perfect; and if you do, I will love you above everyone." She kept the promise—as long as she lived. Even after my offense, she treated me as though I were a god. In her eyes, I had been perfect: I accommodated to toilet and eating and language training earlier than children usually do. I measured up to her moral and social expectations. I became the all-American boy—a scholar, an athlete, a school and campus leader. I became a naval officer, a teacher and coach, a devoted husband and father. For 39 years I lived entirely within the law. I fulfilled her expectations and she kept the promise.

With no father (my father was beaten to death with a hammer when I was six months old) to rescue me in my most vulnerable years, my obsession (to be loved by everyone as my mother loved me) and my compulsion (to qualify for that love by being perfect) took root. To feel impelled to measure up to and to please others—to be always "right and good and perfect"—to feel right about yourself is a terrifying and precarious existence, and when you fail—catastrophic.

In my 15 years in prison, I refused to think of myself as a convict, an inmate, a number. I accepted responsibility for what I had done; but I fought tooth and toenail to maintain my identity as a person.[1]

A profiler attempting to analyze this case study would be hard-pressed to find any major sociological factors usually associated with homicide. Richard was white, had a middle-class occupation and income, was not a member of a gang, was not involved with a "subculture of violence," and had, if anything, been "overcontrolled" by his parent—his mother. Richard may have been traumatized by the death of his father, and may have been abused in other ways in childhood. However, he appears to be characteristically a "contracultural overconformist," rather than nonconformist. Richard does resemble a "shut in" or "seclusive personality," a term that Faris used to describe schizophrenics in his study to be discussed later.[2]

Richard's case illustrates that there are limitations to the explanatory power of macrosociological variables, although there may have been family group dynamics, or microsociological variables involved in his case. For crimes such as Richard's, individualistic explanations—psychological theories, or even biological approaches—may be needed for a comprehensive analysis of the case.

In this chapter various explanations for homicide—sociological, psychological, and biological—are discussed, as well as the evidence for each explanation. Then some cross-national data, both qualitative and quantitative, will be addressed, in an attempt to enhance understanding of the topic of homicide.

DEFINITION

The term **criminal homicide** or **murder** commonly includes both murder and manslaughter. For tabulation purposes, the FBI includes in its category of "murder and nonnegligent manslaughter" all instances of the "willful (nonnegligent) killing of one human being by another."[3] Not all homicides are murder. Some homicides are justifiable homicides, such as those committed by law enforcement officers in the course of their duties. What people commonly call "murders" are what criminologists call "criminal homicides— unlawful killings, without justification or excuse." These are further subdivided into murder, manslaughter, and negligent homicide.[4]

As defined in common law, murder is "the unlawful killing of a human being with malice aforethought."[5] Another way of understanding the range of acts included in the FBI's categorization is that there are various degrees of murder, from *first-degree murder* to *second-degree murder*. First-degree murder is the most serious of criminal homicides and may carry the death penalty in jurisdictions that have it. Some jurisdictions attach "special circumstances," such as killing by poison, during a kidnapping, by a person serving a life sentence, and so forth before attaching a death penalty. First-degree murder combines the elements of premeditation and deliberation. *Premeditation* means that the killing was contemplated before it was committed, whereas *deliberation* refers to the fact that the crime was planned. For instance, if a gang member drove across town to kill a rival gang member, that would be eligible for treatment as a first-degree murder; if a gang member simply came upon a rival gang member and killed him or her, that act would not be first-degree murder. It might be classified as second-degree murder, which involves malice aforethought, but not premeditation or deliberation. **Manslaughter** refers to homicide without malice, and thus is differentiated from murder; however, it is often included in statistics describing murder, such as those gathered by INTERPOL. *Manslaughter* is further divided between *voluntary* (nonnegligent) and *involuntary* (negligent) *manslaughter*. *Voluntary manslaughter* would be illustrated by the killing of someone during a fight, while *involuntary manslaughter* would be indicated by deaths resulting from drunken driving.[6] Both are punishable by imprisonment, but normally the former may result in a longer term of imprisonment than the latter.

Terms such as malice aforethought, premeditation, and deliberation are vaguely defined in law and often overlapping. It should be observed that the decision of "murder" versus "manslaughter" ultimately results from a "social definition" by a jury during the prosecution of the crime. For instance, if the prosecution could convince a jury that the accused deliberately got drunk and had an automobile accident in order to kill his wife who was a passenger in his car, then the crime of involuntary manslaughter could be elevated to first-degree murder. On the other hand, if the prosecution feels that evidence is lacking to prove first-degree murder, then it may plea bargain a case down to second-degree murder or even manslaughter.

Curiously, it is possible for a person to be charged with first-degree murder, even if he or she commits an act without intent, malice aforethought, premeditation, or deliberation in the special case of **felony murder.** Felony murder occurs when a death results during the commission of another felony, such as rape or robbery. Even if a person is killed through the accidental discharge of a weapon during a rape or robbery, the charge of felony murder could be made for both the perpetrator and any accomplices to the act.[7]

EXTENT AND TRENDS

The murder rate in the United States in 2004 was 5.5 per 100,000 inhabitants. The murder rate in the United States peaked at 10.2 per 100,000 inhabitants in 1980, declined until 1984–85, rose again to 9.8 in 1991, and has been declining since 1991, as shown in Table 6–1.

Ironically, the public fear of crime and violence has been increasing during the same period of time that the homicide rate has been declining. The Gallup Report has included data on this subject for the years 1982 to 2002. In telephone interviews with a random sample of adults in the United States 18 years and older, the respondents were asked "What do you think is the most important problem facing the country today?" Starting in 1982, 3% of the respondents answered "crime, violence" to this question. This figure rose to 9% in 1993 and then jumped to 37% in 1994. It then leveled off to 20% in 1998, followed by a decline to 1% in year 2002, being replaced by 22% indicating "terrorism" as the most important problem in 2002.[8]

Why did the fear of violent crime rise during this period, despite the decline in homicide? One explanation is that coverage of sensational crime stories in the mass media has inflamed public opinion, and there is plenty of evidence that the number of violent crime stories seems to run parallel to the fear of crime. For instance, during the peak years of 1994 and 1995, crime stories featured on network TV broadcasts also peaked in volume, probably accounted for largely by the national obsession with the O. J. Simpson murder trial, as seen in Table 6–2.

However, another explanation is that public fear has to do with the type of offender and nature of the crimes committed (i.e. that people fear that they or someone they are intimate with will be killed by a "marauding stranger"). There is evidence that, though homicide in general declined,

Table 6–1 **Homicide Victimization in the United States, 1950–2002**[9]

Year	Homicide Rate	Number of Homicides	Year	Homicide Rate	Number of Homicides
1950	4.6	7,020	1977	8.8	19,120
1951	4.4	6,820	1978	9.0	19,560
1952	4.6	7,210	1979	9.7	21,460
1953	4.5	7,210	1980	10.2	23,040
1954	4.2	6,850	1981	9.8	22,520
1955	4.1	6,850	1982	9.1	21,010
1956	4.1	6,970	1983	8.3	19,308
1957	4.0	8,060	1984	7.9	18,692
1958	4.8	8,220	1985	8.0	18,976
1959	4.9	8,580	1986	8.6	20,613
1960	5.1	9,110	1987	8.3	20,096
1961	4.8	8,740	1988	8.5	20,675
1962	4.6	8,530	1989	8.7	21,500
1963	4.6	8,640	1990	9.4	23,438
1964	4.9	9,360	1991	9.8	24,703
1965	5.1	9,960	1992	9.3	23,760
1966	5.6	11,040	1993	9.5	24,526
1967	6.2	12,240	1994	9.0	23,326
1968	6.9	13,800	1995	8.2	21,606
1969	7.3	14,760	1996	7.4	19,645
1970	7.9	16,000	1997	6.8	18,208
1971	8.6	17,780	1998	6.3	16,974
1972	9.0	18,670	1999	5.7	15,522
1973	9.4	19,640	2000	5.5	15,586
1974	9.8	20,710	2001	5.6	16,037
1975	9.6	20,510	2002	5.6	16,204
1976	8.8	18,780	2003	5.7	16,528
			2004	5.5	16,137

stranger killings and multiple murders increased during this same period of time, providing a semirational basis for the public fear of crime. During the period from 1976 to the early 2000s, the FBI reported a decline in homicides committed by "intimates."[10] By implication, the number of crimes committed by "strangers" to the victim has been increasing. At the same time, the number of victims per homicide incidents increased. Many of these "multiple murders" may qualify for the term "marauding stranger," being carried out by *mass murderers* and *serial killers*. The percentage of the number of victims killed in a single homicide event has increased from 1976 to 2000, whereas the number of homicide offenses with only one victim dropped during that period of time. The trend toward "stranger killings" may also be indicated by clearance rates which dropped from 64.8% in 1995 to 62.6% in 2004.[11]

Why did the increased number of news stories related to coverage of the O. J. Simpson trial inspire so much fear of crime, as measured by public opinion polls? In this photo, O. J. Simpson tries on one of the leather gloves prosecutors say he wore the night his ex-wife, Nicole Brown Simpson, and Ron Goldman were murdered. The fear of crime engendered by this trial may have triggered a deeper-lying fear in the predominantly white American public, of "black peril," the perception that even blacks they previously thought could be trusted could not always be trusted; and, furthermore, given excellent legal representation, they could commit crimes such as double murder and "get away with it."

Source: Sam Mircovich/AP Wide World Photos

Table 6–2 **Number of Crime Stories Featured on National Network TV Broadcasts[12]**

Year	Stories
1990	757
1991	630
1992	830
1993	1,698
1994	1,949*
1995	2,574*
1996	1,227
1997	1,617

*O. J. Simpson trial

E. Fuller Torrey described the deep-seated fear of crime and unpredictability of when and where it might happen:

> . . . as noted by a New York Times columnist in 1995 in response to the Reuben Harris case (a former mental patient who pushed a woman to her death into the path of an ongoing subway train): "If you are a New Yorker the fear is there somewhere, maybe buried deep beneath the surface of consciousness, or maybe right out there in the open. . . . The fear is that from out of the chaos some maniac will emerge to pointlessly, stupidly, inexplicably hurl you, blast you, cast you into oblivion."[13]

TYPES OF MURDER

Criminology texts have traditionally identified a variety of forms of murder, including "typical" killings, mass murder, serial murder, "buddy" killings, gang murder, spree killings, thrill killing, and cult killings (see text box).

However, global study leads to the discovery of a number of types not usually mentioned in American texts, such as **dowry murders,** honor killings, and female infanticide. These must not be ignored by American criminology because such killings may be committed by immigrants residing within the United States. Also, the exploration of these foreign types of murder may reveal the motivation for killings that occur by nonimmigrants within the United States. A study of the comparative literature also enhances understanding of a wide variety of other types of murder, including parricide, feticide, and erotophonophilia (lust murder). Although many of these types of murder are usually associated with the perpetrator/victim framework, international study reveals that violence by police is a major form of homicide in many countries throughout the world. While this is often thought of as "legal, sanctioned, and rational violence,"[14] police are often involved in the killing of political enemies of the existing regime, complicity with organized crime, and predatory crimes such as rape and robbery, ending in a murder as a means of

BOX 6–1

Types of Murder

Mass murder: The killing of four or more people at a singular location, as one identifiable event (e.g., the sequential murder of eight student nurses in Chicago by Richard Speck in July of 1966).[15]

Serial murder: A term for a number of similar killings by one offender or a group of offenders. According to the FBI, serial murder is the killing of several victims in three or more separate acts.[16]

Spree killing: The killing at two or more locations with almost no time break between murders, (e.g., the sniper killings by John Allen Muhammad and John Lee Malvo in the Washington, DC area in 2002).[17]

Buddy killing: The killing by two or more individuals acting in concert (e.g. the Hillside Strangler murders, perpetrated by Kenneth Bianchi and his cousin Angelo Buono).[18]

Female infanticide: Intentional causing the death of a female human infant.[19]

Lust murder: A homicide in which the offender stabs, cuts, pierces, slashes, or otherwise mutilates the sexual organs or areas of the victim's body, usually done by a sane criminal motivated by the sheer excitement of the act (e.g., the murder of 14-year-old Bobby Franks on May 21, 1924 by Nathan Leopold and Richard Loeb).[20]

BOX 6-2

Dowry Murders in India

Dowry disputes are a serious problem in India. Although providing or taking dowry is illegal under the Dowry Prohibition Act, dowry is still practiced widely. In the typical dowry dispute, a groom's family members harass a new wife whom they believe has not provided a sufficient dowry. This harassment sometimes ends in the woman's death, which family members often try to portray as a suicide or kitchen accident; research suggests that a significant percentage of kerosene attacks are also due to domestic violence. Although most dowry deaths involve lower and middle-class families, the phenomenon crosses both caste and religious lines. According to National Crime Records Bureau statistics, 6,917 dowry deaths occurred in India in 1998. In December 2001 in Bihar, police searched for a judge who allegedly had chained up his daughter-in-law in his home and physically abused her over a dowry dispute.[21]

silencing possible witnesses to crimes. On a global basis, murder by cop should not be ignored as a major form of homicide, nor should it be ignored within the United States.

Each of the aforementioned types of murder requires different kinds of explanation. So a full discussion of murder involves a description of the various types, their etiology, and explanations.

TYPICAL MURDERS

Murder typically occurs between persons who know each other. Nearly half of all murders involve family members, friends, and acquaintances, whereas only a small minority of murders involves strangers.[22] It has been said that the family is the most violent group in society. Invariably, murder results from an argument, often over a trivial matter. Several theories are presented to explain the murders that occur between intimates. One is *routine activities theory.* This theory holds that crime is a normal outcome of routine activities of life, when there is a motivated offender and suitable target and an absence of protection by capable guardians.[23] Evidence for this theory is given in the timing of murder. The motivated offenders and suitable targets are the family members. If murder is most frequent during times when family are at home, then the theory is supported. Indeed, murder occurs most often during summer months and the Christmas holiday season, during dinner hours, and on weekends, when families are most likely to get together. This family togetherness explanation presents an odd paradox, which is that people are most likely to be killed by those closest to them, and during family gatherings. However, closeness alone cannot explain murder, because murder is a relatively rare event, and family life is society-wide in nature. Murder is associated with a variety of social variables, other than close relationships, that need to be factored into the equation to explain murder. Murder is primarily a phenomenon that occurs in large cities, and increases with the size of cities,[24] although it also tends to be higher in rural areas than in intermediate-sized cities.[25] Murder also tends to have its highest rates in Southern states[26] and is twice as prevalent in the South as in other regions in the United States.[27] Murder tends to be high in some third-world countries, such as Colombia, Honduras, and Nicaragua, and is generally inversely related to modernization. Within the United States, it is highest among African American urban

BOX 6–3

Culture Clash led to "Honor Killing" of Teen Daughter

A Kurdish Muslim immigrant has been jailed for life by a British court for slitting his 16-year-old daughter's throat in an **honor killing** after she embraced Western culture and began dating a Christian. Abdalla Yones, 48, cut his daughter Heshu's throat and left her to bleed to death. He had subjected her to months of beatings before killing her in a frenzied knife attack. Yones, who until last week denied murdering Heshu, asked the Old Bailey to impose the death sentence but was told that was not possible under English law. He was jailed for life. Sentencing him, Judge Neil Denison said the killing was "a tragic story arising out of irreconcilable cultural differences between traditional Kurdish values and those of western society." Scotland Yard described Heshu's death as an honor killing brought about by a "clash of cultures" between Yones—a refugee from Iraqi Kurdistan, where such murders are common—and his Westernized daughter.[28] In Turkey, a country that borders Iraq, two articles of the Turkish Penal Code provide for a reduction of sentence when killing is committed to purify the honor of the family. These articles include Article 453, which pertains to the murder right after birth of an illegitimate baby and Article 462, which reduces punishment by seven eighths when a killing is done in relation to an adultery or fornication.[29]

males who have a chance of 1 in 24 of being murdered during their lifetimes. It is high among African American females who have a 1 in 98 chance of being murdered during their lifetimes. It is also high among Native American males, who have a 1 in 57 chance of being murdered during their lifetimes.[30] Murder is higher among males, nonwhites in general, the age group 20 to 24, and in the lower socioeconomic class.[31] Murder seems to increase during times of prosperity and decrease during depression. The victim of homicide is very likely to be a male and of the same race as the offender. He is likely to be killed by a gun in an interaction in which he has affected the emotions of the other party. Alcohol and other drugs are often likely to have been involved in the situation.[32]

THEORY

Murder is clearly the most serious of crimes not only in the FBI's list of Index crimes, but also in public opinion. Many texts and articles treat murder more or less as synonymous with crime itself. Accordingly, there are a large number of theories that have been developed to explain differential rates of criminal homicide (which are subsequently referred to as "murder"). Because of its importance, there have probably been more theories advanced to explain murder than any other crime. Extant theories of homicide include subculture of violence, strength of relational systems, lack of external restraint, firearms availability, media influence, culture of honor, brain pathology, genetic defects, personality traits, child abuse, inconsistent discipline, childhood trauma, instinctual drives, being of male gender, exposure to violence, membership in social movements, the culture of the South, membership in a gang (social learning), residing in a violent society, substance abuse, and even prohibition of drugs. The following discussion proceeds from biological to psychological to sociological explanations. Among the sociological explanations, coverage proceeds from microsociological explanations to macrosociological explanations.

Instinct Theory

In Freud's theory, human beings are born with life instincts (eros) and death instincts (thanatos) that are in constant conflict with each other. These instincts constitute the id, which through the process of socialization, comes to be regulated by the ego and superego.[33] Failure to develop the superego or ego may mean the person cannot handle hostility. Murder and other forms of aggression may result. The personality possibilities for murderers are variable, depending on the extent of socialization. On a continuum, they range from *presocial criminals* and *psychopaths,* who have not developed superego controls, to *accidental* or *situational criminals,* or *acting out neurotics,* who have developed normal egos and superegos, but have developed an obsessive compulsion to kill because of situational pressures.[34] The latter explanation fits the case study of Richard that began this chapter. Generally speaking, criminal homicide results from insufficient ego and superego, because the aggression is directed toward another person or persons, whereas if the superego is strong, the aggression is directed toward the self, possibly resulting in suicide. In "normal" individuals who have a well-developed ego and superego, a sudden release of aggressive impulses might result from the use of drugs or alcohol. Drugs or alcohol might serve as an "un-inhibitor," breaking down superego controls, and indeed, alcohol is a factor in a majority of homicides.[35]

Recently, there have been a number of evolutionary theories developed suggesting that violence in humans has served a function in the evolution of the species. One of the earliest of these theories was developed by Konrad Lorenz, who was a medical doctor and scientist in Germany during the Nazi era. Possibly as a product of this experience, Lorenz suggested that humans possess the same violent instincts as lower animals. However, humans are lacking in the restraint against fatal violence that lower animals apparently possess. Thus, humans, more commonly than lower animals, are capable of killing their own kind in war or in interpersonal conflicts, making the extinction of the human species a definite possibility.[36]

Another theme in evolutionary theories is that violent behavior is predominantly a trait of males. Aggressive males are those most likely to produce children, and they display that aggression during the youthful period when they are at the peak of their virility.[37] Buss and Duntley[38] developed an even more elaborate evolutionary theory that they term **homicide design theory.** They suggest that murder serves adaptation in several ways: through protecting self and kin from injury or death, through depriving rivals of access to valuable mates, through gaining access to contested resources, through terminating prenatal offspring of rivals, through eliminating genetically unrelated stepchildren, through removing key antagonists, and through eliminating future competitors of one's children.

Attempts to prove instinct theories have the same disadvantage as Freudian theory in that "instinctual drives" are posited that cannot be measured. Thus, the theories themselves cannot be tested, although predictions drawn from the theories can yield testable propositions.

The Brain and the Criminal

In Chapter 5, recent biological theories and studies were reviewed, including twin studies, adoption studies, chromosome and hormone studies, as well as brain and neurotransmitter studies. Many of these studies seem to have targeted violent offenders. For instance, the chromosome studies of males with an extra Y chromosome (XYY) posited that such males would have an excess of testosterone and thus would be more aggressively violent. However, it was found that males with an extra Y chromosome were actually *less* likely than the general population of prison to commit violent offenses. It was also found that drugs that lower testosterone, like Depo-Provera, though lowering sexual crimes, are unsuccessful in decreasing violent crimes.

Probably the most promising biocriminological studies mentioned in Chapter 5 were the studies assessing brain functioning that have yielded diagnostic classifications such as minimal brain dysfunction (MBD) and "attention deficit/hyperactivity disorder" (ADHD). A study by Pallone and Hennessy[39] found brain pathology in murderers to be 32 times higher than in the general population. Brain studies have focused upon the frontal lobe, which is important for regulating and inhibiting behavior, and the temporal lobe, which relates to subjective consciousness, emotionality, and response to environmental change.[40] Studies using PET scans and SPECT scans have indicated damage to either the frontal and/or temporal lobe in violent offenders in general and homicide offenders in particular.[41] Such findings are of such significance that they cannot be dismissed or ignored in any complete analysis of murder.

Revelation of such findings does not suggest that criminology may necessarily return to biological determinism, with its implications of racism, eugenics, genocide, and so forth. Brain pathology may very well be of environmental origin, traced to poor prenatal care of the mother, drug use of the mother during pregnancy, child abuse, and even neighborhood violence. The virtue of brain pathology studies may be that they could provide the answer as to how environmental problems lead to extreme behavior such as murder, and could possibly lead to important treatments. For instance, Van Winkle argued that brain damage can result from suppression of emotions during fight or flight reactions. Such brain damage can be treated by "release of anger" therapies such as "primal therapy," practiced by the Canon Foundation in Wernersville, Pennsylvania.[42] Reference to environment as an underlying cause, however, does not imply that brain pathology does not have a genetic component. In fact, one of the authors of brain scan studies discussed earlier (Adrian Raine) published a study with a well-known proponent of genetic predisposition of brain pathology—Sarnoff Mednick.[43] Sarnoff Mednick proposed a theory as to how brain damage might lead to violent criminal behavior in individuals who have a genetic susceptibility. He hypothesized that susceptible individuals inherit an autonomic nervous system (ANS) that is slower to be aroused or react to stimuli, causing the individuals to control aggressive behavior slowly, if at all.[44] In a later study, Raine found frontal lobe damage in 26 out of 38 murderers, only 12 of whom were victims of former child abuse. He argued that brain damage accounts for the murders by individuals who come from good homes. As with Mednick's ANS theory, Raine argued that the damaged

BOX 6–4

Maternal Smoking and Violent Crime in Finland

A study done in Finland tested the hypothesis that maternal smoking during pregnancy is associated with greater risk of criminal behavior of the offspring in adulthood. The findings were that, compared to the sons of mothers who did not smoke, the sons of mothers who smoked during pregnancy had more than a two-fold risk of having committed a violent crime or having repeatedly committed crimes by age 28, even when other biopsychological risk factors were controlled.[45]

prefrontal cortex pertains to homicide because that portion of the brain inhibits the functions of the limbic system, a far deeper area of the brain, giving rise to aggressive behavior. The orbital frontal cortex is involved in fear conditioning. Fear conditioning is making an association between antisocial behavior and punishment, which is key to developing a conscience in humans. Raine found no higher levels of head injuries in the subjects from good homes, suggesting either a prenatal or genetic component in the brain damage.[46] Mednick had similarly published findings suggesting a hereditary component.[47] A theory similar to Mednick's and Raine's pertaining to low arousal levels was published by Hans J. Eysenick and Lee Ellis. Eysenick argued that those with low arousability are less able to learn prosocial behavior and more likely to learn criminal behavior.[48] Ellis suggested that those with "suboptimal arousal levels" are more likely to engage in risk taking and thrill seeking, including breaking the law, to compensate for low arousal levels.[49] One is tempted to suggest that these findings may bear a pertinent relationship to Gottfredson and Hirschi's self-control theory. As presented in Chapter 5, Gottfredson and Hirschi posited a theory that crimes provide short-term gratification and are committed by people who lack the self-control to resist this mode of gratification because they have lacked effective parenting during their formative years. Raine[50] argued that persons with poor self-control might have had effective parenting, but they have failed to develop self-control because of brain damage in the regions of the brain that pertain to that development.

Although the recent biological studies are enticing, and may someday lead to some treatments for violent and other criminal behaviors, research has not yet established the validity of biological theories. Various reviews of these studies have found problems with the methodology, sampling, and measurement in biocriminological studies.[51] Akers and Sellers concluded that "The more recently and rigorously studies are conducted, the more likely they are to find the weaker effects of genetic factors on crime than did the older and more poorly designed studies." Furthermore, they argued that, "The greater the extent to which a biological theory proposes to relate normal physiological and sensory processes to social and environmental variables in explaining criminal behavior, the more likely it will be empirically supported and accepted in criminology."[52]

In any event, while the recent findings by biocriminologists are interesting, biological determinism is a thing of the past. In fact, as will be shown in cross-cultural analysis discussed later, biological findings can scarcely explain the immense differences in homicide rates between countries. Some Latin American countries, such as Colombia, have homicide rates over 10 times

BOX 6–5

Low Heart Rate and Aggression in Children in Mauritius

A study done in Mauritius tested the hypothesis that low resting heart rate at age 3 predicts aggression at age 11 years. The study assessed resting heart rate at age 3 years in a sample of 1,795 male and female children and then assessed aggressive behavior using a Child Behavior Checklist at age 11 years. Aggressive children had lower heart rates than nonaggressive children and, conversely, those with low heart rates were more aggressive than those with high heart rates. It was suggested that low resting heart rate reflects fearlessness and stimulation-seeking and is an important early biological marker for later aggressive behavior.[53]

that of the United States, and yet it is not believable that their populations have genetic defects or even environmental hazards causing brain damage or some other biological problem that accounts for those differences.

Approximately 10% of state inmates are being administered psychotropic medication in prison, according to a recent Justice Department report.[54] Judging from the rate at which inmates are administered "meds" in state institutions, one might surmise that it is widely believed that the inmates are mentally ill.

The Psychology of Murder

Coverage of psychological approaches to murder are often brief in criminology texts, most of which are written by sociologists, who favor sociological theories. Yet the psychology of murder has a very extensive literature and gets a tremendous amount of exposure in the mass media, usually following news stories on high profile killings. Typically, psychologists and psychological profilers, such as former FBI profiler Jack Douglas, are interviewed at length both on local news programs and national 24-hour news broadcasts on CNN, FOX, and MSNBC.

Experts are called into court, consulted by the police, and interviewed in the mass media frequently to answer questions about (or feed public curiosity about) serial killings, mass murders, killings of celebrities (or by celebrities), and child abduction killings, often because a suspect is not yet in custody and the crime needs to be solved. Thus, psychological theories are widely believed to have potency. Psychological accounts typically hold that the killers are either mentally ill or have a character disorder indicative of psychopathy.

Again, sociological criminologists have side-stepped psychological thinking based on a belief that most murders are committed by essentially normal individuals driven by rage during family conflicts or influenced by peers to participate in gang killings. Based upon existing research, it may not be possible to determine the extent to which murder is either the product of a "normal" personality versus abnormal psychology. However, coverage of the latter is well-justified by the considerable volume of literature. Regardless of the direction of findings, environmental factors need not be ruled out as leading to either outcome—normal or abnormal. Frequently, psychological studies have focused on **mass murderers,** who are typically construed as "mentally ill." Psychological studies have also described "serial killers" who are often viewed as possessing a psychopathic personality. Of course, both personality types have been involved in killings of other types. Because of the linking of topics, the studies of violence by the mentally ill are presented in conjunction with studies of mass murder, and discussions of serial killers are associated with the topic of psychopathy.

Mass Murderers

The term "mass murder" is defined as "the killing of more than three individuals at a single time."[55] The killings need not occur in the same location, but the time limit is usually 24 hours. Mass murderers, as differentiated from serial killers, engage in a single, uncontrollable outburst that is termed "simultaneous killing." Jack Levin and Alan Fox have published a number of books and articles on both mass and serial killers. They differentiate four types of mass murderers. These include (a) *revenge killers,* who seek to get even by targeting victims such as estranged wives (and their children) or an employer and "his" employees; (2) *love killers,* depressed people who may commit suicide and take other loved ones with them; (3) *profit killers,* covering up a crime through eliminating witnesses; and (4) *terrorist killers,* who are sending a message (which can include gang killers and cult killers).[56] Levin and Fox argue that most mass murderers are not mentally ill, but instead are ordinary citizens driven to extreme acts and motivated by frustration, isolation, blame, loss, and failure. They group these acts as having three types of contributing factors, which include predisposing factors (long-term problems), precipitating factors (short-term triggers), and facilitating factors (situational factors that increase the likelihood of violence).

There is no way to know whether or not mass murderers have (or had) a mental disorder, for two reasons. Frequently, the question becomes a basis for adversarial conjecture in court with the defense maintaining insanity and the prosecution denying it. Most important, however, individuals who would have been treated or hospitalized in the past for mental illness are left untreated and undiagnosed today. This is due to the **deinstitutionalization movement** that occurred over the past 50 years in America. This movement may have contributed to an increase of mass murders, uncommon in the past, including school killings, workplace violence, and even family violence. It hardly seems coincidental that the variety of bizarre mass murders was unheard of prior to the deinstitutionalization movement, a major change that occurred in the United States starting in the early 1960s, and one that requires further discussion here.

The "Sling Blade" Phenomenon

In a 1996 feature film staring Billy Bob Thornton, a mental patient named Karl Childers, now a grown man, is released from a psychiatric hospital where he has been hospitalized since the age of 12 for the murder of his mother and her lover. After his release, he returns to his hometown and becomes involved in a situation similar to that of his childhood. He commits murder again and is reinstitutionalized.

Although this scenario is extreme, it is credible in light of what has happened to the residents of mental hospitals since the 1960s. That is a sociological phenomenon that deserves discussion in any commentary on murder (not to mention crime in general). The deinstitutionalization movement has had a two-pronged impact upon mentally disordered violent, and potentially violent, criminals. First, it has led to the release of such people as the character Karl Childers, described in the movie *Sling Blade,* into the community. Second, it has decreased the probability of treatment for potentially psychotic killers through instituting legal barriers to involuntary hospitalization of such individuals.

Since the 1960s, there has been a tremendous decrease in the number of individuals housed in state psychiatric hospitals. In 1955, state mental hospitals housed 558,239 mentally ill individuals. By 1997, the population was less than 70,000.[57] This emptying of public psychiatric hospitals has been referred to as "the second-largest social experiment in twentieth-century America, exceeded only by the New Deal."[58] Though well-intended at its inception, the deinstitutionalization movement has led to homelessness for the mentally ill, a decline in psychiatric care for them, a displacement of the mentally ill to jails and prisons, and a rise in crimes committed by the mentally ill, including murder.

Who is responsible for the deinstitutionalization of the mentally ill in America? Some blamed John F. Kennedy. Others held Ronald Reagan responsible, and still others pointed the finger at social scientists and civil libertarians who agitated for closing down the state mental hospitals during the 1960s. The history of deinstitutionalization will be discussed and then the consequences will be assessed, especially for rising rates of mass murder.

During the 1960s, a body of literature developed that supported a movement to decrease the use of mental hospitals for treatment of the mentally ill, particularly the state-run mental hospitals. Sociologist Erving Goffman, in his book *Asylums*,[59] described state mental hospitals as "total institutions" in which work, sleep, and play occur in the same location under a single authority, in the company of others. The incoming patient is subjected to a degrading "stripping process" and then, after admission, subject to a caste-like hierarchy in which the patient has the lowest status. The patient follows several stages, including situational withdrawal, rebellion, colonization, and conversion, resulting in the patient's institutional dependency and a negative self-concept. Although Goffman's work was largely theoretical, an actual participant observation study of state mental hospitals was done by Psychiatrist D. L. Rosenhan and fellow researchers after they got themselves admitted to 12 different mental hospitals by pretending to be psychotic.[60] They noted dehumanizing treatment and both physical and sexual abuse at those hospitals, which were reported as "dangerous routines" of state institutions in testimony before the U.S. Senate.[61] Also during the 1960s, mental illness was trivialized by a group of "labeling theorists" who actually denied the existence of mental illness. These included psychiatrist Thomas Szasz, who argued that "Mental illness is a myth, whose function it is to disguise and thus render more palatable the bitter pill of moral conflicts in human relations."[62] Similarly, Thomas Scheff characterized the mentally ill as relatively harmless "residual rule-breakers" whose behavior cannot be compared to serious rule breaking that society has more clearly defined, including "crime, perversion, and immoral acts."[63] As perhaps the most extreme expression of the labeling approach, British psychiatrist R. D. Laing actually glorified the mentally ill, referring to them as "supersane" individuals, oriented to "inner" space and time and more sane than normals. He felt their psychosis was a sane response to an insane world.[64] Laing ran a small group home in which psychiatric patients could live freely, engaging in deep thinking without the use of psychotropic drugs and with a minimum of psychiatric assistance. His unique program reportedly cured most of the patients who stayed at his home.[65]

While many of these writings were based upon empirical observation, actually only one scientific study was done before the deinstitutionalization movement began (and it was cited frequently in prodeinstitutionalization literature). "Published in England in 1960 by Dr. John Wing, the study found that 20 schizophrenic individuals, selected because they were functioning at a high level and were able to work, did relatively well when moved from a psychiatric hospital to supervised community living facilities."[66]

President John F. Kennedy, a Harvard graduate, may have been influenced by some of the aforementioned literature, or he may have viewed mental illness as a civil liberties issue. He may also have been personally interested in enacting mental health legislation, because his sister, Rosemary, suffered from mental retardation and mental illness.[67] Kennedy appointed an "Action for Mental Health" committee that advocated community-based treatment centers, and Kennedy later promulgated the idea of community mental health centers in his speech, "The Dream." He fostered the belief that the institutional care of patients, not the disease itself, was the major problem and that the solution was prevention through community mental health centers.[68] He set the goal of a 50% reduction of custodial care for mental patients within a decade. The result was the Community Mental Health Centers Act (CMHC Act) of 1961, officially beginning deinstitutionalization. This was followed in 1962 by government-funded Aid to the Permanently and Totally Disabled, an early form of Supplemental Security Income. In 1963, Kennedy signed legislation for the creation of CMHCs, which made mentally ill individuals eligible for federal benefits to pay for rent, food, and other needs.[69] In 1968, the Lanterman-Petris-Short Act was passed in California, restricting grounds for involuntary hospitalization and its length. At the same time, civil liberties lawyers and the New York Civil Liberties Union influenced the development of minimum staff-to-patient ratios, "least restrictive setting" mandates, "refusal of treatment" mandates, and "dangerous to self or others" criteria as the test for involuntary commitment. The population of state mental hospitals fell precipitously under these restrictions, but ironically so did the proportion of patients treated at CMHCs for mental illness, for various reasons. One reason was that state hospitals were never mandated by the National Institute of Mental Health (NIMH) or any legislation to refer patients to CMHCs. Another reason was that CMHC directors had a misguided concept of their mission; that is, they believed their mission was to deal with social issues such as rent inflation and civil rights, and/or to treat the "worried well" rather than the seriously mentally ill, whom they found to be onerous and difficult to work with. Also, many of the mentally ill chose not to seek treatment at CMHCs for reasons of autonomy or because they believed they did not need support.

The community mental health movement might have been successful had there been leadership, either at the Presidential level or from the NIMH or Congress, to remedy the problems with the CMHCs. However, leadership was, regrettably, in the opposite direction owed to the budget-cutting efforts of Ronald Reagan, both during his Governorship of the State of California (1967–1975) and during his years as President of the United States (1981–1989). The passage of the Lanterman-Petris-Short Act of 1968 in California was thought to be a major victory for the deinstitutionalization movement. It provided a legal basis for treatment, strengthened patients' rights protections, regulated involuntary commitment criteria, and set the stage for community-based mental health services. California Governor Ronald Reagan saw the act as justification for social service spending cuts. He authorized the release of patients and dismantling of state facilities, and he shifted the burden for mental health services to county and local governments, who lacked the resources to provide the community support systems recommended by researchers.[70] Although the Lanterman-Petris-Short Act and Governor Reagan's budget cuts applied only to California, they set a precedent for other states to emulate.[71]

An opportunity to remedy the problems with the CMHCs was developed during the Carter administration (1977–1980). In 1977, President Carter appointed a Commission on Mental Health whose recommendations led to the Mental Health Systems Act of 1980. This act provided funding for CMHCs and continued federal government support for such programs. However, when Ronald Reagan became President, he rescinded the Mental Health Systems Act (in 1981), because it conflicted with the financial goals of his New Federalism program to reduce social programs and transfer responsibility of many government functions to the individual states.[72] During Reagan's presidency, government funding for public programs declined precipitously, although privatized psychiatric care increased. At the same time, homelessness and imprisonment of the mentally ill also increased precipitously. It is estimated that approximately one third of the homeless are former mental patients who had no place to go when the nation's psychiatric hospitals were emptied as a result of deinstitutionalization.[73] A 1995 New York study reported that 38% of discharged psychiatric patients "have no known address within six months of their release."[74] In the absence of CMHCs, others are living in board-and-care homes. These house the formerly institutionalized as well as the new generations of chronically mentally ill. Still others live in single-room-occupancy hotels. These dwellings are not secure facilities and the residents are free to leave. For a variety of reasons, many mentally ill persons will drift from these facilities into homelessness and, to support themselves, to crime. Many of the mentally ill will end up in jail, having committed misdemeanors like disorderly conduct or trespassing. However, a small number do commit serious crimes, including murder, often as a result of not receiving medication for their illnesses at the time of their crime.

While observations about the plight and crimes of the mentally ill since deinstitutionalization have found a forum mostly on the Internet, a 215-page report on the subject of the mentally ill in prison was released by Human Rights Watch on October 22, 2003. The Human Rights Watch report was based on more than two years of research and hundreds of interviews with prisoners, correctional officials, mental health experts, and attorneys. Some of the more significant findings from the report are addressed in Text Box 6–7.[75]

In New York, crimes by the mentally ill have become a continuing commentary on the perversity of deinstitutionalization.

Mary Ventura, three weeks after being discharged from a psychiatric hospital, pushed a woman she did not know into the path of a subway train. Reuben Harris, with 12 previous psychiatric hospitalizations, pushed another woman to her death in the same manner. Juan Gonzalez, who had been psychiatrically evaluated four days earlier, killed two and injured nine others on the Staten Island Ferry. Kevin McKeiver, well known to the city's psychiatric services, stabbed to death a woman who was walking her dogs in Central Park. Christopher Battiste, psychiatrically treated at city hospitals twice in the previous two months, bludgeoned to death an 80-year-old woman on the steps of a church. Jorge Delgado, previously hospitalized seven times for his paranoid schizophrenia, ran naked into St. Patrick's Cathedral and killed an elderly usher. Dennis Sweeney, Louis Lang, Van Hull, Michael Vernon, Steve Smith, Da Pei Wu, Tatiana Belopolsky . . . the tragic litany continues year after year.

BOX 6–6

Female Homicide and Schizophrenia in Finland

A study of 127 female homicide offenders in Finland found that female homicide offenders were 10 times more likely than the general female population to have schizophrenia or a personality disorder. The personality disorders with the most substantially higher odds ratios were alcohol abuse/dependence and antisocial personality disorder.[76]

BOX 6–7

United States: Mentally Ill Mistreated in Prison

- One in six U.S. prisoners is mentally ill.
- The level of illness among the mentally ill being admitted to jail and prison has been growing more severe.
- There are three times as many men and women with mental illness in U.S. prisons as in mental hospitals.
- Fewer than 80,000 people now live in mental hospitals, and the number is continuing to fall.
- The high rate of incarceration of the mentally ill is a consequence of underfunded, disorganized, and fragmented community health services.
- Many people with mental illness—particularly those who are poor, homeless, or struggling with substance abuse problems—cannot get mental health treatment. If they commit a crime, even low-level nonviolent offenses, punitive sentencing laws mandate imprisonment.
- The mentally ill prisoners are likely to be picked on, physically or sexually abused, and manipulated by other inmates, who call them "bugs."
- Mentally ill prisoners can find it difficult if not impossible to comply with prison rules, and end up with higher than average rates of disciplinary infractions. A study in Washington found that although mentally ill inmates constituted only 18.7%, of the state's prison population, they accounted for 41% of the infractions.
- Untrained staff escalate confrontations with mentally ill prisoners, sometimes using excessive force. Several mentally ill prisoners have died from asphyxiation after struggling with guards who used improper methods to control them.

There are an estimated 1,000 such homicides in the United States per year—4 to 5 percent of all homicides. The common denominator is a severely delusional mentally ill person not receiving treatment.[77]

These incidents provide anecdotal evidence of a link between untreated mental illness and violence, but is there any empirical evidence relating these two variables? According to studies on a Website compiled by the "Treatment Advocacy Center" of Arlington, Virginia, while mentally ill individuals who are taking their medication are not more dangerous than the general population, a host of findings indicate that severely mentally ill individuals who are not taking their medication are more dangerous than the general population.[78] Some of these findings are given in the text box.

One might be inclined to take comfort in the finding that the mentally ill who take their medication are not more violent than the general population. However, approximately half of those who were released from mental hospitals do not seek treatment once out of the hospital because they do not believe themselves to be ill.[79] This suggests that same half (or more) of the released mental patients are not taking their antipsychotic medications.

The aforementioned studies provide no proof that mass murderers are typically mentally ill, and proof would be difficult to provide, because mass murderers typically are killed by the police or commit suicide after their crime. However, it is credible that the deinstitutionalization of the mentally ill may account for the rapid increase of mass murders since the inception of the deinstitutionalization movement.

Besides a possible relation to an increase in violent crime, deinstitutionalization has had a possible impact on crime in at least two other ways. One is in terms of the public fear of crime, which in turn fuels "moral panics" leading to extremely repressive law and order "get tough" policies dealing with crime. Not only the violent acts that are recapitulated on the nightly news, but the daily encounters with mentally ill persons in urban areas urinating on the sidewalk, defecating in the gutter, yelling obscenities at passersby, masturbating in front

BOX 6–8

Violence and Untreated Severe Mental Illness

The Epidemiological Catchment Area surveys carried out in 1980–1983 reported much higher rates of violent behavior among individuals with severe mental illness living in the community compared to other community residents. For example, individuals with schizophrenia were 21 times more likely to have used a weapon in a fight.[80]

A 1990 study investigated violent behavior among severely mentally ill individuals in 1,401 randomly selected families who were members of the National Alliance for the Mentally Ill. In the preceding year, 11% of these individuals were reported to have physically harmed another person.[81]

A 9- to 12-year follow-up of 192 men with schizophrenia who were detained by the Secret Service when they presented themselves at the White House with delusional demands found that they had a subsequent arrest rate for violent crimes 1.6 times (no past history of violence) to 4.8 times (with a past history of violence) the general population.[82]

Among 20 individuals who pushed or tried to push another person in front of the subway in New York, all except one was severely mentally ill and offered motives directly related to their untreated psychotic symptoms.[83]

In a carefully controlled study comparing individuals with severe mental illness living in the community in New York with other community residents, the former group was three times more likely to commit violent acts such as weapons use or "hurting someone badly." The sicker the individual, the more likely they were to have been violent.[84]

A four-state (NH, CT, MD, and NC) study of 802 adults with severe mental illness (64% schizophrenia or schizoaffective disorder, 17% bipolar disorder) reported that 13.6% had been violent within the previous year. "Violent" was defined as "any physical fighting or assaultive actions causing bodily injury to another person, any use of lethal weapon to harm or threaten someone, or any sexual assault during that period." Those who had been violent were more likely to have been homeless, to be substance abusers, and to be living in a violent environment. Those who had been violent were also 1.7 times more likely to have been noncompliant with medications. As has been found in other such studies, the women with severe psychiatric disorders were almost as likely to have been violent (11%) as were the men (15%). Because the data on violent behavior were collected by self-report, the authors suggested "that our findings are probably conservative estimates of the true prevalence of violent behavior for persons with SMI." They concluded "that risk of violence among persons with SMI is a significant problem" and "is substantially higher than estimates of the violence rate for the general population."[85]

---

of children, and the like, provide impetus for the fear of crime. The second, and related outcome, is the growth of imprisonment in America. In a state-by-state study of declining mental hospitalization rates between 1971 and 1996, Stephen Raphael found a strong negative effect of hospitalization rates on prison incarceration rates.[86] He estimated that deinstitutionalization accounted for between 48,000 and 148,000 of the inmates in state prison systems in 1996.

There is evidence that only about 5% of all homicides can be accounted for by mental illness.[87] However, if that 5% accounts for a disproportionate share of mass murders, then that 5% could have great significance.

BOX 6–9

Maternal Filicide and Mental Illness in Canada

A study of 34 cases of maternal filicide (child-killing) revealed that 15 of the mothers committed suicide after the filicide and that a psychiatric motive was present in 85% of the cases. The majority of this 85% had received previous treatment for a depressive or psychotic disorder. The majority of the offenses occurred in the family home and the most common methods included carbon monoxide poisoning, use of a firearm, strangulation, drowning, stabbing, and beating, in that order.[88]

BOX 6–10

Psychiatric Admissions in Finland

A study of 5,636 male subjects drawn from the Northern Finland 1966 Birth Cohort, the Finnish Hospital Discharge Register, and national crime registers compared violent and nonviolent offenders in Finland. One third of violent and one fourth of nonviolent male offenders had at least one hospital admission related to a psychiatric disorder before they reached age 32. These rates were significantly higher when compared with males with no criminal records, although the violent offenders received lesser care in terms of number of hospital days, suggesting that they were frequently treated at an inappropriate level of health care.[89]

Paranoid Schizophrenia

Not all mentally ill persons are violent. However, one category of mental illness is distinctive in that the patients are frequently violent—*paranoid schizophrenics.* Paranoid schizophrenics are preoccupied with one or more systematized delusions or with frequent auditory hallucinations related to a single theme. In addition, symptoms characteristic of the disorganized and catatonic types of schizophrenia, such as incoherence, flat or grossly inappropriate affect, catatonic behavior, or grossly disorganized behavior, are absent. Paranoid schizophrenia is characterized by unfocussed anxiety, anger, argumentativeness, and violence. There is often a stilted, formal quality to the personality, or the subject may exhibit extreme intensity in interpersonal interaction.

The impairment in functioning in paranoid schizophrenia may be minimal if the delusional material is not acted upon. Onset tends to be later in life than other types of mental illness, and the distinguishing characteristics may be more stable over time.[90]

Over 60 years ago, Faris and Dunham did extensive ecological studies of schizophrenics in Chicago. Consistent with the Chicago School findings on crime and juvenile delinquency, Faris and Dunham found that hospital admissions for mental illness (mostly psychosis) occurred disproportionately in the most disorganized areas of the city, marked by high rates of broken homes, crime, unemployment, and congested living conditions.[91] Both Faris and Dunham did some ethnographic study of mental illness, in addition to statistical analysis of hospital admissions. Both found that schizophrenics had personal characteristics that resulted in their youthful alienation or isolation from peer groups. Dunham described the catatonic as having such traits as self-consciousness, timidity, cautiousness, an inferiority complex, and inhibition traced to seclusiveness from informal contacts. They were ignorant of subjects of common knowledge to teenagers and conformed to adult standards by being obedient, honest, moral, studious, and intropunitive.[92]

As mentioned at the beginning of this chapter, Faris characterized the schizophrenic as a "shut in" or seclusive personality. Frequently, the schizophrenics had experienced an overprotective, strict socialization typically by a domineering mother in a single-parent home. As a result of this socialization, the schizophrenic became separated from sympathetic social contacts, and this isolation led to eccentricity, illogicality, inappropriateness of emotions, hallucinations, and delusions that were said to characterize schizophrenics as youngsters. Schizophrenics were found to have a history of rejection by peer groups either due to physical unattractiveness or overconventionality of parentally imposed standards, or both.[93]

Faris did a case study of a paranoid schizophrenic patient Albert Ritter (pseudonym), who was known as "the most violent patient on his ward." In the Chicago School, mental patients were often characterized as having being "personally disorganized" as a counterpart to the social disorganization they encountered in their life. However in an article entitled "Reflections of social disorganization in the behavior of a schizophrenic patient," published in the *American Journal of Sociology,* Faris[94] argued that Ritter did not appear to be disorganized. In fact, he was the opposite. Ritter had experienced a series of failures in work and relationships with the opposite sex, leading to his schizophrenia. In response to this, Ritter had developed, through extensive study of the works of philosophers such as Marx, Freud, and Nietzche, an elaborate and orderly system of thought, privately worked out as a solution to a number of severe life problems.

Ritter's solution was to develop a new society based upon principles such as communal sharing of property and "free love." He sought to recruit followers toward the goal of developing a new society, and would give speeches in public places in favor of his philosophy. He would become violent when opposed, and was arrested assaulting somebody who disagreed with him in a street car. Faris pointed out that Ritter, had he been able to recruit followers, may have become a leader of a mass movement, instead of a mental patient, and speculated that this may have occurred elsewhere in the world and throughout history.[95]

Zacarias Moussaoui is the French al-Qaeda member who first denied and then confessed to his role in the September 11, 2001 attacks on the United States. He testified in court, against his lawyers' advice. His lawyers were planning to argue that their client was mentally ill. They intended to state that he was alienated from society as a result of his traumatic childhood, which included five years in orphanages, as well as being raised (in France) by a Moroccan mother separated from a "violent alcoholic" father. One expert witness, a neuroscientist, was prepared to testify that Moussaoui most likely suffered from schizophrenia. For his role in the September 11 terrorist attacks, the jury voted to give Moussaoui life in prison, rather than the death penalty, May 3, 2006.

Source: AP Wide World Photos

BOX 6–11

Cults, Paranoia, and Murder in Guyana

Guyana today has a high rate of murder, ranking 19th in the world, with a murder rate of 16.19 per 100,000 inhabitants. During the 1970s and 1980s, a religious group known as the House of Israel became an informal part of the People's National Congress (PNC) security apparatus and engaged in actions such as strikebreaking, progovernment demonstrations, political intimidation, and murder. The House of Israel was established by an American fugitive, David Hill, also known as Rabbi Edward Washington, who arrived in Guyana in 1972. The cult had no ties to traditional Jewish religion but was a black supremacist movement. In the 1970s, the group claimed a membership of 8,000. The House of Israel had a daily radio program in which it preached that Africans were the original Hebrews and needed to prepare for a racial war. During an antigovernment demonstration, a House of Israel member murdered a Roman Catholic priest because he was on the staff of a religious opposition newspaper, the *Catholic Standard.* Guyana acquired international notoriety in 1978 following a mass murder-suicide at the commune of the People's Temple of Christ, which had been led by the Reverend Jim Jones, of Oakland, California. In 1974 the People's Temple, a utopian commune, leased a tract of land near Port Kaituma in western Guyana to escape from mounting scrutiny of the group by California authorities. The government welcomed the People's Temple in part because of its interest in populating the interior of the country, especially the area claimed by Venezuela, where Jonestown was situated. Members of the People's Temple also became close to PNC leaders, and the group was allowed to function without interference from the government. Allegations of atrocities by commune leaders and charges that the commune was holding people against their will led a United States congressman, Leo Ryan, to go to Jonestown to investigate the allegations of abuse. Fearing that Congressman Ryan's report on the commune would bring unwanted publicity and restrictions on his operations, Jones had the congressman shot as he was boarding an airplane to return to Georgetown. The United States immediately asked Guyana to send in its army. Before the army could reach Jonestown, however, Jones coerced and cajoled over 900 members of the commune to commit murder and suicide.[96]

The relevance of this case study of some 60 years ago to today has to do with what has changed. When Faris interviewed Albert Ritter, Ritter was a patient in a mental hospital. Today, Ritter, as a result of deinstitutionalization, could very likely be walking the streets among the homeless population, and he could become a mass murderer. Mass murders have increased since deinstitutionalization. These mass murders have been the subject of considerable media attention, and they are featured on Internet Web pages. These Websites include lists of "pseudocommando" mass murders, of school killings, and of workplace killings. Such attempted or completed mass murders, rare in the past, have been increasingly common (especially in the 1980s and 1990s) in America.

Pseudocommando mass murderers can be defined as those mass murderers who intentionally and unlawfully kill five or more nonrelations (i.e., strangers or workmates) with a firearm, or a number of firearms, in a single paramilitary-style raid. Pseudocommando mass murders are relatively rare, but they began to increase in the late 1980s. The greatest number of incidences of this type of offence occurred in the United States, particularly in the states of California and New York. The average number of victims for these incidents is 11 killed and 9 wounded. Pseudocommando mass murderers fit the profile of the paranoid schizophrenic in that they tend to be male paranoid loners; aged between 22–47 with a mean age of 35; who are white, single, and have a preoccupation with firearms with a corresponding background in the military or law enforcement. They also tend to commit their raids after long deliberation and then either force the police to kill them

BOX 6–12

Running "Amok" in Laos and North America

The term "amok" is a Malaysian term that means to engage furiously in battle, and refers to a syndrome involving a sudden unprovoked outburst of uncontrollable rage and aggressive behavior, often leading to indiscriminate injury or death to others. Hempel, Levine, and Meloy[97] did a cross-cultural comparison of 18 "grenade amok" attacks between 1959 and 1971 in Laos, compared with 30 North American assaults involving a firearm with or without other weapons. There was evidence in both studies that perpetrators were characterized by social isolation, loss, depression, anger, pathological narcissism, and paranoia, often to a psychotic degree, suggesting that sudden mass assault by a single individual is not a culture-bound syndrome.

in a shootout or commit suicide at the conclusion of their raids. The weapons used by these individuals are most often semiautomatic rifles—especially the AK47 military assault rifle—or semi-automatic pistols. It is also common for a combination of weapons to be used.

A Website contains a list of 43 cases of pseudocommando mass murderers that gives the following information—if known—for each case: name of perpetrator, age of perpetrator, date of incident, location of incident, number of dead and wounded, and the fate of the perpetrator.[98] Out of 43 cases of such mass murders done worldwide, almost half (21) were done in the United States. These included Charles Whitman, the "Texas Tower" killer who killed 16 people and wounded 30 at the University of Texas on August 1, 1966. Also included was James Huberty, who killed 21 and wounded an additional 19 persons at a McDonald's restaurant in San Ysidro, California in July, 1984. In five cases, including the latter two, the police shot and killed the perpetrator at the scene of the crime. In 20 cases, the perpetrator committed suicide after the murders. In three cases, the perpetrator was interned in a mental hospital after the murders. Analysis of these cases by decade is insightful. Only one occurred before 1940. One occurred during the 1940s. None occurred during the 1950s. Two occurred during the 1960s, whereas three occurred during the 1970s. However, during the 1980s 16 occurred, followed by 20 during the 1990s.

A closely related subject is workplace violence, which has also been on the rise since the late 1980s. It seems possible, if not likely, that this surge of workplace violence incidents that has occurred since the late 1980s is increasingly being done by individuals who would have been diagnosed as mentally ill and, specifically, paranoid schizophrenics, prior to deinstitutionalization. The textbox presents a list of traits of individuals who commit workplace violence, which seems to suggest the probability of undiagnosed mental illness in general, and paranoid schizophrenia in particular:[99]

BOX 6–13

Mass Murder Copycat Effect in Australia

The Port Arthur Massacre, a mass murder of 35 people by a lone gunman in 1996 in the island state of Tasmania, resulted in gun control measures nationally for Australia. But it also yielded more murder. There was an immediate increase in firearm homicides during the 5 days following the event, after which homicide resumed its long-term downward trend.[100]

BOX 6–14

Symptoms Warning of Workplace Violence

Weapons: Has recently purchased a weapon, he has a weapon collection, or he makes constant references to weapons.

Others (blame): Blames others and refuses to accept responsibility for his own actions.

Righteous: Expects everything and retains grudges.

Kept contact: If he has been recently fired, he maintains contact with current employees and refuses to let go, appearing more focused on his old job than on finding a new one.

Paranoia: Feels others are out to get him and conspiring against him.

Long history of grievances: Has a history of making complaints, particularly unreasonable or unjustifiable complaints.

Angry: Is angry or depressed.

Crusades: Has undertaken a crusade or a mission at work.

Escalation: Has used threats, intimidations, manipulations, or escalations toward staff or management.

Violence: Has a history of violence or threatening violence.

Inflexible: Resists change or is not prepared to discuss new ideas and concepts.

Other workers: Coworkers are intimidated by him.

Lone gunman: Identifies with other perpetrators of workplace violence or violent crime.

Encounters with police: Has a history of involvement with the police, including crimes of violence and behavioral incidents.

Negative: Is negative about everything.

Criticism: Reacts poorly to criticism and is suspicious of those who offer it.

Events: There have been recent media reports on workplace violence and he relates to the crime or the offender.

Though paranoid schizophrenia is now known to be a phenomenon that often occurs in early adulthood, it has historically been referred to as dementia praecox, a disorder of teenagers. Among high school students, two phenomena have been on the increase in recent years. One is the bullying that occurs between more physically aggressive students, such as athletes and gang members, and students who are perceived as weak and ineffectual, often termed "nerds" and "geeks." Although the bullying itself is a form of workplace violence that usually does not result in death, the "revenge of the nerds" carried out by students who may have an undiagnosed mental illness has been quite deadly and, in some cases, qualifies as "mass murder." A Website provides a list of such recent killings.[101]

Serial Killers

Serial murder is defined as criminal homicide that "involves the killing of several victims in three or more separate events."[102] The exploits of **serial killers** are probably the most fascinating high-profile news stories of all. Serial killers, perhaps because they command so much media attention, also get attention from profilers. Often profilers interviewed in these programs speculate that such killers are likely to be, as described in many textbooks, as "white middle-class men with no physical handicaps, of average or above average intelligence, and of normal heights and weights."[103] Countless so-called profilers were proven wrong when "Beltway Snipers" 41-year-old John Allen

Muhammad and 17-year-old Le Malvo (described as Muhammad's stepson), both of whom are African American, were brought to justice.

Although it is commonly agreed that serial killers are typically psychopathic or sociopathic in their personality type, there are a variety of types of serial killers (making profiling in the absence of information a highly speculative process). Ronald Holmes and J. DeBurger,[104] drawing from an analysis of 400 cases, developed a four-fold typology based upon offender motivation, selection of victim, expected gain, and method of murder. These include *visionary serial killers*, who hear voices and have visions compelling them to murder; *comfort serial killers*, who seek financial gain; *hedonistic serial killers*, who find pleasure in killing; and *power seekers*, who occupy a position of authority over others, and play the role of sadistic tormenter, such as a nurse who poisons a patient, restores the patient to health, poisons again, and continues the cycle until the patient dies. James Fox and Jack Levin classify serial killers as either *thrill motivated, mission-oriented*, or *expedience-directed*. *Thrill motivated serial killers*, the most common type of serial killer, are either sexual sadists or dominance killers. *Mission-oriented serial killers* are either reformers, who want to rid the world of evil, or visionaries, who are generally psychotic—hearing voices commanding them to do certain activities. *Expedience-directed serial killers* seek either profit or financial gain or protection by committing murder to mask other crimes, such as robbery.[105]

Among the types just discussed, although "reformers" may be psychologically normal individuals fighting for a cause and visionaries are psychotic, the remainder of types is typically characterized in the literature as psychopathic.

Making Sense of Senseless Killings

What is a psychopath and what are the causes of psychopathy? Serial killers, as discussed earlier, are typically described in the literature as vicious, sadistic killers, hardly characters that one can sympathize with. For instance the following "profile" of a typical serial killer is given online:

> Serial killers tend to be white, heterosexual males in their twenties and thirties who are sexually dysfunctional and have low self-esteem. Their methodical rampages are almost always sexual in nature. Their killings are usually part of an elaborate fantasy that builds to a climax at the moment of their murderous outburst. Serial killers generally murder strangers with cooling off periods between each crime. Many enjoy cannibalism, necrophilia and keep trophy-like body parts as mementos of their work. Serial killers are sadistic in nature. Some return to crime scenes or grave sites of their victims to fantasize about their deeds. Many like to insert themselves into the investigation of their crimes and some enjoy taunting authorities with letters or carefully placed pieces of evidence.[106]

While juries are likely to condemn such individuals to death sentences, where available, and most people are shocked and horrified by the crimes they commit, it is useful to understand the development of the psychopathic personality. At least some experts believe that psychopathy is a progressive disorder that can be curtailed if caught early enough in the career of the psychopath.

Gary Leon Ridgway, in a white jail uniform, appears in King County Superior Court in Seattle, Washington, on December 18, 2001. Ridgway confessed to more murders (48) than any other American serial killer. He said he murdered prostitutes because he did not want to pay them for sex.

Source: © Greg Gilbert/Reuters NewMedia,Inc./CORBIS

The first step in comprehending the mentality of a serial killer is to understand what constitutes a psychopath. There have been varying definitions of psychopathy over time; however, the meaning of the term has been refined in recent years, along with the understanding about the development of the psychopathic personality. A brief history of the development of the term might be of interest.

Just as criminals were treated brutally in 18th century France, the mentally ill were treated like animals, but their asylums were much worse than zoos. Patients were whipped, chained, and thrown into dungeons. In 1793, Phillippe Pinel (1745–1826) accomplished a revolutionary change in a large asylum he administered by removing chains from the inmates and administering what he called *moral treatment* to them. Pinel was a reformer who sought to improve the treatment of mentally ill in the late 18th century and early 19th century. Pinel believed that morally treating the mentally ill meant treating their emotions. The doctrine of moral treatment utilized "occupation; man's goal directed use of time, interests, energy, and attention; in combination with purposeful daily activity, for treatment."[107]

Probably the earliest attempt to categorize what would come to be known as the psychopathic personality was that of Pinel, who had a patient who showed no remorse or personal restraint. Pinel, coined the term *manie sans delire* (madness without delirium), which indicated that these people display crazy behavior without actually being crazy. This was part of Pinel's classification of mental patients that included melancholy, dementia, mania without delirium, and mania with delirium.[108] Pinel was not exposing a heinous personality type as an explanation of violent behavior. Quite the opposite; he was suggesting that some people being treated barbarically in asylums were not actually insane. J. C. Prichard (1786–1848) replaced the term *manie sans delire* was with the term **moral insanity,** which he described as:

> a form of mental derangement in which the intellectual facilities [are un-injured], while the disorder is manifested principally or alone in the state of feelings, temper, or habits. . . . The moral . . . principles of the mind . . . are depraved or perverted, the power of self-government is lost or greatly impaired, and the individual is . . . incapable . . . of conducting himself with decency and propriety in the business of life.[109]

The link between moral insanity and crime probably first occurred in the trial of Charles Guiteau, who assassinated President Garfield. One psychiatrist for the defense testified that Guiteau suffered from moral insanity, while another called him a "moral imbecile." The term "psychopathic inferiority" was first used by J. L. Koch in Germany in 1888, and came to replace moral insanity as a diagnosis. Even today, many people consider "psychopath" to be a "waste basket category" for abnormal individuals who are neither psychotic nor neurotic. However, this would change in 1941 with the work of Hervey Cleckley.[110] He indicated 16 distinct clinical criteria for distinguishing psychopathy. Among these characteristics, he said that psychopaths had superficial charm and "good intelligence"; were unable to feel guilt or shame; were unreliable; engaged in chronic lying; exercised poor judgment and were unable to learn from experience; were self-centered and lacked the capacity to love; had an impersonal, trivial, and poorly integrated sex life; and had failed to follow any life plan. He also indicated that they had an absence of psychosis or neurosis, and specified that they participated in ongoing antisocial behavior. After Cleckley's work, the official term for psychopath in the first edition of the American Psychiatric Association's *Diagnostic and Statistical Manual of Mental Disorders* changed from psychopath to "sociopathic personality" in 1952. In the second edition of the *Diagnostic and Statistical Manual of Mental Disorders,* published in 1968, the term "sociopathic personality" was changed to "personality disorder, antisocial type" essentially defined following Cleckley's analysis as "unsocialized, impulsive, guiltless, selfish, callous, and failing to learn from experience."

Although there is evidence that a psychopathic personality is characteristic of serious offenders, there is a lack of controlled study to indicate whether or not psychopathic personality (aside from the tautological "ongoing antisocial behavior" component) even correlates with criminal behavior. It may be that people who are remorseless, shallow, manipulative, lying, egocentric, glib, and so forth are quite prevalent in the population but do not engage in criminal activity because of informal or formal controls on their activity, or other factors that cancel out their negative personality traits. Probably a better question to ask is how a person goes from being an ordinary "shallow Hal" to becoming a full-blown serial killer? Thus, the sociopathic personality is not the endpoint of analysis, but just the beginning of it. There are several pathways or "careers" that people take to the level of a serial killer, and understanding these pathways is probably the best way to prevent such crimes.

Becoming a Serial Killer

Numerous studies indicate a relationship between having been a victim of child abuse and, later in life, becoming a child abuser and/or violent criminal.[111]

However, child abuse does not bear a one-to-one relationship to later adult violence. Not all violent adult criminals were abused as children, and not all abused children become violent adult criminals (just as not all psychopaths become serial killers). There may be a process that one goes through in becoming a serial killer. This process has been described by criminologist Lonnie Athens as *violentization*.[112] *Violentization* is a form of socialization that occurs in four stages, according to Athens. These begin with *brutalization* and *subjugation,* followed by *violent coaching, belligerency,* and *virulency.* Athens, a product of the violent underclass in Richmond Virginia, developed his **violentization theory** through qualitative interviews of violent, convicted, incarcerated prisoners.[113] During the *brutalization stage,* the subject is forced into *subjection* by a member of his/her primary group, or may experience personal horrification by the violent subjugation of a member of his/her primary group. Subsequently, violent *coaching* takes place by someone who insists that the subject must defend himself/herself, possibly glorifying violence through storytelling or even coercing the subject through threatening to "stand up and fight, or I'll beat you myself." Next, in the *belligerency stage,* the subject resolves to do something about his former violent subjugation by physically attacking people who unduly provoke him, which is a highly emotion-laden resolution. The subject then engages in violent performances against individuals who provoke him or her and acquires a reputation as "dangerous" or "crazy," a reputation akin to "celebrity" status. The subject then becomes filled with feelings of exultancy (vainglorification) and concludes that since his earlier violence, he should perform even more impressive violent feats in the future, that he is invincible, and that he may attack with lethal force even with little or no provocation (*virulency stage*). Having reached this stage, the subject is now a dangerous, violent criminal, according to Athens.

Sociological Theories of Murder

There are numerous sociological and pseudosociological theories of murder that are cited in leading textbooks. Many of these are "common sense theories" that haven't really been related to sociological theory. Most are provincial in the sense that they haven't really been tested through cross-national comparison beyond a study or two in one or two foreign cultures. The more formal sociological theories include the subculture of violence theory, external restraint theory, and containment theory, and popular theories include gun control (or lack of it), alcohol and drug use, exposure to violence in the media or family, and membership in a gang or social movement. A couple of theories—victim precipitation and regional variation—are discussed as variations of the subculture of violence theory.

Subculture of Violence Theory

Probably the leading sociological theory is termed the **subculture of violence theory** by Marvin Wolfgang and Franco Ferracuti.[114] This theory is less provincial than many criminological theories in that the authors argue that the subculture of violence can be found in other countries, namely in Colombia, Sardinia, Mexico, Albania, Italy, and India. The subculture of violence is a subculture emerging among youthful, black, urban males, and the subculture has its own codes and characteristic set of beliefs and attitudes.

> A male is usually expected to defend the name and honor of his mother, the virtue of womanhood . . . and to accept no derogation about his race

(even from a member of his own race), his age, or his masculinity. Quick resort to physical combat as a measure of daring, courage, or defense of status appears to be a cultural expression, especially for lower socioeconomic class males of both races.[115]

In this subculture, personal assaults are not seen as wrong or antisocial, but in fact are socially approved and even expected under some conditions. Wolfgang and Ferracuti describe this subculture in psychoanalytic terms as a "collectivization of the id" whereby basic urges and impulses are less inhibited, needs are satisfied immediately, and social regulation is weak. There are several important hypotheses derived from this theory:

1. The greater the degree of integration of the individual into this subculture, the higher the likelihood that his behavior will often be violent.
2. There is a direct relationship between rates of homicide and the degree of integration of the subculture of violence.
3. Persons not members of the subculture of violence who nonetheless commit crimes of violence have psychological and social attributes significantly different from violent criminals from the subculture of violence; that is, violent criminals from a culture of nonviolence have more psychopathological traits, more guilt, and more anxiety about their violent behavior.
4. The development of favorable attitudes toward, and the use of, violence in a subculture usually involves learned behavior and a process of differential learning, association, or identification.

Wolfgang and Ferracuti's theory can be seen in this last proposition as a variant of Sutherland's "differential association" theory and suffers the same criticisms as that theory. One criticism, as stated by the authors, is that the theory doesn't explain the violence of "loners" who are not members of the subculture (who populate the list of serial and mass murderers discussed earlier). Another criticism is that the theory takes the subculture of violence as a given and does not try to explain its origin. It contains a nearly racist assumption that the subculture of violence is one that has developed among blacks in the United States, completely ignoring the fact that before the development of black ghettos in urban areas of the United States, white Irish, English and other gangs made up the bulk of the violent subculture. Implicit is the assumption that blacks, or at least "people of color," are responsible for most violent crime. Cross-national study challenges this theory in that many predominantly white countries, such as Russia and many former Soviet countries such as Estonia, not to mention Scotland, have high rates of murder.

As suggested earlier, participation in a "subculture of violence" is not so much a "racial trait" as it is a manifestation of being a member of an underclass in a society characterized by inequality. It is entirely possible that Americans of African descent could be replaced by white Russians or Ukrainians as the bottom underclass in America's future. As a matter of fact, more recent studies using more sophisticated measurement and stronger research designs have revealed that the racial composition of an area does not have a significant influence on the homicide rate for either whites or blacks.[116] In addition, there is considerable evidence contradicting the notion of a black subculture of violence. One survey study found that white males were more likely than black males to give violent responses in response to a defensive situation and there were no racial differences in responses to offensive situations.[117] Studies also find that gang members in lower class neighborhoods both know and accept the norms of the dominant culture.[118]

One variation on the subculture of violence theory is Wolfgang's theory that murder is often *victim-precipitated,* which means that the victim is a "direct, positive precipitator of the crime" in the sense that the victim is the first to display and use a deadly weapon, strike a blow, and commence the interplay of resort to physical violence.[119] Wolfgang found that approximately one in four murders is victim precipitated. Victim studies have provided the basis for linking this theory with the subculture of violence, as they find that victims are typically part of the same subculture as their offenders (viz., the subculture of violence). However, victim precipitation theory introduces a new dynamic into subcultural theory, notably gender. Wolfgang found as many as 60% of cases where women had killed their husbands as victim precipitated, but only 9% of situations where men had killed their wives as victim precipitated. Subsequent study has indicated that slightly more than 50% of all homicides committed by women, but only 12% of those committed by men, are victim-precipitated.[120]

Another variation of the subculture of violence theory ironically holds murder rates to be high among white people in the South. Raymond Gastil found a relationship between high murder rates and residence in the South, as well as an influx of Southerners in other regions of the United States.[121] He attributes this high homicide rate to a Southern culture that includes a frontier mentality, mob violence, night riders, personal vengeance, personal honor, firearms, and an inclination to defend family and home against threat reminiscent of medieval European knights. As with the subculture of violence theory, Gastil's theory has been challenged for not controlling for the influence of structural variables, such as poverty, as alternative explanations for regional differences in the homicide rate.[122]

External Restraint Theory

While the subculture of violence theory is discussed in virtually every contemporary text on criminology, one theory of homicide that seems to have been omitted from contemporary discussion is Henry and Short's **external restraint theory.**[123]

Henry and Short proposed a theory that was rooted in psychoanalytic theory but that also took into account certain social correlates. By trying to view both homicide and suicide in a unified framework, they provided insights that expanded the reach of frustration-aggression theory to international comparisons. Henry and Short stated that there are three major the

BOX 6–15

Murder in Pakistan

A study based upon interviews with 600 incarcerated offenders in the New Central Jail of Multan, Pakistan found that murder is most commonly committed by young males from the lower end of the socioeconomic system. Murder was typically a vengeful response to a challenge to one's honor, in keeping with the subculture of violence theory.[124]

independent variables to be related in discussing homicide and suicide: (a) amount of frustration, (b) the "strength of relational systems," and (c) the degree of external restraint. Strength of the relational system is defined as "involvement in social or cathetic relationships with other persons." The relational system of the married is stronger than the relational system of the unmarried and stronger among rural people than among urban. "Strength of external restraint" is defined as the degree to which behavior is required to conform to the demands and expectations of other persons and varies inversely with position in the status hierarchy, that is, socioeconomic class system.[125] With these definitions in mind, Henry and Short hypothesized:

1. Suicide varies inversely with the strength of the relational system and homicide varies positively with strength of the relational system.
2. Suicide varies inversely and homicide varies positively with the strength of external restraint over behavior.

In terms of the correlates of homicide, external restraint explains the greater homicide rate of males, nonwhites, the young, and the lower socioeconomic class, whereas strength of relational systems explains the higher incidence of homicide in the South and rural areas.

Henry and Short attempted to test strength of relationships using data available on marital status, but concluded that no conclusions could be made because available data failed to distinguish between those who were single, widowed, and divorced and those who were married.

Containment Theory

A theory of internal and external containment was proposed by Reckless as an alternative to the Henry and Short formulation.[126] *External containment* refers to the holding power of the group whereby society and particularly nuclear groups contain, steer, shield, divert, support, reinforce, and limit their members. External containment is related to such factors as meaningfulness of roles; availability of supportive relationships conferring a sense of belonging and identity; and degree of isolation and homogeneity of culture, class, and population. High containment is found in folk societies and religious sects, such as the Jews, Quakers, Mennonites, and Amish. The Hutterites of North America, a communal Christian sect, are a case in point. Despite some evidence of mental disorder among the Hutterites and strong evidence of "themes of violence, murder, and stealing occurring in response to Thematic Apperception Tests for almost every Hutterite respondent who took these and other projective tests," these tendencies are not acted on overtly or directly. Antisocial behavior and violence are rare among Hutterites. Reckless attributes

BOX 6–16

Homicide/Suicide in Finland

A study in Finland drawing upon data for years 1960 to 1974 found that the percentage and rate of homicide/suicide had been consistently highest among the middle classes and lowest among the unemployed and working classes. Explanations of these unusual social class characteristics of the offender included stressful life events and alcohol consumption.[127]

this lower level of overt aggression to the high level of external containment as shown in strong taboos against violence and childhood socialization against fighting. Thus, among the Hutterites, there is a strong relational system, and strong external restraint—conditions Henry and Short link with high rates of homicide—and yet the Hutterites fail to show that form of aggression.

Guns, Drugs, and Gangs

The War on Drugs

As discussed in the previous section, there is a probable link between terrorism and the drug trade, and the term "narcoterrorism" describes this link. One interesting theory suggests that attempts to prohibit drugs or alcohol (i.e, prohibition efforts, such as the "War on Drugs") actually have an influence on homicide rates within the United States. Kirby R. Cundiff published online a paper entitled "Homicide Rates and Substance Control Policy." Cundiff argues that prohibition of drugs and alcohol actually increases murder rates within the United States:

> One theory of violent crime in the United States is that the prohibition of alcohol or drugs drives up the prices of these substances. This creates a highly profitable profession that can only be engaged in by persons who are willing to risk violent confrontation with law enforcement officials. Since this profession is outside the normal court system, violence with competitors is used as a mechanism for settling disputes. Drug and alcohol consumers could also resort to theft and violence to pay for the high cost of the substances they desire. If this theory is correct, there should be a strong correlation between the homicide rate and law enforcement activity to enforce the prohibition of alcohol or drugs.[128]

Using data sets derived from FBI records, Census, and other data, Cundiff performed multiple and simple regression analysis between the per-capita homicide rate and proxies for the U.S. government's substance control policy. Cundiff concluded that with the exception of the time period 1975–1997, during all other time periods the correlation between the homicide rate and substance control proxies are excellent. (It should be noted that the 1975–1997 "exception" encompasses the time period during which the present day "War on Drugs" occurred. It essentially began during the Nixon administration, was expanded during the Reagan administration, and continued up to and including the Clinton administration.)

In addition to the new theory about the War on Drugs, some additional ad hoc theories are frequently developed in criminology texts pertaining to the guns, drugs, and gangs often associated with murder. Somehow these factors have developed theoretical importance by virtue of their frequency of discussion in the mass media, though no systematic sociological theory has developed pertaining to these factors, with the possible exception of differential association theory. At face value, these "factors in crime" are essentially neutral. Guns may be used legally by law enforcement, the military, or in self-defense, or illegally as part of a criminal act. Drugs (including alcohol) may lead individuals to a state of agitation that may incite violence or may induce drowsiness, sleep, or even anesthesia for purposes of surgery. Gangs may (and typically are) organized for noncriminal social purposes, and/or for drug consumption, theft, or violent crime. Although cross-national studies have yet to extensively assess these three variables as independent variables contributing to homicide, one cannot deny that these factors are undeniably linked in the literature with violent crime, and they deserve some discussion.

Guns

One report (*Small Arms in the Pacific*) states that "In the United States, four percent of the world population possesses 50% of the planet's privately owned firearms."[129] Gun control advocates argue that this factor alone accounts for the fact that the United States has had a much higher rate of murder than other countries of the same level of economic development. On the other hand, opponents of gun control point to Switzerland as an example of a country where gun ownership is nearly universal, yet the murder rate is very low.[130] However, statistics on the use of handguns in crime are persuasive in the argument that the availability of firearms is a contributing factor in murder. Approximately 66% of all murders and around 41% of all robberies involve firearms.[131] Violence among intimates, such as family members, is 12 times more likely to result in death if a handgun is used than if no firearms are involved.[132] Similarly, if guns are used in robberies, they are three times more likely to be fatal than robberies with knives and 10 times more likely to be fatal than robberies with other weapons.[133]

While these domestic statistics are impressive, cross-national data are even more informative. In a study published in 1993, rates of homicide and suicide with a gun were studied for 11 European countries, Australia, Canada, and the United States. A positive correlation was found between the rates of household gun ownership and the national rates of homicide.[134] A study of fewer nations published in 1981 made some even more interesting comparisons. The study found that in 1980 New York had almost 10 times as many murders as comparably populated London, where there has been gun control for 60 years. Although the non-gun homicide rate for the United States is three times that of England, Germany, Denmark, Norway, Poland, Greece, and Japan, gun homicide is an astounding 50 times higher than in those other countries.[135] Another more recent study (1998) of 36 countries, using data from health officials on firearm-related homicides and suicides, found mortality rates in the U.S. to be the greatest of all countries studied. The study found that the rate of firearm deaths in the U.S. (14.24 per 100,000 inhabitants) exceeded that of other high-income countries (that averaged 1.76 per 100,000) eightfold. Furthermore, the U.S. rate was 95 times higher than Asia, whose rate was .13 per 100,000 inhabitants. The term "firearm deaths" referred to homicides and suicides, as well as accidental deaths. It was found that suicide and homicide contributed equally to total firearm deaths in the United States (a "high-income country"). However, most firearm deaths were suicides in other high-income counties, whereas most firearm deaths were homicides in upper-middle-income countries.[136] Another study, by the same authors, comparing 26 countries and the United States was published that same year (1998). The study found that firearm-related victimization among children under 15 was five times higher in the United States than for *all 26 other countries combined*.[137]

Certainly the accessibility of guns is a fertile area in which comparative criminological research can help to determine more definitively the causative role that gun availability plays in murder. However, it is doubtful that gun control advocates will be able to prevail in the United States. For one reason, guns are "big business" in the United States. The United States is the single most important small arms producer in the world today. The United States has the largest number of companies (for a single country) that produce small arms and/or ammunition, and it has one of the world's largest domestic markets for small arms.[138]

Another problem with arguments for gun control is the shear number of guns in the United States. U.S. citizens own about 200 million guns.[139] No doubt, people are acutely aware of the problem of existing guns getting into the hands of criminals, even if there were a ban on guns. In a 2004 Harris Poll, about 72% of Americans polled favored a ban on assault rifles. However, the 2004 Gallup Poll revealed that 63% of Americans believe there should not be a law that bans the possession of handguns. This percentage of 63% has increased 10 percentage points from 53% in 1991. The 2004 Gallup Poll revealed that 38% of all Americans have a gun in their homes.[140] The American desire to own a handgun is quite possibly because of the perception that a good share of the 200 million guns Americans possess are in the hands of criminals and juvenile delinquents, and empirical studies support this fear. One anonymous self-report study of 89 male youths in a detention facility in Seattle, Washington revealed that 59% of the youths reported owning a handgun.[141] There is also ample evidence of handgun violence among young offenders. According to a study done in 1995, 16- to 19-year-olds had the highest rate of handgun victimization among all age groups.[142] Also, a well-known finding about juvenile murder may have entered public consciousness. James Fox found that the murder rate for teens aged 14–17 had jumped 172% from 1985–1994, with the role of guns quadrupling in those crimes during that time.[143] Further study revealed that for youthful offenders, access to guns is relatively easy. Guns were acquired from friends, drug users, and drug dealers. It was thought that the guns were originally acquired by theft.[144]

Arguments in favor of gun control in America are often countered by the National Rifle Association (NRA) slogan, "when guns are outlawed, only outlaws will have guns." The slogan, it would seem, is supported by scientific study. In Great Britain, where strict gun control has been in place for 60 years, a study was done of 1,570 arrestees in 16 locations in England and Wales. About 25% of arrestees said they had owned or obtained a gun at some point in their lives, and 10% had done so in the previous year. The most common gun was a handgun, and the most common reason for obtaining a gun was self-protection, particularly during drug dealing or purchasing.[145] These findings are important in terms of policy considerations. In America, particularly, efforts to restrict the supply of guns through legislation would probably have minimal impact upon criminals and juvenile delinquents, because guns are readily available from a variety of sources that include illegal gun traffickers, drug traffickers, friends, and theft.[146]

Guns and Public Policy

Given the prevalence of guns in America, and apparent enhanced prevalence among criminals and juvenile delinquents, what can be done about the problem? There is strong sentiment among many social scientists for an outright ban on guns. The merit of such an approach has been shown by an actual instance within the United States. A law that banned the purchase, sale, transfer, or possession of handguns by civilians was adopted by the District of

Columbia in 1976. This law was followed by an abrupt 25% decline in homicides by firearms and a 23% drop in suicides by firearms the following year.[147] However, even if Congress has no objection to gun control for its immediate environment (District of Columbia), the legislation that it passes for the nation is still influenced by the firearms industry, pro-gun lobbying groups like the NRA, and public opinion, all of which favor legal access to handguns. Thus, legislation passed by Congress, in the final analysis, must pass the test of public opinion. Federal gun legislation has developed incrementally over time, as seen in the text box. These laws have typically been passed in response to some gun-related crisis situation. The Second Amendment was intended to enable Americans to defend themselves, presumably against the British military, and perhaps those who continued to be loyal to Great Britain, after the American Revolution. The laws of the 1930s were a product of President Roosevelt's desire to curtail the gangster violence that had been the product of Prohibition. The 1968 gun control act was, in part, the product of the assassination of President Kennedy, which was carried out by an assailant (Lee Harvey Oswald) who had purchased a rifle through the U.S. mail. The 1990 Crime Control Act was a response to the rising drug-related violence perpetrated by juveniles in the late 1980s. The Brady Handgun Violence Act was spurred by the severe wounding of President Reagan's Press Secretary James Brady, as a result of the attempted assassination of President Reagan by John Hinkley in 1981. The "Assault Weapons Ban" was probably spurred by several paramilitary-style shootings that occurred in the 1990s.

There has been much debate as to whether the roughly 300 state and federal gun laws have had any influence upon the use of guns in crime.[148] Federal laws passed in the mid-1990s may have had an impact upon juvenile drug-related gang violence, because it seems to have leveled off since

BOX 6–17

U.S. Federal Gun Laws[149]

1791 Second Amendment Ratified: "A well regulated Militia, being necessary to the security of a free State, the right of the people to keep and bear Arms, shall not be infringed."

1934 National Firearms Act: A tax of $200 on each firearm sold by gun manufacturers, and all buyers were required to fill out paperwork subject to Treasury Department approval.

1938 Federal Firearms Act: Aimed at persons selling firearms through interstate commerce.

1968 Gun Control Act: License requirements were expanded to include more dealers and more record-keeping was expected of them.

1972 Bureau of Alcohol Tobacco and Firearms (ATF) created: Replacing the Department of Treasury's Alcohol and Tobacco Tax Division, the ATF enforced the Gun Control Act.

1972 Law Enforcement Officers Protection Act: Made it illegal for anyone to manufacture or import armor-piercing ammunition.

1986 Firearms Owners' Protection Act: Eased restrictions on gun sellers and sale of some guns, but imposed additional penalties for persons using a firearm during crimes.

1990 Crime Control Act: Established criminal penalties for possessing or discharging a firearm in a school zone.

1993 Brady Handgun Violence Prevention Act: Imposed a five-day waiting period and background check before a licensed gun importer, manufacturer, or dealer can sell or deliver a handgun to an unlicensed individual.

1994 Violent Crime Control and Law Enforcement Act: The bill banned the manufacture, possession, and importation of new semiautomatic assault weapons and large-capacity ammunition-feeding devices (or magazines) for civilian use.

1994. However, many other factors may be responsible for that trend, such as increased incarceration of offenders. Guns are still considered easy to access by juvenile gang members, as well as by adult criminals. One study critical of the Brady Act compared the 32 "treatment" states directly affected by the Brady Act requirements to 18 "control states" and the District of Columbia, which had equivalent legislation already in place. The study found that implementation of the Brady Act appeared to have been associated with reductions in the firearm suicide rate among those aged 55 and older, but not with decreases in homicide rates or overall suicide rates.[150]

Another controversial approach has been advocated by John R. Lott, Jr., who is a resident scholar at the American Enterprise Institute for Public Policy Research, a conservative "think tank" in Washington, DC. In 1998, Lott published a book entitled, *More Guns; Less Crime: Understanding Crime and Gun Control Laws.*[151] In the book, he reports the analysis of data from reported crime statistics for all 3,054 counties in the U.S., through the years 1977–1992, pertaining to laws regulating the carrying of concealed handguns. He argues that allowing citizens without criminal records or mental illness to carry concealed handguns deters violent crimes. Although Lott admitted that there may a displacement in the form of increasing property crimes involving stealth, he maintained that these crimes are less serious because they do not involve violence or the threat of violence. He found that when state-concealed handgun laws went into effect in a county, murders fell by 8.5%, rapes fell by 5%, and aggravated assaults fell by 7%. Based upon the findings of his study, he estimated that if the entire country had adopted right-to-carry-concealed-handgun laws in 1992, an estimated 1,500 murders and 4,000 rapes would have been avoided. Needless to say, Lott's findings did not stand unopposed. Another study found just the opposite using a state data set with several additional years of information—that crime tended to *increase* more when states adopt shall-issue laws.[152]

In the final analysis, guns in the hands of criminals and juvenile delinquents, possibly funded by the drug trade, can occur anyplace in the world, notwithstanding the presence or absence of laws prohibiting such possession. While supposedly law-abiding citizens may or may not do more good than harm if they are allowed to carry concealed weapons, the removal of possession by delinquents and criminals is the prime objective in dealing with violent crime. The recent Kansas City Gun Experiment provides some food for thought. In this experiment, "hot spots" within Kansas City, (Missouri): were targeted by the police for *directed patrol.* The target area had a homicide rate 20 times higher than the national average. Over a six-month period, in a ten-by-eight-block area, intensive patrol produced a 65% increase in firearms seized by the police, typically as a result of traffic stops. Gun crimes declined in the target area by 49%, with no significant displacement to any patrol beat surrounding the target area. Drive-by shootings dropped from seven to one in

BOX 6–18

Directed Patrol

Directed patrol is defined as a police management strategy designed to increase the productivity of patrol officers through the scientific analysis and evaluation of patrol techniques.[153]

the target area, but doubled from six to 12 in the comparison area (not near the target area).[154]

We may see that there are problems with the implementation of the Kansas City approach to directed patrol. One might say that a police campaign to seize guns provides an extreme contrast to John Lott's approach of allowing citizens to carry concealed weapons. There could be problems implementing a gun seizure program in many states where carrying an illegal concealed weapon is a misdemeanor. If carrying a concealed weapon is a misdemeanor, then the police have no right to seize the weapon, unless the weapon is in plain view or they had observed a crime in progress that would justify a search. Thus, what may be needed are changes in laws that would raise possession of weapons to the level of a felony for persons in special categories such as of documented gang members, persons with a criminal record, and/or juveniles. However, there are issues pertaining to civil liberties that may hamper such efforts.

Drugs

Drug use, especially illegal drug use, has often been linked with homicide in the mass media. A man stole a tank from a military facility in San Diego, driving it on a potentially murderous rampage through downtown San Diego, before the tank became impaled on a freeway divider and the police shot him dead. Reportedly, the man was high on "crystal meth," a drug that first became prevalent in the United States after World War II, when it was trafficked through San Diego as a port of entry. The original Harrison Act of 1914 included cocaine on a list of drugs to be regulated, justified by media stories of its link between murder and cocaine use among African Americans. An anti-marijuana film, "Reefer Madness," discussed an ax murder in which the suspect was high on marijuana. Drug use forecast studies of individuals who have been sent to jail find illegal drugs in blood samples of inmates in major cities ranging as high as 80%. The other side of the coin are those who link violence with drugs, not so much because of the drugs causing violence, but because the prohibition of drugs leads to a profit motivated violent drug trade, that is, the prohibition of drugs and alcohol, not the drugs themselves, causes high rates of homicide.

The relationship between drugs and homicide has also been examined by social scientists. In 1985, Paul J. Goldstein published an important conceptual typology having to do with the relationship between drugs and crime.[155] Goldstein said that drugs could be tied to violent offending through a *psychopharmacological model*, as a result of *economic compulsion*, and through *systematic violence*. The *psychopharmacological model* holds that use of drugs produces violent behavior by lowering inhibitions or elevating aggressive tendencies. *Economic compulsion* occurs when crime is used to support a drug habit, whereas *systematic violence* refers to the link between drugs and trafficking in the form of drug rival wars and murders, as well as murder in the course of robbery of a drug dealer. Goldstein and his colleagues applied this typology to some 414 homicides in New York City during the 1980s. They found that more than half the cases could be classified as systematic, but all of the homicides where alcohol was present were described as psychopharmacological.[156] Goldstein et al. also argued that very few murders are committed by people trying to obtain money to buy drugs. They stated that the notion of "crazed killers" due to substance abuse is a fallacy. They also argued that reports attributing psychopharmacological violence to heroin and/or marijuana users have been discredited. They stated further that heroin, marijuana, and tranquilizers tend to ameliorate violent tendencies, while alcohol, stimulants, barbiturates, and PCP are the drugs that contribute to psychopharmacological violence.

Gangs

Gangs or "ganging" have often been blamed for the high rate of homicide in the United States. Although rates of homicide have declined among adults 35 and older since 1980,[157] rates of murder increased for teens and young adults during that same period of time. In fact, from 1985 to 1994, the rate of murder committed by teens, ages 14–17, increased 172%.[158] This increase in juvenile homicide has been linked to increasing rates of gang membership in the United States. Estimated gang membership rose from 55,000 members in 1975 to 846,000 members in 1996.[159]

While there has been much publicity devoted to school shootings committed by isolated loners, it is probable that the bulk of the increase in juvenile homicides is owed to the increase in gang participation. Reasons for believing that the violence is gang related are several, having to do with area, guns, race, and relationship with the victim. Violence rates are highest in urban areas in which subcultural values support teenage gangs and whose members support the use of violence.[160] Guns are an important indicator of gang involvement, and from 1984 to 1994, the number of juveniles killing with a gun quadrupled.[161] Studies show that male gang members are more likely to own guns, are more likely to have peers who are gun owners, and are more likely to carry guns outside the home.[162] Teen black males have occupied an increasing proportion of the murder rate, rising from around 15% in the early 1980s to over 30% in the mid 1990s, and researchers have found that gang murders were more likely to involve black males than white males.[163] Finally, although the majority of homicide victims are previously known to the offender, there has been an increasing trend in stranger killings[164] and researchers have found that gang killings are more likely than nongang to involve victims and offenders with no prior relationship.[165] One study found that violence is the central activity of gangs, for several reasons, including enabling new members to show toughness during initiation ceremonies, to retaliate against rivals for

BOX 6–19

"Do-it-Yourself Justice" and Homicide in Uganda

One way of looking at gang violence in the United States is that it is "do-it-yourself justice." Gang violence is often in retaliation for violence perpetrated by rival gangs. In many countries that lack adequate policing (which may be the case in urban ghettos in America), mob violence does the job of the police. A study published in 1970 found that the official rate of homicide in Uganda was substantially lower than the homicides known to the police. (Note: in the CCDB, the rate of homicide in Uganda was 10.25 in 2002.) The high unofficial homicide rate was in large part traced to "do-it-yourself justice." Major factors in the violence included a tradition of self-help in personal matters, the condonation of mob violence (such as in the mob assault of thieves), the community need to punish suspects immediately, and an acceptance of violence in marital relationships.[166]

BOX 6-20

Mediation in Sudan

In southern Sudan, tribal feuds, once begun, tend to go on indefinitely and to result in violent outcomes such as homicide. A new approach now being used is to look upon crime, such as homicide, as a dispute to be resolved. Solutions may involve limiting boundaries, fixing routes, digging wells, developing natural resources, and arranging for preventive security measures. Dispute mediation results from a conference held between the tribes, and as a result each tribe pays the other for the losses it caused, thus avoiding perpetuation of the feud. Mediators, who may be tribal members or even a committee, play important roles in proposing a formula that will end the dispute.[167]

actual or perceived grievances, to defend honor when graffiti is defaced by rivals, and to protect turf from incursions by outsiders.[168]

How does youth gang violence fit the economic inequality model discussed? There is considerable evidence that as a backdrop for this growth in gangs and violence, the United States has experienced a change in income distribution. As one text put it, "the rich got richer, and the poor got prison." There is evidence that income inequality in the United States increased 32% between 1961 and 1999.[169] Most of this change occurred during the 1980s and 1990s, a period during which the "War on Drugs," and "America's imprisonment binge" occurred. Although blacks were going to prison in record numbers, leaving their children without parental supervision, juvenile gang members were turning to the drug trade, not only as a means of survival, but also as a means of showing contempt for the rules of the dominant class. The product of this War on Drugs was "terrorism" in the ghetto. While our country is spending billions fighting terrorism abroad, it may be losing its war on domestic terrorism by youthful gangs at home, and we may see increasing rates of violence on the order of those predicted by James Fox "if present trends continue."

COUNTRY PROFILES

According to a widely published criminology text, "The American murder rate always has been high (in the United States). It reached a peak in 1980 and has been declining erratically since then."[170] The question to ask is, "high, compared to what?" As can be seen in Table 6–3, in year 2001, the rate of murder was 5.6 homicides per 100,000 persons in the United States. However, that same year the rate was 114.84 per 100,000 inhabitants in South Africa. The rate in Honduras was 154.02 per 100,000 inhabitants for year 1998 (most recent data reported). The United States ranks 66th in its rate of murder out of 159 countries of the world for which data are available. Even at its high recent rate of 9.8 per 100,000 inhabitants in 1991, the murder rate in the United States was very low compared to these figures for South Africa and Honduras. It should be pointed out that the murder rate for the United States is relatively high compared to other *developed* nations. According to the CIA World Factbook, countries highlighted in Table 6–3 are considered to be "developed nations," based largely upon economic indicators. The United States ranks 5th of 30 developed nations in Table 6–3.

Table 6–3 Countries of the World Ranked by Annual Rate of Murder per 100,000 Population[171]

Country	Rate	Rank
Honduras	154.00	1
South Africa	114.80	2
Colombia	69.98	3
Lesotho	50.41	4
Rwanda	45.08	5
Jamaica	43.71	6
El Salvador	34.33	7
Guatemala	33.34	8
Venezuela	33.20	9
Bolivia	31.98	10
Bahamas, The	27.09	11
Namibia	26.32	12
Ecuador	25.92	13
Nicaragua	24.07	14
Brazil	22.98	16
Russia	22.43	17
Guyana	16.19	19
Mexico	14.11	24
Luxembourg	13.74	25
Sweden	10.01	41
Belgium	6.00	64
United States	5.60	66
Canada	4.10	81
France	4.10	82
Italy	3.80	87
Denmark	3.70	88
Australia	3.60	90
Germany	3.20	97
Liechtenstein	3.00	102
Switzerland	2.90	105
Spain	2.90	107
Greece	2.75	111
Norway	2.66	112
Portugal	2.57	113
Austria	1.96	123
Great Britain	1.63	127
Ireland	1.60	128
New Zealand	1.17	137
Netherlands	1.15	138
Japan	1.05	140

Table 6–3 shows the United States compared to countries of the world in the top 10% with regard to their murder rates. It can be seen that the murder rate for the United States is miniscule compared to these 16 other countries.

Support for the external restraint hypothesis is provided from an analysis using the CCDB developed for this text, as seen in the Table 6–4. In Table 6–4, murder is directly correlated with the percentage of people who are living in poverty and who are unemployed, but also directly correlated with a measure of socioeconomic inequality called the Gini Index. Using World Health Organization (WHO) data, an even stronger correlation between murder and economic inequality ($r = .57$) was obtained. The WHO data were based upon a smaller number of countries (71) compared to the findings from United Nations and INTERPOL data in Table 6–3 that were for 159 countries; however, the WHO data are from medical records, whereas the data in Table 6–3 are derived from police statistics.[172]

Henry and Short argued that those in the underclass would suffer greatest restraint, and these data agree, but the data add a dimension to Henry and Short's analysis—economic inequality. It seems that those in the lowest levels of the socioeconomic system would suffer greatest "external restraint" (limitations on their activities, reduction in life chances and opportunities, etc.) in countries in which there is greatest socioeconomic inequality. The frustration that lower class people endure in these countries is made even more unendurable by the knowledge that those above them flaunt an unshared lavish wealth and lifestyle with impunity. The frustration leads to anger and the anger leads to rage that leads to collective action to redress their lowered status. These findings on the relationship between inequality and violent crime essentially replicate a similar study of some 37 countries.[173]

Although the Henry and Short theory is consistent with the aforementioned homicide data, it is even more helpful in explaining the seemingly anomalous suicide data in that same table. It seems counterintuitive that poverty and unemployment, as well as socioeconomic inequality, would be negatively related to suicide. This means that the people in poor countries with high rates of unemployment and high rates of inequality are less likely to commit suicide. However, Henry and Shorts' hypothesis that suicide varies negatively with the strength of external restraint over behavior is consistent with these data. It would seem, in the words of Emile Durkheim, that "poverty protects" against suicide. If people are restricted in their activity and held in their place, they are less likely to experience the effects of "normlessness." Their life is circumscribed by rules rather than being normless, and perhaps they respond by efforts to "get even" or fight back against the system, than by escaping by "ending it all." People living in countries at the other end of the

Inequality and Murder

Table 6–4 **Correlations between Various Economic Indices and Dependent Variables Murder and Suicide**

	Murder	*Suicide*
Inequality (Gini Index)[174]	.41	−.44
Percentage living in poverty	.26	−.33
Percentage unemployed	.19	−.26

spectrum socioeconomically, where wealth is more abundant and shared more equally, have leisure time to become involved in drug and alcohol consumption, with nobody telling them what to do. Normlessness occurs in this situation rather than the opposite.[175]

Drugs, Alcohol, and Murder

Cross-cultural study of the relationship between drug arrests and murder using the CCDB developed for this text indicated an inverse statistically insignificant relationship of $-.07$ between these two variables. Using data drawn from the WHO,[176] alcohol consumption was also correlated with homicide internationally and a small, statistically insignificant, correlation of .09 was obtained. These findings run contrary to findings by Parker and associates, in a city-by-city and state-by-state study of the relationship between alcohol and homicide. They found a positive relationship between alcohol and homicide, arguing that this relationship results from "selective disinhibition."[177] Alcohol tends to lower people's inhibitions against using violence to achieve their goals. In addition, alcohol's well-known negative effects on people's perception, ability to interpret others' actions and intentions, and judgment make it more likely that interpersonal conflicts arise. This theory is stated as follows:

> These effects of alcohol (lowered inhibitions against violence, altered perceptions, etc.) are more likely to lead to violence in situations in which a complex set of social and psychological circumstances neutralize the normal social and psychological constraints against violence. There is a greater likelihood that these situations, and hence violence, will occur when alcohol is more readily available, such as in areas of high alcohol outlet density—such as liquor stores and convenience stores.[178]

Correlational studies are sometimes persuasive that alcohol causes violence. In light of the negative findings with international statistics, two points should be kept in mind. One is that the correlations between alcohol and violence within the United States could be "spurious correlations." A third variable (e.g., association with violent people) could account for both the alcohol use and violence. Secondly, alcohol is, like heroin, a depressant. When taken in small quantities, it may result in disinhibition, but when taken in large quantities it will result in drowsiness, incapacitation, and sleep. Actually, membership in a gang may be one of the social contexts that result both in alcohol drinking and in violence.

However, from our data it seems that cross-nationally alcohol doesn't have much to do with violence. This could have to do with the cultural differences in the way that alcohol is consumed. For instance, in some countries, such as Italy and Spain, alcohol is consumed frequently with meals, but as part of a meal, and acting inappropriately is frowned upon. In other countries, alcohol may be consumed in the social context of bars and taverns, and rowdy, violent behavior may result from this social situation. In addition, "binge drinking" may occur privately, which may lead to domestic violence and/or child abuse.

As mentioned previously, there seems to be a strong correlation between inequality and murder. This is illustrated by country profiles on South Africa and Colombia that are drawn from the Website that accompanies this text.[179] Although finding a high correlation between murder and extreme inequality is interesting, qualitative analysis is helpful to determine why this relationship

BOX 6–21

Homicide in Russia

Recent data reveal that the current Russian homicide victimization rate is more than 3 times higher than that of the United States.[180] Another study found that there was a positive significant relationship between alcohol consumption and homicide in Russia linked with cultural traditions such as a preference for distilled spirits, a tendency toward binge drinking, and the practice of drinking most often in (semi)private settings, together with the disappearance of the powerful authoritarian regime.[181]

exists. For this purpose, it is desirable to turn to qualitative analysis—country profiles. Both South Africa and Colombia have high rates of inequality and high rates of murder. What about inequality can contribute to widespread instances of murder? No doubt inequality can lead to jealousy, resentment, and anger on the part of the underclass; but how does that get translated into murder? A study in depth of these two countries may yield some insights.

South Africa

South Africa is a good place to start with a description of countries with high murder rates because it has the highest murder rate reported for all major countries of the world. In INTERPOL data, it ranks number one for murder in year 2001. (The data in Table 6–3 for Honduras were for 1998, the year Honduras was devastated by Hurricane Mitch, related to the rise in murder from around 28 per 100,000 for Honduras in 1995 to 154 per 100,000 in 1998. See text box on Honduras.) South Africa has many of the same social problems as the United States, with similar historical origins, except carried to extremes. The social problems include racism, civil disorder, racial conflict, class conflict, and inequality. Like the United States, South Africa is a very wealthy nation, ranking 21st out of 231 countries, with a gross domestic product of $432 billion annually. However, it also ranks high in poverty (50%), unemployment (37%), and inequality. Inequality has been measured by an index called the Gini Index. It can be seen from the aforementioned data that the Gini index is a strong correlate of murder internationally with a correlation of .41, as well as an even stronger correlation of .57 using WHO data on murder. Out of

BOX 6–22

Honduras Highest Rate of Murder in 1998

From 1995 to 1998, the rate of murder in Honduras increased from 28.8 per 100,000 inhabitants to 154.02—highest in the world. This tremendous increase was influenced by the occurrence of Hurricane Mitch in October of 1998. The hurricane left more than 5,000 people dead and 1.5 million displaced, with damages totaling $3 billion. The banana crop, the country's second-largest export, was virtually wiped out. One product of this devastation was loss of employment in a country whose annual per-capita income is approximately $920. Hardest hit were youth, many of whom pursued subsistence through gang crimes and drug trafficking. However, the high rate of murder was owed to the response of security forces to the subsistence crimes of these youth. Casa Alianza reported that 800 children and youth, only some of whom lived on the street, were killed in "social cleansing" between January and May 1998—killings done by vigilante security forces, "death squads," and neighborhood watch groups or Citizen Security Councils that patrolled their neighborhoods.[182]

112 countries for which the "Gini index" has been calculated, South Africa ranks fifth highest with a Gini Index of 59.3 (the United States has a Gini Index of 40.8 and ranks 40th).

The high degree of social inequality that exists in South Africa today is a historical product of colonialism. Starting in 1488, Portuguese, Dutch, French Huguenot refugees, and Germans settled in the Cape of Good Hope, collectively forming the Afrikaner segment of today's population. Subsequent British settlement, stimulated by the discovery of diamond and gold deposits, led to conflict between the Afrikaners and the English, culminating in the Anglo-Boer Wars in 1880 and 1899, won by the British who subsequently formed the Union of South Africa, a dominion of the British Empire.

Despite the founding of the South Africa Native National Congress (ANC) in 1912, whose goals were the elimination of restrictions based on color, the government continued to pass laws limiting the rights of blacks. In 1948, the National Party won the all-white elections and began passing, codifying, and enforcing an even stricter policy of white domination and racial separation known as *apartheid* (separateness). Following protests in the 1960s, the ANC and the Pan-African Congress (PAC) were banned. Nelson Mandela and many other anti-apartheid leaders were convicted and imprisoned on charges of treason. In 1961, South Africa relinquished its dominion status and declared itself a republic, in part because of international protests against apartheid. Following decades of guerrilla warfare and popular uprisings in 1976 and 1985, State President F. W. de Klerk announced the unbanning of the ANC, the PAC, and other anti-apartheid groups, followed in two weeks by the release from prison of Nelson Mandela. A new nonapartheid constitution was promulgated into law in December 1993 and Nelson Mandela became president in the country's first nonracial elections held on April 26–29, 1994.

Although violent crime is extraordinarily high today in South Africa (20 times the rate of the United States), it actually declined significantly during

Nelson Mandela waves to his supporters after giving his victory speech. Mandela and the ANC won a majority of the votes in South Africa's first all-race elections in April 1994.

Source: David Brauchli/AP Wide World Photos

Mandela's 5-year term. From 1995 to 2000, murder declined from 68.09 to 51.39 per 100,000 inhabitants. Mandela's administration focused on social issues that were neglected during the apartheid era such as unemployment, housing shortages, and crime. Mandela's administration began to reintroduce South Africa into the global economy by implementing a market-driven economic plan called Growth, Employment and Redistribution. However, this plan ironically opened South Africa to the drug trade, with the trappings of violent and property crime that goes with it. To heal the wounds created by apartheid, the government created the Truth and Reconciliation Committee under the leadership of Archbishop Desmond Tutu. There was an attempt to forge a single South African identity, resulting in a reduction in political violence after 1994. The GEAR strategy failed to reduce inequality. In fact, unemployment increased to 37% by 2000. Also, many vestiges of apartheid continue in criminal law, the criminal justice system, and in informal norms.

Historically, violence has increased following reforms as a product of white right-wing terrorism in South Africa and this process may be continuing today. White right-wing terrorists include groups such as the White Liberation Army, the White Republican Army, the Boer Republican Army, the White Wolves, and the Order of the Boer Nation, which have claimed responsibility for some 35 bombings. Some of these groups formed an alliance known as the White People's Front in 1992 and threatened further violence as the political transition continued. Many organizations hired private security guards for protection, a move opposed by the ANC as "vigilante" activities. The ANC subsequently formed its own Self-Defense Units to protect ANC supporters. This move was countered by political rivals in Inkatha Freedom Party (IFP) strongholds by forming Zulu Self-Protection Units. Although blacks were barred from gun ownership during the apartheid era, an estimated one half of all white families owned at least one firearm. Although firearms and explosives were the cause of more than one half of the deaths in the early 1990s, spears, knives, and axes—so-called Zulu traditional weapons, which were legal—were responsible for about 20% of violent deaths.

Currently, the high rate of violence in South Africa is related to taxi drivers' street rivalries, vigilante action and mob justice, murders of farm families and of black farm laborers, and witchcraft-related incidents. Human rights organizations have claimed that rural police and courts refuse to arrest or prosecute white perpetrators of crimes against the black workers and farm families. Evidence exists that, of all racial groups, the blacks are the most victimized by

BOX 6–23

Enforcement Terrorism

Wolf characterized murder by law enforcement officers as **enforcement terrorism** and he distinguished it from "agitational terrorism."[183] *Agitational terrorism*, due to control by the police, is committed by organizations consisting of a handful of persons who attempt to highlight their cause through violence. *Enforcement terrorism* is sponsored by the government, is highly efficient, and is posited to maintain social control. Examples of enforcement terrorism include the "white terror" conducted by military intelligence services in Chile, the Death Squad in Brazil; the White Warriors Union in El Salvador; the National Intelligence Directorate (DINA) in Chile; the K.G.B. in the former U.S.S.R.; Operation Condor in Latin America sponsored by Argentina, Bolivia, Brazil, Chile, Paraguay, and Uruguay; "hit teams" composed of elite Israeli and Arab killers; the Libyan Death Squads; and SAVAMA, Ayatollah Khomeini's security agency.

violent crime in South Africa. A 1981 survey revealed that 20% of the black respondents, 10% of colored, 5% of Indian, and 2% of white respondents reported being victims of assault.

The South African Police Service (SAPS), which traces its origin to the Dutch Watch, a paramilitary organization formed by settlers in the Cape in 1655, has as its primary mission quelling unrest and conducting counterinsurgency activities. There is evidence of links between the SAPS and white terrorist organizations. President de Klerk's credibility was severely damaged in July 1991, when official documents leaked to the public confirmed longstanding rumors of police support for the Zulu-dominated IFP in its rivalry with the ANC. In late 1992, the Goldstone Commission concluded that secret cells within the police force had, with the cooperation of military intelligence officials, "waged a war" on the ANC. In 1993, more than 2,000 murders were in Zulu-inhabited areas of KwaZulu and Natal Province, and the Goldstone Commission concluded that the weapons used in the violence against ANC supporters had been supplied by the police. SAPS contribution to the homicide statistics is not just indirect in the form of support for Zulu vigilantes. According to the 2001 Human Rights Report, police use of lethal force during apprehensions resulted in numerous deaths, and deaths in police custody also remained a problem.

Although capital punishment was eliminated in 1995, a new form of execution of prisoners has been developed in South Africa, owed to overcrowding in prison. In 2001, there were 165,000 prisoners in facilities designed to hold only 105,000. Prisoners are often required to sleep in shifts because of a lack of space. Overcrowding is cited as the main reason for the high rate of HIV/AIDS infection in prisons and a reported increase of more than 300% in deaths among inmates. In the first 7 months of the year 2001, 1,101 inmates died of HIV/AIDS, with the rate of infection among prisoners increasing by 36% over the same period in 2000. Press reports indicated that some detainees awaiting trial contracted HIV/AIDS through rape.

The aforementioned paragraphs about South Africa provide a "worst-case scenario" for the production of high rates of murder. Extremely high rates of murder have sociocultural roots in South Africa, roots that lie in the longstanding inequality of the economic system, the development of terrorist organizations and guerrilla activity among competing groups, and through the development of an ineffective and corrupt criminal justice system that provides support in the form of state-sponsored violence for the white majority in South Africa.

Colombia

In Table 6–3, although Colombia is second in the world to South Africa in its murder rate (excluding Honduras), Colombia has (year after year) shown the highest murder rate in the world. Colombia is, perhaps, a case in point of a country's attempt to curtail the drug trade contributing to high homicide rates, because that government has been battling drug cartels, as well as narcoterrorist organizations, for some time and has received U.S. support in its effort. Class conflict has been even more problematic in Colombia, and Colombia's government has been less successful than the other South American governments in suppressing guerrilla organizations, historically, and in dealing with narcoterrorist organizations since the 1960s. As in South Africa, in Colombia the police have supported paramilitary organizations that have attempted to battle left-wing insurgency. Colombia leads the world not only

BOX 6–24

Murder by Cop

In Colombia, the police may serve not merely as a control agency in regard to homicides, but may be responsible for some of them. An analysis of data from the Center for Investigations and Popular Research, published by the Colombian Commission of Jurists, a nongovernmental organization (NGO), claimed that from June 2000 to June 2001, state forces committed 100 reported extrajudicial killings, including deaths that resulted from police abuse of authority. Also, members of the security forces sometimes illegally collaborated with paramilitary forces, and the authorities continue to investigate past cases of collaboration with or failure to prevent massacres by paramilitaries. There were some reports that police and former security force members have committed "social cleansing" killings, some of them directed at children. Death squads have also been reported in Brazil, where young street children and poor people have been summarily executed by the police for crime control purposes. Such police violence is tacitly accepted by the public-at-large, as indicated by the co-existence of private vigilantism.[184]

in its murder rate, but also in kidnappings, cocaine production, previously in marijuana production, and increasingly in heroin production. The chief market for Colombian drugs is the United States, with Colombia benefiting from its proximity to the United States, closest of the South American countries, and easily accessibility to the United States via central America, as well as by sea and air.

Colombia has a history of violence. Resulting from the bitter rivalry between the Conservative and Liberal parties, the War of a Thousand Days (1899–1902) cost an estimated 100,000 lives, and up to 300,000 people died during La Violencia of the late 1940s and 1950s. Starting in the 1960s, a link between the drug trade, terrorism, and murder developed in Colombia. An escalation of Colombian marijuana production began in the mid- and late 1960s as a result of the growing demand generated by the U.S. market. When, in the early 1970s, the United States tightened up drug enforcement along the United States–Mexican border, and Mexico launched a major drive against its domestic producers, the epicenter of marijuana production in the hemisphere rapidly shifted to Colombia, which developed a similar percentage of the cocaine trade in the 1980s. By the end of the decade, Colombia accounted for about 70% of the marijuana reaching the United States from abroad. The drug trade facilitated the development of numerous terrorist organizations in Colombia, including drug cartels, leftist guerrilla organizations, and paramilitary right-wing anti-guerrilla forces. Colombia is a case study and an example relating to the perspective that was previously discussed that, when viewed cross-nationally, murder on a wide-scale basis is closely related to inequality and the resulting development of groups protesting that inequality. Drug cartels that engaged in terrorist acts in Colombia included the Medellin Cartel and the Cali Cartel. The Cali Cartel has its own military wing. The leader of the military wing was recently captured by Colombian authorities. This person, identified as Loiza Ceballos (aka "The Scorpion") is believed to have taken part in the massacre of 100 peasants who refused to cooperate with the cartel. The peasants were murdered with chainsaws.

Colombia's first generation of traffickers, the "cocaine cowboys" typified by Pablo Escobar's Medellin Cartel, trained legions of young assassins, kept mounds of cash in wicker baskets, and concentrated operations in specific regions. Flaunting their wealth and defying authorities, they went down in flames in the early 1990s with the death of Medellin cartel leader Escobar in a police shootout in 1993. This cartel had waged a war on the state that killed hundreds.

Both leftist antigovernment guerrilla organizations and right-wing paramilitary organizations arising to combat the leftist groups have engaged in acts of terrorism and have been financed through drugs. The Leftist groups included the Revolutionary Armed Forces of Colombia (FARC), The 19th of April Movement, the National Liberation Army (ELN), and the Popular Liberation Army. The ELN was formed in 1965 by Cuban-inspired urban intellectuals and is financed through drugs and the Iranian-backed "Hezbollah of Colombia and Venezuela."[185] FARC was established in 1964 as a military wing of the Colombian Communist Party, with 9,000–12,000 armed members, operating with impunity through much of the country. The FARC has become increasingly involved in the illegal drug trade. They have been involved in either the processing or the exporting of cocaine.

The FARC demands as much as $15,000 per flight of every drug-carrying plane that takes off from an airstrip that they guard. The drug cartels are said to be willing to pay the guerrillas $20,000 for every plane or helicopter that is involved in antinarcotics operations and is shot down.[186] Right-wing terrorist groups became increasingly active during the Barco administration and repeatedly targeted for assassination many public officials and guerrilla organizations. Several groups, however, have distinguished themselves for their national-level operations. The most prominent of these were Death to Kidnappers and the Extraditables, both of which had ties to the narcotics traffickers. NGOs have attributed a large majority of political killings, social cleansing killings, and forced disappearances to paramilitary groups. According to military estimates, the United Self-Defense Forces of Colombia (AUC) paramilitary umbrella organization has a membership of 8,000 and 11,000 combatants. The AUC exercised increasing influence during the year 2001 and fought to extend its presence through violence and intimidation into areas previously under guerrilla control, while conducting selective killings of civilians whom it alleged had collaborated with guerrillas. Throughout the country, paramilitary groups killed, tortured, and threatened civilians suspected of sympathizing with guerrillas in an orchestrated campaign to terrorize them into fleeing their homes, to deprive guerrillas of civilian support, and to allow paramilitary forces to challenge FARC and ELN for control of narcotics cultivations and strategically important territories. They also fought guerrillas for control of some lucrative coca-growing regions and engaged directly in narcotics production and trafficking. On the other hand, the FARC and ELN regularly attacked civilian populations, committed massacres and summary executions, and killed medical and religious personnel. In many places, guerrillas collected "war taxes"; forced members of the citizenry into their ranks; forced small farmers to grow illicit crops; and regulated travel, commerce, and other activities.

Commentary

Both South Africa and Colombia demonstrate the conditions leading to extremely high rates of murder. These conditions include extremely high rates of inequality and a history of colonial domination by one race (whites) over another (blacks in the case of South Africa, Indians or Mestizos in the case of Colombia). Although these conditions lead to anger and hatred between the underclass and elites, they are not solely responsible for high rates of murder.

What led to violence in these two countries was the development of opposition groups (pro and antigovernment) with the means to engage in widespread combat. While the Zulus of South Africa may have carried out some murders using knives and spears, semi-automatic guns are much more effective in waging guerrilla warfare, and these are expensive. It takes money to wage civil warfare on the level of South Africa and Colombia. In the case of Colombia, that money was supplied by the trade in drugs, and in South Africa, drugs are augmenting "conflict diamonds" as a source of funding violence.

One point referred to in both the earlier country profiles and text boxes is the role of the police in "extrajudicial killings," as well as the support by the police for progovernment paramilitary and/or vigilante groups. How does this observation apply to the United States? The objection may be raised that police violence and vigilante activity cannot account for America's relatively high rate of murder. It is true that it is difficult to investigate extralegal killings by police in America due to the geographical dispersion of the police as well as the lack of civilian oversight in regard to police activities in the United States. However, vigilante activities in the United States date back to the legendary "lynch laws" of the 19th century. Also, one of the topics of concern in the literature is the police use of force and police brutality. Furthermore, there can be no doubt that vigilante groups, such as the Ku Klux Klan, skinheads, militias, and the Guardian Angels, are quite active in America. Furthermore, retaliatory violence on the part of urban youth gangs is often construed by them as vigilante activity. Thus, it seems logical that investigation of police and/or vigilante violence may yield fresh insights into the relatively high rate of murder in the United States, compared to other developed nations.

The United States

The overall murder rate for the United States is low compared to these other countries, but it is even lower in some of the states. The murder rate is quite low throughout the Midwest in states like Idaho, Iowa, Minnesota, Nebraska, North Dakota, and South Dakota. The murder rate is consistently high in Southern states, as shown in Table 6–5.

In 2001, murder rates varied from a low of .9 in South Dakota to a high of 11.2 in Louisiana, and an even higher rate of 40.6 if the District of Colombia is included. Rather than characterize the entire country as high in homicide, it might be more insightful to ask what factors account for the high rates in the states that have a high murder rate, and the low rates in the states with low murder rates. Similarly, by studying countries with extremely high and low rates of murder, we may have developed insights that help us to account for these variations in murder within the United States.

In this chapter, a number of variables and theories have been reviewed, and data have been analyzed, in regard to murder. Murder has been related to the membership in a subculture of violence, social inequality, firearm ownership, brain damage, membership in gangs, drug abuse, alcohol abuse, and even paranoid schizophrenia. Countries have been studied that are high in murder rates. Various international data have been accessed yielding information about some possible universal correlates of homicide. The country studies and international homicide data seem to indicate that social inequality, as measured by the Gini Index, is the lead variable—the greater the social inequality in a country, the greater the homicide rate. What does this all mean for the United States?

Table 6–5 States of the United States Ranked by Rates of Murder[187]

State	Rate	Rank	State	Rate	Rank
Washington, DC	40.6	1	New Jersey	4.0	27
Louisiana	11.2	2	Ohio	4.0	28
Mississippi	9.9	3	Montana	3.8	29
Alabama	8.5	4	Rhode Island	3.7	30
Nevada	8.5	5	Colorado	3.6	31
Maryland	8.3	6	Wisconsin	3.6	32
Illinois	7.9	7	Kansas	3.4	33
Arizona	7.5	8	Connecticut	3.1	34
Tennessee	7.4	9	Utah	3.0	35
Georgia	7.1	10	Washington	3.0	36
Indiana	6.8	11	Delaware	2.9	37
Michigan	6.7	12	Hawaii	2.6	38
Missouri	6.6	13	Nebraska	2.5	39
California	6.4	14	Minnesota	2.4	40
South Carolina	6.3	15	Oregon	2.4	41
North Carolina	6.2	16	Idaho	2.3	42
Texas	6.2	17	Massachusetts	2.3	43
Alaska	6.1	18	West Virginia	2.2	44
Arkansas	5.5	19	Wyoming	1.8	45
New Mexico	5.4	20	Iowa	1.7	46
Florida	5.3	21	Maine	1.4	47
Oklahoma	5.3	22	New Hampshire	1.4	48
Pennsylvania	5.3	23	North Dakota	1.1	49
Virginia	5.1	24	Vermont	1.1	50
New York	5.0	25	South Dakota	0.9	51
Kentucky	4.7	26			

Fortunately, the U.S. Census has produced some state-by-state data on various indices that can be correlated with the FBI's murder data. Correlations between these variables and murder appear in Table 6–6.

First, as with the world data, murder seems to be strongly correlated with income inequality in the United States ($r = .59$). It is also correlated, to a lesser extent, with unemployment ($r = .48$) and poverty ($r = .44$). Murder is very strongly correlated with the percentage of blacks in a state ($r = .81$), suggesting a possible link between murder and a black subculture of violence. However, murder is even more strongly correlated with the black/white income gap (the difference between black and white income by state). This correlation is .84. This is a measure of income inequality between the races. This suggests that it is the income inequality between the races, rather than race per se, that accounts for the differences in murder rates. Murder is strongly correlated with heroin seizures by law enforcement ($r = .57$), but less strongly with cocaine seizures ($r = .11$). This suggests a possible drug trade connection to murder for heroin but not cocaine. Infant mortality is strongly

Table 6–6 **Murder as Correlated with Various Indicators in State Data**[188]

Infant mortality	.78
Percentage birth to unwed mothers	.76
Heroin seizures (Kg rate)	.57
Cocaine seizures (Kg rate)	.11
Gini Index	.59
Percentage of people living in poverty	.44
Unemployment rate	.48
Male unemployment rate	.39
Female unemployment	.53
Percentage black	.81
Black/White income gap	.84

correlated with murder ($r = .78$) and with percentage of births to unwed mothers ($r = .76$). Infant mortality was intended as a proxy for "child abuse" whereas percentage of births to unwed mothers was intended as a proxy for domestic violence. In the final analysis, it would seem that murder is greatest among unemployed blacks living in poverty, living in an abusive family relationship, with a single mother. These circumstances may lead to murder among intimates, or to street gang involvement in the drug trade, which, in turn, may lead to violent gang activity.

The fact that these variables (except for inequality) do not correlate strongly with murder cross-nationally suggest that there are conditions that are unique to the United States that contribute to the aforementioned profile of murder. Most notable among those conditions have been the history of slavery, the breakup of the black family, a loss of manufacturing and other employment, the War on Drugs, and a high rate of imprisonment of African Americans.

SUMMARY AND CONCLUSION

Murder is the unlawful killing without justification or excuse. Cross-cultural analysis indicates that murder includes types not usually covered in American criminology texts, including *dowry murders, honor killings, feticide,* and others. Within the United States, "typical murders" are typically done between victim and offender who are intimate, from an urban area, and disproportionately African American. Although America is characterized as high in its murder rate in most texts, comparative study reveals that the murder rate of the United States ranks 66th out of 159 countries. The rate of murder for the United States is miniscule compared to countries such as Honduras, South Africa, and Colombia.

In America, murder is considered to be the most serious of crimes and is given considerable attention by scholars and in this chapter. Explanations discussed in this chapter included breakdown of "superego" control, violent instincts, evolutionary adaptation, brain damage, mental illness, psychopathy, the subculture of violence, and external restraint. The deinstitutionalization of the mentally ill in the United States may have been a factor in the rising rate of mass murder, including "pseudocommando" mass murders, school killings, and workplace violence. Serial killings, on the other hand, are linked with psychopathy, which has also been termed "sociopathy." Both mental illness and psychopathy have sociological roots. Mental illness, especially paranoid schizophrenia, is connected with low socioeconomic status. On the other hand, peer socialization is a sociological factor in the development of violent tendencies for psychopathic individuals. Psychopathic individuals can be converted to violent killers through a process of peer socialization called "violentization." In this chapter, additional sociological theories of murder included the "subculture of violence" theory and the theory of external restraint. Murder was found positively correlated with social inequality using an international database linked with this text, a finding that supports and helps refine the **external restraint theory.** Profiles of countries with high rates of murder and high rates of social inequality show why inequality is such an important factor in murder. In these countries, right- and left-wing insurgents, terrorists, and paramilitary groups are prevalent, providing the basis for ongoing civil turmoil. The civil turmoil, especially when supported by a profitable black-market dealing in contraband such as illicit drugs or diamonds, leads to a high rate of murder.

With this background of cross-national study, a similar analysis was done for the United States using data reported for the states by the U.S. Census and the FBI. It was found that murder correlates strongly with infant mortality, percentage birth to unwed mothers, poverty, unemployment, and inequality; however, the strongest correlations with murder are the variables "percentage black" and (even stronger) the "black/white income gap." Although these findings are in agreement with the international findings on social inequality using the CCDB, factors unique to the United States are indicated regarding the involvement of African Americans in murder. These are factors that may be traced to events such as America's history of slavery, the breakup of the black family, the loss of manufacturing and other jobs, the War on Drugs, and the high rate of imprisonment of African Americans in this country.

DISCUSSION QUESTIONS

1. Do you think that recent studies of the brain in relation to murder have nullified environmental explanations of murder? What does cross-cultural analysis show in regard to the question of "nature versus nurture" in relation to murder?

2. In your opinion, was it a mistake to shut down most of the mental hospitals in the United States? Which, if any, mental patients do you think should be hospitalized?

3. Do you think most mass murderers are mentally ill? Discuss the evidence for or against this statement.

4. Do findings regarding recent gang violence support the "subculture of violence" theory? Why do you think that gang violence has recently increased?

5. What do cross-national studies say about murder, suicide, and social inequality? How does "external restraint theory" help to explain these findings? What other factors relating to murder, suicide, and social inequality are shown in the country profiles of South Africa and Colombia?

6. In the text box on Honduras, it was suggested that the high murder rate in Honduras in 1998 was related to Hurricane Mitch and "social cleansing." Is there any evidence that something similar occurred during Hurricane Katrina in the United States? Suggestion: Check the Web on this topic.

7. In the country profiles of Colombia and South Africa, it was shown that the police in those countries were allied with white terrorist organizations. Do you think there is any evidence of similar conduct of the police in the United States today and/or historically?

8. Do you think that the high correlation between the percentage of black individuals and the murder rate in the individual states is unique to America or valid cross-nationally? Please explain your reasons.

SUGGESTED WEBSITES

http://www.city-journal.org/html/7_3_a2.html. Essay about the deinstitutionalization of the mentally ill in the United States and its consequences in terms of violent crime.

http://www.hrw.org/press/2003/10/us102203.htm. Results of a study by Human Rights Watch of the prisoners in the United States who are mentally ill and their treatment in prison.

http://www.mayhem.net/Crime/serial.html. Website that defines serial killing and lists notorious serial killers and mass murderers chronologically.

ENDNOTES

1. Winslow & Winslow, 1974, pp. 320–325.
2. Faris, 1934.
3. FBI, 2004, p. 505.
4. Adler, Mueller, & Laufer, 2001, p. 288.
5. Siegel, 2000, p. 332.
6. Siegel, 2000, p. 333.
7. Adler, et al., 2001, p. 288.
8. Gallup, 2003.
9. BJS, 2002b (years 1950–2002); FBI, 2004, Table 1, p. 72 (for years 2003 and 2004).
10. BJS, 2002a.
11. FBI, 1995, Table 25, p. 201; FBI, 2004, Table 25, p. 266.
12. Shuster, 1998.
13. Torrey, 1997, p. 3.
14. Yablonsky, 1990, p. 216.
15. Falcone, 2005, p. 159.
16. Falcone, 2005, p. 230.
17. Schmalleger, 2005, p. 47.
18. Yablonsky, 1990, p. 229.
19. YourDictionary.com, 2000.
20. Geberth, 1998.
21. From Website linked with this text entitled, "Crime & Society: A Comparative Criminology Tour of the World," for the country India, on the Web at *http://www.rohan.sdsu.edu/faculty/rwinslow/index.htm*l hereinafter referred to as the Comparative Criminology Website.
22. Beirne & Messerschmidt, 1995, p.107.
23. Cohen & Felson, 1979.
24. Beirne & Messerschmidt, 1995, p. 106.
25. Lowney, Winslow, & Winslow, 1981, p. 351.
26. Brown, Esbensen, & Geis, 2001, p. 452.
27. Lowney et al., 1981, p. 351.
28. The Telegraph, London, September 30, 2003.
29. Van Eck, 2000.
30. Brown, et al., 2001, p. 452.
31. Winslow, 1968, pp. 58–59.
32. Lowney et al., 1981, p. 351.
33. Freud, 1922.
34. Winslow, 1970, p. 133.
35. Wolfgang & Ferracuti, 1967.
36. Lorenz, 1966.
37. Daly & Wilson, 1988.
38. Buss & Duntley, 2002.
39. Pallone & Hennessy, 1998.
40. Currans & Renzelli, 2001, p. 54.
41. Volkow & Tancredi, 1987; Raine, 1993.
42. Van Winkle, 2000.
43. Raine, Venables, & Mednick, 1997.
44. Mednick, 1977.
45. Rasanen, Hakko, & Isohanni, 1999.
46. Doctor's Guide Publishing Limited, 1995.
47. Hutchings & Mednick, 1977.
48. Eysenick & Gudjonsson, 1989.
49. Ellis, 1987.
50. Raine, 1993.
51. Fishbein, 1990; Walters, 1992; Walters & White, 1989.
52. Akers & Sellers, 2004, p. 63.
53. Raine et al, 1997.
54. *CNN.com*, 2001.
55. Schmalleger, 2002 , p. 296.
56. Levin & Fox, 1996, p. 66.
57. Torrey, 1997.

58. Torrey, 1997, p. 1.
59. Goffman, 1961.
60. Rosenhan, 1973.
61. Weicker, Jr., 1985.
62. Szasz, 1970, p. 24.
63. Scheff, 1966.
64. Laing, 1965.
65. Mishara, 1983.
66. Torrey, 1997, p. 4.
67. Stubbs, 1998.
68. Isaac & Armat, 1990.
69. Torrey, 1988.
70. Institute for Scientific Analysis, 1999.
71. *Bayvida.com,* 2003.
72. Thomas, 1998.
73. Torrey, 1988.
74. Torrey, 1997.
75. Human Rights Watch, 2003.
76. Eronen, 1995.
77. Torrey, 1997, p. 3.
78. Treatment Advocacy Center, 2003.
79. Torrey, 1997, p. 5.
80. Swanson, Hozer, & Ganju, 1990.
81. Steinwachs, Kasper, & Skinner, 1992.
82. Shore, Filson, & Rae, 1990.
83. Martell & Dietz, 1992.
84. Link, Andrews, & Cullen, 1992.
85. Swanson, Swartz, & Essock, 2002.
86. Raphael, 2000.
87. Torrey, 1997.
88. Bourget & Gagne, 2002.
89. Timonen, Miettunen, & Hakko, 2000.
90. *HealthyPlace.com,* 2000.
91. Faris & Dunham, 1939.
92. Dunham, 1944.
93. Faris, 1934.
94. Faris, 1944.
95. Faris, 1944.
96. Comparative Criminology Website: Guyana.
97. Hempel, Levine, & Meloy, 2000.
98. Knight, 2000.
99. Lancaster, 2002.
100. Carcach, Mouzos, & Gabosky, 2002.
101. *Hology.com,* 2006.
102. Bureau of Justice Statistics, 1988, p. 4.
103. Yablonsky, 1990, p. 231.
104. Holmes & DeBurger, 1985.
105. Fox & Levin, 1999.
106. Mendoza, 2003.
107. Riese, 1969.
108. Riese, 1969.
109. Ozarin, 2001.
110. Cleckley, 1941.
111. Siegel, 2004, p. 324.
112. Athens, 1992.
113. Rhodes, 1999.
114. Wolfgang & Ferracuti, 1967.
115. Wolfgang & Ferracuti, 1967, p. 275.
116. Sampson, 1985.
117. Cao, 1997.
118. Campbell, 1984; Hirschi, 1969; Short & Strodtbeck, 1965.
119. Wolfgang, 1958, p. 252.
120. Rosenfeld, 1997.
121. Gastil, 1971.
122. Loftin & Hill, 1974.
123. Henry & Short, 1954.
124. Kanwar, 1989.
125. Henry & Short, 1954, p. 16, 17.
126. Reckless, 1967.
127. Kivivuori & Lehti, 2003.
128. Cundiff, 2001, p. 1.
129. Alpers, 2003.
130. *GunCite.com,* 2003.
131. FBI, 2004, p. 19, 36.
132. Salzman, Mercy, O'Carrol, Rosenburg, & Rhodes, 1992.
133. Cook & Moore, 1999.
134. Killias, 1993.
135. Conklin & Seiden, 1981.
136. Krug, Powell, & Dahlberg, 1998.
137. Krug, et al., 1998.
138. Isenberg, 2003.
139. Malcolm, 2002.
140. The Polling Report, Inc., 2005.
141. Callahan, Rivara, & Farrow, 1993.
142. O'Donnell, 1995.
143. Fox, 1996.

144. Webster, Freed, & Frattaroli, 2002.

145. Bennett & Holloway, 2004.

146. Braga, Cook, Kennedy, & Tonry, 2002.

147. Colin, McDowall, & Wiersema, 1991.

148. Bowers, 2003.

149. Gettings, 2005.

150. Ludwig & Cook, 2000.

151. Lott, 1998.

152. Ayres & Donohue, 2002.

153. Schmalleger, 2003, p. 746.

154. Sherman & Rogan, 1995; Sherman, Shaw, & Rogan, 1995.

155. Goldstein, 1995.

156. Goldstein, Brownstein, Ryan, & Belluccio, 1989.

157. Bureau of Justice Statistics, 2002d.

158. Fox, 1996.

159. Siegal & Senna, 2000, p. 328.

160. Messner, 1983.

161. Fox, 1996, p. 1.

162. Bjerregaard & Lizotte, 1995.

163. Maxson, Gordon, & Klein, 1985.

164. Fox, 1996, Figure 9.

165. Maxsong, Gordon & Klein, 1985.

166. Tanner, 1970.

167. Abu, 1985; Ginat, 1984.

168. Decker, 1996.

169. Yun, 2002.

170. Adler et al., 2004, p. 240.

171. Source: CCDB—Includes all countries in top 10%, but only "developed countries" (highlighted) ranked below U.S.

172. Krug, Dahlberg, Mercy, Zwi, & Lozano, 2002, pp. 308–313.

173. Adler et al., 2001.

174. Central Intelligence Agency. (2002). Field Listing—Distribution of family income—Gini index. Retrieved September 9, 2003 from *http://www.odci.gov/cia/publications/factbook/fields/2172.html* The Gini Index measures the degree of inequality in the distribution of family income in a country. The index is calculated from the Lorenz curve, in which cumulative family income is plotted against the number of families arranged from the poorest to the richest. The index is the ratio of (a) the area between a country's Lorenz curve and the 45-degree helping line to (b) the entire triangular area under the 45-degree line. The more nearly equal a country's income distribution, the closer its Lorenz curve to the 45-degree line and the lower its Gini Index (e.g., a Scandinavian country with an index of 25). The more unequal a country's income distribution, the farther its Lorenz curve from the 45-degree line and the higher its Gini Index (e.g., a Sub-Saharan country with an index of 50). If income were distributed with perfect equality, the Lorenz curve would coincide with the 45-degree line and the index would be zero; if income were distributed with perfect inequality, the Lorenz curve would coincide with the horizontal axis and the right vertical axis and the index would be 100.

175. Durkheim, 1893/1947; 1897/1951.

176. Global Alcohol Database, 2003.

177. Parker, 1995.

178. Parker & Rebhun, 1995.

179. Comparative Criminology Website.

180. Pridemore, 2001.

181. Pridemore, 2002.

182. Comparative Criminology Website: Honduras.

183. Wolf, 1981.

184. Comparative Criminology Website: Colombia.

185. Cromwell, 2003.

186. Macko, 1996.

187. Source: FBI, 2001; note that 2001 data were used for the state-by-state comparisons because they are close to the 2000 Census statistics (with which they will be better correlated with than the current 2004 data. The FBI 2001 data were also used for cross-national comparisons, as the year most recently available as of December 26, 2003.

188. The state data and indices can be found on the Website linked with this text at: *http://www.rohan.sdsu.edu/faculty/rwinslow/links/newlinks.html*

—7—

FORCIBLE RAPE

KEY TERMS

female genital mutilation
forcible rape
forcible sex offense
fixated pedophiles
genocidal rape
marital rape
regressed pedophiles

rape culture theory
sex offenses
sexual assault
sexual coercion
sexual harassment
sexual violence
man in the middle

OUTLINE

Definition
Extent and Trends in Rape
Types of Rape and Rapists

Theories of Rape
Country Profiles

LEARNING OBJECTIVES

After reading this chapter, students should be able to:

1. Distinguish between forcible rape and sexual assault and know why Australia and Canada have replaced the term *rape* in favor of *sexual assault*

2. Be aware of the global problem of sexual violence in the form of genocidal rape, sexual harassment, and the sex abuse of children

3. Understand how the incidence of forcible rape depends upon its definition

4. Describe the extent and trends in rape and account for its declining rate and the possible role of the Violence Against Women Act of 1994 in this decline

5. Discuss a wide variety of typologies of rape and rapists

6. Explain rape from various theoretical perspectives

INTRODUCTION

CASE STUDY: Fred, a Rapist[1]

I am a classic case of progressive perversion. Well, originally I started out as a peeping Tom at about 10 to 12 years old, which is normal in that period. I was active in this with four other brothers, but while they grew out of it, I never did. I never got caught but it was close a lot of times. From there I went to simple assaults on women. I didn't beat them up, just reached out and felt them. Like, we used to hitchhike along the road and women would pick us up. We'd feel them up and they'd say, "No, that's naughty" but we'd still continue. Well, as we hitchhiked and felt women up nobody ever blew the whistle on us. Well, anyway, from that I progressed to attempted rapes. I was really afraid to have forcible intercourse with a woman. Sometimes I would beat on the woman, sometimes no. Some women liked to be raped, and a few times the women thanked me afterwards that this was what they were looking for. This really bolstered my ego; I was 16.

I was born and raised on a farm in Iowa. There were seven kids in my family. I was in the middle. At home we were taught nothing about sex. My parents were of German stock and very reserved. Sex was strictly taboo in the house. It was dirty and filthy and not to be talked about. It was strictly physical attraction with no emotion attached. That's the way I was brought up.

I went on to realize that I hated my mother for the way I was treated as a child and that all I wanted was to have control of the situation. My little brother used to beat the shit out of me, and my mother used to sit there and laugh at me. My brothers didn't progress like I did. I stayed home and was a mama's boy. I was small and slender. They were dating, and I was not. I was very withdrawn and nobody gave a shit about me. I felt very inadequate, not able to associate with other people. My mother took me to a family doctor when I was about 15 and found I had a slight case of large nipples. He poked around and made me feel very embarrassed, and I ran out of his office crying. I hated my mother for this and didn't talk to her for a year.

In terms of relations with my peers in school, I was what you'd call a pretty quiet fellow. I didn't date girls—girls were dirty. Mom always degraded the girl, but Dad gave us the car and money when we'd go out. I double-dated and would pick up girls in the pickup truck, but a girl I really liked and respected—well, I'd never tell my parents about her. There was never any sex play when I dated; I was

afraid of intercourse. I was very sensitive and had mixed-up emotions; I thought I couldn't satisfy a woman. I had underdeveloped testicles and penis until the chief medical officer at prison gave me male hormones. At CMC, California Men's Colony in California, the doctor gave me testosterone proof 100—100 milligrams of the hormone every two weeks. This male hormone is made from bulls' testicles. My testicles and penis are fully developed now, and I'm able to function successfully and completely; it's a hell of a feeling.

Getting back to my story, I progressed to simple assaults on women rather than forcible assaults. This was before the Army. I would kidnap the woman and pull her out in the sticks. I didn't have sexual intercourse or attain orgasm. This was the thing that really shook me up. I just pulled off their clothes and touched them and kissed their nipples. There were cases where we'd have oral copulation. At knifepoint, she'd copulate me back, and I still wouldn't have orgasm. I couldn't do anything and would just let them go. I never got caught because this was a small town, and in a small town they never said anything. I would see the victims every day. They kept their secret, and I kept my secret with them, because the virgin really doesn't want to talk about it—the way it was performed and what I made them do. They don't want to retell it in court. Sometimes there was a sexual overtone, an old girlfriend who jilted me or wives who didn't want to tell their husbands.

When I was in the Army (I joined when I was 17), I never stopped these activities. I went to the Army psychiatrist; blah, blah, was all he said and nothing was ever done about my situation. When I was 19 I was going to get married. I was home on a 48-day leave from the Army to get married and the day before the wedding my fiancée got killed. If she was alive today, I'd marry her. She was the only girl my mother ever approved of, too. When I came home from the Army my dad tried to whip me and I beat the shit out of him. He never touched me again. He says the reason for this was because I was the only one of the boys that ever stood up to him, and he respected me for that. Coming from a dad, that's quite a compliment. My dad was very shrewd. In the Army I went to Ranger school, survival school, and learned how to be very, very sneaky. We specialized in guerrilla warfare, and I specialized in hand-to-hand combat. I was a bayonet instructor for four years. Taught judo and now have learned Kung Fu.

This training enabled me to trust and feel in control of myself. Most of my outfit was criminals or ex-cons. They were willing to serve in the Army to keep from going to prison, such as I did. My dad was also a black belt in karate, and he taught us all he knew when we were kids. He taught us when we were about 10. He'd use the handle from a toilet plunger to hit us quite often. To this day I have scars on my hips and on the back of my legs. He beat us until we bled. Both my parents did this; if one of us did something wrong all of us got beatings. It wasn't just the boys, it was the girls too, up to when they were late teenagers.

I committed my first forcible rape when I got out of the service in Tempe, Arizona. After the Army, I progressed from forcible assaults to forcible rapes. The first rape I committed was when I was 23 years old. It was the first time I attained an erection and experienced orgasm. Before this it always shook me up bad not to attain erection and have orgasm. I was standing at a bus stop, not hitchhiking, when a young woman about 35 picked me up. I pulled a knife on her. She had a low-cut summer dress on, no bra or panties. Her nipples were up at this time so I knew she was sexually excited. She looked like she just came from being seduced. She was still sweating; hair matted down and kind of messed up. Her bra and panties were lying in the back seat so I don't know where she'd been. She was married with a daughter 13 years old. When I pulled the knife on her, she said, "What do you want, the car?" and I said, "Yeah, among other things." "I don't have any money; do you want sex?" she said. I told her I was gonna rip her off. She said she'd let me. I put the knife down on the seat and never took it out again until we got out on the desert. I then drove out in the desert about 30 miles and raped her forcibly. I raped her out on an Indian reservation, which made it a Federal crime—kidnap and rape. When we got out there she told me her husband was an invalid in a wheelchair, and I undressed her in the car as we were driving along. Even though she was willing, because a knife was involved it makes it forcible.

(Fred was prosecuted for this rape and went to prison.) The first time I went to prison I went to a mental institution in California. This was a maximum security hospital for sex offenders. I was there four years and eight months. The reason I went there was that I committed a rape in Arizona where I cut her nipple off with a knife. I had the knife under the nipple, and she jerked away and cut it off. I got shook up and told her I was gonna kill her. Cut her a few more times on the breast and in the pubic area.

She was down on her hands and knees looking for her nipple. Said she was gonna put it back on. She was crying about it, so I just took her clothes and left her there—120 degrees in the sun. Ditched her car later. There was an article in the paper about a car being stolen but nothing about the assault at all. I don't know how she got home, but I saw her about two weeks later and she was still blistered up bad. At that time I didn't give a damn whether she lived or died. I would've preferred that she died 'cause it would've left me in the clear. By the way, I wore disposable gloves every time I pulled a rape. No prints. I thought then about killing her, but I didn't. I was deathly afraid of murder. I asked the court to send me to the hospital. I knew that if I killed somebody I would take my own life. I didn't want to do that. I never felt any guilt about it for three years.

I've been in prison twice, four years each. The reason I went the second time was for a simple assault on my sister-in-law. My older brother is a Ph.D. in psychology, and the night I assaulted his wife we sat and talked. He was my parole officer, by the way, which made it pretty rough at home. I was living with them and found myself falling in love with my sister-in-law. When I assaulted my sister-in-law I had intended to rape her but I just couldn't do it. I broke down and cried. She was very susceptible to rape. She was very open-minded. Nothing shook her up. (The way you can tell women that are susceptible to rape is that they are pretty broadminded and pretty sexy. Sometimes a woman who tries to hide sexuality is very susceptible to rape. What she's really saying is, "I'm a woman but I'm not gonna let anybody know about it, but I dare you to find out.") I told her the problems I was having with myself. Regarding alcohol, I was drunk a few times when I pulled my last crimes. I was drunk the night I assaulted my sister-in-law. My granddaddy had a still, and I started drinking when I was a kid. It has aggravated my crimes. I had also, before, assaulted my mother. I raped both my sisters and felt very guilty about it. I thought about suicide many times and tried to take my life once; hung myself and my eyes were starting to pop out when my mother found me. She cut me down and saved my life. She asked me why I did it and I told her to go screw herself, so she kicked me out of the house. I've never been back, for 15 years.

If I had a choice between a passive and aggressive woman, I would choose the passive one first. I'd be reluctant to rape the aggressive one because I want control of the situation, unlike the way it was at home. There I was pretty much the scapegoat.

Fred's self-analysis provides food for thought as we progress through the topics of this chapter. He gives us some insight as to the definition of rape ("Because a knife was involved it makes it forcible."). He illustrates not just one type of rapist, but several. He also relates what is sometimes called "the rapist's delusion" (Some women like to be raped. . .) in the so-called "culture of rape." The details of Fred's childhood illustrate specific theories. Thus, this one case study helps to provide concrete reality to many generalizations as the discussion of the phenomenon of rape develops in this chapter.

DEFINITION

Although the focus will be on forcible rape in this chapter, some other countries and international organizations conceptualize the problem more broadly as sexual violence. Viewing sexual violence that takes place in the world, there are many forms of it that can take place in different circumstances and settings. The following is a list of types of sexual violence compiled in the WHO World Report on Violence and Health.[2] These include:

- Rape within marriage or dating relationships
- Rape by strangers
- Systematic rape during armed conflict
- Unwanted sexual advances or sexual harassment, including demanding sex in return for favors
- Sexual abuse of mentally or physically disabled people
- Sexual abuse of children
- Forced marriage or cohabitation, including the marriage of children
- Denial of the right to use contraception or to adopt other measures to protect against sexually transmitted diseases
- Forced abortion
- Violent acts against the sexual integrity of women, including female genital mutilation and obligatory inspections for virginity
- Forced prostitution and trafficking in persons for the purpose of sexual exploitation

The link between sexual and other assaults requires additional explanation. At its root, rape is primarily a crime of assault or violence. While not all rapes involve violence, they are invariably carried out with the threat of violence. Under law, force must be proved for a crime to be classified as a forcible rape within the United States. Many rapists themselves have come from a family background of child abuse and even sexual assault by female members of their family. In addition to the family basis of rapes and other sexual crimes, there is a link between rape and other forms of assault, as is shown by an examination of international statistics.

In this chapter, sexual assault (including rape and incest) is discussed. Nonsexual assault (including spousal and child abuse), is the subject of Chapter 9. Forcible rape is given priority, because it is ranked as a more serious crime than robbery or aggravated assault by the FBI.

BOX 7–1

Forcible Rape Replaced by Sexual Assault in Canada

As of 1983, the terms *rape* and *indecent assault* were replaced by *sexual assault* in Canada. The definition of sexual assault can be ascertained by combining Sections 265 and 271 of the Canadian Criminal Code: Section 265 (Assault) states that "(1) A person commits an assault when [generally] without the consent of another person, he applies force intentionally to that other person, directly or indirectly, . . .

(2) This section applies to all forms of assault, including sexual assault, sexual assault with a weapon, threats to a third party or causing bodily harm and aggravated sexual assault." In Section 271 (Sexual Assault), the commentary states that, "Sexual assault . . . is not defined, although an essential element, assault, is elsewhere defined for such purposes. In general, it is an assault under Section 265 (1) committed in circumstances of a sexual nature such as to violate the sexual integrity of [the victim]".[3]

INTERPOL collects data both on sexual assaults and forcible rape, since some countries, such as Australia and Canada, only report data for sexual assaults nationally. The Australian Bureau of Statistics defines **sexual assault** as:

a physical assault of a sexual nature, directed toward another person where that person does not give consent; or gives consent as a result of intimidation or fraud; or is legally deemed incapable of giving consent because of youth or temporary/permanent incapacity. Sexual assault includes: rape, sexual assault, sodomy, buggery, oral sex, incest, carnal knowledge, unlawful sexual intercourse, indecent assault, and assault with intent to rape.[4]

Most countries reporting to INTERPOL report data for both sexual assault and rape; however, the United States only reports data for rape. The FBI, over the years, has reported offense data only for forcible rape, not sexual assault, to INTERPOL. The FBI includes other forms of sexual assault under Part II, where such offenses are classified as sex offenses (except forcible rape, prostitution, and commercialized vice) for which arrest data, but not offense data, are reported. The FBI defines **forcible rape** as, "The carnal knowledge of a female forcibly and against her will. Rapes by force and attempts or assaults to rape regardless of the age of the victim are included. Statutory offenses (no force used—victim under age of consent) are excluded." By contrast the FBI defines **sex offenses** (except forcible rape, prostitution, and commercialized vice) as "statutory rape and offenses against chastity, common decency, morals, and the like. Attempts are included."[5] The FBI is moving toward an expanded definition of rape in developing the NIBRS. In the NIBRS, forcible rape is defined as, "The carnal knowledge of a person, forcibly and/or against that person's will; or not forcibly or against the person's will where the victim is incapable of giving consent because of his/her temporary or permanent mental or physical incapacity or because of his/her youth."

The NIBRS does not include a definition of sexual assault, but does have a broader **forcible sex offense** category that includes not only forcible rape, but also forcible sodomy, sexual assault with an object, and forcible fondling.[6]

There is a trend internationally and by states to adopt the sexual assault approach rather than the more narrow "rape" focus in law enforcement. It is

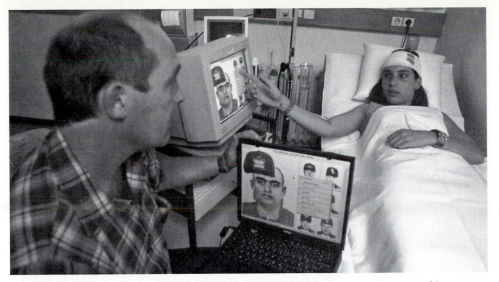

A female assault victim works with a police officer to construct a likeness of her assailant, using computer images to compile facial features and clothing accessories. Better investigation of all violence toward women (rather than just investigation of forcible rape), facilitated by the Violence Against Women Act of 1994, seems to have yielded a decline in all forms of violence against women (as well as forcible rape) in the late 1990s.

Source: Jochen Tack/Das Fotoarchiv, Peter Arnold, Inc.

felt that the broader sexual assault approach encourages victims to report crimes. This is because when a victim reports a rape, she (and it must be a "she" with the FBI's Uniform Crime Report [UCR] definition) must prove that force was used, usually by some evidence that she was injured in some way. This is potentially significant because increased reporting of this crime may be a vital factor in deterrence of the crime.

As mentioned at the beginning of this chapter, the WHO has issued a report that views sexual violence *globally* rather than *parochially*. The WHO report devoted an entire chapter to sexual violence in its various forms and presented perhaps the broadest definition of sexual violence yet to be discussed in this chapter. As discussed earlier, the broader definitions have the advantage of bringing to the surface victimizations that have been ignored, and this can have a positive impact upon lowering the sexual crime rate, and perhaps even the rate of other crimes. In the WHO report, **sexual violence** is defined as "any sexual act, attempt to obtain a sexual act, unwanted sexual comments or advances, or acts to traffic, or otherwise directed against a person's sexuality using coercion, by any person regardless of their relationship to the victim, in any setting, including but not limited to home and work."[7] Some of the types of sexual violence mentioned in that report have not yet been discussed. They include systematic rape during armed conflict, sexual harassment, and sexual abuse of children.

Other Forms of Sexual Violence: Global Perspective

Armed Conflict and Rape

Throughout history, soldiers of conquering armies have assumed that sexual intercourse with their enemies' women was one of the spoils of war. During warfare, rapes of women were socially acceptable as part of the rules of warfare among the ancient Greeks, and even by knights and pilgrims during the Crusades.[8] Some 200,000 Korean women were raped by the Japanese army during World War II, as were some 20,000 Chinese women during the "Rape of Nanking" in 1937. In 1971, Pakistani soldiers raped an estimated 200,000 to 400,000 Bengali women during Bengal's war of independence, after which it became Bangladesh.[9] Rape has also been used in a number of armed conflicts such as those in Algeria, India, Indonesia, Liberia, Rwanda, and Uganda.[10] Data from the Office of the United Nations High Commissioner for Refugees indicated that among the "boat people" who fled Vietnam in the late 1970s and early 1980s, 39% of the women were abducted or raped by pirates while at sea.[11]

The Serbian army recently engaged in **genocidal rape** of Bosnian and Kosovar women during the civil war in the former Yugoslavia. Rape in this case was intentionally used to impregnate Bosnian women with Serbian children. According to Allen, genocidal rape occurred in three forms.[12]

> First, Chetniks or other Serb forces enter a Bosnia-Herzegovina or Croatian village, take several women of varying ages from their homes, rape them in a public place, and depart. Several days later, regular Bosnian Serb soldiers . . . arrive and offer the now-terrified residents safe passage away from the village on the condition they never return. Most accept, leaving the village abandoned to the Serbs and thus furthering the genocidal plan of "ethnic cleansing." Second, Bosnian-Herzegovinan and Croatian women being held in Serb concentration camps are chosen at random to be raped, often as part of torture preceding death. Third, Serb . . . soldiers and militias . . . and Chetniks arrest Bosnia-Herzegovina and Croatian women, imprison them in a rape/death camp, and rape them systematically for extended periods of time. Such rapes are either part of torture preceding death or part of torture leading to forced pregnancy. Pregnant victims are raped consistently until such time as their pregnancies have progressed beyond the possibility of a safe abortion and are then released. In the first case, the death of the victim contributes to the genocidal goal. In the second, the birth of the child [contributes to the genocidal goal by treating] the child to be only Serb and to have none of the identity of the mother.[13]

Although some assume that the United States military would never become involved in wartime rape, it has been charged that U.S. servicemen in Vietnam did, in fact, engage in rape. From the individual rape of barroom girls in Saigon to the mass rape and murder of dozens of civilian women in

BOX 7–2

Violence against Women Byproduct of War in Serbia

A study of questionnaires filled out from calls to the SOS Hotline for Women and Children in Serbia revealed that the frequency and duration of violence toward women was increased as a result of men's participation in the wars in Croatia and Bosnia. The majority of incidents involved physical and verbal/emotional violence, whereas a minority involved sexual and economic violence. A large amount of violence against women was that of sons against their mothers.[14]

the village of My Lai, the Criminal Investigative Division of the United States Army is rife with documentation concerning abuses by Americans. Beyond the brutality of rape, however, was the American military's involvement in the commercial sex business. To maintain soldiers' morale in fighting an unpopular war, the Pentagon knowingly allowed the formation of brothels on base camps throughout Vietnam. Military authorities also organized thinly veiled "sex tours" for Army troops, sailors, airmen, and Marines on leave in Thailand, the Philippines, Taiwan, and other locales.[15]

Wartime rapes have implications for theories discussed in this chapter. Given a situation in which men can rape with impunity, it is evident that a large number of men will participate in this activity, even men whose religious or moral code opposes sex outside of marriage (such as the Pakistani Muslims, as well as the Middle Ages Crusaders). Supported by these instances are the theories that take for granted the willingness to rape on the part of a large proportion of the male population, including routine activities theory, deterrence theory, control theory, and Islamic beliefs.

Sexual Harassment

Sexual harassment is a form of sex discrimination in violation of Title VII of the Civil Rights Act of 1964. Victims of sex harassment can thank Southern politicians for the inclusion of gender in the Civil Rights Act. This is because a group of them pushed to include Title VII (discrimination on the basis of sex) in the Civil Rights Act, hoping that the absurdity of the concept of the sexes as equals would defeat the entire bill.[16] After this, it wasn't until 1980 that sexual harassment actually became a crime. In 1980, the Equal Employment Opportunity Commission (EEOC) of the federal government issued guidelines that determined sexual harassment to be a violation of Title VII. The basis for this ruling was the EEOC conclusion that sexual harassment had been successful in achieving what sexual discrimination had done previously, keeping people out of employment positions solely on the basis of gender. The EEOC defined sexual harassment in its guidelines specifying that employers must prevent "unwelcome sexual advances, requests for sexual favors, and other verbal or physical conduct of a sexual nature."[17] The Supreme Court affirmed the EEOC finding in 1986 in the case of *Meritor vs. Vinson,* followed in 1992 by a Supreme Court decision making sexual harassment in public schools illegal, not only under Title VII but also Title IX (which prohibited gender-based discrimination in schools that receive federal funds).

Because it has been defined as "unwanted or unwelcome conduct that is sexual in nature," the term sexual harassment is extremely vague. It includes "not only sexist jokes and innuendos, 'accidental' collisions and fondling, and constant ogling and pinches, but attempted and completed forcible rape and 'interpersonal coercion.'" Accordingly, there have been widely varying estimates of the extent of sexual harassment in the workplace. These estimates range from 50% to 88% of women being victims, and 31% of men being victims.[18] Recently, the issue of sexual harassment has been highlighted as occurring in schools. One study by the American Association of University Women found that 81% of students experience some form of sexual harassment while in school, with 27% saying it happens often.[19] A large-scale representative study of the United States revealed that 87% of girls and 71% of boys reported having been sexually harassed by another student, whereas rates of sexual harassment perpetrated by teachers were 20% for girls and 8% for boys.[20] Again, the "unwanted sexual behavior" was wide-ranging in nature and varied with gender, as well as the relationship (peer vs. teacher-student). For boys, typical unwanted sexual behavior was name-calling ("Calling me a homo"). For girls the harassment ranged from being groped to being handed a nude drawing of her or a pornographic picture.

Sexual Abuse of Children

As discussed earlier, possibly 20% of girl students in the United States have been sexually harassed by their teachers. However, the situation is even worse in some other countries, particularly in Africa. Internationally, however, sexual harassment that takes place in schools is sometimes of a very serious nature. In an extreme case of violence in 1991, 71 teenage girls were raped by their classmates and 19 others were killed at a boarding school in Meru, Kenya. Also, a report by Africa Rights found cases of school teachers attempting to gain sex, in return for good grades or for not failing pupils, in the Democratic Republic of the Congo, Ghana, Nigeria, Somalia, South Africa, Sudan, Zambia, and Zimbabwe.[21] A recent national survey in South Africa found that schoolteachers were responsible for 32% of disclosed child rapes.[22]

Although the data in the text box suggests that public fear of child abduction and murder may in large part be based upon exaggeration by the mass media, there is one source of information that bears out such concerns—attempted abductions. In a study done in 1992, Finkelhor, Hotaling, and Sedlak found that "stereotypical kidnappings" in which a stranger perpetrator took a child overnight or a distance of 50 miles or more, or killed, ransomed, or evidenced an intent to keep the child permanently, constituted only about 200 to 300 children. However, *attempted* abductions in which an unsuccessful attempt was made to take, detain, or lure a child constituted an estimated 114,600 cases.[23] Thus, while the public fear of child abduction and murder may be excessive, experience with *attempted* child abduction is widespread.

Regardless of conjecture over how many children are abducted and killed every year in the United States, the crime is one that is considered serious in public opinion and therefore merits careful analysis by social scientists. Why would a person resort to the extreme measure of murdering a child? In the case of David Westerfield, his motive probably was to conceal his crime of abduction and/or child rape by "destroying the evidence." Thus, abduction by someone known to the child victim would seem to be a more dangerous situation to the victim than abduction by a stranger. Beyond that, Westerfield's abduction of Danielle van Dam requires an understanding of the motive for the abduction and child molestation.

One study of sexually motivated child abductors compared 97 abducting and 60 nonabducting child molesters who were committed to the Massachusetts Treatment Center and who were in the files of the FBI Academy. The abducting child molesters were more likely to have a low degree of contact with children (outside of their offenses), were more likely to be low in social competence, were less frequently married, were more apt to be classified as sadists, and were more likely to use weapons.[24]

Another study looked at 25 nonfamily child abductors who had murdered their victims and who were serving sentences in several states including Florida,

BOX 7–3

When Sex Abuse Can Lead to Murder

A San Diego County search-and-rescue team canvasses a neighborhood, looking for clues in the disappearance of 7-year-old Danielle van Dam, Tuesday, February 5, 2002. On February 27, 2002, her body was found by a similar team in a rural area in the eastern part of San Diego County. The child's blood was found on the clothing of her neighbor, David Westerfield, as well as in his residence. Westerfield was charged with possession of child pornography, kidnapping, and murder. Danielle's body was found in such a state of decomposition that the identification had to be made with dental records. Westerfield was subsequently sentenced to death for the killing.

Source: Fred Greaves, AP Wide World Photos

Terror struck San Diego, California in 2002 in the form of child abduction, alleged sex abuse, and murder. Seven-year-old Danielle van Dam was first discovered missing from her home on Saturday morning, February 1, 2002. Her father had put her to bed sometime after 10 p.m. on Friday, while her mother was attending a coworker's going-away party at a nearby Poway nightspot. Sabre Springs, where the abduction occurred, is an affluent housing development in the suburbs of San Diego, California. The abduction of Danielle van Dam provided a nightmare scenario— not only in San Diego, but nationally—that a child could be abducted in the middle of the night from her bedroom. Danielle's body was found on February 27, 2002. Ultimately convicted for the abduction and murder of Danielle was the van Dam's neighbor, David Westerfield, a twice-divorced design engineer, who lived alone in a five-bedroom house across from the van Dams. A similar abduction and murder of Polly Klas in 1993 led to the passage of California's "Three Strikes Law," although the van Dam murder situation was quite different. Although Polly Klas's murder was done by Richard Allen Davis, an ex-con who had been arrested 25 times and spent 17 of the previous 20 years in jail, Danielle's murder was done by an upper-middle-class, highly educated engineer with no prior offenses. While the arrest of Westerfield put to rest fears in San Diego that there was a child killer at large, it may have actually increased the fear that child abduction could happen to any family anywhere, regardless of neighborhood.[25]

Unfortunately, child abduction and murder is not a well-researched topic—and noticeably absent in its coverage from most textbooks on criminology, despite its importance. This is not because the act occurs rarely. A study using the FBI's NIBRS found that there were 1,214 kidnappings in 12 states.[26] Lack of coverage probably has to do partly with the fact that perpetrators are rarely caught for this crime and partly because those who are caught vary from each other so much as to defy analysis. The NIBRS study found that the kidnappings were of three types: those perpetrated by (a) a relative of the victim (49%), (b) an acquaintance (27%), and (c) a stranger (24%). Despite the public fear, only one death was associated with these juvenile kidnappings. Child abduction-murders become high-profile cases and occupy the public consciousness through 24-hour news reporting; however, hard research reveals that such killings constitute a small proportion of all killings, even of children. Hotaling and Finkelhor reviewed five studies in an attempt to derive estimates of the number of stranger-abduction murders of children occurring each year in the United States. They found that estimates of the number of stranger-abduction child murders ranged from 46 to 318, with the best guess being between 52 and 158, substantially lower than what the public has perceived.[27]

Texas, New Jersey, and New York. The offenders were typically white, in the mid-to-late 20s, unmarried, and employed in unskilled or semi-skilled occupations. Although 28% had been sexually abused, over half were raised by their biological parents and viewed their home environment as stable through childhood. The study found that the major identifier was that the subjects were not socially integrated into society in terms of education and personal relationships. However, there were no identifiable demographic or behavioral indicators during childhood or adolescence that could predict the later child abductions and murders.[28]

Probably the most extensive study of some 600 child abduction murder cases across the United States was done in late 1993 by the Criminal Division of the Washington State Attorney General's Office, a study that lasted 3.5 years. The purpose of the study was to determine the characteristics of these cases that could help make future law enforcement investigations more efficient and effective. The study found that 76% of the children who were abducted and murdered were females. The victims and killers were strangers in 53% of the cases, and friends or acquaintances in 39% of the cases. Only 9% of the cases involved parents or intimates who killed the child. Younger girls were more likely to be killed by friends or acquaintances, whereas older girls were more likely to be killed by strangers, as were younger boys. In 60% of the cases, more than two hours passed between the time someone realized the child was missing and the time police were notified. In 74% of the cases, the child was dead within three hours of the abduction.[29] Findings of the latter type have led to the development of the "Amber Alert," in which identifying information on suspected child molesters is posted on freeway signs to try to track suspects as quickly as possible.

It is obvious from the aforementioned analysis that very little research has been done to develop a profile of child abductors and murderers. However, some hints at the motivation for such killings can be given from studies that have been done of the motive for child abduction and murder elsewhere in the world.

One interesting journalistic study of pedophiles was done in England and Holland, suggesting a connection between pedophilia, abduction, and pornographic snuff movies. Police in Bristol discovered, through an informant, a ring of pedophiles exiled from England who were running legitimate gay brothels and trafficking in under-aged boys "under the counter." They had branched out into the production of child pornography, and had killed some of the children in snuff films. Boys were being exported from the economic chaotic Eastern Europe, as well as from the streets of London, to be put to work in the sex industry of western Europe.[30]

Although the English story just discussed pertained to homosexual child abductors and murderers, the American studies discussed earlier pertain mostly to heterosexual abusers. This comparison is parallel to a distinction between two main types of pedophiles—**regressed pedophiles** and **fixated pedophiles.** Regressed pedophiles are individuals who have primary orientations toward adult members of the opposite sex but, due to inability to maintain adult relationships, substitute a female child for the adult sexual partner. Regressed pedophiles otherwise maintain fairly normal relations with adult peers. Fixated pedophiles have poor relations with adults and identify with male children, seeking sexual relationships with them. While the primary targets of regressed pedophiles are females, the primary targets of fixated pedophiles are males.[31]

Aside from abduction for sexual purposes, common in the United States, kidnapping for financial gain or for purposes of terrorism is common in countries characterized by social inequality. Colombia is said to be the kidnapping capital of the world and Honduras has an extremely high rate of kidnapping. Iraq has witnessed a rash of kidnappings during the post 9/11 occupation of that country by coalition forces. The purpose in many of these instances is to terrorize agents of foreign governments who the kidnappers view as interlopers. The goal is to redress grievances and to end domination by foreign influences. What is the connection between these kidnappings that arise from inequality and those that are essentially the product of social isolation of individuals who have an aberrant sexual tendency in the United States? Perhaps the connection is that pedophiles in the United States are, in a sense, the lowest of the low, a bottom caste of individuals, even in prison. Their activities are widely condemned in society, and, realizing their lowly status, they may seek a form of redress from ostracism through the revenge killing of children.

EXTENT AND TRENDS IN RAPE

In 2004, there were 94,635 rapes reported to the FBI, with a rate of 32.2 per 100,000 inhabitants.[32] The rate of rape has declined 2.9% in the United States since 1995. Nationally, some 41.8% of rapes were "cleared" in 2004. ("Cleared" means that the police have "solved" the crime by arresting the perpetrator or know who the perpetrator is, but cannot arrest him because he is out of country, dead, etc.) Estimates of the actual incidence of rape vary considerably, primarily because of disagreement over the definition of rape (see text box on Japan). Probably the broadest definition of rape has been suggested by feminists such as Susan Brownmiller. In her book, *Against Our Will: Men, Women, and Rape,* she argues, "If a women chooses not to have intercourse with a specific man and the man chooses to proceed against her will, that is a criminal act of rape."[33] Based upon a broad definition of rape it has been estimated that between 20% to 30% of American girls now 12 years old will suffer a violent sexual attack during their life.[34] Another study of women of all ages done in San Francisco found that 26% of women had been raped and 44% had been victims either of rape or attempted rape.[35] Probably a better "apples with apples" comparison may be done with NCVS victimization data, because the NCVS uses a definition of rape very similar to that of the FBI— "Carnal knowledge through the use of force or threat of force, including attempts." However, the NCVS data includes both males and females.[36] The NCVS reports an average of 108,950 rapes for the years 2003 and 2004. Based upon this figure, the FBI's count of 94,635 rapes represents 86.9% of actual rapes.[37] In UCR statistics, the rate of rape rose during the 1980s and peaked at 42.8% in 1992.[38] Then it fell each year to a low of 31.8% in 2001, rising again to 32.2 per 100,000 inhabitants in 2004.[39] The NCVS also found that rape victimization declined by 75% from 1993–2004. A possible significant factor in this drop has been the increase in reporting of rape.[40] The percentage of rapes reported to the police increased from 33.9% in 1995 to 56.6% in 2002, although the percentage reporting rape declined to 32.7 in 2003.[41]

In terms of clearance rates, nationally, 41.8% of rapes were cleared during 2004. This clearance rate has declined significantly in recent years. In 1988 the clearance rate was 52% for rape. It was 51% in 1995.

Comparison of UCR with NCVS Incidence and Trend Data

Over time there has been a decrease in rape offenses in FBI statistics and in NCVS data. From 1995 to 2004, the rate of rape in UCR statistics declined from 37.1 per 100,000 to 32.2 per 100,000, a decrease of 4.9 per 100,000, or 13.2%. Rape also declined in the NCVS by an even more sizeable degree. Using the NCVS category of "Rape/Attempted Rape" (the FBI includes attempted rapes in its rape figures), the NCVS rate per 1,000 households declined from 1.1 to .5 from 1995 to 2004, a decline of 54.5%. What makes these data puzzling is a study that was released in the NCVS's 2002 report, which showed that the percentage of "rapes/sexual assaults" reported to the police rose tremendously during this same time period.[42] The percentage reporting to the police rose from around 30% in the 1993–1996 period to around 53.7% in 2002. Such an upward spike in reporting would be expected to result in an increase in reported rape offenses. It is also puzzling that clearances for rape declined in the FBI statistics from 51% in 1995 to 41.8% in 2004. It is counterintuitive to think that lower clearance rates are conducive to lower rates of rape. However, it seems logical that the increased reporting of rapes to the police during the 1990s may have a deterrent effect. Offenders' "brushes with law" may have prevented a repetition of such offenses, even if their cases were handled informally by the police.

FBI Demographic Data

The FBI reports victim-offender information for murder, but not rape. However, forcible rape offenses are studied by month, by region, by state, and by population group (city, suburban, and rural). Arrest data are given in the UCR by gender, age, race, and population group. The FBI does not provide any socioeconomic data on the victims or offenders (income, level of education, occupation, etc.). No reason is given for this omission.

According to the FBI, the largest plurality of rapists is in the age range of 15–24. Teens 15–19 years old committed 20.1% of all rapes in 2004, whereas men in their early twenties (20–24) committed another 19.4% of the rapes, with the rate rapidly falling off after age 24. Rape arrests increase steadily during the teen years, peaking at age 18, and then declining progressively each year thereafter.[43]

Race has been a controversial topic in discussing rape. Amir's Philadelphia study found that 77% of the rapists were economically lower class and black; however, he also found that rapes were typically intraracial, with only 3% being a black offender with a white victim.[44] His study was of Philadelphia police statistics for the years 1958 through 1960. Looking at FBI data, blacks constituted 32.2% of the rape arrests in 2004, and that is a decline from 41.9% in 1995. Whites increased in rape arrests from 55.9% in 1995 to 65.3% in 2004.[45]

NCVS Demographic Data

The NCVS is broader in scope and in its definitions than the FBI UCR. It also is more scientific than the UCR in the sense that it is based upon a random sample of households in the United States. Although the NCVS has been published in summary form for the year 2004, the most recent full report including

BOX 7–4

"Black Peril" and Death Penalty for Attempted Rape in Zimbabwe

During British colonial rule in the early 20th century, the struggle for patriarchal white power in predominantly black Southern Rhodesia (now Zimbabwe) led to the introduction of the death penalty for attempted rape to counter the supposed threat posed by black men to white women, a threat known as the "Black Peril." Over the next 30 years, more than 20 men were executed for this crime.[46]

tables is for 2003.[47] In regard to rape, the NCVS provides information on incidence, offender age, alcohol/drug use, gender, multiple victimizations, victim-offender relationships, and weapons used. The report provides information on victim age, ethnicity, gender, income, and race. In addition, the NCVS is a source of information on victim economic and work-time loss, place of occurrence, police response to reported incident, reporting to police, self-protective measures, series victimizations, time of occurrence, and victim-offender relationship (stranger vs. nonstrangers).

As discussed previously, rape has a different definition in the NCVS than in the UCR. While the FBI defines "forcible rape" as "The carnal knowledge of a female forcibly and against her will (including attempts)," the NCVS defines rape as "forced sexual intercourse including both psychological coercion and physical force." The FBI excludes "psychological coercion" and would classify such acts as "Sexual Offenses (Other)." The NCVS also expands upon forced sexual intercourse to include vaginal, anal, or oral penetration by the offender(s), including penetration by a foreign object such as a bottle, and including attempts, as well as male and female victims. In practice, the FBI and most police in the United States exclude anal and oral penetration, penetration with an object, and cases involving males as victims. Then the NCVS adds another category, sexual assault, which includes "completed or attempted unwanted sexual contact, which may or may not involve force, and can include verbal threats." These acts would probably be included in the FBI's category "Sexual Offenses—Other." In describing the findings in the NCVS, the term "rape/sexual assault" is used when the data are for that more general category (when only such data are presented) and the term "rape" is used to refer to "rape and attempted rape."

To summarize NCVS findings, the picture of rape that is drawn with NCVS data is that rape is an intraracial act, disproportionately done during summer months. The victim is typically unmarried, single, or divorced. The perpetrator is usually a friend, relative, or acquaintance of the victim. Victimization is disproportionately experienced by a low-income, young victim (age 15–19), at or near the victim's home. There is typically no weapon used. Stranger rapes are more likely to be reported by the victims than nonstranger rapes.

The rapist, based upon the aforementioned analysis, appears to be the **man in the middle** in the sense that he tends to be not as close to the victim as the murderer (usually friends or relatives), but closer to the victim than the robber (who is usually a stranger). By implication, the rapist would be an "acquaintance," and the event might qualify as "casual sex," and also by implication the victim is partly to blame for getting herself into a situation where she is "vulnerable to rape." However, the NCVS data seem to reveal that the offender is more than just a casual acquaintance. He is frequently a spouse, former spouse, close friend, or jilted close friend.

There is yet another new report that may shed some light on this "man in the middle" controversy. This is entitled the *Full Report of the Prevalence, Incidence, and Consequences of Violence against Women: Findings from the National Violence Against Women Survey,* to be referred to as the NVAW Survey below.[48]

National Violence against Women Survey

The NVAW survey was a national survey of violence against both men and women, including physical assault, rape, and stalking, that was conducted by phone interviews from November 1995 to May 1996. It included a random

Rape victims are said to be victims twice, the first time by the rape perpetrator and the second time by the criminal justice system. In the photo, a rape survivor shows a survivor booklet to a rape victim at a crisis center. Victim-witness programs are helpful in walking victims through the criminal justice process to help them avoid the second form of victimization. Such programs increase the number of rape convictions by ensuring that the victim appears and testifies at the trial.

Source: Michael Newman, PhotoEdit Inc.

sample of 8,000 men and 8,000 women. Its most prominent findings were as follows:

- Fifty-two percent of surveyed women and two thirds of surveyed men said they were physically assaulted as a child by an adult caretaker and/or as an adult by any type of attacker.
- Of the 17.6% of all women surveyed who said they had been the victim of a completed or attempted rape at some time in their life, 21.6% were younger than age 12 when they were first raped, and 32.4% were ages 12 to 17. Thus, more than half (54%) of the female rape victims identified by the survey were younger than age 18 when they experienced their first attempted or completed rape.
- There is a relationship between victimization as a minor and subsequent victimization. Women who reported they were raped before age 18 were twice as likely to report being raped as an adult. Women who reported they were physically assaulted as a child by an adult caretaker were twice as likely to report being physically assaulted as an adult.
- Violence against women is primarily intimate partner violence: 64% of the women who reported being raped, physically assaulted, and/or stalked since age 18 were victimized by a current or former husband, cohabiting partner, boyfriend, or date.

It was based upon the last point that a significant policy recommendation was made: that violence against women, particularly intimate partner violence, should be classified as a major public health and criminal justice concern in the United States.

The NVAW survey can be criticized on numerous grounds: the fact that it was based upon self-reports that can be untruthful, the fact that it was a telephone survey that had a participation rate of only 72%, and the breadth of its definitions. For instance, rape was defined as "an event that occurred without the victim's consent, which involved the use or threat of force to penetrate the victim's vagina or anus by penis, tongue, fingers, or object, or the victim's mouth by penis. The definition included both attempted and completed rape." This definition is so broad that it is comparable to the NCVS's broadest category of "sexual assault," and would combine both of the FBI's classifications of "Forcible Rape" and "Sexual Offenses." So it is not surprising that the NVAW Survey estimated the number of rapes for women annually at 876,064, a number over double that estimated by the NCVS in 1994, which was 432,100 rapes or sexual assaults. The percentage of lifetime victimizations reported for rape were very similar for white and African American women—17.7% versus 18.8%, respectively. The NVAW Survey found that nearly 10% of surveyed women, compared with less than 1% of surveyed men, reported being raped since age 18. Probably the most important finding in the report was that nearly two thirds (61.9%) of the women were raped by a current or former spouse, cohabiting partner, boyfriend, or date. In comparison, 21.3% were raped by an acquaintance, and 6.5% were raped by a relative. As previously discussed, almost identical results were found for the other two categories of the study, assault and stalking. Although the report found that all forms of violence against women were predominantly "intimate partner" acts, 56.2% of males were assaulted by strangers, and a plurality of males (35.3%) were stalked by strangers. Insufficient data on male rapes existed to determine the victim-offender relationship for those acts.

The Violence Against Women Act (VAWA) of 1994, which provided state grants directed toward reducing violence against women, reflected a domestic violence emphasis in its administration of grants to various states. Both FBI and NCVS data show a precipitous drop in rape, assault, and other crimes since the passage of the act.

TYPES OF RAPE AND RAPISTS

Guttmacher divided rapists into three categories: (a) *explosive*—those in whom the rape is an explosive expression of pent-up sexual impulse, (b) *sadistic*—those who want to injure the victim, and (c) *aggressive criminal*—those who are out to "pillage and rob" and for whom rape is just another act of plunder.[49]

Gebhard and his associates provided a five-fold classification: (a) *assaultive*—men whose behavior involves "unnecessary violence" who have a "strong sadistic element" in them; (b) *amoral delinquents*—those who pay little heed to social controls and treat females strictly as sexual objects; (c) *drunken;* (d) *explosive;* and (e) *double standard,* those who divide females into good and worthy of respect versus bad and not entitled to consideration despite resistance.[50] Of these, the first is the most frequent, and all five constitute about two thirds of the rapists Gebhard studied.

A. Nicholas Groth and Jean Birnbaum developed a similar three-fold typology based on the rape situation that involves *anger, power,* or *sadism.* Groth based his typology on empirical evidence gathered in his capacity as a prison psychologist. *Anger rape* involves expressing and discharging pent-up anger and rage, often involving excessive brutality. The *power rape* has as its goal sexual conquest and the use of only enough force to achieve this objective, whereas *sadistic rape* involves both sexuality and aggression. The *power* type constituted about 55% of offenders studied, while the *anger* type characterized about 40%, and the *sadistic* type about 5%.[51]

A four-fold typology similar to Groth's was more recently developed by Hazelwood and Burgess.[52] The four types included *power-assertive, power-reassurance, anger-retaliatory,* and *anger-excitation rapists. Power-assertive rapists* are hypermasculine males who plan their crimes, use both seduction and considerable force to subdue their victims, and typically attack their victims several times during the same incident. *Power-reassurance rapists* are most typical among rapists who attack strangers, are socially and sexually inadequate persons who typically target victims of their own age through stalking, do not consciously degrade their victims, and may attempt to contact the victim after the rape. *Anger-retaliatory rapists* use rape as a means by which a pre-existing anger is expressed, attacking either the actual source of their anger or a representative, often subduing the victim through immediate application of direct and physical force. *Anger-excitation rapists* plan and carefully execute their rapes and are sexually stimulated and/or gratified by inflicting pain and subjecting the victim to degradation and humiliation.

Dennis Stevens developed a typology based upon interviews with 61 serial rapists, including *lust rapes, righteous rapes, peer rapes, control* and *anger rapes, supremacy rapes,* and *fantasy rapes.*[53] The plurality was *lust rapists* (42%) for whom lust was the primary motive for the rape, a minimal amount of force was used, and targets were selected based upon availability. *Righteous rapes,* constituting 15% of the rapists, justified their rapes as based on a "silent deal" of "sex" that had already been negotiated, with sexual intimacy as the primary objective (as in *lust rape*). *Fantasy rapes* (16%) were an attempt to obtain some imaginary goal that had been part of their past, often involving violence. *Supremacy rapes* (13%) and control and anger rapes (6%) involved using more violence than necessary to accomplish the rape, with the rape being secondary in the offender's mind to the violence fueled by anger. *Peer rapes,* which accounted for 3% of the rapists, involved an offender who attributed the rape to friendships and "running with bad company."

Just as the estimates of the incidence and prevalence of rape vary with the definition of rape that is used, so do the typologies of rapes and rapists. As pointed out previously, feminists argued that the FBI's narrow definition of rape should be broadened. First, it did not include all "forcible rapes," because in some states violent forcible rape of a wife was not considered rape. Thus, feminists advocated that the definition should be broadened to include spousal rape, which led to some changes in state laws. Secondly, the traditional

BOX 7–5

Spousal Rape in Japan

Japan is very low in its rate of rape. Japan's rape rate of 1.75 per 100,000 inhabitants is 121st out of 152 countries of the world. One research study, however, found that in Japan, physical abuse of wives and children, including spousal rape, is not defined by the penal code as a crime. Spousal rape is considered to be a private matter and is more broadly tolerated than elsewhere. In Japan, criminal justice agents and health care practitioners respond to spousal rape with indifference or tolerance.[54]

BOX 7–6

Marital Rape and the Law

In 1980, only three states criminalized **marital rape**, while today marital rape is against the law in almost every state.[55] It should also be pointed out that, even today, 33 out of 50 states permit "marital exemptions." For instance, the man is exempt in many states if the wife was legally unable to give consent because she is mentally or physically impaired, unconscious, asleep, and so forth.[56]

definition of rape excludes situations where the woman is coerced economically (i.e. the boss threatens to fire a female employee unless she provides him with sex).[57] Like Brownmiller, Box and Hale defined rape (perhaps even more inclusively than Brownmiller) as "sexual access gained by any means where the female's overt genuine consent is absent."[58] The suggested broadening of the definition of rape was opposed by Finkelhor and Yllo because it dilutes the meaning of the word "rape." They suggest that rape should be differentiated from **sexual coercion.** They suggested that there are two types of sexual coercion—social and interpersonal. *Social coercion* is exemplified by a woman having sex with her husband when she doesn't want to out of a sense of duty, whereas *interpersonal coercion* might result from job threats from a boss (or divorce threats from the husband).[59] These types would be included under the new title used by the NCVS—sexual assault. Besides interpersonal and social coercion, there is a third type of sexual assault—*assault through seduction.*[60] In this situation, the victim initially decides not to engage in sexual intercourse, but is persuaded through psychological means (cajoling, bullying, etc.) to do so anyway.

Adler, Mueller, and Laufer have suggested a three-fold typology of rape that seems to comply with the FBI's NIBRS definition of rape. This includes *stranger rape, predatory rape,* and *date rape. Stranger rape* refers to a situation where the victim has had little or no prior contact with the offender. By contrast, *predatory rape* involves a man who pretends to engage in legitimate dating behavior, but who intends and plans to rape the victim through deception or force. The latter category may be difficult to distinguish from a *date rape* involving a legitimate dating situation gone badly when force is eventually used to gain sex from a woman who is an unwilling participant.[61] *Date rape* has recently been facilitated by a new designer drug named Rohypnol, or "Roofies," a tranquilizer that produces a sedative effect, amnesia, muscle relaxation, and a slowing of psychomotor response. The drug is often dropped into punch at parties and given to females to lower their inhibitions and facilitate sexual conquest, after which the victim may have no memory of the event taking place. This increases the difficulty for prosecution of such offenses by law enforcement.[62]

More in keeping with the sexual assault approach to rape, another current text in criminology adds a number of types to the aforementioned list to include *gang* versus *individual rape, serial rape,* and *acquaintance rape.* The latter, *acquaintance rape,* includes date rape, statutory rape, and marital rape. *Gang rapes* are defined as those involving multiple offenders, whereas *serial rapes* are those that involve rapists who engage in multiple offenses. *Acquaintance rapes* involve someone known to the victim, including family members and friends.[63]

BOX 7–7

Date Rape in Kenya

Although rape is a very serious offense in Kenya, date rape is not a crime. This is because the culture provides that a woman should stay away from a man who has no ties of consanguinity with her. If she is invited by a man who has no blood relationship with her, she should know that a demand for sexual favor will be a likely prospect. If she does not expect to yield to the possible sexual demand of the invitee, she should decline the invitation. Therefore, in Kenya, Ghana, Nigeria, and many other countries in Africa south of the Sahara, it is inherently contradictory and ridiculous for a woman to report that she was raped by her friend or boyfriend who invited her for a date. The cultures of these countries send a message to women, "Beware in responding to a man's invitation. If you accept the invitation, then you pick the consequences."[64]

THEORIES OF RAPE

When applied to the situation of rape, the various theories discussed in Chapters 3, 4, and 5 must be made applicable to the male-female relationship. Existing Western theories discussed in current texts range from biological theories to macrosociological approaches. However, because the perspective in this text is comparative, it seems desirable to include another view that has received a great deal of attention internationally—the Islamic view of rape.

Biological Theories

As in other aspects of human behavior, genetic or physiological explanations have been advanced to explain the act of rape and other acts of human aggression, as discussed in Chapters 3, 4, and 5. These have included theories based upon genes, the size and shape of cranial cavities, body size and shape, and so on. More recently, the XYY chromosome pattern has been advanced. This explanation is based upon the presence of an extra (Y) chromosome among those who are criminally inclined, particularly among those who are involved in sexual offenses and other acts of aggression.[65] Similarly, recent study of testosterone indicates a link between high testosterone and crimes of sex and violence.[66] Study of "hypermasculine men" indicates that such men might be more likely to engage in sexual violence. They have a callous sexual attitude and believe that violence is manly. They are also impulsive, tend to brag about their sexual conquests, and are more likely to lose control, especially when using alcohol, and may view the female as a legitimate target of sexual violence.[67] Those who believe that excess testosterone causes men to rape (whether or not it is linked with an extra Y chromosome) are likely to also feel that rapists can be treated through castration or chemical castration through use of a drug called Depo-Provera, which "removes the biological and chemical tendencies that are intrinsically linked to the desire to rape in males."[68]

Feminist Susan Brownmiller relied heavily upon a biological approach in developing her theory of rape. She referred to the "structural capacity" of men to rape and women's "corresponding structural vulnerability" to build her thesis of the historical, cultural, psychological, and social factors by which men have used rape as a weapon to dominate women.[69] Sociobiological perspectives that focus upon evolution seem to support this feminist view. According to the evolutionary view, the sexual urge in men developed over time as a means of perpetuating the human species, in that forcible sexual contact historically may have helped spread genes and maximize offspring. Thus it is believed, according to this view, that males still have a natural sexual drive to have sex with as many women as possible.[70] By contrast to men, women are more cautious and want stable partners who are willing to make a long-term commitment to child rearing. Because of this difference, sexual tension is produced that causes men to utilize aggressive sexual tactics, especially when the chance of punishment is low.[71] Critics of the biological perspective have argued that rape is a social behavior that is not instinctual, and the theory should be severely criticized for justifying rape as "natural."

Although the XYY chromosome theory has, for the most part, been dismissed, the newer sociobiological/testosterone approaches remain largely untested.[72] There are some human rights concerns in using actual castration as a cure for sex offending, and potential serious side effects from administration of the drug Depo-Provera. It is also difficult to assure that the offender will continue taking the drug.

Many of the psychological theories of rape are related to the psychological typologies discussed earlier. Generally, psychologists view rapists as socially or sexually inadequate in some way that prevents them from normally relating to the opposite sex. There are various versions of this in the psychological literature: (a) The rapist engages in overassertive and overaggressive sexual behavior to hide feelings of sexual inadequacy; (b) he suffers from inner conflict, inner disharmony, and social isolation; (c) he is overly aggressive toward women to conceal a homosexual tendency; (d) he is sexually aroused only when women put up a fight against his advances; (e) he has a sexual desire for his mother (Oedipus complex) and seeks women who remind him of his mother; and (f) he has been sexually aroused or seduced by his mother during childhood, but the sex was also combined with cruelty toward him.[73]

In regard to the sixth point, there have been some interesting corroborating studies. Groth and Birnbaum found that of the serial rapists they interviewed, more than a majority (60%) reported having been sexually abused during childhood, and 20% reported having been sexually abused by a woman.[74] A study done in New Zealand in the Kia Marama Sexual Offenders Unit found that 67% reported childhood sexual abuse, while 30% reported that the primary or sole abuser had been a woman, typically a mother or cousin.[75] Even stronger evidence of heterosexual childhood molestation is given in a study by Petrovich and Templer. They studied 83 rapists in a California prison and found that 59% of them had been molested by an older women when they were children (compared with 3% of college students in another study), and 82% of the female molesters engaged in sexual intercourse with the boys.[76] These findings on "early erotization" and "precocious sexualization" have led to many studies in the field of psychology having to do with the "cycle of violence." These studies indicate that the victims of sexual abuse may internalize the aggressive and erotized aspects of their early sexual experiences and then turn them into preferred patterns of deviant sexual gratification through a process of social learning, imitation, modeling, and the like. Some new treatments have derived from these findings, which have shown some evidence of being effective with juvenile sexual offenders, but not adults.[77]

In terms of personality type, evidence in the literature is conflicting in regard to convicted rapists who have been studied. In one study of rapists and other sex offenders in Sing Sing Prison, psychologists found that none of the inmates had a normal personality and most of them (70%) showed symptoms of schizophrenia.[78] Another study found a high proportion of serial

Psychological Theories

rapits and repeat sexual offenders could be characterized as "psychopathic" in their personality structures.[79] Other studies have found convicted rapists to be essentially "normal" in personality, and studies of acquaintance rapists in college have found them actually more heterosexually successful (rather than sexually inadequate) than other college students.[80] Along these same lines, Yochelson and Samenow view aggressive sexual behavior as only one of several characteristics of "the criminal personality."[81] In their view, rape and homosexual activity are components of a general way of life marked by the inability to form relationships, treating persons as objects, lack of acceptance of responsibility, absence of guilt, and general antisocial behavior. The sexuality of such individuals is such that they use sex to prove their "manhood" and to "conquer" others. The male criminal tends to begin his sexual activity earlier in life, frequently engages in voyeurism and exhibitionism as well as homosexual and heterosexual activity, but has difficulty in maintaining an erection and reaching ejaculation.

Sociological Theories

Except in terms of the development of general theories of crime, there have been very few contributions by sociologists to the understanding of rape. Within sociology, discussions of rape have related it to participation in the "subculture of violence," to social inequality, and to general values within our culture.

Subculture of Violence

Menachem Amir's theory of rape is an application of the subculture of violence theory to rape. The subculture of violence theory was developed by Marvin Wolfgang[82] as well as Wolfgang and Ferracuti.[83] This theory asserts that a subculture that emphasizes violence and masculinity develops in the lowest socioeconomic class of society as a response to powerlessness. In his study of 646 rape cases from the Philadelphia police files for the years 1958 and 1960, Amir found that 77% of the rapists were economically lower class and black, and in 43% of the cases, the rapes were gang rapes. In the lower class, aggression and exploitation of women were viewed as commonplace. In keeping with the subcultural approach, Amir found that of about 95% of the rapes in Philadelphia, both offenders and victims were of the same race, and in only 3% were the rapists black and their victims white. He found that half of the rapes were committed by a person known to or even friendly with the victim.[84] Among Amir's most controversial findings, however, were his findings on victims. He found that 19% of rapes were "victim-precipitated rape." By this he meant that the victim agreed to sexual relations but retracted before the actual act or did not resist strongly enough when the suggestion was made by the offender.[85] Although this finding of 19% victim-precipitation is probably consistent with the notion that the victims and offenders were members of the same subculture, the use of the term "victim precipitation" as used by Amir may be a distortion of the meaning of the term as originally conceived by Wolfgang. As applied to homicide, Wolfgang had viewed the victim as the initial perpetrator or aggressor, who struck the first blow. Applied to rape, a comparable definition would have the female sexually assaulting the male in some way. Thus, Amir's definition of victim-precipitation in rape was a stretch of the meaning of the term, and probably his counting of cases was an exaggeration, as well. Lynn Curtis did a recount using Amir's data and found only 4% of the rapes in his survey were victim-precipitated.[86] As will be discussed later, Amir's findings have been assailed by feminists as "blaming the victim," resulting in the devaluation of the significance of his research generally.

Social Inequality

Julia and Herman Schwendinger developed an approach to rape that was both feminist and sociological. Utilizing a Marxist perspective, they argued that conditions for the prevalence of sexual violence were directly correlated with economic inequality[87] This hypothesis was validated by a subsequent empirical study.[88]

Rape Culture

Sociological study has been done focusing on a hidden "culture of rape," the cultural values within our society that are conducive to rape. Some of this discussion is a prelude to feminist views that will be discussed later.

The **rape culture theory**[89] is a theory akin to social learning theory. The theory holds that there are various attitudes and values in our culture, including popular myths, which make men more inclined to rape. To the extent that men are exposed to these attitudes and values, they will be inclined to engage in the act of rape. People can be exposed to rape culture through family, friends, acquaintances, work, school, the mass media, and even the legal system. Historically, women have been treated as property in the civil law institution of marriage in the sense that a female is treated as her father's property before marriage and her husband's property after marriage. Women who have been raped are popularly viewed as damaged goods—as "ravaged," "ravished," "despoiled," or "ruined," and divorce rates are high following a rape, owed to the husband's devaluation of "his" property (his wife). Women are treated as property when they are deemed "sex objects" in pornography and other media, and when they are "used sex objects" they are devalued through the use of derogatory terms like "cheap women," "loose women," "easy lay," "slut," and the like. Women as property are also treated as sex objects in "masculinity contests," where relations with women are like a game where the object is to "score" with a "piece of meat," "a piece of ass," a "box," and so on. Rape is also encouraged by the rapist's adoption of popular "myths" present in our culture, the most important of which is the myth that women secretly want to be raped. This belief, sometimes termed "the rapist's delusion," is frequently maintained by convicted rapists who maintain that their victims enjoyed their sexual assault. This myth may spill over into jury trials where the victim is often covertly put on trial to prove that she did not give her consent in the form of the "willing victim myth," making the assumption that it is impossible to rape a woman if she resists ("You can't thread a moving needle."). Lastly, in our culture there are relatively rigid sex roles taught from an early age, that it is feminine to be passive, gentle, weak, childlike, dependent on men, and (by implication) submissive to aggressive or violent men. Such women are sought by rapists as "ideal victims" for rape.

Feminist Theories

The Schwendingers' theory, which treats economic inequality to be a cause of rape along with gender inequality, is considered to be a feminist theory but not a "pure" feminist theory because of their inclusion of the sociological variable of inequality. Pure feminist theories hold gender to be the most

BOX 7–8

Political Rape in Zimbabwe

Zimbabwe ranks 10 out of 152 countries that supplied data for rape. A good share of these rapes were termed "politically motivated rapes" by the Amani Trust, which reported that at least six such rapes were committed during the year 2001 but noted that the figure likely is grossly underreported due to cultural taboos. The attacks targeted female farm workers and health workers. No action was taken against the ruling party supporters who conducted 200 reported attacks on schools in June 2000. Teachers were dragged from classrooms, beaten, and stripped naked in front of their students. Health care workers also were targeted for assault, and nurses were raped. During the year 2001, ruling party supporters continued to target teachers whom they suspected of supporting the opposition. Approximately 1,000 rapes were reported in Harare during the first 10 months of the year—a rate that reportedly was higher than the previous year. Six cases of politically motivated rapes were documented during the year 2001; human rights groups estimate that the actual number of politically motivated rapes may number in the hundreds. Women face many obstacles in filing reports of rape; for example, many police stations are not prepared to handle properly the investigation of such cases. In addition, women are reluctant to file reports because of the social stigma of rape.[90]

significant variable in rape. Pure feminists also blame the dominance of men over women down through the ages as the source of rape. Rape, in turn, is one of the many means of keeping women in their subordinate status.

Susan Brownmiller argued that, from prehistoric times until the present, rape has played a critical function. It is nothing more or less than a conscious process of intimidation by which all men keep all women in a state of fear.[91] Fear of rape is a strong consideration in limiting the mobility of women, both geographic as well as social, as well as pursuing other aspects of individual freedom, such as going to school, playing sports, or just taking a walk in the park. To hold a job, women must transport themselves to the work site, either in an automobile or on public transportation, or by walking. One study of the fear of rape among women concluded that rape is a central fear in the lives of a large proportion of women.[92]

Evidence for the theory of economic domination via rape is varied. One argument made is that the majority of rapes involved men raping women, rather than men raping men (or women raping men). Also, anthropological studies are often cited to support the feminist approach. Peggy Sanday studied 156 tribal societies, finding that of 95 tribal societies, 47% were rape-free, 35% intermediate, and 18% rape-prone. In the rape-prone societies, women were characterized by their low status, poor decision-making power, and separation from men.[93] In addition to male dominance, rape-prone societies were characterized by interpersonal violence, and men were more likely to dominate women through rape if they were faced with diminishing food resources or other difficult circumstances.

In his study of the Gusii people in Kenya, anthropologist Robert LeVine attempted to explain the high incidence of rape among the Gusii. He found that females had more restrictions on nonmarital sexual activities than did males, and there were stronger sexual inhibitions in females than in males.[94] LeVine postulated that both sexes would engage in abstinence if both sexes were restricted sexually, whereas both would be promiscuous if both were unrestricted. However, if only females are restricted, then rape of females by males is the result. Thus, the sexual inequality of females is the key cause of rape.

BOX 7–9

Blaming the Victim of Rape in Pakistan

A 1999 study conducted in Pakistan's two largest cities, Karachi and Lashore, indicated that neither marital rape nor statutory rape are considered to be crimes in that country. Victims of nonfamilial sexual violence are deterred from pressing charges by an adverse legal system that detains some victims of rape for months or years prior to trial on charges of illicit sexual intercourse. Another Human Rights Watch report (1992) found that more than 70% of women in police custody in Pakistan are subjected to physical and sexual abuse, but not a single police official has been subjected to criminal penalties.[95] Mehdi (1990) argued that it is practically impossible for a man to obtain "hadd" punishment (stoning, amputation, whipping) in Pakistan because of the high standard of proof, and for punishment of rape under "tazir" (whipping, imprisonment, and fines) the woman runs the risk of being implicated as an accused in fornication/adultery if she fails to convince the court that rape occurred.[96]

As discussed earlier, much of the feminist literature disputes the conventional FBI definition of rape, which requires proof of force before rape can be established in court. Women can be psychological or economically coerced into a rape through sexual harassment, acquaintance rape, and marital rape. In fact, feminists argue that marital rape has only been recently recognized in law, and that most states do not effectively prosecute it. The exemption of marriage derives from the common law notion that wives are the property of husbands. Feminists argue that unrecorded rapes are highly prevalent in our patriarchal society. In fact, such rapes are often not distinguished from consensual sex and are difficult if not impossible to prosecute in court, owed to the way that gender relations are socially constructed as male dominant (and therefore superior) versus female subordinate (and therefore inferior).[97] Various studies have validated this feminist claim that unrecorded rape is widespread in our society. An old study done in 1957 estimated that as many as 20% of college women had experienced rape.[98] More recently, Mary Koss did a study of rape among college students and found that approximately 28% reported having experienced attempted or completed rape since age 14.[99] One study found a higher figure of 78% for those who reported sexual assault.[100]

Although biological, psychological, and sociological studies discussed earlier have focused upon the perpetrator, the rapist himself, many feminists have focused on the victim of rape. In fact, Amir was widely assailed by feminists for his finding that 19% of rapes were victim-precipitated. Feminists argued that a male bias is revealed in the concept of "victim-precipitated rape." Opponents of the victim-precipitation concept argue that the victim has a right to change her mind whenever she pleases, and that the concept of "victim-precipitated rape" is merely adopting the rapist's judgment and rationalizations. Those who believe that rape is "victim-precipitated" are shifting the blame from the offender to the victim. They also argue that males have an uncontrollable sexual urge that, once initiated, must be gratified, regardless of the consequences, making the male, in essence, not responsible. The explosive male sex drive theory is contradicted by the finding that approximately 82% of rapes are either partially or entirely planned, even according to Amir's data.[101] The lack of comparability to victim-precipitation in the situation of murder has been a major basis for the criticism of the concept of victim-precipitated rape. While it is argued that victim-precipitation is relevant to the

BOX 7–10

Rape Suicide in China

A historical study of rape victims in Qing China during the years 1744–1903 found that in 40% of 1,841 rape cases examined, the rape victims committed suicide. Confucian tradition controlled women's sexuality and demanded their chastity. Accordingly, stringent rape laws made it difficult for victims to proclaim their innocence unless the rape resulted in serious injury or death. Thus, many victims committed suicide after their rape to implicate and avenge their perpetrators.[102]

crime of murder, it is clearly incorrect to apply the concept to rape. As Box and Hale stated, "By what stretch of the imagination do rape victims initiate the sexual assault? Do they actually start to assault sexually the persons who subsequently assault them sexually?"[103]

In fact, our legal system has traditionally taken into account "victim-precipitation" in rape cases to the extent that reputation and degree of consent of the victim have been admissible as a defense.[104] Brownmiller, in opposition to Amir, suggested her definition of rape ("a woman chooses not to have intercourse with a specific man and the man chooses to proceed against her will"), and excluded the defenses of initial consent, contributory provocation, degree of resistance, lack of penetration, and marital relationship.[105] She subsequently proposed legislation that would cover all sexual assaults, be "genderless," include rape in marriage, and vary penalties according to the severity of injury inflicted and threat employed. She advocated the certainty of prison as a deterrent to rape.[106] In essence, Brownmiller was espousing "deterrence theory" as a remedy to the problem of rape. Actually, feminists have been quite effective in spearheading the development of laws such as those advocated by Brownmiller.

The Rape Victim
Although field data pertaining to feminist theories are not sufficient to prove or disprove these theories, the efficacy of laws advocated by feminists may provide some evidence for or against the theories. Feminists have shifted the focus away from the "rapist's perspective" to the point of view of the victim of rape. Rape victims are sometimes treated especially harshly by the legal system, in which victims are considered to be nothing more than a "piece of evidence." Given this system, and the presumptions that the victim "brought it on" herself, the victim becomes an "object" or "thing" to be utilized as evidence.[107] Complaints have arisen of maltreatment by police who are attempting to "get the facts," to push for the pressing of charges, and to initially determine the honesty of the victim as a witness.[108]

Other reactions have arisen in response to treatment by physicians and hospital personnel. These persons must serve a dual role of treating physical injury that the rape victim may have incurred, on the one hand, but, usually with police officers waiting nearby, they are required to serve as "detectives" who must gather evidence about which they may later be required to testify in court.[109] They must obtain a medical and sex history, examine the vagina for evidence of sperm and pubic hair, and, frequently, gather the victim's clothing and hair samples for additional evidence. Furthermore, they may be required to determine the degree of intoxication and the mental state of the victim, as well as prescribe medication and follow-up treatment for possible venereal disease, infections, and pregnancy.[110] In addition, the victim is required to prepare for trial and to undergo a public court proceeding in which the defense attorney attempts to build a case of "reasonable doubt" by cross-examination concerning the degree of consent involved and one's behavior prior to the incident, including alcohol use and past sexual or other personal history.[111] The result of this entire prosecution of rape is often called "rape trauma," or the feeling of having been raped again, but this time by the legal system, and the results are often negative in terms of reactions to the victim as a "spoiled woman." In fact, in 75% to 85% of the cases where the woman who has been raped is married, her marriage ends in divorce within two years following the sexual assault.[112]

It was pointed out in Chapter 3 that Islamic law, based upon the Koran, considers crimes against morality to be the most serious of crimes—*Hudud*—and some are subject to the death penalty. Fornication is subject to flogging as a punishment, whereas rape and adultery are subject to the death penalty, death by stoning.

Islamic Theory of Rape

"Blaming the victim" seems to be characteristic of Islamic countries. Although Islamic scholars consistently maintain that women are equal to men in Islamic countries, there are aspects of the treatment of women in Islamic countries, such as the wearing of the *hijab*, that human rights advocates view as forms of subjugation. Women (potential rape victims) are expected to prevent sexual assault through covering their bodies and faces and those who fail to do so are considered to be "asking for it," as illustrated from the following quote:

> The women, who uncover their beauty and show off their bodies and made-up faces for all to enjoy, expose themselves to be harmed by wolves in human clothing. Allah enjoined *hijab* on the Muslim woman to protect her from harm. He knows his creation, and knows that when women make a dazzling display of themselves, with immodest clothes, perfumed bodies, and made-up faces, it serves to increase the sexual deviance of the overall society.[113]

One consideration pertaining to the status of women is that in court, it takes the testimony of "two virtuous women" to equal that of one man. Another is the requirement that women, as discussed earlier, wear a veil, sometimes called a *burqa, hijab,* or *niqaab.* While the Koran may provide for equality of women, when Islamic law is applied broadly in a nation, harsh restrictions seem to be applied to women. This was seen during the Taliban era in Afghanistan. Taliban leaders had as their objective to set up a pure Islamic state. In Afghanistan, female education, from kindergarten through graduate school, was banned. Employment for women was banned, and it was illegal to wear makeup, nail polish, or jewelry; to pluck eyebrows; or cut hair short; and to wear colorful or stylish clothes, sheer stockings, white socks and shoes, or high-heeled shoes. It was illegal for women to walk loudly, talk loudly, or laugh in public. In fact, one of the Taliban edicts was that "Women, you should not step outside your residence."

The *burqa* covered the women from head to toe, with only a heavy gauze patch across the eyes, making it hard to see and completely blocking peripheral vision. As a result, a large number of women were hit by vehicles. In addition to public veiling, the government ordered all exterior windows of homes to be painted black, and even public transport such as buses were required to have all windows (except driver's) covered if a woman was on board. It was illegal for women to talk to men. The penalty for talking to a man other than father or husband was flogging for a single woman, and a possible death penalty for a married woman.[114]

The Islamic scholar Naik has justified the use of the veil as a means of preventing rape. Naik argues that the veil prevents molestation, and adds:

> The Qur'an says that *hijab* has been prescribed for the women so that they are recognized as modest women and this will also prevent them from being molested. . . . Suppose two sisters who are twins, and who are equally beautiful, walk down the street. One of them is attired in the Islamic *hijab*, i.e., the complete body is covered except for the face and the hands up to the wrists. The other sister is wearing western clothes, a mini skirt or shorts. Just around the corner there is a hooligan or ruffian who is waiting for a catch, to tease a girl. Whom will he tease—the girl wearing the Islamic *hijab* or the girl wearing the skirt or the mini? Naturally he will tease the girl wearing the skirt or the mini. Such dresses are an indirect invitation to the opposite sex for teasing and molestation. The Qur'an rightly says that *hijab* prevents women from being molested. . . . Under Islamic Sharia, a man convicted of having raped a woman is given capital punishment. . . . Implementation of Islamic Shariah will reduce the rate of rapes naturally [and] as soon as Islamic Sharia is implemented positive results will be inevitable. If Islamic Sharia is implemented in any part of the world, whether it is America or Europe, society will breathe easier. Hijab does not degrade a woman, but uplifts a woman and protects her modesty and chastity.[115]

If this line of reasoning sounds familiar, it could be because of its resemblance to Cohen and Felson's "routine activities theory."[116] The theory postulates that crime will occur if there are three elements: (a) motivated offenders, (b) suitable targets of criminal victimizations, and (c) an absence of capable guardians of persons and property. The earlier discussion, like routine activities theory, assumes that there are motivated offenders, but suggests a way to hide suitable targets—under a veil, and as was the case with the Taliban, or behind blackened windows or blankets.

Deterrence Theory

As discussed in Chapter 5, there has been a resurgence of interest in "deterrence theory," which was first developed during the late 18th century by Beccaria and Bentham. In the earlier discussion of feminist theory, it would seem that as gender equity improves for women (e.g., an increase in female income relative to men), rape also increases. If women desire to decrease their chances of rape, obtaining economic equality may be an ineffective method for achieving the goal of less sexual assault. Perhaps joining the workforce increases a woman's chance of sexual harassment, stalking, and even possibly domestic violence in the home. However, there is another form of equality that does seem to be an efficient means by which women can reduce their chances of rape and other forms of sexual assault—*by seeking equality before the law*. Since 1981, rape convictions have nearly doubled in the United States from around 100 per 1,000 rapists to about 200 per 1,000 rapists.[117] One recent factor that has contributed to deterrence (and an increasing conviction rate for rapists and other sexual assaulters) has been the Violence Against Women Act of 1994, which provided state grants directed toward reducing

BOX 7-11

***Delegacias de Policia* in Brazil**

In response to a history of tolerance for violence against women and demands of feminist activists, Brazil established its first all-female-staffed police stations (*Delegacias de Policia*) in 1985. These stations now number 260 throughout the country. An examination of INTERPOL data for Brazil reveals that although reported rapes increased from 8.11 per 100,000 to 15.95 in 2001, aggravated assaults decreased from 255.67 to .61 per 100,000 during those same years. The rise in reported rapes, no doubt, reflects the willingness of victims to report rapes and this, in turn, helps support a declining assault rate.[118]

violence against women. Grants include funds to end violence against women with disabilities, encourage arrest policies and enforcement of protection orders, reduce violent crimes against women on campus, assist sexual assault and domestic violence coalitions programs, improve legal assistance to victims, stop abuse and sexual assault against older individuals, and aid tribal and Indian women. The text box shows a list of states and the changes in rape rates that have occurred from 1995 to 2001, according to the UCR. A study was made of how VAWA funding influenced rape and other violent crimes against women by "The Snapshot Project," a project of the Institute for Child and Family Policy at the Edmund S. Muskie School of Public Service, University of Southern Maine.[119] Some sample statements made in that report for states that significantly decreased their rates of rape are shown in the text box.

It should be noted that though all states received VAWA funding of some sort, not all of them had declining rates of rape. It is possible that in some states, the VAWA funds were not applied effectively, or some change occurred in those states that caused rape to increase, despite funding. However, we have noted that on average there has been a tremendous drop in rape in the United States since VAWA. It seems unlikely that this is a coincidence.

Probably the most important observation from the aforementioned findings is that the states most successful in reducing rape were targeting domestic violence against females (rather than rape or sexual assault, per se) in their observations. There are several possibilities that may be happening. It is subsequently noted that, internationally, assault was the strongest correlate of rape of all of the major crimes, with a Pearson correlation of .66 (see Table 7–2). What this seems to suggest is that in a lot of cases, when the police go after perpetrators of aggravated assault, they also reduce the rate of rape. Also, aggravated assault is a crime often committed by people close to the victim. Rape is sometimes an act of revenge perpetrated by a former boyfriend or husband. So the tie between assault and rape seems to be a logical one; however, that can only account for some of the cases of rape. Probably the most important outcome of targeting domestic violence is that the police, courts, and hospitals set up procedures that curtail the "dual victimization" that traditionally occurred in the case of the rape victim. Medical personnel who are trained to deal with the injuries of domestic violence victims, and who are accustomed to serving as expert witnesses in court, can just as easily deal with sexual assault or rape victims. Fairly sophisticated technology (e.g., culposcopes) was provided by VAWA funding to detect physical trauma to victims of domestic violence. That same technology provides needed technical resources for proving that force was indeed used in the act of rape.

BOX 7–12

Decreased Rape Rate Statements

- **Delaware (−34.2%):** From 1996 to 1997, there was a 67% increase in total calls/contacts to the Rape Crisis Program. That number has increased slightly each year. Since its creation in 1996, the Sexual Assault Nurse Examiners program has conducted 629 hospital accompaniments for sexual assault victims.

- **Maryland (−36%):** The findings from Maryland focus almost entirely on domestic violence toward women rather than rape or sexual assault. Nevertheless, the drop in the rate of rape for Maryland was extraordinary. Some of the points made were: From fiscal year 1997 to fiscal year 1999, the domestic violence homicide rate decreased 40% (in Baltimore City). From fiscal year 1998 to fiscal year 1999, the domestic violence homicide rate decreased 45% (in Montgomery County). Before the Pro-Prosecution training for law enforcement and prosecutors was implemented, the nol pros (*nolle prosequi*, or refusal to prosecute) rate was 56%. Approximately one year after Pro-Prosecution was implemented, the rate dropped to 32%. It currently stands at 3%. This was attributed to the separate Domestic Violence Unit at the Montgomery County Police Department and an improved supplemental report that was devised by this department to assist officers responding to domestic violence calls. Conviction rates for domestic violence offenses have increased 53%, from 38.5% in fiscal year 1996 (pre-grant) to over 59% in fiscal year 2000.

- **New York (−21.1%):** The SAFE program at St. Luke's-Roosevelt Hospital trained 55 practitioners (doctors, nurses, physician's assistants, and midwives) to conduct forensic examinations. In the first year and a half of the program, they treated 166 sexual assault victims in the Emergency Department. More than 63% of those victims reported their cases to the police. The conviction rate in the Kings County D.A.'s office for felony sexual assault was 87.5% in 1999, as compared to an average of 46% in New York State in 1996. In the first two years of Project SAVE, advocacy and counseling for sexual assault victims increased three-fold. In the year before VAWA funding, the New York Prosecutor's Training Institute (NYPTI) at Albany, New York did not conduct any training on domestic violence or sexual assault. In 1998, NYPTI conducted two domestic violence/sexual assault courses for 135 prosecutors. In 1999, NYPTI conducted 14 domestic violence/sexual assault courses for 1714 prosecutors.

- **South Carolina (−28.1%):** Three hundred summary court judges have been trained on domestic violence; prior to VAWA there was no judicial training. Seventy-nine cases have been opened for prosecution since June of 1998; prior to VAWA, domestic violence prosecutions were rare. There was a 174% increase in victims served (321 victims in 1999). In 1999, over 900 students received education regarding dating violence, sexual assault, and stalking; prior to VAWA funding, there were no programs in the Pee Dee area addressing violence against women on campus. SAFE Homes-Rape Crisis Coalition used STOP funding for a Domestic Violence Criminal Court Advocate Program. Prior to receiving VAWA funds, advocates attended 62 criminal court hearings. That number increased to 648 in 1997, 1,171 in 1998, and 1,511 in 1999. Stronger relationships with the Solicitor's Office, police, and judges have resulted in increased cooperation from victims and a positive change in the way victims are perceived and treated.

- **Vermont (−37.9%):** Conviction rates for aggravated domestic assault increased from 48% in 1995 to 60% in 1999. Prosecution of domestic violence cases has increased significantly under VAWA activities, with a rate of 3.9 charges filed per 1,000 in 1994 versus 5.4 charges per 1,000 filed in 1998. The number of alleged perpetrators charged with domestic violence offenses has quadrupled since 1993. Since VAWA, there has been a dramatic shift in sentencing practices for defendants convicted of felony domestic assault. Sentences of incarceration-only have increased from 39% in 1994 to 67% in 1999. Sentences of probation-only have decreased from 17.3% in 1994 to 4.7% in 1999.

In the United States there has been a tremendous increase in prosecutions and convictions for rape over the past 20 years, and a concomitant increase in the willingness of victims of rape to come forth and testify against their rape perpetrators. The resulting reduction in reports of rape (both in the FBI reports and the NCVS) suggests that rape is one act that is amenable

In keeping with the studies of states effectively using VAWA grants, a police officer in this photo conducts an interview with a victim of domestic violence. As suggested in the VAWA study, attention to domestic violence seems to be a key in reducing rates of forcible rape.

Source: Mark Burnett, Stock Boston

to penal sanction. Rates of rape are still high in the United States, at least when compared with those reported by many traditional and Islamic countries. However, rape reduction occurs in Islamic countries at the cost of human liberty. Although the "Islamic solution" to rape is unlikely to take place in America, vigorous prosecution can be used within the United States and possibly by other countries to curtail this serious crime. In summary, the VAWA program entails a vigorous effort to train law enforcement officers, prosecution, judges, medical personnel, and potential victims. All are trained in the appropriate treatment of victims of rape and other violence toward women. The existence of the program helps to carry the message that violence toward women is a serious crime for which penal sanction is necessary.

This suggested link between domestic violence and rape may indicate that rape is an outcome of a "subculture of violence." It seems likely that in neighborhoods where males are assaulting women and children, they may also be assaulting other males in bars, nightclubs, and so forth, and even on the street (in defense of "turf"). Defense of "turf" among gang members has the goal of preventing outsiders' access to their girlfriends, wives, siblings, and children, for sexual purposes. Though Fred the rapist was not a gang member, Fred was violently abused as a child and pursued a "career" of physical and sexual assault upon women as a result. In many ways, rape is part of a general milieu that includes aggravated assault, child molestation, child battering, and spousal abuse. Often instances of child molestation are, in fact, cases that should have been classified as rape, because they have all of the elements of rape; however, the legal system has traditionally prosecuted them through the "family court" or "juvenile court," in a separate jurisdiction that under federal law treats the event with the "least restrictive measures." Child testimony is often not believed, and the court typically reunites the family with an order for them to seek counseling. Often it is only after several instances have been noted by the court that the child is removed from the home, and still the parent perpetrator is not prosecuted. This situation of neglect by the juvenile justice system may itself be the precursor for the high rate of rape and sexual assault that exists in the United States.

COUNTRY PROFILES

Internationally, the United States has a very high rate of rape, especially when compared with other developed nations, as can be seen in the Table 7–1.

The table shows that the United States ranks 14th out of 152 countries of the world in rape. The rate of rape for the United States was 31.77 per 100,000 inhabitants, compared to an average of 12.31 per 100,000 inhabitants for all countries of the world for which data were available. The U.S. rate of rape is more like that of "third world" countries such as Rwanda and Namibia than to other developed nations. Other developed nations have a rape rate of half or less than that of the United States. Clearance rates are relatively low for the United States, compared to other countries. The average clearance rate for rape was 71.32 in the world, compared to 44.3 for the United States. Table 7–1 will be useful to guide us to countries with high and low rates of rape for comparative analysis.

It can be seen from Table 7–2 that rape is correlated very strongly internationally with rates of aggravated assault ($r = .66$). This suggests that when the

Table 7–1 Countries of the World Ranked from High to Low in Rates of Rape[120]

Country	Rate	Rank	Country	Rate	Rank
South Africa	121.13	1	Luxembourg	8.78	56
St. Vincent & the Grenadines	111.44	2	Austria	7.12	60
Gabon	105.07	3	Switzerland	6.61	63
Antigua & Barbuda	84.51	4	Liechtenstein	6.06	68
Botswana	68.46	5	Russia	5.64	74
Anguila	66.67	6	Italy	4.05	86
Grenada	60.00	7	Portugal	3.90	87
Swaziland	59.82	8	Andorra	3.03	99
Bahamas, The	55.85	9	Spain	2.96	100
Zimbabwe	38.38	10	Greece	2.29	105
Namibia	36.89	11	Japan	1.75	121
Rwanda	35.93	12	Nepal	0.77	138
Jamaica	35.00	13	Georgia	0.75	139
United States	**31.77**	**14**	Indonesia	0.63	140
Sweden	23.39	21	Gambia	0.53	141
New Zealand	22.48	22	Azerbaijan	0.47	142
Belgium	18.82	26	Mali	0.46	143
France	17.63	30	Cameroon	0.45	144
Great Britain (England & Wales)	16.50	34	Madagascar	0.39	145
Norway	15.12	36	Myanmar	0.32	146
Iceland	14.53	37	Syria	0.29	147
Finland	11.18	44	Yemen	0.29	148
Ireland	11.06	46	Burkina Faso	0.24	149
Germany	10.45	48	Kuwait	0.20	150
Netherlands, The	10.36	49	Saudi Arabia	0.14	151
Israel	10.11	50	Egypt	0.02	152
Denmark	9.22	53			

Table 7–2 International Intercorrelation Matrix for the FBI's Index Crimes

	Murder	Rape	Robbery	Aggravated Assault	Burglary	Larceny	Auto theft
Murder	1	.35	.25	.14	−.01	−.03	−.06
Rape	.35	1	.36	.66	.39	.22	.04
Robbery	.25	.36	1	.13	.31	.26	.08
Aggravated assault	.14	.66	.13	1	.51	.18	.17
Burglary	−.01	.39	.31	.51	1	.5	.43
Larceny	−.04	.22	.26	.18	.5	1	.16
Auto theft	−.06	.04	.08	.17	.43	.16	1
Index	.01	.35	.36	.43	.82	.8	.61

police make arrests for aggravated assault, they may be netting many of the same perpetrators who engage in rape, and vice versa. Rape is also correlated internationally with robbery and burglary, but not to the extent of its correlation with assault.

Although the fear of rape may be a mechanism that keeps women "in their place," the issue discussed here is whether or not there is a correlation between gender economic inequality and rape. As can be seen from Table 7–3, which shows an index of gender empowerment (income equality between males and females), gender empowerment appears to be a direct correlate of rape, rather than an inverse correlate as posited by some feminist theory (based upon the assumption that gender inequality is a factor that can lead to rape).

Internationally, rape is a moderately strong correlate of economic inequality, as measured by the Gini Index. This refers to economic inequality for both sexes—male and female. However, inequity between male and female income has, to some extent, a reverse effect. It would seem that as women achieve economic mobility, they become even more vulnerable to rape. The international statistics cited earlier do not invalidate the feminist theory that gender economic inequality is a cause of rape, because these data only pertain

Table 7–3 Rape as Correlated with Various Indicators for the Countries of the World

Gini Index	.29
Percentage living in poverty	.08
Percentage unemployed	.14
Lack of freedom	−.20
Percentage Islamic	−.31
Drug arrests	.22
HIV/AIDS	.58
Gender empowerment	.20
Percentage convicted	−.30
Rate juveniles admitted to prison	.34
Adult alcohol consumption	.23
Beer consumption	.22
Wine consumption	.14
Spirit consumption	.15

to officially recorded rape. Men rape women and children when they are economically frustrated, as indicated by the moderate Gini Index correlation with rape ($r = .29$). Table 7–2 also indicates that men rape women and children when they are involved in other crimes, such as robbery, burglary, and especially aggravated assault. This tendency to rape is correlated with the rate at which juveniles are admitted to prison ($r = .34$), suggesting a possibility that predatory sexual attitudes are a product of juvenile imprisonment. There also seems to be a connection between drug arrests, alcohol consumption, and rape. Routine activities theory would suggest that females become vulnerable targets for rape when they engage in drug and alcohol consumption, particularly at bars and clubs. The data in Table 7–3 also suggests that women and children become targets for HIV/AIDS as a result of a sexual encounter with a rapist as well. The correlation between the rate of rape and the rate of HIV/AIDS is strong ($r = .58$). In some instances, the females who become infected are children who are sought by rapists who fallaciously believe that the children are less likely to be infected (or even that having sex with a virgin is a "cure" for AIDS).

Although the price females pay for an active public social life and economic career mobility may be an increased chance of being raped, a counter-offensive directed at male perpetrators seems to be emerging in the United States, as well as an increasing number of countries that are developing policies to prevent violence against women. The success of the counter-offensive is shown in the inverse correlation between rates of conviction and rates of rape cross-nationally ($r = -.30$). This means that the greater the rate of conviction for rape, the less the rate of rape. Thus, while the informal means of control such as the wearing of veils may be a useful method of deterring rape in undeveloped countries, effective criminal justice remedies may be the preferred and equally effective alternative in developed countries.

International data provide insight as to factors that are involved in various crimes cross-nationally. However, country profiles provide a better knowledge of why these factors contribute to a crime. In this case, the profiles can provide an idea of the kind of cultural milieu that contributes to rape. That is,

BOX 7–13

Prison Rape[121]

In December 2000, the Prison Journal published a study based on a survey of inmates in seven men's prison facilities in four states. The results showed that 21% of the inmates had experienced at least one episode of pressured or forced sexual contact since being incarcerated . . . over 50% had submitted to forced anal sex at least once . . . at least 140,000 inmates have been raped . . . a broad range of factors that correlate with increased vulnerability to rape. These include youth, small size, and physical weakness; [and] being white. . . . The perpetrators also tend to be young, if not always as young as their victims. . . . They are frequently larger or stronger than their victims, and are generally more assertive, physically aggressive, and more at home in the prison environment. They are "street smart"—often gang members. They have typically been convicted of more violent crimes than their victims. . . . Prisoners refer to the initial rape as "turning out" the victim. . . . Stigmatized as a "punk" or "turn out," the victim of rape will almost inevitably be the target of continuing sexual exploitation . . . becoming another inmate's "property" . . . literally the slaves of the perpetrators . . . replicating the financial aspects of traditional slavery. . . . Their name may be replaced by a female one. . . . some experts believe that the experience of rape threatens to perpetuate a cycle of violence, with the abused inmate in some instances turning violent himself. Another devastating consequence of prisoner-on-prisoner rape is the transmission of HIV, the virus that causes AIDS.

"rape culture" can be viewed objectively by looking at a country other than our own. Profiled later is a country that is internationally high in rape. Although South Africa is perhaps highest in the world in its rate of rape, that country is profiled in Chapter 6. However, there is a country that is near South Africa that provides an excellent description of how "rape culture" develops—Swaziland. The study of Swaziland will provide a summary description of why rape is so high in that country, with the hope of deriving insights that we can apply to the United States.

Swaziland

Although Table 7–1 shows Swaziland among the top countries of the world for rape with a rate of 59.82 for year 2001, in year 2000 Swaziland had the highest rate of rape in the world with a rate of 127.69 per 100,000 population. Swaziland is a country that has been analyzed quite extensively to help in understanding why the rate is so high.

Swaziland may be characterized as a patriarchal society. It is governed by a traditional monarchy at the national level and by chiefs at the local level. The Swazis derive their name from King Mswati II. It was under his leadership that in 1840 the Swazis migrated and expanded their territory north of Zululand in Mozambique. As a result of Mswati's request for British assistance against Zulu raids into then-Swaziland, the British assumed control of Swazi interests by 1902. While the British expected Swaziland would eventually be incorporated into South Africa, after World War II South Africa's intensification of racial discrimination induced the United Kingdom to prepare Swaziland for independence. As independence approached in the 1960s, several political parties were formed and jostled for independence and economic development. However, these largely urban parties had few ties to the rural areas, where the majority of Swazis lived. King Sobhuza II and his Inner Council formed the Imbokodvo National Movement (INM) and faced an election in mid-1964 against four other parties. The INM won all 24 elective seats in Parliament. After independence was achieved in 1968, King Sobhuza repealed the constitution, dissolved parliament, assumed all powers of government, and prohibited all political activities and trade unions from operating. Sobhuza's successor, Prince Makhosetive, enthroned as Mswati III in 1986, abolished the Liqoqo, a supreme traditional advisory body, and in 1987 a new parliament was elected and a new cabinet was appointed. In June, 2000, the King issued Decree No. 2, which reasserted and strengthened his absolute authority, provided further restrictions on freedom of speech and the press, reinstated a nonbailable offense provision, and provided a mechanism to neutralize the powers of the judiciary and Parliament. All but the nonbailable offense provision was subsequently repealed by the King, after the government received strong condemnation from foreign governments and domestic civil rights groups.

Chiefs have been custodians of Swazi law and custom and have been responsible for the day-to-day running of their chiefdoms. They have also been responsible for maintaining law and order in their respective chiefdoms. They have had their own community police. The police may arrest a suspect and bring the suspect before an inner council within the chiefdom for trial. Chiefs have been an integral part of society and have acted as overseers or guardians of families within the communities. Chiefs have traditionally reported directly to the King. Local custom mandates that chieftaincy was hereditary.

In Swaziland, domestic violence against women, particularly wife beating, has been common, despite traditional restrictions against this practice.

BOX 7–14

HIV/AIDS and Rape in Sub-Saharan Africa and the Caribbean

Many countries in sub-Saharan Africa and the Caribbean have high rates of rape. They also tend to have high rates of HIV/AIDS. In Table 7–3, there is a strong correlation between rape and HIV/AIDS ($r = .58$). Could there be a causal connection between these two variables? South Africa has the highest rate of rape in Table 7–1, and 20.1% of its population is HIV/AIDS infected. There is a myth in Africa, especially South Africa, that having sex with a virgin will cure AIDS. This is an extension of a traditional African belief that sleeping with a virgin is a cure for curses and illness.[122] A Johannesburg city council study found that of about 28,000 men, 1 in 5 believed in the virgin-AIDS cure.[123] According to a WHO Fact sheet (June, 2000), there is a connection between rape and HIV/AIDS in that "Men are seeking younger and younger partners in order to avoid infection and in the belief that sex with a virgin cures AIDS and other diseases."[124] Also, biologically, women who are forced to have sex are more vulnerable to HIV infection because "microlesions which can occur during intercourse may be entry points for the virus; very young women [are] even more vulnerable in this respect," and "Coerced sex increases risk of microlesions."

Although urban women have a right to charge their husbands under both the Western and the traditional legal systems, rural women often have no relief if family intervention does not succeed. This is because traditional (chieftain) courts can be unsympathetic to "unruly" or "disobedient" women and are less likely than modern courts to convict men for wife beating. Rape is common and regarded by many men and the police as a minor offense. Women are inhibited from reporting such crimes by a sense of shame and helplessness, especially when incest is involved. Even in modern courts, sentences are light, typically resulting in several months in jail, a fine, or both.

Women occupy a subordinate role in society. In both civil and traditional marriages, wives are treated as legal minors. A woman generally requires her husband's permission to borrow money, open a bank account, obtain a passport, leave the country, gain access to land, and, in some cases, take a job. An unmarried woman requires a close male relative's permission to obtain a passport.

The dualistic nature of the legal system (Western and tribal) complicates the issue of women's rights. Because uncodified law and custom govern traditional marriage, women's rights are often unclear and change according to where and by whom they are interpreted. In traditional marriages, a man may take more than one wife. Traditional marriages consider children to belong to the father and to his family if the couple divorces. Children born out of wedlock are viewed as belonging to the mother. Under law, a woman does not pass citizenship automatically to her children. Inheritances are passed through male children only.

Just as in the United States, where various myths and fallacies are part of "rape culture," there are comparable fallacious beliefs in Swaziland that are being combated by action groups. A widespread fallacy exists that mistreatment of women and children is sanctioned by Swazi tradition. In 2002, it was in the high mountains and narrow canyons of Hhohho, where up to 70% of small landholder farms illegally cultivate marijuana, that the sensational court case of rapist Jasper Nxumalo was publicized. Nxumalo defended himself against charges of raping his nine-year-old daughter, alleging that the

Bible sanctioned his "family's tradition" of the headman having intercourse with a daughter to achieve a male heir. He claimed that his father, grandfather, and great grandfather had all done the same. His daughter, whom he had abused for four years, became pregnant and gave birth at age 13. Nxumalo was convicted and sentenced to a nine-year prison sentence.[125] Activists have researched Swazi society history and have found no basis for beliefs such as this. Instead, the society-wide pattern of abuse of women and children is attributed to changes in the economy.

Swaziland has a Gini Index (income inequality) of 60.3 (where 39.3 is average for the countries of the world). In the past, rural Swazis lived in multigenerational polygamous farms, which depended on all family members, and thus empowered women and even children. However, today the wage-earning father has replaced the communal system, giving the father more power, but putting him under more pressure, with resulting family strife (including abuse) when he is unable to provide. Recently there was an upswing in abuse cases when Swazi miners lost their jobs in South Africa, and they were sent home to unemployment. In the case of a 16-year-old girl at a halfway house, her father raped and impregnated her. This occurred after he lost his mining job in South Africa. He was angry all the time when he returned home. Her father would not leave, and he beat her until she had sex with him.[126]

The high rape figures given for 2000 followed by a drop for 2001 may be a sign of a rising trend in law enforcement as well as the courts having an impact on the rate of rape. The Swaziland Government has maintained that the spike in rape cases in 2000 and again in 2002 has been indicative of an increase in effective prosecution of rape, with an actual decline of actual rapes as a result of increasing law enforcement effectiveness.[127]

What the Swaziland example appears to indicate is that a combination of factors seem to have produced the highest rate of rape in the world. These include a patriarchal tradition supporting "rape culture myths"; a criminal justice system that ignored or trivialized rape as a crime, particularly for rural women and children; and a growing economic inequality in the country, resulting in abusive relations within traditional families.

Although Swaziland and South Africa have perhaps the highest rates of rape in the world, it would be insightful to analyze countries that have the lowest rates. As it turns out, many of them have had a high Islamic population for some time or have recently "gone Islamic." As was shown in Table 7–3, there is a fairly sizable negative correlation between percentage Islamic in a country and rape ($r = -.31$). This means, in essence, that the larger the proportion of the population that professes Islam as a faith, the less the reported rape in a country. While this correlation is not high enough to hold Islamic belief as a "cure" for rape, the relationship between Islamic belief and reduction in rape is certainly worth careful consideration.

It can be seen from Table 7–1, which lists countries in ascending order by the reported rate of rape, that many of those listed in the "low rape" range are Islamic countries.

In fact, there are no Islamic countries above the average rate of rape for the world's countries (which is 12.31 per 100,000 inhabitants). It should also be noted that these are typically poor countries, but with relatively little economic inequality. They are also below average in terms of the gender equality scores. With these statistics in mind, one of these countries, Egypt, will be profiled next.

Egypt   In 1994, Egypt reported the lowest rate of rape in the world, a rate of .02 per 100,000 inhabitants, in its report to the United Nations. (No report has been given either to the United Nations or to INTERPOL since then.) Given that Egypt has a low rate of reported rape, analysis is made as to why this might be true, but then some evidence will be presented that the rate of rape may not be as low as given in the official reports.

With a population of 68 million people, Egypt is the most populous country in the Arab world, with a high population density of 3,820 persons per square mile in inhabited areas. Egypt is a poor country with a GDP per capita of $3,900 (with $9,100 being average for the countries of the world); however, income inequality is not great. Egypt has a Gini Index (of income inequality) of 28.9, compared to a 39.9 average for the countries of the world. Ninety-four percent of the population is Islamic in religion, mostly Sunni. However, a plethora of Muslim sects have for years created civil disorder within Egypt.

Egypt is widely known for a civilization that dates back to antiquity. It had organized agriculture by 6000 B.C. and was united under a ruler by 3100 B.C. It had a legal system similar to that of nearby Babylonia, where the earliest Code of Hammurabi ("eye for an eye, tooth for a tooth") dated back to 1800 B.C. Egypt was invaded and conquered by Arab forces in 642 A.D., after which Arabization and Islamization and Arab language replaced the indigenous Coptic tongue and belief system. For the next 1,300 years, a succession of Arab, Mameluke, and Ottoman caliphs, beys, and sultans ruled the country. The Ottoman Turks controlled Egypt from 1517 until 1882, except for a brief period of French rule under Napoleon Bonaparte. In 1805, Mohammed Ali, commander of an Albanian contingent of Ottoman troops, was appointed Pasha, founding the dynasty that ruled Egypt until his great-great grandson, Farouk I, was overthrown in 1952. In 1882, British forces crushed a revolt against the Ottoman rulers, marking the beginning of British occupation and the virtual inclusion of Egypt within the British Empire. In deference to growing nationalism, the UK unilaterally declared Egyptian independence in 1922, but subsequently continued to dominate Egypt's political life. In the pre-1952 revolution period, three political forces competed with one another: the Wafd, a broadly based nationalist political organization strongly opposed to British influence; King Fuad, whom the British had installed during World War II; and the British themselves, who were determined to maintain control over the Suez Canal. Other political forces emerging in this period included the Communist Party (1925) and the Muslim Brotherhood (1928), which eventually became a potent political and religious force. During World War II, British troops used Egypt as a base for Allied operations throughout the region.

In 1952, a group of disaffected army officers led by Lt. Col. Gamal Abdel Nasser overthrew King Farouk, whom the military blamed for Egypt's poor performance in the 1948 war with Israel. Nasser established a socialist government and, in response to his neutrality vis-à-vis Russia, he nationalized the privately owned Suez Canal Company, after the United States and the World Bank withdrew their offer to help finance the Aswan High Dam in 1956. Subsequently, Egypt was invaded in October, 1956 by France, Britain, and Israel. Nasser's foreign and military policies helped provoke the Israeli attack of June 1967 that destroyed Egypt's armed forces along with those of Jordan and Syria. Israel also occupied the Sinai Peninsula, the Gaza Strip, the West Bank, and the Golan Heights. Nasser, nonetheless, was revered by the masses in Egypt and elsewhere in the Arab world until his death in 1970.

Nasser's successor, Anwar el-Sadat, shifted Egypt from a policy of confrontation with Israel to one of peaceful accommodation through negotiations, culminating in the Camp David accords in September, 1978, signed by Egypt and Israel during U.S. President Jimmy Carter's presidency. He also attempted to increase civil liberties in Egypt, but his efforts were met by increased sectarian violence that ultimately resulted in his assassination by Islamic extremists on October 6, 1981. Sadat was succeeded by Hosni Mubarak, who has been reelected to the presidency every six years until now.

During his administration, Mubarak has had to contend with religiously inspired activism that has been a source of much of the internal violence, particularly that occurring during the 1980s. In general, Egypt's security forces demonstrated a capacity to suppress widespread violence among Muslim extremists. As of early 1990, most observers believed that the majority of the population had rejected these radical but factionalized fringe groups and that these groups presented no immediate threat to the political system. However, the continuation of civil disorder has forced the perpetuation of "police state" tactics of torture, prolonged detention, and imprisonment, reminiscent of that which was in place during the Nasser regime. Under provisions of the Emergency Law, which has been in effect since 1981, the police may obtain an arrest warrant from the Ministry of Interior upon showing that an individual poses a danger to security and public order. This law allows the authorities to detain an individual without charge, and there is no maximum limit to the length of detention if the judge continues to uphold the legality of the detention order or if the detainee fails to exercise his right to a hearing. In addition to the Emergency Law, the Penal Code also gives the State broad detention powers and it may detain a suspect for a maximum of six months pending investigation. The Penal Code contains several provisions to combat extremist violence. These provisions broadly define terrorism to include the acts of "spreading panic" and "obstructing the work of authorities." Human rights groups have reported that hundreds, perhaps thousands, of persons detained under the Emergency Law have been incarcerated for several years without charge.

With this background and history in mind, how, amidst this turmoil, might a low rate of rape be explained for Egypt. The possible answer is twofold: part of the answer lies in the criminal justice system and the other pertains to the tribal customs and Islamic law that are applied in Egypt. Egypt, over time, has developed a very efficient criminal justice system. The Nasser and Sadat administrations initiated a number of police and law enforcement reforms that professionalized the police. The police were organized at the national level, but a director of police, reporting to the Ministry of Interior, commanded all police within each governorate. In urban areas, police had modern facilities and equipment, such as computers and communications equipment. Almost all commissioned officers were graduates of the Police College at Cairo, and all police had to complete a three-month course at the college. Egypt based its criminal codes and court operations primarily on the Napoleonic model; hence, there are no juries, resulting in a higher conviction rate than common law systems that do employ juries. Rape is a capital crime that carries a possible death sentence, rarely carried out. The government prosecutes rapists, and punishment for rape more typically ranges from three years in prison to life imprisonment with hard labor. If a rapist is convicted of abducting his victim, he is subject to execution. In 1987, Egypt executed two individuals for abduction and rape. In 1999, the government abolished an article of the

Penal Code that permitted a rapist to be absolved of criminal charges if he married his victim. However, marital rape is not illegal. Clearance rates for major crimes are high. The police claim to have solved more than 90% of the major crimes and 75% of the thefts. Although criminal court procedures have been substantially modified by the heritage of Islamic legal and social patterns, a woman's testimony is equal to that of a man's in court. While prisons are overcrowded, the government has renovated and built several prisons in recent years, and provides separate prison facilities for men and women, and for juveniles and adults.

In addition to the effectiveness of the legal system in regard to rape, there are strong norms regarding premarital chastity that stem from the Islamic beliefs. "Honor killings" (a man murdering a female for her perceived lack of chastity) are known to occur, but are not common. In practice the courts sentence perpetrators of honor killings to lighter punishments than those convicted in other cases of murder. Besides fear of being murdered by a family member, females are influenced toward premarital chastity by another widespread practice—**female genital mutilation** (FGM)—the surgical removal of the clitoris. Despite a 1996 decree banning FGM issued by the Minister of Health, a study conducted in 2000 estimated the percentage of women who have ever been married and have undergone FGM at 97%.[128] Although religious leaders have stated repeatedly that FGM is not required by religious doctrine, illiteracy impedes some women from distinguishing between the deep-rooted tradition of FGM and religious practices. Moreover, FGM is an important part of maintaining female chastity, which is a part of religious tradition, and the practice is supported by some Muslim religious authorities and Islamist political activists.

Given the above emphasis upon chastity for both genders, causing both males and females to avoid situations where rape is likely, as well as the extremely efficient (though probably human rights neglecting) criminal justice system of Egypt, it seems credible that Egypt would have a very low rate of rape. However, recent news reports suggest that the actual rate of rape in Egypt may be very much underreported. One online news source suggests that rape is on the increase in Egypt. This is due to economic difficulties of young men affording marriage and frustration with the cultural prohibition on sex before marriage. News stories of rape have exceeded the numbers of

BOX 7–15

Female Genital Mutilation

FGM comprises various forms: *clitoridectomy* (partial or total removal of the clitoris), *excision* (removal of the clitoris and labia minora), and *infibulation* (removal of the clitoris, labia minora, and majora, and stitching of the vulva with a little passage for menstrual blood and urine). FGM is still widely practiced in countries of North Africa, the Middle East, and South East Asia. Some developed countries now include in their criminal codes references to the unlawfulness of such practices (e.g., Sweden, United States, United Kingdom). Many other countries do not make specific reference to FGM, but the practice is dealt with under other legal provisions regarding violence and/or medical care. The report of the Special Rapporteur estimated in 1994 that approximately 100 million women had been sexually mutilated, the majority of them living in 26 African countries and some in Asia, with an increase of "cases" among immigrants in Europe, Australia, Canada, and the United States. With respect to FGM, Focus on Women states: "Globally, at least 2 million girls a year experience genital mutilation, approximately 6,000 new cases every day, five girls every minute."[129]

rapes reported internationally, and in fact the rate of court convictions reported by Egypt to the United Nations in 1994 (the same year it reported a rape rate of .02 to the United Nations) was 2.33 per 100,000 population. This rate is 1,165 times the officially reported rape of .02 reported in Table 7–1. Also, according to an unofficial, unpublished survey by the state-run National Center for Criminal and Social Research, an estimated 10,000 rapes are committed in Egypt each year, but only a handful are formally reported to the authorities. In addition to the humiliation that victims face with the criminal justice system being a deterrent to reporting, up until the abolishment of section 291 of the Penal Code that permitted the rapist to avoid prosecution through marrying his victim, rapes that involved this legal loophole went unreported. The law benefited the victim through avoidance of the humiliation of reporting the crime of rape and the possibility of "honor killing," and, of course, benefited the rapist by insulating him from prosecution. Frequently, though, the rapist got the best of the deal, due to Egypt's biased divorce laws. While men in Egypt can divorce a woman by simply repeating "I divorce you" three times, women can only obtain divorce if the husband agrees or if they have proof of spousal abuse, congenital disease, abandonment, remarriage to a second wife or failure to provide support.[130] So not only could the rapist exploit the law by evading prosecution for rape, but he could also extort the victim for money. Some victims who married the rapist with the intent to divorce were forced to pay the rapist for his consent to divorce. In the case of victims who were looking for security in such a marriage, the rapist could and often did divorce her as soon as he was cleared of charges.

If the aforementioned estimate of 10,000 rapes annually is correct, given Egypt's population of 68 million, the true rate of rape in Egypt would be 14.7 per 100,000. That rate would still be less than half that of the United States rate of 31.77 per 100,000. In the United States, women only report their rape in 54% of the cases. Using that same figure of 54%, the comparable rate of rape for Egypt would be 7.9 per 100,000 inhabitants. Inasmuch as the average rate of rape for the countries of the world is 12.2, this rate would still be low. Based upon Egypt's male-dominated patriarchal Islamic religious system, it is credible that the rate of rape might be higher than reported by that country. However, other factors militate against rape, including stringent religious control, a low rate of economic inequality, and an efficient criminal justice system. For Western countries such as the United States, although it is unlikely that a fundamentalist religious orientation will come to prevail, there is a possibility that the criminal justice system could be "tuned up" to improve the deterrence of rape. A large number of countries are in the same category as Egypt, namely, predominantly Muslim with a low rate of rape and crime in general. There are also a good number of Muslim countries who do not report any statistics to the United Nations or INTERPOL at all, possibly reflecting either their lack of development or xenophobic suspicion of "Western" institutions like the United Nations and INTERPOL. Virtually all Muslim countries who report to the UN or INTERPOL report rates of rape way below the average for the world (which is 12.31), typically from .02 to 3.73. Malaysia and the United Arab Emirates report slightly higher (but below average) rates of 5.78 and 5.95, respectively. All of these countries, with the exception of Bahrain, which is a country that accommodates Western "vices" for tourism purposes and is a military ally of the United States, have low crime rates. Index totals range from 4.72 per 100,000 for Mali to 728.4 for Maldives. (We are excluding Jordan, because it is only 70% Islamic, and Bahrain.) These "low crime" Islamic countries include Afghanistan, Albania, Algeria, Azerbaijan, Bangladesh, Brunei, Comoros, Djibouti, Egypt, Gambia, Guinea, Indonesia, Iran, Iraq, Jordan, Lebanon, Libya, Malaysia, Maldives, Mali, Mauritania, Morocco, Niger, Oman, Pakistan, Qatar, Saudi Arabia, Senegal, Sierra Leone, Somalia, Sudan, Syria, Tajikistan, Tunisia, Turkey, Turkmenistan, United Arab Emirates, Uzbekistan, Western Sahara, and Yeman. Of these, Afghanistan, Guinea, Iran, Sierra Leone, Somalia, Turkmenistan, and Western Sahara do not report crime statistics to the UN or INTERPOL.

The United States   State-by-state analysis reveals a tremendous variation between states in rates of rape. Although 13 states increased in reported rape during 1995–2001, the remaining 37 states experienced a decrease in reported rape. Rape ranged from 78.9 in Alaska to 15.1 in New Jersey. During the period 1995–2001, the average decline in rates of rape for the United States was 9.8%.

Within the United States, what correlations are revealed by a state-by-state analysis? Rape does not seem to correlate as strongly as some of the other crimes (murder, robbery, burglary) with various Census indices, as seen in Table 7–4.

Most of the correlations are consistent with international statistics, except the Gini Index, which is the opposite of that shown internationally for rape. The correlation between the Gini Index and rape within the United States is −.14. This means that rape is inversely correlated with economic inequality (or directly correlated with economic equality) within the United States (although it is a low-level correlation). Contrasting with murder statistics, there is no correlation with percentage black or the black/white income gap. Rape seems to be correlated moderately with male unemployment, and not female unemployment, and it does not correlate with poverty. Rape correlates moderately with the rate of divorce and weakly to percentage birth to unwed mothers, as well as to cocaine seizures, but not heroin seizures. Perhaps the vigorous reporting of and prosecution of rape that has occurred since 1994 has had an impact on these factors within the United States. Thus, proactive prosecution on the part of female victims of rape may have nullified

Table 7–4   **Rape as Correlated with Various Demographic Indicators for American States**

Divorces	.20
Marriages	.07
Infant mortality	.01
Percentage birth to unwed mothers	.13
Child abuse	−.14
Heroin seizures (Kg rate)	.04
Cocaine seizures (Kg rate)	.15
Gini Index	−.14
Percentage people living in poverty	−.01
Unemployment rate	.17
Male unemployment rate	.21
Female unemployment	.09
Percentage black	−.04
Black/white income gap	−.01

some of the usual causes of rape. In the United States today, men don't rape "because they can't." Given the increasing opportunities for consenting sexual activity outside of marriage in America, would-be rapists may be finding sufficient opportunities for sexual gratification without the use of force. And if they still have an urge to "take out their aggressions on someone," they may be turning to other forms of crime (assault, robbery) to vent their frustrations.

SUMMARY AND CONCLUSION

A case study such as Fred's (at the beginning of this chapter) is quite extensive and detailed. As such, it can serve as a vehicle for summarizing the contents of this chapter.

First, in terms of the definition of rape, most of Fred's early deviant sexuality did not meet the legal standard for "forcible rape," but rather might have qualified as sexual assault or even sexual harassment. As such, Fred did not receive a prison sentence until he had committed an extreme act of forcible rape—with a knife.

A large number of typologies were described in this chapter. In terms of the typologies, Fred does not fall consistently into one of the types described. If anything, he could be said to progress from one type to another. For instance, in Groth and Birnbaum's typology, Fred may have progressed from *power,* to *anger,* to *sadism.* So Fred's case reveals that a rapist can fall into any of a variety of types, depending upon the stage of development.

Turning to theoretical perspectives, the psychological theories seem to hold some merit in Fred's case. Fred certainly engaged in over-assertive and overaggressive sexual behavior to hide feelings of sexual inadequacy, and he suffered from inner conflict and social isolation (contemplating and attempting suicide on one occasion). Fred's early voyeurism, heterosexual activity, and difficulty in maintaining an erection and ejaculating brings to mind Yochelson and Samenow's description of *the criminal personality.* In fact, he indicated that he preferred a passive woman, because he needed to remain in control. In terms of sociological theories, Fred seems to best fit the "culture of rape theory." Fred seems to have adopted the cultural myth that some of the victims enjoy being sexually assaulted. His early "simple assaults" may have been done in the company of peers who encouraged each other to "score." However, his later actual rapes were individual acts of aggression.

One consideration not mentioned earlier is the failure of the criminal justice system in Fred's history of countless sexual assaults and rapes. Fred mentioned that prison had benefited him, and had he been caught and treated at an earlier age, he might have been deterred and/or reformed. In addition to the legal considerations, there is no concern with the victims in Fred's dialogue. What happened to all of them? Concern about all of these issues has been advanced by feminist theories.

Among the sex crimes, although forcible rape is the focus of the FBI and law enforcement in the United States, globally a variety of forms of sexual violence are recognized. These include not only forcible rape but forced marriage, forced abortion, forced prostitution, and FGM. In the United States, forcible rape offenses have been declining recently (despite declining clearance rates for that crime), but America still ranks 14th out of 152 countries in the world in its rate of rape. Examination of NCVS data reveals a possible reason for declining rates of rape—a sizable increase in the reporting of that offense by victims to the police. Examination of survey data highlights the significance of prior acquaintance between victim and offender in the crime of rape.

The feminist argument that gender economic inequality fosters rape was contradicted by data from the CCDB that showed the opposite—that rape is positively correlated with gender equality or empowerment. On the other hand, there is evidence that lack of "equality before the law" is a factor in rape because, internationally, rates of conviction are inversely correlated with rape—the lower the rates of conviction, the higher the rates of rape. A country profile of Swaziland illustrated the relationship between legal impunity of offenders and high rates of rape.

Islamic beliefs regarding rape were also discussed in this chapter, namely that rape can be prevented if women cover their bodies with a *burqa* or *hijab*. This explanation was supported with a moderate inverse correlation ($r = -.31$) between percentage Islamic and rates of rape, using the CCDB. A country study of Egypt, a country that reported the lowest rate of rape in the world, is given as a case in point.

The assumption that men are "naturally" motivated to engage in rape, made by biological theory, feminist theory, Islamic beliefs, and routine activities theory seems to be borne out by comparative study. Men can and do engage in rape of enemy women during wartime. Men (and to a lesser extent, women) also engage in sexual harassment in the workplace, and even in schools. To make matters worse, sexual abuse of minors can culminate in murder, under circumstances that require further study.

DISCUSSION QUESTIONS

1. How does the NCVS definition of forcible rape differ from the FBI's definition?

2. Why is the rapist sometimes referred to as "the man in the middle"?

3. What were the major findings of the NVAW survey? What criticisms were made of this study?

4. In terms of types of rapes and rapists, how would you classify Fred, a Rapist (Case Study)? What theory or theories seem to fit his case?

5. What problems do you think exist in enforcing marital rape laws?

6. What is the sociobiological perspective on rape and how has it been criticized?

7. Considering all of the evidence and arguments, what theory do you think works best in terms of the goal of reducing rapes?

8. Do you think that Swaziland is a good example of a "rape culture"? Why or why not?

9. Egypt reported the lowest rate of rape in the world. Do you think this is true? Why or why not?

10. Do you think that rape is a major cause of HIV/AIDS in Africa? Why or why not?

11. Do you accept the analysis that today in America men are less likely to rape than they were in the past because they are deterred from doing so by legal constraints? Explain.

SUGGESTED WEBSITES

http://www.hrw.org/ Website maintained by Human Rights Watch that includes reports on prison conditions, HIV/AIDS, treatment of the mentally ill, and a broad array of human rights issues.

http://www.aic.gov.au/publications/ Website that contains links to a large number of Australian government publications on crime, including the Australian rationale for focusing upon sexual assault, rather than forcible rape.

http://en.wikipedia.org/wiki/Child_sexual_abuse Article that provides a survey of literature on the topic of child sexual abuse, with numerous links to other sites.

http://www.irf.net/irf/main.htm Website for Islamic Research Foundation and source of articles on Islamic views on crime, such as Dr. Zakir Naik's views on rape.

http://muskie.usm.maine.edu/snapshot/profiles.html Website for the Snapshot Project, giving state profiles and findings related to VAWA funding.

http://www.truthorfiction.com/rumors/a/aids-virgins.htm Website pertaining to the widespread belief in Africa that having sex with a virgin will cure AIDS, and its cultural background.

http://www.africahome.com Website providing links to news stories about Africa.

http://www.state.gov/g/wi/rls/rep/crfgm/ 10096.htm State Department's Website pertaining to the practice of female genital mutilation in Egypt.

ENDNOTES

1. Winslow & Winslow, 1974.
2. Krug, Dahlberg, Mercy, Zwi, & Lozano, 2002, pp. 149–150.
3. Cohen & Longtin, 1993.
4. Australian Institute of Criminology, 2002, p. 8.
5. Federal Bureau of Investigation (FBI), 2004, p. 505.
6. Schmalleger, 2002, p. 43.
7. Krug et al., 2002, p. 149.
8. Siegel, 2004, p. 329.
9. Neill, 2000.
10. Krug et al., 2002, p. 156.
11. Swiss & Giller, 1993.
12. Allen, 1996.
13. Bradford, 1996.
14. Mrsevic & Hughes, 1997.
15. Neill, 2000, p. 4.
16. Hall, 1994.
17. Beirne & Messerschmidt, 1995, p. 136.
18. Schur, 1984, pp.136–137.
19. Murray, 2001.
20. Timmerman, 2003.
21. Krug et al., 2002, p. 155.
22. Krug et al., 2002, p. 156.
23. Finkelhor, Hotaling, & Sedlak, 1992.
24. Lanning & Burgess, 1995.
25. A full chronology of the events involving the murder of Danielle Van Dam is given on the Courttv Website: *Courttv.com*, 2006.
26. Finkelhor & Ormrod, 2000b.
27. Hotaling & Finkelhor, 1990.
28. Beyer & Beasley, 2003.
29. Wooley, 2002.
30. Davies, 2000.
31. Wikipedia, 2004c.
32. FBI, 2004, p. 27, 266.
33. Brownmiller, 1975, p. 8.
34. Johnson, 1980, pp. 136–145.
35. Russell, 1983.
36. Schmalleger, 2002, p. 43.
37. BJS, 2004a, p. 3.
38. Disaster Center, The, 2005.
39. FBI, 2001, p. 29; FBI, 2004a, p. 27.
40. BJS, 2004a, Table 3, p. 5.
41. BJS, 1995, Table 91; BJS, 2002e, Table 91; BJS, 2003, Table 91.
42. BJS, 2002e, Table 91.
43. FBI, 2004, p. 292–293.
44. Amir, 1971.
45. FBI, 2004, p. 298.
46. McCulloch, 2000.
47. BJS, 2003; BJS, 2004b.
48. Tjaden & Thoennes, 2000.
49. Guttmacher, 1951.
50. Gebhard, Gagnon, Pomeroy, Christenson, & Hoeber, 1965.
51. Groth & Birnbaum, 1979.
52. Hazelwood & Burgess, 1995.
53. Stevens, 1999.
54. Yokihama, 1999.
55. Siegel, 2004, p. 333.
56. New Criminologist, 2002.
57. Box & Hale, 1983.
58. Box & Hale, 1983, p. 125.
59. Finkelhor & Yllo, 1985.
60. Beirne & Messerschmidt, 1991, p. 72.
61. Adler, Mueller, & Laufer, 2001.
62. Staten, 1996.
63. Siegel, 2004, pp. 331–333.
64. Ebbe, 1993a.
65. Jacobs, Brunton, & Melville, 1965.
66. Dabbs, 1995.
67. Downs & Gold, 1997.
68. Amlin, 2003, p. 1.
69. Brownmiller, 1975, pp. 4–7.
70. Symons, 1979.
71. Ellis & Walsh, 1997.
72. American Psychiatric Association, 1970.
73. Goldner, 1972.
74. Groth & Birnbaum, 1979.
75. Birks, 1996.
76. Petrovich & Templer, 1984.
77. Shaw, 1999.

78. Thio, 1995, p. 147.

79. Porter, Fairweather, Drugge, Herve, Birt, & Boer, 2000.

80. Thio, 1995, p. 148.

81. Yochelson & Samenow, 1976.

82. Wolfgang, 1958.

83. Wolfgang & Ferracuti, 1967.

84. Amir, 1971, pp. 233–234.

85. Thio, 1995, p. 154.

86. Curtis, 1974.

87. Schwendinger & Schwendinger, 1983.

88. Smith & Bennett, 1985.

89. Thio, 1995.

90. Comparative Criminology Website: Zimbabwe.

91. Brownmiller, 1975, p. 15.

92. Warr, 1985.

93. Sanday, 1981.

94. LeVine, 1959.

95. Human Rights Watch, 1992; See also Human Rights Watch, 1999.

96. Mehdi, 1990.

97. MacKinnon, 1989.

98. Kanin, 1957.

99. Koss, Gidycz, & Wisniewski, 1987.

100. Muehenhard & Linton, 1987.

101. Amir, 1971, p. 142.

102. Li, 1999.

103. Box & Hale, 1983, p. 135.

104. Amir, 1971, 265–266.

105. Brownmiller, 1975, pp. 422–433.

106. Brownmiller, 1975, pp. 425–426.

107. Ziegenhagen, 1977, p. 2.

108. Holmstrom & Burgess, 1978, pp. 34–60.

109. Holmstrom & Burgess, 1978, pp. 63–117.

110. Bode, 1978, pp. 126–127.

111. Burgess & Holmstrom, 1976, p. 24.

112. Gordon & Riger, 1989.

113. Joan, 1999.

114. Goodwin, 1998.

115. Naik, n.d., p. 3.

116. Cohen & Felson, 1979.

117. BJS, 1996.

118. Hauzinger, 1998; Hautzinger, 2002; Comparative Criminology Website: Brazil.

119. Muskie, 2000; based upon the success of the 1994 VAWA, VAWA II was passed in 1998, providing continued funding for this project. For more information go to: *http://www.now.org/issues/violence/vawa/vawa1998.html*

120. Data for the United States are for 2001, which was the most recent date shown by INTERPOL as of December 26, 2003. The same rule (most recent year available) was used for other countries. The table includes the United States (2001) and all higher ranked countries, all developed countries, and the bottom 10%.

121. Human Rights Watch, 2001.

122. Lee, 2004.

123. *TruthOrFiction.com*, 2002.

124. World Health Organization, 2000.

125. Integrated Regional Information Networks (IRIN), 2002.

126. IRIN, 2002.

127. Prime Minister, 2003.

128. Office of the Senior Coordinator for International Women's Issues, 2001.

129. Patrignani, 1995.

130. Gubash, n.d., 2003.

8

ROBBERY

KEY TERMS

addict robber
alcoholic robber
broken windows theory
carjacking
drug robbers
economic abundance theory
home invasion robberies
intensive offender

occasional offender
opportunist robber
power-control theory
professional robber
robbery
state-raised youth
strong-arm robbery
target hardening

OUTLINE

Definition
Extent and Trends in Robbery
Types of Robbers

Profiling Robbery
Theories of Robbery
Country Profiles

LEARNING OBJECTIVES

After reading this chapter, students should be able to:

1. Define robbery and distinguish it from other property crimes
2. Perceive how professional robbery careers may be an outgrowth of socialization of offenders in juvenile institutions as "state-raised youth"
3. Distinguish between professional robbers and other types of robbers
4. Understand the role of the criminal justice system in deterring robbery, as well as ways in which the American criminal justice system has failed in this regard

5. See a relationship between drug interdiction and high rates of robbery
6. Draw a relationship between the black/white income inequality in America and high rates of robbery among inner-city blacks
7. See the relationship between cross-national events, such as the drug trade and immigration of refugees, and high rates of robbery in the United States

INTRODUCTION

I come from a wealthy family. My parents were show business people. Looking back, maybe I knew more and experienced more than most kids my age, but I didn't understand it better. I've experienced the total criminal justice system; being through everything past and present that they have to offer. I started at eight years old.

My criminal career was, I think, an accident. I came from a good home and went to a Catholic school and had pretty nice experiences as a child. At some point in time, however, things happened. I trace my beginning in this to riding my bicycle on the sidewalk and in doing this I ran into an elderly old lady and knocked her down. At this point it became hit-and-run bicycle. This got me to the attention of the police. It wasn't too bad an experience because they didn't do too much. They told me I couldn't ride my bike for 30 days. I lost the shock of the thing after a few days and soon was back on the street riding with another fellow on a Sunday morning and it was raining, so we went into an old garage and started a small fire, which soon spread and burned the building down. Now I'm an arsonist. This time they sent me to juvenile hall and locked me up. The first thing they do in any jail, and a thing that I can't help but equate with the criminal justice system, is that they take all your clothes off. A great deal of my life I've spent running around naked. The "home away from home" (juvenile hall) wasn't a bad place but it was a scary place for an eight-year-old boy. I met kids there that were much more sophisticated than I. I didn't like it so I ran home. I ran away with a fellow who was older than I, and stealing a car came very natural to him. It didn't really seem like a very big thing. He knew how to start it and drive it and at that age it was exciting to have such a big, powerful object under your control. Out of this I learned how to steal cars. I ran with a gang, and we'd steal cars and joyride. Some of my gang I'd met in juvenile hall; some I'd met out. Some were on their way in; they'd just been a little bit slicker than me and hadn't got caught. We used to steal the night watchman's car at the old brewery. We did it every night and finally got caught.

My timing is terrible, because I seem to get arrested at a point in time when the authorities want to try new things. So at 10 years old they sent me to reform school. I started out in state reform school, which is our junior reform school. When I arrived, it was at its low. They beat the kids, locked them in stand-up lockers, literally tortured them to death. They had just finished beating one kid to death when I got there, and were hanging him in his room trying to feign suicide. There was an investigation and all kinds of things happened. Father Flanagan of Boy's Town fame was brought out there to try to bring some semblance of order to the place.

His philosophy was that there was no such thing as a bad boy. I ran away from him 13 times. Each time we would pray together and I would swear to him and God that I would not go and sin again, and then in just a short time I'd run. I think he modified his statement after me. I am the only one in the history of State to ever be taken home in handcuffs. They turned me loose to my parents, saying that I was just too much for the reform school. During my 13 escapes I'd steal cars, and when I was released, I went on stealing them. I just fell in love with stealing cars; some I would try and take back to where I'd stolen them. At one point in time they told me that I had run some 120 car thefts that they knew about; there were some that they didn't know about.

Because of further activity, mostly car theft, I was again apprehended. This was at a time when California was recognizing that they had a juvenile delinquency problem. Then, about 1940, there was a movement to do something about the juvenile problem. Someone hit on the idea that the best thing to do with kids who exhibited the same kinds of behavior I did and had some kind of genetic failing that would be impossible to cure was to pass a law called 7050 of the Penal Code, in which it would give the state the right to sterilize these kinds of people and thereby breed them out of existence. They went all over the landscape collecting juveniles and shipping them off to insane asylums across the country. I was sent to [names school]. I'm reluctant sometimes to go into detail about the treatment there because of so many girls present, but this place was not to be believed. The things they did to people were crazy. They beat people, they killed people, they performed weird operations on people, they forced people to have abnormal sex, perverted sex, and they put liniment in your rectum; and this was just standard treatment. I was terrified, and I managed to escape from there—and this is what you're going to find out, is that I'm probably one of the best escape artists. Everyone thinks I'm so slick and keen. Actually, I'm just scared to death and find a way out.

One of the control features at the school was that they kept everybody naked. We're back to that again! I think there's some kind of psychological hold on people if they're running around naked and the authorities have clothes on. They seem to mean more to you. So when I ran from there, I had to run naked. I ran three days and three nights through those mountains naked and with a shaved head—that's another thing they do. During this time in the mountains, I broke into this cabin for food and clothes, and I found a rifle. Until that time, I had never come into contact with a rifle, but I knew by instinct that this was power. Then I got the idea that this gun would make all the difference . . . and I made a plan, and went back to the school. I went back to the ward they had had me on; I stuck up the guards; I turned everybody loose—if you can imagine 350 naked bodies running all over the countryside—I did things to those guards that they had done to me and some things that you wouldn't believe; and every time I think about it I feel good. I really did bad things to them and it really caused quite an uproar—I pushed the war news right off the front page. I really created a stink, but it did do one thing; it brought an investigation to the school, one of the superintendents of 20 years was fired, several of the guards were imprisoned. It was just a snake pit and they cleaned it out.

When this happened, I was 12 or 13. I'd been at the game a long time. After this thing they took me back and damned-near killed me. My family got a court order finally; they moved me back home by ambulance. They had beaten me for days, in shifts. Why I lived I don't know, but I think one of the things was that I just hated them. I found that hate's a powerful weapon, if you can control it. My problem was that I couldn't control it very well. After a while I got well, in terms of my body. By that time my mind was pretty sick. I appeared in front of the local judges, and they said, "While there certainly are some extenuating circumstances, and I think you were even justified in some of the things you did, we just can't turn you loose on society." So they decided that they were going to do me a favor. They were going to send me to a school of industry. Now, this is the senior reform school. I arrived there and it was definitely different. It was really a clever place. They had developed a system there where the guards didn't beat you. They had other cadet officers work their fellow prisoners over. And it worked because there was a quasimilitary type of thing where if you wanted to be captain of a company, the way to become captain was to beat the present captain up. And for being captain you got more credits, and if you got more credits that meant you went home quicker. It

was that kind of a game. When you arrive there, the four cadet officer prisoners take you into the shower and strip you naked—you're back to that again—and give you a good thrashing. The thing that they missed about me was that they were amateurs at this beating game and they hadn't really even hurt me. So I went through all their Mickey Mouse routine, and finally I got my chance to go out on what they call recreation hour. And one of the games we used to play was one guy took a bat and hit the ball out and you tried to catch it. Well, I worked like hell to catch a ball, so that I would have my turn at bat. And when I got my hands on that bat, I went after those four guys who had done this to me and really hurt them. I never had any more trouble at the school. I got to be captain; I got to do anything I wanted. I found out that if you're a bigger animal in the jungle than the other animals, then you do well. I used this philosophy throughout my criminal career. I got through two sessions there. I got through one and they let me out, but by then I was really committed to this thing. I had learned to burglarize and all sorts of things.

Now I am in my teens and it suddenly occurs to me that I've got the label of having been in an insane asylum; they'd performed weird operations on me (I really thought that my manhood was in question); I'm a reform school ex-inmate; I'm a thief; I'm an arsonist. Christ, I'm all sorts of things, and I haven't made a nickel. So I decided that, well, if this is what I am and this is what I'm going to be, then I had better try and be a little more professional about it. I hooked up with a guy much older than I and started committing armed robberies. And I was quite successful, and I guess I was a pro 'cuz I didn't just run into gas stations. I planned them; I executed them with what I like to call professionalism. Fortunately, I had been taught by a much older guy who had been a robber all his life, and his philosophy was that a good robbery was one in which you don't hurt anybody. I had trouble learning this because I had a lot of hate and hostility in me. He pointed out to me that to take it out on some broad that's a teller at a bank is really kinda dumb. You don't even know her. I think in some ways, I learned more about being a human being from a bank robber than I ever did from my parents, the institutions, and a lot of other things.

I decided that this was going to be my life. I had everything that I wanted—lots of money, pretty long-legged girls, fancy cars, the works. I robbed banks, supermarkets, and department stores. I'm one of the few people who can say honestly that I've been able to do anything I wanted. The problem is that the retirement system in this life is terrible. I finally got caught, and the sentence for armed robbery is state prison.

Banks I robbed twice; the third time I couldn't beat the security. My idea of robbing a bank is not what you read in the paper, where you run up to the teller and give her a note asking for all her money because she'll give $1,500. Some place in that bank might be $15 million. My attitude was that you rob the whole bank. This doesn't mean the branch downtown, because that's too huge. You find rural banks. The one I said that I didn't rob was in Salinas, and I had taken a job as a women's shoe salesman. The store just happened to be right across the street from the bank, so I could watch it all the time, and the store also did business with that bank. That job was the most horrifying experience I've ever had! I spent months looking at this bank and I couldn't beat their security. I could have robbed the bank probably, but not in the way that I wanted to. I'm greedy and if I can't have it all, I don't want any. It's hard to describe techniques. You look for flaws, for ways to get away, you cover every contingency that one can think about. There's always the X factor that you can't control and that's what usually gets you caught. That's what got me caught. Like, for instance, you get all the money into your car and then the thing won't start. I always figured that getting caught was one of the occupational hazards. And I was prepared to pay that price. I finally reached a point where I think I had received more time than anyone in this country has ever been given, except for the gas chamber. I went up with robbery on the habitual criminal act—I had

more life sentences than this whole room could probably do—and they sent me to Folsom State Prison. After appealing the case all the way to the Supreme Court, it dawned on me that I was either going to have to do all these life sentences, which meant 15 or 20 years before I even thought about getting out. I could have killed myself—I thought about that, but I'm chicken!—or I could escape. And the more I looked at it, the more the escape route seemed interesting enough to try. Nobody had ever escaped from Folsom as a maximum security prison before, so that made it quite a challenge.

(Ray described how he escaped with a partner via swimming the American River that flows by Folsom; however, after evading a search party of some 650 people, he had his comeuppance after breaking into a Japanese American's farm house when the couple returned to the house. They refused to obey Ray's orders, so he left them. They called the police, and Ray was captured and returned to prison. He was berated by fellow convicts for not killing the couple, which led to his change of heart.) I'd always wanted the acceptance of these people (fellow convicts), I'd always earned it, and if I had to kill that old man and woman for these guys to like me, I had to question what I was, what I had become, and where I was going. If there's a turning point in somebody's life, I would say that that was the beginning of mine. I decided to try to get my things together. I started reading, going to school, doing many things that I'd neglected.

This was the story of Ray Johnson, who at the time of the interview, was an ex-convict "doing good," in John Irwin's terminology.[1] Ray was atypical of robbers today (although not of professional robbers) in that he was white and from an affluent family background. In prison, Ray had obtained treatment by a psychiatrist, and met a female social worker in prison whom he later married. With her help and the help of others, Ray got out and remained free until he passed away. He obtained employment as a consultant; wrote a book about himself (*Too Dangerous to Be at Large*); and became a "celebrity convict" on the speaker circuit, including Johnny Carson's Tonight Show.

Ray was essentially what John Erwin termed a **state-raised youth.**[2] His angry personality developed as a result of the abusive treatment he received in custody as a youth. Ray's case study illustrates the development of a professional robber, and that development largely illustrates differential association theory, as well as labeling theory. But there is more to Ray's case, having to do with **power-control theory,** guns, his mind-set to be the "biggest animal in the jungle," as well as his later schooling by a professional robber not to hurt anybody during the course of a robbery. "Old-style professional criminals" may be a vanishing breed among American robbers; however, we cannot ignore them in a global study of crime. They could be more prevalent in other countries, and may make a comeback in our country. In fact, a recent rash of **home invasion robberies** (HIR) by Asian gangs seems to bear the mark of professionalism, to be discussed near the end of this chapter. This case study thus serves as a good introduction to many of the aspects of robbery that will be discussed later, but first it is necessary to start from the top with the basics.

Just as with aggravated assault, most criminology texts treat robbery as just another violent crime and refer readers to the various theories that were formulated to explain murder for an explanation of robbery. However, there are a wide variety of types of robbery, including **strong-arm robbery,** where no weapon is used other than the offender's own body. Thus, to liken all robberies to murder is to overstate the homicidal intent of most robberies.

In some ways, robbery is the most important of the Index crimes. It is one crime that is highly feared by the public in which the fear is perhaps justifiable. This is because it is a crime that can occur without warning, and it is a crime that is typically done by a stranger. Although it is not true that everyone stands the same chance of being robbed, nearly everyone recognizes a vulnerability to robbery, explaining the general public concern about this crime.[3] Of the crimes of violence, it is a crime in which the average victim incurs the most injury per incident, outside of murder. To allay this fear, the crime should be prosecuted vigorously by law enforcement, and yet the crime of robbery has a clearance rate that stands at only 26.2%.[4]

DEFINITION

Robbery is probably one of the least ambiguously defined terms in the FBI's UCR. It involves "attempted or actual theft of property or money by force or fear," or in more detail: The taking or attempting to take anything of value from the care, custody, or control of a person or persons by force or threat of force or violence and/or by putting the victim in fear.[5]

Because of the violence or threat of violence involved in robbery, as well as the theft or property component, robbery is considered to be a dual crime—both a crime against property and a crime against person (or violent crime). Whether robbery ought to be grouped with violent crime or property crime is obviously a matter of conjecture. One view is that robbery should be put in the company of property crimes because lethal injury is not part of the motivation in the crime of robbery and is an outcome of the crime in a declining number of cases.[6] In 2001, the UCR noted that robbery was the circumstance in which murder took place in 7.6% of the cases of murder, down from 10.3% of the cases in 1991. One reason for the declining lethality of robbery has been (ironically) the *increasing* use of firearms by robbers. In 2004, firearms were involved in 40.6% of robberies, compared to 33% in 1988.[7] The robber's possession of a gun seems to result in less victim resistance (which would provoke the robber to attack). Thus, the robber's possession of a gun reduces the probability of victim injury. This is so even when controlling for victim resistance.[8]

However, the use of guns in a robbery increases the risk of death in those robberies. Zimring found a .68 correlation between the percentage of robberies involving a gun and robbery death, although the death rate was small—1 in 100 gun robberies resulting in death.[9] According to Berne and Messerschmidt,

The increasing use of firearms in robbery, as well as the desperation of robbers, is illustrated by this crime shootout in the wake of a botched bank robbery in Hollywood, California, February 28, 1997. Two robbers (dressed like commandos) were killed, at least one was arrested and six officers and two civilians wounded after multiple suspects entered a Bank of America and attempted to rob it.

Source: Reuters/KNBC–TV, Getty Images, Inc./Hulton Archive Photos

"the primary motive of the robbery offender is not violence, but economic gain. Thus, sociologically it is better to designate robbery a property crime and not a crime of violence."[10] Robbery differs from other crimes of violence in that the majority of offenses involve offenders who are strangers to the victims, whereas for rape and assault, the offender is often known to the victim.[11]

It should be acknowledged that a strong case can be made for treating robbery primarily as a violent crime because of the actual violence used. The 2001 NCVS found that the percentage of all victims who sustained physical injury was actually greater for robbery (38.3%) than for assault (25.4%), and the percentage receiving hospital care was greater for robbery (12.2%) than for assault (5.8%). The percentage of victims who sustained physical injury from robbery has increased from 27.4% in 1995 to 35.9% in 2003, and the percentage of victimizations in which victims received hospital care has increased from 5.5% in 1995 to 12.5% in 2003.[12] Thus, it is a truism that robbery is a violent crime and one that is becoming increasingly so (though declining in lethality).

Is robbery a violent crime or a property crime? The obvious answer to this question is that it is *both*. The issue of grouping presents itself typically as a textbook management issue—namely, whether to put robbery in the chapter on property crime or violent crime. However, the approach taken in this text is to address each of the FBI's Index crimes against person separately, each with its own chapter. Certainly robbery and the other Index crimes against person are important crimes that are discussed in a vast and growing literature, and they merit their own chapters.

In light of the aforementioned statistics, should a person fear being injured more from robbery than from assault? The correct answer is no, according to a BJS study published in 1997. This was a report of the findings of a 1994 survey estimating the number of persons treated in hospital emergency departments (ED) in the United States for nonfatal injuries. The study found that among the 1.4 million ED violence victims, 94% had been injured in an assault, 2% during a robbery, and 5% in a rape or sexual assault.[13] This is because assaults are far more frequent than robberies. In 2004, the FBI reported 401,326 robberies and a rate of 136.7 per 100,000 inhabitants, while there were more than double that number of aggravated assaults—854,911 offenses and a rate of 291.1 per 100,000 inhabitants.[14] The FBI reported an additional 1,285,501 arrests for "other assaults," but did not report the number of crimes reported for these assaults. According to the NCVS, these FBI figures are underestimates of both robberies and assaults. The NCVS for 2004 estimated that there were 501,820 robberies, making the FBI estimate of robberies 80% of the total. The 2004 NCVS estimated aggravated assault at 1,030,080, making the FBI estimate for aggravated assault 83% of the total. The NCVS 2004 estimation of 3,440,880 simple assaults has no counterpart in FBI data; however, the combined assault total in the NCVS of 4,470,960 victimizations for assault (both simple and aggravated) is a contrast to 501,820 robbery victimizations.[15] Thus, there are approximately seven times as many assaults as robberies.

Recent trends in robbery have been significantly downward. Starting in 1984, the FBI reported that the rate of robbery increased from 205.7 to a peak of 272.7 in 1991, falling steadily to a low of 145.0 in year 2000.[16] The rate of robbery declined between 1995 and 2004 from 220.9 to 136.7 per 100,000 inhabitants.[17] The NCVS found that robbery declined from a rate of 6.0 per 1,000 households in 1993 to a rate of 2.1 in 2004.[18] Clearance rates for robbery increased slightly from 24.7% in 1995[19] to 26.2% in 2004.[20]

TYPES OF ROBBERS

Although the rates of robbery are declining, NCVS findings are that the proportion of robberies that result in injury is increasing. Overall the result is less people being injured, but for the average victim of robbery, the chances were greater of being injured in 2004 than in 1993, with 38.1% being injured in 2004 and 28.3% being injured in 1993.[21] This suggests that there has been a shift in the type of offender and/or in the victim/offender relationship during the eight-year-period. There are a number of typologies in the literature, including both robbers and the victim-offender relationship in robbery. A review of these typologies can be helpful in understanding the changing rates of robbery and of robbery injuries that take place in the United States.

Prior to the 1960s, the prevailing viewpoint on robbery was traced to Sutherland's characterization of the "professional thief," related to Sutherland's differential association theory. Sutherland's book, *The Professional Thief,* described the life of a thief who was active in the period between 1905 and 1925.[22] In the book, professional thieves were described as highly skilled and highly specialized. They typically planned their crimes carefully, and they would try to avoid violence in the commission of their crimes (to avoid the attraction of law enforcement). They enjoyed a sense of identity and solidarity with other thieves, and they had a code of honor that entailed a "no ratting" rule. This "honor among thieves" rule held that thieves who were caught by the police would never inform upon their accomplices. Ray Johnson's autobiography at the beginning of this chapter is a good illustration of Sutherland's characterization of the professional thief. Based upon the prominence of Sutherland's view, robbers were for some time divided into only two types—professionals or amateurs—in the criminological literature.

Sutherland's view was considered gospel in criminology until 1967. That was the year The President's Commission on Law Enforcement and Administration of Justice released a Task Force Report based upon the Commission's pilot field-research study in four cities—Atlanta, Chicago, New York, and San Francisco—during the summer of 1966. The consultants located and talked with professional criminals, with a total of 50 being interviewed. The Commission defined *professional crime* as "crime committed for personal economic gain by individuals whose major source of income is from criminal pursuits and who spend the majority of their working time in illegal enterprises."[23] The study found, contrary to Sutherland's findings, the typical professional was a small-time operator. His preoccupation was the "hustle," which means moving around bars and being seen; it means asking "what's up?" It means connecting in the morning with two others who have a burglary set up for the evening, calling a man you know to see if he wants to buy 10 stolen alpaca sweaters at five dollars each, and scouting the streets for an easy victim. It means being versatile: passing checks, rolling a drunk, driving for a stickup, boosting a car, burglarizing a store. It is a planless kind of existence, but with a purpose—to make as much money as can be made each day, no holds barred. The Commission further found that associations among professionals tended to be unstable, in part because of the diversity of their activities. The Commission also found that there was no evidence of an ethical "no ratting" code. The professional criminals interviewed took it for granted that others would do whatever is necessary to avoid imprisonment or reduce a sentence. They also expected that their colleagues would and have cheated them and even told of being victimized by their colleagues in the past. The Commission noted that Sutherland's characterization of the professional thief pertained only to the more successful of professional criminals. Thus, the "run-of-the-mill" career criminal should be characterized differently.

Probably the most widely cited typology of robbers was developed by John Conklin. The typology, based upon a study of robbers, was done in the 1960s. Conklin's study specifically rejected the hypothesis that increased rates of drug addiction had contributed to higher rates of robbery and found as late as 1968 that nine tenths of adult robbery suspects had never been arrested for drug offenses. Conklin linked robbery increases with increasing rates of gun ownership, as well as *relative deprivation* (a person's sense that he is economically not as well off as people in his reference group). Conklin then developed a typology that included a greater variety of types than "professional" versus "amateur." He developed a four-fold typology of robbers to include: (a) the **professional robber,** a career criminal committed to robbery over the long-term and who seeks large sums of money in carefully planned robberies; (b) the **opportunist robber,** who is not involved in a career of crime but seeks a small amount of money to buy "extras"; (c) the **addict robber,** who needs enough money to support his habit; and (d) the **alcoholic robber,** who robs on impulse and has few plans for the money he steals. Conklin's finding that the median amount of money gained in robberies from 1964 to 1968 was less than $50 indicated that the majority of robbers were not professionals.[24] In fact, Conklin's view was that the opportunists were the most common type of robbers, not the drug addicts (for the reasons of their fewness). Conklin did not provide in his typology for the type of professional "hustler" as described by the President's Commission, because the opportunist and alcoholic robbers were clearly not professional criminals, and the drug addict was considered to account for a minor portion of all robberies. One point possibly overlooked by Conklin was the possibility that a relatively few drug addicts, by virtue of the expense of their habit, might account for a larger share of robbery.

A more recent typology of bank robbers was developed by James Harlan from an in-depth analysis on the backgrounds and crimes of 500 armed bank robbers convicted in New York between 1964 and 1976. A dramatic change occurred in the offender makeup during this period. In the 1960s, 63% of the robbers were white males, older (over 25), married, poorly educated, and lacking in employable skills. Few were first offenders or drug addicts. Starting in the 1970s, 61% of the bank robbers were black males who were young, single, unattached, and poorly educated with no employable skills. They were typically unemployed (69%), had some prior arrest record (81%), and a sizable number were drug addicts (39%). The robberies were typically armed robberies that were unsophisticated, committed by gangs, averaging slightly more than $3,000, and typically resulting in apprehension within 30 days.

Bank robbery suspects have a high rate of apprehension, according to FBI Statistics. One reason for this is security cameras. In this photo, a bank robber is being videotaped during a bank robbery. This picture was obtained from a copy of the camera tape.

Source: LiHua Lan/Syracure Newspaper, The Image Works

Offenders could be broken down into four types: (a) *heavy career types*, with a lifetime commitment to crime through engaging in thefts of various kinds; (b) the *compulsive type*, engaging in bank robbery to obtain funds for drug abuse, mainly heroin; (c) the *casual type*, who dabbles in crime periodically but does not have a career commitment; and (d) the *amateur type*, a first-time offender who may have engaged in only minor offenses before the bank robbery.[25]

Another study done in Montreal, Quebec City and other Canadian cities yielded a four-fold typology of robbers based upon interviews with 39 robbers in the mid-1980s. This included: (a) the *chronic offender*, a multi-recidivist criminal who commits many other offenses besides robbery, is poorly prepared, and obtains moderate amounts of money; (b) the *professional*, a career criminal who is better prepared and makes high profits; (c) the **intensive offender**, a short career criminal who is poorly prepared, commits robberies in quick succession, and obtains modest gains; and (d) the **occasional offender**, who also has a short career, plans little, and obtains minimal profits.[26]

A third study done in Holland in 1989–1991 explored the motives and choices of 43 robbers, excluding muggers, housed in 5 Dutch prisons. The result was a three-fold typology including (a) *beginners*, who were relatively unprepared, and selected their object and the moment of the robbery based on expected loot and possibilities for flight, and were prepared to use violence when necessary; (b) *desperation robbers*, who lacked a significant criminal career, were relatively unprepared, but chose an object and a moment for the robbery that enabled them to use minimum force; and (c) *professional robbers* who had been criminally active for a long time, were prepared to use physical violence when needed, but (like beginners) selected their object and the moment of the robbery on the basis of the expected loot and possibilities for flight.[27]

It can be seen that typologies of robbers have developed over time to include a variety of types besides the highly skilled professional and amateur, including desperation, chronic, intensive, occasional, compulsive, casual, opportunist, drug addict, and alcoholic robbers. It would seem that the profiling of robbers has changed over time and from place to place.

While there are numerous typologies of robbers, there has been very little study of the victim. However, one study done in Nigeria led to the development of a typology of victims (see text box).

Another basis for typing robbery has to do with the type of weapon used against the victim. According to the UCR for 2004, firearms were used in 40.6% of robberies, followed by "strong-arm robberies" (41.1%) in which no weapon was used. Knives or cutting instruments were used in 8.9% of robberies and

BOX 8–1

Victims of Robbery in Nigeria

A study of 670 armed robberies that occurred in a wave of armed robberies after the Nigerian Civil War (July 1967–January 1970) provided a nine-fold typology of *victims*, ranging from the guileless to those who seem to invite victimization. In order of frequency, the types are (a) neutral victims (43.6%), who take all precautions and cannot be held responsible for their victimization; (b) reckless victims (19.1%); (c) individuals careless with their property (11.3%); (d) victims disregarding professional hazards (7.6%); (e) victims publicly displaying their wealth (6.7%); (f) Good Samaritans (5.5%); (g) victims engaging in loose talk (3.3%); (h) credulous victims (2.1%); and (i) officials not taking adequate security measures (0.8%).[28]

other weapons were used in 9.4% of the cases. This represents no upward trend in the firearms that were used in 41% of the robberies in 1995, whereas strong-arm robberies were 40.7% of robberies that year, followed by 9.1% knives or cutting instruments, and 9.2% other weapons. However, the 40.6% firearms use in 2004 is a big jump from the distant past. In 1987, 33% of all robberies reported were committed through the use of firearms, whereas 44% involved strong-arm tactics, 13% involved knives or cutting instruments, and 10% used other weapons.[29]

Another study based upon data gathered from 1993–1996 on convenience store robberies yielded a 10-fold typology of robbery situations in general. These included mugging/personal robberies, home invasion robberies, carjackings, purse snatches, fast-food robberies, bank robberies, convenience store robberies, gas station robberies, robberies of other businesses, taxi cab robberies, and "other" types.[30] Though "situation-based" as opposed to "depth-interview-based," such as the offender typologies reviewed earlier, this typology includes a couple of important "emerging types" of robberies—home invasion robberies and carjackings—that merit some discussion later.

Situation-based data for robberies are given in the UCR for 2004.[31] The robberies in descending order of frequency include street/highway (42.8%), miscellaneous (17.4%), commercial houses (14.7%), residences (13.8%), convenience stores (6.1%), gas or service stations (2.7%), and banks (2.4%). This represents a decline in street/highway robbery, from 62.9% in 1995, with all other categories increasing. Commercial house robberies rose from 10.7% in 1995 to 14.7% in 2004. Residential robberies rose from 9.9% in 1995 to 13.8% in 2004. Convenience store robberies rose from 2.9% in 1995 to 6.1% in 2004. Gas or service station robberies increased from 1.5% in 1995 to 2.7% in 2004, whereas bank robberies rose from 1.1% in 1995 to 2.4% in 2004.

The proliferation of typologies of both robbers and their victims probably provides a basis for the understanding of robbery, in getting the "big picture" of what robbery is all about today in the United States and/or throughout the world. How can the typical robber be characterized today? To find out, it is necessary to look at studies that describe the backgrounds of robbers (profiles) as well as to discuss theories of robbery, look at countries that have extremely high rates of robbery, and look at some national and international statistics.

PROFILING ROBBERY

Factors associated with robbery have been the subject of numerous studies.[32] Some of these studies describe characteristics of offenders while others characterize the targets or victims or robbery. Summing up the plethora of factors described in these studies, robbery offenders seem to be increasingly young, male, black, involved in street culture, involved with drugs and/or alcohol, residing in the inner city, relying upon guns in the conduct of robbery, and violently disposed toward victims. Victims seem to share many of those same characteristics, with the addition of short-term residency and unmarried or divorced marital status. The trend in unarmed "muggings" seems to be down, owed perhaps to the availability of weapons among inner-city youthful gang members. There have been many attempts to make sense of these various facts through theoretical explanations of robbery that are discussed next.

THEORIES OF ROBBERY

The police clearance rate for robbery is only 26.2%, the rate of crimes that are "solved" by the police by an arrest of the assumed perpetrator. Thus, compared to other violent crimes, police are extremely ineffective in catching robbers. One way to cut down on the rate of robbery might be to increase police effectiveness and one way to do this is to develop a better understanding of the crime. Police investigation usually begins with a theory or expectation on the part of the police that murder or assault is likely to have been done by a family member, that rape is likely to have been done by an acquaintance, and so forth. But since robbery is typically done by a stranger, the police frequently "have no clue." Studies show that unless a robbery is solved quickly, the crime typically becomes a closed or unsolved case. However, "smart policing" can involve the better use of forensic evidence, psychological profiling, computer databases, police informants, and more that can result in additional arrests for this crime. In discussing theory, part of the objective is to help in the development of a better orientation toward crime (i.e., better theories about "who done it").

Theories of robbery include racial inequality, income inequality, deterrence theory, "broken windows" theory, economic theory, routine activities theory, economic abundance theory, and even the War on Drugs theory. These theories are not mutually exclusive.

A study that probed several of these factors simultaneously was done by Blau and Blau.[33] Using FBI data from 125 American Standard Metropolitan Statistical Areas (SMSAs), Blau and Blau tested a hypothesis that variations in rates of urban criminal violence are a result of differences in economic inequality and poverty. They found that criminal violence is positively related to location in the South, to the proportion of blacks in an SMSA, and to poverty. Probing further, they found economic inequality increases rates of violence. Once economic inequality is controlled, poverty no longer influences the rates, nor does Southern location. Also, the proportion of blacks in the population has little influence. Thus, they concluded that the primary variable in violence (including robbery) is income inequality. Blau and Blau did not focus specifically on robbery in their study. However, Sampson's 1983 test of their theory of economic inequality found that the correlation between violent crime and inequality was greater for crimes of theft, including robbery, than for other crimes of violence. Also, he found that neighborhood racial and age heterogeneity is strongly related to interracial and inter-age rates of criminal encounters.[34] After further analysis, Sampson found that income inequality has a direct positive effect on black offending rates for serious crime, whereas black poverty had no effect. On the other hand, he found that although white poverty was positively correlated with white violence, inequality also significantly increased white robbery and burglary rates.[35]

Deterrence theory in the case of robbery would hold that to the extent that punishment is swift and certain, and (recently) severe, then rates of robbery will decline. Conflict theorist William Chambliss proposed a form of this theory when he discussed "instrumental" versus "expressive offenses."[36] He concluded that research findings show a low deterrent effect of legal punishment for offenses that involve a high commitment to crime as a way of life combined with involvement in an act that is "expressive" in the sense of being an end in itself (e.g., murder and drug addiction). On the other hand are acts in which the commitment of the agent to crime is low and the act is "instrumental" (i.e., a means to some other end). These crimes have a high

BOX 8–2

State Terrorism and Robbery

Violent crime, including "kondoism," or armed robbery with violence done by gangs of people, was reportedly prevalent in Uganda during the period immediately after independence from British rule in 1962. The violent crime was dealt with by "state-terrorism" during the brutal reign of Idi Amin, which began in 1971. Police procedure under Amin provides insight as to why reported rates of robbery might be low in some countries with repressive regimes. During the early years of the Amin regime, the Police Safety Unit (PSU) and the Military Police also acquired reputations as terrorist squads operating against their compatriots. In 1972 the PSU, which was created as an armed robbery investigative unit within the civil police organization, was equipped with submachine guns. Amin ordered PSU agents to shoot robbers on sight, and PSU agents became known among many Ugandans as roving death squads.[37]

capability of being deterred by the legal system. Robbery is said to be a good example of an "instrumental crime" in the sense that it is typically not done "for the fun of it" but as a means to another end (money, drugs, etc.).[38] Wilson and Boland developed a deterrence theory of robbery based on a study of the rate of robbery in 35 large American cities. They found that the "legalistic model of policing" as indicated by aggressive police activity and measured by police resources (patrol units on the street) and police activity on the street (moving citations issued) had the effect of lowering rates of robbery, independent of various socioeconomic factors.[39] This study was replicated by Sampson and Cohen for 171 U.S. cities in 1980, and it was found that overall, proactive policing appeared to have a direct inverse effect on aggregate robbery rates, independent of known determinants of crime, such as poverty and region, and the inverse effect was largest for adult and black offenders.[40] Another study found that deterrence as indicated by police clearance rates had a positive effect in reducing rates of robbery.[41]

Unfortunately, application of deterrence theory in the case of robbery is not shown by America's criminal justice system. Clearance rates have remained steady at about 25% for the past decade. There is evidence of a 50% to 60% attrition rate (failure to convict) after arrest.[42] Furthermore, cases that do result in felony conviction may be "pled out." The result is often more lenient misdemeanor convictions and sentences of "local time" or probation rather than state prison. In California, a study done in 1980 indicated that jury trials for robbery had become rare and that most were the product of a plea bargain with the prosecution. This resulted in a lighter sentence, which was not likely to be state imprisonment.[43] Curiously, the opposite treatment of robbery by the New York City Police Department resulted in positive results in a 1979 experiment called the Felony Case Preparation Project. That experiment featured postarrest investigation of felony arrests resulting in an improved indictment rate for arraigned robbery arrests from 39% to 66%. The conviction rate rose from 51% to 74%; and the incarceration rate rose from 30% to 44%. Sentences of five years or longer rose from 8% to 30%.[44] Another apparently successful "experiment" in reducing robbery was Florida's mandatory gun law (use a gun, go to prison). This statute mandated that the charges for the offense cannot be dropped once they are officially filed and that the trial judge must sentence those found guilty to a minimum of three years. Findings indicated that the law did reduce the amount of armed robbery, homicides committed with a firearm, total robbery, and total homicides.[45]

The ineffective criminal justice system insofar as robbery is concerned can fuel the flames of this crime. From the point of view of robbers, robbery may seem to be a "perfect crime" that can be done with impunity. This was revealed in a study by Richard Wright and Scott Decker who interviewed 86 active armed robbers in St. Louis, Missouri, all but three of which were African Americans. The plurality of this group (31%) had committed more than 49 robberies during their lifetime, yet one third of the group had never been arrested, and another 26% had one or more arrests but no convictions. Thus, a majority had committed numerous robberies without conviction. Their success in not being convicted may have been due to the fact that most (85%) committed street robberies, often focusing upon victims who would not report the crime to the police, such as drug dealers and married men looking for illicit sex. They also focused upon targets that were "easy," such as white men, women, and the elderly.[46] In addition to the knowledge that arrest and prosecution are unlikely in the case of street robbery, robbers are encouraged by the fact that only around 60% of victims of robbery report that crime to the police.[47]

The sense of immunity from prosecution was also indicated in a 1996 study of 310 male convenience store armed robbers incarcerated in 20 prisons in Maryland, Texas, and Washington.[48] Even though nearly half had been previously incarcerated (and were incarcerated at the time of the study), 83% of the sample said they had not expected to be caught. Perhaps the offenders felt that they "had a good thing going" with convenience store robberies. When compared with inmates in Erickson's earlier 1985 research ($N = 187$), the convenience store robbers committed more crimes and were less likely to be deterred. This increase in volume of robberies may have been related to the fact that escape route had replaced money as the most important factor considered by the robbers. Also, they robbed for less money than the 1985 cohort. The motivations for the crime included money, drugs, thrill, power, anger, and peer pressure.

Failure of the criminal justice system to cope with robbery may have led to a growth of situational theories. That is because those theories provide for the **target hardening** capability of victims of crime, without law enforcement involvement. One early theory in this school of thought was Leroy Gould's **economic abundance theory,** which posited that the abundance that occurred from 1944 to 1965 alone can explain the variation in rates of property crime. Simply stated, this theory holds that people steal because there is more to steal. As a result, there is more opportunity to steal.[49] Another influential analysis of the victim-offender relationship that may have led to situational analysis was David Luckenbill's study of 261 cases of robbery. Luckinbill discovered that there were typically four stages in robbery: (a) the offender establishes a co-presence with the victim, (b) the offender and victim develop a co-orientation toward a common robbery frame, (c) one or both opponents (offender and victim) transfer the material goods, and (d) the offender leaves the setting.[50] Cohen, Cantor, and Kleugel applied routine activities theory to show how this process could be prevented or interrupted through target hardening and enhancing property guardianship.[51] Thus, robbery can be reduced through enhanced victim awareness of vulnerability, as well as provision of extra guardianship, as in surveillance cameras, private security guards, reduced store hours, and so forth. Studies that have been done seem to validate the routine activities approach to robbery, including studies of (a) temperature, time of day, and day of the week,[52] (b) street robberies near a "face block" (i.e., corner lots with both sides of a city block near intersections) as opposed to robberies on a face block,[53] and (c) informal surveillance.[54]

Closely related to the routine activities approach has been Wilson and Kelling's **broken windows theory.**[55] This theory maintains that the poor physical appearance of a neighborhood can indicate a breakdown in community cohesion and provides an open invitation to criminals of all types, including drunks, prostitutes, robbers, and burglars. Application of the "broken windows" approach by the New York City Police has been credited during the 1990s with the decreasing rates of violent crime in New York City, including murder down by 70%, robbery down by more than 60%, and violent crimes down by more than 50%.[56]

Although Blau and Blau's 1982 study focused upon income inequality rather than poverty as the cause of robbery, a recent study of juveniles has brought economic theory to attention again. The study obtained data drawn from the National Longitudinal Study of Adolescent Health ($N = 16,478$ U.S. high school students). The study found that an increase in local unemployment contributed to the propensity to commit robbery, burglary, and theft for males, and assault and burglary for females. The authors concluded that employment opportunities and increased family income should be effective tools in reducing juvenile crime.[57] It seems credible that at a certain point in a youngster's development, career choices are made. For youth living in a ghetto or barrio, from which manufacturing jobs have recently declined significantly, the tendency might be to turn to drug sales and other crimes as an alternative career. What then is the link between unemployment, drug sales, and robbery? There is a growing literature on that subject, which is discussed next.

Critics of the "War on Drugs" have argued that the crackdown on drugs has led to an increase in robbery in two ways. One is a reduction in prison sentences for robbers to make room for the increased population of drug offenders.[58] Critics have also argued that harsher enforcement of drug laws has resulted in robberies motivated by the drug addict's need to get the money to pay for artificially higher priced drugs.[59] There is quite a bit of literature that

BOX 8–3

The Swiss Paradox: Low Robbery but High Burglary

Switzerland's rate of robbery in 2002 was 33.4 per 100,000 inhabitants—possibly the lowest rate for developed countries, whereas its burglary rate was 830.8, ranking 29 out of 147 countries, higher than the United States. A possible explanation for this paradox is Switzerland's drug policy that emphasizes four pillars—prevention, treatment, harm reduction, and law enforcement. On the one hand, Switzerland has a prescription program for heroin users, as well as a needle exchange program. A significant percentage of Switzerland's some 30,000 addicts are allowed to obtain heroin legally and provided free of charge, in some cases, by the government. On the other hand, Switzerland regards itself as a devotee to the War on Drugs, in terms of interdiction and money laundering. The latter efforts may have kept the price of illegal drugs high, thus prompting high rates of burglary for the purpose of obtaining revenue to support drug consumption. However, the heroin prescription relief for addicts may very well have targeted heroin, the drug of choice for robbers, or would-be robbers, thus keeping that crime low.[60] One study done in Switzerland and published in 1998 found that the number of heroin patients involved in muggings has decreased by more than 80% since the program of prescription heroin began in 1992. In addition to robbery, it was found that users had previously raised cash through selling hard drugs to consumers from their own social network. Thus, the heroin prescription may be vital to breaking the link between dependence and resale to new consumer recruits.[61] Another two-year study of prescription heroin in Switzerland, which included psychiatric and social assessment in addition to heroin administration, found that there was a significant decline in the consumption of illegal drugs and a massive decline in illegal activities among the 800 participants.[62]

BOX 8–4

Portugal, Robbery, and the War on Drugs

From 1995 to 2001, Portugal went from being a country with a very low crime rate of 529.3 per 100,000 inhabitants to a much higher rate of 1,776.35 per 100,000 inhabitants. Most of this increase was due to property crime. Robbery increased by 137%, burglary by 167%, larceny by 287%, and motor vehicle theft by 371%. One change that happened was that Portugal increased its drug enforcement efforts. The rate of drug offenses increased from 27.72 per 100,000 inhabitants in 1995 to 54.54 per 100,000 inhabitants in 2001, an increase of 96.8%. There is evidence of increased interdiction. Though heroin use has remained constant over the past several years, authorities seized twice as much heroin in the first half of 1998 as they did in the first half of 1997, and 1.5 times as much cocaine. These property crime increases may be linked to the rising price of drugs on the black market, because addicts must turn to crime (or more crime) as a source of revenue to support their habits. The combination of property and drug crime prosecutions led to an increase in incarceration in Portugal from 91.46 per 100,000 to a peak of 149.28 per 100,000 inhabitants in 1998. Independent reports and NGOs indicated that prisons were overcrowded, juveniles were at times held with adults, pretrial detainees were held with convicted criminals, drug addiction was prevalent in prison, and illicit drugs were available in prison on a widespread basis. The combination of conditions seems to suggest that in Portugal's prisons, recently, related to the War on Drugs, more and more inmates were graduating from the status of petty thieves to armed robbers (in much the same manner as Ray Johnson was indoctrinated as a "state raised youth"). The robbery rate in Portugal's neighbor Spain is extraordinary, considering Spain's otherwise low rate of crime. Spain's robbery rate in 2001 was 250.04 and Spain ranked 9 out of 152 countries in the world that reported data. Spain has for some time been waging its own War on Drugs, with drug offense rates peaking in 2000 at 251.89 per 100,000 inhabitants.[63]

indicates a significant correlation between drug addiction and robbery in the United States, but not necessarily in other countries. According to one study done in Britain, there was little evidence to suggest that drugs played a primary role in street robbery there.[64] Karl-Heinz Reuband reported that German addicts are less likely than American addicts to engage in robbery, even in the absence of methadone programs, possibly due to the greater availability of welfare and medical care programs in Germany.[65] However, numerous studies done in the United States have found a correlation between drug use and robbery.[66]

Some case studies help reveal the reason for the connection between drug addiction and robbery in America.

- Ron Santiago, a 42-year-old black man of Cuban ancestry, indicated that robbery and legitimate jobs were the initial way he obtained money to support his addiction to heroin. He became a dealer after he tired of robbing. At age 16, he had gone to prison, where he learned the best means for scoring dope from Spanish gangs that he joined to survive in prison.[67]
- After a childhood with an alcoholic father and suicidal mother, Jim Dycus became immersed in a life of drugs and addiction. He had to commit crimes, including robberies, to support his $300-a-day habit. He nearly died when he was shot in the head by a policeman during a botched robbery attempt.[68]
- Jack Abbott was admitted to a juvenile correctional institution at age 12 for "failure to adjust to foster homes." Abbott came to use and abuse drugs in prison and, later in life, after an escape from prison, became a bank robber.[69]

The War on Drugs Theory would explain the link between robbery and drug addiction in the United States. The resulting high cost of drugs drives

BOX 8-5

Drug Sales and Property Crime in Australia

A study determined income generation patterns among 202 active heroin users in South West Sydney, Australia. This study revealed that drug market activities account for a greater proportion of drug user income than do other offenses. The study revealed that law enforcement crackdowns on opportunities for generating income from the drug market actually increase property crimes by heroin users.[70]

addicts to commit desperate crimes, such as robbery, to support their habits. However, the Jack Abbott story suggests that a related factor linking robbery with drug addiction in the United States is America's high rate of imprisonment itself. There is evidence that the experience of being in prison encourages drug use,[71] and one study even found that 22% of inmates in the study had begun using drugs in prison.[72] Thus, the growth of imprisonment that has resulted from the War on Drugs may contribute to the link between robbery and drug addiction through actually adding to the amount of addiction among the criminal population. This contributes to rates of robbery outside of prison when the released and often unemployable inmates must support their habits through criminal means. In addition, the techniques of committing the crime of robbery may have been acquired through time spent in incarceration.

COUNTRY PROFILES

From the aforementioned analysis, it can be seen that plenty of attention has been paid by criminologists to robbery, both in terms of profiling robbers and the development of theories of robbery. If anything, this diversity of factors and explanations probably does more to add confusion about robbery than to enhance understanding and a sense of closure on the topic. Hopefully, cross-cultural analysis will be helpful in that respect, starting with a country that has the highest rate of robbery in the world—Costa Rica.

The countries of the world ranked for rate of robbery are shown in Table 8–1. (Developed countries are highlighted.)

Although Latvia appears to be the number one country for robbery, the robbery rate of 554.58 reported for Latvia seems to be an anomaly and not characteristic of Latvia.[73]

Table 8–2 shows some correlations between various international indices from the CCDB. Some of these correlations are the opposite of those using official statistics within the United States. From the profiling done earlier in this chapter, it would be expected that poverty, unemployment, and youth would be positively correlated with robbery. However, in Table 8–2, they are negatively correlated with robbery (using cross-national data). Admittedly, the correlations for percentage living in poverty and percentage unemployed are small correlations, but they are, nevertheless, negative. Median age is positively correlated with robbery rates, which suggests that robbery is positively correlated with a larger percentage of persons in the population that are old rather than young. This makes some sense in terms of situational theories in the sense that older people are "easier" victims of crime, because they cannot usually resist against a younger offender. Similarly, *gender empowerment*

Table 8–1 **Countries Ranked for Rate of Robbery**[74]

Country	Rate	Rank	Country	Rate	Rank
Latvia	554.60	1	Finland	53.06	63
Costa Rica	515.70	2	Ireland	48.10	65
South Africa	468.90	3	Norway	47.47	66
Bahamas, The	457.20	4	New Zealand	46.33	67
Puerto Rico	437.60	5	Switzerland	33.40	72
Trinadad & Tobago	329.70	6	Israel	30.30	74
Estonia	321.80	7	Iceland	19.62	88
Bahrain	263.40	8	Greece	16.63	89
Spain	25.00	9	Belgium	8.73	101
Swaziland	229.10	10	Liechtenstein	6.06	111
France	224.40	11	Japan	5.02	119
Mexico	219.50	12	Andorra	1.52	135
Belize	208.00	13	Vietnam	1.48	136
Uruguay	195.20	14	Burundi	1.42	137
Great Britain (England & Wales)	182.70	15	Bangladesh	1.38	138
Guyana	179.10	16	Azerbaijan	1.36	139
Barbados	159.40	17	Qatar	1.34	140
Russia	148.90	18	American Samoa	1.19	141
United States of America	**149.00**	**19**	Thailand	1.07	142
Portugal	133.30	23	Cameroon	0.97	143
Australia	121.70	28	Nepal	0.90	144
Netherlands, The	117.20	32	Egypt	0.66	145
Luxembourg	96.61	36	United Arab Emirates	0.55	146
Sweden	95.83	38	Brazil	0.52	147
Canada	88.20	42	Saudi Arabia	0.14	148
Austria	85.84	43	Syria	0.07	149
Germany	71.41	52	Mali	0.05	150
Italy	69.92	53	Burkina Faso	0.04	151
Denmark	59.67	58	Myanmar	0.04	152

is positively correlated with robbery, suggesting that a larger percentage of women in the workforce makes them vulnerable targets of crime. Deterrence theory seems to be supported in the moderate correlations between both *lack of freedom* and *percentage Islamic,* both of which are proxies for a strong legal system. *Alcohol consumption* seems to be a fairly strong correlate of robbery, particularly *spirit consumption.* This could mean that alcohol consumption leads to a large robbery offender group who have a "party lifestyle," and/or a large victim group of inebriated victims who are vulnerable to robbery. In Chicago School studies, youths who robbed drunks in the city were referred to as "jackrollers." This concept helps to explain the correlation between the *rate juveniles are admitted to prison* and robbery. As indicated in the case study of Ray, a Bank Robber, at the beginning of this chapter, youthful offenders often learn the "tricks of the trade" of robbery during their stay in detention centers and correctional facilities.

Table 8–2 Robbery Correlated with International Indices

Gini Index	.12
GDP	.05
GDP per capita	.14
Percentage living in poverty	−.14
Percentage unemployed	−.09
Lack of freedom	−.35
Percentage Islamic	−.29
Rape rate	.36
Aggravated assault rate	.13
Drug offense rate	.10
Gender empowerment	.12
Rate juveniles admitted to prison	.24
Adult alcohol consumption per capita	.38
Beer consumption per capita	.18
Wine consumption per capita	.24
Spirit consumption per capita	.42
Net migration rate	−.11
Median age	.19

An FBI photo taken by a Gilmore Bank surveillance camera shows a woman at gunpoint during a robbery. An African American woman bank robber pins an elderly white woman to the floor with a gun at her head in the Gilmore Bank in Los Angeles. Consider this dramatic photo in relation to the factors correlated with robbery in Table 8–4.

Source: Contact Press Images, Inc.

BOX 8–6

Underreporting Crime in Nigeria

In a country profile of Nigeria, Obi N.I. Ebbe explains why crime statistics reported by the police underreport crime even more than in more developed nations. "Systematic record keeping of crime data in Nigeria is still very cumbersome for the Nigerian Police Force, although the NPF Headquarters is making some effort to improve. The amount of robbery and burglary recorded by the Nigerian police captures only about 30% of the number of robberies or burglaries actually committed because many of the crimes are not detected or reported. Additionally, over 60% of the crimes that should be kept in police records are disposed without being recorded at the informal, customary courts. These facts and biases in police crime records should be considered when analyzing Nigerian crime data." Thus, the extremely low crime rates of underdeveloped countries should not be taken at face value.[75]

In sum, the international data seem to point to the importance of deterrence theory, situational theory, and possibly labeling theory as a basis for explaining robbery. Deterrence theory is suggested with the social control variables (lack of freedom, percentage Islamic). Situational theory might apply to the victimization of elderly, inebriated persons and working women. Labeling theory might apply to the youthful offenders learning to rob from other offenders in a correctional setting. Not mentioned was a very low positive correlation with social inequality. However, inequality may be greater for selected groups in society, such as minorities, who may commit more than their share of robberies. Given these preliminaries, let us take a look at a couple of countries that are high in robbery to see how these variables might work within those countries.

Costa Rica

Costa Rica is a country that is insightful to study because, though its robbery rate is extremely high, it has a very low crime rate overall. However, it has a rising rate of robbery, and from the aforementioned analysis is second among the 152 countries in the country database for which data have been reported on robbery. So from looking at Costa Rica, it might be possible to isolate some key factors in the crime of robbery. Taking a quick look at the demographic data for Costa Rica, how is Costa Rica unusual? The CIA's World Factbook indicates that the population of Costa Rica is 94% white in race. However, it has been estimated that from 10% to 15% of the population is Nicaraguan, of fairly recent arrival and primarily of mestizo origin. The Spanish named this country Costa Rica, which means "rich coast" in English; however, there was relatively little gold or silver in Costa Rica.

Costa Rica became a largely agrarian economy and an egalitarian tradition also arose. Yet widening class distinctions were brought on by the 19th century introduction of bananas and coffee cultivation and the consequent accumulation of local wealth. Today, Costa Ricans have a gross domestic product (GDP) per capita slightly below the average for the countries of the world in the CCDB. The per capita GDP is $8,500 compared to an average of $8,961 in the CCDB. Twenty one percent of the population lives in poverty, which is below the average (39%) for the countries in the CCDB. The unemployment rate is low (6.3%) compared with 16% for countries in the CCDB. However, the Gini Index of 45.9 is relatively high, compared to the 39.9 average for the countries in the CCDB. Thus, a considerable amount of income inequality has been a recent trend (despite the egalitarian tradition). Adult per capita alcohol consumption is moderate at 4.3 liters of ethanol per year, compared with the 4.5 liters per capita average for all countries. However, the largest component of this alcohol consumption is "spirit" consumption, with a rate of 3.6 liters of ethanol per capita per year. That rate is more than double the average in the database for the countries of the world (1.7 liters of ethanol per capita per year). The rate of heroin seizures per capita is also high at .23 kilograms per 100,000 inhabitants, compared to .006 Kg average for the countries of the world.

One interesting facet of the Costa Rica crime picture is the comparatively lenient treatment of robbery. Robbery in Costa Rica is punished according to a specific formula, which is based on the offender's economic situation. Penalties are calculated with a formula that uses the base income of the offender to calculate sentences and fines. If the value of the articles stolen or damaged does not exceed three times the base figure of the offender's annual income, then the sentence is set accordingly at somewhere between six months to three years. The sentence of three to nine years is commonly given when injuries have occurred or the amount of the theft or loss was larger than three times the base income of the offender.

The areas of Costa Rica that have the greatest concentration of criminal activity are those within the Great Metropolitan Area. The cities of San Jose, parts of Cartago, Heredia, and Alajuela form most of this area. These cities, which are densely populated, have a greater percentage of total crime than the outlying rural areas. The port cities of Limon and Puntarenas experience a great amount of drug-related incidents. Assault and robbery are more common because their populations are of a more transient nature. Petty crimes, mugging, shoplifting, and fraud are prevalent in cities such as San Jose and the rest of the greater metropolitan area. In recent years, the cities have seen a large increase in juvenile criminal gang activities. These young criminal children, generally called "chapulines" or grasshoppers, are a phenomenon that reflects the breakdown of the family unit in Costa Rica. An interesting description of these chapulines appears on a travel website (see textbox).

BOX 8–7

The *Chapulines* of Costa Rica[76]

Costa Rica is generally considered to be a very safe country and Costa Ricans on the whole are honest and friendly people. Any crime that does exist tends to be opportunistic, rather than involving out-and-out assault. The main things travelers have to worry about in the city are street mugging and pickpocketing. In downtown San Jose, you need to be wary at all times. Street crime, especially chain and watch snatching and pickpocketing, can be a problem, especially in isolated or poor sections of the city. Gangs of kids called *chapulines* (grasshoppers), too young to prosecute under Costa Rican law, turned into a major problem a few years back. Travelers were given the following advice: "Wear a money belt, and never carry anything of value in an outside pocket; it is also wise not to wear jewelry or carry expensive equipment, such as cameras while walking around downtown. Do not carry large wads of bills and do not show all your bills when paying for what you buy. Other good advice includes: Do not get drunk in public so as not to invite mugging, do not argue with inebriated persons, do not walk around in secluded areas or in the city during the night. If you decide to take a companion up to your room, be forewarned that prostitutes are notorious for cleaning out their customer's pockets before leaving."

The textbox succinctly reveals and combines the numerous factors that seem correlated with robbery in Costa Rica, some of which were profiled previously. Such factors include juvenile street crime in poor sections of urban areas, the vulnerability and culpability of people who are inebriated, and the role of (legalized) prostitutes in robbery. There is little if any discussion of the role of prostitutes in robbery in the criminological literature. However, various in-class presentations by prostitutes and drug users have revealed that there is a widespread scam perpetrated in the United States as well as other countries. It has been described as "the Murphy game" or the "Murphy." The Murphy game is played on individuals who are lured up to hotel rooms by prostitutes. It is named after the Murphy Bed, a bed that was kept in a closet during the day, but can be extended into the room for sleeping purposes by night. In the Murphy, the prostitute typically works as an accomplice to a robber (frequently her pimp) who hides in the closet of her hotel room. Upon the prostitute's signal, the robber jumps out of the closet (like a Murphy Bed) and intimidates or assaults the prostitute's client for whatever money or valuables the client possesses.

As pointed out in the text box, Costa Rican criminal justice disregards the problem presented by juvenile delinquents (the chapulines), because they are too young to prosecute under Costa Rican law. Also, Costa Rican criminal justice appears to provide excessive lenience in other areas. The general practice in Costa Rica is to set bail or release all suspects. In fact it is estimated that 85% of those awaiting trial are released on their own recognizance. As discussed earlier, imprisonment terms for robbery are relatively short; furthermore, time off for good behavior and participation in work programs is offered. An inmate is also eligible to apply for *benificio* or benefit after 50% of the sentence has been served. While in prison, inmates are not required to work, and during leisure time, television sets are available and radios and other personal property are allowed. Family visits and conjugal privileges are permitted. As noted earlier, these lenience factors indicate the strong possibility that narcotics and other contraband are prevalent in prison. In fact, illegal narcotics are said to be readily available in the Costa Rican prisons, and drug use is common.

As discussed previously, domestic violence seems to be a precursor to juvenile delinquency in the sense that children from such families may make gang membership their family surrogate and/or they may run away from such home environmental circumstances, after which they must commit crimes (robberies, prostitution) to survive on the streets. Indeed, the government of Costa Rica has identified domestic violence against women and children as a serious societal problem. According to data compiled by the judicial branch in 2000, 32,646 reports of domestic abuse were received, 6,209 more than in 1999. However, 70% of the cases were dropped because the women decided not to pursue prosecution. In terms of child abuse, the autonomous National Institute for Children (PANI) has increased public awareness of abuse of children, which remains a problem. From January to June 2001, the Institute intervened in 3,640 cases of abandonment, 1,246 cases of physical abuse, 573 cases of sexual abuse, and 941 cases of psychological abuse of children. Abuses appear to be more prevalent among poor, less educated families. Traditional attitudes and the inclination to treat such crimes as misdemeanors sometimes hamper legal proceedings against those who commit crimes against children. There is evidence that children are being exploited sexually. The PANI has identified street children in the urban areas of San Jose, Limon, and Puntarenas as being at the greatest risk for child prostitution. An International Labor Organization study of four San Jose neighborhoods in 1998–1999 identified at least 212 minor girls working as prostitutes, but other countrywide estimates are higher. A PANI study estimated that some 40 families in August 2000 supported themselves by "renting" their children to sex tourists. In 2000, the police arrested five men involved in a so-called Costa Rican Association of Pedophiles for sexually exploiting four children. The children were given cocaine and marijuana before they were exploited, and they were to receive about $21 (5,000 colones) payment for having sex with pedophiles. After the arrest, the children were returned to their families, who live in the poorest sections of San Jose. Costa Rica is a transit and destination country for trafficked persons, including persons from Africa, Asia, Bolivia, China, Columbia, Cuba, the Dominican Republic, and the Middle East. There also have been reports of girls from the Philippines being trafficked to the country for the purpose of sexual exploitation.

Drug trafficking seems to be a significant factor related to rising crime rates in Costa Rica, as shown rather dramatically in Figure 8–1.

By virtue of its location in the Central American isthmus, Costa Rica is an important transshipment country for the smuggling of cocaine from South America to the United States, as demonstrated by these record seizures during both 1997 and 1998. Costa Rica is also a temporary storage area for cocaine being smuggled to the United States and Europe. During the first 11 months of 1998, authorities seized record amounts of cocaine—over eight metric tons—as well as 18 kilograms of heroin. As is typical with countries involved in the drug trade, drug abuse among the citizens of Costa Rica has become an increasing problem. Costa Ricans have become increasingly concerned over local consumption, especially of crack cocaine. Abuse appears highest in the Central Valley (including the major cities of San Jose, Alajuela, Cartago, and Heredia), the port cities of Limon and Puntarenas, the north near Barro del Colorado, and along the southern border. It seems likely that the considerable drug seizures were both indicative of high prevalence of the use of cocaine (and possibly heroin) in Costa Rica, as well as productive of drug-related crimes. The seizures themselves would have the effect of driving up the street price of the drugs, making it necessary for addicts to commit more serious

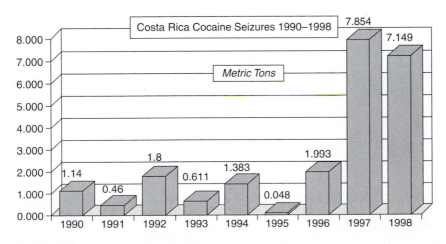

Figure 8–1
Costa Rica Cocaine Seizures 1990–1998[77]

crimes than petty thefts or drug sales (viz., robbery) to sustain their habits. United Nations data on robbery for these years (1990–1998) correlated positively with the cocaine seizure rates in Figure 8–1 ($r = .21$).

The Bahamas   The Bahamas are a group of islands with the nearest island located some 40 miles from the Florida coast. The population of these islands is small, estimated at 300,529 in 2002, compared to Costa Rica, with a population of 3,834,934 in 2002. The Bahamas have a higher standard of living than Costa Rica, with an income of $17,000 GDP per capita compared to $8,500 for Costa Rica. Also noteworthy is the much higher alcohol consumption in The Bahamas totaling 15.26 liters per capita compared to 4.39 for Costa Rica. The unemployment rate is about the same for the two countries at 6.3% for Costa Rica and 6.9% for The Bahamas. Poverty and income inequality data are not available for The Bahamas. The racial composition of The Bahamas is nearly the reverse of the 90% white in Costa Rica. Blacks constitute 85% of the population of The Bahamas, whereas Asians constitute 12 percent and (non-black) Hispanics constitute 3%. Like Costa Rica, The Bahamas are heavily involved in the drug trade, but with a greater emphasis on the trade in cocaine than Costa Rica, and with practically no evidence of heroin traffic. Considering the fact that the population of The Bahamas is less than one tenth that of Costa Rica, cocaine seizures for 1997 of 2.58 and 3.68 tons, respectively, compared to 7.85 and 7.15 tons for Costa Rica, indicates that the cocaine trade is substantially greater on a per capita basis in The Bahamas than in Costa Rica.

Christopher Columbus actually made his first landfall in the Western Hemisphere in The Bahamas in 1492. After the decimation of the Indian population by the Spanish slave traders, The Bahamas became a British Crown Colony in 1717. Its first Royal Governor was a former pirate named Woodes Rogers, who ironically brought law and order to The Bahamas in 1718 when he expelled the buccaneers who had used the islands as hideouts. Loyalists from the United States settled in The Bahamas after the American Revolution, bringing with them black slaves to provide labor for cotton plantations. The plantations died out after emancipation, but the islands served as a base for American rumrunners during the post-World War I era of Prohibition. Hence, The Bahamas have a legacy of piracy and smuggling.

Starting in the 1950s, the black Bahamians and their Progressive Liberal Party (PLP) opposed the ruling white-controlled United Bahamian party. The PLP won control of the government in 1964, led by Prime Minister Lynden O. Pindling, and the country gained full independence within the Commonwealth on July 10, 1973. As a result of allegations of widespread government corruption related to money from drug trafficking in 1983, Pindling resigned and was subsequently succeeded as Prime Minister by Hurbert Ingraham of the Free National Movement.

BOX 8–8

Security in The Bahamas

An estimated 85% of households in The Bahamas have security bars, alarm systems, or some form of security.[78]

The Bahamas rank number four of the world's countries in the CCDB in its rate of robbery with a rate of 457.19 per 100,000 inhabitants in 1999; however, this rate is down from an even higher rate of 566.21 in 1998. The Bahamas have a problem of overcrowded prisons, as well as indications of high rates of domestic violence and child abuse. Another chronic problem is ethnic conflicts with a minority of some 20% to 25% Haitians, many of whom are illegal aliens. A major factor in crime in the country is the country's involvement in drug trafficking, as well as the involvement of its banking industry in money laundering. Strategically located on the air and sea routes between Colombia and the United States, The Bahamas encompass hundreds of small, deserted islands used for transshipment and temporary drug storage. Traffickers are increasingly using tactics that make it difficult for U.S. and Bahamian law enforcement to intercept their shipments. Among these are the ever-increasing use of Cuban airspace and territorial sea to evade law enforcement officers; the use of very high-speed, low-profile boats; and the use of well-hidden compartments on large coastal freighters.

Although there is evidence of a considerable trade in drugs, Bahamian law enforcement receives considerable support from the United States in countering the drug traffic and enjoys periodic success in drug seizures. The Bahamas have a national police force called the Royal Bahamas Police Force (RBPF). The RBPF maintains internal security, and the small Royal Bahamas Defense Force is responsible for external security. The Drug Enforcement Unit (DEU) of the RBPF is the lead institution for drug law enforcement. The DEU works closely with the U.S. Justice Department's Drug Enforcement Administration (DEA) on drug investigations. The DEU also receives training and equipment through the U.S. State Department's International Narcotics Control program.

During 1998, the government of the Commonwealth of The Bahamas arrested 1,982 persons on drug charges and seized 3.68 metric tons of cocaine and 2.86 metric tons of marijuana. The seizures of cocaine in The Bahamas from 1990 to 1998 are shown in Figure 8–2.

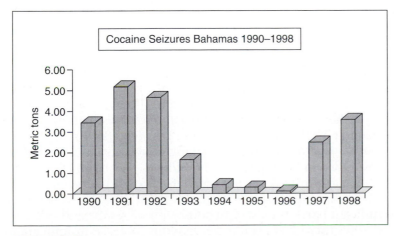

Figure 8–2
Cocaine Seizure Rates for the Bahamas, 1990–1998[79]

Table 8–3 **Robbery Rates and Cocaine Seizure Rates by Year for The Bahamas**

Year	Robbery Rate	Metric Tons of Cocaine Seized
1990	492.96	3.53
1991	600.77	5.26
1992	630.88	4.80
1993	601.12	1.80
1994	200.00	0.49
1995	371.94	0.39
1996	466.9	0.12
1997	518.33	2.58
1998	566.21	3.68

There is a strong correspondence between the robbery rates for those years and the seizure rates for cocaine, as seen in Table 8–3.

Drawing upon United Nations robbery data for the years 1990–1996 and INTERPOL data for 1997–1998, the Pearson correlation between the robbery rates and cocaine seizures by year in Table 8–3 was .72. While these findings are "food for thought," caution should be used in generalizing these findings to the United States or to other countries. The same strength of correlation does not seem to apply to other countries for which data are available (nor does it apply to the United States, as will be discussed later). The drug trade is an inordinately major criminal enterprise for The Bahamas. Two possible explanations for the link between robbery and cocaine seizures in The Bahamas are worth considering. One possibility is that when the supply of cocaine is severely curtailed, criminals must turn to other criminal enterprises, such as robbery, as their source of income. Another possibility is that cocaine use is extensive within The Bahamas, and when interdiction efforts are successful, the price of the drug rises, causing users to resort to desperate measures, such as robbery for money (or of drug dealers themselves) to obtain the quantity of the drug that they desire. In any event, it would seem that in The Bahamas, stringent efforts by law enforcement to reduce drug trafficking and drug abuse are positively correlated with higher rates of a seemingly more serious crime—robbery.

The United States

The United States has much in common with both Costa Rica and The Bahamas, although it seems more like a blend of the two countries. One important difference however is the size of the United States with its 50 states, each of which geographically and in population is as large as, or larger than, many countries of the world. In terms of racial composition, the United States resembles Costa Rica in having some 77% whites, but has a larger black population (13%) than Costa Rica. In terms of national background, the United States has been described as a "nation of immigrants." However, up until recently, significant barriers existed to admission of Asians and other nationalities. Since 1995 there has been a tremendous increase in immigration, both legal and illegal, of Asians, Hispanics, and other nationalities, made possible by the size and openness of America's borders of some 12,034 kilometers as well as 19,924 kilometers of coastline. The population as of 2003 was 290 million people, almost 10 times that of Costa Rica. The United States is a federation of some 50 states and one district (the District of Columbia) with a separate Federal government. Its legal system is a common law type, descended from that of England, but the county's criminal justice system lacks the unification of that of Great Britain. Each of the states has its own police, court, and correctional system, resulting in jurisdictional disputes that may hamper prosecution of crimes, particularly crimes that cross state borders. The United States has the largest and most technologically powerful economy in the world, with a per capita GDP of $37,600 with a purchasing power parity of $10.4 trillion, more than double that of the next largest economy, China, which has a population of 1.3 billion people. One important key to understanding crime in America, however, is that income is not shared equally. Although the Gini Index of income inequality for the United States (40.8) is just above average for the world (39.9), there is considerable variation in this index by states, ranging from a high of 47.6 for Louisiana to a low of 38.5 for Vermont. Also, the percentage living in poverty varies from a high of 17.6% in Mississippi to a low of 5.6% in New Hampshire. Moreover, there is an important racial disparity in income in the United States. In 1996, the real family income of whites was $44,756, compared to $26,522 for blacks. In regard to drugs, the United States is on the receiving end of cocaine, heroin, marijuana, and methamphetamine shipped from Columbia, Mexico, the Caribbean, Southeast Asia, and other countries, and the various states also serve as transshipment points as well as storage locations. Major ports of entry for illegal drugs are the Southerly coastal states of Florida, Mississippi, and Texas; the Western state of California; and the Northeastern state of New York (which also serves as a major shipping port and port of entry for many immigrants).

Inequality, Race, and Domestic Violence

Abundant data are available on the Internet on many of the aforementioned variables. As has been done in previous chapters, these variables have been intercorrelated on a state-by-state basis (i.e., using the state data as "cases" for analysis). The intercorrelation array for robbery appears in Table 8–4. Independent variables included in this table are infant mortality as a proxy for child abuse, percentage born to unwed mothers as a proxy for domestic partner abuse, the Gini Index as a measure of income inequality, as well as economic indicators as measures of the percentage of people living in poverty, unemployment rate, and male and female unemployment rate. In addition, percentage black in a state and the *difference* between black and white family incomes for the state are also included as independent variables. In addition to the aforementioned demographic factors, the per capita rates for heroin and cocaine seizures were also included as independent variables. The dependent variable in this table is the rate of robbery as reported to the FBI for 2001.[80] The best correlates of robbery in this table were infant mortality, percentage born to unwed mothers, the heroin seizure rate, the Gini Index, female unemployment, the percentage black, and (more strongly) the black/white income gap. It should be noted that, although the per capita rate of heroin seizures correlated strongly with robbery ($r = .65$), the rate of cocaine seizures did not correlate strongly ($r = .10$). It would appear from

Table 8–4 **State Correlates of Robbery Rates**

Divorces	−.18
Marriages	−.15
Infant mortality	.66
Percentage born to unwed mothers	.73
Child abuse	.21
Heroin seizures per capita	.65
Cocaine seizures per capita	.10
Gini Index	.58
Percentage living in poverty	.30
Unemployment rate	.48
Male unemployment rate	.41
Female unemployment rate	.52
Percentage black	.79
Black/white income gap	.89

Table 8–4 that robbery is a problem that has very much to do with race, as well as family problems, in the United States. By far the primary variable in robbery is the black/white income gap, with a Pearson r of .89. Robbery, it would seem, is a means of offsetting this income gap, especially when heroin

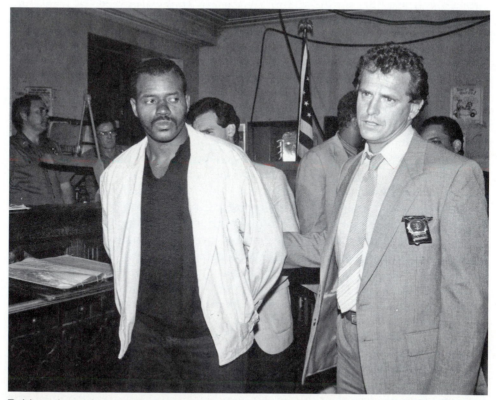

Robbery is a crime of racial economic inequality. A young black man, Terrence Troy Pusey, 24, left, of Queens, is escorted by a police officer in New York. Pusey is charged with the armed robbery of a Texas couple who surrendered $80,000 in cash and jewelry in their room at New York's Plaza Hotel.

Source: David Bookstaver, AP Wide World Photos

becomes unavailable (either as a means of generating income or as a drug to consume). The preponderance of cases are those in which child abuse is a factor ($r = .66$) and domestic abuse is indicated ($r = .73$). It would seem that the War on Drugs, as well as the trend toward imprisonment for drug offenses, may have exacerbated the conditions under which this "racial profile" exists in the United States. Discussed in later chapters is the question of whether or not this is a worldwide phenomenon, one that occurs in many other countries, or a situation that exists more or less "only in America."

The Changing Face of Robbery

The application of target hardening opportunity theories that was discussed in the section on theories of robbery may have had some harmful side-effects. For instance, the development of better car burglar alarms, steering column locking devices, and auto theft tracking technology (e.g., "LoJack") may have led to a trend toward more life-threatening auto robberies, referred to as carjackings. Similar use of home security in the form of burglar alarms, surveillance cameras, rapid response private security, deadbolt locks, and the like may have led to the growth of **home invasion robberies (HIRs).** These are robberies in which the perpetrators deliberately confront the residents in their home. Furthermore, enhanced department store merchandise electronic security may have helped to decrease shoplifting, but at the same time may have encouraged a surge in convenience store holdups.

The term **carjacking** refers to a completed or attempted robbery of a motor vehicle by a stranger to the victim.[81] It differs from other motor vehicle thefts because the victim is present and the offender uses or threatens to use force. Klaus did a study of the incidence of carjackings in the United States from 1992–1996 as reported in the NCVS. She found that an average of about 49,000 attempts or completed carjackings occurred in the United States in each of the years examined. This estimate of 49,000 is up from 35,000 completed and attempted carjackings that occurred each year between 1987 and 1992.[82] About half of these were completed carjackings. Seven in 10 completed carjackings involved firearms, compared to two in 10 attempted carjackings. Most of the carjackings did not result in injury to the victim, although 60% of carjackings involve assaults,[83] and injuries have been found to occur in one third of the cases.[84] All of the completed carjackings were reported to the police, whereas more than half of the attempts were reported. The latter statement is also true of auto thefts, one of the most reported of all crimes, because the victims will not be compensated by their insurance companies unless they report the crime to the police. Carjackings are most likely to occur at night in parking lots or garages, or on the street.[85] Peak carjacking hours were between 8 p.m. and 2 a.m., with the crime occurring most frequently on the weekend, on a public street.[86] Offenders are disproportionately between the ages of 21 and 29, while victims are disproportionately residents of a central city, as opposed to suburbanites or rural residents.[87] All of the carjackers reportedly are males, and about 60% had one or more accomplices.

HIR is not a completely new crime. In fact, a HIR was portrayed in Truman Capote's classic true-crime book *In Cold Blood*, in which two killers invaded a home in rural Kansas in 1959. The robbery ended in the murder of the entire family. However, HIRs have been a relatively recent threatening new crime trend attributed to immigrant Southeast Asian gangs in America. Curiously, Asian groups at one time were held up as an example of an exception to the Chicago school's "transitional areas" of crime. Asians were said to live in culturally different insulated groups ("Oriental enclaves") that maintained low rates of crime and delinquency despite exposure to poverty, discrimination, exploitation, and disadvantageous conditions.[88] Such may have been the case during the 1960s, when the Chinese population of the United States was fairly stable because of a ban on Chinese immigration that had been in place since the Chinese Exclusion Act of 1882.

Perhaps based upon the "Oriental enclave" assumption that Asians had a low crime rate, a number of acts were passed to facilitate Asian immigration into the United States, beginning with the Immigrant Act of 1965. This legislation was followed by the Indochina Migration and Refugee Assistance Act of 1975, the Refugee Act of 1980, and others. These acts rested on the assumption that Asians immigrate from stable, continuous, traditional cultures. However, most of the post-1965 Asian immigrants came from societies disrupted by colonialism, as well as the French and American wars in Southeast Asia.[89] During the past 25 years, refugee youth from such war-torn countries as Laos, Cambodia, and Vietnam have formed the basis for Asian gangs that have specialized in home invasion robberies. The "Asian Gangster Guy" was described in the following way on one Website:

> Usually seen: at the local billiards hall, at the local video arcade, at the bowling alley, at the college recreation room (ditching class) and at the Korean Karaoke bar. . . . Usually wears: ultimately insanely huge baggy pants, Nike visor (upside down), Nike warm-up jacket, pager/beeper/cellular phone (it has to be exposed so everyone can see it!). Also, he wears too many designer clothes just for their labels (Hilfiger, Nautica, CK, Ralph Loren, and JNCO) . . . accessories: earrings and a hoe. . . A great Street Fighter and Tekken player. . . . No matter who's around (parents, aunts, uncles, cousins, teachers), he always has to act hard and tough. Gives that bad impression to everyone . . . Very good at the art of the home-invasion robbery.[90]

One account of HIR in the United States traces its origin to the South Florida "cocaine cowboys" of the late 1970s and early 1980s who used HIR as an effective method to obtain large amounts of cash and drugs from rival dealers.[91] Another account traces invasion robberies to those conducted in the Tenderloin district of San Francisco in the early 1980s by gang members whose roots were in Vietnam, Cambodia, and Laos. Gang members initially chose HIR of immigrants from their own country. The reason for this was because of their awareness that the victims were distrustful of banks and kept their wealth (money, jewels, and gold) hidden at home. HIRs declined after a 1995–1996 crackdown on gangs involved in the "gray market" robberies of computer chips (gray referring to the color of the computer chips) from companies in the Bay Area. Many of the robberies go unreported because victims are not only compatriots, but they are also players in the drug trade who prefer to settle the scores on the street.[92] The link developed by these sources between robbery and the drug trade helps to shed light upon the strong correlation ($r = .65$) shown in Table 8–4 between heroin seizures and robbery.

Discussion of Asian gangs in the criminal justice literature began in the late 1980s and early 1990s. One study based upon law enforcement sources portrayed the Asian gangs as "home invaders," who travel across the United States robbing, terrorizing, and intimidating Asian families.[93] A couple of interview studies have been completed, one of which was done in San Francisco, California, based on face-to-face interviews with 73 representatives of several different gangs. That study found that gang membership was traced to a breakdown in the traditional family structure. The gang members had experienced victimization and abuse in their families, which prompted the youth to seek gang membership as a source of support.[94] Another ethnographic study resulting from 64 face-to-face interviews of Asian gang members found that the gang members were not found to participate in formally organized and hierarchically controlled criminal enterprises.[95] In fact, rather than participating on the level of soldiers in an organized crime family, the youthful Asian gang members appear to resemble the old-fashioned "professional criminals" that Sutherland described—professional thieves operating in small groups; displaying considerable geographic mobility; and exhibiting considerable skill, planning, and organization. The following description of home invaders indicates a high level of planning and coordination in their operations:

> Home invaders prefer to make direct entry into a targeted residence. In fact, the entry is often dynamic—relying on sheer force, false pretense, or various forms of impersonation. The violence associated with home invasion robbery generally occurs during the initial confrontation with victims, in order to establish control quickly and to limit the likelihood of later identification by the victims. . . . Unlike the majority of burglars, home invaders carry items that connote control and confrontation, such

Asian male and female Cambodian immigrants, members of a gang called Tiny Rascals, hold weapons and flash gang signs, emulating black and Hispanic gangs, in Long Beach, California. The TRG is considered to be the largest Asian gang in the United States. They are highly mobile and engage in home invasion robberies and carry out drug sales, extortion, and other crimes for profit.

Source: A. Ramey, PhotoEdit, Inc.

Table 8–5 **Robbery Percentage Distribution by Type for 1995 and 2004**[96]

Type	1995	2004	Difference
Street/highway	54.3	42.8	−21.2
Commercial house	12.3	14.7	19.5
Gas or service station	2.3	2.7	17.4
Convenience store	5.2	6.1	17.3
Residence	10.8	13.8	27.8
Bank	1.6	2.4	50.0
Miscellaneous	13.4	17.4	29.9
Total	100.0	100.0	

as firearms, handcuffs, masks, and tape. Because the threat level inside a residence is rarely known in advance, the offense almost always is committed by more than one offender. These offenders often develop well-organized plans and divide specific tasks among themselves. One or more of the home invaders usually control the victims while the other offenders systematically ransack the residence. Home invaders usually target the resident, not the residence. They may make their selection in a variety of ways, often choosing women, senior citizens, or drug dealers.[97]

There is evidence that the number of HIRs is dropping, but home invasions are now being committed increasingly by criminals of all ethnicities. At the same time, many Asian gang members have moved on to less risky but more profitable crimes, such as computer chip theft, forgery, and credit card fraud.[98]

Although most types of robbery dropped during the 1990s until 1999, all except street robberies rose after 1999 until 2004 to a point higher than the rate in 1995, as can be seen in Table 8–5. Gas station/convenience store robberies increased by 17%, and residential robberies rose 27.8%. Commercial house robberies also increased 19.5%, and bank robberies increased by 50%. Declining were "street robberies," by 21.2%. Although the number of robberies declined during this period from 580,545 in 1995 to 401,326 in 2004, the dollar loss actually increased during this time from an estimated $507 million in 1995 to $525 million in 2004. The value of property stolen averaged $873 per robbery in 1995, but $1,308 per robbery in 2004.[99]

BOX 8–9

"Express Robbery" in Mexico

While Mexico's high rate of robbery may be related to the drug trade, it may also be related to tourism. Robbery, predominantly pickpocketing, is prevalent at tourist destinations, airports, and bus stations in Mexico, and on the metro in the capital, Mexico City.

There have been many incidents, particularly in Mexico City, of "express kidnapping" where individuals are forced to withdraw funds at automatic teller machines to secure their release. Passengers have also been robbed in taxis. Taxis should only be used from authorized taxi ranks (sitios).[100]

This increase in commercial robbery produces a bigger yield in terms of dollars, but at a greater risk of arrest, particularly in the case of bank robberies. According to the FBI, over 80% of bank robbers are identified and arrested. Also, 88.8% of those arrested for this crime and prosecuted in Federal courts are convicted.[101] Thus, it would seem that, more and more, robbers are fitting the profile of the "drug addict" robber, as suggested by Table 8–3, desperate for money to supply a drug habit that becomes more and more expensive proportionate with the success of law enforcement interdiction efforts.

Although active **drug robbers** (those who take money and drugs from dealers by force or threat of force) probably pursue their robberies without the event being known to the police, a recent description of drug robbers seems to fit the "mind set" of the desperate robbers as described earlier. Jacobs, Topalli, and Wright interviewed 25 currently active drug robbers; largely African American males aged 15 to 46, contacted in the streets of St. Louis, Missouri. The robbers developed an orientation consisting of intimidation, anonymity maintenance, and hypervigilance as part of retaliatory threat management. However, all three elements declined along with a record of past successes—less discretion, less precision, and less vigilance; furthermore, the vast majority of subjects were characterized by fatalism coupled with heavy drinking, hard drug use, and fiscal desperation.[102]

While such experiments have been forbidden by law in America, the Swiss conducted a study to evaluate programs implemented in several Swiss cities to medically prescribe heroin and other opiates to about 1,000 seriously addicted drug users. Data were obtained from interviews with 319 participants, as well as from police files and the national register of convictions. All indicators consistently pointed to a substantial reduction in criminal involvement after entering the program, particularly for larceny, burglary, and robbery, and also for trafficking in drugs.[103] If drug addiction is, indeed, at the root of robbery and other major crimes today, the results of research such as this should be studied carefully to see if medically supervised drug use can provide an effective and long-term offset to serious crimes against person and property.

BOX 8–10

Opium Wars Come Back to Haunt the United Kingdom

Great Britain is a country that trafficked in opium from India to China during the 19th century via its English East India Company, and fought two wars with China (Opium Wars) over its right to peddle opium to the Chinese. Now Britain is on the receiving end of the opium trade, primarily originating in the same region of the world from which England based its 19th century drug trade—the golden crescent of southwest Asia, notably Afghanistan and Pakistan. Just as China tried to do then, England has attempted to prohibit the trade in heroin, among other opiate derivatives. Although England had a practice of prescribing heroin to addicts from the 1920s to the 1960s, in response to political pressure from the United States, heroin maintenance was severely curtailed in 1971 with the passage in England of the Misuse of Drugs Act. The result was an unregulated illicit market and a jump in the number of heroin users from fewer than 2,000 in 1970 to upward of 300,000 today.[104] Along with that increase in addicts was a significant jump in crime, particularly property crime in England. From 1981 to 1995, according to victim surveys done in England, robbery rose 81% (4.2 per 1,000 population rising to 7.6) and burglary doubled in England (40.9 per 1,000 households rising to 82.9).[105]

SUMMARY AND CONCLUSION

Robbery may be defined as attempted or actual theft of property by force or fear. Robbery is unique in being both a crime of violence and a crime against property. This chapter began with the case history of Ray Johnson, a person who progressed from juvenile delinquency to a career as a professional bank robber as a result of his socialization as a "state-raised youth." Professional thieves, a category originally identified by Sutherland, appear to be diminishing in number. Robbery declined from a peak of 272.7 per 100,000 inhabitants in 1991 to 148.5 per 100,000 in year 2001. Despite this downward trend, an increasing proportion of robberies result in injuries to the victim. Another trend has been the recognition by researchers of a greater variety of types of robbers than just "professionals" and "amateurs." Included in the list of robber types today are desperation, chronic, intensive, occasional, compulsive, casual, opportunist, drug addict, and alcoholic robbers. Today's robber tends to be increasingly violently disposed, armed, young, black, and involved with street culture, drugs, and alcohol. Related to these trends are increasing unemployment, increasing income inequality, a lack of deterrence of robbery by the criminal justice system, and the negative impact of the War on Drugs. These causative factors have had the greatest impact upon male, black youths. Country profiles of two countries emphasized the negative effect of a lenient justice system (Costa Rica) and a link with drug interdiction (The Bahamas) as factors in the high rates of robbery in these countries. Analysis for the United States using Census data by state indicated that factors strongly correlated with robbery recently were income inequality, child abuse, children born to unwed mothers, and heroin, but not cocaine seizures. The strongest correlation with robbery rates was that of black/white income inequality with a Pearson correlation of .89. These correlations suggest that robbery in the United States is very much a product of racial income inequality, compounded by the related problems of heroin addiction vis à vis the high cost of heroin on the black market.

The aforementioned analysis seems to indicate that crimes are interrelated in a kind of "system of crime." Government policy may move in the direction of suppressing one kind of crime (e.g., drug abuse). The unanticipated consequence of this policy may be an increase in another form of crime (e.g., robbery). The trend toward mass incarceration of offenders and toward longer sentences is based upon the belief that both crimes—robbery and drug abuse—can be addressed by incarcerating all of the criminals. However, if the social conditions that lead to crime (e.g., family violence, economic inequality) continue to exist, the next generation of youth who are subjected to those conditions will simply replace those that have been put in prison. Furthermore, unless all prisoners are locked up for life, the larger prison population periodically yields larger numbers of angry persons getting out of prison, bitter about their treatment in prison. As a result, they will be inclined to take revenge through perpetrating progressively more violent crime. If the convicts have engaged in substance abuse in prison without treatment for that abuse, they will emerge with a drug addiction that generates an enhanced need for income, which (in the absence of good job prospects) may have to be attained through crime. Thus, the application of deterrence theory by itself may not be sufficient to reduce rates of robbery, especially if the theory is applied to only a small fraction of offenders, leaving the remainder to play the odds and continue with robberies unabated.

DISCUSSION QUESTIONS

1. Among the theories covered in this text, which theory do you think is best illustrated by the life story of Ray, a Bank Robber?

2. Do you think that robbery should be treated primarily as a crime against persons or a crime against property?

3. Among the various types of robbers, which type do you think is predominant today?

4. Why do you think clearance rates for robbery are so low? What about conviction rates—why do you think they are also so low in the United States?

5. What do you think comparative study tells us about the causes of robbery in America today?

6. How do you account for the new trend in "home invasion robbery"?

SUGGESTED WEBSITES

http://www.lycaeum.org/drugwar/dupe.html Web-site documenting the history of the War on Drugs and its relationship to politics, CIA secret wars, the mass media, and race.

http://www.lindesmith.org/global/ Website dedicated to the legacy of Alfred Lindesmith, describing the reach of the United States in criminalizing drug use and trafficking in countries around the world.

http://www.smartraveller.gov.au/zw-cgi/view/Advice. Website focusing upon crime threats, such as robbery, kidnapping, and purse snatching, which travelers should consider when traveling to foreign countries.

http://www.infocostarica.com/travel/safety.html. Web-site giving current warnings about crime threats in Costa Rica.

ENDNOTES

1. Irwin, 1970.
2. Irwin, 1970.
3. Langan, 1978.
4. FBI, 2004, p. 266.
5. FBI, 2004, p. 505.
6. Felson & Messner, 1996.
7. FBI, 2004, p. 36; FBI, 1989.
8. Kleck & DeLone, 1993.
9. Zimring, 1977.
10. Beirne & Messerschmidt, 1995, p. 145.
11. Bureau of Justice Statistics (BJS), 2003, Table 27.
12. BJS, 1995, 2003, Tables 75 and 79.
13. Rand, 1997.
14. FBI, 2004, pp. 31, 37.
15. BJS, 2004b, p. 2, Table 1.
16. FBI, 2000, p. 66.
17. FBI, 2004b, p. 31.
18. BJS, 2004b, Table 3, p. 5.
19. FBI, 1995, p. 201.
20. FBI, 2004, p. 266.
21. Calculations based upon BJS, 2004b, Table 3.
22. Sutherland, 1937.
23. Winslow, 1968, p. 164.
24. Conklin, 1972.
25. Haran, 1982.
26. Gabor & Normandeau, 1989.
27. Kroese & Staring, 1993.
28. Nkpa, Nwokocha-K.U. 1976.
29. Yablonsky, 1990, p. 76.
30. Petrosino & Kass, 2000.
31. FBI, 2004, p. 32.
32. Ball, 1991; Birkbeck, 1983; Boggess & Bound, 1997; Bureau of Justice Statistics, 2001, 2002e, 2003b, 2004c; Camp, 1968; Carrington, 2001; Corbo & Coyle, 1990; Corman & Mocan, 1996; Costanz, Bankston, & Shihadeh, 2001; Davison & Smith, 2001; Ekpenyong, 1989; Engbersen & van der Leun, 2001; Fajnzylber, Lederman, & Loayza, 2002; Harlan, 1982; Inciardi, Horowitz, & Pottieger, 1993; Kevin, 1995; Klein, Bartholomew, & Bahr, 1999; Kruize, 2001; Landau and Fridman, 1993; Martell, 1991; Miller, 1998; Morrison & O'Donnell, 1994; Mundt,1990; Puerto Rico Criminal Justice Information System, 1983; Queensland Office of Economic & Statistical Research, 2001; Sampson, 1985; Savolainen, 2000; Smith, 2003; Topalli, Wright, & Fornango, 2002; Welford, MacDonald, & Weiss, 1997; Wright & Decker, 1997; Zimring & Zuehl, 1986.
33. Blau & Blau, 1982.
34. Sampson, 1983.
35. Sampson, 1985.
36. Chambliss, 1967.
37. Comparative Criminology Website: Uganda.
38. Trasler, 1986.
39. Wilson & Boland, 1978.
40. Sampson & Cohen, 1988.
41. Sullivan, 1985.
42. Feeney, Dill, & Weir, 1983.
43. California Legislature Joint Committee for Revision of the Penal Code, 1980.
44. McElroy, Cosgrove, & Farrell, 1981.

45. DeZee, 1982.

46. Wright & Decker, 1997.

47. BJS, 2003, Table 91.

48. Erickson, 1996.

49. Gould, 1969.

50. Luckinbill, 1981.

51. Cohen, Cantor, & Kleugel, 1981.

52. Cohn & Rotton, 2000.

53. Smith, Frazee, & Davison, 2000.

54. Bellaire, 2000.

55. Wilson & Kelling, 1982.

56. Kelling & Sousa, 2001.

57. Mocan & Rees, 1999.

58. *Kykeon@lycaeum.org*, 1991.

59. Hornberger, 2000.

60. Comparative Criminology Website: Switzerland.

61. Killias & Rabasa, 1998.

62. Brehmer & Iten, 2001.

63. Comparative Criminology Website: Portugal.

64. Barker, Geraghty, & Webb, 1993.

65. Harrision, 1992.

66. Barton, 1980a; Barton, 1980b; Barton, 1982; Chaiken & Chaiken, 1985; Feeney & Weir, 1974; Inciardi, Horowitz, & Pottieger, 1993; Kmet, 1981.

67. Hills & Santiago, 1992.

68. Dycus & Dycus, 1988.

69. Abbott, 1981.

70. Maher, Dixon, & Hall, 2002.

71. Swann & James, 1998.

72. Korte, Pykalainen, & Seppala, 1998.

73. Latvia has faithfully reported complete statistics to INTERPOL starting in 1995, and since that year the rates of robbery per 100,000 inhabitants have been 35.78 in 1995, 40.98 in 1996, 33.43 in 1997, 24.77 in 1998, 110.48 in 1999, 136.11 in 2000, and 554.58 for 2001. For purposes of holding constant the data for analysis, new data were not entered into the database after October 2003; however, it should be noted that Latvia returned to a robbery rate of 108.15 in 2002, confirming the finding that an uncharacteristic robbery rate was reported for Latvia in 2001. Accordingly, a country profile on Latvia will not be done for purposes of analyzing robbery, because that country is not consistently high in robbery.

74. NOTE: Includes the United States and all countries ranking higher in robbery, all developed nations, and countries ranked in the bottom 10%. (Countries highlighted are developed nations.)

75. Ebbe, 1993b.

76. Infocostarica Staff, 2003.

77. Source: Bureau for International Narcotics and Law Enforcement Affairs, U.S. Department of State. (1999a).

78. Retrieved 4/13/2002 from *http://www.safe-bahamas.com/facts.lasso*

79. SOURCE: Bureau for International Narcotics and Law Enforcement Affairs, U.S. Department of State. (1999b).

80. FBI, 2001.

81. Klaus, 1999.

82. Rand, 1994.

83. Donahue, etal., 1994.

84. New York State Department of Correctional Services, 1995.

85. Rand, 1994.

86. Donahue, et al., 1994.

87. Rand, 1994.

88. Winslow, 1968, pp. 156–157.

89. Braziel, 2000.

90. Vinnie, 2003.

91. Hurley, 2003.

92. Zamora, 2000.

93. Burke & O'Rear, 1990.

94. Toy, 1992; Toy, 1993.

95. Joe, 1994.

96. FBI, 1995, p. 27, Table 2.20; FBI, 2004, p. 34, Table 2.20.

97. Hurley, 2003.

98. Carney, 1997.

99. FBI, 1995, p. 27; FBI, 2004, p. 34.

100. *Smartraveller.gov.au*, 2004.

101. Haran & Martin, 1984, p. 47.

102. Jacobs, Topalli, & Wright, 2000.

103. Killias & Rabasa, 1998.

104. Drug Policy Alliance, 2003.

105. BJS, 1998a, 1998b.

9

ASSAULT

KEY TERMS

aggravated assault
assault
battery
carnal abuse
chastisement
coverture
garrison communities

hate crimes
power-control theory
road rage
rule of thumb
simple assault
witchcamps

OUTLINE

Definition
Extent and Trends
Need for a Theory of Assault

Themes in Assault Studies
Types of Assault
Theory

LEARNING OBJECTIVES

After reading this chapter, students should be able to:

1. Define the term "assault"

2. Show an awareness of various types of assault, including those not taken seriously in our society

3. Describe the trends in both simple and aggravated assault and factors that may be related to these trends

4. Account for the relatively high rate of aggravated assault in the United States compared to other developed countries

5. List the factors related to assault in the United States, as well as assault-related factors found in other countries that have a high assault rate

6. Discuss the general theory of assault developed by Thio (power-control theory)

INTRODUCTION

CASE STUDY ONE: Domestic Violence

An 18-year-old woman presented to her family physician for an initial obstetric examination, accompanied by her 27-year-old boyfriend. Initial history revealed that she was at 16 weeks of gestation and living in a mobile home with her partner. She was strongly considering giving up the baby for adoption because of "financial and other" reasons. Answers to screening violence history questions indicated that she had been beaten by her father from preschool age until she was 13 years of age; her parents then divorced. The patient stated that her present partner had "slapped her around" on several occasions and that once she was "accidentally dragged by his truck" during an argument. He had slammed the driver's door, started the truck and put it in gear, reportedly without realizing that her dress was caught in the car door. On further questioning the patient stated that she was not happy in this relationship and in fact did not feel safe. However, she stated that she "had no place else to go" and expressed optimism about the future because her partner had begun to attend church and stated that he wanted to be a good father.[1]

CASE STUDY TWO: Elder Abuse

Several years ago I listened to an interview with an older, abused woman who had filed for divorce. She had been a stay-at-home mom, and had no resources of her own. Her husband, not wanting to lose his power over her, played the part of the innocent "Mr. Nice Guy" in court. The judge refused to believe the woman and did not grant the divorce. At the end of the interview the woman said, "The only choice I have is to go back to him unless I want to become a bag lady."[2]

CASE STUDY THREE: Child Abuse

This boy, born in 1990, was placed in the custody of his mother after his parents' divorce, with overnight visits with his father. When he was less than two years old, he began reporting ongoing sodomy by his father. He had a cluster of symptoms indicative of sexual abuse, including rectal bleeding, nightmares, night terrors, enuresis, encopresis, sexualized behavior, depression, extreme dissociation, intense anger, flashbacks, physical pains, insomnia, diarrhea, and stomach aches. The child disclosed the abuse to five teachers, the family physician, therapists, police, family, and friends. There were over 62 reports of suspected abuse in seven years. Child Protective Services investigated and substantiated seven reports of child sex abuse. The child wrote and talked to the judge, asking to live with his mother and grandmother. Instead, the court repeatedly placed him in the custody of his identified perpetrator. He called 911 for help from his father's house, and his therapist called the police to help him, and was put into expensive private foster care, rather than with his nonoffending mother. He was able to stay with his mother while she was dying. Four months after her death, he was forcibly removed from his nonoffending grandmother's care by armed police. He was placed in expensive foster care again for over six months, and is now forced by Juvenile Court to live with his identified perpetrator permanently. The child's attorneys did not represent his wishes, and functioned as de facto attorneys for the accused perpetrator.[3]

These three case studies indicate that assault frequently takes place in the home. The pregnant 18-year-old woman said that her present partner had "slapped her around" and that she was "accidentally dragged by his truck." The second case study of elder abuse revealed how the lack of outside resources can trap an elderly person in a relationship in which she is subject to assault. Resources have been made available to women through VAWA and other legislation in recent years. However, the assumption may be made that a woman once freed of a relationship can get a job and live independently. However, such may not be the case for the senior citizen. The third case includes a situation that has not yet been addressed in public policy—the return of an abused child to an abusive parent where he will be assaulted perpetually. Although the term "assault" often brings to mind a street fight or bar brawl, there is growing evidence that much assault occurs "behind closed doors" in a family or household situation. Furthermore, additional evidence is developing to show how many assaults that take place outside the home environment can be traced back to the violence that previously occurred between family members.

DEFINITION

There are numerous different definitions of assault and its subtypes in various government documents. The term **assault** as it is used in these documents also includes **battery.** Because these crimes are associated, it is assumed that they are the same thing, but they are not. Many states list the crime as "assault and battery." For instance, in California assault and battery is defined as follows:

> Under California law, assault and battery are separate crimes, although often they are charged together. Assault is defined as an unlawful attempt to violently injure another person.
>
> Battery means unlawfully and willfully using force or violence against another person. Other laws make both assault and battery more serious crimes if the offender uses a firearm or other deadly weapon, commits the crime with the intent to commit mayhem or rape, or if the assault or battery is against a government officer or an elderly person. Under California law, transmission of HIV may constitute an aggravated battery.[4]

The FBI's UCR includes battery in its definitions of two forms of assault, aggravated and simple. **Aggravated assault** in the UCR is defined as: "An unlawful attack by one person upon another for the purpose of inflicting severe or aggravated bodily injury. This type of assault usually is accompanied by the use of a weapon or by means likely to produce death or great bodily harm." By contrast, **simple assaults** in the UCR are defined as "Assaults and attempted assaults where no weapons are used and which do not result in serious or aggravated injury to the victim."[5]

The NCVS is based upon a survey, so it incorporates definitions that are slightly different from the FBI definitions. The NCVS defines aggravated assault as "a completed or attempted attack with a weapon, whether or not an injury occurred. It is also an attack without a weapon in which the victim is seriously injured." In the NCVS, a simple assault is defined as "an attack without a weapon resulting either in no injury, minor injury (such as bruises, black eyes, cuts, scratches, or swelling), or an undetermined injury requiring less than 2 days of hospitalization. Simple assault also includes attempted assaults without a weapon."[6] While the NCVS definition for aggravated assault is virtually identical to the FBI's definition, the NCVS definition for simple assault contains some specifics (e.g., less than two days hospitalization) not contained in the FBI definition of simple assault.

Table 9–1   **Violent Crimes by Weapons Used.**[7]

Crime	Firearms	Sharps	Other Weapon or Weapon Not Stated	Strong-Arm or No Weapon Used
Murder	66.0	13.2	14.1	6.6
Aggravated assault	19.3	18.6	35.6	26.6
Simple assault	0.0	0.0	9.0	91.0
Rape	3.1	5.9	6.9	84.1
Robbery	40.6	8.9	9.4	41.1

Most texts in criminology have treated assault as being explained by the same causal factors as murder, both in terms of the offense and offender population. A strong case can be made that "aggravated assaulters" are in most ways very similar to murderers. However, if the discussion is opened up to include "simple assaults," then the profile of the typical assaulter is quite different from that of murderers.

The question of motive may be raised to differentiate between assaulters and murderers, as related to the weapon used, as shown in Table 9–1. There is a difference in weapons used between assault and murder. In the vast majority of assaults, which are termed *simple assaults* or *other assaults* by the FBI, there is no weapon used. Even in "aggravated assaults," the weapon array used is quite different from that in murder.

Table 9–1 reveals that, in terms of weapons use, simple assault has more in common with rape than it does with either murder or robbery. Although 66% of murders involved firearms, only 19.3% of aggravated assaults involved firearms. Furthermore, in cases of aggravated assaults, use of the weapon was only threatened in the majority of cases, with only 16.2% of the cases was actual injury incurred, according to NCVS findings.[8] If simple assaults are included, then the differences between assault and murder are even greater. In terms of motive, then, it seems likely that in the vast majority of cases of assault, the motive was not to kill the victim but some other goal, such as to subordinate, exact revenge, punish, inflict pain, express frustration, enjoin conformity, self-defense, and so forth.

EXTENT AND TRENDS

In FBI statistics, there were 1,726,054 persons arrested for assault in 2004. Of these 440,553 were "aggravated assaults" and 1,285,501 were "other assaults"[9] In 2004, there were 854,911 aggravated assault offenses reported to the police.[10] In 2004, the NCVS estimated the number of aggravated assaults at 1,030,080, indicating the FBI's report of aggravated assaults is 83% of the total offenses.[11] In 2004, there were 1,367,009 violent offenses in the UCR. Thus, "aggravated assaults" were 62.5% of all violent crimes.[12] In the NCVS, aggravated assaults are about 60.7% of violent crimes (excluding simple assault).[13]

What percentage of major crimes are assaults? The answer is that it depends. If we count only aggravated assaults in the list of major crimes, the answer is only about 4%; however, if we include simple assaults the answer is about 14% using NCVS figures.[14] If we use FBI data, the 854,911 aggravated assaults reported are about 7.3% of major offenses.[15] If we add the 1,285,501 arrests for "other assaults" to the 894,911 offenses reported, then assaults become 16.6% of the total. Thus, assault is either a tiny proportion of all crime, or a fair proportion of all crime, depending upon which approach is used.

Aggravated assault, particularly as defined by the FBI is, for all practical purposes, "attempted murder" because the FBI stipulates that "this type of assault is usually accompanied by the use of a weapon or other means likely to produce death or great bodily harm."[16] Thus, it is usually explained by the same theories that are used for murder (e.g., the subculture of violence theory). However, the NCVS has given more significance to simple assault, by including statistics on it along with other serious crimes in "Table 1," the main table of its report. (The NCVS also includes statistics on "sexual assault" as well as rape.) The FBI is moving in the direction of treating "simple assault" more seriously by treated it as a "Class A" offense (most serious) in the new NIBRS. Thus, this chapter includes both "aggravated assault" and "simple assault" in the analysis, including the discussion of extent and trends in this section.

FBI Data

Since 1981, the rate of aggravated assault increased progressively from 289.3 per 100,000 inhabitants in 1981 to a high of 441.9 in 1992.[17] After this, the rate declined each year until 2004 when the rate was 291.1 per 100,000 inhabitants.[18] The FBI arrest rate for "other assaults" grew from 216.8 in 1980 to 466.5 in 2001 and then declined slightly to 439.0 in 2004.[19] It is interesting to note that for the period 1980 through 2001, the increase in the aggravated assault offense rate was only 10.1%, whereas the increase in the "other assault" arrest rate was 115.2%. Cohen, Kauder, and Ostrom suggested that the increase in the arrest rate for other assaults, rather than indicating a crime epidemic, instead indicates an aggressive intervention and mandatory arrest policy for domestic violence crimes.[20]

NCVS Data

Assault trends in the NCVS are shown in Figure 9–1.

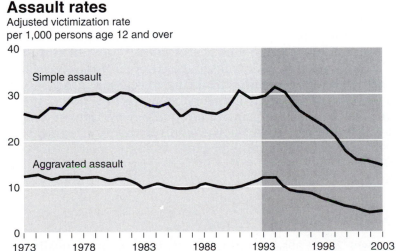

Assault rates

Adjusted victimization rate
per 1,000 persons age 12 and over

Simple assault

Aggravated assault

Figure 9–1 Assault Victimization Trends from the NCVS[21]

Figure 9–1 shows a pattern that has a minor similarity to the FBI trends in assault as described earlier in the sense that the trends spiked upward in 1993. However, the trend chart differs from the FBI trends described earlier in regard to aggravated assault, which has progressively declined in the NCVS data since 1973. Simple assault is shown to rise in the chart up until 1993. Both simple and aggravated assaults declined precipitously since 1993 in the NCVS data. Aggravated assault declined from a rate of 8.7 to 4.3 per 1,000 households from 1995 to 2004 in NCVS data, a decline of 50.6%. During that same time period, simple assault declined from 28.9 in 1995 to 14.2 per 1,000 households in 2004, a decline of 50.9%.[22]

If the NCVS data are to be accepted at face value, it would seem that some major change occurred after 1993 that made a considerable impact upon the incidence of simple assault. We explore that possibility later.

NEED FOR A THEORY OF ASSAULT

Although it is true that, in general, aggravated assault and murder can probably be explained by the same body of theories, it seems that it would be valuable to explain assault first, and then, drawing on the theories of homicide, show how assault can progress to homicide in a small percentage of the cases. If all forms of assault are involved, assault is different from murder. Assault is different from murder not only in terms of its greater frequency, but in that, demographically, it is more a crime that is done by the "average American" to other "average Americans," if one takes into consideration the huge volume of simple assaults.

In the UCR, aggravated assault is by far the most frequently occurring violent crime. In 2004, there were 16,137 murders, 94,635 forcible rapes, 854,911 aggravated assaults, and 401,326 robberies per 100,000 people in the United States. Thus, there were more aggravated assaults than all of the other violent crimes combined. In terms of arrests, in 2004 there were an estimated 1,726,054 arrests for simple and aggravated assaults, more than any other crime except drug abuse violations.[23] For this reason alone, assault deserves some attention. Unfortunately, because assault has been the "neglected child" of the major crimes, there have been few attempts to explain it in the criminological literature (apart from referring to theories of murder). It may be necessary here to begin to build a theory of assault. To do that we need to look at the various types of assault. We also need to do some profiling. We will see that there is a theory called power-control theory that has potential for being developed into a theory of assault. Given the power-control theory as a starting point, the country profiles that are on the comparative criminology Website may be of assistance in expanding upon the power-control theory. Countries that are high in rates of assault may provide clues as to the factors that contribute to that crime.

THEMES IN ASSAULT STUDIES

There are over 2,500 abstracts in *Criminal Justice Abstracts* dealing with the topic of assault. A review of these abstracts was done, and it was found that there are numerous themes in the criminological literature on assault, as follows:

- Assault is often a routine part of marriage and intimate partner relationships.

- In many (if not most) societies historically and even today, occasional assault in the form of **chastisement** or even physical abuse of the wife and children by the male is expected as part of the husband's traditional role as head of the household.

- A family or intimate partner situation is a relationship in which people spend a disproportionate share of time, compared to relationships with strangers. Thus, odds are greater that assault will occur. In fact, conflict that may result in assault may be a normal part of improving communication and therefore intimacy within a family.

- Most of the literature on assault pertains to family or intimate partner relations. Out of 2,581 sources (articles, books, etc.) referenced in *Criminal Justice Abstracts* using the term "assault" for the years 1968–2003, *only seven* pertained to "stranger assault."

- Most topics discussed in textbooks under the caption "assault" pertain to family issues. These topics include the nature and extent of assault, history of assault, spouse abuse, intimate partner assault, child abuse, abuse of the elderly, and sexual abuse.

- Murder as an outgrowth of domestic violence is rare and usually involves extraordinary stresses such as alcoholism, drug addiction, job loss, gang participation, mental illness, and the like.

- Domestic violence on average is by less lethal means than those used in murder.

- Even in stranger violence, the basis for the violence may pertain to an intimate relationship or potential intimate relationship. For instance, often stranger violence is preceded by an insult to one's manhood, which if done in front of a girlfriend, date, or intimate partner, may result in violence.

- Even in prison, violent assault has to do with intimate relationships. When an inmate's manhood is challenged, if he fails to dominate through violent retaliation, he may be sexually and physically assaulted. Often weak men in prison are forced to seek the protection of a strong male, in return for which he becomes involved in an intimate relationship with the strong male, as his property ("bitch" or "punk").

- People who take it upon themselves to "call out" or challenge a strange male and challenge his masculinity or right to possess a woman may be aggressive because of prior intimate relationships, such as child abuse, a broken marriage, or even a prison relationship. They may also be seeking an intimate relationship with a woman accompanying another man or with the man himself (homosexual relationship).

- The perspective on assault suggested in the aforementioned review of studies departs from the usual "assault as murder" approach. Instead, assault seems to be mostly a "family" concern, or at least an outgrowth of a relationship between "intimate partners" forming an informal family or common law marriage.

TYPES OF ASSAULT

When the subject of assault is broadened to include not just aggravated assaults, but also simple assaults, there are a wide variety of types of assault that can be included in the discussion. The scope of assault then ranges from the "rough play" of children, to spouse abuse (domestic violence), to child abuse, to street fighting or bar fighting that can occur between friends, acquaintances, and strangers—and even "road rage." As we go along we will develop profiles for these various types of assault, toward the goal of developing a "theory of assault." We will also find that there are typologies developed for almost each topic—types of spousal abusers, types of child abuse, and so forth.

One point that seems to resonate in discussions on the prevalence of assault is that assault is often not taken seriously. A man was only "chastising" his wife, or disciplining his child. Teenagers assaulting each other are often characterized as engaging in "horseplay." In terms used by labeling theorists, assault is often a form of *primary deviance,* and it is not reacted to informally, or by formal agencies of social control. Assault can even constitute a recreational activity in the form of aggressive games, such as football, hockey, and soccer. Assault as "primary deviance" may be a good point of departure for the development of a "theory of assault," because that is one way in which it surely differs from murder which almost invariably considered "secondary deviance."

Assault as Play

Much (if not most) assault takes place in everyday life and goes unnoticed by law enforcement. As indicated by NCVS statistics, children are most victimized by assault. In schools, smaller and younger children are assaulted by schoolyard bullies during sometimes unsupervised "recess" breaks. A "game" frequently played during these recess periods is "dodge ball" in which a "team" of children form an inner circle surrounded by a larger group of children who then throw a volleyball as hard as they can at the inner group of children, scoring points if they hit one of the children. These games frequently result in injury:

> . . . there is a movement afoot to ban dodge ball, a staple of the playground for generations. Dodge ball, it seems, is bad. There are liability concerns, critics say, and the game provides a poor cardiovascular workout. The real deal-breaker, though, is that the game can hurt children's feelings, not to mention their teeth. The man taking aim at dodge ball—a.k.a. murder ball, killer ball, bombardment—is Neil Williams, chairman of the physical education department at Eastern Connecticut State University in Willimantic. . . . It wasn't until he became a physical education teacher years later that he underwent a radical conversion. His moment of epiphany came when he coaxed an overweight girl with John Lennon-style glasses and a rosy complexion out of the back of the room to join in a dodge ball game. Within minutes, a young boy slammed her in the face with the red rubber ball. "He hit her so hard, it broke her nose. There was blood streaming down her face," remembers Williams. "Most of the kids stood around laughing. And I thought to myself, 'What am I doing setting up an activity where this is not only possible, but predictable?'"[24]

BOX 9–1

School Bullying: International Perspective

A recent study found the prevalence of school bullying in elementary schools to be 11.3% in Finland, 49.8% in Ireland, and 19% in the United States. School bullies tend to be academically poor, not bonded with school, and absentee compared with other students. Reduction of bullying involves a whole-school approach that includes providing better recess supervision, forming a bullying prevention co-ordinating group, encouraging parent-teacher meetings, establishing classroom rules and meetings about bullying, and requiring talks between victims and bullies.[25] Another study done in Sweden indicated that bullying in school is strongly linked to violent behavior and weapon carrying on the streets, both among boys and girls, part of a more general violent and aggressive behavior pattern that may continue into adulthood.[26]

School Bullying

Children have had to deal with assaulting bullies who take their lunch money, accost them in the schoolyard during recess, push them against lockers, challenge them to fight, call them names like "nerd" and "geek," and turn them upside down into trash barrels, for as long as there have been schools. Beyond the schoolyard, children are most frequently the victims of assault after school as they make their way home, being beaten by bullies or even their "friends." Juvenile gangs often initiate new gang members by "jumping them in." Jumping in involves the new gang member being beaten up by the entire gang, usually starting with a fist fight with an individual gang member, and ending with the new gang member knocked down (or out) sustaining multiple injuries.

Frequently, even as a family recreational activity, children play aggressive games such as Paintball:

> As the popularity of paintball has increased over the past several years, so have eye-related injuries. The game is played with gelatin balls measuring about .68 of an inch in diameter that are filled with water-soluble paint. When fired through a gun at 300 feet/second, they turn into small missiles. Injuries with this sport are often serious because the paintball fits perfectly in an eye socket, increasing the risk of perforating the globe. . . . According to American Sports Data Inc., the number of paintball players has increased to over 6.4 million in the past ten years. An estimated 2,000 eye injuries were treated in emergency rooms between 1997 and 1999, but that number excludes private office visits, an impossible number to track. Interestingly, most injuries don't occur mid-game. Instead, they're more likely to occur at the very end of the game when the goggles have been removed because the player is hot, or just finished playing.[27]

Games that "Kill"

There has also been concern about computerized games that often involve vicariously assaulting persons on the computer screen. Listed here are some of those games:

- Doom 1
- Freedom Force (05/30/02)

BOX 9-2

Hooliganism: Violence as "Play" in Belgium

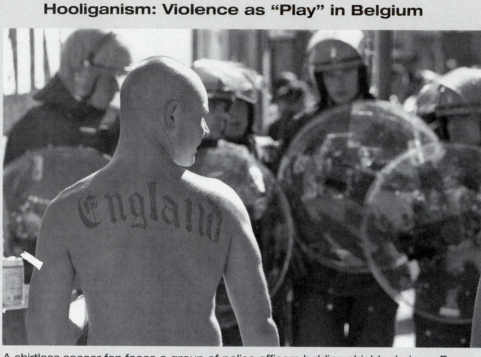

A shirtless soccer fan faces a group of police officers holding shields during a European Soccer Championship match in Belgium in 2000.

Source: Sebastian Bolesch/Das Fotoarchiv, Peter Arnold, Inc.

A study of football hooliganism in Belgium was done using data from a variety of sources regarding 679 soccer matches played from 1991 to 1999. In this activity, major teams are supported by hard-core hooligan groups and the major risk occurs when two teams meet in which each is supported by hard-core hooligans and is directly proportional to team success. Hooliganism is a male group phenomenon similar to a war game in which the individual pleasure of violence and fighting finds expression in Belgium.[28] Peter Marsh used the term *aggro* for such assaults as hooliganism.[29] Aggro, he said, is a ritual form of expressing aggression in a relatively harmless manner, and can be traced back to the practice in Roman circuses of having opposing "teams" chant and fight each other. Similar forms of aggression are found among New Guinea tribesmen today in the form of social rituals.

- Freelancer (05/07/03)
- Mafia (10/03/02)
- MechCommander 2 (11/16/01)
- Medal of Honor: Allied Assault (04/15/02)
- Mortyr
- Neverwinter Nights (08/15/02)
- No One Lives Forever: The Operative (12/10/01)
- No One Lives Forever 2: A Spy in Harms Way (11/04/02)
- Serious Sam: The Second Encounter (06/28/02)
- Soldier of Fortune
- Soldier of Fortune II: Double Helix (06/12/02)
- Splinter Cell (04/09/03)

- Star Wars: Galactic Battlegrounds (03/04/02)
- Star Wars: Rebellion (09/26/02)
- Star Wars: The Phantom Menace
- Swat 3 (04/09/02)
- Warcraft
- Warcraft 2: Tides of Darkness
- Warcraft 3: Reign of Chaos (07/25/02)

Most of these games involve the player pretending to use weapons to defeat an enemy. Some of these games have been used to recruit people into the army[30] and to sell guns to young people.[31]

Brainwashed to Kill

Grossman did a study to determine whether the ability of humans to viciously kill other humans is innate or learned behavior, basing his analysis upon interviews, first-person reports, and historical studies of war. He concluded that soldiers are overwhelmingly reluctant to kill even during war, and that modern armies use operant conditioning techniques to overcome this reluctance. He found that soldiers willing to fire their rifles have increased from 15% to 25% in World War II to 50% in Korea and over 90% in Vietnam, but with a consequence of postcombat stress. He argued that contemporary media in the form of violent movies, entertainment and news television, and point-and-shoot video games have replicated the conditioning techniques used by the military, resulting in an increased willingness of youth to pull the trigger as an automatic response.[32]

War and Domestic Violence

Does participation in a war cause an increase in interpersonal violence within the United States? Bebber studied the rate of violence in the United States following four military strikes by the United States: the invasion of Granada in 1983, the bombing of Libya in 1986, the Persian Gulf incident in 1988, and the invasion of Panama in 1989. The study found that an increase in the rate of violence greater than that of the previous appeared after each of the military episodes but not at any other time. This relationship was significant at the .01 level.[33]

Road Rage

Although the prevalence of guns in the United States may account for the high rate of murder in America, most every working adult is in possession of an even deadlier weapon—his or her automobile. Road rage in its various forms accounts for an estimated 1,200 deaths and an average of 1,500 injuries every year. Road rage actually became prevalent starting in the late 1980s, as a result of increasing freeway congestion. In Southern California, an area riddled with freeways and lacking in other forms of mass transit, the freeways are frequently referred to on the radio as "parking lots."

Road rage has been studied in detail by Louis Mizell and Company in a study sponsored by the American Automobile Association (AAA) Foundation

A man behind the steering wheel of a car exhibits road rage when he gesticulates angrily at another driver (blurred motion).
Source: Sean Murphy, Getty Images, Inc.– Stone Allstock

for Traffic Study.[34] **Road rage** was defined as "any display of aggression by a driver." Road rage is often used to refer to "the more extreme acts of aggression, such as physical assault," that occur as a direct result of a disagreement between drivers. In 1995, AAA commissioned a survey of 526 motorists. The study indicated that almost 90% of motorists had experienced "road rage" incidents within the last 12 months. Sixty percent admitted to losing their tempers behind the wheel. The forms of road rage, in rank order, included aggressive tailgating (62%), headlight flashing (59%), obscene gestures (48%), deliberately obstructing other vehicles (21%), verbal abuse (16%), and physical assault (1%). Mizell found that the majority of aggressive drivers were profiled as relatively young, relatively poorly educated males who have criminal records, histories of violence, and drug or alcohol problems. He also found that many had recently suffered an emotional or professional setback, such as losing a job or girlfriend, going through a divorce, or having suffered an injury in an accident. Often friends and relatives described these individuals as "odd," "disenfranchised," or "loners." Mizell and Company analyzed the reasons for violent disputes associated with at least 25 incidents that resulted in death or injury, which were quoted:

> "It was an argument over a parking space."
> "He cut me off."
> "She wouldn't let me pass."
> A driver was shot to death "because he hit my car."
> "Nobody gives me the finger."
> A shooting occurred "because one motorist was playing the radio too loud."
> "The bastard kept honking and honking his horn."
> "He/she was driving too slowly."
> "He wouldn't turn off his high beams."
> "They kept tailgating me."

In 4,400 of the 10,037 aggressive driving incidents studied by Mizell and Company, the perpetrator used a firearm, knife, club, fist, feet, or other standard weapon for the attack. However, in 2,300 cases the perpetrator used an even more powerful weapon, his or her automobile. In 37% of the cases a firearm was used, but in 35% the weapon was the vehicle itself. Analyzing the reasons for the aggressive driving, the study found involvement in domestic violence in 322 cases, racism and hate in 38 cases, "crash and rob" robbery in 94 cases, assault on law enforcement personnel in 221 cases, assault on crowds of people in 22 cases, females as perpetrators in only 413 cases, and probable insanity in 103 cases. . . . "when a 'crazy' climbs aboard a bulldozer, tank, or tractor-trailer, the potential for death and destruction increases dramatically."[35]

In a most spectacular example, Shawn Timothy Nelson, 35, a divorced, alcoholic, drug-taking plumber, had been watching his life crumble around him. He lost his job, his girlfriend left him, he broke his neck in an accident, and he had recently been evicted from his house. So what the heck: He stole a 57-ton U.S. Military M-60 tank. On May 17, 1995, in San Diego, Nelson entered a National Guard Armory, started up the heavily armed tank, and headed out for the highway. Barreling through six miles of residential roads and with 20 police cruisers trailing helplessly behind, Nelson mashed 20 cars, flattened vans, knocked over telephone poles, and squashed a telephone booth and bus bench. The power lines that were knocked down left 5,000 homes without electricity. Fortunately the tank weapons—a 105 mm cannon, 7.62 mm machine gun, and a 12.7 mm anti-aircraft gun—were not loaded. Leaving behind a trail of destroyed vehicles, spouting hydrants, sideswiped bridges, and nail-biting insurance agents, Nelson's rampage finally came to a halt when his tank became immobilized astride a concrete highway divider. At that point, four police officers leaped onto the tank, opened the hatch with bolt cutters, and shot Nelson to death.[36]

Throughout much of history, men have been allowed to beat their wives and children as a form of social control and discipline. Although this practice has been curtailed in America (with some exceptions), men continue to chastise their wives through beatings in many underdeveloped countries. During the reign of the Taliban in Afghanistan, videotape footage of "religious police" beating women in public was smuggled out of that country by the Revolutionary Association of the Women of Afghanistan (RAWA) and seen worldwide on television, particularly after the Twin Tower's terrorism on September 11, 2001. While many in the West were shocked by such violence against women, before an accusing finger is pointed at the Taliban, our own history, both ancient and recent, should be examined.

Much of the common law of England (the root of American common law) was taken from the laws of Rome, as well as the canon law of the Catholic Church. Early Roman law upheld a man's right to beat, divorce, or murder his wife for offenses committed by her which offended his honor or threatened his property rights. Because the Old Testament maintained, by virtue of the fact that Eve, the first woman, was virtually created from the rib of Adam, women were held to be subservient and subordinate to men within the family. Women were supposed to adhere to virtues that included docility,

"Legalized Assault"— Spousal Abuse

BOX 9–3

Chastisement versus Spousal Abuse in Sierra Leone and Singapore

Sierra Leone is a polygamous society in which customary law recognizes a husband's right to physically chastise his wives for dereliction of domestic duties, flirting with other men and adultery; however, English law that was imposed on this society and continues to apply to the independent state recognizes spousal abuse, including marital rape, as a criminal assault, resulting in a conflict between the legal system and customary law.[37] On the other hand, in Singapore, which has one of the lowest crime rates in the industrialized world,[38] there is strong public support for police intervention in cases of wife assault and serious treatment of these cases by judges.[39]

chastity, and passivity, and the unruly wife was subject to death by mutilation or stoning. The Catholic Church perpetuated this subjugation of women by endorsing the Rules of Marriage, a 15th century publication that encouraged a husband to beat his wife with a stick upon commission of an offense.[40]

The English principle of **coverture** established that a woman could not own property free from her husband's claim or control and that women themselves were to be treated as "property." Rape in common law was a crime against the husband, father, or fiancé of the victim, with compensation due the male for damage to his "property."

In fact, the term **rule of thumb,** owes its origin to an English common law sanctioning wife beating. This law decreed that a man might use a "rod not thicker than his thumb" to chastise his wife. This rule was adopted in the early 19th century by American states, formally recognizing the husband's right to beat his wife.41

Even after World War II, English courts found in favor of husbands who beat their wives as a punishment for misbehavior.[42]

This "women as property" concept is still very salient in the minds of many men, despite the fact that virtually every state legislature has recognized domestic violence as a criminal act.[43] Most states now have made it a crime for a man to rape his wife, and women now possess legal status and rights separate from their husbands. Police departments have only recently begun to vigorously arrest wife beaters, perhaps motivated less from concern for the woman than lawsuits based on equal protection claims for a failure to protect.

Given that the laws have recently changed and that the police are now being proactive in pursuing domestic abusers, is spousal abuse still prevalent? Starting with the NCVS report for 2003, 2.2% of aggravated assaults were done by spouses, with an additional 1.8% done by ex-spouses. If simple assaults are included, of which 2.6% were done by spouses and an additional 1.2% were done by ex-spouses, then the total spousal abuse increases to 4.8% for spouses and 3% for ex-spouses, or 7.8% combined.[44] The NCVS for 1995 found higher figures for aggravated and simple assault. From 1995 to 2003, assault by spouses declined from 6.7% to 4.8%. If ex-spouses are included, then spousal assault declined from 9% to 7.8%.

Although the aforementioned discussion of the history of laws regarding wife beating suggests that these assaults are man beating wife, studies have suggested that when it comes to assault, there is more gender equity than might be assumed. While the NCVS sample hasn't been large enough to break down spousal assaults by gender, a study done in 1995–1996, by the National Violence against Women Survey (NVAW), did so. Although intimate partner rapes were exclusively done by men against women, only two-tenths of 1% of the sample of 8,000 women had experienced intimate partner rape in the past 12 months. With physical assault, the percentage of women victimized was 1.3%, but .9% of men said they had been physically assaulted by a current or former intimate partner. The NVAW study differed from the NCVS study in including not just spouses but same-sex partners and cohabiting partners.[45]

In the study of family violence published in 1990, Stets and Straus found that there was indeed "gender equity" in terms of victim precipitation. Men claimed they struck the first blow in 44% of the cases, their female partners in 44% of the cases, and "couldn't remember" in 12% of the cases. The women claimed men hit them first in 43% of the cases, that they struck the first blow in 53% of the cases, and "couldn't remember" in 5% of the cases. However, more women (137) were severely assaulted than men (95) and a higher percentage of women (7.3%) than men (1%) needed medical attention.[46]

Approximately 7.8% of assaults in 2003 were spousal (current or ex-spouse). They by no means account for the biggest share of assaults. And this figure is down from 11.7% in 2001, continuing the decline shown in Figure 9–1 for assaults generally. Furthermore, in a spousal relationship, the genders have obtained relative parity in terms of perpetrating assault. It seems possible that the decreases shown in the NCVS survey may actually be a manifestation of the same increased reporting that has occurred with the police. Remember that the big picture is that all violent crimes have declined roughly 50% since 1993 in the United States. If the NCVS data are valid, then the decline in spousal abuse may be a key element in the overall decline in violence.

However, NCVS data may underestimate the frequency of spouse abuse. Based upon NCVS estimates, there were 220,030 spousal assaults (current and ex-spouse; simple and aggravated) in 2003. According to the 1990 Census, there are approximately 50 million people married in the United States, making the NCVS assault estimate to be less than five-tenths of 1% of marriages. Future research may show even higher frequencies of spouse abuse than the national studies (NCVS and NVAW). The NVAW Survey was a telephone survey, as is the NCVS in large part. It seems credible (if not inevitable) that husbands (and wives) when asked over the phone, "do you beat your wife/husband," might tend to underreport such activity (if not hang up the phone). It is possible that more information would be revealed in an in-person interview. In fact, high incidence findings were revealed by earlier research by Straus, Gelles, and Steinmetz.[47] They used a household interview technique to survey 2,143 adults representing a cross-section of families in 103 counties in the United States. They used an 18-item Conflict Tactics Scale (CTS) that included three distinct methods of resolving conflicts: rational discussion and argument, verbal and nonverbal expressions of hostility (i.e., insults or acts that symbolically hurt other family members, such as smashing or kicking an object), and physical force or violence. Violence was classified as normal (i.e., slapping) or severe (i.e., punching, kicking, biting, hitting with an object, beating, or threatening to use a knife or gun). They found that of the adults interviewed, 28% reported that the husband had acted violently toward his wife during the survey year, 1975. Among the husbands interviewed, 12.1% said they had acted violently toward their wives during the survey year, whereas 11.6% of the wives had acted violently toward their husbands.

These figures suggest that spousal violence involved approximately one fourth of the marriages, using the 28% figure reported by adults interviewed. The 1975 survey, termed the National Family Violence Survey ($N = 2,143$), was followed by the National Family Violence Resurvey ($N = 6,002$), conducted in 1985. The 1985 survey found that one in six couples experienced at least one physical assault during the survey year.[48] These findings were comparable with those of a cohort study done in Dunedin, New Zealand, of 1,037 men and women born between 1972 and 1973, interviewed with their intimate partners at age 21. That study found that between one fifth and one third of all study members reported they had experienced one or more of the behaviors on the CTS physical abuse scale in the past year.[49]

Whether or not larger percentages of spousal abuse admissions are revealed in future government reports, spousal abuse may account for a bigger cut of the assault pie in a number of ways. It may relate to child abuse. It may also influence children in such families to engage in abuse of siblings. It may also influence children in such families to be violent toward peers and others outside the family. Also, spousal abuse may relate to criminal assault by the spousal partners outside of the family, assault upon friends, acquaintances, and strangers. These displacement effects of spousal abuse are discussed more fully later. But before moving on to other topics, yet to be discussed are types of spousal abusers and explanations of spousal abuse.

Types of Spousal Abusers

Domestic violence calls to police are one of the most frequent categories of police calls. Such violence often accounts for 50% of calls to police on late-night shifts.[50] Police responses to domestic violence calls are also an area of ambivalence on the part of police because of the potential danger involved.[51] The issue of legal typing of domestic violence is a critical decision that is made in the field at the discretion of the police who respond to the call. If the police classify the situation as involving a simple assault or no assault at all, then they typically do not arrest the alleged perpetrator, because simple assault is a misdemeanor and police may not arrest misdemeanants unless they directly observe the crime in progress. However, if the police deem the situation as involving an aggravated assault, then they must make an arrest in many, if not most, jurisdictions, particularly under recently enacted legislation.

Beyond the legal typing of felony versus misdemeanor, a few typologies of spousal abusers have been developed by researchers.[52] A survey of literature on typology research on perpetrators of spouse abuse indicates that three types can be distinguished on the basis of severity of partner abuse perpetrated: generality of the violence (e.g., toward women and toward others) and psychopathology/personality disorders.[53] Based on these variables, three types proposed were (a) the *family-only perpetrator*, involving less severe violence, little psychological or sexual abuse, and few or no symptoms of psychopathology; (b) the *dysphoric/borderline perpetrator*, who produces moderate to severe violence, largely confined to the family, and is generally distressed, dysphoric, or emotionally volatile; and (c) the *generally violent/antisocial perpetrator*, who engages in moderate to severe partner abuse, commits the most violence outside the family, has an extensive history of criminal involvement, is an alcohol and drug abuser, and has an antisocial personality disorder or psychopathology.

BOX 9-4

Domestic Violence Laws Strict in Sweden

Rates reported to the United Nations for Sweden for crimes of violence for 1997 were low—1.77 for murder, 37.93 for major assaults, and 14.71 for rapes, a fraction of those crimes reported by the United States. The probable reason is that Sweden gives high priority to violent crimes in its civil law system, particularly those against women and children. The government has longstanding programs to deal with violence against women. The law provides complainants with protection from contact with their abusers, if so desired. In some cases, the authorities help women obtain new identities and homes. The government provides electronic alarms or bodyguards for women in extreme danger of assault. Both national and local governments help fund volunteer groups that provide shelter and other assistance to abused women, and both private and public organizations run shelters. There is a hotline for victims of crime, and police are trained to deal with violence against women. The authorities strive to apprehend and prosecute abusers. Typically the sentence for abuse is a prison term—14 months on average—or psychiatric treatment. Although prostitution is legal in Sweden, the purchase or attempted purchase of sexual services is illegal. The law prohibits parents or other caretakers from abusing children mentally or physically in any way. Parents, teachers, and other adults are subject to prosecution if they physically punish a child, including slapping or spanking. Children have the right to report such abuses to the police. The authorities generally respect these laws, and the usual sentence is a fine combined with counseling and monitoring by social workers. However, if the situation warrants, authorities may remove children from their homes and place them in foster care.[54]

Jacobson and Gottman did a study of 200 couples in dangerous relationships. They categorized the batterers as two types, *Pit Bulls* and *Cobras*. The *Pit Bulls* are insecure individuals, many of whom have had batterers as fathers and who confine their violence to family members. They were found less likely to have criminal records, but more explosive in their violence, more controlling of their wives, inclined to jealous rages and attempts to deprive their wives of independence, and, although easier to leave in the short run, they may be more dangerous in the long run, becoming obsessed with their spouses, stalking, and harassing them. The *Cobras* have a history of antisocial behavior, including drugs and alcohol abuse. They come from violent, traumatic childhoods and are likely to be violent outside their marriages. *Cobras* (like the snake for which they were named) remain initially calm during abuse, and were found to have heart rates that decrease during abusive incidents. However, they are more dangerous than *Pit Bulls*. When they strike, their violence is swift and ferocious, making it more difficult for wives to leave them than with the *Pit Bulls*. However, once the wives leave the *Cobras,* there is less danger because *Cobras* generally stop pursuing their spouses after a short while and pursue other situations that they can control.

Arresting Perpetrators of Domestic Violence

Neil Jacobson has criticized both the justice system and a patriarchal culture that have condoned spousal abuse and the idea that men are justified in dominating women. He expressed the view that sentences for batterers should be longer and that punishment instead of therapy should be given to the perpetrators. He argued, "We should put our money elsewhere, into treatment programs to rebuild women's lives and into education programs to alert them to the signs of domestic violence."[55]

When police answer calls regarding domestic violence, they are walking into a virtual minefield of difficult decisions, as well as danger. Quick access to criminal records via computer, and some social science training, as well as practical experience, can help police conduct a successful intervention. There is some controversy over the mandate to arrest that has become routine in some departments, primarily because the research basis for this mandate is controversial. One well-known experiment done in the early 1980s that had a tremendous impact on police treatment of domestic violence was the Minneapolis Domestic Violence Experiment. This experiment provided three alternative approaches in cases of domestic violence. In the first, the batterer was arrested. In the second, the partners were required to separate for a specific period of time. In the third, a mediator intervened between the two partners. During the next six months, the offenders who were arrested had the lowest recidivism rates (10%), the separated offenders had the highest rates (24%), and the offenders who submitted to mediation had rates somewhere in between (19%).[56] As a result of this one study, mandatory arrest has become policy in many departments across the country. However, a number of studies have been done since the Minneapolis experiment that failed to show that arrest lowers recidivism rates in domestic violence cases.[57] More specifically, these studies found that arrest did not lower recidivism in the inner city, with offenders who had a prior conviction record, and among the unemployed. However, arrest did lower recidivism among the employed. More research is needed to see if sophisticated typing of domestic violence perpetrators, as well as longer sentences (than overnight in jail) as well as follow-up services provided to victims of domestic violence (counseling, shelters, legal help, etc.), may help to improve recidivism outcomes, as well as prevent future violence to victims of domestic violence.

BOX 9–5

Mandatory Caning for Domestic Violence in Singapore

In Singapore, the rates for all types of violent crime are low. In 2001, the rate for murder was .80, the rate for rape was 2.81, the rate for robbery was 15.18, and the rate for aggravated assault was 1.77 per 100,000 inhabitants. For aggravated assault, Singapore ranked (from high to low) 151 out of 163 countries of the world. One possible reason for this low rate of violence is the focus in the laws of Singapore upon violence against women. The Penal Code and the Women's Charter criminalize domestic violence and sexual or physical harassment. A victim of domestic violence can obtain court orders barring the spouse from the home until the court is satisfied that the spouse has ceased his aggressive behavior. Court orders for protection against violent family members have increased in recent years, in part because the definition of violence includes intimidation, continual harassment, or restraint against one's will. The Penal Code prescribes mandatory caning and a minimum imprisonment of two years for conviction on a charge of "outraging modesty" that causes the victim fear of death or injury. The press gives fairly prominent coverage to instances of abuse or violence against women. There are several organizations that provide assistance to abused women. The government actively enforces the law against rape, which provides for imprisonment of up to 20 years and caning for offenders. The Penal Code mandates caning, in addition to imprisonment, as punishment for some 30 offenses involving the use of violence or threat of violence against a person, such as rape and robbery, and also for such nonviolent offenses as vandalism, drug trafficking, and violation of immigration laws.[58]

Profiling Domestic Violence

Although a fairly good effort has recently been devoted to estimating the problem of domestic violence, as shown by the NCVS, NVAW, and other surveys discussed earlier, and some good preliminary typologies have been developed, no systematic theory of domestic violence has yet been developed, as is also true with assault in general. However, etiological studies of spouse and intimate partner abuse may provide guidance in developing a theory of spouse abuse.

The factors associated with partner violence include lower socioeconomic status, poor school achievement on the part of the male perpetrator, poor communication skills on the part of the perpetrator, personality disorders or psychopathology on the part of the male perpetrator, chronic alcohol abuse on the part of the perpetrator, alcohol abuse on the part of the victim, having been battered as a child on the part of the perpetrator, a history of paternal violence in the woman's family of origin, prior or present military service on the part of the male perpetrators, a history of violence against other children prior to age 15, violence against victims outside the family, mental illness among 65% of the female victims and 88% of the male perpetrators, and the male tendency to secrete adrenaline when sexually threatened.[59]

Child Abuse

Straus and Gelles argued that the family is the focus of risk for those who are being physically assaulted, particularly for women and children. Women and children, they said, are statistically more at risk of assault in their own homes than in the streets of any American city.[60] Support for their thesis is given in a recent study by the FBI in its newly developed NIBRS. In an Appendix to the 1998 UCR, the FBI provided a special report entitled, "Incidents of Family Violence: An Analysis of 1998 NIBRS Data," based upon data submitted by 14 states during 1998. Using all four of the violent Index crimes, the study revealed that 27% of violent crimes involve victims and offenders who are related.[61] Only 12% involved strangers to the victims, whereas 48% were acquaintances of the victim. These data provide further evidence that family relations are key in the crime of assault, though the home is not necessarily the location for a majority of all assaults. Nevertheless, there are a number of ways that violent family relations can spill over into the surrounding community. Spouses who are fighting can take their aggressions out on others at work (work place violence) or on the road (road rage). Children who are quarreling with their siblings or are violently abused by adult caretakers can similarly take their aggressions out on peers or outside of school. If the family is large, the children can even form the nucleus of a violent delinquent gang. Children may leave the family (or be kicked out) and become street children. They may become involved in child prostitution, perhaps in an exploitative relationship with a pimp. The child may be assaulted by the pimp, and may employ various strategies at the direction of the pimp to get more money from each "trick," including robbery of customers. Both male and female runaways may become involved in prostitution. Commonly, teenage male prostitutes cater to homosexual male pedophiles whom they may mug in conjunction with the sexual exchange. These are only a few examples of the "ripple effect" of family violence. Studies of this ripple effect will be discussed later.

BOX 9–6

Child Selling

In many countries, children are sold by their parents for adoption or, in some cases, illicit purposes. In a study on the trafficking and sale of Argentinean children for domestic and foreign adoption, based upon interviews with 283 professionals and affected families, 134 cases of child-selling in Argentina were identified, of which 15 cases were affirmed to be sales to foreign parties. The purchase price ranged from $500–$2,000.[62]

Although violence against women has received considerable attention, including increased reporting by women and likely prosecution of perpetrators by law enforcement, such has not been the case with child abuse. While it is true that child abuse receives occasional sensational media coverage, given estimates of two to three million children that are abused yearly, child abuse has not been prosecuted vigorously, primarily because abused children are usually dealt with by social workers who refer very few perpetrators for prosecution, focusing upon the victim "in the best interests of the child." Social workers typically return abused children to their family, and even when they remove the child from the family they are enjoined to place the child in the "least restrictive and most home-like setting." This practice began with the Child Abuse Prevention and Treatment Act (CAPTA) of 1974, also known as the Mondale Act, after one of its sponsors.

BOX 9–7

Camel Jockeys: Unrecorded Child Abuse in the United Arab Emirates

There are reportedly hundreds of underage camel jockeys working in the United Arab Emirates who are subjected to harsh conditions. Some press reports claim that 2,000 boys have been trafficked to the country over the last 2 years, although this figure appears to be inflated. The largest concentration of camel jockeys is located in Abu Dhabi Emirate, which is home to the country's largest camel racing tracks and associated stables and training facilities. Credible sources report that almost all camel jockeys are children under the minimum employment age. Reports indicate that small, organized gangs provide the stables with the young boys, who generally are between the ages of 4 and 10. The gangs obtain the youths, usually from poor families in Pakistan and Bangladesh, by kidnapping or, in some instances, buying them from their parents or taking them under false pretenses, and then smuggling them into the country. The boys are often underfed and subjected to crash diets to make them as light as possible. Boys of 4 to 5 years of age are reported to be preferred; although older boys aged 6 to 8 also are used, depending on their size. Some children have reported being beaten while working as jockeys, and others have been injured seriously during races. Labor regulations prohibit the employment of persons under the age of 15, and a 1993 Presidential Decree prohibits camel jockeys under the age of 15 or who weigh less than 99 pounds. However, these laws are not enforced. Rather, the government defers control of camel racing events and the enforcement of rules concerning camel racing, including labor laws prohibiting child labor, to the Camel Racing Association, which is under the chairmanship of Shaikh Hamdan bin Zayid Al-Nahyan, Minister of State for Foreign Affairs. Many persons who own the camels and employ the children come from powerful local families who have ties to the government and are, in effect, above the law. The camel owners are not prosecuted for violations of the labor laws; consequently, the demand for child jockeys continues unrestricted.[63]

Types of Child Abuse

The CAPTA is federal legislation that defines child abuse and neglect. States use it as a guideline for their own laws. There are four basic types of abuse:

1. *Physical abuse,* where the child is punched, kicked, bitten, beaten, burned, or shaken.
2. *Child neglect,* which can be *physical, emotional,* or *educational. Physical neglect* involves a delay in seeking medical attention for the child or abandonment of the child. *Emotional neglect* includes refusing to give the child affection and attention as well as spouse abuse in front of the child. *Educational neglect* includes allowing truancy and not allowing the child to attend special education programs.
3. *Sexual abuse* includes incest, intercourse, rape, sodomy, and commercial exploitation.
4. *Emotional abuse* includes instances when parents cause serious behavioral, emotional and cognitive problems to their children.[64]

Unintended Consequences

This act was passed at a time when there was great public concern about "runaway" abused children; however, it had some unintended consequences. One was the possible overreporting of childhood injuries that were not, in fact, actual cases of child abuse. This overreporting was due to the "mandatory reporting" requirements on the part of child care professionals required by CAPTA.[65] Another unintended consequence, a very negative one, resulting from CAPTA was to shield abusers from law enforcement because investigation of child abuse now became a function of *child-protection agencies* rather than law enforcement agencies.

The key difference is that for child-protection agencies, unlike the police, the focus is not on the perpetrator (i.e., the parent) but on the victim (i.e., the child). Hence it is the child who is removed, not the parent, when the situation is dangerous. This concentration on the child instead of on the one who causes harm is part of the problem. It is the result of treating child maltreatment, with rare exceptions, outside of the bounds of criminal prosecution, for behavior that if perpetrated against anyone other than a relative would result in assault charges. Under CAPTA, there was a required confidentiality of records: "States were only allowed to release information to other governmental agencies with a need to know such information. Now child abusers are only guaranteed punishment if they harm someone not related to themselves."[66]

Richard Gelles noted the tragic consequences of the policy of treating the victim and not the perpetrator. Gelles argued that the standard policy for helping children is to provide families with counseling and resources in hopes of ending the abuse, followed by returning children to their parents. However, nearly half of the children who are killed by their parents every year are murdered after they or their families have come to the attention of child welfare agencies.[67]

Thus, while the extent of child abuse "victimization" as reported to the National Child Abuse and Neglect Data System (NCANDS) was an estimated 3 million referrals of child abuse, the number of child abuse perpetrators is "covered up" by the social service system. Because of rules of confidentiality, the number of such perpetrators cannot even be estimated, let alone such offenders prosecuted. The NCANDS reported that about 1,300 children died of child abuse in 2000, and it is unknown how many of the perpetrators were prosecuted.[68] NCANDS also stated that reports of maltreatment (child abuse) were at a "reduced" level of 12.2 reports of maltreatment per thousand children, down from a high of 15.3 per thousand in 1993. There is really no way to even estimate actual child abuse rates, because the victims are hidden behind the wall of family privacy, and it would be difficult (if not impossible) to interview the victims anyway due to their immaturity. It is likely that child abuse reporting rates were higher in 1993, but declined due to decreasing substantiation rates. Substantiation rates are the rates with which the abuse is judged by social workers to be true or "founded" rather than "unfounded." It is known that substantiation rates have declined from a high of 61% in 1976 to a current low of 31%.[69]

Gelles and Straus attempted to compare abuse statistics from their two national representative sample studies done in 1985 and 1975. They found that the rate of severe violence toward children was 47% lower in 1985 than 1975. They offered four possible explanations for the change including: (a) increased reluctance to report, (b) differences in the method of study, (c) reductions due to prevention and treatment efforts, and (d) reductions due to favorable changes in American society and family patterns.[70]

Drawing from the same survey data, Hampton, Gelles, and Harrop found that in comparing the rates of physical violence in black and white families from the 1975 to the 1985 study, the rate of severe violence toward black women declined by 43%, but the rates of severe violence toward black children and men were higher (48% and 42%, respectively).[71] These findings, particularly on black children and men, may pertain to the increasing involvement of black youth and males in homicide and assault that occurred during that period of time, related to the growth in gangs, the drug trade, and increasing imprisonment of black youth and males.

Who are the Perpetrators?

Given that there is not much information about child abuse perpetrators (based on confidentiality norms promulgated by the "child abuse establishment"), what can be surmised from the literature about who the perpetrators are? A 1998 study using the FBI's NIBRS data is insightful. Although the NIBRS study in 1998 did not reveal anything about the gender of the offender, it did reveal the gender of the victim for crimes within families. Females were a majority of the victims in family murder (56%), family rape (97%), family aggravated assault (60%), and family simple assault (72%). According to the NIBRS, 35% of the cases of family violence overall involved spouses,[72] but the figures rise to over 53% if cases are included where the victim is both a victim and perpetrator (such as family disputes where both husband and wife are involved). Given that at least a plurality and possibly a majority of family violence is spousal, and the majority of victims are female, it seems likely that the perpetrator is male in the majority of cases. This statement is subject to revision over time, because the proportion of female perpetrators in spousal relations seems to be increasing, especially in simple assaults. Also, in single parent homes (usually female), the female is likely to be the perpetrator. Studies seem to suggest, however, that male perpetrators inflict more injury than female perpetrators. This is certainly true in murder, where the key is male familiarity with firearms, the weapon of choice in 57% of family murders in the NIBRS study[73] and in 66% of murders reported in the 2004 UCR. Finkelhor and Ormrod did some further analysis of the 1998 NIBRS data and found that male offenders are responsible for three-fourths of the child abuse incidents reported to the police, including 92% of sexual assaults and 68% of physical assaults.[74]

Again, in the absence of any systematic theory of assault (other than theories of murder), it is necessary to try to explain child abuse based upon a study of the factors involved in it. Other than the National Family Violence Survey (First and Second), it is necessary to derive information from other studies. Factors said to be involved with child abuse include poverty or low socioeconomic status, being a single mother, spouse abuse, young parental age, less parental education, large families, history of spouse abuse in the family, history of parents' own child abuse as a child, blended families in which children are living with an unrelated adult, isolation from friends, neighbors, and relatives; and alcoholism and drug abuse.[75]

Once again, alcohol abuse seems related to yet another form of family violence. The NIBRS study found alcohol was "suspected" in 17% of family-related murders, 8.2% of rapes, 21% of aggravated assaults, and 20% of simple assaults. Alcohol was higher in family-related violence compared with nonfamily violence in all offenses except rape, in which it was less of a factor than in nonfamily violence.

All of the factors listed earlier as instrumental in child abuse are sources of stress. The picture that comes through of the "typical" abusive situation is a poor, uneducated, young, single mother, herself an alcohol abuser, with a history of being abused as a child, cut off from contact with friends, neighbors, and relatives by an alcoholic, abusive intimate partner. To maintain his control, the spouse (or intimate partner) beats his wife (or intimate partner) and children (and prospective children during pregnancy). This may be the same individual who gets in fights in the neighborhood, at bars, at work, and elsewhere. If these assumptions are true, there should be a link between child abuse and the overall rates of assault.

It seems likely that the NIBRS may provide vital data on the link between family violence and violence outside the family in the future; however, it is necessary to rely upon small-scale surveys until then. A study done in Dunedin, New Zealand found that a history of violence against other victims was one of the strongest links to partner violence.[76] Murray Straus has done studies of the relationship of family violence to nonfamily violence. In one study, Straus drew data from two surveys, one a survey of 555 students at a State University in New England. The second study involved personal interviews with a national probability sample of 2,143 families. He found that teenage boys, but not girls, who had been hit by their parents during the year covered by the survey, had a higher rate of violence against nonfamily members than other boys. Straus also found that the overall crime rate was elevated for couples who engaged in violent acts against each other.[77] In another student survey of 437 students in two New England colleges, Straus and Lincoln asked respondents to recall events in which members of their family had committed a crime together.[78] Some 96% of the families of the 437 students had committed one or more crimes, the most frequent of which was underage

Family Assault and Assault Outside the Family

drinking (49%). Around 6% had committed serious crimes with another family member, the most common of which was assault (4%). In a review of three data sets from general populations (two national U.S. household surveys and a student survey), Hotaling, Straus, and Lincoln found a link between physical assaults in the family and assaults and other crime outside the family, and this applied for both victims and offenders; that is, both victims of family violence and family violence offenders were more likely to perpetrate assaults outside the family than those who were not victims or offenders in family violence.[79]

Stranger Violence

As discussed earlier, fights between strangers may often have a link with a family tie in the sense that males often challenge each other for "possession" of an intimate sex partner. The person being insulted is called a name such as "wimp," "nerd," "pussy," "punk," "bitch," "mama's boy," "sissy," "little girl," "fag," and so forth. In many instances (such as in a bar or club or at the beach), the insult may pertain to a man's right to possess "his woman" or girlfriend. The challenger may be a former boyfriend (who could be a stranger to the person being insulted) or just a stranger who believes himself superior to a male who is accompanying a female he wants. Popular culture in America has been permeated with examples of this situation, ranging from Popeye cartoons to "Charles Atlas" ads in which a bully at the beach kicks sand in the face of the 98-pound weakling, and the bully gets the girl. In the movie *Urban Cowboy*, a man is accompanied by a female to a cowboy bar. The man is beaten up by a bully at the bar and "his" woman goes home with the bully. Further ethnographic study or survey research is needed to determine the "family connection" of stranger violence to domestic problems. What percentage are "bar fights" where the partners to the conflict are competing for the affections of a third-party female?

To what extent are "drive-by shootings" and other forms of gang violence motivated by the gang member's defense of family and "rights" to intimate sexual partners? To what extent are the perpetrators of stranger violence embroiled in domestic violence at the time or reacting somehow to past family violence (e.g., child abuse)? Given that more study of these questions is needed, this section can be concluded with a suggested hypothesis—that assault in general is strongly associated with domestic violence.

Policy Implications

In this chapter, much emphasis has been placed upon the link between assault (both sexual and physical) and relationships between intimate partners. It was shown that a national policy of addressing domestic violence has coincided with a reduction in violent crime generally, both in FBI statistics and in NCVS data. Women have been empowered both within the legal system and in dealing with abusive male partners. Cross-national data from the CCDB and numerous surveys have indicated the role of alcohol in matters of physical abuse within the family. It will be shown that prohibition of alcohol proved to be unenforceable when it was tried in the United States. However, much can be done in terms of harm reduction with the distribution of alcohol, as well as provision of social services for abusers of alcohol. Also, more can be done to expose and prosecute domestic abusers of children, rather than shielding them with codes of confidentiality, while treating only the victims of child abuse. Just as rapists of female victims are now being successfully prosecuted, and this is leading to heightened rates of reporting of the offense by women, the enhanced prosecution of child rapists and physical assaulters may help to further reduce violent crime in America.

THEORY

The factors discussed earlier do not constitute a theory, and a systematic theory of assault (apart from theories of homicide) has yet to be developed. In an apparent attempt to "put it all together," one text resorted to sociobiology:

> Some people view spousal abuse from an evolutionary standpoint: males are aggressive toward their mates because they have evolved with a high degree of sexual proprietariness. Men fear both losing a valued reproductive resource to a rival and making a paternal investment in a child that is not their own. Violence serves as a coercive social tool to dissuade interest in other males and to lash out in jealousy if threats are not taken seriously (that is if the woman leaves). This explains why men often kill or injure their ex-wives; threats lose their effectiveness if they are merely a bluff.[80]

Most sociologists would view this sociobiological theory as a form of "reductionism." Resorting to sociobiology as an explanatory framework for domestic violence stands as testimony to the absence of any specific theory to explain the phenomenon. The real question is what makes people act like animals in the jungle? A clue may be in the factorial studies discussed earlier. It may be noted that there were more studies emphasizing a link between domestic violence and alcohol abuse than any other single factor.

There is a theory that ties all of these factors together, though not one linked in current criminology textbooks with assault. It is **power-control theory.** This theory explains both spouse abuse and child abuse. It has been developed as a theory by Alex Thio in a textbook on deviant behavior.[81] This theory states that powerful people are more likely to commit deviance than powerless people, although the crimes of powerful people are more often "low consensus" deviance whereas the crimes of powerless people are "high consensus." "Low consensus" refers to crimes that are not widely viewed as serious crime (e.g., white-collar crime and wife beating). Thio also maintains that the powerful have greater access to both legitimate and illegitimate opportunities.

Given that we live in a patriarchal society, what kinds of men are more likely to (get caught) beating their wives? According to Thio:

> Basically, it is those who have lost control of their lives to poverty, unemployment, drug abuse, and alcoholism. Deprived of the sense of power over their lives, those men are understandably more receptive to the patriarchal idea that men should dominate and control their wives. But since they do not have money and other precious resources that rich men can use to control their wives, the poor men are compelled to resort to violence as a way of controlling their wives.[82]

Thio also uses power-control theory to explain child abuse. Just as lower class spouse abusers are likely to use the one area of their life in which they are powerful (the spousal relationship), lower class parents (often single moms) are likely to use their relationship with their children as a means in which to assume some power. The opportunity to engage in child abuse is facilitated by the sanctified privacy of the home and the social acceptability of spanking as a means of correcting the misbehavior of children. Then, Thio says, the parents obtain, it would seem, a "license to kill":

> The more a parent uses the (legitimate) opportunity to punish the child physically, the more that parent uses the (illegitimate) opportunity to abuse the child. At the same time, being powerful, the parents who abuse their children are also likely to see their abusive behavior as legitimate rather than criminal. This is particularly true of authoritarian fathers, who in effect exercise more power over their children than do other fathers.[83]

Curiously, Thio also explains "alcoholism" using the same power-control theory. "Societies and individuals with accentuated needs for personalized power are more likely to drink more heavily in order to get the feeling of strength they need so much more than others."[84]

Thus, the man who is frustrated by poverty and unemployment, working with a limited education, finds a compensating sense of power in heavy alcohol consumption and in beating his wife and kids. It would seem that consumption of alcohol would help to lower inhibitions against wife and child abuse, so that the alcohol would typically precede the assaultive behavior. A study based upon a nationally representative sample of 2,143 couples has provided some evidence in favor of the power control theory, finding that equalitarian couples had the lowest rates of conflict and violence, whereas male-dominant and female-dominant couples had the highest rates.[85]

COUNTRY PROFILES

In Table 9–2, some of the countries at the top of the list developed sovereignty after the initial list of countries was made for the comparative criminology Website in 2000 (e.g., St. Vincent & the Grenadines). Country profiles have not been developed for those countries. Other countries near the top of the list (e.g., Australia, Belgium, and Sweden) have included major and minor assaults in their report of "major assaults" to INTERPOL or the United Nations. Excluding these countries, four countries were selected for analysis. These countries are Botswana, Ghana, Jamaica, and Namibia. Note that none of these countries are developed nations (developed nations are highlighted). All four of these countries have assault rates higher than that of the United States. The first two, Botswana and Ghana, have exceptionally high assault rates, but do not have especially high murder rates. This makes it possible to isolate factors that make for high assault rates without high murder rates. Analysis will begin with those two countries.

Using the CCDB developed for this text, correlation coefficients between various international indicators with rates of aggravated assault were computed. All four crimes of violence are included in the table to see how aggravated assault is similar or different from the other three. The results can be seen in Table 9–3.

Table 9–2   Countries Ranked by Rate of Aggravated Assault[86]

St. Vincent & the Grenadines	1322.73	Italy	53.17
Grenada	1304.21	Monaco	46.67
Turks & Caicos	764.44	Israel	42.22
Australia	736.79	Finland	38.06
Dominica	682.39	Great Britain	30.07
Sweden	667.42	Japan	26.68
South Africa	597.74	Denmark	24.08
Belgium	552.99	Spain	21.23
Namibia	533.60	Andorra	19.70
Antigua & Barbados	478.87	Iceland	18.16
Swaziland	466.27	Portugal	8.13
Ghana	448.42	Austria	2.59
Saint Kitts & Nevis	434.00	Latvia	2.24
Anguila	377.78	Azerbaijan	2.11
Botswana	369.30	Oman	1.87
Jamaica	352.25	Burkina Faso	1.77
Montserrat	345.45	Singapore	1.77
Nicaragua	329.10	China	1.49
United States	**318.55**	Brunei	1.45
Netherlands	242.77	Mali	1.45
France	211.26	Nepal	1.26
Germany	153.97	Cameroon	1.17
Canada	148.52	Bulgaria	1.12
Liechtenstein	127.27	Tonga	1.08
New Zealand	101.73	Brazil	0.61
Luxembourg	92.56	Bahrain	0.52
Ireland	85.88	Egypt	0.37
Switzerland	83.64	Saudi Arabia	0.12
Norway	77.43	Syria	0.06
Greece	69.79		

It can be seen cross-nationally that beer, wine, and overall alcohol consumption correlate well with rape, robbery, and aggravated assault, but not at all with murder. Heavy drinkers are sometimes said to have a "Jekyll and Hyde" personality, being especially mean and abusive when they are drunk. It would seem that of all the factors discussed earlier, alcohol abuse seems to have the most potential as a "key" variable in domestic violence (and one variable that is most amenable to government policy intervention). A plausible scenario in the millions of nightly episodes (frequent domestic violence police calls are by night), is that the husband arrives home drunk or begins "serious drinking" when he gets home. His personality is transformed, a fight ensues, and abuse is the outcome. A growing number of studies have shown a significant correlation between the number of retail outlets for alcohol and the rate of violent crime, especially assault. Although Prohibition

Table 9–3 Correlations between Various Indicators and Rates of Violent Crime for Countries of the World

	Murder	Rape	Robbery	Aggravated Assault
Gini Index	.41	.29	.12	.09
GDP per capita	−.15	.06	.14	.13
Percentage living in poverty	.26	.08	−.14	−.03
Percentage unemployed	.19	.14	−.09	.05
Lack of freedom	−.11	−.20	−.35	−.29
Percentage Islamic	−.22	−.31	−.29	−.26
Drug arrests	−.06	.22	.10	.24
HIV/AIDS	.25	.58	.15	.43
Murder rate	1.00	.35	.25	.14
Rape rate	.35	1.00	.36	.66
Robbery rate	.25	.36	1.00	.13
Burglary rate	−.02	.40	.32	.51
Larceny rate	−.03	.22	.26	.19
Auto theft	−.06	.04	.08	.17
Index	.00	.35	.36	.43
Gender empowerment	−.20	.20	.12	.21
Rate juveniles admitted to prison	.28	.34	.24	.17
Adult alcohol consumption per capita	.04	.23	.38	.20
Beer consumption per capita	.02	.22	.18	.28
Wine consumption per capita	−.03	.14	.24	.21
Spirit consumption per capita	.11	.15	.42	−.03
Net migration rate (in or out)	−.07	.14	.00	.29

was a "failed experiment" in the United States, limiting consumption has been tried elsewhere. For instance, in Sweden, alcohol is sold only in government-run stores and customers are limited in their purchase to three bottles of wine, especially on Saturdays. While the Swedish rates of assault are currently very high, the short-term effect of the Swedish experiment of limiting alcohol in the early 1980s was to cut the assault rate in half.[87]

Table 9–3 shows other differences between aggravated assault and murder. The Gini Index correlates strongly with murder, but not with aggravated assault. Likewise, murder correlates with poverty and unemployment, but aggravated assault does not. Aggravated assault seems to be correlated with drug arrests, internationally, whereas murder is not. Aggravated assault is not strongly correlated with the murder rate, but is very strongly correlated with the rape and burglary rate. Aggravated assault is a very strong correlate of the Index of crime, while murder is not. Aggravated assault is positively correlated with gender empowerment, while murder is negatively correlated with gender empowerment. Alcohol consumption, particularly beer and wine, is a moderate correlate of aggravated assault internationally, whereas the correlation between alcohol consumption and murder is practically zero.

Table 9–3 differentiates between assault and murder. This indicates that it is possible to have a theory of assault that is separate from homicide, if assault is viewed cross-culturally. One major difference between murder and assault is the frequency of assault. There are around 40 times as many assaults as murders. Obviously, a huge number of assaults stay at that level and do not progress to murder. Although assault is probably an everyday event in many societies (including our own), murder as an outcome is rare, and it seems logical that other factors than, say heavy drinking and family fighting, lead to murder. Often it is a series of problems and failures that culminate in murder, such as being fired from one's job, divorcing or breaking up with one's intimate partner, losing money in the stock market, having a mental illness, and so forth, that seem to be productive of murder. People who are drunk all the time frequently are abusive and injurious to others and themselves. However, if a person is intoxicated, he or she may be too drunk to actually kill someone. The literature on assault seems to indicate that spousal or partner violence is primary in the sense that "violence begets violence." A video shown in psychology classes illustrating "frustration-aggression theory" shows the husband coming home from work and hitting his wife, then the wife hits the child, then the child kicks the dog, then the dog chases the cat. This somewhat humorous scenario serves as a model of what likely happens in society, although social learning theory can be used to explain the same events. Social learning theory would posit that dad hits mom (or mom hits dad), the children see this going on and they become aggressive toward each other, as well as others outside the family, based upon the training in how to handle personal relations they received from their parents as "models of aggression." The same person that responds to alcohol through abusing his wife may be abusive in other settings (bars, clubs, restaurants, boating, golfing, etc.). While alcoholism or heavy drinking cannot be "blamed" on the spousal relationship, it is certainly intertwined, and because domestic violence calls are of considerable frequency (especially after hours and on weekends), the best chance for intervention is based upon the "going public" exposure of a call to the police.

Although society has less of a chance of intervening in cases of child abuse (because of the privacy of family lives), it is an important area to study because it has the potential for generalizing to other forms of aggression—juvenile delinquency and later intimate partner abuse.

Botswana

The Batswana, a term inclusively used to denote all citizens of Botswana, also refers to the country's major ethnic group (the "Tswana" in South Africa), which came into the area from South Africa during the Zulu wars of the early 1880s. Prior to European contact, the Batswana lived as herders and farmers under tribal rule. In the late 19th century, hostilities broke out between the Batswana and Boer settlers from the Transvaal. After appeals by the Batswana for assistance, in 1885 the British government put "Bechuanaland" under its protection. The Batswana resisted incorporation into the Union of South Africa and obtained independence from Britain in 1961. However, the 1961 constitution provided an overrepresentation of Europeans in the Legislative Council, which had only 10 Batswana of 34 members, whereas Batswanans constituted 99% of the population. However, Britain accepted proposals for democratic self-government in 1964, and the seat of government was moved from Mafikeng, in South Africa, to the newly established Gaborone in 1965. Botswana has shared with South Africa a legacy of high rates of murder, rape, and, particularly, aggravated assault. INTERPOL data for 1995 and 1996 reveal an upward trend in rape, but a downward trend in murder (from 15.55 to 12.87 per 100,000 population) and aggravated assault (from 416.16 to 369.30). Two factors seem relevant to these statistics—the legal system and the treatment of women and children.

Botswana has a dual legal system, combining Roman Dutch law with customary law. It wasn't until 1943 that customary law became regulated, and customary law is still the law applicable to tribesmen (i.e., members of a tribe or tribal community in Botswana).

Customary Courts

Today, the law of Botswana provides for the right to a fair trial. However, the civil courts remain unable to provide for timely, fair trials in many cases due to severe staffing shortages and a backlog of pending cases. Most trials in the regular courts are public, although trials under the National Security Act may be held in secret. Those charged with noncapital crimes are tried without legal representation if they cannot afford an attorney. As a result, many defendants may not be informed of their rights in pretrial or trial proceedings. Most citizens encounter the legal system through the customary courts, under the authority of a traditional leader. These courts handle minor offenses involving land, marital, and property disputes. In customary courts, the defendant does not have legal counsel, and there are no precise rules of evidence. Tribal judges, appointed by the tribal leader or elected by the community, determine sentences, which may be appealed through the civil court system. The quality of decisions reached in the traditional courts varies considerably. Customary courts continued to impose corporal punishment sentences in the form of lashings on the buttocks, generally against young offenders in villages for crimes such as vandalism, theft, and hooliganism. In communities where chiefs and their decisions are respected, plaintiffs tend to take their cases to the customary court; otherwise, persons seek justice in the civil courts.

Women as Property

Domestic violence against women remains a serious problem. Under customary law and in common rural practice, men have the right to "chastise" their wives. Women in Botswana do not have the same civil rights as men. A married woman is "common property" and is held to be a legal minor. She requires her husband's consent to buy or sell property, apply for credit, and enter into legally binding contracts. Police rarely are called to intervene in cases of domestic violence. Reports of sexual exploitation, abuse, and criminal sexual assault are increasing, and public awareness of the problem generally is growing. The national police force has begun training officers in handling domestic violence problems to make them more responsive in such cases. Although the government has become far tougher in dealing with criminal sexual assault, societal attitudes toward other forms of domestic violence remain lenient. Half the murders of women in the country were linked to histories of domestic violence. Human rights activists estimate that 6 women in 10 are victims of domestic violence at some time in their lives. Rape is another serious problem, and the government acknowledged in 1999 that, given the high incidence of HIV/AIDS, sexual assault has become an even more serious offense. By law the minimum sentence for rape is 10 years, with the minimum increasing to 15 years with corporal punishment if the offender is HIV-positive, and to 20 years with corporal punishment if the offender knew of his or her HIV status. In 1999, a High Court ruled unconstitutional a provision in the law that allowed the detention of rape suspects without bail. The law does not address the issue of marital rape. A 1999 study of rape by the police service urged police to develop improved methods of rape investigation, including the use of DNA tests in all rape cases. The police force purchased new equipment, and officers were trained to use it during the year. Women's groups acknowledged an improvement in the treatment of alleged victims by police officials during rape investigations; however, they noted that police still lack basic investigative knowledge of rape cases.

Sexual Harassment

Sexual exploitation and harassment continue to be problems as well, with men in positions of authority, including teachers, supervisors, and older male relatives, pressuring women and girls to provide sexual favors. Greater public awareness and improved legal protection have led more victims of domestic violence and sexual assault to report incidents to the authorities. In 1999 the Women's Affairs Department submitted the Report on the Study of Socio-Economic Implications of Violence Against Women in Botswana to the Attorney General's office, which is working with other ministries to further study these problems. In May 2000 the Department held a national workshop on violence toward women and issued another report on using an integrated approach among all interested parties to gender-based violence.

HIV/AIDS

It was estimated in 2000 that 38.5% of adults between the ages of 15 and 49 were infected with HIV/AIDS, and due largely to deaths from HIV/AIDS, 78,000 orphans were reported by UNICEF. Increasing numbers of children, mostly believed to be orphans, were observed begging or engaging in prostitution in urban areas. Relatives denied orphans infected with HIV/AIDS their inheritance rights. There is no societal pattern of abuse against children, although incest and other forms of child abuse have received increased attention from the media and from local human rights groups. The problem of sexual harassment of students by teachers is a national concern. Reports of rape and sexual assault of young women, and cases of incest and "defilement" of young girls appear with greater frequency in the news. The age of sexual consent is 16. Child prostitution and pornography are criminal offenses, and the law stipulates a 10-year minimum sentence for "defilement" of persons under 16 years of age. Intergenerational sex (sexual relations between older men and young girls) and the problems of teenage pregnancy caused by older men received extensive media attention during the year 2000.

Ghana The Gold Coast was renamed Ghana upon independence in 1957 because of indications that present-day inhabitants descended from migrants who moved south from the ancient kingdom of Ghana. The first recorded English trading voyage to the coast was made by Thomas Windham in 1553. During the next three centuries, the English, Danes, Dutch, Germans, and Portuguese controlled various parts of the coastal areas. In 1821, the British government took control of the British trading ports on the Gold Coast. In 1844, Fanti chiefs in the area signed an agreement with the British that became the legal stepping-stone to colonial status for the coastal area. A new constitution, approved on April 29, 1954, established a cabinet consisting of African ministers drawn from an all-African legislature chosen by direct election. In the elections that followed, the Convention People's Party (CPP), led by Kwame Nkrumah, won the majority of seats in the new Legislative Assembly. In May 1956, Prime Minister Nkrumah's Gold Coast government issued a white paper containing proposals for Gold Coast independence. The British government stated it would agree to a firm date for independence if a reasonable majority for such a step were obtained in the Gold Coast Legislative Assembly after a general election. This election, held in 1956, returned the CPP to power with 71 of the 104 seats in the Legislative Assembly. Ghana became an independent state on March 6, 1957, when the United Kingdom relinquished its control over the Colony of the Gold Coast and Ashanti, the Northern Territories Protectorate, and British Togoland.

Starting with the CPP government of Kwame Nkrumah, Ghana went through a series of military coups, each of which was followed by attempts at constitutional democracy. The present day "Fourth Republic" might be considered to be one such attempt at democracy.

The crime rate for Ghana is extremely low, totaling 461.28 for 2000. However, the bulk of this crime rate is attributed to "major assaults" in INTERPOL data. The rate for major assaults was 448.42 for Ghana in year 2000 (compared to 323.62 for the United States, which is considered to have a high assault rate). Like Botswana, the high assault rate may be traced in part to the legal system and criminal codes, as well as the treatment of women and children. The assault rate is exacerbated by police practices, as well as an abusive prison system.

Traditional Law

Prior to the advent of British imperial rule, traditional law, which sought to maintain social equilibrium and to ensure communal solidarity, governed social relations among Ghana's peoples. Among the Talensi ethnic group of northern Ghana, for example, homicide was viewed as a transgression against the earth, one's ancestors, and the victim's lineage. Deterrence from crime and rehabilitation of an offender were not objectives of the legal system. Among the Ashanti, the same concern with social equilibrium and communal solidarity prevailed. Serious crimes such as murder, unintentional homicide, suicide, sexual offenses, treason, cowardice in war, witchcraft, and crimes against the chief were termed *oman akyiwad,* offenses that threatened the mystical communion between the community, on the one hand, and one's ancestors and Ashanti gods, on the other. The authorities punished such behavior with a sentence of death in the case of murder or by the sacrifice of an appropriate animal in the case of lesser offenses. *Efise,* or minor crimes, did not rupture this relationship; hence, an offender could repay his debt to society with a ritual *impat,* or compensation.

Criminal Code of 1960

The British imposed criminal laws and penal systems upon Ghana's traditional society designed to "keep the multitude in order," rather than to preserve the equilibrium between man and traditional gods. The development of penal law, however, was uneven. From 1828 to 1842, a council of merchants exercised criminal jurisdiction in and around British forts on the coast. The council often abused this power, thereby alienating many Ghanaians. After creating the Colony of the Gold Coast in 1874, the British gradually reformed and improved the legal and the penal systems. After more than a century of legal evolution, the application of traditional law to criminal acts disappeared. Since 1961 the criminal law administered by the court system has been statutory and based on the Criminal Code of 1960. This code is founded on British common law, doctrines of equity, and general statutes that were in force in Britain in 1874, as amended by subsequent Ghanaian ordinances.

"Machomen"

The criminal justice system imposed by the British (with the exception of assault) has been effective in keeping the crime rate low. Qualifications for police work are relatively high, and police are trained in academies, including the Elmira Police Depot for rank-and-file personnel and the Accra Police College for officers. Nevertheless, the police are believed to engage in beatings of suspects in police custody and have required bribes from motorists at illegal barrier road stops that they create. Also, private police have themselves engaged in assaults. There were several cases of police being arrested and standing trial for abuses, including robbery and extortion. "*Machomen*" (party thugs) and land guards, private security enforcers hired by citizens to settle private disputes and vendettas, have caused injury and property damage. The *machomen* are not constituted legally, but organized privately and operate outside the law. Police arrested a land guard in the Greater Accra Region who was accused of involvement in a killing over a land dispute. The land guard was remanded into custody and was awaiting trial at year's end.

Types of Offenses

Four degrees of offenses are recognized in Ghana. *Capital offenses,* for which the maximum penalty is death by hanging, include murder, treason, and piracy. *First-degree felonies,* punishable by life imprisonment, are limited to manslaughter, rape, and mutiny. *Second-degree felonies,* punishable by 10 years' imprisonment, include intentional and unlawful harm to persons, perjury, and robbery. *Misdemeanors,* punishable by various terms of imprisonment, include assault, theft, unlawful assembly, official corruption, and public nuisances. Increased penalties apply to individuals with a prior criminal record.

Although rapes have been vigorously prosecuted as second-degree felonies (intentional and unlawful harm to persons), assaults are typically prosecuted under traditional tribal law, which usually results in a minor sanction of compensation, if any.

Traditional Courts

The traditional courts are the National House of Chiefs, the regional houses of chiefs, and traditional councils. The traditional courts are constituted by the judicial committees of the various houses and councils. All courts, both superior and inferior, with the exception of the traditional courts, are vested with jurisdiction in civil and criminal matters. The traditional courts have exclusive power to adjudicate any cause or matter affecting chieftaincy as defined by the Chieftaincy Act of 1971. The law gives village and other traditional chiefs power to mediate local matters and enforce customary tribal laws dealing with such matters as divorce, child custody, and property disputes. However, a number of laws passed during the years 1981 to 1992, as well as the 1992 Constitution, have steadily eroded the authority of traditional rulers and vested it in civil institutions, such as courts and district assemblies.

Harsh Prisons

Currently, prisons in most cases are maintained very poorly and conditions are harsh; 106 inmates died of various diseases in the country's prisons in 2000. However, according to the Commission for Human Rights and Administrative Justice (CHRAJ) Year 2000 Inspection Report, which was not released publicly by year's end, 2001, prison conditions have improved over previous years. The Director General of Prisons has described the prisons as overcrowded and underfinanced and has stated publicly the need to improve living conditions for the prisoners. Three of the country's largest facilities, which were intended to hold 1,600 inmates, currently hold approximately 3,800. The Ghana Prisons Service 2000 Annual Report stated that the average number of prisoners in lock-up on a monthly basis was 9,507, an increase of 3.5% from 1999. Bedding was available for only 30% of the inmates, and there was no funding for clothes. Medical facilities are inadequate and the prisons supply only the most basic medicines. Overcrowding contributed to a high prevalence of communicable diseases. Juvenile offenders are supposed to be sent to a dedicated facility; however, this facility is underutilized, and the CHRAJ and the Prisons Service confirmed reports of some children as young as 14 years old housed with the general prison population. Women are housed separately from men; pretrial detainees are housed with convicted prisoners.

Violence against Women

Violence against women, including rape and domestic violence, remains a significant problem. A 1998 study revealed that particularly in low-income, high-density sections of greater Accra, at least 54% of women have been assaulted in recent years. A total of 95% of the victims of domestic violence are women, according to data gathered by the International Federation of Woman Lawyers (FIDA). These abuses usually go unreported and seldom come before the courts. The police tend not to intervene in domestic disputes. However, 1998 legislation doubled the mandatory sentence for rape. The media increasingly report cases of assault and rape. The police administration's Women and Juvenile Unit (WAJU) handles cases involving domestic violence, child abuse, and juvenile offenses. Located in Accra and Kumasi, the

WAJU works closely with the Department of Social Welfare, FIDA, and the Legal Aid Board. During the year, the Accra Branch of this unit recorded 658 cases, including 204 defilement cases, 58 rapes, 5 cases of incest, 28 indecent assaults, 232 instances of assault and wife battery, and 9 abductions.

Mysterious Murders

In late 1998, a series of "mysterious" murders of women began to occur in the Mateheko area of Accra. Three of the 20 murders reportedly involved husbands' suspicion of their wives' infidelity. The men subsequently were arrested, but they were not convicted. There were more than 30 murders between 1993 and 2000, which were referred to as "serial murders." Police instituted evening roadblocks throughout Accra in an attempt to catch the murderers. In March 2000, the Ministry of Interior offered a $10,000 reward to any member of the public who provided information leading to the arrest of any of the murderers. In July 2000, a group of seven organizations, including FIDA, Amnesty International, The Ghana Employers Association, and The Association of Business and Professional Women, issued a joint statement reflecting their disappointment at the police's lack of success, and encouraging the government to seek international help to solve the murders. In December 2000, this group, known as Sisters Keepers, marched peacefully to the Castle and submitted a petition to the President calling for the Minister of Interior and the Inspector General of Police to resign because of their failure to solve the murders. On May 8, a suspect whom police had arrested in February, confessed to eight of the murders. In October the Office of the Attorney General directed that the suspect be charged with murder. He remained in police custody at year's end.

In 1998, Parliament passed legislation that amended the 1960 Criminal Code to provide additional protection for women and children. The legislation added new definitions of sexual offenses and strengthened punishments for others. The provisions of the bill ban the practice of "customary servitude" (known as *Trokosi*); protect women accused of witchcraft; double the mandatory sentence for rape; raise the age of criminal responsibility from 7 years to 12; criminalize indecent assault and forced marriages; and raise punishments for defilement, incest, and prostitution involving children.

Elder Abuse in "Witchcamps"

Belief in witchcraft is still strong in many parts of the country. Rural women can be banished by traditional village authorities or their families for suspected witchcraft. Most accused witches are older women, often widows, who are identified by fellow villagers as the cause of difficulties, such as illness, crop failure, or financial misfortune. Many of these banished women go to live in **witchcamps,** villages in the north populated by suspected witches. The women do not face formal legal sanction if they return home. However, most fear that they may be beaten or lynched if they return to their villages. For example, in January two elderly women in Komenda, Central Region, were accused of being witches by their nephew and subsequently were abducted and tortured to obtain confessions. One of the women died two weeks later. The CHRAJ was investigating the case at year's end.

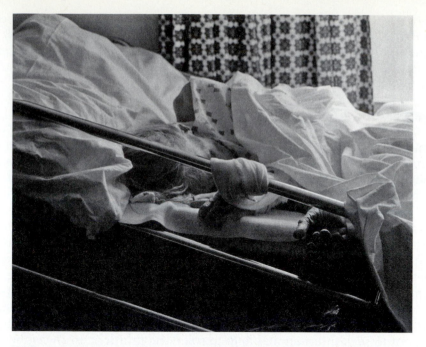

While "witchcamps" in Ghana may seem strange to Americans, a similar practice of "banishment" is practiced with some elderly women in the United States. In the photo, restrained by a metal bar and tied with cloth restraints, an elderly patient is confined to her bed in a Midwestern nursing home.

Source: James R. Polk, AP Wide World Photos

Female Genital Mutilation

There are several traditional discriminatory practices that are injurious to the health and development of young girls. In particular, female genital mutilation (FGM), which is condemned widely by international health experts as damaging to both physical and psychological health, is a serious problem. A 1998 study estimated that between 9% and 12% of women have undergone FGM, but some estimates are as high as 30%. A Ministry of Health survey conducted between 1995 and 1998 found that FGM is practiced among nearly all the northern sector ethnic groups, up to 86% in rural parts of the Upper West and Upper East Regions. A 1998 study reported that 51% of all women who had undergone FGM were excised before the age of 1, and 85% of total excisions were performed on girls under the age of 15. A 1999 survey indicated that more than 50% of the women who had undergone FGM indicated that they disapproved of the practice.

Sexually Assaulting Teachers

There are frequent reports of teachers sexually assaulting their female students. The girls are often reluctant to report the attacks to their parents, and social pressure often prevents parents from going to the police and other authorities. In April, 2001, a math tutor at Aburi Girl's Secondary School, Eastern Region, fled after being accused of assaulting at least 17 girls. Students reportedly told the school administration, including the headmistress, about the assaults, but they were rebuffed and no action was taken; the teacher has not been arrested.

The Ghana Education Service ordered the headmistress on leave while it conducted an investigation. The investigation was pending at year's end 2001.

Shrine Servitude

Trokosi, also known as *Fiashidi*, is a religious practice involving a period of servitude lasting up to three years. It is found primarily among the ethnic Ewe group in the Volta Region. A virgin girl, sometimes under the age of 10, but often in her teens, is given by her family to work and be trained in traditional religion at a fetish shrine for a period lasting between several weeks and three years as a means of atonement for an allegedly heinous crime committed by a member of the girl's family. In exceptional cases, when a girl of suitable age or status is unavailable, a boy can be offered. The girl, who is known as a *Trokosi* or a *Fiashidi*, then becomes the property of the shrine god and the charge of the shrine priest for the duration of her stay. As a charge of the priest, the girl works in the shrine and undergoes instruction in the traditional indigenous religion. In the past, there were reports that the girls were the sexual property of the priests; however, although instances of abuse may occur on a case-by-case basis, there is no evidence that sexual or physical abuse is an ingrained or systematic part of the practice. Shrine priests generally are male, but may be female as well.

Commentary

Botswana and Ghana both report high rates of aggravated assault, but do not report correspondingly high rates of murder. One common factor stands out in the development of high rates of assault in these two countries—lenient treatment of assaulters. Most of the assaults are committed by men against women—"because they can." In Botswana, customary courts deal with most cases of domestic violence informally and leniently, and men are allowed to "chastise" their wives who are "legally minors." In Ghana, assault is considered

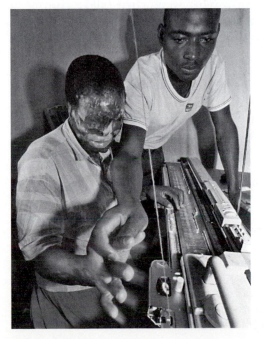

In Handicapped Project Uganda, Kampala, a woman disfigured by acid thrown at her by her husband is attending a project for disabled women. She is learning how to use a knitting machine.

Source: Jorgen Schytte, Peter Arnold, Inc.

to be a "misdemeanor," and, as in Botswana, assault is typically prosecuted under tribal law, resulting in minor punishment for the perpetrator, if any. In both Botswana and Ghana, police tend not to intervene in cases of domestic violence. In Botswana, sexual harassment and sexual exploitation by teachers and others in positions of authority are prevalent and done with impunity. In Ghana, police (both public and private) themselves have frequently engaged in assaults.

Assault in the form of rape has led to the spread of HIV/AIDS in Botswana, which has an extraordinarily high rate of infection from that disease (38.5% of adults between the ages of 15 and 49). Resulting fatalities have left some 78,000 orphans, who are effectively banished to living on the streets. In Ghana, elderly women who are deemed "witches" are banished to "witchcamps," a unique form of elder abuse in that country.

While these countries seem to feature and tolerate domestic abuse of women, the British-imposed legal system, still intact since pre-independence days, has led to the reporting of these domestic violence assaults internationally to INTERPOL.

Jamaica

Arawaks from South America settled in Jamaica prior to Christopher Columbus' first arrival on the island in 1494. During Spain's occupation of the island, starting in 1510, the Arawaks were exterminated by disease, slavery, and war. Spain brought the first African slaves to Jamaica in 1517. In 1655, British forces seized the island, and in 1670, Great Britain gained formal possession. Sugar made Jamaica one of the most valuable possessions in the world for more than 150 years. The British Parliament abolished slavery as of August 1, 1834.

Colonial Slave Courts

Slaves were treated brutally by the British who established "slave courts" in the 18th century that labeled any resistance on the part of the slaves as crimes. These courts resulted in ritualized punishments of the slaves, allowing "what was otherwise naked violence" and sustaining the "outsider" status of slaves as subordinate to white colonists.[88] During the era of slavery, physical and sexual abuses were part of the public and private lives of large Jamaican plantations.[89] After a long period of direct British colonial rule, Jamaica gained a degree of local political control in the late 1930s and held its first election under full universal adult suffrage in 1944. Jamaica joined nine other UK territories in the West Indies Federation in 1958, but withdrew after Jamaican voters rejected membership in 1961. Jamaica gained independence in 1962, remaining a member of the Commonwealth.

Emigration

Historically, Jamaican emigration (migration out of the country) has been heavy. Since the United Kingdom restricted emigration in 1967, the major flow has been to the United States and Canada. About 20,000 Jamaicans emigrate to the United States each year; another 200,000 visit the United States annually. New York, Miami, Chicago, and Hartford are among the U.S. cities with a significant Jamaican population. Remittances from the expatriate communities in the United States, United Kingdom, and Canada, estimated at up to $800 million per year, make increasingly significant contributions to Jamaica's economy.

Crimes of Violence High

Jamaica has had high rates of violent crime. In 2001, the murder rate was 43.71, the rape rate was 35.00, the major assault rate was 352.25, and the robbery rate was 80.93. Since 1995, murder has increased from a rate of 31.20, and rape has increased from a rate of 30.68, but assault and robbery have decreased from 595.32 and 176.96, respectively. Thus, Jamaica is presently high in major assault, but recently was much higher. Factors that account for the high rates of violence include poverty and inequality, corrupt and abusive police force, an overcrowded court system, poor prison conditions, abuse of women and children, hotly contested elections, and drug trafficking gangs.

   In terms of economic indicators, the Gini Index (socioeconomic inequality) is 37.9, which is below average for the countries of the world. However, 91% of the population is black, and 34.2% live below the poverty line, which is also below average for the world (39%). Also, Jamaica has suffered from depressed economic conditions that include: high interest rates; increased foreign competition; a pressured, sometimes sliding exchange rate; a widening merchandise trade deficit; and a growing internal debt resulting from government bailouts of various ailing sectors of the economy. These depressed conditions have led to increased civil unrest, including violent crime, as well as excessive out-migration. The net migration rate for Jamaica (the difference between the number of persons entering and leaving a country during the year per 1,000 persons) is a deficit of –5.78 (more leaving the country than entering). Only 15 countries in the world have a larger deficit net migration. This high out-migration rate is significant as a response to economic conditions because it pertains to the drug trade, which has had a causative impact on the country's crime rate, as will be discussed later.

Order Maintenance Policing

The police force in Jamaica (Jamaica Constabulary Force) is a carryover from the colonial period, when members of the public were treated like subjects rather than citizens, and has an "order maintenance" style of policing that has served as a source of its legitimacy deficit.[90] The police frequently employ lethal force in apprehending criminal suspects. In 2002, there were 149 deaths, including 16 police officers, during police encounters with criminals, compared with 163 such deaths in 2001. The police are combating well-armed gangs that traffic in narcotics and guns, and the gangs are often better equipped than the police. Gangs conduct coordinated ambushes of joint security patrols that are targeted assaults against police officers and their families. In addition to police killings, vigilantism and spontaneous mob killings occur in response to the crime problem. The police do not consider such murders a priority and rarely press charges.

Members of the Rastafarian community complain that law enforcement officials unfairly target them. However, it is not clear whether such complaints reflect discrimination on the basis of religious belief or due to the group's illegal use of marijuana, which is used as part of Rastafarian religious practice. Because Rastafarianism is not recognized as a religion under the law, Rastafarians had no right to prison visits by Rastafarian clergy.

Child Abuse in Prison

Prison conditions in Jamaica are poor. Overcrowding, inadequate diet, poor sanitary conditions, and insufficient medical care are typical. Though the constitution prohibits it, children as young as 12 and 13 are detained for months at a time in filthy and overcrowded lockups. Often they share cells with adults accused of serious crimes who sometimes physically and sexually abuse the children. Children are also sometimes severely abused by police officers and guards.[91] The law requires police to present a detainee in court within a reasonable time period, but the authorities continue to detain suspects beyond such a period, which the government attributes to an overburdened court system.

"Yardie" Gang Members

Reasons why people leave Jamaica include the high crime rate, poverty, poor health care, as well as an inefficient criminal justice system. There is one particular group of migrants that are significant to the understanding of violent crime in Jamaica, not to mention the United States and United Kingdom where they migrate. These groups are called "Yardies" or "Posses"; they are violent, drug trafficking, gun-toting gangs whose growth can be traced to Jamaican politics.

Since independence, two political parties have rivaled each other in closely contested elections—the Jamaica Labour Party (JLP), and the Democratic Socialist Party (PNP). The JLP, formed by Sir Alexander Bustamante, was the majority party during the first two governments, whereas the PNP, started by Norman Manley, who was succeeded by his son Michael after his death in 1969, held power from 1972 to 1980. The JLP favored a free market economy compatible with conservative corporate America; however, poverty continued during the early JLP years as there was no "trickle down effect" despite the expansion of mining, tourism, manufacturing, and construction.

During the 1972 to 1980 period during which the PNP held power, Michael Manley attempted to retain some profits from industry for Jamaica, to obtain worker benefits, and to move toward socialism through working collaboratively with noncapitalist countries, This action resulted in the development of a plan by the United States CIA to topple the regime. A violent election in which almost 700 people lost their lives resulted in the return to power by the JLP in 1980. After nearly a decade of economic problems, the PNP and Manley returned to power in 1989 with a more conservative open market approach. After Manley's retirement in 1992, he was succeeded by P. J. Patterson (Protect Jamaica Patterson) who became Jamaica's first black Prime Minister.[92] Patterson continued for an unprecedented four terms as Prime Minister, with an election victory in year 2002 in which the PNP won

34 of the 60 seats in the October elections, while the JLP held 26 seats. Fairly stringent improvements in the electoral system, including the introduction of new voter's identification cards, the inclusion of voter's pictures on the voter's list, and fingerprinting of voters at registration, have helped to reduce fraudulent voting, which was more prevalent in the 1997 elections.

Garrison Communities

During the various elections, much of the violence has been perpetrated by the Yardies or Posses. According to one news source, 43 people were killed in the run-up to the October 2002 election by these gangs. Reportedly, many areas in the nation's capital, Kingston, were in a state of war as rival armed gangs loyal to one or another of the two ruling parties launched attacks on each other's territory and candidates. Motorcades for both Prime Minister candidates were fired upon, and one PNP candidate, Jennifer Edwards, was shot at while campaigning in a JLP stronghold and then slashed with a knife. She was able to seek refuge in a safe house until police could escort her from the area.[93] As a result of election violence, the downtown urban ghettos have become **garrison communities** where residents have resorted to barricading their streets with abandoned cars, concrete posts and tree stumps to prevent drive-by shootings. The "Yardies" were an outgrowth of Jamaican violent elections, starting out as gangs who would be given guns and money by political parties to ensure that certain communities would stay loyal or vote in a particular way. When the party supporting a particular gang lost power, the gang members moved abroad (to America and the United Kingdom, in particular) where they sold drugs, and then sent money to Jamaica to continue the fight.[94] Jamaica posses in the United States sold Jamaican *ganja* (marijuana and hashish) during the 1970s, but subsequently trafficked in cocaine in cooperation with Colombian narcotics cartels. Yardies were said to be responsible almost single-handedly for the explosion in crack cocaine use in the United States during the 1980s.[95] The posses established working relationships with West Coast street gangs, as well as traditional organized crime groups.[96] It should be pointed out that the previously noted plan by the CIA to topple the PNP regime of Michael Manley has generated considerable comment on the Internet, particularly because then yet-to-become-Vice-President and then-President George Bush was director of the CIA from January 1976 to January 1977. Furthermore, there are accusations that it was CIA backing for Jamaican posses in the fight against Manley that may have accelerated the posses' involvement in the distribution of crack cocaine in the United States, as well as posse involvement in violent crime in the United States. Following are some of those comments:

- "Election-related gang warfare using automatic weapons began in earnest during the 1976 campaign, when the CIA, under its Director, George Bush, carried out a widely reported drive to destabilize the Manley government."[97]
- "CIA involvement in the arming of the JLP-linked gangs was revealed by the former agent Philip Agee. By the end of the 1970s, JLP and PNP politicians brought the CIA stooge Edward Seaga to office, and Jamaica became a sweatshop for American manufacturers, with Nike paying 20 cents an hour to handpicked cheap labor. Seaga turned the police and army onto

the gun gangs whose expansion he'd overseen. By the mid-1980s, the Americas Watch human rights monitoring group estimated that one-third of the island's homicides were committed by the police. The gangs moved to New York and Miami, and many of them became street soldiers for the Cali cartel."[98]

- The CIA employed Charles "Little Nut" Miller as a political thug attached to Edward Seaga's JLP Party and later as a member of a vicious Jamaican "posse" drug gang in the U.S. Now an influential local soft-drink and chicken distributor, Miller is cast by U.S. official sources as an ingenious former federal witness-turned-fugitive who has learned the inner workings of U.S. anti-drug intelligence, law enforcement and judiciary. . . . Working for what he called "the underworld section" of Jamaica's Labor Party in Kingston [allied to Edward Seaga], he stuffed ballot boxes, intimidated voters, shot and wounded a clerk during a robbery and spent years in prison. . . . He also testified, according to court records and documents, that he escaped the Jamaican prison using political connections in 1983 and came to the United States, where he became a trusted member of a brutal Jamaican drug gang known as the Shower Posse. The gang's trademark was spraying victims—from California to Miami to New York—with machine-gun fire, often killing and maiming bystanders. . . . He said he was present the day posse leaders opened fire with machine guns in a Florida crack house, killing five people–including a pregnant woman found in a praying position— and shooting the sole survivor in the mouth.[99]

- "For most of the 1980s, The Shower Posse's reach stretched from coast to coast, dominating the cocaine trade and leaving a trail of unsolved murders in its wake. . . ." "A Frankenstein monster created by Uncle Sam. . . ." "The Shower Posse's leaders was buying guns in the U.S. like they were going out of style in '79 and '80. . . ." "The CIA had taught him how to make 'boms' and kill people. . ." "They were very dangerous, The Shower Posse, the deadliest. . . ." "The Shower Posse and others like it were in the employ of some of Jamaica's top politicians. Shower's juice flowed from its roles as bodyguards, hit men, intimidators and ballot stuffers for the Jamaican Labour party, which had the overt and covert backing of the American embassy. In return the Shower Posse's dope business received political protection. It was as if the Crips or the Bloods worked for the Democrats or the Republicans. . . ."[100]

One point is clear from the intertwining connections between Jamaican politics and American crime—*that we cannot accurately assess "where crime is coming from" in the United States without a global view of crime.*

Carnal Abuse

Getting back to the analysis of high assault rates in Jamaica, there is evidence that domestic violence, probably traced back to the colonial days of slavery, is a significant backdrop behind Jamaican violent crime. The U.S. Department of State's Country Reports on Human Rights Practices—2002 reported that:

Social and cultural traditions perpetuate violence against women, including spousal abuse. . . . But many women were reluctant to acknowledge or report abusive behavior, leading to wide variations in estimates of its extent . . . there were numerous reports of rape and incest, especially in inner cities. NGOs reported that inner city "dons" or community leaders and sometimes even fathers initiated sex with young girls as a right.

There were 270 reported cases of **carnal abuse**—sex with girls under 16—during the year.[101]

A 2001 study done at a womens' counseling organization and shelter in Kingston, Jamaica, revealed some interesting statistics. Women who were counseled at the center in 1999 provided information in response to questionnaires completed by trained center staff. An analysis of 187 questionnaires for which the perpetrator was a male intimate partner revealed that 89% had a high level of physical injury and a low level (26%) of reporting violent crime to the police. The use of alcohol or psychoactive drugs doubled the risk of cutting injuries, but 71% of those injured did not report the incident to the police, even though 75% of the victims sought medical care.[102]

Hate Crimes

Gang violence is not limited to rival gangs, political groups, women, and children in Jamaica. There are also **hate crimes** against gays and lesbians. Country Reports 2002 discussed this briefly:

> The Jamaica Forum for Lesbians, All Sexuals, and Gays released testimony alleging human rights abuses, including police harassment, arbitrary detention, mob attacks, stabbing, and harassment of gay patients by hospital staff, and targeted shootings of homosexuals. In October (2002) the United Kingdom granted three gay men asylum based on their fear of persecution in Jamaica, and other such asylum applications reportedly were pending. Individuals committed acts of violence against suspected homosexuals; for example, in May (2002) a neighbor broke into a private home and caught two boys in a homosexual act. He called other neighbors who joined him in the home. The neighbors beat the boys until they fled, leaving their clothes behind.[103]

This hatred of homosexuals has worked its way into pop culture in Jamaica in the form of lyrics in songs by Reggae bands. A story on a homosexual advocacy Website, GayToday, reported that three Music of Black Origin (MOBO) Award nominees were subject to arrest on charges of inciting the murder of lesbian and gay people.

The gay human rights group OutRage! is urging the Metropolitan Police to bring hate crime charges against Elephant Man, Bounty Killer, and Beenie Man—all of whom are nominated for a MOBO Award in the category "Best Reggae Act." "These singers are three of the most popular entertainers in Jamaica, and have a big following in the black community in Britain." "The MOBO Awards are scheduled to take place at the Royal Albert Hall in London on September 25 (2003)." "Britain's Attorney-General, Lord Goldsmith, and the former Solicitor-General, Lord Falconer, have both given their legal opinion that it is possible under British law to prosecute singer's who incite homophobic violence." "The three reggae singers have released songs variously urging the beating, shooting and burning of lesbians and gay men. These songs abuse gay people using the derogatory Jamaican patois slang, *batty man,* and *chi chi man* (the equivalent of poof, bender, and faggot)." "OutRage! is calling for the three reggae stars to be prosecuted under either the Public Order Act, the common law offence of inciting violence and murder, or the solicitation to murder clause of the Offences Against the Person Act." "It also wants prosecutions bought against the singer's record companies: Jet Star, Greensleeves, Octave, VP, Shanachie, Tvt and Artists Only Records." "It is also pressing for charges against UK retailers that sell these singers' incitement-to-murder songs, including Amazon, HMV and Virgin record stores."[104]

Namibia   Namibia, a fourth country located in Africa, should provide an interesting addition to the previous country profiles, because its assault rate is actually the highest of all the countries that have been analyzed (533.60 per 100,000 inhabitants) and the rate rose to this level in 1999 from a lower rate in 1996 (498.97). Although the robbery rate increased from 1996–1999, the murder and rape rates declined. It might be informative to find out why assault and robbery go up, whereas murder and rape are declining in Namibia.

The violence in Namibia is partially explained by its recent nation building, by the extreme inequality that exists there, by the violence on the part of the police, by the inadequacy and overcrowding in the court and corrections systems, by domestic violence against women and children, by the movement of money and diamonds out of Namibia, and by its accessibility to drug trafficking.

Civil Disorder

Namibia was originally inhabited by Bushmen, the Damara, the Bantu-speaking Ovambo and Herero, and the Nama. Because the Namib Desert constituted a formidable barrier to European exploration, it was not until the late 19th century that colonization by Europeans developed, and the area then known as South West Africa was shared by the British and the Germans. After Germany's defeat in WWI, South Africa undertook administration of South West Africa in 1920. During the 1960s, as the European powers granted independence to their colonies in Africa, South Africa refused to grant independence to Namibia. In 1966, the UN revoked South Africa's mandate and that same year the pro-independence South West Africa People's Organization (SWAPO) began guerrilla attacks on Namibia, infiltrating the territory from bases in Zambia and later in the southern part of Angola. South Africa agreed to yield to international pressures in granting independence to Namibia in 1978. However, South Africa held elections in 1978 in Namibia without United Nations supervision, elections that were boycotted by SWAPO and a few other political parties. South Africa then continued to administer Namibia through its installed multiracial coalitions. It wasn't until 1989 that "free and fair" elections were held, as judged by the United Nations. In the 1989 election, almost 98% of the registered voters turned out and SWAPO got 57% of the vote, just short of the two-thirds necessary to have a free hand in drafting the constitution. The Democratic Turnhalle Alliance, the opposition party, received 29% of the vote. A constitution was drafted, based on the 1982 document, Constitutional Principles, and adopted in 1990. Though independence from South Africa was achieved in

1990, the decade of the 1990s was characterized by fighting between Angolan Armed Forces (FAA) and Forces from the National Union for the Total Independence of Angola (UNITA) that crossed into Namibia. Namibian police arrested and detained UNITA forces and reportedly tortured and beat citizens and Angolan refugees who were suspected of complicity with UNITA. In 1999, after the government decided to allow the FAA to launch anti-UNITA attacks from the country's territory, there was extensive cross-border fighting, which resulted in civilian deaths and injuries. In 1999 there were reports that security force officers killed eight Caprivi Liberation Army (CLA) rebels and several civilians, and beat, arrested, and detained suspected CLA rebels and sympathizers during operations against the CLA and after a 1999 CLA attack at Katima Mulilo. In 2000, senior civilian and military government officials made public statements acknowledging that security forces abused and killed civilians in the Kavango and Caprivi regions during security operations in response to cross-border UNITA attacks in Namibia. In 2001, security forces were charged with assault and torture, and many victims initiated civil suits against the government.

The border conflict resulted in violent assaults against Namibian civilians, rapes, and kidnappings. During several cross-border attacks into the northern area of the country, UNITA kidnapped Namibian citizens and took them to Angola. There were reports that some of the kidnapped persons were raped or forced to serve as combatants or porters. There were also reports that FAA soldiers abducted Namibian citizens. On February 12, 2001, FAA soldiers reportedly abducted two Namibians after looting the village of Mutwarantja east of Rundu. The soldiers took them across the Okavango River into southern Angola and shot them.

Justice Delayed

Although the police forces have been heavily involved in border disputes that resulted in violent crimes, the court and prison systems in Namibia are in the early stages of development. The lack of qualified magistrates, other court officials, and private attorneys has resulted in a serious backlog of criminal cases. So, while there is a court system consisting of three levels (30 magistrates courts, the High Court, and the Supreme Court), delays in trials of up to one year or more result from lack of personnel. Also, most rural citizens are processed through the traditional courts, which deal with minor criminal offenses such as petty theft and infractions of local customs. Prisons are described as Spartan, though clean and orderly. However, prison guards allegedly sometimes abuse female prisoners, who are held separately from male prisoners. Also, although the government has made efforts to separate youthful offenders from adult criminals, in many rural areas juveniles continue to be held with adults.

Domestic Violence

Domestic violence against women, including beating and rape, is widespread. Traditional attitudes regarding the subordination of women exacerbate problems of sexual and domestic violence. However, there has continued to be an improvement in the attention paid to the problems of rape and domestic violence. Government ministers joined in public protests against domestic violence, and the President, members of his Cabinet, and parliamentarians continued to speak out against it. During the year 2001, convicted rapists and abusers received longer prison sentences than in previous years. NGOs expressed concern that the court system does not have mechanisms to protect vulnerable witnesses. The government worked on establishing judicial procedures to address the problem. Police stated that more women came forward to report cases of rape and domestic violence. In 2000, the National Assembly passed (and the President signed) the Combating of Rape Act, which defines rape in broad terms, and allows for the prosecution of rape within marriage.

In 2000, the police began a special training course on gender sensitivity. Centers for abused women and children in Oshakati, Windhoek, Keetmanshoop, Walvis Bay, and Rehoboth are staffed with specially trained female police officers to assist victims of sexual assaults. In 2000, safe houses opened in Mariental, Swakopmund, and Tsumeb. Reports continued that women were kidnapped, raped, or otherwise abused by armed men along the border with Angola in the Kavango and Caprivi regions. The government claimed that the abuses were carried out by UNITA rebels; however, human rights groups reported that some of the incidents were perpetrated by Angolan government soldiers.

Child Abuse

Child abuse is a serious and increasingly acknowledged problem. The authorities vigorously prosecuted cases involving crimes against children, particularly rape and incest. The law criminalizes crimes against children and protects children under 18 years from sexual exploitation, child pornography, and

BOX 9–8

How Diamonds Bought Arms for Angolan Rebels

In May 1999, the Security Council authorized an investigation into how Mr. Jonas Savimbi and his UNITA guerrillas were able to re-arm and resume the Angolan civil war despite years of United Nations economic, military, and diplomatic sanctions. Investigators got a major break in October 1999, when government forces captured UNITA's principal supply base at the remote central Angolan town of Andulo and many senior members of the rebel movement defected or were captured. From seized documents and interviews, the Security Council was able to assemble a detailed picture of Mr. Savimbi's sanctions-busting operations.

According to former rebel officials, UNITA would identify a need for war munitions and solicit competitive bids from several prospective suppliers. Once a price was agreed on, the successful bidder would be provided by UNITA with a false government weapons-purchasing document, called an end-user certificate, from corrupt officials in one of several neighboring states. The certificate would be used to purchase the munitions from suppliers in Europe for shipment by air direct to Andulo or to depots in surrounding countries for delivery later. According to the report, the list of corrupt officials included the heads of state of several African countries.

UNITA paid for war material with uncut diamonds from UNITA-controlled mines. In a typical transaction, an arms dealer and the dealer's diamond expert would fly to Andulo and meet with Mr. Savimbi and UNITA's diamond expert. They would agree on the number of stones needed to cover the purchase price. These were then handed to the supplier for sale on the international market. In most cases, lax regulation and the industry's traditional secrecy assured that no questions would be asked about the origins or ownership of the precious stones. According to United Nations investigators, UNITA used this global barter arrangement to maintain a steady flow of weapons, including tanks, missiles, and artillery, to its forces in the field.[105]

child prostitution. The age of sexual consent is 16 years. In 2001, courts handed down longer sentences against child rapists than in previous years, and the government provided training for police officials to improve the handling of child sex abuse cases. Centers for abused women and children were working actively to reduce the trauma suffered by abused children. The Legal Assistance Center launched a national campaign to revise legislation on child "maintenance" in 1999. The Child Maintenance Bill was sent to the Cabinet for discussion in 1999; however, by year's end 2001, no movement was made toward tabling it in Parliament. The bill would require divorced spouses to provide maintenance allowances for their children.

Red Eye Gang

A gang known as the Red Eye Gang has existed in Namibia for some time. The identities of members of the gang are a matter of speculation, whisper, and rumor. However, some of the persons thought to be members of the gang are known to lead flamboyant lifestyles without keeping regular employment. They are also known to associate with well-known illegal diamond dealers. The Red Eye Gang is generally linked to illegal diamond dealing. In a number of cases, Namibian residents or nationals have been involved with foreign nationals in the commission of cash-in-transit armed robberies, diamond dealing, and drug-trafficking. Such cases have often been very serious, involving huge sums of money or large quantities of drugs such as cocaine, methaqualone (quaaludes), and marijuana. Famous cases of cash-in-transit armed robbery include the Karibib Heist, involving one million Namibian dollars, and the Brakwater Heist of over six million Namibian dollars. Both were believed to have been inside jobs where security forces colluded with the robbers, and frequently the criminals have been from South Africa. Many criminals abscond to Angola, a country with which Namibia does not have formal extradition arrangements, as well as South Africa, where many Namibians still hold citizenship, which makes extradition nearly impossible. Just as lax border controls and huge open spaces hamper prosecution of robbery suspects, the same conditions make Namibia vulnerable to drugs transiting the country. There is evidence that unknown quantities of cocaine are smuggled through Namibia to markets in South Africa; these shipments originate in Brazil and are shipped to Angola for transit through Namibia.

Commentary

Of the four countries discussed earlier, two of them are high in all violent crimes—Jamaica and Namibia—whereas two—Botswana and Ghana—are high primarily in reported rates of assault. All four countries have high assault rates. The one common denominator in all four countries is high rates of domestic violence toward women and children, passed down through tradition. In three out of four of these countries (Botswana, Ghana, and Namibia), domestic violence is largely ignored by the formal criminal justice system and handled largely by customary or traditional courts, which deal with domestic disputes as disputes over "property," which is what women are considered to be in these countries. In Botswana, the law allows a man to "chastise" his wife, who is considered to be his property and legally a minor. In Ghana, assaults are dealt with as minor offenses by traditional courts, and women are subject to various forms of humiliation, including banishment as "witches," FGM, *Trokosi* or forced servitude to a fetish shrine, and forced marriage. In Namibia, traditional courts handle domestic disputes, and traditional attitudes support subjugation of women. Although there is little evidence of customary or traditional courts dealing with marital disputes in Jamaica, there is considerable evidence of domestic violence in that country. Possibly because of the legacy of slavery, as in the United States, families have been disorganized and any vestige of tribal community has been destroyed, only to be replaced by "garrison communities." In Jamaica, the legacy of domestic violence and sexual abuse may date back to the physical and sexual abuse that occurred on plantations during the British colonial rule in the 19th century.

Recent contacts with dominant foreign countries seem to be exacerbating factors in Jamaica and Namibia, yielding record rates of murder, rape, and assault. The violence by "gun-toting" posse gangs during Jamaican elections peaked in the 1980 election, in which at least 700 people were killed by these gangs and the police, perhaps as result of U.S. CIA intervention opposing the "communist inspired" candidate Michael Manley and the PNP. Unfortunate "blowback" (to use the CIA term) to the United States followed, when Jamaican posses immigrated to the United States to participate as traffickers in the crack cocaine drug explosion of the 1980s. For Namibia, it was its contact with South Africa that added fuel to the fire of violent crime. The country was born of guerrilla warfare waged by its now-leading party (previously a guerrilla insurgency group), the SWAPO. More recently, as of 1990, the newly independent nation of Namibia has had to deal with Angolan insurgency by UNITA. UNITA has been fighting an Angolan civil war with the Angolan Armed Forces within Namibian borders. There is also a well-entrenched system of organized crime within Namibia engaged in diamond and drug smuggling, robbery, and other financial crimes. There is often a connection between insurgency and various forms of smuggling (diamonds, drugs, etc.) as sources of revenue to fund the insurgency. For instance, "conflict diamonds" were found by United Nations investigators to allow rebel leader Jonas Savimba to re-equip his UNITA forces and resume the Angolan civil war in 1998, despite years of United Nations arms and financial sanctions.[106] In a sense, it is also true that drug-smuggling has funded insurgency in Jamaica. The "Yardie" gangs have immigrated to the United States and Canada, where they (largely through drug-trafficking activities) earn a good share of the some $800 million per year that is sent back to Jamaica by expatriate communities. This money, in turn, helps to fund the "Yardie" insurgency in Jamaica. Thus, the extremes of violence within foreign countries and the United States are best curtailed through tracing and suppressing international lines of support for organized crime, as well as insurgency activities.

Policy Implications   The perspective that seems to be emerging from these country studies, however, is that assault is largely an issue that is consistently linked with domestic violence. This may seem like circular or tautological reasoning—tracing a crime to a crime itself. However, what seems to be the case is that assault in general is rooted in domestic violence, especially that done to women and children by men. The root cause of this domestic violence ultimately may be historical inequality, slavery, traditional views, and the like. However, the perspective that seems to emerge is that domestic violence is the most fruitful target for law enforcement, as well as NGOs, to deal with the larger problem of assault, as well as rape. Much can be done (and has already been done in the United States since the passage of the Violence against Women Act of 1994 and VAWA II in 1998) domestically to dramatically impact the overall rate of assault (and rape) through adopting a public policy of curtailing domestic violence. This is doubly true because the targeting of domestic violence helps to break the cycle of violence. Families in which there is spousal abuse are often also families in which there is child abuse. A significant percentage of children who have been abused become abusers themselves later on in life, and this abuse ranges from being the neighborhood bully to being a serial killer.

The United States

By providing a different perspective on assault than "assault as murder," it is not intended that assault be trivialized or that it should not be taken seriously. Quite the contrary is true. Assault can and does sometimes progress to murder, but most assaults do not. However, it seems that assault, even "simple assault," is important enough on its own to deserve independent explanation. It would seem that assault is "the common cold of violent crime," the most frequently occurring violent crime, both in FBI and NCVS data, and yet it is the most neglected area of criminology. If a "cure for the common cold" of crime (assault) cannot be found, then at least a means of treating it should be sought, to prevent it from progressing to even more serious "ailments" (i.e., crimes such as murder, rape, and robbery). Thus, through focusing on assault it may also be possible to reduce those even more serious crimes.

In a sense, criminology is lagging behind law enforcement in its treatment of assault. The police are detaining and locking up stalkers and spouse abusers. Both federal and state laws have recently been developed to address domestic violence, yet most criminological texts barely scratch the surface of the huge volume of crime that pertains to assault. Fortunately, the Internet contains a burgeoning literature on that subject, which may help to inform criminology texts of the future.

Table 9–4 may be helpful in summarizing the assault profile for the United States. It contains data on simple as well as aggravated assaults, as well as the other Index crimes. All are correlated with major census indices that might be factors in the crimes. It can also be seen in Table 9–4 that aggravated assault within the United States seems to follow the same pattern of correlations as murder. In other words, aggravated assault is like murder in terms of correlated demographic factors *within the United States*. Why is this table so different from the international table (Table 9–3)? In Table 9–4, both murder and assault are positively correlated with infant mortality, percentage born to unwed mothers, heroin seizures, the Gini Index, poverty, unemployment, percentage black, the black/white income gap, and consumption of alcohol.

In the international table (Table 9–3), murder is correlated with the Gini Index, but assault is not. Murder is correlated with unemployment and poverty, but assault is not. Assault, both aggravated and simple, is correlated with alcohol consumption and drug arrests, but murder is not.

Table 9–4 Correlations of Census Indicators by FBI Index Offenses, Including Aggravated and Simple Assault

State	Murder	Rape	Robbery	Aggravated Assault	Burglary	Larceny	Motor Vehicle Theft	Other Assaults
Divorces	−0.13	0.20	−0.18	−0.08	0.35	0.07	−0.12	0.15
Marriages	−0.11	0.07	−0.15	−0.08	0.19	0.27	−0.06	−0.10
Infant mortality	0.78	0.01	0.66	0.59	0.42	0.29	0.40	0.31
Percentage born to unwed mothers	0.76	0.13	0.73	0.72	0.54	0.35	0.58	0.30
Child abuse	0.05	−0.14	0.21	0.19	0.15	−0.06	0.15	−0.14
Heroin seizures (Kg rate)	0.57	0.04	0.65	0.50	0.22	0.31	0.58	0.09
Cocaine seizures (Kg rate)	0.11	0.15	0.10	0.14	0.36	0.11	0.07	0.20
Gini Index	0.59	−0.14	0.58	0.57	0.51	0.24	0.43	0.10
Percentage people living in poverty	0.44	−0.01	0.30	0.46	0.54	0.28	0.19	0.03
Unemployment rate	0.48	0.17	0.48	0.54	0.32	0.22	0.45	0.10
Male unemployment rate	0.39	0.21	0.41	0.49	0.16	0.15	0.37	0.02
Female unemployment rate	0.53	0.09	0.52	0.53	0.50	0.29	0.50	0.19
Percentage black	0.81	−0.04	0.79	0.66	0.45	0.29	0.51	0.42
Black/white income gap	0.84	−0.01	0.89	0.66	0.24	0.31	0.71	0.27
Beer consumption per capita	0.19	0.21	0.15	0.18	0.15	0.18	0.24	0.33
Wine consumption per capita	0.36	0.04	0.49	0.27	−0.10	0.03	0.53	0.14
Spirits consumption per capita	0.45	0.19	0.45	0.28	−0.11	−0.01	0.40	0.33
All beverages per capita	0.41	0.19	0.43	0.29	−0.03	0.07	0.45	0.35

What seems to be happening is that certain factors, notably those connected to race—poverty, unemployment, born to unwed mothers, percentage black, participation in the drug trade, and so forth—seem to be correlated with both assault and murder *within the United States, but not worldwide.* It seems that the targeting of blacks may be a unique focus of American law enforcement and prosecution. Thus, the correlations that are found principally in the United States could be as a result of a "self-fulfilling prophecy." If criminological theory is built upon the assumption that these correlations are indicative of true causes, then criminologists are being routed in the wrong direction in the search for causes. This is an instance of the way that criminological theory and textbooks based upon it have been provincial.

By contrast, if assault is studied using international data, other factors, such as patriarchy, failure of law enforcement to prosecute domestic violence, alcohol and drug consumption, the activities of rival political factions, an inadequate court system, poor prison conditions, and so forth may be revealed as more important variables than the race-linked variables prominent in American criminology. Consideration of these more fundamental variables may lead to a reorientation of criminological theory and policy based upon it. Resulting reformulation of U.S. criminal justice policy, in turn, may lead to a reduction of crime, as well as costly law enforcement, court administration, and imprisonment.

SUMMARY AND CONCLUSION

A developing theme in this chapter is that assault is an important crime that may be the key to other crimes because of the family nexus of assault and the "ripple effect" to other crimes. Aggravated assault is distinguished from simple assault, the former involving the use of a weapon and/or serious injury, with the latter involving neither. While most texts explain assault using theories of homicide, there are some problems with this approach. Assault has a very low correlation with murder internationally, and statistical differences between murder and assault in FBI and NCVS data are noted in this chapter, particularly in the victim-offender relationship. Of crucial significance is the possible motive for these two crimes. In murder the motive is to kill the victim, whereas in assault the motive may be various—to subordinate, to get revenge, to punish, to vent frustration, to prove "manhood," and so forth. Although theories of assault are not found in the literature apart from theories of murder, the view developed in this chapter is that assault should be explained separately from murder. The development of a "theory of assault," in turn, may be a key to explaining other derivative crimes.

In this chapter, an attempt was made to develop such a theory, starting with a study of various forms of assault in everyday life. The forms include "assault as play," school bullying, "road rage," spouse abuse, child abuse, and elder abuse. The major typologies pertaining to assault refer to forms of domestic violence. In Chapter 7, it was pointed out that criminalization of domestic violence in state and federal law may have led to a significant drop in rape, as well as other crimes during the 1990s in the United States. Factors related to domestic violence were discussed in this chapter, and they include, for both victim and offender, low economic status, school failure, poor communication skills, chronic alcohol abuse, and an abusive childhood history. Although violence against women has been addressed by federal and state law, child abuse has yet to be effectively addressed. Currently, child abuse, based upon federal mandates, is dealt with by social workers rather than prosecutors. Abused children are typically returned to the abusive home, and perpetrators are not prosecuted.

A theory that seems to fit the demographic profiles both of spouse abuse and child abuse is termed power-control theory. According to this theory, assaults that take place within the family (whether spouse or child) are attempts to "grab power" where none exists in the life of the perpetrator. This theory is distinct from theories of murder that have been developed, and may be helpful not only in explaining family violence, but derivative crime that stems from family violence.

Four countries that have high assault rates were profiled to determine the factors that contribute to high rates of assault in those countries, in order to assess and elaborate power-control theory. The four countries studied included Botswana, Ghana, Jamaica, and Namibia. In three of these countries (Botswana, Ghana, and Namibia), customary law permits men to "chastise" their wives with impunity, and the men are given lenient treatment in customary or traditional courts. Jamaica and Namibia have both high murder and assault rates, related to civil turmoil stemming from foreign entanglements. The civil turmoil in both Jamaica and Namibia contributes to abusive family relationships.

These country profiles suggest the importance of domestic violence as the key variable in the crime of assault, validating, to some extent, the power-control theory. In the four countries studied, men who are frustrated by economic inequality engage in domestic violence as an outlet for their anger and rage. They may also seek to offset their economic disadvantage through gang membership, organized crime, or guerrilla warfare, made more lethal through weapons supplied by "developed countries."

DISCUSSION QUESTIONS

1. Do you agree that a separate "theory of assault" should be developed, apart from "theories of murder"? Why or why not?

2. Do you know of any instances in which aggressive games, such as Dodge ball and Paint-ball, resulted in actual assaults upon a player

or players? Have you witnessed any instances of aggressive driving or road rage?

3. Do you favor stricter laws regarding violence against women and children, similar to those in Sweden?

4. Do you think that assault in general is strongly associated with domestic violence? Explain.

5. What are the major factors associated with assault discussed in this chapter?

6. How did the U.S. involvement in Jamaican politics lead to an increase in violent crime both there and in the United States during the late 1970s and 1980s?

SUGGESTED WEBSITES

http://www.protectiveparents.com/cases.html Website documenting numerous selected samples of real California Family Law cases (categorized by county), in which children are taken away from safe parents, and forced to live with abusive parents.

http://www.ncsconline.org/D_Research/CSP/ Highlights/LLCrimeTrendsV6N2pdf.pdf Online reprint of an article entitled "A Renewed Interest in Low-Level Crime," from the journal *Caseload*

Highlights, suggesting the crime deterrence effects of police prosecution of Part II offenses such as "simple assaults."

http://www.mustardseed.com/locations/jamaica.html Website presenting some significant facts about Jamaica, its history, and national heroes.

http://www.aaafoundation.org/resources/index.cfm? button=agdrtext#Road%20Rage Website providing a compilation of articles on road rage.

ENDNOTES

1. Eyler & Cohen, 1999.
2. Gentzler, Jr., 1999.
3. California Protective Parents Association, 1999.
4. Schneider, 1997.
5. FBI, 2004, p. 505.
6. BJS, 2001, p. 14.
7. Source: Murder, robbery, and aggravated assault, FBI, 2004, pp. 19, 36, and 38; rape and simple assault, BJS, 2003, Table 66; the data for rape include sexual assaults.
8. BJS, 2004b, Table 66.
9. FBI, 2004, p. 280, Table 29.
10. FBI, 2004, p. 37.
11. BJS, 2004b, p. 2, Table 1.
12. FBI, 2004, p. 11.
13. BJS, 2003, Table 1.
14. BJS, 2004b, p. 2, Table 1.
15. FBI, 2004—total offenses (11,632,049) include violent offenses (1,367, 009) plus property offenses not including arson (10,265,040), pp. 11, 41, 62.
16. FBI, 2004, p. 37.
17. FBI, 2001, p. 64.
18. FBI, 2004, p. 72.
19. Cohen, Kauder, & Ostrom, 2000; FBI, 2001, p. 235, Table 30; FBI, 2004, p. 281, Table 30.
20. Cohen et al., 2000.
21. BJS, 2004a.
22. BJS, 1995, p. 8; BJS, 2003, Table 1.
23. FBI, 2004, p. 280, Table 29.
24. Miller, 2002, pp. 1–2.
25. Dake, Price, & Telljohann, 2003.
26. Andershed, Kerr, & Strattin, 2001.
27. EyeWorld, 2000.
28. Vreese, 2000.

29. Marsh, 1978.
30. Letters to the Editor, 2002.
31. McDonald, 2000.
32. Grossman, 1995.
33. Bebber, 1994.
34. Mizell, 1996.
35. Mizell, 1996, p. 6.
36. Mizell, 1996.
37. Thompson & Erez, 1994.
38. Wilbanks, 1995.
39. Choi & Edleson, 1995.
40. Bin, 1999.
41. Dowd, n.d.
42. Siegel, 2004, p. 345.
43. Gelles, 2004.
44. BJS, 2003, Table 34.
45. Tjaden & Thoennes, 2000.
46. Stets & Straus, 1990.
47. Straus, Gelles, & Steinmetz, 1980.
48. Straus & Gelles, 1988.
49. Moffitt & Caspi, 1999.
50. Sanford Police Department, 1996.
51. Kinego, 2003.
52. Gondolf, 1988; Jacobson & Gottman, 1998; Sanders, 1992.
53. Holtzworth-Munroe, & Stuart, 1994.
54. Comparative Criminology Website: Sweden.
55. Schwarz, 1998.
56. Sherman & Berk, 1984.
57. Dunford, Huizinga, & Elliott, 1990; Frisch, 1992; Garner, Fagan, & Maxwell, 1995; Hirschel, Hutchinson, & Dean, 1992.
58. Comparative Criminology Website: Singapore.
59. Alarondo & Sugarman, 1996; Dutton, 1988, p. 15; Hamberger & Hasting, 1986; Hamberger & Hasting, 1988; Hotaling & Sugarman, 1986; Hotaling & Sugarman, 1990; Holtzworth-Munroe, 1992; Jacobson & Gottman, 1998; Kantor & Strauss, 1989; McCord, 1988; Miller, Nochajski, Leonard, Blare, Gonddi, & Bowers, 1990; Moffitt & Caspi, 1999; Siren, 2002; Straus & Sweet, 1992; Sugarman & Hotaling, 1989; Wolfgang & Ferracuti, 1967.
60. Straus & Gelles, 1990.
61. FBI, 1998.
62. Defence for Children International, 1989.
63. Comparative Criminology Website: United Arab Emirates.
64. Zaczkiewicz, 1998.
65. Thio, 1995, p. 122.
66. Orr, 1999, p. 2.
67. Gelles, 1996.
68. National Child Abuse and Neglect Data System, 2002.
69. Orr, 1999, p. 1.
70. Gelles & Straus, 1987.
71. Hampton, Gelles, & Harrop, 1989.
72. FBI, 1998, p. 280.
73. FBI, 1998, p. 282.
74. Finkelhor & Ormrod, 2001.
75. Adler, Mueller, & Laufer, 2004, p. 251; Appel & Holden, 1998; Gelles, 1989; Gelles, 1992; Ingis, 1978, p. 53; Rumm, Cummings, Kraus, Bell, & Rivara, 2000; Straus, Gelles, & Steinmetz, 1980; Straus & Gelles, 1990.
76. Moffitt & Caspi, 1999, p. 6.
77. Straus, 1985.
78. Straus & Lincoln, 1985.
79. Hotaling, Straus, & Lincoln, 1989.
80. Wilson & Daly, 1996, as quoted in Siegel, 2004, p. 346.
81. Thio, 1995.
82. Thio, 1995, p. 124.
83. Thio, 1995, pp. 122–123.
84. Zeisel, 1982, as quoted in Thio, 1995, p. 396.
85. Coleman & Straus, 1986.
86. Includes top and bottom 10% and developed nations.
87. Agren, 1997.
88. Paton, 2001.
89. Daniels & Kennedy, 1999.
90. Harriott, 1998.
91. Human Rights Watch, 1999b.
92. Mustard Seed Communities, 2003.
93. Thompson, 2002.
94. Thompson, 2002, p. 2.
95. Small, 1995.

96. Gay & Marquart, 1993.

97. Gunst, 1989.

98. Shalif, 1997.

99. Conscious Rasta Press, 1998.

100. Blake, 1999.

101. U.S. Department of State, 2002.

102. Sharon, 2001.

103. U.S. Department of State, 2002.

104. GayToday, 2003.

105. Fleshman, 2001.

106. Fleshman, 2001.

10

SNEAK THIEVES: BURGLARY, LARCENY, AND MOTOR VEHICLE THEFT

KEY TERMS

burglary
curtilage
Easterlin hypothesis
fences
grand theft
inchoate offense
larceny
larceny-theft

life-as-party
motor vehicle theft
personal theft
sneak thief
sneak thieves
stealthy theft
theft
victim-offender mediation

OUTLINE

Definition
National Stealthy Theft Statistics
Types of Stealthy Theft

Profiling Stealthy Theft
Theory
Country Profiles

LEARNING OBJECTIVES

After reading this chapter, students should be able to:

1. Draw a distinction between robbery and the three crimes of stealthy theft described in this chapter (burglary, larceny-theft, and motor vehicle theft)

2. Define the three acts of stealthy theft using both the FBI and NCVS definitions

3. Understand the similarity between the three acts of stealthy theft

4. Understand why individuals who may engage in larceny-theft in this country would probably prefer burglary if they lived in a developing country

5. Describe the trends as well as changing demographics of the stealthy theft crimes in both FBI and NCVS statistics

6. Characterize the variety of types of burglars, larceny-thieves, and motor vehicle thieves

7. Develop an improved understanding of stealthy theft in terms of social characteristics of the thieves and causes of their behavior

INTRODUCTION

CASE STUDY ONE: Pete, a Burglar

Pete is 29 years old and he started using solvents and taking cannabis at the age of 13. Significantly, because of his early brush with crime his father disowned him and what relationship they had, had been particularly volatile.

While in a young offenders' institute at the age of 18 he was introduced to heroin and in his early 20s progressed to using crack cocaine and heroin. In recent years he has been renowned as a prolific house burglar, committing crime to fund his £500-a-day ($950 USD) habit.

His most recent conviction resulted in a 31-month sentence for 24 burglaries. Following his release, he was recalled to prison for re-offending within two

and a half weeks. He is currently in a drug treatment center in Devon, England, undergoing a three-month primary drug treatment program.

He has just signed up for a second stage treatment that will last for another six months. Following his arrival at the center he wrote this letter to two probation officers who have been dealing with his case. "I would just like to take this time to give you a big thank you. . . . I feel very happy today because I was allowed to talk to my father and just the tone of his voice said it all. He is so supportive and happy for me and I owe that thanks to you for persuading them to give me this opportunity. I can't thank you enough. Keep up the excellent work."[1]

CASE STUDY TWO: Wes, a Shoplifter

I've had a long career as a shoplifter, so it seemed ironic that I'd find myself in a department store seeking out a store detective. I stole my first candy bar when I was nine and I loved it. It was exciting and thrilling and it was gleefully wrong. Now I wanted to find out more about the people who were trying to stop me. My stepbrothers introduced me to shoplifting.

They'd steal candy bars and Playboys just to see if they could. They taught me that the more cavalier your theft, the harder to detect. I was better at it than they were. I never got caught, but my brothers were busted numerous times. Although they graduated to petty theft and larceny, I stuck with the small stuff now and again, eventually losing the habit.[2]

CASE STUDY THREE: Lucy, a Shoplifter

At a support group meeting in suburban Detroit, Lucy, a real estate agent and divorced mom, talks about her experiences as a shoplifter. It's a high so good that Lucy can't get enough of it, but a shame so great that she's never told her three grown children. Why would a successful businesswoman risk everything to steal something she could easily buy? "They feel compelled because something has happened, usually just prior to their taking that item, in their life, something that usually involves a major stress or trauma that they have not dealt with properly," says psychologist Will Cupckik. He says these ordinarily law-abiding people are trying to replace something

they've lost in their lives. For some people it can become an addiction, like drugs, alcohol, gambling, food, or sex. After years of shoplifting, Lucy was finally caught and is now on probation. "What precipitated (my shoplifting) was number one, the death of my dad, and number two, a huge—this is no excuse—but a huge loss in the market. That makes me real mad," Lucy says. Though they never talked about it, Lucy learned to shoplift by watching her mother. She remembers "just looking around the corner and seeing something fall into her purse." Eventually Lucy's mother, who had been battling depression, killed herself over a shoplifting incident.[3]

CASE STUDY FOUR: Dorah, a South African Shoplifter

Dorah Itumeleng Mora (42) pleaded guilty to two counts of theft in the Benoni Magistrate's court in July this year. Mora has been convicted of shoplifting 11 times since 1981. Her lawyer, S. Ibrahim, told the

court that Mora claimed to be a "kleptomaniac." According to Ibrahim, Mora had previously seen a Benoni psychiatrist for her problem. She was later unable to afford his services and so was not treated.

Ibrahim argued that prison was not the best solution for Mora and that she should be given medical treatment for her condition instead. The Magistrate, H. de Kock, asked Mora why she had not asked the court for help during her earlier cases. She said she had tried, but her requests "fell on deaf ears." Her two most recent crimes both occurred at Benoni Lakeside Mall. She stole food and cosmetics from the Lakeside Checkers and clothing from the Lakeside Wool-worth's. Prosecutor J. Ntabani argued that Mora deserved a "stiff sentence." Ntabani said, "Prices of goods in shops are very high, to cover the cost of theft. If this lady is locked up maybe those prices will drop." Mora is a mother of four and is separated from her husband. She works part-time as a domestic worker but has no stable income. Three of her children are still at school, while her oldest child, a 20-year-old daughter, is physically disabled.[4]

CASE STUDY FIVE: Jason, a Canadian Car Thief

Jason Richardson just got out of jail. He's sticking to the rules of probation. He wants to be a chef. At 31, he's turning his life around—but this is not a life he's ever known. Jason is an ex-car thief and armed robber. It all started when he was just 12. "My parents were drug addicts," he says with a shrug. "There really wasn't another way of life. That's how it was. You seen that, you did that, and, you know, I progressed with my friends to stealing cars." The first car that kicked off nearly 20 years of theft was a Datsun. It was a car his brother had stolen, and Richardson drove it around New Westminster, using one foot on the accelerator and a crutch for the brakes and the clutch. In fact, it was the fact that Jason only had one leg that initially made him start stealing cars. "At that time it was a convenience," he says. "I was handicapped, I lived all over the place and my parents moved around quite a bit so really it was a convenience to steal a car to get around." From there, he started stealing cars for drugs and to facilitate robberies. He stole hundreds of cars. Any car without an alarm or club was a possibility. And he never thought about his victims. . . . "That was a time in my life when I was a bad person. I'm not a bad person anymore," Jason says with a smile.[5]

As may be discerned from the wide variety of case studies presented here, we are including numerous crimes in this chapter under the heading **sneak thieves,** or **stealthy theft.** The term **sneak thief** refers to a "burglar who steals by sneaking into houses through open doors, windows, etc."[6] We are going to use the term sneak thief in a broader sense to refer to thieves who commit their acts of theft by stealthy or secretive means. They could be stealing an automobile in the middle of the night, shoplifting in a store when they think that no one is watching, or breaking into a house when they are sure that the residents are at work or school. This chapter will include burglary, larceny-theft, and motor vehicle theft. These are different forms of theft that are nonviolent in nature, and there is little or no contact between the offender and his or her victim or victims. In contrast to robbery, in which there is a direct personal confrontation, the nonviolent crimes committed by sneak thieves have very low clearance rates. In 2004, the clearance rate for burglary was 12.9, for larceny-theft 18.3, and for motor vehicle theft 13.0. By contrast, robbery had a clearance rate of 26.2.[7]

The clearance rates of these three theft crimes are low precisely because they are done secretly and furtively, so that the victim cannot identify the offender. Most important, however, is that we think these three crimes can be explained by the same body of theories. We also suspect that these are also levels of crime that are often done by the same individuals, with similar backgrounds.

Two teenage sneak thieves are shoplifting in a hardware store. One of the boys furtively slips a handful of steel wrenches into the pocket of his jacket with the assistance of a friend who is serving as a lookout.

Source: Jim Smith/Photo Researchers, Inc.

DEFINITION

The term **theft** refers to "the unlawful taking of another's property or services."[8] In this chapter we use the term *stealthy theft* or *sneak thief* to refer to three forms of impersonal, unlawful taking—burglary, larceny-theft, and motor vehicle theft. As we discuss these topics, it will be shown that they have much in common, and are distinct from robbery, which is a violent crime. It will be shown that these three forms of theft using cross-cultural data correlate very well with each other, but not very well with robbery. It will also be shown that these three variables correlate *negatively* with the Gini Index of economic inequality in international data, whereas robbery correlates *positively* with the Gini Index. All three forms of theft contain an element of stealth, and offenders consistently attempt to get away with the theft without any contact or with minimal contact with the victim. In robbery, on the other hand, the victim is contacted directly, and sometimes very aggressively.

Motor vehicle theft is actually a form of larceny, even though it is reported separately in the UCR and NCVS. It is reported separately because of the sizable value of motor vehicles, as well as the volume of such crimes—not because it is not a larceny. It should also be pointed out that the distinction between burglary and larceny-theft is not as great as is often thought. For instance, if a household employee takes something from the owner's house, the theft is classified as a *larceny-theft,* because the employee has a legal right to be there. Similarly, if a shoplifter gets caught with stolen merchandise in a store after hours, the thief can be charged with burglary (because the person has no legal right to be there).[9] On the other hand, in one case at a Chevron gas station, at 7:10 p.m. in the evening a suspect who asked for a pack of cigarettes and then ran out the door with them without paying, was also booked on a charge of burglary.[10] In actual field practice the term "burglary" is quite often used if an act involves after-hours theft.

BOX 10–1

Burglary and Larceny-Theft in the United States Compared with Argentina

Larceny-theft may occur frequently in developed countries because the opportunity for theft is greater than it is in developing nations. A comparative study was done of theft versus burglary in the United States compared with Argentina. It was found that shoplifting and auto theft were greater in the U.S. because of the physical design of supermarkets and department stores and because autos were more readily available in U.S. than in Argentina. In Argentina, property crime was more likely to take the form of burglary from the homes of employers, because that opportunity was more readily available.[11]

Burglary is a crime that declines as compared with other forms of theft as countries become more affluent. In developing nations, there are fewer stores and shopping centers, so theft tends to take the form of burglary from the homes of wealthy persons. In developed nations, there are "big box stores" that are generally understaffed, and these stores often anchor large shopping malls, with a choice of merchandise from all over the world. Lots of merchandise is on display in these warehouse/stores and shopping malls, where customers are expected to serve themselves. There customers often do so without paying for the merchandise. A growing number of thieves in developed nations find it easier and less risky to shoplift, rather than to burglarize from homes (see text box on Argentina).

Thus, the distinction between these three crimes (burglary, larceny, and motor vehicle theft) is often not great. However, it is important to define these three forms of (nonviolent) theft as precisely as possible, starting with burglary.

Burglary

The term "burg" refers to "an ancient or medieval walled fortress or walled town."[12] It was assumed that the owner of the burg could defend it during the day. Thus, the common law definition of burglary (which came into existence around 1527) was "the breaking and entering of a dwelling house of another in the nighttime with the intent to commit a felony."[13] Current definitions of burglary are broader in nature and include daytime burglaries, other structures than a dwelling, and include attempts as well as completed burglaries. Burglary is an example of an **inchoate offense,** a word that means "incomplete or partial."[14] The FBI defines **burglary** as "The unlawful entry of a structure to commit a felony or a theft. Attempted forcible entry is included."[15] The use of force to gain entry is not required to classify an offense as burglary in the FBI viewpoint. The FBI divides burglary into three subclassifications: forcible entry, unlawful entry where no force is used, and attempted forcible entry.[16] Although NCVS definitions are usually broader than those of the FBI, in the case of burglary, the NCVS definition is more restricted than the FBI's in the sense that the NCVS definition is limited to *residential* burglary, as follows:

> **Burglary** is the unlawful or forcible entry or attempted entry of a residence. This crime usually, but not always, involves theft. The illegal entry may be by force, such as breaking a window or slashing a screen, or may be without force by entering through an unlocked door or an

open window. As long as the person entering has no legal right to be present in the structure, a burglary has occurred. Furthermore, the structure need not be the house itself for a burglary to take place; illegal entry of a garage, shed, or any other structure on the premises also constitutes household burglary. If breaking and entering occurs in a hotel or vacation residence, it is still classified as a burglary for the household whose member or members were staying there at the time the entry occurred.[17]

By court precedent, the definition of a dwelling has been extended to the **curtilage,** a term dating back to the 14th century in England referring to "a piece of ground (as a yard or courtyard) within the fence surrounding a house."[18] Originally this referred to attached servants quarters, barns, carriage houses, and so forth, but today the term has been extended to include even open fields next to a house.[19]

It may be observed that burglary does not always involve theft; however, as the earlier NCVS quote states, "The crime usually, but not always, involves theft." By virtue of the FBI's hierarchy rule, which mandates that only the most serious felony is reported in the UCR, official national statistics on burglary exclude rapes, robberies, aggravated assaults, and murders, because those are more serious offenses. Thus, larceny-theft is the major felony that would normally be linked with burglary in official statistics.

Larceny

Larceny refers generally to the taking of property from a person without that person's consent with the intention of depriving that person permanently of the use of the property.[20] Larceny, in contrast to burglary, does not involve the use of forced entry or other means of illegal entry.[21] It also does not involve a direct personal, forceful confrontation with the victim at the time of the act, although thieves may be caught during or after the act by police or security personnel. If the thief must be forcefully subdued by the police or security personnel, the larceny can be prosecuted as a robbery. This lack of force (toward property or person) makes larceny less frightening than burglary or robbery and may also be a reason that the crime tends to be treated as a less serious offense than burglary.

Although the case can be made that identity theft, credit card fraud, check forgery, and other "paper crimes" are forms of larceny, such crimes are not included in police reports as larceny, and are not tabulated either by the FBI or in the NCVS as larcenies. The FBI classifies these paper crimes as Part II offenses, meaning that they are less serious than larceny. While the dollar amount a victim may lose from paper crimes often is quite sizable, the case can be made that such crimes are typically less serious than larceny, because there is no actual physical contact or potential physical contact of the criminal with the victim. Thus, with larceny, there is the possibility of the crime developing into a personal, violent crime. A contemporary example of this is carjacking, of which there are some 50,000 committed every year and approximately 1% of which result in a murder of the victim. Historically, larceny has included "a trespassory taking and carrying away of personal property belong to another."[22] This indicates that the offender is in physical contact with the property. In this chapter, discussion is limited to such crimes. Paper crimes, even those done by career criminals, are discussed in Chapter 14.

Fairly precise definitions of larceny are given in the UCR and the NCVS. The FBI uses the term *larceny-theft* instead of larceny. **Larceny-theft** is the unlawful taking, carrying, leading, or riding away of property from the possession or constructive possession of another. It includes crimes such as shoplifting, pocket-picking, purse-snatching, thefts from motor vehicles, thefts of motor vehicle parts and accessories, bicycle thefts, and so forth, in which no use of force, violence, or fraud occurs. Motor vehicle theft is also excluded from this category inasmuch as it is a separate Crime Index offense.[23]

The NCVS has a different way of viewing "larceny" from the FBI. The term larceny is not used in the NCVS, and theft is distinguished from **personal theft. Theft** in the NCVS is defined as:

> the taking of property or cash without personal contact. Incidents involving theft of property from within the sample household would classify as theft if the offender has a legal right to be in the house (such as a maid, delivery person, or guest). If the offender has no legal right to be in the house, the incident would be classified as a burglary.[24]

In the NCVS, purse-snatching and pocket-picking are classified separately from theft as personal theft and are listed under "personal crimes."[25] Because the NCVS is based upon interviews with a random sample of households, the data are somewhat biased in favor of crimes committed within homes, as opposed to businesses, because the subjects are asked about personal victimization. Unless the victim is an owner of a home-based business, he or she may not report such victimization.

A young man grabs the strap of a woman's handbag on a sidewalk in London, England, during a purse-snatching attempt. Because of the contact between offender and victim, the NCVS classifies purse-snatching separately from "theft." Purse-snatching is listed in the NCVS under "personal crimes" as a "personal theft."

Source: Getty Images, Inc./Image Bank.

Motor Vehicle Theft The FBI defines **motor vehicle theft** as "the theft or attempted theft of a motor vehicle. This offense category includes the stealing of automobiles, trucks, buses, motorcycles, motorscooters, snowmobiles, etc. The definition excludes the taking of motor vehicles for temporary use by those persons having lawful access."[26] The FBI also excludes from the category of motor vehicle theft motor vehicles that would not normally travel surface streets and highways, such as trains, airplanes, bulldozers, most farm and construction machinery, ships, boats, and spacecraft, the theft of which would be classified as "larceny-theft."[27] In addition, a bicycle is not considered to be a motor vehicle, even if a motor is retrofitted to the bicycle.

Like the UCR, the NCVS separates motor vehicle theft from ordinary theft. *Motor vehicle theft* in the NCVS is defined as "the stealing or unauthorized taking of a motor vehicle, including attempted thefts. A motor vehicle is defined as an automobile, truck, motorcycle, or any other motorized vehicle legally allowed on public roads and highways."[28] The latter definition may be slightly broader than the FBI's definition of motor vehicle theft, possibly including tractors and other construction vehicles that can be operated on the highway.

NATIONAL STEALTHY THEFT STATISTICS

There are many findings in the UCR and NCVS regarding incidences and trends, as well as factors involved in the crimes that are discussed for these crimes compared to each other. To avoid confusion, we use the FBI term larceny-theft for both FBI data and NCVS data on "theft," because we are using the term stealthy theft as a general term for all three crimes against property—burglary, larceny-theft, and motor vehicle theft.

FBI Statistics   **Extent and Trends**

Burglary rates have been declining since they peaked in 1980 in the United States. The FBI has published its UCR online since 1995. Comparisons made for those two years (1995 and 2004) show a continued downward trend in the number and rate of burglaries. There were 2,594,995 burglaries in 1995, compared with 2,143,456 in 2004, with rates per 100,000 inhabitants of 987.6 in 1995 and 729.9 in 2004.[29] This represents a drop of 26.1% in the rate of burglary. Burglaries in 2004 constituted 18.3% of all Index crimes. Clearance rates for burglary also dropped during this period from 13.4% to 12.9%.[30] The trends can be seen in Table 10–1. Robbery has been included in this table for comparison purposes. It can be seen that robbery offenses reported have dropped much more than burglary, as well as larceny-theft and motor vehicle theft.

Larceny is by far the most prevalent of the Index crimes, with a rate of 2,365.90 in 2004. Yet, the clearance rate for larceny-thefts reported to law enforcement in 2004 was 18.3%,[31] down from a rate of 19.6 in 1995.[32] Although the FBI tabulates "larceny-theft" separately from motor vehicle theft, the category "larceny-theft" still constitutes 59.4% of all Index crimes. As shown in Table 10–1, larceny-theft has decreased since 1995 by 22.3%. It has decreased consistently since its peak year in 1991.[33] However, larceny-theft has not decreased as much as total Index crimes since 1995.

Table 10–1 **Theft-Related Offenses in the UCR, 1995 and 2004**[34]

Offense	No. Year 1995	Rate Year 1995	No. Year 2004	Rate Year 2004	Trend
Robbery	580,545	220.9	401,326	136.7	−38.1
Burglary	2,549,995	987.6	2,143,456	729.9	−26.1
Larceny-theft	8,000,631	3044.9	6,947,685	2,365.9	−22.3
Motor vehicle theft	1,472,732	560.5	1,237,114	421.3	−24.8
Total Index Offenses	13,867,143	5277.6	11,695,264	3,982.6	−24.5

Motor vehicle theft constituted 10.6% of all index offenses in year 2004. The rate of motor vehicle theft in 2004, as shown in Table 10–1, was 421.3 per 100,000 inhabitants. The clearance rate in 2004 for motor vehicle theft was 13%, down from 14.1% in 1995.[35] Also, as shown in Table 10–1, motor vehicle theft dropped 24.8% between 1995 and 2004, a greater drop than other larceny-thefts (22.3%) discussed previously. Motor vehicle theft has been declining steadily since its peak year in 1991.[36] Motor vehicle theft has decreased more than total Index offenses.

With all of the crimes in Table 10–1, despite declines in crime, dollars lost have generally increased. In 1995, losses from robbery were estimated at $507 million, with an average value of $873 per robbery, whereas in 2004, the loss from robbery was estimated at $525 million, because of a much higher average loss per robbery of $1,308.[37] The loss from burglary was $3.3 billion in 1995 and $3.5 billion in 2004. The yield per burglary was $1259 per burglary in 1995, compared with $1,642 per burglary in 2004.[38] The loss from larceny-theft was $4.3 billion in 1995 and $5.1 billion in 2004. The yield per larceny-theft was $538 in 1995 and $727 in 2004.[39] The loss from motor vehicle theft was $7.6 billion in both 1995 and 2004. The loss from vehicle theft remained constant, despite a decline in offenses, based upon a rise in the value per vehicle from $5,129 in 1995 to $6,108 in 2004.[40]

Hot Season Crimes

Both in 1995 and in 2004, burglary, larceny-theft, and motor vehicle theft all peaked during the hot summer months of July and August.[41] It should be noted that this pattern is the opposite of robbery, which peaks during the winter months.[42] This "hot season" finding may be due to additional leisure time for youth, but can also be attributed to the use of air conditioning systems. Air conditioners often make a loud noise that can obscure the sounds of burglary and other theft-related activity.

Demographic Comparisons

In 1995, burglary was predominantly done by adults, who were involved in 79% of burglary offenses cleared, with persons under 18 (juveniles) accounting for 21% of burglaries cleared by arrest.[43] In 2004, adults were involved in 84% of burglaries, whereas juveniles accounted for only 16% of all burglary clearances.[44] In 1995, juveniles accounted for 36.2% of arrestees compared to 27.2% in 2004.[45] (The higher number of juvenile arrestees than clearances is because more than one person can be arrested for the same crime.) In 1995 the peak age for burglary was 16, whereas in 2004 the peak age for burglary was 18.[46] Males comprise a large but declining percentage of burglary arrests, being 88.9% of arrestees in 1995 versus 85.7% in 2004.[47] By race, blacks are a declining minority of burglary arrestees. In 1995, 67% of arrestees were white compared to 31% who were black, while in 2004, 70.9% of burglary arrestees were white, compared to 27.2% who were black.[48]

To sum up the FBI characterization, the burglar is predominantly of male gender, adult in age, and of white race. Burglaries are committed disproportionately to percentage in the population, by blacks and juveniles. According to the year 2,000 census, African American persons constituted 12.3% of the U.S. population. Juveniles (persons under 18 years old) constituted 25.7% of the U.S. population.[49] However, in both proportion of clearances and arrests, males, blacks and juveniles are a declining proportion of all burglary arrests, while females are trending upward in their arrest rate for this crime.

Officially, larceny-theft is predominantly an adult crime and increasingly so over time. In 1995, 74% of larceny-thefts cleared by arrest were persons 18 or over (adults).[50] In 2004, adults constituted 80.2% of larceny-thefts cleared by arrest. In 1995, the percentage of all larceny-theft arrests for those under 18 was 33.6%, whereas in 2004, persons under age 18 constituted 27.3% of those arrested for larceny-theft.[51] In 1995, the peak age for larceny-theft was 16, while in 2004 the peak age was 17.[52] In 1995, females constituted 33.2% of larceny-theft arrests, whereas in 2004, females arrested for larceny-theft constituted 38.2% of the total.[53] In 1995, blacks constituted 32.4% of larceny-theft arrests, while in 2004 blacks constituted 28.2% of larceny-thefts.[54]

Thus, larceny-theft, according to the FBI statistics, is a crime done predominantly by white, adult males, but disproportionately by teenagers and blacks, although both groups are trending downward. It is also a crime that is committed by a growing number of females and in a percentage (38.2%) uncharacteristic of females, who constituted 11% of arrests for violent crime and 20% of arrests for property crime in 2004.[55] Females are trending upward in their relative participation in the crime of larceny-theft.

In 1995, 74.4% of offenses cleared by arrest for motor vehicle theft involved adults, whereas in 2004, 83.6% of offenses cleared by arrest for motor vehicle theft involved adults.[56] In 1995, 42% of those arrested for motor vehicle theft were under 18, while persons under age 18 constituted 26.5% of those arrested for motor vehicle theft in 2004.[57] In 1995 the peak age for motor vehicle theft was 15, whereas in 2004, the peak age for motor vehicle theft arrests was 16.[58] In 1995, females comprised 13.1% of motor vehicle theft arrests, while in 2004, females arrested comprised 17.1% of motor vehicle theft arrests.[59] In 1995, blacks constituted 38.3% of arrests for motor vehicle theft, whereas in 2004 blacks constituted 34.2% of motor vehicle theft arrests.[60]

Thus, motor vehicle theft is an offense committed predominantly by white, adult males, but disproportionately by teenagers and blacks although their participation is declining. The percentage of motor vehicle theft arrests has increased for females (although females are still a small percentage of those arrested for motor vehicle theft—17.1%).

Thus, all three theft crimes share very similar demographics, being committed predominantly by white, adult males, but disproportionately by teenagers and blacks whose participation is declining, while females are trending upward in arrest rates for all three crimes. Robbery demographically has differed from the three theft crimes in its domination by blacks who constituted a majority of arrests for robbery in both 1995 and 2004.[61] Adult blacks constituted a declining majority of robbery arrests from 59.1% in 1995 to 50.5% in 2004; however, juvenile blacks became an increasing majority of robberies done by juveniles from 60.2% of robberies in 1995 to 63.5% in 2004.

Trends over Time

Although burglary, larceny-theft, and motor vehicle theft have much in common in terms of 10-year trends, season of the year, and demographic characteristics, they have varied in terms of trends since 1960. Table 10–2 below shows the rate highlighted for the peak years for each of these crimes.

Burglary offenses peaked in 1980 and have fallen consistently since that year, whereas larceny-theft and vehicle theft peaked in 1991, and have fallen since that year. It is a point to ponder as to why burglary peaked over 10 years before the other two theft crimes. It may be that the "get tough" approach to crime begun during the Reagan presidency that resulted in massive warehousing of career criminals may have had its effect first upon burglary, which is typically treated as a more serious crime than larceny-theft or even motor vehicle theft.

Next, the findings of the NCVS for 1995 and 2004 are compared to those of the FBI, just discussed, for those years, and additional findings unique to the NCVS are presented.

NCVS Findings

Extent and Trends

NCVS data concur with the FBI findings about the decline in burglary, theft (larceny-theft), and motor vehicle theft rates, as seen in Figures 10–1, 10–2, and 10–3; however, the FBI data showed burglary rising until 1980 and then falling off, and showed larceny-theft and motor vehicle theft rising until 1991 and then falling off. However, the NCVS trends for burglary and larcency-theft were continuously downward since 1973, with only motor vehicle theft trending like the FBI data.

In 2004, the NCVS provided an estimate for household burglary of 3,427,690.[62] The UCR's estimate for all burglaries (residential and nonresidential) is 2,143,456, which is 62.5% of the NCVS's estimate for household burglary alone. In 1995, the NCVS estimated the volume of burglaries to be 4,822,480.[63]

Table 10–2 **Peak Years for Three Theft-Related Crimes**

Year	Burglary	Larceny-Theft	Vehicle Theft
1960	508.6	1,034.70	183.0
1980	1,684.1	3,167.00	502.2
1991	1,252.0	3,228.80	658.9
2004	729.9	2,365.90	421.3

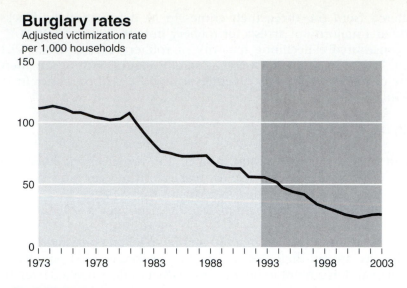

Burglary rates
Adjusted victimization rate
per 1,000 households

Figure 10–1
Burglary rates from 1973 to 2003.[64]

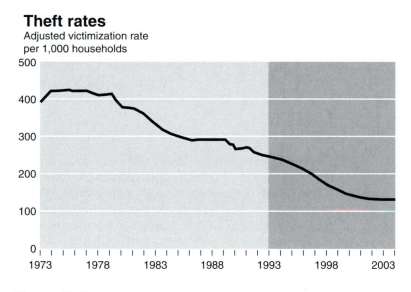

Theft rates
Adjusted victimization rate
per 1,000 households

Figure 10–2
Trends in theft (larceny-theft) reported in the NCVS from 1973 to 2003.[65]

The rate of burglary estimated for 2004 by the NCVS is a 37.4% drop from the figure given for 1995. This is a greater drop than that of the FBI, which was a drop of 26.1% between 1995 and 2004.

It can be seen from Table 10–3 that the rate of robbery declined by a much higher rate in the NCVS than the three stealthy theft offenses in this chapter (60.4%). Comparing the NCVS data for 1995 through 2004, one trend is noteworthy. The youngest age group (12–19) dropped from a rate of 152.4 to 66.6 during the years 1995–2001, a drop of 56.1% compared to a drop of

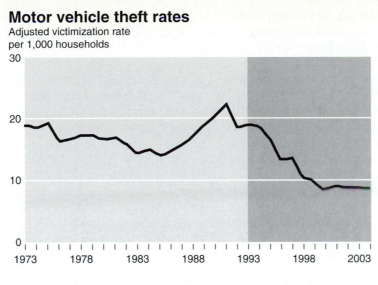

Motor vehicle theft rates

Adjusted victimization rate
per 1,000 households

Figure 10–3
Motor vehicle theft trends reported in the NCVS from 1973 to 2003.[66]

Table 10–3 **Theft Offenses in the NCVS, 1995 and 2004[67]**

Offense	Rate Year 1995	Rate Year 2004	Trend
Robbery	5.3	2.1	−60.4
Purse-snatching/pocket-picking	1.7	0.9	−47.1
Household burglary	47.3	29.6	−37.4
Completed	39.9	25.1	−37.1
Forcible entry	14.8	9.5	−35.8
Unlawful entry without force	25.2	15.7	−37.7
Attempted forcible entry	7.4	4.5	−39.2
Motor vehicle theft	16.2	8.8	−45.7
Completed	10.8	6.7	−38.0
Attempted	5.5	2.0	−63.6
Larceny-theft	216.0	122.8	−43.1
Completed	207.6	117.0	−43.5
Less than $50	80.9	35.5	−56.1
$50-$249	74.5	41.9	−43.8
$250 or more	40.9	28.2	−31.1
Attempted	8.4	5.4	−35.7

38.2% for other age groups.[68] However, the rate of burglary victimization for the youngest age group rose again to 94.8 in 2003.[69] Comparing the races, both white and black burglary victimization declined by about 37% for each racial group between 1995 and 2003.[70] Victimization for those with income less than $7,500 declined about 19% between 1995 and 2003.[71]

Data reported in the NCVS, as explained previously, reflect different definitions of theft. Personal theft (purse-snatching/pocket-picking) is separated from larceny-theft in data tabulation. In terms of incidence, the NCVS estimate of

14,211,940 for all larceny-thefts[72] is more than double the FBI's figure of 6,947,685 for 2004, suggesting that the FBI significantly underestimated larceny-theft. The FBI's figure for larceny-theft for 2004 is 47.9% of all larceny-thefts recorded by the NCVS.

The NCVS data seen in Table 10–3 indicate that larceny-theft declined 43.1% from 1995 to 2004, a figure double that estimated in the UCR (22.3). There are interesting details in the NCVS not found in the UCR. Purse-snatching and pocket-picking have declined even more than larceny-theft, with a drop of 47.1% for these personal thefts.

In agreement with the FBI data, motor vehicle theft in the NCVS declined more than other thefts (45.7% for motor vehicle theft vs. 43.1% for larceny-theft), but particularly so with "attempted motor vehicle thefts," which dropped 63.6%. Again, the 10-year drop shown in the NCVS for motor vehicle theft (45.7%) is nearly double the decline estimated by the FBI (24.5%) during the 1995–2004 time period. The latter finding seems to point to the impact of vehicle security devices, such as Lojack®, alarms, The Club®, and so forth in preventing the completion of the act of vehicle theft.

From 1995 to 2003, estimated loss increased for two out of five of the NCVS theft-related crimes. Burglary decreased from $3.6 billion in 1995 to $3.3 billion in 2003. Larceny-theft loss declined from $6 billion in 1995 to $4.9 billion in 2003. Purse-snatching increased from $11 million in 1995 to $14 million in 2003. Pocket-picking increased from an estimate of $11 million in 1995 to $20 million in 2003. Robbery declined from $566 million in 1995 to $501 million lost in 2003.[73]

In 2003, 60.5% of purse-snatchings and 35.5% of the pocket-pickings were reported to the police. However, only 31.8% of larceny-thefts were reported.

Demographic Comparisons

The NCVS gives no data on the victim-offender relationship or the offender in crimes against property, because the NCVS is based upon reports taken from victims. Victims can only guess characteristics of offenders in crimes against property, when they have not seen the offender. So there are no offender data in the NCVS for burglaries, larcenies, and auto thefts. The NCVS mainly provides information about the victim, reported as rates per 1,000, that can be summarized here.

In 2003, victims of burglary were disproportionately black rather than white (38.8 vs. 28.4 per 1,000).[74] Rates are not given in the NCVS on victimization for burglary by gender. By income, the largest rate of victimization is reported by those who earn less than $7500 per annum (58 per 1,000), declining progressively with higher incomes.[75] Young people age 12 to 19 are the most victimized age group, with a rate of 94.8 per 1000 households as opposed to progressively lower rates for other age groups.[76]

For the crime of purse-snatching/pocket-picking (i.e., "personal theft"), about 66% of the victims were white and 25.5% were black.[77] A total of 75.7% of the victims were female.[78] The largest rate for this crime in 2003 was for the age group 20 to 24.[79] Victims of personal theft were also found to be disproportionately young.[80] In terms of income, the largest rate of 1.2 per 1,000 households is given for those earning less than $7,500, declining with each higher category of income.[81]

For larceny-theft, 82% of the victims were white, while 13.4% of the victims were black.[82] No rates were reported in the NCVS on larceny-theft by gender. Young people age 12–19 were most frequently the victim of theft, with the rate declining with each higher age group.[83] For whites, theft was directly proportional with income, with the higher income whites experiencing the most theft. For blacks, theft victimization increased up to the middle income bracket ($35,000–$49,999), declining with incomes $50,000–74,999, but then increasing with income of $75,000 or more.[84]

Victims of motor vehicle theft were found to be disproportionately black, young, and middle income.[85] No rates were reported in the NCVS on motor vehicle theft by gender. The highest rate for motor vehicle theft victimization, 16.5 per 1,000 households, was for households whose head was age 12–19. The highest rate of motor vehicle theft, 12.3 per 1,000 households, was for households in the medium income bracket of $25,000–$34,999.[86]

In terms of locality of the various property crimes by race (white and black), all three crimes are greatest in urban localities, second in suburban localities, and least in rural areas, with one exception. Motor vehicle theft has its highest rate, 21.4 per 1,000 households, for blacks who live in suburban areas, followed by blacks who live in urban areas (15.2) and blacks who live in rural areas (3.7).[87] Rates of both robbery and purse/pocket theft are greatest in urban areas, second in suburban areas, and least in rural areas.[88]

Although the NCVS typically reports criminal victimization in terms of rates in various demographic categories, this method of reporting can be misleading as to the overall distribution of crime. To show the distribution of various theft-related crimes, we computed frequencies and percentages for the demographic variables race, gender, age, and income. The percentages for each theft-related crime are given in Table 10–4. From this table it can be seen that whites are proportionately higher in victimization from the property-theft crimes as compared with the personal-theft crimes. Females are disproportionately victimized by burglary and purse/pocket theft, while males are more highly victimized by larceny-theft, vehicle theft, and, especially, robbery. Middle-aged persons (age 35–49) are disproportionately victimized by the property theft crimes, while young people (age 12–34) are more highly victimized by robbery and purse/pocket theft. In terms of income, the highest income category ($75,000 or more) is most victimized by larceny-theft, vehicle theft, and purse/pocket theft, whereas the lower to middle income ($15,000–$24,999) group is most frequently victimized by burglary and robbery.

Motor Vehicle Theft

Table 10–5 shows figures from the NCVS for motor vehicle theft as compared with the number reported in the UCR for 1995–2004. The FBI figure for motor vehicle theft for 2004 is 1,237,114, whereas while the NCVS 2004 estimate is *less*—1,014,770. This discrepancy is possibly due to sampling error on the part of the NCVS and the fact that auto thefts are one of the few crimes that have a high rate of reporting by victims to the police. Also, the NCVS data are the result of a household survey, so they may underrepresent commercial auto thefts (fleets of trucks or cars owned by companies, the government, universities, etc.). However, another interesting possibility is that the "stolen" cars never existed in the first place (see text box). Another plausible explanation is that due to faulty methodology—namely surveys done primarily over the phone—the NCVS is underestimating crime generally. This table reveals that the NCVS figure for motor vehicle theft was less than that of the FBI in eight of the past 10 years.

Table 10–4 **Characteristics of Victims of Property Crime Shown as Percentages for Each Demographic Category, from 2003 NCVS[89]**

	Burglary	Larceny-Theft	Vehicle Theft	Robbery	Purse/Pocket Theft
Race					
White	79.2	82.0	71.9	62.5	66.0
Black	15.9	13.4	20.7	28.3	25.5
Other	4.9	4.5	7.3	9.2	8.4
Total	100.0	99.9	99.9	100.0	99.9
Gender					
Male	48.5	54.0	54.1	61.3	24.3
Female	51.5	46.0	45.9	38.7	75.7
Total	100.0	100.0	100.0	100.0	100.0
Age					
12–19	2.7	1.6	1.6	28.7	26.3
20–34	28.6	29.5	30.6	37.7	38.8
35–49	39.4	40.2	42.1	18.7	17.9
50–64	20.2	21.1	19.9	10.9	7.6
65 and over	9.0	7.6	5.8	4.0	9.3
Total	99.9	100.0	100.0	100.0	99.9
Income					
Less than $7,500	10.8	6.1	3.8	14.7	6.6
$7,500–14,999	14.0	9.2	7.9	12.5	11.5
$15,000–24,999	17.4	13.9	13.1	19.3	11.3
$25,000–34,999	15.0	13.1	17.0	10.5	12.8
$35,000–49,999	14.7	17.3	16.4	13.2	14.8
$50,000–74,999	13.5	17.0	14.8	13.8	11.6
$75,000 or more	14.6	23.4	27.1	16.0	31.5
Total	100.0	100.0	100.1	100.0	100.1

Table 10–5 **Comparison of FBI and NCVS Estimates for Motor Vehicle Theft[90]**

Year	FBI	NCVS
1995	1,472,441	1,653,820
1996	1,394,238	1,387,440
1997	1,354,189	1,433,370
1998	1,242,781	1,137,940
1999	1,152,075	1,068,130
2000	1,160,002	937,050
2001	1,228,391	1,008,720
2002	1,246,646	988,760
2003	1,261,226	1,032,470
2004	1,237,114	1,014,770

BOX 10–2

Sale of Nonexistent Vehicles in South Africa

In South Africa, an area of concern has been insurance fraud, whereby nonexistent vehicles are created on paper through skillful forging of vehicle paper work. The vehicle is then insured and conveniently "stolen" or "hijacked." To combat this crime, most insurance companies now require a pre-acceptance inspection of the vehicle to confirm its existence. South Africa is an "Old Commonwealth" country and has many of the same problems such as auto theft, drugs, and immigration crime, that are reported in England. Fourteen percent of crime in South Africa is committed by illegal immigrants, including murder, drug trafficking, and arms smuggling—possible reasons for an increase in xenophobia in the country. Vehicle theft is connected to the smuggling of drugs, firearms, and people in a form of "barter trade," whereby one illegal product is exchanged for another, in countries such as the Democratic Republic of the Congo and Zambia. In South Africa, car thieves are increasingly becoming organized and linked to overseas syndicates.[91]

TYPES OF STEALTHY THEFT

Burglary

Although the potential for violence probably is the reason that burglary is considered a serious crime, burglary by itself is a nonviolent crime against property. Studies discussed later indicate that burglars go to some effort to avoid interaction with people, whereas robbers more or less deliberately seek out interaction with people. Burglary is done stealthily, while robbery is sometimes a very public act. In any event, there is ample basis for developing typologies of burglars that are independent of typologies of robbers or other property offenders. The very secrecy of acts of burglary is probably the reason that better typologies have not been developed. Burglary typologies (up until recently) have not progressed much beyond distinguishing between "professional thieves" as described by Sutherland and amateur burglars.

Neil Shover described the "good burglar" in his dissertation research, based upon a study of prison inmates,[92] and later likened his "good burglars" to Sutherland's characterization of professional thieves.[93] Indeed, up until recently the study of burglars has been limited to those who have been arrested, detained, and/or convicted and incarcerated. Ethnographic research by Wright and Decker, through use of the "snowball technique" of locating actual working burglars, has done much to open up the field of investigation into careers of burglars.[94] As a result of a study conducted through interviews with convicted burglars, Neil Shover developed a typology of burglars, including low-level, middle-range, and high-level burglars.[95] The typology is based on several variables, including age of the offender, identification with crime, use of alcohol or drugs, type of target selected for burglaries, and connections with fences (people who buy stolen goods). *Low-level burglars* are typically juveniles who are less likely to plan their burglaries and are easily deterred from a target by security devices such as burglar alarms. They usually do not pull off highly profitable burglaries and lack the connections to move large volumes of stolen goods. *Middle-range burglars* are older than juveniles, though they are likely to have a history of burglary as a juvenile. They may be periodically employed in legitimate jobs but have a substance abuse problem greater than the other two types. They select targets based upon both the profitability and risks involved but are not as easily deterred by security devices as are the low-level burglars.

They are limited in their yield from sometimes very successful burglaries that they have committed because they lack the necessary connections that enable them to fence stolen goods on a large-scale basis. *High-level burglars* resemble Sutherland's "professional thief" in that they plan their crimes, they work in organized crews, they are connected with reliable sources (tipsters) who help to identify targets, they earn a good living from crime, and they are able to pursue theft on a large-scale basis because they possess connections with fences adequate to dispose of the stolen goods.

Types of "Fences"

Although Shover's typology of burglars seems to be insightful, even more types of *fences* have been described. **Fences** are individuals who purchase stolen goods, and a typology of fences was developed by Cromwell, Olson, and Avary, based upon interviews with 30 active burglars and shoplifters, an analysis of statements given to police by 190 arrested burglars and shoplifters in west Texas, and some 310 hours of interviews with professional and nonprofessional fences as well as 19 amateur receivers (fences) who purchase stolen property for personal consumption.[96] It is important to study fences, not just regarding burglary, but in relation to all forms of theft including larceny-theft, robbery, and motor vehicle theft. Ways of turning stolen goods into cash, as seen earlier, are what differentiates the small-time burglar from the big-time professional. The question Cromwell, Olson, and Avary were asking was, "Who are these fences?" The typology they developed differentiated the "receivers" on the basis of four criteria—the frequency, scale, purposes, and level of commitment to purchase stolen property. Based upon these criteria, they found that there were six levels of receivers or fences: professional fences, part-time fences, associational fences, neighborhood hustlers, drug-dealers who barter drugs for stolen property, and amateurs. *Professional fences* have as their principle enterprise the purchase and redistribution of stolen property. Although they may operate other businesses as fronts for their fencing activities, they are proactive in establishing a reliable and persistent flow of stolen merchandise. They buy and sell stolen goods on a large scale basis and have a reputation among law breakers as reliable fences. Professional fences tend to prefer doing business with professional thieves who won't inform on them in the event of arrest. *Part-time fences* are differentiated from professional fences by the lesser frequency of purchases, volume of business, degree of commitment to fencing enterprises, and the fact that they do not depend on fencing as their principal means of a livelihood. *Associational fences* are persons whose legitimate occupations place them in close association and interaction with thieves, including police officers, criminal defense attorneys, and bail bond agents. *Neighborhood hustlers* buy and sell stolen property as one of many "hustles" or small-time criminal enterprises, providing a marginal living outside of legitimate employment. They may be thieves themselves, and typically they work out of the trunk of a car or from their home. They may not have a reputation for reliability among criminals and may be described as "snitches" or informants. Thus, they are limited to buying from juveniles, drug addicts, and novice thieves who are unable to market their stolen goods to professional fences (because they are not trusted by the professional fences). *Drug dealer fences* sell drugs and trade in stolen goods, often accepting stolen goods in exchange for drugs, knowing that they can market the stolen goods for more than what the drugs are worth. Finally, *amateur receivers* are consumers who, when approached by the thieves in a public place and anonymously will purchase the stolen goods. They are persons with whom the thief has developed a relationship and who buy stolen property regularly, at a bargain rate. Most buy for personal consumption. However, some of the amateurs resell the goods to friends and coworkers, and others sell the "hot" merchandise at garage sales or through flea markets. Cromwell, Olson, and Avary's typology seems to call into question the age-old supposition that theft could be reduced significantly through legal action against fences, because they found that receiving stolen goods as "part-time crime" is ubiquitous.

Types of Larceny-Theft

Larceny can vary from a very petty crime like stealing a candy bar to a very serious crime such as the theft of a valuable art object. Because of the broad span of objects that can be stolen and the frequency of this crime, it is the most common crime in the United States.

Larceny-theft is often trivialized as an unimportant crime. This fact alone may help to account for the prevalence of larceny-theft in the United States and many developed countries. However, trivializing larceny-theft may be a mistake because, according to some studies, larceny-theft may very well be a "gateway crime," a juvenile prelude to a career in crime or a lifetime of participation in crime. In the FBI's Index crimes, motor vehicle theft is listed separately, although motor vehicle theft is actually a form of larceny. The FBI lists motor vehicle theft separately in the UCR because it is both a frequent crime and one that is typically a costly one and can usually be considered **grand theft.** Grand theft is usually defined by state law as involving theft of items ranging in value from a low of $50 to $150 upward. Actually, because inflation plays havoc with crime statistics, the FBI abandoned attempts to distinguish between petit larceny and grand larceny.[97]

Although motor vehicle theft is a form of larceny, it is dealt with separately from larceny in this chapter, for several reasons. Motor vehicle theft is

A young male shoplifter checks to make sure nobody is looking while he stuffs a DVD into his jacket at a video store.
Source: David Young-Wolff/PhotoEdit, Inc.

Table 10–6 **Trends in Larceny-Thefts Known to Police with Projected Rate of Larceny-Theft for each Category, Years 1995–2004.**[98]

Category	Percentage 1995	Rate 1995	Percentage 2004	Rate 2004	Trend 95–04
Pocket-picking	0.6	18.3	0.4	9.5	−48.2
Purse-snatching	0.6	18.3	0.6	14.2	−22.3
Shoplifting	15.1	459.8	14.5	343.1	−25.4
From motor vehicles (except accessories)	24.3	739.9	25.3	598.6	−19.1
Motor vehicle accessories	12.1	368.4	10.8	255.5	−30.6
Bicycles	6.3	191.8	3.6	85.2	−55.6
From buildings	12.5	380.6	12.4	293.4	−22.9
From coin-operated machines	0.6	18.3	0.7	16.6	−9.3
All others	27.9	849.5	31.6	747.6	−12.0
Total	100.0	3044.9	99.9	2365.9	−22.3

separated from larceny-theft not just in the UCR, but also in INTERPOL and United Nations statistical reports. Furthermore, larceny-theft and motor vehicle theft as crimes each have been the subject of a considerable volume of literature. Motor vehicle theft is also a special type of larceny in that it tends to be a crime done by males. Larceny, by contrast, seems to be a "gender equity" crime, with a higher representation of females in official statistics.

The FBI definition of larceny-theft discussed earlier includes a wide variety of types of larceny-theft. To enhance understanding of larceny in general, Table 10–6 shows all categories of larceny-theft and the projected rate of crime for each category. While "thefts from motor vehicles" was the largest category of larceny in 2004, with a rate of 598.6 per 100,000 inhabitants, shoplifting was the second largest category with a rate of 343.1 per 100,000 inhabitants. All of the subcategories of larceny have declined since 1995, but at different rates. Pocket-picking, motor vehicle accessories, and bicycle theft have declined the most. However, purse-snatching, theft from coin-operated machines, and "all others" have declined less than the overall rate for larceny.

Besides the types of offenses described in Table 10–6, there are several additional typologies of larceny-thieves as offenders in the literature. As discussed in previous chapters, the early literature, based upon Sutherland's discussion of the professional thief, distinguished between amateur thieves and professionals.

Sutherland's characterization of professional thieves as being specialized, highly skilled, nonviolent toward victims, and honorable in not informing on other thieves began to break down with the study of thieves by the President's Commission on Crime in 1967. Criminals that departed from Sutherland's characterization (and yet were chronic or career criminals) started to appear in the literature. These types lie somewhere between Sutherland's pure professional thieves and true amateurs. Shover distinguishes between professional criminals and persistent thieves, who continue in "common law property crimes despite their, at best, ordinary levels of

BOX 10–3

Personal Theft in France

The rate of larceny-theft in France is 2768.4, and France ranks 8th of 145 countries in the world for larceny-theft. What is noteworthy about France is that much of the larceny-theft takes the form of personal theft—pickpocketing and purse-snatching. A tourism Website provides the following account of personal theft in France:

> Gangs of thieves operate on the rail link from Charles de Gaulle Airport to downtown Paris by preying on jet-lagged, luggage-burdened tourists. Often, one thief distracts the tourist with a question about directions while an accomplice takes a momentarily unguarded backpack, briefcase or purse. The Number One Subway Line, which runs by many major tourist attractions, is the site of many thefts. Pickpockets are especially active on this metro line during the summer months. Many thefts occur at the major department stores where tourists often leave wallets, passports, and credit cards on cashier counters during transactions. In hotels, thieves frequent lobbies and breakfast rooms, and take advantage of a minute of inattention to snatch jackets, purses and backpacks. Many Americans have reported thefts occurring in restaurants, where purses are stolen from the back of a chair or from under the table during the meal. Thefts from cars stopped at red lights are common, particularly in the Nice-Antibes-Cannes area, and in Marseille. In "snatch and grab" thefts, the thief is usually a passenger on a motorcycle. Similar incidents have also occurred at tollbooths and rest areas. Purse-snatching and pickpocketing occur throughout southern France.[99]

success."[100] *Persistent thieves* are so deemed because of their party lifestyle, which helps explain their persistence, regardless of risks of arrest:

> It is a lifestyle distinguished in many cases by two repetitively cyclical phases and correspondingly distinctive approaches to crime. When offenders' efforts to maintain the lifestyle (i.e., their party pursuits) are largely successful, crimes are committed in order to sustain circumstances or a pattern of activities they experience as pleasurable. By contrast, when offenders are less successful at party pursuits, their crimes are committed in order to forestall or avoid circumstances experienced as threatening, unpleasant or precarious (e.g., addiction to drugs or alcohol, unemployment, loss of support by friends and family, etc.).[101]

Shover and Honaker expanded their discussion of the preoccupation of persistent property offenders with **life-as-party**[102]:

> persistent property offenders spend much of their criminal gains on alcohol and other drugs. The proceeds of their crimes . . . typically are used for personal, non-essential consumption (e.g., "nights out"), rather than, for example, to be given to family or used for basic needs. Thieves spend much of their leisure hours enjoying good times. . . . Life as party is enjoyed in the company of others. Typically, it includes shared consumption of alcohol or other drugs in bars and lounges, on street corners, or while cruising in automobiles. . . . Crimes that once were committed for recreational purposes increasingly become desperate attempts to forestall or reverse uncomfortable or frustrating situations. Pursuing the short term goal of maximizing enjoyment of life, legal threats can appear to the offender either as remote or improbable contingencies when party pursuits fulfill their recreational purposes or as an acceptable risk in the face of continued isolation, penury, and desperation.[103]

Another term intermediary between amateur and professional criminals is the term *occasional offenders*, which refers to criminals whose crimes "occur on those occasions in which there is an opportunity or situational inducement to commit the crime."[104] Although opportunities to engage in larceny present themselves to members of all social classes, situational inducements may vary. Situational inducements are short-term influences, such as financial problems and peer pressure, that increase risk-taking. Situational inducements may be more common among unemployed people and/or people living in poverty, as well as young people generally.

There has been some effort by criminologists to develop typologies pertaining to one subtype of larceny—shoplifting. Mary Owen Cameron pioneered the analysis of shoplifters in her ethnographic study in which she characterized shoplifters as either boosters or snitches. *Boosters,* a small percentage of those apprehended for shoplifting, are professional shoplifters who sell the items that they steal, whereas *snitches,* the majority of those caught shoplifting, steal to satisfy their own needs, often stealing items of small value.[105] However, since Cameron's work, there have been a couple of attempts to develop more detailed typologies of shoplifters, based upon their motivation. Richard Moore developed a five-fold typology of convicted shoplifters which included impulsive, occasional, episodic, amateur, and semi-professional shoplifters.[106] *Impulsive shoplifters* were inexperienced shoplifters who rarely planned the offense, while *occasional shoplifters* were more experienced shoplifters who also rarely planned their offense, but were motivated by peer pressure. *Amateur shoplifters* shoplifted regularly and sought to maximize profit and minimize risk. *Semiprofessional shoplifters* had the greatest skill of all types and stole for resale to others. *Episodic shoplifters* were those with psychological problems. The largest group were the amateur shoplifters, who constituted over half of the sample, whereas episodic shoplifters, were the smallest group. Occasional shoplifters were approximately 15% of the sample, whereas semiprofessional shoplifters were about 12% of the sample.

McShane and Noonan developed a four-fold typology based upon a "cluster analysis" of 75 subjects who were apprehended for shoplifting, including rebels, reactionaries, enigmas, and the infirm. *Rebels* were young females with a sizable prior history of offending. *Reactionaries* were more likely than the rebels to be more highly educated older, married, and males, but, like the rebels, were economically able to pay for the stolen merchandise. *Enigmas* were demographically similar to the reactionaries, but lacked psychosocial stressors more characteristic of the reactionaries. *The infirm* described a type of shoplifter who was more likely to be female than male, and to have experienced previous episodes of chronic illness. The most prevalent of these types were the enigmas (41.43%), followed by reactionaries (27%), and rebels (19%).[107]

Types of Motor Vehicle Theft

There has been some effort by criminologists to develop typologies pertaining to motor vehicle theft. One study done in the Netherlands contained a three-fold typology of car thieves. The first type of car thief uses the car for only a short time for transportation. The second type steals a car in conjunction with another criminal offense, possibly to transport stolen goods after a burglary. The third type of theft is done to sell the car.[108]

Probably the most extensive typology of vehicle theft, which seems to build upon the aforementioned typology, was developed by McCaghy and Associates. Based upon an examination of data from police and court files, McCaghy and Associates concluded that there are five types of auto

BOX 10–4

Joyriders Beaten in Northern Ireland

In Northern Ireland, car theft is attractive to adolescents as a source of excitement, a way of impressing friends, and a possible source of financial gain. In 1987, paramilitary organizations carried out 60 punishment beatings and 124 punishment shootings on car thieves there, yet the problem persists.[109]

theft—joyriding, short-term transportation, long-term transportation, profit, and commission of another crime.[110] *Joyriding* is typically the theft of automobiles by teenagers motivated by a desire for power, prestige, and the sexual potency often associated with an automobile. Whereas *short-term transportation* simply involves getting from one place to another, *long-term transportation* usually involves theft for permanent use by the offender. *For-profit* auto thieves include highly organized professionals who alter the identification tags of the vehicles and resell them. Included in this category are *jockeys,* car thieves who are routinely involved in "steal-to-order jobs." The term *jockeys* is based upon the speed with which they carry out their car thefts.[111] Also included in the category of *for-profit* auto thieves are amateur auto strippers who "part out" cars for use on their own cars or for resale. Finally, auto thieves use the stolen car to *commit another crime,* such as robbery, to ensure their anonymity during the crime.

Dark Figures of Crime

Although the typologies of burglary, larceny-theft, and motor vehicle theft are helpful in providing an expanded and detailed understanding of these stealthy theft crimes, it is obvious that more work is needed, especially of an ethnographic or qualitative nature, to improve knowledge of these important and prevalent crimes. Probably one reason these crimes are not better researched is that for all of these crimes the clearance rates are very low. This leaves a very large "dark figure" with roughly 85% of these crimes unsolved. It is possible (if not probable) that a larger number of persons who commit stealthy theft crimes are never caught. This large group may actually constitute the majority of persons who commit this crime, persons whose characteristics we can only guess. Such guesswork may be aided by a careful study of existing statistics, especially those from self-reports, but also from comparative analysis, which is made in this chapter.

PROFILING STEALTHY THEFT

Profiling Burglary

There are numerous factors associated with burglary, some of which have already been discussed, along with additional factors that have been revealed by criminological studies. Factors found to be positively related to burglary include the unemployment rate; reduction in cost of living Aid to Families with Dependent Children (AFDC) payments per recipient; larger households; a disproportionately large population of young people; houses with back alley access; houses with low surveillability; businesses at the center of a recreational activity node; businesses close to alcohol outlets, including strip clubs, bars, and convenience stores; businesses located greater than three blocks from heavily traveled thoroughfares; businesses located in wealthy communities; retail businesses located in office parks; establishments in business less than one year; an absence of burglar alarms; absence of night lighting; households of single parents with children; households with youthful occupants; households in the inner city; areas of mixed land use (commercial, single, and multiple dwellings); areas of temporary residences; households with Asian occupants; households with low occupancy levels (between 9 to 11 a.m. and 1 to 3 p.m.); the absence of watchdogs; the presence of obstructed windows; use of drugs by burglars and to help them carry out burglaries; an ambient temperature, at least up to 85 degrees Farenheit; and targets located 1.6 miles from the burglar's residence.[112]

Profiling Larceny   Larceny has been associated in various studies with certain factors, which include: increased levels of policing; offenders being teenage girls; offenders' illicit drug use, particularly methamphetamine, PCP, and crack cocaine; offenders' unemployment; the introduction of legalized gambling; economic development or "modernization"; offenders being of female gender; confusion and chronic shortages following a war; an architectural location of rooms in a hospital near an escape route, rooms located along hallways, and controlled access areas facilitating employee theft; gentrification of a neighborhood; victims being guests in a hotel; victims being of female gender; offenders having a significant other involved in shoplifting; victims and offenders being tourists; juveniles being truant from school; victims being college students, especially if a fraternity or sorority member; offenders being black in race in cases of purse-snatching; victims (of purse-snatching) being white and aged; and offenders being adolescents (shoplifting).[113]

BOX 10–5

Latvia Declares War on Drugs and Reaps "Reward"—Higher Property Crime

Following reinstatement of the independence of Latvia from Russia, Latvia joined the War on Drugs by signing three United Nations drug Conventions indicating the passage of laws to fight against drugs by Latvia's parliament. Starting in 1995, INTERPOL data indicate that drug offenses increased from a rate of 10.71 per 100,000 inhabitants to 27.78 in 2000, an increase of 159%. During that same period of time, robberies increased 280%, burglaries increased 112%, and larcenies increased 63% in Latvia, whereas murder and assault actually declined. In the CCDB, drug arrests correlate strongly with burglary ($r = .48$), larceny ($r = .40$), and motor vehicle theft ($r = .59$). One explanation—as drug enforcement increases the cost of drugs to users, they must turn to property crimes to afford their habit.[114]

BOX 10–6

Truancy and Shoplifting

A study of crime among truants done in Dayton, Ohio, revealed that of 1,930 juveniles arrested during the years 1979–1980, 225 were truant from school at the time they were arrested. Over half of the truants were arrested for the crime of larceny, the majority of which were for shoplifting.[115]

Motor vehicle theft has been associated in various studies with certain specific factors, including decreased arrest rates or lack of deterrence; offenders being of male gender; offenders being hard drug users; offender unemployment and unfavorable future work prospects, especially in youthful offenders; offenders being juveniles or young adults; offenders being members of documented gangs; economic development or "modernization"; the absence of a parts-marking program; offenders being African American males; older, Japanese manufactured vehicles with theft-vulnerable door and ignition locks; vehicles in the United States that are vehicles made in Mexico; unemployment and unfavorable future work prospects, especially in youthful offenders; cars being stolen from parking lots in the late evening and early hours of the morning; perception on the part of offenders that car theft is not a serious offense; declining incidence of auto theft associated with the availability of Lojack (hidden radio-transmitter device used for retrieving stolen vehicles); and victim residence on a block near a high school.[116]

The general drift of the aforementioned findings is that burglary, larceny-theft, and motor vehicle theft are associated with law enforcement leniency in regard to the crime, unemployment, and economic development. Young people of high school or college age are likely to be both victims and offenders in burglary, larceny-theft, and motor vehicle theft. Black males are disproportionately involved in purse-snatching and motor vehicle theft. Females are more involved in larceny-theft, particularly shoplifting, than they are in other crimes. Burglary and larceny-theft are crimes of opportunity in regard to their prevalence with vulnerable targets (the aged, tourists, hotel guests), as well as lack of guardianship (urban areas, gentrified neighborhoods, targets near escape routes). However, as discussed later, even though routine activities theory has certainly been a major approach in the literature in dealing with stealthy theft, there are many other theories that have been of relevance to stealthy theft. These include deterrence theory, anomie theory, and others to be discussed later. Situational theories seem to carry with them an assumption that there is little society can do to prevent a particular crime, so individuals must do what they can to protect themselves through target hardening, neighborhood guardianship, and the like. However, along with these approaches, there may be much that can be done on a policy level based upon alternative theoretical approaches to reduce the overall rate of larceny.

Situational Theories

The focus on target vulnerability in the aforementioned findings suggests the omnipresence of *routine activities theory* as an underlying approach assumed in these studies. To review, routine activities theory was the theory developed by Cohen and Felson in 1979 postulating that crime is likely to occur when a motivated offender and a suitable target contact each other in the absence of a capable guardian.[117] To some extent, routine activities theory is an outgrowth of the Chicago School theory of social disorganization. It is in the socially disorganized neighborhoods that most of these factors converge. The slums are areas with high unemployment rates and youthful occupants, often single parents with children, dependent upon AFDC. These are certainly areas of mixed land use and temporary residences, ranging from rented dwellings to flop houses. Back alleys characterize housing in the inner city and are largely absent from suburban housing. Residents and businesses alike typically are lacking in burglar alarms or night lighting, but are likely to be characterized by gun ownership. The theory of social disorganization designated these areas as being weak in social control as well as "collective efficacy." Because many of the residents are single mothers who work, leaving children with grandparents or in daycare, their households have low occupancy during working hours, leaving residences without guardianship during the day (low surveillability). In the inner-city areas, alcohol outlets are prevalent, as are commercial establishments and office parks. Residing in these neighborhoods are offenders and ex-offenders who have a substance abuse problem that, given periodic unemployment, makes burglary a necessary means of gaining the dollars necessary to support a drug and/or alcohol habit.

Bursick and Grasmick described the relationship of routine activities theory to social disorganization theory, stating that routine sustenance activities of residents mediate the effects of social organization in regard to victimization patterns by providing different levels of guardianship.[118] Routine activities in inner-city neighborhoods display a lack of guardianship, with motivated offenders nearby. Thus, burglary is a predictable outcome.[119]

Closely related to routine activities theory was the emergence of situational approaches to crime prevention that developed in the early 1970s. C. Ray Jeffery developed an approach to crime prevention called *Crime Prevention through Environmental Design* (CPTED).[120] Another example of this approach was the work of Oscar Newman in his 1973 book, *Defensible Space*.[121] Newman advocated architecture that encouraged guardianship and protected potential victims. Thus, he opposed high-rise apartments, because they required extended stairways and/or elevator rides where criminality could occur. CPTED involves altering environments to decrease victimization, whereas *defensible space* refers to improved architectural designs to enhance security. Both approaches have been linked with rational choice and routine activity theories to form a new and influential approach called *situational crime prevention*.

Clarke and Homel have documented some 16 techniques of situational crime prevention that include: target hardening (e.g., steering locks); access control (e.g., entry phones); deflecting offenders (e.g., street closures); controlling facilitators (e.g., credit card photos); entry/exit screening, formal surveillance (e.g., cameras); surveillance by employees; natural surveillance (e.g., street lighting); target removal (e.g., removable car radios); identifying property; reducing temptation (e.g., off-street parking); denying benefits (e.g., PIN for cell phones); rule setting; strengthening moral condemnation; controlling disinhibitors (e.g., ignition interlock); and facilitating compliance (e.g., trash bins).[122] In the sense that these various procedures are an application of routine activities and rational choice theories, evidence of the effectiveness of these procedures can be construed as supporting the base theories. Thus, numerous studies listed earlier pertaining to factors in burglary have been construed as providing support for these approaches.

Situational crime prevention is applied in this confrontation between a male store manager and a startled teenage boy attempting to steal a compact disk in the "Rock and Soul" section of a music store.

Source: Bill Aron/PhotoEdit, Inc.

BOX 10–7

Drug Use in the Netherlands

Those who support the "drugs cause crime" school of thought might point to Holland, a country known for its lenient policy in regard to drug use. In 2002, according to INTERPOL data, the Netherlands had an extremely high rate of burglary and larceny, with rates of 3,276.94 and 2,373.13 per 100,000 inhabitants, respectively. In the Netherlands, sale and use of small amounts of soft drugs (hashish and marijuana) is tolerated in coffee houses throughout the country. Upon closer examination, INTERPOL data reveal that larceny had risen dramatically from a rate of 389.09 in 1995 to 2,373.13 per 100,000 inhabitants in 2002, whereas the rate of burglary was high in both years (3,064.74 in 1995 and 3,276.94 in 2002). The stereotypical view that the Netherlands is a haven for drug users, however, is based upon a misconception.

Prohibited by law in the Netherlands are drug *trafficking offenses*—importations, exportation, and transportation, according to the Opium Act of 1976. Thus, although Dutch lawmakers have favored "normalizing" drug offenders through the decriminalization of marijuana and hashish and through "harm reduction" programs for hard drug users, they have given high priority to fighting narcotics trafficking. Furthermore, in 1998, control over "coffee shops" increased, leading to a significant fall in their number from about 200 to 62. Thus, drug addicts, even in Holland, increasingly have to obtain their drugs on the black market at high prices and must turn to crimes such as burglary and larceny to provide revenue for their increasingly expensive habits.[123]

Economic Model

The situational approaches discussed so far take for granted the criminal motivation of offenders. Thus, theories that emphasize motivational characteristics of the offender might be taken as competing theories. Such theories, when applied to burglary, do not assume that almost everybody would engage in burglary if he or she could get away with it. Instead they view the offense as driven by causes that motivate the offender to commit the crime. One study testing an economic model of crime found that family poverty and local unemployment increased the propensity to commit burglary among both males and females.[124] Similarly, DeFronzo's study, cited earlier, of the negative relationship between AFDC and burglary supports the economic opportunity model.[125] Several studies have shown a positive relationship between unemployment and burglary.[126] In regard to the variables poverty versus economic inequality, Sampson found that income inequality has a direct positive effect on black and white offending rates for burglary, but poverty has no effect.[127] Another study based upon data from 113 major cities found a direct positive relationship between burglary and poverty, joblessness, and income inequality. This study traced these social problems to economic restructuring, resulting in a decline in manufacturing jobs from 1970 to 1990.[128]

Easterlin Hypothesis

Another approach to burglary is a demographic theory formulated by economist Richard Easterlin.[129] This approach predicts a positive relationship between the relative size of a birth cohort and burglary. According to the **Easterlin hypothesis,** a larger birth cohort or "baby boom" results in excess unemployment and poverty for that cohort when it reaches adulthood, due to a heightened competition for jobs. This in turn fuels crime as an alternative source of income. Some evidence for this theory is shown later in the country profile of Australia. Support for this hypothesis for the crime of burglary was also given in studies by O'Brien[130] and Savolainen.[131]

Although the studies described earlier used official data or conviction as a criterion of the rate of burglary, one study using self-report data found no urban-rural difference for youths in regard to burglary and other crimes.[132]

While the aforementioned studies focused upon economic variables as causative of burglary, other studies have found drug use[133] and possible involvement with alcohol, as indicated by density of liquor outlets, as causative factors in burglary.[134]

The studies and theories of burglary discussed earlier portray burglary as a crime of urban, inner-city, poverty-stricken, jobless offenders, and victims from the same areas. However, some disquieting facts about burglary should raise concern about the validity of these observations as a basis for theory building. One fact is that the clearance rate for burglary is only around 13%, according to the FBI.[135] Thus, 86% or 87% of burglaries are not accounted for. A recent examination of victimization data has revealed that 72% of households within the United States are burglarized at least once over the average lifetime.[136] It seems likely that important data have been omitted from studies dependent upon official reports, data about the unrecorded burglaries that take place everywhere, not just in the inner city. Some of these burglaries may be committed by middle and upper class offenders who never come to the attention of police, so study of their motivations, modus operandi, targets, and social characteristics cannot be made. As has been previously discussed, confining study to the statistics drawn from law enforcement sources within the United States may lead to provincial theorizing.

Probably more studies testing or relating to routine activities theory have been done in regard to larceny-theft than any other theory.[137] This is the theory that is probably most cited in the literature, for various reasons. One reason is that the police have been unsuccessful in providing guardianship, as indicated by the low clearance rates for larceny in United States data. As a result of this, attempts at deterrence have been generally abandoned, because if police catch few thieves, there is little hope of deterring them through legal means.

Another reason for the popularity of routine activities theory is that larceny-theft has been shown to be a crime done by a large number of people in society, especially young people, confirming the theory's assumption of the omnipresence of the motivated offender. One study done in 1980 found that out of 100,671 students surveyed in the United States, 49% of the total sample admitted to having shoplifted at least once; 30% indicated that they would continue to shoplift; and 40% had shoplifted in the last two years.[138] A national survey of school violence in a representative sample of 1,234 public schools in 1997 found that theft or larceny (116,000 incidents) was second to physical attacks or fights (190,000 incidents) among crime incidents reported.[139] Another study found that two thirds of 606 college students surveyed admitted that they had been involved in at least one shoplifting offense.[140]

If guardianship by law enforcement has failed to deter larceny and motivated offenders are widespread in the population, then the emphasis must be upon either enhanced guardianship or target hardening. Enhanced guardianship can be provided by private security in stores or neighborhoods, as well as through informal efforts, such as Neighborhood Watch. Private security is expensive, both for stores and homeowners, and in stores, major shoplifting takes place despite the presence of private security guards. Neighborhood Watch programs depend upon volunteer efforts on the part of neighborhood residents, but in developed countries such residents are often absent during the day due to employment or other activities outside the home.

Thus, in regard the crime of larceny, the omnipresence of motivated offenders plus the doubtfulness of guardianship leaves only the third variable of routine activities theory, a suitable target, available for possible intervention through "target hardening." By default, target hardening has become the major method of curbing larceny in the United States and other developed countries that have high rates of larceny. The two major subjects for target hardening pertaining to larceny have been automobiles and stores. Auto security will be discussed later; however, there are a variety of store security measures that are of interest. Although small independent stores typically

BOX 10–8

Consumer Misbehavior in Britain

Britain has a high rate of larceny, despite a considerable investment in retail security. A consumer survey was done on a sample of 417 consumers using Northhampton shops March to April 1997. Of those interviewed, 32% admitted to shoplifting behavior, with 7% having shoplifted during the previous year. Reasons stated were lack of moral concern about the behavior, peer influence, and the perception that shoplifting is a low-risk, low-cost crime.[141]

rely upon store clerks to detect shoplifting, large retailers utilize more costly measures that include plain-clothes floor detectives, video surveillance cameras, and electronic article surveillance devices attached to products that cause alarms to go off if not deactivated by the cashier. Expensive items may be secured in locked enclosures or by locked cables or hanger locks.[142] Store security tags include radio frequency tags, electromagnetic strips, and acousto-magnet tags. Although these tags can foil the novice shoplifter, techniques for defeating these tags through slitting or demagnetizing are well known and even published on the Internet.[143]

Improvements in store security have probably had less of an impact upon shoplifting than auto theft prevention devices. Larceny-theft declined 22.3% from 1995 to 2004. However, the decline in larceny-theft was less than the decline in total Index offenses (24.5%). In terms of larceny-theft, the United States ranks 11th out of 145 countries for which data are available (see Table 10–8). Thus, improvement in store security has not succeeded in curtailing this crime.

The major point emerging from the discussion of situational theories and the development of largely physical security measures to curtail larceny-theft is that the larceny-theft has not been eliminated or even significantly reduced as a result of the application of this single theory. In fact, the dollars lost because of larceny-theft increased by nearly one billion over the 1995–2004 period. Thus, it is worthwhile to explore alternative theories that have appeared in the literature. Alternative theories include the Durkheimian-modernization hypothesis, Merton's anomie theory (disadvantaged-group hypothesis), deterrence theory, the "baby boom" theory (Easterlin's theory), the war on drugs, and psychoanalytic theory (kleptomania).

Durkheimian-Modernization Hypothesis

In cross-national research on homicide and theft in 51 nations, one study found a strong positive correlation between gross national product levels and theft rates, a finding the researchers said supported the Durkheimian-modernization hypothesis. Increased property crime, it was concluded, was at least as much because of increased opportunities for crime as because of a breakdown of social control. The researchers concluded that a comprehensive explanation of modernization and larceny should include elements of both the Durkheimian-modernization hypothesis and routine activities approaches. In another study related to this explanation, it was found that burglary, the major property crime in the 1970s, was being replaced in its prevalence by larceny-theft in Puerto Rico in recent years. This trend occurred along with increasing social change and an increase in the gross national product in Puerto Rico.[144] In the comparative study of the United States versus Argentina cited in the text box, property crime in Argentina was more likely to take the form of burglary from the homes of employers, compared to the United States, where larceny-theft was the more prevalent crime due to the greater availability of retail outlets and automobiles.[145]

Easterlin Hypothesis

As discussed in the section on burglary, Easterlin's theory proposed that relative cohort size has an indirect but sizable effect on age-specific crime rates.

BOX 10–9

Death Penalty for Shoplifting in 18th Century England

The criminal statutes of the early 1700s in England endorsed the "bloody code," in which an offender could be sentenced to death for a minor offense such as pickpocketing or shoplifting. These brutal punishments were eliminated through the legislative efforts that stemmed from the Enlightenment and legal utilitarianism of the early 1800s.[146]

The theory states that if an age cohort is especially large ("baby boom"), when approaching adulthood members of the cohort will experience shortages due to competition for scarce resources and employment. The result is that crime is resorted to by some members of the cohort as an alternative means to achieve income.[147] One study using data gathered from the UCR for 1960, 1965, 1970, 1972, 1977, 1982, and 1987 supported Easterlin's theory for larceny-theft, but not for motor vehicle theft.[148]

Deterrence Theory

The need for enhanced application of deterrence theory has been suggested by several studies. One study, which used a general equilibrium model of larceny, provided a behavioral framework that was used to estimate the effects of government policies on the commission of larceny. Using data from cities in Los Angeles County, the simulations show that longer prison sentences and higher conviction rates for criminals are the most effective methods to reduce larceny, whereas subsidized leisure activities, increased police expenditures, and income transfers have little effect on larceny.[149]

Another study, cited previously, found that 43% of shoplifters felt that store personnel were too "soft" on shoplifters in general. Of the 17% who were "caught" at shoplifting, 46% were "lectured" by store personnel, 36% were detained, 40% were detained and their parents were contacted, 16% were arrested by the police, 7% were taken to court, and 5% were sentenced or fined by the court.[150] These findings will prove to be relevant in regard to the country profile of Sweden to be presented later in this chapter.

The War on Drugs

Although the movement to curtail illegal drugs is not unique to developed nations, attempts at interdiction and control of illegal substances certainly have been spearheaded by Western countries, particularly the United States. As with homicide and other crimes, there has been a growing movement of those who blame the war on drugs for the escalating larceny rates in countries in the West. There is concern that attempts to cut off the supply of illegal drugs through interdiction efforts has only been successful in driving the price of the drugs higher. People habituated or addicted to the drugs, then, particularly if they are unemployed or unable to obtain the desired drugs on their income, feel they must turn to crime such as larceny to procure their drugs. Evidence for this theory is twofold. First, there appears to be a high prevalence of drug use among those who commit larceny, and, vice versa, a high

BOX 10–10

Shoplifting Number One Crime for German Drug Addicts

A study done in Germany involved interviews with 100 addicts in institutions. Heroin was the dominant drug: 80% named it as their favorite. The most frequently occurring of their 173,000 offenses per year were some 27,000 instances of shoplifting.[151]

rate of larceny for those who are drug users. In London, England, according to the Office of the National Drug Control Policy, drug users are 16 times more likely to commit theft or larceny than non-drug users.[152] Numerous studies have shown that a majority of persons convicted of larceny test positive in jail for drugs and/or alcohol.[153] However, these studies can be used both by people who advocate the war on drugs and those who oppose it. Advocates of the war on drugs claim that the drugs influence the offenders to commit the thefts (therefore the drugs should be banned). Opponents of the war on drugs counter that the thefts are committed by the offenders to obtain money to pay high black market prices for the drugs. In the United States, it is impossible to do scientific testing to determine which argument is correct, because drugs such as crystal methamphetamine, cocaine, and heroin are universally banned. However, in Switzerland, a program was implemented in several cities to medically prescribe heroin and other opiates to about 1,000 seriously addicted drug users. Based upon interviews with 319 participants, all indicators pointed to a substantial reduction of criminal involvement, particularly for larceny, burglary, and robbery, after entering the program.[154]

Kleptomania

As a point related to the last cited study on shoplifting, we might ask, "To what extent is shoplifting driven by a neurotic compulsion or kleptomania?" As with the sociological theories discussed earlier, theories pertaining to kleptomania have, up until recently, been largely discarded as obsolete. The Freudian theory of kleptomania was adhered to by followers of Freud in the first part of the 20th century. However, in the last half of the 20th century, Freudian theory was often characterized as ridiculous. In the 1960s, when feminist theories started to emerge, Freudian theory came to be construed as male chauvinist or antifemale in nature.

Kleptomania was first defined by Andre Mathey as "A unique madness characterized by the tendency to steal without motive and without necessity. The tendency to steal is permanent and not at all accompanied by mental alienation. Reason preserves its domain. It resists this secret compulsion; but the thieving tendency triumphs. It subjects the will."[155]

Mathey coined the term "klopemania," which meant stealing insanity. Two decades later the term was changed to "kleptomania," which also meant "stealing insanity," by C. C. H. Marc, who added the following characteristics to its description:

• Irresistible impulses to steal objects of trivial value and that made no economic sense for the thief. (The stolen objects were often immediately discarded.)

- A sense of exhilaration and relieve of tension triggered by the acts of theft.
- Found more often among women.[156]

Kleptomania is described by Mathey and Marc as characterizing people of high social and economic status, including European royalty, and it came to be used as a defense in legal proceedings. Starting in the 1830s, French alienists (psychiatrists) actively courted, and received, an active role in the legal defense of upper class women accused of shoplifting. If their patients' actions were found due to "moral insanity," their clients could avoid degrading legal sentences.

Although French psychiatrists eventually came to dismiss kleptomania as a legal excuse for the self-indulgence of wealthy ladies, French psychiatry was increasingly removed from the mainstream and lost international influence. Instead the Germans and Austrians moved to the forefront, starting with the work of Sigmund Freud. Freudian theory held that shoplifting in girls is driven by an unconscious "penis envy," and the objects they acquire are substitutes for a penis—lipstick, bottles of perfume, soap, pens, pencils, and so forth. Wilhelm Stekel, a follower of Freud, maintained that acts of kleptomania were symbolic behavioral expressions of disturbed mental states developing because of frustrated sexual desires. The objects of shoplifting, he said, had a symbolic meaning. "A shoplifted pencil represented a penis, an umbrella a male erection, a glove a condom, a music box female genitalia, and so forth."[157]

From the 1930s through 1950s, when referred for treatment by the courts, kleptomaniacs usually received Freudian psychotherapy. However, starting in the 1970s, doubts developed concerning the reality of kleptomania as a disease. A large-scale study of shoplifters in Great Britain was critical of Stekel's concept of sexual symbolism. It also found that, while one in five apprehended shoplifters was "a psychiatric case," only a few exhibited symptoms of kleptomania.[158] A similar finding was produced by Cameron in her book, *The Booster and the Snitch,* cited previously. As later stated by Abelson, kleptomania came to be based upon a dated and degraded view of women that no reasonable person could assume.[159] Subsequently, kleptomania, present in the first edition, was dropped from the second edition of the American Psychiatric Association's *Diagnostic and Statistical Manual of Mental Disorders (DSM).*

However, despite declarations of the extinction of the concept of kleptomania, researchers continued to report cases of kleptomania. Subsequently, the third edition of the *DSM* contained an entry on kleptomania and continued in the fourth edition (*DSM-IV;* a description very similar to that of Mathey and Marc). Since then, a steady stream of work on kleptomania has been published. However, today, although Freudian treatments are marginal, current therapies include cognitive, behavioral modification, and pharmacological therapy, as well as those therapies pertaining to comorbidity with eating disorders.[160] In terms of incidence, authorities declare kleptomania to afflict no more than 3% to 8% of apprehended shoplifters.[161] However, because kleptomaniacs may shoplift more frequently than other shoplifters, they may account for a significant percentage of all reports of shoplifting. Stekel described a particular kleptomaniac who:

> on certain days . . . stole from many stores without experiencing that feeling of relief and satisfaction which eventually culminated in a sense of

complete gratification; on such occasions she rushed from store to store and kept stealing, until the acquisition of some particular article brought on the yearned for gratification.[162]

Today, although "consumer behavior perspectives are grounded in both rational choice or 'feelings, fantasies, fun' perspectives," kleptomania may be re-emerging as a concept that has withstood the "test of time," according to Fullerton and Punj. An interesting study published in 1997 found that "kleptomania" may be even broader in scope than the 8% cited at the high end by Fullerton and Punj. With subjects recruited through newspaper advertisements, Interviews were conducted with 37 persons who satisfied the *DSM-IV* criteria for kleptomania. The subjects were compared with 50 shoplifters immediately after their arrest for that crime. Although the kleptomaniacs rated a feeling of inner tension before the theft higher than the arrested shoplifters, there were no differences between the groups in degree of planning, psychological imbalances, and the need for the stolen item in question. Also, the arrested shoplifters rated high in the feeling of inner tension before the theft, as well as the feeling of relief during the theft, and impulsivity. The authors suggested possible medical treatment of all shoplifters with antidepressives, as well the use of educational programs such as Shoplifters Anonymous.[163] Another study recommended the Youth Emotional Shoplifting program of Shoplifters Anonymous as an effective treatment program for juveniles.[164] It should be pointed out that the concept of "kleptomania" has its close counterpart in Gottfredson and Hirschi's concept of "self-control," which was found to be significantly correlated with shoplifting in a study of 548 first-time shoplifting offenders.[165]

The question of "what works" in curbing shoplifting and other forms of larceny is addressed near the end of this chapter. Although empirical studies can lead to hints on this subject, another approach is to see what works and what doesn't work by studying countries high and low in the crimes of larceny. This is done in the country profiles discussion later.

Motor Vehicle Theft

Many of the theories discussed previously in regard to larceny-theft also apply to motor vehicle theft, because vehicle theft is a form of larceny. These include routine activities theory and other situational theories with their emphasis upon target hardening. Automobiles have been a major subject for target hardening, as suggested in the Lojack study cited earlier.

Improvements in security for automobiles have included steering shaft locks, cutoff switches, improved alarm systems, and electronic tracking systems, such as LoJack, and the "Unbrakeable Autolock." The Unbrakeable Autolock prevents the brake pedal from being depressed, thus preventing the automobile from being put into gear (for most cars built after 1990).[166] Other physical security devices include smart keys, kill switches, steering wheel locks, tire locks, steering column collars, window etching, and theft deterrent decals.[167] Smart keys have special coded computer chips or audio frequencies that must be used to start the engine. Kill switches use a special key to stop the flow of electricity or fuel to the engine. Tire locks are similar to the steel boots used by police departments to prevent the car from being driven. Steering wheel locks, such as The Club®, attach to the steering wheel and prevent it from turning. Steering column collars fit around the whole steering column, including the ignition, to prevent thieves from hot-wiring a car. Window etching involves having the vehicle's identification number etched into a window to make it difficult for a thief to resell the car or its parts. Theft deterrent decals warn a thief of car security devices, such as a car alarm, whether or not such devices exist.

The effectiveness of these physical security devices for automobiles may relate to the decline in rates of motor vehicle theft. As shown in Table 10–1, the rate of motor vehicle theft declined 24.8% from 1995 to 2004, a greater drop than the drop in the rate of larceny-theft (22.3% drop) and total index offenses (24.5% drop). However, this figure is offset somewhat by the increased rate of carjackings, which amount to around 50,000 per year. These are recorded as robberies and were discussed in Chapter 8. Carjackings may occur in part because of the difficulty that offenders have in stealing automobiles protected by security devices. The increased use of physical security devices may also account for the lower rates of motor vehicle theft for persons under 18 years of age in 2001 (33%) compared to the rate for 1995 (42%). There has been some evidence that, along with the development of physical security devices for automobiles, an increasing percentage of auto thefts that are done by professionals has occurred. Edelman noted as far back as 1980 that motor vehicle theft, once the province of joyriding teenagers, has been taken over by experienced professionals with ready-made markets. Edelman based this observation on the 10-year decline in recovery rates for automobiles (from 90% to 60%) and clearance rates for auto thieves (from 28% to 15%).[168] It should also be noted that, although auto thefts have dropped, the United States still ranks 13th in the world (out of 140 countries providing data) in its rate of motor vehicle theft (see Table 10–8).

The major point emerging from the discussion of situational theories and the development of largely physical security measures to curtail motor vehicle theft is that, although auto theft appears to have dropped, the crime has not been eliminated as a result of various target hardening techniques. Also, the dollar loss from vehicle theft has remained the same from 1995 to 2004. Thus, it is worthwhile to explore alternative theories that have appeared in the literature. Alternative theories include the Durkheim-modernization theory, Merton's anomie theory (disadvantaged-group hypothesis), deterrence theory, the "baby boom" theory (Easterlin's theory), the "favored group hypothesis," and the war on drugs. There has been no mention of "kleptomania" in the literature on auto theft. While these theories were discussed at some length previously, one theory seems to have special applicability to motor vehicle theft—the Durkheimian-modernization theory.

Durkheimian-Modernization Hypothesis

Perhaps related to the Durkheimian-modernization loss of control hypothesis discussed earlier is the "favored group" hypothesis. This was developed in regard to auto thefts by Wattenberg and Balistrieri.[169] In their 1948 research, they found that the 230 white youths charged with auto theft in their study in Detroit differed from the 2,544 juveniles charged with other types of offenses in that they came from relatively affluent neighborhoods. The finding that auto thieves were likely to be white and to come from a higher economic stratum than other delinquents was a finding of four other studies.[170] In the study done in Toledo in which they derived the five-fold typology discussed earlier, McCaghy et al. disputed the findings of the aforementioned four studies. McCaghy et al. found that of the 103 arrests they studied in 1975–1976, 55.9% of those arrested were white and 42.2% were black, whereas the population was only 13.8% black. They also found that half of those arrested came from areas with a lower median income level than the areas in which they were arrested.[171] Although the findings of McCaghy et al. were consistent with theories such as Merton's anomie theory that postulate a "disadvantaged group hypothesis," the "favored group hypothesis" studies that supported Wattenberg and Balistrieri's findings provided a stark contrast. It is, however, possible that there is no need to pit one school against the other. Both can be correct.

Adolescent Social System Theory

Herman Schwendinger developed a theory of middle class delinquency based upon the analysis of adolescent social systems. These teen social systems were autonomous from the adult social system in middle class, urban, industrialized, large school districts. Schwendinger stated that delinquency would be greatest for those who participate in insider groups of low status, and, to a lesser extent, of high status within the high school social system.[172] Thus, it is participation in these status groups, rather than parental socioeconomic status, that is the strongest correlate of delinquency. Schwendinger's findings from ethnographic work done in Los Angeles, California were replicated in a self-report study done in Long Beach, California by Robert Winslow. Winslow found that the low-status insiders in the high school social system had the highest rate of self-reported delinquency, followed by the high-status insiders. Further, Winslow found that status within the adolescent social system was not correlated with parental socioeconomic status. The development of adolescent social systems in the schools studied by Winslow was related to school attendance area socioeconomic heterogeneity, with the most heterogenous schools having the more highly developed adolescent social systems.[173] Thus, the prevalence of theft in developed nations may be related to the autonomy of youth, which, in turn, may be facilitated by the automobile.

We look at deterrence theory in the country profile on England, where youthful auto thieves are often given a "caution" for their first offense, or a "summary judgment" for subsequent offenses, with very little use of penal sanction for this offense.

COUNTRY PROFILES

Burglary   Table 10–7 reveals some correlations between various international indices from the comparative criminology database. Some of the correlations in the international database are the opposite of those found using data drawn from official statistics within the United States.

Although robbery and murder are *positively* correlated with the Gini Index of inequality, the crimes of stealthy theft—burglary, larceny-theft, and motor vehicle theft—are *negatively* related to that same index ($r = -.34, -.34$, and -32, respectively). This means that for stealthy theft, the greater the inequality, the less the burglary. Stealthy theft is negatively correlated with percentage unemployed (burglary $= -.32$, larceny $= -28$, and vehicle theft $= -.31$), whereas robbery has a low negative correlation with percentage living in poverty ($-.14$). Similarly, stealthy theft is negatively related to percentage unemployed (burglary $= -.32$, larceny $= -.28$, and vehicle theft $= -.31$), whereas robbery has a very low negative correlation with this variable ($-.09$). What

Table 10–7 Theft-Related Crimes as Correlated with Various International Indices

	Robbery	Burglary	Larceny-Theft	Vehicle Theft
Gini Index	0.11	−0.34	−0.34	−0.32
GDP	0.05	0.04	0.20	0.20
GDP per capita	0.15	0.48	0.63	0.62
Percentage living in poverty	−0.14	−0.32	−0.28	−0.37
Percentage unemployed	−0.09	−0.26	−0.28	−0.31
Lack of freedom	−0.35	−0.54	−0.46	−0.50
Percentage Islamic	−0.29	−0.39	−0.28	−0.28
Murder rate	0.25	−0.01	−0.05	−0.05
Rape rate	0.36	0.40	0.20	0.15
Robbery rate	1.00	0.32	0.19	0.31
Aggravated assault rate	0.14	0.51	0.31	0.25
Burglary rate	0.32	1.00	0.61	0.56
Larceny rate	0.19	0.61	1.00	0.65
Vehicle theft rate	0.31	0.56	0.65	1.00
Drug offense rate	0.10	0.51	0.46	0.46
Gender empowerment	0.13	0.58	0.55	0.47
Rate juveniles admitted to prison	0.24	0.03	−0.04	−0.07
Alcohol consumption per capita	0.39	0.60	0.44	0.49
Beer consumption per capita	0.19	0.59	0.50	0.47
Wine consumption per capita	0.24	0.48	0.38	0.51
Spirit consumption per capita	0.43	0.30	0.11	0.15
Net migration rate	−0.11	0.11	0.20	0.11
Median age	0.19	0.44	0.51	0.50

these data mean is that stealthy theft is greatest in countries in which there is the least amount of poverty, the least amount of unemployment, and the least amount of inequality. The positive correlation with GDP per capita ($r = .48$) may help to shed some light on these anomalies. Burglary, larceny-theft, and vehicle theft are greater in countries in which there is more wealth per person—more to steal.

All forms of theft correlate negatively and moderately with indices of control in Table 10–7. These measures include lack of freedom and percentage Islamic. The greater the control in terms of lack of freedom or percentage Islamic, the less the crime in terms of robbery, burglary, larceny-theft, and vehicle theft.

In trying to determine if these crimes are similar or different with respect to each other, it is useful to intercorrelate them with respect to each other and the other Index crimes, also shown in Table 10–7. Robbery is the only theft crime that correlates positively with murder ($r = .25$), whereas the stealthy theft crimes have zero correlations with murder (burglary $r = −.01$; larceny-theft $= −.05$; vehicle theft $= −.05$). The stealthy theft crimes correlate better with aggravated assault than robbery (burglary $= .51$, larceny-theft $= .31$, and vehicle theft = .25, with robbery only .14). The stealthy theft crimes correlate strongly with each other, with correlations ranging from .56 to .65. They correlate about half as well with robbery, with correlations ranging from .19 for larceny and robbery to .31 for auto theft and .32 for burglary and robbery. Robbery and burglary both are moderately correlated with forcible rape, (.36 and .40, respectively), whereas larceny-theft and vehicle theft are weakly correlated with rape (.20 and .15 respectively). It seems that the stealthy theft crimes correlated best with robbery where one facilitates the other. The fairly strong correlation between burglary and rape may have to do with the fact that a burglar may encounter a female during the act of burglarizing, so the opportunity arises to rape as well as rob. The moderate correlation between vehicle theft and robbery may have to do with the fact that the vehicle theft facilitates the robbery in the sense that a stolen car can be used as a getaway car whose license plate cannot be used to identify the thief.

Other variables that correlate strongly with the stealthy theft crimes but not as much with robbery include the drug offense rate, gender empowerment, beer consumption, wine consumption, and median age. Robbery has a small but positive correlation with the rate juveniles are admitted to prison, while the stealthy theft crimes have zero correlations with this variable. Robbery correlates more strongly with spirit consumption per capita than the stealthy theft crimes. Robbery also correlates negatively with the net migration rate (more people leaving the country than coming in), whereas the stealthy theft crimes correlate positively with the net migration rate (more people coming in than leaving). The latter finding may pertain to the fact that the stealthy thieves are not identified during the course of their crime, while robbers may be identified and therefore may have to leave the country to avoid capture by law enforcement.

How do these findings relate to the various theories we have studied? In keeping with the Durkheimian-modernization hypothesis, the three acts of stealthy theft are strongly correlated with the GDP per capita. Support is given for deterrence theory in the inverse correlations pertaining to lack of freedom and percentage Islamic. Stealthy theft is inversely related to lack of freedom in terms of civil and political liberties. This means, in essence, the greater the freedom, the greater the stealthy theft. Also, Islamic countries have greater success in curbing stealthy theft. The greater the percentage

BOX 10–11

Economic Equality Not a Cure for Crime in Romania

Communism indeed led to socioeconomic equalitarianism in Romania. Today the country has a Gini Index of 31.1 (the average for all countries is 39.9). According to the Partidul Comunist Român or Romanian Communist Party, the socialist system eliminated the root cause of lawlessness—economic inequality—and therefore crime started to disappear. Articles in the Romanian press, however, indicated that crime remained a significant, if not growing, problem in 1989. The phenomenon of economic crime was the byproduct of Romania's inefficient, overly centralized economy. Unrealistic prices and exchange rates led to widespread corruption, shortages, a black market, speculation, and hoarding. In 1987, courts sentenced 300 citizens for economic crimes or the "illegal acquisition of wealth" and confiscated goods. There were indications that apprehension of economic "criminals" was difficult and that a prosecutorial backlog of such cases existed in 1989.[174]

Islamic in a country's population, the less the stealthy theft. Sharia law in Islamic countries features harsh physical punishments for theft, including amputation. Thus, a prospective burglar or shoplifter who may think that he or she might be able to get away with a stealthy crime might think twice about the consequences of the theft if caught.

More difficult to explain with Table 10–7 are the negative correlations pertaining to the Gini Index, percentage of people living in poverty, and percentage of unemployment. According to these findings, the less the inequality in a country, the less the poverty and the less the unemployment, the greater the amount of larceny. These findings run directly contrary to findings within the United States and other countries that these factors are directly correlated with larceny. To find out how these anomalies work, it will be necessary to look at countries as cases in point. For the same reason, the anomalous finding that the median age in a country is a direct correlate of stealthy theft, the opposite of that found with FBI statistics cited earlier, is a finding that will have to be interpreted via country studies.

The fairly strong correlation in Table 10–7 between gender empowerment and stealthy theft is not surprising of light of liberal feminist theories that crime increases with female emancipation. However, it is an interesting finding, nonetheless, that needs further exploration.

Selection of Countries for Profiling

In this chapter, we have not just one crime, but three crimes for country ranking. Yet it is still desirable to present all of the countries in one table, because they are closely related. For this purpose, we have prepared a table (Table 10–8) that shows the countries ranked for "stealthy theft," a variable that is constructed from the sum of the three stealthy theft crime rates in much the same way as the FBI Index is constructed from the sum of the Index crimes. The stealthy theft crimes include only burglary, larceny-theft, and motor vehicle theft. In Table 10–8, countries are ranked from high to low in terms of their ranks for stealthy theft. In this table, countries that are ranked high in stealthy theft are given a rank of "1" or "2" and countries that have low rates of crime are given low ranks (e.g., 60). Also presented in that table are the country's ranks for the three crimes individually (burglary, larceny-theft, and vehicle theft). Thus, in searching for countries to profile we are looking for countries with high ranks (1–5) to represent those with high rates of stealthy theft. We are also looking for countries with low ranks to profile. In this chapter, we have a chance to compare countries on the low end that are on the same level of development as the countries that have high rates of stealthy crimes.

In terms of burglary, Turks & Caicos is number one in rank in Table 10–8; however, it is a new country for which we do not have adequate qualitative or quantitative information to do a country profile. Australia is a country for which a country profile is available on the Comparative Criminology Website. It is just below Turks & Caicos as the second highest country in the world in its rate of burglary. The latest data for Australia available at the time of this writing were for year 2000. In 2000, Australia reported a burglary rate of 2280.82 per 100,000 inhabitants. This compares with a rate of 740.8 per 100,000 inhabitants for the United States. With a rate of burglary nearly three times that of the United States, Australia is a suitable subject for extensive analysis.

Table 10–8 Countries of the World Ranked from High to Low on Rate of Stealthy Theft, Including Ranks on Burglary, Larceny-Theft, and Vehicle Theft

Country	Stealthy Theft	Burglary	Larceny-Theft	Vehicle Theft
Sweden	1	15	1	9
Denmark	2	6	2	6
Australia	3	2	4	2
Great Britain (England & Wales)	4	12	5	3
New Zealand	5	9	6	4
Netherlands	6	41	3	22
Finland	7	10	10	8
Turks & Caicos	8	1	23	83
Gibraltar	9	26	7	17
France	10	34	8	10
Germany	11	16	12	43
Canada	12	23	13	5
United States of America	**13**	**32**	**11**	**13**
Bermuda	14	4	21	53
Norway	15	81	9	7
Israel	16	27	17	11
South Africa	17	24	14	23
Austria	18	20	16	60
Luxembourg	19	21	18	33
Estonia	20	7	31	25
Puerto Rico	22	30	27	12
Hungary	23	35	20	41
Malta	24	19	33	20
Barbados	26	18	34	44
Slovenia	27	45	24	49
Dominica	29	8	116	47
Zimbabwe	30	51	22	91
Ireland (Northern)	31	37	26	103
Andorra	32	46	25	45
Japan	34	68	19	59
Switzerland	35	29	112	1
Poland	36	28	37	31
Spain	37	42	35	16
Bahrain	39	59	29	26
Lithuania	40	47	36	28
Bulgaria	42	56	42	32
Monaco	43	73	32	50
Belgium	44	33	136	18
Russia	45	55	40	64
Mauritius	47	83	30	95
Portugal	49	53	60	19
Uruguay	50	62	47	34
Romania	51	60	44	66
Czech Republic	52	38	80	24

Countries high in larceny-theft are, for the most part, developed nations, whereas those low in larceny are undeveloped countries and Islamic countries. Countries that rank high in larceny are for the most part Scandinavian countries, with Sweden reporting the highest larceny rate in the world. An analysis using data from the ICVS showed Sweden to be 2nd in larceny out of 19 countries in Europe and the New World. Sweden was 11th in rate of larceny out of 55 countries in the world in the ICVS. Thus, Sweden seems to be a suitable subject for a country profile on larceny-theft.[175]

In terms of countries low in burglary and larceny-theft, it seems appropriate to compare countries at a similar level of development as Australia and Sweden. Many of the countries at the bottom of the larceny list are Islamic countries and/or countries with a low gross national product. If there is little property to steal, whether it be auto accessories or store merchandise, it seems likely that the major reason for the low larceny rate in developing countries is the absence of opportunity to steal, rather than a lack motivation on the part of potential criminals. Of course, strict Islamic law, which mandates cutting off the hand of the thief, may very well be a deterrent to theft. (See text box on Justice in Saudi Arabia.) However, mutilation is not a viable option as a criminal justice penalty in most Western countries, because of their concern with human rights. For comparison, it seems desirable to focus on European countries. Portugal seems like an appropriate country to compare with Sweden. Portugal has a low rate of larceny of 310.48 per 100,000 inhabitants (compared to 6988.7 for Sweden). Portugal is near the bottom of the "stealthy theft" list and ranks low in larceny-theft (60). Portugal is also relatively low in burglary, with a rank of 49. A country profile is done for Portugal representing the low end of burglary and larceny-theft for Europe.

BOX 10–12

The "Bloody Codes" of Saudi Arabia

The country with the lowest rate of burglary in the world, according to the Comparative Criminology Database, is Saudi Arabia. Saudi Arabia is said to be the only country today that totally applies the Islamic system of justice, "Sharia."[176] Theft is punishable by amputation of the right hand, administered under anesthetic in Saudi Arabia. Aggravated theft (including burglary) is punished by cross-amputation of a hand and a foot. Amnesty International reported four cross-amputations in 1986 and less than 10 hand amputations in 1990. More recently, Amnesty International has expressed concern about the increasing rate of judicial amputations in Saudi Arabia:

On May 13, 2000 cross amputations (amputation of the right hand and left foot) were carried out on Kindi Amoro Muhammad, Nurayn Aladi Amos and Abdullah Abu-Bakr Muhammad, Nigerian nationals convicted of armed robbery and assault with seven Nigerians executed on the same day. In June two Nigerian men had their right hands amputated following conviction for theft: on 1 June Muhammad Othman Adam in Mecca, and on 4 June Sanussi Sani Muhammad.[177]

Offenses that may be related to burglary, drunkenness, and drug smuggling, are also punished severely in Saudi Arabia. Drunkenness is punished by flogging with a cane, usually from 30 to 120 strokes. First-time drug smugglers face prison terms, floggings, and fines, or a combination of all three punishments. Those convicted for a second time face execution. By the end of 1987, at least nine persons were executed for offenses that involved drug smuggling.[178]

Great Britain ranks high in both larceny-theft and motor vehicle theft. Switzerland, which is considered to have an overall low crime rate, has, surprisingly, the highest rate of motor vehicle theft of all countries. However, this high rate for vehicle theft is doubtful because it is inconsistent with that reported by Switzerland to the United Nations. Australia, which ranks second in automobile theft in INTERPOL data, has already been selected for profiling in regard to burglary. Thus, it seems appropriate to include Great Britain as a country high in motor vehicle theft. In United Nations data, Great Britain has typically been ranked 1st of all countries in that crime. It can be seen that Great Britain, the "mother country" of the United States, ranks 5th in larceny and 3rd in motor vehicle theft, quite a bit higher than the United States, which ranks 11th in larceny and 13th in motor vehicle theft.

In terms of countries low in motor vehicle theft, it seems appropriate to compare countries at a similar level of development as Britain, rather than third world countries, for reasons stated earlier for burglary and larceny-theft. It seems desirable to compare two developed European countries. Thus, for comparison, a European country that is relatively low in vehicle theft is desired. Austria is a country that is relatively low in motor vehicle theft with a rate of 48.71 per 100,000 inhabitants, compared with Britain's rate of 650.47 per 100,000 inhabitants. Thus, Austria is compared as a country on the low end, with Great Britain as a country on the high end, in regard to the crime of motor vehicle theft.

Australia

Australia is currently at the top of the world in its rate of burglary, which in 2000 was 2280.82 per 100,000 inhabitants. This finding seems to hold true according to reported official data and by country comparisons using victimization surveys. Within Australia, burglary is a matter of great concern, being the most common business and residential crime. Australia serves as a case-in-point of the observations made earlier about socioeconomics, substance abuse, and burglary. Australia has a low rate of income inequality (Gini Index = 35.2). It has a low rate of unemployment (6.3%) and a high GDP per capita of $27,000. However, it has an extremely high rate of alcohol consumption of 10.25 litres per capita of ethanol, consumed primarily in the form of beer (5.18 litres) and wine (3.41 litres), with spirits constituting the smallest component of consumption (1.7 litres). Because Australia is a "destination country" for drugs, particularly heroin from Southeast Asia and cocaine from South America, it is plausible that heroin and cocaine use are prevalent in Australia.

Convict Colony

It seems to be no surprise that Australia has a high rate of alcohol consumption, because it was once used as a "convict colony" where Britain exiled many of its convicted criminals, not long after the 1743 Gin Riots. During the 1740s in England, the British were consuming 8,000,000 gallons of gin a year. It seems probable that many of the convicts sent to Botany Bay in Australia were also heavy drinkers. Although it is true that colonial America was also a destination for British convicts, that practice ceased after the American Revolution ended in 1783. The practice of sending convicts to Australia, however, continued until 1850. By then, more than 150,000 had been sent to the two colonies that comprised Australia. In 1850, the sending of convicts to Australia was abolished. As convicts completed their sentences, the convicts agitated for land and opportunities, and were known as *emancipists,* opposed by the free settlers, who were known as *exclusives.* Owed to a movement toward free trade, which nullified the need for colonies from 1842 to 1850, Australian colonies received constitutions and were given legislative councils (preventing a war of independence that might have unified the Australian colonies).

White Australia Policy

Australia had its own gold rush in the 1850s, which resulted in an influx of Chinese immigrants attracted by gold, a movement that was opposed by the white settlers who sought to exclude all but Europeans from Australia. This became known as a "White Australia policy," a policy that endured up until recently in Australia. Seemingly, this policy also applied to the Aborigines who, as the frontier pushed inland, were often poisoned, hunted, abused, and exploited by the settlers.

The White Australia policy was discarded during the 1950s through 1970s. Australia remains part of the British Commonwealth, after a national referendum failed to win a majority vote to change Australia's form of government to a republic.

Australia's legal system is similar in its decentralization to that of the United States. The Commonwealth of Australia is a federalist government composed of a national government and six state governments. If territories are included, there are, in effect, nine different criminal justice systems in Australia—six state, two territory, and one federal. The eight states and territories have powers to enact their own criminal law, whereas the Commonwealth has powers to enact laws. Criminal law is administered principally through the federal, state, and territory police. There is no independent federal corrective service. State or territory agencies provide corrective services for federal offenders. The government of the Commonwealth is responsible for the enforcement of its own laws. Local governments can pass legislation, known as bylaws. These generally include social nuisance offenses, as well as traffic and parking rules. The legal system is adversarial in nature and places a high value on the presumption of innocence.

The decentralization of Australia's legal system applies to the three branches of the criminal justice system—police, courts, and corrections. Australia has one police force for each of the six states and the Northern Territory. There is also a Commonwealth agency, known as the Australian Federal Police, which provides police services for the Australian Capital Territory and is also involved in preventing, detecting, and investigating crimes committed against the Commonwealth, including drug offenses, money laundering, organized crime, and fraud. However, because of the findings of several Royal Commissions in the late 1970s and early 1980s that revealed the extent of organized crime in Australia, the Commonwealth government, in July 1984, established the National Crime Authority (NCA). The NCA is the only law enforcement agency in Australia not bound by jurisdictional or territorial boundaries. Its single mission is to combat organized criminal activity. Australia has a hierarchical system of courts with the High Court of Australia operating at the top. The High Court of Australia is the final court of appeal for all other courts. It is also the court that has sole responsibility for interpreting the Australian Constitution. Within each state and territory there is a Supreme Court and, in the larger jurisdictions, an intermediate court below it, known as the District Court, District and Criminal Court, or County Court. Below the intermediate courts there are Magistrates Courts at which virtually all civil and criminal proceedings commence. Approximately 95% of criminal cases are resolved at the Magistrates Courts level. Prisons are the responsibility of states or territories. There are no federal penitentiaries or local jails. The rate for imprisonment in Australia was 148 per 100,000 inhabitants.

Australian Burglary Data

As stated earlier, the rate of burglary reported by Australia to INTERPOL for 2000 was 2280.82 per 100,000 inhabitants. Often the reported rates are not in agreement with victimization studies; however, that is not the case with Australia. The ICVS published in 1992 showed Australia and New Zealand as highest in self-reported burglary of 21 countries surveyed. Australia reported a rate of 4.03% victimized once or more per annum, whereas New Zealand reported a rate of 4.30% per annum. (Note that New Zealand is also ranked high in Table 10–8, ranking 9th of the countries of the world in burglary.) The United States reported a rate of 3.48% per annum.[179] Victimization rates for burglary have increased since 1993 from 6.8% to 7.6% (including both break-in and attempted break-in).[180] The most recent crime survey data for Australia come from the ICVS that was conducted in March 2000. About one in five persons reported being a victim of personal crime in 1999. Just over 4% of households reported being a victim of a completed burglary (break-in) annually. About one in five households reported being a victim of a household crime in 1999.[181] Burglary has been cited as the most common crime affecting businesses, of which 27% are victimized.[182] Also, one Australian study found the most common crime with regard to households affected is burglary.[183]

Burglary is described in FBI statistics as predominantly an adult crime in the United States. However, in Australia burglary is predominantly a crime committed by youth aged 15 to 19. That age group has a rate of burglary close to 3600 per 100,000 population in the period of 1995 to 2000, compared to half that rate for those age 20 to 24, declining to near zero for those 25 and over.[184] In 2001, the main offenses for which male offenders were sentenced in Australia included burglary (12%), robbery (14%), and sex offenses (13%).[185] The police clearance rate for burglary (crimes resulting in arrest) is only 7% (compared to 14% for the United States).

Australia seems to provide many of the elements of the Shover and Honaker's life-as-party atmosphere, especially for youth.[186] It currently has a high rate of alcohol consumption. It is an affluent country with leisure time and money that can be spent on drugs, which are trafficked to Australia, from South America and Southeast Asia, on both sides of the island continent. Australia has an excellent climate and geography for beach-going teenagers and young adults, and as is discussed later, and a recent "baby boom" combined with economic recession provides the basis for a fairly sizable youth culture of party-eligible individuals.

Alcohol consumption in Australia is high. It is interesting to compare the age distribution in Australia for alcohol-caused "acute condition deaths" with those for burglaries. The term *acute conditions* refers to causes such as falls, assaults, road injuries, fire injuries, and drowning (as opposed to "chronic conditions," such as cirrhosis of the liver). The age distribution for deaths is similar to the age distribution for burglary, rising rapidly to nearly 80 deaths for ages 15–19 to over 100 deaths for ages 20–24, declining rapidly thereafter.[187] One Australian study found that liquor outlets were particularly vulnerable to burglary, with 37% experiencing at least one incident of burglary per year and 24% being burgled more than once.[188]

Although Australia has a low rate of inequality and unemployment, this observation may not be true for all age groups. Just as in the United States, in Australia there is a link between property offenses such as burglary and factors such as a local concentration of public housing, male unemployment, and income inequality within Australia.[189] In explaining the rise in burglary in Australia that took place from 1973 to 1992, both in police and victimization data, Chappel and Wilson made the following observation:

> To complicate the analysis, the economic recession (of 1990–1991) provides a range of other factors to be considered. It occurred as the baby-boom-echoers were leaving school and looking for jobs, delaying their financial independence and greatly enhancing the frustrations normally felt by adolescents anxious to begin life as adults. It has left many thousands of them with time on their hands, and a proportion of them may have turned to crime which, in better economic circumstances, they might not have become involved in. Coinciding, as it has, with the increased promotion of alcohol to young people, through such devices as aggressive sporting sponsorships, this may be ultimately an explosive mixture.[190]

This statement is almost identical to the hypothesis formulated by Richard Easterlin, sometimes called "the Easterlin effect," as described earlier.

During roughly the same period described by Chappel and Wilson, Australia became "party central" for young people, a Mecca for surfers and drinkers. In fact, one website lists 490 beaches in Australia that are considered good for surfing.[191] Australia draws tourists from all over the world during the months that are winter months in the northern hemisphere (the summer months in Australia). Not surprisingly, these months are "the peak period for recorded statistics on a range of crimes including burglary, personal thefts, and assaults."[192]

To test the hypothesis that there is a positive relationship between surfing and burglary, the Australian states were listed with corresponding rates of burglary and surfing beaches, listed in the surfing Website cited earlier. Table 10–9 was produced. A positive correlation between the number of surfing spots and burglary was obtained ($r = .20$). The number of "surfing spots" is a very crude measurement of the surfing population density. Many of the beaches listed on the Website are virtually deserted, whereas others may be attended by large crowds of beachgoers. The surfing spot Website indicated beaches for which a camera is sometimes present, which were tabulated as "surfing hotspots," possibly indicating a larger population of surfers. The variable "surfing hotspots" correlated more strongly with burglary ($r = .33$).

Besides high consumption of alcohol as a factor in youthful participation in burglary in Australia, another factor in the exceedingly high rate of burglary in that country may be the availability of illicit drugs. In South Australia and the

Table 10–9 **The Number of Surfing Beaches and Rates of Burglary by State in Australia[193]**

State	Burglary Rate	Surfing Spots	Surfing Hotspots*
New South Wales	2701.9	211	107
Victoria	1608.7	95	32
Queensland	2082.9	39	22
South Australia	1883.0	27	13
Western Australia	3145.3	102	57
Tasmania	2995.6	16	7

*As indicated by camera view of beach noted.

Australian Capital Territory, marijuana has been partly decriminalized, and Tasmania is one of the world's major suppliers of licit (legal) opiate products (although reportedly the government maintains strict controls over areas of opium poppy cultivation and output of poppy straw concentrate). More important, Australia is a destination country for illicit narcotics, especially Southeast Asian heroin and South American cocaine. Studies of convicted offenders in Australia have found an association between heroin use and burglary.[194]

Sweden   It hardly seems coincidental that Sweden and Great Britain both have high rates of larceny-theft. Sweden, in fact, is an English-speaking bilingual nation, with nine years of English being required in Swedish schools. Moreover, Swedes are descendents of the Scandinavian Normans who conquered Britain in 1066 and their leader, William the Conqueror, ascended to the crown. William unified Britain into a feudal kingdom and had a profound influence upon the institutions that remain characteristic of Britain. Among these are the political, administrative, cultural, and economic center in London; a separate but established church; a system of common law; distinctive and distinguished university education; and representative government.

Sweden seems to incorporate most of the factors indicated in Table 10–7 and in the direction shown in the table. Sweden has a very low rate of inequality, with a Gini Index of 25 (compared to roughly 40 for all nations in the CCDB). Sweden is a wealthy country, with a GDP per capita of $25,400, compared to about $9,000 average for other countries. A figure is not given for percentage living in poverty, and it is claimed that nobody in the Swedish welfare state lives in poverty. The rate of unemployment is 4% compared to an average of about 16% for other countries. It rates a "1" on the freedom scale (most free) for both political rights and civil liberties. The percentage Islamic in the country is rated at 0%. In terms of gender empowerment, Sweden is probably number one in the world, with virtually half of the labor force being women. Also, Sweden has had a declining rate of morbidity, aided by its publicly funded health care system, resulting in a growing population of senior citizens. The average age in Sweden is 40, compared to about 26 for other countries of the world.

How can these positive traits be translated into a negative fact of crime? Though Sweden is comparatively low in violent crime, its high rates of property crimes result in its being number one in the world in overall crime as measured by the FBI Index of 9604.57 per 100,000 inhabitants.

There are some negative facts that may be symptomatic of the underlying causes of crime in Sweden. Swedish consumption of wine, beer, and spirits is at a much higher rate than that of other countries, despite government attempts to regulate alcohol through limiting its sales to state-run stores on a quota system. Sweden also has a high rate of drug offenses, around 364 per 100,000 compared with about 147 average for other world countries.

To begin to understand the high rate of larceny-theft in Sweden, it is necessary to look at the very nature of larceny-theft itself. Looking back upon FBI statistics for the United States, larceny-theft is seen as disproportionately a crime of youth. The same is true in Sweden, and possibly even more so than in America. Table 10–10 may help to cast light on the problem,

Table 10–10	**Juvenile Percentage of all Crime by Country in United Nations 1997 data[195]**
Japan	48.74
Hong Kong	30.73
Germany	29.16
Albania	28.99
Tonga	27.23
Sweden	25.34
New Zealand	22.89
Canada	21.85
Latvia	19.52
United States of America	18.74
Netherlands	17.50
Lesotho	15.33
Finland	14.24
Poland	14.15
Cyprus	13.61
Lithuania	12.97
Maldives	12.36
Romania	11.01
Argentina	10.77
Malaysia	10.47
Ukraine	9.21
Croatia	8.50
Israel	7.94
Chile	7.55
Kazakstan	7.12
Tajikistan	6.59
Norway	5.39
Thailand	3.65
Italy	2.44
India	0.48

Note: Included were all countries above the United States, but only every other country below.

showing that Sweden ranks 6 out of 50 countries in the rate with which juveniles contributed to the crime problem. This table shows the percentage of persons brought into formal contact with the criminal justice system who are juveniles (under 18 years of age) and is drawn from United Nations data for 1997 (most recent year for which complete information is available on this subject). According to this table, juveniles constitute 25.34% of the crime contacts in Sweden, compared to 18.74% for the United States. There are countries with higher police contact, but lower larceny-theft rates in this table. Japan has a larceny-theft rate of 1550.4 per 100,000 inhabitants and ranks 19th in the world, yet half of the police contacts in that country are with juveniles. Quite possibly, in Japan the police make proactive contacts with juveniles, but their treatment after formal contact is quite different from the treatment in Sweden. Thus, the treatment of juveniles in Sweden might be the first subject that needs to be addressed in understanding the high larceny-theft rate; or rather, the *lack of treatment* of juveniles in Sweden is what needs to be addressed. In Sweden, the age of criminal responsibility is 15 (compared to age 8 for the United States). It is also unusual for young people under the age of 20 to be sent to prison. Instead, young people are typically given the sanction of a "day fine" (proportionate with their earnings), typically by a prosecutor, without any judicial proceedings.[196] Despite the fact that "Young people up to the age of 20 are the most criminally active group in Swedish society in terms of crimes per capita,"[197] there is little or no deterrence of this group in Sweden in the form of imprisonment. Persons under age 20 in Sweden exist in a legal limbo in which their criminal actions are met with, at worst, a modest fine, similar to that of a traffic citation in the United States.

Aside from placing youth in a "no limits" state of mind in regard to the crime of larceny-theft, what other factors pertaining to youth in Sweden contribute to that crime? It could be that youth in Sweden are, as Merton said of American youth, imbued with high aspirations of success. The largest category of youth surveyed in Sweden rated "traveling and seeing the world by age 25" and "owning own home by age 35" as among their desires. Yet in Sweden, "some are more equal than others." In an egalitarian society such as Sweden, incomes are limited for all. Managers of companies typically make nearly the same wages as workers. Income is taxed at a rate—nearly 50%—that would be unacceptable to most Americans. Thus, wealth, or even home ownership, is difficult to achieve. Most young adults in Sweden live in urban apartments, whereas only their elders—parents and grandparents, have the privilege of home ownership, boats, and expensive cars. If there is resentment and jealousy in Sweden, it is resentment of the privileges enjoyed by the elderly. And the elderly constitute a viable target for theft. It is they who own the stores from which items can be shoplifted, and it is they who own the expensive motor vehicles that can be stolen.

But more is happening in Sweden than mere resentment of the senior citizens who are a growing privileged class in that country. There are some social and economic trends among youth that have contributed to the country's growing crime rate. One of the trends has been gender equality, along with its corresponding trends in child care, competition for jobs, divorce, and single parenthood. The divorce rate in Sweden in 1996 was 64%

of marriages, placing Sweden third in the world for divorce.[198] Although divorces characterize nearly two-thirds of all marriages in Sweden, the United States compares favorably with a "mere" 49% or half of marriages that end in divorce. However, while it would seem that divorce is what characterizes Swedish partnerships, such is not the case. One survey of 891 women aged 25–34 in Sweden revealed that only 28% had been married, but 59% were currently or previously cohabiting. Thus, cohabitation is the prevailing mode of intimate partnership for young Swedes.[199] The survey found that the majority of first-born children were born during a cohabiting partnership. The reason for cohabitation indicated in studies cited was unemployment or blue-collar employment of the male partner, with the unmarried couples disproportionately from the lower socioeconomic groups. Thus, the decline in rates of marriage may have something to do with economic trends in Sweden, which are discussed later. However, it should be pointed out that the widespread nature of cohabitation in Sweden prompted the passage in 1987 of a Cohabitees Act by the Parliament. The act included provisions concerning the property of cohabiting unmarried couples and strengthened inheritance rights of the financially weaker partner upon death of the other partner.[200]

Although women make up more than half of the population and almost half of the labor force in Sweden, women still do most of the work in the home and assume most of the responsibilities for child care.[201] As a consequence of this full-time or part-time employment of women, many of whom have children, there is an increasing reliance upon day care for children for these employed mothers. There is also increased stress caused by the extra work load involving housekeeping and child care for working mothers.

In a country in which equality of opportunity is primarily determined by age, rather than merit because wages are essentially the same for the custodian as they are for the computer engineer, high aspirations are not easily met. For males, there is increasing competition for jobs from females whose equality of opportunity has been written into law. There is also competition for jobs resulting from outsourcing of jobs, as well as by immigrants coming into the country. Sweden admitted a large number of refugees during the first half of the 1990s (primarily from the former Yugoslavia)[202] and has traditionally had an open door policy toward immigrants.[203] As a result, during the first half of the 1990s Sweden faced a high rate of unemployment (for Sweden) of approximately 8%. Hardest hit by the recession of the 1990s were those entering the job market—young people and immigrants. The number of persons outside the labor force aged 20–25 more or less doubled in the period from 1990 to 1997.[204] The declining employment for young people has influenced the trend toward cohabitation, and along with that a decline in the birth rate. Women have delayed having a first child to a median age of 28 years, particularly women of low incomes. The declining birth rate, combined with a 17% increase in elderly pensioners from 1990 to 1998, had important implications for the welfare state, necessitating changes impacting working and unemployed youth the most, especially single mothers. Levels of health insurance benefits, as well as unemployment insurance benefits, were lowered several times during the decade, as were parental leave benefits. In addition, cuts were made in day care. The average expenditure per child in pre-school care was cut by about 14%, which resulted in an increase in the number of children per group or per staff member in childcare facilities. Similarly, total expenditures on schools, calculated per pupil, declined during the 1990s, as did teacher density per 100 pupils. During the 1990s, an increasing number of schools run by nonpublic bodies tripled, and the proportion of pupils who qualified for secondary education declined as well.[205]

Conventional wisdom and social science explanations for crime in Sweden have traditionally focused upon indulgence in alcohol as an explanation for crime.[206] Levels of drug usage among Sweden's young people are low from an international perspective, but young people consume more alcohol than youth in other countries. An international survey revealed that young Swedes consume more than average quantities of alcohol. The percentage of 15- to 16-year-old boys and girls who have been drunk more than 10 times in a year was just under 20% in Sweden compared with an average of 10% in 22 other countries involved in an international survey.[207] In Sweden, there are strict laws against drunk driving, resulting in imprisonment for adult offenders. Similarly, the low percentage of youth using illegal drugs may be a product of strict laws concerning illegal drugs. Yet there is evidence that there was a dramatic increase in heavy drug use among young adults (aged under 24) with a more than 100% increase from 1992 to 1998.[208]

However, concern about the consequences of young people self-medicating with alcohol or illicit drugs would seem to coexist with a societal indifference to the plight of youth. In Sweden, the "classless society," youth constitute the lowest of social classes, the *lumpenproletariat* of Sweden, confronting an apparently permanent "glass ceiling" to their aspirations of home and family, while facing the uncertainty of fragile cohabiting partnerships. Some may also seek much touted consumer goods through the alternative means of shoplifting and other property crimes.

So far in our analysis, not much has been said about adults in Sweden, who commit the majority of larcenies. Probably the majority of larcenies in Sweden are done by young adults and immigrants who face increasing unemployment and dwindling opportunities. While penal sanction is nearly absent for minors in Sweden, adults who commit larceny-theft also enjoy a lenient civil law system.

Sweden has a civil law criminal justice system that is comparatively swift and certain with regard to crimes that are of high priority. Persons and their households can be searched without a warrant. If they are detained for trial they are not entitled to bail, although they are entitled to an attorney. There are no juries. Those who go to trial are tried by a panel of judges, which usually consists of two attorneys and three lay persons. Victims have more rights in Sweden than in the United States, and they can appeal a not-guilty verdict to higher court.[209]

Swedish law, in regard to the prosecution of crime, is tough on crime— but not all crime. Priority is given to violent crimes,[210] drunk driving, and drug offenses. In prison data from 1993 cited by Wikstrom and Dolman, violent crimes constituted 17.1% of annual prison admissions, fraud 8.2%, drunken driving 18.5%, drug offenses 9.4%, and robbery 3.0%. Property crimes were 22.7% of annual admissions, which is a low percentage considering the status of Sweden as being number one in the world in reported rate of larceny-theft. As mentioned earlier for juveniles, larceny-theft is treated preponderantly with the sanction of a fine. Out of 164,380 persons sanctioned or prosecuted, 111,560 were given fines, whereas only 15,872 were sanctioned by a prison sentence, and a comparatively smaller number, 6274, were given probation as a sanction. Separate from the 164,380 sanctioned or prosecuted, 199,144 were given "on-the-spot" fines by the police.

Although Sweden has a prison population rate of only 75 per 100,000 population[211] (compared to a prison population of 702 per 100,000 in the United States),[212] the apparently effective emphasis upon the prosecution of violent crime in Sweden results in a low public fear of crime,[213] at the same time that there is apparent vulnerability to property crime. The vulnerability to property crime, however, may be indicated by studies in Sweden demonstrating vulnerability to crime by selected groups in the population that might be most vulnerable to property crime, such as women and the elderly, who show higher fear of crime levels in Sweden.[214]

While the problems of young people coping with hard economic reality in the early 1990s were undoubtedly a contributing factor to their high rates of larceny-theft. However, there is evidence that there was a considerable decline in theft among youths aged 15–17 during the late 1990s. In fact, theft among teenagers has declined to a level comparable to that of the 1950s (though this level was still enormous compared to pre-WWII levels).[215] The high level of larceny-theft in Sweden, despite diminishing levels of youth crime, is probably accounted for by the rising number of immigrants. A description of the immigration problem in Sweden can help us to understand why "net migration" (more "in-migration" than "out-migration") in Table 10–7 correlates positively with stealthy theft.

Foreign prisoners constitute 27.2% of the prison population in Sweden.[216] This is so despite the fact that people born in another country numbered about 950,000 of Sweden's 8.8 million inhabitants, or approximately 11%.[217] Immigrants generally have higher crime rates than indigenous Swedes, particularly for violence and theft. Immigrants also rank high in Sweden as victims of violence.[218] These last two statements point to the problems related to the high rate of crime for foreigners in Sweden. The term *foreigners* is used in preference to *immigrants,* because persons of foreign birth have not enjoyed easy access to citizenship in Sweden since the country's adoption of its first Aliens Act in 1914. However, over the years Sweden has been a haven for refugees, beginning in late 1942 and thereafter. Those who seek refuge in Sweden are typically allowed to stay. During the 1950s, and even more in the 1960s, foreigners were welcomed into the country to compensate for the labor shortage that was great in Sweden during that time. In 1975, Sweden adopted an immigration policy departing from its prior policy of assimilationism. The three principles incorporated in government policy with regard to foreign workers was equality, freedom of cultural choice, cooperation, and solidarity. In the 1970s and the 1980s, a huge increase of refugees included asylum seekers totaling between 10,000 and 30,000 per year. They came from countries such as Iran, Iraq, Chile, Argentina, Peru, and Eritrea. The most recent surge of refugees provided sanctuary numbered more than 170,000 people fleeing from the war in the former Yugoslavia. Many refugees ended up living in suburban "ghettos" (ethnic enclaves) of major cities, especially Stockholm, Gothenberg, and Malmo. During the 1970s, this influx of refugees contributed some 6 billion SEK annually to the public coffers because the immigrants of that period contributed by working in the manufacturing and construction sectors. However, today the opposite situation prevails. Approximately 20 billion SEK per year net compensation to immigrants occurs in the form of transfer payments such as social assistance, housing allowances, and unemployment benefits. As a result of high unemployment among today's immigrant groups, many immigrants have taken early retirement, and they depend to a large scale upon public benefits.[219] Many of the immigrants, as a result of the multicultural national policy, do not speak Swedish and do not participate in Swedish institutions and organizations, and they remain in segregated suburban areas. These areas are characterized by a shortage of private and public services, an impoverished physical environment and low levels of education, as well as low incomes. They are also characterized by high crime rates.[220] The crime rates include high rates of theft and violence. Some of the violence is in the form of hate crimes perpetrated upon the immigrants by Swedish citizens.[221]

Immigrants, many of whom are alien refugees, find themselves in the situation of being marginalized in Sweden. They are treated in a discriminatory fashion both in their attempts to obtain employment in a high-tech contemporary society, applying for jobs for which they are increasingly unqualified owing to their lack of education and Swedish language skills. They are also the target of xenophobic hate crimes on the part of Swedish citizens. Furthermore, they experience cultural conflict, coming from traditional cultures that emphasize premarital chastity and marriage, when they encounter the "culture shock" of a Swedish society in which divorce is the norm and cohabitation is practiced by the majority of youth. Immigrants also face a society in which theft is leniently sanctioned, typically with "day-fines," a stark contrast with punishments meted out in their country of origin, punishments ranging from amputation to "murder by cop" and even genocide. Even the prospect of being confined in one of Sweden's prisons may fail to provide deterrence for people who have obtained sanctuary from war-torn Baltic States. Sweden's prisons are characteristically small "open" institutions where security is lax, 90% of the inmates serve terms of less than one year, all inmates are employed and can earn wages the same as workers on the outside, frequent furloughs home are considered a right for most inmates, and conjugal visits are routine for all prisoners.[222] Thus, in Sweden, theft for the growing segregated class of unemployed foreigners has become a viable option to employment, which is lacking for them. And the theft, as well as usurpation of welfare benefits by foreigners, motivates hate crimes directed at the foreigners by Swedish citizens. The hate crimes, in turn, may enhance the resentment felt by the foreigners which may, in fact, contribute to their tendency to grab all that they can in the form of theft, as well as welfare benefits.

Portugal

Portugal has been selected as a country to study illustrating low rates of larceny-theft, not because it is lowest in the world, but because it is one of the lowest of the European nations. In the case of larceny-theft, how does Portugal differ from Sweden (the country that reported the highest rate of larceny-theft in the world)? Portugal reported a larceny-theft rate of 310.48 per 100,000 inhabitants, compared with Sweden's rate of 6988.81. Both countries are "civil law" countries with national police and court systems. The income level is lower in Portugal (GDP per capita = $18,000 compared to $25,400), and Portugal is less egalitarian than Sweden, with a Gini Index of 35.6, compared to 25 in Sweden. The rate of unemployment is roughly the same in the two countries—4.7% for Portugal versus 4% for Sweden. Portugal is not quite as committed to gender equity as Sweden, with a gender empowerment rating of .53 compared to Sweden's .68. Both countries are given a "1" for freedom in both political rights and civil liberties, and neither country has a significant Islamic population. The average age is slightly lower in Portugal (37.6 compared with Sweden's 40.1). Alcohol consumption is actually considerably higher in Portugal than in Sweden, especially wine consumption, no doubt related to the fact that that wine is a major product of Portugal.

Three factors stand out, however, in comparisons between these two countries—drug offenses, migration, and religion. Although Sweden reports a relatively high rate of drug offenses (363.73 per 100,000 inhabitants), Portugal reports a low rate (42.49). In 2002, the net migration rate for Portugal was half that of Sweden (.49 per 100,000 inhabitants for Portugal compared with 1.00 per 100,000 inhabitants for Sweden). Finally, religion is a significant factor differentiating these two countries. Sweden is a Protestant country with 84% of its population adhering to the Lutheran faith, whereas 94% of the Portuguese population is Roman Catholic.

In regard to the religious differences between Sweden and Portugal, one might be inclined to jump to the conclusion that the two religions differ in their view of theft, and that results in the differences between the two countries. However, it seems more likely that the religious differences are symptomatic of important demographic differences between the two countries, namely in divorce rates, marriage rates, and cohabitation rates. Marriage rates are greater for Portugal, while divorce and cohabitation rates are greater for Sweden. Although the divorce rate in Sweden is 64%, it is only 21% in Portugal.[223] Differences between Sweden and Portugal for cohabitation are even greater, with approximately 59% of Swedes unmarried and currently or previously cohabiting, compared with only 7% of the Portuguese in the sample.[224]

A possible explanation for the greater theft rate among Swedes may have to do with the "financial marginalization" that young Swedes face. A comparative study of Sweden and nine additional European countries asked a representative sample of unemployed youth questions on an 11-item scale measuring that dimension: "During the last 12 months, which of the following have you had to give up due to lack of money: warm meals, essential clothes for yourself or your family, paying rent and bills on time, visiting the cinema, theatre or concerts, having friends to your home," and so forth. The study found that Swedish youth expressed nearly twice the rate of financial deprivation of youth in Portugal, possibly traced to the fact that 95% of the Portuguese youth continued to live with their parents as compared to only 45% of the Swedish youth.[225] Thus, it seems likely that Swedish youth, having left their parents' home, supported by government benefits, actually face more severe financial deprivation, when unemployed, than Portuguese youth, who live until an older age in their parents home, awaiting secure employment prior to marriage. So, if financial marginalization is a factor in theft, then the Portuguese youth, though facing a lower standard of living than Swedish youth, suffer less financial deprivation than the Swedish youth because of parental support.

The lower rate of immigration in Portugal than in Sweden might influence theft rates in the sense that immigrants, too, must face unemployment and may need to engage in theft to obtain needed necessities. They would also compete for jobs with nonimmigrants, driving up the youthful rate of unemployment and enhancing the tendency of youth to engage in theft to obtain necessities.

The last item worthy of comment is the difference between Sweden and Portugal in the rate of drug offenses. As explained previously, drug offenses are treated harshly in Sweden, often resulting in imprisonment. Such is not the case in Portugal. In Portugal, incarceration of drug users is rare, and addiction is treated by Portuguese law as an illness. The Portuguese government prefers to see addicts in drug therapy programs rather than in prison. Judges have the power to offer convicted drug users a choice between shorter prison sentences or longer therapy programs, and often do.[226] The drug of choice in Portugal is said to be heroin, which originates in North Africa and South America. Over time, drug consumption has remained consistently flat. However, Portugal was a party to the 1988 United Nations Drug Convention, and in the first half of 1998, authorities seized twice as much heroin as they did in the first half of 1997. Interestingly, the rate of larceny-theft in Portugal rose from 233.43 per 100,000 inhabitants in 1995 to 903.51 per 100,000 inhabitants in 2001, after which it fell back to 310.48 in 2002. One can only wonder if the declining supply of heroin resulting from the 1998 interdiction efforts might have driven up the price of heroin, resulting in an increase of theft by heroin addicts to cover the increased costs of the drug. In the same way, the vigilant efforts of the Swedish government to stem the tide of illicit drug consumption through interdiction efforts, as well as high volume imprisonment of substance abusers, may have unintended effects. These include driving drug prices higher, as well as exposing substance abusers to criminal norms and values that may be even more prevalent in the prison subculture than on the street.

Great Britain Great Britain is the island containing England, Wales, and Scotland whereas the United Kingdom (UK) contains Great Britain and Northern Ireland. All of the following references to England or Great Britain will include Wales and Scotland, but not Northern Ireland.

Great Britain has much in common with Sweden. In a sense, Sweden is a "mother country" of England, as a result of the tremendous influence of the Norman Conquest upon Britain, starting in the 11th century. It is not surprising, then, that England shares a common problem with Sweden, a high rate of larceny-theft, and, in particular, motor vehicle theft. Great Britain is high in larceny-theft, and third in the world for motor vehicle theft in the CCDB. By other analyses, Britain is *highest* in the world for vehicle theft. According to one account:

> Motorists in Britain are twice as likely to have their cars stolen as anyone else in Europe. An average of 22 cars were stolen per 1,000 on British roads in 1995, twice as many as in the second-worst European country, France. 'The UK remains the car-crime black spot of Europe,' said Graham Johnston of insurers Eagle Star, which commissioned the survey. England and Wales were the worst areas, with almost 23 thefts per 1,000. In Scotland the figure was 15.5 and in Northern Ireland it was 14.6. This compared with just one and a half cars stolen per 1,000 in Austria, which had the lowest incidence of car crime in Europe. . . . Drivers in Britain are almost 15 times more likely to have their cars stolen than motorists in Austria.[227]

England has been found to be number one in motor vehicle theft in the ICVS for 1989, 1992, 1996, and 2000.[228]

Britain shares some of the economic characteristics of Sweden, but is has not adopted all of the "welfare state" approaches taken by Sweden. In the

CCDB, Great Britain shows a GDP of $1.47 trillion, but with a population of about 62 million, this results in a high GDP per capita of $24,700. The rate of inequality for Great Britain as measured by the Gini index is 36.1, lower than the world average of 40; however population below the poverty line stands at 17%. The unemployment rate is 5.1%. Although Britain still rates a "free" mark in the freedom index, it earns a 1 (most free) for political rights, but a 2 for civil liberties, thus averaging 1.5 for these two indices. Like Sweden, Britain is committed to equality of the sexes, but has a slightly lower gender empowerment index of .60 as compared with Sweden's .66. Britain has an aging population with an average age of 38.4, but not as old as Sweden's average of 40.1. Alcohol consumption is higher in all categories (beer, wine, and spirits) in Britain than in Sweden, and the overall consumption of alcohol per capita is 9.73, compared with Sweden's 5.71. Reported drug offenses are less in Britain (217.83 per 100,000 inhabitants) than in Sweden (363.73 per 100,000 inhabitants). Over the years, Sweden has attempted to curtail alcohol consumption with a quota distribution through state-run liquor stores, whereas Britain has not. Also, as discussed earlier, Sweden has been proactive in arresting and imprisoning illegal substance abusers, perhaps to a greater extent than Britain.

Thus, there are similarities and differences between the two countries, with the similarities accounting for high rates of larceny-theft in both countries. However, the differences may help to account for the higher rate of auto theft in Britain than in Sweden or other countries in Europe. In terms of correlations in Table 10–7, motor vehicle theft mirrors all of the correlations found with larceny-theft in general, in the same direction and strength. Factors that stand out as drawing higher correlations for motor vehicle theft are percentage living in poverty (of which Britain has more than Sweden) and, among the different forms of alcohol, wine consumption per capita, in which Britain has essential parity with Sweden (2.29 for Britain compared with 2.19 for Sweden). There is evidence of an even higher rate of immigration in Britain, with a rate of 2.2 migrants per 1,000 inhabitants compared with 1 migrant per 1,000 inhabitants in Sweden.

Though England has not accepted the euro as currency, it was one of the original signators of the Treaty on European Union (commonly called the Maastricht Treaty) in 1991, along with Belgium, Denmark, France, Germany, Greece, Ireland, Italy, Luxembourg, the Netherlands, Portugal, and Spain. The Maastrict Treaty permitted relaxed border controls. Also, customs and immigration agreements were modified to allow European citizens greater freedom to live, work, and study in any of the member states.[229] Car theft became an extensive problem in the European Union, where the number of stolen cars almost tripled between 1989 and 1993.[230]

England is in some way closer in proximity to Europe than Sweden. Although Sweden's access to the European continent is exclusively by ferry (excluding the polar transit), England has been virtually unified with France, in particular, by virtue of the Channel Tunnel, also called the Euro Tunnel or Chunnel, which was completed in 1994.

Besides membership in the European Union (EU), numerous factors have been associated with the high rate of auto theft in England. Factors associated with auto theft include being a teen or juvenile, the influence of peer groups, youth unemployment, unemployment in general, multigenerational unemployment, immigration (especially illegal immigration), a high rate of drug trafficking, a high rate of human trafficking, and involvement of organized crime. Also, there is a strong interrelationship between some of these factors (e.g., auto theft, drug trafficking, and human trafficking). In addition to the aforementioned factors, several factors are developed in the discussion later, based upon the country study on the Comparative Criminology Website. These include the history of England, the system of justice, the court system, and the development of policing in England.

Government statistics in England indicate that over 50% of car thefts are committed by juveniles age 10 through 17 in England and Wales.[231] Further evidence of the juvenile involvement in vehicle theft is given in the relatively high rate of recovery of stolen vehicles in England, which is around 70% (although that figure is said to be declining).[232] There is evidence that since the European Union's 1998 legislation making the fitting of electronic immobilizers mandatory on all new cars in the United Kingdom, there has been a reduction in vehicle theft rates.[233] Data in the CCDB indicate that the rate of motor vehicle theft decreased between 1996 and 2001 from 933.67 to 650.47 per 100,000 inhabitants, a decrease of 30.3%. This downward trend is suggestive that a good number of vehicle thefts were previously done by teenage "joyriders" who steal cars on impulse and for the excitement of the activity itself.[234] These thefts tended to be from car lots and at night. One study found that the employment of "crime prevention attendants" in parking lots reduced car theft by 66%.[235] Further evidence of the involvement of young offenders was found in a study of reconvictions. Reconvictions were associated with younger offender's age in this study, and motor vehicle theft was the offense most associated with reconviction (62%).[236] However, the involvement of youth in vehicle theft in England is not necessarily a transitory phenomenon that is lowered by "aging out." One study of 100 car thieves found that their primary reason for starting to steal cars was peer influence, boredom, and potential excitement. However, this initial involvement in car crime tended to be with other more experienced offenders. This apprenticeship typically lasted from six months to a year, after which the thieves became more skilled and confident.[237]

A possible reason for the juvenile involvement in car theft is a lack of deterrence on the part of the juvenile justice system in England. If a juvenile admits to his crime and there is supporting evidence, he may typically receive a "caution."[238] Another explanation for youth involvement (as well as adult involvement in theft) in the United Kingdom is unemployment.[239] Unemployment is aggravated by the fact that in England, youth complete their secondary education at age 16, and nearly 30% of the age cohort leaves school at 16 years old, rendering them exposed to the job market or unemployment.[240]

The earlier discussion of "juvenile" involvement in the crime of vehicle theft in England is not meant to indicate that the crime should be trivialized as "joyriding" in that country, or that juvenile involvement is the entire story. Despite the fact that auto theft has declined in England (apparently due to antitheft devices), England is still near the top or at the top of the world's countries in this crime (depending upon the data source). The resilient nature of vehicle thieves in England is indicated by the increase in offenses aimed at stealing keys through house burglary, as well as renting cars with the intention of stealing, and robbery by carjacking (which now accounts for 1% to 2% of all vehicle thefts).[241]

Along with the finding that auto theft is largely the province of young males in England is a great concern that results from increasing rates of auto theft among immigrants. Foreigners in the United Kingdom constitute 10.8% of the prison population of 75,045 inmates.[242] However, the foreign population of the United Kingdom represents only 4% of the total population of the country.[243] Although immigrants typically commit crime at a lower rate than nonimmigrants in Britain, there is one crime for which immigrants are imprisoned at a much higher rate in Britain—drug offenses. In England in 1995, 98% of all incarcerated immigrants had been convicted of drug offenses.[244] No data are available on immigrant involvement with the crime of motor vehicle theft, but the last statement would indicate that imprisonment of immigrants for this offense would be miniscule in England (i.e., included in the 2% for all other crimes besides drug offenses). However, the prevalence of arrest for drug offenses among immigrants could obscure an actual higher rate of motor vehicle theft. This is because, while drug offenses are typically prosecuted as "indictable" (more serious) offenses,[245] unauthorized taking of a motor vehicle was downgraded from an indictable to a summary offense in the Criminal Justice Act of 1988.[246] The Aggravated Vehicle Taking Act of 1991 created a new and separate indictable offense of "theft of motor vehicle," separate from "unauthorized taking of a motor vehicle," which is a summary offense. However, the Criminal Justice Act of 1991, implemented in October 1, 1992, discouraged the use of custody for nonviolent offenses, generally prevented judges from taking account of previous conditions of more than two current offenses, required that persons age 17 should be dealt with as juveniles rather than adults, and reduced maximum prison sentences for nonresidential burglary and theft.[247] For vehicle theft offenders given a sentence, the average time served per conviction for vehicle theft was lenient—about 37 days in 1999.[248] On the other hand, prison sentences for drug offenses in England are quite sizable. Under England's Misuse of Drugs Act of 1971, the maximum sentences available on indictment for possession of drugs are seven years for Class A, five years for Class B, and two years for Class C. Examples of Class A drugs are heroin, cocaine, and hallucinogens. Examples of Class B drugs are amphetamines and cannabis. Class C drugs include Valium, Librium, and steroids. When tried on indictment, the maximum sentences for supplying Class A, B, or C drugs are life imprisonment, 14 years, and 5 years, respectively.[249] Thus, while immigrants arrested for vehicle theft would, along with nonimmigrants, be dismissed or given a very light sentence, they would be most likely to be sentenced to prison if they also had Class A, B, or C drugs in their possession at the time of the arrest. It is not known what proportion of the drug offenders was caught in conjunction with an auto theft. Although auto theft is "trivialized" and nearly "decriminalized" in England, possession of illicit drugs is considered among the most serious of offenses.

The whole issue of auto theft is essentially treated as a minor offense by the criminal justice system. On the other hand, the prosecution of crimes of immigrants is often treated as racially inspired or a result of xenophobia in scholarly publications.[250] The implication that the bulk of imprisonment of immigrants in England is the result of racism is shown in the following quote from a university research study.

In England, where the question of so-called street crime tends to be confounded in public perception as well as in the practices of the police, with the visible presence and demands of subjects of the Empire from the Caribbean. Blacks are seven times more likely to be incarcerated than their white or Asian counterparts (and West Indian women ten times as likely). In 1993, persons of West Indian, Guyanese, and African ancestry made up 11 percent of all prisoners, while they represent a mere 1.8 percent of the country's population ages 18 to 39. The over-representation is especially flagrant among prisoners put away for possession or distribution of drugs, of whom more than half are black, and among those in for burglary, where the proportion approaches two-thirds.[251]

It would seem that any kind of actual data on motor vehicle theft by immigrants in England is somehow lost in the process that results from the de facto decriminalization of auto theft by legislators, on the one hand, and the humanitarian concerns of academics for the rights of immigrants as victims of crime or as unfortunate targets of racial profiling by law enforcement. The topic of vehicle theft by immigrants in England has, in essence, been rendered taboo.

However, there is an indirect reference to immigrant involvement in auto theft in the literature on organized crime, especially that pertaining to transnational organized crime (that violates the laws of two or more countries). This discussion pertains to England's involvement in the European Union, and the increase of vehicle theft that took place in conjunction with that development. The essence of the discussion seems to suggest that vehicle theft is a key element in a cluster of crimes that includes motor vehicle theft, trafficking in stolen automobiles, drug trafficking, and even human trafficking. As a result of the open borders policy made possible by the European Union, motor vehicles are stolen in England (and other European countries) and are driven across many international borders, even before the owners discover or report the theft. The vehicles are driven to countries such as Poland, the Baltic Republics and on rarer occasions to Slovakia and Hungary, where they are renovated or "laundered" and, given new vehicle identification and documentation. Many are then shipped to Eastern European countries that have a high demand for these vehicles, such as Russia. To make the theft even more productive, the proceeds from the sale of these automobiles may be used as a source of "seed money" to purchase illicit drugs, which, in turn, are smuggled back to England, either by themselves or in conjunction with the smuggling of illegal aliens.[252] Thus, the crime of auto theft may be a key crime, at least for the small-time operator, in funding a whole circuit of profitable crimes. It may also be an enhancement when used by larger organized crime syndicates. Named as involved in the trade in stolen cars have been Russian groups, Turkish groups that also traffic in 75% to 85% of the heroin and other opiates in Europe, Jamaican "posses" or "yardies," Hell's Angels biker gangs, and Iranian groups.[253]

In sum, it would seem that the high rate of vehicle theft in England is associated with several factors. These include problems of youth unemployment, and a lack of deterrence of vehicle theft by the criminal justice system, as well as with an enhanced profitability of the crime brought on by Britain's membership in the EU. Vehicle theft may have also been increased by England's own war on drugs. This is because the profitability of professional trafficking in stolen automobiles is enhanced by the added incentive of return trip smuggling of drugs and/or illegal aliens. England's "soft" policy on vehicle theft has been a facilitator, just as its "hard" policy on drugs has been

BOX 10–13

"Coyote" Car Thieves in the United States

Arizona has a vehicle theft rate of 983.6 per 100,000 inhabitants, the highest of any state in the United States. Smuggling experts believe that a major portion of theft of vehicles is done by "coyotes," individuals who transport illegal aliens into to the United States from Mexico for a fee. One indication of this activity is the increasing theft of SUV and extended-cab pickups, which are ideal for clandestinely transporting people and drugs from the Mexican border. The increase in vehicle thefts by coyotes has indirectly been a product of the U.S. government's policy of seizing vehicles used by drug smugglers. Now the human smugglers rely more on using stolen vehicles than buying them. Smuggling organizations typically pay gangs and street criminals to steal vehicles for them. They then hire "mules" (drivers) to drive the vehicles to the border to transport undocumented immigrants to the United States. The stolen vehicles are also used by the mules to transport drugs into the United States.[254] The increased smuggling in Arizona is a likely effect of the recent enhanced border enforcement in California (Operation Gatekeeper) and Texas (Operation Forerunner). The California Highway Patrol has a Foreign Export and Recovery team, which intercepts stolen vehicles headed across the border for sale in Mexico and Central and South America.[255] In Phoenix, coyotes may steal cars on the streets, selecting from cars with keys in the ignition or with unlocked doors; however, they also hire thieves to get jobs at auto dealerships. The thieves then make duplicates of keys and steal vehicles after hours.[256]

---

an enhancer, along with participation in organized crime by individuals from Commonwealth countries.

Historically, Britain developed from an ancient tribal country, to a colony of the Roman Empire, then to a kingdom of feudal warlords under William the Conqueror, to an empire in the 19th century that stretched over one fourth of the earth's surface. Although the Empire was largely dismantled during the 20th century, Britain still remains a permanent member of the United Nations Security Council, a founding member of NATO, and of the Commonwealth, as well as the EU. The latter two memberships (Commonwealth and EU) have resulted in a considerable immigration of visitors, persons seeking citizenship, and refugees seeking asylum. Current demographic trends include a disproportionate number of British citizens emigrating, combined with a disproportionate number of New Commonwealth residents and residents immigrating to England. Commonwealth nations are former colonial possessions of England who are now independent and sovereign nations who voluntarily associated with each other and with England after sovereignty.[257] Members enjoy privileged access to each other's markets, as well as free or preferred right of migration from one Commonwealth country to another. New Commonwealth countries refers to British Dependent Territories such as Anguilla, Bermuda, British Virgin Islands, Cayman Islands, Falkland Islands, and Gibraltar.[258] Also included are Jamaica, Barbados, The Bahamas, and Belize, among others. Commonwealth countries also include some 16 African states ranging from Botswana to Zimbabwe. England enjoys considerable economic benefit through free and preferred trade with its Commonwealth of nations; however, as suggested previously, there may be some negative consequences in terms of crime that relate to the relative freedom of Commonwealth members to migrate to England. Presently, England has a relatively high net migration rate of 2.19 migrants per 1,000 population.

In a sense, England's history of colonial domination has come to haunt this country. Former British "subjects," many of whom are descendents of slaves under colonial domination, may freely migrate to England. Many of these migrants may come from a background of poverty and unemployment in home countries such as Jamaica and The Bahamas. When they arrive in England, they may observe the relative affluence of that country and compare it with their own abject poverty. They also may become aware of the leniency of a court system that typically dismisses vehicle theft as a "summary offense." As a consequence, the "underclass" of these Commonwealth countries visiting or living in England may seek redress through crime. They may acquire "seed money" through trafficking in cocaine and heroin from Colombia, or if they are from Asian countries, heroin and opium from South Asia.

Although England has provided plenty of opportunity for the theft of expensive automobiles, combined with limited sanctions, it has developed a weapon to control the "dangerous classes" of individuals from impoverished Commonwealth nations—namely, drug legislation. England's drug legislation developed on a track similar to that in the United States, as discussed earlier, with prison sanctions for both possession and trafficking in drugs. During the 1980s, there was considerable cooperation between the conservative Thatcher administration in England and the Reagan administration in the United States. England became a partner in the war on drugs in 1988, when the United Kingdom became a party to the 1988 United Nations Drug Convention. Yet today England is a gateway country for Latin American cocaine entering the European market, a major consumer of synthetic drugs, a major consumer of Southwest Asian heroin, and a money laundering center.[259] However, the side effect of this emphasis upon drugs and lack of emphasis upon auto theft has been an increasing rate of vehicle theft, and, unfortunately, an increasing problem of drug trafficking, as well as other forms of smuggling. England, like an increasing number of countries in Europe, is experimenting with alternatives to imprisonment for drug offenders, such as methadone maintenance and prescription heroin. However, along with this "decriminalization" of drugs, there may need to be a "criminalization" of vehicle theft, because the crime may very well provide "seed money" for drug trafficking and many other crimes.

Austria   Austria is said to have the lowest rate of vehicle theft in Europe.[260] For Austria, the rate of motor vehicle theft shown in the CCDB is 48.71 per 100,000 inhabitants, compared with 650.47 for England. Austria seems like a good "apples with apples" comparison with England for this crime because there are many similarities between the two countries. Austrians enjoy approximately the same level of income as residents of England, with a GDP per capita of $27,700 (compared with $27,000 for England). Austria has a Gini Index of 31, making it a more egalitarian nation than England, with a Gini Index of 36.8. Beer, wine, and spirit consumption is actually higher in Austria than England, but the net migration rate is very similar to that of England (2.44 for Austria, compared with 2.2 for England). The drug offense rate is similar for the two countries—271.06 per 100,000 inhabitants for Austria compared to 217.83 per 100,000 inhabitants for England.

Although the rates of unemployment for the two countries are about the same (5.20 for England vs. 4.80 for Austria), there is a sizable difference in the percentage of population living in poverty. Although 17% of the inhabitants of England are estimated to be living in poverty, only 3.9% of Austrians live in poverty. Thus, there is a difference in the sharing of wealth between the two countries, with less people ending up at the bottom of the economy in Austria than in England.

In terms of religion, there is a difference between England and Austria. The predominant religion in Austria is Roman Catholic, while it is Protestant (predominantly Anglican) in England. The divorce rate in England is 53%, whereas it is 38% in Austria.[261] Cohabitation is actually slightly higher in Austria (35% currently or previously cohabiting) than in England (34% currently or previously cohabiting).[262] Thus, while family support, as discussed in regard to larceny-theft earlier, might be somewhat higher in Austria than in England, differences are not as dramatic as in the comparison between Sweden and Portugal.

Besides greater equality, less poverty, and better family support, there are two other factors that may be significant. One is the treatment of drug addiction by the criminal justice system. The other is the use of a relatively new experimental program called **victim-offender mediation** (VOM).

There is a difference in drug policy in Austria compared with England. Austrian authorities view drug addiction as a disease rather than a crime. This orientation results in a focus upon demand reduction, treatment, and counseling, as well as on "harm reduction." Although the use of heroin for therapeutic purposes is generally not allowed, substitution programs, such as methadone, have been in place for over a decade. The Narcotic Substances Act, which went into effect January 1, 1998, focuses on therapy for drug users while maintaining severe penalties for drug dealers. While drug dealers may face up to 20 years in prison, first-time users of cannabis may avoid criminal proceedings if they agree to therapy.[263]

What seems noteworthy about Austria is its use of VOM, initially with juveniles. The Juvenile Justice Act of 1988 made victim-offender reconciliation possible at the prosecutor and court level.[264] Since then, Austria has played a pioneering role in developing a mediation model for juveniles.[265] VOM has been utilized there with juveniles for more than 10 years.[266] As of 2000, there were 17 VOM programs in Austria, and word of the success of the Austrian program had led to the growth of VOM programs in other countries, including Australia, Belgium, Canada, Denmark, Finland, France, Germany, Italy, New Zealand, Norway, South Africa, Scotland, Sweden, and the United States.[267] In VOM, victim and offender meet in the company of a mediator or mediators, and typically with a parent or parents present as well, in the case of juveniles. A dialogue takes place in which both the victim and offender tell their story, with the goal of negotiating a restitution plan, and ultimately a written agreement. Although the victim will subsequently receive restitution, and the offender may obtain diversion from sanction as a result of fulfilling the agreement, there is a sense of emotional gratification from the process, both on the part of the victim and offender.

In the earlier discussion, because vehicle theft was revealed to be predominantly a youthful offense, if not a juvenile offense, in the majority of cases, the use of VOM in Austria may help to account for that country's extraordinarily low rate of vehicle theft. This is so despite the fact that Austria has all of the conditions that makes that country a ripe target for auto theft—high level of income; expensive cars; membership in the EU; and being surrounded by countries that traffic in persons, cars, drugs, and so forth.

In the discussion of the treatment of vehicle theft in England, it was pointed out that vehicle theft in that country is typically dealt with by a "summary" judgment, usually in a magistrate's court. Often for juveniles vehicle theft is dealt with through the administration of a "caution" by the police. Although the Austrian experience using VOM also qualifies as a noncustodial sanction, some intervention is taking place (compared to virtually no intervention in the British system). It seems that the low rate of vehicle theft in Austria may indicate the effectiveness of this procedure in dealing with a crime that, though typically considered to be a minor crime by offender and agents of the legal system, may be a "gateway" offense in the case of many youthful offenders, who later may become involved in a broader array of crime.

Stealthy Theft in the United States

Looking at the data for the United States, as can be seen from Table 10–11, there are both similarities and differences in the variables that correlated with robbery and burglary. Robbers and burglars are similar in terms of the family abuse variables of infant mortality and birth to unwed mothers. In addition, robbery and burglary are similar in terms of female unemployment and income inequality as measured by the Gini Index. However, robbers differ from burglars in cocaine versus heroin statistics. Robbery is positively correlated with heroin seized, as is vehicle theft, whereas burglary correlates moderately with cocaine seizures. Certain economic indicators (percentage unemployed, percentage male unemployed, and percentage female unemployed) are strongly positively correlated with robbery and vehicle theft. Percentage

Table 10–11 **Various Demographic Indices as Correlated with State FBI Data for Theft-Related Crimes**

	Robbery	Burglary	Larceny-Theft	Vehicle Theft
Divorce	−0.18	0.35	0.06	−0.12
Infant mortality	0.66	0.42	0.29	0.40
Marriages	−0.15	0.19	0.27	−0.06
Birth to unwed mothers	0.73	0.54	0.35	0.58
Child abuse victimization	0.21	0.15	−0.06	0.15
Kg heroin seized per capita	0.65	0.22	0.31	0.58
Kg cocaine seized per capita	0.11	0.36	0.11	0.06
Gini Index	0.58	0.51	0.24	0.43
Percentage living in poverty	0.30	0.54	0.28	0.19
Percentage unemployed	0.48	0.32	0.22	0.45
Percentage male unemployed	0.41	0.16	0.15	0.37
Percentage female unemployed	0.52	0.50	0.29	0.50
Percentage black	0.79	0.45	0.29	0.51
Black/white income disparity	0.89	0.24	0.31	0.71
Beer consumption per capita	0.15	0.15	0.18	0.24
Wine consumption per capita	0.49	−0.10	0.03	0.53
Spirit consumption per capita	0.45	−0.11	−0.01	0.40
Alcohol consumption per capita	0.43	−0.03	0.07	0.45
Hispanic migration rate	−0.17	0.29	0.02	−0.15
Mexican American population	0.14	0.11	0.02	0.20
Juvenile population	0.24	0.14	−0.05	0.18

living in poverty correlates moderately with burglary, but less so with the other theft crimes. The strongest correlate of robbery was the black/white income disparity (.89), which was also the strongest correlate of vehicle theft (.71). The latter finding probably reflects the fact that the majority of robbery arrests are of blacks whereas the majority of burglary arrests are of whites within the United States.

Looking again at the data on burglary, burglary is more a crime committed by whites than robbery, yet probably whites who have some problems—divorce, unwed mothers, living in poverty, unemployment, and living in a state where there is considerable inequality. If we follow the Australian pattern, we are describing white young males who are adapting to problems of breaking into the job market. The high correlation with cocaine seems to suggest "party culture," as it does in Australia. However, the strongest correlations for beer, wine, and spirits are for vehicle theft.

There is even some evidence that in the United States, "party culture" extends to a surfing lifestyle, as it does in Australia. An ethnographic study was done of surfers in San Diego, California, following the lives of around 72 surfers from 1970 to the 21st century. It was found that many of the devoted surfers were chronically unemployed and engaged in heavy drinking at "kegger parties" at people's homes or on the beach. The surfers were also involved with drugs other than alcohol, predominantly hallucinogens (42%), stimulants (29%), sedatives (26%), cocaine (40%), opiates (10%), and glue/paint (6%). Despite coming from affluent family backgrounds, many of the surfers engaged in thefts as a means of supporting their lifestyle (surfing and "partying"). The most important factor in the backgrounds of the surfers was the lack of "fathering." Typically, their parents had been divorced and they had been raised by their mothers without much contact with their biological father.[268] (Note the resemblance between the lifestyle of surfers to that of Pete, described in the case study at the beginning of this chapter.)

Although the surfing lifestyle just described is only one instance of the party lifestyle, there is some evidence that surfers as a social type are not confined to coastal communities in the United States. In fact, there is a Website that lists "surfing camps" for almost every state in the union.[269] If surfing at one time was a California lifestyle, it is one that is emulated by youth elsewhere.

Surfing is only one "escape mechanism" where youth who are stranded at the bottom of a job market can find refuge. Youth culture, generally includes a variety of pastimes, including hanging around shopping malls, skateboarding, sports, video gaming, compulsive gambling, and gang membership. Each of these "lifestyles" if pursued extensively may require financial support. If legitimate employment is not available, then burglary may be a valuable method of obtaining funds to support the leisure lifestyle.

How does the United States compare in larceny-theft with the picture that has been drawn for the countries of the world, with Sweden as an example? An outstanding factor in larceny-theft, comparatively, appears to be unemployment of youth and immigrants. There also appears to be a correlation with the drug trade, with the possibility that larceny-theft goes up along with increasing interdiction efforts on the part of the government. As the price of drugs rises, drug addicts make up the difference in cost through more crime, including larceny-theft. The study of Sweden pointed to these factors, and also pointed to the role of single parenthood as a possible factor. The data in Table 10–11 show how these factors manifest themselves in America.

Although divorce is not a correlate of larceny-theft, several factors indicative of single and young parenthood are factors. These include births to unwed mothers and infant mortality. In regard to single parenthood, it is interesting that female unemployment correlates about twice as much as male unemployment with larceny-theft. Race does correlate with larceny-theft, with a .29 correlation between percentage black in a state and the larceny rate. However, the black/white income disparity is an even stronger correlation (.31). A weaker correlation was drawn with the Gini Index of economic equality (.24). A very similar correlation (.31) is shown between kilograms of heroin seized per capita and larceny-theft. There isn't much of a correlation between alcohol consumption and larceny-theft, except with beer consumption, which has a low correlation (.18) with larceny-theft. Percentage living in poverty seems to be a moderate correlation with larceny-theft (.28).

Looking at some new variables suggested by the international data, the Hispanic migration rate and the Mexican population by state was correlated with the larceny-theft rate. Both were null correlations (.02 and .02). To test if youth is a factor, the percentage of population by state that are juveniles was correlated with larceny-theft, resulting also in a null correlation (−.05).

Thus, larceny-theft in the United States seems to be very much a problem of black Americans, particularly female black Americans, and not so much a problem of youth. It should be remembered that the United States is not an egalitarian society in the sense that Sweden is. Youth have high aspirations in America, but in some ways they have an opportunity to accrue considerable wealth through pursuing business opportunities, high-tech careers, or even in the trades. At the same time, many youth face low wage jobs and unemployment. It seems that the persons with the worst situation in America are unemployed black females who are also unmarried and mothers. Curiously, in Table 10–11, marriage—not divorce—correlates positively with larceny-theft. Married people living in poverty and with low wage jobs, or possible unemployment, particularly if there are children to support, may have the most inclination to engage in shoplifting or other petty theft to provide needed goods or income. This finding is consistent with Mary Cameron's findings on boosters and snitches. Snitches (amateur shoplifters) were typically lower middle class housewives or teenage girls. If this combination (poverty, being black, being unemployed) occurs among individuals who also participate in the drug trade, particularly in heroin, then a major drop in the supply of heroin may result in the need to engage in theft to offset income lost from the lost drug sales.

Throughout this chapter, there has been evidence that larceny-theft is not taken seriously by agents of the criminal justice system. In Sweden, offenders are let go with a "day-fine" and in the United States, shoplifters are typically given a verbal reprimand by store security. Only a small percentage ever go to court for the offense. Larceny-theft has typically been an offense that has been the target of "radical nonintervention," a term coined by Edwin M. Schur, during the era when labeling theory was popular. Schur's application of the term *radical nonintervention* began with the premise that we should "leave kids alone wherever possible."[270]

However, there is some evidence that stealing appears to be a "gateway crime," one that leads to a progression to a criminal career. One study done in Texas found that youths arrested for stealing were more likely than other offenders to have subsequent charges, including assault offenses and multiple charges.[271] More research is certainly warranted on this point, because larceny-theft seems to be universally trivialized. Intervention of some type may be desired with this offense. Intervention in the form of the death penalty (practiced in England during the 18th century) or amputation practiced today in some Islamic countries is not what is being suggested. However, some intervention may be needed. There are a number of ways to intervene in the criminal career of a juvenile that, although not involving the possible harming influence of detention or institutionalization, still constitute a sanction. Many intervention programs conducted by police or probation authorities require going to meetings, engaging in community service, parent participation, and the like.[272] Another mild sanction for juvenile delinquency, VOM, has been pioneered in Austria and is now being used in Finland, other European countries, and the United States. An additional treatment program called "Shoplifters Anonymous" was shown by one study to have a success rate of 95% to 99%, in terms of juveniles not being rearrested for shoplifting within the next 6 to 24 months.[273]

The FBI data on vehicle theft seem to point to some interesting observations about this crime in relation to the drug trade, race, and Hispanic ethnicity. Vehicle theft has a .58 correlation with Kg heroin seized per capita. This finding is suggestive of a connection between the drug trade and auto theft. Just as in Great Britain, where stolen vehicles are used to traffic in persons as well as drugs, the same observation may be true in America. The correlation between black ethnicity and vehicle theft and the even stronger correlation between the black/white income disparity and vehicle theft, combined with the observation about heroin seizures, seems to suggest that these crimes are connected. For instance, blacks may steal a car or truck to transport drugs. The car is reported stolen, and the police may identify the stolen vehicle. Upon searching the vehicle the police may find a quantity of heroin and apprehend the suspects both for vehicle theft and for trafficking heroin. Similarly, the small correlation (.2) between vehicle theft and the number of Mexican Americans by state may be indicative of the "coyote" phenomenon, described in the text box. Mexican Americans who have smuggling connections in Mexico may steal vehicles to transport persons and/or drugs into the United States.

The observations drawn about FBI data should be tempered with the caveat that these generalizations must be looked upon with suspicion. There is a strong possibility that racial profiling accounts for many of the correlations, particularly because the clearance rates for the stealthy theft crimes are so low. Overall, about 85% of these crimes are not solved. Ethnographic field studies of the "party culture" (such as that described in this chapter) are needed to determine the hidden components of these crimes.

SUMMARY AND CONCLUSION

In terms of the volume of crime, the crimes described in this chapter constitute the majority of Index offenses. As such, we have included a number of case studies representing the variety of crimes we have referred to as stealthy thefts, the perpetrators of which we refer to as sneak thieves. Stealthy theft includes three Index crimes (burglary, larceny-theft, and motor vehicle theft), but excludes robbery, which involves direct confrontation between the offender and victim. This chapter opened with a case study of Pete, a "prolific" burglar (24 burglaries). Pete was "disowned" by his father at the age of 13 due to his illicit use of cannabis and solvents. Institutionalized at age 18, he became addicted to heroin and crack cocaine. He committed burglaries to fund his addiction. Three additional case studies at the beginning of the chapter suggest several factors influencing theft or larceny-theft. These include imitation of others (stepbrothers, mother), financial troubles (no stable income, financial losses), and family problems (divorce, physically disabled child, death of father). This chapter included one case study of vehicle theft—Jason, a Canadian car thief (son of drug addicted parents), who progressed from pre-teen joyriding to a career of car theft, combined with robbery and drug offenses.

In the United States, burglary is broadly defined as unlawful or attempted entry, whether forcible or not, of any structure with intent to commit a felony, and that entry might include areas around the structure, as well (curtilage). Larceny-theft is defined as the intended permanent taking of actual physical property, without force or illegal entry. Motor vehicle theft is technically a form of larceny. Unlike the UCR, the NCVS distinguishes between personal theft (purse snatching and pocket-picking) and theft that involves no personal contact.

The importance of the crimes in this chapter pertains not to the seriousness of these crimes but to the sheer volume or extent of such crimes. Together the three forms of stealthy theft constitute 88.3% of Index crimes. In terms of trends, all three crimes have declined in both volume and rates over the past 10 years. Burglary and motor vehicle theft have declined more than total Index offenses, whereas larceny-theft has declined less than total Index offenses. Despite a decline in rates and volume, dollars lost from these crimes have not declined, primarily because the value of items stolen has increased or because higher valued items have been targeted by thieves (or both).

Some comparisons were made between the three stealthy theft crimes in this chapter and robbery, the subject of Chapter 8. The stealthy crimes involve offenders who are predominantly white, adult males, whereas robbery is done predominantly by teen or young, black, adult males. All three stealthy theft crimes are most prevalent during the hot summer months of July and August, while robbery is a winter crime. The most profound difference between the stealthy theft crimes and robbery were shown in the international correlations. Robbery is correlated positively cross-culturally with the Gini Index of inequality, whereas burglary, larceny, and vehicle theft were correlated negatively with that same index. Thus, it seems that the stealthy theft crimes are crimes of opportunity in egalitarian, affluent societies, while robbery is more a crime of desperation whose purpose is to offset inequality.

Typologies of the three stealthy theft crimes tend to resemble each other, developing over time from Sutherland's distinction between professional and amateur crime, including subtypes in between the two extremes.

Etiological studies of stealthy theft crimes portray them as disproportionately prevalent among youth and inner-city poorly protected neighborhoods characterized by poverty and unemployment. The low clearance rates of these crimes suggest police ineffectiveness and a lack of deterrence by the criminal justice system opening the way for situational theories that offer "target hardening" strategies in lieu of police protection. However, some alternative theories of stealthy theft have emerged in the criminological literature including Easterlin's hypothesis of the "baby boom" for burglary, psychological theories of "kleptomania" pertaining to shoplifting, and a "favored group hypothesis" for vehicle theft.

The country profiles in this chapter were intended to shed some light on the "dark figure" crimes, the stealthy theft crimes of burglary, larceny-theft, and vehicle theft with low clearance rates. In Australia, we found a "party culture" of youth indulging in alcohol, drugs, and surfing, a lifestyle supported by burglary and other stealthy theft crimes of young people who are part of a "baby boom generation." In Sweden, we found that youth and immigrants who are just entering the job market in an affluent egalitarian society are the bottom social class with severe limits to their aspirations of home ownership, family, and travel. A lenient justice system that features "day fine" sanctions for theft-related crimes facilitates the use of such crimes by youth and immigrants to redress their status differentials, resulting in the world's highest rate of larceny-theft for that country. Great Britain has for some time been the target of sneak thieves, as indicated by the omnipresence of CCTV monitors in that country. Factors involved in the prevalence of vehicle theft include a lenient treatment of motor vehicle thieves (who typically receive a "caution" in court); a high rate of unemployment for youth; and a high rate of commerce with EU countries and Commonwealth countries, the latter of which is facilitated by the new English Channel tunnel to numerous countries in Europe where vehicles can be sold to fences and/or "barter traded" for illicit drugs or even human trade to be transported back to Great Britain to complete a profitable cycle of transnational crime.

Two European developed countries with low rates of stealthy theft were profiled for comparison—Portugal and Austria. Both are Catholic countries in which children typically live with their parents until marriage, in contrast to Australia, Sweden, and Great Britain where adult children are typically out on their own, cohabiting instead of getting married, and experience a psychological state of poverty because their basic physical needs are not provided for. Both Portugal and Austria treat drug offenses differently than the other three countries in the sense that drug abuse is treated using a harm reduction approach rather than imprisonment. Austria has pioneered the use of VOM with motor vehicle thieves, helping to account for the fact that Austria has the lowest rate of vehicle theft in Europe.

Looking at American offense statistics by state, stealthy theft appears in FBI statistics to be disproportionately a "black problem," related to heroin and alcohol abuse and unstable relations between the sexes (as indicated by the link with unwed motherhood). Underlying this "black problem" is a stronger correlation between the black/white income disparity and robbery and motor vehicle theft, and to a lesser extent burglary and larceny-theft. Always present, however, is the possibility that this racial link with these stealthy theft crimes is a product of racial profiling by the police—a classic case of "driving while black." Based upon our international research, it seems likely that the police may find a large chunk of the "dark figure" of burglaries, larcenies, and motor vehicle thefts among the white middle class "boys and girls next door" living a "party lifestyle" in the suburbs. More ethnographic research is needed with the middle class joyriders, as well as the Mexican American "coyotes," both of whom may employ the automobile in conjunction with other and possibly transnational crimes (drugs, robbery, burglary, etc.).

DISCUSSION QUESTIONS

1. Do you think that burglary generally is a more serious crime than larceny-theft and motor vehicle theft as discussed in this chapter? Why or why not?

2. Why do you think that the three stealthy theft crimes have dropped in recent years?

3. Burglary, larceny-theft, and motor vehicle theft are "hot season crimes," while robbery typically peaks in the winter. What is your explanation for this difference?

4. The majority of persons arrested for stealthy theft crimes are white, whereas the majority arrested for robbery are black. How do you account for this racial difference?

5. Why do you think that the three stealthy theft crimes declined much more in the NCVS statistics than those of the FBI?

6. Why do you think females are trending upward in the three stealthy theft crimes?

7. How would you characterize the shoplifting case studies at the beginning of this chapter in terms of the stealthy theft typologies presented in this chapter (i.e., which types seem to fit each case)?

8. Based upon your reading of the etiological studies, the theories, and the county profiles, which theory or theories do you think best explain(s) burglary, larceny-theft, and motor vehicle theft? Explain your reasoning.

SUGGESTED WEBSITES

http://www.discoverfrance.net/France/consulate_info.shtml   Website maintained by the French consulate containing crime travel warnings, as well as educational programs offered by major universities.

http://magazines.ivillage.com/goodhousekeeping/consumer/cars   A good list of security devices that can be obtained for cars.

http://www.abs.gov.au/Ausstats   Australia's equivalent of the U.S. Census bureau of population statistics.

http://www.aic.gov.au/publications/facts   Australia's equivalent of the FBI Web page with links to annual reports on crime.

http://www.kcl.ac.uk/depsta/rel/icps/worldbrief/world_brief.html   Website giving prison statistics for all countries of the world that can be accessed by clicking the country on a world map.

http://ncis.gov.uk   British Website that is a good source of e-papers on transnational organized crime in Europe.

http://www.vehicle-documents.it/index-inglese.htm   Website providing a worldwide database for vehicle identification.

ENDNOTES

1. Avon and Somerset Constabulary: Prolific Offenders Unit, 2004.
2. Modes, 2000.
3. *CBSNEWS.com*, 2002, November 7.
4. Duncan, 2003, August 20.
5. CBC News, 2003, October 28.
6. Stein, 1970, p. 1347.
7. FBI, 2004, p. 266, Table 25.
8. Falcone, 2005, p. 252.
9. *Groups.google.com*, 2006.
10. City of El Cerrito Police Department, 2006, Report no. 06–03886.
11. David & Scott, 1973.
12. Merriam-Webster Online, 2006a.
13. La Fave & Scott, 1972, p. 708.
14. Schmalleger, 2003, p. 146.
15. FBI, 2004, p. 45.
16. FBI, 2004, p. 45.
17. BJS, 2001, p. 14.
18. Merriam-Webster, 2006b.
19. Schmalleger, 2003, p. 631.
20. Brown, Esbensen, & Geis, 2001, p. 497.
21. Schmalleger, 2002, p. 333.
22. Adler, Mueller, & Laufer, 2004, p. 290.
23. FBI, 2004, p. 49.
24. BJS, 2001, p. 14.
25. BJS, 2001, P. 3.
26. FBI, 2004, p. 55.
27. Schmalleger, 2003, p. 58.
28. BJS, 2004c, Appendix: Survey Methodology.
29. FBI, 1995, p. 38; FBI, 2004, p. 45.
30. FBI, 1995, p. 199, Table 25; FBI, 2004, p. 266, Table 25.
31. FBI, 2004, p. 266, Table 25.
32. FBI, 1995, p. 199, Table 25.
33. FBI, 1995, p. 58, Table 1; FBI, 2004, p. 73, Table 1.
34. FBI, 1995, pp. 5, 26, 38, 49; FBI, 2004, pp. 31, 45, 49, 55; Index computed from sum of Index offense rates (excluding arson).
35. FBI, 2004, p. 266, Table 25.
36. FBI, 1995, p. 58, Table 1; FBI, 2004, p. 73, Table 1.
37. FBI, 1995, p. 27; FBI, 2004, p. 34.
38. FBI, 1995, p. 39, 196, Table 23; FBI, 2004, pp. 45, 259, Table 23.
39. FBI, 1995, p. 44; FBI, 2004, p. 52.
40. FBI, 1995, p. 50; FBI, 2004, p. 57.
41. FBI, 1995, p. 39, Table 2.26, p. 44, Table 2.27; p. 50, Table 2.29; FBI, 2004, p. 46, Table 2.25, p. 50, Table 2.26, p. 56, Table 2.28.
42. FBI, 1995, p. 27, Table 2.19; FBI, 2004, p. 32, Table 2.18.
43. FBI, 1995, p. 42, 205, Table 28.
44. FBI, 2004, p. 273, Table 28.
45. FBI, 2004, p. 284, Table 32. (This table contains data for both 1995 and 2004.)
46. FBI, 1995, p. 218, Table 38; FBI, 2004, p. 290, Table 38.
47. FBI, 1995, p. 225, Table 42; FBI, 2004, p. 297, Table 42.

48. FBI, 1995, p. 227, Table 43; FBI, 2004, p. 298, Table 43.

49. U.S. Census Bureau, 2006.

50. FBI, 1995, p. 205, Table 28.

51. Computations based upon FBI, 2004, p. 284, Table 32.

52. FBI, 1995, p. 219, Table 38; FBI, 2004, p. 290, Table 38.

53. Computations based upon FBI, 2004, p. 285, Table 33.

54. FBI, 1995, p. 226, Table 43; FBI, 2004, p. 298, Table 43.

55. FBI, 2004, p. 280, Table 29; FBI, 2004, p. 285, Table 33.

56. FBI, 1995, p. 205, Table 28; FBI, 2004, p. 273, Table 28.

57. FBI, 1995, p. 218, Table 38; FBI, 2004, p. 290, Table 38.

58. FBI, 1995, p. 218, Table 38; FBI, 2004, p. 290, Table 38.

59. FBI, 1995, p. 225, Table 42; FBI, 2004, p. 297, Table 42.

60. FBI, 1995, p. 226, Table 43; FBI, 2004, p. 298, Table 43.

61. FBI, 1995, p. 227, Table 43; FBI, 2004, p. 299, Table 43.

62. Catalano, 2005, p. 2, Table 1.

63. BJS, 1995, p. 8, Table 1.

64. BJS, 2005a.

65. BJS, 2005b.

66. BJS, 2005c.

67. BJS, 1995, p. 8, Table 1; BJS, 2004b, p. 5, Table 3.

68. BJS, 1995, Table 19; BJS, 2001, Table 19.

69. BJS, 2003, Table 19.

70. BJS, 1995, 2001, 2003, Table 16.

71. BJS, 1995, 2003, Table 20.

72. BJS, 2004b, p. 2, Table 1.

73. BJS, 1995, Table 82; BJS, 2003, Table 82.

74. BJS, 2003, Table 16.

75. BJS, 2003, Table 20.

76. BJS, 2003, Table 19.

77. BJS, 2003, Table 5.

78. BJS, 2003, Table 2.

79. BJS, 2003, Table 3.

80. BJS, 2003, Table 3.

81. BJS, 2003, Table 14.

82. BJS, 2003, Table 16.

83. BJS, 2003, Table 19.

84. BJS, 2003, Table 22.

85. BJS, 2003, Tables 16–19.

86. BJS, 2003, Table 20.

87. BJS, 2003, Table 55.

88. BJS, 2003, Tables 52–54.

89. Data on race were derived from BJS, 2003, Table 16 for property crimes (burglary, larceny-theft, and vehicle theft) and Table 5 for personal crimes (robbery and purse/pocket theft); data on gender were derived from Table 93a for property crimes and Table 2 for personal crimes; data on age were derived from Table 19 for property crimes and Tables 96 and 3 for personal crimes; data on income were derived from Table 20 for property crimes and Table 14 for personal crimes. Frequencies were given in Tables 2, 5, and 17. For Tables 3, 14, 19, and 20, frequencies were computed from a formula—frequency = (total number of households × rate of crime)/1000. For Table 93a, frequencies were computed from another formula—number of households reporting crime/fraction reporting to police. Totals given are typically less than those reported in Table 1 because of incomplete data for a particular demographic category.

90. FBI, 2004, p. 73, Table 1; BJS, 1995, 1996b, 1997, 1998b, 1999, 2000, 2001, 2002e, 2003, 2004c Table 1.

91. Mdluli-Sedibe, 1999.

92. Shover, 1971.

93. Sutherland, 1937.

94. Wright & Decker, 1994.

95. Shover, 1991.

96. Cromwell, Olson, & Avary, 1993.

97. Brown, et al., 2001, p. 497.

98. Rates were computed by multiplying the total amount of larceny-theft by the percentage given in the UCR for the different forms of larceny-theft and multiplied by 100. Data for 1995 were taken from FBI, 1995, p. 44, Table 2.28. Data for 2004 were taken from FBI, 2004a, p. 50, Table 2.27. Because of rounding, figures may not total 100%.

99. DiscoverFrance, 2003.

100. Shover, 1996, pp. xii–xiii, as quoted in Schmalleger, 2003, p. 331.

101. Shover & Honaker, 1996, p. 14.

102. Shover & Honaker, 1996.

103. Shover & Honaker, 1996, pp. 15–20.

104. Hepburn, 1984, as quoted in Schmalleger, 2003, p. 332.

105. Cameron, 1964.

106. Moore, 1984.

107. McShane & Noonan, 1993.

108. Jacobs, Essers, & Meijer, 2002.

109. Webb & Laycock, 1992.

110. McCaghy, Giordano, & Knicely, 1977.

111. Tremblay, Clermont, & Cusson, 1994.

112. Bichler & Potchak, 2002; Budd, 1999; Capowich, 2003; Clontz, 1995; Cohn, 1990; Corman & Mocan, 2002; Cromwell, Olson, & Avary, 1991; DeFronzo, 1984, 1996; Hakim & Shachmurove, 1996; Ludwig & Cook, 2003; Martin, 2002; Rhodes & Conly, 1981; Stack, 1995.

113. Atkins, 1998; Berger, 1981; Best, Sidwell, & Gossop, 2001; Bowers, 1997; Carlson, 1990; Chesney Lind & Lind, 1984; Chesney Lind & Okamoto, 2001; Covington & Taylor, 1989; Feeney & Weir, 1974; Forston, 1976; Glacopassi & Stitt, 1994; Hayes, 1997, Horwitz, 1986; Kovandzic & Sloan, 2002; Lester, 1995; Neustrom & Norton, 1995; Ortega & Burnett, 1987; Ortega, Corzine, & Burnett, 1992; Parker & Bottomley, 1996; Pelfey, 2000; Poyner & Woodall, 1987; Sherman, 1989; Shichor, 1990; Shikita & Shinichi, 1990; Sigler & Koehlor, 1993; Simon & Landis, 1991; Smith, 1987; White, 1999.

114. Caunitis, 2002.

115. Belger, 1981.

116. Atkins, 1998; Ayres & Levitt, 1998; Chamlin, Grasmich, & Bursik, 1992; Field, Clarke, & Harris, 1991; Fleming, Brantingham, & Brantingham, 1994; Gow & Peggrem, 1991; Higgins, 1997; Katz, Webb, & Schaefer, 2000; Lyengar, 1995; Mayhew, 1991; McCullough, Schmidt, & Lockhard, 1990; Palacios, 1996; Roneck & Lobosco, 1983. Light, Nee, & Ingham, 1993; Thomas, 1990; U.S. National Highway Traffic Safety Administration, 1998; Victoria-Parliament, 2002; Willis, 1983;

117. Cohen & Felson, 1979.

118. Bursick & Grasmick, 1993.

119. Capowich, 1996.

120. Jeffery, 1971.

121. Newman, 1973.

122. Clarke & Homel, 1997.

123. Comparative Criminology Website: Netherlands.

124. Mocan & Rees, 1999.

125. DeFronzo, 1996.

126. Corman & Mocan, 2002; Kohfeld & Sprague, 1988; Yamada, Yamada, & Kang, 1991.

127. Sampson, 1985.

128. Ousey, 1997.

129. Easterlin, 1980.

130. O'Brien, 1989.

131. Savolainen, 2000.

132. Natalino, 1979.

133. Cromwell, Olson, & Avary, 1991.

134. Bichler & Potchak, 2002.

135. FBI, 2004, p. 47.

136. Schmalleger, 2002, p. 340.

137. Included among these studies are Clarke & Mayhew, 1994; Cohen & Cantor, 1980; Ehrhardt & Tewksbury, 1998; Thompson & Fisher, 1996.

138. French, 1981.

139. National Center for Education Statistics, 1998.

140. Klemke, 1992.

141. Farrington, 1999.

142. McGoey, 2004.

143. Oran, 2004.

144. Arthur, 1992.

145. David & Scott, 1973.

146. Follett, 2001.

147. Easterlin, 1980.

148. O'Brien, 1989.

149. Zak, 2000.

150. French, 1981.

151. Kreuzer, Romer, & Schneider, 1991.

152. Kronfeld, 2002.

153. Pelfey, 2000; Best, Sidwell, & Gossop, 2001; Parker & Bottomley, 1996.

154. Killias & Rabasa, 1998a, & 1998b.

155. Mathey, 1816.

156. Marc, 1840.

157. Stekel, 1911.

158. Gibbens & Prince, 1961.

159. Abelson, 1989.

160. Fullerton & Punj, 2004, p. 14.

161. Fullerton & Punj, 2004, p. 14.

162. Stekel, 1922, p. 277.

163. Sarasalo, Bergman, & Toth, 1997.

164. Krasnovsky & Lane, 1998.

165. Xiaogang & Zhang, 1998.

166. Adler et al., 2004, p. 296.

167. *Ivillage.com,* 2004.

168. Edelman, 1980.

169. Wattenberg, & Balliestri, 1951.

170. Cavan & Ferdinand, 1975; Gibbens, 1958; Gibbons, 1977; Sanders, 1976.

171. McCaghy, Giordano, & Henson, 1977.

172. Schwendinger, 1963.

173. Winslow, 1966.

174. Source: Comparative Criminology Website: Romania.

175. Fairchild & Dammer, 2001, pp. 22–23.

176. AlRomaih, 1993.

177. Amnesty International, 2000.

178. Amnesty International, 2000; AlRomaih, 1993; Comparative Criminology Website: Saudi Arabia.

179. Chappel & Wilson, 1994.

180. Australian Bureau of Statistics, 2002.

181. Australian Institute of Criminology, 2001c.

182. Walker, 1994.

183. Minnery, 1988.

184. Australian Institute of Criminology, 2001a.

185. Australian Institute of Criminology, 2001b.

186. Shover & Honaker, 1996, pp. 15–20.

187. Chikritzh, Jonas, Heale, Dietze, Hanlin, & Stockwell, 1999.

188. Patterns of Victimization among Small Retail Businesses, 2002.

189. Carcach & Muscat, 2002.

190. Chappel & Wilson,1994.

191. *Wannasurf.com,* 2003.

192. Walker, n. d.

193. Australian Bureau of Statistics, 1998.

194. Laxley, 2002; Stevenson & Forsythe, 1998.

195. United Nations Office on Drugs and Crime, 2000.

196. Zander, 2001.

197. Zander, 2001, p. 30.

198. Segue Esprit Inc., 2004.

199. Kiernan, 2002.

200. Sweden.se, 2004, p. 6.

201. Sweden.se, 2004, p. 5.

202. Bernhardt, 2001, p. 1.

203. Runblom, 1998.

204. Bernhardt, 2001, p. 3.

205. Bernhardt, 2001, p. 4.

206. For instance, see Von Hofer & Henrik, 2000.

207. Zander, 2001, p. 27.

208. Stalenkrantz, 2004.

209. Wikstrom & Dolmen, 1994.

210. Interpretations of these data reports were given through correspondence with Swedish criminologist Sven Larson of the University of Gothenberg, Sweden. The Swedish civil law system is successful in curbing violent crime, which is not indicated accurately in the data on violent crime presented in the CCDB. The CCDB includes only the most recent data on crime, and in the case of Sweden, the data used were those reported to INTERPOL for 2001. The most recent data reported to the United Nations by Sweden were for year 1997. INTERPOL does not audit data reported to it by member countries, and Sweden routinely reports to INTERPOL both attempted and completed criminal homicides as "murders." Although the murder rate indicated in the CCDB from INTERPOL data for year 2001 was 10.01 per 100,000 inhabitants, the Swedish rate for "intentional homicides completed" reported to the United Nations in 1997 was only 1.77. Just as with murder, the 2001 INTERPOL report of 667.42 per 100,000 inhabitants for "serious assault" in the CCDB was padded by the inclusion of both "simple assaults" and "aggravated assaults" in this figure for Sweden. Although INTERPOL data contains no distinction between simple and aggravated assaults, United Nations data does include such a distinction—between "major assaults" and "total assaults." The 1997 United Nations Swedish report for "major assaults" of 37.93 per 100,000 inhabitants is probably more accurate as a record of "aggravated assaults" for Sweden than the INTERPOL data.

211. International Centre for Prison Studies, 2004a.

212. The Baltimore Sun, 2003.

213. Von Hofer, 1999.

214. Smith, Torstensson, & Johansson, 2001.

215. Estrada, 2004.

216. International Centre for Prison Studies, 2004a.

217. Jederlund, 1998.

218. Martens, 1997.

219. Jederlund, 1998, p. 2.

220. Jederlund, 1998, p. 3.

221. Jederlund, 1998, p. 4.

222. Serril, 1977.

223. Segue Esprit Inc., 2004.
224. Kiernan, 2002.
225. Hammer, 2004,
226. Comparative Criminology Website: Portugal.
227. World's Vehicle Documents, 2001.
228. Kesteren, Mayhew, & Nieuwberrta, 2000. Mayhew & Van Dijk, 2000; Phillips, Cox, & Pease 1996.
229. Urwin, 2004, p. 1.
230. World's Vehicle Documents, 2001, p. 2; Neilson, 2000.
231. Richardb, 2003.
232. National Criminal Intelligence Service, 2004.
233. Brown & Thomas, 2003.
234. Gow & Peggrem, 1991.
235. Laycock & Austin, 1992.
236. Oldfield, 1996.
237. Light, Nee, & Ingham, 1993.
238. Richardb, 2003.
239. Carmichael & Ward, 2001.
240. Hammer, 2004.
241. National Crime Intelligence Service, 2004, p. 12.
242. International Centre for Prison Studies, 2004b.
243. Nationmaster.com, 2004.
244. Simon, 2004, June 24.
245. Jason-Lloyd, 1998.
246. Farrington & Jolliffe, 2004, p. 17.
247. Farrington & Jolliffe, 2004, p. 26.
248. Farrington & Jolliffe, 2004, p. 28.
249. Jason-Lloyd, 1998.
250. Garden, 2001.
251. Wacquant, 1999, p. 2.
252. World's Vehicle Documents, 2001.
253. Sands, 2002, p. 8–10.
254. Gonzalez, 2004, April 15.
255. California Highway Patrol, 2003.
256. Myers, 2004, October 10.
257. Wikipedia, 2004d.
258. Office for National Statistics, 2004.
259. Comparative Criminology Website: Great Britain.
260. World's Vehicle Documents, 2001.
261. Segue Esprit Inc., 2004.
262. Kiernan, 2002.
263. Comparative Criminology Website: Austria.
264. Troppenhaur & Seipel, 1994.
265. McGeorge, 2001.
266. Kilchling, 2004.
267. Umbreit, 2000.
268. Lowney, 2001.
269. Surfing camps are described in the Website: http://www.mysummercamps.com/camps/arizona-surfing-camps.html
270. Schur, 1973.
271. Taylor, Kelly, & Valescu, 2001.
272. See for instance a list of diversion and intervention programs on the Florida State Attorney's Website at http://www.coj.net/Departments/State+Attorneys+Office+/Diversion+Programs+for+Juveniles.htm (Retrieved October 29, 2004).
273. Krasnovsky & Lane, 1998.

KEY TERMS

Black Hand
clustered hierarchy
black market
consigliere
core groups
criminal networks
Golden Crescent
Golden Triangle
La Cosa Nostra
Mafia
omerta

organized crime
outlaw motorcycle gangs
regional hierarchy
snakehead
soldati
standard hierarchy
transnational organized crime
Triads
Tongs
Yakuza

OUTLINE

Definition

Types of Organized Crime

Global View of Organized Crime

LEARNING OBJECTIVES

After reading this chapter, students should be able to:

1. Understand the confusion that develops from the variety of definitions of organized crime that are used by authors, organizations, and law enforcement agencies

2. Define organized crime in a way that enables the term to be operationalized and used in a court of law

3. Distinguish between the Mafia and La Cosa Nostra, as described by the Kefauver Crime Commission and the McClellan Commission, respectively

4. Identify the numerous ethnic groups and nationalities that are involved in organized crime today

5. Name the five different organized crime structures involved in transnational organized crime

6. Trace the history of organized crime in China, Hong Kong (now part of China), Taiwan, Japan, the United States, Mexico, Italy, Russia, and Nigeria

7. Understand how organized crime is used, in Daniel Bell's words, as a "queer ladder of social mobility," for various ethnic groups at different times, but primarily African Americans and Hispanic Americans today

INTRODUCTION

I lived in a section of New York City known as Fordham. I owned and operated an auto repair shop in New York. During the course of my business, I repaired police cars and through this association was able to "fix tickets." I also repaired cars owned by gangsters. I am related by marriage to a man who owned a bakery in whose ovens the mob disposed of its bodies. I witnessed the assassination of a gangster and was told to keep my mouth shut about it. I did so and was rewarded by the syndicate for having done so.

As a child growing up, I lived near a corner store that was a pastry shop in an Italian neighborhood. That pastry shop was where all the gangsters and top hoods came who were in the area to do their business. And they did this business with kids running in and out buying lemonades. The barber shop was another place where gangsters did business, and this was well known. The police department would walk in and out to collect their fees. I was only a little boy, but I was seeing things and getting wiser, and my eyes were opened up slowly but surely toward organized crime (OC) and how it works. Some of the boys I worked with, incidentally, were part of this crime syndicate. All the other boys in the neighborhood were always involved in petty gang thievery, but I managed to stay clear of it, but always keeping an eye on crime and how it operated. The police were always in with the crime syndicate. The payoff was being made. People always talked about wanting to get rid of crime, yet people sort of embraced themselves with the crime machine. No matter what they did—there were people who wanted to make a living so they did with bootlegging, and this is how the system began to grow. And they also had the protection racket going. The small businessman couldn't operate unless he had the protection of insurance. If they didn't buy insurance, owners of the stores received a beating by strangers that were sent in from other areas.

This all occurred during the 1920s. I was born in 1912, so I was going to school around World War I. People think that OC is dominated by the Italians, but this is not necessarily so. The main syndicate is the Mafia, which people say has changed its name and is now La Cosa Nostra (LCN), but it is still the Mafia. It's only moved into a different racket. And LCN, so to speak, is now just the plain hoodlums. They are now not allowed to associate with the Mafia because Mafia is now big business and they can't afford to associate with hoodlums because they are now part of the society. Yes [names a well-known bank] is part of the syndicate; so are your biggest bankers. If you want to get rid of OC in the United States today, you must get rid of the United States because that is who controls the government, controls everything that exists in the country today, is crime. Politics are part of your crime syndicate. Crime is so prevalent among politicians because they are the ones who are allowing it to go on.

The Mafia is not just here in this country. They are in every country in the world. They are in Taiwan, Japan, and Hong Kong. As a matter of fact, they've got a big business going in Japan. It's not a local organization. It's a worldwide organization. Each man answers to himself in that it is not done collectively. They come with teletype machines and they do it through the teletype when they operate. The way to trace them is they control the money. They can stir up money in any part of the world if they want, and make you believe you are fighting a war for some reason or other. The main operators are out in the suburbs, the bigger wheels. They are in politics. The main organization, the Mafia itself, originates in Palermo, and that organization is still alive. They are not the controlling interest of the world because every country now has its own, which is linked with the international Mafia. Now you have INTERPOL, which is the international police, to cope with them, but they are bought and sold also, so they can't do anything either.

I am an Italian American from New Orleans, and I did some time in prison for robbery. At one time I owned a bar and was associated with the syndicate in New Orleans. I worked with a wire service that was associated with an organization, like most bookie joints are. It was my job to keep those bookies who weren't associated with the syndicate out of business. They were very generous. They gave me a salary, and I could also keep their bankroll when I closed them down.

I find that even with all the elaborate investigating equipment of the FBI, they find it hard, if not impossible, to get a clear picture of what constitutes OC, how it comes about, and what its purposes are.

I don't believe in the theory of a national conspiracy—that it is a complex organization with tentacles stretching out into every city. It's developed on a local level and always on a local level there is someone who controls, someone with the most influence and who loosely bosses the criminal endeavor such as prostitution, drugs, stolen goods . . . this type of thing. I know two of the men who were at the Appalachia meeting. I think that what was actually happening was an attempt to organize on a national scale, and it was broken up. Nothing was ever accomplished, and there were no more attempts.

Valachi was an old-line, minor criminal. I'm not sure why Vito Genovese swore him dead. I am sure that he did swear him dead, but Valachi was looking for some reason to keep alive and he tried to get this by giving Bobby Kennedy and others some reason. I think that he had a great imagination, and there was probably some truth in everything that he said, but I think he exaggerated them. I don't doubt that he was a gunman. He hadn't done anything recently, if you remember. The information was 15 years old. I don't think that he was much more than I was when I was involved, just a gunman, and a muscle man.

What's happened today is that the Al Capone era is over and done with. You now have highly educated men in high places and they make far more money legitimately than they do illegitimately, I think. It might be questionable how they gained control of this company or that company, but what they do is offer legitimate organizations through which illegitimate acts can be carried out. For instance, I know of an old bank that used to be on my criminal route. This bank will exchange money for securities, bonds, monies that you shouldn't legally have—for a percentage. There's millions of dollars every year just in percentages. But it always develops on a local level and local crime leaders get hold of something, then willingly give up their money to have certain officials elected and thereby get control of legitimate companies and control of the government until it pyramids and those officials finds a tremendous influence and power. He has his hands in elected officials for mayor, state governor, and even Congress. Now when you talk about the Mafioso or LCN, which I personally think was invented by Valachi, these people who control at a local level have knowledge of each other. Sometimes they're even related by blood or marriage. The thing, though, that prevents this so-called national conspiracy, is the great amount of suspicion that they have in regard to their ability and power. It's inconceivable to me that the people I know could ever get together and appoint an absolute boss over them. It's contrary to their personality. It's contrary to the Italian personality since we're probably talking more about Italians.

The Mafia started in this country in New Orleans, brought from Sicily by the dock men. Then it spread because this guy would leave and then another and so on. But they didn't leave like a conspiracy. They just went. They developed a personal thing. It wasn't "our thing." It was my thing. They were able, of course, to call on each other for assistance in influencing different things, but that's as far as the alliance goes.

They don't have to use the strong arm anymore, because they can will the law. They have control of the people who write, interpret, and enforce the laws. And they do this. I'd say some 60% of the Congress has obligation to some particular crime boss, and it's the same in the Senate. There are several top businessmen in several large cities that I know of that, although they aren't prime leaders, they are associated with the syndicated activities in their areas. They do favors and provide fronts. This includes bankers and corporation heads.

It is basically true that the syndicate is in reality breaking laws that shouldn't have been laws in the first place—against drugs, gambling, and prostitution. They always appealed to human weaknesses. The public helps make a young man ambitious, like the kid telling me that he'd rather be a Mafia Don than President because he could tell the President what to do. Being successful at crime doesn't discount you anything. You get all the respect, prestige, and material goods anyway. The key is being successful. You'd be surprised at how much this influences the guys I worked with. What a lot of these burglars and gunmen want is to be noticed by some Don who'll say, "Hey man, you're just what I need." The public adds to that, the movies add to that, and yellow newspapers add to that. Then after you condone this big man up here, and you punish this little man down here, and then when you let him out you treat him like some kind of alien being. Society doesn't want to take responsibility for creating this little man.

The only people who can effectively end OC are those people of the community where OC exists. I'm talking about elected officials who must be able to say, "I don't care if you can make me a cinch for this election; I would rather not win than be indebted to you." And then expose them. Or even use them to get into office and then expose them. We're talking about honesty, courage, awareness, and involvement as opposed to ignorance, apathy, and self-seeking rather than for the good of the whole. Also, I mentioned revamping corrections and the justice system. Planting the seed and hoping that it will flourish and that someday we can successfully accomplish this change.[1]

The aforementioned case studies were college class lectures by informants that were located by students working in community-based organizations that provided services for ex-offenders. Most of the concerns addressed by these speakers were about the Italian Mafia or LCN. As the discussion progresses during this chapter, it is shown that OC involves many other ethnic groups as well as nations, especially when viewed on a global basis. However, concern about the Sicilian Mafia was a starting point for discussion of OC in criminology and criminology texts. So discussion of the Mafia or LCN is covered initially in this chapter, followed by the evolution of OC in this country and globally.

DEFINITION

One of the most remarkable aspects of this topic is the variety of definitions of **Organized Crime** (OC) that are presented in various published sources. In a Website devoted to the topic of definitions of OC, Klaus von Lampe has provided a collection of 60 definitions whose authors are shown in Table 11–1. A content analysis of these 60 definitions would be useful to derive a definition that can be used for the following analysis. The following are elements that are commonly mentioned in these numerous definitions:

- A nonideological enterprise carried on through a corporate hierarchy involving division of labor and three or more levels or ranks, such as suppliers, manufacturers, wholesalers, and retailers, resulting in insulation of key members from identification and prosecution.
- Pursuit of profit or power through traffic in or provision of illegal goods or services in great public demand (vice) or through racketeering (organized extortion).
- Conspiracies (usually done by top leadership) and the provision of reciprocal services by criminals, their clients, and politicians.
- Use of threats, force or violence, or corruption of public officials.
- Use of an informal, though effective, means of communication known as the "grapevine".
- Persistence of conspiratorial activity through time (at least one year) regardless of change in personnel.
- Attempts at cartelization or monopolization of markets.
- Because of scope or scale of operation, the organization eludes control by local law enforcement.
- Lifetime careerist orientation among participants.
- A goal of bringing unlawful gains into the legal economy through money laundering.
- Ethnic ties that result in restricted membership.
- Cooperation of respectable society (active or passive).

Apart from these key characteristics of OC, many definitions (particularly those by government groups) include a list of characteristic activities of organized criminal groups, such as trafficking in illegal drugs, illegal gambling, usury, and prostitution. However, additional illegal activity attributed to OC

Table 11–1 Definitions of Organized Crime[2]

American Definitions of Organized Crime, by Author/Source:	Definitions of OC From Other Countries:
Howard Abadinsky	Australia
Jay Albanese	Queensland CrimeCommission
Joseph Albini	Pat O'Malley
American Heritage Dictionary	Belgium
Alan Block	Black et al./Annual Report Organized Crime
Block and Chambliss	
California Control of Profits of OC Act	Canada
California Commission on OC	Samuel Porteous
Comptroller General	Alfried Schulte-Bockholt
Donald Cressey	Croatia
Finckenauer and Voronin	Ministry of Interior
Frederic Homer	Germany
Francis Ianni	Bundeskriminalamt
ITT Research Institute	Link to other German definitions (in German)
Robert J. Kelly	
Kenney and Finckenauer	Klaus von Lampe
Lasswell and McKenna	Great Britain
Donald Liddick	Home Office/National Crime Intelligence Service (NCIS)
Alfred Lindesmith	
Peter Lupsha	Greece
William McCulloch	Nestor Courakis
Raymond Michalowski	India
Missouri Task Force	Maharashtra Control of Organized Crime Act, 1999
National Advisory Committee	
New Mexico's OC Commission	Italy
Omnibus Crime Control and Safe Streets Act	Adamoli et al.
	Vincenzo Ruggiero
Oyster Bay Conferences	Federico Varese
Richard Poff	The Netherlands
Gary Potter	Petrus C. van Duyne
Peter Reuter and Jonathan B. Rubinstein	Fijnaut et al.
	Van Traa Commission
Robert Rhodes	Weenink et al.
Ralph Salerno and John S. Tompkins	Poland
Thomas C. Schelling	Emil Plywaczewski
Thorsten Sellin	**International Agencies**
Larry Siegel	Council of Europe
Dwight C. Smith	INTERPOL
Task Force 1967	United Nations
U.S. Attorney General (1959)	**Others**
	Encyclopaedia Britannica

includes arson for profit, hijacking, insurance fraud, loan sharking, labor racketeering, smuggling, operating vehicle theft rings, and systematically encumbering the assets of a business for the purpose of defrauding creditors. The definition also may include terrorism, fraud, corruption of public officers, extortion of money, shoplifting, stealing automobiles, and robbing banks.

It can be seen from this wide array of crimes that are said to indicate OC, that the term OC is vaguely defined. Often this "list of crimes" is a method of defining OC by government agencies or legislators frustrated in their attempt to define OC. In the United States, lawmakers seem to be saying "forget all this definition business, you know what we mean—we mean the Mafia . . . La Cosa Nostra." Consider the following quotes from U.S. government sources:

- OC . . . is a confederation of some 24 families consisting of up to 5,000 individuals. The families are organized along military lines and receive general guidance from a selected group of family bosses called the *Commission*.[3]
- Today the core of OC in the United States consists of 24 groups operating as criminal cartels in large cities across the nation. Their membership is exclusively men of Italian descent, they are in frequent communication with each other, and their smooth functioning is insured by a national body of overseers. To date, only the FBI has been able to document fully the national scope of these groups, and FBI intelligence indicates that the organization as a whole has changed its name from Mafia to LCN.[4]

Although the existence of organized crime is not denied in this text, it seems that the definition should be narrowed—not only for legal purposes, but also for scientific purposes. Obviously a definition that includes practically anything and everything has no usefulness. Application of such definitions in the past have led to witch hunts and McCarthyism. Vague definitions can also result in racial profiling or ethnic profiling. Thus, it is important to craft a definition of OC carefully. Even laws on the books today result in severe consequences if the person arrested is deemed to be participating in OC. These include longer prison sentences and confiscation of property.

Thus, what is sought in this text is a clear (and operational) definition of OC that may even have potential for legal application. Some of the definitions reviewed by Von Lampe were definitions given by Commonwealth nations such as Australia and Canada, which stipulated that "indictable offenses" must be part of the conspiracy. That is a clue, but not quite sufficient to differentiate OC from the cheating scam described earlier. "Indictable offenses" are the rough equivalent to "felonies," which are considered to be "serious crimes." However, "felonies" can include "petty theft with a prior" in some states—thus are not always serious offenses. Going one step further, what really seems to make OC a serious offense is the threat of force or actual use of force or violence (extortion). Thus, extortion is the delimiting essential component in OC. The following, then, is suggested as a definition of OC.

OC *refers to a conspiratorial enterprise pursuing profit or power through provision of illegal goods and/or services, involving systematic use of force or threat of force.*

Because participation in such an enterprise carries penalties greater than participation in a common individual crime, proof must be given that conspiracy or collusion exists; that illegal goods and/or services are provided; and that force, or threat of force, is used. This definition pays no reference to many of the attributes given in the bullet points earlier, including step hierarchy, nonideological enterprise, corruption of public officials, informal "grapevine," evasion of local law enforcement, lifetime career orientation, money laundering, attempts to monopolize, ethnic ties, and cooperation of respectable society. Many of these attributes characterize almost all crime or deviant behavior and are not necessarily components of the definition of OC. In regard to the assumption of "hierarchy," it is shown that there are many forms of OC today that are nonhierarchical in nature. These are emerging new forms of OC that include "core groups" and "criminal networks," to be discussed later.

TYPES OF ORGANIZED CRIME

As suggested earlier, one way of typing OC is by type of illegal activity involved in the organized criminal enterprise. Some of these illegal enterprises were discussed earlier and include trafficking in illegal drugs, illegal gambling, usury, arson for profit, hijacking, insurance fraud, loan sharking, labor racketeering, operating vehicle theft rings, and so forth. Much of the discussion about OC in government, the media, and academia has been about ethnicity. In fact since the 1950s, discussion has centered about allegations that OC in America consists of a Sicilian American Mafia or an organization controlled by Americans of Sicilian descent—LCN. Over time, a typology of OC has evolved from this discussion, including not just Sicilians, but also Chinese, Mexicans, Japanese, Russians, Israeli, Colombians, Jamaicans, and more. That discussion is summarized subsequently. However, another recent approach to typing OC has been according to organizational structure. A pioneering effort in typing organizational structures in OC was introduced in a pilot survey done by the United Nations Office on Drugs and Crime, and is summarized later.

Organized Crime as the "Mafia"

The belief that there is a nationwide crime syndicate controlled by Sicilians (with roots in Sicily) that dominates OC in this country dates back to the 19th century. In 1890, New Orleans Superintendent of Police David Peter Hennessey was murdered. Hennessey had been investigating the activities of the Matranga brothers, a gang of Sicilians who allegedly gained complete control of the New Orleans waterfront in 1890. Residents assumed Sicilians to be responsible and 19 gang members were arrested, and then subsequently acquitted. An irate crowd lynched 11 of the 19, resulting in an international incident, and considerable coverage in the news media blaming the event on the **Mafia** or **Black Hand.** The allegation in the news media led to a strong reaction in the Italian community, and many Italian community leaders vehemently denied the existence of the Black Hand. In 1907, however, these leaders organized the White Hand Society, a society whose acknowledged purpose was to combat the Black Hand, thus themselves confirming the existence of the Black Hand.[5]

It is possible that the Mafia as a large-scale organization did not exist in this country before all the national publicity. However, it appeared to flourish from 1910 to 1920 but then became less influential in the 1920s when the Black Handers joined with the mainstream of American gangsterism. The *Mafia* became a popular term during the 1950s, when the Kefauver Crime Committee began to uncover testimony about a national crime syndicate in this country, based in Sicily and dominated by Sicilian Americans.

Behind the local mobs that make up the national crime syndicate is a shadowy, international criminal organization known as the Mafia, so fantastic that most Americans find it hard to believe it really exists. The Mafia, which has its origin and its headquarters in Sicily, is dominant in numerous fields of illegal activity—principally narcotics—and it enforces its code with death to those who resist or betray it.[6]

The Mafia was said to have arisen in Sicily during the early part of the 19th century. It began as a protective organization of the peasant classes formed to resist oppression by the feudal land barons. The Mafiosi (members of the Mafia), however, launched a reign of terror—murder, rape, robbery, extortion, and kidnapping. Landowners acquiesced to Mafia demands and made deals with the Mafiosi to protect their estates, and the Mafiosi in turn became crueler tyrants over the peasants than the gentry ever were.

Based largely on testimony by Harry Anslinger, Commissioner of the Narcotics Bureau at the time, the Kefauver Committee uncovered several alleged characteristics of the Mafia: (a) a secret code called *Omerta,* or "death to informers"; (b) an inner circle of OC known as the "family"; and (c) a Mafia grand council that governed local families. Evidence for this view consisted of testimony by Anslinger and other Narcotics Bureau agents, systematic denials of the existence of the Mafia by alleged gangsters who testified ("evidence" for the code of Omerta), and reference to various violent crimes that "had all of the earmarks of the Mafia." The international head of the Mafia in Italy was believed to be Charles (Lucky) Luciano, who, after serving 10 years in prison, was deported to Italy by Thomas E. Dewey. Additional evidence of a national conspiracy was produced by a meeting of some 75 leaders of crime cartels in November, 1957, at the home of Joseph Barbara in the small New York town of Appalachian. Although the purpose for the meeting was never revealed, Joseph Bonanno and 26 others were convicted of obstruction of justice for refusing to reveal the purpose of the meeting, a conviction later overturned by the U.S. Supreme Court.[7]

Organized Crime as "La Cosa Nostra"

While the term Mafia, as used by the Kefauver Committee, referred to a national organization rooted in Sicily, the term **La Cosa Nostra** (LCN) conveyed another perspective. LCN implied a national organization of Sicilian origin, but centralized and controlled in the United States, and with a somewhat unique organizational structure. This perspective came to light largely as a result of the testimony of Joseph Valachi before the McClellan Committee in 1963.[8] Valachi, by his own testimony a *soldati,* or soldier, in the Vito Genovese family, revealed in detail the organizational structure of LCN; named the major bosses and numerous subordinates; and told the history of LCN and how it became transformed from the Sicilian-based Mafia to LCN, its Americanized counterpart. Based largely on the McClellan Commission findings, Valachi's testimony, and a consultant paper by Donald Cressey, a President's Crime Commission gave a detailed description of LCN in an attempt to bring its existence to public attention.[9] As discussed previously, the Commission pinpointed the structure of LCN to 24 exclusively Italian groups, with 5,000 individual members, operating as crime cartels in large cities throughout the nation. Together they were said to have controlled most of the illicit gambling and loan sharking in the country, and were heavily implicated in narcotics trafficking and labor racketeering. The Commission estimated the annual income from 7 to 50 billion dollars from gambling, several billion from loan sharking, and 250 million from the heroin trade. In addition, LCN was said to

Joseph Valachi is pictured here testifying before the McClellan congressional committee on organized crime in October 1963. Valachi had been a "soldier" in New York City's Vito Genovese crime family. He was the first Mafia member to acknowledge the existence of the Mafia, describe its structure, and name the major members of La Cosa Nostra (as he called it). Valachi's testimony was followed by his biography in the 1968 book, *The Valachi Papers,* by Peter Maas, and a later movie, with the same title, staring Charles Bronson as Valachi. His testimony also influenced the findings of the 1968 Presidential Commission Report on Organized Crime. Valachi died at La Tuna Correctional Institution in El Paso, Texas, in April, 1971.

Source: AP Wide World Photos.

exercise a virtual monopoly over many legitimate enterprises such as cigarette vending machines and juke boxes. These 24 groups were said to work with and control other racket groups, whose leaders were of various ethnic derivations, in enterprises representing a cross-section of the nation's population groups.

The President's Commission then described the structure of LCN (which became the basis for subsequent Hollywood movies such as *The Godfather* and television productions such as *The Sopranos*).

Each of the 24 groups was known as a "family," with membership varying from as few as 20 men to as many as 700. Each family was headed by one man, the *boss,* whose primary function was to maintain order and maximize profits. His authority in all matters relating to his family was absolute. Beneath each boss was an *underboss,* the vice-president or deputy director of the family. He collected information for the boss, relayed messages to him, and passed his instructions down to his own underlings. On the same level as the underboss, but operating in a staff capacity, was the **consigliere,** who was a counselor or advisor to the boss and other family members, enjoying considerable influence and power. Below the level of the underboss were the *caporegime,* or lieutenants, some of whom served as buffers between top members of the family and the lower echelon personnel. To maintain insulation from the police, the leaders of the hierarchy (particularly the bosses) avoided direct communication with the workers. Although some caporegime served as buffers, others served as chiefs of operating units. The lowest level members of a family were the soldati, the soldiers or "button" men who reported to the caporegime. A soldier may operate a particular illicit enterprise—such as a loan-sharking operation, a dice game, a lottery, a bookmaking operation, or a smuggling operation—or he may "own" the enterprise and pay a portion of its profit to the organization, in return for the right to operate, and perhaps for being backed by the capital and resources of the organization. Beneath the soldiers in the hierarchy are large numbers of employees who are not members of the family and are not necessarily of Italian descent. These are the people who do most of the actual work of the various enterprises. They have no buffers or other insulation from law enforcement. They take bets, drive trucks, answer telephones, sell narcotics, and work in the legitimate businesses.

The soldati sometimes served as "corruptors," functioning to establish relationships with public officials and other influential persons whose assistance was needed. They may also have specialized as "enforcers," whose function was to maim or kill recalcitrant members.

The most threat in terms of conspiracy, according to the President's Commission, was the nationwide centralized control of LCN by a ruling body known as the "Commission." This was an oligarchic body serving as a combination legislature, Supreme Court, board of directors, and arbitration board. It was composed of the bosses of the nation's most powerful families and had authority over all 24. The composition of the Commission was said to vary from nine to 12 men.

The structure and history of LCN were described in even greater detail in Donald Cressey's book *Theft of the Nation,* a book developed from Cressey's consultant paper to the President's Crime Commission. Cressey's information came from "police reports, informants, wire taps, and electronic bugs." LCN, Cressey held, differed from the Sicilian Mafia in several respects. The term LCN came into use when a group of "young Turks" headed by Lucky Luciano emerged triumphant from a struggle with more traditional Sicilian "mustache Pete" leaders, including Salvatore Maranzano and Guiseppe Masaria. The "Commission" was an American innovation and not just a transplant from Sicily. It differed from Italy's counterpart in its more diffuse division of power, resembling a *corsa* or stable union of families within a given district rather than a *consorteria,* or society-wide Mafia. Despite the dispersion of power, however, the members of LCN, Cressey maintained, threatened a behind-the-scenes takeover of the government of this country on the local, state, and federal levels.

Organized Crime as Independent Collectivities

The idea that OC was exclusively dominated by a national crime syndicate of Italian Americans has been questioned, both by academicians and government sources. One of the earliest essays opposing the idea of a dominant Italian syndicate was Daniel Bell's "The Myth of the Mafia."[10] The Crime Commission's portrayal of LCN was also held to question by Ramsey Clark, who was the U.S. Attorney General from 1967 to 1969, during the Presidency of Lyndon Johnson (who appointed the Crime Commission).[11] Also critical of the Italian conspiracy model were Morris and Hawkins in their book, *The Honest Politician's Guide to Crime Control.*[12] The main theme of these analyses was that although OC exists, it is not nationally centralized but consists at best of independent collectivities organized mainly in the major metropolitan areas—local syndicates without any real national or even regional ties to one another. Also, all three sources challenge the notion that OC is dominated by any one ethnic group, either currently or historically.

Bell challenged the Mafia concept of the Kefauver Committee as based upon speculation and unsubstantiated testimony. Bell further argued that OC is not a Sicilian American invention, but is instead part of the American way of life and a "queer ladder of social mobility" used by many newly arriving immigrant groups in this country.

> The salient reason, perhaps, why the Kefauver Committee was taken in by its own myth of an omnipotent Mafia and a despotic Costello was its failure to assimilate and understand three of the more relevant sociological facts about institutionalized crime in its relation to the political life of large urban communities in America, namely: (1) the rise of the American-Italian community, as part of the inevitable process of ethnic succession to positions of importance in politics, a process that has been occurring independently but also simultaneously in most cities with large Italian constituencies; . . . (2) the fact that there are individual Italians who play prominent, often leading roles today in gambling and in the mobs; and (3) the fact that Italian gamblers, and mobsters often possessed "status" within the Italian community itself and a "pull" in city politics. These three items are indeed related—but not so as to form a "plot."[13]

Ramsey Clark was highly critical of the findings of the Commission on OC. He argued that the Commission itself had found evidence of OC in only 25 out of 71 cities surveyed, and that the crimes alleged (narcotics, gambling, prostitution) were of a minor nature. Clark argued that violence was declining among crime bosses, as they "go soft" in comparison to early days, and expressed doubts about the Commission's estimates of earnings by OC. He added that LCN is only part of the picture of OC in America.

> As with all crime, we oversimplify our definition of OC. There is far more to it than La Cosa Nostra. Our society is much too complex to expect only a single syndicate or type of illegal activity. There is no one massive organization that manages all or even most planned and continuous criminal conduct throughout the country. There are hundreds of small operations that engage in organized criminal activity—car theft rings, groups of burglars, safecrackers working together, gangs of armed robbers, combinations that occasionally smuggle and distribute marijuana and dangerous drugs—scattered throughout the nation.[14]

Finally, Morris and Hawkins critically examined, "the major sources of data, stating (a) the Valachi testimony is analogous to the knowledge of Standard Oil, which could be gleaned from interviews with gasoline station attendants"; (b) Cressey's argument that by outlining the detailed structural skeleton of LCN demonstrates the existence of such is a nonsequitur; (c) the Valachi testimony, though it comprised the prime source of the knowledge of the skeletal structure, is uncorroborated by any other testimony; (d) the Valachi testimony contained internal inconsistency, for example, despite a code such as "one for all, all for one," Valachi testified the organization offered him no immunity from prosecution; (e) the Valachi testimony was contradicted by others; (f) with regard to the alleged "meeting at Appalachia" on November 17, 1967, which has been used as "proof of conspiracy," there was (1) conflicting testimony as to how many top leaders were there and (2) the conviction of 20 arrested there was reversed on appeal and conspiracy was not proven legally; and (g) there are members even in the Crime Commission Report who are of non-Sicilian ancestry.[15]

Other Ethnic Groups

Over time, it has become apparent, as maintained by Bell, Clark, and Morris and Hawkins, that OC in America is not the exclusive province of Italian Americans. In 1986, a President's Commission on OC found a wide variety of racial, national, and ethnic groups engaging in syndicated crime in the United States. These included blacks, Canadians, Chinese, Colombians, Cubans, Irish, Italians, Japanese, Mexicans, Russians, and Vietnamese.[16] More and more it is being recognized that OC, rather than being a national crime syndicate of a single ethnic group (Italian Americans), is actually a "transnational" endeavor of a multitude of national, ethnic, and racial groups. The term **transnational organized crime** is used here to refer to crime committed in more than one country, or more specifically according to the Convention against Transnational OC developed by the United Nations in 1998:

> an offence is transnational if "(a) It is committed in more than one state; (b) It is committed in one state but a substantial part of its preparation, planning, direction or control takes place in another state; (c) It is committed in one state but involves an organized criminal group that engages in criminal activities in more than one state; or (d) It is committed in one state but has substantial effects in another state."[17]

Transnational groups include Chinese Tongs and Triads, Medellin and Cali drug cartels of Colombia, Jamaican Posse's, Japanese Yakuza, outlaw motorcycle gangs, Russian Mafiya, and Vietnamese Triad groups and gangs of Vietnamese origin.[18] In 1995, the United Nations identified 18 categories of transnational offenses, whose inception, perpetration, and/or direct or indirect effects involve more than one country. These offenses include:

> money laundering, terrorist activities, theft of art and cultural objects, theft of intellectual property, illicit arms trafficking, aircraft hijacking, sea piracy, insurance fraud, computer crime, environmental crime, trafficking in persons, trade in human body parts, illicit drug trafficking, fraudulent bankruptcy, infiltration of legal business, corruption and bribery of public or party officials.[19]

Transnational Organized Crime

An ad hoc committee of the United Nations developed a five-fold classification of organizational structures of transnational OC groups. The stated purpose of this typology was:

> To counter the public image of organized criminal groups as simply Mafia-type organizations. Law enforcement authorities have long underestimated the harm caused by smaller groups whose capacity to adapt to new markets and profits is higher and whose detection is difficult due to their low profile and loose structure. Important also in this regard is to inform the public more generally about the wide variety of forms that OC takes. Experience has shown elsewhere that awareness raising among the public about the dangers of OC (and how to identify its manifestations) can be an important weapon to fight it.[20]

Accordingly, the research team identified five types of structures found among the 40 OC groups studied. These included the standard hierarchy, regional hierarchy, clustered hierarchy, core group, and criminal network.

The **standard hierarchy** was described as having a single leader, clearly defined hierarchy, strong systems of internal discipline, being known by a specific name, often having a strong social or ethnic identity, using violence as essential to activities, and often having a clear influence or control over defined territory. This was the most common form found in the sample of 40 groups, 13 of which could be classified as fitting the broad profile of this typology. Illegal activities included gambling houses, prostitution, cigarette smuggling, and racketeering. All three groups from China fit this typology, while the other groups who fit the typology were from Eastern Europe—Russia, Bulgaria, Lithuania, and Ukraine.

The regional hierarchy had a single leadership structure and a line of command from the center, but a degree of autonomy at the regional level, a geographic/regional distribution, multiple activities, often strong social or ethnic ties, and violence as essential to activities. Regional hierarchies appear to operate a "franchise model" in which regional groups pay money and give allegiance to use the name of a well-known criminal group. Outlaw motorcycle gangs from Australia followed this model and are prominent in the production and distribution of amphetamines and cannabis. Japanese Yakuza groups in Australia and the Fuk Ching gang in the United States also followed this model.

The **clustered hierarchy** consists of a number of criminal groups with a governing or oversight body. The groups may have a diversity of structures, but generally they are of the standard hierarchy type. Each group has considerable autonomy, but the groups may come together to divide up markets or to regulate conflict between each other. Clustered hierarchies engage in multiple activities and have a relatively wide membership. In the United Nations research, only three groups corresponded to this model—one consisting of former prison inmates in South Africa, another in an Italian dominated network in Germany, and a third in Russia.

The **core groups** type of OC consists of a limited number of individuals who form a relatively tight and structured group to conduct criminal business. Around this "core group" may be a large number of associate members or a network that is used from time to time, depending on the criminal activity in question. There may be an internal division of activities among the core members. Core groups are generally quite small (20 individuals or less) and are more likely to engage in a single or limited number of criminal activities. Internal discipline is maintained through the small size of the group and the use of violence, though violence is not as prominent as in the standard hierarchy. Of the 40 groups on which data were collected, eight were identified as fitting this typology. They had no name and no distinct social or ethnic base. Two groups active in the Netherlands were mainly involved in the trafficking in human beings. Each member has a specific role in the trafficking process (e.g., recruitment, transport, protection, and marketing). Such groups are more horizontally structured than hierarchically ordered.

Finally, **criminal networks** are defined by the activities of key individuals who engage in illicit activity in often shifting alliances. Prominence in the network is determined by contacts and/or skills, and personal loyalties and/or ties are more important than social/ethnic identities. The network connections are maintained based upon a series of criminal projects. Criminal networks maintain a low public profile, and are seldom known by any name. The network reforms after the exit of key individuals. While criminal networks characterized only four of the 40 groups in the research, it is likely that criminal networks are increasingly more common and a growing phenomenon. This is because networks can be more easily reformed if key individuals are arrested than can hierarchical structures, where the loss of a key individual causes major disorganization. Two of the network groups were operating from the Netherlands, and the remaining two were from the Caribbean.

Although the United Nations study was broad in scope and provided five organizational types (as compared to only one in American Mafia studies), similar ethnographic research is needed, ideally focusing upon specific forms of transnational crime. As an example of this, Sheldon Zhang and associates studied Chinese alien smuggling into the United States through interviews with aliens, smugglers, and law enforcement officials in China, Hong Kong, and the United States. The study revealed that the groups emerging were non-Triad organized criminals that resemble the "criminal networks" model discussed earlier. The Chinese alien smuggling groups are best understood as "task forces," or small groups of people assembled to perform a particular piece of work. The task forces are typically linked to international social networks characterized by overlapping, dyadic relationships; a high level of role differentiation; and a limited degree of hierarchy. The groups are highly responsive to changing social, legal, and market constraints.[21]

GLOBAL VIEW OF ORGANIZED CRIME

By definition, OC is not a crime done by individuals, but by groups, whether they be clusters, core groups, networks, or hierarchies. Generally the term OC implies a "conspiracy," and that term is part of the list of attributes bulleted earlier. A possible exception to the conspiracy assumption is the *criminal networks* structure that develops around a host of individuals who have specialized skills sought in a particular enterprise. Criminal networks engage in criminal enterprises and share the proceeds of these enterprises, but without a common "boss" or planning group. What they share in common can be simply a common goal—financial gain through illicit enterprise.

Also, OC does not pertain to a particular crime, but to a wide variety of crimes. Because of the variety of group structures and types of crime, a profile of the "typical" individual who engages in OC cannot be drawn. Research is needed to begin to profile individuals who participate in particular types of syndicated crime. At this point all that can be done is to narrow down discussion to a particular key OC enterprise representative of OC. If one were to choose one particular enterprise of OC that is most representative of OC, and one upon which hard data are available for international comparisons, what would it be? Looking at all of the transnational OC enterprises, the one that qualifies as possibly most lucrative and upon which hard data are available is illicit drug trafficking. Among all of the illicit drugs that are involved in the drug trade, one drug stands out as most indicative of OC—heroin. Heroin is probably the most profitable drug to transport, and the demand for it is constant (probably always trending upward) because it is the most addicting of all drugs. Moreover, heroin seems to be the drug that is most involved with crime, especially if vigorous efforts are made by law enforcement to limit access to it. Heroin addicts must face withdrawal distress, which results in serious illness and possible death in the absence of the drug. Thus, when faced with limitation of their supply of the drug, heroin users will turn to crime, if need be, to obtain whatever funds are needed to feed their addiction. Thus, trade in heroin is "good business" in the sense that a customer base can be assumed.

Previously in this text, the variable kilograms of heroin seized by country was used only as a correlate of various crimes (robbery, burglary, etc.). However, in this chapter, the focus is changed to seeing how countries are ranked by kilograms of heroin seized. Kilograms of heroin seized is used as a proxy for OC, based upon the assumption that heroin trafficking is the most profitable OC enterprise.

In the absence of etiological data on organized criminals, we are back in the business of generating theory for that subject. With the exception of Howard Abadinsky's book, *Organized Crime*, up until now most of the discussion in the literature has pertained to "the nature of OC," as opposed to explaining it. So our task is to contribute to the theory development process started by Abadinsky by looking at countries that appear to be high in OC. What characterizes those countries? Although OC constitutes a vast array of crime, the focus is upon vice, a topic not yet covered in this text. Table 11–2 shows selected countries of the world in the comparative criminology database ranked by kilograms of heroin seized. Included were countries ranked in the top 25% in terms of kilograms of heroin seized in the country and all developed nations.[22]

Table 11–2, ranking countries in terms of heroin seized, is definitely an imperfect index of countries with high OC rates; however, it provides a starting point for research. In a study entitled International Crime Threat Assessment (ICTA), published in 2000, a thorough analysis of OC throughout the world is made.[23] In this study, it was pointed out that not all countries serve as a *home base* for OC. Some countries serve as *transit countries* for items and people shipped by OC, and some countries serve as *client countries*, without significant generation of OC groups other than those involved in receiving the illicit traffic. Many, if not most, countries that serve as *home base countries* for OC groups also serve as *client countries* (e.g., Japan). Of course, criminal organizations may work in all countries, but the critical question to be answered in this chapter is what countries serve as home base countries for criminal organizations, and why? The following countries may be considered *home base* countries for criminal organizations according to the ICTA report and other publications: China, Colombia, Hong Kong (now part of China), India, Italy, Japan, Mexico, Nigeria, Pakistan, Russia, Taiwan, Turkey, and the United States. What do all of these countries have in common? A brief history of the development OC in some of these countries would be insightful.

A quote from the ICTA report regarding Nigeria provides a clue:

Nigerian criminal syndicates centered in Lagos, many of which have global networks, operate with virtual impunity and in an environment of pervasive corruption. *Decades of mostly military rule in Nigeria have exacerbated the problem* [italics added for emphasis], ruining the Nigerian economy and nearly bankrupting the Nigerian government. Moreover, decades of gross economic mismanagement, with which the newly elected civilian government has just begun to grapple, have left not only private citizens but also government and law enforcement officials and junior and

Table 11-2 Countries Ranked for Kg of Heroin Seized

Country	Kg	Country	Kg
China	13200.000	Saudi Arabia	178.825
Pakistan	6931.470	Kyrgyzstan	170.898
Turkey	4392.100	Hong Kong	156.400
Tajikistan	4239.010	Hungary	154.410
Iran	4001.000	Taiwan	153.000
Great Britain	3382.390	Kazakstan	136.700
Italy	2004.590	Macedonia FYR	110.882
United States	1983.700	Singapore	106.678
Bulgaria	1550.630	Sri Lanka	102.216
Russia	1287.230	Myanmar	96.744
India	889.000	Slovenia	88.930
Germany	835.836	Czech Republic	88.590
Colombia	787.600	Panama	87.000
Netherlands	739.000	Argentina	84.683
Spain	630.600	Australia	82.729
Thailand	501.000	Canada	73.979
Uzbekistan	466.601	Norway	67.905
Fiji	357.700	Israel	67.625
France	351.055	Nigeria	46.639
Greece	329.725	Sweden	32.627
Portugal	316.039	Ireland (Northern)	29.527
Austria	288.312	Denmark	25.125
Mexico	263.152	Luxembourg	11.358
Ecuador	254.639	Finland	7.500
Venezuela	228.430	New Zealand	5.526
Switzerland	227.515	Japan	4.944
Malaysia	227.058	Monaco	0.011
Burkina Faso	222.000	Andorra	0.009
Poland	208.106	Liechtenstein	0.003
Belgium	187.739		

noncommissioned military officers with great incentive to engage in criminal activity to make ends meet. Under the recent military regime, many of Nigeria's political and military leaders, government bureaucrats, and business elites routinely accepted and demanded bribe or kickbacks in return for facilitating profitable business activity—whether in the lucrative oil sector, competitive procurement contracts, or the drug trade.[24]

The phrase "decades of mostly military rule in Nigeria have exacerbated the problem" is insightful in that it describes most of the countries listed as home base countries for OC. Certainly, under Communist regimes, China and Russia have had military rule. Hong Kong, India, and Pakistan were subject to British military rule prior to WWII. Mexico, up until recently, has had a one-party, largely military rule. Italy during WWII was under fascist military rule, and Sicily (home base for the Mafia) has been governed by numerous occupations and military rulers over the centuries. Japan, prior to WWII, was subject to military rule, and after WWII, subject to Allied military rule. One is reminded of the development of the black market that took place in the United States during both World Wars as a model of how OC may develop in various countries, related to imposed scarcity of desired goods and services:

> The **black market** is the sector of economic activity in a jurisdiction involving illegal activities. Depending on the sense in which the term is used, this can primarily refer to illegally avoiding tax payments, to the profits of narcotic trafficking, or profits made from theft. It is so called because "black economy," or black market affairs, are conducted outside the law and are necessarily conducted "in the dark," out of sight of the law. The Prohibition period in the United States is a classic example of black market activity, when OC groups took advantage of the lucrative opportunities in the resulting black market in banned alcohol production and sales. In many countries today, it is argued whether a "war on drugs" has created a similar effect for drugs such as marijuana. Black markets have also flourished in some countries during wars, especially WWII, when rationing and price controls were enforced in many countries.[25]

In the country profiles to follow, the format departs from that of previous chapters because of the subject matter—OC. Instead of looking for factors that might be related to a given crime, the emphasis is upon tracing the historical development of OC in different countries. A brief history of the country will be given, with the focus being on the development of OC groups in the country.

China

China is the oldest continuous major world civilization, with records dating back about 3,500 years. Successive dynasties developed a system of bureaucratic control, a Confucian state ideology and common written language that gave the agrarian-based Chinese an advantage over neighboring nomadic and hill cultures. The bureaucracy remained staffed with Chinese, even during periods of conquest, such as that of the Mongols in the 13th century. The last dynasty was that of the Qing (Ch'ing) that resulted from the 1644 overthrow of the Ming dynasty by the Manchu's, which expanded China to many border areas. The Qing dynasty declined during the 19th century, partly as a result of a Russian-supported separatist movement in Xinjiang and conflict with Great Britain. Britain, seeking to offset its balance of trade with China, fought two Opium Wars, which resulted when Britain's desire to continue its illegal opium trade with China collided with imperial edicts prohibiting the addictive drug. China lost the Opium Wars and was forced to cede Hong Kong to Britain in 1842 under the Treaty of Nanking and provided a 99-year lease of the New Territories in 1898, significantly expanding the size of the Hong Kong Colony.

Opposition to the Qing dynasty included some young officials, military officers, and students—inspired by the revolutionary ideas of Sun Yat-sen. The Qing dynasty was also opposed by the Triads, and, in fact, the Triad phenomenon is believed to have originated in opposition to the Qing dynasty. The term **Triads** refers to the Chinese societies' common symbol: an equilateral triangle representing the three basic Chinese concepts of heaven, earth, and man. Sun Yat-sen was a Triad member.[26] The Qing dynasty was overthrown and a republic was created in 1911 as a result of a compromise that allowed high Qing officials to retain prominent positions in the new republic. One of these figures, General Yuan Shikai, was chosen as the republic's first president. After his death in 1916, the republican government was all but shattered, ushering in an era of "warlords" during which China was ruled and ravaged by shifting coalitions of competing provincial military leaders. One of these factions formed the Kuomintang (KMT; "Chinese Nationalist People's Party") led by Sun Yat-sen, which entered into an alliance with the fledgling Chinese Communist Party (CCP) and sought to unite the fragmented nation. After Sun's death in 1925, one of his protégés, Chiang Kai-shek, seized control of the KMT and succeeded in bringing most of south and central China under its rule. Chiang had divided his time between exile in Japan and haven in Shanghai's foreign concession areas. In Shanghai, Chiang cultivated ties with the criminal underworld, dominated by the notorious Green Gang, who he reputedly recruited to fight the CCP in Shanghai. In 1927, Chiang waged war against the CCP and executed many of its leaders. The remnants of the CCP fled, ultimately developing a guerilla base at Yan'an in the northwestern province of Shaanxi. During their "Long March" to Shaanxi, the Communists reorganized under a new leader, Mao Zedong (Mao Tse-tung). Both the KMT and CCP continued a clandestine struggle during the Japanese invasion (1931–1945), though forming a united front to oppose the Japanese invaders. The war between the two parties resumed after the Japanese defeat in 1945.[27]

During the war, many Triad members turned to criminal activities: gambling, loan sharking, extortion, and trafficking in opium from the Golden Triangle of Southeast Asia.

Chiang Kai-shek (1887–1975) was the revolutionary Chinese leader who led the unification of China in the 1920s. He was head of the Nationalist Republic from 1928–1949. After losing China to the Communists in 1949, Chiang maintained the Republic by moving it to the island of Taiwan (Formosa).

Source: Getty Images, Inc.–Hulton Archive Photos.

This activity was strengthened considerably by the activities of Chinese Nationalist forces in the Golden Triangle (see text box) and Chiang Kai-shek was himself a Triad member, who was reputed to have used Triads in his war against the Communists and labor unions.[28] However, Communist forces defeated Chiang's Nationalist Army in 1947 and Triads were suppressed on the mainland with a great deal of violence by Mao Tse-tung. Many Triad members fled to Taiwan with Chiang Kai-shek and remnants of the KMT government, where Chiang proclaimed Taipei to be China's "provisional capital" and vowed to reconquer the Chinese mainland. Even today the KMT authorities on Taiwan still call themselves the "Republic of China." Other Triad members fled to the British colony of Hong Kong, which already had locally organized Triads that dated back to the early 20th century. In the postwar era, they emerged as powerful criminal societies.[29]

In Beijing, on October 1, 1949, Mao Zedong proclaimed the founding of the People's Republic of China. Mao made a strong effort to rid China of bureaucratic agencies and procedures, which he abhorred. His goal was to establish a criminal justice system in the People's Republic of China based upon informal social control. Based upon Maoist teachings, during the Chinese Cultural Revolution from 1966 to 1973, Mao called upon his followers, the Red Guards, to "smash the police and the courts." As a result of Mao's thinking and the action of the Red Guards, the People's Republic of China had no criminal or procedural legal codes, no lawyers, and no officially designated prosecutors until after 1978. While informal control was the goal, in actuality the police were replaced by military control, with arrest power residing in the People's Liberation Army.[30] Thus, the entire period of Communist government in China has been characterized by military control. However, the Cultural Revolution did not occur in a vacuum. It was in part a reaction to advocacy for pragmatic economic policies by Party General Secretary Deng Xiaoping in the early 1960s. During the Cultural Revolution, Deng was accused of dragging

Chairman Mao Zedong (1893–1976) wears a Red Guard armband as he waves to the crowd during a Peking rally in 1966. Following the Communist Party's military victory over the KMT in 1949, Mao led the Communist Party rule of China until his death in 1976.

Source: CORBIS/Bettmann.

BOX 11–1

Golden Triangle and Golden Crescent

The **Golden Triangle** is one of Asia's two primary illicit opium-producing areas. It overlaps the mountains of three countries of mainland Southeast Asia, including Burma (Myanmar), Laos, and Thailand. The term **Golden Crescent** refers to Afghanistan, Iran, and Pakistan.[31]

China back toward capitalism. Ultimately the rift within the party resulted in protests, including the 1989 civil disobedience that took place at Tiananmen Square by students, intellectuals, and other parts of a disaffected urban population. Although the protest at Tiananmen Square was repressed and resulted in martial law and casualties estimated in the hundreds, economic reform continued, culminating in Deng's dramatic visit to southern China in early 1992. His push for a market-oriented economy received official sanction at the 14th Party Congress later that year. A number of reform-minded leaders rose to top positions, and the Politburo publicly issued an endorsement of Deng's policies of economic openness. Since then, leadership has followed in the footsteps of Deng. China is now firmly committed to economic reform and opening to the outside world. The Chinese leadership has identified reform of state industries and the establishment of a social safety network as government priorities. Government strategies to achieve these goals include large-scale privatization of unprofitable state-owned enterprises and development of a pension system for workers.

Reform policies brought great improvements in the standard of living. However, political dissent, as well as social problems such as inflation, urban migration, and prostitution emerged. According to some estimates by experts, there are 4 to 10 million commercial sex workers in the country, along with a female suicide rate that is the highest in the world. While trafficking in persons was previously a domain controlled by Triad groups in Hong Kong, it is now becoming a major enterprise of mainland China syndicates. In August 1998, Chinese Premier Zhu Rongji announced that rampant smuggling was occurring at unprecedented levels in terms of its scope and quantity of products. He blamed smuggling for corrupting government officials, poisoning social morals, and a surge in other crimes. China's high tariffs and taxes, as well as nontariff barriers to trade, make smuggling of foreign-produced automobiles, cigarettes, petroleum products, and other goods extremely lucrative for criminal groups and corrupt officials.[32]

Among the items smuggled into China, heroin may be the most problematic. Before 1990, when most Southeast Asian heroin transited through Thailand, China had few problems with drug trafficking or addiction. Between 1990 and 1998, however, the number of registered drug addicts in China increased by a factor of 10 from some 70,000 to nearly 700,000.[33] Thus, mainland China has become a "client country" for OC groups, including Hong Kong's 14K Triad. China has also become a home base country for mainland criminal groups that are now heavily involved in smuggling. Mainland Chinese groups exploiting widespread corruption have established strong ties of their own to Chinese officials and entrepreneurs. In Fujian Province, Chinese alien smuggling networks operate with the assistance of corrupt officials, local police, and customs officers. Through these activities and the establishment of international networks, mainland Chinese criminal syndicates may be eclipsing the once-dominant role played by Triad members from Hong Kong and Macao. (It should be added that the latter two countries are now part of China, and no longer sovereign nations.) Although the Triad groups in Taiwan and Hong Kong focus on more traditional extortion, gambling, drug trafficking, gunrunning, and alien smuggling enterprises, the upstart Chinese criminal groups from mainland China, on the other hand, are more loosely organized, their members more flamboyant, and their criminal operations often more sophisticated. These groups are also extensively involved in international drug trafficking, alien smuggling, arms trafficking, and money laundering. They have moved more aggressively than the Triads into the more sophisticated and highly profitable areas of credit card fraud, theft of computer chips, software piracy, and other intellectual property violations.[34]

Hong Kong

Hong Kong has human activity dating back over five millennia, including northern Chinese stone-age cultures. The first major migration from northern China to Hong Kong occurred during the Sung Dynasty (960–1279). The British East India Company made the first successful sea venture to China in 1699, and Hong Kong's trade with British merchants developed rapidly soon after. After the Chinese defeat in the First Opium War (1839–1842), Hong Kong was ceded to Britain in 1842 under the Treaty of Nanking. Britain was granted a perpetual lease on the Kowloon Peninsula under the 1860 Convention of Beijing, which formally ended hostilities in the Second Opium War (1856–1860). The United Kingdom executed a 99-year lease of the New Territories in 1898, significantly expanding the size of the Hong Kong colony. Hong Kong reverted from British to Chinese sovereignty on July 1, 1997 (the handover).

In the late 19th and early 20th centuries, Hong Kong became a warehousing and distribution center for UK trade with southern China. After the end of WWII and the Communist takeover of Mainland China in 1949, hundreds of thousands of people fled from China to Hong Kong, including Triad OC members. Hong Kong became an economic success and a manufacturing, commercial, finance, and tourism center. Along with that success came crime. Hong Kong has long been a hub of criminal activity in East Asia—a status that has not changed since China assumed sovereignty over the territory in 1997. The massive volume of trade in containerized shipping through Hong Kong (16 million containers annually) offers substantial opportunity for criminals to smuggle all kinds of contraband, including drugs, arms, and illegal migrants. Hong Kong is one of East Asia's major sanctuaries for heroin drug profits. Heroin traffickers launder proceeds through numerous businesses in Hong Kong that are associated with the Chinese Triads.

Hong Kong's ethnic Chinese OC groups, the Triads, control local criminal activity. As they did during British colonial rule, Triad members continue to infiltrate and cultivate contacts in Hong Kong's civil service, political parties, news media, and stock exchange to protect or further their interests. While they do not monopolize international smuggling and illicit financial transactions, Triad members frequently help broker deals and facilitate shipments of drugs, arms, and other illicit contraband through Hong Kong to overseas destinations.

Hong Kong's two largest Triads are the 14K and the Sun Yee On. Hong Kong police estimate there are 50 to 60 different Triad societies operating in Hong Kong. Currently, Hong Kong's largest Triad, Sun Yee On, is the only one with a true hierarchical structure. By contrast, the 14K Triad, still one of the most powerful, is comprised of more than 15 loosely affiliated groups. In addition to facilitating smuggling, they protect many of the retail businesses involved in the manufacturing and distributing of counterfeit compact discs and are engaged in buying, moving, and selling contraband CDs. Moreover, Hong Kong's lucrative film industry is widely regarded as controlled by the Triads.

Although mainland China's law enforcement system is in a stage of redevelopment (after being entirely destroyed by the Red Guards during the Cultural Revolution), Hong Kong has a much stricter law enforcement environment. It includes an entrenched common law system, a strong rule of law tradition, and well-organized and well-equipped law enforcement bodies. Thus, it is less likely that mainland criminal interests will take a great interest in expanding their operations into Hong Kong as compared to the opposition situation—Hong Kong Triads doing illicit business operations in mainland China.[35]

Taiwan

Taiwan was populated by aboriginal peoples who originated in Austronesia and southern China some 12,000 to 15,000 years ago, while significant migration to Taiwan from the Chinese mainland began as early as 500 A.D. The Dutch first claimed the island in 1624 and administered it until 1661. In 1664, a Chinese fleet led by the Ming loyalist Zheng Chenggong, fleeing from the Manchu invasion at the end of the Ming Dynasty, expelled the Dutch and established Taiwan as a base in his attempt to restore the Ming Dynasty. He died shortly thereafter, and his successors submitted to the Manchu's (Qing dynasty). During the 18th and 19th centuries, migration from Fujian and Guangdong provinces steadily increased, and Chinese supplanted aborigines as the dominant population group. In 1895, Taiwan was ceded to Japan after the first Sino-Japanese war. From 1895 to 1945, Japan developed Taiwan's economy and attempted to "Japanize" the nation, requiring compulsory Japanese education and forcing residents of Taiwan to adopt Japanese names.

At the end of WWII in 1945, Taiwan reverted to Chinese rule. As a result of the Communist takeover of mainland China, two million refugees, predominantly from the nationalist government, military, and business community, fled to Taiwan. Chaing Kai-shek established a "provisional" KMT capital in Taipei. During the immediate postwar period, the Nationalist Chinese (KMT) administration on Taiwan was repressive and corrupt, leading to local discontent. Island-wide rioting was brutally put down by Nationalist Chinese troops, who killed thousands of people.

Nevertheless, the KMT authorities implemented a far reaching and highly successful land reform program on Taiwan that facilitated Taiwan's transition from an agricultural to a commercial, industrial economy. Tremendous prosperity on the island was accompanied by economic and social stability. Along with that business success, OC also thrived, deeply entrenched in Taiwan's business and political sectors. Chiang Kai-shek himself was a Triad member. Accordingly, large ethnic Chinese criminal syndicates such as the

United Bamboo and Four Seas Triads—which followed the ruling KMT party from the mainland to Taiwan in the late 1940s—and Taiwanese criminal gangs have established strong influence in Taiwan's local communities. These groups feed off Taiwan's generally strong economy. They reportedly have been involved in direct extortion of "protection" money from construction firms, engage in bid-rigging for public works projects, and have tried to manipulate the island's stock market. Some Taiwan-based Triads have links to Hong Kong and China, including establishing front companies or investing in specific criminal ventures.[36]

Both the Triads and crime groups originating in mainland China have established relationships with ethnic Chinese crime groups in countries throughout the Pacific Rim, Europe, and the Western Hemisphere. Using traditional Chinese practices of networking, ethnic Chinese crime groups rely on a broad criminal fraternity that can broker contacts in any country where there is a large ethic Chinese community and help facilitate transnational criminal activity. Chinese OC has strong roots in Chinese ethnic enclaves around the world. Local Chinese crime groups—ranging from street gangs to more formally structured groups modeled after, or affiliated with, traditional Triads—typically are extensively involved in local rackets like gambling, loan sharking, narcotics distribution, prostitution, and business extortion.

Ethnic Chinese Global Networks

Although they are closed and secretive to outsiders, Chinese criminal organizations generally have few qualms about cooperating with other ethnic criminal groups in profitable joint ventures. For example, in the United States, Canada, and Europe, Chinese OC groups have worked with Italian and Dominican criminal organizations in trafficking heroin.

Europe and North America are major targets for Chinese criminal networks. Although ethnic Chinese groups are not as powerful as Italian or Russian OC in Europe, they have long-established footholds in the Chinese communities of several European nations from which they appear to conduct most of their illegal operations. International Chinese OC groups are particularly strong in the Netherlands, the United Kingdom, and Germany. Since the late 1980s, Chinese criminal organizations have also established themselves in Central Europe, which has become a major conduit for moving illegal Chinese immigrants to Western Europe.[37] U.S. and Canadian law enforcement reporting indicates that the Big Circle Gang, which is the dominant OC group in China, has in a short time become one of the most active Asian criminal organizations in the world. By the early 1990s, the Big Circle Gang had established criminal cells in Canada, the United States, and Europe. It is extensively involved in drug trafficking; alien smuggling; vehicle theft and trafficking; and various financial, intellectual property rights, and high-tech crimes. Big Circle Gang cells are also highly sophisticated in their use of technology to thwart law enforcement investigations, according to U.S. law enforcement. Since first appearing in the United States in the early 1990s, Big Circle Gang members have been detected in New York, Boston, Seattle, San Francisco, and Los Angeles. The Fuk Ching Gang is most notorious for alien smuggling, including the Golden Venture tragedy in New York in 1993.[38]

BOX 11–2

The Golden Venture Incident

The Golden Venture tragedy occurred in 1993 and was an incident in which some 300 Asian illegal aliens were left stranded on a freighter, the Golden Venture, that eventually became grounded on a sand bar in New York. The passengers were ordered by the crew to jump overboard, resulting in the death of many who either drowned or were killed by the propeller of the ship. The Golden Venture was awaiting orders from a **snakehead** (illegal alien smuggler) of the Fuk Ching Gang. Two factions of the gang were fighting for leadership (and the $3 million value of the human cargo in the ship). Gang warfare ensued, resulting in the death of one faction and jailing of the other faction. As a result, no snakehead was available to provide berthing orders or arrangements to the ship.[39]

Chinese Organized Crime in the United States

Just as in China, Hong Kong, and Taiwan, Chinese OC has a fairly long history within the United States. Chinese immigrants were welcomed to the United States during the mid-19th century to provide cheap labor, particularly in the West during the Gold Rush and in the construction of the first continental railroad. As the numbers of Chinese immigrants increased, anti-Chinese sentiment increased. This occurred particularly in California, where most Chinese had settled. Xenophobic vigilante activity and riots occurred in San Francisco. The result of this anti-Chinese sentiment was the passage of Chinese exclusion legislation, both in California and by the U.S. Congress. The result was the exclusion of all Asians starting in the late 19th century, and the imposition of a quota of 105 Asian immigrants per year in the 1920s. Given the ban on all legal immigration, illegal immigration became the only option for the Chinese, and this was facilitated by the development of large "Chinatown" ethnic ghettos in San Francisco, New York, and other cities. Then and now, illegal immigrants could "disappear" into these enclaves without detection by the police, who lacked familiarity or access to the Chinese population in these settlements. It wasn't until after WWII that immigration laws provided increased quotas for Asians. As pointed out previously, after the 1967 President's Commission characterized the "Oriental Enclaves" as relatively crime-free areas, Asians were stereotyped as hard working, intelligent, and low in crime—the latter of which was soon to be challenged by the arrival of Southeast Asian refugees who formed the nexus of a new Asian crime wave.

Along with the highly productive workforce of Chinese in the 19th century came the simultaneous admission of Triad members from China. In the United States, they were called **Tongs**, a term that means "hall" or "gathering place." Some of the Chinese immigrants were Triad members at home and in the United States engaged in organized criminal activities, including opium trafficking, prostitution, gambling, and extortion. While most Tongs were business, fraternal, or political in character, among the Tongs was a group of "fighting Tongs" who controlled large-scale vice operations and were part of a tight-knit nationwide alliance. Around the turn of the 20th century, Tong wars occurred on the East and West Coasts, one of which in 1909 was between the On Leong and Sip Sing Tongs and claimed an estimated 350 lives. After the passage of the anti-immigration legislation, the influx of Chinese population diminished and the "Tong wars" ceased. However, the Tongs continued to be associated with illegal gambling, particularly Pai Gow, an ancient Chinese domino game.

Contemporary Tongs such as Hip Sing and the On Leong dropped the term Tong from their names because of its association with "Tong wars."[40] Many contemporary Tongs, including the Hip Sing, On Leong, and Tsung Tsin, and the Ghost Shadows and Flying Dragons in New York, Chicago, Boston, and San Francisco, date back to 1965, the year new immigration laws facilitated a large influx of youths from Hong Kong. The result was an increase in violent street crime (robbery, kidnapping, extortion, prostitution, and loan-sharking). In addition, the new gangs were sometimes used by the Tongs to provide security for gambling operations. A 1995 federal indictment indicated that New York's Chinatown was divided into fiefdoms dominated by Tongs aided by their affiliated gangs—the Tsung Tsin Tong and Tung On Tong with the Tung On Boys; the On Leong Tong with the Ghost Shadows; and the Hip Sing Tong with the Flying Dragons. The younger gangs collected protection money from both legal and illegal Chinatown businesses, including 24-hour-a-day gambling dens.[41]

Vietnamese youth gangs, particularly Chinese Vietnamese (Viet Ching, ethnic Chinese born in Vietnam) have also gained a foothold in Chinese ethnic communities and an affiliation with the Tongs. Vietnamese gang members are favored by Tong groups. This is because Vietnamese gangs are reputed to be skilled with and in possession of firearms. One such gang was developed by a member of New York Chinatown's Flying Dragons named David Thai, who was born in Saigon in 1956 and immigrated to the United States in 1976. In 1989, Thai developed a confederation of Vietnamese gangs in New York City named Born to Kill (BTK). The BTK was involved in unrestrained victimization of massage parlors, bars, and Tong gambling dens. The BTK subsequently killed Flying Dragons and Ghost Shadows gang members and committed a string of armed robberies in New England, the South, Canada, and wherever Asian businesses could be victimized. An arrest resulting from a Georgia robbery led to an extensive interagency investigation and successful prosecutions of the gang's leadership. However, not all Vietnamese youth gangs were affiliated with Tongs. Vietnamese gangs in California were highly mobile and constantly changing their gang unit affiliation, a lesson learned from the Vietcong. They engaged in home invasion robberies, usually of Vietnamese families, as well as the armed robbery of computer chips. The computer chips, in turn, were smuggled back to the Far East, eventually to wind up back in computers lawfully imported into the United States.[42]

Japan

Control by the military seems to characterize Japanese history before, during, and after WWII. Of course, after WWII Japan was placed under international control of the Allies through the Supreme Commander, General Douglas MacArthur, of the United States. Prior to the forced opening of the isolationist Japan to the West by Commodore Matthew Perry of the U.S. Navy in 1854, Japan was ruled by shogun warlords. At the top was the shogun himself. Beneath him were the *daimyo*, the local lords who controlled large amounts of land. The *daimyo* had their own collection of samurai, who were the warrior class. The *boryokudan* (violent groups) date back 300 years to the Tokugawa period, when Japan united under a central system of government. With the end of Japanese feudalism, samurai lost their role in life, and many became *ronin*, or masterless samurai, many of whom wandered the countryside as freelance mercenaries. The **Yakuza** were those ronin who became unscrupulous itinerant

BOX 11–3

Yakuza and the Crime Rate

It has been pointed out in previous chapters that Japan has a low crime rate in regard to the FBI Index crimes. However, this discussion of the Yakuza's role in controlling crime suggests that the police have a partner in controlling crime in Japan—the Yakuza. As Abadinsky stated, "The relatively low rate of street crime in Japan is in large part the result of a symbiotic relationship between the Yakuza and the police. The police share the political views of the Yakuza (conservative) and do little against them—police raids are often publicity stunts. The Yakuza reciprocate by keeping "disorganized crime" under control."[43] In addition, the respect generally given for the activities of the Yakuza, including many areas of vice (narcotics, prostitution, gambling, etc.) normally subject to police intervention in Western countries, promotes a "look the other way" approach on the part of the police for these activities. Thus, the relationship between vices, such as drug consumption, and crime may be broken, because illegal commodities can be obtained from the Yakuza routinely at a price not requiring additional criminal activity.

peddlers, professional gamblers, and common criminals, eventually forming structured groups. The term Yakuza is actually derived from an old card game whose object is to draw three cards adding up as close as possible to without exceeding the number 19. "Ya-ku-za" represents the Japanese words for 8, 9, 3, which totals 20, a useless number; hence, Yakuza means "good for nothing."[44]

After 1854, the shogun (military governor of Japan) was forced to resign, and the emperor was restored to power. However, this restoration did not dampen the country's inclination toward war. Japanese leaders of the late 19th century regarded the Korean Peninsula as a "dagger pointed at the heart of Japan." After the Sino-Japanese war with China (1894–1895) and war with Russia in 1904–1905, Japan was ceded the Pescadores Island, Formosa (now Taiwan), and Korea, which it formally annexed in 1910.

Subsequently, Japan adopted a Western legal system and constitutional government along quasiparliamentary lines. Japan became a member of the League of Nations and fought with the Allies (Britain, France, Russia, and the United States) in World War I, and obtained new Pacific island territories as spoils of that war. However, economic and political pressures of the 1930s led to an increasing influence of military leaders. Japan invaded Manchuria in 1931 and set up a puppet state that was called Manchukuo. In 1933, Japan resigned from the League of Nations. Japan signed an "anti-Comintern pact" with Nazi Germany in 1936 and invaded China in 1937, and then attacked the United States at Pearl Harbor, Hawaii, on December 7, 1941. As a result of WWII, Japan was occupied by the Allied military and lost its overseas possessions, including Manchuria, Formosa, Korea, and other territories. After military occupation for seven years, Japan was granted full sovereignty by the U.S. Senate in 1952.

This historical background provided the backdrop for the development of an OC network called the Yakuza, which in Japan provides illegal goods and services not available through legitimate means. The Yakuza has not been of great concern to U.S. law enforcement. This is probably because the Yakuza engages in illicit trade predominantly to and with its home country, Japan, which itself is a very prosperous nation. In terms of Table 11–2, Japan is in the middle of countries with regard to heroin seizures, probably because the illegal drug of choice in Japan overwhelmingly is methamphetamine.

The Yakuza have gained a wide measure of public acceptance in Japan as a result of their traditional roles in arbitrating disputes and loan collection. The Yakuza practice of "sokaiya," corporate extortion, often by threatening to disrupt corporate shareholder's meetings, has been tolerated by Japanese society and has given the Yakuza considerable economic influence. The Yakuza have often been in a better position than the government to respond to civic emergencies, such as bringing relief aid to victims of the 1996 earthquake in Kobe. The Yakuza have been careful to avoid violence against the police and innocent civilians, and they have been able to operate largely in the open, including highlighting the location of their headquarters in local communities.

Although they have engaged in illegal activities in the arenas of drugs, gambling, and corporate extortion, they also engaged in the fraudulent real estate loans during the real estate boom of the 1980s, accounting for 10% to 39% of the banking industry's bad loans.

There are an estimated 3,000 Yakuza groups and subgroups based in Japan, and 60% of the estimated 90,000 members and associates of Yakuza families are affiliated with one of three groups: the Yamaguchi-Gumi, Sumiyoshi-Kai, and Inagawa-Kai. These groups control most criminal activity in Japan, including gun trafficking, drug smuggling, alien smuggling, prostitution, illegal gambling, extortion, and white-collar crime through infiltration of legitimate business. Yakuza groups have used their international networks in Asia, Australia, and the Western Hemisphere primarily to acquire narcotics, guns, or illegal immigrants—particularly women for prostitution—for the Japanese market. Yakuza groups acquire most of their heroin and methamphetamine from Chinese criminal groups in Taiwan and Hong Kong and many have established relationships with South American trafficking organizations for obtaining cocaine. A large share of the methamphetamine consumed in Japan comes from North Korea. China, Taiwan, and Russia are major sources of firearms for the Yakuza. Because of Japan's strict gun control laws, Japanese police officials have estimated that 90% of the illegal weapons seized each year come from overseas. The Yakuza also rely on their international connections for illegal aliens to work in the prostitution, entertainment, and construction enterprises they control in Japan.

Perhaps because the Japanese market for Yakuza trade is so affluent, there hasn't been much evidence of Yakuza trafficking of persons or contraband in the United States. The major threat has been that posed by the investment of Japanese OC groups in legitimate businesses in the United States and Canada. The Yakuza reportedly have invested heavily in U.S. and Canadian real estate, ranging from golf courses to hotels. By playing the stock market, Yakuza groups have also laundered criminal proceeds through U.S. financial institutions, according to U.S. law enforcement.[45]

The United States (Country Profile)

One form of OC has a uniquely American derivation—the **outlaw motorcycle gang**. In a recent video entitled "Methamphetamine: From the Streets of San Diego," the role of "crystal" in that war was documented, and the consequences after the war were discussed. During WWII, methamphetamine was used extensively—by the German troops, by Hitler himself, by Japanese pilots, as well as by American pilots flying long range bombing missions. After the war, San Diego, which was a major navy base, became the location for the development of the methamphetamine trade by biker gangs who had been pilots during WWII. The term *Hell's Angels*, now used by a major biker group, was used during WWII by members of the U.S. Army's 11th Airborne Division, an elite group of paratroopers trained to rain death on the enemy from above. The biker gangs developed the illicit trade in methamphetamine through Asian connections developed during the war and made San Diego "the methamphetamine capital of the world" during the 1980s. After a drug sting operation by law enforcement termed Operation Triple Neck that took place in the East County of San Diego, Mexican cartels took over the methamphetamine production, according to the video.[46]

As mentioned earlier, OC seems to emerge most prevalently in countries with a history of military rule. In this regard, or at least in regard to military conflict, the United States stands out as a country with a considerable history of military conflict. If trafficking in persons can be considered a major form of OC, the United States with its wholesale trafficking in African slaves can be considered to be founded in OC. Participation in military conflict has seemingly been a considerable part of the country's history. As a colony militarily occupied by Great Britain, America's occupation culminated in events such as the Boston Massacre of 1770. The colonists fought and won a war of independence against the British that ended in 1783. A weak federal government was formed under the Articles of Confederation, which eventually was supplanted by the Constitution of the United States, written largely by officers of the Continental Army and officials of the Confederation government with wartime experience. American history has been punctuated by wars at approximate 20-year intervals. Participation in the military is considered by some Americans to be a "rite of passage" from boyhood to manhood.

After the Revolutionary War, war was again waged with Britain in the War of 1812. Under the doctrine of "manifest destiny," war was waged with Mexico in 1846, culminating in the Treaty of Guadalupe Hidalgo of 1848. This treaty ceded numerous southwest and western states to the United States, including Texas, New Mexico, Arizona, California, Nevada, Utah, most of Colorado, and part of Wyoming. Then, from 1861–1865, after seven southern states seceded from the union, the Civil War was fought, resulting in a victory for the north. In 1898, the United States engaged in the Spanish-American war in Cuba, which resulted in the Spanish ceding the Philippines, Puerto Rico, and Guam to the United States, as well as surrendering all claims to Cuba. In 1917, America entered World War I and fought on the side of the Allies, and then returned to war in World War II in 1941, after the Japanese bombing of Pearl Harbor.

During the 20th century, the pace of wartime involvement increased. From 1950 to 1953, America fought the Korean War, followed by an unsuccessful war campaign in Vietnam from 1964 to 1975. The next formal war was the Persian Gulf War in 1991, followed by the war in Afghanistan in 2001 and in Iraq in 2002. Besides these recent war efforts, there were several clandestine operations, starting with the Kennedy Administration, which launched the failed Bay of Pigs invasion of Cuba in 1961. During the Vietnam War, a secret war was conducted in Cambodia during the Nixon administration. During the Reagan Administration, another secret war, termed the Iran-Contra Affair, was fought against the Sandanista government in Nicaragua. All of these covert operations were said to have been launched against Communist governments or insurgents. There were allegations of involvement of OC in connection with these covert operations, such as allegations that "Air America" pilots were flying opium out of Laos as a means of providing funding for the secret war in Cambodia. Former Air America pilots were also alleged to have flown Colombian cocaine into the United States as a means of funding the Iran-Contra offensive.

Clearly, the United States may be characterized as a "military industrial complex" and war is a recurring and current part of American life. A wide variety of video games distributed in America provide training in the use of firearms, and a large share of toys developed for boys focus upon war and combat. If there is a correlation between military control and OC on a cross-cultural basis, then the United States should have more than its share of organized criminal groups. An attempt was made to list organized criminal groups by country, and the results are shown in Table 11–3. This list was compiled primarily from the various sources that have been quoted previously.[47]

One can make the case that many of these OC groups have developed in conjunction with American military involvement. For instance, the early Chinese groups that developed in San Francisco began to emerge after the acquisition of California that resulted from the war with Mexico. Vietnamese and Cambodian gangs may have been the product of the massive immigration (to the United States) of Southeast Asian refugees after the Vietnam War. Jamaican gangs such as the "Shower Posse" may have been the product of covert operations by the CIA in Jamaica during the 1970s. However, the most obvious case for the military connection with OC is made with the biker gangs. Although a large number of the gangs listed in Table 11–3 are the product of countries outside the United States, the biker gangs are home grown. At the same time, they have spread to countries around the world. The most notorious U.S. crime groups operating overseas are outlaw elements of motorcycle gangs, according to U.S. law enforcement agencies. Some of the approximately 900 motorcycle gangs that have been identified as having outlaw elements by U.S. law enforcement have worldwide chapters and are expanding into other countries at a significant rate. Law enforcement authorities in countries where motorcycle gangs have established themselves indicate that the motorcycle gangs are extensively involved in OC and have particularly bad reputations for violence, property crimes, prostitution and extortion rackets, and trafficking in drugs and firearms.[48]

According to Abadinsky, these clubs date from the years after WWII, when veterans of combat, especially those residing in California, sought new outlets for feelings of hostility and alienation. Motorcycle clubs like the "Booze Fighters" and "Market Street Commandos" became a symbol of freedom from social responsibilities. These clubs also offered quasi-military comradery among the members. One group of veterans calling themselves the POBOBs, an acronym for "Pissed Off Bastards of Bloomington," a small southern California town between San Bernardino and Riverside, organized a nameless group in San Bernardino in 1947. In Fontana, in 1948, these dedicated outlaws adopted the name used by WWII fighter pilots—Hell's Angels. The club moved to Oakland in 1957, led by Hubert ("Sonny") Barger, Jr., a high school dropout who had obtained army basic training, but had been discharged for being too young. In 1967, Barger appeared in a film, *Hell's Angels on Wheels*, with Jack Nicholson, which helped to add to the mystique of the outlaw motorcycle club. The Hell's Angels and outlaw clubs that have copied them (the Outlaws, Banditos, and Pagans) exhibit a bureaucratic structure similar to that of the military, consistent with their founders' background as military veterans.[49]

Table 11–3 Organized Crime Groups Listed by Country

Country	Group	Country	Group
Australia	The McClean Syndicate	Holland	Verhagen Group
Bulgaria	VIS-2	Russia	Mafiya
Canada	Hell's Angels	Russia	Sizranskaya Groopirovka
China (mainland)	Big Circle Gang	Russia	Ziberman Group
China (mainland)	Fuk Ching Gang	South Africa	The 28s Prison Gang
China (mainland)	Liang Xiao Min Syndicate	Taiwan	Four Seas Triads
China (mainland)	Liu Yong Syndicate	Taiwan	United Bamboo
China (mainland)	Zhang Wei Syndicate	Thailand	Teng Boonma Group
Colombia	Cali Cartel	Ukraine	Sovlokhov Group
Colombia	Juvenal Group	U.S.	Bandidos (motorcycle club)
Colombia	Medillin Cartel	U.S.	Born to Kill (BTK) (Vietnamese)
Colombia	Ochoa Family	U.S.	Canal Boys (Vietnamese)
Hong Kong	14 K Triad	U.S.	El Rukns/Black P. Stone Nation
Hong Kong	Sun Yee On	U.S.	Flying Dragons (NY Chinese gang)
Italy	Calabrian 'Ndrangheta	U.S.	Fuk Ching Gang
Italy	La Cosa Nostra	U.S.	Gangster Disciples
Italy	Licciardi Clan	U.S.	Ghost Shadows (NY Chinese gang)
Italy	Neapolitan Camorra	U.S.	Green Dragons (Chinese)
Italy	Puglian Sacra Corona Unita	U.S.	Gulleymen
Italy	Sicilian Mafia	U.S.	Hell's Angels
Italy	Clan Paviglianiti	U.S.	Hip Sing (Chinese Tong gang)
Jamaica	Posses	U.S.	Hip Sing Tong
Japan	Inagawa-Kai	U.S.	Junior Black Mafia
Japan	Sumiyoshi-Kai	U.S.	LCN
Japan	Yamaguchi-Gumi	U.S.	On Leong (Chinese Tong gang)
Lithuania	Cock Group	U.S.	Outlaws (motorcycle club)
Macau	Stanley Ho Group	U.S.	Pagans (motorcycle club)
Mexico	Amezcua Contreras Organization	U.S.	Russian Mafiya
Mexico	Herrera Family	U.S.	Shower Posse
Mexico	Arellano-Felix	U.S.	The "Westies" of Hell's Kitchen
Mexico	Carillo Fuentes Organization	U.S.	The Bloods
Mexico	Caro-Quintero Organization	U.S.	The Crips
Mexico	Gulf Cartel	U.S.	Tsung Tsin (Chinese Tong gang)
Mexico	Juarez Cartel	U.S.	Tsung Tsin Association
Mexico	Mocha Orejas Organization	U.S.	Tung On Boys
Mexico	Omar Rocha-Soto Organization	U.S.	Tung On Gang (Chinese)
Mexico	Tijuana Cartel	U.S.	Vice Lords
		U.S.	Zips

While it may seem more usual to characterize the United States as a target for international criminals providing illicit goods and services, the United States also serves as a source country not only of outlaw motorcycle clubs, but also of goods and services banned or heavily taxed in foreign countries. The

United States is one of the world's leading sources of contraband luxury goods, firearms, tobacco products, and alcohol smuggled and sold overseas. Both U.S. and foreign crime groups operating in the United States are involved in stealing cars and other high-priced items and illegally shipping them out of the country. The United States is a primary source for criminal groups involved in the international smuggling of firearms because there are fewer restrictions on the manufacture and sale of firearms than in most other countries. The tremendous volume of goods entering and leaving the United States in legitimate trade provides criminal groups with unparalleled opportunities to smuggle contraband through U.S. ports to overseas destinations. Although the United States is the world's leading importer of illicit drugs, it is also a major source of illegal drugs—some of which are smuggled overseas. The United States is one of the world's leading producers of marijuana, crack cocaine, and methamphetamine.[50]

As mentioned previously, methamphetamine production has increased in Mexico. One reason for this is that many of the precursor chemicals required for production of methamphetamine, as well as cocaine and heroin, can be easily purchased from U.S. sources.[51]

The close relationship between the United States and Mexico suggests that a study of Mexico may be important for a fuller understanding of OC in the United States. Although Colombian drug cartels are discussed in Chapter 6, it is important to do some careful analysis of America's next-door neighbor.

Mexico

Mexico clearly exemplifies a country with a history of military rule.[52] Prior to its occupation by the Spanish, Mexico had a history of highly developed cultures, including those of the Olmecs, Mayas, Toltecs, and Aztecs. Hernando Cortez conquered Mexico during the period 1519 to 1521 and founded a Spanish colony that lasted nearly 300 years. Independence from Spain was proclaimed by Father Miguel Hidalgo on September 16, 1810; this launched a war for independence. An 1821 treaty recognized Mexican independence from Spain and called for a constitutional monarchy. The planned monarchy failed; a republic was proclaimed in December, 1822, and established in 1824. During the interim, General Augustin de Iturbide, who defeated the Spaniards, ruled as Mexican emperor from 1822 to 1823. General Antonio Lopez de Santa Ana controlled Mexican politics from 1833 to 1855. Santa Ana was Mexico's leader during the conflict with Texas, which declared itself independent from Mexico in 1836, and during the Mexican American War (1846–1848). The presidential terms of Benito Juarez (1858–1871) were interrupted by the Hapsburg monarchy's rule of Mexico (1864–1867). Archduke Maximilian of Austria, whom Napoleon III of France established as Emperor of Mexico, was deposed by Juarez and executed in 1867. General Porfirio Diaz was president during most of the period between 1877 and 1911. The Mexican revolution occurred from 1910 to 1920, giving rise to the 1917 constitution and the emergence of popular leaders such as Poncho Villa and Emiliano Zapata. The Institutional Revolutionary Party (PRI), was formed in 1929 as a vehicle for keeping political competition in peaceful channels. The PRI controlled Mexico's national government for 71 years afterwards, until the election of Vincente Fox Quesada of the National Action Party in July 2000.

The military has served actively in policing the country and has had to play an active role in dealing with the insurgents in the state of Chiapas, who in 1994 took up arms against the government. They were protesting alleged oppression and governmental indifference to poverty. The insurgents, termed the Zapatista National Liberation Army, have received peace accords from the Fox government.

Not mentioned earlier in the various military conflicts in Mexico was a civil war that was fought between 1857 and 1860 regarding Catholicism. The Roman Catholic Church's role in Mexican history goes back to 1519. When Cortez landed on the coast of Mexico, he was accompanied by Roman Catholic clergy, and the new Spanish territories were to be conquered in the name of the cross as well as the crown. Between 1833 and the early 1840s, the Mexican government produced various pieces of legislation to limit the power of the church. This legislation was based on the influence of 19th century liberals, trained in law and influenced by the French Revolution. During the presidency of Benito Juarez (1855–1872), laws were passed and the constitution was modified, resulting in the confiscation of all church properties and the suppression of all religious orders, empowering the state governors to designate what buildings could be used for religious services. Mexico's first religious civil war was fought between 1857 and 1860 in reaction to this legislation. Further restrictions continued with the constitution of 1917, leading ultimately to the second Mexican religious war, the bloody Cristero Rebellion of 1926–1929 in western Mexico. The church-state conflict ended with the administration of Manuel Avila Comancho (1940–1946), which offered nonenforcement of key constitutional provisions in exchange for the Roman Catholic Church's cooperation in achieving social peace. By the early 1980s, however, the unspoken consensus supporting the legal status quo eroded, and the Church demanded the right to play a more visible role in national affairs. It became increasingly outspoken in its criticism of government corruption, as well as the lack of democracy in Mexico. Peasants and Indians were said to be an exploited, marginalized mass barely living at a subsistence level and subject to continual repression. Bishops denounced electoral fraud in northern Mexico, and in the south frequently accused the government of human rights violations. The Salinas administration's 1991 proposal to remove all constitutional restrictions on the Roman Catholic Church were approved by the legislature the following year. Today Catholicism remains the dominant religion, adhered to by roughly 90% of the population in Mexico.

The interface between OC and the military history of Mexico is seen in the role of the police. The military serves many policing functions in Mexico. OC in the form of espionage, arms trafficking, and bank robberies fall under the purview of the Federal Judicial Police, which tripled in size between 1982 and 1984. The Federal District police are poorly paid. In 1992 they earned the equivalent of between 285 U.S. dollars and 400 U.S. dollars a month. Double shifts are common, although no extra pay for overtime is provided. Incomes can be supplemented in various ways, including from petty bribes (mordidas) from motorists seeking to park in restricted zones. Junior officers are forced to pass along a daily quota of bribes to more senior officers.

From the 1940s until it was disbanded in 1985, the Federal Directorate of Security was the equivalent of the United States DEA. By the final years of its existence, the directorate had more than doubled in size to some 2,000 personnel. The agency's demise came after it became evident that many of its personnel were in league with the major drug traffickers.

In 2001, the military played a large role in some law enforcement functions, primarily counternarcotics. However, corruption was widespread within police ranks and also in the military. There were numerous reports of executions carried out by rival drug gangs, whose members included both active and former federal, state, and municipal security personnel. Each day during 2001 in Mexico City, one officer was fired for misconduct ranging from armed robbery to beating suspects and accepting bribes.

Mordida, in addition to characterizing the police, also permeates the judicial and correctional system in Mexico. Corruption, inefficiency, impunity, disregard of the law, and lack of training are major problems for the judiciary. Many detainees report that judicial officials often solicit bribes in exchange for not pressing charges. Mexican prisons are typically run by prisoners, displacing prison officials. Violent confrontations, often linked to drug trafficking, are common between rival prison groups. Prisoners complain that they must purchase food, medicine, and other necessities from guards or bribe guards to allow the goods to be brought in from the outside. Inmates in many prisons exercise authority and engage in influence peddling, drug and arms trafficking, coercion, violence, sexual abuse, and protection payoffs to control fellow inmates. In July 2001, the Ciudad Juarez prison director cited a study that showed that as many as 80% of the prisoners in the facility used some type of drug—heroin being the most common.

OC that takes place in Mexico is in the form of trafficking in persons and drug trafficking. These two pursuits are not mutually exclusive, as undocumented migrants may serve as willing or coerced human "mules," who backpack or strap the drugs to their bodies. Mexico is a source country for trafficked persons to the United States, Canada, and Japan, a transit country for persons from various countries, especially Central America and China, and a destination country for children trafficked from Central America, especially from Honduras to Tapachula, Chiapas. There are no specific laws that prohibit the trafficking of persons in Mexico.

Taking full advantage of the approximately 3,300 kilometer (2,051 mile) border between Mexico and the United States, as well as the massive flow of legitimate trade and traffic, well-entrenched polydrug-trafficking organizations based in Mexico have built vast criminal empires that produce illicit drugs, smuggle hundreds of tons of South American cocaine, and operate drug distribution networks across the continental United States. Mexico is the primary transit route for South American cocaine, and a major source of marijuana and heroin, as well as a major supplier of methamphetamine to the illicit drug market in the United States. Mexico has also become a major money laundering center and a significant international placement point for U.S. dollars. Drug cartels launder the proceeds of crime in legitimate businesses in both the United States and Mexico, favoring transportation and other industries that can be used to facilitate drug, cash, and arms smuggling or to further money laundering activities.

Drug cartels led by Colombian drug lords are said to operate throughout Mexico. These include the Juarez Cartel, operating in 15 states; the Tijuana Cartel, headed by the Arelano Felix brothers, operating in 11 states; the Colima Cartel, run by the Amezcua brothers, operating in 11 states; the Valencia Mendoza Cartel, operating in 4 states; the Gulf Cartel, headed by Juan Garcia Abreyo (now serving a life sentence in Houston, Texas); and the Miguel Caro-Quintero Cartel, operating in Sonoma. These cartels smuggle drugs that include marijuana, Colombian cocaine, Mexican-grown heroin, and methamphetamine. Persistent corruption at all levels of the justice system and frequent changes in personnel have combined to hinder Mexico's ability to meet the goals of its antidrug strategy.

Historically, Mexico has been a hideaway for bandits and a staging area for cross-border smuggling. The urban sprawl that straddles both sides of the border in twin cities like San Diego/Tijuana and El Paso/Juarez has complicated the problem. Both Tijuana and Juarez, on the Mexican side, became "boom towns" during Prohibition in the United States. The city of Juarez became an entertainment destination for many Americans living near the border. Juarez established a streetcar system to facilitate the movement of American tourists to various nightclubs, restaurants, casinos, and brothels, a phenomenon that still exists today.[53] Prior to U.S. Prohibition, Tijuana was a rural area, with a climate suitable for the cultivation of grapes, tomatoes, and onions. However, during Prohibition Tijuana became a popular location for Americans seeking alcohol, receiving thousands of tourists on a regular basis. During WWI and WWII, U.S. military personnel were stationed in San Diego, and Tijuana provided access to prostitutes as well as alcohol for underage soldiers, sailors, and Marines, as well as nightclubs, bullfights, horse races, and every other kind of entertainment imaginable.[54] Just as the U.S. military helped enhance the economy and illicit enterprises of Tijuana during WWI and WWII, soldiers stationed at El Paso's Fort Bliss helped Juarez's entertainment based economy during the war years.[55] It is shown later that there has been a link between the military of both countries (United States and Mexico) and the development of OC in Mexico. These two border cities have been a location for major OC activity. In the case of the wartime participation, one major driving force between the development of OC activity was the U.S. military "looking for a good time" and the Mexican military helping to provide it.

Mexican drug traffickers have trafficked in Mexican-grown heroin, cocaine from Colombia, and, most recently, methamphetamine. More than half of the cocaine smuggled into the United States comes from Mexico. Mexican traffickers now dominate the methamphetamine production and distribution in the United States, which previously was controlled by outlaw U.S. motorcycle gangs. Besides drug smuggling, Mexican criminal groups are involved in illegal alien smuggling, product piracy, and cross-border trafficking—from the United States into Mexico—of stolen vehicles, firearms, tobacco, alcohol, and other contraband. Mexico is also the top money-laundering country in Latin America. President Vincente Fox in 2000 called "narcocorruption" a "national cancer" and promised to launch an aggressive campaign against Mexico's drug-trafficking organizations, as well as restructure the country's antidrug forces. However, rooting out corrupt officials and reversing ingrained patterns of institutional corruption will be difficult and meet significant bureaucratic and political obstacles.[56] It can be seen from Table 11–3 that Mexico is second only to the United States in the number of OC groups listed. It should be added that Mexican American gangs in the United States are numerous and are not listed in Table 11–3. However, one multinational group deserves some mention—the so-called 18th Street Gang. While Hispanic gangs in Southern California number in the thousands, most are territorial and exclusive to members living in a specific area, and are accordingly called "homeboys." On the other hand, the 18th Street Gang, which began in the 1960s in the downtown Rampart area of Los Angeles, has grown to be one of California's largest street gangs, with over 20,000 members. Members of the gang often tattoo "18", "666," or "XVIII" on their bodies, and are considered to be the most violent and aggressive of street gangs. What is unique about

18th Street is that it is nonterritorial and heavily populated with illegal immigrants, as well as numerous Asian, black, native American, and white members. The gang has a relatively high level of organization, credited to the gang's close relationship with Mexican and Colombian drug cartels.[57]

So far, coverage of many groups that impact OC in the United States has focused upon Chinese and other Asian groups, biker groups, and Mexican organizations. However, coverage would not be complete in this chapter without returning to a couple of countries high on the list of heroin seized—Italy and Russia. Italy was covered earlier as an alleged source of most OC in America, according to the investigations of Estes Kefauver. However, law enforcement's apparent success in combating these traditional Mafia or LCN groups was tempered by a concern about the new groups arriving on the scene—Chinese, Asian, Mexican, and biker groups. However, there is no reason to believe that the Italians have entirely disappeared from OC activity, so our concerns turn there next. Focus then shifts, to Russian OC. Less is known about Russian OC, because Russia was behind the "Iron Curtain" before 1991, when the Berlin Wall fell and new leadership declared openness with the West. Many former Soviet Union states were given sovereignty. However, Russian OC is shown to be a significant and world-threatening problem, so coverage will include what is known at this time.

Italy

OC in the United States commonly connotes that which derived from Italy, and more particularly Sicily, the island off the south coast of Italy. Sicily is also closest of any part of Italy to the continent of Africa. The Sicilian Mafia, as discussed previously in this chapter, was said to be the source of the American Mafia, which was later called LCN. However, there were and are other criminal organizations in Italy—the Camorra, the 'Ndrangheta, and the Sacra Corona Unita. All of these organizations developed in the south of Italy. In reality, the American Mafia drew from many of these organizations and regions.[58]

In a sense, Italy could be considered the epitome of a country having a history of military rule, and the Mafia developed in large part as an adaptation to military rule. The peninsula was unified under the Roman Empire and the neighboring islands came under Roman control by the third century B.C. Roman Catholicism developed during this period. The Roman Emperor Constantine I was converted to Catholicism in 312 A.D. and with his Edict of Milan (313 A.D.) he ended the persecution of Christians. After the collapse of the Roman Empire in the 5th century A.D., the peninsula and islands were subject to a series of invasions, and political unity was lost. Italy became a frequently changing succession of small states, principalities, and kingdoms, which fought among themselves and were subject to ambitions of foreign power. Popes of Rome ruled central Italy. Rivalries between the Popes and Holy Roman Emperors, who claimed Italy as their domain, often made the peninsula a battleground. Invasions more typically occurred in the south of Italy, because the Roman Catholic Church had greater control in Rome and the north. It was in the south, or Mezzogiorno, that organized criminal groups developed over the centuries. The groups that would become OC groups were initially secret societies that developed as part of a resistance to the rule of foreign emperors. Secrecy was ensured by the limitation of membership of the secret societies to family members, or blood ties.

The evolution of the resistance movements into criminal societies in the south was also rooted in Italian history. The Mezzogiorno never enjoyed a

Renaissance, but remained mired in feudalism and dependent on agriculture, with a legacy of repression. Just as in the United States, in Italy the northern region became industrialized, while the south remained agricultural during the 19th century. After the 1860 revolution against (Spanish) Bourbon rule, Italy united. However, under this unification little changed for the common people of the Mezzogiorno. Instead of foreign repression, the peasants of the south were repressed by other Italians. The new states political foundation was an alliance between the northern industrial bourgeoisie and the southern landed aristocracy. The members of the landed aristocracy of the southern estates were, for the most part, absentee landlords who preferred to reside in the urban areas of Palermo, Naples, or even northern Italy. They hired or rented their estates to *gabelloto,* a manager who had already gained the reputation of *umo inteso,* a "strong man." The *gabelloto* ultimately developed an organization that evolved into a network known as the Mafia. The *gabelloto,* assisted by *famiglia* (family members), *amici* (friends), and *campieri* (lawfully armed mounted guards), ruled over the estate (*latifondo*) with brute force, protecting it from bandits, peasants' organizations, and unions. The *gabelloto* typically did not appear at the *latifondo* but left day-to-day operation to the *campieri,* who themselves could become *gabelloto.* The *gabelloto* was a patron to the peasant laborers on the *latifondo,* controlling access to scarce resources and mediating between official government power and the peasantry through the exercise of force. On the other hand, he fought land reform, labor unions, and revolution, in league with the landlords.[59]

The term *mafia* developed in Sicily, during a time of Arab rule. Originally, the term mafia did not connote a secret criminal organization, but rather it meant a state of mind involving guardianship and defense against the arrogance of the powerful. However, there certainly were *mafiosi,* who exploited the gap left by an ineffective state, providing a form of rudimentary order on the anarchy of Sicilian life. In southern Italy, mistrust and suspicion permeated personal and business relationships. The mafioso, in this context, provided himself as guarantor. For legitimate enterprises, he provided insurance against untrustworthy suppliers. He was also the guarantor for illegitimate entrepreneurs, who could not turn to the police or courts to remedy their grievances.

The Mafia developed in Sicily as a criminal organization due to its unique history, which was characterized by a succession of occupying regimes dating from ancient history. Sicily was colonized by the Phoenicians and Punic settlers from Carthage (Africa) and by Greeks, starting in the 8th century B.C. Following the First Punic War between Rome and Carthage that ended in 242 B.C., all of Sicily was in Roman hands, although Sicily continued to periodically revolt against the Roman Empire. The empire did not make an effort to Romanize the island, and the island remained largely Greek. As the Roman Empire ebbed, Sicily fell in 440 A.D. to the Vandal king Geiseric, then to Ostogothics, followed by the Byzantines in 535 A.D. The Byzantines ruled until the Arab conquest of 827–965 A.D. The Arabs were followed by the Normans, who conquered and ruled from 1060–1266. Sicily was then conquered by the French, who ruled until 1479. After 1479, Sicily was ruled by the kings of Spain, followed by rule by the Austrian Hapsburgs, who in 1734 formed a union with the Bourbon-ruled kingdom of Naples. Sicily was joined with the Kingdom of Italy in 1860. Sicily had bypassed the industrial growth that had transformed the larger urban areas of Northern Italy, and remained with vestiges of feudalism, out of which emerged the Sicilian Mafia.[60]

The rise of Mussolini in the 1920s was an important turning point for the Mafia and Italian American OC. Although other OC in the south of Italy became Fascist almost overnight, the Mafia in Sicily continued to be defiant. Mussolini responded by providing emergency powers to Prefect Cesare Mori of Lombardy, who sent a small army of agents who essentially purged the island of mafiosi, torturing, killing, and sending many to prison, in many cases based on information from the landowners, who knew that the Fascists would replace the Mafia as intermediaries and maintainers of Sicilian law and order. While Mori claimed to have destroyed the Mafia, in reality they were simply driven underground, and re-emerged as soon as Fascism fell in 1943.[61]

Repressive government in the south of Italy may have been a factor leading to the immigration of some four million Italians to America between 1891 and 1920, the overwhelming majority coming from the Mezzogiorno. In the urban slums of America, the Mafia organizational structure facilitated even more rampant criminal activity for the American Mafia than had occurred in Italy. Members of the Unione Siciliana (American Mafia) thrived during Prohibition as "alky cookers" or bootleggers. The American Mafia drew not only from Sicily, but from other parts of southern Italy. The defeat of Italian fascism in WWII allowed Italy's largest criminal organizations—the Sicilian Mafia, Calabrian 'Ndrangheta, Neapolitan Camorra, and Puglian Sacra Corona Unita—to extend their influence into urban areas of Italy, which, in turn, provided these OC groups greater access to the outside world. Many of Italy's banking, commercial, and port facilities fell under the influence or control of OC. These four major Italian OC groups comprise 540 crime families and more than 21,000 members. The Sicilian Mafia is the oldest, most powerful, and most hierarchical of Italy's criminal organizations.

These organizations have been weakened by a series of sweeping prosecutions and convictions in both Italy and the United States. However, testimony of informants indicates that Italian criminal organizations have responded by making organizational and operational adjustments, including restructuring into smaller compartmentalized cells that have tightened security and allowed the continuation of widespread criminal activities. As a result, Italian OC groups have moved well beyond their home regions in southern Italy and are now firmly entrenched throughout Europe, in Central and South America, the Caribbean, Canada, and the United States. They are able to move highly profitable contraband products including drugs, arms, and cigarettes, and launder illicit proceeds on a global basis. They maintain worldwide legitimate business holdings, particularly in real estate and entertainment enterprises such as gambling casinos in Germany, France, Monaco, Spain's Costa del Sol, and the Caribbean. These holdings also serve as a conduit for money laundering.

Drug trafficking remains an important source of revenue for Italian crime syndicates. Although they have traditionally procured Southwest Asian heroin from Turkish traffickers, they have more recently established heroin-trafficking links to Russian, ethnic Albanian, and Asian crime groups. They also collaborate with South American traffickers to acquire cocaine. Italian OC groups were responsible for 85% of the U.S. heroin trade in the 1960s and 1970s, and they continue to be involved in smuggling drugs into the United States, but on a smaller scale. The reduced Italian participation is a result of the "French connection" prosecution in Italy, Turkey, and the United States, targeting Italian networks supplying heroin to the United States in the 1970s and 1980s. Much of this trade has been supplanted by Mexican OC groups, discussed earlier. To fill the diminished market in the United States, Italian groups have developed mutually beneficial relationships with Russian criminal organizations (in transitioning former Communist countries) that help facilitate their drug and arms trafficking operations. They have moved aggressively into the legitimate economy of many formerly Communist countries, including Hungary, Poland, the Czech Republic, Bulgaria, and Romania, taking advantage of poor regulations guiding privatization of national assets and capitalization of banks to purchase or invest heavily in banks, financial institutions, and businesses, and to defraud fledgling stock markets. These activities have enabled criminal organizations to operate companies as fronts for smuggling contraband between East and West and for laundering illicit proceeds.

The developing link between Italian and Russian OC has resulted in the growth of the "Balkan route" for trafficking in drugs, persons, and other contraband to Western Europe (and as has been shown, the return of proceeds sometimes in the form of stolen vehicles). This new venture and partnership for Italian syndicates suggests that the influence of Russian OC is now of greater significance than in the past.[62] Russian OC seems logically to be the next subject of study.

Russia   Although Americans generally think that Russia (now termed the "Russian Republic") was dominated by a military dictatorship during the 69 years of Soviet rule, less known is the fact that Russia was highly militaristic under the Tsars. Ivan III (1462–1505), in fact, referred to his empire as "the Third Rome," and a century later the Romanov dynasty was established under Tsar Mikhail in 1613. Peter the Great (1689–1725) created Western-style military forces and developed expansionist policies that were continued by Catherine the Great, who established Russia as a continental power. The military capability of Russia was shown by the defeat of Napoleon in 1812, when he attempted to conquer Russia after occupying Moscow, setting the stage for Russia to share with Austria-Hungary a domination of the affairs of Eastern Europe for the next century. In 1860, Russia expanded across Siberia all the way to the port of Vladivostok, which was secured on the Pacific coast in 1860. However, Russia's economy failed to compete with those of Western countries. Imperial decline was evident in Russia's defeat in the unpopular Russo-Japanese war in 1905, and subsequent opposition was suppressed. Popular anger was manipulated by the Tsars through diversion into anti-Semitic pogroms, in the absence of much needed economic reform. These problems, combined with the ruinous effects of WWI, sparked a March, 1917 uprising that led Tsar Nicholas II to abdicate the throne. A provisional government headed by Alexander Kerensky was overthrown by Vladimir Lenin's Bolshevik Party on November 7, 1917. Civil war broke out in 1918 between Lenin's "Red" army and various "White" forces and lasted until 1920 when, despite foreign interventions, the Bolsheviks triumphed. After the Red army conquered Ukraine, Belorussa, Azerbaijan, Georgia, and Armenia, in 1922 a new nation was formed—the Union of Soviet Socialist Republics (USSR).[63]

During the 69 years of the USSR, millions died in political purges, the vast penal and labor system, or state-created famines. However, during this time an underground economy continued to provide goods and services not provided by the government. The ancient organization that ran the black market in Russia came to be known as the *Mafiya*.[64]

The term Mafiya was used in Russia beginning in the 1970s. The term was based upon images of the American Mafia described in the mass media. More specifically, the term Mafiya refers to Communist Party barons accused of corruption, black market speculators, and the groups of criminal entrepreneurs and corrupt officials who came to prominence in the post-Soviet era.[65] Both under the rule of the Tsars and the Communist state, Russians had to endure totalitarianism that made them distrustful of government. This distrust for government is a breeding ground for OC, because people turn to gangsters as guarantors for business deals or as a source of goods and services. While the former Soviet Union did not have OC similar to the American system, it did have an extensive professional criminal underworld, the *vorovskoy v. zakone*, literally translated "thieves in law," and also known as *vorovski mir* (thieves' world). The vory actually began in prison and originally developed during the Stalinist era. Stalin tried to crush the thieves through execution and imprisonment. Membership in the *vorovskoy v. zakone* required three sponsors. Participants were required to undertake a ceremony with an oath of allegiance. Also, members had to be free of regular employment, paying taxes, and membership in the Communist Party (i.e., no involvement with conventional society). The other term for this group, *vorovski mir*, referred to a criminal society in the model of Camorra. This organization was run from prison by crime bosses who planned and organized operations across the country, with lieutenants, called *brodyagi* (vagabonds), who conducted formal dealings with the outside. With the collapse of the Soviet Union, vory groups developed as an important element of Russian OC—the Mafiya.[66] However, prison gangs are only part of the Mafiya. The Mafiya includes not only ex-prison gang members but also the *nomenklatura capitalists*, Soviet party elites who have participated in illegal activities, including bank fraud, to become wealthy business owners. It also includes members of the Red Army who have been caught in smuggling rings, as well as cabinet ministers and police officials discovered working for disreputable commercial firms.[67]

One is tempted to cast the Russian Mafiya as Russia's version of the Sicilian Mafia. However, that would be an incorrect interpretation. The Mafiya has been referred to as "the most disorganized form of organized crime"—a loose series of networks of criminal entrepreneurs rather than any formal structure. These networks form long- and short-term affiliations on the basis of common backgrounds, friendships, hometowns or region, or ethnic identity, but do not fit into formal hierarchies. They are prone to internal disagreement and bloodletting, but they are also extremely flexible and responsive to the market.

The Russian model is best understood as OC, white-collar crime, and political crime all rolled into one. This is because it developed in a society in which all forms of private enterprise were illegal. Thus, the gangs operate across a spectrum, from entirely legitimate enterprise (formerly illegitimate), through "gray" or paralegal business into overtly criminal activities. For instance, a mobster may set up a private bank using money embezzled from Communist Party funds in 1990, but is now operating above board as a property company. However, this company may also launder drug money and serve as a front for protection racketeering. Thus, it is difficult to tell a gangster from a businessman, a distinction that people doing business in Russia may see as irrelevant. The Russian Mafiya is highly diversified, with activities ranging from contract killing to cybercrime, but also includes legal and paralegal businesses.[68]

The Mafiya is all-pervasive within the Russian economy. According to the Russian Ministry of Interior, (MVD), there are 89 major criminal communities in Russia that are comprised of about 1,000 smaller criminal groups. Eleven of these communities make up 243 groups with some 50,000 members who also operate in 44 other countries. The U.S. government estimates that there are about 200 sophisticated OC groups in Russia with a broad range of operations, some of which extend beyond Russia's borders in some 60 different countries.[69] According to one Russian estimate, the underground economy accounted for 40% of the country's GDP in 1996. A 1997 study by then-President Boris Yeltsin's staff found that 70% to 80% of private businesses paid extortion fees to OC amounting to 10% to 20% of their revenue. According to published Russian figures, 79 Russian bankers and at least twice as many businessmen were assassinated in contract killings between 1994 and 1997. In 1999, there were 155 contract killings in Russia, according to published figures. In the absence of effective legal protections, Russian businesses often rely on criminal groups and pay significant fees for protection, debt collection, capital, and information gathering. Representing their business "clients," criminal groups often play a role in negotiating contracts or resolving business disputes, which often end violently.[70] In other words, they serve as a surrogate justice system.

In addition to servicing business interests, the Russian Mafiya has a lucrative "bread and butter" drug smuggling business in Russia that has been facilitated by the elimination of travel controls and opening of borders with Europe. By 1999, according to Russian data, there were 350,000 officially registered drug users in Russia, of which 175,000 were considered drug addicts. The MVD and Health Ministry estimate that the actual totals are 10 times greater—more than 3 million users and almost 2 million addicts. Three million users would be 2% of the Russian population. Afghanistan opium cultivation increased tremendously after the dissolution of the Soviet Union in 1991. In addition to participation of Party officials in OC, there have been significant reports of participation of the Russian military in the trafficking in drugs and other contraband. Press reporting from the region says that Russian troops in Tajikistan have accepted large bribes to facilitate the movement of Afghanistan-produced narcotics into Central Asia and are themselves involved in drug trafficking. In the most notable incident, Tajikistan officials seized 109 kilograms of opium from a Russian border guard's helicopter in August, 1996. With close ties to corrupt officers and soldiers in the Russian armed forces, Russian OC groups are also heavily involved in illicit arms trafficking. Most Russian criminal arms deals involve sales within Russia and other countries of the former Soviet Union, including combatants in ethnic conflicts in Chechnya, Georgia, Armenia, and Azerbaijan.[71]

Mafiya activities in Russia and former Soviet countries present an indirect threat to United States citizens in the way that they contribute to destabilization of those countries, as well as a breakdown in government attempts to establish democracy. However, the Mafiya contains another very direct threat in that Mafiya members have immigrated to the United States and are conducting their criminal activities on U.S. soil. The background provided earlier is important in providing an understanding that Russian OC takes a different form than Mexican or Italian OC, and it would be a mistake for American law enforcement to respond to it using the same methods as with those groups. Russian OC, in addition to the usual smuggling and extortion crime usually associated with OC, has a strong business or "white-collar crime" component.

Thus, the tools of law enforcement must go beyond the usual wire taps and undercover work normally used in dealing with OC when approaching Russian OC. More sophisticated techniques must be employed for dealing with the use of computers, for instance, in cybercrime. The most frequent violations found in U.S. investigations involving Russian OC were for crimes that border on "white-collar crime"—fraud and money laundering.[72] Russian OC has been a growing law enforcement problem in the United States since small groups began establishing a foothold in this country in the late 1970s.

This timeline seems curious, especially in light of the fact that *perestroika* (openness, or more generally liberalization and democracy) occurred starting in 1991, during the administration of Boris Yeltsin. However the 1970s were significant, according to Robert Friedman who wrote a book on the subject, because the 1970s were a period of détente with the Soviet Union, a policy of the Nixon Administration.[73] In 1974, the Jackson-Vanik Amendment to the Trade Reform Act (Title IV) forbid granting of the Most Favored Nation status (now known as Normal Trade Relations) to countries with a poor record of human rights—chiefly the right to emigrate (migrate out of the country) freely and inexpensively. The thrust of the legislation was clearly anti-Russian, and Henry Kissinger, then U.S. Secretary of State, was so alarmed that he flew to Moscow and extracted from the Kremlin a promise that "the rate of emigration from the USSR would begin to rise promptly from the 1973 level."[74] Friedman revealed in his book that a major byproduct of the Nixon détente and the Jackson-Vanik Amendment was that the Russians opened prison doors in the gulag, and thousands of hard-core criminals left for the United States. He added that a product of this was an explosion of the members of the Jewish Mafia in Brighton Beach, New York during the 1970s and 1980s, when 40,000 Jews from Russia settled there.[75] Because of its reputation as a seat of the Organizatsiya, as the Russian Jewish mob was called, Brighton Beach came to be known as Little Odessa. Odessa was a Black Sea port in the Ukraine where many Russian mobsters spent vacation time and settled.[76]

Friedman also stated that more than 800,000 Russian Jews settled in Israel since the first massive wave of immigration in the 1970s, taking advantage of Israel's most sacred law—the Right of Return, which guarantees citizenship and freedom of Jews who return to their ancestral homeland. Friedman indicated that about 10% of the Russian immigrants were criminals. Israel was an attractive destination for several reasons. It was a good place for money laundering, because banks can accept large cash deposits with no questions asked. Israeli police officials estimated that Russian mobsters poured from 4 to 20 billion dollars into Israel's economy, and purchased factories, insurance companies, and a bank. After two decades of unimpeded growth, the Russian Mafiya, Friedman contended, turned Israel into its very own "mini-state."[77]

In a book on the Mafia, Finckenauer and Waring contended that Russia released not only its "suffering" Jews into America, but also sent their Afghan war veterans and KGB thugs as a fifth column, after giving them false Jewish identities.[78]

Friedman maintained that the Mafiya has become bigger, more brutal, better armed, and richer than other crime cartels. The Russian mob, he said, is involved in trafficking of drugs, money, handguns, assault carbines, submachine guns, antiaircraft missiles, helicopters, plutonium, enriched uranium, and submarines. The latter item (submarines) was discussed in an interview with Ludwig Fainberg (aka "Tarzan"), a Russian mob nightclub owner who arranged the sale of a Russian submarine, complete with captain and crew, to Colombian drug runners. The actual sale of the submarine to Colombian drug runner Juana Almeda was interrupted by DEA agents who arrested Tarzan.[79] Fainberg was deported to Israel with 1,500 dollars in his pocket after spending a mere 33 months in the Miami Federal Detention Center. As he awaited deportation, Fainberg told Friedman that, given what he knows about the sex industry, he'll soon be rich again (he had owned a strip club in Miami known as "Porky's"). But he added that he regretted leaving America. He said, "I love this country. . . . It's so easy to steal here."[80] Israel has a policy of not extraditing its citizens, so it may prove a "safe haven" to Fainberg, as it has for other Russian criminals, and a place where he can continue his activities on an international basis.

In Russia, there are, according to Russian police, three forms of organized criminal activities: (a) criminal gangs of thugs—the violent enforcers that collect protection money, run prostitution rings, sell counterfeit goods, peddle drugs, and sell weapons; (b) big businessmen whose methods are rough, who avoid paying taxes when they can, and make liberal use of bribery; and (c) those who obtain government property, or commodities like oil or diamonds, from corrupt officials at controlled or very low prices, and sell the contraband on the open market at a vast profit. Probably the biggest area of concern since the Soviet breakup has been the *mafia in uniform*. The term refers to a large number of service men, some still in the military, who engage both in drug consumption, as well as drug and other illicit trafficking. Many of these men acquired drug habits during the nine years of war in Afghanistan. They are now poorly paid, badly housed, and demoralized. Smuggling crimes of all types (particularly drug and arms trafficking), the massive diversion of equipment and materials, illegal business ventures, and coercion and criminal violence, all occur under the umbrella of military OC. Furthermore, an increase in the number of "contract killings" has the mark of military involvement. With the fall of communism, ex-KGB officers, veterans of the Afghan war, and unemployed military officers formed expedient alliances with the gangster thugs and black market profiteers who carried out work-violence, threats, and intimidation.[81]

Afghanistan was Russia's Vietnam in the sense that members of Russia's military were criminalized, both by the loss of morale, but also by contact with opium, of which Afghanistan provides some 72% of the world's supply. (The criminalization of American Vietnam veterans will be discussed later.) Once again, the theme of this chapter, that military rule is the seed of OC, seems to hold true in Russia, as well as all of the countries discussed earlier. It also seems that addiction to heroin may be an engine driving OC in that it provides not only a motivation for participation in crime, but also a lucrative source of revenue through the illicit trade in heroin.

The last country that is profiled in this chapter is Nigeria, the country that was mentioned at the beginning of this analysis as having decades of military rule. It is also a country described as having networks of organized criminal groups in many countries of the world. Nigeria is described before concluding this chapter, and serves as a link with African American crime. Just as Chinese, Vietnamese, and Latin American illegal immigrants have "disappeared" into ethnic communities, the same can be said of Nigerians, as well as Jamaicans, and others of African descent, who can blend into America's African American ghettos.

Nigeria was briefly discussed as a country with a significant participation in OC, a fact that was related to its history of military rule, corruption, and economic problems. Nigeria is a coastal country located in central West Africa. Historically, it has been a center for trade, not only of goods, but of slaves. After 1000 A.D., in what is now Nigeria, the North African Berbers and forest people exchanged slaves, ivory, and kola nuts for salt, glass beads, coral, cloth, weapons, brass rods, and cowrie shells (used as currency). In the 17th through 19th centuries, European traders established coastal ports for the increasing traffic in slaves destined for the Americas. It is suggested later that this legacy of trafficking in persons—the slave trade—may be related to the current day traffic in another commodity—heroin.

Nigeria has a history of military rule, first under the British from 1914 to 1960. After independence, Nigeria has been ruled successively by militarily controlled governments, with occasional attempts at democracy, usually marred by rigged elections. The country has a poor, mostly rural, economic system with a recorded GDP per capita of $250, with much of the country's wealth concentrated in the hands of a small elite group.

This inequality is due to corruption, nontransparent government contracting practices, a banking system that favors the wealthy, and regulatory and tax regimes that are not always enforced impartially. Law enforcement in the country is disorganized by a "tripartite" system of criminal law and justice: the Criminal Code, based on English common law and legal practice; the Penal Code, based on Maliki Law, which is Islamic; and customary law, based upon the customs and traditions of the people. The British-based Criminal Code is often in conflict with both customary law and the Penal Code, creating additional confusion. Reportedly, most crimes (60%) that should be kept in police records are disposed of without being recorded at the informal, customary courts.[82]

As in Israel, the law prohibits expulsion of citizens, and there is no forced exile of criminals. The succession of military regimes has made for a large number of Nigerians living abroad, fearing persecution by previous military regimes. Prostitution is said to be rampant in Nigeria, particularly in urban areas, and there is an active market for trafficking in women to Europe and elsewhere. No law makes trafficking in persons a crime, and there is a steady flow of Nigerian women lured and sold into prostitution in Europe, particularly Italy, the Netherlands, Spain, and the Czech Republic. Nigerian girls are sold into sexual slavery and trafficked throughout England. The girls reportedly request asylum at British airports and are taken into the care of social services or foster care. A few weeks later, the girls disappear and reportedly are trafficked to European countries, in particular Italy, where they are forced into prostitution. Additionally, there was evidence of trafficking of children to the United States and Europe, primarily to reunite children with their undocumented parents abroad.

BOX 11–4

Child Trafficking Linked with Heroin Trade in Nigeria

Prince Nnaedozie Umegbolu, a 12-year-old Nigerian American kid, was made to swallow 87 condoms filled with heroin white traveling from Lagos to New York. His Georgia-based African American mother Alissa Walden says her son was made to work as a mule for Nigerian drug dealers because he was desperate to return to the United States. The boy's father, Chukwunweike Umegbolu, 40, of Atlanta, has served 7 years of a 10-year sentence for his role in a heroin ring that trafficked more than $33 million into Atlanta.[83]

BOX 11–5

Trafficking in Wildlife Linked with Drug Trade

LONDON—Although conservation groups are working hard and spending millions to save endangered species, their efforts are being undermined by organized gangs conducting a hybrid drug and wildlife trade. Live snakes stuffed with condoms full of cocaine are shipped across borders; live snails packed with heroin travel by air. The WWF and TRAFFIC investigators found that about half the wildlife criminals prosecuted in the United Kingdom have previous convictions for drugs, violence, theft, and firearms offenses, a pattern that they say shows up around the world. In Brazil, recent estimates suggest that up to 40% of illegal drug shipments are combined with wildlife. The U.S. Fish and Wildlife Service reports that more than a third of cocaine seized in the United States in 1993 was associated with wildlife imports. Legal shipments of wildlife are used to conceal drugs as customs officers at Heathrow discovered in 1996 while inspecting a consignment of live snails. They were packed with heroin. In 1993, a U.S. Customs inspector in Miami noticed an unnatural bulge in a live boa constrictor that was part of a shipment of 312 animals from Colombia. Officers found cocaine-filled condoms that had been inserted into 225 of the snakes. A total of 39 kilograms (86 pounds) of cocaine was recovered from the reptiles, which all died. Venomous snakes are used by criminals to guard or conceal drug caches and consignments.[84]

There have been allegations based upon statements made by returnees that immigration officials actively cooperate with crime syndicates. Nigeria also remains the hub of African narcotics trafficking. Nigerian polycrime organizations operate extensive global trafficking networks, control the sub-Saharan drug markets, and account for a large part of the heroin imported to the United States. There is an interesting connection between trafficking in persons and the heroin trade. Traffickers can get double duty out of persons who are trafficked to foreign countries, because drugs can be secreted on their person or can be ingested by the couriers in a condom tied shut. The text box describes the remarkable case of a child who "paid his way" to America to be reunited with his mother through swallowing 87 condoms filled with heroin. In 1998, the Nigerian Drug Law Enforcement Administration scored a key success at Lagos Airport by breaking up a well-organized ring that had been smuggling heroin to the United States concealed in the wheelchairs of Nigerian Special Olympics participants. There is evidence that the technique of smuggling described in the text box (condoms full of drugs) has even been used by Drug traffickers in conjunction with the legal (or illegal) traffic in wildlife, as discussed in the text box.

According to the ICTA, Nigeria is involved in international criminal activity coming from Africa. Powerful and sophisticated criminal syndicates based in Nigeria have extensive networks that reach into the Western hemisphere, Europe, Russia, and the New Independent States, Southeast and Southwest Asia, Australia, and Africa. Worldwide, there are hundreds of Nigerian criminal cells located primarily in major metropolitan centers in North America, Europe, and Asia. Recent estimates suggest that more than 500 Nigerian crime cells are operating in at least 80 countries. Nigerian criminals take advantage of large West African ethnic communities in major cities to establish the infrastructure needed to support a wide range of criminal activities—foremost among them drug trafficking and sophisticated schemes to defraud individuals, businesses, and governments—that reap billions of dollars in illicit proceeds. Nigerian crime groups also facilitate illegal immigration of Nigerian nationals to metropolitan areas around the world, whom they then use for filling high-risk, low-level roles in drug trafficking. The United States and Britain are the primary targets of Nigerian criminal activity, with Nigerian crime cells elsewhere in the world purchasing drugs or providing financial and logistical support. Between 25% and 30% of the heroin seized at U.S. international airports in recent years was taken from couriers employed by Nigerian trafficking groups, according to U.S. Customs data.[85]

Nigerian criminal syndicates are among the world's most active traffickers in Asian heroin—particularly to the United States. Producing no heroin of their own, Nigerian traffickers have well-established networks in Southeast and Southwest Asian countries to acquire the drug. The steady and virtually uninterrupted flow of Nigerian-controlled heroin from these source regions is facilitated by criminal cells in transit countries along the way. Nigerian traffickers typically smuggle only small quantities of drugs, using both express mail services and thousands of individual couriers in an effort to overwhelm market country customs and law enforcement capabilities and to lessen the cost of any seizures. They tend to avoid sending drug couriers on direct flights from drug-producing and key transit countries to market countries, relying instead on a widely diverse number of routes transiting airports throughout Asia, Africa, and Latin America.

In planning their drug courier runs, Nigerian traffickers make careful study of customs and security procedures in producer, transit, and market country air and sea ports. They readily adapt to international law enforcement measures against them. Nigerian traffickers, for example, are now recruiting "low-profile" couriers who are less likely to draw the attention of international customs agents. These include whites, women (often with children), and the elderly. To avoid scrutiny at U.S. international airports, Nigerian traffickers sometimes deliver drugs to Canada or Mexico for overland transshipment to the United States.

This discussion of Nigeria may raise more questions than it answers. Some may wonder, what does this have to do with American criminology? What do the Nigerians have to do with crime in America? Is there a connection between Nigerians and African Americans? The answer may come in the form of an answer to a point made about the history of Nigeria and having to do with "roots." Many African Americans have roots in Nigeria and surrounding countries because they were the victims of the "trafficking in persons" (i.e., slavery) that took place not so long ago in America—before the civil war. Some extremely elderly African Americans may even have living great-grandparents living in Nigeria. Curiously, a DNA study tracing family ties to Africa revealed that Nigeria was one of the countries from which many African Americans derived.[86] Thus, there may remain some family ties that facilitate today's trafficking in persons from Nigeria.

As is discussed in the next section on the OC picture in the United States, the heroin trade in America appears to be heavily dominated, not by Chinese, Italians, or even Mexican Americans, but by African Americans. The Nigerian connection may be explanatory, and this information suggests that blacks in America are prominent in American OC, not just at the lowest level of street trafficking, but also at the highest level of OC. Furthermore, their participation is highly sophisticated and global in nature.

OC in the United States

Assumptions have been made throughout this chapter to analyze the concept of OC. At the beginning of the chapter it was pointed out that OC, unlike the single crimes described in previous chapters, is extremely difficult to define. For one thing, OC theories are conspiracy theories, and conspiracies are difficult to prove. A second problem is that a host of crimes are included under the umbrella of OC, with varying characteristics. Another difficulty, as elaborated on in this chapter, is that a variety of organizational structures characterize OC—ranging from rigidly hierarchical organizations to loose networks. The loose networks, particularly, run far afield from the rigid hierarchy employed in the traditional theory of OC that focused upon the Sicilian-based Mafia. Thus, OC is difficult to study empirically. A compromise was made to operationalize OC, notably to pick one crime that most characterizes OC and do international comparisons with that. The crime was heroin trafficking and the index used was kilograms of heroin seized. It was also pointed out that this is a highly imperfect index of OC because it includes host or home base countries, transit countries, and client or target countries. Seizures of heroin could take place in countries that are on the receiving end of the heroin trade, but with no particular OC network within the country, other than for distribution. However, ranking countries by kilograms of heroin seized provided a starting point for analysis. Qualitative sources, including government reports and country profiles, were used to describe countries at the high end in terms of kilograms of heroin seized. More analysis is needed (both quantitative and qualitative) to distinguish the client countries from the home base countries to develop a good index of OC cross-nationally, but this analysis is beyond the domain of this text.

Turning to the task of analyzing OC within the United States, a similar analysis can be done using data by states. States within the United States are ranked in terms of kilograms of heroin seized, as shown in Table 11–4. Left out of Table 11–4 were Arkansas, Colorado, Idaho, Iowa, Kentucky, Maine, Mississippi, Montana, Nebraska, New Hampshire, North Dakota, South Dakota, Tennessee, West Virginia, and Wyoming, which had no reported heroin seized. Intuitively, looking at the table, this appears to be a reasonably good

Table 11–4 **States Ranked by Kg of Heroin Seized**

State	Kg
New York	181.9
Florida	148.6
California	84.7
Washington	84.0
Texas	49.6
New Jersey	20.3
Illinois	13.9
Pennsylvania	13.2
District of Columbia	9.1
North Carolina	6.7
New Mexico	6.0
Virginia	5.8

Table 11–4   (*Continued*)

Arizona	5.7
Nevada	5.3
Kansas	5.1
Maryland	4.8
Michigan	4.6
South Carolina	4.4
Louisiana	2.7
Connecticut	1.9
Oregon	1.7
Alabama	1.2
Minnesota	1.2
Georgia	1.1
Hawaii	1.1
Massachusetts	1.1
Ohio	1.0
Indiana	0.9
Rhode Island	0.5
Wisconsin	0.4
Delaware	0.3
Missouri	0.2
Oklahoma	0.2
Alaska	0.1
Utah	0.1
Vermont	0.1

index of OC. The big OC syndicates mentioned in the literature are located in New York, New Jersey, Florida, California, and Illinois. But as with the international data, there is the problem of host, transit, and client states. For instance, New York (although the location of traditional Italian Mafia families) may actually rank higher than it should because it is a major port of entry into the United States. Washington State may also be primarily a transit state, because it not only is an ocean port state, but also a border state with Canada. Thus, kilograms of heroin seized is only a rough empirical guide to OC. With that caveat in mind, the correlations between kilograms of heroin seized (and kilograms of heroin seized per capita) can be viewed as rough indices for attempting to understand OC in the United States. An attempt to validate these indices was made, correlating the number of gang cities (cities that report gang activity) by state with both heroin kilograms seized and heroin kilograms per capita seized. The correlations were low to moderate, as seen in Table 11–5. Much more work on construct validity is needed, because the variable "number of gang cities" itself is an imperfect measure of OC.

If the assumption that heroin seized is a rough indicator of OC activity is accepted, then what does Table 11–5 tell us? The table may look familiar because is bears a resemblance to the table of state correlations for murder in Chapter 6, especially in regard to the correlations with heroin kilograms per capita. From this table it looks very much as though black ethnicity and variables related to black ethnicity (infant mortality, unwed mothers, poverty,

Table 11–5 Kg Heroin Seized and Kg Heroin Seized per Capita by Various State Demographic Variables

State Database Variable	Heroin Kg	Heroin Kg per Capita
Divorce	−0.01	−0.11
Infant mortality	−0.14	0.27
Marriages	−0.04	−0.09
Births to unwed mothers	0.10	0.43
Child abuse victimization	0.64	0.26
Kg cocaine seized per capita	0.36	0.19
Gini Index	0.27	0.35
Percentage living in poverty	0.13	0.22
Unemployment	0.23	0.47
Male unemployment	0.19	0.39
Female unemployment	0.26	0.50
Percentage black	0.08	0.40
Black/white income disparity	0.18	0.61
Beer per capita	−0.14	0.03
Wine per capita	0.22	0.48
Spirits per capita	−0.03	0.33
Alcohol per capita	−0.01	0.32
Hispanic migration rate	−0.25	−0.34
Hispanic population	0.35	0.08
Juvenile population	0.63	0.22
Number of gang cities	0.35	0.17

and unemployment) is a major correlate of OC as measured by kilograms of heroin and kilograms of heroin per capita. Particularly important in this table, however, is that the strongest variable is the black/white income disparity. Mexican American ethnicity is a low correlate of heroin kilograms per capita, but it should be noted that it is a moderate correlate of heroin kilograms seized. A good guess as to the difference has to do with the location of the Hispanic population, which is disproportionately in California, Arizona, and Texas, so there may have been some big seizures in those border states that bring the correlation up more so than with the heroin kilograms per capita variable. The black population is spread much more evenly around the country, so its participation per capita has a greater chance, on a state-by-state basis, to show up in relation to kilograms per capita seized.

All issues considered, it appears from Table 11–5 that OC is very much an African American enterprise in American society. Early black participation in OC had to do with black exclusion from the mainstream. Prior to the civil rights movement of the 1960s, black Americans were frequently denied access to bank loans, good jobs, nice homes, insurance, influential political positions, advanced educational opportunities, and equal social treatment and benefits. Gunnar Myrdal, a Swedish economist who made insightful observations on the situation of blacks in America, referred to blacks as a quasicaste in a society that held up the "American dream" as accessible to all.[87] Given this exclusion, the American equivalent to apartheid in South Africa, it is understandable that blacks would turn to OC as a rational alternative to poverty and unemployment. There is evidence that blacks did so and were quite effective in OC in the early days of its development in America. It is also evident that American criminologists have also minimized the efficacy of blacks in their pursuit of organized criminal endeavors. Lombardo, for instance, pointed out that:

> Though a number of authors have recognized black participation in the policy (lottery) gambling racket, they also argue that African-Americans lacked the political associations and organizational skills necessary to participate in criminal activity on the same level as the once prominent Italian American crime syndicates.[88]

Lombardo also quoted other authors on the issue of the capability of African Americans to succeed at OC. He quoted Shatzberg and Kelly in their book entitled, *African-American Organized Crime*, who maintained that:

> Throughout the early period of white gang development, African-Americans were not visible in the structure of any significant organized criminal process. Indeed, African-American criminals who entered the twentieth century had no documented history of a leadership role or any significant active affiliation with any organized criminal group.[89]

Through a qualitative detailed analysis of African American OC groups, Lombardo provided strong evidence that African Americans developed sophisticated OC groups in Chicago independently of Italian American OC. Furthermore, they eventually played an active role in the activities of the Chicago Outfit, the traditional Italian American OC group in Chicago. He argued that there were several black crime bosses who developed extensive political connections as far back as the 1890s. Blacks literally developed the "policy game" or numbers racket, and black nightclubs dominated the illicit distribution of alcohol during Prohibition, where whites would "go slumming" looking for alcohol, prostitutes, and "jazz" when it was introduced in Chicago.[90] Policy bankers who accumulated financial assets often became the source of loans for blacks unable to obtain financing from white-dominated financial institutions.[91] Policy banks also came to own many legitimate businesses using the capital they had accumulated from the numbers game. The black policy racket even survived an attempted takeover by Al Capone, who made a deal with the black underworld to leave the numbers game to African Americans in exchange for their staying out of the beer business.[92]

Another approach to black OC was authored by Francis Ianni in 1974. Ianni followed Daniel Bell's thesis of "ethnic succession," and argued that a "black Mafia" would emerge to replace the traditional Italian American OC, using OC as a means of social mobility. The Italians, like the Irish before them, had, using OC as a stop-gap, found jobs, educated their children, and moved to the suburbs.[93] Ianni maintained that childhood gang and prison gang participation served as the basis for networks that will (he predicted) emerge as a militant black criminal empire forged out of the wreckage of the crumbling Italian dynasty.

There were several major areas of black involvement of a resistance, criminal, or protest nature at the time of Ianni's publication that may have helped bring reality to Ianni's prophecy. One was the civil rights movement, which grew increasingly militant during the 1970s with the emergence of quasi-military black civil rights groups such as the Nation of Islam, the Black Panthers, and the Symbionese Liberation Army (SLA). Another was black participation in the Vietnamese war. Other expressions of black militancy were the prison riots that took place during that time, including the Attica riot of 1971. The military order of the Black Panthers, the Nation of Islam, the SLA, and even combat platoons in Vietnam may have provided prototypes for black criminal organizational enterprises of the 1980s, 1990s, and up until today. Blacks also brought back one additional "asset" from Vietnam—enhanced knowledge of Southeast Asian drug networks. In addition, an estimated 20% to 33% of service personnel came home from that war addicted to heroin.[94]

The question of whether or not black gangs are forms of OC is subject to question. Just as with early studies of African American OC, studies of black gangs on the West Coast question their ability to organize. For instance, a study of drug sales and violence among San Francisco Crips (black gangs), concluded that:

> most gangs do not have the skills or knowledge to move to other communities and establish new markets for drug sales. While it is true they can and do function on their own turf they are often like fish out of water when they go elsewhere. . . . They are not like OC figures (Mafia and Colombian cocaine cartels) who have capital, knowledge and power . . . while it might be romantic to think that the L.A. Bloods and Crips are exceptional, I will remain skeptical that they are more competent than other gangs.[95]

However, other studies have found the opposite—that there are high levels of mobility among "entrepreneurial" California gang members traveling long distances to establish drug distribution outlets and maintaining close ties to their gangs of origin.[96] Further evidence that the black gangs are more than just groups of youthful neighborhood "chums" is shown in the growth, migration, and proliferation of these gangs. One study found 274 black gangs in 17 cities and 5 unincorporated areas in Los Angeles County—198 Crip-affiliated and 74 Blood-affiliated (the terms Crip and Blood are discussed later). There is evidence that there was little or no black gang activity during the 1960s, which was a decade during which civil rights and political activism attracted the attention of would-be gang members.[97] In terms of growth of gangs, Miller's 1996 compilation of data from several sources indicated that in the 1970s, street gangs existed in the United States in 201 cities, climbing to 468 cities in the 1980s, and to 1,487 in the 1990s.[98] In regard to proliferation of these gangs, one study found that nearly three fourths of the 792 cities that responded to a 1992 mail survey reported that at least some indigenous gangs adopted gang names generally associated with Los Angeles or Chicago (e.g., Bloods, Crips, Vicelords, Gangster Disciples, or Latin Kings).[99]

Abadinsky maintained that the heroin trade is a major enterprise for black gangs, of which he mentions Jamaican Posses such as the "Shower Posse," Crips, and Bloods of Los Angeles; and the Gangster Disciples, and El

Rukn/Black P. Stone Nation of Chicago. He also adds that the rise of this lucrative trade was coincidental with the Vietnam War.

There are important black criminal organizations in the heroin business, particularly in New York, Detroit, Chicago, Philadelphia, and Washington, DC. Although blacks have traditionally been locked out of many activities associated with OC (e.g., labor racketeering and loansharking) by prejudice, dope is an equal opportunity employer. African American criminal groups made important strides in the heroin business when the Vietnam War exposed many black soldiers to the heroin markets of the Golden Triangle—previous black groups were dependent on OC families for their heroin. As a result of their overseas experience, black organizations were able to bypass traditional OC and buy directly from suppliers in Thailand.[100]

Interestingly, there is a military connection to the Crips and Bloods. As mentioned earlier, the 1960s were characterized by the emergence of black militant organizations, including the Black Panther Party (BPP). The BPP was founded in Oakland in 1966 with a large membership of returning black Vietnam Vets who were angry at having fought for Vietnamese civil rights while being denied their own back home. In addition, they objected to the disproportionate number of their black brothers who were being drafted and dying in a war that they considered unjust.[101] Black militant organizations like the BPP were suppressed in the late 1960s through the actions of the federal and local police.[102] A 15-year-old student at Fremont High School started the first new street gang on 78th Street in Los Angeles in 1969. Members wore the BPP black leather jackets and called themselves Baby Avenues. Later, they became known as the Avenue Cribs, a comment on their youthfulness. In addition to their black leather jackets, they were in the habit of often walking with canes, and wearing an earring in their left ear lobe. The name was changed to Crips, based upon a newspaper story describing the robbery of a group of elderly Japanese women who described the perpetrators as young cripples that carried canes.[103] As mentioned earlier, the term Crips now describes some 198 gangs in Los Angeles, and is considered an umbrella for those organizations, rather than a term for one particular group. The Bloods, on the other hand, is an umbrella term for some 98 groups in Los Angeles, and many elsewhere. The Bloods were originally a group of gangs who unified to defend themselves against the Crips. Bloods identify with the color red, while Crips identify with the color blue. The term *Blood* has a link to Vietnam. The term most likely originated with black Vietnam vets, who referred to each other as "blood" as a greeting. The original Bloods centered on Piru Street in Los Angeles, and the original Blood gangs were probably the Pirus and Bounty Hunter Bloods. Crips and Bloods brought hand signs into greater use and sophistication, and this, too, was probably derived from the Vietnam War. In the Vietnam War, black soldiers routinely greeted each other with a complex, stylized ritual termed the *dap*. Soldiers developed daps according to where they were from, what unit they were with, their political views, and so forth. When these black Vietnam Vets returned, many were bitter about how they had been treated and used in the military, as well as angry about the contempt that returning servicemen experienced. While they lacked marketable skills for legitimate jobs, their military training (and access to drug markets) made them ripe for another form of employment—with criminal gangs.

Although the rise of black gangs in America seems, in part, to be a byproduct of the Vietnam War, there are obviously other factors that seem to account for the growth of black gangs. A major factor has been increased segregation in America. While de jure segregation of schools ended with court decisions that had begun with the 1954 case of Brown v. Board of Education of Topeka, there is evidence that de facto segregation has actually increased in America. In fact, after the Supreme Court authorized "forced busing" in its 1971 Swann v. Charlotte-Mecklenburg Board of Education decision, there was increased "white flight" from the cities. Where serious attempts were made to force busing, such as in Boston, the whites reacted by rioting, protesting, removing their children from public schools and placing them in private schools, and by moving out of the city to the suburbs.[104] In addition to these maneuvers, whites also control school boards who perpetuate segregation by drawing school district lines and locating new schools so that students are segregated.[105] Although participation in and bitterness in regard to the Vietnam War may have spurred some blacks to join gangs and participate in an alternative occupation of trafficking in drugs, the continued increase in the growth in gangs in the decades after the Vietnam War must reflect the growing bitterness and alienation that has been produced by the abandonment of the American Dream. With the increasing globalization that has resulted in a decline in manufacturing jobs, as well as increased "ghettoization" of blacks, participation in gangs and the drug trade has become a rational and predictable outcome, an outcome only furthered by the War on Drugs.

Military Rule and Organized Crime: A Review

To review, there are several ways that military rule can contribute to the development of OC.

1. The military provides a hierarchical model that has been adopted historically by traditional OC groups.
2. Military experience exposes participants to foreign criminal networks.
3. Soldiers can experience psychological or physical pain resulting from wounds or injury leading to use of and possible addiction to narcotics such as heroin, as well as alcohol.
4. Morale problems resulting from a perception of forced participation in an unjust war effort can contribute to secretive participation in crime.
5. Participation in foreign wars can lead to parental absence, leading to juvenile delinquency on the home front.
6. Wartime restrictions on civilian access to goods needed in the war effort can lead to a Black Market for those goods.
7. Corruption of military personnel can result from an "end justifies the means" mentality that may be the product of battle experiences.
8. Isolation from needed sex partners leads to pursuit of surrogates through prostitution.
9. Migration that occurs after war results in a body of refugees seeking asylum that may turn to crime for survival purposes.
10. Wartime occupation may result in the development of resistance groups that grow into OC groups over time.

SUMMARY AND CONCLUSION

This chapter began with case studies of two informants, Ralph and Tony. As a child, Ralph had observed police being bribed, businesses paying protection money, and bootlegging activities in New York City during the 1920s. Tony had owned a bar and worked as an enforcer for the New Orleans crime syndicate. Tony indicated that Italian immigrants had started LCN in New Orleans and it spread to other parts of the country as the immigrants migrated. Both Ralph and Tony stated that crime bosses have, in their opinion, "gone legit." They no longer have to use strong-arm methods because they own legitimate businesses and control the people who "write, interpret, and enforce the laws."

In this chapter, we defined the term OC as "a conspiratorial enterprise pursuing profit or power through provision of illegal goods and/or services and involving systematic use of force or threat of force." The terms Mafia and LCN have characterized popular and public concepts of OC in the United States since the 1950s. However, criticisms of the widely held view that Italian Americans control OC in this country emerged in the 1960s. Of these criticisms, Bell's contention that OC is subject to "ethnic succession" is probably the most significant. More recently, it has been acknowledged, even by a 1986 President's commission, that OC is the province of a variety of ethnic and national groups and that it is transnational in nature. A United Nations study found that there are at least five different organizational structures involved in OC, of which "core group structures" and "criminal networks" involve little or no hierarchy.

An attempt was made to operationalize the term OC through limiting the definition to one measurable variable—the traffic in heroin. Countries discussed in the criminological literature and/or high in heroin trafficking were selected for profiling, including China, Hong Kong (now part of China), Italy, Japan, Mexico, Nigeria, Russia, Taiwan, and the United States.

What these countries have in common is a "history of military rule." In China, Triad OC groups developed as an underground secret society opposing oppressive governments and as a black market organization providing desired goods and services (drugs, prostitution, etc.). In China in the 1990s, free trade enabled the drug trade and trafficking in persons to flourish as new groups of "networking" smugglers from mainland China emerged. Like China, Japan has a military history that dates back to Samurai warriors of the Middle Ages. The Samurai were models for today's Yakuza OC groups, which carry on an illicit trade that is largely confined to providing goods and services for Japan itself, particularly the drug amphetamine. Mexico's long military rule has as its legacy corruption in the form of the bribe (mordida), accepted routinely in Mexico by underpaid police. Mexican gangs then transport illegal drugs and aliens into the United States with little police intervention. Italy historically has been occupied by a succession of military governments, especially in Sicily, where the Mafia began as a resistance movement to various military regimes. Mafia members have recently migrated, especially to countries that were formerly part of the Soviet Union, sometimes referred to as the Newly Independent States where law enforcement is lax and corruptible. The Italian Mafia has collaborated with the Russian "Mafiya" in joint ventures such as narcotics trafficking and vehicle theft. The Russian Mafiya developed at several levels—as a secret society of criminals in prison (vory); as a black market business that moved goods and services during the austere Soviet era; as Communist Party officials engaging in corrupt practices; and as alienated, underpaid members of the military who were exposed to drug trafficking and other OC through their travels, notably in Afghanistan. The United States has never had "military rule" per se, but frequent wartime involvement has, at times, led to priority being given to military considerations. The United States is a point of origin for one particular form of OC—outlaw motorcycle gangs, whose members initially were veterans of WWII who trafficked amphetamine after the war.

Finally, Nigeria was discussed as a country both with a history of military rule and slave trading. Military rule led to a large number of expatriates forming a nexus of some 500 criminal cells in 80 countries, including the United States, where one fourth of all airport heroin seizures are attributed to Nigerians.

Correlational analysis using U.S. data suggests that OC in America may be on the way to becoming a largely black enterprise. This growth may be linked to the involvement of black Americans with wars in Korea and Vietnam, where drug connections in Golden Triangle countries were established. Thus, it seems possible that the emerging nationwide networks of rival black gangs (i.e., the Crips and Bloods) may be, in fact, the New Mafia, an instance of what Daniel Bell termed ethnic succession.

DISCUSSION QUESTIONS

1. Do you believe the Mafia or LCN exists or existed previously in this country, or do you think it is or was a "myth," as Daniel Bell suggested?

2. Do you think that Prohibition and, today, the War on Drugs, have contributed to the development of OC groups in the United States, or have reduced OC?

3. What bearing does a "history of military rule" have on the development of OC in a country? Explain in detail, giving examples from the country studies in this chapter.

4. What factors do you think account for the development of border towns, such as Juarez and Tijuana, as locations for major OC activity in Mexico?

5. Do you believe that African Americans and Hispanic Americans are controlling most OC in the United States today? Why or why not?

SUGGESTED WEBSITES

http://da_wizeguy.tripod.com/omerta/id10.html
Mafiosi dictionary including terms used by the Italian Mafia and the Russian Mafiya.

http://www.american.edu/projects/mandala/TED/hpages/crime/Russian.htm   Website on Russian Mafiya.

http://clinton4.nara.gov/WH/EOP/NSC/html/documents/pub45270/pub45270index.html   Volume entitled *International Crime Threat Assessment* providing a complete study of OC from a global point of view.

http://www.infoplease.com/spot/slavery2.html
Website that describes research on the west African roots of most slaves brought to America. "Most blacks brought to the United States came from what are now Nigeria, Benin, Togo, Ghana, and Sierra Leone, all of which are in West Africa. Smaller numbers came from Senegal, the Gambia, the Congo River basin, and Angola."

http:/www.museumca.org/picturethis/5_4.html
Websites containing images pertaining to various civil rights movements throughout American history

ENDNOTES

1. Winslow & Winslow, 1974, pp. 69–79.
2. Von Lampe, 2003.
3. Rep. William McCullough in U.S. House of Representatives, 1970: 78, as quoted in Von Lampe, 2003, p. 8.
4. Task Force Report, 1967, 1, 6, as quoted in Von Lampe, 2003, p. 11.
5. Nelli, 1969.
6. Kefauver, 1951, p. 14.
7. Schmalleger, 2002, p. 371.
8. Cressey, 1969.
9. President's Commission on Law Enforcement and Administration of Justice, 1967.
10. Bell, 1965.
11. Clark, 1970.

12. Morris & Hawkins, 1969.
13. Bell, 1965, p. 141.
14. Clark, 1970, pp. 57–58.
15. Winslow & Winslow, 1974, p. 68.
16. President's Commission on Organized Crime, 1986, pp. 75–128.
17. Transnational Organized Crime Convention, Article 3 (2) as cited in United Nations Office on Drugs and Crime, 2002.
18. Faculty.ncwc.edu, 2004.
19. United Nations Office on Drugs and Crime, 2002, p. 4
20. United Nations Office on Drugs and Crime, 2002, p. 33.
21. Zhang & Chin, 2003; Zhang & Gaylord, 1996.
22. Wikipedia.org, 2005b.
23. Clinton Administration, 2000.
24. Clinton Administration, 2000, pp. 100–101.
25. Wikipedia, 2004a.
26. Abadinsky, 1997.
27. Comparative criminology website: China.
28. Abadinsky, 1997, p. 274.
29. Abadinsky, 1997, p. 275.
30. Schmalleger, 2003, p. 663.
31. Chouvy, 2002.
32. Clinton Administration, 2000, pp. 89–91.
33. Clinton Administration, 2000, p. 93.
34. Clinton Administration, 2000, p. 95.
35. Clinton Administration, 2000, p. 93.
36. Clinton Administration, 2000, pp. 94–95.
37. Clinton Administration, 2000, p. 95.
38. Clinton Administration, 2000, p. 97.
39. Goodling, 1998.
40. Abadinsky, 1997, p. 277.
41. Abadinsky, 1997, p. 279.
42. Abadinsky, 1997, p. 281.
43. Abadinsky, 1997, p. 270.
44. Abadinsky, 1997, p. 268–269.
45. Clinton Administration, 2000, p. 100.
46. KPBS, 2004.
47. Abadinsky, 1997; Clinton Administration, 2000; United Nations Office on Drugs and Crime, 2002. In addition, a list of Mexican organizations was drawn from About.com, 2002.
48. Clinton Administration, 2000, pp. 119–121.
49. Abadinsky, 1997, pp. 227–229.
50. Clinton Administration, 2000, pp. 118–119.
51. Clinton Administration, 2000, pp. 118–119.
52. Comparative Criminology Website: Mexico.
53. Anthony, Brooks, & Lo, 1999.
54. Patel, 2000.
55. Anthony, Brooks, & Lo, 1999.
56. Clinton Administration, 2000, pp. 115–118.
57. Lewis, 2001.
58. Clinton Administration, 2000, p. 62.
59. Abadinsky, 1997, p. 108.
60. Wikipedia, 2004e.
61. Abadinsky, 1997, pp. 113–114.
62. Clinton Administration, 2000, pp. 64–66.
63. Comparative Criminology Website: Russia.
64. Arvantides & Butcher, 1997.
65. Tripod, 2004.
66. Abadinsky, 1997, p. 215.
67. Arvantides & Butcher, 1997.
68. The Committee Office, House of Commons, 1999.
69. Clinton Administration, 2000, p. 72.
70. Clinton Administration, 2000, p. 70.
71. Clinton Administration, 2000, p. 75.
72. Clinton Administration, 2000, p. 76.
73. Friedman, 2000a.
74. Vanknin, 2002.
75. Friedman, 2000b.
76. Friedman, 2000, April 10.
77. Friedman, 2000c.
78. Finckenauer & Waring, 2001.
79. Friedman, 2000b.
80. Friedman, 2000b, p. 5.
81. Kagner, 1999.
82. Comparative Criminology Website: Nigeria.
83. Gardiner, Lowe, & Goode, 2002.
84. Environmental News Service, 2002.
85. Clinton Adminstration, 2000, p. 104.
86. Infoplease, 2004.
87. Myrdal, 1944.
88. Lombardo, 2002, p. 33.
89. Schatzberg & Kelly, 1996, 11, as quoted in Lombardo, 2002, p. 33.
90. The term "go slumming" came into use during this time, according to Lombardo, 2002, p. 40.
91. Lombardo, 2002, p. 51.
92. Lombardo, 2002, p. 52.

93. Ianni, 1974.

94. Brecher & Editors of Consumer Reports Magazine, 1972; McCoy, 1972, 1991 and 1997.

95. Waldorf, 1993.

96. Skolnick, 1990; Skolnick, Correl, Navarro, & Rabb, 1990.

97. Alonso, 2004.

98. Miller, 1996.

99. Maxson, 1998.

100. Abadinsky, 1997, pp. 283–284.

101. Oakland Museum of California, 2003.

102. Alonso, 2004, p. 4.

103. Alonso, 2004, p. 5.

104. Hubbard, 1999.

105. World Book, Inc., 2003.

KEY TERMS

Black Codes
Controlled Substances Act
decriminalization
depressants
drug abuse
drug addiction
drug trafficking

hallucinogens
interdiction
narco-terrorism
Schedule I–V drugs
Slave Codes
stepping-stone theory
stimulants

OUTLINE

Introduction
Classes of Drugs
Racism and the Drug Laws
History of Drug Abuse Legislation

The Addict and the Law
Arguments For and Against Decriminalization
Extent and Trends in Drug Trafficking
Country Profile

LEARNING OBJECTIVES

After reading this chapter, students should be able to:

1. Distinguish between the three major categories of psychoactive drugs—depressants, stimulants, and hallucinogens—and list examples of each

2. Identify and define the various classes of drugs in the U.S. Controlled Substances Act and list examples of drugs that are Schedule I, II, III, IV, and V

3. Trace the history of drug laws in the United States

4. Discuss the view that the drug laws have been used as a weapon in group conflict in the United States as a means of suppressing racial and ethnic minorities

5. Understand how, after the Civil War, the Black Codes, passed in the South to replace the Slave Codes, often had the effect of re-enslaving African Americans

6. Understand how drug laws at the national and state level came to have a similar effect as the Black Codes

7. Describe how events in the history of Pakistan resulted in its becoming a country with the world's highest rate of heroin seizures and the largest number of terrorist organizations

INTRODUCTION

I come from an upper middle class family. I started having what you call problems, or what I call symptoms, at about seven or eight years old. I went on into grade school, and about eighth grade I think it was, I started experimenting with drugs—cough syrup, pills, diet pills out of the medicine cabinet. I went on into high school and my freshman year of high school started smoking weed, and the first time I had a lid, and after that was gone a group of us started making runs across the border down here bringing kilos so it started being an every day sort of thing. I lived in the San Francisco Bay area. So we were trafficking in weed, there's fighting, a lot of truancy, drinking, minor scrapes with the law. The last day of my junior year I was expelled from high school for fighting with a couple of my teachers because I didn't like their ideas and they didn't like mine, I guess. So at this time I was about 17 years old, and I did get a job laying carpets, though I didn't stay at it very long.

When I was 17, I took my first shot of heroin on a trip to Mexico with some friends. I wasn't going to get hooked because all the [educational] films were showing it was your mainliners who were getting hooked, so I just took a skin pop, which everybody knows is not dangerous. So it took me about 20 minutes to get hooked for life instead of about three seconds if I'd have put it right in the sewer. This went on for quite some time, a number of years, actually, with a number of dry out periods. I probably should have been put in jail, but coming from a middle class family, that helped me stay out. At this time when you checked into the hospital they didn't have to call the police, so it was quite some time before I did end up in some kind of jail. I think the first time was here in San Diego on a smuggling charge that I bought my way out of. [After a third arrest] I was finally going to have to do some time, so in order to beat this time I went to the U.S. Federal Narcotic Hospital in Fort Worth, Texas. I was hooked pretty bad at this time and probably would have been real sick, but they took about 11 or 12 days and they brought me down with this methadone. I came out of there and I stayed clean for about 30 days, which was about the longest period I had stayed clean during this time. After this I went back to using again. I was caught and sentenced to 10 years in the hospital over here at the California Rehabilitation Center (CRC). After 18 months there, I got parole. And this time I think I stayed clean until about 2:00 in the afternoon the day I got out. The reason it took so long was because

I had to get from Riverside back to San Francisco. I was out for about 40 days and got sent back to CRC. After a year there I was released, but after about 40 days I was picked up in a flophouse with what they say was an overdose of narcotics. There are things in this apartment that I am in from a drug store burglary. So I was convicted of these. Actually, I wasn't convicted—I actually pled guilty, which was a bad mistake and nobody should ever do it, in my opinion, to the drug store burglary and was sentenced to state prison for six months to 15 years. I ended up doing three and a half years. I came out 17 months ago with a five-year parole with narcotics testing, and I could probably think of some way to beat the urine analysis, but I'm so sick and tired of being in jail and things like that that I think I'm about ready to quit. Right now I think my attitude has changed quite a bit and I've stopped trying to fight these people, though actually the motives for a lot of the things I do are revenge.

I can give you what I feel a few of the reasons are [for my drug addiction and crime]. I don't really think it was because my mother put me on the potty crooked when I was two, but this family situation I grew up in was a bad situation. This father of mine, and I'm still a little sorry I didn't kill him, said that none of my friends were good enough for my family type setting, and none were good enough for me. I think as these friends were being eliminated that I kept looking for a worse and worse type of friend, if you want to call it that, but people who are more out of society, or dropping out of society.

The reason that I relapsed each time I got out of prison was that drugs are so good. The feelings that I get out of drugs are so good and I would do it in a minute if they legalized narcotics; I would start shooting heroin right now today. An addict would rather take narcotics than have sex or get into bed with somebody. It is the most pleasurable thing in his life. I would like to add I am just barely functioning in society today. As to what I do, I'm down at the Salvation Army in a rehabilitation program and this is where Dr. Winslow picked me up. I never went in (to rehab) on my own choice. It was always something else—police pressure, family pressure—police pressure really is the only thing that has ever made me dry out. I think I did dry out once or twice for lack of drugs, but I just didn't have the money, didn't have somebody that was clean enough to make the border run down here; their arms are looking so bad they can't cross any border.

[Regarding the **stepping stone theory** that marijuana leads to heroin use] No, I don't think this is true, but you're placing you young people in a position where they're traveling in circles where these things are available. Your curiosity, it might just be curiosity, or actually I think that a kid smoking weed is trying to tell you something. He may not like society. He may not like his family, but he might not be so messed up that he can't go on and become one of you people here in the State University and function in society, and most of them will. We're talking about a really small percentage of them who will be jammed up and in bad trouble that they can't get out of.

Some addicts can find their way like through rehab while another finds it through AA and another might see the light and have Jesus Christ come into his life and be saved by a religious trip. To this day I haven't found my particular bag for what is going to cure me. There are a lot of us like me, hostile, bitter people who just can't go for any of these other programs. One answer is legalizing narcotics—heavy narcotics—and take the profit out of the 50 cents worth of pot or that these addicts are paying $200 a day for. These existing addicts let them shoot themselves to death. These guys are gone anyway for all practical purposes, and they are just walking death. As long as I don't bother anybody else in society I don't feel anyone should impress their morals on me. The thing would be set up so you aren't going to be starting new addicts. Like any narcotics you are giving—say to me, you are putting it right in the sewer in my arm and you're setting it up so you can't start new addicts by taking the profit out of it. When we die off you may not have any addicts left (and the crime that goes with it). I'm a narcotics dealer; it's my basic bag. But I've committed about every crime there is—armed robbery, burglary. . . . My point of view is that there is nothing bad about heroin. It produces narcosis or whatever some of these fancy words are and actually makes a passive type person; he is not usually involved in aggressive type crimes. There is no sexual drive so I say I doubt they can dig up an addict with a history of sexual offenses.

How I made my money and how successful I was I haven't yet discussed. When I got out of high school I was using. I was supporting a family. I did start a state-sponsored, four-year apprenticeship as an electrician. I took four years of night school plus eight hours a week of on-the-job training. And I was functioning so I had a working income that was pretty good. I wasn't maintaining my habit with that. I was maintaining my living expenses with that—money to support my family. I had a wife and two children. My wife was a little grasshopper herself, but she didn't go on to become an addict. I was selling about $200 a week worth of narcotics and supporting my habit. . . . Actually an addict that is living in a family-type setting like I was, working, keeping reasonable hours, eating three times a day, is not going to get in too bad of physical shape. My family is all gone now, because my life took a turn for the worst after I was busted for smuggling.[1]

In this chapter, and the next two, a variety of criminal enterprises are discussed. What do all of these criminal enterprises have in common? Actually, none of these crimes is listed in Part I of the UCR. Thus, in some regards they are not considered to be serious crimes. As discussed in Chapter 2, Sellin and Wolfgang did a study in which they tried to operationalize seriousness of delinquent acts. Their findings were based upon the rating of 141 juvenile offense descriptions in terms of seriousness by several subsamples that included university students, police officers, juvenile police officers, and juvenile court judges.[2] They found that items that lacked victimization in terms of bodily injury, property damage, and/or theft were rated low in seriousness. As may be surmised, Sellin and Wolfgang's findings correspond reasonably well with the FBI's distinction between Part I and Part II offenses. Thus, the Index crimes are rated as serious offenses by the general public, but the others are not. It is a point to ponder that many of the crimes discussed in this and the next two chapters have been treated as serious crimes by Congress and most state legislatures, despite the fact that the FBI treats them as Part II offenses. It is shown that the expanded list of felonies (omitted from Part I) may be related to "interagency conflict" within the U.S. federal bureaucracy. The list of Part I felonies was formed under the direction of J. Edgar Hoover, who was the founder of the FBI. Drug and sex trafficking offenses were not included as Index Offenses (Part I) when the UCR began publication in 1930, and it remains that way today. During all of these years, the UCR has included drug and white-collar offenses as Part II (non-index offenses). Other federal law enforcement agencies developed side-by-side with the FBI to deal with these Part II offenses. The most notable of these agencies was the Federal Bureau of Narcotics (FBN), which was developed more or less in the shadow of the FBI. Its founder and chief, from 1930 until his retirement in 1962, was Harry Anslinger, who managed to get Congressional approval for laws pertaining to "narcotic" drugs. The most significant of these laws were the Harrison Act of 1914 (passed before formation of the FBN) and the Marijuana Tax Act of 1937. These laws, which were replicated in state legislation, made possession and sale of a wide variety of drugs felonies. However, the drug felonies never made the FBI's seven major crimes list of Index crimes.

The fact that these crimes are treated by the FBI as Part II offenses is significant. Although Part I includes crimes reported to the police (whether or not an arrest is made), Part II only includes crimes that resulted in an arrest. This distinction is important in terms of comparative criminology. Looking at the INTERPOL data for frauds, counterfeit currency offenses, and drug offenses, it can be seen that the United States has nothing to report in regard to "cases known to the police," as well as related categories (attempts, cases solved, and rate per 100,000 inhabitants). Based upon the weakness of the FBI method of data keeping, only arrests can be reported to INTERPOL for these crimes. The same problem is reflected in U.S. reporting of information to the United Nations for similar crimes. As a result of this omission, international comparisons for drug offenses cannot be made using INTERPOL data or United Nations crime data between the United States and other nations of the world (although we draw upon United Nations drug seizure data for country comparisons).

Non-index crimes are the subject of this chapter and the next two chapters, and the discussion involves a long list of crimes. Included in this chapter will be crimes that have not been covered in previous chapters. The list of crimes covered in this and the next two chapters are crimes that some have argued should not be crimes (e.g., prostitution, possession of marijuana). In fact, some of these crimes are "winked at" in the sense that a popular perception exists that "everybody does it," such as drunkenness, avoiding taxes, taking illicit drugs, and so forth. In some instances, young people seek to "hang out" with persons who provide these illicit services who are considered to be "cool," in the case of a friend who can supply drugs, or a "nice guy," in the case of a mobster, such as John Gotti. Gangsters in the past have been romanticized through the "Bogart" image of them conveyed in Hollywood movies, and people sometimes enjoy going to bars and restaurants where such people are known to frequent.

Drug trafficking is a major category discussed throughout the text. Here, a more detailed description of the various drugs that are trafficked in the United States is made. Various terms involving drugs are defined, the history of the legal approach to the drug is discussed, and the origins of drugs, in or outside of the United States, is traced. Various drugs are considered illicit in the United States. It is necessary to describe these drugs and their effects. Then, the legal history of these drugs is explored, including the chronology of the legislation concerning these drugs. Commentary is made on source countries at different times, as well as the alleged relationship of the drug laws to the treatment of various ethnic groups. Finally, a country profile of Pakistan helps to show the many factors related to drug trafficking today, through cross-national comparison.

Before discussing the history of illegal drugs, a brief discussion of pharmacological and social issues regarding the definition of **drug abuse** is desirable. In some ways it is true that the pharmacological effect of drugs has little to do with whether or not they are declared illegal. There are three general categories of drugs, both legal and illegal—stimulants, depressants, and hallucinogens. The category **depressants** includes a cross-section of drugs, legal and illegal, prescription, and nonprescription. The category includes alcohol and inhalants, which can be purchased legally in the United States without a prescription. It includes tranquilizers such as Halcyon, Valium, Librium, and Xanax. It also includes opium, codeine, morphine, heroin, methadone, Demerol, and Percodan. **Stimulants** include caffeine, nicotine, methylphenidate (Ritalin), Methedrine, Dexedrine (amphetamine), and cocaine. Caffeine can be legally obtained by anybody in the United States, whereas tobacco can be legally obtained by adults. **Hallucinogens** include lysergic acid diethylamide (LSD), phencyclidine (PCP), mescaline or peyote, methylenedioxymethamphetamine (MDMA, or Ecstasy), and cannabis.[3]

Of these drugs, heroin and most of the hallucinogens are banned by law as "Schedule I" offenses under Title II of the 1970 Comprehensive Drug Abuse Prevention and Control Act. Title II is also called the **Controlled Substances Act** (CSA). There are five schedules under this act, based upon whether or not the drug has a current accepted medical use and whether or not the drug has a high potential for abuse. **Schedule I drugs** are designated by this act to have no current accepted medical use and to have a high potential for abuse. These include heroin, methaqualone, LSD, MDMA (Ecstasy), peyote, psilocybin, marijuana, hashish, hash oil, and various amphetamine variants.[4] Since these drugs are deemed to have no accepted medical use, they cannot legally be prescribed by a doctor, according to federal law, so any possession of these drugs is illegal.

State and local laws tend to be consistent with the federal laws, with the exception of alcohol and marijuana. With regard to alcohol, local ordinances still prohibit alcohol in hundreds of "dry" counties across the United States.[5] Many of these dry counties (alcohol not for sale) are located in the South in states such as Kentucky and Mississippi. Mississippi has 44 "wet" counties, 26 "dry" counties, and 8 counties that have never held an alcohol legalization vote.[6] By contrast, since 1978, when New Mexico's state legislature enacted the nation's first law recognizing marijuana's medicinal values, 34 states have followed suit with similar state actions.[7] Because the state laws of these 34 states permit medicinal marijuana, if the person is caught with marijuana by local or state police in these states (and meets the conditions required by the state, such as a doctor's prescription), then the person could avoid arrest for possession of marijuana. In addition, there are 10 states that have decriminalized possession of up to one ounce of marijuana. In these states, possession of small quantities of marijuana is a civil, rather than a criminal offense. Offenders may be given a citation or fined, and their marijuana is confiscated. Possession of larger amounts is still considered a criminal offense because it indicates intent to sell.[8]

In states such as California where marijuana is decriminalized, offenders face the odd circumstance of having the possible penalty depend upon which law enforcement agency apprehends them. If caught by a federal law enforcement agent (DEA, FBI, Immigration and Naturalization Service [INS] etc.), persons apprehended for possession of less than an ounce of marijuana could face a sentence of not less than five years. If caught by local police the person would at worse face a fine, but generally no sanction at all.

BOX 12–1

Doctors Behind Bars

In February 1999, Dr. Frank Fisher, a general practitioner in Shasta County, California, was arrested by agents from the California state attorney general's office and charged with drug trafficking and murder. The arrest was based on records indicating that Dr. Fisher had been prescribing high doses of narcotic pain relievers to his patients, five of whom died. He lost his home and his medical practice and served five months in jail before it was discovered that the patients had died from accidents or from medical illnesses, not from the narcotics he prescribed. All charges were dropped last year, and Dr. Fisher now has his medical license back. Yet his ordeal lingers as a cautionary tale of what can happen to doctors who treat pain aggressively. . . . A 1998 survey of more than 1,300 physicians by the New York State Medical Society found that 60% were moderately or very concerned about the possibility of being investigated by regulatory authorities for prescribing opiates for noncancer pain. A third said they prescribed lower quantities of pills and lower dosages "frequently" because of the possibility of eliciting an investigation. When asked how often they avoided prescribing a preferred drug for noncancer pain, because doing so required triplicate forms, half said "frequently."[9]

Schedule II–V controlled substances have current accepted medical uses, and are therefore available by prescription. **Schedule II drugs** are considered to have a high potential for abuse and are considered to be addictive.[10] Included in this class are cocaine, codeine, Demerol, opium, morphine, PCP, and certain stimulants such as Ritalin and phenmetrazine (Preludin). Prescriptions to Schedule II drugs are nonrefillable and vendors are required to have vault storage and keep thorough records.[11] Persons caught with these drugs who do not have a prescription for them are subjected to the same penalties as for Schedule I drugs.

Schedule III, IV, and V drugs have accepted medical use, but medium, low, and lowest potential for abuse, respectively. Included in Schedule III are low-dose opium products such as Vicodan and Tylenol with codeine, anabolic steroids (added in 1991), amphetamines, and barbiturates. Schedule IV includes depressants and minor tranquilizers such as Halcyon, Librium, Valium, and Xanax, along with some stimulants. Schedule V includes cough medicines and antidiarrheals containing small amounts of opium, morphine, or codeine. Maximum federal penalties for Schedule III, IV, and V drugs are imprisonment for five years, three years, and one year, respectively.

Aside from the possible impact upon criminality that drug prohibition may create, other criticisms have been made of the aforementioned classification system. One main criticism already discussed has been the inclusion of nonaddicting hallucinogens, such as marijuana, in Schedule I, while addicting drugs, such as alcohol and nicotine, are available over the counter.[12] It has also been suggested that not only marijuana, but also heroin, may have an accepted medical use. In Great Britain, heroin has been found to be effective with patients experiencing extremely severe pain, such as that resulting from terminal cancer.[13]

RACISM AND THE DRUG LAWS

Probably the most damning criticism of the rank order of drugs in the CSA, as well as other antidrug legislation in the United States, is that the ranking was influenced by racism. The legislation that preceded and followed the CSA has been assailed for being connected with the politics of the time and being developed as a weapon in group conflict. A brief history of these drugs and drug laws helps to show the basis for the allegation of racism and the politics of drug legislation. The major drug laws that have been developed by the federal government are listed in Table 12–1.

There is much criminological literature devoted to the issue of racism or xenophobia forming the context for much of antidrug legislation. It should be pointed out that before 1914, none of the drugs listed in the 1970 CSA were illegal. Opium was primarily used, not by impoverished racial minorities, but disproportionately by white, middle aged, middle class women.[14] However, opium, and two other drugs—cocaine and marijuana—came to be associated with use by ethnic groups. All three, as it turns out, were used to relieve pain associated with strenuous manual labor. Opium was the drug of choice for Chinese workers who performed much of the labor of developing America's first coast-to-coast railroad system in the 19th century.[15] Cocaine was provided to African American dockworkers,

Table 12–1 **Timeline of Significant Drug Laws[16]**

Year	Event	Effect
1906	Pure Food and Drug Act	Gave FDA power to regulate food and drugs
1909	Opium Exclusion Act	Prohibited importation of opium, except for medical purposes
1914	Harrison Tax Act	Outlawed the opiates and cocaine
1922	Narcotic Drug Import and Export Act	Outlawed narcotics except for legitimate medicinal use
1924	Heroin Act	Outlawed the manufacture of heroin
1937	Marijuana Tax Act	Applied controls over marijuana similar to narcotics
1938	Food, Drug and Cosmetic Act	Defined "drug" as effecting a body in absence of disease
1942	Opium Poppy Control Act	Prohibited growing poppy without license
1951	Durham-Humphrey Amendment	Set guidelines for prescription drugs
1951	Boggs Amendment to Harrison Act	Set mandatory sentences for narcotics violations
1956	Narcotics Control Act	Set more severe penalties for narcotics violations
1965	Drug Abuse Control Amendments (DACA)	Set strict controls over amphetamines, barbiturates, LSD, etc.
1966	Narcotic Addict Rehabilitation Act (NARA)	Allowed treatment as an alternative to jail
1968	DACA Amendments	Sentence suspended/record expunged if no violations within one year
1970	Comprehensive Drug Abuse and Control Act	Replaced/updated all previous laws—narcotics/dangerous drugs
1972	Drug Abuse Office and Treatment Act	Established federally funded prevention/treatment programs
1973	Methadone Control Act	Regulated methadone licensing
1973	Heroin Trafficking Act	Increased penalties for distribution
1973	Alcohol, Drug Abuse & Mental Health Association (ADAMHA)	Consolidated NIMH, NIDA, and NIAAA under umbrella organization
1973	Drug Enforcement Administration (DEA)	Bureau of Narcotics/Dangerous Drugs became DEA
1974	Drug Abuse Treatment and Control Amendments	Extended 1972 act
1978	Drug Abuse Treatment and Control Amendments	Extended 1972 act
1978	Alcohol and Drug Abuse Education Amendments	Set up education programs within Department of Education
1980	Drug Abuse Prevention, Treatment, & Rehabilitation Amendments	Extended prevention education and treatment programs
1984	Drug Offenders Act	Set up special programs for offenders and organized treatment
1986	Analogue (Designer Drug) Act	Made use of substances like existing illicit drugs illegal
1988	Anti-Drug Abuse Act	Established oversight office: National Drug Control Policy
1992	ADAMHA Reorganization	Transfers NIDA (National Institute of Drug Abuse), NIMH (National Institute of Mental Health), and NIAAA (National Institute of Alcohol Abuse and Alcoholism) to NIH and incorporates ADAMHA's programs into the Substance Abuse and Mental Health Services Administration (SAMHSA)

around the turn of the 20th century, to facilitate longer working hours and greater productivity.[17] Marijuana was a drug used by Mexican farm labor in the west and southwest of the United States to ease pain and promote sleep at the end of a day of working in the fields.[18]

HISTORY OF DRUG ABUSE LEGISLATION

Despite the fact that the drugs were used to ease pain or increase productivity of hard working laborers, when it came time for xenophobia and racism, guilt by association with these drugs was used as a weapon in group conflict. After the transcontinental railroad was completed and the gold mines ceased to be productive in California, Chinese laborers were no longer needed and legislation was passed toward the goal of excluding them. During the depression of 1875–1880, Chinese laborers became an obstacle to the economic survival of white workers. Although the Chinese laborers were previously free to smoke opium as they pleased, in the mid-1870s the situation was different, and whites organized against opium-smoking Chinese. Starting in 1875, San Francisco and several other cities enacted anti-opium laws outlawing opium "dens" (smoking houses), legally repressing the Chinese and serving the interests of the white working class.[19] In 1882, the U.S. Congress lent its support to the anti-Chinese sentiment by passing the Chinese Exclusion Act, which prohibited Chinese immigrants from becoming citizens of the United States. In 1909, Congress enacted the Opium Exclusion Act, which prohibited the importation of opium and any of its derivatives, except for medical purposes.

Narcotics addicts in Hong Kong heat a dab of opium over the flame of an oil lamp until it is dry enough to smoke from a pipe. The smoking of opium was introduced to China by British and other European sailors who had learned to use a pipe to smoke tobacco from Native Americans. In the late 1800s, opium dens were prevalent in the United States in San Francisco, which was a major port of entry for the traffic in opium. The dens were known as joints or dives and the pipe used to smoke the opium was termed a yen. The term "dive" was derived from "divan" referring to Turkish smoking rooms, later to mean a sofa or couch upon which such smoking is sometimes done. The term "yen" came to connote a "craving or yearning."

Source: Getty Images, Inc.–Hulton Archive Photos.

While intergroup conflict was taking place between whites and Chinese in California during the late 1800s, in the South the conflict was between whites and blacks. The whites were passing apartheid laws to curb the voting rights of blacks, who were slaves before the Civil War, and lynching was also used as a sanction for perceived black misbehavior. The media began to report the use of cocaine by the black population (who were given cocaine to "improve their productivity" by employers, as pointed out earlier). While whites consumed cocaine in social settings in a popular new beverage called Coca Cola (which originally contained cocaine), use of the drug by blacks was considered to be dangerous—since, based upon the Lombrosian thinking of the time, they were thought of as subhuman to begin with:

> The drug produces several other conditions that make the "fiend" a peculiarly dangerous criminal. One of these conditions is a temporary immunity to shock—a resistance to the "knock down" effects of fatal wounds. Bullets, fired into vital parts, that would drop a sane man in his tracks, fail to check the "fiend"—fail to stop his rush or weaken his attack. A recent experience of Chief of Police Lyerly of Asheville, N.C., illustrates this particular phase of cocainism. The Chief was informed that a hitherto inoffensive Negro was "running amuck" in a cocaine frenzy. . . . Knowing that he must kill the man or be killed himself, the Chief drew his revolver [a heavy army model . . . large enough to kill any game in America], placed the muzzle over the Negro's heart and fired—"intending to kill him right quick"—but the shot did not even stagger the man. And a second shot that pierced the arm and entered the chest had just as little effect in stopping the Negro or checking his attack.[20]

Just as Congress had come to the rescue of whites in the West with the Opium Exclusion Act of 1909, additional legislation was passed in 1914 to serve the interest of whites both in the West and the South—The Harrison Tax Act. This law made it illegal for anybody to possess opium or cocaine unless prescribed by a physician. Chinese and blacks, who had been free to use these substances previously, could now be imprisoned for doing so.

In one form or another, this law has helped re-enslave blacks by the thousands in the United States, and in the late 1800s black prisoners were leased out as chain gangs to white "masters" after their incarceration under the Harrison Act or similar acts duplicated at the state level. In a sense, the Harrison Act provided a Black Code on the federal level comparable to those that had been passed in the South after slavery:

> After the Civil War, the 13th Amendment officially abolished slavery for all people except those convicted of a crime. Legally allowing any such individual to be subjected to slavery and involuntary servitude opened the door for mass criminalization. . . . When African Americans were no longer legally held as slaves or property, there was a tremendous increase in the number of African American convicts. Before the Civil War, laws called the **Slave Codes** governed the rights of slaves and all African Americans in the South. When slavery was legally abolished, the Slave Codes were rewritten as the **Black Codes,** a series of laws criminalizing legal activity for African Americans. Through the enforcement of these laws, acts such as standing in one area of town or walking at night, for example, became the criminal acts of "loitering" or "breaking curfew" for which African Americans were imprisoned. In the late 19th-century South, . . . [the] convict lease system

functioned with the Black Codes to re-establish and maintain the race relationships of slavery by returning the control over the lives of these African-Americans to white plantation owners. This is illustrated by the fact that in 1878, Georgia leased out 1,239 convicts, 1,124 of whom were African Americans. Through the convict lease system, bidders paid an average $25,000 a year to the state, in exchange for control over the lives of all of the convicts. The system provided revenue for the state and the profit of unwaged, unprotected workers for plantation owners or private industries.[21]

Full social control of the "Black Peril" in the South and the "Yellow Peril" in the West was achieved in regard to opium and cocaine as a result of a series of Supreme Court decisions between 1919 and 1922 that made it illegal for physicians to prescribe narcotics (opium and cocaine) to patients.[22] Thus, simple possession of these drugs would henceforth be a criminal offense, prescription or no prescription. Furthermore, this series of decisions meant that it was impossible for addicts to obtain their drugs legally, resulting in an illegal drug trade charging users up to 50 times more than the legal retail drug price.[23] Under these circumstances, African Americans who became addicted to either cocaine or some form of opium (including heroin and morphine) would most likely need to pursue a life of crime to provide the income to support the addiction. And this life of crime would very likely result in slavery through imprisonment.

Although these actions at the federal level appeased whites in the South and West, economic depression once again created intergroup conflict during the Great Depression of the 1930s. However, this time the conflict was between whites and Mexicans in the Southwest. The Mexicans competed with U.S. whites for scarce jobs by working for lower pay. Once again, drug legislation came to the rescue. One weapon in group conflict with the Mexicans was marijuana, since the drug was commonly used by Mexican field workers. Thus, a way to exclude the Mexicans was to pass laws against marijuana (which was done in many Southwest states) and then arrest and deport Mexicans caught with the drug. To get this legislation passed, Mexicans who used marijuana were demonized:

> Probably the best single statement was the statement of a proponent of Texas' first marijuana law. He said on the floor of the Texas Senate, and I quote, "All Mexicans are crazy, and this stuff (referring to marijuana) is what makes them crazy." Or, as the proponent of Montana's first marijuana law said, . . . and I quote, "Give one of these Mexican beet field workers a couple of puffs on a marijuana cigarette and he thinks he is in the bullring at Barcelona."[24]

While state and local legislation served to harass Mexicans in the Southwest states, police, prosecutors, and politicians from these states pressed for federal intervention to control the "degenerate and violent Mexican." The responsibility for the production of federal legislation against marijuana fell to Harry Anslinger, who became Commissioner of the FBN. Anslinger was successful in getting Congress to pass the Marijuana Tax Act of 1937, which put marijuana into the class of federally forbidden narcotics. Anslinger reportedly had the support not only of whites in the Southwest, but also of the Hearst syndicate of newspapers, which published a series of stories about the horrors of marijuana:

> News stories were manipulated to aggrandize and exaggerate the supposed "horrors" of recreational marijuana use. The story of an auto accident where one marijuana cigarette was found would dominate front

American syndicated newspaper owner William Randolph Hearst (1863–1951) is said to have backed yellow journalism newspaper articles that supported FBN bureaucrat Harry Anslinger's campaign to criminalize hemp. In these articles, Hearst popularized use of the term, "marijuana," the Mexican term for hemp. It is alleged that Americans might have had second feelings about the anti-marijuana campaign if they had known that the media campaign was against hemp. Hemp is a plant that, since antiquity, has been used in the manufacture of clothes, rope, twine, cordite, sails, and paper products. Hemp paper was reportedly used by Thomas Jefferson to draft the Declaration of Independence.

Source: Getty Images, Inc.–Hulton Archive Photos.

page headlines for weeks while alcohol related accidents—which outnumbered marijuana 1,000 to 1—were briefly mentioned and buried in the back pages. The rape of a white woman by a "Negro," previously attributed by Hearst publications to cocaine use was, by these same publications, suddenly attributed to the use of marijuana.[25]

It has been alleged that William Randolph Hearst had a vested interest in providing "anti-hemp" newspaper stories, because Hearst was in the paper manufacturing business and in the timber business as well. Hearst popularized the Mexican term for hemp (marijuana) in his many sensational stories, while never using the word hemp. Thus, most Americans never associated marijuana with hemp, or with "extract of cannabis" used as a medicine previously.[26] Harry Anslinger had served for several years in the ill-fated Prohibition division in the Department of the Treasury. After the narcotics sector of the Prohibition division was rocked by scandal, Anslinger was appointed head of the newly created FBN in 1930, where he remained until his forced retirement (by President Kennedy) in 1962. Anslinger managed a publicity campaign, with the help of Hearst and others, that led to the passage of the Marijuana Tax Act. Before the passage of the Marijuana Tax Act, Anslinger promulgated propaganda about the drug and campaigned for the passage of the Uniform Narcotic Drug Act, which was proposed in 1932, to be passed by state legislatures. By 1937, every state had enacted some form of legislation relating to marijuana, and 35 had enacted the Uniform Act, which included marijuana as a "narcotic" prohibited by law, with criminal penalties.[27] The FBN was involved in the creation of the final draft of the Uniform Narcotic Drug Act and conducted a campaign in newspapers and legal journals to boost public support for the Uniform Act. Harry Anslinger himself co-authored an article entitled "Marijuana: Assassin of Youth," published in July, 1937, containing some inflammatory rhetoric including alleged incidents of an association between marijuana use and robbery, murder, suicide, insanity, and "hot jazz." Some excerpts from the article are indicative of the allegations made:

BOX 12–2

Reefer Madness

A propaganda film from 1936 that has become a cult hit because of its dated outlook on marijuana use, *Reefer Madness* is the height of camp entertainment. Framed as a "documentary," the film is narrated by a high school principal imparting his wisdom and experiences with the demon weed. The bulk of the film focuses on almost slapstick scenes of high school kids smoking pot and quickly going insane, playing "evil" jazz music, being committed, and going on a murder spree. Meant to be an important and affecting cautionary tale, this dated black-and-white film's true value is in its many entertaining moments of unintended hilarity.[28]

THE sprawled body of a young girl lay crushed on the sidewalk the other day after a plunge from the fifth story of a Chicago apartment house. Everyone called it suicide, but actually it was murder. The killer was a narcotic known to America as marijuana, and to history as hashish. It is a narcotic used in the form of cigarettes, comparatively new to the United States and as dangerous as a coiled rattlesnake. . . . THERE was the young girl, for instance, who leaped to her death. [After smoking marijuana at parties, falling behind in her studies, and becoming worried.] With every puff of the smoke the feeling of despondency lessened. Everything was going to be all right—at last. . . . Without hesitancy she walked to a window and leaped to her death. Thus can marijuana "solve" one's difficulties. . . . An entire family was murdered by a youthful addict in Florida. . . . The boy said he had been in the habit of smoking . . . "muggles," a childish name for marijuana. [The members of the military order of Assassins in ancient Persia] were confirmed users of hashish, or marijuana, and it is from the Arabic "hashshashin" that we have the English word "assassin." . . . It would be well for law enforcement everywhere to search for marijuana behind cases of criminal and sex assault. During the last year a young male addict was hanged in Baltimore for criminal assault on a 10-year-old girl. His defense was that he was temporarily insane from smoking marijuana.[29]

The timing of Anslinger's "Assassin" article, published in July of 1937, coincided perfectly with the passage of the Marijuana Tax Act, which Congress passed one month later, in August of 1937.

Anslinger had the backing not only of the Hearst syndicate, but also of Hollywood film producers with the production of the 1936 propaganda film *Reefer Madness*. Through these various mass media and political manipulations, Anslinger managed to create what was later termed a "moral panic" regarding the criminal potential of marijuana, considered previously to be a weed that grew wild, even in Washington, DC, and a fairly harmless, nonaddicting medicine. As a result of Anslinger's "bureaucratic virtuosity," his fledgling FBN, with 300 employees and a budget of a little over $1 million, would one day evolve into the DEA, which today is an enormous law enforcement agency at the federal level, with approximately 10,000 employees and a budget of over $2 billion.[30] In addition to his personal propaganda campaign, Anslinger testified before Congress that the Marijuana Tax Act should be passed, based upon the model of the National Firearms Act (which required an unavailable federal tax stamp for machine gun sales). Anslinger stated that the drug, marijuana, makes people insane, can cause murderous behavior, and is used by school children.[31] The following are excerpts from his actual testimony:

Mr. Chairman, my name is H. J. Anslinger; I am Commissioner of Narcotics in the Bureau of Narcotics, in the Treasury Department. Mr. Chairman and distinguished members of the Ways and Means Committee, this traffic in marijuana is increasing to such an extent that it has come to be the cause for the greatest national concern. This drug is as old as civilization itself. Homer wrote about [it], as a drug that made people forget their homes, and that turned them into swine. In Persia, a thousand years before Christ, there was a religious and military order founded which was called the Assassins and they derived their name from the drug called hashish which is now known in this country as marijuana. They were noted for their acts of cruelty, and the word "assassin" very aptly describes the drug. Marijuana is the same as Indian hemp, hashish. . . . It is known as cannabis, cannabis Americana, or Cannabis Sativa. Marijuana is the Mexican term for cannabis indica. We seem to have adopted the Mexican terminology, and we call it marijuana, which means good feeling. In the underworld it is referred to by such colorful, colloquial names as reefer, muggles, Indian hay, hot hay, and weed. It is known in various countries by a variety of names. . . . As a matter of fact the staminate leaves are about as harmless as a rattlesnake. . . . But here we have [a] drug that is not like opium. Opium has all of the good of Dr. Jekyll and all the evil of Mr. Hyde. This drug is entirely the monster Hyde, the harmful effect of which cannot be measured. . . . It affects different individuals in different ways. Some individuals have a complete loss of sense of time or a sense of value. They lose their sense of place. They have an increased feeling of physical strength and power. Some people will fly into a delirious rage, and they are temporarily irresponsible and may commit violent crimes. Other people will laugh uncontrollably. It is impossible to say what the effect will be on any individual. . . . It is dangerous to the mind and body, and particularly dangerous to the criminal type, because it releases all of the inhibitions. . . . The use of cannabis, whether smoked or ingested in its various form[s], undoubtedly gives rise to a form of addiction, which has serious social consequences (abandonment of work, propensity to theft and crime, disappear-ance of reproductive power). . . . Here is a gang of seven young men, all seven of them, young men under 21 years of age. They terrorized central Ohio for more than two months, and they were responsible for 38 stick-ups. They all boast they did those crimes while under the influence of marijuana. . . . There was one town in Ohio where a young man went into a hotel and held up the clerk and killed him, and his defense was that he had been affected by the use of marijuana. . . . As to these young men I was telling you about, one of them said if he had killed somebody on the spot he would not have known it. In Florida a 21-year-old boy under the influence of this drug killed his parents and his brothers and sisters. The evidence showed that he had smoke[d] marijuana. In Chicago recently two boys murdered a policeman while under the influence of marijuana. Not long ago we found a 15-year-old boy going insane because, the doctor told the enforcement officers, he thought the boy was smoking marijuana cigarettes. They traced the sale to some man who had been growing marijuana and selling it to these boys all under 15 years of age, on a playground there. . . . Young men between the ages of 16 and 25 are frequent smokers of marijuana; even boys of 10 to 14 are initiated (frequently in school groups); to them as other[s]; marijuana holds out the thrill. Since the economic depression the number of marijuana smokers has increased by vagrant youths coming into contact with older psychopaths.[32]

Anslinger's testimony was excerpted here because of its tremendous importance in terms of drug policy for the United States. It was his testimony and the ultimate passage of the Marijuana Tax Act that ultimately culminated in the War on Drugs, because marijuana was a drug that was so freely abundant that it could and did result in the imprisonment of an estimated 20 million people in the United States.[33] In a sense, the politics that led to the Marijuana Tax Act served as a model for successful future antidrug legislation. Marijuana would become a focal point for the youthful rebellion that occurred in the 1960s, which in turn would spur even more repressive drug legislation in the 1970s, 1980s, and 1990s, which has also been attributed to racism.

The Marijuana Tax Act was draconian legislation, not only in its provisions, but in the way in which it was administered by the FBN under Anslinger's direction. The Act ostensibly was a tax act, with penalties of five years' imprisonment and/or a $2,000 fine for evading the purchase of a Treasury Department tax stamp. However, under the Act, the FBN was given absolute policing power, and physicians who wished to prescribe marijuana under the 60-odd pages of "Regulations No. I," had to provide a maze of affidavits, depositions, sworn statements, and constant Treasury Department police inspections in every instance of transmitting the drug, making it in essence impossible for physicians to comply with the law. Furthermore, Anslinger's administration of the new law, given absolute power, was indeed heavy handed. From the passage of the bill in 1937 through 1939, more than 3,000 doctors were prosecuted. Although the AMA had actually provided testimony opposing Anslinger's testimony before Congress, in 1939, the AMA made peace with Anslinger by coming out in opposition to marijuana, and during the next 10 years only three doctors were prosecuted by the FBN.[34] In addition, Anslinger actually used his influence to ban a 1946 law enforcement training film on the subject of drug addiction produced by the Canadian Film Board with the assistance of the Royal Canadian Mounted Police.[35]

One would imagine that seemingly dictatorial power being displayed by an agency of the government would have met opposition by social scientists—and it was—by one social psychologist named Alfred Lindesmith. It was Lindesmith and Lindesmith alone who dared to oppose Anslinger, and Lindesmith's dialogue with Anslinger is important enough to merit discussion, because it has to do with the nature of addiction. Lindesmith treated addiction as an illness, whereas Anslinger linked addiction with criminality.

THE ADDICT AND THE LAW

Alfred Lindesmith (1905–1991) was a University of Chicago trained social psychologist who had been a student of Herbert Blumer, Ernest Burgess, Louis Wirth, W. I. Thomas, and Edwin Sutherland, from whom he derived the "symbolic interactionist" approach to social psychology. Lindesmith developed the symbolic interactionist approach to social psychology in his Ph.D. dissertation and in his text on social psychology. Lindesmith's social psychology involved a rejection of instinct theory. He maintained that all human behavior is learned behavior, including addiction.[36] In describing **drug addiction,** Lindesmith maintained that there was a strong learned and self-labeling component to it. He distinguished between physical addiction and psychological addiction. He indicated that a person could take a physically addicting drug and not become a drug addict. For instance, if a person is administered morphine in the hospital to relieve the pain of injury, and then later experiences "withdrawal distress" from the morphine, he or she will not necessarily become addicted. This is because the person may not be aware that the pain he or she is experiencing is, in fact, withdrawal distress.

Lindesmith indicated that there are essentially five steps in addiction. First, the person must take an addicting drug. Second, the person must experience withdrawal distress. Third, the person must associate the withdrawal distress with the absence of the drug. Fourth, the person must then obtain and take more of the addicting drug. Fifth, the person then associates relief from the withdrawal distress with taking more of the drug.[37] It turns out that Lindesmith's ideas were not well liked by Harry Anslinger, the "moral entrepreneur," who by this time had obtained considerable power in regard to the dissemination of information regarding drugs, and Lindesmith was targeted. Anslinger was particularly angered by Lindesmith's publication of an article entitled "Dope Fiend Mythology," in the *Journal of Criminal Law and Criminology*. The difference of view was, as stated previously, that Lindesmith viewed addiction as a medical problem, while Anslinger sought to portray it as primarily criminality. Not only was a counter-Lindesmith media campaign launched by Anslinger, but Lindesmith was personally harassed and subject to investigation by the FBN. The power of Anslinger and the FBN was shown by its suppression of the 1946 Canadian film, *Drug Addict*, as discussed earlier. The film largely supported Lindesmith's view through several themes:

1. Addicts and traffickers are recruited from all races and classes;
2. High-level drug traffickers are white;
3. Law enforcement only targets low-level dealers;
4. Addiction is a sickness;
5. Addiction to legal and illegal drugs is essentially the same;
6. Cocaine is not necessarily addictive; and
7. Law enforcement control of drugs is, in the final analysis, impossible.[38]

Lindesmith was aware of the importance of the film, not only for its intended audience, but also for its damning rebuttal of the misinformation campaign carried out by Anslinger and the FBN. However, Lindesmith was never able to overcome opposition from Anslinger, the FBN, and supporters of Anslinger that included the Women's Christian Temperance Union, many churches, and many drug companies. The film *Drug Addict* is to this day technically banned in the United States.

Anslinger went on to testify before the Kefauver Committee, suggesting that drug trafficking was controlled by OC. As a result of this testimony, the Kefauver Committee recommended the passage of the Boggs Amendment to the Harrison Act, sponsored by Congressman Hale Boggs, one of Anslinger's strongest supporters.[39] The Boggs Amendment established mandatory minimums of two years for a first offense for selling narcotics, five years for a second offense, and 10 (to 20) for third and subsequent repetitions.[40] In addition to his success in establishing tough sentences for selling drugs, Anslinger argued with conviction to Congress that marijuana could be used by Communists, who would sell it to American solders to sap their will to fight.[41] As head of the U.S. delegation to the United Nations Drug Convention, Anslinger obtained the United Nations Single Convention Treaty on Narcotics, which classified marijuana as a criminal narcotic.[42] Thus, America's drug policy became that of the United Nations through the efforts of Anslinger.

Lindesmith's protest against Anslinger and the FBN did not receive much public support until the 1960s, when Vietnam War protests, combined with the civil rights movement and civil disobedience regarding marijuana resulted in an anti-establishment movement among youth. The **decriminalization** movement resulted in lowering penalties for possession of less than an ounce of marijuana in 11 states. However, fear over the civil turmoil of the 1960s culminated in the election of Richard Nixon in 1968. During the Nixon administration, the 1970 Comprehensive Drug Abuse and Control Act included the Drug Schedules I–V and recriminalized marijuana as a Schedule I offense. President Jimmy Carter (1976–1980) followed Gerald Ford, who replaced Nixon after the Watergate scandal, and supported decriminalization. However, subsequent presidents have all favored increasingly harsher penalties for drugs, based upon the perceived voter support for these positions.

ARGUMENTS FOR AND AGAINST DECRIMINALIZATION

Much academic literature provides a rationale for legalization, decriminalization, or "repeal" of various drug laws, especially those concerning marijuana. An excellent analysis of the arguments in favor of legalization and decriminalization has been provided by Schmalleger:

- Legal drugs would be easy to track and control. The involvement of organized criminal cartels in the drug-distribution network could be substantially curtailed.
- Legal drug sales could be taxed, generating huge revenues.
- Legal drugs would be cheap, significantly reducing the number of drug-related crimes committed to feed expensive drug habits.
- Because some people are attracted to anything taboo, legalization could, in fact, reduce the demand for drugs.
- The current war on drugs is already a failure, and prohibiting drugs is too expensive in terms of tax dollars, sacrificed civil liberties, and political turmoil.
- Drug dealers and users care little about criminal justice sanctions. They will continue their illegal activities no matter what the penalties.
- Drug use should ultimately be a matter of personal choice.[43]

Regardless of the eloquence, rationality, and proof provided by advocates of decriminalization and/or legalization, it may be observed that drug laws never seem to become more lenient in the United States. Legislators seem to vie with each other in respect to being "tough on drugs" and politicians who even breathe a word in regard to "decriminalization" commit political suicide. Drugs and being tough on drugs have become a political wedge issue that works well in getting votes. Opponents of decriminalization include Christian evangelicals, parents who fear the influence of the drug subculture upon their children, a relatively indifferent group of voters who agree that "drugs are bad," and employees of the DEA and other law enforcement agencies.

Probably the most comprehensive compilation of *anti-legalization* arguments came from the DEA itself. In 1994, the DEA held a two-day conference in Quantico, Virginia, called the Anti-Legalization Forum. The conference was attended by five city police officials, representatives of the Office of National Drug Control Policy, the National Institute on Drug Abuse, National Families in Action, the California Office of Criminal Justice Planning, the Michigan Office of Drug Control Policy, the DEA, the Kennedy School at Harvard University, and other local and state officials. The conference resulted in a 41-page guide entitled, "How to Hold Your Own in a Drug Legalization Debate" for officials, police officers, and citizens who are invited to debate against the legalization of drugs.[44] The report outlined 10 anti-legalization position statements drafted by the seminar participants. For each of the statements, the manual spelled out arguments for and against the claim. The 10 anti-legalization arguments were as follows:

- Crime, violence, and drug use go hand-in-hand.
- We have made significant progress in reducing drug use in this country. Now is not the time to abandon our efforts.
- Legalization of drugs will lead to increased use and increased addiction levels.
- Any revenues generated by taxing legalized drugs would quickly evaporate in light of the increased social costs associated with legalizing drugs.
- There are no compelling medical reasons to prescribe marijuana or heroin to sick people.
- Legalization and decriminalization of drugs have been a dismal failure in other nations.
- Alcohol has caused significant health, social, and crime problems in this country, and legalized drugs would only make the situation worse.
- Drug control spending is a minor portion of the U.S. budget, and compared to the costs of drug abuse, spending is minuscule.
- Drug prohibition is working.
- Drug legalization would have an adverse effect on low-income communities.[45]

Those who favor decriminalization are a sizable group of marijuana advocates tainted as "potheads," some members of ethnic and racial minority groups who were alleged to have brought on the drug epidemic, civil libertarians who are concerned about the abridgement of constitutional rights such as freedom against unlawful search and seizure, and a dwindling group of academics carrying the Lindesmith torch who argue for a "rational" approach to drugs. Some have also argued that there is a curious conspiracy between those who make the laws and those who profit from the illegality of drugs, notably drug traffickers.[46]

The position on these issues taken in this text is, whether or not various drugs cause crime, the use of drugs by itself is not a serious criminal offense because a crucial element of crime is missing—harm or victimization to others besides oneself—as long as the drug is being self-administered. Volumes have been written by criminologists about drugs, and criminology texts often devote considerable coverage to the topic, including a full discussion of definitions, typologies, extent, trends, etiological studies, theories, and so forth. However, illicit drug use is, like alcohol use during Prohibition, widespread in America and in other countries.

Since the focus of this chapter is upon the drug trade, it is necessary to refer the reader to other sources, such as those referred to in earlier footnotes, for a fuller knowledge of illicit drug abuse as "deviant behavior."

The focus here is the extent and trends in *drug trafficking* in the United States, but not the causes of drug use, drug addiction, or even "drug offenses" as measured by police data. International data that are available via INTERPOL or the United Nations are incomplete on the subject of "drug offenses" and, as mentioned previously, the United States cannot be compared with other countries because of the nature of FBI record keeping on this subject.

We are not attempting to deny that there is a link between drugs and crime. Quite the contrary, there very often is such a link, as shown by Drug Use Forecast studies of jail inmates.[47] However, there is no way to know (because the scientific study of many drugs is typically forbidden) whether the drugs cause the crime, if drugs facilitate the crime, if the crime was motivated to obtain funds to support an addiction, or any other linkages. Indeed, it seems quite likely that if someone is going to commit a crime, he or she may shoot drugs, smoke marijuana, or take a stiff drink to bolster the courage needed to commit an aggressive act, shoplift goods, or break into a residence. People may also use illicit drugs prior to engaging in a legitimate occupation or recreational activity, for somewhat the same reason, as illustrated by the case study of Rick, the drug addict. The use of drugs in the commission of a crime can, perhaps, be considered an aggravant (or mitigant) in a court of law. However, until scientific evidence proves that a drug is in itself the motivation for commission of a serious crime, then the mere possession of small quantities or use of a drug does not constitute a crime of the seriousness of those discussed in previous chapters.

In regard to the arguments for and against decriminalization, it may be necessary to regulate the possession of certain drugs by law; however, the evidence presented later seems to suggest that a greater emphasis should be placed upon the prosecution of *drug traffickers* and less emphasis should be placed upon the prosecution of persons who possess small quantities of drugs for personal consumption. From an examination of countries of the world in previous chapters, it seems that countries that apply a drug policy such as this (tough on drug traffickers—forbearing on minor substance abusers) seem to have the least problems pertaining to drug abuse leading to participation in such serious crimes as burglary, robbery, and larceny.

EXTENT AND TRENDS IN DRUG TRAFFICKING

A variety of drugs are trafficked into the United States. Drugs that are trafficked on the black market into the United States are those that have been federally banned, including cocaine, heroin, and marijuana. Also included is a new category of "designer drugs," called MDMA or Ecstasy.

There are a number of ways to assess traffic, which include quantities seized, the street price of drugs, the amount of drug consumption, and the rate of drug overdoses. The resources devoted to combating drug traffic on a national scale have increased dramatically over time. While Harry Anslinger started his FBN with 300 employees and a budget of around $1.4 million, the DEA began operations in 1973 with 2,775 employees and a budget of $65.2 million. Currently, the DEA has a budget of over $2 billion and around 10,000 employees.[48] More resources have been expended at the state level. The critical question to be asked is, has this investment paid off in terms of declining supply, increasing prices, declining demand for illicit drugs, and a decline in rates of drug overdoses?

It is certainly clear that the War on Drugs has resulted in a massive increase in the number of people incarcerated in prisons and jails, as shown in Figure 12–1. As of June 1996, there were 1.7 million Americans behind bars and 5.5 million under some form of control by the justice system. This was a 12-fold increase from 1980 to 1995. At the federal level, 85% of the increase in the federal prison population was due to drug convictions.

This table indicates that arrests were being made, and convictions were resulting in imprisonment for drug offenses. However, are these arrests and convictions resulting in a successful decrease in the supply of drugs through successful interdiction efforts? Actually, the UCR for 2004 show that only 18.3%

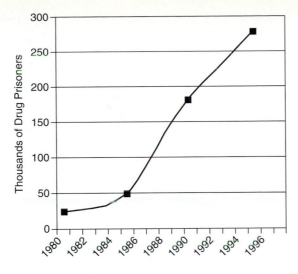

Figure 12–1
Incarceration for drug arrests.[49]

of all drug arrests reported in the United States are for "sale/manufacturing" of illicit drugs, whereas 81.7% are for simple possession. Even more interesting is the breakdown by drug. Marijuana possession accounts for 39.2% of all drug arrests, while heroin or cocaine and their derivatives account for only 22% of all drug arrests. Thus, the War on Drugs, even as recently as 2004, was still very much a war on marijuana possession, just as it was in the late 1930s when Harry Anslinger was conducting his personal crusade against marijuana.[50] These data suggest that a small minority of arrests actually pertain to drug interdiction or cutting off supply, less than 20%. Could these relatively few arrests be of high level traffickers? Evidence is to the contrary. One way to address this question is to take a look at the price of drugs. Based upon the law of supply and demand, if the supply goes up, the price goes down (given a constant demand). From 1981 to 1997, the price for 5 oz. of cocaine went from $275 to $87, and the purity rose from 48% to 66%. The price of 5 grams of heroin declined from $3,374 to $1,175, and the purity increased from 7% to 47%. On the other hand, the price of marijuana rose from $2.56 per pound to $4.57, suggesting that **interdiction** efforts (preventing the drug from entering the country illegally) have been somewhat successful with that drug.[51] One cause for concern during the period since the Reagan administration's efforts to eradicate illegal drug use has been a rise in the number of drug overdose deaths, as shown in Figure 12–2. This alarming increase in drug overdose deaths corresponds almost perfectly with the increase in incarceration for drug arrests shown in Figure 12–1.

Three observations can be made about this increase. One point indicated here is that "dangerous drugs" (i.e., drugs that kill the user) are evidently increasingly available. Another concern about this figure is that the purity of dangerous drugs may be increasing (as suggested in the tremendous increase in the purity of heroin), such that users may overdose as a result of injecting more of the drug than they expect. A third observation is that with the rising price of marijuana, along with increasing arrests for this offense, marijuana users may be switching to other, more dangerous drugs.

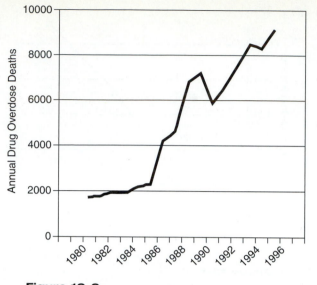

Figure 12–2

Increase in drug overdose deaths.[52]

If heroin has increased in purity, why might this be so? A 2001 U.S. government report suggests there may be a "Canadian connection" that pertains to the increased purity and, perhaps, increased supply of drugs on the street today—particularly heroin. First, the report found that the number of hardcore heroin addicts in the United States increased from an estimated 630,000 in 1992 to 980,000 in 1999. In Canada, the number is estimated at 25,000 to 50,000 heroin addicts. As pointed out in Chapter 11, Canada has also been a preferred destination country for Asian traffic in persons. The report stated that, although most of the heroin in the United States is smuggled directly from Colombia or Mexico, approximately 25% travels through Canada en route to U.S. markets.[53] The report pointed out that there is a Border Patrol deficit between the Canadian and Mexican borders. There are only 300 U.S. Border Patrol (USBP) agents to patrol a 6,000 kilometer border with Canada, compared to 8,000 USBP agents to patrol an approximately 3,000-kilometer border between the United States and Mexico. Drugs in backpacks may accompany human traffic across the Canadian border as a means of payment for passage. Conceivably the recent influx of illegal Asian immigration may have brought with it an increased traffic in a renewed influx of the potent "China white" heroin.

Although the rising price of marijuana may be indicative of a decreasing availability of that drug, another indication is actual use. In this regard, the availability of marijuana to youth has been a major target of rhetoric as well as interdiction efforts. Has the usage of marijuana by youth declined, as a result of arrests, imprisonment, and marijuana confiscation? Figure 12–3 is instructive on this matter.

Figure 12–3 presents information from the National Survey on Drug Use and Health, formerly called the National Household Survey on Drug Abuse. This is an annual household survey of approximately 67,500 civilian persons in the United States aged 12 and older.[54] The trend chart shows that, evidently, adults aged 18 or older have declined in their marijuana use since the 1970 Controlled Substances Act was passed; however, there has been no decline

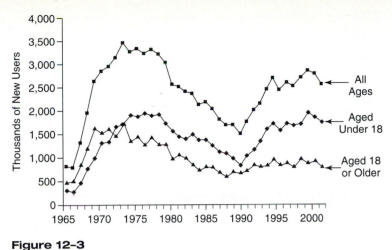

Figure 12–3
Annual numbers of new users of marijuana: 1965–2002.[55]

in first use of marijuana among juveniles, persons under 18. In fact, the current juvenile use rivals that of its all time high during the late 1970s. For cocaine, no trend chart was shown in the report, and first use was said to occur at age 18 or later for 70% of cocaine initiates in 2002. Cocaine trends were said to be similar to those for marijuana shown in Figure 12–3. The incidence of cocaine use generally rose throughout the 1970s to a peak in 1980 (1.6 million new users) and subsequently declined until the early 1990s. Cocaine initiation steadily increased after 1973, averaging over a million new users per year from 2000 to 2002. From 1995 through 2002, the annual number of new heroin users ranged from 121,000 to 164,000, 75% of whom were 18 years or older and 63% of whom were male. As described earlier, the estimated number of heroin addicts increased by one-third from 1992 to 1999.

The fall in new marijuana use among adults, compared with the rise in cocaine and heroin, suggests a switch to drugs that are easier to smuggle. However, the term "adult" includes young people of college age. In this regard, Figure 12–4 may be of interest. Figure 12–4 suggests that if young adults are shying away from marijuana (which is classified as a hallucinogen), they are not avoiding hallucinogens altogether. The overall trend in LSD was upward until 2000; however, another drug called MDMA or "Ecstasy" seems to have replaced LSD almost entirely. The traffic in MDMA has increased dramatically. For instance, from 1999 to 2000 seizures of MDMA increased from 3.5 million tablets to 9.3 million tablets. MDMA is said to be produced primarily by clandestine laboratories in the Netherlands and Belgium, and is smuggled into the United States by express mail, courier, and, indirectly, through transit countries, including Canada. The primary outlets for MDMA in both the United States and Canada are dance clubs and "raves" (all-night dance parties), which normally are attended by people of college and high school age.[56]

Has the war on drugs been successful in the United States? Data presented earlier indicate that in terms of the rising supply, increasing drug overdose deaths, increasing use of marijuana and MDMA among youth, and increasing cocaine and heroin use among adults, the illicit traffic in drugs has been seemingly

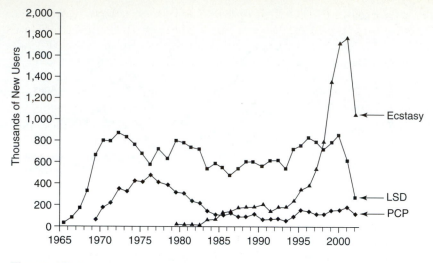

Figure 12–4

Annual numbers of new users of ecstasy, LSD, and PCP: 1965–2002.[57]

impervious to interdiction efforts on the part of law enforcement, as was pointed out in the banned Canadian film, *Drug Addict.*

At this point, based upon similar evidence of the harm caused by the War on Drugs, many texts provide recommendations concerning "harm reduction" measures that can be taken at the federal, state, and local level. That approach will not be taken in this text. Volumes have been written on this subject including numerous government commission reports, and countless blogs on the Internet, which seem to be "preaching to the choir" of those who favor legalization or decriminalization. It would seem that, in so far as politicians and government officials are concerned, nobody is listening. Academicians who missed their opportunity to join Alfred Lindesmith when he was taking on the federal government antidrug bureaucracy (and Harry Anslinger) have waited too long. The drug war resonates well with the majority of voters and no self-respecting politician who values his or her political career would dare step out of line by crusading to legalize or decriminalize any drug, despite the obvious counter-productiveness of interdiction efforts. In addition, the War on Drugs works well in another respect, which is to suppress the "dangerous class" of minorities—blacks and Hispanics—who have filled America's prisons and jails in inordinate numbers during America's war on drugs.

COUNTRY PROFILE

Pakistan Pakistan is part of the "Golden Crescent" (Afghanistan, Iran, and Pakistan) that encompasses the poppy producing areas of Southwest Asia that are the world's main source of illicit opiates. In Chapter 11, countries were ranked in terms of kilograms of heroin seized (in the most recent year recorded). Pakistan was second only to China, with 6,931.47 kilograms seized. More recently, in 2003, Pakistan was number one in the world in seizures of heroin, constituting 35% of the world's seizures, with Iran the next highest at 17%.[58] While Afghanistan produces the opium, most processing takes place in small, mobile laboratories in the Afghan-Pakistan border areas.[59] Also indicative of the traffic in heroin, Pakistan is one of the countries hardest hit by narcotics abuse in the world. The number of chronic heroin abusers in Pakistan increased from about 20,000 in 1980 to more than 1.5 million in the late 1990s.[60] Pakistan's fellow Muslim state/neighbor Afghanistan produced two-thirds of the world's opium poppies in 2004.[61] However, the growers of opium are said to receive the smallest share of the profits from that crop, whereas traffickers receive the largest share.[62] While China was profiled in Chapter 11 (related to the topic of organized crime), Pakistan seems to be a suitable country to profile in this chapter, focusing on the drug trade.

It is interesting to note that, just as Pakistan is number one in the world for heroin seized, it is also number one in the world in the number of terrorist organizations that exist in a single country. According to data published by the Terrorism Research Center, Pakistan has 67 terrorist organizations within its borders. That is 11 more organizations than the next highest country, India, which has 56 terrorist organizations.[63] The 67 terrorist organizations in Pakistan are listed in Table 12–2.

Two questions are to be answered regarding these findings. Why does Pakistan have such a high amount of heroin traffic, and why is it, by far, the country with the highest number of terrorist organizations? Further, are these two findings coincidental, or is there an interconnection between the number of terrorist organizations in Pakistan and heroin traffic? To address these questions, it is necessary to learn about the history of Pakistan and its relationship with other countries, including the United States.

Historical Development of Pakistan

Pakistan is a relatively new country, having become a sovereign nation in 1947. Pakistan is similar to other countries in Chapter 11 that are "home-base" nations for OC in the sense that it has had a "history of military rule." Prior to 1947, Pakistan was part of India, a country that itself could be characterized as having a history of military rule, dating back to ancient times. Much of that military rule was by Muslims.

The initial entry of Islam into India came in the first century after the death of the Prophet Muhammad. The Umayyad caliph in Damascus sent an expedition to Balochistan and Sindh in 711 A.D. led by Muhammad bin Qasim (for whom Karachi's second port is named). The expedition went as far north as Multan, but was not able to retain that region and was not successful in expanding Islamic rule to other parts of India. Coastal trade and the presence of a Muslim colony in Sindh, however, permitted significant cultural exchanges and the introduction into the subcontinent of Muslim teachers. Muslim influence grew with conversions.

Almost three centuries later, the Turks and the Afghans spearheaded the Islamic conquest in India through the traditional invasion routes of the northwest. Mahmud of Ghazni (979–1030) led a series of raids against Rajput kingdoms and rich Hindu temples and established a base in Punjab for future

Table 12–2   67 Terrorist Organizations in Pakistan

Al Badr	
Al Barq	Jamiat ul Mujahideen (JUM)
Al Jehad	Jammu and Kashmir Freedom Force
Al Jehad Force	Jammu and Kashmir Liberation Front (JKLF)
Al Jihad	Jammu and Kashmir National Liberation Army
Al Mujahid Force	Jammu and Kashmir Students Liberation Front
Al Mustafa Liberation Fighters	Jihad Force
Al Qa'nun	Kashmir Jehad Force
Al Umar Mujahideen	Lackawanna Six
Al-Fatah	Lashkar e Jabbar (LJ)
Al-Qaeda	Lashkar e Jhangvi (LJ)
Allah Tigers	Lashkar-e-Tayyiba (LeT)
Baluch Students Organisation (BSO)	Mahaz e Azadi
Baluch Students' Organisation - Awami (BSO-A)	Markaz Dawa al Irshad
Baluchistan Liberation Army (BLA)	Mohajir Qaumi Movement (MQM)
East Turkestan Islamic Movement	Muslim Janbaz Force
God's Brigade	Muslim Mujahideen
Haqiqi Mohajir Quami Movement (MQM-H)	Mutahida Majlis e Amal (United Action Forum)
Harakat ul Jihad I Islami (HUJI)	Muttahida Jehad Council (MJC)
Harakat ul Mujahidin (HUM)	Muttahida Quomi Mahaz - MQM (A)
Harkat ul Ansar (HA)	Nadeem Commando (NC)
Hizb ul Mujahedin	People's League
Hizb-I Islami Gulbuddin (HIG)	Popular Front for Armed Resistance (PFAR)
Hofstad Network	Sipah e Mohammed Pakistan (SMP)
Ikhwan ul Mujahideen	Sipah I Sahaba Pakistan (SSP)
Ikhwan-ul-Muslimeen	Taliban
Intigami Al-Pakistani	Tehreek e Jaferia Pakistan (TJP)
Islambouli Brigades of al Qaeda	Tehreek e Nafaz e Shariat e Mohammadi (TNSM)
Islami Inquilabi Mahaz	Tehrik e Hurriat e Kashmir
Islami Jamaat e Tulba	Tehrik e Jehad
Islamic Movement of Uzbekistan (IMU)	Tehrik e Jehad e Islami
Islamic Students League	Tehrik e Nifaz e Fiqar Jafaria
Jamaat I Islami	Tehrik ul Mujahideen
Jamaat ul Fuqra (JF)	Virginia Jihad Network

incursions. Mahmud's tactics originated the legend of idol-smashing Muslims bent on plunder and forced conversions, a reputation that persists in India to the present day.

During the last quarter of the 12th century, Muhammad of Ghor invaded the Indo-Gangetic Plain, conquering in succession Ghazni, Multan, Sindh, Lahore, and Delhi. His successors established the first dynasty of the Delhi Sultanate, the Mamluk Dynasty (mamluk means "slave") in 1211. The territory under control of the Muslim rulers in Delhi expanded rapidly. By mid-century, Bengal and much of central India was under the Delhi Sultanate. Several Turko-Afghan dynasties ruled from Delhi: the Mamluk (1211–1290), the Khalji (1290–1320), the Tughlaq (1320–1413), the Sayyid (1414–1451), and the Lodhi (1451–1526). As Muslims extended their rule into southern India, only the Hindu kingdom of Vijayanagar remained immune, until it too fell in 1565. Although some kingdoms remained independent of Delhi in central India and Bengal, almost all of the area in present-day Pakistan came under the rule of Delhi.

The sultans of Delhi enjoyed cordial, if superficial, relations with Muslim rulers in the Near East but owed them no allegiance. The sultans based their laws on the Quran and the *sharia*. They permitted non-Muslim subjects to practice their religion only if they paid *jizya* or head tax. The sultans ruled from urban centers—while military camps and trading posts provided the nuclei for towns that sprang up in the countryside. Perhaps the greatest contribution of the sultanate was its temporary success in insulating the subcontinent from the potential devastation of the Mongol invasion from Central Asia in the 13th century. The sultanate ushered in a period of Indian cultural renaissance resulting from the stimulation of Islam by Hinduism. The resulting "Indo-Muslim" fusion left lasting monuments in architecture, music, literature, and religion. The sultanate suffered from the sacking of Delhi in 1398 by Timur (Tamerlane) but revived briefly under the Lodhis before it was conquered by the Mughals.[64]

Analyzing this long history, it seems accurate to state that the resulting Muslim Mogul Empire militarily dominated India and, in fact, most of South Asia (including much of present-day Pakistan) during the 16th and 17th centuries.[65]

British traders first arrived in South Asia in 1601, but the British Empire did not consolidate control of the region until the latter half of the 18th century. After 1850, the British or those influenced by them governed virtually the entire subcontinent. During the century of British control, the position of Muslims declined sharply because the British belief in democracy resulted in power being shifted to the more populous Hindus. By the 1940s, the Hindus were better educated than Muslims and better positioned to take control of the country, once the British left. The British legacy of parliamentary democracy in India further cemented Hindu dominance over Muslims in India.

The attrition of Muslim hegemony should be considered vis-à-vis the Muslim concept of *jihad*, or the "striving." "There are two forms of *jihad*: the inner one is the battle each Muslim wages with his or her lower self; the outer one is the battle which each Muslim must wage to preserve the faith and its followers. People who fight the outer jihad are *mujahidin*."[66]

In India, the Muslims, under British rule, had fought a losing jihad to preserve the faith and its followers. Concern about Hindu domination of the Indian National Congress Party led Muslims to form the all-India Muslim League in 1906. Starting in the 1930s, the idea of a separate Muslim state emerged. In 1940, Muhammad Ali Jinnah, leader of the Muslim League, formally endorsed the "Lahore Resolution," calling for the creation of an independent state in regions where Muslims constituted a majority. In June, 1947, the British Government declared it would bestow full dominion status upon two successor states—India and Pakistan. Under this arrangement, the some 650 "princely states" could freely join either India or Pakistan.[67] However, the resulting dispute over territory that continues into the present has formed a basis for current-day resistance movements that have been labeled "terrorist organizations" by INTERPOL, the United Nations, the United States, Great Britain, and other developed countries. Pakistan initially (in 1947) was divided between West Pakistan (present-day Pakistan) and East Pakistan (consisting of a single province, which is now Bangladesh). The Maharaja of

Kashmir was reluctant to make a decision on accession to either Pakistan or India. However, after armed incursions into the state by tribesmen from the North-West Frontier Province in Pakistan (in 1947), the Maharaja signed accession papers allowing Indian troops into much of the state. Pakistan has contested this accession from 1947 up to the present time.

Pakistan after Partition

Beginning in 1947, the government of Pakistan has been characterized by political instability and military rule through martial law. Military rule in the form of martial law has occurred frequently in the short history of Pakistan. In 1958, President Iskander Mirza, with the support of the army, suspended the 1956 constitution and imposed martial law. Twenty days later the military sent Mirza into exile, after which the country was run by military dictatorships until 1971. In 1971, Zulfikar Ali Bhutto, who had founded the Pakistan Peoples Party, became President and the first civilian Chief Martial Law Administrator. Bhutto carried out populist reforms, nationalizing major industries and the banking system. Bhutto was ousted by the military and arrested in 1977, and General Muhammed Zia ul-Haq became Chief Martial Law Administrator. Zia conducted a criminal investigation of Bhutto, who was subsequently convicted of the murder of a political opponent, was sentenced to death, and was hanged in 1979. Zia then pursued an "Islamization" program, which he said, based upon a referendum, was approved by a 63% majority of voters, which he interpreted as approval of his presidency. Zia died in a plane crash in 1988, and Benazir Bhutto (daughter of Zulfiker Ali Bhutto) formed a government. She was replaced by Nawaz Sharif, leader of the centrist Pakistan Muslim League (PML). Sharif's economic reform program involved privatization and deregulation. Sharif was dismissed by the President in 1993, and was followed, once again, by Benazir Bhutto as leader of a coalition government.[68] Accordingly, Benazir Bhutto's government was dismissed in 1996 by the President Leghari on the basis of corruption, mismanagement, and extrajudicial killings in Karachi. Bhutto was followed, once again, by Nawaz Sharif. Sharif attempted to replace the Chief of Army Staff Genera Pervez Musharraf in 1999, but the army moved quickly to depose Sharif. Musharraf then declared a state of emergency and appointed an eight-member National Security Council to function as Pakistan's supreme governing body, and in 2001, named himself as president and was sworn in. After the terrorist attacks in the United States on September 11, 2001, Musharraf pledged cooperation with the United States in its "War on Terror." He pursued a program of shutting down terrorist training camps in Pakistan.[69]

Historically, then, Pakistan has frequently been governed by the military, followed by attempts to form coalition governments by parliamentary leaders. How does this pattern of military rule and regime change pertain to drug trafficking and terrorism described at the beginning of this country profile? There are several considerations to be brought into the discussion. The first concerns the variety of dissident groups that were brought together as a result of partition into a "multipartite state." The second has to do with Pakistan's relationship to other countries, focusing on India and the United States. A third factor has to do with the symbiotic relationship between terrorism and the drug trade (i.e., narco-terrorism) and the government's relationship to both. The last has to do with unexpected consequences having to do with extreme changes in civilian government, ranging from Zulfikar Ali Bhutto's populist attempts to nationalize industry and banking to the other extreme of Zia's Islamization program.

Multipartite State

The CIA's *World Factbook* for 2006 lists 24 different political parties in Pakistan. The number of political parties represented in Pakistan provides a reason for the difficulty that major leaders have had in forming parliamentary coalitions.

Similarly, in terms of languages spoken in Pakistan, the following are listed in the CIA *World Factbook* for 2006—Punjabi 48%; Sindhi 12%; Siraiki (a Punjabi variant) 10%; Pashtu 8%; Urdu (official) 8%; Balochi 3%; Hindko 2%; Brahui 1%; English (official and most commonly used language of Pakistani elite and most government ministries), Burushaski, and other, 8%.

Ethnic groups in Pakistan consist of the Punjabi, Sindhi, Pashtun (Pathan), Baloch, and Muhajir (immigrants from India at the time of partition and their descendants).

Religions in Pakistan include Muslim 97%, further subdivided into Sunni Muslim 77%; Shi'a Muslim 20%; as well as Christian, Hindu, and other 3%.

The vast array of political parties, languages, and ethnic groups in Pakistan can help to explain the basis for civil disorder; however, in terms of religious affiliation, the country is overwhelmingly Muslim (97%). The Sunni's constitute a majority and the Shi'a a minority of Muslims in Pakistan. Sectarian differences may account for some of the divergent terrorist organizations in Pakistan. Shites may receive support from nearby countries, such as Iran, and (now) Iraq. Sunni terrorist organizations may receive support from predominantly Sunni countries, such as Syria and Jordan. However, sectarian divisions alone do not account for the large number of active terrorist organizations in Pakistan—67. Additional factors may have contributed to the growth of a large contingent of terrorist organizations that have developed in one country. International relations may provide part of the answer, particularly between Pakistan, Afghanistan, India, and the United States.

Influence of the United States

According to a number of journalistic accounts, the terrorism problem that Pakistan must now face was actually an indirect byproduct of a secretive operation of the U.S. government that took place between 1978 and 1992. During that time, "the U.S. government poured at least $6 billion (some estimates range as high as $20 billion) worth of arms, training, and funds to prop up the *mujahidin* (Islamic holy warrior) factions in Afghanistan."[70] The purpose was to oust a government in Afghanistan that was backed by the Soviet Union. The Soviet-backed People's Democratic Party of Afghanistan had seized power in Afghanistan in April, 1978. Washington's backing for the *mujahidin* was based upon a strategy developed by President Jimmy Carter's national security advisor, Zbigniew Brzezinsky, and was continued by successors. The plan was to spread Islamic fanaticism into the Muslim Central Asian Soviet republics to destabilize the Soviet Union. The plan coincided with Pakistan dictator General Zia ul-Haq's own ambition to Islamize the whole region.

Norm Dixon, journalist for the *Green Left Weekly* in Australia, in his article, "How the CIA created Osama bin Laden," indicated that in 1986 CIA Chief William Casey committed the CIA to support a long-standing Inter-Services Intelligence (ISI; Pakistan's CIA) proposal to recruit from around the world to join the Afghan jihad. Reportedly, at least 100,000 Islamic militants flocked to Pakistan between 1982 and 1992. Dixon also cited John Cooley, a former journalist with the U.S. ABC television network and author of *Unholy Wars: Afghanistan, America and International Terrorism.* Cooley maintained that Muslims recruited in the United States for the *mujahidin* were sent to Camp Peary, the CIA's spy training camp in Virginia, where the trainees were taught "sabotage skills." The program was part of a Washington-approved plan called "Operation Cyclone." Washington, Dixon added, favored a *mujahidin* faction led by Gulbuddin Hekmatyar, who was also reputed to be a close associate of Osama bin Laden. Hekmatyar was also known for his participation in the cultivation and trafficking in opium, which became a booming business that supplied 60% of U.S. drug users with their drugs. Recruits, money, and equipment were distributed in Pakistan, according to Dixon, to the *mujahidin* factions by an organisation known as Maktab al Khidamar (MAK). MAK was a front for Pakistan's CIA, which received the vast bulk of CIA and Saudi Arabian covert assistance for the Afghan resistance.[71]

Although there are many more aspects to Dixon's article pertaining to terrorists who later attacked the United States, those are discussed more fully in Chapter 15, which focuses on terrorism. At this point, it is sufficient to conclude that this covert U.S. aid in Operation Cyclone, run through the Pakistan ISI, may have been a factor in the proliferation of Islamic "freedom fighters" (now known as terrorist organizations) within Pakistan. However, there is another story pertaining to Pakistan's poor relations with India. The conflict between India and Pakistan also may have fueled the fire of terrorism in Pakistan.

India, Terrorism, and Organized Crime

Since the creation of Pakistan, Pakistan and India have fought four wars. The first (1947–1948) arose over Kashmir, in Northwest India. The 1965 war involved fighting on the West Pakistan-India border that spread to Kashmir and to the Punjab. The third, in 1971, involved a civil war between East and West Pakistan. After 10 million East Pakistani Bengalis fled to India, India attacked both East and West Pakistan. This war culminated in the independence of East Pakistan, which became Bangladesh. All three wars were resolved through United Nations intervention.[72] The fourth war, which was fought in 1999 and was known as the Kargil conflict, also over Kashmir, was settled as a result of U.S. diplomacy.[73]

Some of the terrorist groups in Pakistan have committed bombings and other acts of terror in India. Relations with India have also been jeopardized on several occasions by the Indian belief that Pakistan is harboring an Indian fugitive from justice, Dawood Ibraham. Dawood is wanted in India for a series of bombings that killed 300 people in Mumbai (Bombay) in 1993.[74] Along with territorial issues such as Kashmir and the issue of terrorist groups in Pakistan, the subject of Dawood's residency in Pakistan has been a constant source of conflict and a subject of recent bilateral talks between India and Pakistan.[75] The Dawood story raises the interesting possibility that in Pakistan there are not only a large number of terrorist organizations, but OC, as well.

Dawood, the son of a Muslim policeman, formed a gang in India called D Company in the 1970s. His syndicate smuggled black-market gold and consumer goods and took over the movie industry (Bollywood). In 1985, Dawood fled to Dubai, United Arab Emirates, where he ran high-stakes gambling rings, fixed cricket matches, and engaged in narcotics and arms trafficking. He also pushed his syndicate into construction, real estate, and underground banking (*hawala*).[76] Dawood invested his wealth in real estate and construction in India. He and his family are estimated to own assets worth $430 million.[77] After expanding his empire in Dubai, Dawood moved from Dubai to Pakistan in 1993.[78] When rioting targeted Bombay's Muslims in 1993, Dawood arranged for the smuggling into India of tons of explosives provided by Pakistan's spy agency, the ISI, according to both U.S. and Indian law enforcement. As a result of the bombings that followed, Dawood became India's most wanted man. Dawood moved to the port city of Karachi, and his connections with the ISI guaranteed him control over the nation's coastal smuggling routes. For 12 years after moving to Karachi, Dawood ran shipping and trucking lines that smuggled arms into India and heroin into Europe. He also maintained ties to several terrorist groups, including al Qaeda, with whom he shared his smuggling routes.[79]

Not only has Dawood Ibraham, a gangster of Muslim faith, turned terrorist, there is evidence that terrorist organizations are transforming themselves into criminal gangs:

> Understanding Dawood's operations is important, experts say, because they show how growing numbers of terrorist groups have come to rely on the tactics—and profits—of organized criminal activity to finance their operations across the globe. An inquiry by *U.S. News,* based on interviews with counter-terrorism and law enforcement officials from six countries, has found that terrorists worldwide are transforming their operating cells into criminal gangs. "Transnational crime is converging with the terrorist world," says Robert Charles, the State Department's former point man on narcotics. Antonio Maria Costa, the head of the United Nations Office on Drugs and Crime, agrees: "The world is seeing the birth of a new hybrid of organized-crime-terrorist organizations. We are breaking new ground."[80]

Thus, there is an important interplay between terrorism and OC, an interplay that has been termed **narco-terrorism.**

Narco-terrorism

The Drug Enforcement Administration defines **narco-terrorism** as

> A subset of terrorism, in which terrorist groups, or associated individuals, participate directly or indirectly in the cultivation, manufacture, transportation, or distribution of controlled substances and the monies derived from these activities. Further, narco-terrorism may be characterized by the participation of groups or associated individuals in taxing, providing security for, or otherwise aiding or abetting drug trafficking endeavors in an effort to further, or fund, terrorist activities.[81]

This definition was given by Asa Hutchinson, who was the 2002 DEA Administrator, before the Senate Judiciary Committee Subcommittee on

Technology, Terrorism, and Government Information in 2002. Hutchinson acknowledged that, under Taliban rule, Afghanistan was a major source of illicit opium and that Osama bin Laden was involved in the drug trade:

> The Islamic State of Afghanistan is a major source country for the cultivation, processing, and trafficking of opiate and cannabis products. Afghanistan produced over 70 percent of the world's supply of illicit opium in 2000. Morphine base, heroin and hashish produced in Afghanistan are trafficked worldwide. Due to the warfare-induced decimation of the country's economic infrastructure, narcotics are a major source of income in Afghanistan. U.S. intelligence confirmed a connection between Afghanistan's former ruling Taliban and international terrorist Osama bin Laden and the al-Qaeda organization. The DEA has received multi-source information that bin Laden has been involved in the financing and facilitation of heroin trafficking activities. While the activities of the two entities do not always follow the same course, we know that drugs and terror frequently share the common ground of geography, money, and violence. In this respect, the very sanctuary previously enjoyed by bin Laden was based on the existence of the Taliban's drug state, whose economy was exceptionally dependent on opium.[82]

According to Hutchinson, the DEA was aware of the existence of drug laboratory sites in Afghanistan and Pakistan:

> DEA sources have reported the observation of numerous inactive laboratory sites in Afghanistan and Pakistan, a number of significant opium dealers, large stockpiles of opium, and active opium markets in Jalalabad and Ghani Khel. The laboratories known to this point are concentrated in the regions bordering the Northwest Border Province of Pakistan, especially in Nangarhar, Laghman, and Konar Provinces in the Konduz and Badakhshan Provinces.[83]

In his testimony before the Senate Judiciary Committee, Hutchinson displayed a table showing the decline in opium production in Afghanistan from the 3,656 metric tons of opium produced in 2000 to 74 metric tons produced in 2001. An important question remained as to whether this was a short-term trend related to the U.S. military occupation of Afghanistan, or a long-term trend. In fact, after 2001 there was a phenomenal increase in opium cultivation in the three years that followed. In 2004, Afghanistan opium poppy cultivation was estimated at 131,000 hectares, a 64% increase from 2003 and an all-time high for Afghanistan. Furthermore, the United Nations survey revealed the encroachment of opium poppy cultivation into previously unaffected areas of the country. It is now found in all 32 provinces of the country. Table 12–3 shows the trend in metric tons for Afghanistan.

As explained at the beginning of the country profile, Pakistan was shown to be number one in the world in seizures of heroin, the primary product of opium. Resurgence in production of the opium poppy in Afghanistan facilitates trafficking in heroin by OC and/or terrorist organizations in Pakistan.

Fringe Politics

Pakistan's multipartite parliament has periodically produced a governing coalition (followed by periods of military rule). However, what has emerged

Table 12–3 **Afghanistan Estimated Opium Production, 1994–2004**[84]

1994	1995	1996	1997	1998	1999	2000	2001	2002	2003	2004
3,400	2,300	2,200	2,800	2,700	4,600	3,300	185	3,400	3,600	4,200

in that country have been governments at one extreme or the other. The "nearly-socialist" government of Zulfikar Ali Bhutto attempted to nationalize major industries (including oil) as well as banks during the 1970s. On the other hand, the right-wing government of General Muhammad Zia ul-Haq attempted to move the country in the direction of "Islamization." Both extremes had consequences in terms of drug trafficking and terrorism.

When Bhutto tried to nationalize Pakistan's banks, he met resistance from Agha Hasan Abedi, whose United Bank had expanded rapidly in Pakistan. In 1972, Bhutto placed Abedi under house arrest. During his house arrest, Abedi developed a plan for a bank that was not subject to nationalization, a bank later to be called the Bank of Credit and Commerce (BCCI). After he was freed from house arrest, Abedi received backing for the development of BCCI from Sheik Zayed bin Sultan Al Nahyan of Abu Dhabi in the United Arab Emirates and the Bank of America in the United States. Initially, the bank was based in Abu Dhabi and profited greatly from the Arab oil embargo in 1973, when tremendous profits poured into the BCCI. Abedi managed to avoid scrutiny from auditors and banking regulators in the countries where he operated by locating his legal headquarters in two countries known to have the barest of regulatory interference—Luxembourg and the Cayman Islands in the Caribbean—both of which were secrecy havens. By 1982, BCCI had 59 branches in Europe, 93 in the Middle East, 58 in Africa, 34 in the Far East and Southeast Asia, and 15 in North America and the Caribbean. In the United States, through covert measures, BCCI took over Financial General Bank and quickly changed its name to First American Bank. BCCI became a cash conduit for drug traffickers, terrorists, despots, arms merchants, and other scam artists and lawbreakers. BCCI was welcomed back to Pakistan after the Zia takeover and Bhutto execution. Among the uses of BCCI in Karachi was the laundering of drug money that was eventually believed to have been used in financing terrorist groups involved in the New York 1993 World Trade Center bombing.[85]

Although Bhutto's socialist nationalization attempts had the unanticipated consequence of the development of a money laundering global bank, BCCI proved to be a tool for drug traffickers and terrorist organizations. However, Zia's right-wing Islamization program also had unintended outcomes. An unexpected outcome of Zia's Islamization was that by relying on a policy grounded in Islam, the state fomented factionalism. By legislating what was Islamic and what was not, Islam itself could no longer provide unity because it was then being defined to exclude previously included groups. Thus, disputes between Sunnis and Shia, ethnic disturbances in Karachi between Pakhtuns (area residents prior to partition) and *muhajirs* (Muslims from India), increased animosity toward Ahmadiyyas (said to be a pseudo-Islamic cult), and the revival of Punjab-Sind tensions—can all be traced to the loss of Islam as a common vocabulary of public morality.[86]

SUMMARY AND CONCLUSION

The story of Rick, a drug addict, begins the chapter. Rick dabbled in drugs and had "minor scrapes with the law" during his childhood and teen years. Though Rick's first experience with heroin was only a "skin pop," he was, in his own words, "hooked for life" as a result of the experience. In the four years after high school, Rick supported a wife and two children on his earnings from legitimate employment as an apprentice electrician, while his heroin addiction was supported by smuggling and selling drugs. After Rick was caught smuggling, his life was characterized by increased use of heroin, periods of abstinence during institutionalization in hospitals and correctional institutions, and relapse upon release, as well as increasing participation in crime (e.g., armed robbery, burglary). Rick advocated legalization of drugs to "take the profit out of it" and to end the vicious cycle of addiction and crime.

This chapter begins a series of three chapters that cover "Part II" crimes in the *Uniform Crime Reports*. The designation of Part II suggests that the FBI does not take these crimes seriously enough to rate them Index crimes. This treatment on the part of the FBI results in a pitfall to comparative analysis. Because the FBI has no offense data to report for these crimes, the United States is one of the few countries that has no "offense" data to report to INTERPOL and the United Nations for drug offenses and white-collar crimes. Only "arrest" data are reported to those agencies for these crimes. Thus, offense data cannot be compared internationally. However, because drug offenses, such as possession of certain drugs, are of questionable seriousness, the orientation in this chapter was to focus on drug trafficking, rather than drug abuse, as an offense, because drug trafficking can harm large numbers of people. It was pointed out that the designation of drugs as illegal in the United States has little to do with their pharmacology. Of the three basic classes of drugs—stimulants, depressants, and hallucinogens—the government identification of drugs as "dangerous," and therefore illegal, seems to have no particular rationale. Adults can purchase alcohol, tobacco, caffeine-laced drinks, glue, and other inhalants "over the counter." However, possession of other drugs that have similar ill-effects, such as marijuana, cocaine, and opium, are a basis for arrest and state or federal imprisonment of five years or more. Marijuana, especially, has been a "hot button issue." In recent years, many states have decriminalized marijuana or even legalized it for medical use. The result is a jurisdictional conflict between state and federal law enforcement agencies. Outside of the United States, even heroin has, in recent years, been lawfully administered. Heroin has been approved for use as a pain reliever for terminal cancer patients in Great Britain and for treatment of heroin addiction in Switzerland and an increasing number of European countries.

Searching for an explanation for the orientation of U.S. drug laws, one theory is that the drug laws have been a useful tool in intergroup conflict between the dominant white majority and minority groups. The drug laws have resulted in the imprisonment and/or deportation of Chinese and Mexican immigrants, and disproportionately, to the widespread incarceration of African Americans.

Another explanation for the development of the drug laws was the desire for bureaucrats like Harry Anslinger to create a federal drug bureaucracy empire—in his case the FBN, forerunner to the DEA, today. Anslinger was opposed by social psychologist Alfred Lindesmith. Lindesmith fervently argued that addiction was a disease, as opposed to a form of criminal behavior, as it was portrayed by Anslinger.

While the criminality of various drug offenses is debatable, the most important focus for law enforcement is interdiction and drug trafficking (rather than locking people up for possession). In this regard, law enforcement has a poor record in the United States. Over 81% of drug arrests in the United States are for "possession," predominantly of marijuana. Only 18.3% are for "sale/manufacturing." There is evidence that the supply and purity of heroin and cocaine is increasing over time. The increasing supply is indicated by the plummeting price for those drugs over the last few years. The increasing purity is indicated by the skyrocketing rate of drug overdose deaths. By many indicators, the War on Drugs has failed to decrease the supply and consequences of drug trafficking.

Finally, a country profile of Pakistan revealed some of the consequences of America's War on Drugs—notably funding terrorism. A large number of predominantly Muslim terrorist organizations have developed in Pakistan, many of them subsidized by the proceeds of heroin trafficking. Evidence in this chapter indicated that the drug trade provided funding both for the terrorists who perpetrated the bombing of the World Trade Center in 1993 and for the *mujahideen* members of Osama bin Laden's al-Qaeda organization who destroyed the World Trade Center on September 11, 2001.

DISCUSSION QUESTIONS

1. Recalling the case study of Rick, the drug addict, what do you think of Rick's contention that heroin should be legalized?

2. Do you think that addictive drugs such as alcohol and cigarettes should remain legal while other addictive drugs such as opium and heroin should continue to be banned by federal law? Why or why not?

3. What role, if any, do you think that racism has played in the development of America's drug laws?

4. Harry Anslinger testified before Congress that marijuana use makes people murderous, insane, suicidal, and delinquent. Do you think that these allegations are true of the drug? Why or why not?

5. What were the consequences of the passage of the Marijuana Tax Act in 1937 in terms of prisoners and the growth of the federal drug control bureaucracy?

6. Do you think that marijuana should be legalized or decriminalized? Do you think it should be available by prescription from doctors? Why or why not?

7. Focusing on the country profile of Pakistan, do you see a relationship between the War on Drugs and the War on Terrorism? What policy changes, if any, would you suggest regarding the U.S. relations with Pakistan?

SUGGESTED WEBSITES

http://www.unodc.org/unodc/de/world_drug_report.html The World Drug Report 2005 provides one of the most comprehensive overviews of illicit drug trends at the international level.

http://www.csdp.org/edcs/theneed.htm Website containing charts, graphs, and information pertaining to reforming America's drug control strategy.

http://www.drugabusestatistics.samhsa.gov/ Website of the Substance Abuse and Mental Health Services Administration (SAMHSA), Office of Applied Studies (OAS). Provides the latest on alcohol, tobacco, marijuana, and other drug abuse; drug-related emergency department data; and the nation's substance abuse treatment systems.

http://www.usdoj.gov/dea/ Website of the Drug Enforcement Administration (DEA).

http://www.a1b2c3.com/drugs/mj004.htm Website providing a history of marijuana legislation from 2000 B.C. up until the 1990s.

ENDNOTES

1. Excerpted from Winslow & Winslow, 1974, pp. 116–135.
2. Sellin & Wolfgang, 1964.
3. McKim, 1991.
4. Brocato, 2003.
5. Hanson, 2004.

6. Salter, 2004.

7. Alliance for Cannabis Therapeutics, 1999.

8. Suellentrop, 2001.

9. Satel, 2004.

10. Schmalleger, 2003, p. 629.

11. Brocato, 2003.

12. Thio, 1988, p. 339.

13. Tweed, 2004.

14. Goode, 1984, p. 218.

15. Smith, 1998.

16. Keel, 2004.

17. Binger, n. d.

18. Whitebread, 1995; *Studyworld.com*, 2004.

19. Helmer, 1975, p. 32.

20. Cohen, 2003.

21. Browne, 1995.

22. Beirne & Messerschmidt, 1995, p. 185.

23. Ray, 1983, p. 36.

24. Whitebread, 1995.

25. *Onlinepot.org*, 2004.

26. McWilliams, 1996.

27. Bonnie & Whitebread, 2002.

28. *Reefer-Madness-Movie.com*, 2004.

29. Anslinger & Cooper, 1937.

30. Drug Enforcement Administration, 2004.

31. A&E Television Network, 2000.

32. Schaffer Library of Drug Policy, 2004.

33. A&E Television Network, 2000.

34. McWilliams, 1996, p. 9.

35. Galliher, Keys, & Eisner, 1998.

36. Lindesmith, & Strauss 1949.

37. Lindesmith, 1968, p. 4.

38. Galliher, Keys, & Eisner, 1998, p. 4.

39. King, 1972.

40. One interesting irony was pointed out by a student who was a law enforcement officer. During the 1950s, when the Boggs Amendment was in place, the average time served for "murder" was approximately seven years. Thus, the best choice for a third-time offender caught selling cocaine or heroin was to kill the arresting officer, because even if caught for murder he would only do 7 years as opposed to 10 years for the drug offense.

41. Herer, 2003.

42. ParaScope, Inc., 1999.

43. Schmalleger, 2005, p. 709.

44. Drug Enforcement Administration, 2003.

45. Criminal Justice Policy Foundation, 1994.

46. Chambliss, 1989a.

47. Office of National Drug Control Policy, 1997.

48. Drug Enforcement Administration, 2004.

49. Source: BJS, Trends in the U.S. Correctional Populations, 1995.

50. FBI, 2004, Table 4.1, p. 278.

51. Faley, 1998.

52. Network Reform Groups, 1999.

53. National Drug Intelligence Center, 2001, pp. 7–8.

54. This is a project of the Substance Abuse and Mental Health Services Administration part of the U.S. Department of Health and Human Services. The survey was initiated in 1971 and is the primary source of information on the use of illicit drugs, alcohol, and tobacco by the civilian, noninstitutionalized population of the United States aged 12 years old and older. The survey interviews approximately 67,500 persons each year.

55. Substance Abuse and Mental Health Services Administration, 2004, p. 43.

56. National Drug Intelligence Center, 2001, pp. 13–14.

57. Substance Abuse and Mental Health Services Administration, 2004, p. 44.

58. United Nations Office on Drugs and Crime, 2005, p. 54.

59. United Nations Office on Drugs and Crime, 2003a.

60. United Nations Office on Drugs and Crime, 2003b, p. 2.

61. UNODC, 2005, p. 41.

62. BBC News, 1998.

63. The Terrorism Research Center, 2006.

64. Library of Congress, 1994a.

65. Comparative Criminology Website: Pakistan.

66. Library of Congress, 1994c.

67. The term "princely states" was actually a misleading British term for the states that were actually ruled by kings (or terms equivalent to); Haynes, 1999.

68. Based upon the Eighth Amendment to Pakistan's Constitution, the President can dissolve the National Assembly for various reasons.

69. U.S. Department of State, 2006. Background Note: Pakistan.

70. Chossudovsky, 2001; Dixon, 2001; Friends of Liberty, 2002; Rana, 2003; Sadat, 2001.
71. Dixon, 2001.
72. *Answers.com*, 2003.
73. *YesPakistan.com* Staff, 2002.
74. BBC News, 2005.
75. Xinhua, 2005; Chellappan, 2004; *Rediff.com*, 2003.
76. *Usnews.com*, 2005.
77. Kaplan, 2005.
78. Swami, 2003.
79. *Usnews.com*, 2005.
80. Kaplan, 2005.
81. Hutchinson, 2002.
82. Hutchinson, 2002, p. 2.
83. Hutchinson, 2002, p. 3.
84. United Nations Office on Drugs and Crime, (UNODC), 2004, p. 4.
85. Pallone, 1994; Committee Against Corruption in Saudi Arabia, 1998.
86. Library of Congress, 1994b.

————13—

THE SEX TRADE

KEY TERMS

cyberporn
erotica
forced prostitution
Mann Act
obscenity
pornography
prostitution

red-light districts
regulationist movement
sexual slavery
social purity movement
trafficking in women
whorehouse riots

OUTLINE

Prostitution Defined
Types of Prostitutes
Prostitutes and the Law
Sex Trafficking of Women in the United States
New Types of Prostitution

Pornography Defined
Types of Pornography
Pornography and Violence
Country Profiles

LEARNING OBJECTIVES

After reading this chapter, students should be able to:

1. Define prostitution and pornography
2. Describe how the criminalization of prostitution (previously legal) has changed prostitution in the United States
3. Understand some of the difficulties police have when dealing with prostitutes,

as well as when the police are assisting prostitutes who are victims of crime

4. Indicate how the globalization of commerce has increased the traffic in women for sexual exploitation in the United States and in the European Union countries

INTRODUCTION

My offenses were several narcotic offenses. Cops picked me up on several suspicions of grand theft. They do this in order to nail prostitutes. Couple of burglaries; everything but murder. Of course I didn't do any of these things. I turned tricks for years at 5th and Market. I made a lot of money and I made little money. I've been hungry. I think when people take to talking about prostitutes they think about Cadillacs and the handsome men who they dine out with. They forget about the times when they have two black eyes and walk the streets hungry. You look so bad that nobody wants to turn a trick with you. I know girls out on the street who are prostitutes because they like to gamble or take dope or whatever. There's no urgent reason for them being out there, but yet they're there—hustling all day and all night. Some have pimps, some don't. I guess there are just as many different reasons for being a prostitute as there is [sic] for being anything else. It took me years and years of therapy at California Rehabilitation Center, a place for narcotics addicts, to realize that my reason was linked to attention-getting. I dug the attention from men, the easy money. You can't beat the hours. The actual sex part took about 30 seconds.

Everyone who wants a whore goes to 5th and Market. It's that simple. We call it whoring; you guys call it prostitution. People come mostly in their cars. I found that mostly in L.A. I worked there for a while, too. And there you just stand on a corner and they holler, "How much?" and you holler back your price and that was it. That doesn't happen too often down here.

(Hate men?) Oh, I don't I really don't. I don't know if I'm an oddity or what, but uh. It was funny. I was very moralistic as a kid. I kept my cherry until I was 17. I was not going to lose it until I got married. And when I did lose it, it was out of curiosity and because all my friends had. When I was in high school I was 5 foot 2 by 5 foot 2 and wore glasses. I just wasn't too lovely. So when the other girls started dating, I started running with the rough group and acting like I didn't care. I guess we attracted each other cuz I was so hostile. I took it out on the teachers or anybody else that was around. I got into the group fairly easily. I had a boyfriend before I got sent up when I was 14 that I had known before. But, heck, we only kissed a couple of times. And then I got sent away, and I never saw him again until I was 17. And when I got out, all my fat had gone away. And I was lovely, like a butterfly. And all the men wanted me and, I was in my glory. I got sent up when I was 14, and I didn't come out until after I was 17—to Norwalk and then to Las Willicas, then to Ventura without getting out. I was sent up for "incorrigibility." I just needed 24-hour-per-day supervision is what it amounted to. That's what they said anyway. I had been sent to juvenile hall 12 times for everything from shoplifting to runaway to, you name it almost. By the time I got out I thought I was gay cuz I had never had a man. I was always carrying on with my women. Then I met my son's father, and we started dating.

I had been with this man for three months who is my son's father. And so anyway, I went ahead, had sex, got pregnant, and had the baby, and then he went to the joint for the fifth time. I was just lost. I was just 18. I just went crazy. I started getting high, getting it on with anyone and everyone, and just giving it away, when and if I felt like it. One night this dude came up to me and offered some money to sleep with him. I thought, well I'm broke, so I just jumped into the car and didn't even think. The idea of hustling had never 'til that time crossed my mind. When I was giving it away, I thought that it was all right as long as I wasn't a dirty prostitute. Now that I'm a dirty prostitute, anyone who gives it away was crazy! So I went and turned my first trick. I think it was just an accident. It looked good to me. I didn't have any money. I was on welfare, trying to raise a baby, getting high, running the streets. I'd say 75% of all prostitutes are either on drugs or are alcoholics.

The women I met were not suckered into the profession. I knew exactly what I was getting into. You do hear about girls being kidnapped and being put in houses and forced to be prostitutes, but it just doesn't happen around here. . . . I got kidnapped once and taken to L.A.—you might say. I took off with a girl to L.A.—I get on my kicks where I think I hate men—and it turned out that she was working for these seven men in this organization. And each of them had anywhere from five to 20 girls, and half of them were prostitutes and half of them were boosters [shoplifters]. And it turned out that she was some kind of a recruiter. So they kept me in a pad for a few days, and I turned a few tricks. As soon as they learned to trust me they cut me loose and I took off and came back down here. You can't keep anyone prisoner, not if they don't want to be. I don't think these guys were Mafia, and if I did I wouldn't talk about it! This organization that I was talking about, I think was just a group of businessmen who got together, and got some girls together—and some of them are just plain housewives—introduce them to their business associates and collect a cut.

We have a code among us like cocktail waitresses—"If you leave my tricks alone, I'll leave your tricks alone." So that way it's safe for any of my tricks to go out on the street and ask, "Is Sandy here?" and they'll say, "Oh, she went to so-and-so place" or have him call me or that I'll be right back.

I laughed at the other girls giving their money to their pimps. But then it happened to me. He just caught me at the right time. Things were going bad. I was working for minimum wage, getting strung-out, living at home—my mother and I cannot get along when we live together—my parole officer was putting pressure on me. The pimp just said, "Come on, baby." And I said, "Right on." And I was gone. And I didn't get away for three months. I had to turn myself in to get away from him. He took all of my earnings. He left me money to eat on. Never enough to get anywhere far. When I was working, he was with me. When the trick and I were in the hotel room, he was right outside the door. You've got to remember, you're there, with no clothes on, with a man that could be anything—a sex maniac, a murderer. Some of them want to pay you, screw you, and then take back the money they gave you and the rest you've made if you've got any. One time I had a guy pull a gun on me. Boy did I give him the money back—FAST! But with Ed outside the door, all I had to do was raise my voice and he was right there. He'd knock on the door and that was usually enough to frustrate the trick and make him want to get out of there quick. Good protection. However, I wasn't scared of anybody. You've got to remember that I was strung-out most of the time and didn't have sense enough to be scared. I was superwoman!

I contracted syphilis in about my fourth year. When I worked down on 5th and Market, the sailors and screwballs are not too clean. You catch clap pretty often. As a matter of fact, I hustled for nine years with nothing but a douche bag, and I never got pregnant. I think that somehow I had gotten things infected once to the point that it made me sterile. When I went to honor camp for a year recently, they unsterilized me. The first thing I did when I got out was get pregnant. No, you don't avoid disease. I am one of the lucky ones. I can damn near always tell if I have something. Within 24 hours, my discharge starts. And until my discharge starts, no one else can get it. So very seldom did I purposely go out and trick when I knew I had a disease. And I was dating this one dude who I was planning to marry. I had a steady job and had stopped tricking and was doing real good, and then I had to tell my boyfriend about my disease. That was a bummer, too.

I never saw my father to this day. My mother and I get along just fine when we live separately. When I was a child growing up, she worked all day. When I was in kindergarten I used to dress myself, fix my own breakfast, and go to school downtown. I've always taken care of myself. I have one brother who is six years younger than me. My baby brother, 6 feet 4 inches, all 200 and some pounds of him. We get along fine. Maybe I picked on him a little too much when we were kids, I don't know. He picked on me a lot too, though. Both my brother and I did get in trouble; I'm still having trouble with the law. My brother's been clean now for, gosh, I guess he still pops a few pills once in a while and smokes a little weed, but other than that, no trouble with the law for almost two or three years. He's a big foreman in Los Angeles, doing great. Two or three years ago when he was in trouble with the law, he thought that I was what was happening. I was big Sis. He enjoyed telling his girlfriends, "My sister's been to the joint three times." It made him look big cuz his scene was looking big and bad. He loved it. But now I'm a dirty rotten so-and-so, cuz he's straightened out—a complete switch about.

Romance and prostitution don't go together too well. You kid yourself. That pimp I had, I tried to believe desperately that I loved him—I couldn't think of any other reason why I was there. But how can you love somebody who puts scars on your body and tells you, "Bitch, if you don't make a certain amount of money you don't live anymore," and then takes all of your money. And that's the way they do it. He used to whip on me. He took me off the streets because we fell in love, so here I am living in a hotel and he's still hanging around with all of his pimp friends and evidently, well, they like to talk about what big men they are, how much money their whores make, and who made the most, who did the biggest boost that night, or whatever their thing is. And evidently, somebody said something to him about him taking me off the street and the fact that he only had me, when he usually keeps three or four of them. And so he came home and whipped me. He couldn't tell his friends, "So what," or whatever. He had to take it out on me. Oh, he whipped good on women. It was something else.

I never hustled when I had a man—ever. I'm so aggressive it's going to be my way or no way at all, so that things never lasted very long. I'd either get mad and throw him out or he'd just get to where he couldn't take it anymore. It just gets to a point where it won't work. And my relationships usually last anywhere from two weeks to three months. Three months, that's definitely love! I've only had a couple of those three monthers.

I think the police punished me because I told them to go screw themselves. See, back then, there weren't too many white girls going with black men. And I was 18, and I used to give the traffic department something like $10,000 a year. They used to screw with me and insist that I went with black men for drugs, not because I wanted to. And they couldn't get it through their heads that I preferred black men. They couldn't get a burglary conviction cuz I didn't steal. They did get me for narcotics, so after my first narcotics beef they started slapping them to me hot and heavy. I have 18 of them, not convicted of all of them, but Jesus Christ! And when they started catching me, I mean attitude hostile, cursed me out all the way to the station, tried to kick me in the left knee, etc. Right now if you picked up my rap sheet, it looks horrible, I swear.

Being a prostitute is kind of like being a dope addict. You don't become close with your connection, not really close. It's got to be business. He's got to have your money. You don't make friends with other dope addicts because they want your dope. And you don't make close friends with people who don't do dope because you're on a different keel. With prostitution, you'd think that we were blood sisters, that we were raised together, that we never left one another except to turn tricks, but that's just the act, the facade we put on. I would never go to one of them and say, "Boy, I feel really blue, depressed," or "so-and-so happened today." You would tell them that, but what they would say would be so superficial you might as well, you just wasted breath. "Oh, yeah. Well, that's too bad. Excuse me, I've got to go."

With the tricks, I managed to develop some real good relationships. I like those men out there—those poor misled husbands. They're honest and generally very, very nice. Only about 25% come on bad. Seventy percent I guess were husbands I guess offhand. Of course, you get the money before you even undress! Well, that too depends, cuz if you're trickin' with a regular, you don't have to worry. But a first or one-night thing, you get the money before you take off a hairpin! You'll not get it back any other way, because he doesn't want to spend it, but he wants you worse than he doesn't want to spend it—or a piece of ass, not necessarily you.

I think that I'm probably to the point where I feel a little bit old, a little bit used, and I'm a little uptight about that. Twelve of my years have been given to the state, and I'll never see that again. I've got scars, inside and out. I don't know what I'm waiting for. I really don't. I'm on parole. I'm on probation. I still get therapy and I sit and help everybody else. I don't get helped. I still get high—on uppers and downers, no heroin and no weed. I don't know why no weed, I just don't use it. I don't get anything. I don't hear anybody giving me anything to take the place of dope. So I sneak around, and I keep a full bottle of urine at all times so that if my parole officer slips up on me, I'll have it. And it's really a bummer. I don't know where I'm going. I don't even know what I want.[1]

Trafficking in persons has been referred to in previous chapters, but in this chapter the focus is on the consequences of this trade within the United States and Europe in the form of prostitution and pornography.

Prostitution and pornography are considered minor crimes and are either classified as misdemeanors or, in most European Union countries, such as Sweden and the Netherlands, not considered crimes at all.[2] A large percentage of the U.S. population participate in these crimes (watching pornography, engaging in the services of prostitutes), and thus the activity would qualify as minor deviance rather than criminality in terms of the lack of any actual victim. Of course, crimes can occur in conjunction with these activities. A person can be robbed while patronizing a prostitute and can be a victim of identity theft using his credit card to procure pornography over the Internet. However, these are robbery and identity theft (and often more serious crimes than prostitution) and should be discussed (and prosecuted) separately.

The sex trade becomes "real crime" when participants are forced against their will to participate. It occurs when a woman is trafficked as an illegal alien in New York City and is told she must pay $45,000 to the "snakehead" who provides her passage there, or else face a threat of bodily harm to her or members of her family in her home country. It occurs when a girl runs away from home and takes a bus to a large city where she is greeted by a pimp who provides her with

Prostitution becomes "real crime" when children are forced against their will to engage in it. Children are often trafficked internationally for this purpose. Seen here is a young Asian child clutching a bouquet of flowers in a red lit bar in a sex district. Pedophiles fly to countries such as Thailand and Cambodia, where such red-light districts are tolerated, to engage in "sex tourism."
Source: Loretta Rae, CORBIS/Bettmann.

room and board, as well as drugs. Subsequently, the girl is told she must earn her keep by working the streets, and she joins the pimp's stable of prostitutes working in involuntary servitude. **Sexual slavery** also occurs when a child or young girl is forced to participate in the production of a pornographic movie by a pimp, a family member, or abductor. These are all instances of when the sex trade becomes real crime, which could by definition be prosecuted as "forcible rape" (but rarely is because of the social definitions of participants as "deviants" or "juvenile delinquents"). Thus, the focus of this section is upon coercive sexual traffic in the United States, when prostitution results in "slavery."

PROSTITUTION DEFINED

Because the authors of this text take the viewpoint that prostitution is at best a minor crime, the literature on prostitution is only briefly summarized, and then focus is given to the "real crime" aspects of the traffic in prostitution—notably **trafficking in women** and children for purposes of sexual exploitation.

One indication that prostitution is a form of deviant behavior that borders on a legitimate occupation is the historical prevalence of the behavior and difficulty in defining the term. **Prostitution** is said to be the second oldest profession, after priesthood.[3] Probably the most quoted definition of prostitution is that of anthropologist Paul Gebhard: "A prostitute is an individual who will engage in sexual activity with strangers or other persons with whom the individual has no affectional relationship in exchange for money or other valuable materials that are given at or near the time of the act."[4] The difficulty with this definition is that it also includes *casual sex,* in which sex is exchanged for dinner and a few drinks between a couple that just met in a bar, or it could include a spouse having sex with a husband she has come to hate in return for some jewelry. The latter instances of "prostitution" would not be recognized as such, even though they conform to Gebhard's definition. They are instances of *primary deviance.* Primary deviance is rule breaking that is not considered to be deviance by participants or society. What people think as prostitution is, in reality, *secondary deviance.* In Lemert's terminology, these are individuals who have been labeled by others as prostitutes and who think of themselves as such. But it seems there are always "shades of gray" in the wide variety of forms of prostitution.

TYPES OF PROSTITUTES

Of the various types of prostitutes, streetwalkers, brothel prostitutes, and call girls would be popularly identified as prostitutes (and define themselves accordingly). However, some prostitutes maintain a "front" of legitimacy and are less recognizable. These include bar girls or B-girls, who work in bars drinking and waiting to be picked up by customers; escort services; masseuses; and girls who work in photo studios and allow customers to put paint on their bodies.

Arrests for prostitution have been declining since the HIV/AIDS epidemic was recognized in the United States in the early 1980s. In 1995, the FBI reported 25,098 arrests for "prostitution and commercialized vice," whereas in 2004, the figure was 17,725.[5]

PROSTITUTES AND THE LAW

Another interesting aspect of prostitution in the United States is that it is not illegal in all states and has not always been criminalized. Throughout the 1800s, female prostitution was considered to be sinful behavior in the United States, but it was not classified as a criminal offense. During the early 1800s, vigilante groups engaged in the infamous **whorehouse riots,** destroying houses of prostitution and battling female prostitutes in street fights. As a result, female prostitution did not end but was segregated within the **red-light districts** of the growing urban slums. Subsequently, *regulationists* sought to control female prostitution as a public health issue, requiring police supervision and medical examinations for female prostitutes rather than complete suppression of prostitution itself. However, this **regulationist movement** didn't get very far. Only one city (St. Louis) ever tried it, and only for four years. Feminists opposed the regulationists on the grounds that medical examination of the prostitutes but not their male customers was discriminatory, and they launched a movement called the **social purity movement** that sought to abolish female prostitution itself.[6] Subsequently, the majority of state legislatures passed laws making brothels and red-light districts illegal. In many respects, the prohibition of prostitution resembled the attempt at prohibition of alcohol that would take place during the same period of the early 1900s. Just as prohibition of alcohol resulted in a black market for that drug, prostitutes continued to ply their trade even after the brothels were declared illegal. Instead, rooming houses, hotels, and massage parlors became prominent sites for prostitution. Madams would send "call girls" out upon request to wealthy clients. However, the majority of poor women were required to turn to streetwalking to seek out clientele and in many cases to turn to pimps for protection. In some instances this relationship turned violent, and the women were subjected to **forced prostitution,** often being physically victimized by their pimps.[7] Based upon this often abusive relationship between pimps and prostitutes, radical feminists such as Kathleen Barry argued that female prostitution is intrinsically a form of female slavery:

> Because it is invisible to social perception and because of the clandestine nature of its practices, it is presently impossible to statistically measure the incidence of female sexual slavery. But considering the arrested sexual development that is understood to be normal in the male population and considering the numbers of men who are pimps, procurers, members of syndicate and freelance slavery gangs, operators of brothels and massage parlors, connected with sexual exploitation entertainment, pornography purveyors, wife beaters, child molesters, incest perpetrators, johns (tricks) and rapists, one cannot help but be momentarily stunned by the enormous male population participating in female sexual slavery.[8]

Although Barry's rhetoric effectively dramatizes the plight of many prostitutes who may be victims of male exploitation, her argument probably overstated the extent to which females were subjected to sexual slavery in the United States in 1979 (the year of Barry's publication). However, it should be added that Barry's characterization may have been prophetic in the sense that it is increasingly true of prostitution today.

In 1969, sex researcher Paul Gebhard reported that only 4% of U.S. prostitutes are forced into prostitution.[9] Many female prostitutes have published statements contrary to the previously quoted feminist viewpoint, which they view as patronizing and condescending. For instance, Margo St. James, founder of COYOTE (Call Off Your Old Tired Ethics), a female prostitute union, has argued that:

> In private the whore has power. She is in charge, setting the terms for the sexual exchange and the financial exchange. In public, of course, she has absolutely no rights—no civil rights, no human rights. Prostitution laws are how women are controlled in this society.[10]

Beirne and Messerschmidt cite several other published statements by prostitutes that contradict the notion that prostitutes in the United States are, for the most part, sex slaves of anybody, pimps or otherwise.[11]

BOX 13-1

Addiction and Prostitution

In a study of 60 women who had been drug users, prostitutes, or both, Paul Goldstein found that different drugs were used by different types of prostitutes. Heroin was most clearly associated with low-level prostitutes whereas stimulants were used by high-class prostitutes. Among lower class prostitutes, addiction occurred before prostitution, while for high-class prostitutes, prostitution occurred before addiction.[12]

Whether or not the statements made by prostitutes in Gebhard's research or those quoted by Beirne and Messerschmidt can be trusted is a matter of conjecture. Prostitutes could be enslaved by a pimp, based on his providing needed addictive drugs, or due to her fear of his violence. The problem in documenting instances of slavery for prostitutes is that the police do not take complaints from prostitutes seriously and rarely if ever file or record complaints of victimization by prostitutes. According to a participant-observation study done in 1982, prostitutes are subjected to widespread abuse that includes rape, robbery, extortion, assault, and murder. Police were found to be unresponsive to prostitutes' complaints of victimization, often refusing to file crime reports. When complaints were filed, district attorneys refused to prosecute.[13] It would seem that prostitutes were somehow, on a de facto basis, exempted from the VAWA. Thus, pimps and customers alike are free to submit prostitutes to a wide range of acts of serious victimization, ranging from rape to murder. The police refusal to take complaints of prostitutes seriously is the subject of criticism by the academic community and is considered a product of prejudice on the part of the police. However, police often respond that the professors need to "walk a mile in their shoes" to understand their perspective on prostitutes. Prostitutes are often seen as "troublemakers" by the police, who suspect them to be covertly involved in numerous crimes, such as robbery (as exemplified by the "Murphy game," discussed in Chapter 8), illicit drug activity, shoplifting goods (boosting), and a variety of other offenses. Thus, when a prostitute comes into a police station with a complaint of rape or violence, the police may typically feel that the woman "brought it on herself" through her illegal activity.

One can sympathize with the ambivalence of police to pursue charges pertaining to rape made by prostitutes. Under existing laws, proof must be made both that consent was not given and that violence was involved. Extensive forensic investigation is often involved in proving that violence was involved, and it is relatively easy to impeach a prostitute as a victim-witness because the fact that she makes a living providing sex in exchange for money would seem to imply the presence of consent.

BOX 13–2

Drug Addiction, Pimps, and Prostitution in Israel

An interview study was done in Israel with 10 prostitutes and 11 pimps, ranging in age between 18 and 42. It was found that both pimps and prostitutes begin using drugs after taking up delinquent activity as a part of the delinquent subculture.[14]

BOX 13–3

Police Abuse of Prostitutes

Because prostitution in the form of "solicitation of sex" is illegal in the United States, police often engage in practices that amount to routine, spontaneous, and uncoordinated harassment, dispersal, and "street-sweep" tactics by sector cars, roving police vans, and unmarked vehicles.[15] A study done in Los Angeles found that even though prostitutes were victims of major crimes including rape, robbery, assault, and murder, police often refused to file crime reports, and, where complaints were filed, district attorneys refused to prosecute.[16] Even the **Mann Act** (sometimes termed the *White Slave Traffic Act*) passed in 1910, which made it a federal crime to transport individuals under the age of 18 across state lines to engage in sexual activity, has been used abusively by law enforcement. One study found that in the enforcement of the Mann Act, the major prosecution was of female victims of trafficking whom the act was designed to protect.[17]

However, when it comes to violence, the situation may be quite different. Prostitutes have often been the target of notorious serial killers, dating from Jack the Ripper to the more recent Green River Killer. Gary Ridgway, who confessed to killing 48 women, was identified as the Green River Killer. Ridgway chose prostitutes with whom he could have sex for free (after killing them). Ridgway picked prostitutes because he was aware that they had so little legal protection, and in fact, he felt he was doing the police a favor by killing the prostitutes. He was quoted as stating:

> I picked prostitutes as my victims because I hate most prostitutes and I did not want to pay them for sex. . . . I also picked prostitutes as victims because they were easy to pick up without being noticed. I knew they would not be reported missing right away and might never be reported missing. I picked prostitutes because I thought I could kill as many of them as I wanted without getting caught. [In Ridgway's mind, he even believed that he was helping the police out, as he admitted in one interview with investigators.] . . . I thought I was doing you guys a favor, killing prostitutes. . . . Here you guys can't control them, but I can.[18]

While police avoidance of dealing with prostitute reports of rape may be understandable in terms of the legal entanglements, police nonintervention in the cases of reports of violence on the part of prostitutes is less justifiable. Reports of violence to the police by prostitutes may be crucial, not only in dealing with the crime of violence, but also in dealing with the sex industry itself. Recent studies have shown evidence of coercion as a means of inducting women into the sex trade. A 2002 report published by the Coalition against Trafficking in Women found that approximately 86% of U.S. prostitutes interviewed reported being physically abused by pimps and traffickers, and half of the women in the study described frequent and sometimes daily assaults.[19]

Prostitute serial killer Gary Ridgway in court on November 5, 2003, in the King County Courthouse in Seattle, listens to the plea agreement being read into the record. Ridgway pleaded guilty to 48 counts of murder. In exchange for providing information to help locate the remains of his victims, prosecutors agreed not to seek the death penalty. Ridgway admitted to investigators that he killed prostitutes to avoid paying them for sex and stated that he actually thought he was helping the police curb prostitution. It should be pointed out that Ridgway was playing "judge and jury" in regard to his victims' identities as career prostitutes, inasmuch as some of them were poor girls and young women who were runaways.

Source: AP Wide World Photos.

BOX 13–4

"Baby Pros" and the Cycle of Victimization

An interview study of 21 juvenile prostitutes and 100 girls in detention characterized them as "throw-away children" whose families had disintegrated and who have no home to which to return. The abusive relationship that the girls experienced with pimps was essentially a replay of the abusive relationship they had experienced earlier in their homes, which included sexual advances by older men at an early age.[20] During another study of drug abuse among children and teenagers, nine girls between the ages of 8 and 12 were encountered who admitted involvement in prostitution and/or pornography. They were neither runaways nor "throwaways," but had been introduced to their careers by relatives. The children were motivated largely by fear of rejection, and drug use did not appear to be associated with the sexual activities. Also, they did not appear traumatized by their early involvement with sex. In this study, family child abusers and pimps were one and the same.[21]

Although the profession of prostitution described by Gagnon and others during the "heyday" of sexual liberation of the 1960s and 1970s may have been entered voluntarily, the situation may have changed today. Then, the business may have been a means of developing freedom for girls running away from abusive family situations, or women freeing themselves from oppressive marriages. However, the sex trade today has evolved into an international criminal business enterprise in which women are involuntarily conscripted for participation. The report cited earlier, *Sex Trafficking of Women in the United States*, the most extensive survey published to date, provides some useful information on how women are lured into prostitution, and then eventually trapped or made into sexual slaves. The report includes the trafficking in women to the United States for purposes of prostitution, but also includes a similar process of recruitment by pimps within the United States. A summary of the findings of this report is given as an important addition to knowledge of prostitution, both global and domestic.

SEX TRAFFICKING OF WOMEN IN THE UNITED STATES

In *Sex Trafficking of Women in the United States*, published by the Coalition against Trafficking in Women, Raymond and Hughes revealed the strong possibility that many women are subject to trafficking and sexual slavery in the United States.

What was unique about the report, compared to other studies of trafficking in women, was that it included not only women trafficked from countries outside of the United States, but also U.S. citizens trafficked for prostitution *within* the United States. In the empirical literature, trafficking in women is often presented as a problem in countries outside the United States, with the United States less visible as a site for transnational and domestic trafficking in women. Several factors have recently promoted sex trafficking, including gender-based social and economic inequality, male demand for sex, "sex tourism," the globalization of trade, the expansion of transnational sex industries through increasingly sophisticated predatory recruitment techniques and networks, and military occupation and conflict. Profits from sex trafficking exceed those from drug trafficking in many countries, yet penalties for human trafficking are far less punitive in most countries than penalties for drug trafficking. There are an estimated 50,000 women and children trafficked each year into the United States. *Sex Trafficking* reports numerous instances drawn from police reports of both international and domestic trafficking for sexual exploitation as seen in the text box.

The study did not purport to constitute a census or even random sample of prostitutes in the United States. Prostitutes interviewed included international ($N = 15$) and U.S. ($N = 15$) women who had been or are presently in

BOX 13–5

Sex Traffic Incidents in the United States

1990   **Houston, Texas, Cantina Case.** Several Honduran women were exploited in a smuggling operation that guaranteed them safe passage and "jobs" for a fee of $450. The women were trafficked and forced to dance and have sex in a cantina.

1991   **Love Shack Brothel.** In Oceanside, California, police shut down a prostitution ring that catered to 300 migrant farm workers. The women, who were trafficked to the United States from Mexico, were placed in makeshift shacks furnished only with mattresses.

1994   **Chinatown, New York City Bowery Street Brothel.** A routine inspection by city housing authorities uncovered a brothel in which over 30 women of Thai origin were imprisoned. In a subsequent raid of the premises, INS officials found barred windows, armed guards, and squalid conditions.

1995   **Seattle Brothel.** Police raided a house in Seattle, Washington, suspecting that it was a brothel, and found five young prostituted Asian women aged 20–27, trafficked from New York City just weeks before the bust who may have been connected to another trafficking incident in Brooklyn.

1996–1997   **Cadina Trafficking Case.** Two 15-year-old Mexican girls escaped from a brothel in Miami and fled to the Mexican consulate. Investigation revealed a well-organized trafficking network from Veracruz, Mexico to Texas, Florida, and South Carolina, which enslaved over 20 young Mexican women in 18 months. The women endured repeated rapes, beatings, and were forced to undergo abortions.

1997   **Portland, Oregon, Child Trafficking and Prostitution Case.** Two Canadian girls, aged 13 and 14, were placed in protective custody after one managed to call 911. The two had been purchased for $3,000 in Canada by two American men who intended to take the girls to San Diego and force them to serve in the escort business.

1999   **Evans Family Trafficking Network.** The FBI uncovered an interstate trafficking ring based in Minneapolis, Minnesota, organized by members of the Evan family. The ring had been operating for 17 years. The ring trafficked young teenage girls forced into prostitution and controlled with repeated rapes, beatings, and death threats, then trafficked to other states.

1999   **Acapulco Pedophile ring.** A Denver schoolteacher and five other Americans brought boys from Mexico to have sex with the men who exchanged pornographic photographs and videos via the Internet.

2000   **Berkeley Landlord Case.** A prominent Berkeley, California, landlord was convicted of the carbon monoxide poisoning of two of his tenants, which included three teenage girls purchased in India and brought to the United States for sexual exploitation. One poisoned girl was pregnant when she died.

the sex industry in the United States who had sought the assistance of non-profit organizations. However, the study also included interviews with law enforcement officials ($N = 32$) who have experience and expertise in sex-industry-related cases and/or immigration; social service workers ($N = 43$) who provide services to women prostitutes; as well as academic researchers, investigative journalists, and health care workers ($N = 13$). The method used was qualitative, including interviews with all 128 individuals, as well as a study of men's writings, downloaded from the Internet, on their experiences with women prostitutes.

NEW TYPES OF PROSTITUTION

A major theme in the study was that prostitution is not limited to the usual types discussed in the literature—street prostitution, massage parlors, call girls, brothel prostitution, and so forth. Instead, prostitution today is an integral part of a growing sex industry in the United States that includes street prostitution; escort services; massage parlors; health clubs; brothels in hotels, rented houses and legitimate front businesses; strip clubs; go-go bars; peep shows; after-hours clubs; makeshift operations in beauty parlors, restaurants and warehouses; saunas; "chicken shacks" (dwellings used for quick prostitution transactions); trailer brothels in migrant farm worker camps; adult entertainment theaters; private residences; rent-by-the hour hotels; and makeshift brothels in gambling halls.

Men Who Manage Prostitutes

Controllers and operators of the sex industry range from family members of the prostitutes to prominent local community members, including judges and lawyers, to Organized Crime (OC) groups. OC networks were instrumental in recruiting 60% of the international and 40% of the U.S. women. U.S. servicemen were also involved in recruiting Asian women, especially from Korea, Vietnam, and Japan, into the sex industry in the United States. The servicemen often marry prostitutes who work around military bases abroad, bring them to the United States, and pressure them into prostitution. The majority of international (75%) and U.S. (64%) women reported that people who recruited and/or trafficked them were connected to pimps in the sex industry. Recruiters, traffickers, and pimps are involved in other criminal activity, such as fraud, extortion, migrant smuggling, theft, and money laundering, in addition to trafficking for purposes of prostitution. Most of the networks were small, with only one to five people involved. Husbands and boyfriends acted as pimps for some of the international (20%) and U.S. (28%) women.

Recruitment of Women into Prostitution

Women were recruited into prostitution in a variety of ways. The promise of an opportunity to make a lot of money was made to many of the international (73%) and U.S. (33%) women. Many women reported circumstances of poverty, economic desperation, lack of sustainable income, and, for many Russian women, the political and economic breakdown of their country. Crises drove even professional women into subordination, as indicated by a report of a trafficked Russian woman who had been a physician in Russia. However, with most women it was not the poverty, per se, but that the poverty was taken advantage of by recruiters, traffickers, and pimps, which ultimately led to their prostitution. The women were "preyed upon with promises," as one social service provider commented, not only of the money itself, but the "fantasy of a lifestyle" complete with house, car, and living happily ever after.

Pimps also recruit young, vulnerable U.S. women in malls and clubs by befriending them and creating emotional and drug or alcohol dependencies to entrap them. Coercion and violence also are used with U.S. women. Women from countries outside the United States answered ads for jobs in the United States, and others entered the country independently, arranging for their own legitimate or illegitimate travel documents. However, women who enter the country legally but overstay their tourist visas find that only illegal employment is open to them, and pimps take advantage of the situation to lure the women into the sex industry. Other international women were brought into the country through marriage to U.S. men, often arranged by mail order bride agencies, after which many were abused, sexually exploited, and recruited or coerced into prostitution.

Military Link with Recruitment

Other international women entered the United States through marriage to U.S. military personnel. Between the early 1950s and the early 1990s, over 100,000 Korean women immigrated to the United States as wives of U.S. servicemen. Many of these women had been prostitutes in Korea, known as *kitjich'on* or military camp town prostitutes. An estimated 80% of marriages between Korean women and American servicemen resulted in divorce, and a large number of the women entered the sex trafficking circuits in the United States. U.S. servicemen have been paid by traffickers to marry women in Korea and bring them to the United States for use in massage parlors and brothels here. In addition, some servicemen are reported to be involved in direct trafficking of women, not only from Korea, but also from Vietnam and Okinawa, Japan. The rise in numbers of sex establishments around military bases has been linked to the Vietnam war period. At that time, Fayetteville, North Carolina, with the largest military base in the United States, became known as "Fayettenam." The red-light district of the town came to resemble the prostitution areas for the U.S. military on rest and recreation (R & R) leave in Saigon. Street prostitution is also common in military towns. Prostitution around military bases is facilitated in two ways by military personnel. Military men marry prostitutes around military bases abroad, bring them back to the United States, and coerce them to engage in prostitution. Some military spouses directly prostitute women in establishments near the base. Other international military wives become victims of domestic violence and ultimately become displaced or homeless. Having no English language and work skills, no ability to access resources, and not understanding their legal rights, they are often lured by the want ads in Korean newspapers advertising work in massage parlors. The massage parlors appear to be well organized and financed, as indicated by their ability to secure consistent and successful legal representation.

Malls as "Pimping Grounds"

U.S. women are recruited to prostitution in various venues. As one social service provider said, "Pimps can smell vulnerability." The Mall of America in Minnesota, the largest shopping complex in the United States, was described by social service providers as one of the largest pimping grounds in the state, where recruiters prey on young, suburban, and rural teens who congregate there. Pimps also recruit women in clubs, create emotional and/or chemical dependencies, and then convince them to earn money for the pimp by prostitution.

Sexual slavery is indicated not only by the methods of controlling the women, but also by the methods of movement and methods of initiation of the women. More of the U.S. women (62%) than international women (29%) were domestically trafficked. Constant movement of women has a three-fold purpose: to provide a change of women for male buyers, who constantly demand new women; to prevent women from establishing any contacts who could provide them with assistance; and to escape detection from law enforcement. Of interest in this regard is that San Francisco, California, serves not only as an entry point into the United States, but also as a destination point for domestic movement of international women. This is because city officials in San Francisco voted to make it a "sanctuary city," which means that police are not allowed to question people regarding their immigration status, and are not even allowed to call the INS, unless the case involves a felony.

Twenty percent of the international women and 28% of the U.S. women had intimate relationships with the men who pimped them, a relationship that evolved typically from battering—both emotional and physical coercion—to pimping. Women are often coaxed, coerced, and/or raped by a pimp, and then cajoled or forced into having sex with his "friends." The seduction and seasoning can be quick or gradual, and is masked by a confusing mix of flattery, attention, "protection," and, most often, violence and exploitation. One U.S. woman talked about her husband, who sold her to his friends, and forcibly initiated her into having anal sex with him when she refused to comply with his friends' demands. Pimps often develop a system whereby they control a group of women by "family" hierarchy, with designated primary girlfriends, "wives," or satellite girlfriends. The main wife or girlfriend of the house is trained to be in charge and helps initiate the other women into prostitution and monitor their movements.

Pornography was used as an "educational tool" with half of the international women. One international woman stated that her pimp made her watch pornography in the beginning. Another reported that she had to watch pornography, because "my clients asked me to do as they did it on the screen." One U.S. woman remembered that as early as age three, she was used in pornography. She was made to perform at "pornofests" from age 3 to 12 that were held in rural Minnesota barns, basements, and private residences with up to 50 men in attendance. Some U.S. teenage girls were lured and photographed by older men in "compromising positions." Then the men threatened to send the photographs to their parents if they refused to have sex with them.

For some, stripping was the entrance point into the sex industry, after which they were constantly pressured into prostitution. Strip clubs initially hire young women to serve drinks and then pressure them into dancing and eventually into prostitution to make more money for the club. The women said the pressure is constant, and both subtle and direct. Women in the strip clubs soon learn that it's the prostitution, not the stripping, that brings in the money. "the dancing itself doesn't bring in that much money . . . it's the prostituting that does, and within six months on average, women get drawn into prostitution from stripping. Stripping is often the deceptive stepping stone to a worse end."[22]

Sexual Slavery

Pornography as "Educational Tool"

Stripping as a Stepping Stone

Methods of Initiation

Besides movement, intimidation, and "brain washing" through pornography methods of introduction to prostitution, methods of control are more clearly indicative of involuntary servitude (i.e., they were not free to leave the sex industry). These include denying freedom of movement, isolation, controlling money, threats and intimidation, drug and alcohol dependencies, threatened exposure of pornographic films, and physical and sexual violence.

There are various ways in which women were said to have been denied freedom of movement. As mentioned earlier, international women were held captive by accumulated debt. Undocumented international women also faced jail if they left, had no means of transportation home, and may not have known how to get home. Many also did not speak English and could not read or write. In some instances, they were locked inside, a condition that may be a carryover from an abusive childhood. Guards and other prostituted women provided surveillance over the women's activity. In one instance, a woman was kept in a hotel, naked.

In most cases, women have little control of their money. Seventy-nine percent of the U.S. women and 36% of the international women had money withheld from them. Money left over would go for food, laundry, lubricants, and condoms. In effect, the women were not receiving any money. Reportedly, a pimp monitors the tips women receive, even when they work in main-stream clubs, to make sure that the right amount of money gets turned over to him, and to the establishment as well.

Abuse of the Women

Eighty-six percent of U.S. women and 52% of the international women reported being physically abused by pimps and traffickers. One half of the U.S. women and one third of the international women described frequent, some-times daily assaults. Eighty percent of U.S. women and 50% of international women reported psychological abuse. Ninety percent of U.S. women and 47% of the international women reported verbal threats. Seventy percent of U.S. women and 40% of international women reported being sexually assaulted in prostitution at the hands of pimps and traffickers, and about that same percent-age had been victims of sadistic sex. One woman said, "I've been beat with hang-ers, tied to a bedpost, beaten for being with a trick too long. I was robbed and raped by a trick and then beaten by the pimp for letting it happen." Thirty-three percent of the international women and 61% of the U.S. women had weapons, such as guns, knives, sticks, ropes, and in one case, a sword, used against them.

International and U.S. women described other types of violence such as stalking, robbery, murder attempts, harassing phone calls, kidnapping, killing of a pet, and being sold.

Seventy-seven percent of social service providers were aware of the phys-ical violence that women suffered in the sex industry, whereas less than half (48%) of law enforcement officers were aware of the violence against women in the sex industry. Eighty-three percent of the social service providers were aware of the sexual violence perpetrated against women in the sex industry, while only 28% of law enforcement officials were aware of such incidents. One official (a female) went so far as to express the opinion that women in prostitution cannot legally be raped. These differences in knowledge in regard to victimization of sex industry workers indicate a crucial lack of knowledge on the part of law enforcement officials (when compared with victim and social service provider reports).

Violence against international women was probably underreported by them to the research team for various reasons, including problems recalling incidents, failure to recognize behavior as violent, reluctance to discuss the violence, normalizing and minimizing the violence, trauma, and shame.

Other Methods of Control

The international women often arrive in the United States with a debt owed to the trafficker for their passage, ranging from $2,000–$47,000, based upon country of origin (e.g., $40,000 for Chinese women as compared with $2,000 for Mexican women). Thus the need to repay this debt served as a strong motivator to the international women that U.S. women did not face, and threats by traffickers to harm or seek money from family members in their home country served as a further motivator. Additional expenses for food, lodgings, clothes, drugs, alcohol, and interest on the debt continued in a vicious cycle that perpetuated bondage for the international women. Ironically, one threat used by the pimps and traffickers was to report the women to the police or to the INS, even though they themselves were breaking the law.

Drugs and alcohol were also used for control, according to 50% of the international women and 71% of the U.S. women. One international woman said a pimp injected her with a drug, and another said her pimp made her drink, especially after a fight.

Another method of control was pornography. A significant number of both international women (36%) and U.S. women (65%) were used in the making of pornography, and/or threatened with it. Some indicated that they had been blackmailed by their pimps who threatened to show the pornographic films to the victims' parents. One woman trafficked for marriage testified that her husband placed pornographic pictures of her on the Internet. Reportedly, girls who are illegal aliens are required to participate in pornography by club managers who threaten to turn the girls in to the INS if they do not.

Buyers

Some generalizations were made in *Sex Trafficking* about the "buyers" who purchase the services of the prostitutes. Brothels housing international women tended to cater to buyers in specific immigrant or migrant worker communities, with some brothels having selective entrances for men from their own ethnicity, nationality, or race. Buyers came from all ages (15–90) and socioeconomic classes, and the majority of men were married. A number of African American women in the sex industry commented that the majority of their "customers" were white, mostly married, and from the suburbs. Some claimed that police were frequent customers, in exchange for dropping charges of prostitution against the women. U.S women reported higher rates of violence from buyers than international women.

Forty-three percent of international women became pregnant as a result of sexual exploitation in prostitution and 20 percent gave birth. Fifty percent of U.S. women became pregnant and 42% gave birth. One international woman commented that her oldest son wants to kill her trafficker when he grows up.

The majority of international (82%) and U.S. (58%) women said that men expected them to comply with all their requests, and men in their writings confirm this. Men generally expected and were willing to pay more for sex without a condom.

Buyers subjected women to physical violence, sexual assault, and other forms of threats and violence. These forms of violence were reported by a majority of U.S. women but a minority of international women. Around half of the women had received head injuries, as well as mouth and teeth injuries, and 56% of the U.S. women required emergency room treatment for injuries and illnesses sustained while in the sex industry. Most of the women contracted sexually transmitted infections while in the sex industry.

Coping with Stress

Emotional distress was another outcome, with 80% of both the international and U.S. women feeling depressed. Also, a large percentage of U.S. women (but not international women) experienced anger and rage, as well as suicidal thoughts. Some 63% said they had tried to hurt or kill themselves. The vast majority of international (87%) and U.S. (92%) women used drugs or alcohol to cope while they were in the sex industry, and half began using drugs and alcohol *after* they entered the sex industry to numb themselves to the trauma of unwanted sex. (The latter point contradicts the theory that drug and/or alcohol addiction normally causes the women to engage in prostitution.) Around half of the women had tried, sometimes multiple times, to leave the sex industry, but various factors had prevented this including economic necessity; drug dependency; and pimps who beat, kidnapped, and/or threatened them or their children.

The majority of women, both international and U.S., said that prostitution should not be legalized or recognized as a form of work, and said they could not recommend prostitution to any other women.

The report, *Sex Trafficking of Women in the United States,* contains some recommendations that include a three-fold antitrafficking plan that incorporates prevention, protection for victims, and prosecution of traffickers. The report concluded that trafficking cannot be separated from prostitution. "Most trafficking is for prostitution, and operates within the context of domestic sex industries."[23] Thus, antitrafficking policies and programs must address organized prostitution and domestic trafficking. Easing of rules of evidence is recommended in prosecuting traffickers (e.g., having police testimony admissible in lieu of sex worker testimony). On the other hand, penalties should be eased for trafficking victims, such as providing them a new "T" visa, which would be valid up to three years. Also recommended was stepped-up prosecution of buyers, including car forfeitures/confiscations of men arrested for soliciting, publication of buyers' names in the newspapers, and more "John schools" where first offender buyers are "educated" about the harm of prostitution to the women, the neighborhood, and themselves. Lastly, more funding from the VAWA should be made available for research, education, training, and services for trafficking victims.

BOX 13–6

"John School" in Toronto

Outside the United States, prostitution in many countries is legal or decriminalized, but prospective patrons who solicit women for prostitution are subject to arrest. In Toronto, Canada, men charged with being a male client of a female prostitute can be diverted into a one-day educational program that focuses on the social harms caused by the sex trade. Upon completion, the original prostitution charge is withdrawn. Follow-up study revealed that participants are more likely to admit they have a sex addiction and less likely to report favorable attitudes toward prostitution. Only 1 in 10 indicated that he will continue to use prostitutes in the future.[24]

As mentioned previously, recruiters, traffickers, and pimps are involved in other criminal activity, as well as legitimate business as a means of laundering money. Their involvement in the plural enterprises of smuggling drugs and women, as well as prostitution and pornography, can yield significant funds, which can then be invested, through various means, in legitimate enterprises. Commercial sex in the United States today is available through strip shows, go-go bars, pornographic magazines and videos, phone sex lines, the Internet, massage parlors, escort services, and sex tours. The connection between the sex and Internet industries shows how the sex industry is able to adapt from its more stereotypical, seedy, backstreets image into a modern diversified enterprise. In a sense, the pimps and buyers are the driving force funding the development and expansion of commercial sex on the Internet.

In addition, organized traffickers and smugglers often expand their illegal activities into legitimate businesses such as travel agencies, language schools, vocational institutes, and shipping companies. This legitimate status wins traffickers and profiteers respectability and power, and it also provides a vehicle for laundering money from other illegal activities. As a show of this respectability and power, a network of pimps annually congregate at a "players' ball" in Las Vegas. They vote for the "best pimp of the year," which is based upon how many women they maintain or recruit.[25]

U.S. women and international women had knowledge of specific forms of criminal activity in which their recruiters, traffickers, or pimps were engaged (in addition to migrant smuggling, trafficking, and prostitution). These include gambling, extortion, money laundering, arms dealing, auto theft and export, robbery, immigration fraud, identification documents forgery, check forgery, carjacking, labor exploitation, welfare fraud, racketeering, tax evasion, bank fraud, pornography, and insurance scams.

Traffickers and pimps were also actively involved in legitimate endeavors, often as a cover for illegal activities. These include clubs, bars, restaurants, bakeries, construction companies, travel agencies, hotels, beauty salons, computer hardware stores, telecommunications services, gas stations, convenience stores, limousine services, employment agencies, farming, and real estate.

PORNOGRAPHY DEFINED

So far, pornography has been discussed as an educational tool for the indoctrination of novice prostitutes and a sideline for pimps, traffickers, and participants in OC. However, it has grown into a major quasilegal industry on its own. Although pornography seems to have for some time been of concern to conservative politicians, it has often been trivialized by social scientists. The advent of **cyberporn** may cause social scientists to change their orientation toward pornography.

The sale, distribution, or exhibition of pornographic material is prohibited by statutes in all states. In addition, federal law prohibits interstate commerce in such materials, as well as the use of the mail, telephone, radio, and television for its dissemination.[26] Yet the pornography industry has grown, according to some estimates, with proceeds of up to $12 billion within the United States and $56 billion for all countries of the world.[27] How could a criminal enterprise that is so extensively regulated by law become so profitable (and as will be discussed later, become a major mainstream industry)? The answer lies in the vagueness of the definition of pornography, as well as in the willingness (or unwillingness) of public officials and law enforcement to enforce the laws that are on the books. Another answer has to do with the clout of those involved in the industry, who according to some accounts include not only pimps and traffickers, but major OC families, as well as big business.

Pornography is defined by state and local ordinances, but the ultimate arbiter of what constitutes pornography is the U.S. Supreme Court. In Supreme Court decisions, the term *obscenity* is often used for what is commonly termed pornography. The major constitutional issue regarding pornography concerns the First Amendment right to free speech. For many years the Supreme Court assumed, without deciding, that laws generally prohibiting dissemination of obscenity were consistent with the free speech guarantees of the Constitution. In 1957, in the case of *Roth v. United States,* the Court held that such laws were constitutional, but required that they utilize a narrowly restrictive standard of what is "obscene." In 1969, in *Stanley v. Georgia,* the Supreme Court modified the premise of the Roth decision to some extent by upholding the right of the individual to read or view concededly "obscene" material in his or her own home. Subsequently, some lower courts held that the *Stanley* decision gives constitutional protection to some distribution of obscenity, as well as to its private possession. Courts also held unconstitutional: (a) the federal importation prohibition of some distribution of obscenity, (b) the federal mail prohibition as applied to the mailing of obscene material to persons who request it, and (c) a state prohibition applied to films exhibited to adults at theatres to which minors are not admitted.[28] In 1973, the Supreme Court provided a legal definition of obscenity in the case of *Miller v. California*. The court held in that case that a work (books, films, etc.) may be subject to state regulation. The test of **obscenity,** according to that decision was:

a. whether "the average person, applying contemporary community standards" would find that work, taken as a whole, appeals to the prurient interest . . .
b. whether the work depicts or describes, in a patently offensive way, sexual conduct specifically defined by the applicable state law, and
c. the work, taken as a whole, lacks serious literary, artistic, political, or scientific value.[29]

By trying to define obscenity, it would seem, the Supreme Court opened the way for litigation as to whether or not a particular media form constitutes pornography. The difficulty of proof and cost of litigation constitutes a barrier to local law enforcement agencies in prosecuting pornography. Thus, the distribution of pornography continues, albeit on a sub rosa level, throughout the United States, and the difficulty of local law enforcement in prosecution has been enhanced by the increasing participation of wealthy corporate entities in the distribution of pornography.

TYPES OF PORNOGRAPHY

Although social scientists have not devoted much effort to providing a taxonomy of pornography, a typology was developed by Kerby Anderson, who devoted a web page to the topic. He wrote:

> The first type of pornography is *adult magazines*. . . . The magazines which have the widest distribution (e.g., *Playboy, Penthouse*) do not violate the

Miller standard of obscenity and thus can be legally distributed. But other magazines which do violate these standards are still readily available in many adult bookstores. The second type of pornography is *video cassettes*. These are rented or sold in most adult bookstores and have become a growth industry for pornography. . . . These videos display a high degree of hard core pornography and illegal acts. The third type of pornography is *motion pictures*. . . . Pornographic movies are being shown and distributed carrying R and NC-17 ratings. Many of these so-called "hard R" rated films would have been considered obscene just a decade ago. A fourth type of pornography is *television*. As in motion pictures, standards for commercial television have been continuously lowered. But cable television poses an even greater threat. The FCC does not regulate cable in the same way it does public access stations. Thus, many pornographic movies are shown on cable television. . . . A fifth type of pornography is *cyberporn*. Hard core pictures, movies, online chat, and even live sex acts can be downloaded and viewed by virtually anyone through the Internet. A final type of pornography is *audio porn*. This includes "Dial-a-porn" telephone calls which are the second fastest growth market of pornography. Although most of the messages are within the Miller definition of obscenity, these businesses continue to thrive and are often used most by children.[30]

PORNOGRAPHY AND VIOLENCE

"Moral entrepreneurs" may wish to make pornography against the law simply because it does not conform to their concept of traditional morality. However,

The Hustler store, owned by *Hustler Magazine* publisher Larry Flynt, is shown here on September 5, 2003, on Sunset Boulevard in West Hollywood, California. The store sells sex toys, sex videos and DVDs, sex magazines, clothing, and other sexually-oriented merchandise and devices.

Source: © Andrew Holbrooke/CORBIS, All Rights Reserved.

the concern to most criminologists is whether pornography is linked in a causal way to serious crime such as those discussed in the chapters (Chapters 6–10) on the Index crimes, and especially violent crimes. Another consideration is whether or not access to pornography can be a corrupting or traumatic experience for children that might lead them to commit criminal acts, presently or in the future.

Two Presidential Commission reports have been written on that subject in the United States and numerous studies have been done. It would be useful to summarize those studies and reports, starting with the first Commission report.

The Johnson Commission Report

The first Presidential Commission was appointed in response to concern on the part of U.S. Congress members about the *Stanley v. Georgia* decision of 1968, which enabled people to read and look at whatever they wished to in the privacy of their own home. Congress authorized two million dollars to fund a Presidential commission to study pornography in the United States and recommend what Congress should do about it. Eighteen members of the commission were appointed by President Lyndon Johnson, and all served to the end of the commission's existence except Judge Kenneth Keating, who was replaced by Charles H. Keating, Jr. (who was not related to Kenneth Keating).[31] Charles H. Keating, Jr. was appointed by President Richard Nixon, who succeeded Johnson. Keating was a lawyer and banker who, in the 1950s, founded the Cincinnati antipornography organization, Citizens for Decent Literature, later called Citizens for Decency through Law. As it turned out, Keating unsuccessfully attempted to stop publication of the commission's recommendations with a restraining order. Having failed in that effort, he filed a dissenting report.[32]

The Commission used the more neutral term **erotica** in place of pornography in its reports and interviews. The Commission found that a very high proportion of both adult men (85%) and women (70%) reported experience with erotica at some time during their lives. Adult experience was infrequent—about once a year, although the incidence was higher for adolescents. What was depicted, usually, was sexual intercourse, and movies were the main medium in which this was depicted. About one man in six and one in 20 women had seen one or more "stag movies" or "skin flicks" within the past two years. Friends were the predominant source of these movies and viewing pornographic films was mainly a social activity. Although men were likely to have seen the films with friends, women most likely saw them with their spouses. Demographically, the people with most recent experience with erotica were young, with some college training, lived in the Northeast, were likely to have "liberal" sex attitudes, tended to be activists in regard to social issues, and were heavy consumers of print media and movies. Patrons of adult bookstores and movie theatres were found to be predominantly white, middle class, middle aged, married males, dressed in business suits or neat casual attire. Patrons appeared to have had fewer sex-related experiences in adolescence than the average American male but to be more sexually oriented as an adult. However, they had about the same degree of enjoyment of sexual intercourse as non-patrons and had no interest in materials about deviant sexual activities, such as sadomasochism or pedophilia. Some 40% to 60% of the Americans surveyed said they felt that reading or viewing erotica does not have an effect on people. However, there were a variety of views of the effects of erotica. Diverse views included the belief that sexual materials provide information about sex, provide entertainment, lead to a moral breakdown, improve sexual relationships of married couples, lead people to commit rape, produce boredom with sexual materials, encourage innovation in marital sexual technique, and lead people to lose respect for women. People were more likely to report having personally experienced desirable effects from erotica, but said that they felt it had undesirable effects on others.

Empirical studies by psychiatrists, psychologists, and sociologists on the effects of exposure to erotica were addressed by the Commission. The findings were that (a) women are aroused as much as men by such material; (b) persons who are college educated, religiously inactive, and sexually experienced report the most exposure to and arousal by erotica; (c) subjects given repeated exposure to erotic visual stimuli over 15 days showed a marked reduction in sexual arousal and interest in such materials; (d) a majority of persons questioned indicated no substantial change in masturbatory or coital behavior after exposure to erotica although slight increases did occur in some individuals within 48 hours of exposure; (e) exposure to erotic stimuli appears to have little or no effect on established attitudes toward sexuality or sexual morality; and (f) delinquent and nondelinquent youth report similar experiences.

The Commission observed that much of the "problem" regarding erotica stems from the inability or reluctance of people in our society to be open or direct in dealing with sexual matters. Because of its importance, if sexual information cannot be obtained from legitimate sources, it will be sought from illicit sources, which may present sex in a "warped context." Therefore, the Commission recommended: (a) a massive sex education effort, (b) continued open discussion on issues related to obscenity and pornography, (c) the development of factual information, and (d) the organization of citizen groups to aid in implementing the previous recommendations. Further, the Commission called for a repeal of federal, state, and local legislation prohibiting the sale, exhibition, or distribution of sexual materials to consenting adults. However, the Commission also recommended that the commercial distribution or display for sale of certain sexual materials be prohibited for minors. It also recommended prohibition of public displays of sexually explicit pictorial material and supported existing federal laws regarding the mailing of unsolicited advertisements of a sexually explicit nature.[33]

Reaction to the Johnson Commission Report

The Commission findings and recommendations did not stand without dissent. As mentioned earlier, Charles Keating dissented, as did two other Commission members. Subsequently, the Senate also dissented, voting 60–5 (with 35 abstentions) to reject the findings and recommendations of the Commission. In addition to opposition by antipornography religious conservatives, feminists developed a curious alliance with the conservatives in regard to pornography. During the period from 1970 to 1986, women began to organize to protest pornography. They argued that pornography is sexist and degrading to women, showing them as stupid objects being manipulated for men's pleasure. As feminist Susan Brownmiller stated, "Nowhere is it written that you can exploit a woman's body because of the First Amendment."[34]

With the election of Ronald Reagan as President in 1980, the United States entered an era of conservative moral realignment and assertion of traditional moral values. Reagan signed the Child Protection Act of 1984 and announced his intention to set up a commission to study pornography. The result was the appointment of a panel by Attorney General Edwin Meese in May of 1985. The panel consisted of 11 members, the majority of whom had established records as antipornography crusaders.[35]

The Meese Commission Report

The Meese Commission gathered data from public hearings and meetings in Washington, DC, Chicago, Los Angeles, Miami, and New York in 1985 and 1986. The commission concluded that circulation of materials that graphically portray sexual violence is one of several factors that increases the probability of rape. With regard to the effects of nonviolent, sexually explicit material, the consensus of the commission, with some dissents, was that viewing nonviolent, sexually explicit material similar to widely circulated adult magazines is statistically related to a higher probability of rape. Pornography was said to increase the probability of rape in two ways: (a) through the simple arousal properties of such materials and (b) through their disinhibiting qualities, which have a capacity of changing attitudes toward sexual aggression. Despite stating that evidence was far from conclusive, the Meese Commission made several far-reaching recommendations for changes in federal laws. These recommendations included: (a) enacting a forfeiture statute to reach the proceeds and instruments of offenses against federal obscenity laws; (b) eliminating the necessity of proving interstate commerce in obscenity, instead requiring that distribution of obscene material "affects" interstate commerce; (c) and amending Title 18 of the U.S. Code to proscribe obscene cable television and transmission through the telephone or other common carriers. The Commission made similar sweeping recommendations for harsher state legislation, as well.[36]

Reaction to the Meese Commission Report

The Meese Commission report was immediately assailed by critics, including Commission members and social scientists who had testified at hearings of the Commission. The major point of attack was that experimental evidence was lacking for the link made by the Commission between pornography and sexual violence. The Commissioners justified the linkage by saying, "We see no reason, however, not to make these assumptions . . . that are plainly justified by our own common sense."[37] Critics included two female members of the Commission, Judith Becker, director of the Sexual Behavior Clinic at the New York State Psychiatric Institute, and Ellen Levin, editor of *Woman's Day* Magazine. They objected to "efforts to tease the current data into a causal link" between pornography and violence.[38] Several social scientists who testified objected to misrepresentation of their work in the Commission's Report. Edward Donnerstein, Neil Malamuth, and Murray Strauss all issued statements that they felt gave a more accurate portrayal of the evidence. They refuted the Commission's contention that, since the 1970 President's Commission report, sexually violent materials had increased in the most prevalent forms of pornography.[39]

Since the release of the Meese Commission report, there have been numerous publications critical of the report. Shirley Feldman argued that the causal link between pornography and sexual violence was unsupported by the evidence, and that longitudinal research is needed on this topic.[40] Nobile and Nadler, journalists in sexual politics, attended the public hearings and interviewed commission members, concluding that the report was extremely biased and lacking in intellectual depth.[41] Another report by Tom W. Smith that analyzed the statistical methods used by the Commission was highly critical. Smith questioned the Commission's analysis of public opinion, which he said was marred by several factors: (a) inappropriate comparisons between variant samples and inappropriate wording of questions, (b) omitting statistical tests of significance when comparing survey results, and (c) failure to use the best available data.[42]

Barry Lynn of the American Civil Liberties Union faulted the report for critical defects in the methods to collect and evaluate testimonial and other evidence. He stated that the faulty procedures included a predominance of antipornography witnesses and uncritical questioning of such speakers. He charged that the Commission made a lopsided effort to locate expert witnesses, had an inordinate focus on aberrant sexual practices and criminal activity, and showed a limited focus on social science research showing insignificant consequences of pornography. He added that the Commission failed to balance and reconcile conflicting evidence and used expansive definitions of child pornography and OC. In sum, Lynn concluded that these procedures seriously tainted the integrity and credibility of the Commission's final recommendations.[43]

Empirical Studies of the Effects of Pornography

Before and after the publication of the Meese Commission report, there have been studies and articles on both sides of the controversy pertaining to whether pornography causes violent crime. One recent study in Japan found that the dramatic increase in available pornography and sexually explicit materials, and the liberalization of restrictions on other sexual outlets, was accompanied by a significant decrease in sex crimes in every category, from rape to public indecency, from 1972 to 1995. The study found that the number of juvenile victims and offenders had also decreased during that same time period.[44] These are findings similar to those reported with the increase in sexually explicit materials in Denmark, Sweden, and West Germany.[45] George Thomas argued that, within the United States, rates of rape have decreased, while availability of pornography increased.[46] Studies using FBI data have shown a lack of correlation between access to pornography and rape.[47] In addition, experimental studies have shown a lack of correlation between exposure to pornography and increased violent behavior.[48]

Feminist Studies

Despite the weight of studies just discussed, there is still considerable concern about the danger aspect of pornography, particularly on the part of feminists. One opinion study done in Ohio found that the sample of 449 adults interviewed by phone was sharply divided in regard to the issue of legalization.[49] One self-report study done in England found that, although pornography could not be shown to be a cause of violence, its use is associated with some forms of violence against women.[50] It could be that the feminists are reflecting upon unrecorded rape or sexual violence in their concern about pornography. One experimental study of battered women in Canada found that the partners of battered women read or viewed significantly greater amounts of pornographic materials than did the partners of the women in the comparison group (of college students). Furthermore, 39% of the battered women compared to 3% of the controls had been disturbed by their partner trying to get them to do what the men had seen in pornographic pictures, movies, or books.[51] Another study done in Toronto involved telephone interviews with 604 currently or formerly married or cohabiting women aged 18 to 50. Overall, 35% of the respondents reported having been physically abused, and 6% had been disturbed by a partner asking them to perform acts that the partner had seen in pornographic material. Women who had been physically abused were three times as likely to have been so disturbed (10.4%) than were women who had not been physically abused (3.6%).[52] A similar finding occurred in a more recent study, which added that use of pornography is associated with an increased frequency of violence, and it was also associated with an increase in the sadistic nature of the violence.[53] These studies follow the lead taken in the pioneering studies of marital rape done in San Francisco by Diana Russell. In an earlier study, Russell found that 14% of her sample of 930 women had been victims of completed or attempted marital rape.[54] In Russell's perspective, pornography plays an active role in marital and other rapes in three ways. First, it predisposes men to want to rape women. Second, it undermines some men's internal inhibitions against acting out their rape desires. Third, it subverts some men's social inhibitions against acting out the desire.[55] Russell's theory was supported in a self-report study of 515 male undergraduates at a southeastern U.S. university. The study found a strong bivariate association between rape and rape proclivity and the use of almost all forms of pornography. The strongest correlation with rape and rape proclivity was exposure to hard-core violent and rape pornography.[56] Another survey of 2,972 college men found a reliable association between frequent pornography use and sexually aggressive behavior. It was also found that the way aggressive men interpret and react to the same pornography differs from that of nonaggressive men.[57]

Although correlational study suggests the two variables (rape and pornography) are related, still unresolved is the question of causation. That is, did the male students increase their rape proclivity after viewing the pornography, or was the pornography just a part of their rape proclivity? Longitudinal and experimental study is needed to determine the answer to this vital question.

The overriding question raised in the preceding paragraphs is whether or not covert forms of sexual coercion, which could include rape and child molestation, are increased by the availability of pornography. And the stakes are getting higher in regard to this issue. As mentioned earlier, there has been an explosion of access to pornography, by child and adult alike, by virtue of its availability on the Internet. Lawrence Stanley has cautioned against "moral panic" having to do with the production and sale of child pornography.[58] However, there is evidence that access to pornography today is a far cry from the annual viewing of a "stag film" discussed by the 1970 President's Commission.

Child Pornography

Besides the possibility that online porn access triggers forms of partner abuse or rape, the Internet also presents a considerable threat in terms of child pornography, which is said to be a two- to three-billion-dollar-a-year business. Pedophiles utilize the Internet in several ways including: (a) to traffic in child pornography, (b) to engage in sexual communication with children, (c) to locate children to molest, and (d) to communicate with other pedophiles.[59] Children can also be contacted in Internet chat rooms by child molesters who might entice them into meeting for purposes of sex. More frightening is the possibility that pedophiles can use the Internet as a means of obtaining sexual images of a child whose computer has a web camera. These screen captures can be saved by the pedophile, and then shared or sold on the Internet.[60] In regard to access to pornography, the Website *ProtectKids.com* has assembled some startling statistics that pertain both to children and adults:

- There are 1.3 million porn Websites.
- The cybersex industry generates approximately $1 billion annually and is expected to grow to $5 to $7 billion over the next 5 years (projection made in 2002).
- 74% of commercial pornography sites display free teaser porn images on the homepage.
- 25% prevent users from exiting the site (mousetrapping).
- Only 3% require adult verification.
- "Sex" is the number one searched topic on the Internet.
- 60% of all Website visits are sexual in nature.
- More than 20,000 images of child pornography are posted on the Internet every week.
- More than half of all illegal sites reported to the Internet Watch Foundation are hosted in the United States.
- Approximately 20 new children appear on the porn sites every month—many kidnapped or sold into sex.
- One in five children who use computer chatrooms has been approached over the Internet by pedophiles.
- Among teens online, 70% have accidentally come across pornography on the Web.
- Nine out of 10 children aged between eight and 16 have viewed pornography on the Internet, in most cases accessed unintentionally using innocent sounding words to search for information or pictures.
- Cybersex is the crack cocaine of sexual addiction.
- 25 million Americans visit cybersex sites between 1 to 10 hours per week. Another 4.7 million visit in excess of 11 hours per week.
- At least 200,000 Internet users are hooked on porn sites, X-rated chat rooms, or other sexual material online.[61]

BOX 13–7

Porn Profits Go Mainstream

According to *Money Magazine* journalist Mary Thompson, adult entertainment has become of interest to mainstream businesses. "As adult entertainment moves from seedy side streets to Main Street, companies with household names are making money from the business. . . . Demand for adult entertainment video is growing in large part because consumers no longer have to stop by the video store to watch pornography on Saturday night. More and more consumers are watching it from the privacy of their homes or hotel rooms without ever stepping foot outside. Liberty Media's On Command unit and Lodgenet Entertainment provide systems that let hotel guests pay to watch adult entertainment or mainstream movies. The companies then turn over some of the revenues to the hotel companies or their franchises that offer these systems. The hotel chains include companies like Hilton, Starwood, Wyndham, and Marriott. . . . Adult entertainment does mean added revenue for cable and satellite companies like Time Warner, Comcast, Cox Communications, Cablevision, Echostar, and News Corp.'s DirecTV. They air content from companies like Playboy, New Frontier Media, and Private Media. The content providers divvy the revenues with the cable companies. "They're getting closer to 20 percent to 25 percent revenue split where the cable company gets about 75 percent to 80 percent of the revenue," says Alan Bezoza, an analyst with Friedman Billings Ramsey. . . . Adult entertainment comprises 30 percent of video-on-demand requests and is expected to grow to 50 percent five years from now."[62]

The Internet porn industry is growing exponentially. There is evidence that pornography is serving as a source of profits for "mainstream" companies (see textbox). However, even feminists are divided as to the imposition of legal control. One study found that feminists are divided between those who join with religious fundamentalists in wanting to impose legal control over pornography and anticontrol feminists, who give a higher priority to individual rights and freedom.[63]

Reform Measures

One approach to this dilemma, suggested by a Canadian study, has been a three-tier system of controls. The most serious criminal sanctions would apply to material in the first tier, including visual representation of minors engaging in sexual conduct and material that encourages the sexual abuse of children. Less onerous criminal sanctions would apply to the second tier—depictions of sexually violent behavior—and defenses of artistic merit or scientific purpose would be available. Material on the third tier, visual pornographic material or performances, would only attract criminal sanctions when displayed in public without warning for minors.[64]

Although the crimes against children and violence against women discussed in this chapter may seem shocking and a justifiable cause for quick and repressive action, caution should be taken in the derivation of penal sanctions. Child molesters and sadistic spouse or partner abusers facing long prison sentences, as well as the pornographers themselves, may take steps to "destroy the evidence" by murdering their victims if penalties are excessive. Laws have been passed, such as the Boggs Amendment discussed in Chapter 12, imposing minimum mandatory sentences that are, in some cases, higher than the penalty that a perpetrator would suffer for murder itself. Such penalties make murder a "rational choice" in such cases. Also, extremely repressive efforts to abolish the sex trade can backfire. One study found that prostitutes in Amsterdam, where sex work is "normalized" through legalization of prostitution, are more likely to appeal for law enforcement assistance in instances of abuse or crimes committed against them. By contrast in the United States, where prostitution is illegal and criminalized, sex workers are likely to face further abuse if they attempt to report crime victimization to the police.

It would seem that we are living in a "brave new world" of cybercrime, one that is out of control. However, cybercriminals leave a digital fingerprint that can be used in tracing and identifying them. Yet in many respects, law enforcement must catch up with the perpetrators in its "computer forensic technology." Pornographers, in addition to being a driving force behind as much as half of the Internet, are on the leading edge of technological innovation, power, and sophistication.[65] Up until today, the Internet has been the "Wild West" in regard to sexual exploitation. However, regulation, such as that suggested in the Canadian report, seems to be called for.

COUNTRY PROFILES

So far, the emphasis in this chapter has been upon the trafficking of women to the United States and within the United States. Prostitution and pornography are examples of "low-consensus deviance," meaning deviance the seriousness of which is not agreed upon by the public.[66] Trafficking in women, it is suggested, is "high-consensus deviance" for which there is little disagreement that it is a serious offense.

The approach taken in this text has been to present country profiles on countries that are either high or low in a given type of crime. We have studied international databases to determine which countries are high or low with regard to a particular criminal activity. It would be ideal for our purposes if we could find a source that lists the "rate of prostitution" in various countries of the world, based upon estimates of the number of prostitutes in those countries. INTERPOL and the United Nations have not provided such information. In fact, the most comprehensive attempt to evaluate prostitution in countries of the world is published on an nongovernmental Website.[67]

Outside of the United States, probably the most extensive research on prostitution has been done in EU countries. Prostitution is legal in most of those countries. It is legal in Austria, Belgium, Denmark, Finland, France, Germany, Greece, Italy, Luxembourg, the Netherlands, Portugal, Spain, Sweden, and the United Kingdom. Prostitution is illegal in only one EU country—Ireland.[68] There is greater concern among EU countries with criminalizing trafficking in women for sexual purposes than prostitution, per se. The reason that this is taken more seriously than prostitution in the EU is that trafficking almost invariably results in victimization conditions that are akin to slavery.[69] Furthermore, the women who are victimized by trafficking are frequently subjected to serious crimes such as assault, forcible rape, robbery, and kidnapping. Possibly because prostitution is legal in most EU countries, they have become destination countries for trafficking. The EU country with the largest number of prostitutes is Germany, with an estimated 200,000 to 400,000 prostitutes.[70] Besides Germany, the EU countries ranked by the estimated number of prostitutes were the United Kingdom (80,000), Italy (60,000), and the Netherlands (25,000).[71] Great Britain was profiled in Chapter 10 as a country high in vehicle theft, attributed in large part to the international traffic in vehicles facilitated by a recent reduction in trade barriers in the EU, itself in addition to the fluidity of trade barriers in the vast English Commonwealth. It was suggested that the stolen vehicles, when driven to countries in Europe, such as Poland, could be converted to cash "seed money," allowing the thief to increase profits through trafficking drugs and other commodities back to England. One such "commodity" is "women."

In Chapter 11, Italy was profiled in relation to the topic of OC. It was suggested that the Sicilian Mafia and other organized crime groups in Italy have recently diversified their interests to the eastern bloc of European countries. Trafficking women back to Italy is the outcome of connections in east Europe made by Italian criminal organizations.

Although the Netherlands has been sensationalized as having a major sex industry, with its shop windows and sex clubs, the extent of prostitution in Germany, on the order of 10 to 20 times that in Holland, is less well known. Both countries are briefly profiled in this chapter.

The fall of the Soviet empire has been discussed previously as a factor related to increasing crime in the EU. In Chapter 10, Poland was discussed as a country where motor vehicles were stripped for parts and/or given a new identity, and then trafficked to Russia, in particular. Poland is also a way-station for women trafficked from the Ukraine and Russia. In Poland, women are initiated into prostitution through assault and rape. During the last decade of the 20th century, an estimated 400,000 women under the age of 30 left Ukraine, with an estimated 40% at risk of becoming a victim of trafficking.[72] Ukraine seems to have replaced Thailand and the Philippines as the epicenter of the global business in trafficking in women.[73] However, the latter two countries continue to have high estimates of the number of prostitutes within their own borders. The Philippines has an estimated 300,000 women in prostitution, with 75,000 prostituted children. Estimates of women in prostitution in Thailand range from 300,000 to 2.8 million, of which a third are minors and children.[74] Of interest, also, are Bangladesh and India. It is estimated that 200,000 women and girls have been trafficked from Bangladesh to Pakistan, while in India, there are an estimated 2.3 million prostitutes.[75] Bangladesh and India were discussed at length in Chapter 12, on the drug trade. While these developing countries have high rates of prostitution, we focus in this chapter on two developed nations—the Netherlands and Germany—to derive comparisons that are most relevant to the United States.

Trafficking in Women: Overview

Before profiling the Netherlands and Germany, an overview of general aspects of trafficking in women is needed. This overview covers the nature, extent, types of trafficking networks, and causes of trafficking in women, which are illustrated in the country profiles.

Trafficking in Women as Slavery

On the surface, the term "trafficking" suggests a relatively benign process of transporting a woman from point A to point B on a fee-for-service basis. However, trafficking in women almost invariably involves forcing women into prostitution, pornography, compulsory marriage, or slavery.[76] Women are recruited by answering job advertisements that are placed by employment agencies in destination countries, through marriage agencies, and through the Internet. Typically, young males of the same nationality contact the women in their home country.[77] In one case, for example, a Ukrainian divorced young mother agreed, as a result of a suggestion by a distant relative, to go to Germany where she was promised a job with a good salary. She was given a foreign passport and then traveled to Poland, where her passport was confiscated. She was then pushed into an unknown building where she was raped, beaten, and deprived of food. She was then sent to Germany, where she was resold by Turkish men. She was then put into brothels to serve clients. She was subsequently deported to Ukraine where, after a medical examination, it was discovered she had become infected with a sexually transmitted disease during her sex slavery in Germany.[78]

In addition to being forced to work in the sex industry, the victims' "recruiters" deduct the cost of their transport and other "fees" from their earnings. The fees, in addition to costs of passports, visas, and transportation, also include rent for living quarters as well as the cost of food, condoms, medicine and health care, and interest on the accumulating debt of the women.[79] While the debt mounts, some 50% to 60% of the prostitutes' earnings go to pimps and club or brothel owners.[80] The women are told that if they escape, the police will not understand their story in a foreign language and they will face deportation or prison. This belief is reinforced by the women's frequent observation of police participating as clients in the bars or brothels where they work. Often, the women are photographed having sex with customers, and told that the photos will be sent to their families back home if they do not cooperate.

Extent of Sex Trafficking in the EU

A good indication of the extent of trafficking is indicated by the percentage of women working as prostitutes in EU countries that are *not* their own countries of origin. The percentage of women working as prostitutes coming from eastern Europe were 70% in the Netherlands, between 60% and 80% in Germany, 80% in Austria, and 80% in Italy.[81]

Types of Sex Trafficking Networks

Networks involved in sex trafficking in western Europe range from small-scale to large-scale. *Large-scale networks* can exert total control over women who are trafficked because they have political and economic contacts in the countries of origin, transit, and destination. Large-scale networks keep the women under their own control, placing them in clubs and brothels owned by the network. Large-scale networks utilize stops at transit countries to obtain false travel documents. *Small-scale networks,* on the other hand, recruit one or two women at a time, transport the women to a destination country, and then deliver them to a club or brothel owner who has placed an order for the women.[82] Dutch authorities have indicated that trafficking in women is increasingly controlled by east European criminal groups.

Women from Romania are being taken to Italy, Greece, and Turkey. Women from Russia and Ukraine (controlled by Russian and Ukrainian networks) are being trafficked to Poland, Hungary, and the Baltic states before being sent on to Western Europe (mainly to Germany and the Netherlands). For example, in the case of Germany, visas are not required for nationals from Poland, the Czech Republic, Hungary, and Slovakia, so Ukrainian women enter Germany with forged Polish, Czech, Slovak, or Hungarian identity documents. Further transportation into another EU country is easy (because of limited border restrictions between EU countries).[83]

The "red Mafia" has added women to the list of goods it can smuggle across borders and this has resulted in a rise in the global "slave trade." The advantage of smuggling women is that although sentences for drug trafficking are increasingly severe, laws and law enforcement are lacking for trafficking in women. The money obtained from trafficking in women can be reinvested in other enterprises such as drug smuggling, arms dealing, or trading in stolen cars.[84] It should be noted that trafficking in women can very easily work in tandem with drug smuggling, since drugs can be concealed in women's vaginas and/or anuses, and/or forcing the women to swallow packets of the drugs.[85]

Causes

What makes women from the Newly Independent States (NIS) of Eastern Europe vulnerable to the sex trade? One factor has been termed the *feminization of poverty* in the former USSR countries.[86] After the fall of the Soviet "welfare state," women lost the advantages of socialism that included guaranteed employment, health care, and child care. Today, women account for between 70% and 95% of official unemployment figures in the NIS. Other factors in sex trafficking include relaxation of visa requirements, permissive legislation, and the physical appearance of women from the NIS. The physical appearance of women from the NIS is European, and therefore less likely to arouse the suspicion of border guards. Also, the women are less likely to be recognizable by the police as illegal immigrants while they reside in Western Europe.

Given these generalizations about European trafficking in women, two brief country profiles for major destination countries in Europe are developed, one for the Netherlands and the other for Germany. The Netherlands is discussed first, because it is probably the number one European destination that comes to mind when one thinks of "legalized prostitution" or "sex tourism." However, it has been discovered that the number of prostitutes in Holland is miniscule compared to Germany. Germany is reportedly the European country most highly populated with sex workers who have been trafficked into the country. So, after a discussion of prostitution and trafficking in the Netherlands, Germany is profiled and given the most detailed analysis of the two countries.

The Netherlands Prostitution has never been illegal in the Netherlands. Since 1988, it has been officially defined as a legal profession and prostitutes joined the Service Sector Union. Brothels advertise openly. In the urban areas and near the borders to Germany and Belgium, there is street prostitution, window prostitution (prostitutes rent a small room and solicit from behind a window, usually in the red-light districts), sex clubs and bars, escort services, and call girls.[87]

The Dutch Government has actually pursued an anticrime policy through its approach to prostitution:

> The Dutch Government believes that by decriminalizing prostitution, licensing brothel operators, and improving working conditions and health care for prostitutes, while at the same time prohibiting the employment of minors and illegal immigrants, prostitution will be less susceptible to criminal organizations trafficking in women and children.[88]

In light of its "open door" policy regarding prostitution, the estimated number of prostitutes in the Netherlands (between 20,000 and 30,000) seems fairly moderate. Yet, the Netherlands has, like other EU countries, been confronted with the problem of trafficking of women into the country, particularly since the end of the Soviet Union. According to the Foundation against Trafficking in Women and the Dutch police, the majority of women working in the prostitution business in the Netherlands are from the former eastern bloc.[89] Just as Holland's initial legalization policy was intended to curb OC, recent legislation by the Dutch Government was intended to target the trafficking problem. The Government now includes in its license requirements the provision that sex club owners may not hire illegal immigrants as prostitutes. The Netherlands also provides for a temporary residence permit for victims of trafficking to enable them to press charges against their traffickers. The Dutch penal code was revised in 1994, increasing its maximum sentence for trafficking from five to six years of imprisonment, while the sentence for trafficking in children is now 10 years.[90]

Germany

The German Federal Office of Criminal Investigation estimates the number of prostitutes in Germany at approximately 200,000, with about 50,000 coming from the central and eastern European countries (CEECs). Another police source claims that the total number of prostitutes in Germany is closer to 400,000.[91] The majority of trafficked women from the CEECs are Polish, followed by women from Russia, the Baltic states, the Czech Republic, Slovakia, Bulgaria, Romania, and the formerly Yugoslav states.[92] It would seem that with a population of about five times that of the Netherlands (roughly 82 million compared with 16 million), Germany has 10 to 20 times the number of prostitutes as the Netherlands (a country often thought to be a haven for prostitutes).

What are the factors that might account for Germany's exceptionally high number of prostitutes and its being a destination point for a large number of women victims of sexual trafficking? There are several significant historical factors related to the high level of prostitution and sexual trafficking that exists in Germany today. One factor, a familiar one from Chapter 11 on OC, is Germany's history of military rule. Along with the totalitarian rule during the Hitler era came its legacy of the use of slavery and mass extermination. Another factor is the partitioning of Germany after WWII and the conflict that resulted, problems similar to those resulting from the partitioning of Pakistan from India described in Chapter 12. In addition, the legal approach taken by Germany (which enables prostitution and trafficking, through nonenforcement of the laws) should be included as part of the discussion. Finally, child-rearing practices in Germany may have some relevance to prostitution, because Germany is considered to be a country where child abuse is a problem.[93]

History of Military Rule

Historically, the development of the German empire in 1871, under the leadership of Otto von Bismarck, resulted in Emperor William II's expansion of the military, culminating in WWI. The post-war Weimar Republic (1919–1933) was a peaceful, liberal democratic regime. However, hyperinflation, combined with world economic depression and resentment toward the conditions of the Versailles Treaty, led to the rise of the National Socialist (Nazi) Party, led by Adolf Hitler. Hitler blamed Germany's ills on the influence of Jewish and non-German ethnic groups. With one third of the vote won by the Nazi Party during the 1932 elections, Hitler was nominated as Reich Chancellor on January 1933, and subsequently assumed the office of President, as well, after the death of President Paul von Hindenburg in 1934. The Nazis implemented a program of genocide, at first through incarceration and forced labor and then by establishing death camps. Nazi expansionism led to WWII, which resulted in the destruction of Germany's political and economic infrastructures and led to its division and occupation by the United States, United Kingdom, USSR, and France. During the 1950s, East Germans fled to the West by the millions, and subsequently a wall was built by the German Democratic Republic (GDR; East Germany) to slow down the flood of refugees. The Berlin wall remained until November 1989, when the Soviet empire collapsed.

Prostitutes in Germany provided for the needs of German military during WWII and, in the post-war period, troops of the occupying nations. During WWII, although prostitution was officially condemned by the Nazis, prostitutes were found to be useful to the military.

Pimps who were arrested were sent to concentration camps but prostitutes were not, in spite of the denunciation of them. In fact, Reinhard Heydrich, who was head of the SS Security Service, had established the Salon Kitty, in Berlin, as a high-class brothel for important officials. Rooms were wired to see if any secrets were given out. By 1939, medically supervised brothels were allowed throughout Nazi-controlled territories.[94]

Sexual slavery was evident in the treatment of Jewish women during WWII. During the Nazi occupation of Poland during the early 1940s, members of the Gestapo would enter the Warsaw ghetto and rape Jewish women. Jewish women were also subjected to forced sterilization via toxic chemicals placed in their food and the use of X-rays to burn and destroy the women's ovaries. Women were also raped in concentration camps, and brothels were set up for soldiers and select prisoners in these camps. The brothels were actually designed for organized rape, where women lacked control over their bodies. In addition to forced sex in concentration camp brothels, women, while imprisoned, would commonly prostitute themselves, asking for favors in return, including the favor of letting them live another day.[95]

The epitome of sexual slavery was purported to have been perfected in Nazi Germany. The process, termed *Marionette Programming,* was designed to create sex slaves who believed themselves to be puppets ("marionettes") controlled by cruel masters. The value of a mind-controlled sex slave was multifaceted. They could be used to satisfy the perversions of people in positions of power without jeopardizing that power, because a person under mind control would not be likely to expose the event to public scrutiny.[96]

Partitioning

The more or less artificial partitioning of Germany by the allies after WWII resulted in a confusing tangle of family and gender orientations vis-à-vis the state that may have contributed to the high rates of prostitution in Germany today.

In German society, women traditionally had a subordinate relationship with men. For centuries, a woman's role in German society was summed up and circumscribed by the three 'K' words: *Kinder* (children), *Kirche* (church), and *Kuche* (kitchen).[97] After WWII, traditional marriage again became society's ideal, despite the shortage of men. Employment and social welfare programs remained predicated on the male breadwinner model. West Germany turned to migrants and immigrants, including large numbers of German Democratic Republic (GDR), or East German, refugees, to satisfy its booming economy's labor requirements. Women became homemakers and mothers again and largely withdrew from employment outside the home. This post-WWII emphasis meant that a large number of women, who were unable to find a husband and who were unable to find a job, might be forced to turn to prostitution or other illegal activities as a means of subsistence. The availability of a large supply of women supporting themselves through prostitution might serve as an attraction, not only for the multitude of military personnel stationed in Germany, but also for husbands seeking sexual diversity.

In the GDR, women remained in the workforce, supported by a Soviet-style system that mandated women's participation in the economy and provided educational and vocational opportunities to women. Laws were rewritten to accommodate working mothers, abortion was legalized and funded by the state, and a day-care network for children was put in place to permit women to be both mothers and workers. The GDR depended upon women for staffing its labor force (while they still maintained the household), a situation made more critical by the fact that most of those fleeing to West Germany were men.[98]

Although West German women began to seek equal rights to employment in the late 1970s, discrimination in income, employment, and in public office holding still persists today. The tearing down of the Berlin wall in 1989 had a greater impact upon the East German women than those in the west. Some reports indicated that two thirds of working women in the new states were unemployed, and many more were turned into part-time workers as a result of privatization, downsizing of firms, and elimination of support services such as day-care and after-school centers. Just as a large surplus of women in West Germany after WWII faced unemployment and turned to prostitution as a way out, women from the east faced the same choice after the fall of the USSR. The opening of the borders between east and west resulted in a dramatic change from the lack of erotic imagery, taboo in the GDR. "Sex could now be consumed in the form of magazines, peep shows, videos, and resorting to prostitutes."[99] In addition, GDR women could now be sought to engage in prostitution or other sex commerce with men from the west. Data are not yet available on the subject of how many women prostitutes are from East Germany, but it is likely that a good share of the 400,000 estimated prostitutes in Germany may include a sizable number of women from the GDR. Like the Netherlands, Germany has a large number of women being trafficked to Germany as a destination country, estimated between 2,000 and 20,000 per year. Approximately 80% of trafficking victims come from Eastern Europe and countries from the former USSR.[100]

The Law Regarding Prostitution and Trafficking in Germany

In Germany, prostitution is legal, while pimping and promoting prostitution are illegal. For trafficked women, however, prostitution is typically illegal. This is because most trafficked women enter Germany with a three-month tourist visa. After expiration of the visas, the women then work illegally. German law stipulates that migrants who enter the country or stay illegally may be punished with fines, deportation, or imprisonment. This illegality of foreigners becomes a loophole making them vulnerable to exploitation by traffickers. Women are lured to Germany by traffickers using fake employment offers, arranged marriages, fraud, and coercive measures. Once the victimized woman's visa expires, the traffickers can use further leverage by threatening to contact the police, with the possibility that the women might be charged with a criminal offense and incarcerated. In Germany, little in the way of witness protection is provided for the women victims of trafficking or their children (unlike the Netherlands). According to the International Organization for Migration, in Germany there is an extremely low rate of convictions for trafficking in women. This is due to the frequent lack of evidence, absence of witness testimony, and the difficulty of proving trafficking. At the same time, trafficked women working illegally in Germany are rarely arrested.[101] Thus, lenient law enforcement in Germany that seldom sanctions either illegal immigrant prostitutes or their traffickers helps to perpetuate the flow of women and organized criminal groups into Germany. In Berlin, many brothels, sex clubs, massage parlors, and saunas are owned and operated by foreign organized criminal groups from Russia, Turkey, or the former Yugoslavia.[102]

Child Prostitution and "Kiddie Porn"

Although international databases are not yet established comparing countries in terms of child prostitution, trafficking in children, or utilization of child pornography, the U.S. State Department's Human Rights Report for Germany does show some statistics for Germany:

> Child abuse was a problem that received widespread media attention. In 2004 there were 15,255 cases of sexual abuse of children and 199 cases of serious sexual abuse of children for the purpose of producing and publishing pornographic material. There were 4,819 cases of possession or distribution of child pornography reported in 2004, a 60 percent increase from 2003, which police attributed to the filing of more complaints due to better information and increasing public awareness. German law provides for the protection of children from pornography and sexual abuse. The maximum sentence is one year's imprisonment for possession of child pornography and five years in prison for distribution. The law makes the sexual abuse of children by citizens abroad punishable even if the action is not illegal in the child's own country. The government effectively enforced these laws.[103]

There is no way to know whether the previously cited statistics are significant when compared to other countries of the world. However, there seems to be a growing perception that Germany is a major client country for both child prostitutes and child pornography. According to a study presented in Berlin by the United Nations children's organization and End Child Prostitution, Child Pornography and Trafficking of Children for Sexual Purposes (ECPAT), an anti-child exploitation group:

> Prostitution rings are bringing minors from throughout the Czech Republic and other central and eastern European countries to the German border. German police psychologist Adolf Gallwitz said the border region had become "the biggest brothel in Europe," adding that pedophilia there was "increasing at an incredible rate." Gallwitz estimated that there were about 100,000 German sex tourists who travel to the Czech Republic, about half of whom were interested in children.[104]

Germany is also a source country for *pedophile activism,* also known as the *childlove movement.* This movement seeks the social acceptance of adults' sexual activity with children, along with change in age-of-consent laws and mental illness classifications.[105] In 1993, the Krumme 13 organization obtained considerable (mostly negative) press coverage in the years 2001 through 2005. In 2005, the organization won a penal court case that a textual depiction of a sexual relation between an 11-year-old boy and a 30-year-old man in the Pedosexual Resources Directory was not child pornography.[106]

Besides the aforementioned statistics on arrests for child sexual abuse and child pornography, the estimated number of German pedophile sex tourists going to the Czech Republic, and the discussion of pedophile activism, it seems likely that if the overall number of prostitutes in a country is as high as that of Germany, estimated at more than 400,000 prostitutes, then a sizable number of those prostitutes are likely to be underage, child prostitutes. Careers in prostitution often may begin during the teenage years.

If child prostitution, trafficking, and pornography are high in Germany, what factors make that country especially high in these deviant activities? The answer to this question may also be related to another historical phenomenon—Nazism in Germany—and that answer is the high rate of child abuse in that country.

Child Abuse, Child Prostitution, and Nazism in Germany

Lloyd deMause is a psychoanalyst who is the director of The Institute for Psychohistory, located in New York and editor of *The Journal of Psychohistory*. DeMause developed the thesis that the cause of Nazism and the origins of the Holocaust was rooted in abusive child rearing practices in Germany and Austria at the end of the 19th century, practices which stemmed from Evangelical Lutheran beliefs about child-rearing that were prevalent at the time. These child-rearing practices, mostly done by mothers, included sexual abuse.

Lloyd deMause believed that the Nazi regime and the Holocaust were a result of widespread child abuse that took place around 1900 within Austrian and German families. He characterized the German family as a totalitarian nightmare of murder, neglect, battering, and torture. He added that sexual molestation and beatings took place at home and at school.[107] Boys were the

Prostitutes, some of them very young, attempt to lure passing motorists May 18, 2002, in Dubi, Czech Republic, near the border to Germany. The United Nations International Children's Emergency Fund (UNICEF) released a damning report October 28, 2003, claiming that the Czech border region with Germany has become a haven for pedophiles and sex tourists whose victims are often children sold into sex slavery.

Source: Sean Gallup/Getty Images, Inc.

preferred gender at child birth, and girls experienced a childhood that was exceedingly harsh, dominated by memories of paternal brutality or negligence, drunkenness and violence, and a father's incestuous advances. German fathers' orientation toward their children was: "I don't want to be loved . . . I want to be feared!" DeMause quoted one father's feelings about childrearing:

> It is good to hate. To hate is strong, manly. It makes the blood flow. It makes one alert. It is necessary for keeping up fighting instincts. To love is feebleness. It enervates. You see all the nations that talk of love as the keynote of life are weak, degenerate. Germany is the most powerful nation in the world because she hates. When you hate, you eat well, sleep well, work well, fight well.[108]

Child-rearing around the end of the 19th century, according to deMause, was characterized by infanticide, wet nursing and swaddling of infants, and beating of children. Child-rearing was overwhelmingly the job of the mother. Infanticide was common, particularly with female babies. The best figures for German infanticide indicated that the rate of infanticide at the end of the 19th century was 20%. Children growing up would see the mothers strangling about 40% of their new siblings. They would also see dead babies everywhere in latrines and streams. From witnessing death, the children grew up with the feeling that they better not be "bad" or their parent(s) might kill them too.

Because hand-fed babies died at a rate three times that of breast-fed babies, mothers also contributed to the death of infants through refusing to breast feed them. Wealthy mothers would send their newborn to wet nurses, who were commonly called *Engelmacherin,* or "angelmakers," because they were often paid to kill the children sent to them.[109]

Children were feared and hated by mothers in Germany. *Kinderfeindlichkeit* or "rage toward children" was widespread.[110] Mothers swaddled their children, wrapping them like a mummy in yards of bandages, strapping them into a crib in a room with curtains drawn to keep out the lurking evils. Children were sometimes given away or sold to relatives, neighbors, courts, priests, foundling homes, schools, friends, and strangers who used the children as beggars.

DeMause traced these abusive patterns of child-rearing, in part, to Lutheran teachings. Martin Luther (1483–1546) was quoted as characterizing children as "useless eaters," who were "obnoxious with their crapping, eating and screaming."[111] DeMause characterized German parents as the most authoritarian batterers in Europe, quoting Luther's opinion that "I would rather have a dead son than a disobedient one."[112]

When it came to beating of children, German parents were experts. DeMause quoted autobiographical studies by Scheck and Ende on this subject.[113] It was found that 89% of children studied had been beaten at the beginning of the 20th century, over half of these with canes, whips, or sticks. Children were even battered while they were in the womb in the form of spousal abuse; some 20% to 30% of pregnant women were assaulted by their spouses. Children were beaten whenever they cried for anything, as soon as they were out of swaddling bands. These were not just spankings but whippings. Adolph Hitler reported that, during his childhood, he received daily whippings of sometimes over 200 strokes with a cane, which sometimes put him into a coma. Children were also frightened by endless ghost stories, and parents would sometimes dress in terrifying costumes, pretending to be a messenger of God who would punish children for their sins.[114]

Germany may be experiencing a new era of sexual license today, characterized by freedom to access the sexual services of prostitutes, both adult and childhood, and to access pornography. This sexual freedom, too, can be traced to the authoritarian family.

German children were also used by parents and servants as sexual objects from an early age. German doctors often said "nursemaids and other servants carried out all sorts of sexual acts on the children entrusted to their care, sometimes merely in order to quiet the children; sometimes 'for fun.' . . . Nurses put crying children to sleep by stroking their genitals." Children were used like a comfort blanket: "If the father goes away on a journey, the little son can come to sleep in mother's bed. As soon as father returns, the boy is banished to his cot, next to the parents' bed, where he will continue to observe their intercourse. "It was unheard of for children to have their own beds," but even in wealthy families parents bring their children to bed with them. After using them sexually, they then would threaten to punish the child for their sexuality."[115]

In the United States, children growing up in such environments often run away from home, and then turn to prostitution as a means of subsistence. It is quite possible that a similar process exists in Germany, contributing to the exceptionally high rate of prostitution among children and (later) adults.

SUMMARY AND CONCLUSION

In the case study at the head of the chapter, Sandy said she had been convicted, not of prostitution, but of a series of narcotic offenses. She explained her prostitution as a means of getting attention from men and obtaining "easy money." Sandy came from a broken home, having never met her father. She had to take care of herself from an early age because her mother worked full-time. Sandy had been overweight and wore glasses as a teenager, and associated with "a rough group," which led to her conviction for "incorrigibility" at age 14 and a sentence of three years in the California Youth Authority (CYA; a juvenile prison in California). After her time in the CYA., she had a slim figure and was attractive to men. She became an unwed mother by an ex-convict boyfriend. After her boyfriend went to prison (for the fifth time), she turned to prostitution. While she denied being coerced into prostitution, she recounted experiences of being kidnapped by a white slave ring and transported to Los Angeles. She believed that the police harassed her partly because of her attitude and because she was a "white girl going with a black man."

Prostitution refers to having sex in exchange for money or property with strangers or people with whom the person has no affectional ties. There are a wide variety of prostitutes, ranging from street prostitutes to "call girls," who cater to an affluent clientele. Part of the reason for the wide variety of types is the history of prostitution in the United States. Although prostitution is now illegal in all states, this was not always the case. Up until the 1800s, there was one major type of prostitution—brothel prostitution. However, prostitution was thought of as sinful. In response to the "whorehouse riots" by vigilantes against the prostitutes in the 1800s, prostitutes were segregated into "red-light districts." At that time, "regulationists" advocated medical and police supervision of prostitutes. However, feminists argued against this approach, because it put the onus on the women rather than the men. Feminists launched the abolitionist movement to outlaw prostitution in the early 1900s, in much the same way that Prohibitionists sought to outlaw alcohol around the same time. The abolitionists won over the regulationists, and prostitution was declared illegal throughout the country. However, this did not decrease the prevalence of prostitution. Instead, prostitutes continued to practice the sex trade covertly in rooming houses, massage parlors, on the street, in bars, and, based upon phoned requests to the madam, as "call girls." Another important change that occurred was that the pimp began to replace the madam as a manager of prostitutes. Although feminists have alleged that prostitution constitutes sexual slavery, prostitutes have argued that it is the criminalization of their activity that enslaves them by depriving them of their rights—civil and human. Over time what seems to have happened is that both sides have been proved right. Prostitutes are treated badly by the justice system, and because of their criminal status, they have often been driven to sexual slavery. A recent report indicates that 86% of U.S. prostitutes have been abused by their pimps or traffickers, with half experiencing frequent or daily assaults. Prostitution has gone from being a small-time business run by women to a major commercial enterprise run by men. Today the men, who include pimps and traffickers, use various techniques to subjugate the women to conditions like slavery. The men use not only violence, but drugs as a means of enticement and control, pornography as a means of socialization and blackmail, and geographic mobility as a means of isolating the women into a state of captivity.

Trafficking in women and children for purposes of prostitution is a growth industry. However, traffic in their images by way of pornography has proven, potentially, to be even more profitable. If a pimp videotapes an act of prostitution, he can reap not only the proceeds of the sexual transaction itself, but potentially thousands of dollars through distribution of the videotape via the Internet.

Two Presidential Commission reports have been produced on the subject of pornography. The first "liberal" report, published in 1970, found pornography to be essentially innocuous and recommended repeal of censorship laws for private use of erotic materials for consenting adults. The second "conservative" Meese Commission report, published in 1986, found that pornography may lead to sexual aggression and recommended enhanced enforcement and harsher penalties for distribution of pornography. Although the majority of social scientific studies have supported the first commission report and opposed the second, there has been a curious alliance between feminists and the conservatives who authored the 1986 Meese Commission Report. In support of these feminist views have been several studies of battered women, as well as self-report studies that indicate the potential of pornography to drive men to increased sexual aggression. Some alarming statistics were discussed in this chapter regarding Internet pornography, child pornography, and child access to "cyberporn" via the Internet. There is also evidence that the Internet is being used by child molesters for child access and exploitation.

A study similar to *Sex Trafficking of Women in the United States* was done for the European Union entitled, *Trafficking in Women: Working Paper.* The study found that most women trafficked to the EU countries are from eastern bloc former Soviet countries as well as Russia. All EU countries, with the exception of Ireland, have legalized prostitution. Germany has, by far, the greatest number of prostitutes (as high as 400,000) of the EU countries, 10 to 20 times the number of prostitutes in Holland. Germany's record of prostitution and high rate of trafficking in women seems to be related to its history of military rule, the partitioning of Germany after WWII, lax law enforcement in regard to prostitution and trafficking in women, and a legacy of abusive child-rearing practices.

DISCUSSION QUESTIONS

1. Sandy the prostitute (case study) said that she didn't believe "forced prostitution" could occur in Southern California. Do you agree or disagree. Why or why not?

2. Do you believe that prostitution should be legalized in the United States? What advantages or disadvantages do you foresee could result from legalization?

3. What role, if any, do you think that child abuse plays in causing prostitution?

4. In recent years, how has prostitution expanded in terms of jobs that involve prostitution or are related to prostitution?

5. How has the management of prostitution changed in the United States from the early days of brothels up to and including the present time?

6. What, if any, do you think is the relationship between the military and prostitution? Discuss this question in relation to America's

participation in wars throughout American history, including WWII, the Korean war, the Vietnam war, the Gulf war, and other "secret wars"?

7. Do you think that the term "slavery" is too strong a term to describe the situation of women described in the report, *Sex Trafficking in the United States.* Why or why not?

8. What changes in the laws do you think are needed to reduce trafficking in women?

9. Do you agree with the idea of arresting clients of prostitutes? Why or why not?

10. Compare and contrast the findings and recommendations of the Johnson Commission with the Meese Commission on the topic of pornography.

SUGGESTED WEBSITES

http://action.web.ca/home/catw/attach/ReportOct2002.pdf Website for the Coalition Against Trafficking in Women.

http://action.web.ca/home/catw/attach/sex_traff_us.pdf The report, *Sex Trafficking of Women in the United States* (141 pp.), downloadable in pdf format.

http://www.europarl.europa.eu/workingpapers/libe/pdf/109_en.pdf The report *Trafficking in Women: Working Paper.* Published by the European Parlia-

ment Directorate-General for Research. Similar to *Sex Trafficking of Women in the United States,* except that it covers trafficking of women to European Union countries, instead of the United States.

http://www.sexatlas.com/wsg/index.php Website containing statistics on prostitution and laws pertaining to prostitution for most countries of the world

ENDNOTES

1. Winslow & Winslow, 1974, pp.241–256.
2. Galiana, 2000, pp. 35–59.
3. Thio, 1988, p. 193.
4. Gebhard, 1971, p. 258.
5. FBI, 2004, p. 285, Table 33.
6. Messerschmidt, 1987, p. 244.
7. Beirne & Messerschmidt, 1995, pp. 203–204.
8. Barry, 1979
9. Gebhard, 1969, pp. 28–30.
10. St. James, 1987, p. 86.
11. Beirne & Messerschmidt, 1995, pp. 205–206.
12. Goldstein, 1978.
13. Jean, 1982.
14. Friedman & Peer, 1970.
15. Cohen, 1980.
16. Lee, 1982.
17. Becknam, 1984.
18. Talvi, 2003.
19. Coalition Against Trafficking in Women, 2001; Raymond & Hughes, 2001, p. 60, 62.
20. Bracey, 1979.
21. Inciardi, 1984.
22. Raymond & Hughes, 2001, p. 58.
23. Raymond & Hughes, 2001, p. 94.
24. Scot, Fischer, & Webster, 2002.
25. Raymond & Hughes, 2001, p. 49.
26. Adler, Mueller, & Laufer, 2004, p. 373.
27. Thompson, 2004; Asher, 2001.
28. Winslow, 1972, pp. 269–270.
29. *Miller v. California,* 1973.
30. Anderson, 1997.
31. Edwards, 1992.
32. Wikipedia, 2004b.
33. President's Commission on Obscenity and Pornography, 1970.
34. Sellen & Young, 1987.
35. Wilcox, 1987.
36. Attorney General's Commission on Pornography, 1986.
37. Attorney General's Commission on Pornography, 1986, p. 325.
38. Edwards, 1992, p. 4.
39. Edwards, 1992, p. 5.

40. Feldman, 1986.
41. Nobile & Nadler, 1986.
42. Smith, 1987, p. 250.
43. Lynn, 1986.
44. Diamond & Uchiyama, 1999.
45. Kutchinsky, 1976; Baun, 1976; Esses, 1985.
46. Thomas, 1993.
47. Gentry, 1989; Gentry, 1991; Scott & Schwalm, 1988.
48. Smith & Hand, 1987; Howard, Liptzin, & Reifler, 1973; Langevin, 1988.
49. Bohsui & McCaghy, 1993.
50. Howitt & Cumberbatch, 1990.
51. Sommers & Check, 1987.
52. Harmon & Check, 1989.
53. Bergen & Bogle, 2000; Cramer, McFarlane, & Parker, 1998.
54. Russell, 1982.
55. Russell, 1988.
56. Boeringer, 1994.
57. Malamuth, Addison, & Koss, 2000.
58. Stanley, 1989.
59. Durkin, 1997.
60. Saytarly, 2004.
61. Hughes, 2001.
62. Thompson, 2004.
63. Cowan, Chase, & Stahly, 1989.
64. Canada Special Committee on Pornography and Prostitution, 1985.
65. Asher, 2001.
66. Thio, 1988, p. 22.
67. *Sexatlas.com*, 2006b.
68. Galiana, 2000, pp. 35–59.
69. Galiana, 2000, p. 3.
70. Galiana, 2000, p. 41.
71. Cockayne, 2002, p. 12.
72. Galiana, 2000, p. 74.
73. Galiana, 2000, p. 74.
74. CATWAP, 1999.
75. CATWAP, 1999.
76. Galiana, 2000, p. 4.
77. Galiana, 2000, pp. 8–9.
78. Galiana, 2000, p. 9.
79. Galiana, 2000, p. 12.
80. Global Survival Network, 1997.
81. Galiana, 2000, p. 5.
82. Galiana, 2000, p. 10.
83. Galiana, 2000, p. 11.
84. Calabresi, 1998.
85. Lancashire, Legg, Lowe, Davidson, & Ellis, 1988.
86. Galiana, 2000, p. 5.
87. *Sexatlas.com*, 2006a.
88. Comparative Criminology Website: The Netherlands.
89. Galiana, 2000, p. 54.
90. Galiana, 2000, p. 55.
91. International Organization for Migration, 1999; Spiegel Online, 2006.
92. Galiana, 2000, p. 42.
93. U.S. Bureau of Democracy, Human Rights, and Labor, 2006.
94. Bullough, 1994.
95. Morrissette & Manitoba, 2004.
96. Twyman, 2001.
97. Comparative Criminology Website: Germany.
98. Comparative Criminology Website: Germany.
99. Sharp, 2004.
100. Comparative Criminology Website: Germany.
101. Galiana, 2000, p. 43.
102. Galiana, 2000, p. 43.
103. U.S. Bureau of Democracy, Human Rights, and Labor, 2006.
104. Taipei Times, 2003.
105. Wikipedia, 2006c.
106. Wikipedia, 2006b.
107. deMause, 1999, p. 2.
108. deMause, 1999, p. 3.
109. deMause, 1982, pp. 117–123.
110. Ende, 1979, p. 250, as quoted in deMause, 2005, p. 7.
111. deMause, 1999, p. 4.
112. deMause, 1999, p. 5.
113. Scheck, 1987, p. 402; Ende, 1979, p. 260.
114. deMause, 1999, p. 7.
115. deMause, 1999, p. 7.

14

WHITE-COLLAR CRIME

KEY TERMS

advance fee swindle
antitrust violations
bankruptcy fraud
check kiting
collective embezzlement
computer crime
corporate crime
embezzlement

fraud
fraud offenses
iatrogenic deaths
identity theft
investment fraud
Ponzi scheme
white-coat crime
white-collar crime

OUTLINE

Definition
Types of White-Collar Crime
Theory

White-Collar Criminal Enterprises
Country Profile: The United Arab Emirates

LEARNING OBJECTIVES

After reading this chapter, students should be able to:

1. Define white-collar crime as it was first defined by Sutherland, criticize that definition, and suggest definitions of white-collar crime that answer those criticisms

2. List the common elements found in all white-collar crimes

3. Group white-collar crime by types based on Edelhertz's and Barnett's classification schemes

4. Explain white-collar crime using various theoretical perspectives

5. Discuss how and why corporations proliferated in the United States, as well as

how and why they developed considerable immunity from criminal prosecution

6. Describe and give examples of various white-collar crimes such as antitrust violations, food and drug violations, securities fraud, immigration fraud, bribery, bankruptcy frauds, and Ponzi schemes

7. Indicate awareness of and the cost of the savings and loan crisis of the 1980s, when 1,043 thrifts went bankrupt, as well as reasons why the crisis occurred

8. Discuss the United Arab Emirates and possible reasons that country has the third highest fraud rate in the world

INTRODUCTION

Both my parents are devout, fine, generous people. I attended the public schools in New York. I don't recall any traumatic experiences in my early childhood outside of the various neighborhood fights. The discipline in my family, which was rare, involved not receiving my weekly five cents allowance. My relationship with my brother (three years my senior) was never very close, mainly because of the friction of an older brother not wanting his younger brother to tag along. He was what I looked upon as a symbol of authority—he drove, worked, and overall did things before me. He was a great mixer and social person whereas I shied away from crowds. I was a good student in junior high and high school. I never smoked, drank, or used drugs—I still don't. I never saw the inside of a police station until I was 38 years old; that was 10 years ago.

I married at the age of 34 and at the time of my offense I had two girls, four and five. I should spend some time talking about my wife. She is nine years my senior, which may have had an effect somewhere along the line. She wasn't a disciplinarian and let the girls turn the house inside-out. During a day's work at the office, I'd get four or five calls from her telling me that Ann did this or Sally did that. This was very embarrassing because I'd constantly be called from a board meeting to the phone. Our sexual life was very poor, so over the course of time I made modifications and when you're involved in this situation you have costly expenditures. This was at the time I committed this offense and the things leading up to it. I didn't want to mention this, but I feel this is a part of it.

In our corporation I was the assistant vice-president. The pressures of a corporate executive are very strong. . . . When you are making this kind of income, you must eat, dress, and socialize expensively. I loathed the patronizing of certain people, but the job made it necessary. I might be evaluated . . . as being antisocial. I have very few friends because this is the way I want it.

The event which caused my condition of crime—I was involved in a financial speculation. You can buy a certain stock on margin; you don't pay for the full price of the stock—you pay a part. As long as the stock is going up, the stock broker who you bought from will carry your account. But should that stock decline, you have to make up the margin immediately—if you don't, he will sell you out. Consequently, with my expenses of a mistress and various other things, I

reached a point where I didn't give a damn. I suddenly realized one day at lunch that my home life was practically nil and the answer to my problems might be to appropriate a large sum of money so I could look at the world and say, "Go to hell." My objective was to go to a foreign country with my family. I would not leave them high and dry. It was that afternoon at lunch that I decided to carry out this fantasy. I did not anticipate that my wife, though her mind was cluttered with problems and ill emotions, would not take part in this type of undertaking. My kids were, of course, too young to understand. It was then that I decided to take as much money as I could. I am not an expert or authority on embezzlement, although in the course of my imprisonment, I did rub shoulders with perhaps half a dozen embezzlers. These other men had spent many months planning. I completed my actions in 90 days—maybe my corporation was more conducive to such a theft.

Let me give you a brief explanation of the mechanics of embezzlement. The structure of a corporation may be condensed into AR and AP. AR stands for accounts receivable; this means the money which is due the company. This does not apply usually in embezzlement. AP, accounts payable, the money which we as a corporation owed, is the area I concentrated on. Basically, the way I completed my theft was that I created a pseudo accounts payable. I created fictitious creditors of my company. In the course of 75 days, I had taken approximately $193,000 out of the company. I created these companies out of state in a little town about 300 miles northeast of New York City. I opened up a fictitious bank account in that town using these small company names. My company wrote a check to these fictitious companies and every week I'd go to these banks and extract the money I had defrauded from my employer. I was the comptroller of the corporation, which is the chief financial officer. He decides how much money will be spent, paid, invested, etc. Therefore, it wasn't too difficult to get away with embezzlement for a while. Thinking back on another of the reasons I stole from my company was the fact that I was passed over for vice-president of the company in favor of a very incompetent man.

An interesting aspect of my case is the area of my trial, sentencing, and prison. . . . The jury system, when you take 12 people who are supposedly your peers and you realize that they're not your peers you begin to wonder. I recall four of the people who were on my jury and their occupations. One was a taxicab driver, another was a factory worker, a housewife, and the fourth a post office clerk. . . . My attitude toward the judicial process was laughable. I didn't contemplate suicide in my 14 months at Sing Sing. During that time three people committed suicide. . . . Out of the 3,500 men in there were about five with which I could carry out a reasonably intelligent conversation.

Embezzlement is definitely a very serious offense . . . no matter how you rationalize it. A good comment on the subculture is that in 99% of these cases the embezzler is a loner. They will do everything possible to remain as anonymous as humanly plausible. In answer to the question of whether someone in the organization prompted me or similar offenders into embezzlement—the answer is no.

Basically, I think I was caught because I subconsciously wanted to get caught. As far as the laws of extradition, Brazil represents a haven as well as Israel. I had enough funds to leave. I told my wife of the possibility of leaving the country, although I never told her why. She had no knowledge of my crime until the police came around. She, of course, refused to leave the country. An independent audit came in . . . during a period of time in which I had taken off several days. . . . See, there are two areas of embezzlement. A man has to have the means of acquiring the money. Authority, also. The second factor is that embezzlement by its very nature involves dealing with written matter and writing is as traceable as fingerprints. That's how they got me.[1]

CASE STUDY TWO: James, an Identity Thief

In his book, *Your Evil Twin: Behind the Identity Theft Epidemic,* Bob Sullivan describes the case of James Rinaldo Jackson, whom he describes as "identity thief to the stars." Jackson impersonated movie stars and Wall Street tycoons during his 20-year career of crime. Jackson, while an inmate at the Millington, Tennessee, federal prison camp, sent a Federal Express package to Terry Semel who was the CEO of a Hollywood studio. The package contained a letter from Jackson pitching a script for a movie. It also contained a copy of Semel's Social Security number (SSN), bank account number, credit card number, and part of his credit report. The package contained similar information on a number of movie stars and producers, including Steven Spielberg. The letter also contained a warning that these famous people were on a hit list for potential massive fraud.

Jackson was serving time in the federal prison camp for massive fraud involving identity theft. At the time of his arrest, he was in possession of a $55,000 Cadillac Allante and a $40,000 Lexus, purchased using fictitious Social Security numbers. He also carried numerous credit cards under assumed names, including business executives of major U.S. corporations.

Jackson's technique of identity fraud was illustrated by his blatant impersonation of film director Steven Spielberg, while Jackson was behind bars in the federal prison. After obtaining a cell phone smuggled in by being thrown over the fence of the minimum security facility by a family member, Jackson set out to "prove he could do it" again. First he called the Screen Actors Guild and obtained the name of the guild's health care provider. He then obtained information by dialing the provider's toll-free number through impersonating an administrator for a medical provider seeking to verify coverage for billing purposes. Operators working for the medical provider provided SSNs, date of birth, addresses, and other private information. Jackson, armed with this information, next called American Express, saying he had left home without his card and was able to ascertain the $100,000 balance of Spielberg's account.

After his release from prison in 1998, Jackson never got the movie deal, but reportedly continued to defraud some of the people on the "hit list" he had earlier revealed to Semel.

Sullivan traced Jackson's identity theft career to his childhood. James Rinaldo Jackson was born in Memphis, Tennessee in the 1960s, of mixed racial parentage—father white and mother black. In school Jackson was teased for his interracial background. After acquiring a guitar as a Christmas present, he impersonated the Beatles (John, Paul, and Ringo) and later Elvis Presley. Identifying with Elvis became an obsession, and James ended up in detention for disturbances he created by breaking out into Elvis songs during school.

Jackson's father died just as he reached high school. It occurred to James that he could help his mother by pretending to be other people. He was successful at a scam involving calling rock-and-roll radio stations that were giving away prizes to "caller number 10." He beat the system by speed dialing from 10 phone lines that he had set up in his home, giving various names and addresses around town, and then stealing from the respective mailboxes to collect his winnings.

After high school, Jackson waited table at the University Club of Memphis, where he learned to imitate the talk of powerful people who dined there. Subsequently, he followed a career of rigging rental car accident claims. Then by chance, while driving a delivery vehicle for Federal Express, he met a Nigerian con artist who explained the technique of tricking customer service operators in the insurance industry into divulging data on anyone. James used this approach to obtain full digital dossiers on numerous corporate CEOs. Using this information, Jackson applied for credit, made purchases, and made cash withdrawals impersonating these people. After a run of about 10 years of fraud and identity theft, Jackson was finally arrested for assuming the identity of a Federal Express employee with the same name (Jackson) for purposes of obtaining an employee discount for air travel.[2]

White-collar crimes are not considered to be Part I Index offenses in the FBI's UCR. They are considered to be Part II offenses (usually crimes that are less serious and less reliably reported than Index offenses); thus, only arrest data for such crimes are published by the FBI. As a result of this omission, data reported to INTERPOL and the United Nations for these crimes for the United States are only for arrests rather than "cases known to the police." Fortunately, the new NIBRS database has remedied many of the problems of the old UCR, and a new list of white-collar crimes based upon the NIBRS is presented in this chapter.

Many scholars have argued that some of the Part II offenses are, in fact, serious offenses in terms of the property loss, dollars loss, or even lives lost. In fact, Sutherland based his whole analysis of white-collar crime upon the allegation that the offenses he described (though many were not described as "crime" in law) should, in fact, be considered crimes.

However, the fact is that many of the offenses discussed by Sutherland were not described as crimes in state and federal legislation, possibly because of corruption or short sightedness on the part of Congress or state legislators. "Paper crimes" were not taken seriously by the lawmakers who felt that they could be controlled by fines or by trade associations. The problem is that, although individual acts of white-collar crime are often trivial, hundreds if not thousands of people are often victims of these crimes. Thus, the impact of these acts on society can be considerable.

White-collar crime is considered to be "nonconsensual deviance," crimes about which public opinion is divided. That is the subject of this chapter, and it includes a long list of crimes. Included in this chapter are crimes that have not been covered in previous chapters. This list also includes crimes that are not considered crimes in many foreign countries (e.g., influence peddling, insider trading). Also, included are crimes about which minimum information is available in the literature—little or no data, few articles or books published.

It is important to explore the full range of white-collar crimes that are described in the criminological literature. These are often trivialized (not taken seriously) by law enforcement and the public, alike, because there is no physical contact between victim and offender. However, some of these crimes can have even more serious consequences for society than many of the "public order" crimes that have been discussed in previous chapters, as well as many of the Index crimes. The seriousness of these crimes is discussed in conjunction with a description of them.

The term white-collar crime was first introduced by Edwin Sutherland during his presidential address at the American Sociological Society Meeting in 1939. At the time, the Society (and its attendant publication the *American Journal of Sociology*) was heavily dominated by populists of the Chicago School. Sutherland, son of a Baptist minister and former divinity student at the University of Chicago, may have been "preaching to the choir." So far as law enforcement was concerned, little in the way of white-collar crime was prosecuted. That is still true today. White-collar crime has even been considered a form of "victimless" crime, because financial institutions or the public at large share the cost of such crimes as antitrust violations, check fraud, embezzlement, and so forth. Even the presentation of this subject to undergraduate students in criminology classes seems to provoke yawns and glazed-over expressions. However these indications of boredom often change to fright when it comes to personal topics such as identity theft and/or stolen personal identification numbers (PINs), because these are crimes with which many students have personal experience, knowledge, or concern.

Although white-collar crime is not being trivialized here as a "victimless crime," its placement in this chapter (as one of many criminal enterprises) is based upon a recognition that while white-collar crime is wide-ranging in nature, such crimes are often viewed by their victims as not worthy of reporting to law enforcement agencies. Therein lies the threat of white-collar crime. It is shrugged off by most victims who may be ashamed that they were duped, or, in the case of large businesses, concerned that their corporate image may be tarnished. As in all crime, impunity can lead to prevalence of the practice, not just by individuals who wear a suit to work, but also by common criminals, including ex-offenders who know a good thing when they see it. As is discussed shortly, there are a variety of definitions, including those that limit white-collar crime to individuals of high social status. However, over time criminologists have come to recognize that white-collar-type offenses occur occupationally from the bottom of the economic ladder to the top. White-collar crimes can even include crimes of those not employed legitimately (such as James, the Identity Thief in Case Study Two). From the individual's point of view, it really doesn't matter to the victim of a white-collar crime if the person who has perpetrated the crime is a corporate executive or someone just released from prison.

It is useful to discuss how the concept of white-collar crime has evolved over time and to cover the variety of types of white-collar crime. Some discussion will be made of the extent and trends in this crime, the major forms of white-collar crime, and some of the explanations of white-collar crime that have been developed. Many of these are new crimes. Because they are so poorly regulated, the number of white-collar crimes seems to be limited only by the inventiveness of the criminal mind. The mere task of listing current white-collar crimes is a daunting one.

Although law enforcement is reluctant to arrest a merchant who has misrepresented the price of a product or a medical doctor who charges for services not rendered, the only deterrence that is available is consumer awareness of the scams that are taking place. Thus, that is the theme of much of this chapter.

Sutherland originally defined the term **white-collar crime** in a way that limited it to "persons of high social status":

White-collar crime may be defined approximately as a crime committed by a person of respectability and high social status in the course of his occupation. Consequently, it excludes many crimes of the upper class, such as most of their cases of murder, adultery, and intoxication, since these are not customarily a part of their occupational procedures. Also, it excludes the confidence games of wealthy members of the underworld, since they are not persons of respectability and high social status.[3]

Sutherland's use of the term *approximately* indicated that this definition was a work-in-progress. He later cautioned that his concept of white-collar crime "is not intended to be definitive, but merely to call attention to crimes that are not ordinarily included within the scope of criminology."[4] Sutherland later broadened the definition to include those in the middle, "wage-earning class, which wears good clothes at work, such as clerks in stores," and those in the upper class such as "business managers and executives."[5] The intent of Sutherland's definition was to make a theoretical point—in essence that crime was not exclusively a lower class phenomenon, but that official statistics erroneously made it seem that crime was concentrated mainly in the lower socioeconomic class of society. Sutherland believed that the statistics were distorted by the fact that upper class persons could use their political influence to escape arrest and conviction and because the laws that apply to business and the professions excluded criminal punishments, in favor of administrative or civil sanctions.[6]

Sutherland's concept of white-collar crime was initially challenged based upon its scope. Critics contended that many so-called white-collar crimes are not crimes but just sharp practices that are a normal part of a profit-pursuing business world. Other critics contended that sociologists should not play judge because a person isn't actually criminal until convicted in a criminal court. John Conklin argued against the "high social status" aspect of Sutherland's definition and singled out embezzlement and employee theft as the kinds of white-collar crime that lower status personnel in a business organization may perpetrate.[7]

Probably the best response to the criticisms of Sutherland's definition was given in a revised definition of white-collar crime developed by Herbert Edelhertz, former chief of the Fraud Section of the Criminal Division of the U.S. Department of Justice. Edelhertz developed an all-inclusive definition of *white-collar crime* as "an illegal or series of illegal acts committed by nonphysical means and by concealment or guile, to avoid the payment or loss of money or property, to obtain money or property, or to obtain business or personal advantage."[8] Beyond this comprehensive definition, Edelhertz provided a list of common elements that are found in all white-collar crime:

1. Intent to commit a wrongful act or to achieve a purpose inconsistent with law or public policy.
2. Disguise of purpose or intent.
3. Reliance by perpetrator on ignorance or carelessness of victim.
4. Acquiescence by victim in what he believes to be the true nature and content of the transaction.
5. Concealment of crime by (a) preventing the victim from realizing that he has been victimized; or (b) relying on the fact that only a small percentage of victims will react to what has happened, and making provisions for restitution to or other handling of the disgruntled victim; or (c) creation of a deceptive paper, organizational, or transactional facade to disguise the true nature of what has occurred.[9]

Edelhertz's analysis (as much prophetic as analytic) was that white-collar crime has spread based upon computerization of "faceless" transactions, obsolescence of products, extension of credit to "have nots," increased affluence enabling fiduciaries to violate the terms of their trust, and so forth.[10] Edelhertz developed a 61-item list of white-collar crime in four basic types, which appear in the text box, extending Sutherland's concept to include individual as well as organizational crimes, crimes done in the course of occupations or incidental to business operations, as well as white-collar crime as a business itself. It can also be seen that Edelhertz's typology encroaches upon OC. This overlap with organized crime was not by coincidence inasmuch as Edelhertz believed that there is an intimate connection between white-collar crime and OC. In the early 1980s, under Edelhertz's direction, the Arizona Organized Crime Project succeeded in combating OC in Arizona by making white-collar crime enforcement the centerpiece of its efforts against OC.[11] Even though some new types of white-collar crime have appeared since Edelhertz formed his list (e.g., ATM crime), his types are still quite comprehensive. We cover many of Edelhertz's types later in the chapter, going from the more general corporate types of crime to individual crimes, and Edelhertz's types serve as a good checklist to follow.

BOX 14–1

Edelhertz's Types of White-Collar Crime[12]

A. Crimes by persons operating on an individual, ad hoc basis.

1. Purchases on credit with no intention to pay, or purchases by mail in the name of another.
2. Individual income tax violations.
3. Card frauds.
4. Bankruptcy frauds.
5. Title II home improvement loan frauds.
6. Frauds with respect to social security, unemployment insurance, or welfare.
7. Unorganized or occasional frauds on insurance companies (theft, casualty, health, etc.).
8. Violations of Federal Reserve regulations by pledging stock for further purchases, flouting margin requirements.
9. Unorganized "lonely hearts" appeal by mail.

B. Crimes in the course of their occupations by those operating inside business, government, or other establishments, in violation of their duty of loyalty and fidelity to employer or client.

1. Commercial bribery and kickbacks (i.e., by and to buyers, insurance adjusters, contracting officers, quality inspectors and auditors, etc.).
2. Bank violations by bank officers, employees, and directors.
3. Embezzlement or self-dealing by business or union officers and employees.
4. Securities fraud by insiders trading to their advantage by the use of special knowledge, or causing their firms to take positions in the market to benefit themselves.
5. Employee petty larceny and expense account frauds.
6. Fraud by computer, causing unauthorized payouts.
7. "Sweetheart contracts" entered into by union officers.
8. Embezzlement of self-dealing by attorneys, trustees, and fiduciaries.
9. Fraud against the Government such as padding payrolls, conflict of interest, and false travel expense claims.

C. Crimes incidental to and in furtherance of business operations, but not the central purpose of the business.

1. Tax violations.

BOX 14–1 (*continued*)

2. Antitrust violations.

3. Commercial bribery of another's employee, officer, or fiduciary (including union officers).

4. Food and drug violations.

5. False weights and measures by retailers.

6. Violations of Truth-in-Lending Act by misrepresentation of credit terms and prices.

7. Submission or publication of false financial statement to obtain credit.

8. Use of fictitious or over-valued collateral.

9. Check-kiting to obtain operating capital on short-term financing.

10. Securities Act violation (i.e., sale of nonregistered securities to obtain capital, false proxy statements, etc.).

11. Collusion between physicians and pharmacists to cause the writing of unnecessary prescriptions.

12. Dispensing by pharmacists in violation of law, excluding narcotics traffic.

13. Immigration fraud in support of employment agency operations to provide domestics.

14. Housing code violations by landlords.

15. Deceptive advertising.

16. Fraud against the government, including false claims, false statements, and moving contracts in urban renewal.

17. Labor violations (Davis-Bacon Act).

18. Commercial espionage.

D. **White-collar crime as a business, or as the central activity.**

1. Medical or health frauds.

2. Advance fee swindles.

3. Phony contests.

4. Bankruptcy fraud, including schemes devised as a salvage operation after insolvency of otherwise legitimate business.

5. Securities fraud and commodities fraud.

6. Chain referral schemes.

7. Home improvement schemes.

8. Debt consolidation schemes.

9. Mortgage milking.

10. Merchandise swindles (gun, coin, general merchandise, buying or pyramid clubs).

11. Land frauds.

12. Directory advertising schemes.

13. Charity and religious frauds.

14. Personal improvement schemes (diploma mills, correspondence schools, modeling schools).

15. Fraudulent application of, use, and/or sale of credit cards, airline tickets, and so forth.

16. Insurance frauds including phony accident rings, looting of companies by purchase of over-valued assets, and so forth.

17. Vanity and song publishing schemes.

18. Ponzi schemes.

19. False security frauds (i.e., Billy Sol Estes or De Angelis type schemes).

20. Purchase of banks, or control thereof, with deliberate intention to loot them.

21. Fraud against the government such as income tax refund swindles, AIDS frauds, Federal Housing Authority frauds, and so forth.

22. Executive placement and employment agency frauds.

23. Coupon redemption frauds.

24. Money order swindles.

A more recent compilation by Cynthia Barnett of white-collar crimes, related to the FBI's NIBRS, added some additional categories of white-collar crime. Her full list is shown in the text box.

Considering that Edelhertz's list was published in 1970, and that many of the categories listed are probably subtypes of the list given by Edelhertz, it would seem that the Edelhertz formulation has withstood the test of time. New in the list are some "high-tech" crimes, various forms of "identity theft," counterfeiting/forgery, recently legislated consumer and environmental crimes, and crimes that have made news headlines recently. Barnett utilized the FBI's offense-based definition of *white-collar crime:*

Those illegal acts which are characterized by deceit, concealment, or violation of trust and which are not dependent upon the application or threat of physical force of violence. Individuals and organizations commit these

BOX 14–2

Barnett's Typology of White-Collar Crime[13]

Academic crime
Adulterated food, drugs, or cosmetics
ATM fraud
Computer crime
Corrupt conduct by juror
Counterfeiting/forgery
Defense contract fraud
Ecology law violations
Election law violations
Environmental law violations

Health and safety laws
Health care provider's fraud
Impersonation
Jury tampering
Mail fraud
Sports bribery
Subornation of perjury
Telemarketing or boiler room scams
Telephone fraud
Travel scams
Unauthorized use of a motor vehicle (entrusted vehicle misappropriated)
Wire fraud[14]

---

acts to obtain money, property, or services; to avoid the payment or loss of money or services; or to secure personal or business advantage.[15]

The list of offenses provided by Barnett included five types of white-collar crime: fraud, bribery, counterfeiting, forgery, and embezzlement. **Fraud offenses** were subdivided into five classifications of fraud including (a) false pretenses/swindle/confidence game, (b) credit card/ATM fraud, (c) impersonation, (d) welfare fraud, and (e) wire fraud. Barnett provided definitions of all of these types of white-collar crime, which can be seen in the text box.[16]

BOX 14–3

Definitions of White-Collar Crime

Bribery: The offering, giving, receiving, or soliciting of any thing of value (i.e., a bribe, gratuity, or kickback) to sway the judgment or action of a person in a position of trust or influence.

Counterfeiting/Forgery: The altering, copying, or imitation of something, without authority or right, with the intent to deceive or defraud by passing the copy of thing altered or imitated as that which is original or genuine; or the selling, buying, or possession of an altered, copied, or imitated thing with the intent to deceive or defraud.

Embezzlement: The unlawful misappropriation by an offender to his or her own use or purpose of money, property, or some other thing of value entrusted to his or her care, custody, or control.

Fraud Offenses: The intentional perversion of the truth for the purpose of inducing another person or other entity in reliance upon it to part with some thing of value or to surrender a legal right.

False Pretenses/Swindle/Confidence Game: The intentional misrepresentation of existing fact or condition, or the use of some other deceptive scheme or device, to obtain money, goods, or other things of value.

Credit Card/ATM Fraud: The unlawful use of a credit (or debit) card or automatic teller machine (ATM) for fraudulent purposes.

Impersonation: Falsely representing one's identity or position, and acting in the character or position thus unlawfully assumed, to deceive others and thereby gain a profit or advantage, enjoy some right or privilege, or subject another person or entity to an expense, charge, or liability that would not have otherwise been incurred.

Welfare Fraud: The use of deceitful statements, practices, or devices to unlawfully obtain welfare benefits.

Wire Fraud: The use of an electric or electronic communications facility to intentionally transmit a false and/or deceptive message in furtherance of a fraudulent activity.

Barnett indicated that white-collar crime accounted for only 3.8% of the incidents reported to the FBI for NIBRS reports from 1997 to 1999.[17] This finding supports those who feel that white-collar crime is not taken seriously, at least so far as the FBI is concerned.

The report indicated that in a large proportion of cases of white-collar crime, victims refuse to cooperate with investigators and prosecutors refuse to prosecute. Unwillingness to cooperate may be indicative of personal embarrassment. It may also suggest that a deal was made with the criminal perpetrator, settling the matter out of court. In any event, these data may indicate that the white-collar offenses are "trivialized" by victims and offenders alike.

However, public concern about white-collar crime may be about to turn to justifiable fear, according to a survey published in 2000. This survey indicated that public opinion may be changing in favor of less lenient treatment of white-collar criminals. The survey presented a variety of injury scenarios to the respondents comparing a street crime (e.g., armed robbery) to a white-collar crime (e.g., adulteration of a food or drug product). The study found that typically half of the respondents rated the white-collar crime as serious as or more serious than the street crime. The study found that 36% of those surveyed had been victimized by white-collar crime in the past year, but only 41% of the victims reported the incident to any law enforcement or regulatory agency. Only one in 10 victimizations was ever reported to law enforcement or consumer protection agencies. Most important, the respondents for the most part disagreed with the more lenient treatment by the criminal justice system of white-collar criminals as compared with street criminals.[18]

These findings are perhaps the first to indicate that public opinion is changing based upon a heightened public awareness or the widespread experience of those surveyed of actual victimization by white-collar crime.

As a matter of fact, that study found that victimization was greatest among those surveyed in the youngest age group (18–39), as opposed to those aged 60 and over, which is often thought to be the most likely victim age group for scams.

What is probably common to this young adult group is its experience with technology, including ATM machines, computers, and cell phones. It could be that the new vigilance found in the respondents in this study can be attributable to their direct experience. They may have been, in some way, defrauded through identity theft, scams, and schemes that have resulted from these new technologies. After a brief discussion of theoretical explanations of white-collar crime, a discussion of many of these scams and schemes is described.

THEORY

What motivates white-collar criminals like Albert, the embezzler, and James, the identity thief, whose stories were told at the beginning of this chapter? A variety of theories have been offered by Sutherland, Cressey, Thio, and others. Because white-collar crime, like OC, includes a range of crimes and people who commit them, it is likely that no one theory will sufficiently cover them all. So it is best to explore the whole range of theories.

We should also consider the possibility that some white-collar crimes are actually motivated by normal motivation and conformity to the requirements of "legitimate" employment (e.g., the sales personnel instructed to lie to customers by their employers).

Sutherland, in his book, *White-Collar Crime*, viewed participation in white-collar crime as a product of indoctrination into the subcultural ways of businessmen, in keeping with his theory of differential association:

> As part of the process of learning practical business, a young man with idealism and thoughtfulness for others is inducted into white-collar crime. In many cases he is ordered by the manager to do things which he regards as unethical or illegal, while in other cases he learns from those who have the same rank as his own how they make a success. He learns specific techniques of violating the law, together with definitions of situations in which those techniques may be used. Also, he develops a general ideology.[19]

After Sutherland applied his theory of differential association to white-collar crime in general, much of the theoretical work that followed Sutherland's work focused upon the crime of embezzlement, for various reasons. One reason may have been the potential for significant loss from such crimes, whereas another may have been the availability of data on this crime in the UCR. However, probably the major reason for the focus upon embezzlement may have been its concentrated study by Donald Cressey, former student and co-author of Sutherland's *Principles of Criminology*. Cressey developed a theory of embezzlement that contradicted Sutherland's differential association theory of white-collar crime. Lastly, embezzlement seems to contain the key elements of white-collar crime as discussed by Edelhertz, Barnett, and others. Thus, focusing upon theories embezzlement is pretty close to explaining white-collar crime generally. However, before discussing Cressey's theory, other theories of embezzlement that predated and led up to Cressey's work are discussed.

Svend Riemer developed a second theoretical approach to white-collar crime that also focused upon embezzlement. Riemer's theory was a variation of opportunity theory. It states that there are opportunities inherent in trust positions that result in temptations if trustees develop antisocial attitudes. The antisocial attitudes make normative violation possible if the incumbents define a need for extra funds or extended use of property as an "emergency" that cannot be met by legal means.[20] It should be noted that this theory postulates a special case of opportunity theory where the deviancy is not induced by a low social position, but by anticipated decline in social status based upon a potential "sudden reversal" of fortune.

Very closely related to Riemer's approach is a tension-reduction psychological theory developed by Lottier. Lottier studied a group of 50 embezzlers convicted by a Detroit court and who had undergone psychiatric examination. The embezzler, according to Lottier, is an individual who has not found other ways to relieve or internalize tension. In addition to the normal biological drives, businesspeople have heightened anxiety and tension due to their competitive, aggressive behavior and position of trust. When this tension is increased in a particular situation and the individual does not have other means with which to discharge this tension, he or she seeks relief through embezzlement. The embezzlement is not merely a relief from financial burdens, but a reduction of other psychic and sexual tensions as well.[21]

Although Lottier's theory is technically a psychological theory, it can also be seen as a variety of strain theory, which is very closely related to the anomie approach employed by Merton, but also provides an interesting prelude to Cressey's theory that focuses on psychological isolation (despite the fact that Cressey was a sociologist and follower of Sutherland).

Cressey had an opportunity to interview a group of 133 embezzlers imprisoned at Joliet, Illinois; Chino, California; and Terre Haute, Indiana. In the course of doing so, he developed a method, which he termed *analytic induction*. Analytic induction was a method of utilizing interviews to give theories an "acid test." Through the interview process, if even a single case of the phenomenon at hand is inconsistent with the theory, then the theory must be rejected. As Cressey explained his method:

> First, a rough definition of the phenomenon to be explained is formulated. Second, a hypothetical explanation of the phenomenon is formulated. Third, one case is studied in light of the hypothesis with the object of determining whether the hypothesis fits the facts in that case. Fourth, if the hypothesis does not fit the facts, the hypothesis is re-formulated or the phenomenon to be explained is re-defined, so that the case is excluded. The definition must be more precise than the first one. Fifth, practical certainty may be attained after a small number of cases has been examined, but the discovery by the investigator or any other investigator of a single negative case disproves the explanation and requires re-formulation. Sixth, this procedure of examining cases, re-defining the phenomenon, and re-formulating the hypothesis is continued until a universal relationship is established, each negative case calling for a re-definition or re-formulation. Seventh, for purposes of proof, cases outside the area circumscribed by the definition are examined to determine whether or not the final hypothesis applies to them.[22]

Cressey defined **embezzlement** as criminal violation of financial trust whereby, "First, the person must have accepted a position of trust in good faith. Second, the person must have violated that trust by committing a crime."[23]

After interviewing 133 embezzlers, Cressey rejected both differential association and opportunity theory. In regard to differential association theory, Cressey found embezzlers who said they knew of no one in their business or profession who was carrying on practices similar to theirs. Regarding economic strain, Cressey encountered cases who had experienced grave financial difficulties earlier in their occupational careers, but had not taken to theft as a solution.

Cressey's final generalization emphasized the situational factor of psychological isolation and posited three conditions considered essential to leading a person to violate a financial trust:

1. When the person conceives of himself as having a financial problem that is nonshareable.
2. When the person becomes aware that his nonshareable problem can be secretly resolved by violation of his financial trust.
3. When the person is able to apply to his own conduct rationalizations that enable him to adjust his conception of himself as a trusted person to his conception of himself as a user of the entrusted funds or property.[24]

Cressey's polite reference to a "non-shareable problem" has been more bluntly defined as "bookies, babes, and booze," and in fact the term *embezzlement* derives from the French term *bezzle,* which means "drink to excess, gluttonage, revel, waste in riot, and plunder."[25] Certainly, the term *nonshareable problem* could include drug addiction, as well as "booze," or even losses through speculating in the stock market, as well as "bookies." Cressey's explanation of embezzlement seems to fit the case of Albert the embezzler quite adequately. However, in some ways Cressey's theory is lacking. Through its focus upon individual cases, Cressey's theory has ended up as a psychological theory, quite similar to Lottier's theory, discussed previously (with the exception of the rationalization proviso in Step 3 of Cressey's universal generalization).

From the comparative criminological perspective, how does Cressey's theory help to explain embezzlement cross-nationally? Sociological variables that would help predict the prevalence of embezzlement in different societies are left out of the theory. Of course, Cressey would be the first to admit that sociological generalizations were not his goal—although his method did prove to be a vehicle for rejection of sociological theories (differential association, opportunity) that are not applicable to the cases at hand. However, to develop sociological theories that are compatible with Cressey's "psychological isolation theory," it is necessary to turn to other sources. Thio has actually suggested that "the higher one's position is in a company, the more likely one is to commit a crime, because of easier access to the company's resources."[26] According to that theory, the larger the number of highly paid corporate executives in a country, the greater the white-collar crime. Certainly, this is an interesting theory, although one that is impossible to test given the limitations of official statistics. Another possible way of operationalizing Cressey's theory would be to develop an index of "nonshareable problems" that could refer to the volume of vices that are occurring in society and correlate that index with official measurement of white-collar crime. A kind of "vice index" could include the volume of prostitution, amount of drug addiction, rate of alcohol consumption, dollars lost gambling, dollars lost speculating in investments, and so forth. However, the secretive nature of much if not most of this activity probably would result in extremely inaccurate measurement. Nevertheless, it seems likely that countries that have high rates of embezzlement would be characterized by high rates of participation in gambling, alcohol consumption, prostitution, drugs, and other "nonshareable problems."

While Cressey may have done an adequate job of profiling embezzlers, it seems likely that white-collar crime today is such a vast criminal enterprise that one explanation will not suffice for all forms of its occurrence. Cressey's method may be very useful in exploring other white-collar crimes, besides embezzlement. But for now, it seems that the book should not be closed on explanations of white-collar crime. Some forms of white-collar crime may very well result from the learning of illicit practices from others involved in a legitimate enterprise. Others may be the result of economic and psychological stress, such as that suffered by James (the identity thief) in the case study discussed at the beginning of the chapter. However, other practices might border on conformity, in the sense that employees are simply doing what they are told to do by their managers (as mentioned by Sutherland). In any event, it seems likely that collar crime is a growing phenomenon, and one that is not amenable to law enforcement control, either because of indifference or ineptitude on the part of the police. Thus, the most important goal that can be sought is to reveal various white-collar criminal enterprises by describing them, to help raise public awareness so that potential victims can avoid such victimization. Thus, the remainder of this chapter is devoted to a description of various white-collar criminal enterprises, from among those listed earlier by Edelhertz and Barnett. Along the way, as various forms of white-collar crime are described, we may gain knowledge of factors involved in white-collar crime that may help in the development of a theory or theories of white-collar crime.

Edelhertz's typology of white-collar crime was incredibly comprehensive, especially considering the fact that it was published in 1970, essentially before the advent of many technological innovations, such as the personal computer, the Internet, and cell phones, which facilitate widespread white-collar crime. Edelhertz's types are used below to provide an overview of crimes in the category of white-collar crime. Coverage includes categories that are not self-explanatory, such as "purchases on credit with no intention to pay." Also discussed are topics that might seem self-explanatory, such as income tax violations, but which have some counterintuitive facts about them that should be brought to light. The crimes of recent derivation added by Barnett are amended to Edelhertz's typology under the classification that seems appropriate to these crimes.

Edelhertz's typology, especially with the addition of Barnett's types of white-collar crimes, includes an overwhelming number of separate crimes. Thus, it seems difficult to determine a starting point for analysis. This bewildering number of white-collar crimes didn't just emerge suddenly or spontaneously. They developed over time. More important, they were not a product of the street-crime underworld, or even of OC. They were a byproduct of the development of America's business community, which may be described for the most part as a corporate community that is moving in the direction of being a multinational corporate community. Thus, a brief description of the development of America's corporations may be insightful in understanding the rise of white-collar crime.

History of Corporations in the United States

In 1995, the U.S. economy hosted around 4.3 million corporations (including individuals who have incorporated), which produced far more goods and services than proprietorships and partnerships, combined.[27] Most Americans view corporations as major employers and a fact of life in the United States today. However, historically this was not always the case. Just as America has multinational corporations that represent it around the world, the same was true for Great Britain in pre-Revolutionary America. Major British corporations included the Massachusetts Bay Company, the Hudson's Bay Company, and the British East India Company, which were used by the British kings to control the affairs of the colonies, as well as to extract resources and taxes. It was the attempt by the British East India Company to impose duties on its incoming tea that inspired the Boston Tea Party, which helped spark the American Revolution. The Declaration of Independence, in 1776, freed Americans as much from the British corporations as it did from British rule. After the Revolution, Americans remained wary of corporations for the next 100 years. Corporations, during this period, were kept in tow, chartered by individual states rather than the federal government. The two hundred or so corporations operating in the United States were not allowed to participate in the political process. They were not allowed to buy stock in other corporations, and they were automatically dissolved if they engaged in activities that violated their charters. However, this situation of tightly controlled state-based corporations changed drastically after the Civil War. Just as OC (as discussed in Chapter 11) was related to a history of military rule, so, it seems would be white-collar crime. Corporations made enormous profits from procurement contracts during the Civil War. They also took advantage of the disorder and corruption of the postwar era to bribe legislators, judges, and even presidents.[28] Corporations abused their charters and became conglomerates and trusts. They created factory systems and company towns where they set wages, hours, production processes, and machine speeds. They forced a nation of farmers to become wage earners, fearful of unemployment, and hired private armies to keep the workers in line. Legislatures gave corporations limited liability, longer charters, and decreased citizen oversight. Judges repeatedly gave privilege after privilege to corporations, including the power of eminent domain for some corporations. Judges also eliminated jury trials to determine corporation-caused harm and to assess damages and took from the legislatures the right to oversee corporate rates of return. Finally, in 1886 the Supreme Court ruled in *Santa Clara County v. Southern Pacific Railroad* that a private corporation was a "natural person" under the U.S. Constitution, protected by the Bill of Rights and the 14th Amendment. "Corporate power, now virtually unchecked, owned resources, production, commerce, trade, prices, politicians, judges and the law."[29] As a consequence of these developments in the 19th Century, America became the world's corporate giant with a gross national product of over $10 trillion per year. At the same time, corporate owners and managers were no longer responsible for criminal acts committed by the corporations. Corporations today can continue in perpetuity even if they exceed their charter's authority and if they cause public harm. Up until the 20th century, it was thought that the owners, managers, and the corporation itself as a "person" could not be charged with a crime in a court of law. Typically, when such crimes are charged, sanctions are usually lenient.[30]

Crimes Committed by Corporations

Edelhertz listed some 18 acts in Category C, "Crimes incidental to and in furtherance of business operations," which describe corporate and business crimes. **Corporate crime** can be defined as "a violation of a criminal statute either by a corporate entity or by its executives, employees, or agents acting on behalf of and for the benefit of the corporation, partnership, or other form of business entity."[31] Corporations are legally considered "persons" in courts of law. They could theoretically be guilty of any crime, including murder. Generally, however, the corporate hierarchy provides a shield of deniability for the top corporate officers. To prove that a crime has occurred, it is necessary to prove *"mens rea"* or intent on the part of corporate officers, and possibly the entire board of directors. In a court of law it is necessary to prove that company officials had advance knowledge and/or even ordered employees to engage in illegal behavior, distribute adulterated food or drugs, offer a bribe to another company or government official, and so forth. Because it is difficult to prove advance knowledge or involvement by corporate officers through the unanimous vote of a criminal trial jury, such cases are generally the subject of civil law procedures and sanctions in the form of fines. In civil court, only probable cause needs to be shown, and jury decisions need not be unanimous. The growing epidemic of corporate involvement in criminal activity is discussed next in various forms of corporate crime.

Corporate Tax Violations

Ironically, under the Internal Revenue Code, if a person willfully fails to file a tax return, he or she has committed a misdemeanor; however, if a person files a fraudulent tax return, he or she has committed a felony.[32] Failure to file a tax return is considered by the Internal Revenue Service (IRS) to be a form of "passive neglect," considered a misdemeanor. However, if upon filing a return a tax payer is found to have willfully underreported income and/or failed to report taxable income, then the crime becomes a felony.[33] Willfulness would be indicated by a "paper trail" such as two sets of books or attempts to hide assets as shown by a rapid increase in a taxpayer's net worth.

The IRS published a Web page in January 2003 pertaining to tax fraud in the restaurant industry. Violations most frequently committed included deliberately underreporting or omitting income, overstating the amount of deductions, keeping two sets of books, making false entries in books and records, claiming personal expenses as business expenses, claiming false deductions, failing to pay employment taxes, and hiding or transferring assets or income. For fiscal year 2003, some 82 businesses were investigated, out of which 62 were prosecuted and 42 were convicted. Incarceration resulted in 81% of the cases. An example of a corporate offender was the following:

> On March 12, 2002, Kengo I. Nozaki was sentenced in the District of Hawaii, to 2 1/2 years in prison. Nozaki filed false corporate tax returns for 1992 for Kapiolani Enterprises, Inc., doing business as Kengo's Royal Buffet, as well as filing false personal income tax returns for 1993 and 1994. Nozaki was originally indicted on August 12, 1999 on three counts of filing false returns for these years. According to the evidence produced at trial, Nozaki skimmed approximately $112,000 during 1992; $166,000 during 1993 and $68,000 during the first half of 1994 while he was the manager of Kengo's Royal Buffet, a restaurant located on Kapiolani Boulevard. These skimmed monies were not reported on Nozaki's personal tax returns or on the corporate tax return.[34]

Two observations can be made about the aforementioned account of IRS investigations for fiscal year 2003. First, the investigation of 82 businesses in the United States, a country that accommodates 4.3 million corporations, is not just miniscule—it is microscopic. Kengo's Royal Buffet is not among the Fortune 500 corporations in the United States. The reason that big businesses are rarely prosecuted is because the tax laws are replete with special advantages, loopholes, and benefits for big business. Major corporations have the power to obtain tax breaks and loopholes specific to their industry that make most corporate tax avoidance completely legal. Because of this, the tax burden carried by the major corporations declined from about 25% of all federal revenues in 1950 to about 7% in the 1990s.[35]

Antitrust Violations

Antitrust violations stem from the Sherman Act of 1890 and the Clayton Act of 1914. These acts outlawed restraint of trade, attempts to monopolize, and mergers and acquisitions that have the effect of lessening competition. Examples of antitrust violations include bid rigging and price fixing schemes that involve conspiracies.[36] The U.S. Department of Justice will prosecute instances of antitrust violation, relying upon complaints received from consumers or businessmen. It is possible for an individual consumer to "get justice" through providing "whistler blower" information to the Department of Justice (see text box "Detecting Signs" below). However, it is more likely that only corporate competitors will have the resources and time to devote to such an undertaking. An example of this is the ongoing antitrust litigation against Bill Gates, the former CEO of Microsoft, Inc. In 2004, Gates was fined $800,000 for acquisition of more than $50 million in voting stock in ICOS, a drug maker on whose board of directors Gates holds membership.[37]

Commercial Bribery

Commercial bribery of another's employee, officer, or fiduciary (including union officers) is considered to be an unfair trade practice that gives an advantage to one competitor over fellow competitors by secret and corrupt dealings with employees and/or agents of prospective purchasers.[38] By itself, such bribery is said to be a minor crime. For instance in the Pennsylvania Penal Code, it is treated as a "misdemeanor of the second degree."[39] It is difficult to prosecute such crimes because finding witnesses who are willing to "blow the whistle" is difficult. It is also difficult to link such crimes to corporate CEOs or managers, since they can deny any involvement in such crimes, even if they ordered employees to engage in such illicit activities. At the federal level, bribery charges are often combined with other more serious allegations such as mail fraud, racketeering, and income tax evasion. For instance, two insiders at Mercy Hospital and Allegheny Power in Pennsylvania were indicted in 2005 by a federal grand jury and charged with conspiracy, mail fraud, accepting kickbacks, and racketeering. The first, Jeffrey L. Davidson, was former head of maintenance and construction at Mercy, and the second, Brian Ramsey, was a

BOX 14–4

Detecting Signs of Antitrust Violations

Price Fixing

- Any evidence that two or more sellers of similar products have agreed to price their products in a certain way, to sell only a certain quantity of their product, or to sell only to certain customers in certain areas.
- More than one seller of very similar products sold under different brand names make equal and substantial price changes at the same time.
- A seller tells you "We can't sell this product to you. We have an agreement with (their competitor) that only they can sell to you."

Bid Rigging

- Far fewer bidders than normal submit bids on a project or sale upon which they would normally bid.
- Several bidders submit identical, to the penny, bids on the same project or sale.
- A company that has previously been awarded contracts for a certain service or in a particular area is always the low bidder on new projects for that service or area.
- A certain group of bidders seem to be awarded contracts on a regular or rotating basis.
- An unusual and unexplainable large dollar difference is evident between the winning bid and all other bids–the "low ball" bid.
- A certain bidder bids far higher on some projects than others for no apparent logical reason.[40]

former leader in the building services department at Allegheny Power in Greensberg, Pennsylvania. Davidson was charged with accepting kickbacks, including remodeling on his house, the use of a vacation home, and an $89,432 payment at the closing of escrow on a home in Murrysville in 1999. Ramsey was charged with accepting kickbacks that included home construction services; a $10,000 down payment on a sport utility vehicle; and paid vacations to the Caribbean, Aruba, and Orlando, Florida, in the 1990s. The federal prosecutors are relying on government witnesses that included owners of La Marca Corporation of Monroeville and a carpenter, all of whom have pled guilty to federal charges.[41]

Although the federal prosecutors were able to indict these "middle managers," bribery that is done by U.S. companies in foreign countries is often beyond the domain of U.S. prosecutors. Probably for that reason it is engaged in freely by U.S. corporations abroad. One study of 34 U.S. corporations involved in paying overseas bribery found that while the bribes totaled $93.7 million, the companies obtained total sales revenues of $679 billion.[42] How corrupt is the United States, compared with other countries of the world? A study by Transparency International, an organization that studies bribery in countries around the world through conducting surveys of business persons, shows that the United States is about 7.5 on a scale of 10 in terms of bribery (where a score of 10 indicates lowest corruption and a score of 1 indicates highest corruption).

Table 14–1 **Corruption Index 2004 from Transparency International (Lower Score = More Corruption)[43]**

Finland	9.7
Iceland	9.5
Switzerland	9.1
Netherlands	8.7
Germany	8.2
Ireland	7.5
United States	**7.5**
Japan	6.9
Portugal	6.3
Bahrain	5.8
Jordan	5.3
South Africa	4.6
Mauritius	4.1
Ghana	3.6
Syria	3.4
Turkey	3.2
Russia	2.8
Palestinian Authority	2.5
Pakistan	2.1
Turkmenistan	2.0
Nigeria	1.6
Bangladesh	1.5
Haiti	1.5

There is no way of knowing how much of this perception is related to business deals that are consummated in foreign countries. There is some evidence that much of the corruption concerns military contracts, both domestically, and abroad. During the 1970s, around the time of the Nixon Watergate scandal, numerous corporations, including Exxon, Gulf, Mobil, Northrop, United Brands and other corporate giants made under-the-table bribes to intermediaries for foreign leaders in Netherlands, Iran, France, Germany, Saudi Arabia, Brazil, Malaysia, and Taiwan.[44] The domestic issue of procurement fraud and inflating pricing has been a recurring issue with military contractors during the entire cold war era. In 2000, Senator Tom Harkin and U.S. Representative Peter DeFazio released a list of procurement fraud cases among the top 100 defense contractors from January 1995 to September 1999, a list compiled by the General Accounting Office (GAO), the investigative arm of Congress, at Harkin's and DeFazio's request. The GAO fraudulent contractor list of cases, charges, and outcomes included:

- Eight criminal cases in which companies pled guilty and paid fines totaling $66 million.
- 95 civil cases, including 94 settlements and one judgment, in which awards totaled $368 million.
- Multiple charges of procurement fraud, defective pricing, cost/labor mischarging, substitution/nonconforming product, undelivered product, contractor/subcontractor kickbacks, misuse/diversion of government furnished materials, and others.
- Involvement in these crimes included many of the largest U.S. company contractors, including Lockheed Martin, McDonnell Douglas (now part of Boeing), Raytheon, and General Dynamics.[45]

Sanctions were lenient. No jail time was served by any of the company officers and not one of the companies in the list was debarred from obtaining federal contracts because of the fraud.

Although bribery of public officials is sometimes classified as a political crime, it also seems logical to classify it as a white-collar crime because money changes hands, usually for the gain of a business or corporate interest, as described earlier. Bribery has been the basis for 42% of the criminal indictments directed toward Congressional office holders since 1940.[46]

A clear instance of bribery of congressional officials was demonstrated by an FBI sting operation known as ABSCAM. The FBI created a front named Abdul Enterprises, Ltd. and agents working on the case posing as representatives of Kambir Abdul Rahman, a fictitious Arab sheik who was seeking Washington favors. Eight officials, including one senator, and several representatives, were persuaded to sponsor special bills or use their influence in exchange for cash payments or other rewards. All were convicted of a variety of crimes, and the senator was given six years in jail and a $40,000 fine.[47]

Food and Drug Violations

One of the first major movements to oppose corporate hegemony in America was that of a group of journalists, novelists, and critics who, in the first decade of the 20th century, were termed the muckrakers. The word *muckrakers* derives from the term *muckrake* that was used by President Theodore Roosevelt

Theodore Roosevelt (1858–1919), shown here giving a campaign speech, was elected the Republican Vice-President in 1901, succeeding to the presidency after the assassination of William McKinley on September 14, 1901. Though nominally a Republican, Roosevelt pursued a progressive antitrust agenda to help the common man and became known as a "trust buster," bringing successful suits against 44 major corporations. While many businesses attacked Roosevelt as a socialist, he said he was trying to offer the common man a Square Deal that provided a balance between business and labor. His 1906 speech describing journalists as muckrakers indicated that his campaign against big business was coming to an end.

Source: CORBIS/Bettmann.

in a 1906 speech in which he compared this group of authors to a character from Bunyan's *Pilgrim's Progress* who could look no way but downward and was interested only in raking the filth with a muckrake in his hand.[48]

The muckrakers included authors and journalists such as Lincoln Steffens, Ida Tarbell, David Graham Phillips, Samuel Hopkins, and Upton Sinclair. Their articles attacked a variety of corporate trusts, including the beef trust, Amalgamated Copper, and the life insurance trust. Particularly relevant to food safety was Sinclair Lewis's novel *The Jungle* (1906), which was a brutally graphic exposé of the Chicago stockyards. Lewis described the area of the Chicago stockyards (aka Packingtown) as a place where immigrants were mercilessly exploited, women were forced into prostitution, and older men, unable to work, were left to starve. Food production described by Lewis included tubercular beef and the grinding up of poisoned rats. Workers who fell into vats emerged as Durham's Pure Leaf Lard. Within six months of the publication of *The Jungle,* the Pure Food and Drug Act (June 30, 1906) and a Meat Inspection Act were passed. The acts forbade foreign and interstate commerce in adulterated or falsely labeled food and drugs, with possible sanctions of product seizures, fines, and jail for offenders.[49]

It would seem that food adulteration laws have continued to be passed, unopposed by corporate interests or big business, including the relatively recent Food Quality Protection Act of 1996, which curtailed the use of many

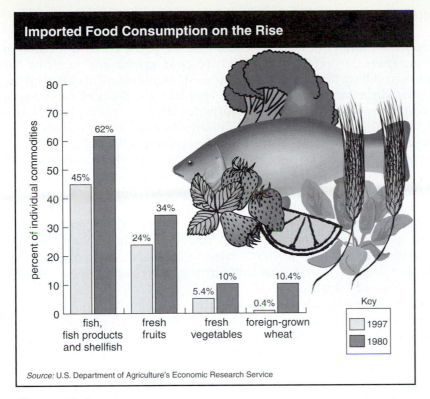

Imported Food Consumption on the Rise

(chart y-axis: percent of individual commodities)

- fish, fish products and shellfish: 45% (1997), 62% (1980)
- fresh fruits: 24% (1997), 34% (1980)
- fresh vegetables: 5.4% (1997), 10% (1980)
- foreign-grown wheat: 0.4% (1997), 10.4% (1980)

Key
- 1997
- 1980

Source: U.S. Department of Agriculture's Economic Research Service

Figure 14–1

Imported food consumption, 1980–1997

Source: http://www.fda.gov/fdac/features/2001/101_food.html

insecticides, fungicides, and rodenticides. Even corporate moguls have to eat from the common food supply. However, in an era of multinational corporations, the issue of food adulteration, seemingly, has morphed itself into a broader issue of food quality. There has been a sizable increase in food imports into the United States, as seen in Figure 14–1. Sixty-two percent of all fish and fish products eaten by Americans came from abroad in 1997, up from 45% in 1980.

Thirty-four percent of fresh fruit consumption in the United States was from foreign countries in 1997, compared with 24% in 1980. Likewise, foreign fresh vegetable consumption almost doubled in 1997 to 10% as compared with 5.4% in 1980. Lastly, foreign grown wheat grew to 10.4% in 1997, compared with 0.4% in 1980.[50] While the upside of this growing trend toward food imports is an availability of inexpensive food products, the downside is the possibility of a diminishing quality of imported foods. Food and Drug Administration (FDA) inspection is next to impossible for growers in remote foreign countries, so the use of chemicals and pesticides banned in the United States is entirely possible abroad. Some importers routinely wash salad leaves in chlorine, possibly to cover up the prior use of pesticides. Salads are then cut and bagged using vacuum cushioning that protects the leaves, a process that destroys nutritional levels.[51] In addition to destruction of food quality, there has been, over time, a tendency for consumers to purchase convenience foods from vending machines and fast food restaurants. These foods are the stock-in-trade of multinational corporations, whose profits advance, along with the growing trend in obesity.

White-Coat Crime

There are a number of forms of fraud that are involved with the health profession. These are referred to as **white-coat crime** and take the form of fraudulent billing for services not rendered, medications never administered, and procedures not performed. They also take the form of "overdoctoring," which means the performance of surgeries that were not needed, unnecessary hospitalization, and the prescription of drugs that are unnecessary. In some instances, the overdoctoring, or "defensive medicine," is a result of fears of lawsuits. This fear causes physicians to take every precaution to rule out the later discovery of an untreated disease, for which the physician could be held responsible. In other instances, unnecessary hospitalizations, surgeries, procedures, and prescriptions are the result of a physician's greed. Although a physician can rationalize that he or she is working in the patient's best interest (or to prevent lawsuit), it is nonetheless true that in the United States physicians are paid on a fee-for-service basis. It is always possible that some physicians may be overzealous in their recommendation of surgery, particularly if they need the money.

In an excellent analysis of fraud in the health profession, entitled *Death by Medicine,* authors Gary Null, Carolyn Dean, Martin Feldman, and Debora Rasio provide a thorough analysis of these forms of fraud. Null et al. also provide an analysis of some of the factors facilitating health care fraud, notably the corrupting influence of pharmaceutical companies, along with the companies that have developed new diagnostic tools and devices. They estimated the number of people in America having in-hospital adverse drug reactions to prescribed medicine at 2.2 million, the number of unnecessary antibiotics prescribed annually for viral infections at 20 million, the number of unnecessary medical and surgical procedures performed annually at 7.5 million, and the number of persons exposed to unnecessary hospitalization annually at 8.9 million. Their principle finding was that in 2001 *iatrogenic deaths* estimated at 783,936 were the leading cause of death in the United States, followed by heart disease (699,697 deaths) and cancer (553,251). **Iatrogenic deaths** are those induced in a patient by a physician's activity, manner, or therapy, a term used especially if there is an infection or other complication of treatment. Over a 10-year period (1992–2001), they estimated the number of iatrogenic deaths at 7.8 million, more than all the casualties from all of the wars that America has fought in its entire history. They also estimated that a total of 164 million people, approximately 56% of the U.S. population, have been treated unnecessarily by the medical industry.[52] Null et al. caution that even these high figures are probably underestimates because doctors are afraid they will be sued if they report an error. The errors are usually reported by the patient or the patient's surviving family.

Null et al. argue that medicine is not taking into consideration major factors that contribute to illness, which include stress; insufficient exercise; excessive caloric intake, especially of highly processed foods grown in denatured and chemically damaged soil; and exposure to tens of thousands of environmental toxins. Instead of seeking the minimization of these disease-causing factors, according to Null et al., the medical profession in America causes more illness through medical technology, diagnostic testing, overuse of medical and surgical procedures, and overuse of pharmaceutical drugs.

What causes this widespread overmedication is next analyzed by Null et al. They argue that they are fully aware that "what stands in the way of change are powerful pharmaceutical companies, medical technology companies, and special interest groups with enormous vested interests in the business of medicine. They fund medical research, support medical schools and hospitals, and advertise in medical journals."[53] There are various routes by which the pharmaceutical companies are able to buy their way in to profits. Field representatives of drug companies provide more than free samples of their drugs. They also spend over $2 billion a year for over 314,000 events that doctors attend. They also sponsor clinical trials of new drugs, and it was found that when a drug company funds a study, there is a 90% chance that the drug will be perceived as effective whereas a non-drug-company-funded study will show favorable results only 50% of the time.[54] One study found a tremendous increase in drug-industry-funded university research, which rose from $292 million in 1981 to $2.1 billion in 1991.[55]

The major problem with clinical trials (predominantly done with company funding) is that the drugs are typically tested on people who are fairly healthy and not taking medications that can interfere with the findings. However, once these drugs have been approved as safe during clinical trials, they enter a new phase of drug testing called Post-Approval. In this phase, the documentation of side effects takes place—after the drug has hit the market. A report cited from the U.S. General Accounting Office (GAO) "found that of the 198 drugs approved by the FDA between 1976 and 1985 . . . 102 (or 51.5%) had serious post-approval risks . . . including heart failure, myocardial infarction, anaphylaxis, respiratory depression and arrest, seizures, kidney and liver failure, severe blood disorders, birth defects and fetal toxicity, and blindness."[56] In a sense, upon completion of drug-company-sponsored clinical trials, "testing" is continued subsequently using the entire U.S. population (or those who see doctors) as experimental research subjects.

In addition to engineering the administration of potentially unsafe drugs to the entire population, pharmaceutical companies have, in recent years, been permitted to promote these drugs through television advertisements. People told to "ask your doctor" about a drug that helps with one or another problem often do, perhaps assuming that such ads must have been reviewed by the FDA. Doctors in private practice are then faced with a choice of acquiescing to their patients' demands or taking up valuable clinic time trying to talk patients out of unnecessary drugs. One might assume that the American Medical Association (AMA) would provide some ethical restraint. However, it appears this is not the case. In 1964, the Surgeon General published a report condemning smoking. The AMA refused to endorse the report, saying that more research was needed. Over the next nine years, the AMA received a payment of $18 million from a consortium of tobacco companies. Furthermore, the *Journal of the American Medical Association,* began accepting tobacco advertisements in 1933, and a state journal, the *New York State Journal of Medicine,* began to run Chesterfield Cigarette ads.[57]

While drug companies who manufacture unsafe drugs have been fined by the FDA (Shering-Plough Corp $500 million in 2002, Abbott Laboratories Inc. $100 million, and Wyeth Laboratories, Inc. $30 million in 2000), company executives have not been sent to jail, despite the lethality of drugs that may have been produced.[58]

Besides serving as a medium for potentially lethal drugs, physicians have contributed to death through unnecessary surgeries that grew from 2.4 million resulting in 11,900 deaths in 1974 to 7.5 million resulting in 37,136 deaths in 2001.[59] It has been estimated that 30% of controversial surgeries are unnecessary. Controversial surgeries include Cesarean section, tonsillectomy, appendectomy, hysterectomy, gastectomy (for obesity), and breast implants. The escalation of surgeries was even driven by television advertising, such as the "modeling" of gastric bypass for obesity by Hollywood personalties.[60]

Besides unnecessary surgeries, physicians contribute to morbidity and mortality through authorizing the use of untested technologies. In 1978 the U.S. Office of Technology Assessment (OTA) reported that "Only 10 percent to 20 percent of all procedures currently used in medical practice have been shown to be efficacious by controlled trial."[61] In 1995, the OTA compared medical technology in eight countries, noting that few medical procedures in the United States had been subjected to clinical trial.[62] The report laid the blame for the dissemination of technologies regardless of their clinical value squarely at the feet of the medical free enterprise system. "Health care technology and its assessment in eight countries" was the last report prepared by the OTA, which was shut down in 1995.[63]

Although the Null et al. report focused upon medical malpractice as a cause of death and disease in America, it also included a section on insurance fraud by doctors. "When doctors bill for services they do not render, advise unnecessary tests, or screen everyone for a rare condition, they are committing insurance fraud." The cost of insurance fraud was estimated by the GAO at $12 billion for 1998. In 2001, the federal government won or negotiated more than $1.7 billion in judgments, settlements, and administrative impositions in healthcare fraud cases and proceedings.[64] Another report published in 1998 estimated the total cost of health care fraud on the part of physicians and other health care professionals at up to $100 billion a year.[65] While physicians may commit fraud, particularly in billing government agencies, fraud is also committed by other "white-coat" professionals, including pharmacists and medical laboratories. In 1992, more than 1,000 Federal agents and 120 other law enforcement officers carried out early morning raids in over 50 cities nationwide as part of Operation Goldpill, resulting in the arrest of over 200 pharmacists and others who were charged with fake prescriptions; false Medicaid billings; unnecessary medical testing; excessive billing; and the illegal diversion, repackaging, and distribution of prescription medicine to street dealers and corrupt pharmacists.[66]

Check Kiting

Check kiting can be used by businesses or by individuals. The common practice of allowing depositors to have access to deposited funds facilitates this practice. In the typical scenario, a nonsufficient fund check written by the malefactor is written on an account from one financial institution and then deposited into an account at another institution. A check drawn on the second account is then used to cover the resulting overdraft on the first account. Cash advances are then obtained, taking advantage of the "float" caused by the normal delays in collection systems.[67] This scheme is used by professional criminals who typically use fictitious identification and run up each account in three or more banks to a large sum such as $50,000, making a substantial withdrawal at the end of a week. At this point, the criminal leaves town with the money to be used as "seed money" for another crime.

Check kiting can involve substantial losses to financial institutions. "A small credit union in northern Illinois took a $4 million kite loss and had to close its doors. Within the last five to seven years we've seen kites in excess of $10 million to $20 million."[68] Kiting can also be a tool used by businesses. In fact, a good share of kiting is done by individuals that have businesses that don't have enough income or revenue to pay debts until they receive payments owed to them.

Securities Fraud

Laws to prevent securities fraud were largely passed after the stock market crash on October 26, 1929. At the federal level, these laws included the Securities Act of 1933 and the Securities Exchange Act of 1934. These acts sought to prohibit manipulation and deceptive practices by companies and brokers. The 1934 act established the Securities and Exchange Commission (SEC). The SEC can initiate civil suits and administrative actions. It can also refer criminal cases to the U.S. Department of Justice.[69] The stock market crash that lasted from January 15, 2000 to October 9, 2002 is said to have been the 10th worst stock market crash in U.S. history.[70] This recent crash, said to have been initiated by the combination of the tech bubble bursting and the September 11 terrorist attack, may have also raised some concerns about fraudulent practices utilized by such corporations as Adelphia Communications, AOL Time Warner, Arthur Anderson, Brystol-Myers Squibb, CMS Energy, Duke Energy, Dynegy, El Paso, Enron, Global Crossing, Halliburton, Homestore.com, Kmart, Merck, Mirant, Nicor Energy, LLC, Peregrine Systems, Qwest Communications International, Reliant Energy, Tyco, WorldCom.Inc, and Xerox.[71] Some of these, such as Aldelphia, AOL Time Warner, Homestore.com, Qwest, and WorldCom.Inc might qualify as "dot com" corporations, whereas most of the others are energy companies. Most of these corporations, in some form or another, inflated assets, cash flow, revenue, or energy-trading activity resulting from "round-trip" or "wash" trades. The latter trades are defined as "prearranged buy-sell trades of energy with the same counter-party, at the same price and volume, and over the same term, resulting in neither profit nor loss to either transacting party."[72]

Probably the most outrageous of the corporate scandals listed here was that of Enron Corporation, which reportedly "boosted profits and hid debts totaling over $1 billion by improperly using off-the-books partnerships; manipulated the Texas power markets to win contracts abroad; and manipulated California energy markets."[73] Enron was said to be responsible for the California energy crisis of 2000–2001 through "megawatt laundering," which refers to selling California's electricity across state boundaries and then reselling it back to California at higher prices.[74] After reaping significant income from sale of its stock and energy at high prices, Enron declared bankruptcy on December 2, 2001.

In the aftermath of the bankruptcy, "Enron officials have acknowledged that the company has overstated its profits by more than $580 million since 1997."[75] One might ask, what happened to the money that Enron had obtained through misleading stockholders and engaging in gouge pricing? The answer is that much of the money went to top Enron executives who cashed out more than $1 billion in stock near its peak. In addition, 600 employees deemed critical to its operations received more than $100 million in bonuses in November prior to the December bankruptcy. As for its 20,000 "noncritical employees," who were barred from selling Enron shares from their retirement accounts when the stock

On Tuesday, March 19, 2002, two workers take away Enron's "crooked E" sign after it was removed from the outside of the ballpark for the Houston Astro baseball team, formerly known as Enron Field. The Enron collapse was said to be the largest corporate failure in U.S. financial history. Enron declared bankruptcy in December 2001 after, it is alleged, Enron executives "cooked the books" to show exaggerated profits and, consequently, company stock prices were driven upward. On the eve of the bankruptcy, Enron Chief Executive Officer Kenneth Lay sold off his own stock in Enron. Kenneth Lay was reported dead as a result of a heart attack on July 5, 2006, although conspiracy theorists have contended that his death was faked.

Source: David J. Phillip, AP Wide World Photos.

price plunged, they lost not only their jobs but their life savings.[76] In addition, because Enron was at one time the seventh largest corporation in the world, thousands of stockholders also lost their investment in its entirety.

Immigration Fraud

"Six months to the day after Mohamed Atta and Marwan Al-Shehhi flew planes into the World Trade Center, the Immigration and Naturalization Service notified a Venice, Florida, flight school the two men had been approved for student visas."[77] Although this obvious and embarrassing bureaucratic blunder was done by the INS, that agency was not actually responsible for the presence in the United States of the 19 individuals who perpetrated the terrorist attacks of September 11, 2001. According to an investigation by the 9/11 Commission, all 19 were traveling on tourist visas that had apparently been issued by the State Department in foreign countries (although visas for six of the terrorists appeared to be "doctored" or "manipulated in a fraudulent manner").[78] The 9/11 Commission found that there were several points of vulnerability that had to do with immigration controls. The Commission found that the September 11 hijackers:

- Included known al-Qaeda operatives who could have been watchlisted.
- Presented passports manipulated in a fraudulent manner.
- Made detectable false statements on visa applications.
- Made false statements to border officials to gain entry into the United States.
- Violated immigration laws while in the United States.[79]

Regardless of how the terrorists got into the United States, the whole issue of immigration fraud came to light as a result of the September 11 terrorist attacks. In 2002, Congress authorized the GAO to conduct a study of immigration fraud. Its report was entitled, *Immigration Benefit Fraud: Focused Approach is Needed to Address Problems.* In the study, the GAO found that the INS does not know the extent of the immigration benefit fraud problem. However, they found that INS officials indicate that the problem is pervasive, significant, and increasing.[80] The term *benefit application fraud* refers to schemes such as marriage fraud and occupational preference fraud. In *marriage fraud,* an ineligible alien makes a false claim to marriage to a U.S. citizen, and an *occupational preference fraud* involves businesses in the United States that falsely claim aliens are needed for employment because of their education, technical knowledge, or experience and that such people are not available in the U.S. workforce. The benefit application fraud category also includes nonimmigrant visa fraud in which the alien stated intent to stay temporarily in the United States on business, as a student, or for temporary or seasonal work. The alien then continues the stay permanently. Another even more vexing benefit fraud relates to asylum applications, because applicants can satisfy their burden of proof through credible testimony alone. Benefit application fraud is distinguished from document fraud that involves the counterfeiting, sale, or use of documents, such as birth certificates, passports, or visas, to circumvent U.S. immigration laws. The GAO report found that the INS faced an enormous work load of about four million applications in fiscal year 2000. The INS has only four operations units that perform analysis for fraud detection, with a total of about 40 positions. In addition, benefit fraud is a comparatively low priority within the INS. A major problem that persists is that ineligible aliens who are denied benefits at one Service Center can apply for and receive benefits at another service center before the information system is updated. Also, different offices often do not share information because they have information systems that are not compatible with one another.

The GAO cited several instances of benefits fraud. In 1998 and 1999, some 45% of claims made on 3,247 petitions suspected of applicant fraud in Chennai, India were found to be of questionable validity, and 21% of the work experience claims made to the INS were confirmed to be fraudulent. An INS California Service Center found visa fraud in about 90% of L-1A visa petitions filed by foreign companies that send executive or managerial personnel to a U.S. subsidiary. Fraud unit officials in the Los Angeles District Office stated that immigrant benefit fraud is rampant across the country. A Miami fraud unit stated that fraud is out of control. A Nebraska Service Center official told GAO investigators that 20% to 30% of all applications filed are fraudulent. In one case, an immigration consulting business filed 22,000 applications for aliens to qualify for visas under the extended legalization program (for residents who had resided in the United States unlawfully since January 1, 1982). Nearly 5,500 of the aliens' claims were fraudulent and 54 individuals perpetrating the fraud were successfully prosecuted.

The GAO report, though inconclusive, suggests that a large volume of individuals are immigrating to the United States (four million applications), some if not many by illegal means. The report indicated that INS officials believe that the problem is pervasive and serious, and that some aliens are using the benefit application process to enable them "to carry out illegal activities, such as crimes of violence, narcotics trafficking, and terrorism."[81]

In the final analysis, a large number of immigrants, either undocumented or those who are seeking visas, come to the United States seeking employment. They seek employment, not only as hotel and restaurant employees, domestic service workers, and as agricultural workers, but also as employees of large corporations, who are interested in hiring workers who will work for low wages and few, if any, benefits.

The employment of legal or undocumented migrants by U.S. corporations is not a matter of public record. However, a new policy enables the INS to raid companies and deport their undocumented employees, a policy bolstered when Congress passed the 1996 Illegal Immigration Reform and Immigrant

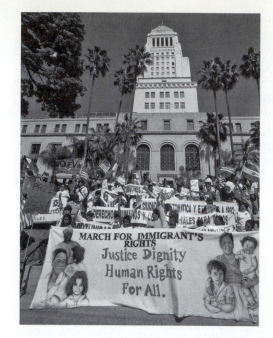

A mostly Hispanic crowd with signs and flags demonstrate in favor of legal and illegal immigrant rights in Los Angeles, California. On Saturday, March 25, 2006, an estimated 500,000 persons marched in Los Angeles, and others demonstrated in cities around the nation to protest legislation passed by the House of Representatives (HR 4437). HR 4437 would strengthen border security and make it a felony to aid undocumented workers. The sheer number of persons who have appeared at these rallies attests to the widespread nature of the white-collar crime—immigration fraud—committed by the employers of undocumented workers and others who have assisted illegal immigration.

Source: A. Ramey/PhotoEdit, Inc.

Responsibility Act. As a result, companies as far north as Chicago, Illinois have been the successful subjects of raids—including Preferred Meal Systems, a company that processes school lunch foods, Arc Tronics Inc., an electronics assembly plant in Elk Grove Village, Illinois; Chicago Textile and Fashion, Inc.; and VICOM, a pie-making production facility.[82] Of those raided, the INS did not levy a fine in half of the cases closed between 1989 and 1997. The 71 sanctioned companies paid a modest total of $324,902 in penalties.

It seems that the "corporate friendly" environment that provides corporate immunity from prosecution may contribute to the illegal immigration problem. There is no question that America's borders are quite porous, not only in terms of people crossing the border, but also to automobiles and goods. A good number of these automobiles are stolen and goods are often smuggled contraband (both in and out of the United States), as discussed in previous chapters. In a single year, 475 million people cross America's borders, as do 125 million vehicles. More than 20 million shipments arrive at 3,700 terminals located in 301 ports of entry. In recent years, more than 1.7 million undocumented immigrants have walked or ridden across the Mexican and Canadian borders.[83]

As we have seen in countries like Sweden, Hungary, and Germany, an unfortunate byproduct of the perception that immigrants are usurping "benefits" that are denied citizens of a country is the emergence of xenophobic vigilante activities that can turn violent. The vigilantes (in other countries) that have been discussed in this text often serve as proxies for the police when the police are perceived to be ineffective. In some cases in other countries, the vigilantes work along with the police. The recent concern about the flow of immigrants into this country, a concern enhanced by the fear that the immigrants might be connected to terrorist organizations, has led to the development of such activity in Arizona in the form of a group of some 500 citizens, the "Minutemen" of Arizona, who have anointed themselves civilian border patrol agents, determined to stop the immigration flow that evades federal authorities. The organization, which calls itself the Minuteman Civil Defense Corps, has its own web page and considers its area of operations the

American border territory immediately adjacent to the U.S. border fence with Mexico within Cochise County, Arizona. The Minutemen claim they have recorded 4,609 peaceful, nonviolent assists with USBP and Customs agents of people illegally crossing the U.S. border with Mexico since November 2002.[84]

The immigration problem may be related to the drug problem and the development of multinational gangs in cities like Los Angeles. The immigration problem may also lead to a job availability issue for millions of Americans who are displaced in their employment by immigrants at all levels of employment, from harvesting crops to high-tech careers. However, the events of September 11 highlight the potential for unchecked illegal immigration to bring forward "sleeper cells" of terrorists who can launch well-coordinated surprise attacks from within the United States at any time. Thus, a "paper crime" problem (of immigration fraud) can very quickly become a political crime problem of international terrorism.

The aforementioned analysis has only sampled the crimes that are committed incidental to corporate business operations. It may be necessary for large businesses to periodically engage in criminal activity in the course of doing business. However, in an environment in which such criminal activities are perceived to be routine in business, some smaller scale operators may go one step further. They may conclude that it may be more cost effective simply to pretend to conduct a legitimate business, knowing very well that a scam or confidence activity is really what is being done. The aura of respectability and, in some cases, the protection of incorporation provides an incentive to the production of criminal business enterprises. Some of these have been described in the literature, as follows.

White-Collar Crime as a Business, or as the Central Activity

Advance Fee Swindles

The email in the text box is typical of numerous email offerings (received by almost everybody with an email address) that could lead to an **advance fee swindle**.

BOX 14–5

Advance Fee Swindle

To: (email address)
Subject: GOOD DAY
FROM: DR. Abu Abu
AUDITOR GENERAL (Central Bank Of Nigeria)

Dear Sir/Madam,

Good day to you. I am Dr. Abu Abu the Auditor General of the Central Bank of Nigeria. I have the privilege of contacting you based on the deal which I feel you would be interested in. There is a particular sum of money ($50.8M) which has been floating in the suspension account of the apex bank and the funds has [sic] remained unclaimed over a decade.

I have the intention of investing in any lucrative business through you in your country and I would appreciate if both of us could seal this deal and I would use my share to invest through you in any investment or any other viable business venture that would be determined by you. If you are interested, kindly get across to me so as to enable [sic] furnish you with the modalities on how the funds could be wire [sic] to your nominated bank account. Be rest assured [sic] that this deal is risk free because I am an insider.

Best Regards
Dr. Abu Abu

There are different names for the scam suggested by the letter in the text box, sometimes called "Advance Fee Fraud"; "419 Fraud," after the relevant section of the Criminal Code of Nigeria; "The Nigerian Connection"; or just "419," used by the Nigerians themselves. This scam has been estimated to be yielding $1.75 billion from the wallets of people nationwide,[85] and over $5 billion since the world wide scam began in the early 1980s (along with the development of the personal computer).[86] According to the United States Secret Service, the 419 schemes frequently use the following tactics:

- An individual or company receives a letter or fax from an alleged "official" representing a foreign government or agency.
- An offer is made to transfer millions of dollars in "over-invoiced contract" funds into your personal bank account.
- You are encouraged to travel overseas to complete the transaction.
- You are requested to provide blank company letterhead forms, banking account information, telephone/fax numbers.
- You receive numerous documents with official looking stamps, seals, and logos testifying to the authenticity of the proposal.
- Eventually you must provide upfront or advance fees for various taxes, attorney fees, transaction fees, or bribes.
- Other forms of 419 schemes include: cash on delivery of goods or services, real estate ventures, purchases of crude oil at reduced prices, beneficiary of a will, recipient of an award, and paper currency conversion.[87]

In the earlier "Dr. Abu Abu" letter, no advance fee was required; however, the information required to "wire" funds from the Nigerian bank would, no doubt, be personal account information (account number, password, or other personal information) on the recipient's bank account. Given such information, the fraud perpetrator could and would most likely remove funds from the victim's bank account, rather than deposit funds.

Most people who read the description of the Nigerian Advance Fee Scam may be thinking to themselves, "I would never fall for such an obvious ripoff." However, it is important to remember that the scam is broad-based in its appeal and it is constantly changing in its approach. According to the U.S. Secret Service Website, there are seven major categories that form the basis of this enticement:

- Disbursement of money from wills
- Contract fraud
- Purchase of real estate
- Conversion of hard currency
- Transfer of funds from over-invoiced contracts
- Sale of crude oil at below market prices

As in many scams, one major enticement made by the advance fee scam is a big return on investment. Particularly vulnerable to such an offer would be people who are computer literate, who are used to online banking, and, in fact, participate in online trading. For many Americans, moving money with the "click of a mouse" has become an everyday event. Furthermore, vulnerable targets of this scam may have become accustomed to 20% yearly returns in the mid-1990s, so the thought of a big return from a foreign investment seems credible. Even people who have steered clear of the stock market may be vulnerable, because they feel cheated after rolling over certificates of deposit that once yielded 8% into ones gaining 2% or less.[88]

The intended victim may receive an unsolicited letter by mail from a Nigerian claiming to be a senior civil servant. It may be remembered that Nigeria was highlighted in Chapter 11 on OC as being a home base country for many OC groups who traffic in heroin, other illicit commodities, as well as in persons. It may be further recalled that such participation in OC is traced to a history of military rule in Nigeria. The Nigerian advance fee scam may play upon that same theme. The sender may declare that he is a senior civil servant in one of the Nigerian Ministries, usually the Nigerian National Petroleum Corporation. The letter may refer to investigations of previous contracts awarded by prior regimes alleging that many contracts were over-invoiced. Rather than return the money to the government, the sender says he wants to transfer the money to a foreign account. Sums ranging from $10 million to $60 million will be transferred and the recipient is usually offered a commission of up to 30% for assisting in the transfer.

Victims who remain skeptical are almost always asked to travel to Nigeria or to a border country to complete the transaction. They are told that a visa will not be necessary to enter the country, and the con artist then bribes airport officials to allow the victim to pass through Immigration and Customs. However, it is a serious offense in Nigeria for a foreigner to enter without a valid visa. Thus, the victim's illegal entry will likely be used by the con artists as leverage to coerce the victims into releasing funds. Furthermore, violence and personal threats of physical harm may be employed to further pressure victims. In June of 1995, an American was murdered in Lagos, Nigeria, while pursuing a 419 scam, and numerous other foreign nationals have been reported as missing. Those involved in perpetrating advance fee scams also appear to be involved in other criminal activity including credit card fraud, false identity fraud, forgery, and immigration fraud involving counterfeit passports and visas. The criminals involved may also have connections with OC groups such as international drug traffickers.[89]

Bankruptcy Fraud

Bankruptcy refers to the declaration of insolvency on the part of a debtor. As a result of bankruptcy proceedings, a debtor's property is usually liquidated and divided among his creditors to pay his debts. Bankruptcy, per se, is a legal proceeding; however, it can become fraudulent (**bankruptcy fraud)** when a debtor falsely claims bankruptcy through concealing his or her company's assets.[90] The interesting question to ponder is, how can a person (or company) profit from bankruptcy? The bankruptcy law was intended to help a person or business make a "fresh start," as well as to fairly allocate assets to creditors. However, fraudsters[91] have found ways to turn the bankruptcy proceeding into a means to obtain illegal profits through two major tactics, termed "bustouts" and "bleedouts." In a *bustout*, a company is set up or purchased with the intention of declaring itself bankrupt, after purchasing merchandise on credit and disposing of it immediately (sometimes below cost) for cash or credit (quickly converted to cash). Instead of paying the creditors for the merchandise, the business is declared bankrupt. The cash is transferred to the accounts of relatives or accomplices who are shown on the books as creditors, leaving little or nothing left to divide among the real creditors. The cash can then be used to purchase other businesses. *Bleedouts* are similar to bustouts, except that they involve the depletion of assets by insiders over a relatively long period of time.[92]

A recent big business example of bankruptcy fraud is exemplified by the case of WorldCom, Inc. In 2004, WorldCom, Inc., a telecommunications company, filed for bankruptcy after investors lost nearly $200 billion as a result of that company's overstatement of billions of dollars in income. The company agreed to pay a $750 million fine to settle its civil fraud suit (fraud is both a tort and a crime) with the Securities and Exchange Commission (SEC). The bankruptcy settlement was said to have erased much of its $41 billion in debt. WorldCom, Inc. planned to change its name officially to MCI (a long distance carrier that WorldCom, Inc. had purchased previously), which is expected to emerge from the bankruptcy with about $5.5 billion in debt, and "one of the strongest balance sheets in the telecommunications industry."[93]

When bankruptcy frauds result in the termination of a business, severe consequences occur, not only for the creditors and stockholders in the company, but also for the employees. Brown et al. provided a list of "red flags" that can be used to tell if a company bustout or bleedout is pending:

Bernard J. Ebbers, a former WorldCom chairman, and Scott Sullivan, former Chief Financial Officer of WorldCom, are sworn in before Congress during hearings in 2002 (where they invoked the Fifth Amendment and refused to testify). Ebbers was convicted in 2005 and given a 25-year sentence for his role in a massive account fraud that led to the collapse of WorldCom, which, combined with the collapse of Enron, sounded a death knell for the 1990s stock market boom. Ebbers' defense team blamed fired CFO Scott Sullivan for the massive fraud at the company. However, Sullivan served as the prosecution's star witness against Ebbers, telling the court that Ebbers had pressured him into falsifying earnings and expense numbers.

Source: Shawn Thew/AFP Photo. Agence France Press/Getty Images, Inc.

- Well-established company with good credit recently taken over by a new group trying to hide the change in ownership
- Warehouse full of high-volume, low-cost items
- Disproportionate liabilities to assets
- Mainly temporary employees
- Leased equipment
- Cash paid up front to rent location
- Same individuals involved in previous "failed companies"
- Unusual banking activities (e.g., "check kiting")

The trend in federal legislation is to prevent abuses of the bankruptcy laws. For instance, the Bankruptcy Reform Act of 1994 included provisions to expedite bankruptcy proceedings and to encourage individual debtors to use Chapter 13 to reschedule their debts rather than Chapter 7 to liquidate.[94]

Ponzi Schemes

Ponzi schemes work on the "rob-Peter-to-pay-Paul" principle, using money from new investors to pay off earlier investors, until the whole scheme collapses.[95] The originator of this scheme was Carlo "Charles" Ponzi, who was born in Parma, Italy in 1882 and emigrated to the United States in 1903. As a young man, Ponzi worked at odd jobs, but had acquired a criminal record and served time both in Canada in 1908 for forgery and in the United States in 1910 for immigration fraud. In 1917, Ponzi moved to Boston, where he was employed typing and answering foreign mail. In August of 1919, Ponzi received a letter from a gentleman in Spain that included an international postal reply coupon, which Ponzi surmised had been purchased in Spain for about one cent in American funds. Yet, when the coupon was cashed, Ponzi was able to exchange it for six American one-cent stamps. Ponzi imagined that he could have agents working in Spain purchase the coupons, which would then be sent to him. He projected that he could redeem the coupons for six times their purchase price. Subsequently, in 1919, Ponzi filed an application with the city clerk in Boston establishing his business as "The Security Exchange Company." He offered investors the opportunity to double their money in 90 days. Though early investors were paid off (to make the scheme look legitimate), an investigation later found that Ponzi had purchased only $30 worth of the international mail coupons. Ponzi was deluged with funds from investors, with an estimated income of $1 million per week at the height of his scheme. However, on August 10, 1920, Ponzi was declared bankrupt by the auditors, banks, and newpapers, and on August 13, 1920, Ponzi was arrested by federal authorities, released on $25,000 bond, and was then rearrested by Massachusetts authorities and rereleased on an additional $25,000 bond. He served three and a half years in federal prison for using the mails to defraud and was then sentenced to an additional seven to nine years by Massachusetts's authorities. He jumped bail, but then resurfaced in Florida where, using the assumed name of Charles Borelli, he was indicted for fraud involving a pyramid land scheme. He jumped bail again, but eventually was caught and sent back to Boston to complete his jail term. After seven years, he was released and deported to Italy in 1934.[96] The term *pyramid scheme* describes Ponzi's second career (selling swamp land in

Florida). A pyramid scheme is very similar to the classic Ponzi scheme, as explained on a SEC Website:

> In the classic "pyramid" scheme, participants attempt to make money solely by recruiting new participants into the program. The hallmark of these schemes is the promise of sky-high returns in a short period of time for doing nothing other than handing over your money and getting others to do the same. The fraudsters behind a pyramid scheme may go to great lengths to make the program look like a legitimate multi-level marketing program. But despite their claims to have legitimate products or services to sell, these fraudsters simply use money coming in from new recruits to pay off early stage investors. But eventually the pyramid will collapse. At some point the schemes get too big, the promoter cannot raise enough money from new investors to pay earlier investors, and many people lose their money.[97]

Purchasing Banks with Deliberate Intention to Loot Them

The savings and loan (S&L) crisis of the 1980s and early 1990s resulted in the failure of 1,043 thrifts, with total net assets of over $500 billion. (The term *thrifts* refers to an organization "that primarily accepts savings account deposits and invests most of the proceeds in mortgages."[98]) The resources of the Federal Savings and Loan Insurance Corporation (FSLIC) were overwhelmed, so U.S. taxpayers were required to pay approximately $124 billion and the thrift industry to pay another $29 billion to back up commitment to insured depositors.[99] Some analysts attribute this loss to the deregulation of thrifts that took place in the early 1980s.[100] However, a U.S. House committee found that over 75% of all S&L insolvencies were linked to serious misconduct by senior insiders or outsiders.[101] (The misconduct of "outsiders" here refers individuals doing business with the banks, such as persons who received fraudulent loans based upon a friendship with a bank officer.)

Less than 20% of these bank failures were caused solely by economic factors, according to a 1988 finding of the comptroller of the currency.[102]

Many of the bank failures that occurred during the 1980s took the form of "bankruptcy fraud," as described earlier. A bank failure that could serve as a forerunner for many of the S&L failures of the 1980s occurred in San Diego, California, in the early 1970s. Banks were less tightly regulated then than were the S&Ls, and illegal activity occurred at United States National Bank (USNB), which was controlled by C. Arnholt Smith. Smith had built a conglomerate that controlled many of San Diego's prime businesses, including a taxicab firm, a tuna cannery, a luxury hotel, a shopping center, a shipbuilding yard, and the USNB. Smith had clout in San Diego, and he also was well connected with the Nixon White House through campaign contributions and a personal friendship with Nixon.[103] When Nixon began his downfall with the Watergate scandal, Smith received the attention of federal regulators who revealed that Smith had systematically looted his bank of $170 million by making bad loans to companies controlled by himself and his friends, many of them connected to the Mafia.[104] Smith's USNB, with nearly a billion dollars in deposits, collapsed in October 1973, which, at that time, was the biggest bank failure in United States history.[105]

Several books and articles were written relating the S&L "bustouts" to OC and to CIA covert operations. These publications included conflict sociologist Gary W. Potter's 1991 article entitled, "The single greatest case of fraud in the history of crime," in the *Seattle Times*.[106] The book *Inside Job*, by Pizzo, Fricker & Muolo, revealed the relationship between the S&L crisis and, not only CIA operations, but also junk bonds promoted by so-called distinguished brokerages, as well as mobsters and politicians.[107] Another more recent book by William K. Black, entitled, *The Best Way to Rob a Bank is to Own One*, provided an insider's account of the looting of the S&Ls and described Charles Keating's junk bond scam. It provided a new term, *control fraud*, to describe the looting of a company for personal profit.[108] Keating was appointed to the Johnson Commission on Pornography by President Nixon, and had founded an antipornography organization in Cincinnati, Ohio. Keating, however, had no reservations against participating in fraud. In 1993, Keating was convicted in a state court of fraud, racketeering, and conspiracy for having duped Lincoln Savings and Loan's customers into buying worthless junk bonds of American Continental Corporation, a real estate firm that Keating ran in Phoenix, Arizona. Lincoln Savings went bankrupt in 1989.[109]

Occupational Crimes

The term *occupational crimes* refers to Edelhertz's category "B" white-collar crimes, which he defined as "crimes in the course of their occupations by those operating inside business, government, or other establishments, in violation of their duty of loyalty and fidelity to employer or client."[110] This definition is close to Sutherland's original definition of white-collar crime, except for his stipulation that it included only persons of respectability and high social status. Today criminologists generally recognize that occupational crime can include both white- and blue-collar workers. Omitting reference to social status, Gary S. Green published a book entitled *Occupational Crime*.[111] Green defined *occupational crime* as "any act punishable by law that is committed through opportunity created in the course of an occupation which is legal."[112] Green's definition seems to be an improvement upon Sutherland's because it includes criminal actions of people working at all status levels. However, the definition, otherwise, is as ambiguous as Sutherland's definition. The definition could include serious Index crimes ranging from theft to murder. A disgruntled employee who murders fellow workers or a supervisor or workers who pilfer goods would be included in this definition. It may be remembered that Edelhertz included in his definition of white-collar crime the stipulation that they be committed by "nonphysical means" and by "concealment or guile." It would seem that Edelhertz's refinement is necessary in distinguishing white-collar from common-law crimes. Thus, it is possible to develop an explanation of white-collar crime that is different from explanations of other types of crime. If fact, in discussing "theory" regarding white-collar crime, we found that Cressey did develop a unique "psychological isolation" explanation for embezzlement that actually contradicted the "differential association theory" of his co-author and mentor Edwin Sutherland.

Thus, in this section on occupational crime we discuss three general occupation-linked crimes. These include embezzlement, securities fraud, and computer fraud. All three of these crimes are "paper crimes" or today's functional equivalent, "cybercrimes," which may lack a paper trail.

Embezzlement

The term *embezzlement* may be defined as "the unlawful appropriation and or conversion of money or other assets placed in one's care to his or her gain."[113] Embezzlement is a "gray area" crime that can include employee theft. The difference between embezzlement and larceny is that in embezzlement the perpetrator comes into possession of the property legally, but fraudulently assumes rights to it.[114] In England, where common law developed, a special situation occurred when property was misappropriated by unfaithful servants, employees, agents, trustees, or guardians. They could be charged only in civil courts for a tort, rather than in criminal courts for larceny, which was a crime. To remedy this situation statutes were passed in England and the United States that made embezzlement a distinct crime, or expanded the definition of larceny to include cases of misappropriation of property.

Albert the embezzler, the case study at the beginning of this chapter, engaged in fraud when he authorized the transfer of money to "shell corporations" that he had created for himself near upstate New York. However, persons who are arrested for embezzlement are not necessarily high-level executives with a company, as Albert was. As stated in an online Chamber of Commerce newsletter:

> Embezzlement is as random as the people who take the money. Organizations large and small, corporate and family-owned, profit and non-profit have all been "hit" by embezzlement. The term "embezzlement" is being used here in the strict sense of referring to someone who has absconded with money and has tried to cover it up, or has taken it over a course of time.[115]

Criminologists tend to focus their attention upon high-profile embezzlement schemes by top-level managers. In fact, some recent theorizing about embezzlement has been devoted to the **collective embezzlement** by top management in the savings and insurance industries, defined as "the siphoning of company funds for personal use by top management at the expense of the institution itself and with the implicit or explicit sanction of its management."[116] Factors in these large-scale instances of embezzlement are the 1980s deregulation of the S&Ls combined with protective insurance and guaranty funds, a "casino" economy where profits are made from speculative investment (not production), extensive networks among insiders and affiliated outsiders, and a government response of containing the financial crisis rather than punishing wrongdoers.[117]

The concept of collective embezzlement was suggested by Calavita, Tillman, and Pontell[118] as the antithesis of Cressey's psychologically isolated embezzler, discussed earlier in this chapter. Yet, Cressey's characterization of embezzlers, drawing upon his method of analytic induction, was based upon interviews with convicted embezzlers. Thus, Cressey may have been in contact with the "average" embezzler, or at least the average person convicted of embezzling. Who are the average embezzlers today? Although no recent study has been done of incarcerated embezzlers comparable to Cressey's, the chances are that persons who have been caught and imprisoned today for embezzlement are, in reality, employee thieves. At the federal level, the theft of mail by an officer or employee of the United States Postal Service is defined as "embezzlement" by Section 1709 of Title 18, United States Code.[119] In the restaurant business, they are the bartenders, waiters, and waitresses who tear order tickets, underring sales, and pocket the difference.[120] In the retail trade, employee theft (that would be prosecuted as embezzlement) is estimated to be the source of 48.5% of inventory shrinkage, as compared with 31.7% for shoplifters (who would be prosecuted for larceny).[121] The embezzlement arrest trend for the years 1995 to 2004 was essentially stable, with a 1995 rate of 5.9 per 100,000 inhabitants, compared with 6.0 per 100,000 inhabitants in 2004.[122] However, during that same time period, the rate of arrests for larceny-theft declined from a rate of 592.7 per 100,000 inhabitants in 1995 to a rate of 412.0 in 2004.[123] It should be noted that the rate of those arrested for larceny-theft was 80 to 100 times that of those arrested for embezzlement. Business employees have an obvious advantage with their knowledge of store security procedures, which shoplifters may not have, making it much more difficult to catch store personnel for theft of property or money.

An interesting study using FBI and census data to do correlation analysis for the crime of embezzlement was published in 2002.[124] The study found that two variables, percentage of divorced males and percentage of females in poverty, were the only significant predictors of embezzlement.[125] These findings are consistent with the theme developed in the last few paragraphs that the average embezzlers are low-level employees of retail trade businesses.

Securities Fraud

Previously, the topic of "securities fraud" was discussed as a form of corporate crime. However, on another level there are a bewildering number of schemes and scams to which customers can be exposed when trying to invest in stocks, bonds, and commodities. Securities fraud scams are the other side of the coin of corporate fraud. They consist of individual transactions that are essentially fraudulent carried out on a daily basis.

Fraud isn't just a practice that is confined to the world of work. It begins in school. In school, various forms of cheating have increased among students over time. In a study by McCabe and Trevino, it was pointed out that cheating in the form of copying from another student during an exam has doubled from 26% in 1961 to 52% in 1991.[126] Another study of 6,000 students attending 31 different universities found that business students reported cheating more than other majors.[127] If college cheating has increased, and it appears to have doubled in 30 years, one might wonder why this trend has occurred. In that period of time, cheating has increased from about one fourth of students to a majority.

Donald M. McCabe, founder of the Center for Academic Integrity at Duke University and co-author of the cheating study cited earlier, says that a reason for the widespread cheating is that professors are becoming "more intimidated by students and worry about offending them and making them unhappy. . . . Faculty are also worried that if they challenge a student, it is they—not the student—who will wind up being put on trial."[128]

Simply listing all of the schemes, scams, and frauds that take place in the world of work today is a challenging task. A Website entitled "Crimes of Persuasion" has been developed to provide such a list. Drawing from the "Crimes

Telemarketers making cold calls in boiler rooms often target senior citizens. The Federal Trade Commission has developed a Senior Sentinel project to help combat an estimated $40 billion in telemarketing fraud losses, much of which is suffered by the elderly. In a typical scam, the telemarketer makes an unsolicited call to a senior citizen, usually over 70 years of age, and tells the consumer that he or she has been selected to receive a valuable prize or award, such as a new car or a large sum of money; however, to receive the prize he or she has to purchase products, such as perfume, calendars, caps, or other merchandise. The scam victim typically pays an inflated price for the products, and the prizes, if received, have little or no value.
Source: Jeff Greenberg/PhotoEdit, Inc.

of Persuasion" Website, we briefly cover some of the schemes, scams, and frauds that pertain to securities.

According to the Website, **investment fraud** includes, "blind pools, commodities, futures, options, films, foreign currency, gemstones, FCC licenses, high-tech, promissory notes, prime bank, real estate, T-bills, bonds, CD's, and viatical settlements."[129] Ownership of securities has grown from one American in 18 in 1980 to one in three by 1999. During the 1990s, mutual funds were showing annual returns of 30% to 40%, and the bull market on Wall Street encouraged investors to take great risks to get big returns. This risk-taking orientation led many investors to be susceptible to the pitches of con-artists.[130]

Blind pools are securities that are sold to the public without indicating to the investors what the specific use of the proceeds will be. One major purpose for a blind pool is to raise funds to acquire a private firm so that the firm can go public without the regulatory scrutiny of state and federal agencies. Acquisition of the private firm can result in increased stock prices for the blind pool investors, and the initial promoters sell their shares at the increased value, leaving the new investors to fend for themselves. When conducted in this manner, blind pools are essentially a variation of the bankruptcy fraud scheme discussed previously.[131]

Quite a few of the investment frauds listed earlier function like blind pools, attracting investors based upon the good reputation of the manager of the investment firm. For instance, a foreign exchange investment fraud was run by J. David Dominelli in San Diego, California during the 1970s. Dominelli had acquired a good reputation for his skill trading in foreign currencies while he worked at Bache Investments in San Diego. Dominelli started his own investment firm, named J. David & Company. The company, required a $50,000 minimum from each investor, carried on a classic Ponzi scheme and defrauded investors (who lost about $80 million) until the company was forced into bankruptcy in February 1984.[132] On June 26, 1985, Dominelli was sentenced to 20 years in prison for four felony counts of fraud and tax evasion.[133]

Computer crime

Computer crime is a broad category that includes a wide and growing variety of crimes involving computers. Computer crime may be defined as "any violation of a federal or state computer crime statute."[134] Computer crime is divided into five general categories:

1. Theft of services
2. Illegal use of computer data for personal gain
3. Improper use of computers for numerous types of financial processes
4. Use of a computer to damage another's assets (e.g., planting a damaging virus to destroy data)
5. The theft of software via unlawful copying[135]

Computer crime might be seen as a potentially "perfect" white-collar crime. As more people become computer literate, more and more white-collar crimes will be done with computers. We are making the assumption that the essence of white-collar crime is "tricking victims out of their money, or its equivalent in property, services, rights and anything else that can be converted to money." In other words, we are saying that white-collar crime is in essence *fraud,* which may be defined as "The knowing and unlawful deception of another with intent to cause him or her to unwittingly surrender property, rights, emoluments, or pecuniary interest."[136] Given that the essence of white-collar crime is fraud, another question needs to be answered in characterizing computer crime as the ultimate white-collar crime. The question is "What is money?" This might seem to be a peculiar question, because most people assume that the term *money* means physical currency—dollars in the United States. Schmalleger makes an important point about money in his textbook, *Criminology Today:*

> Although most people probably think of money as dollar bills, money today is really only information—information stored in a computer network, possibly located within the physical confines of a bank, but more likely existing as bits and bytes of data on service providers' machines. Typical financial customers give little thought to the fact that very little "real" money is held by their bank, brokerage house, mutual fund, or commodities dealer. Nor do they consider the threats to their financial well-being by activities like electronic theft or the sabotage of existing accounts. Unfortunately, however, the threat is very real. Computer criminals equipped with

enough information, or able to ferret out the data they need, can quickly and easily send vast amounts of money anywhere in the world.[137]

Consider the email in Figure 14–2, similar to one that has been sent to numerous email recipients. The actual name of the bank was deleted and the letters XXX were substituted. The email was identified as "spam" by an antivirus program.

Figure 14–2
Example of "Phishing" scam

From: "XXX Savings"<abuse@xxxsavings.com>
Subject: New Message From Online Banking

XXX Savings Institution

XXX Savings Institution - **Unauthorized charge to your credit card**

We recently reviewed your account, and we suspect an unauthorized ATM based transaction on your account. Therefore as a preventive measure we have temporary limited your access to sensitive XXX Savings Institution features. To ensure that your account is not compromised please login to your XXX Savings Institution Online Banking, verify your identify and your online accounts will be reactivated by our system.

SERVICE: XXX Savings Institution Online Banking and Bill Pay services.

What you need to do:

- Go to: https://www.xxxsavings.com/
- Enter your user ID and Password (that you selected during the online enrollment process).
- Enter the requested information and your Online Banking and Bill Pay services will be reactivated.

Note: XXX Savings Institution & Loan customers are not held liable for any fraudulent charges to their accounts .

****
IMPORTANT CUSTOMER SUPPORT INFORMATION
****

We are committed to delivering you a quality service that is reliable and highly secure. This email is one of many components designed to ensure your information is safeguarded at all times.

Please do not reply to this message. For any inquiries, contact Customer Service.

The email raises fear by indicating that an unauthorized ATM-based transaction on the recipient's account had occurred. Then it directs its intended victim to "login," entering the user ID and Password. Once the user has logged in, additional information will be requested. Once that information is given, (supposedly) the online banking and bill paying services will be reactivated.

A certain percentage of individuals contacted by this fraudulent email may have accounts at the XXX Savings. On a Website published by the actual bank, this email is described as a phishing scam. The term *phishing* is defined as "The act of sending an e-mail to a user falsely claiming to be an established legitimate enterprise in an attempt to scam the user into surrendering private information that will be used for identity theft." The e-mail directs users to visit a Website where they are asked to update personal information, such as passwords and credit card, social security, and bank account numbers, that the legitimate organization already has. The fraudulent email was sent from a Website that looked legitimate. However, the information entered on this Website can be stored and used to raid the victim's account through funds transfer.[138]

While phishing scams are a threat to persons who engage in online banking, credit card purchases over the Internet can result in *credit card fraud,* which is defined as "the illegal appropriation of another's credit card, credit card number, or identity."[139] This can happen when online customers do business with Websites that are not secure. Secure Websites have firewall, antivirus, and antispam security features and can be identified by https:// instead of http:// as the protocol prefix in their addresses. Websites that are not secure are subject to invasion by *hackers* (persons who use computers for exploration and exploitation)[140] who can obtain credit card and other information on the customers of those Websites. Once the fraudster has obtained a name and credit card number, he or she can make purchases by phone, over the Internet, and even by regular mail. The purchases can be small, in which case they may not be recognized when the victim receives his or her monthly statement from the credit card company. However, large purchases can also be made by an identity thief using a credit card, as was illustrated by the case study of James, the identity thief, at the beginning of this chapter.

Even when credit card purchases are made with secure Websites, one's credit card number can still be acquired by cybercriminals as a result of spyware. *Spyware* is defined as:

> Any software that covertly gathers user information through the user's Internet connection without his or her knowledge, usually for advertising purposes. Spyware applications are typically bundled as a hidden component of freeware or shareware programs that can be downloaded from the Internet. . . . Once installed, the spyware monitors user activity on the Internet and transmits that information to the computer criminals. Spyware can also gather information about e-mail addresses and even passwords and credit card numbers.[141]

Spyware can determine an online shopper's credit card number and then transmit the number to a credit card fraudster. One such spyware application is called Credit Card Number Finder, a program that can pass along your credit card number to a hacker who has accessed your computer.[142] Spyware, more often than not, is accessed as a result of browsing pornography and gambling sites, according to an article in *Network World:*

Today most spyware infiltrations follow a different course: Users browsing the Web unknowingly launch "drive-by" downloads as they peruse sites affiliated with spyware makers. What those spyware-dumping sites often have in common is pornographic content. "We've gotten to a point where, statistically, virtually all of the spyware that you get is being planted onto a system by browsing the Web," says David Perry, global education director for security vendor Trend Micro. "The most available Web sites to undertake this kind of thing are those Web sites that are willing to do anything to make a buck off of you. And those have a tendency to be pornography and gambling sites."

When users browse such sites, they wind up silently installing adware, keystroke loggers, Trojans and other nefarious programs. A person browsing pornographic Web sites from an unprotected machine could pick up 50 or 60 pieces of spyware in just 30 minutes, according to Perry. Habitual porn surfers can find their PCs quickly disabled from all the programs running in the background. The problem is so widespread among consumers that one computer repair consultant says the first thing he looks for when a customer complains of poor PC performance is pornography. "Almost universally, it's what the problem is," says the consultant, who asked not to be identified. "A computer I just did had 36 instances of viruses and 700 pieces of malware installed. And gee, they wondered why their computer wouldn't work. Absolutely it's porn-related."[143]

Besides the aforementioned phishing and spyware scams that affect all computer users, there are numerous other types of computer crimes. David Carter, a professor in the School of Criminal Justice at Michigan State University, itemized these types in a 2001 FBI Law Enforcement Bulletin:

1. **Computer as the Target:** Crimes in which the computer is the target include such offenses as theft of intellectual property, theft of marketing information (e.g., customer lists, pricing data, or marketing plans), or blackmail based on information gained from computerized files (e.g., medical information, personal history, or sexual preference). These crimes also could entail sabotage of intellectual property, marketing, pricing, or personnel data or sabotage of operating systems and programs with the intent to impede a business or create chaos in a business' operations. Unlawful access to criminal justice and other government records is another crime that targets the computer directly. This crime covers changing a criminal history; modifying want and warrant information; creating a driver's license, passport, or another document for identification purposes; changing tax records; or gaining access to intelligence files.

2. **Computer as the Instrumentality of the Crime:** In common law, instrumentality refers to the diversion of a lawfully possessed item, that is, an instrument, to facilitate committing a crime. In this category, the processes of the computer, not the contents of computer files, facilitate the crime. Essentially, the criminal introduces a new code (programming instructions) to manipulate the computer's analytical processes, thereby facilitating the crime. Another method involves converting legitimate computer processes for illegitimate purposes. Crimes in this category include fraudulent use of ATM cards and accounts; theft of money from accrual, conversion, or transfer accounts; credit card fraud; fraud from computer transactions (stock transfers, sales, or billings); and telecommunications fraud.

3. **Computer is Incidental to Other Crimes:** In this category of computer crime, the computer is not essential for the crime to occur, but it is related to the criminal act. This means that the crime could occur without the technology; however, computerization helps the crime to occur faster, permits processing of greater amounts of information, and makes the crime more difficult to identify and trace. Such crimes include money laundering and unlawful banking transactions, bulletin board services[144] supporting unlawful activity, organized crime records or books, and bookmaking. In one case, a suspect committed murder by changing a patient's medication information and dosage in a hospital computer.

4. **Crimes Associated with the Prevalence of Computers:** The simple presence of computers, and notably the widespread growth of microcomputers, generates new versions of fairly traditional crimes. In these cases, technological growth essentially creates new crime targets. Software piracy/counterfeiting, copyright violation of computer programs, counterfeit equipment, black market computer equipment and programs, and theft of technological equipment fall into this category of computer crime.[145]

The number of ways that computers have been involved with crime, as described earlier, is simply astounding. In the United States, thought to be the hub of computer innovation since the advent of Bill Gates's Microsoft empire, legislation lists are reaching epic proportions, at both the state and federal level. The reader may be referred to two Websites on legislation for further information—the first for federal computer intrusion laws[146] and the second for computer-crime-enacted legislation at the state level.[147] The legislation and court decisions referenced on these lists recommend sanctions ranging from community service to 20 years in prison for various computer offenses from computer hacking to stalking, harassment, and possession of child pornography. However, in addition to the "too little, too late" aspect of much of this legislation, a primary consideration is not addressed by judges or legislators—computer criminals have and probably will continue to have the ability to play the game of "catch me if you can." The Internet has been likened to the Wild West in which outlaws could carry out crimes and then return to their hideouts in the badlands beyond the reach of law enforcement (i.e., "nobody knew their address"). Every computer that accesses the Internet also has an address or Uniform Resource Locator (URL); however, the programs and data from each computer can be sent to other computers all over the world through the medium of Internet Service Providers (ISP) whose computers provide the service of facilitating the traffic of programs and data by virtue of their permanent connection to the World Wide Web. The ISPs may deny culpability, saying that they were unaware that criminal content was being transmitted by their customers or stored on their computers; however, just as with other forms of smuggling, laws are needed that target the traffickers themselves—the Internet Service Providers or ISPs—in a similar way as laws target smugglers of drugs, persons, guns, and other illicit items.

However, it isn't sufficient to target only ISPs within the United States. This is because America is not the only country with computer capability. David Carter, cited earlier, states:

> Americans must be concerned about the growth of computer-related crime capabilities emerging outside U.S. borders because of the ease of information exchange and the high concentration of computer-driven businesses and

research projects in the United States. However, it appears that the area of most rapid growth will be in Europe as a result of the treaties signed to create the European Community. Among the important elements of the act that established the basis for unification are open communications, a single, European-wide communication protocol, a strong profit-oriented market spanning 12 countries, open borders, unification of technology standards, and easier banking, including monetary transfers between countries. . . . While businesses can make great use of these unifying measures, so can criminals. Emerging international crime-related issues most probably will accompany the unification of Europe. These issues include industrial espionage (competitive intelligence), economic/political espionage, expansion of international organized crime beyond traditional areas, and theft of technological hardware.[148]

Crimes by Persons Operating on an Individual, Ad Hoc Basis— Identity Theft

Most of the crimes grouped under Edelhertz's Category A crimes (crimes by persons operating on an individual, ad hoc basis) are related to the term commonly used today—**identity theft.** We touched upon the topic of identity theft in the last section on computer crime. Identity theft differs from some of the scams described earlier, including credit card fraud, in that the offender assumes the victim's commercial identity and conducts business or even crime in the name of the person whose identity is stolen. The criminal acquires the victim's full name, address, birth date, SSN, and bank account numbers.[149] In addition to phishing scams, such as the one described earlier, according to the U.S. Federal Trade Commission report, *ID Theft: What's It All About,* identity thieves use a variety of methods to gain access to your personal information.[150] For example, they may:

- Get information from businesses or other institutions by stealing it while they're on the job.
- Bribe an employee who has access to these records, hack these records, and con information out of employees.
- Steal your wallet or purse.
- Steal your personal information through email or the phone by saying they're from a legitimate company and claiming that you have a problem with your account. This practice is known as "phishing" online, or "pretexting" by phone.
- Steal your credit or debit card numbers by capturing the information in a data storage device in a practice known as "skimming." They may swipe your card for an actual purchase, or attach a device to an ATM machine where they may enter or swipe your card.
- Get your credit reports by abusing the authorized access that was granted to their employer, or by posing as a landlord, employer, or someone else who may have a legal right to your report.
- Rummage through your trash, the trash of businesses, or public trash dumps in a practice known as "dumpster diving."
- Steal personal information they find in your home.
- Steal your mail, including bank and credit card statements, credit card offers, new checks, and tax information.
- Complete a "change-of-address form" to divert your mail to another location.

Once identity thieves have your personal information, they may use it to commit fraud or theft. For example, they may:

- Call your credit card issuer to change the billing address on your account. The imposter then runs up charges on your account. Because the bills are being sent to a different address, it may be some time before you realize there's a problem.

- Open new credit card accounts in your name. When they use the credit cards and don't pay the bills, the delinquent accounts are reported on your credit report.

- Establish phone or wireless service in your name.

- Open a bank account in your name and write bad checks on the account.

- Counterfeit checks or credit or debit cards, or authorize electronic transfers in your name and drain your bank account.

- File for bankruptcy under your name to avoid paying debts they've incurred under your name, or to avoid eviction.

- Buy a car by taking out an auto loan in your name.

- Get identification such as a driver's license issued with their picture, in your name.

- Get a job or file fraudulent tax returns in your name.

- Give your name to the police during an arrest. If they don't show up for the court date, a warrant for arrest is issued in your name.

It has been difficult to estimate the extent of identity theft since, as of 1998, no U.S. federal agency has overall *primary jurisdiction* for investigating all forms of this fraud.[151] The U.S. Postal Inspection Service (USPIS) has primary jurisdiction in all matters infringing on the integrity of the U.S. mail. The USPIS is the law enforcement arm of the U.S. Postal Service. If identity theft resulted from the theft of mail, the crime is reported to the local postal inspector.[152] Under the federal *Identity Theft and Assumption Deterrence Act (1998),* the Federal Trade Commission (FTC) is responsible for receiving and processing complaints from people who believe they may be victims of identity theft. The FTC provides informational materials and refers complaints to appropriate entities. In addition to the local post office, complaints may be referred to the FBI, the U.S. Secret Service, the Social Security Administration, or the IRS.[153] The Secret Service reported that arrests in these cases considered to be directly associated with identity fraud totaled 8,806, 8,686, and 9,455, respectively, for fiscal years 1995, 1996, and 1997. Another report by the GAO found more damaging data reported by other agencies. Consumer reporting agencies regard the number of seven-year fraud alerts placed on consumer credit files to be the most reliable indicator of identity theft. These alerts increased from 65,600 in 1999 to 89,000 in 2000 for one agency. Allegations involving social security number misuse increased from 11,000 in 1998 to 65,000 in 2001. FBI arrests for identity-theft-related crime have increased from 579 in 1998 to 691 in 1999. The USPIS has noted a 67% increase in identity theft from 1999 to 2000.[154] One article suggested that a major reason for the "dot-com burst" (the failure of business that depended upon merchandise orders over the Internet in the late 1990s and early 2000s) was the concern on the part of potential Internet customers that information they transmitted by the Internet could result in credit card fraud, vendor privacy breaches, and personal identity theft.[155]

On a daily basis, people are offered the opportunity to view their credit report online. According to a government Website, criminals are obtaining passwords to download credit files (which give all identification information). For instance, the Ford Motor Credit Corporation in Grand Rapids, Michigan had its branch's password and code used for approximately 10 months to download approximately 15,000 credit reports from Experian. Similar instances occurred with other credit card companies, permitting identity theft on a wide-scale basis.[156]

When this identity information is used fraudulently, the burden of proof is on the victims to produce evidence that the transactions were done by someone other than themselves.

Local police departments usually will not take the time to investigate a white-collar crime. So the victim is often alone and must crusade to restore his or her credit rating. There are Websites that help walk the victims through the processes of redeeming their credit; however, the process sometimes takes hundreds of hours, and expensive travel and correspondence. What has been attempted elsewhere (e.g., in the United Kingdom), are efforts to tighten up the process of issuing documents commonly used as evidence of identity. In addition, an "entitlement card scheme," which results from the submission of rigorous evidence of one's identity, is being tried there.[157]

Improved identity cards are a sensitive issue, and opponents consider them an invasion of privacy or a prelude to a "Brave New World" with the government monitoring citizen's personal information. With the U.S. rate of imprisonment at the highest level in the country's history and also highest for all countries of the world, the threat of such schemes increases. Prisons are schools for crimes where inmates often share their secrets, searching for the "perfect crime." Assuming the identity of some "fat cat" whom the inmate resents and whom the inmate might perceive was instrumental in his or her being put in prison for an offense that they consider trivial, might be considered sweet revenge. As more and more inmates are being locked up for "street crimes," their orientation may very well change to the more leniently punished "white-collar crimes" that they know can be pursued with relative ease. Thus, rigorous efforts to produce more adequate identification for the citizens of the United States seem to be an imperative need.

COUNTRY PROFILE: THE UNITED ARAB EMIRATES

A theme developed throughout this chapter is that white-collar crime consists of a myriad of criminal enterprises. It has also been suggested that much, if not most, white-collar crime involves **fraud**, a term defined by the United Nations as "the acquisition of another person's property by deception."[158] The crime of *fraud*, therefore, might make a good index for the more general offense of "white-collar crime." The United States does not report a figure for fraud to INTERPOL for "cases known to the police," although the United States does report arrest data to INTERPOL. However, the United States did report a rate figure for total recorded frauds to the United Nations for 1999, a rate of 133.74 per 100,000 inhabitants. Despite uncertainty as to what that rate figure indicates, we used that rate estimate for the United States in the CCDB. For other countries, we used the most recent data available for the crime of fraud to construct a fraud database. The rates of fraud for the United States and all countries rated above the United States in fraud are shown in Table 14–2.

Table 14-2 **Countries Ranked from High to Low**
          in Rate of Fraud per 100,000 Inhabitants

Country	Rate of Fraud
Bermuda	1339.54
Germany	1124.33
United Arab Emirates	1073.72
New Zealand	744.62
Great Britain	613.09
France	593.01
Cayman Islands	534.29
Sweden	474.03
Poland	436.47
South Korea	402.66
Hungary	355.22
Austria	348.88
Finland	344.42
Gibraltar	313.33
Luxembourg	295.91
Canada	284.19
Norway	268.71
Slovenia	249.34
Liechtenstein	212.12
Cyprus	182.10
Iceland	180.92
Andorra	169.70
Estonia	168.58
Israel	158.89
Lebanon	152.58
Monaco	146.67
Switzerland	141.06
South Africa	136.49
Denmark	133.76
Mauritius	129.08
Fiji	117.65
United States	113.52

The table shows Bermuda to have the highest rate of fraud, followed by Germany, and then the United Arab Emirates (UAE). As previously discussed, the data for the United States are suspect in this table because our country only reports data for arrests, not for all offenses reported. However, some countries stand out as having extraordinarily high rates of fraud. Because both Bermuda and Germany have been profiled previously, we focus here on the UAE. The UAE was mentioned briefly in relation to the Bank of Credit and Commerce International (BCCI) banking scandal. That country has also been in the news lately in terms of attempts on the part of a UAE-based business, Dubai Ports World, to acquire managerial control of six U.S. ports. Issues raised by critics of the port deal have been the UAE's connections and support for terrorist organizations, drug trafficking, and money laundering.[159] All of these concerns seem to make the UAE an appropriate country to profile in this chapter on white-collar crime.

To find clues about why the UAE is so high in fraud, correlation analysis is needed, and is shown in Table 14–3, in which fraud is internationally correlated with various independent variables.

Fraud correlates with these variables in very much the same way as the stealthy theft crimes discussed in Chapter 10. In fact, the strongest correlation of the seven major crimes is between the rate of larceny and the rate of fraud. The UAE is a wealthy country, with a very high per capita income of $29,100. In Table 14–3, fraud is strongly correlated with GDP per capita. Per capita income in the UAE is close to the per capita income in the United Kingdom, which is $30,900. Like the stealthy theft crimes, fraud is negatively related to percentage living in poverty and percentage unemployed. In other words, this means that countries that have high rates of affluence and employment also have high rates of fraud. Fraud is more likely to occur if there are rich and employed people around to cheat out of their money. These are all clues as to the underlying factors related to the high rate of fraud in the UAE. However, a full country profile is needed to see how all of the variables work together.

In the UAE, there is a dual system of Shari'a law courts and civil law courts. As discussed previously, under Shari'a law, theft-related crimes can be punished by amputation.[160] Crimes involving theft are infrequent in the UAE compared with other countries of the world. The rate of robbery in 2000 was .55 per 100,000 inhabitants, burglary 5.61, theft of motor vehicles 28.62, and other thefts 319.73. Normally in a country with abundant wealth such as the UAE, theft-related crimes would be prevalent; however, the potential of severe punishment probably serves to suppress these crimes. People may be tempted by the abundance of merchandise in shopping malls in a country

Table 14–3 **Fraud as Correlated with Various International Indices**

Gini Index	−.34
GDP	.09
GDP per capita	.55
Percentage living in poverty	−.38
Percentage unemployed	−.26
Lack of freedom	−.33
Percentage Islamic	−.15
Murder rate	−.10
Rape rate	.07
Robbery rate	.09
Aggravated assault rate	.04
Burglary rate	.43
Larceny rate	.50
Auto theft rate	.34
Index rate	.52

where wealth is flaunted in shopping venues such as Dubai's Gold Souq jewelry store, which offers jewelry from all over the world. (Dubai is a major port city, but the name Dubai also refers to the second largest of the UAE's emirates. An emirate is a small state ruled by a hereditary chief called an "emir."[161]) "Dubai promotes shopping opportunities through the Dubai Shopping Festival and various other shopping events run throughout the year."[162] It also offers a plethora of luxury hotels, discos, pubs, night clubs, and sporting activities. The covert method of money and property acquisition—fraud— would seem to be a cautious means of illicitly acquiring money and goods. Just as in the United States, frauds sometimes are classified as crimes and sometimes as torts to be tried in civil court. However, perhaps even more often, they are not defined by the authorities as frauds at all. Moreover, the perpetrator of the fraud may be difficult if not impossible to find.

Part of the reason for the widespread fraud in the UAE is that it is a relatively new country, achieving independence from Britain in 1971. After the discovery of petroleum in the 1950s, the country went through a period of rapid social change, becoming a modern, wealthy, developed country.

The territory that is now known as the United Arab Emirates was once known as a "haven for pirates." Originally the area was populated by a seafaring people who converted to Islam in the 7th century.[163] They formed tribally organized sheikhdoms along the southern coast of the Persian Gulf and the northwestern coast of the Gulf of Oman.[164] In the 9th century, a dissident and heretical sect (the Karmathians) established an independent communist community that controlled the area, and its army conquered Mecca.[165] When the Karmathian sheikhdom disintegrated, around 1000 A.D., its people became pirates. The area became known as the *Pirate Coast,* as raiders based there harassed foreign shipping from the 17th century to the 19th century. After the decline of the Karmathian sheikhdom, the Qawasim tribes in the area of the present-day UAE adopted the ideas of the Wahhabi Islamic movement. The Wahhabis opposed all that was not orthodox in Islam. It particularly opposed non-Muslim elements such as the increasing European presence in the Persian Gulf. Qawasim piracy resulted in an increased British presence in the Gulf area.[166]

In 1819, British expeditions formed to protect the India trade from the pirate raiders along the coast. The British had previously asked the sultan in Oman (to whom the pirates owed allegiance) to control the pirates. After it became evident the sultan was unable to do so, the British attacked Qawasim strongholds in the present-day area of the UAE. The British had no desire to take over the desolate Gulf territory. Their objective was simply to protect shipping to and from their possessions in India. Pirate raids continued until 1853, when the sheikhs signed a treaty with the United Kingdom, under which the sheikhs agreed to a "perpetual maritime truce" and formed the "Trucial Sheikhdoms." Parties to the truce were tribal leaders who had not been involved with piracy and who promised to suppress all piracy. In return, the Trucial Sheikhdoms would receive the protection of the British military.

When the British-Trucial Sheikhdoms treaty expired in 1971, the sheikdoms became fully independent. The UAE is actually a federation of the seven emirates (Abu Dhabi, Ajman, Dubai, Fujayrah, Ra's al Khaymah, Sharjah, and Umm al Qaywayn) established after independence in 1971.[167] None of the emirates has any democratically elected institutions or political parties. Each emirate is run by a single royal family and associated tribe and clans.

The emirs' rule is based upon a consensus established by tribal counsels and advisory bodies whose members are drawn from outside the royal family.[168]

The city of Abu Dhabi is the federal capital of the UAE, and the city of Dubai is the largest city in the country. Both city names, Dubai and Abu Dhabi, are also the names of emirates. About 85% of the country's oil is located in the emirate of Abu Dhabi, and the UAE has proven oil reserves that make up nearly one-tenth of the world's total.[169] Abu Dhabi is the largest and richest emirate, representing 82% of the total land area of the UAE.[170]

Before independence, in 1966, Sheikh Zayed Bin-Sultan Al Nuhayyan (Zayed) took over as ruler of Abu Dhabi. After independence, Zayed became Head of State of the entire UAE.[171] Zayed also became the prime sponsor of the Pakistani banker Agha Hasan Abedi, when Abedi opened his Bank of Credit and Commerce International (BCCI) in Abu Dhabi in 1972. In Abu Dhabi, the BCCI provided a place for Pakistani immigrant workers to cash their checks. Although the initial capital for the bank consisted of $2.5 million from the Bank of America and about $20 million from Zayed, huge revenues accumulated in the bank during the Arab Oil Embargo by the Organization of Petroleum Exporting Countries, of which the UAE was a member. The BCCI participated in funding drug traffickers, terrorist organizations, and gun runners until its collapse in 1991. At that point, the Zayed owned 77.4% of the bank's shares. In 1993, Abu Dhabi sued BCCI's executives for damages, and in 1994, 11 of the 12 former BCCI executives were accused of fraud and convicted in Abu Dhabi, given prison sentences, and ordered to pay compensation. In 1996, two of the BCCI executives were cleared of fraud charges on appeal. Abedi had resigned as the President of BCCI in 1990 and his health began to deteriorate. He escaped prosecution and retired to Pakistan, where he died in 1995.[172]

The BCCI scandal, in the form of money laundering, fraudulent loans, and embezzlement left a "trail of fraud" that continued in the UAE into the last decade of the 20th century. Abedi approached Sheikh Zayed in 1972, one year after the UAE's independence in 1971, when the country was guided primarily by its new Constitution and by Shari'a law. In a comparatively short period since its establishment, the UAE made important strides in regulating its economy. Laws passed in the 1980s included the Labor Law of 1980, the Agency Law of 1981, the Maritime Law of 1981, the Commercial Companies Law of 1984, the Insurance Law of 1984, the Civil Transactions Law of 1985, and the Penal Code Law of 1987. Laws promulgated in 1992 (one year after the demise of BCCI) included the Law of Criminal Procedures; the Law of Evidence; the Trade Marks Law; the Law for the Protection of Intellectual Property and Author's Rights; and the Regulation and Protection of Industrial Property of Patents, Drawings, and Industrial Designs.[173]

In 2001, on the occasion of the birth anniversary of the Prophet Mohammed, President Zayed pardoned approximately 6,000 prisoners (of which 2,000 were women), approximately 55% of the 11,000 inmates in UAE jails. The decree included prisoners convicted of embezzlement, drug-related offenses, brawling, drinking, fighting, engaging in premarital sex, swindling, and violation of immigration laws. The pardon did not include prisoners convicted of murder, rape, and kidnapping. In 2004, UAE President Sheikh Zayed died and was succeeded by his eldest son, Sheikh Khalifa.

Because of the wealth resulting from oil production, the UAE became a three-class society consisting of royals at the top, citizens of the UAE in the middle, and foreign workers (who constitute 80% of the inhabitants of that country) at the bottom. According to the CIA's *World Factbook* for 2006:

> The UAE is a drug transshipment point for traffickers given its proximity to Southwest Asian drug producing countries; the UAE's position as a major financial center makes it vulnerable to money laundering; anti-money-laundering controls improving, but informal banking remains unregulated.[174]

Drug trafficking and other crimes are said to be confined mainly to the expatriate community.[175] According to the U.S. State Department's human rights report, cited on the Comparative Criminology Website for the UAE, the country is also a transit point for precursor chemicals intended for the illicit drug manufacture elsewhere, primarily in Afghanistan. The law in the UAE does not prohibit trafficking in persons, although child smuggling, prostitution, and pornography are crimes. The report indicated that trafficking in women for the purposes of sexual exploitation is a problem in the UAE. Prostitution is illegal; however, it has become an increasingly open phenomenon in recent years, particularly in Dubai. The traffic in children is also a problem. "Camel jockeys," many of whom were lured to Abu Dhabi under false pretences, are typically under the Abu Dhabi legal age of 15. However, the laws, regarding either child smuggling or the age of camel jockeys, are not enforced. Rather, the Government defers control of camel racing to the Camel Racing Association, chaired by (prior to his death) by Sheikh Zayed.

Foreign workers, who constitute 98% of the work force, are paid the equivalent of three to five U.S. dollars per day, and in cases of workers from India and Bangladesh, newspaper reports have documented cases of laborers claiming their employers had not paid them for long periods of time.

Not too long ago, the UAE had a reputation for being a safe harbor for pirates of another kind than those who founded the country—"infringers and their pirated products." "In the past year (2005), raids were successfully carried out and led to a number of people being arrested, large numbers of personal computers and pirated software being confiscated and pirated goods destroyed, and fines imposed on individuals and companies."[176] Part of the reason for the "safe harbor" in UAE was that the country lacked laws that prohibited the theft of intellectual property. "In 1992, the first copyright, patents, and trade marks laws were introduced. In 1996, the UAE became a member of the World Trade Organization and a signatory to the TRIPs Agreement.[177]

In Dubai, the "Jebel Ali Free Trade Zone" is an established, successful free trade zone. The emirate now has ambitious plans to establish the Dubai Internet City—the world's first free trade zone for E-commerce.[178] E-commerce can and does include e-fraud. Nigerian advance fee scams discussed earlier in this chapter don't come just from Nigeria. Some come from the UAE, as seen in the text box.

The data and qualitative analysis presented earlier is not intended as an indictment of the UAE for the crime of fraud. If anything, the authorities in that country should be credited for their *truthfulness* in reporting the statistics on fraud to INTERPOL. From all reports available, it would appear that the UAE is striving to develop laws and sanctions to cope with the social problems that rapid modernization brings with it.

BOX 14–6

Advance Fee Fraud—Yousif Abdullah Fahad, UAE (2006)[179]

From: Yousif Abdullah Fahad yafahad@netscape.net
Date: Jan 24, 2006 9:24 PM
Subject: HELP THE NEEDY

My names are Yousif Abdullah Fahad, A Businessman in the United Arab Emirates. I have been diagnosed with prostate cancer and esophageal cancer that was discovered very late due to my laxity in caring for my health. It has defied all form of medicine, treatment and right now, I have only about a limited time to live according to medical experts.

I have not particularly lived a good life, as I never really cared for anyone not even myself but for the money I make from my business. Though I was wealthy, I was never generous because I was always hostile to people and only focus on my business. But now I regret all this as I now know that there is more to life than just wanting to have or make all the money in the world. I believe when God gives me a second chance to come to this world I would live my life a different way from how I have lived it before.

Now that I know my time is near, I have willed and given most of my assets to my immediate and extended family members and as well as schools in the United Arab Emirates. I have decided to give alms to the less privileged and some charity organizations, I want this to be one of the last good deeds I have done on earth.

So far, I have distributed funds among some charity organizations in the United Arab Emirates, and some other countries in Asia. Now that my health has deteriorated badly, I can't do this my self any more. Some time ago I asked members of my family to donate some money to less privileged homes in Iran and East Europe, which was in my account in Dubai but they refused and kept the money to themselves.

Hence, I don't trust any member of my family, as they seem not to be contented with what I gave them. The last of my money which is a great sum of money that I deposited with a finance company in Europe. I want you to help me make claim of this deposit and distribute it among the less privilege and charity organizations and let them know that it was I Yousif Abdullah Fahad that is making this donation.

I am sending you this email message from my hospital bed where I wait for my time to come. I pray that God use you to support and assist me with good heart.

I will appreciate your utmost confidentiality in this project until the task is fulfilled as I don't want anything that will jeopardize my last wish. and also I will be contacting with you by email as I don't want my relation or anybody to know because they are always with me.

Yours truly,
Yousif Abdullah Fahad

The following conditions (historical and contemporary) appear to have contributed to the high rate of fraud reported by the UAE to INTERPOL.

1. The UAE has a history of piracy-at-sea by Qawasim tribe members, who were influenced by the Wahhabi fundamentalist Islamic movement. They were said to have been engaging in jihad (holy war) to combat the European influence.[180]

2. After being defeated by the British navy, a treaty was signed in 1859, by which the emirates became the "Trucal Sheikhdom," controlled and defended by Britain. Under an 1859 truce agreement with Britain, the tribal leaders (emirs) controlled the pirates and the civilian population, mostly through a continuation of Shari'a law and courts.[181] Starting in the 1950s, the discovery of oil brought wealth to the emirs, who demanded a 50% share from foreign governments whose companies were employed to find the oil and market it.

3. Wealth, as a result of rapid growth and modernization in the area, brought with it power and eventual independence in 1971.[182]

4. In 1971, the "Trucal Sheikhdom" became the United Arab Emirates, a country led by Sheikh Zayed until his death in 2004.

5. Zayed entrusted his wealth to the Pakistani banker Abedi and his bank, BCCI.

6. The bank served not only the emirs, but also traffickers in drugs and women and children from Pakistan and other countries of the "Golden Crescent" and other Southwest and Southeast Asian countries who became 98% of the workforce of the UAE.

7. The fraudulent business dealings of BCCI ended with the collapse of that bank in 1991; the emirs, especially Zayed, were major victims of that bank's "bankruptcy fraud."

8. Starting in the 1980s, laws were promulgated pertaining to "white-collar crime." In 1992, several laws were passed to deal with "high-tech" crimes, in the wake of the 1991 BCCI bankruptcy.

9. Today the UAE remains a three-class system, with the royals and their tribes at the top, the affluent citizenry in the middle, and the great mass of immigrants who comprise 98% of the labor force at the bottom.

The frauds carried out by the masses of diaspora (people settled far from their ancestral homelands[183]) from Pakistan, Afghanistan, India, and Bangladesh can be characterized as "crimes of accommodation," based upon resentment and subsistence needs. Unfortunately, the emirs who continue to rule the UAE are discovering that control of the multitude of frauds that take place in that country is not responsive to royal edict, despite a huge volume of laws to deal with fraud that were developed during the 1980s and 1990s. Perhaps what they are discovering is that the establishment of democratic institutions, such as the "rule of law," also requires the establishment of democratic government.

SUMMARY AND CONCLUSION

This chapter opened with two case studies. The first case study pertained to an embezzler who defrauded a business in which he was an accountant for reasons that Cressey termed "non-shareable problems"—in this case mounting debt and a mistress. In the second case study, the identity thief was able to use the identification information of celebrities to make large purchases. He traced his career in identity theft to "identity problems" related to the fact that he had been a child from a biracial marriage.

Edwin Sutherland coined the term white-collar crime to point to the largely ignored crimes the wealthy committed in the course of their occupations. Critics of Sutherland argued that his definition of white-collar crime was too narrow. They maintained that white-collar crime frauds could occur at all occupational status levels, as well as in or outside of occupations. Herbert Edelhertz, former chief of the Fraud Section of the Criminal Division of the U.S. Department of Justice, provided an improved definition of white-collar crime that emphasized "nonphysical means" and "concealment and guile," without mentioning occupation or status level. In 1970, Edelhertz published a comprehensive 61-item list of white-collar crimes. In 2002, the list was updated to reflect new "high-tech" crimes by Cynthia Barnett, who drew upon definitions developed for the FBI's new NIBRS research.

Discussed in this chapter were various theories of white-collar crime including differential association (Sutherland), opportunity theory (Riemer), tension-reduction (Lottier), and psychological isolation (Cressey). A wide variety of white-collar crime enterprises were discussed, including the types of white-collar crime mentioned by Edelhertz and Barnett.

Corporate crime was the first general type of white-collar crime to be addressed. Studying the history of corporations in America proved insightful. Corporations were shunned by the early colonists, based upon their struggle with English corporations. Nevertheless, corporations obtained a foothold in America because of their great profits from the Civil War. This money was used to bribe judges and legislators. The chief product of corporate efforts to make government more "corporate friendly" was the 1886 Supreme Court decision, *Santa Clara County v. Southern Pacific Railroad*. This case concluded that a corporation is a "natural person." This decision provided criminal impunity to corporations that were thought to be incapable of crime because they lacked "*mens rea.*" As a consequence, America became the home to over four million corporations (including individuals who are "incorporated"), many of which committed major offenses against the public. It wasn't until the turn of the 20th century, with the Presidency of Theodore Roosevelt, the "trust buster," that corporate America came under regulatory control. However, today corporations seem to continue to commit criminal offenses that include tax violation, price fixing, bid rigging, bribery, adulteration of food, check kiting, securities fraud, and immigration fraud (as a means of exploiting the cheap labor of undocumented immigrants). Today, there are blurred distinctions between Edelhertz's "corporate crime" and "white-collar crime as a business." The WorldCom.Inc scandal is an example of a huge corporation that engaged in a "bankruptcy fraud," accompanied by insider trading for its executives, and then emerged as a new company, MCI, with a "strong balance sheet."

The distinctions between Edelhertz's major types of white-collar crime continue to blur when we turn our attention to "occupational crime." Occupational crimes today are typically frauds that are carried out by telemarketers in "boiler rooms" or through deceptive email or "popup" advertisements on personal computers. The employees of white-collar crime businesses, many of them college graduates, possess computer skills that prove to be an enhancement when it comes to hacking into people's computers for fraudulent purposes.

This chapter concluded with a country profile on the UAE, a country whose ruling family provided the working capital that started the infamous BCCI bank. The country's discovery of oil in the 1950s led to its independence and great wealth. This wealth is shared generously among the citizens of the seven emirates but not with the foreign workers. The foreign workers constitute 80% of the population of the UAE. Citizens of the UAE live a lavish lifestyle, supported by the labor of foreigners, who constitute 98% of the work force. The states of the UAE are ruled by the emirs and are not democracies in the Western sense, although members of tribes enjoy a measure of democracy through participation in tribal councils. However, the great mass of foreign workers do not share the wealth nor do they participate in tribal councils. It was the immigrant banker, Agha Hasan Abedi, who perpetrated the white-collar crime of the century, developing the bank called BCCI in the UAE and in the end engineering a massive bankruptcy fraud, victimizing the royalty of the UAE.

Although the UAE has promulgated numerous laws to combat white-collar crime and has signed major treaties, the emirs have been unsuccessful at thwarting the frauds that continue in the UAE. The high rate of fraud reported to INTERPOL by the UAE's law enforcement agencies seems to relate to the country's absence of laws regarding fraudulent activity. In addition, the country has no laws pertaining to trafficking in persons. Many of the laws pertaining to "white-collar crime" were developed in the 1980s and 1990s. Thus, the laws concerning fraud are very recent, and law enforcement agencies in the nation have not yet developed the necessary infrastructure to prosecute these crimes. As such, the UAE continues to be a major transit center, not only for trafficked persons, but also for illegal drugs, arms, and money. Along with this traffic comes the fraud and fraud-related crimes that, frequently, are the "crimes of accommodation" of the Diaspora living in the United Arab Emirates—many of whom are immigrants from India—as well as countries that were part of India prior to WWII—Pakistan and Bangladesh.

DISCUSSION QUESTIONS

1. Which of the various definitions of white-collar crime do you think is best and why?

2. Do you think that white-collar crime should be considered a serious crime in the United States? Why or why not?

3. How can Cressey's theory of embezzlement be used to explain the case of Albert, the embezzler, the case study given at the beginning of this chapter?

4. Why do you think corporations became so prevalent and powerful in the United States?

5. What does the term "collective embezzlement" refer to, and why do you think it has become so prevalent over the past 30 years?

6. Do you agree that more and more jobs these days are requiring employees to engage in unethical practices, if not outright fraud? Why or why not?

SUGGESTED WEBSITES

http://www.cybercrime.gov Website of the Computer Crime and Intellectual Property Section (CCIPS) of the Criminal Division of the U.S. Department of Justice, containing links to articles on computer crime, intellectual property crime, and identity theft.

http://www.crimes-of-persuasion.com/index.htm
A Website that describes "schemes, scams, and frauds." The Website explains how con artists steal victims' savings and inheritance through telemarketing fraud, investment schemes, and consumer scams.

http://www.crime-research.org/ An Australian Website that focuses on computer forensics, a promising new career in law enforcement, with links to such topics as cybercrime, Internet fraud, cyberterrorism, and child pornography.

http://www.whitecollarcrimefyi.com/index.html
Good general source for general discussion of white-collar crime, including definition, history and definitional debate, punishment, and in excess of 20 different types of white-collar crime.

http://www.sec.gov/index.htm Website for the Security and Exchange Commission.

http://www.sec.gov/index.htm Website for the Federal Deposit Insurance Corporation; historical account of the S&L crisis of the 1980s.

http://www.irs.gov/compliance/enforcement/article/0,,id=121259,00.html Internal Revenue Service's Website providing links to descriptions of a number of tax frauds, including corporate fraud, money laundering, and tax scams.

http://www.ftc.gov/bcp/conline/pubs/credit/idtheft.htm Website describing how to find out if you have been a victim of identity theft and what to do about it.

ENDNOTES

1. Winslow & Winslow, 1974.
2. Sullivan, 2004.
3. Sutherland, 1949, p. 9.
4. Sutherland, 1949, p. 9.
5. Thio, 1988, p. 420.
6. Yablonsky, 1990, pp. 330–331.
7. Thio, 1988, pp. 410–421.
8. Edelhertz, 1970, p. 3.
9. Edelhertz, 1970, p. 12.
10. Edelhertz, 1970, pp. 5–8.

11. Edelhertz, Cole, & Berk, 1983.
12. Edelhertz, 1970, pp. 73–75.
13. Barnett, 2002, p. 7.
14. Barnett, 2002, p. 7.
15. Barnett, 2002, p. 1.
16. Barnett, 2002, Glossary.
17. Barnett, 2002, p. 2.
18. Rebovich & Layne, 2000.
19. Sutherland, 1961, p. 240.
20. Riemer, 1941, p. 411.
21. Lottier, 1942, pp. 843–844.
22. Cressey, 1953, p. 16.
23. Cressey, 1953, p. 20.
24. Cressey, 1953, pp. 16–20.
25. Bloch & Geis, 1962, p. 291.
26. Thio, 1995, p. 342.
27. Watts, 2005.
28. Lasn, 1999.
29. *ReclaimDemocracy.org*, 2005.
30. Gilbert Geis found in a 1961 case involving price fixing in violation of the Sherman Antitrust Act of 1890, the defendants pled guilty to the charges and were given a fine plus 30 days in jail for seven of the defendants; Geis, 1968.
31. Benson, Cullen, & Maakstad, 1993, as quoted in Schmalleger, 2002, p. 362.
32. Adler, Mueller, & Laufer, 2004, pp. 328–329.
33. Siegel, 2003, p. 396.
34. Internal Revenue Service, 2003.
35. Fredrichs, 1996, p. 85.
36. *About.com*, 1999a.
37. CNNMoney, 2004.
38. *Fritz-reuter.com*, 2005.
39. Martin, 2003.
40. *About.com*, 1999b.
41. Ove, 2005.
42. Jacoby, Nehemkis, & Eells, 1977, p. 119.
43. Transparency International, 2004.
44. Coleman, 2002, p. 42.
45. DeFazio, 2000.
46. Coleman, 2002, p. 47.
47. DeFazio, 2000.
48. Columbia Encyclopedia, 2001.
49. Houghton Mifflin, 2005.
50. Cohn, 2001.
51. Lawrence, 2004.
52. Null, Dean, Feldman, & Rasio, 2003, p. 4.
53. Null et al., p. 6.
54. McKenzie, 2002.
55. Crossen, 1996.
56. Null et al., 2003, p. 13.
57. Weiner, 1996.
58. Null et al. 2003, p. 17.
59. Null et al., 2003, p. 18.
60. Leape, 1989.
61. Office of Technology Assessment, U.S. Congress, 1978.
62. Tunis & Gelband, 1995.
63. Null, Dean, Feldman, & Rasio, 2003, p. 20.
64. Null, Dean, Feldman, & Rasio, 2003, p. 28.
65. Rosoff, Pontell, & Tillman, 1998, p. 318.
66. FBI, 1992.
67. Idaho Credit Union League and Affiliates, 1999.
68. Bruce, 2002.
69. Adler et al., 2004, pp. 321–322.
70. *About.com*, 2006.
71. Patsuris, 2002.
72. Degenhardt, 2002.
73. Patsuris, 2002.
74. BBCNEWS, 2002.
75. *CNN.com*, January 13, 2002.
76. *CNN.com*, 2002.
77. Potter & Phillips, 2002.
78. 9/11 Commission, 2004a.
79. 9/11 Commission, 2004b, p. 13.
80. U.S. General Accounting Office, 2002b.
81. U.S. General Accounting Office, 2002, p. 1.
82. Gordon, 1997.
83. Data from Nye, Jr., 2002, p. 56, as quoted in Reich, 2004, p. 166.
84. Minuteman Civil Defense Corps., Inc., 2005.
85. Dinnen, 2002.
86. The 419 Coalition, 2000.
87. U.S. Secret Service, 2002.
88. Dinnen, 2002.
89. Gup, 1995, pp. 120–125.
90. Cornell Law School, 2005.
91. The term "fraudster" is commonly used on the Web to refer to "someone who commits fraud," WordWeb Online, 2005.

92. Brown, Netoles, Rasnak, & Tighe, 1999.

93. *Bankruptcylawfirms.com,* 2006.

94. *Bankruptcylawfirms.com,* 2005.

95. U.S. Securities and Exchange Commission, 2001.

96. Silverman, n. d.

97. U.S. Securities and Exchange Commission, 2004.

98. National Information Center, 2006.

99. Curry & Shibut, 2000.

100. Federal Deposit Insurance Corporation, 2002.

101. Pizzo, Fricker, & Muolo, 1989, p. 305.

102. Pizzo et al., 1989, p. 305.

103. Potter, 1999.

104. Bauder, 2005; Potter, 1999.

105. Potter, 1999.

106. Potter, 1991.

107. Pizzo et al., 1989.

108. Black, 2005.

109. Wikipedia, 2006b.

110. Edelhertz, 1970, pp. 73–75.

111. Green, 1990.

112. Green, 1990, p. 12.

113. Falcone, 2005, p. 83.

114. White Collar Crime FYI, 2006.

115. South Dakota Chamber of Commerce and Industry, 2001.

116. Calavita & Pontell, 1990, p. 94.

117. Calavita & Pontell, 1991; Pontell, Calavita, & Tillman, 1994.

118. Calavita, Tillman, & Pontell, 1997.

119. U.S. Postal Inspection Service, 2006.

120. CNNMoney, 1997.

121. Hollinger, 2003; also see *About.com,* 2004.

122. FBI, 1995, p. 209, Table 30; FBI, 2004a, p. 281, Table 30.

123. FBI, 1995, p. 209, Table 30; FBI, 2004a, p. 281, Table 30.

124. Hochstetler, Kerley, & Mason, 2002.

125. Hochstetler et al., 2002.

126. McCabe & Trevino, 1996, p. 31.

127. Meade, 1992.

128. Idea House, 2001.

129. Henderson, 2006b, 2006d.

130. Henderson, 2006c.

131. Henderson, 2006a.

132. Bauder, 1985.

133. *Nytimes.com,* 1985.

134. Schmalleger, 2006, Glossary p. G-2.

135. Falcone, 2005, p. 50.

136. Falcone, 2005, p. 97.

137. Schmalleger, 2006, p. 486.

138. Webopedia, 2006.

139. Falcone, 2005, p. 60.

140. Schmalleger, 2006, p. G-6.

141. Webopedia, 2006.

142. Tenebril, 2006.

143. Bednarz, 2005.

144. Bulletin Board Services (BBSs) were computers set up by using a modem and phone lines to welcome anyone who called. Users could converse on the BBSs and exchanges files. During the 1990s, the world of the BBS faded, changed, and became part of the present networked world; Scott, 2006.

145. Carter, 2001.

146. *Usdoj.gov,* 2003.

147. National Conference of State Legislatures, 2001.

148. Carter, 2001.

149. U.S. General Accounting Office, 1998.

150. Federal Trade Commission, 2003.

151. U.S. General Accounting Office, 2002a, p. 2.

152. Federal Trade Commission, 2005.

153. Usdoj, 2006.

154. U.S. General Accounting Office, 2002a.

155. Pflaum, 2002.

156. U.S. Department of Justice United States Attorney Southern District of New York, 2002.

157. U.K. Home Office, 2002.

158. Center for International Crime Prevention Office for Drug Control and Crime Prevention and Statistics Division Department of Economic and Social Affairs, United Nations, 1995, p. 20.

159. *CNN.com,* 2006.

160. In 1993, a foreign national was sentenced to the amputation of his hand for stealing; U.S. Department of State, 1994.

161. Peck, 2006.

162. *Arabianbiz.com,* 2000.

163. Infoplease, 2006.

164. Comparative Criminology Website: United Arab Emirates.

165. *AllRefer.com,* 2005.

166. Ciao Atlas, 1993.

167. BBCNews, 2006.

168. Ciao Atlas, 1993.

169. Peck, 2006, p. 2.

170. *Arabianbiz.com,* 2000.

171. *Arabianbiz.com,* 2000.

172. Khan, 1995.

173. Gulf Legal Services Ltd, 2001.

174. Central Intelligence Agency, 2006.

175. Peck, 2006, p. 3

176. Haidar, 2006.

177. Haidar, 2006.

178. *Arabianbiz.com,* 2000; Haidar, 2006.

179. *Rjohara.net,* 2006.

180. *Ciao.com,* 1993.

181. *Ciao.com,* 1993.

182. Peck, 2006, p. 1.

183. Merriam-Webster Online, 2006.

15

TERRORISM

KEY TERMS

Air America
black bag job
fatwah
narcoterrorism
French connection
Iran-Contra affair
Operation Cyclone

Operation Mockingbird
political crimes
Project Paperclip
state-based terrorism
state organized crime
state white-collar crime
terrorism

OUTLINE

When White-Collar Crime Becomes Political Crime

Terrorism Defined

Extent and Trends in Terrorism

Types of Terrorists

Profiling Terrorists

Theories of Terrorism

Measurement of Terrorism

Testing the Theories

Prevention and Control of Terrorism

Country Profile: Turkey

USA PATRIOT Act

LEARNING OBJECTIVES

After reading this chapter, students should be able to:

1. Define terrorism and distinguish between terrorism and resistance to occupation by a foreign country

2. Describe the extent and trends in victimization by terrorism of U.S. citizens in foreign countries

3. Recount various types of terrorists and explain the increased lethality of the "new terrorism"

4. Discuss various theories of terrorism and, in terms of correlations discussed in this chapter, assess the theories

5. Compare two countries with the same number of resident terrorist organizations (Turkey and the United States) and, despite its high amount of heroin trafficking, explain why Turkey does not have *more* terrorist organizations

INTRODUCTION

CASE STUDY: Ismail Abu Shanab, Terrorist[1]

[NOTE: The interview with Ismail Abu Shanab was actually drawn from two interviews, one by Abeja Hummel in 2000 and another by Paul Hilder in 2002]

I feel it is good to present our case to Americans . . . in the United States that there is a lot of misunderstanding and ignorance about the Middle East. The Israeli press . . . brainwashes Americans by the media they own and control, telling them that they are the victims and Palestinians are the terrorists, while the real truth is vice versa . . . we can solve the refugee problems, and they withdraw to the 67 borders and release all prisoners, I think these are acceptable to the Palestinians to start living together . . .

Hamas began in 1987 as a popular organization to resist the occupation. . . . The people themselves developed their own means of struggle. First, they were without anything in their hands. Then they developed stones, then a knife, like the ones in the kitchen. Then they developed a gas bomb. Fourth, they started to get guns, as far as they can, because they are not easy to get. Until they found that, in all circumstances, they die. So the best way to face death is to make your enemy suffer like you are suffering . . . and it started the car bombs and bombs in bags around the body. This is the utmost we can do to face people with tanks, to face people with all military means. . . . [Whether or not the bombings will continue] will all depend on the Israelis. . . . I cannot imagine how Palestinians can sit with Israelis while, at the same time, the Israelis are expanding their settlements on Palestinian land.

[The Israelis] are like a nail in the wood. The nail in the wood will not withdraw by itself. You cannot talk to the nail: "Just, please, get out." . . . This nail will never be drawn without resistance, without force. This is the conviction of Hamas . . .

When President Clinton tried to put the parties together and bring pressure to bear on them, we thought there was an American effort toward a solution. But . . . the Bush administration . . . tends toward securing the Israelis and giving them a green light to attack. [As to the September 11 attacks] It was a plot by some Zionist lobbyists outside, handed to bin Laden. I'm totally sure about this. What happened was much bigger than what bin Laden could do. . . . The creation of Israel was a tool of colonialism to get rid of Jews from the community of Europe. They disturbed its unity: Christians hated them. . . . The colonialists consider the Israelis part of the colonial strategy. But if they suffer, they will suffer alone. The Europeans will not suffer with them. They will give them money, they will give them support. If

Trying to remove the "nail in the wood" (as Hamas leader Ismail Abu Shanab refers to the Israelis), blasts are set off by Muslim militant suicide bombers, exploded back to back in a bus in downtown Jerusalem and at a bus stop in Ashkelon, killing at least 25 and wounding scores. The wreckage of the bus in downtown Jerusalem is being inspected by Israeli police officers, soldiers, medics, and burial society members.

Source: Eyal Warshavsky/AP Wide World Photo.

they succeed, give them money. If they fail, let them go to hell.

But the Zionist lobbyists in the United States are still in control of the administration of Bush. . . . They want to attack Iraq. They want to control the whole region. So they want a strong Israel, not a stable Israel. But the Americans will pay money for this, and they consider everything by dollars.

Ismail Abu Shanab, a founder of the Islamic militant group Hamas, was interviewed by Abeja Hummel on February 2, 2000 in the Gaza Strip. At that time she described Ismail as the spokesman for the Hamas political wing, a description similar to that of Paul Hilder in the 2002 interview also quoted earlier. Himmel interviewed Shanab in what she described as an almost empty office in a dreary building in downtown Gaza City. She said that she had a hard time reconciling her image of a terrorist with the man she had in front of her whom she described as wearing a suit and tie. Ismail, she said, turned out to be an engineer who went to college in Colorado. She also described Ismail as "a really nice guy."

In the interview done by Paul Hilder in 2002 (which begins [The Israelis] are like a nail in the wood), Hilder said that just three days before the meeting, Salah Shehadeh, leader of Hamas's military wing and formerly Abu Shanab's cellmate, was assassinated with a one-ton bomb. It demolished a refugee-camp block and killed 14 civilians. But Hilder said he felt no fear. Abu Shanab was the most moderate leader of Hamas's political wing, not at that time a target. This was Hamas's ceasefire negotiator, a man who advocated engagement in parliamentary process, who was openly prepared to entertain the two-state solution.

On August 21, 2003, "five Israeli missiles incinerated Ismail Abu Shanab in Gaza City, killing one of the most powerful voices for peace in Hamas and destroying the ceasefire that Palestinian leaders believed would avert civil war."[2]

This chapter might be viewed as an extension of the chapter on murder, although **terrorism** is shown to be multidimensional, including the whole array of crimes discussed in this text. A separate chapter on terrorism and political crime is provided here primarily because of the significance of recent events, and, in particular, the mass murder that occurred on September 11, 2001. Terrorism has been prevalent since the turn of the 21st century, and of growing concern is a brand of terrorism that has been labeled "the new terrorism," which has arisen since the 1970s. The name Osama bin Laden is widely known now, a name almost synonymous with terrorism today. He tops the FBI's list of "most wanted, not only for the Twin Towers attacks, but also for other terrorist acts." A brief list of these events is provided here:

- On September 11, 2001, 19 terrorists hijacked four passenger planes, two from American Airlines and two from United Airlines. In an unprecedented act of terrorism, the hijackers crashed two planes into New York City's 110-story twin towers of the World Trade Center, killing over 3,000 civilians. One American Airlines plane crashed into the Pentagon, killing more than 100 people. The fourth plane crashed in a rural area in Pennsylvania. The passengers probably prevented the hijackers from attacking another building in Washington. Osama bin Laden is suspected to be the key financier and instigator of these terrorist attacks.[3]

While the events of September 11 captured the attention of the whole world, Osama bin Laden is also held responsible for numerous other "spectacular" acts of terrorism during the past decade including the:

- 1993 World Trade Center bombing
- 1993 ambush in Somalia that killed 18 U.S. troops
- 1996 truck bomb attack on Kobar Towers, a U.S. military residence in Dhahran, Saudi Arabia
- 1998 U.S. embassy bombings in Kenya and Tanzania
- 2000 bombing of the USS Cole in Yemen

Osama bin Laden also has issued religious edicts declaring war on America and calling on "every Muslim who believes in God and wishes to be rewarded to comply with God's order to kill the Americans and plunder their money wherever and whenever they find it."[4]

Terrorism generally pertains to acts of murder or attempted murder, thus meriting inclusion in Chapter 6. However, terrorism also includes other crimes that were covered in this text, including assault, robbery, extortion, abduction, counterfeiting, and even drug trafficking (narcoterrorism). Furthermore, there is substantial literature on the topic to provide the basis of a chapter on terrorism.

After the September 11 terrorist attacks on the Twin Towers and the Pentagon, many Americans wondered why such unprovoked attacks should be directed at the United States. Their reactions were expressed in a patriotic Website:

America is the most benign super power that has ever existed on the face of the earth. We rebuilt Europe and Japan after WWII, pouring billions into their war ravaged lands, leaving them to self-determination, and then removing their debts. No other power in the history of the world has shown this kind of compassion to its vanquished. Today, we pour billions into impoverished, third world countries.[5]

Although these statements about American altruism are true, there is another, darker side to American foreign involvement. During the Cold War era that commenced after WWII, it has been alleged that agencies of the American government carried out secret wars, election rigging, and other foreign interventions without the knowledge of the American people. A lot of these activities involved American corporate interests abroad, so the next section is entitled "When White-Collar Crime becomes Political Crime."

WHEN WHITE-COLLAR CRIME BECOMES POLITICAL CRIME

Political crimes are generally defined as "those crimes or prohibited acts directed at the established political order, its laws, and institutions."[6] Beirne and Messerschmidt argued that the concept should be broadened. They said the state and its representatives often initiate illegal attacks upon legally functioning subordinate groups. They developed a four-fold typology of political crime that includes:

1. Violent political crimes against the state
2. Nonviolent political crimes against the state
3. Domestic political crimes by the state
4. International political crimes by the state

We have given many examples of each category throughout this text. However, the fourth category has been of greater emphasis in this text because of the comparative emphasis. This approach pertains to how international activities of one nation can influence crime in another nation or group of nations.[7]

In regard to the United States in its dealing with foreign countries, there has been much analysis of the role that the United States has played in pursuing its free trade and business agenda in countries outside the United States. A great deal of interest has been focused, in particular, upon the role that the CIA has played in the affairs of foreign countries. Chambliss characterized the activities of the CIA with the term **state organized crime**. We prefer to refer to such foreign policy endeavors as **state white-collar crime**, essentially because they are carried out in pursuit of American business interests. While the CIA, at times, has formed alliances with organized crime groups to carry out its agenda, the activities of the CIA have more typically benefited American business interests abroad. The white-collar criminality comes into play when politicians violate the public trust, or even accept bribes, in return for their support of particular business interests. We show that such foreign activities on the part of the CIA have been unsavory, to put it mildly, often leaving a legacy of hatred and resentment of the United States in countries where these activities have been conducted. A brief profile of CIA operations abroad may be insightful in showing the extent of the problem. An excellent chronicle of the CIA's involvement in clandestine activities at home and abroad is provided by whistleblower Steve Kangas. His essay, *Timeline of CIA Atrocities,* was published online prior to his 1999 unsolved killing outside the office of billionaire Richard Mellon Scaife, who was said to be Kangas' nemesis. Steve Kangas (1961–1999) was found dead, shot twice in the head, on the 39th floor in the bathroom of the offices of Richard Mellon Schaife.[8] Kangas, known as an "Internet warrior," had served in U.S. Army intelligence. After serving in the army he became a Doctoral Candidate at the University of California at Santa Cruz (UCSC) in economics and political science. He characterized this transition in the following sentence: "Going from the Army to UCSC was like going from conservative heaven to liberal heaven at warp speed."[9]

Kangas' "tell all" analysis of the role of the CIA in foreign policy begins his *Timeline* article:

> CIA operations follow the same recurring script. First, American business interests abroad are threatened by a popular or democratically elected leader. The people support their leader because he intends to conduct land reform, strengthen unions, redistribute wealth, nationalize foreign-owned industry, and regulate business to protect workers, consumers and the environment.
>
> So, on behalf of American business, and often with their help, the CIA mobilizes the opposition. First, it identifies right-wing groups within the country (usually the military), and offers them a deal: "We'll put you in power if you maintain a favorable business climate for us." The Agency then hires, trains and works with them to overthrow the existing government (usually a democracy). It uses every trick in the book: propaganda, stuffed ballot boxes, purchased elections, extortion, blackmail, sexual intrigue, false stories about opponents in the local media, infiltration and disruption of opposing political parties, kidnapping, beating, torture, intimidation, economic sabotage, death squads and even assassination.
>
> These efforts culminate in a military coup, which installs a right-wing dictator. The CIA trains the dictator's security apparatus to crack down on the traditional enemies of big business, using interrogation, torture and murder. The victims are said to be "communists," but almost always they are just peasants, liberals, moderates, labor union leaders, political opponents and advocates of free speech and democracy. Widespread human rights abuses follow.[10]

Kangas goes on to add that the CIA actually teaches this scenario in a special school at the "School of the Americas," in Fort Benning, Georgia, where Latin American military officers are taught how to conduct coups, including the use of interrogation, torture, and murder. He alleges that by 1987, six million people had died as a result of CIA covert operations,[11] and quotes former State Department official William Blum in calling this an *American Holocaust.* He states further that, although the CIA justifies these actions as part of its war against communism, the nations that are targeted often are instituting only liberal or moderate social reforms that threaten U.S. business interests.

Ironically, Kangas pointed out that the dictators installed by the CIA often become arrogant and defiant of Washington's will, leaving the United States the choice of "impotence or war." Examples of the United States having to resort to the war option now include General Noriega of Panama and Saddam Hussein of Iraq. The United States is now facing the "impotence option" with regard to Iran after the Islamic overthrow of the CIA installed Shaw of Iran. A chronicle of CIA initiatives is instructive in terms of explaining the present threat of terrorism that America faces. The September 11 attack was not the only terrorist attack on the United States. Also, the majority of terrorist attacks abroad have targeted U.S. companies, officials, and/or individuals.

Many if not most Americans were incredulous after the September 11 attacks and wondered why anybody would want to perform such an atrocity against a country that supports freedom and democracy around the world. However, they may be surprised to find that the opposite has often been the case. Agents of the U.S. government have, in fact, supported tyranny and oppression throughout the world when they felt it was in the national interest of the United States to do so. The American people have not been informed of this support for tyranny because CIA operations were typically "covert operations." However, Kangas also argued that the CIA recruited American news organizations and journalists to become spies and disseminators of propaganda. Kangas assembled a list of historical events (timeline), the occurrence of which we have attempted to verify and expand to include information from other sources. Some of these occurrences have been reported previously in this text.

- 1942, Office of Strategic Services (OSS) created: President Franklin D. Roosevelt asks New York Lawyer William J. Donovan to draft a plan for an intelligence service. The OSS was established in June, 1942, with a mandate to collect and analyze strategic information required by the Joint Chiefs of Staff. The OSS was also authorized to conduct special operations not assigned to other agencies. Because the FBI had been responsible for intelligence work in Latin America, the OSS received complete jurisdiction over all other foreign intelligence activities.[12]
- 1943, Italy: Donovan (head of the OSS) recruits the Roman Catholic Church to serve as a center for the spy operations in Fascist Italy.
- 1945, OSS is abolished: In October, 1945, the OSS was abolished and its functions were transferred to the State and War Departments. Donovan had proposed the development of a civilian agency that would have authority to conduct "subversive operations abroad."
- 1946, Central Intelligence Group: In response to the post-WWII debate between agencies regarding who should handle foreign operations, in January, 1946, President Harry S. Truman established the Central Intelligence Group, whose purpose was to coordinate existing departmental intelligence between the State Department, FBI, and other agencies. It was during this period that the U.S. intelligence community developed **Project Paperclip**, a program that brought selected German scientists to work for America during the "Cold War." Truman ordered the exclusion of anyone who had been a member of the Nazi Party. However, dossiers were rewritten, at the direction of Allen Dulles (who became the CIA Director in 1947). As a result, a number of Nazi scientists were admitted to the United States. These included Arthur Rudolph (who later designed the Saturn 5 rocket used in the Apollo moon landings) and Wernher von Braun (who became director of the National Aeronautic and Space Administration's Marshall Space Flight Center). Also recruited was General Reinhard Gehlen, one of Hitler's

chief intelligence officers, who had built an intelligence network in the Soviet Union. After the war, Gehlen was employed by Dulles, who provided Gehlen with a private intelligence facility in West Germany called the Gehlen Organization. The Gehlen Organization supplied the United States with major intelligence on the Soviet Union and served as a bridge between the abolishment of the OSS and the creation of the CIA. Gehlen also set up "rat lines" to get Nazi war criminals out of Europe so that they wouldn't be prosecuted. One of these was Klaus Barbie (the butcher of Lyons) who helped governments set up death squads in Argentina, Chile, El Salvador, and elsewhere.[13]

- 1947, Greece: President Truman requests military aid to Greece to support anti-communist right-wing forces. This action puts in place a policy that will prevail for the rest of the Cold War, whereby Washington and the CIA will back notorious Greek leaders with deplorable human rights records.

- CIA created: The CIA and the National Security Council are created under the provisions of the National Security Act of 1947. The charter allows the CIA to perform "other functions and duties" that may be requested by the National Security Council, opening the door to covert action. The two principle operating divisions of the CIA were the Office of Policy Coordination (OPC) and the Office of Special Operations (OSO). The OPC was responsible for directing political subversion, and the OSO was responsible for espionage and intelligence collection.[14]

- 1948, Italian election: In its first covert political action, the CIA offset Soviet funding of the communist party of Italy through a **black bag job** of its own, passing money to candidates for the Christian Democratic Party.[15] The Christian Democratic Party went on to win its greatest election victory in April, 1948.[16]

- Late 1940s, Operation Mockingbird: Headed by Frank Wisner, Allan Dulles, Richard Helms, and Philip Graham (publisher of the *Washington Post*), the CIA recruited American news organizations and journalists to serve as informants and disseminate propaganda. The early **Operation Mockingbird** influenced 25 newspapers and wire agencies that consented to serve as organs of CIA propaganda. Many of these were already run by men with conservative views, including William Paley (CBS), C. D. Jackson (*Fortune*), Henry Luce (*Time*), and Arthur Hays Sulzberger (*New York Times*). Eventually, the CIA's media assets included ABC, NBC, CBS, *Time, Newsweek,* Associated Press, United Press International, Reuters, Hearst Newspapers, Scripps-Howard, and Copley News Service.[17]

- 1953, Iran: The CIA overthrows the democratically elected Prime Minister of Iran, Mohammed Mossadegh, after he nationalized several foreign-owned oil companies (despite his government's offer to compensate the oil companies). The CIA replaces the Mossedagh government with the monarchy of Shah Reza Pahlavi, who promises that U.S. oil companies will have control over 50% of Iran's oil production. The CIA helps create, train, and finance SAVAK, a brutal secret police force loyal to the Shah that on June 5, 1953 murdered 6,000 Iranian citizens in one day. The ultimate cost of the coup was the revolution of 1979 that installed the virulently anti-American government of the Ayatollah Khomeni. This new government was heavily engaged in sponsoring terrorism, as well as seizing of hostages as part of a bizarre conspiracy involving U.S. intelligence during the Reagan administration, the **Iran-Contra Affair** (see text box).[18]

BOX 15–1

Iran-Contra Affair

The Contras were the armed opponents of the Left-wing Sandinista government in Nicaragua. The Reagan Administration supported the Contras covertly through various measures, one of which was the diversion of some $18 million from a $30 million sale of arms to Iran.[19]

- Operation MK-ULTRA: After reports of North Korea's brainwashing program, the CIA began experiments in mind control. The most notorious experimentation involved using LSD on unwitting subjects, most often prisoners or patrons of brothels set up and run by the agency. Two-way mirrors were installed in the establishments to allow observation of the drug's effects, and agents referred to this branch of MK-ULTRA as "Operation Midnight Climax." Besides LSD, the research included parapsychological phenomenon, hypnosis, telepathy, precognition, photokinesis, and "remote viewing."[20]

- 1954, Operation "Success" in Guatemala: After its early 1950 successful coup and installation of the Shah in Iran, the CIA turned its attentions to Guatemala, and its leader, Jacobo Arbenz, democratically elected with 65% of the vote. Arbenz's fatal flaw was that he favored land reform in a country in which 3% of the landowners held 70% of the agricultural land, and he nationalized 1.5 million acres of arable land, including land owned by the U.S.-based and Rockefeller-owned United Fruit Company, in which CIA Director Allen Dulles owned stock. The CIA financed a rebel "army" in neighboring Honduras, and Arbenz fled the country. The U.S.-sponsored dictator, Castillo Armas, who replaced Arbenz, canceled the land reform program and broke up the peasants' agricultural cooperatives. Hundreds of Guatemalans were rounded up and killed, and during the next 30 years repressive operatives of successive military regimes murdered more than 100,000 civilians.[21]

- 1961, The Bay of Pigs and Operation Mongoose: The CIA launched an invasion of 1,500 Cuban exiles to overthrow Castro. However, the invasion failed due to poor planning, security, and backing. The expected popular uprising against Castro never happened and a promised air strike never occurred. However, fearing another attack, Castro sought and obtained a Soviet missile defense system, provoking the "Cuban missile crisis."

- 1963, Kennedy Assassination: After Kennedy was assassinated, the CIA backed military coups/or assassinations occurred in countries with democratically elected leaders, including the Dominican Republic (1963), Ecuador (1963), Brazil (1964), Indonesia (1965), Greece (1967), Cambodia (1970), Bolivia (1971), Chile (1973), Panama (1989), and Haiti (1990). The CIA has also participated in the form of *black bag jobs* (black bags filled with money for candidates) in elections in various countries, including Jamaica (1980) and even Australia (1970). In Jamaica, CIA involvement led to election-related violence, as discussed in Chapter 9.

Human rights advocates may view the CIA covert operations over the years as wrong; however, on the other side are those who would argue that the CIA intervention in these foreign countries has been in the "national interest" of the United States.

After reading about all of these CIA exploits in foreign countries, some may wonder, "What does all this have to do with crime?" which, after all is the subject of this text. Previously in this text, we saw the effects of the "blowback" from the Jamaican posses who had previously served as political henchmen in Jamaica. The posses may have been a major factor in the crack epidemic of the 1980s, not to mention the epidemic of "drive-by-shootings" that erupted during that time. Yet some may counter that "blowback" is the price we must pay for our high standard of living (i.e., we must use whatever muscle we have to access the resources and/or services of the people who live in the developing world).

In reply, we can only argue that the predatory policy on the part of the CIA makes for a continuing crime problem in a variety of ways:

1. Forcing countries to accept our terms under brutal dictatorships often results in political instability and civil disorder in those countries, and rebel groups may fund their insurgency through illicit traffic in drugs and other illicit commodities, with the United States as a major marketplace for the illicit traffic.
2. Brutal dictatorships create a refugee problem of people escaping from such oppression, and the United States is often a target destination for human traffic.
3. To fund clandestine wars, the CIA has often found it necessary to fund its activities through illicit means—most particularly, through the drug trade and money laundering (as discussed later).

The drug trade and money laundering have both been a source of crime problems for the United States. Insofar as the wisdom of interfering in the internal affairs of developing nations to benefit U.S. business interests, it seems that this strategy is a "double-edged sword." Citizens of countries angered by our participation in their oppression and exploitation may ultimately install a democratically based government. When they do, it seems likely that U.S. interests will be excluded from these countries altogether. Furthermore, the bitterness that the citizens feel as former members of our "colonies" makes them more likely to join the ranks of international terrorists, thus contributing to the present major problem facing our nation.

The CIA is sometimes referred to as a "shadow government" organization and a carry-over from WWII. During WWII, its predecessor, the OSS, carried on a number of clandestine covert operations that were enabled by the War Powers Act, which allowed the Executive Branch to carry on spy-type activity, based upon a national emergency. Normally in peacetime, such organizations are suspended; however, after WWII the threat of the Cold War justified a continuation of such functions by the CIA and other organizations that report directly to the President. According to a watchdog organization (*AboveTop Secret.com*), the functions of the CIA are that it:

commands, often controls, and sometimes coordinates, the gathering of secret overseas information gathered by spies (HUMINT), electronic surveillance (SIGINT), and other means; carries out covert unconstitutional paramilitary counterinsurgency operations and preemptive political pacification projects in violation of international law, as well as counter-intelligence sting operations against foreign agents; engages in domestic surveillance, and manipulation of the U.S. political process, "in the national interest" in direct violation of its congressional charter; operates proprietary "false front" companies for profit; [and] conducts a major share of international trans-shipment of illegal drugs, using National Security cover and immunity.[22]

In regard to the issue of CIA drug trafficking, false front companies, and money laundering, the following instances have been cited:

- **Military Intelligence Operations WWII**: The help of mob boss Lucky Luciano was utilized by having his network of pimps, prostitutes, and dockworkers prevent the sabotage of New York docks during the war.[23] In Italy, Vito Genovese, who was living in self-imposed exile, served as an "unofficial advisor to the American military government" after the invasion of Sicily. He also found and installed right-wing politicians loyal to OC who served to offset potential gains by socialists and communists in Italy. The right wing politicians also gave OC a "free ride" for almost four decades.[24]

- **The French Connection**: Corsican OC figures were recruited by U.S. intelligence during the 1950s to help deal with dockworkers in France. The socialist dockworkers were opposed to the French war with Vietnam, which was seeking independence from France. The Corsicans created "goon squads" that attacked union picket lines and harassed and even assassinated union leaders, breaking the union. While the French were allowed to resume their war in Vietnam, the Corsicans were granted the right to use Marseilles as a heroin trafficking center, creating the infamous "French Connection." The latter would supply U.S. heroin needs for the next 20 years.[25]

- **Air America**: In the 1950s, the CIA provided direct support to Kuomintang (Chinese Nationalist) opium growers in Thailand and Burma in hopes that their armies would someday attack Communist China, setting up front air transport companies that flew opium out of the Golden Triangle to Thailand or Taiwan. This support largely accounted for the explosion of heroin addiction in the United States in the 1960s. During the 1960s, the number of known addicts grew from 65,000 to over 500,000.[26] Later, during the Vietnam War, the CIA financed a renegade 36,000-man secret Laotian army of Hmong (or Meo) tribe members, commanded by Vang Pao. The tribesmen were traditionally opium poppy farmers, whose trade was disrupted by the war, so the CIA supplied them with a fleet of aircraft called Air America to transport their opium from the Laotian hills to a CIA base at Long Tieng, Laos, where it was refined into heroin, and then transported to South Vietnam, where it was sold to U.S. troops, 20% of whom became heroin addicts.[27]

- **Operation Cyclone**: Zbigniew Brzezinsky, National Security Adviser to President Jimmy Carter, in 2002 revealed that President Carter secretly authorized $500 million to create an international terrorist movement that would spread Islamic fundamentalism in Central Asia and "destabilize" the Soviet Union. They called this plan Operation Cyclone and poured $4 billion into setting up Islamic training schools in Pakistan. Young zealots were also sent to the CIA's spy training camp in Virginia, where future members of al-Qaeda were taught "sabotage skills."[28] The Mujahadeen financed their war through drug trafficking, in this case heroin, while the CIA had reopened trade routes through Pakistan to supply the Mujahadeen with weapons. The Afghani rebels smuggled the drug into the world market, making the areas they controlled the world's leading source of heroin exports in the United States and Europe.[29]

- **Iran-Contra Affair:** During the 1980s, the Reagan administration backed a coalition of paramilitary groups known as the "contras" who were trying to overthrow the left-wing Sandinista government in Nicaragua. Some of the contras were trained in Honduras by CIA operatives. After the Democratic Congress refused to fund the the war in Nicaragua by passing the Bolland Amendment, drug money became involved in funding the insurgency. The Reagan administration, which launched a War on Drugs in America, actually facilitated the drug trade to fund the contras in three ways:

  1. Direct funding from major cocaine traffickers
  2. "Guns-for-drugs" scheme involving the cocaine cartels
  3. Direct drug trafficking by some of the contra leadership[30]

TERRORISM DEFINED

The term *terrorism* is difficult to define, because the definition depends upon one's point of view. The old adage, "One man's terrorist is another man's freedom fighter," clearly indicates the problem in forming a definition. In fact, it has been suggested that the American Revolution was the result of the actions of war-seeking groups of American men who used weapons of terrorism against all who opposed them.[31]

The issue of definition in the case of terrorism is crucial, as is discussed later, particularly after the events of September 11. At this writing, the national government has passed significant legislation to combat terrorism, and, in fact, has declared a "war on terrorism." Under the "rule of law" in our society, there can be no crime without first a law; however, if the law is unclear as to the definition of a particular crime, then the government, as represented by the police, can engage in arbitrary action and individual liberty can be threatened. The following are definitions of terrorism that have been used by the FBI:

- Terrorism is defined in the Code of Federal Regulation as "the unlawful use of force and violence against persons or property to intimidate or coerce a government, the civilian population, or any segment thereof, in furtherance of political or social objectives."[32]
- The FBI defines a terrorist incident as "a violent act or an act dangerous to human life, in violation of the criminal laws of the United States, or any state, to intimidate or coerce a government, the civilian population, or any segment thereof, in furtherance of political or social objectives."[33]

In terms of law enforcement in the United States, the definitions given by the FBI are important because the FBI is the prosecuting authority at the national level. Thus, any ambiguities in these definitions can have consequences in terms of the arrest of potentially massive numbers of persons in or outside of the United States. Note that the first definition includes force and violence against property as well as persons. Thus, tearing down a sign or spray painting graffiti could be construed as an act of terrorism by the FBI. The second definition is even more vague, including not only violent acts, but any act dangerous to human life. Thus, if a group, staging a protest demonstration, blocks a public highway, and someone has an accident with injury, the protesters could be charged with terrorism. The danger in such vague definitions is that the FBI might be locking up persons who are simply opposed to the current government in power, potentially facilitating a tyrannical government. The USA PATRIOT Act of 2001, to be discussed later, augmented the existing definitions of terrorism to include definitions of terrorist acts against mass transportation systems and harboring or concealing terrorists. If a person willfully "wrecks, derails, sets fire to, or disables a mass transportation vehicle or ferry" and does a variety of acts affecting mass transport, or "attempts, threatens or conspires to do any of the aforesaid acts," he may be fined or imprisoned under the USA PATRIOT Act. Although this delineation helps to clarify the definition of terrorism through indicating specific acts, there is still vagueness in the latter clause involving threats and conspiracies. More work is needed on the definition of terrorism to prevent arbitrary use and to make prosecution less subject to challenge in court.

A definition that combines the elements of many definitions of terrorism is given by the Terrorism Research Center, an independent institute that has assembled an excellent database on international terrorism:

> *Terrorism* (is) the systematic use of physical violence—actual or threatened—against non-combatants but with an audience broader than the immediate victims in mind, to create a general climate of fear in a target population, in order to effect some kind of political and/or social change.[34]

In addition to being inclusive, this definition is consistent with data produced by the Terrorism Research Center that is discussed later in this chapter. This definition overcomes limitations of the FBI's definitions in that it does not include "violence against property" (which could include minor acts of vandalism) and it specifies "noncombatants" as the target (a point not made clear in the FBI definitions).

Reflecting upon this definition, it can be seen that terrorism probably is as old as mankind. In ancient times, warring armies raped, pillaged, and plundered civilians and their property during the middle ages and before. During the American Civil War, William Tecumseh Sherman utilized a total-war strategy that targeted soldiers as well as all civilians, man, woman and child, in the American South.[35] Similarly, the Allies used a strategy of "total war" against the Nazi Regime in Germany to break the will of the enemy during World War II. Even bioterrorism is ages old. The ancient Scythe dipped their arrow heads in putrefied blood, and the Mongols won against the Genovese in 1344 by catapulting corpses infested with the plague.[36]

While terrorism, loosely construed, has occurred throughout history, there have been attempts in the literature to more specifically characterize terrorism today. Hazelip studied the works of 12 advocates of terrorism, from Yassir Arafat to Leon Trotsky, and deduced 12 tenets or principles of terrorism from their writings:[37]

1. Violence is necessary to overthrow oppression.
2. There is no limit to the extent of violence justified.

3. Actions should clearly convey their purpose.
4. Reprisal killings are counter-productive.
5. Ruthlessness and extraordinary violence are essential to terrorist success.
6. Government failures can be used to gain popular support.
7. Terrorism exposes the repressive side of government.
8. Terrorists aim to incapacitate government directly or indirectly.
9. Secrecy is important to terrorist operations.
10. Systematic planning and execution is critical to terrorist success.
11. Small-scale, persistent attacks are the most effective.
12. Terrorists are dedicated to destruction for the sake of their cause.

A more simplified version of these characteristics was published by Gwynn Nettler.[38] He said that there are six characteristics in all forms of terrorism:

1. There are no moral limitations upon the degree or type of violence that terrorists can use (no rules).
2. No distinctions are made in killing between children and adults, soldiers and civilians (no innocents).
3. Kill one, frighten 10,000 (economy).
4. Terrorists pursue publicity, and publicity encourages terrorism (publicity).
5. Terrorism gives meaning and significance to the lives of terrorists (meaning).
6. Beyond the immediate goal of destructive acts, the long-term goals of terrorists are often poorly conceived or impossible to implement (no clarity).

Obviously, volumes could be and have been written about the topic, because terrorism is a subject that has a wide variety of definitions and is done all over the world. However, the thrust of this chapter concerns terrorist acts directed at United States citizens. This does not mean that the study is parochial. This limitation is simply to keep the definition consistent with the other topics of the text. This text focuses upon criminal acts (murder, rape, robbery, etc.) done against citizens of this country. The discussion is not limited to this focus, however. A country profile is included in this chapter pertaining to terrorism done against citizens of other countries. By analyzing the factors involved with terrorism in other countries, insights are obtained that are relevant to the study of terrorism with regard to citizens of the United States.

EXTENT AND TRENDS IN TERRORISM

The Twin Towers/Pentagon attacks of September 11 constitute the popular connotation of terrorism in America today. However, the number of terrorism incidents involving Americans during the period from 1970 until today has been great. Most of the incidents were experienced by diplomats, government officials, and persons doing business in countries outside of the United States. Also, a plurality of international terrorism attacks in the world has been against United States citizens or property. In 1980, there were 760 incidents involving terrorist attacks. Of these, 1.8% (90) were in North America, but worldwide 36.6% (278) were against United States citizens or property. The forms of attack were explosive bombs, bomb threats, hijacking, and skyjacking. The countries in which attacks occurred against U.S. citizens were, in rank order, Turkey (36), West Germany (19), El Salvador (19), Philippines (18), Colombia (13), Greece (13), Uganda (13), and Guatemala (11).[39] A Rand report published in 1979 found that terrorist attacks on the American business community increased 400% since 1970.[40] From 1970 to 1978, United States businesses were the victims of 2,427 out of 5,529 terrorist attacks worldwide. Thousands of business executives and other personnel were held hostage, wounded, or killed.[41]

A congressional hearing in 1984 noted that terrorist activity against United States had increased 60% in 1982, and that more people were killed or injured by terrorists in 1983 than any year since countries began keeping records. The committee's concern was a possible link between terrorism and drugs, or **narcoterrorism**.[42]

In the mid-1980s, Mueller and Adler called attention to the threat of another form of terrorism—piracy.[43] They pointed to the attacks on refugees fleeing Southeast Asia, particularly off the coast of Singapore and to the disappearance of hundreds of vessels in the Caribbean. They said that an average of one substantial vessel per week had been disappearing, with a total of 23,000 vessels lost in 1985, compared to 800 in 1975.

The Rand Corporation has been monitoring international terrorism events since 1968. Findings are that international terrorism incidents increased from 121 in 1968 to 345 in 1985, then falling to 239 in 1990, rising again to 380 in 1991 (the year of the first Gulf War). After that, international terrorist acts fell gradually to a low total of 11 in 1997, but rose in 1998 to 1,256, followed by a decline to 988 in 2000, rising to 1,705 in 2001, 2,642 in 2002, and 1,355 in 2003.[44] Hoffman analyzed these trends and found that there has been a change not only in the incidence of terrorism but in the orientation and lethality.[45] He argued that traditional terrorism was radical leftist and secular in nature (i.e., Marxist, Leninist/Maoist/Stalinist movements). The purpose was to victimize targets (through kidnapping, assassination, bombing, etc.) that were blamed for economic exploitation or political repression to attract attention to themselves and their causes. The traditional groups generally issued communiqués taking credit for, as well as explaining in considerable detail, their actions. The "new terrorists" have been evident since the early 1990s (coincidental with the emergence of some 25 new Muslim nations). These new terrorist groups are religious in nature, with a less-cohesive and more diffuse organizational structure. It is rare for these new terrorists to claim credit for their acts of terrorism, and the acts have been progressively more lethal in nature. Hoffman characterized their acts of terror as typically in the form of "spectaculars"—dramatic, attention-riveting, and highly lethal. The reason for this increasing lethality is the need to get the attention of the jaded media and the increasing adeptness of terrorists at killing. Also involved is the terrorists' desire to get the backing and support of rogue states for which the terrorists secretly play the role of "surrogate warriors." The new terrorists are frequently of Shiite Islamic faith and have access to inexpensive lethal means of terrorism. Also a factor is the increasing sophistication and operational competence of professional terrorists.

Hoffman provided a list of terrorist incidents that were examples of the new terrorism. He prophetically indicated that the (then, in 1999) most recent embassy bombings were financed by millionaire Saudi Arabian dissident, Osama bin Laden, who was leading a worldwide campaign against the United States. Bin Laden's opposition to the United States was based upon its support for Israel and the continued presence of American military forces in Saudi Arabia. Bin Laden's influence added a new dimension to the lethality, imparting a religious fervor to his war on America as a *fatwa,* or Islamic religious edict. He also was able to augment the size of a terrorist organization (usually 20–400) to an estimated 4000–5000 well-trained fighters.

TYPES OF TERRORISTS

The FBI distinguishes between domestic terrorism and international terrorism. Domestic terrorism is terrorism by a group or individual based and operating entirely within the United States or its territories, whereas international terrorism occurs outside the United States or transcends national boundaries in terms of the means with which it is accomplished.[46] However, criminological literature offers many other typologies. Possibly as a reflection of the varying definitions of terrorism, there are a significant number of typologies in the literature. In 1977, Rayne identified five types of terrorists: (a) the politically motivated, (b) the minority group, (c) the purely criminal, (d) the religiously motivated, and (e) the mentally deranged.[47] It should be observed that political motivation is now included in the definition of terrorism, but that Rayne was providing an early preview of religiously motivated terrorists that Hoffman has found to be the trend today. Another very insightful early typology (in light of Hoffman's findings) was published by H. H. A. Cooper in 1978.[48] Cooper indicated that organized terrorists are generally highly disciplined and dedicated to the pursuit of specific objectives, and they limit their violence in the pursuit of those objectives. However, groups that serve as surrogate agents for nation states may escalate their violence because of the restrictions they must respect, and the most dangerous include three groups: (a) maverick terrorists, mercenary groups with a nihilistic creed and no expectation of attaining political power, (b) splinter groups forced into a position of desperation, and (c) solitary psychotic or psychopathic imitators. The religious terrorists described by Hoffman could fit any of these categories.

BOX 15–2

Police Terrorism in Sri Lanka

In countries with high murder rates, police are not passive investigators who merely respond to an offense reported to them. They are often part of the process. Sri Lanka is an Asian country which had a murder rate of 10.22 per 100,000 inhabitants in 1998, high by Asian standards and for a country with an otherwise very low crime rate. In recent years in Sri Lanka (formerly Ceylon), the police representing the Sinhalese majority have abused Tamil rights in that country. Tamils are a Muslim minority whose forebears were brought from India in the late 19th century to work on the tea and rubber plantations. The Tamils have their own language. The Sinhalese are the largest ethnic group. They have their own language, and over 90% of the Sinhalese are Buddhists. The Sri Lankan National Police have been battling a Tamil terrorist organization, the Tigers of Tamil Eelam ("LTTE" or "Tigers"), with conflict escalating in the 1990s. In 1993 the Tigers assassinated the Prime Minister of Sri Lanka, Ranasinghe Premadasa. This conflict has led to participation in extrajudicial killings on the part of the police (similar to Wolf's enforcement terrorism). In October 2000, while police allegedly looked on, 27 young Tamil males held at the Bindunuwewa rehabilitation camp for former child soldiers were hacked and clubbed to death by local villagers; 15 others were injured. Police allegedly took part in the killings and did nothing to prevent the villagers from entering the detention camp. At his sentencing for the 1998 rape and murder of Krishanthi Kumaraswamy, a Tamil schoolgirl, former Lance Corporal Somaratne Rajapakse, claimed knowledge of mass graves at Chemmani in Jaffna containing the bodies of up to 400 persons killed by Sri Lankan security forces in 1996. The other five defendants convicted in the Kumaraswamy killing also later claimed knowledge of mass graves in the Chemmani area, where they allegedly had buried between 120 and 140 bodies on the orders of their superiors.[49]

Several authors have distinguished between government-sponsored terrorism and that done by nongovernment groups; however, a typology especially relevant to criminal justice was developed by John Wolf in 1981.[50] Wolf referred to government terrorism as enforcement terrorism, used by nations to maintain social control. Examples included the "white terror" of Chile's military intelligence services, the Death Squads in Brazil, the White Warriors Union in El Salvador, and the KGB in the USSR. As discussed in the text box and later in this chapter, many countries that report extremely low crime rates may be characterized by enforcement terrorism. Nongovernment terrorism, which Wolf characterized as agitational terrorism, is done by small groups of individuals who want to alter the country's status quo, but must do so within restricted time and space perimeters and must restrict their organizational membership to a handful of persons. It should be observed that agitational terrorism is more prevalent today, because it may be supported by the majority of the civilian population in a country, or a nearby country in which the terrorists are given refuge.

Harvey Kushner provided a similar discussion of the "new terrorism," but with a broader reach than that of Hoffman.[51] He said the new terrorist, often a freelancer or someone involved with a loosely affiliated group, is more difficult to spot, track, intercept, and combat than the traditional terrorist. The "new domestic terrorist" movement (in the U.S.) includes Christian Identity advocates, Ku Klux Klan members, militias, Freemen, skinheads, survivalists, Populists, gun enthusiasts, militant anti-abortionists, tax protesters, and neo-Nazis. In some countries, such right-wing groups work in concert with the government and police as a covert means of supporting the status quo. It is probably not beyond credibility to assert that such organizations have served as surrogates for the police in the United States in the not too distant past.

As suggested earlier, much of the "new terrorism" in other nations has been the product of the emerging independence of Islamic countries. Pluchinsky suggested that on the horizon is another type of terrorism, blood feud terrorism, which entails retaliatory acts of violence to satisfy the vengeance code of a clan.[52] Blood feud terrorism seems likely in the 15 newly independent states of the former Soviet Union. These include Dagestan, Chechnya, Ingushetia, North Ossetia, Georgia, Azerbaijan, and Tajikistan. These areas may replace the Middle East as the primary generator of international terrorism, according to Pluchinsky.

Siegel has condensed many of the aforementioned typologies into a sevenfold typology including revolutionary, political, nationalist, cause-based,

When Rape Is Terrorism

A study based upon 250 interviews with Bosnian refugees in Croatia and Austria determined that there were four distinct types of rape during wartime: (a) rape as bounty, (b) rape as a formally forbidden but de facto tolerated outlet for soldiers, (c) rape as a breakdown of the command structure and the morale of the troops, and (d) rape as part of a deliberate assault strategy.[53] Another study found that the Serbs had adopted an official policy that not only permitted but also recommended "genocidal rape" to further military and political goals. This policy involved a strategy of systematic terror based upon raping and murdering women as well as impregnating them to provide a new source of Serbian citizens.[54]

environmental, state-sponsored, and criminal terrorists.[55] Revolutionary terrorism uses violence to replace the existing government through frightening and inciting the government to use repressive measures that can be exposed by the terrorists as oppressive. Political terrorists seek to shape the existing government so that it accepts its views. Timothy McVeigh's Oklahoma City bombing was an instance of political terrorism. Nationalist terrorism is directed at promoting the interests of a minority ethnic or religious group that believes it has been mistreated by majority rule and seeks to form its own independent homeland. The Palestinians and the Kurds represent groups who have engaged in terrorist acts for this purpose. Cause-based terrorism is directed at individuals or governments that are objectionable to the terrorists. Osama bin Laden's al-Qaeda organization is an example that seeks to impose its own religious code on the world or certain regions of the world. Environmental terrorism typically involves arson or vandalism to promote the cause of environmentalism (and thus is a form of cause-based terrorism). State-sponsored terrorism is that done by a repressive government regime to force its citizens into obedience. Criminal terrorism involves the use of terrorist acts, such as kidnapping, for profit or gain. Criminal terrorism can be done by other types of terrorists.

Aside from the general typologies discussed earlier, terrorism has been characterized by the various forms it takes. The forms include bombings, kidnappings, assassinations, facility attacks, lock-ins, robberies, extortion, hijacking, skyjacking, hostage-taking, and rape.

It should be added that mentioned in criminological literature are some forms of terrorism that stretch to its limits the definition of terrorism, including workplace terrorism, patriarchal terrorism (by husbands to wives), and agricultural terrorism.

Shown here is the Alfred P. Murrah Federal Building in Oklahoma City, Oklahoma, bombed on April 19, 1995, an instance of political as well as domestic terrorism. It was the deadliest terrorist attack on United States soil prior to the events of September 11, 2001, killing 168 people. Timothy McVeigh, a decorated Gulf War veteran, was convicted and executed for the crime. McVeigh used a truck, loaded with 5,000 pounds of fertilizer, as a bomb. McVeigh's motivation, in his words, was "necessity," arguing that his bombing was a justifiable response to what he believed were the crimes of the U.S. government at Waco, Texas, where 76 Branch Davidian members died in a confrontation with U.S. federal agents on April 19, 1993.

Source: Paul Moseley/Fort Worth Star Telegram. SIPA Press.

PROFILING TERRORISTS

There have been some attempts to develop a psychological and/or sociological profile of the typical terrorist. These attempts may be useful in regard to the goal of developing theories of terrorism, discussed later in this chapter. Osama bin Laden is probably the number one terrorist being profiled today. Although bin Laden's background does not resemble that of common criminals that have been described in this text, there are elements in his biography that are similar to those found in the profiles of other terrorists.

> Osama bin Laden was born in the city of Riyadh, Saudi Arabia, probably in 1957. . . . His father, Muhammad bin Laden, was a small-time builder and contractor. . . . His father had more than 50 children from several wives. The oil boom of the 1970s changed Muhammad bin Laden's fortunes . . . he soon developed a special relationship with the upper-most echelons of the House of al-Saud as both a superior builder and the provider of discreet services, such as the laundering of payments to "causes." . . . the House of al-Saud contracted with the bin Laden company to refurbish and rebuild the two holy mosques in Mecca and Medina. Osama . . . went to high school in Jeddah and then studied management and economics at King Abdul Aziz University in Jeddah. . . . While in high school and college, Osama often visited Beirut [Lebanon], frequenting flashy nightclubs, casinos, and bars. He was a drinker and womanizer, which often got him into bar brawls. Ultimately, however, Osama bin Laden was not an ordinary Saudi youth having a good time in Beirut. In 1973 Muhammad bin Laden was deeply affected spiritually when he rebuilt and refurbished the two holy mosques, and his father's renewed spirituality greatly affected Osama. Even during his brief trips to Beirut, Osama began to show an interest in Islam. He started reading Islamic literature and soon began his interaction with local Islamists. In 1975 the outbreak of the Lebanese civil war prevented further visits to Beirut. The Saudi Islamists claimed that the agony of the Lebanese was a punishment from God for their sins and destructive influence on young Muslims. Osama bin Laden was strongly influenced by these arguments.[56]

Although Osama bin Laden's childhood could hardly be described as deprived or impoverished, the family situation would certainly draw comment by profilers had Osama been raised in the West. As the Gluecks' study[57] and many other studies pointed out, children raised in large families are prone to delinquent behavior. One reason given is that there is a breakdown in control in such families because the amount of attention given to each child declines proportionately to the number of children. Sibling rivalry may erupt into violent behavior that cannot be effectively contained, particularly if the father figure is absent. Such a childhood could pave the path for violence in adult years.

In gang neighborhoods, large families can form the nexus of delinquent gangs. A family of 50 siblings could form the core not just of a gang, but of a social movement. However, other factors led to Osama bin Laden's lethality as a terrorist in his subsequent career, first as a freedom fighter, and later as a terrorist, as well. While his early work was in support of the Saudi royal family, it is shown that his increasing radicalism led to his isolation and alienation and ultimate expulsion from his home country as a social pariah, thus driving his terrorism to the desperation of a "maverick" or "splinter" group, as previously described by Cooper.

In college, Osama adopted the main trend of many educated Muslims at the time, Muslim Brotherhood. Through Hajj visits to Mecca and at King Abdul-Aziz University in Jeddah, Osama was mentored by two distinguished teachers in Islamic studies. Starting in the early 1980s, Osama visited Pakistan secretly during the Soviet invasion. There he was taken to see the refugee camps and to meet some Islamic leaders whom he had already encountered at various Hajj meetings. Upon returning to Saudi Arabia, Osama collected a huge amount of money and material that he subsequently supplied to his connections in Pakistan. In 1982, Osama decided to go to Afghanistan, bringing with him plenty of construction machinery, which he put at the disposal of the local mujahedeen. In 1984, he set up a guesthouse in Peshawar, Afghanistan, which was to serve as a way station for Arab mujahedeen on their way to training camps or the front to fight the Soviets. In 1986, he set up his own camps inside Afghanistan, building more than six camps within two years. Ultimately he was to establish more than 50 camps in that country. The whole complex (guesthouse and camps) was termed Al-Qa'edah, which in Arabic means "The Base." After the Soviet withdrawal from Afghanistan in 1989, Osama experienced his first chastisement by the Saudi government. Upon his return to the kingdom, he was banned from travel. The reasons for the ban were, perhaps, his intentions to start a new "front" of jihad in South Yemen, his lectures and speeches warning of impending invasion by Saddam Hussein (at a time when the Saudi regime was on very good terms with Saddam). Osama felt vindicated when Saddam invaded Kuwait, and recommended the development of an all-Arab force of mujahedeen to defend the kingdom. Instead, he was shocked to learn that the Americans had been invited to defend Saudi Arabia. In response to this, Osama obtained a **fatwah** (in Islam, a legal opinion or ruling issued by an Islamic scholar[58]) from one of the senior scholars to the effect that training and readiness is a religious duty. He circulated the fatwah and convinced some 4,000 people to obtain training in Afghanistan. The Saudi regime, displeased with Osama's activities, limited his movement to Jeddah only and raided his farm in the suburb of Jeddah, further alienating bin Laden. In 1991, Osama was able to obtain permission to leave the country through connections of one of his brothers with the Saudi royal family, and he left for Pakistan. There he notified his brother that he was not coming back and apologized for letting his brother down with the royal family. He left immediately for Afghanistan where more than once, the Saudis tried to kidnap or kill him in collaboration with the Pakistani intelligence service. He managed to escape these attempts by virtue of leaks from friends connected with the Saudi royal family and Pakistani government, but eventually departed from Afghanistan for Sudan in a private jet, wearing a disguise. In Sudan, Osama found a safe refuge and was treated as a welcome guest by the Islamic government. He provided aid in construction as well as financing for that government through his Saudi connections. While in Sudan, he once again escaped a Saudi-based assassination attempt. During his stay in Sudan, between 1992 and 1994, the Saudi government froze his assets and in 1994 publicly withdrew his citizenship. Sudan subsequently was exposed to considerable international pressure for hosting bin Laden and bin Laden fled in 1996 to Jalalabad in Eastern Afghanistan. There he issued his first anti-American message, a Declaration of War, limited to expelling American forces from the Arabian Peninsula. He was given refuge in Afghanistan, personally sponsored by Mullah Omer, the leader of the Taliban. This did not stop assassination attempts by the Saudis, one of which took place in early 1997 prompting bin Laden's move to Qandahar, the stronghold of the Taliban, after news of the latest assassination attempt was leaked to him. In 1997, a commando attempted kidnapping of bin Laden by the Americans was foiled after information was again leaked to bin Laden, and he went public, causing the Americans to cancel their plans. Bin Laden enjoyed sanctuary in Afghanistan up until the Americans invaded the country after the destruction of the World Trade Center. The Taliban protected him because they saw him as a saint. Providing bin Laden sanctuary performed the functions of protecting a distinguished Muslim who gave up wealth to help his brother Muslims in Afghanistan, as well as performing the tribal duty of protecting a decent [sic] refugee. Contrary to speculation, bin Laden has never had any relation with America, the CIA, or other American departments.[59] (For another version of the latter statement, see text box.)

BOX 15–4

The CIA's "Operation Cyclone" and Osama bin Laden

Although Osama bin Laden has been implicated in the 2001 terrorist destruction of the World Trade Center in New York City, various news articles have also implicated the United States CIA (indirectly) in the development of his terrorist network. One author, Norm Dixon, alleged that bin Laden's terrorist network was more or less a direct product of a covert CIA operation called "Operation Cyclone." Dixon maintained that between 1978 and 1992, the U.S. government provided between $6 billion and $20 billion worth of arms, training, and funds to support the mujaheddin in Afghanistan in their efforts to oust the Pro-Soviet People's Democratic Party of Afghanistan and the Soviet occupying forces. The strategic plan, authored by U.S. President Jimmy Carter's national security advisor, Zbigniew Brzezinski, was to foster an international movement to spread Islamic fanaticism into the Central Asian Soviet republics to destabilize the Soviet Union. The CIA funneled its support through Pakistan's CIA, the Inter-Service Intelligence Directorate (ISI), which in turn distributed money, recruits, and equipment to the mujaheddin factions through an organization known as Maktab al Khidamar (MAK; Office of Services). According to bin Laden's CIA biography, bin Laden was running the MAK in 1984. One faction favored by Washington was headed by Gulbuddin Hekmatyar, an Islamic extremist and close associate of Osama bin Laden. In 1992, Hekmatyar became prime minister of the new Taliban government in Kabul after his forces rained U.S.-supplied missiles and rockets on that city. Hekmatyar was also well known for his participation in the trafficking in opium in Afghanistan, resulting in a boom in opium production in the Afghanistan-Pakistan border region. Brzezinski's plan coincided with desires of then Pakistan military dictator General Zia ul-Haq's to develop an Islamic domination of the region, and the CIA lent support to a longstanding ISI proposal to recruit from around the world to join the Afghan jihad. Some 100,000 Islamic militants flocked to Pakistan between 1982 and 1992, with some 60,000 attending fundamentalist schools in Pakistan. At the same time, Muslims were recruited in the United States for the mujaheddin and were sent to Camp Peary, the CIA's training camp in Virginia. There, young Afghans, Arabs from Egypt and Jordan, and even some African American "black muslims" were taught "sabotage skills."[60]

Regardless of which version of Osama bin Laden's biography is true, it can be seen that there are considerable differences between the background of this man and that of ordinary criminals discussed throughout this text. One of the earliest studies profiling terrorists closely captured bin Laden's personality. The study was based upon an analysis of 350 terrorists during the years 1966 to 1976. The typical terrorist was found to be a single male, age 22 to 24, with at least a partial university education, employed in law, medicine, teaching, engineering, or technical occupations. The terrorists came from middle or upper class families, but gained an anarchist or Marxist world view and were recruited into terrorist operations while attending a university.[61] In a subsequent analysis, Kampf suggested that the artificial environment of universities contributes to the appeal of terrorism for youths going through adolescence in the modern world.[62]

From the psychodynamic point of view, terrorists have been characterized in terms of narcissistic personality disturbances.[63] While narcissism may describe the personality of terrorist leaders, the "logic of religious violence" in which images of cosmic war are related to political battles may appeal to marginalized, alienated, and unempowered groups of individuals, particularly youth.[64] Religious terrorist organizations can offer special appeal to youth in that they offer community, comaraderie, simplicity, and a mutual feeling of the righteousness of cause.[65]

The attempts at profiling that have been done indicate that there are both similarities and differences between terrorists and ordinary criminals. In the opening interview with Hamas spokesman Ismail Abu Shanab, he was revealed to be a college-educated, "really nice guy," and it was said that most of what he said "made sense." That very concisely indicates why terrorism is very difficult to explain, and, as is discussed later, defies conventional explanations of crime that are presented in this text—including inequality, poverty, unemployment, drug and alcohol addiction, an ineffective criminal justice system, and the like. Some attempts at correlation analysis using the CCDB are done near the end of this chapter.

Exiled Saudi dissident Osama bin Laden, the prime suspect behind the September 11, 2001, terrorist attacks in the United States, holds a Kalashnikov assault rifle in 1998 at a meeting in an undisclosed location in Afghanistan. In the background is a banner with a verse from the Koran, Islam's holy book. This photo was offered to The Associated Press on September 22, 2001, by a Pakistani photographer who wished to remain anonymous.

Source: AP Wide World Photos.

Searching for the sources of terrorism is a challenge for criminological theory. A common view is that terrorism is caused by poverty, and that to rid the world of terrorism, we must first proceed to eradicate poverty. Klaus Teopfer, executive director of the United Nations Environment Program, was quoted shortly after the collapse of the World Trade Center as saying that although poverty wasn't a factor on its own, "it can fan the flames of hate and ignite a belief that terrorism is the only solution to a community's or nation's ills."[66] Along the same lines of argument, Jeffrey Nedoroscik observed that the presence of a large, dissatisfied, underemployed, or unemployed segment of the population in Egypt made that sector easily susceptible to the ideas of Islamic fundamentalist groups, some of which were empowered by Osama bin Laden.[67] Thus, based upon views drawn from these "economic strain theories," it may be hypothesized that terrorism is positively correlated with poverty and unemployment.

While it may be true that terrorists may utilize poverty and other sources of grievance to inflame potential followers, it has been argued that poverty by itself is no predictor of terrorism. Albert Parry held that while it is common for sociologists to suggest that terrorism would abate if we put an end to oppression, history is our witness that not all revolutions come on empty stomachs but often on full ones. He said that people who are subjected to starvation have no energy and no time for revolt.[68]

Related to the oppression of poverty is a perspective that terrorism arises from social inequality, that terrorism is a response by frustrated, powerless people to oppression, and that powerful people are the targets of that terrorism.[69] It can be hypothesized, then, based upon this view drawn from "critical criminology," that terrorism is positively correlated with social inequality.

Yet another theory is that social injustice is the root of terrorism, and that the attainment of social justice is a necessary prelude to world peace and advancement.[70] According to this view, countries in which there is greatest oppression by the criminal justice system should experience the greatest amount of terrorism. On the other hand, many researchers contend that terrorism is most prevalent within Western liberal democracies, or liberal states. In these nation-states, force is strictly governed by the doctrine of "minimal force," applied as proscribed by the "rule of law."[71] It may be hypothesized, based upon the first view drawn from "social justice theory," that "lack of freedom" in terms of civil and political liberties is positively correlated with terrorism. However, based upon the opposing viewpoint that liberal democracy supports the

BOX 15-5

The Drug Trade and al-Qaeda

Adam Robinson wrote a biography of Osama bin Laden, based upon interviews with bin Laden's family and research conducted in Saudi Arabia, Lebanon, Bahrain, Oman, and other countries. He concluded that the burgeoning opium drug trade financed al-Qaeda's decade-long war against the United States.[72]

BOX 15–6

Terrorism in Lebanon

The definition of terrorism is fraught with controversy, particularly in the Middle Eastern context. But by almost any definition, Lebanon is an epicenter of terrorist activity. Assassination is an occupational hazard for politicians. The slaying of Prime Minister Karami on June 1, 1987, when a bomb exploded aboard his helicopter, was but another in a long string of political murders. Car bombings, known in the Lebanese lexicon as "canned death," were occurring almost on a daily basis. The United States embassy had twice been attacked by suicide truck-bombers. And the hijacking of TWA Flight 847 in June 1985 was only the most brazen of a long series of airliner hijackings originating in Beirut. Over the years, literally hundreds of groups have claimed responsibility for various acts of terrorism committed against civilian targets. Most of the names, however, were merely code words meant to conceal the true identity of the organization behind the attack. In the judgment of most informed observers,

a few men or families have been responsible for masterminding the majority of terrorist operations. For example, the Lebanese Armed Revolutionary Faction, a terrorist organization that assassinated United States and Israeli officials in Western Europe in 1982 and 1984 and staged numerous other attacks, was eventually revealed to be run by a single Maronite extended family, the Abdallah clan from the northern Lebanese town of Al Qubayyat. In March 1987, ringleader George Ibrahim Abdallah was sentenced by a French court to life imprisonment. Likewise, virtually all of the Shia terrorist attacks against Western interests in Lebanon since 1982, claimed in the name of the Islamic Jihad Organization and a dozen other groups, have been attributed by intelligence experts to two related Shia families—the Mughniyyahs and the Musawis. Two leaders of these families—Imad Mughniyyah and Husayn al Musawi—were widely believed to be responsible for holding 23 Westerners hostage in 1987.[73]

---

development of terrorist organizations, the number of terrorist organizations in a country would be inversely correlated with the lack of freedom.

Another interesting theory relates the War on Drugs to terrorism. According to Steven Wisotsky, the War on Drugs creates a black market in illegal drugs, making them highly profitable for traffickers, and that same black market promotes and finances—among other things—terrorism.[74] According to Richard Clutterbuck, 30,000 Colombians have died violent deaths from terrorism financed by the drug trade.[75] Based upon these views regarding the link between the drug trade and terrorism, one could hypothesize that the greater the trafficking in illegal drugs in a country, the greater the terrorism.

Beyond the black market in drugs as a funding source for terrorism, some authors have suggested that terrorism may be state sponsored. One theory states that the former Soviet Union sponsored (with direct and indirect support) some of the groups that have used terrorist tactics.[76] This theory can no longer be tested with current data, because of the dissolution of the Soviet Union in 1991. Since that event, the major **state-based terrorism** has been linked with the newly emerging Islamic nation-states. It is alleged that Islamic states such as Iran, Iraq, Saudi Arabia, and so forth have secretly sponsored terrorist organizations that act as their surrogates in combating the economic and political dominance of the West, and the United States in particular.[77] It may be hypothesized that if the Islamic state support theory is correct, then there should be a positive correlation between the percentage of people of Islamic faith in the population of a country and terrorism.

MEASUREMENT OF TERRORISM

Using international data sources, an attempt is made to assess hypotheses drawn from the various theories stated earlier. For purposes of this study, the independent variables poverty, unemployment, inequality, lack of freedom, percentage Islamic, and heroin seized are derived from data available on the World Wide Web. Data by country for population below the poverty line, unemployment, inequality, and percentage Islamic were retrieved from the CIA World Factbook 2002.[78] Data on "lack of freedom" were based upon an index developed by Freedom House combining ratings for political rights and civil liberties for the countries of the world.[79] The measure used for inequality, published in *The World Factbook,* was the "Gini Index."[80] Data on heroin seizures were derived from a publication entitled *Global Illicit Drug Trends 2003.*[81]

However, to be developed here is a measure of terrorism. One measure of terrorism that is available is the number of terrorist organizations in a particular country. Data for this variable are given on The Terrorism Research Center's Website.[82] This measure has the advantage of being a current index consisting of groups active today. The measure would also seem to provide an intuitively reasonable operational definition of terrorism.

TESTING THE THEORIES

In searching for an understanding of the causes of terrorism, Table 15–1 provides some interesting data. Internationally, the number of terrorist organizations in a country appears to be negatively associated with the percentage of people living in poverty. This means, in essence, the less the poverty the more the terrorism, although this is a very low minus correlation ($r = -0.13$). This correlation runs contrary to the explanation that poverty incites terrorism. Seemingly, there are slightly more terrorist organizations in affluent countries than in poor countries. There appears to be no correlation between percentage unemployed and the number of terrorist organizations by country, evidence also contrary to the unemployment/terrorism link. Furthermore, there is no correlation between inequality (as measured by the Gini Index) and the number of terrorist organizations. Thus, reduction of world poverty, unemployment, and inequality would not curtail the problem of terrorism, according to these findings. Critical theories, as well as strain theories, do not seem to serve well in dealing with the problem of terrorism.

There is some evidence for the social justice theory in the aforementioned data. The "lack of freedom" index, which measures lack of civil and political liberties, is positively correlated with the number of terrorist organizations ($r = .11$), although the correlation is low.

There does seem to be some evidence for the "Islamic conspiracy theory" in the correlation between percent Islamic by country and number of terrorist organizations ($r = .27$).

However, the strongest correlation in Table 15–1 is that between the number of kilograms of heroin seized by country and the number of terrorist organizations, supporting the theory that the illicit traffic in heroin, though not a "cause" of terrorism, may provide a funding source for terrorist organizations ($r = .39$).

Table 15-1 Number of Terrorist Organizations per Country by Selected Independent Variables

Percentage living in poverty	−0.13
Percentage unemployed	−0.06
Gini Index	−0.08
Lack of freedom	0.11
Percentage Islamic	0.27
Kilograms of heroin seized	0.39

PREVENTION AND CONTROL OF TERRORISM

After the World Trade Center and Pentagon terrorist attacks on September 11, President George W. Bush declared that a "War on Terrorism" would be the theme of his administration. Toward that goal, the United States launched an offensive against Afghanistan with the objective of killing or capturing Osama bin Laden and wiping out al-Qaeda, his terrorist organization. Subsequently, the United States invaded Iraq, capturing its President, Saddam Hussein, and killing his two sons, as well as countless numbers of military personnel and civilians in that country. During the period from 2001 to 2003, as discussed earlier, terrorist attacks actually increased. Still to be answered is whether America's military means of "counter-terrorism" have succeeded in lessening the threat of international terrorism to United States citizens. In this section, attention is directed to "what works" and what doesn't work in regard to programs to prevent and/or control terrorism.

Victims often suffer posttraumatic stress whenever they are the subject of crime, particularly a violent crime, and in a sense many Americans have suffered from a kind of posttraumatic stress after the events of September 11. First, they experienced the shocking loss of thousands of lives in a single act of mass murder. This was quickly followed by a sense of extreme vulnerability (to terrorism), not previously known to United States citizens. How could a group of only 19 individuals commit such atrocities, armed only with a determined will and box cutters as weapons? The September 11 killings were almost immediately followed by an Anthrax scare in which several people working for the government were victimized through exposure to powdered Anthrax, which was delivered anonymously via the U.S. mail.

The U.S. government response to both of these threats was swift and decisive. At 9:26 a.m. on September 11, all civilian air traffic was grounded as a deterrent to further attacks. Post office security measures were implemented. The Government Printing Office that produces the FBI's UCR and thousands of other government documents ceased doing any business by mail.

In addition, Congress very quickly put together the PATRIOT Act and the President developed a Department of Homeland Security to better coordinate law enforcement activities at the federal level.

Since the implementation of these reforms, international terrorist attacks have declined on U.S. soil. It is difficult to objectively assess the efficacy of these recent efforts in the long term, however. A look at terrorism control efforts in other countries may be insightful because those accounts can be viewed by us, as objective outsiders, more or less neutrally. The effort to evaluate

BOX 15-7

Belgium: The Epicenter of Terrorism in Europe

Since 2001, a significant number of terrorist plots in Europe were disrupted. Many of these plots had their roots in Belgium, with nearly every major thwarted terrorist plot within Europe traced in some fashion to Belgium. Because of Belgium's role in the diamond trade, as well as having one of the three busiest ports in Europe, funding for terrorism is seen as easily accessible. For a number of years, a major concern has been the proliferation of fraudulent Belgian identity documents. There have been entire criminal enterprises dedicated to handling stolen blank Belgian passports.

Stolen Belgian passports have been found in al-Qaeda safehouses all over Europe. Terrorist cells in Belgium have been able to grow due to the weaknesses in Belgium's bilingual criminal justice system and the manipulation of the pan-European trend of immigration by al-Qaeda cells. It is known that those engaging in terrorism have little to fear from an ill-equipped police force, and they know that if apprehended they will not be tortured, executed, or deported. The Belgium legal system is viewed as mild and meek. However, Belgium has undertaken successful programs to catalogue all the missing Belgium passports and issue new documents designed to reduce tampering, and Brussels has begun a tightening of its antiterror laws.[83]

efficacy of control procedures begins with a review of such procedures in foreign countries.

Improvements in the efficiency of a country's criminal justice system seem to have been a good starting point for terrorism control efforts. It should be pointed out that many European countries have centralized civil law systems (which America does not) making them in some ways more efficient criminal justice systems than the American system, even before reform measures were taken. The decentralization of American criminal justice, both in law enforcement and adjudication, is an issue that needs to be addressed.

West Germany, which has a civil law system, responded to terrorism in the mid 1970s with three levels of antiterrorist legislation. First, legislation was enacted in 1975 that improved and sped up the trial process and prevented the sabotage of trial proceedings by defendants or defense attorneys. In 1976, statutes were enacted making it a crime for anyone to organize so as to threaten the West German Constitution, and specific acts were identified as related to this crime. In 1978 legislation was enacted concerning search warrants, police checkpoints, apprehending suspects, and defense attorneys' conduct.[84] Similar reforms were instituted in Italy.[85] Subsequent research (done in 1980) indicated that terrorism was nearly under control in West Germany and Italy. Terrorists had been reduced to a fugitive status and the terrorist acts that occurred were aimed solely at freeing or improving the lot of already imprisoned terrorists. Particularly noteworthy for West Germany was the effectiveness of certain police and investigative techniques and strategies, particularly the use of small antiterrorist squads and detailed investigative patterns. Also mentioned was the successful West German coordination of state, federal, and international functions during a terrorist attack.[86] Terrorist activities were said to decline in Italy largely because of public disapproval; preventive action; emergency legislation that provided for harsher punishments and greater investigative powers for the police, prosecution, and judiciary; and collaboration on an international level between the police organizations and jurisdictional authorities of several countries.[87] A report critical of the American response to terrorism indicated that the United States suffered from Balkanization, meaning that responsibility for managing terrorism attacks is so divided among federal, state, and local agencies that it is frequently difficult to determine who is in charge.[88] By contrast, an international coordinating group known as TREVI (Terrorism, Radicalism, Extremism, International) dedicated to coordinating police action to combat terrorism was set up by the 12 member states of that organization back in 1975.[89]

A theme in the earlier analysis, particularly of effective antiterrorism measures in West Germany and Italy, has been the need for increasing effectiveness of the criminal justice system, as well as interagency and international cooperation and coordination. What seems to be suggested is the need for a "two-track" system of justice, one for common criminals and the other for terrorists. Thus, emergency legislation would apply to terrorists, providing swift justice, but with less regard to constitutional or due process concerns. In fact, Wolf indicated specifically that the vulnerability of democratic nations is that they lend credibility to terrorists' claim as legitimate political forces by not implementing legislation to eradicate the terrorists, fearing that rigid control measures would be viewed as a threat to civil liberties.[90]

Although our usual method of analysis is to profile a country that is high in its rate of a particular crime, we already did that in Chapter 12, with the topic of terrorism. Pakistan, the country profiled in Chapter 12, has the highest rate in the world in both heroin trafficking and the number of terrorist organizations in a single country. However, another country, Turkey, is worthy of study in terms of terrorism. Turkey is third in the world for heroin seized, below China and Pakistan. However, Turkey hosts only six terrorist organizations compared to over 10 times that many for Pakistan (67). Turkey has the same number of terrorist organizations as the United States (6). Turkey borders both Iraq and Iran, another reason to expect it might have a large number of terrorist organizations. Turkey provides a good contrast with the United States in terms of legal systems, because Turkey has a civil law system, and the United States has a common law system. Another factor to consider is that Turkey has been dealing with terrorism for a longer period of time than the United States.

In regard to the "nice guys finish last" critique of Western democracy, it might be valuable to compare the efficacy of antiterrorism efforts in Turkey with the United States. Turkey is a country that is struggling to be a democracy, while contending with a preponderantly Islamic population and at least six terrorist organizations within its territory. The United States is a country with a democratic tradition of over 200 years, a preponderant Christian population, but also a country that is contending with at least six terrorist organizations within its borders. Turkey developed an Anti-Terrorism Act in 1991, 10 years before the USA PATRIOT Act was developed by the United States Congress after the September 11 attacks in 2001. Thus, Turkey has some 10 years of experience utilizing an act similar to the USA PATRIOT Act in combating terrorism. Turkey's experience may be useful in the development of America's terrorism control efforts.

COUNTRY PROFILE: TURKEY

In many ways, terrorism has been a much greater problem in Turkey, and over a longer period of time, than it has been in the United States. There are as many terrorist organizations in Turkey as in the United States, and yet Turkey has a population one fourth that of the United States. Most important, Turkey has, since the 1920s, been struggling to become a parliamentary democracy and to be admitted to the European Union (EU).

Westerners may think of Turkey as an Islamic country where the women all wear veils and the men wear turbans. They may also think of

Turkey as a country in which travelers caught with drugs will be subject to barbaric punishments in prison, as dramatized in the movie *Midnight Express*. Though 99.8% of the population are of Muslim faith (mostly Sunni), religious head coverings were banned by law 50 years ago, and the government continues to enforce this ban at universities and in public buildings. Although torture may continue to be used by the police in Turkey today, beatings and other severe punishment in prison have decreased considerably in Turkey in recent years.

Ataturk and "Kemalism"

Before World War I, Istanbul, formerly Constantinople, a city in northwestern Turkey, was the capital of the Byzantine Empire, and subsequently the Ottoman Empire, which controlled vast stretches of North Africa, southeastern Europe, and Western Asia, including Iraq, Syria, Iran, Saudi Arabia, Tunisia, and Algeria. The Ottoman Empire sided with Germany during WWI and lost territories as a result of the loss to the allies. After the war, a nationalist movement headed by Mustafa Kemal, a Turkish WWI hero later known as "Ataturk," founded the Republic of Turkey in 1923. Ataturk ousted the Greek forces and abolished the temporal and religious ruling institutions of the old Ottoman Empire. He instigated many reforms, known as "Kemalism," favoring secularism, nationalism, and modernism, turning to the West for inspiration and support. Kemalism resulted in abolishment of Sharia law and in 1925 veils and turbans were banned in public places. A civil legal system, based upon the Swiss Civil Code, the Italian Penal Code, and the Swiss Code of Civil Procedure, was instituted in 1926. Women were given the right to vote in 1930. Turkey sided with the allies near the end of WWII and became a charter member of the United Nations. Under the Truman Doctrine of 1947, Turkey received guarantees of security by the United States and large-scale U.S. military and economic aid. Turkey joined the North Atlantic

Mustafa Kemal Ataturk (1881–1938), a Turkish general, nationalist leader, and the first President of Turkey. In the 1920s, Ataturk emerged as a charismatic military commander who crushed the Greek invaders of his country, leading the nation to full independence. As President, he put an end to the six-century-old Ottoman dynasty and created the Republic of Turkey in 1923. He then transformed the country's legal system whereby religious laws were abolished and a secular system of jurisprudence (Kemalism) was introduced.

Source: Getty Images, Inc.–Hulton Archive Photos.

Treaty Organization (NATO) in 1952 and is currently an EU candidate. Today Turkey is a constitutional republic with a multiparty parliament.

From 1984 to 1999, the Turkish government engaged in armed conflict with the terrorist Kurdistan Workers Party (PKK), whose goal was the formation of a separate state (Kurdistan) in southeastern Turkey. Despite the end of the war, a state of emergency, declared in 1987, continued in the four southeastern provinces that faced substantial PKK terrorist violence. Under this state of emergency, the regional governor may exercise certain quasi-martial law powers. It is in exercising these powers that the police in Turkey have allegedly committed human rights abuses, including torture.

 Although incommunicado detention facilitated the use of torture in the past, its use has declined along with the decline in PKK violence. Recurrent terrorist incidents, however, have helped to perpetuate the practice of torture. During 2001, the European Court of Human Rights ruled against Turkey in eight cases in which 18 persons had been killed in detention or taken into custody and then disappeared. Commonly employed methods of torture include: systematic beatings; stripping and blindfolding; exposure to extreme cold or high-pressure cold water hoses; electric shocks; beatings on the soles of feet and genitalia; hanging by the arms; food and sleep deprivation; heavy weights hung on the body; water dripped onto the head; near-suffocation by placing bags over the head; vaginal and anal rape with truncheons and, in some instances, gun barrels; squeezing and twisting of the testicles; and other form of sexual abuse.

Terrorism in Turkey

Official statistics in Turkey indicated a doubling of prison admissions between 1984 and 1991. This increase was due almost entirely to a rapid rise in the number of persons jailed "according to special laws," meaning those convicted of terrorism or illegal political activity. While the number of prison admissions in numerous categories of ordinary crime, actually fell from 1984 to 1991 the number entering prisons under special laws rose rapidly, from 7,514 in 1985 to 32,645 in 1991. This period corresponded to the spiraling Kurdish dissidence and the strict laws then in effect dealing with "thought crimes." This period of rising terrorism culminated in the Anti-Terror Law of 1991. Although this law formally ended capital punishment and nullified the "thought crimes" articles of the penal code, it introduced a broad and ambiguous definition of terrorism. This enabled the government to use the law not only to combat alleged terrorism but also to impose sentences of two to five years on ordinary citizens for written and oral propaganda, as well as meetings and demonstrations aimed at "damaging the indivisible unity of the state." This law also gave legal sanction to incognito detention. Although persons detained for individual crimes under the Anti-Terror Law must be brought before a judge within 48 hours, anyone charged with crimes of a collective political or conspiratorial nature may be detained for up to 15 days (and up to 30 days in the 10 southeastern provinces) under a state of emergency declared in early 1995. The law does not guarantee access to counsel and leaves the decision to prosecutors, who routinely deny access. Persons accused of terrorism are tried in one of eight state security courts, each composed of five members—two civilian judges, one military judge, and two prosecutors. There is no jury, the hearings can be closed, and testimony gathered during police interrogation in absence of counsel may be admitted.

Anti-Terror Law of 1991

Narcoterrorism
It is believed that funding for insurgency activity by the PKK is supported by the narcotics trade. Turkey plays a major role in moving heroin and hashish from Pakistan, Afghanistan, and Iran to destinations in Europe. In spite of Turkey's efforts, it is believed that little of the heroin passing through the country is seized because of insufficient staff to screen cargoes adequately, particularly at the key transfer point of Istanbul. As much as 75% of the heroin seized in Europe has a "Turkish connection," having either passed through Turkey, been processed there, or been seized in connection with Turkish criminal syndicates.

Thus, the cycle of terrorism funded by the illicit drug trade (which leads to torture by the police and other oppressive aspects of the criminal justice system) will continue to challenge Turkey's desire to be accepted as a democratic nation-state.[91]

Commentary on Turkey
Looking at the numbers, Turkey, although it has six active terrorist organizations within its borders, seems to have avoided the proliferation of terrorist cells that has occurred in Pakistan. It may be remembered that, during the 1970s, in Pakistan the right-wing government of Muhammad Zia ul-Haq attempted to move the country in the direction of "Islamization." Zia's plan had the unintended effect of fomenting factionalism and increasing the number of terrorist organizations, many of which evolved as religious sects within that country. However, since Ataturk's Kemaism movement toward modernism and a secular state, religion and the state remain separate in Turkey. While tough legislation and punitive treatment may have been a factor in suppressing the violence of terrorist groups, the separation of religion and state may have been the major reason that terrorist groups did not proliferate in Turkey.

The previous paragraph is a description of modern Turkey. Turkey has been routinely criticized by developed nations, including those in the EU, and the United States in its Human Rights Reports, for its treatment of prisoners. But consider the behavior of officers from a developed nation who took suspects into custody in a Mideast country (see Text Box 15–8).

As may have been guessed, these are quotes from the International Committee of the Red Cross (ICRC) on the treatment by U.S. and Coalition forces of prisoners of war in Iraq. Much of the abuse took place at the "Abu Ghraib Correctional Facility." The report indicated that coalition military intelligence officials estimated that 70% to 90% of prisoners detained had been arrested by mistake. Thus, they were neither "enemy combatants" nor "prisoners of war." The behavior of coalition interrogators and guards was reported, with photos and videotapes, by CBS News on April 28, 2004. It is evident from this report that even officials from a developed country such as the United States could engage in the barbarous behavior that has long been associated with Turkish prisons.

Although it may be true that these activities occurred during a military campaign in Iraq, what is illustrated is that these behaviors may very well be "normal" or at least routine responses in dealing with terrorists (or perceived terrorists). Because the terrorists use "any means necessary" to achieve their goals, then counter-terrorism often involves "fighting fire with fire," in essence using terrorism to counter terrorism. Evidence for the view that torture may be defined by the public as normal, or at least justifiable, is given in a Fox News opinion poll taken in March 2003. Respondents were asked whether they favored or opposed allowing the government to use any means necessary, including torture, to obtain information from prisoners to protect the United States from terrorist

BOX 15–8

International Red Cross Report on Torture

Reportedly, "arresting authorities entered houses after dark, breaking down doors, waking up residents roughly, yelling orders, forcing family members into one room under military guard. . . . Sometimes they arrested all adult males present in a house, including elderly, handicapped or sick people." Subsequently, when the suspects were taken to detention centers, "the methods of ill-treatment exhibited most frequently during interrogation included:

- Hooding, used to prevent people from seeing and to disorient them, and also to prevent from breathing freely;
- Beatings with hard objects (including pistols and rifles), slapping, punching, kicking with knees or feet on various parts of the body (legs, sides, lower back, groin);
- Pressing the face into the ground with boots;

- Being stripped naked for several days while held in solitary confinement in an empty and completely dark cell that included a latrine;
- Being paraded naked outside cells in front of other persons deprived of their liberty, and guards, sometimes hooded or with women's underwear over the head;
- Being attached repeatedly over several days, for several hours each time, with handcuffs to the bars of their cell door in humiliating (i.e., naked or in underwear) and/or uncomfortable position causing physical pain;
- Exposure while hooded to loud noise or music, prolonged exposure while hooded to sun over several hours, including the hottest time of the day when temperatures could reach 122 degrees Fahrenheit or higher.
- Being forced to remain for prolonged periods in stress positions such as squatting or standing with or without the arms lifted."[92]

attack.[93] The largest percentage (44%) favored the use of torture, whereas 42% opposed it. Of the remainder, 5% said it depends, and 9% were unsure.

It may be useful to examine the responses that have been taken by the United States government since the September 11 attacks. The skyjacking of passenger airlines and subsequent destruction of the World Trade Center Twin Towers and part of the Pentagon Building led to a state of fear in America, as well as a frenzy of legislation, both at the state and federal level, to combat terrorism. Probably the most significant piece of legislation was the USA PATRIOT Act. Some analysis of that legislation and its consequences would be useful in more fully understanding the control measures that have been taken in the United States.

BOX 15–9

Does Terrorism Work?

A hero to modern Algerian nationalists, Abd al-Qadar was an Islamic holy man who, from 1834 to 1847, used hit-and-run tactics to oppose the French, who annexed Algeria in 1834. It was not until after al-Qadar was subdued in 1847 that France colonized Algeria. The French colonists, though a numerical minority, became elites in Algeria. They developed a modern economy, producing wine and citrus fruit crops for export to France. The Muslims were a growing numerical majority and suffered subjugation by the French. During the 1950s, the National Liberation Front (FLN) sought Algerian independence through coordinated attacks on public buildings, military and police posts, and communications installations. The FLN strategy combined Abd al-Qadir's guerrilla tactics with deliberate use of terrorism, immobilizing superior French forces and, with murders and kidnappings, creating a climate of fear. The French responded by bringing in reinforcements of 400,000 French troops to wage counterterrorism by raiding Muslim villages and slaughtering the civilian population. Ultimately, the French government and General Charles De Gaulle, the wartime leader of the Free French, faced with international criticism of the brutal counter-terrorist tactics, realized that the war with terrorists was unwinnable. In 1962 a cease-fire was arranged between government and FLN representatives, and a referendum was held in Algeria in which the vote was overwhelmingly for independence. The French citizens began a mass evacuation, and most had left the country before the end of the year.[94]

The USA PATRIOT Act actually refers to an acronym for its full name, the Uniting and Strengthening America by Providing Appropriate Tools Required to Intercept and Obstruct Terrorism Act. This bill was passed on October 24, 2001, only five weeks after the terrorist attacks on September 11. This was emergency legislation with sunset provisions that became inactive on December 31, 2005. The bill was 342 pages long and was difficult to read because it consisted largely of amendments of more than 15 different federal statutes, which the reader would also need to have access to in order to make sense of the bill. The bill essentially strengthened the FBI's ability to pursue terrorists and augmented that agency's technical and tactical operations support by $200 million for each of the fiscal years 2002, 2003, and 2004. It also augmented the President's emergency powers, such that any person, including citizens of the United States, can be identified by the President as an "enemy combatant," subject to indefinite preventive detention. Persons so identified by the President can be held without representation by an attorney and without their identities being made public for the duration of the war on terror. Since the war on terror may go on for a long time, such individuals could be detained for an indefinite period of time, conceivably for life.

The USA PATRIOT Act strengthened the FBI's ability to engage in surveillance to identify terrorists and to gather more complete evidence against them. It also increased the likelihood of gaining a conviction against them.

The USA PATRIOT Act is broad in its scope. The bill allows preventive detention of noncitizen terrorist suspects, it permits nationwide execution of warrants in terrorism cases, it outlaws money-laundering in the United States of proceeds from cybercrime, and it prohibits individuals from supporting terrorist organizations and from participating in foreign crimes of violence or political corruption.

Most controversial of the bill's provisions are those having to do with surveillance. Under the bill, "sneak and peek" search warrants allow officers to search the home of suspected criminals, plant listening devices, and seize physical objects or electronic communications without telling the target of the investigation until an unspecified later time. It permits "roving" surveillance of persons rather than particular telephones, allowing investigators to listen to any phone the target might use. Lastly, it expands the government's ability to look at records of an individual's activity being held by a third party, such as doctors, bookstores, universities, and even Internet service providers.[95]

Arguments in Favor of the USA PATRIOT Act

Since its passage, the USA PATRIOT Act has been the subject of debate, both pro and con. A Department of Justice Website has compiled a comprehensive list of arguments favorable to the Act, as follows.

Congress enacted the USA PATRIOT Act by overwhelming, bipartisan margins, arming law enforcement with new tools to detect and prevent terrorism: The USA PATRIOT Act was passed nearly unanimously by the Senate 98-1, and 357–66 in the House, with the support of legislators from across the political spectrum.

The Act improves our counter-terrorism efforts in several significant ways:

1. The PATRIOT Act allows investigators to use the tools that were already available to investigate organized crime and drug trafficking. The act

(a) allows law enforcement to use surveillance against more crimes of terror; (b) allows federal agents to follow sophisticated terrorists trained to evade detection . . . able to use "roving wiretaps"; (c) allows law enforcement to conduct investigations without tipping off terrorists, using delayed notification search warrants; (d) allows federal agents to ask a court for an order to obtain business records in national security terrorism cases.

2. The PATRIOT Act facilitates information sharing and cooperation among government agencies so that they can better "connect the dots" . . . enabling the law enforcement, intelligence, and national defense communities to talk and coordinating their work

3. The PATRIOT Act updated the law to reflect new technologies and new threats. . . . Allows law enforcement officials to obtain a search warrant anywhere a terrorist-related activity occurred. . . . Allows victims of computer hacking to request law enforcement assistance in monitoring the "trespassers" on their computers.

4. The PATRIOT Act increased the penalties for those who commit terrorist crimes. The act prohibits the harboring of terrorists. It enhanced the maximum penalties for various crimes likely to be committed by terrorists, including arson, destruction of energy facilities, providing material support to terrorists and terrorist organizations, and destruction of national defense materials. It enhanced a number of conspiracy penalties, including for arson, killings in federal facilities, attacking communications systems, material support to terrorists, sabotage of nuclear facilities, and interference with [airline] flight crew members. The act punishes terrorist attacks on mass transit systems. It punishes bioterrorists. It eliminates the statutes of limitations for certain terrorism crimes and lengthens them for other terrorist crimes.[96]

Arguments against the USA PATRIOT Act

The major criticism of the USA PATRIOT Act, as well as its successor, PATRIOT Act II, has been from organizations and individuals concerned with civil liberties for citizens of the United States. They have expressed concern about the potential erosion of civil liberties that the acts invite. There has also been concern about human rights losses for noncitizens of the United States. In some cases, actual examples of the loss of civil liberties by U.S. citizens and/or human rights for noncitizens have been alleged. The following is a partial list of such arguments and allegations:

- According to Human Rights Watch, "the country has witnessed a persistent, deliberate, and unwarranted erosion of basic rights against abusive governmental power that are guaranteed by the U.S. Constitution and international rights law . . . government practices including the secret incarceration of post-September 11 detainees and immigration proceedings closed to the public; custodial interrogations without access to counsel; arbitrary prolonged confinement including detention without charge; as well as the deplorable conditions—including solitary confinement—as well as the physical abuse to which some detainees have been subjected . . . questioning led to the arrest and incarceration of as many as 1,200 non-citizens although the exact number remains uncertain. Of those arrested, 752 were charged with immigration violations. Arresting persons of interest in the September 11 investigation on immigration charges, such as overstaying a visa, enabled the Department of Justice to keep them jailed while it continued investigating and interrogating them about possible criminal activities—a form of preventive detention not permissible under U.S. criminal law. . . . While the alleged visa violations provided a lawful basis for seeking to deport these noncitizens, the Justice Department's actions constituted an end run around constitutional and international legal requirements governing criminal investigations. . . . While an immigration law violation may justify deportation, it does not in itself justify detention after arrest . . . only if there is evidence of the individual's dangerousness or risk of flight. In effect, 'special interest' detainees have been presumed guilty until law enforcement agents concluded otherwise."[97] The report further stated that "The U.S. government has not charged a single one of the thousand-plus individuals detained after September 11 for crimes related to terrorism."[98]

- In specific rebuttal to the arguments given in the Department of Justice Website cited earlier, Jim Dempsey of The Center for Democracy and Technology made several points.[99] First, he said that Congress acted under intense pressure and without serious debate and deliberation when it passed the PATRIOT Act. "leaving members and their staff with literally not enough time to read what was in the lengthy bill." Second, that the Justice Department "had the ability to use wiretaps, including roving traps, in criminal investigations of terrorism, just as in other criminal investigations, long before the PATRIOT Act." However, Dempsey said that he objected to the standard for sneak and peek searches in the PATRIOT Act because "the standard is so loose that it could arguably be used in almost every criminal case." Further, Section 215 of the USA PATRIOT Act "permits the FBI to obtain a side range of business records—including library, bookstore, medical, travel and other records—in any intelligence investigation, under a legal standard so low that it essentially results in a judicial rubber stamp. The FBI doesn't even have to name the person whose records it is seeking, but rather it can sweep up entire data bases indiscriminately." In regard to the facilitation of information sharing and cooperation among government agencies, the Center indicated, "In fact, there was never a legal bar to intelligence agencies sharing information with prosecutors. Intelligence and law enforcement officials weren't sharing information and using their existing powers not because of legal barriers, but because of their overly strict interpretation of then-existing law, cultural problems, and turf wars among agencies."

- In July, 2003, the American Civil Liberties Union filed the first lawsuit against the USA PATRIOT Act, claiming that Section 215 of the law is unconstitutional because it "vastly expands the power of the FBI to obtain records and other 'tangible things' of people not suspected of criminal activity." "To obtain a Section 214 order, the FBI needs only assert that the records or personal belongings are 'sought for' an ongoing foreign intelligence, counterintelligence, or international terrorism investigation." "The FBI is not required to show probable cause—or any reason—to believe that the target of the order is a criminal suspect or foreign agent." Although the results of the lawsuit are pending, "the House of Representatives voted to bar the Justice Department from executing such searches under the act."[100]

- Columnist Wayne Madsen of *The Miami Herald* argued that, because of its vagueness, the PATRIOT Act could be used to deprive citizens who engage in "eco-terrorism" of their constitutional rights.[101] He said that "Congress hastily passed the anti-terrorist PATRIOT Act in October 2001 during a time when it was under siege by a real bio-terror anthrax attack. . . . Following an arson attack against a condominium under construction in San Diego, the vandalism of sport utility vehicles in four Los Angeles area auto dealerships and the freeing of 10,000 minks from a farm near Seattle, the Justice Department is labeling such attacks 'eco-terrorism.' " He added that "It is a hallmark of totalitarian regimes around the world to elevate simple crimes to 'crimes against the state.' . . . But to argue that these groups pose the same level of threat as al-Qaeda and Jemaah Islamiya is ludicrous. The environmental vandals are not in the category of worldwide networks that aim to kill thousands by setting off bombs and releasing dangerous toxins. . . . If Ashcroft and his friends get their way and pass new anti-terrorist legislation, American citizens who support environmental causes could find themselves declared as 'enemy combatants,' thrown into the brig without having the right to see a lawyer and, according to one provision in a version of the proposed Patriot II, could have their U.S. citizenship taken away, even if they are native born." Lastly, Madsen argued that, "Those who spray-paint cars are not terrorists. There are state and local laws on the books to deal with vandalism. Setting buildings on fire is arson, and we have plenty of laws to deal with arsonists. Freeing minks that then go about eating parakeets and chickens, although abhorrent, does not constitute terrorism."
- It has been further argued with regard to the unanimity with which Congress passed the USA PATRIOT Act, that three states and a large number of cities and counties (including Los Angeles and New York City) have approved resolutions calling for a repeal of the act.[102]
- Professor of Law Patricia Williams maintained that the USA PATRIOT Act would enable spying on citizens and noncitizens alike, and that it would enable profiling based on looks and ethnicity, detention without charges, searches without warrants, and even torture and assassination. Further, she argued that preventing surprise attacks of such sophistication may never be possible anyway.[103]
- While many Americans may be comfortable with the fact that the USA PATRIOT Act has predominantly been used in regard to noncitizens, there have been cases in which innocent American citizens have become subject to its provisions. These are the subject of the text box.

In remarks before a Town Hall meeting in Austin, Texas on Tuesday, September 16, 2003, William Rivers Pitt made the following comments on the USA PATRIOT Act: "If you murder the idea that is America, you have murdered America itself. You can keep all of our roads, our cities, our crops, our people, our armies—you can keep all that, but if you murder the fundamental idea that is America, you have murdered America itself in a way that ten thousand September 11ths could never do. No terrorist can end this country. No terrorist can destroy the ideals we hold dear. Only we can do that, we who are most comforted by that blanket of freedom, and I fear that we have begun to do so with the passage of this thing they call the PATRIOT Act. There are

BOX 15-10

Worst Case Scenario

Waking up with his wife dead was only the beginning of Steve Kurtz's troubles. Within a few days of her untimely passing, the FBI had raided his Buffalo home. Health workers dressed in hazmat moon suits had turned the place into a quarantine zone. Now, Kurtz's livelihood may be in jeopardy, too. Kurtz is a University of Buffalo professor and artist specializing in biotechnology-inspired works: "subversive remixes" of big pharma corporate materials, and kits to see if food is genetically modified. Chicago's Museum of Contemporary Art, New York's New Museum, and the Corcoran Gallery in Washington, DC, displayed his art. . . . Earlier this month [May 2004], Kurtz woke up to find his wife, Hope, dead of apparent heart failure. In shock, he called the police. But when the officers came over, they saw strange things: test tubes, Bunsen burners, Petri dishes, and the like. So they brought in the local counter-terror task force and the FBI. Kurtz was detained on the way to the funeral home. His house was cordoned off, while the county health department searched for chemical or biological agents. . . . And Kurtz's equipment was all confiscated, for further testing and investigation. The artist was planning to use some of that gear in a new show at the Massachusetts Museum of Contemporary Art, slated to open Sunday. . . . Other works—including a book in progress—are also on hold. And Kurtz has a $10,000 mountain of legal bills; he's retained celebrity lawyer Paul Cambria (Larry Flynt and DMX's defender) to represent him.[104]

hundreds and hundreds of sections to the PATRIOT Act. My personal favorite is Section 213. Legal scholars have dubbed this the "Sneak and Peek" provision. Section 213 of the PATRIOT Act gives authority to agents of the Federal government to enter your home, search your belongings, tap your phone, tap your computer so every keystroke and Website and email is recorded. They can do this without getting a warrant, and without ever letting you know they were there."[105]

BOX 15-11

How the Drug Trade Sponsored Terrorism in Afghanistan, Uzbekistan, and Tajikistan

There is evidence of a direct link between the drug trade and terrorist activities of the Islamic Movement of Uzbekistan (IMU) in Afghanistan, Uzbekistan, and Tajikistan. In 1991, some unemployed young Muslims seized the Communist Party headquarters in the eastern Uzbekistan city of Namangan, in retaliation for the mayor's refusal to give them land on which to build a mosque. The leaders of this group were Tohir Yuldeshev and Jumaboi Khojaev. Yuldeshev was a 24-year-old college dropout and well-known mullah (religious cleric) in the Islamic underground movement. Khojaev was a former Soviet paratrooper who had fought against the mujahidin in Afghanistan and gained a high regard for them during that experience. Khojaev later adopted the alias Juma Namangani and eventually fled to Tajikistan after the splinter movement, Adolat, founded by Yuldeshev and Khojaev, was banned by Uzbekistan's President Karimov. In Tajikistan, Namangani fought in the civil war, and after the civil war, settled with his family and some 50 of his supporters at a farm in the village of Hoit. There he allegedly became involved in the transportations of heroin as a way of feeding his growing camp of followers, which included many of Central Asia's Islamic radicals. Proceeds from drug smuggling were used to finance the group which, in 1998, became known as the Islamic Movement of Uzbekistan (IMU). The organization reportedly handles 70% of the heroin and opium traffic through Central Asia. The IMU's creation was announced from Kabul by Namangani and Yuldeshev, where Yuldeshev met Osama bin Laden. Osama bin Laden is believed by the United States to have provided most of the funding for setting up the IMU. During the years 1999, 2000, and 2001, the IMU carried on various punitive terrorist campaigns in Uzbeklistan, Kyrgyzistan, and Tajikistan including car bombings and kidnappings.[106]

On March 9, 2006, President Bush signed the USA PATRIOT Improvement and Reauthorization Act of 2005. The Senate had rejected attempts to reauthorize the key surveillance provisions of the USA PATRIOT Act. The 16 provisions in question included those authorizing secret searches of records and roving wire-taps. These provisions (including sections 201, 202, 203(b), 206, 207, 209, 212, 214, 215, 217, 218, 220, 223, 224, and 225) are set to expire December 31, 2006.[107] However, the Reauthorization Act has been criticized for a new provision—*SEC. 605. THE UNIFORMED DIVISION, UNITED STATES SECRET SERVICE*—that actually creates a "secret police."[108] Section 605 reads as follows:

> There is hereby created and established a permanent police force, to be known as the "United States Secret Service Uniformed Division." Subject to the supervision of the Secretary of Homeland Security, the United States Secret Service Uniformed Division shall perform such duties as the Director, United States Secret Service, may prescribe. . . .[109]

USA PATRIOT Improvement and Reauthorization Act of 2006

SUMMARY AND CONCLUSION

The chapter opened with an interview with a terrorist—Ismail Abu Shanab—who was described as a "really nice guy," an engineer who went to college in Colorado. This case study included statements made in interviews done in 2000 and 2002. Ismail, described as a "moderate" Hamas leader, advocated co-existence between Israel and Palestine. Ismail maintained that "human bomb" terrorism was done out of a fatalistic sense that the bomber is going to die anyway. He maintained that the Israelis had invaded, and continue to occupy, Palestine with support of colonial powers, including the United States. Most significant, he believed the September 11 World Trade Center and Pentagon attacks were backed by the Israelis to get the United States to help fight enemies of the Israelis—including Saddam Hussein. Ismail was killed by an Israeli missile attack in 2003.

One problem with terrorism is that it is ambiguously defined, even in definitions used by the FBI. A definition of terrorism used by the Terrorism Research Center narrows the definition to "the systematic use of violence against non-combatants to instill a climate of fear." This definition is, in a sense, both delimiting and more general—delimiting in the sense that it excludes property crimes and acts of war, but more general in the sense that it can include age-old tactics such as the deliberate bombing of civilians used even by the United States and its allies during WWII. Thus, it does not denote merely Islamic terrorism.

Terrorist attacks have increased sizably since the 1970s, and the plurality have been directed against United States citizens abroad—especially diplomats and persons doing business. While "traditional terrorism" was Marxist-Leninist in ideology, since the dissolution of the Soviet Union, the "new terrorism" has been inspired by the Islamic faith. Along with this trend has been increasing lethality, as exemplified by the September 11 attacks. However, Islamic terrorism is still only one of countless forms of terrorism today, including revolutionary, political, nationalist, cause-based, environmental, criminal, religious, enforcement, maverick, splinter, and even psychotic terrorism. The United States must confront not just Islamic terrorism, but terrorism done by the "unibomber," Theodore Kaczynski, the unsolved anthrax distribution killings that took place immediately after the September 11 attacks, and potential terrorism by the United States government itself (counter-terrorism).

Profiling studies reveal that "typical terrorists" differ from "common criminals" in being single males, from a college or university background, and in professions such as engineering or medicine. They are described as narcissistic, marginalized, alienated, and imbued with a radical belief system, frequently acquired during university years. The profile seems to fit Osama bin Laden. The significance of bin Laden is that he personally has organized terrorist groups, normally consisting of small isolated cells, into a worldwide multinational organization, thousands strong.

Explanations of terrorism, including poverty, unemployment, inequality, social injustice, Islamic fundamentalism, and the War on Drugs are examined through use of correlation analysis. Poverty, unemployment, and inequality were not correlated with the number of terrorist organizations in a country. However, measures of social injustice, percentage of Islamic population of a country, and kilograms of heroin seized were positively correlated with the number of terrorist organizations, with the last measure being the strongest ($r = .39$). To prevent and control terrorism in the United States, the literature seems to point to streamlining and centralizing the criminal justice system in dealing with terrorism, goals being sought in the USA PATRIOT Act and the development of the Department of Homeland Security. However, critics of these measures have cautioned that authoritarian state tactics may be the outcome, as exemplified by the abusive interrogation and detention procedures used at Abu Graib Correctional Facility by Coalition forces in Iraq. It is not known what abuses have occurred with some 1,200 persons detained under the USA PATRIOT Act because their detention is shrouded in secrecy.

The United States can benefit from the experience of other countries in fighting terrorism, namely Turkey. Turkey has been a parliamentary democracy since the 1920s, but has had to combat terrorism within its borders, particularly that of a Kurdish separatist organization, the PKK. The use of torture and incommunicado detention by Turkish authorities has drawn disapproval of Turkey by human rights organizations. PKK terrorism in Turkey appears to draw financial support from the drug trade, particularly in heroin and hashish, which are trafficked through Turkey with European destinations. The drug trade appears to fund not only Turkish terrorism, but also terrorism in the South Asian countries of Afghanistan, Pakistan, and Iran, where al-Qaeda is most active.

Thus, for both Turkey and the United States, efforts to combat terrorism invite a re-examination of policy regarding the War on Drugs. Some of the goals of the War on Drugs have been incompatible with the goals of the War on Terrorism. Drug interdiction efforts, it would seem, have in reality resulted in higher prices on the international drug market for the contraband trafficked in the drug trade, particularly heroin. It might be appropriate, comparing the magnitude of the threat of international terrorism with that offered by heroin abuse, to consider a reorientation of policy in regard to heroin trafficking. To cut the profit from the heroin trade that can be used to fund terrorism, it might be worthwhile to consider approaches to the problem of heroin abuse other than interdiction efforts. An example of such alternative procedures is broadening the use of heroin prescription programs for registered heroin addicts. Such programs have been the favorable subject of experimentation in Switzerland and a growing number of European countries.[110]

Cutting off the funding for terrorist organizations is just the first step in reducing the threat of terrorism. It is also the first step in reducing the "siege mentality" that has led to antidemocratic counterterrorism measures in democratic countries like the United States, as well as countries that are aspiring to have democratic governments, such as Turkey.

DISCUSSION QUESTIONS

1. What do you think of (terrorist case study) Ismail Abu Shanab's characterization of Israel and his characterization of Hamas members as "freedom fighters" rather than terrorists?

2. Were you surprised at Steve Kangas's allegations that the CIA has used covert measures in foreign countries to install right-wing dictators who would support American business interests? If you don't believe Kangas's allegations, explain why. If you do, how do you relate his allegations to terrorism in the world today?

3. How can terrorism be distinguished from "acts of resistance" or "freedom fighting" during occupation by a foreign country?

4. In terms of extent of victimization, how do U.S. citizens traveling in foreign countries compare with citizens of other countries? Please explain why you think this is so.

5. What have been the trends in terrorism during the last two decades of the 20th century? How do you account for these trends?

6. In the correlation analysis in Table 15–1, what variables showed the strongest correlation with the number of terrorist organizations in a country? How do you account for these correlations?

7. Do you think that civil law countries, such as Germany and Italy, were swifter and more

effective in curbing terrorism than the United States has been? Why or why not?

8. What aspects of the U.S. criminal justice system, in your opinion, need to be improved to cope with the threat of terrorism? What needs to be done to improve them?

SUGGESTED WEBSITES

http://www.terrorism.com/modules.php?op=modload & name=Countries & file=index Website that lists terrorism events and terrorist organizations by country.

http://conspiracyarchive.com/ Website describing a large number of conspiracy theories, such as "How the CIA created Osama bin Laden," "Operation Paperclip," and so forth.

http://www.globalterrorism101.com/UTTerroristCells .html Website for *World Conflict Quarterly*—News, analysis, and articles on terrorists and terrorism.

http://www.serendipity.li/cia/cia_time.htm Website of Steve Kangas, Timeline of CIA Atrocities, summarized briefly in this chapter.

ENDNOTES

1. Hummel, 2000; Shanab & Hilder, 2002.

2. McGreal, 2003.

3. Gerber, 2001.

4. Hartwig, 2001.

5. Head, 2002.

6. Falcone, 2005, p. 200.

7. Beirne & Messerschmidt, 1995, p. 286.

8. Bashford, 1999.

9. Kangas, 1999.

10. Kangas, 2002.

11. Ratcliffe, 1999. A document declassified in 1977, Appendix C of the National Security Code (NSC 542), entitled the National Security Council directive on covert operations defined "covert operations" as "all activities conducted pursuant to this directive which are so planned and executed that any U.S. Government responsibility for them is not evident to unauthorized persons and that if uncovered the U.S. Government can plausibly disclaim any responsibility for them. Specifically, such operations shall include any covert activities related to: propaganda, political action; economic warfare; preventive direct action, including sabotage, anti-sabotage, demolition; escape and evasion and evacuation measures; subversion against hostile states or groups including assistance to underground resistance movements, guerrillas and refugee liberation groups; support of indigenous and anti-communist elements in threatened countries of the free world; deceptive plans and operations; and all activities compatible with this directive necessary to accomplish the foregoing. Such operations shall not include: armed conflict by recognized military forces, espionage and counterespionage, nor cover any deception for military operations."

12. Pike, 1996.

13. *ConspiracyArchive.com*, 1999.

14. Wolf, 2004.

15. *CNN.com*, 1995.

16. Wikipedia, 2005a.

17. Constantine, 2000.

18. Potter, 2005b.

19. Wolf, 1999.

20. Elliston, 1996.

21. Doyle & Kornbluh, 1997.

22. Boylan, 2003.

23. Simon & Eitzen, 1993, p. 81.

24. Simon & Eitzen, 1993, p. 81.

25. Potter, 2005a.

26. Kwitny, 1987; McCoy, 1972.

27. Kwitney, 1987, p. 51.

28. Friends of Liberty, 2002.

29. Potter, 2005b.

30. Cockburn, 1987, p. 17.

31. Reith, 1975.

32. FBI, 1999, p. i.

33. FBI, 1999, p. ii.

34. Terrorism Research Center, 2004.

35. Carr, 2002.

36. Mollaret, 2002.

37. Hazelip, 1980.

38. Nettler, 1982.

39. *Executive Protection and International and Transnational Terrorism,* 1981.

40. McGuire, 1979.

41. Alexander & Kilmarx, 1979.

42. U.S Senate Committee on Labor and Human Resources Subcommittee on Alcoholism and Drug Abuse, 1984.

43. Mueller & Adler, 1985.

44. Rand Corporation, 2003.

45. Hoffman, 1999.

46. FBI, 1999, p. ii.

47. Rayne, 1977.

48. Cooper, 1978.

49. Comparative Criminology Website: Sri Lanka.

50. Wolf, 1981.

51. Kushner, 1998.

52. Pluchinsky, 1998.

53. Benard, 1994.

54. Allen, 1996.

55. Siegel, 2004, pp. 355–359.

56. Bodansky, 2001.

57. Glueck & Glueck, 1950.

58. *WordReference.com,* 2005.

59. Frontline, 2001—anonymous interview.

60. Dixon, 2001.

61. Russell & Miller, 1977.

62. Kampf, 1980.

63. Pearlstein, 1991.

64. Juergensmeyer, 2000.

65. Levine, 1999.

66. Chretien, 2002.

67. Nedoroscik, 2002.

68. Parry, 1976.

69. Taylor, 1978.

70. Hippchen, 1981.

71. Georges, 1981.

72. Robinson, 2001.

73. Comparative Criminology Website: Lebanon.

74. Wisotsky, 1983.

75. Clutterbuck, 1995.

76. Jenkins, 1981; Sterling, 1981.

77. Wolf, 1989.

78. Central Intelligence Agency, 2002.

79. In the table developed by Freedom House (1999), scoring was done by a survey team at Freedom House. A score of 1 refers to most free whereas a score of 7 refers to least free in terms both of political and civil liberties. Because high scores indicate low freedom, the scores generated by Freedom House are taken to indicate "lack of freedom" for purposes of the correlation analysis done here.

80. The Gini Index measures the degree of inequality in the distribution of family income in a country. The index is calculated from the Lorenz curve, in which cumulative family income is plotted against the number of families arranged from the poorest to the richest. The index is the ratio of (a) the area between a country's Lorenz curve and the 45-degree helping line to (b) the entire triangular area under the 45-degree line. The more nearly equal a country's income distribution, the closer its Lorenz curve to the 45-degree line and the lower its Gini Index (e.g., a Scandinavian country with an index of 25). The more unequal a country's income distribution, the farther its Lorenz curve from the 45-degree line and the higher its Gini Index (e.g., a Sub-Saharan country with an index of 50). If income were distributed with perfect equality, the Lorenz curve would coincide with the 45-degree line and the index would be zero; if income were distributed with perfect inequality, the Lorenz curve would coincide with the horizontal axis and the right vertical axis and the index would be 100.

81. United Nations Office on Drugs and Crime, 2003. Data were given for the years 1996 to 2001. For purposes of developing the database on drug seizures, data were for the most recent year for which a seizure was made. The actual data used for the analysis are given as a link on the following Website: *http://www.rohan.sdsu.edu/faculty/rwinslow/index.html*

82. The Terrorism Research Center, 2004.

83. National Criminal Justice Reference Service, 2002.

84. U.S. Senate Judiciary Committee Criminal Law and Procedures Subcommittee, 1978.

85. Colin, 1985; Hewitt, 1984.
86. U.S. House Committee Subcommittee on Civil and Constitutional Rights, 1981.
87. Grassi, 1990.
88. Buckelew, 1984.
89. Kube & Kuckuck, 1992.
90. Wolf, 1989.
91. Comparative Criminology Website: Turkey.
92. International Committee of the Red Cross, 2004.
93. FOX News/Opinion Dynamics Poll, 2003, March 11–12.
94. Encarta, 2001.
95. Reichel, 2005, pp. 95–100.
96. U.S. Department of Justice, August 21, 2003.
97. Human Rights Watch, August 2002, pp. 3–4.
98. Human Rights Watch, 2002, p. 12.
99. Dempsey, 2003.
100. Bohn, 2003.
101. Madsen, 2003.
102. Howlett, 2003.
103. Williams, 2001.
104. Defensetech, 2004.
105. Pitts, 2003.
106. Center for Defense Information, 2002.
107. *Npr.org,* 2006.
108. Roberts, 2006.
109. Thomas (Library of Congress), 2006.
110. Brehmer & Iten, 2001; Killias & Rabasa, 1998a; 1998b.

GLOSSARY

addict robber   A robber who needs enough money to support his drug habit.

advance fee swindle   A scheme where an individual or company receives a letter, fax, or email from an alleged "official" representing a foreign government or agency. An offer is made to transfer millions of dollars in "over-invoiced contract" funds into the victim's personal bank account. The victim provides upfront or advance fees for various taxes, attorney fees, transaction fees, or bribes, and receives nothing in return.

adversarial system   A system used in the Anglo-American common law tradition whereby the prosecution and defense serve as opponents or adversaries before the court. In this system, the judge or jury determines who the winner of this contest is by awarding a guilty or not guilty verdict. This system is a stark contrast to the inquisitorial system used in many European countries that derived from Roman civil law, whereby the judge is more active in investigating whether a law has been violated.

aggravated assault   A completed or attempted attack with a weapon, whether or not an injury occurs. It is also an attack without a weapon in which the victim is seriously injured.

Air America   Allegedly, in a secret war carried on by the Central Intelligence Agency (CIA) during the Vietnam War, the CIA financed a renegade 36,000-man Laotian army of Hmong (or Meo) tribe members, commanded by Vang Pao. The tribesmen were traditional opium poppy farmers, whose trade was disrupted by the war, so the CIA supplied them with a fleet of aircraft called Air America that transported opium from the Laotian hills to a CIA base at Long Tieng, Laos, where it was refined into heroin, and then transported to South Vietnam, where it was sold to U.S. troops, an estimated 20% of whom became heroin addicts during the Vietnam War.

alcoholic robber   A robber who robs on impulse and has few plans for the money he steals.

anomie theory   As initially used by Emile Durkheim in the 19th century, the term *anomie* referred to a state of society in which the various functional parts of society are poorly regulated, a state of society that results in conflict. In 1937, Robert Merton developed an American version of anomie theory referring to a state of society whereby there is a disjunction between what the culture encourages (economic success) and the means available to make economic success possible, resulting in a variety of deviant adaptations (innovation, ritualism, retreatism, and rebellion) for members of the society lacking in such means.

antitrust violations   White-collar crimes defined by the Sherman Act of 1890 and the Clayton Act of 1914. These acts outlawed restraint of trade, attempts to monopolize, and mergers and acquisitions that have the effect of lessening competition. Examples of antitrust violations include bid-rigging and price-fixing schemes that involve conspiracies.

assault   An unlawful attempt to violently injure another person.

atavism   A reversion to an earlier form of the human species as indicated by stigmata of degeneracy, which are traits of that earlier form (e.g., Neanderthals).

bankruptcy fraud   A fraudulent bankruptcy in which a debtor falsely claims bankruptcy by concealing his or her company's assets. Money is usually transferred to the accounts of co-conspirators who are falsely shown as creditors on the books of the company declaring bankruptcy.

battery   Unlawfully and willfully using force or violence against another person.

black bag job   A covert action undertaken by a police force or intelligence agency not known to its target. Allegedly, during the 1948 Italian election, in its first covert political action, the CIA offset Soviet funding of the communist party of Italy through a black bag job, passing money to candidates for the Christian Democratic Party. The Christian Democratic Party went on to win its greatest election victory in April 1948.

Black Codes   A series of laws criminalizing legal activity for African Americans after the Civil War (to replace the Slave Codes). Acts such as standing in one area of town or walking at night, for example, became the criminal acts of "loitering" or "breaking curfew," for which African Americans were imprisoned. In the late 19th-century South, the convict lease system functioned with the Black Codes to re-establish and maintain the race relationships of slavery by returning control over the lives of these African Americans to white plantation owners.

Black Hand   A criminal and terrorist secret society that was active in Sicily in the late 19th century and in the United States in the early 20th century. In the United States it was especially active in New Orleans and New York City. Its method of operation was to threaten death to members of the Italian population with letters marked with a black hand. The Black Hand was blamed for the 1890 murder of New Orleans chief of police Daniel Hennessy.

black market   The sector of economic activity in a jurisdiction involving illegal activities. Depending on the sense in which the term is used, this can primarily refer to illegally avoiding tax payments, to the profits of narcotic trafficking, or to profits made from theft. It is so called because "black economy" or black market affairs are conducted outside the law and are necessarily conducted "in the dark," out of sight of the law. The Prohibition period in the United States is a classic example of black market activity, when organized crime groups took advantage of the lucrative opportunities in the resulting black market in banned alcohol production and sales. In many countries today, it is argued that a "war on drugs" has created a similar effect for drugs such as marijuana. Black markets have also flourished in some countries during wars, especially World War II, when rationing and price controls were enforced in many countries.

born criminal   A term referring specifically to Lombroso's theory that persons born with physical traits (stigmata) resembling an earlier, less developed form of human beings are criminalistic by nature.

broken windows theory   A theory developed by Wilson and Kelling that maintains the poor physical appearance of a neighborhood can indicate a breakdown in community cohesion and provides an open invitation to criminals of all types, including drunks, prostitutes, robbers, and burglars.

burglary The unlawful entry of a structure to commit a felony or a theft. Attempted forcible entry is included.

carjacking A completed or attempted robbery of a motor vehicle by a stranger to the victim. Carjacking differs from other motor vehicle thefts because the victim is present and the offender uses or threatens to use force.

carnal abuse The injury to the genital organs of a female while attempting, but not completing, penetration.

case law The body of law, based upon a collection of reported cases created by appellate decisions on specific issues, that serves as a guide to decision making, especially in the courts.

chastisement The physical punishment of disobedient wives and children by the male expected as part of the husband's traditional role as head of the household, historically and in many developing nations today. In fact, the term *rule of thumb* was derived from English common law whereby a man might use a "rod not thicker than his thumb" to chastise his wife. This rule was adopted in the early 19th century by American states, formally recognizing the husband's right to beat his wife.

check kiting A scheme used by professional and white-collar criminals who typically use fictitious identification and run up accounts in two or more banks through successively making deposits with overdraft checks to an account in each bank from one or more of the other banks. A large sum of cash is then withdrawn from each bank by such criminals who subsequently move to a new town or state.

Chicago School of Criminology A school of criminology that developed at America's first department of sociology at the University of Chicago and was influenced by the Progressive movement. The major emphasis of the Chicago School was contrary to the Social Darwinism that was influential in Europe at the time, and crime was seen as an outcome of natural processes like that of animal and plant ecology, rather than heredity. Applied to crime, the ecological theory hypothesized that crime would be greatest in the inner city, regardless of which ethnic or racial group lived there.

chronic offender The term refers to repeat offenders. Wolfgang and associates operationalized the term to mean offenders with five or more offenses, finding that 6% of the offenders in their study of juvenile offenders in Philadelphia were chronic offenders. These "chronic 6%" were responsible for 51.9% of all offenses, 71% of the homicides, 73% of the rapes, 82% of the robberies, and 69% of the aggravated assaults committed by the cohort.

civil law legal system A system of law originating in Roman law (and generally a derivative of the 19th-century Napoleonic Code) that includes a comprehensive system of rules, usually codified or passed by a legislative body, which are applied and interpreted by judges.

Classical School An approach to criminology developed during the 18th century Age of Enlightenment by Cesare Beccaria in Italy and Jeremy Bentham in England positing that crime is a product of rational choice and hedonistic pursuit and should be countered with punishment that is swift, certain, and just exceeds the pleasure of the crime, opposing the use of torture that was common in Europe and the New World at the time.

clearance rates   The number of offenses that have been solved divided by the total number of offenses known to the police times 100 (to indicate the percentage cleared). Crimes are considered solved when the police arrest the offender or as a result of exceptional means (e.g., the offender is known but it has been found that he or she has died or left the country).

collective embezzlement   The siphoning of company funds for personal use by top management at the expense of the institution itself and with the implicit or explicit sanction of its management.

common law legal system   A system of law characterizing countries with a history as British territories or colonies that places great emphasis upon non-statutory law (i.e., judge-made law) including precedent derived from case law, as well as common law in England in which unwritten judicial decisions were based on tradition, custom, and precedent.

comparative criminology   The study of criminology in two or more nations with the goal of developing theories of crime and criminal justice that are cross-nationally valid. An even more general definition is the study of criminology in two or more cultures, with the goal of developing universal generalizations about crime and criminal justice.

computer crime   Any violation of federal or state computer crime statutes. Computer crime is divided into five general categories: (a) theft of services, (b) illegal use of computer data for personal gain, (c) improper use of computers for numerous types of financial processes, (d) use of a computer to damage another's assets (e.g., planting a damaging virus to destroy data), and (e) theft of software through unlawful copying.

conflict theory   Conflict theory developed from the writings of Karl Marx and Frederick Engles who argued that under capitalism, the working class was oppressed by the ruling class, the bourgeoisie, and that revolution was necessary to develop a classless society. American criminologist Richard Quinney applied the theory to criminology by observing that the criminal justice system under capitalism is an instrument of the state and ruling class to maintain and perpetuate the existing social and economic order. Contemporary less revolutionary forms of conflict theory include critical criminology and peacemaking criminology.

consigliere   A member of an Italian organized crime family who is a counselor or advisor to the boss and other family members, enjoying considerable influence and power.

constitutional theory   A theory developed by William Sheldon in the early 20th century that a person with a predominantly mesomorphic (muscular with massive skeleton) body type or constitution is more inclined to engage in delinquency than individuals with other body types (ectomorphic or endomorphic).

containment/control theories   These theories were rooted in Freudian theory, on the one hand, and the Chicago School, on the other. The central premises of these theories are that the breakdown in personal and/or social controls over individual behavior is the primary cause of crime and that this breakdown is primarily the result of early childhood family disruption.

Controlled Substances Act   This refers to Title II of the 1970 Comprehensive Drug Abuse Prevention and Control Act.

core group   A type of organized crime that consists of a limited number of individuals who form a relatively tight and structured group to conduct criminal business. Around this "core group" may be a large number of associate members or a network that is used from time to time, depending on the criminal activity in question. There may be an internal division of activities among the core members. Core groups are generally quite small (20 individuals or less) and are more likely to engage in a single or limited number of criminal activities.

corporate crime   A violation of a criminal statute either by a corporate entity or by its executives, employees, or agents acting on behalf of and for the benefit of the corporation, partnership, or other form of business entity.

coverture   The English principle that established a woman could not own property free from her husband's claim or control and that women themselves were to be treated as "property."

crime   A type of behavior defined by law as deserving punishment, including imprisonment, as well as possible fine and for which there is no legally acceptable justification or excuse.

criminal   A person convicted of a criminal offense in a court of law.

criminal behavior   Behavior in violation of criminal law whether or not the person or persons involved have been convicted in a court of law.

criminal homicide   Unlawful killing, without justification or excuse, a term including murder, manslaughter, and negligent homicide.

criminal network   A type of organized crime defined by the activities of key individuals who engage in illicit activity in often shifting alliances. Prominence in the network is determined by contacts and/or skills, and personal loyalties and/or ties are more important than social/ethnic identities. The network connections are maintained based upon a series of criminal projects. Criminal networks maintain a low public profile and are seldom known by any name. The network reforms after the exit of key individuals.

criminology   The scientific study of the causation, prevention, treatment, and control of crime and criminal behavior, as well as the rehabilitation and punishment of offenders. Prior to the use of the scientific method by Lombroso in the 19th century, the Classical School applied pure reason rather than the scientific method to study crime.

critical criminology   Critical criminology refers to a theory known variously as Marxist, conflict, or radical criminology. It includes peacemaking, radical feminism, left realism, and postmodernism. Key concepts include the role of government, capitalism, and political power in relation to crime rates.

curtilage   A piece of ground (as a yard or courtyard) within the fence surrounding a house. Originally this referred to attached servants quarters, barns, carriage houses, and so forth, but today the term has been extended to include even open fields next to a house.

cyberporn   Hard-core pictures, movies, online chat, and even live sex acts that can be viewed or participated in using a computer connected to the Internet. Computer files containing sexual media can be downloaded and viewed by virtually anyone through the Internet.

dark figure of crime   A term first used by Sutherland and Cressey in discussing problems with police-based data, notably that some crimes have a low rate of crime being reported to the police. The *dark figure* refers to the difference between the true rate of a crime and the rate of the crime reported to the police. Thus, rape is said to have a very large dark figure, because rape victims may be fearful or embarrassed to report the crime, whereas auto theft has a very small dark figure, because victims of auto theft must report the theft to obtain insurance compensation.

decriminalization   The removal by a legislature of an act previously deemed criminal from the jurisdiction of the criminal justice system, frequently through deeming it an infraction punishable only by a fine.

deinstitutionalization movement   A movement to cut down on the number of individuals housed in state psychiatric hospitals that began with the Community Mental Health Centers Act of 1961, a product of the John F. Kennedy administration. Kennedy had set the goal for a 50% reduction of custodial care for mental patients within a decade. Between 1955 and 1997, the population of state mental hospitals declined from 558,239 to 70,000 mentally ill individuals.

depressants   Chemical agents that diminish the function the central nervous system, thus producing a drowsy or calm feeling, relieving anxiety or insomnia. An overdose can produce dangerously slow breathing and heart rates, and may result in death. The category of depressants includes a cross-section of drugs, legal and illegal, prescription and nonprescription. Alcohol and inhalants are depressants that can be purchased legally in the United States without a prescription. Other depressants are available as prescription drugs or administered by a medical doctor. These include tranquilizers such as Halcyon, Valium, Librium, and Xanax, as well as opium, codeine, morphine, heroin, methadone, Demerol, and Percodan.

differential associations theory   A theory developed by Edwin Sutherland that criminal behavior is learned in interaction with intimate personal groups, and such learning involves all the mechanisms involved in other learning.

diyya   In Islamic law, *diyya* crimes involve money to be paid in compensation in cases where the harm was unintentional or the evidence is inconclusive, as opposed to *qisa* crimes, which involve retribution as a punishment for the crime.

dowry murders   Dowry refers to the money or property a woman brings to her husband at marriage. In India, dowry disputes result in an estimated 6,917 dowry deaths yearly. Harassment of a new bride for payment of dowry may end in the bride's death, which family members often try to portray as a kitchen accident or suicide.

drug abuse   The use of a drug for a purpose other than that for which it is normally prescribed or recommended. For certain drugs, such as heroin and LSD, which are illegal substances, any use of the drug is considered to be drug abuse.

drug addiction   According to Alfred Lindesmith, a person becomes an addict if he or she has completed five essential steps. First, the person must take an addicting drug. Second, the person must experience withdrawal distress. Third, the person must associate the withdrawal distress with the absence of the drug. Fourth, the person must then obtain and take more of the addicting drug. Fifth, the person then associates relief from the withdrawal distress with taking more of the drug. The continuation of drug addiction probably requires a sixth step, that the person is able to obtain more of the drug on a regular basis. Other elements are generally included in the definition of drug addiction: (a) an increasing body tolerance leading to a tendency of the addict to increase dosage, (b) psychological dependence, and (c) physiological dependence.

drug robbers   Robbers who take money and/or drugs from drug dealers by force or threat of force.

drug trafficking   Manufacturing, distributing, dispensing, importing, and exporting (or possession with intent to do the same) of a controlled or counterfeit substance.

Easterlin hypothesis   This approach predicts a positive relationship between the relative size of a birth cohort and the rate of crime. According to this hypothesis, a larger birth cohort or "baby boom" results in excess unemployment and poverty for that cohort when it reaches adulthood, due to a heightened competition for jobs. This in turn fuels crime as an alternative source of income.

econometric theory   One type of neoclassical theorizing is that done by economists who have essentially tried to operationalize or provide a formula for Bentham's "hedonistic calculus," as illustrated by the work of Gary Becker, as well as Schmidt and Witte.

economic abundance theory   A theory developed by Leroy Gould that posited the economic abundance that occurred from 1944 to 1965 can explain the variation in rates of property crime during that time. Simply stated, this theory holds that people steal because there is more to steal, and thus more opportunity to steal.

embezzlement   The unlawful misappropriation by an offender to his or her own use or purpose of money, property, or some other thing of value entrusted to his or her care, custody, or control.

enforcement terrorism   Murder by law enforcement officers sponsored by the government that is highly efficient and is posited to maintain social control.

erotica   A term used in place of pornography in the 1970 President's Commission Report on Obscenity and Pornography.

ethnocentric viewpoint   A viewpoint characterized by, or based on, the attitude that one's own group is superior to another group or other groups. For instance, theories such as the "black subculture of violence" may lead to the ethnocentric belief that whites are superior to blacks because of the apparent higher violent crime rate of blacks compared to whites in the United States.

eugenics movement   A movement based upon eugenics, the science that involved sterilizing individuals that were deemed biologically inferior, to improve the human race. The movement was popular in the United States during the 1920s through the 1940s, as well as in Nazi Germany where it culminated in the holocaust.

external restraint theory   A theory developed by Andrew Henry and James Short specifically to explain homicide and suicide. Drawing upon frustration-aggression theory, Henry and Short postulate that homicide correlates positively with the strength of external restraint. External restraint refers to the degree to which behavior is required to conform to the demands and expectations of others.

factual guilt   The admitted or actual commission of a crime, regardless of whether or not a prosecuting attorney can prove the crime in court (or a defense attorney can gain an acquittal).

fatwah   A legal opinion or ruling issued by an Islamic scholar.

felony   A crime punishable by death or incarceration in a state or federal prison (as opposed to a jail or local detention facility) and for a period of one year or more.

felony murder   A death results during the commission of another felony, such as rape or robbery. Even if a person is killed through the accidental discharge of a weapon during a rape or robbery, the charge of felony murder could be made for both the perpetrator and any accomplices to the act.

female genital mutilation   The surgical removal of the clitoris.

feminist theory   Feminist theories are essentially rejective of traditional criminological causation theory as gender based and male dominated. Some of these theorists argue that the major criminological theories are "for men only"—they apply only to males and have little or no relevance for explaining female criminality or delinquency.

fence   As a verb, to buy or sell stolen goods. As a noun, one who buys stolen goods to sell for a profit. The *defense* of secrecy is said to be the original basis for the use of this term.

Five Pillars of Islam   The core mandates of the Muslim religion, which are: (a) *shahada:* belief in one God; (b) *al-Salat:* prayer five times per day at dawn, noon, afternoon, sunset, and night; (c) *al-Sayam:* fasting during the month of Ramadan; (d) *al-Hajj:* pilgrimage to Mecca once in a lifetime; and (e) *al-Zakat:* charity, or taking from the rich and giving to the poor.

fixated pedophiles   As compared with regressed pedophiles who otherwise maintain fairly normal relations with adult peers, fixated pedophiles have poor relations with adults and identify with male children, seeking sexual relationships with them. Whereas the primary targets of regressed pedophiles are females, the primary targets of fixated pedophiles are males.

forced prostitution   Sexual slavery, generally of females or children, resulting from such coercive measures as frequent assault, international or interstate trafficking, physical isolation, threats to family, and/or deprivation of funds.

forcible rape   The carnal knowledge of a person, forcibly and/or against that person's will, or not forcibly or against the person's will where the victim is incapable of giving consent because of his or her temporary or permanent mental or physical incapacity or because of his or her youth.

forcible sex offense   A category of sex offenses in the National Incident-Based Reporting System that includes not only forcible rape, but also forcible sodomy, sexual assault with an object, and forcible fondling.

fraud   The knowing and unlawful deception of another with intent to cause him or her to unwittingly surrender property, rights, emoluments, or pecuniary interest.

French Connection   Allegedly, Corsican organized crime figures were recruited by U.S. intelligence during the 1950s to help deal with dockworkers in France who were opposed to the French war with Vietnam. The Corsicans were said to have created "goon squads" that attacked union picket lines, harassed, and even assassinated union leaders, breaking the union. Although the French were allowed to resume their war in Vietnam, the Corsicans were granted the right to use Marseilles as a heroin trafficking center, creating the infamous "French Connection." Marseilles would supply U.S. heroin needs for the next 20 years.

garrison communities   Streets that have been barricaded with abandoned cars, concrete posts, and tree stumps to prevent election-related violence such as drive-by shootings by rival gangs of politically connected posses or "yardies" in the urban ghettos of Kingston, Jamaica.

genocidal rape   The United Nations definition of genocide refers to the "intent to destroy, in whole or in part, a national, ethnical, racial or religious group, as such," and five acts described in sections a, b, c, d and e. A crime must include *both elements* to be called "genocide." The acts are (a) killing members of the group, (b) causing serious bodily or mental harm to members of the group, (c) deliberately inflicting on the group conditions of life calculated to bring about its physical destruction in whole or in part, (d) imposing measures intended to prevent births within the group, and (e) forcibly transferring children of the group to another group. Genocidal rape occurs when in warfare enemy women are killed after being raped or raped to impregnate them for the purposes of blurring ethnic identity in the subsequent offspring.

Golden Crescent   A term referring to the first of Asia's two primary illicit opium-producing areas. The three countries are Afghanistan, Iran, and Pakistan.

Golden Triangle   A term referring to the second of Asia's two primary illicit opium-producing areas, overlapping the mountains of three countries of mainland Southeast Asia, including Burma (Myanmar), Laos, and Thailand.

grand theft   The term is usually defined by state law as involving theft of items ranging in value from a low of $50 to $150 upward. Because currency inflation plays havoc with crime statistics, the FBI has abandoned attempts to distinguish between petit larceny and grand larceny.

hallucinogens   A variety of drugs that alter perceptions, thoughts, and feelings, including LSD, mescaline, MDMA (ecstasy), PCP, and psilocybin (magic mushrooms).

hate crime   A criminal offense committed against a person or property that is motivated, in whole or in part, by the offender's bias against a race, religion, disability, ethnicity/national orientation, or sexual orientation.

hedonistic calculus   Jeremy Bentham developed a theory called utilitarianism that postulated that humans seek to maximize pleasure and avoid pain. The hedonic calculus includes the quantification of seven features of pleasure to which attention must be paid to assess how great it is. These features include: intensity, duration, certainty, propinquity, fecundity, purity, and extent. Applied to crime, Benthan proposed that the hedonistic calculus could be used to devise penalties (pain) that just exceed the hedonistic pleasure of a crime.

home invasion robbery   A theft involving violence that occurs in a residence that the offender knows or offenders know is occupied for the purpose of obtaining money or property in the possession of the residents or that the residents can obtain, such as through opening a safe.

homicide design theory   Buss and Duntley's theory that murder is an evolutionary adaptive trait of males. Murder serves adaptation in several ways: through protecting self and kin from injury or death; through depriving rivals of access to valuable mates; through gaining access to contested resources; through terminating prenatal offspring of rivals; through eliminating genetically unrelated stepchildren; through removing key antagonists; and through eliminating future competitors of one's children.

honor killings   The killing of a female justified on the basis that the female brought dishonor upon the family through some moral indiscretion, such as premarital loss of virginity or adultery.

hudud crimes   Hudud crimes are considered to be the most serious crimes in the Islamic system of jurisprudence. Hudud crimes are those described in the Koran (Holy Book) and the Sunna (writings) of the Prophet, and include adultery, theft, banditry (robbery), and defamation. Three additional crimes, transgression, drinking alcohol, and apostasy, are considered by the majority of Muslim scholars to be hudud crimes as well. Adultery carries a maximum penalty of death by stoning (similar to the penalty for adultery in the Puritan Massachusetts Code of 1648 in America). Theft is punishable by amputation of the hands. Banditry can result in death by crucifixion, and defamation (false accusation of unchastity) may be punished by whipping. Lesser punishments are specified for the remaining hudud crimes.

iatrogenic deaths   Those induced in a patient by a physician's activity, manner, or therapy, a term used especially if there is an infection or other complication of treatment.

identity theft   A crime in which the offender assumes the victim's commercial identity and conducts business or even crime in the name of the person whose identity is stolen.

inchoate offense   A term that means incomplete, unfinished, or partial. Such offenses need not require the demonstration of *actus reus* to be classified as a crime. Examples include attempted, but unsuccessful, breaking and entering and conspiracy to commit murder that was not carried out.

Index crimes   The term *Index crimes* refers to eight major crimes included in Part I of the Uniform Crime Reports (UCR), including criminal homicide, forcible rape, robbery, aggravated assault, burglary, larceny-theft, auto theft, and arson, in descending order of seriousness. The term "Index" as applied to arson is a misnomer, because arson has not been included in the overall rate of crime since it was added to Part I by an act of Congress in 1979. Furthermore, the FBI ceased reporting the overall rate or Index of crime in the 2004 UCR.

integrated theory   Some criminologists have attempted to renew interest in extant criminological theories by providing composite or integrated theories, combining different theories into one sequential model. The idea is to provide theories with greater explanatory value through the use of multiple variables that are said to be causative of crime. This approach departs from the "general theory" orientation of Sutherland and Merton, tending toward the eclecticism that Sutherland and Merton tried to avoid. Integrated theories are also called integrative, integrating, mixed, synthetic, and convergent theories. Instead of viewing various theories, such as control theory, differential association, and strain theory as competing theories, the integrating theories are attempts to combine the theories into a single, usually sequential, developmental theory. The theory can then be tested, often using multivariate statistical analysis (regression, path analysis, factor analysis) to determine which variables account for the greatest percentage of variance.

intensive offender   A short-term career criminal who is poorly prepared, commits robberies in quick succession, and obtains modest gains.

interdiction   The interception of illicit drugs being transported over the nation's borders.

international crime   A major criminal offense as designated by the United Nations for the protection of interests common to all of humankind (e.g., genocide).

investment fraud   A fraud that occurs when an advisor, brokerage firm, or stockbroker advises against the Securities and Exchange Commission's guidelines designed to ensure that investment advice is given fairly and consistently to investors.

Iran-Contra affair   Allegedly, the Reagan Administration covertly supported the Contras, a coalition of paramilitary groups who were trying to overthrow the left-wing Sandinista government in Nicaragua, through various measures, one of which was the diversion of some $18 million from a $30 million sale of arms to Iran.

Islamic law system   A system of laws, also termed *Shari'a law*, which means "way" or "path," that is based upon the Muslim religion, drawing upon the Koran, the holy book of Islam. The fundamental premises of this system are that God's will is revealed in the Koran and that society's laws must conform to God's will as revealed in the Koran. In Arab countries, there is a considerable diversity of opinion in the interpretation of the Koran, sometimes resulting in sectarian violence (similar to the conflicts that occurred during the Puritan experiment in colonial America).

labeling theory   A theory derivative of symbolic interaction theory of the Chicago School popularized during the 1970s by the work of Howard S. Becker.

Becker argued that through labeling, individuals so labeled were driven to the status of outsiders whereby they accept the deviant label as a master status and pursue crime as a way of life. Labeling theory was influential in leading to the diversion movement of the 1970s.

La Cosa Nostra A national organization of Sicilian origin, but centralized and controlled in the United States, and with a somewhat unique organizational structure. This perspective came to light largely as a result of the testimony of Joseph Valachi before the McClellan Committee in 1963.

larceny The taking of property from a person without that person's consent and with the intention of depriving that person permanently of the use of the property.

larceny-theft The FBI uses the term *larceny-theft* instead of *larceny* to refer to the unlawful taking, carrying, leading, or riding away of property from the possession or constructive possession of another. The category includes crimes such as shoplifting, pocket-picking, purse-snatching, thefts from motor vehicles, thefts of motor vehicle parts and accessories, bicycle thefts, and so forth, in which no use of force, violence, or fraud occurs. Motor vehicle theft is also excluded from this category inasmuch as it is a separate Index Crime offense.

legal guilt The guilt of a crime established by a court of law. Legal guilt can occur without factual guilt in our adversarial system if the legal skills of the prosecution exceed those of the defense and a judge or jury finds an innocent person guilty. This can occur as a result of a plea bargain whereby an innocent person confesses to a crime he or she did not commit in exchange for being released from detention or other incentives.

life-as-party Shover and Honaker's theory that persistent property offenders spend much of their criminal gains on alcohol and other drugs. The proceeds of their crimes are typically used for personal, nonessential consumption (e.g., "nights out"), rather than, for example, to be given to family or used for basic needs. Thieves spend much of their leisure hours enjoying good times. Life as party is enjoyed in the company of others.

Mann Act An Act of Congress, sometimes termed the *White Slave Traffic Act,* passed in 1910, which made it a federal crime to transport individuals under the age of 18 across state lines to engage in sexual activity.

manslaughter Homicide without malice aforethought. *Malice aforethought* refers to intentional predetermination to commit the crime. Manslaughter is differentiated from murder; however, it is often included in statistics describing murder. Manslaughter is further divided between voluntary (nonnegligent) and involuntary (negligent) manslaughter.

marital rape Unwanted sexual acts committed by a spouse or ex-spouse, occurring without consent and/or against a person's will, obtained by force, or threat of force, intimidation, or when a person is unable to consent.

mass murder The killing of more than three individuals at a single time. The killings need not occur in the same location, but the time limit is usually 24 hours. Mass murderers, as differentiated from serial killers, engage in a single, uncontrollable outburst that is termed *simultaneous killing.*

mesomorphy In William Sheldon's constitutional theory, mesomorphy refers to a body type characterized by square masculinity and skeletal massiveness, in between the frail thinness of ectomorphs and the plump roundness of endomorphs. In terms of personality, mesomorphs are active, assertive, aggressive, and noisy, with a lust for power and love of dominating others, traits that are conducive to delinquency.

moral insanity   A term coined by J.C. Prichard (1786-1848) describing a form of mental derangement in which the intellectual facilities are uninjured, whereas the disorder is manifested principally or alone in the state of feelings, temper, or habits. The moral principles of the mind are depraved or perverted, the power of self-government is lost or greatly impaired, and the individual is incapable of conducting himself with decency and propriety in the business of life.

motor vehicle theft   The theft or attempted theft of a motor vehicle, including automobiles, trucks, buses, motorcycles, motorscooters, snowmobiles, and so forth. The definition excludes the taking of motor vehicles for temporary use by those persons having lawful access. The definition also excludes motor vehicles that would not normally travel surface streets and highways, such as trains, airplanes, bulldozers, most farm and construction machinery, ships, boats, and spacecraft, the theft of which would be classified as "larceny-theft." In addition, a bicycle is not considered to be a motor vehicle, even if a motor is retrofitted to the bicycle (per FBI definition).

murder   The unlawful killing of a human being with malice aforethought, also known as *criminal homicide.*

narcoterrorism   A subset of terrorism, in which terrorist groups, or associated individuals, participate directly or indirectly in the cultivation, manufacture, transportation, or distribution of controlled substances and the monies derived from these activities. Further, narcoterrorism may be characterized by the participation of groups or associated individuals in taxing, providing security for, or otherwise aiding or abetting drug trafficking endeavors in an effort to further, or fund, terrorist activities.

obscenity   A term used interchangeably with the term *pornography.* The Supreme Court ruled in the 1973 case of *Miller v. California* that for something to be deemed obscene, it must be shown that the average person, applying contemporary community standards and viewing the material as a whole, would find (a) that the work appeals predominantly to "prurient" interest; (b) that it depicts or describes sexual conduct in a patently offensive way; and (c) that it lacks serious literary, artistic, political, or scientific value.

occasional offender   An offender who has a short career, plans little, and obtains minimal profits.

omerta   A secret code involving "death to informers" that existed within the Mafia according to Kefauver Committee testimony by Harry Anslinger, Commissioner of the Narcotics Bureau at the time.

Operation Cyclone   Allegedly, a CIA operation developed by Zbigniew Brzezinsky, National Security Adviser to President Jimmy Carter. The plan was to develop an international terrorist movement that would spread Islamic fundamentalism in Central Asia and "destabilize" the Soviet Union. Approximately $4 billion was said to have been poured into setting up Islamic training schools in Pakistan. Also allegedly, CIA's spy training camps in Virginia were put to use, where future members of Al Qaeda were taught "sabotage skills." The Mujahadeen financed their war through drug trafficking, primarily in heroin, after the CIA reopened the trade route to supply the Mujahadeen with weapons.

operational definitions   In science, an operational definition refers to the data to be used to measure a concept or variable. For instance, in many studies police data are used to measure rates of crime, but such measures have been subject to much criticism by social scientists.

Operation Mockingbird   Allegedly, in the late 1940s the CIA recruited American news organizations and journalists to serve as informants and disseminate propaganda. Early MOCKINGBIRD influenced 25 newspapers and wire agencies that consented to serve as organs of CIA propaganda. Eventually, the CIA's media assets included ABC, NBC, CBS, Time, Newsweek, Associated Press, and United Press International.

opportunist robber   A robber who is not involved in a career of crime but seeks a small amount of money to buy "extras."

opportunity theory   Opportunity theory is another name for Robert K. Merton's anomie theory, which is also sometimes termed *strain theory*. This theory posited that the lack of opportunity for access to the means to achieve economic success in American society was a primary cause of crime.

organized crime   A conspiratorial enterprise pursuing profit or power through provision of illegal goods and/or services, involving systematic use of force or threat of force.

outlaw motorcycle gangs   A particular form of organized crime said to have originated in the United States, whose members initially were veterans of WWII who trafficked amphetamine after the war. Outlaw motorcycle gangs from Australia followed the regional hierarchy model and are prominent in the production and distribution of amphetamines and cannabis.

paradigm shift   A paradigm is a school of thought within a discipline that provides scientists with a model for choosing problems to be analyzed, methods for analyzing them, and the theoretical framework to explain them. Paradigm revolutions would include the change from the classical school to the positivist school and, finally, the Marxist/radical school. The term paradigm shift refers to major changes that have taken place within sociological thought from the Chicago School, to opportunity theory, to labeling theory, and finally to Marxist/conflict theory.

Part I offenses   In the UCR, Part I offenses include Index Crimes of criminal homicide, forcible rape, robbery, aggravated assault, burglary, larceny-theft, auto theft, and arson, in descending order of seriousness. For these offenses, the UCR includes both "crimes reported to the police" data and arrest data.

Part II offenses   In the UCR, Part II offenses include numerous crimes considered to be less serious than Part I offenses. Such crimes include minor misdemeanors such as vandalism, prostitution, and violation of liquor laws. However, Part II also includes many white-collar crimes, such as forgery/counterfeiting, fraud, and embezzlement. For these crimes the UCR includes only arrest data. The United States is one of few developed nations that have no "crimes reported to the police" data to report to the United Nations and INTERPOL for these white-collar crimes.

peacemaking criminology   Peacemaking criminologists, such as Hal Pepinsky and Richard Quinney, argue that crime is a form of violence and suffering, but to respond to crime with violence in the form of punishment is counterproductive, as violence begets violence. Instead, they advocate peacemaking in the form of bringing offenders and victims together for mediation, conflict resolution, and reconciliation. They also favor nonpunitive approaches including having the offender apologize to the victim, make restitution by paying the victim and/or community back through fee or service, and requiring the offender to make charitable contributions.

personal theft   A term used in the NCVS for purse-snatching and pocket picking, which are classified separately from theft in the NCVS and are listed as "personal crimes."

political crime   Those crimes or prohibited acts that are directed at the established political order, its laws, and institutions, as well as crimes of the state that include domestic political crimes by the state, and international political crimes by the state.

Ponzi scheme   An investment fraud that works on the "rob-Peter-to-pay-Paul" principle, offering high returns by using money from new investors to pay off earlier investors inciting a speculative frenzy, until the whole scheme collapses.

pornography   A term synonymous with obscenity. The Supreme Court ruled in the 1973 case of *Miller v. California* that for something to be deemed obscene, it must be shown that the average person, applying contemporary community standards and viewing the material as a whole, would find (a) that the work appeals predominantly to "prurient" interest; (b) that it depicts or describes sexual conduct in a patently offensive way; and (c) that it lacks serious literary, artistic, political or scientific value.

positivist criminology   As developed by Belgian statistician Adolphe Quetelet, the term *positivism* referred to the collection of data to uncover, explain, and predict the ways in which observable facts followed uniform patterns. Though national crime data were scarce in the early 19th century, early criminologists such as Quetelet, Tarde, Verkko, and Durkheim used government statistics to do comparative studies of crime.

power-control theory   A liberal-feminist theory of delinquency, developed by Hagan, Simpson, and Gillis, which argues that females will be more equal to males in their delinquency (as a form of risk-taking) in equalitarian families and less delinquent relative to male siblings in patriarchal families. Thio provided a power-control theory of assault which stated that men who have lost control of their lives to poverty, unemployment, drug abuse, and alcoholism are more receptive to the patriarchal idea that men should resort to violence, if need be, to dominate and control their wives and children.

primary data   Preferable in science, these are facts and observations gathered by a researcher expressly to test the hypotheses of a study.

professional robber   A career criminal committed to robbery over the long term who seeks large sums of money in carefully planned robberies.

progressivism   In the early 20th century, progressives rejected the Social Darwinist argument that criminality was traced to the biological inferiority of the poor. Instead, they believed that the poor were driven by their environment into a criminal way of life. The Progressives pushed for government programs to save the poor by providing social services, including schools, clinics, recreational outlets, settlement homes, foster care, and reformatories.

Project Paperclip   In January, 1946, President Harry S. Truman established the Central Intelligence Group, whose purpose was to coordinate existing departmental intelligence between the State Department, FBI, and other agencies. It was during this period that the U.S. intelligence community allegedly developed Project PAPERCLIP, a program that brought selected German scientists to work for America during the "Cold War." Truman ordered the exclusion of anyone who had been a member of the Nazi Party. However, dossiers were rewritten at the direction of Allen Dulles (who became the CIA Director in 1947). As a result, a number of Nazi scientists were admitted to the United States. These included Arthur Rudolph (who later designed the Saturn 5 rocket used in the Apollo moon landings) and Wernher von Braun (who became director of NASA's Marshall Space Flight Center). Also recruited was General Reinhard Gehlen, one of Hitler's chief intelligence officers who built an intelligence network in the Soviet Union.

prostitution   Engaging in sexual activity with strangers or other persons with whom the individual has no affectional relationship in exchange for money or other valuable materials that are given at or near the time of the act.

provincial theories   The term *provincial* refers to being confined to a province or region. In this text, we used the term provincial to refer to theories that have been tested only in the United States.

psychoanalytic theory   The theory developed by Sigmund Freud that asserts there are three components to the personality—the id, the ego, and the superego—and they develop in the same sequential order. The id is composed of instinctual impulses, typically of a sexual nature, developing through five stages, in which id impulses seek gratification. The superego consists of internalized moral standards taught primarily by parents. If the superego does not develop sufficiently, then the id impulses are manifested in criminality.

psychological trait theory   A theory that attempts to identify a criminal type in psychological terms. Examples of such character types include mental illness (psychosis or neurosis), psychopathy, retardation, and other character disorders.

rape culture theory   The theory that there are various attitudes and values in a country's culture, including popular myths, which make men more inclined to rape. To the extent that men are exposed to these attitudes and values, they will be inclined to engage in the act of rape.

rational choice theory   In this theory, crime is considered a steadfast, rational choice made by criminals. No matter what was done to rehabilitate criminals, they would choose crime. From an early age, they would find that they could not make it in school or succeed in legitimate employment, and after a succession of arrests, they would become confirmed criminals.

red-light districts   Neighborhoods where prostitution is practiced frequently, a term that resulted from the 19th century practice of placing a red light in the window to indicate to customers the (often illegal) nature of a business.

regional hierarchy   A type of organized crime that has a single leadership structure and a line of command from the center, but a degree of autonomy at the regional level, a geographic/regional distribution, multiple activities, often strong social or ethnic ties, and violence as essential to activities. Regional hierarchies appear to operate on a "franchise model" in which regional groups pay money and give allegiance to use the name of a well-known criminal group.

regressed pedophiles   Regressed pedophiles maintain fairly normal relations with adult peers, whereas fixated pedophiles have poor relations with adults and identify with male children, seeking sexual relationships with them. The primary targets of regressed pedophiles are females, whereas the primary targets of fixated pedophiles are males.

regulationist movement   A 19th century movement in the United States that sought to control female prostitution as a public health issue, requiring police supervision and medical examinations for female prostitutes rather than complete suppression of prostitution itself.

reintegrative shaming   This theory, developed by John Braithwaite, posits that not all labeling of criminal offenders makes them into hardened criminals. *Reintegrative shaming,* in contrast with *disintegrative shaming,* is that done by members of the community as an expression of disappointment in the individual who has done wrong. The offender is not treated as a "bad person," but a "good person" who has done wrong, reaffirming the offender's morality. Community disapproval may range from a mild rebuke to degradation ceremonies. These are followed by gestures of reacceptance of the offender into the community of law-abiding citizens.

restorative justice theory   This theory in providing remedial measures for crime departs from Becker's version of labeling theory which seemingly rejected "cause and cure" approaches altogether.

road rage   The term generally refers to any display of aggression by a motor vehicle driver, but is more commonly defined as more extreme acts of aggression, such as physical assault, that occur as a direct result of a disagreement between drivers.

robbery   The taking or attempting to take anything of value from the care, custody, or control of a person or persons by force or threat of force or violence and/or by putting the victim in fear.

routine activities theory   A theory, developed by Lawrence Cohen and Marcus Felson, which postulates that crime will occur if three elements are present: (a) *motivated offenders,* (b) *suitable targets* of criminal victimization, and (c) *an absence of capable guardians* of persons and property. This theory is sometimes called *lifestyle theory,* because it focuses upon the relationship between a victim's daily activities and vulnerability to crime.

Schedule I-V Drugs   The five schedules (I-V) or categories under the Controlled Substances Act, based upon whether or not the drug has a current accepted medical use and whether or not the drug has a high potential for abuse.

scientific method   The scientific method is a body of techniques for testing hypotheses about variables to predict the relationship between one variable and another variable. An ideal of science is the controlled experiment in which all but two variables are held constant. Then one (independent) variable can be introduced and the change in the second (dependent) variable can be observed in hopes of determining a causal relationship between the first and second variable. In a social science such as criminology, controlled experiments are rare and surveys are more typical. Using survey data, social scientists use multivariate statistical techniques to attempt to control the variables involved in the study. Comparative criminologists suggest cross-national analysis as an important "other" variable to be introduced in multivariate analysis.

secondary data   Considered less preferable in science than primary data. Secondary data are information previously collected for a different, and often government-related, purpose, and for different reasons than to test an investigator's hypotheses or theory. An example of secondary data in criminology would be police-based data and census data.

self-control theory   As an outgrowth of containment and control theory, in Hirschi's 1990 publication with Michael Gottfredson, a General Theory of Crime was proposed that is based upon one type of control only—self-control. Gottfredson and Hirschi argue that crime provides short-term gratification and is committed by people who lack the self-control to resist this mode of gratification because they have lacked effective parenting during their formative years. In addition to not being able to resist crime, such persons will fail in school, in employment, and in intimate relations. Policy consequences of the theory are unclear.

serial killing   Criminal homicide that involves the killing of several victims in three or more separate events.

sex abuse   The forcing of undesired sexual acts by one person upon another, including a broad list of acts such as rape or sexual assault, verbal sexual statements or stalking, and violation of a position of trust for sexual purposes.

sex offenses   In the UCR, the FBI defines sex offenses (except forcible rape, prostitution, and commercialized vice) as statutory rape and offenses against chastity, common decency, morals, and the like. Attempts are included.

sexual assault   A physical assault of a sexual nature, directed toward another person where that person does not give consent; or gives consent as a result of intimidation or fraud; or is legally deemed incapable of giving consent because of youth or temporary/permanent incapacity. Sexual assault includes: rape, sexual assault, sodomy, buggery, oral sex, incest, carnal knowledge, unlawful sexual intercourse, indecent assault, and assault with intent to rape. The term *sexual assault* is used for crime reporting purposes in place of forcible rape by Canada and Australia.

sexual coercion   Finkelhor and Yllo suggest that rape should be differentiated from sexual coercion. They suggested that there are two types of sexual coercion—social and interpersonal. Social coercion is exemplified by a woman having sex with her husband when she doesn't want to out of a sense of duty, whereas interpersonal coercion might result from job threats from a boss (or divorce threats from the husband).

sexual harassment   Unwanted sexual advances, including demanding sex in return for favors.

sexual slavery   Sexual access through rape or other forms of sexual violence with a person who exercises all of the powers attaching to the right of ownership of the victim's body. A major form of sexual slavery is the trafficking of women and children.

sexual violence   The World Health Organization defines sexual violence as a broad category including rape within marriage or dating relationships; rape by strangers; systematic rape during armed conflict; unwanted sexual advances or sexual harassment, including demanding sex in return for favors; sexual abuse of mentally or physically disabled people; sexual abuse of children; forced marriage or cohabitation, including the marriage of children; denial of the right to use contraception or to adopt other measures to protect against sexually transmitted diseases; forced abortion; violent acts against the sexual integrity of women, including female genital mutilation and obligatory inspections for virginity; and forced prostitution and trafficking in persons for the purpose of sexual exploitation.

simple assault   An attack without a weapon resulting either in no injury, minor injury (such as bruises, black eyes, cuts, scratches, or swelling), or an undetermined injury requiring less than two days of hospitalization. Simple assault also includes attempted assaults without a weapon.

situational choice theory   Cornish and Clarke's situational choice theory involves a view of criminal behavior as the outcome of decisions and choices by the offender. This theory features environmental contingencies that can serve as a deterrent to crime. These are choice structuring properties that provide opportunities, costs, and benefits attached to specific crimes.

Slave Codes   Codes that, before the Civil War, governed the rights of slaves and all African Americans in the South. They were criticized by the abolitionists for their brutality. For instance, if a slave was killed by his master while the master was administering punishment, the master was exempt from prosecution.

snakehead   A Chinese illegal alien smuggler.

sneak thieves   Persons who commit their acts of theft by stealthy or secretive means. They could be stealing an automobile in the middle of the night, shoplifting in a store when they think no one is watching, or breaking into a house when they are sure that the residents are at work or school. The term *stealthy theft* is used to describe the illegal activities of sneak thieves.

Social Darwinism   A theory developed by Herbert Spencer, it was an attempted adaptation of Darwin's theory of the survival of the fittest to human societies, classes, and races. The theory, particularly during the 19th century, was used to justify social inequality. It has also been used to justify laissez-faire capitalism, imperialism, and racism.

social disorganization   The breakdown of effective social control, social bonds, and primary group associations in neighborhoods and communities said to lead to the development of high rates of juvenile delinquency and crime in these areas.

social ecology theory   A theory developed by Robert E. Park in the early days in the Chicago School of criminology. Park observed that like any ecological system, urban development was patterned and could be understood by social processes such as invasion, conflict, accommodation, and assimilation. Park added that principles of animal and plant ecology could be applied to the distribution of human population in a city.

social learning theory   A theory developed by Ronald Akers' that is a broadened version of Sutherland's differential association theory, incorporating variables from learning theory and social control theory.

social purity movement   A 19th-century movement which sought to abolish female prostitution itself. Major proponents of the social purity movement were feminists who opposed the regulationist movement on the grounds that medical examination of the prostitutes but not their male customers was discriminatory.

social reaction theory   A theory akin to labeling theory, developed by Edwin Lemert. He said that primary deviance can develop for a wide variety of reasons—biological, psychological, and/or sociological. However, secondary deviance is more important because it is intensified deviance. Secondary deviance develops as a means of defense, attack, or adaptation to the problems caused by society's reaction to the primary deviance.

socialist law systems   A term for the legal system that is used in Communist states, arising in some ways from a distrust of law and criminal justice itself (as an arm of the former bourgeoisie elite and aristocracy). Socialist law resembles civil law systems (i.e., codified law), but differs in its concept that most commercial private property (the means of production) should be owned by the state, as well as the belief that the purpose of law is to restructure society in favor of the proletariat, or working class.

soldati   The lowest level members of an Italian organized crime family, the soldiers or "button" men who report to the caporegime (lieutenants). A soldier may operate a particular illicit enterprise—such as a loan-sharking operation, a dice game, a lottery, a bookmaking operation, or a smuggling operation—or he may "own" the enterprise and pay a portion of its profit to the organization, in return for the right to operate, and perhaps for being backed by the capital and resources of the organization. The soldati sometimes serve as "corruptors," functioning to establish relationships with public officials and other influential persons whose assistance is needed. They also can specialize as "enforcers," whose function was to maim or kill recalcitrant members.

somatotyping   A school of criminology that draws a relationship between body build and behavioral tendencies and temperament.

standard hierarchy   A type of organized crime characterized as having a single leader, a clearly defined hierarchy, strong systems of internal discipline, being known by a specific name, often having a strong social or ethnic identity, using violence as essential to activities, and often having a clear influence or control over a defined territory.

state-based terrorism   This term includes enforcement terrorism, used by nations internally to maintain social control. Examples included the "white terror" of Chile's military intelligence services, the Death Squads in Brazil, the White Warriors Union in El Salvador, and the K.G.B. in the U.S.S.R. State-based terrorism also includes the secret or open funding and/or training of terrorists for foreign missions by national governments.

state organized crime   The participation of a national government, covertly or overtly, in organized crime.

state-raised youth   According to John Irwin, these are offenders who more or less "grew up" within various juvenile correctional facilities and prisons (in addition to juvenile detention centers, foster care homes, group homes, etc.), rarely spending any significant amounts of time in free society. Their world view is distorted, stunted, and incoherent. The prison world has become their only meaningful world.

state white-collar crime   The participation by a national government, covertly or overtly, in white-collar crime to further the nation's business interests, at home in foreign countries.

stepping stone theory   A theory promulgated by the DEA and FBI that the use of certain nonaddicting drugs, such as marijuana, can serve as a gateway to the use of addicting drugs, such as heroin.

stigmata of degeneracy   According to Lombroso, traits indicative of atavism or throwbacks to earlier forms of the human species, include sloping foreheads; ears of unusual size; excessively long arms; receding chins; excessive cheek bones; twisted noses; fleshy, swollen, and protruding lips; premature and abundant wrinkling of the skin; inability to blush; anomalies of the hair; extra fingers, toes, or nipples; ambidexterity; insensitivity to pain; and excessive tattooing.

stimulants   Chemical substances that increase the activity of the sympathetic nervous system, thus producing a sense of euphoria or the feeling of being more awake, including caffeine, amphetamines, cocaine, Ritalin, and MDMA (ecstasy). Stimulants are used as recreational drugs. They are also used as therapeutic drugs to increase alertness, boost endurance and productivity, and suppress appetite.

strain theory   Another term for the opportunity theory or anomie theory that was developed initially by Robert K. Merton. Merton hypothesized that the lower class in American society experienced "structured strain" because they are imbued by the culture of American society with high aspirations for material success, but lack the institutional means to attain this success.

strong-arm robbery   A robbery in which no weapon is used other than the offender's own body.

subculture of violence theory   According to Wolfgang and Ferracuti, the subculture of violence is a subculture emerging among young, black, urban males, and the subculture has its own codes and characteristic set of beliefs and attitudes. A male is usually expected to defend the name and honor of his mother, the virtue of womanhood, and to accept no derogation about his race (even from a member of his own race), his age, or his masculinity. Quick resort to physical combat as a measure of daring, courage, or defense of status appears to be a cultural expression, especially for lower socioeconomic class males of both races.

symbolic interactionism   A theory akin to labeling theory and social reaction theory. Founded by George Herbert Meade and Charles H. Cooley of the Chicago

School, social interaction was fully expressed by Alfred Lindesmith and associates in their text on social psychology. In opposition to Social Darwinism, they argued that all human behavior is learned and there are no human instincts. Lindesmith also advanced the theory that drug addiction is learned behavior that should be treated as an illness rather than a crime.

target hardening   Making it difficult for offenders to successfully engage in criminal acts by increasing the protection of the money, property, or persons at risk through use of surveillance cameras, private security guards, alarms, improved locks, and other measures.

terrorism   The systematic use of physical violence—actual or threatened—against noncombatants but with an audience broader than the immediate victims in mind, to create a general climate of fear in a target population, to effect some kind of political and/or social change.

theft   This is a term used in the National Crime Victimization Survey (NCVS) to refer to the taking of property or cash without personal contact. Incidents involving theft of property from within the sample household would classify as theft if the offender has a legal right to be in the house (such as a maid, delivery person, or guest). If the offender has no legal right to be in the house, the incident would be classified as a burglary. The NCVS distinguishes between theft and personal theft, which refers only to pocket-picking and purse-snatching.

Tongs   Starting in the 19th century in the United States, Triad members from China were called Tongs, a term that means "hall" or "gathering place" The Tongs engaged in organized criminal activities, including opium trafficking, prostitution, gambling, and extortion.

trafficking in women   The recruitment, transportation, transfer, harboring, or receipt of women, by means of the threat or use of force or other forms of coercion, of abduction, of fraud, of deception, of the abuse of power or of a position of vulnerability, or of the giving or receiving of payments or benefits to achieve the consent of a person having control over another person, for the purpose of exploitation. Exploitation shall include, at a minimum, the exploitation of the prostitution of others or other forms of sexual exploitation, forced labor or services, slavery, or practices similar to slavery, servitude, or the removal of organs.

transnational crime   A criminal act occurring and against the laws of more than one sovereign nation, or having an impact upon a foreign nation, usually undertaken and supported by organized criminal group, (e.g., money laundering, international terrorism, and drug trafficking).

transnational organized crime   An ad hoc committee of The United Nations discovered that transnational organized crime groups have more than one organizational type, contrary to the image of organized crime as being hierarchically structured like the Sicilian Mafia in the United States. Accordingly, the research team identified five types of structures found among the 40 organized crime groups studied. These included the standard hierarchy, regional hierarchy, clustered hierarchy, core group, and criminal network.

trend analysis   In comparative criminology, trend analysis consists of observing the increase or decrease in crime in various countries before and after the introduction of a given variable. For instance, Switzerland has been experimenting for years with the administration of "prescription heroin" to registered drug addicts, finding that when all variables are controlled, the rate of robbery has declined in that country.

Triads Triad phenomenon is believed to have originated in opposition to the Qing dynasty in China. The term Triad refers to the Chinese societies' common symbol: an equilateral triangle representing the three basic Chinese concepts of heaven, earth, and man. The Qing dynasty was overthrown and a republic was created in 1911. After an "era of warlords," Triad member Sun Yat-sen created the Kuomintang (KMT or Chinese Nationalist People's Party) by forming a coalition with the Chinese Communist Party and sought to unite the country. After Sun's death in 1925, one of his proteges, Chiang Kai-shek (also a Triad member), seized control of the KMT and brought most of south and central China under its rule. During World War II, many Triad members turned to criminal activities: gambling, loan sharking, extortion, and trafficking in opium from the Golden Triangle of Southeast Asia. However, Communist forces defeated Chiang's Nationalist Army in 1947 and Triads were suppressed on the mainland. The Triads subsequently fled with Chiang to Taiwan and to the British colony of Hong Kong. In the postwar period, the Triads emerged as powerful criminal societies.

universal generalizations The term *universal generalization* refers to a scientific law, which is an hypothesis, or group of related hypotheses (theories), that has been confirmed through repeated experimental tests. In comparative criminology, the term universal generalization refers to an hypothesis or theory that has been confirmed through testing in a variety of cultures or nations throughout the world.

utilitarianism A theory of human nature developed by Jeremy Bentham, which served as the philosophical basis for the Classical School of criminology, based upon the premise that good can be judged by whatever brings the greatest happiness to the greatest number of people. It is the business of government to promote happiness for the greatest number by rewarding and punishing.

victim-offender mediation A rehabilitation program in which victim and offender meet in the company of a mediator or mediators, and in the case of juveniles, typically with a parent or parents present as well. A dialogue takes place in which both the victim and offender tell their story, with the goal of negotiating a restitution plan, and ultimately a written agreement. Although the victim will subsequently receive restitution, and the offender may obtain diversion from sanction as a result of fulfilling the agreement, there is a sense of emotional gratification from the process, both on the part of the victim and offender.

violentization theory A process that one goes through in becoming a serial killer, described by criminologist Lonnie Athens as violentization. Violentization is a form of socialization that occurs in four stages, according to Athens. These begin with brutalization and subjugation, followed by violent coaching, belligerency, and virulence.

white-coat crime This refers to a number of forms of fraud that are involved with the health profession, such as fraudulent billing for services not rendered, medications never administered, and procedures not performed, as well as the performance of surgeries that were not needed, unnecessary hospitalization, and the prescription of drugs that are unnecessary along with fee-splitting with the pharmacist.

white-collar crime An illegal or series of illegal acts committed by nonphysical means and by concealment or guile, to avoid the payment or loss of money or property, to obtain money or property, or to obtain business or personal advantage.

whorehouse riots   Disturbances that took place in the United States during the early 1800s by vigilante groups that destroyed houses of prostitution and battled female prostitutes in street fights. As a result, female prostitution did not end but was segregated within the red-light districts of the growing urban slums.

witchcamps   Villages in the northern part of Ghana populated by suspected witches. In Ghana, belief in witchcraft is still strong in many parts of the country. The witchcamps are populated by rural women banished by traditional village authorities or their families for suspected witchcraft. Most accused witches are older women, often widows, who are identified by fellow villagers as the cause of difficulties, such as illness, crop failure, or financial misfortune.

Yakuza   With the end of Japanese feudalism, samurai lost their role in life, and many became *ronin,* or masterless samurai, many of whom wandered the countryside as freelance mercenaries. The Yakuza were those ronin who became unscrupulous itinerant peddlers, professional gamblers and common criminals, eventually forming structured groups. The term *Yakuza* is actually derived from an old card game whose object is to draw three cards adding up as close as possible to without exceeding the number 19. "Ya-ku-za" represents the Japanese words for 8, 9, 3, which totals 20, a useless number; hence, Yakuza means "good for nothing." This historical background provided the backdrop for the development of an organized crime network called the Yakuza, which in Japan provides illegal goods and services not available through legitimate means. The Yakuza has not been of great concern to U.S. law enforcement. This is probably because the Yakuza engages in illicit trade predominantly to and with its home country.

REFERENCES

419 Coalition, The. (2000). Nigeria-The 419 Coalition Website. Retrieved May 17, 2005, from http://home.rica.net/alphae/419coal/

9/11 Commission. (2004a). *Staff Statement No. 1: Entry of the 9/11 hijackers into the United States.* Retrieved May 15, 2005, from http://news.findlaw.com/hdocs/docs/terrorism/911comm-ss1.pdf

9/11 Commission. (2004b). *The 9/11 Commission Report: Final Report of the National Commission on Terrorist Attacks upon the United States: Executive summary.* Retrieved May 15, 2005, from http://a257.g.akamaitech.net/7/257/2422/22jul200411300/www.gpoaccess.gov/911/pdf/execsummary.pdf

A&E Television Network. (2000). *Hooked: Illegal drugs and how they got that way—Volume One. Marijuana and methamphetamine* (Documentary).

Abadinsky, H. (1997). *Organized crime.* Chicago: Nelson-Hall.

Abbott, J. H. (1981). *The belly of the beast: Letters from prison.* New York: Random House.

Abelson, E. (1989). *When ladies go a-thieving: Middle class shoplifters in the Victorian department store.* New York and Oxford, UK: Oxford University Press, as cited in Fullerton & Punj, p. 13.

About.com. (1999a). *Antitrust laws: How to identify and report violations.* Retrieved May 14, 2005, from http://usgovinfo.about.com/library/weekly/aa111499.htm

About.com. (1999b). *Antitrust laws: How to identify and report violations.* Retrieved May 14, 2005, from http://usgovinfo.about.com/library/weekly/aa111499p2.htm

About.com. (2002). *Drug cartels.* Retrieved November 14, 2004, from http://gomexico.about.com/cs/?once=true&

About.com. (2003). *Islam in the World: Country index.* Retrieved December 7, 2003, from http://atheism.about.com/library/FAQs/islam/blfaq_islam_countries.htm

About.com. (2004). *Retail theft report.* Retrieved December 21, 2004, from http://retailindustry.about.com/od/statistics_loss_prevention/l/aa011124a.htm

About.com. (2006). 2000 to 2002 stock market crash. Retrieved 9/3/06, from http://mutualfunds.about.com/cs/history/p/crash10.htm

Abu, G. M. M. (1985). Policies for the prevention and control of violence: A case study from the Sudan. *International Review of Criminal Policy, 37,* 24–27. Retrieved June 26, 2004, from the Criminal Justice Abstracts database at http://spweb.silverplatter.com/calstate

Adler, F. (1975) *Sisters in crime: The rise of the new female criminal.* New York: McGraw-Hill.

Adler, F. (1983). *Nations not obsessed with crime.* Littleton, CO: Fred B. Rothman.

Adler, F., Mueller, G. O. W., & Laufer, W. S. (2001). *Criminology and the criminal justice system* (4th ed.). New York: McGraw-Hill.

Adler, F., Mueller, G. O. W., & Laufer, W. S. (2004). *Criminology and the criminal justice system* (5th ed.). New York: McGraw-Hill.

Administrative Office of Pennsylvania Courts. (2004). *Glossary of legal terms.* Retrieved February 20, 2005, from http://www.courts.state.pa.us/Index/Aopc/Glossary/a.htm

Agren, G. (1997). *The new Swedish public health policy.* National Institute of Public Health (Sweden). Retrieved December 20, 2003, from http://www.fhi.se/shop/material_pdf/Nyafoh.pdf

Aichorn, A. (1936). *Wayward youth.* New York: Viking.

Akers, R. L. (1997). *Criminological theories* (2nd ed.). Los Angeles, CA: Roxbury.

Akers, R. L. (2000). *Criminological theories* (3rd ed.). Los Angeles, CA: Roxbury.

Akers, R. L., & Sellers, C. S. (2004). *Criminological theories* (4th ed). Los Angeles, CA: Roxbury.

Aldarondo, E., & Sugarman, D. B. (1996). Risk marker analysis of the cessation and persistence of wife assault. *Journal of Consulting and Clinical Psychology, 64*(5), 1010–1019.

Alexander, F., & Healy, W. (1935). *Roots of crime.* New York: Knopf.

Alexander, Y., & Kilmarx, R. A. (Eds.). (1979). *Political terrorism and business: The threat and response.* New York: Praeger.

Alic, M. (1995). Sheldon, William Herbert (1898–1977). *Gale encyclopedia of psychology.* Retrieved October 11, 2003, from http://www.findarticles.com/cf_dls/g2699/0006/2699000622/p2/article.jhtml

Allen, B. (1996). *Rape warfare: The hidden genocide in Bosnia-Herzegovina and Croatia.* Minneapolis: University of Minnesota Press.

Allgeier, A. R. (1994). Nazis and sex. In V. L. Bullough & B. Bullough (Eds.), *Human sexuality: An encyclopedia.* Retrieved May 13, 2006, from http://www2.huberlin.de/sexology/GESUND/ARCHIV/SEN/CH18.HTM#b1NAZIS%20AND%20SEX

Alliance for Cannabis Therapeutics. (1999). *Legislative actions and voter initiatives.* Retrieved December 5, 2004, from http://www.marijuana-as medicine.org/Alliance/leg-tall.html

Alliance of Sodomy Supporters. (1998). *United States sodomy laws.* Retrieved January 30, 2005, from http://www.sodomy.org/laws/

AllRefer.com. (2005). *Karmathians, Islam.* Retrieved May 23, 2006, from http://reference.allrefer.com/encyclopedia/K/Karmathi.html

Alonso, A. A. (2004). *African-American street gangs in Los Angeles.* Retrieved November 30, 2004, from http://www.nagia.org/Crips_and_Bloods.htm

Alpers, P. (2003). *Small arms in the Pacific.* Pacific Islands Forum Secretariat, Suva, Fiji. Retrieved September 25, 2003, from http://www.forumsec.org.fj/news/2003/Apr/April%2003.htm

AlRomaih, Y. A. (1993). *Social control and delinquency in Saudi Arabia.* (Doctoral Dissertation, Washington State University). Ann Arbor, MI: University Microfilms International. Retrieved June 26, 2004, from the Criminal Justice Abstracts database at http://spweb.silverplatter.com/calstate

American Psychiatric Association. (1970). No definite link found between XYY and crime. *APA Monitor,* 1, 5.

Americans.net. (2005). Harrison Narcotics Tax Act, 1914. Retrieved February 19,/2005, from http://www.historicaldocuments.com/HarrisonNarcotics TaxAct.htm

Amir, M. (1971). *Patterns in forcible rape.* Chicago: University of Chicago Press.

Amlin, K. (2002). *Chemical castration: The benefits and disadvantages intrinsic to injecting male pedophiliacs with Depo-Provera.* Retrieved October 14, 2003, from http://serendip.brynmawr.edu/biology/b103/f02/web1/kamlin.html

Amnesty International. (2000). *Saudi Arabia: Executions of Nigerian men and women.* Retrieved May 23, 2004, from http://web.amnesty.org/library/Index/engMDE-230492000

Andershed, H., Kerr, M., & Stattin, H. (2001). Bullying in school and violence on the streets: Are the same people involved? *Journal of Scandinavian Studies in Criminology and Crime Prevention, 2*(1), 31–49. Retrieved June 26, 2004, from the Criminal Justice Abstracts database at http://spweb.silverplatter.com/calstate

Anderson, K. (1997). *The pornography plague.* Retrieved December 31, 2004, from http://www.probe.org/docs/porplag.html

Anslinger, H. J., & Cooper, C. R. (1937, July). Marijuana: Assassin of youth. *The American Magazine, 124*(1). Article retrieved December 9, 2004, from http://www.redhousebooks.com/galleries/assassin.htm

Answers.com. (2003). *Indo-Pakistani wars.* Retrieved May 9, 2006, from http://www .answers.com/topic/india-pakistan-wars

Anthony, R., Brooks, A., & Lo, K. (1999). *History of Ciudad Juarez, Chihuahua.* Retrieved November 23, 2004, from http://www-personal.umich.edu/~kenlo/econdev/elpasohistory.html

Anti-Defamation League of B'nai B'rith. (1995). *The Skinhead international: A worldwide survey of neo-Nazi Skinheads.* New York: Anti-Defamation League of B'nai B'rith.

Appel, A. E., & Holden, G. W. (1998). The co-occurrence of spouse and physical child abuse: A review and appraisal. *Journal of Family Psychology, 12*(4), 578–599.

Arabianbiz.com. (2000). United Arab Emirates—Contemporary vision Arabian tradition. Retrieved April 19, 2002, from http://www.arabianbiz.com/travel/uae/uae.asp

Arenz, M. (2003). *Stone tablets wield "magical powers" say town leaders.* Retrieved May 5, 2004, from http://www.ridiculopathy.com/news_detail.php?id=877

Arrigo, B. A., & Bernard, T. J. (1997). Postmodern criminology in relation to radical and conflict criminology. *Critical Criminology, 8*(2), 39–60.

Arthur, J. A. (1992). Social changes and crime rates in Puerto Rico. *International Journal of Offender Therapy and Comparative Criminology, 362,* 103–119.

Arvantides, C., & Butcher, J. (1997). *Global organized crime: The Russian Mafiya.* Retrieved November 25, 2004, from http://american.edu/TED/hpages/crime/Russian.htm

Asher, G. (2001). *E-pornography offers opportunity for research.* Retrieved December 31, 2004, from http://www.slis.indiana.edu/news/story.php?story_id=360

Athens, L. (1992). *The creation of dangerous violent criminals.* Urbana, IL: University of Chicago Press.

Atkins, R. A. (1998). *Economic analysis of criminal procedure: Mapping out the aftermath of the exclusionary rule.* Ann Arbor, MI: University Microfilms International.

Attorney General's Commission on Pornography. (1986). *Final report.* Washington, DC: U.S. Government Printing Office.

Australian Bureau of Statistics. (1998). Recorded crime, Australia–1997, Cat No 4510.00. Retrieved December 23, 2003, from http://www.law.ecel.uwa.edu.au/crc/stats/Stats97/ch%201/ch1_text.htm

Australian Bureau of Statistics. (2002). *Crime and justice: Crime and safety.* Retrieved April 12, 2002, from http://www.abs.gov.au/Ausstats

Australian Institute of Criminology. (2001a). *Australian crime—facts and figure 2001: Alleged offenders.* Retrieved April 26, 2002, from http://www.aic.gov.au/publications/facts/2001/sec4.html

Australian Institute of Criminology. (2001b). *Australian crime—facts and figures 2001: Corrections.* Retrieved April 27, 2002, from http://www.aic.gov.au/publications/facts/2001/sec6.html

Australian Institute of Criminology. (2001c). *Australian crime—facts and figures 2001: Volume of crime.* Retrieved April 26, 2002, from http://www.aic.gov.au/publications/facts/2001/sec1.html

Australian Institute of Criminology. (2002). *Australian crime—facts and figures 2001.* Retrieved October 12, 2003, from http://www.aic.gov.au/publications/facts/2001/sec3.html

Avanesov, G. (1982). *The principles of criminology.* Moscow: Progress.

Avon and Somerset Constabulary. (2004). *Prolific Offenders Unit—Case study.* Retrieved May 15, 2004, from http://www.avonandsomerset.police.uk/prolific_offenders_unit/case_study.asp)

Ayres, I., & Donohue, J. J. (2002). *Shooting down the more guns, less crime hypothesis.* Cambridge, MA: National Bureau of Economic Research.

Ayres, I., & Levitt, S. D. (1998). Measuring positive externalities from unobservable victim precaution: An empirical analysis of Lojack. *Quarterly Journal of Economics, 113*(1), 43–77.

Ball, J. C. (1991). The similarity of crime rates among male heroin addicts in New York City, Philadelphia and Baltimore. *Journal of Drug Issues, 21*(2), 413–427.

Baltimore Sun, The. (2003, June 1). *U.S. prison population largest in world.* Retrieved October 10, 2004, from http://www.charleston.net/stories/060103/wor_01jailbirds.shtml

Banas, D. W., & Trojanowicz, R. C. (1985). *Uniform crime reporting and community policing: An historical perspective.* Retrieved March 13, 2005, from http://www.cj.msu.edu/~people/cp/uniform.html

Bankruptcylawfirms.com. (2005). *Bankruptcy history: About bankruptcy history from Act of 2005 to Act of 1978.* Retrieved May 30, 2006, from http://www.bankruptcylawfirms.com/History-Bankruptcy.cfm

Bankruptcylawfirms.com. (2006). *WorldCom bankruptcy news: Senate Judiciary Committee urged to strip WorldCom's Assets.* Retrieved May 19, 2006, from http://www.bankruptcylawfirms.com/WorldCom-Broke-Bank.cfm

Barak, G. (Ed.). (2000). *Crime and crime control: A global view.* Westport, CT: Greenwood.

Barker, M., Geraghty, J., & Webb, B. (1993). *The prevention of street robbery: Crime prevention unit series paper 44.* London: UK Home Office Police Department.

Barnett, C. (2002). *The measurement of white-collar crime using Uniform Crime Reporting (UCR) data.* Washington, DC: U.S. Department of Justice, Federal Bureau of Investigation, Criminal Justice Information Services (CJIS) Division. Retrieved December 4, 2004, from http://www.fbi.gov/ucr/whitecollarforweb.pdf

Barry, K. (1979). *Female sexual slavery.* Englewood Cliffs, NJ: Prentice Hall.

Barton, W. I. (1980a). *Drug abuse history and criminality of inmates of local jails: Results of the 1978 LEAA survey of inmates of local jails in the U.S.* Washington, DC: U.S. Drug Enforcement Assistance Administration.

Barton, W. I. (1980b). Drug histories and criminality: Survey of inmates of state correctional facilities, January 1974. *International Journal of the Addictions New York, 15*(2), 233–258.

Barton, W. I. (1982). Drug histories and criminality of inmates of local jails in the United States (1978): Implications for treatment and rehabilitation of the drug abuser in a jail setting. *International Journal of Addictions, 17*(3), 417–444.

Bashford, D. (1999). *Who killed Steve Kangas?* Retrieved April 30, 2005, from http://www.psnw.com/~bashford/kang-ev0.html

Bassett, P. M. (n. d.). (Christian) *Fundamentalism.* Retrieved June 2, 2005, from http://mb-soft.com/believe/text/fundamen.htm

Bauder, D. (1985). *Captain money and the golden girl.* San Diego: Harcourt Brace Jovanovich.

Bauder, D. (2005, June 2). Cover story: Captain money and the golden girl. *SanDiegoReader.com.* Retrieved May 19, 2006, from http://www.sdreader.com/php/cover.php?mode=article&showpg=1&id=20050602

Baun, A. (1976). Public expectations and police role concepts: Denmark. *Public Chief, 43*(5), 40–44.

Bayvida.com. (2003). *The history of involuntary treatment in California.* Retrieved July 19, 2003, from http://www.bayvida.com/health/help1.asp

BBC News. (1998, May 9). *Afghanistan's opium harvest.* Retrieved May 9, 2006, from http://news.bbc.co.uk/1/hi/programmes/from_our_own_correspondent/90211.stm

BBC News. (2002, May 7). *Enron "manipulated energy crisis."* Retrieved May 22, 2005, from http://news.bbc.co.uk/1/hi/business/1972574.stm

BBC News. (2005, August 3). *Musharraf invited to Miandad party.* Retrieved May 9, 2006, from http://news.bbc.co.uk/1/hi/world/south_asia/4741845.stm

BBC News. (2006, January 4). *Timeline: United Arab Emirates.* Retrieved May 23, 2006, from http://news.bbc.co.uk/1/hi/world/middle_east/country_profiles/828687.stm

Bebber, C. C. (1994). Increases in U.S. violent crime during the 1980s following four American military actions. *Journal of Interpersonal Violence, 9*(1), 109–116.

Becker, G. S. (1968). Crime and punishment: An economic approach. *Journal of Political Economy, 76,* 169–217.

Becker, H. S. (1953). Becoming a marihuana user. *American Journal of Sociology, 59,* 235–243.

Becker, H. S. (1963). *Outsiders: Studies in the sociology of deviance.* New York: The Free Press.

Becker, H. S. (2003). *Howie's homepage.* Retrieved December 8, 2003, from http://home.earthlink.net/~hsbecker/

Becknam, M. D. (1984). The White Slave Traffic Act: The historical impact of a criminal law policy on women. *Georgetown Law Journal, 72*(3), 1111–1142.

Bednarz, A. (2005). An unseemly marriage: Porn sites and spyware go hand in hand on the Web. *Network World.* Retrieved May 22, 2006, from http://www.networkworld.com/news /2005/110705widernet.html

Beirne, P., & Messerschmidt, J. (1991). *Criminology.* New York: Harcourt Brace Jovanovich.

Beirne, P., & Messerschmidt, J. (1995). *Criminology* (2nd ed.). New York: Harcourt Brace Jovanovich.

Belger, H. E. (1981). *A study of the criminal activity of juveniles during truancy.* Ann Arbor, MI: University Microfilms International.

Bell, D. (1965). *The end of ideology.* New York: Free Press.

Bellair, P. E. (2000). Informal surveillance and street crime: A complex relationship. *Criminology, 38*(1), 137–169.

Benard, C. (1994). Rape as terror: The case of Bosnia. *Terrorism and Political Violence, 6*(1), 29–43.

Bennett, R. R., & Lynch, J. P. (1990). Does a difference make a difference? Comparing cross-national crime indicators. *Criminology, 28*(1), 153–182.

Bennett, T., & Holloway, K. (2004). Possession and use of illegal guns among offenders in England and Wales. *Howard Journal of Criminal Justice, 43*(3), 237–252.

Benson, M. L., Cullen, F. T., & Maakestad, W. J. (1993). *Local prosecutors and corporate crime.* Washington, DC: National Institute of Justice, 1993.

Bentham, J. (1969). An introduction to the principles of morals and legislation. In M. P. Mack (Ed.), *A Bentham reader.* New York: Pegasus.

Bergen, R. K., & Bogle, K. A. (2000). Exploring the connection between pornography and sexual violence. *Violence and Victims, 15*(3), 227–234.

Bernhardt, E. (2001). *The situation of families in Sweden in the 1990s.* Retrieved October 8, 2004, from http://europa.eu.int/comm/employment_social/eoss/downloads/gm_01_sweden_bernhardt_en.pdf

Best, D., Sidwell, C., & Gossop, M. (2001), Crime and expenditure amongst polydrug misusers seeking treatment. The connection between prescribed methadone, crack use and criminality. *British Journal of Criminology, 41*(1), 119–126.

Beyer, K. R., & Beasley, J. O. (2003). Nonfamily child abductors who murder their victims: Offender demographics from interviews with incarcerated offenders. *Journal of Interpersonal Violence, 18*(10), 1167–1188.

Bichler, R. G., & Potchak, M. C. (2002). Testing the importance of target selection factors associated with commercial burglary using the blended approach. *Security Journal, 154,* 41–61.

Bin, L. (1999). *Masculine sexuality and violence.* Retrieved October 14, 2003, from http://hyper.vcsun.org/HyperNews/battias/get/pace356/rsch/12.html?nogif)

Binger, N. (n. d.) *The War on Drugs: A domestic policy failure (Documentary).* Retrieved December 7, 2004, from http://www.unc.edu/~binger/WOD.html

Birkbeck, C. H. (1983). Victimization surveys in Latin America: Some first experiences. *Victimology, 8*(3–4), 7–22.

Bjerregaard, B., & Lizotte, A. (1995). Gun ownership and gang membership. *Journal of Criminal Law and Criminology, 86,* 37–58.

Black, W. K. (2005). *The best way to rob a bank is to own one.* Austin: University of Texas Press.

Blake, D. (1999). *Shower Posse: The most notorious Jamaican criminal organization* [Book Review]. Retrieved October 17, 2003, from http://www.headstartbooks.com/cstudies/carribbean.htm

Blau, J. R., & Blau, P. M. (1982). The cost of inequality: Metropolitan structure and violent crime. *American Sociological Review, 47*(1), 114–129.

Blinne Blogg, The. (2004). *Why Democrats don't get evangelicals.* Retrieved February 27, 2005, from http://www.blinne.org/blog/2004/11/why_democrats_d.html

Bloch, H., & Geis, G.. (1970). *Man, crime, and society.* New York: Random House.

Bodansky, Y. (2001). *Bin Laden: The man who declared war on America.* New York: Prima Publishing/Random House.

Bode, J. (1978). *Fighting back: How to cope with the medical, emotional and legal consequences of rape.* New York: Macmillan.

Boeringer, S. (1994). Pornography and sexual aggression: Associations of violent and nonviolent depictions with rape and rape proclivity. *Deviant Behavior, 15*(3), 289–304.

Boggess, S., & Bound, J. (1997). Did criminal activity increase during the 1980s? Comparisons across data sources. *Social Science Quarterly, 78,* 725–739.

Bohn, K. (2003). *ACLU files lawsuit against PATRIOT Act.* Retrieved June 8, 2004, from http://www.cnn.com/2003/LAW/07/30/patriot.act/

Bohsui, W., & McCaghy, C. H. (1993). Attitudinal determinants of public opinions toward legalized pornography. *Journal of Criminal Justice, 21*(1), 13–27.

Bonger, W. (1916). *Criminality and economic conditions.* Boston: Little, Brown.

Bonnie, R. J., & Whitebread, II, C. H. (2002). Passage of the Uniform Narcotic Drug Act: 1927–1937. Retrieved December 9, 2004, from http://www.drugtext.org/library/reports/vlr/vlr3.htm

Borricand, J. (1995). *France. World Factbook of Criminal Justice Systems.* Retrieved May 28, 2005, from http://www.ojp.usdoj.gov/bjs/pub/ascii/wfbcjfra.txt

Bourget, D., & Gagne, P. (2002). Maternal filicide in Quebec. *Journal of the American Academy of Psychiatry and the Law, 30*(3), 345–351.

Bowers, D. (1997). Political culture and felony sentencing: An examination of trial courts in 300 counties. *Criminal Justice Policy Review, 8*(4), 343–364.

Bowers, S. (2003). *Study disputes claim of 20,000 U.S. gun laws; research of federal and state gun laws yields 300 relevant statutes.* Retrieved June 11, 2005, from http://www.scienceblog.com/community/older/archives/K/4/pub4873.html

Box, S., & Hale. C. (1983). Liberation and female criminality in England and Wales revisited. *British Journal of Criminology, 22*(3), 35–49.

Boylan, R. (2003.) *The secret shadow government: A structural analysis.* Retrieved June 19, 2005, from http://www.abovetopsecret.com/pages/secgov.html

Bracey, D. H. (1979). "Baby-pro": Preliminary profiles of juvenile prostitutes: *Criminal Justice Center Monography Number, 12,* 86–87. New York: John Jay Press.

Bradford, D. G. (1996). [Review of the book *Rape warfare: The hidden genocide in Bosnia-Herzegovina and Croatia,* by Beverly Allen]. Retrieved October 27, 2003, from http://www.airpower.maxwell.af.mil/airchronicles/bookrev/allen1.html

Braga, A. A., Cook, P. J., Kennedy, D. M., & Tonry, M. (2002). The illegal supply of firearms. In *Crime and justice: A review of research, Vol. 29,* (pp. 319–352). Chicago: University of Chicago Press.

Braithwaite, J. (1989). *Crime, shame and reintegration.* New York: Cambridge University Press.

Braithwaite, J. (1995). Reintegrative shaming, republicanism, and policy. In H. Barlow (Ed.), *Crime and public policy: Putting theory to work* (pp. 191–204). Boulder, CO: Westview.

Braithwaite, J. (1999). In Michael Tonry (Ed.), *Crime and justice: A review of research, 25,* 1–127.

Braziel, J. E. (2000). *History of migration and immigration laws into the United States.* Retrieved October 12, 2003, from http://www.umass.edu/complit/aclanet/USMigrat.html

Brecher, E. M. (1972). *The Consumer Union Report on Licit and Illicit Drugs: Chapter 8. The Harrison Narcotic Act (1914).* Retrieved February 19, 2005, from http://www.druglibrary.org/schaffer/Library/studies/cu/cu8.html

Brecher, E. M., & Editors of Consumer Reports Magazine. (1972). *The Consumer Union report on licit and illicit drugs.* Retrieved November 29, 2004, from http://www.drugtext.org/library/reports/cu/CU20.html

Brehmer, C., & Iten, P. X. (2001). Medical prescription of heroin to chronic heroin addicts in Switzerland: A review. *Forensic Science International, 121*(1–2), 23–26. Retrieved June 26, 2004, from the Criminal Justice Abstracts database at http://spweb.silverplatter.com/calstate

Brians, P. (1998). *The Enlightenment.* Retrieved February 19, 2005, from http://www.wsu.edu:8080/~brians/hum_303/enlightenment.html

British Museum. (1977). *Sir Francis Drake.* London: British Museum Publications.

Brocato, D. A. (2003). *Drug schedules.* Retrieved December 5, 2004, from http://www.addictions.org/schedules.html

Brown, J. B., Netoles, B., Rasnak, S. T., & Tight, M. (1999). *Identifying bankruptcy fraud.* Retrieved May 19, 2006, from http://www.crfonline.org/orc/pdf/ref11.pdf

Brown, R., & Thomas, N. (2003). Aging vehicles: Evidence of the effectiveness of new car security from the Home Office Car Theft Index. *Security Journal, 16*(3), 45–53.

Brown, S., Esbensen, F., & Geis, G. (2001). *Criminology: Explaining crime and its context* (4th ed.). Cincinnati, OH: Anderson.

Browne, J. (1995). *The labor of doing time.* Retrieved December 7, 2004, from http://www.prisonactivist.org/crisis/labor-of-doing-time.html

Brownmiller, S. (1975). *Against our will: Men, women, and rape.* New York: Bantam.

Bruce, A. A., & Schehr, R. C. (1998). Restoring justice for juveniles: A critical analysis of victim-offender mediation. *Justice Quarterly, 154,* 629–666.

Bruce, L. (2002). *Anatomy of check-kiting fraud.* Retrieved May 14, 2005, from http://origin.bankrate.com/brm/news/chk/20021203b.asp

Buckelew, A. H. (1984). *Terrorism and the American response.* San Rafael, CA: MIRA Academic.

Budd, T. (1999). *Burglary of domestic dwellings: Findings from the British Crime Survey.* London: UK Home Office.

Bullough, V. L. (1994). Nazis and sex. In Bullough, V. L., & Bullough, B. (Eds.), *Human Sexuality: An Encyclopedia.* Retrieved May 13, 2006, from http://www2.huberlin.de/sexology/GESUND/ARCHIV/SEN/CH18.HTM#b1-NAZIS%20AND%20SEX

Bureau for International Narcotics and Law Enforcement Affairs, U.S. Department of State. (1999a). *International Narcotics Control Strategy Report, 1998.* Washington, DC. Retrieved November 21, 2003, from http://www.state.gov/www/global/narcotics_law/1998_narc_report/camex98.html

Bureau for International Narcotics and Law Enforcement Affairs, U.S. Department of State. (1999b). *International Narcotics Control Strategy Report, 1998.* Washington, DC. Retrieved November 21, 2003, from http://www.state.gov/www/global/narcotics_law/1998_narc_report/baham98.xls

Bureau of Justice Statistics. (1988). *Report to the nation on crime and justice* (2nd ed.). Washington, DC: U.S. Government Printing Office.

Bureau of Justice Statistics. (1995). *Criminal victimization in the United States, 1995: A national crime victimization survey report.* Retrieved August 23, 2002, from http://www.ojp.usdoj.gov/bjs/pub/pdf/cvus95.pdf

Bureau of Justice Statistics. (1996a). *Convictions per 1,000 offenders.* Retrieved November 4, 2003, from http://www.ojp.usdoj.gov/bjs/pub/html/cjusew96/cpo.htm

Bureau of Justice Statistics. (1996b). *Criminal Victimization in the United States, 1996: Statistical Tables.* Retrieved September 1, 2006, from http://www.ojp.usdoj.gov/bjs/pub/pdf/cvus96.pdf

Bureau of Justice Statistics. (1997). *Criminal Victimization in the United States, 1997: Statistical Tables.* Retrieved September 1, 2006, from http://www.ojp.usdoj.gov/bjs/pub/pdf/cvus97.pdf

Bureau of Justice Statistics. (1998a). *Crime and justice in the United States and in England and Wales, 1981–96: Crime rates from victim surveys.* Retrieved June 13, 2004, from http://www.ojp.usdoj.gov/bjs/pub/html/cjusew96/crvs.htm

Bureau of Justice Statistics. (1998b). *Criminal Victimization in the United States, 1998: Statistical Tables.* Retrieved September 1, 2006, from http://www.ojp.usdoj.gov/bjs/pub/pdf/cvus98.pdf

Bureau of Justice Statistics. (1999). *Criminal Victimization in the United States, 1999: Statistical Tables.* Retrieved September 1, 2006, from http://www.ojp.usdoj.gov/bjs/pub/pdf/cvus99.pdf

Bureau of Justice Statistics. (2000). *Criminal Victimization in the United States, 2000: Statistical Tables.* Retrieved September 1, 2006, from http://www.ojp.usdoj.gov/bjs/pub/pdf/cvus00.pdf

Bureau of Justice Statistics. (2001). *Criminal victimization in the United States, 2002: Statistical tables.* Washington, DC: U.S. Department of Justice. Retrieved November 3, 2003, from http://www.ojp.usdoj.gov/bjs/pub/pdf/cv01.pdf

Bureau of Justice Statistics. (2002a). *Homicide trends in the U.S.: Intimate homicide.* Retrieved October 11, 2003, from http://www.ojp.usdoj.gov/bjs/homicide/intimates.htm

Bureau of Justice Statistics. (2002b). *Homicide trends in the U.S.: Long term trends. Retrieved* October 21, 2003, from http://www.ojp.usdoj.gov/bjs/homicide/hmrt.htm

Bureau of Justice Statistics. (2002c). *Homicide trends in the U.S.: Multiple victims and offenders.* Retrieved October 19, 2003, from http://www.ojp.usdoj.gov/bjs/homicide/tables/multivictab.htm

Bureau of Justice Statistics. (2002d). *Homicide trends in the* U.S.: *Age trends.* Retrieved November 3, 2003, from http://www.ojp.usdoj.gov/bjs/homicide/teens.htm

Bureau of Justice Statistics. (2002e). *National crime victimization survey: Criminal victimization 2002.* Retrieved November 3, 2003, from http://www.ojp.usdoj.gov/bjs/pub/pdf/cv02.pdf

Bureau of Justice Statistics. (2003). *Criminal victimization in the United States, 2003: Statistical tables.* Retrieved September 10, 2005, from http://www.ojp.usdoj.gov/bjs/pub/pdf/cvus03.pdf

Bureau of Justice Statistics. (2004a). *Assault rates declined since 1994.* Retrieved June 16, 2004, from http://www.ojp.usdoj.gov/bjs/glance/aslt.htm

Bureau of Justice Statistics. (2004b). *National crime victimization survey: Criminal victimization 2004.* Retrieved December 5, 2005, from http://www.ojp.usdoj.gov/bjs/pub/pdf/cv04.pdf

Bureau of Justice Statistics. (2004c). Criminal Victimization in the United States, 2004: Statistical Tables. Retrieved September 1, 2006, from http://www.ojp.usdoj.gov/bjs/pub/pdf/cvus04.pdf

Bureau of Justice Statistics. (2005a). *After many years of declining, burglary rates have stabilized.* Retrieved April 17, 2005, from http://www.ojp.usdoj.gov/bjs/glance/burg.htm

Bureau of Justice Statistics. (2005b). *After many years of declining, theft rates stabilized in recent years.* Retrieved April 17, 2006, from http://www.ojp.usdoj.gov/bjs/glance/theft.htm

Bureau of Justice Statistics. (2005c). *After declining since 1992, motor vehicle theft rates leveled off after 2000.* Retrieved April 27, 2006, from http://www.ojp.usdoj.gov/bjs/glance/mvt.htm

Burgess, A. W., & Holmstrom, L. L. (1976). Rape: Its effect on task performance at varying stages of the life cycle. In M. J. Walker & S. L. Brodsky (Eds.), *Sexual assault: The victim and the rapist* (pp. 23–34). Lexington, MA: D.C. Heath.

Burke, T. W., & O'Rear, C. E. (1990). Home invaders: Asian gangs in America. *Police Studies, 13*(4), 154–156.

Burnham, B. (1997). *A short history of the collection of UN crime and justice statistics at the international level.* Retrieved April 3, 2004, from http://www.uncjin.org/Special/history.html

Bursik, R. J., Jr., & Grasmick, H. G. (1993). *Neighborhoods and crime: The dimensions of effective community control.* New York: Lexington.

Buss, D. M., & Duntley, J. D. (1999). *Murder by design: The evolutionary psychology of homicide.* Retrieved August 20, 2006, from http://homepage.psy.utexas.edu/homepage/Group/BussLAB/pdffiles/Human%20Nature%20and%20Culture.pdf#search=%22Buss%20Duntley%20Murder%20by%20Design%22

Calabresi, M. (1998, November 30). The Dons of the East: A growing wave of organized crime moves westward from the ex-communist countries of eastern Europe. *Time International,* p. 20.

Calavita, K., & Pontell, H. N. (1990). "Heads I win, tails you lose": Deregulation, crime and crisis in the savings and loan industry. *Crime and Delinquency, 36*(3), 309–341.

Calavita, K., & Pontell, H. N. (1991). "Other people's money" revisited: Collective embezzlement in the savings and loan and insurance industries. *Social Problems, 38*(1), 94–112.

Calavita, K., Tillman, R., & Pontell, H. N. (1997). The savings and loan debacle, financial crime, and the state. *Annual Review of Sociology, 23,* 19–38.

Calhoun, C. (2003). *Robert K. Merton remembered.* Retrieved April 6, 2003, from http://www.asanet.org/footnotes/mar03/indextwo.html

California Crime Control and Violence Prevention Commission. (1981). *An ounce of prevention: Toward an understanding of the causes of violence.* Sacramento: [s.n.]

California Highway Patrol. (2003). *Safety, service, & security.* Retrieved October 10, 2004, from http://www.chp.ca.gov/html/border.html

California Legislature Joint Committee for Revision of the Penal Code. (1980). *Plea bargaining.* Sacramento, CA.

California Protective Parents Association. (1999). *Case studies.* Retrieved June 16, 2005, from http://www.protectiveparents.com/cases.html

Callahan, C. M., Rivara, F. P., & Farrow, J. A. (1993). Youth in detention and handguns. *Journal of Adolelscent Health, 14,* 350–355.

Cameron, M. O. (1964). *The booster and the snitch: Department store shoplifting.* New York: Free Press of Glencoe.

Camp, G. M. (1968). *Nothing to lose: A study of bank robbery in America* (Doctoral Dissertation, Yale University). Ann Arbor, MI: University Microfilms.

Campbell, A. (1984). *The girls in the gang.* New York: Basil Blackwell.

Canada Special Committee on Pornography and Prostitution. (1985). *Pornography and prostitution in Canada.* Ottawa: Canadian Publishing Center.

Canivell, J. M. (1993). *Spain. World factbook of criminal justice systems.* Retrieved May 28, 2005, from http://www.ojp.usdoj.gov/bjs/pub/ascii/wfbcjspn.txt

Cao, L., Adams, A., & Jensen, V. J. (1997). A test of the black subculture of violence thesis: A research note. *Criminology, 35,* 367–379.

Capowich, G. E. (1996). *Neighborhood dynamics and crime: Testing the systemic model of neighborhood victimization* (Doctoral Dissertation, University of Maryland at College Park). Ann Arbor, MI: University Microfilms International.

Capowich, G. E. (2003). The conditioning effects of neighborhood ecology on burglary victimization. *Criminal Justice and Behavior, 30*(1), 39–61.

Carcach, C., Mouzos, J., & Grabosky, P. (2002). The mass murder as quasi-experiment: The impact of the 1996 Port Arthur Massacre. *Homicide Studies, 6*(2), 109–127.

Carcach, C., & Muscat, G. (2002). Location quotients of crime and their use in the study of area crime careers and regional crime structures. *Crime Prevention and Community Safety: An International Journal, 4*(1), 27–46.

Carlson, W. R. (1990). Crime prevention through environmental design: A micro-environmental study of theft within a hospital setting. *Security Journal, 1*(5), 276–286.

Carmichael, F., & Ward, R. (2001). Male unemployment and crime in England and Wales. *Economics Letters, 73,* 111–115.

Carney, S. (1997, December 11). *Crime: Police see new perpetrator profiles for robbery, once a trademark of Asian gangs. Flare-up has occurred in last few months.* Retrieved November 23, 2003, from http://www.pacificnet.net/jue/humor/docs/invasion_home.html

Carr, C. (2002). *The lessons of terror: A history of warfare against civilians: Why it has always failed and why it will fail again.* New York: Random House.

Carrington, P. J. (2001). Population aging and crime in Canada. *Canadian Journal of Criminology, 43*(3), 331–356.

Carter, D. L. (2001). Computer crime categories: How techno-criminals operate. *FBI Law Enforcement Bulletin.* Retrieved May 22, 2006, from http://nsi.org/Library/Compsec/ crimecom.html

Catalano, S. M. (2005). *Crime victimization, 2004: Bureau of Justice Statistics National Crime Victimization Survey.* Retrieved December 5, 2005, from http://www.ojp.usdoj.gov/bjs/pub/pdf/cv04.pdf

CATWAP. (1999). Statistics on trafficking and prostitution in Asia and the Pacific. Retrieved April 28, 2006, from http://salidumay.org/discussions/articles/stats_prostitution.htm

Caunitis, J. (2002). *Drugs in Latvia: Situation Report. State Center for Drug Abuse Prevention and Treatment: Nordic Council of Ministers.* Retrieved May 16, 2004, from: http://www.nmr.lv/eng/activities/docs/DRUGS_IN_LATVIA.doc

Cavan, R. S., & Ferdinand, T. N. (1975). *Juvenile delinquency.* Philadelphia: Lippincott.

CBC News. (2003, October 28). *The thief.* Retrieved September 30, 2004, from http://www.cbc.ca/consumers/market/files/cars/gta/thief.html

CBSNEWS.com. (2002, November 7). *Addicted: Shoplifting for thrills.* Retrieved September 20, 2004, from http://www.cbsnews.com/stories/2002/10/17/48hours/main525948.shtml

Center for Defense Information. (2002). *In the spotlight: Islamic Movement of Uzbekistan* (IMU). Retrieved May 27, 2004, from http://www.cdi.org/terrorism/imu.cfm

Center for International Crime Prevention Office for Drug Control and Crime Prevention and Statistics Division Department of Economic and Social Affairs, United Nations. (1995). *Questionnaire for the Sixth United Nations Survey of Crime Trends and Operations of Criminal Justice Systems, covering the period 1995–1997.* Retrieved April 3, 2005, from http://www.unodc.org/pdf/crime/sixthsurvey/que.pdf

Central Intelligence Agency. (2002). *The world factbook 2002.* Retrieved July 28, 2003, from http://www.odci.gov/cia/publications/factbook/index.html

Central Intelligence Agency. (2005). *The world factbook 2005: Field Listing—Legal System.* Retrieved February 28, 2006, from http://www.odci.gov/cia/publications/factbook/fields/2100.html

Central Intelligence Agency. (2006). *The world factbook 2006.* Retrieved May 24, 2006, from http://www.cia.gov/cia/publications/factbook/

Chaiken, M. R., & Chaiken, J. M. (1985). *Who gets caught doing crime?* Washington, DC: U.S. Bureau of Justice Statistics.

Chambliss, W. J. (1967). Types of deviance and the effectiveness of legal sanctions. *Wisconsin Law Review, 3,* 703–719.

Chambliss, W. J. (1989a). *On the take: From petty crooks to presidents* (Rev. ed.). Bloomington, In: Indiana University Press.

Chambliss, W. J. (1989b). State organized crime. *Criminology, 27,* 183–208.

Chamlin, M. B., Grasmich, H. G., & Bursik, R. J., Jr. (1992). Crime aggregation and time lag in macro-level deterrence research. *Criminology, 30*(3), 377–395.

Chappel, D., & Wilson, P. (1994). The facts and figures that describe Australia's crime patterns and trends. Abbreviated from D. Chappel & P. Wilson (Eds.), *Trends in crime and criminal justice in the Australian criminal justice system—the mid-1990s.* Retrieved April 12, 2002, from http://members.ozemail.com.au/~born1820/auscjs.htm

Chellappan, K. (2004, 23 June). True follower of Gen Zia. *Asianet News.* Retrieved May 7, 2006, from http://www.asianetglobal.com:8080/asianet/2004/news/detailedstory.jsp?catId=7&newsId=19

Chen, X. (2002). Social control in China: Applications of the labeling theory and the reintegrative shaming theory. *International Journal of Offender Therapy and Comparative Criminology, 46*(1), 45–63.

Chesney-Lind, M. (1989). Girls' crime and woman's place: Toward a feminist model of female delinquency. *Crime and Delinquency, 35,* 5–29.

Chesney-Lind, M., & Lind, I. Y. (1984). *Visitors as victims: Crimes against tourists in two Hawaii counties.* Manoa: Youth Development and Research Center, School of Social Work, University of Hawaii, Manoa.

Chesney-Lind, M., & Okamoto, S. K. (2001). Gender matters: Patterns in girls' delinquency and gender responsive programming. *Journal of Forensic Psychology Practice, 1*(3), 1–28.

Chikritzh, T., Jonas, H., Heale, P., Dietze, P., Hanlin, K., & Stockwell, T. (1999, December). Alcohol-caused deaths and hospitalizations in Australia, 1990–1997. *National Alcohol Indicators, 1.*

Choi, A., & Edleson, J. L. (1995). Advocating legal intervention in wife assaults; results from a national survey of Singapore. *Journal of Interpersonal Violence, 10*(3), 243–258. Retrieved June 26, 2004, from the Criminal Justice Abstracts database at http://spweb.silverplatter.com/calstate

Chossudovsky, M. (2001). *Who is Osama bin Laden?* Retrieved May 4, 2006, from http://www.globalresearch.ca/articles/CHO109C.html

Chouvy, P.-A. (2002). Golden triangle. In L. D. Christensen (Ed.), *Encyclopedia of modern Asia* (pp. 442–443). Chicago: Scribners. Retrieved April 30, 2006, from http://www.pa-chouvy.org/drugtradeinasiaPRINT.html

Chretien, J. (2002). United Nations Report: Linking poverty to terrorism starts at the United Nations. Retrieved June 5, 2004, from http://www.canadafreepress.com/archives/2002/un91602.htm

Christianson, K. O. (1974). Seriousness of criminality and concordance among Danish twins. In R. Hood (Ed.), *Crime, criminology and public policy* (pp. 63–77). New York: Free Press.

Ciao Atlas (1993). *Trade in the Gulf.* Retrieved May 17, 2006, from http://www.ciaonet.org/atlas/countries/ae_data_loc.html

City of El Cerrito Police Department. (2006). *Directory of prior reports—Report no. 06–03886.*

Clark, R. (1970). *Crime in America.* New York: Pocket Books.

Clarke, R. V. (1983). Situational crime prevention: Its theoretical basis and practical scope. In M. Tonry & N. Morris (Eds.), *Crime and justice: An annual review of research, Vol. 4,* (pp. 225–256). Chicago: University of Chicago Press.

Clarke, R. V. (1992). *Situational crime prevention: Successful case studies.* Albany, NY: Harrow and Heston.

Clarke, R. V., & Homel, R. (1997). A revised classification of situational crime prevention techniques. In S. P. Lab (Ed.), *Crime prevention at a crossroads.* Cincinatti, OH: Anderson.

Clarke, R. V., & Mayhew, P. (1994). Parking patterns and car theft risks: Policy-relevant findings from the British Crime Survey. In R. V. Clarke (Ed.), *Crime prevention studies, Vol. 3,* (pp. 91–108). Monesey, NY: Criminal Justice Press.

Cleckley, H. M. (1941). *The mask of sanity.* St. Louis, MO: C.V. Mosby.

Clinard, M. B., & Quinney, R. (1973). *Criminal behavior systems: A typology.* New York: Holt, Rinehart and Winston. Inc.

Clinton Administration. (2000). *International crime threat assessment.* Retrieved November 4, 2004, from http://clinton4.nara.gov/WH/EOP/NSC/html/documents/pub45270/pub45270index.html

Cloward, R. A., & Ohlin, L. E. (1960). *Delinquency and opportunity: A theory of delinquent gangs.* New York: Free Press.

Clutterbuck, R. (1995). *Drugs, crime and corruption: Thinking the unthinkable.* New York: New York University Press.

CNN.com. (1995). *CNN Cold War—Interview: F. Mark Wyatt.* Retrieved May 1, 2005, from http://www.cnn.com/SPECIALS/cold.war/episodes/03/interviews/wyatt/

CNN.com. (1999, January 26). *Vatican issues first exorcism ritual since 1614: Rites seek to bring church up to date with science.* Retrieved July 25, 2003, from http://www.cnn.com/WORLD/europe/9901/26/exorcism/

CNN.com. (2001, July 15). *Report: 16 percent of state prison inmates mentally ill.* Retrieved July 14, 2003, from http://www.cnn.com/2001/US/07/15/prisons.mental.health/

CNN.com. (2002, January 13). *Explaining the Enron bankruptcy.* Retrieved May 22, 2005, from http://archives.cnn.com/2002/US/01/12/enron.qanda.focus/

CNN.com. (2003, November 18). *Supreme Court strikes down Texas sodomy law.* Retrieved January 30, 2005, from http://www.cnn.com/2003/LAW/06/26/scotus.sodomy/

CNN.com. (2006, February 22). *Lou Dobbs tonight: White House refuses to back down on UAE Ports deal.* Retrieved May 23, 2006, from http://transcripts.cnn.com/TRANSCRIPTS /0602/22/ldt.01.html

CNNMoney. (1997). *Arresting employee theft.* Retrieved May 20, 2006, from http://money.cnn.com/1997/11/13/smbusiness/theft_a/

CNNMoney. (2004). *U.S. fines Bill Gates $800,000.* Retrieved May 14, 2005, from http://money.cnn.com/2004/05/03/technology/gates_penalty/

Coalition Against Trafficking in Women. (2001). *Coalition Report: 2001.* Retrieved December 14, 2004 from http://action.web.ca/home/catw/attach/ReportOct2002.pdf; A list of publications was retrieved December 17, 2004, from http://www.catwinternational.org/

Cockayne, A. (2002). *Prostitution and sexual exploitation in the European Union.* Retrieved May 12, 2006, from http://www.ex.ac.uk/~watupman/undergrad/aac/word_format.doc

Cockburn, L. (1987) *Out of control.* New York: Atlantic Monthly Press.

Cohen, A. K. (1955). *Delinquent boys: The culture of the gang.* New York: Free Press.

Cohen, B. (1980). *Deviant street networks: Prostitution in New York City.* Lexington, MA: Lexington.

Cohen, D., & Longtin, S. (1993) *Canada.* Retrieved April 16, 2002 from http://www.ojp.usdoj.gov/bjs/pub/ascii/wfbcjcan.txt

Cohen, L. E., & Cantor, D. (1980). The determinants of larceny in empirical and theoretical study. *Journal of Research in Crime and Delinquency, 17*(2), 140–159.

Cohen, L. E., Cantor, D., & Kluegel, J.R. (1981). Robbery victimization in the U.S: An analysis of a nonrandom event. *Social Science Quarterly, 61*(4), 644–657.

Cohen, L. E., & Felson, M. (1979). Social change and crime rate trends: A routine activities approach. *American Sociological Review, 44,* 588–608.

Cohen, P. (2003). *Cocaine and cannabis: An identical policy for different drugs?* Retrieved December 7, 2004, from http://www.cedro-uva.org/lib/cohen.drugs.iii.html#p2

Cohen, T., Kauder, N., & Ostrom, B. J. (2000). A renewed interest in low-level crime. *Caseload Highlights: Examining the Work of State Courts, 6*(2). Retrieved June 16, 2005, from http://www.ncsconline.org/D_Research/CSP/Highlights/LLCrimeTrendsV6N2pdf.pdf

Cohn, E. G. (1990). Weather and crime. *British Journal of Criminology, 30*(1), 51–64.

Cohn, E. G., & Rotton, J. (2000). Weather, seasonal trends and property crimes in Minneapolis, 1987–1988. A moderator-variable time-series analysis of routine activities. *Journal of Environmental Psychology, 20,* 257–272.

Cohn, J. P. (2001). The international flow of food: FDA takes on growing responsibilities for imported food safety. *U.S. Food and Drug Administration FDA Consumer Magazine.* Retrieved May 15, 2005, from http://www.fda.gov/fdac/features/2001/101_food.html

Coleman, D. H., & Straus, M. A. (1986). Marital power, conflict, and violence in a nationally representative sample of American couples. *Violence and Victims, 1*(2), 141–157.

Coleman, J. W. (2002). *The criminal elite: Understanding white-collar crime.* New York: Worth Publishers.

Colin, L., McDowall, D., & Wiersema, B. (1991). Effects of restricting licensing of handguns on homicide and suicide in the District of Columbia. *New England Journal of Medicine, 325*(23), 1615–1620.

Colin, R. O. (1985). The blunt instruments: Italy and the police. In J. Roach & J. Thomaneck (Eds.), *In police and public order in Europe* (pp. 185–214). London: Croom Helm.

Columbia [sic.]. (2003). Retrieved July 31, 2003, from http://www.cromwellintl.com/security/nu/co.html

Columbia Encyclopedia. (2001). *Muckrakers.* Retrieved May 15, 2005, from http://www.bartleby.com/65/mu/muckrake.html

Committee against corruption in Saudi Arabia (CACSA). *A bad monarchy is a government without a country.* Retrieved November 2, 1998, from http://saudhouse.com/building.htm

Committee Office, House of Commons, The. (1999). *Memorandum Submitted by Dr. Galeotti to the Senate Committee on Foreign Affairs, The United Kingdom Parliament.* Retrieved November 26, 2004, from http://www.parliament.the-stationery-office.co.uk/pa/cm199899/cmselect/cmfaff/815/9102605.htm

Comparative Criminology Website. See Winslow, 2003.

Conklin, B. R., & Seiden, R. H. (1981). Gun deaths: Biting the bullet on effective control. *Public Affairs Report Berkeley California, 22*(5), 1–7.

Conklin, J. E. (1972). *Robbery and the criminal justice system.* Philadephia: Lippincott.

Conscious Rasta Press. (1998). *CIA and Reggae. Part 3 of a series excerpted from high crimes of murder.* Retrieved November 11, 2003, from http://www.7mac.com/7MAC/academy/CIA_reggae5.htm

ConspiracyArchive.com (1999). Retrieved April 30, 2005, from http://conspiracyarchive.com/NWO/project_paperclip.htm

Constantine, A. (2000). *Tales from the crypt: The depraved spies and moguls of the CIA's Operation MOCKINGBIRD.* Retrieved May 1, 2005, from http://www.apfn.org/apfn/mockingbird.htm

Cook, P. J., & Laub, J. H. (1998). The unprecedented epidemic in youth violence. In M. Tonry & M. H. Moore (Ed.), *Youth violence* (pp. 27–64). Chicago: University of Chicago Press.

Cook, P. J., & Moore, M. H. (1999). Guns, gun control, and homicide. In M. D. Smith & M. A. Zahn (Eds.), *Studying and preventing homicide: Issues and challenges* (p. 252). Thousand Oaks, CA: Sage.

Cooley, C. H. (1902). *Human nature and social order.* New York: Scribner.

Cooper, H. H. A. (1978). Terrorism: New dimensions of violent criminality. *Cumberland Law Review, 9*(2), 369–390.

Corbo, C. A., & Coyle, E. (1990). *Mandatory sentences for firearms offenses in New Jersey.* Newark, NJ: Data Committee, Criminal Disposition Commission.

Corman, H., & Mocan, H. N. (1996). *A time-series analysis of crime and drug use in New York City—NBER Working Paper, #5463.* Cambridge, MA: National Bureau of Economic Research.

Corman, H., & Mocan, N. (2002). *Carrots, sticks, and broken windows.* Cambridge, MA: National Bureau of Economic Research.

Cornell Law School. (2005). *Bankruptcy fraud.* Retrieved May 19, 2006, from http://www.law.cornell.edu/wex/index.php/Bankruptcy_fraud

Cornish, D. B., & Clarke, R. V. (1985). Modeling offenders' decisions: A framework for research and policy. In M. Tonry & N. Morris (Eds.), *Crime and Justice, Vol. 6.* Chicago: University of Chicago Press.

Cornish, D. B., & Clarke, R. V. (1986). *Introduction.* In D. B. Cornish & R. V. Clarke. *The reasoning criminal: Rational choice perspectives on offending* (pp. 1–18). New York: Springer-Verlag.

Cornish, D. B., & Clarke, R. V. (1987). Understanding crime displacement: An application of rational choice theory. *Criminology, 25*(4), 933–947.

Costanz, S. E., Bankston, W. B., & Shihadeh, E. (2001). Alcohol availability and violent crime rates: A spatial analysis. *Journal of Crime and Justice, 24*(1), 71–83.

Courttv.com. (2006). *Danielle Van Dam murder case.* Retrieved April 1, 2006, from http://www.courttv.com/trials/westerfield/

Covington, J., & Taylor, R. B. (1989). Gentrification and crime: Robbery and larceny changes in appreciating Baltimore neighborhoods during the 1970s. *Urban Affairs Quarterly, 25*(1), 142–172.

Cowan, G., Chase, C. J., & Stahly, G. B. (1989). Feminist and fundamentalist attitudes toward pornography control. *Psychology of Women Quarterly, 13,* 97–112.

Cox, J. A. (2003). Bilboes, brands, and branks: Colonial crimes and punishments. *CW Journal.* Retrieved February 27, 2005, from http://www.history.org/Foundation/journal/spring03/branks.cfm

Cramer, E., McFarlane, J., & Parker, B. (1998). Violent pornography and abuse of women: Theory to practice. *Violence and Victims, 13*(4), 319–332.

Cressey, D. R. (1953). *Other people's money.* Glencoe, IL: Free Press.

Cressey, D. R. (1969). *Theft of the nation.* New York: Harper and Row.

Criminal Justice Policy Foundation. (1994). *DEA guide tells "how to hold your own in a drug legalization debate."* Retrieved May 10, 2006, from http://www.ndsn.org/nov94/debate.html

Cromwell, B. (2003) *Colombia.* Retrieved July 31, 2003, from http://www.cromwell-intl.com/security/nu/co.html

Cromwell, P. F., Olson, J. N., & Avary, D. W. (1991). *Breaking and entering: An ethnographic analysis of burglary.* Newbury Park, CA: Sage.

Cromwell, P. F., Olson, J. N., & Avary, D. W. (1993). Who buys stolen property?—A new look at criminal receiving. *Journal of Crime and Justice, 56*(1), 75–95.

Crossen, C. (1996). *Tainted truth: The manipulation of fact in America.* New York: Touchstone.

Crowe, R. R. (1972). The adopted offspring of women criminal offenders. *Archives of General Psychiatry, 27,* 600–603.

Cundiff, K. R. (2001). *Homicide rates and substance control policy.* Retrieved July 29, 2001, from http://www.independent.org/tii/WorkingPapers/DrugWar.html

Curran, D. J., & Renzetti, C. M. (1994). *Theories of crime.* Boston: Allyn and Bacon.

Curran, D. J., & Renzetti, C. M. (2001). *Theories of crime* (2nd ed.). Boston, MA: Allyn and Bacon.

Curry, T., & Shibut, L. (2000). The cost of the savings and loan crisis: Truth and consequences. *FDIC Banking Review.* Retrieved May 20, 2006, from http://www.fdic.gov/bank/analytical/banking/2000dec/brv13n2_2.pdf

Curtis, L. A. (1974). Victim precipitation and violent crime. *Social Problems, 21*(4), 594–605.

Dabbs, J., Jr. (1995). High testosterone linked to crimes of sex, violence. *Crime Times, 1*(3), 2. Retrieved September 5, 2005, from http://216.117.159.91/crimetimes/95c/w95cp4.htm

Dake, J., Price, J. H., & Telljohann, S. K. (2003). The nature and extent of bullying at school. *Journal of School Health, 73*(5), 173–180.

Daly, K. (1989). Neither conflict nor labeling nor paternalism will suffice: Intersections of race, ethnicity, gender, and family in criminal court decisions. *Crime and Delinquency, 35,* 136–168.

Daly, K., & Chesney-Lind, M. (1988). Feminism and criminology. *Justice Quarterly, 5,* 497–535.

Daly, M., & Wilson, M. (1988). Homicide. New York: Aldine de Gruyter.

Daniels, C., & Kennedy, M. V. (Eds.). (1999). *Over the threshold: Intimate violence in early America.* New York: Routledge.

Darwin, C. (1999a, June). *Origin of the species.* Retrieved December 7, 2003, from http://www.literature.org/authors/darwin-charles/the-descent-of-man/index.html

Darwin, C. (1999b, June). *The Descent of Man.* Retrieved December 7, 2003, from http://www.literature.org/authors/darwin-charles/the-descent-of-man/index.html

David, P. R., & Scott, J. W. (1973). A cross-cultural comparison of juvenile offenders, offenses, due processes, and societies: The cases of Toledo, Ohio, and Rosario, Argentina. *Criminology, 11*(2), 183–205.

Davies, N. (November 27, 2000). *When sex abuse can lead to murder. The Guardian.* Retrieved June 13, 2004, from http://www.guardian.co.uk/child/story/0,7369,403435,00.html

Davison, E. L., & Smith, W. R. (2001). Informing community policing initiatives with GIS assisted multi-source data and micro-level analysis. *Journal of Crime and Justice, 24*(1), 85–108.

Decker, S. H. (1996). Collective and normative features of gang violence. *Justice Quarterly, 13,* 251–261.

DeFazio, P. (June 7, 2000). *Harkin and DeFazio release list of fraud cases among top 100 Pentagon contractors.* Retrieved May 16, 2005, from http://www.house.gov/defazio/060700DERelease.shtml

Defense for Children International: Argentina Secretariat for Human Development and Family Welfare. (1989). *Trafficking and sale of children in Argentina.* Geneva, Switzerland: DCI International Secretariat.

Defensetech. (2004). *FBI nabs Buffalo man for "biotech" art.* Retrieved June 10, 2004, from http://www.defensetech.org/archives/000933.html

DeFronzo, J. (1984). Climate and crime: Tests of an FBI assumption. *Environment and Behavior, 16*(2), 185–210.

DeFronzo, J. (1996). AFDC, a city's racial and ethnic composition, and burglary. *Social Service Review, 70*(30), 464–471.

Degenhardt, H. F. (2002). *Dynegy settles securities fraud charges involving SPEs, round-trip energy trades.* Retrieved May 22, 2005, from http://www.sec.gov/news/press/2002-140.htm

deMause, L. (1982). *Foundations of psychohistory.* New York: Creative Roots.

deMause, L. (1999). The cause of Nazism. *Digital Archive of PsychohistoryArticles and Texts.* Retrieved May 13, 2006, from http://www.geocities.com/kidhistory/nazism.htm

deMause, L. (2005). *The childhood origins of the Holocaust*—speech given on September 28, 2005 at Klagenfurt University, Austria. Retrieved May 13, 2006, from http://www.nospank.net/demause9.htm

Dempsey, J. (2003). *Setting the record straight: An analysis of the Justice Department's PATRIOT Act Website.* Washington, DC: The Center for Democracy and Technology. Retrieved June 8, 2004, from http://www.cdt.org/security/usapatriot/031027cdt.shtml

DeZee, M. R. (1982). *Law, police and criminal choice: A box-tiao intervention analysis of Florida's mandate* (Doctoral Dissertation, Florida State University). Ann Arbor, MI: University Microfilms International.

Diamond, M., & Uchiyama, A. (1999). Pornography, rape, and sex crimes in Japan. International *Journal of Law and Psychiatry, 22*(1), 1–22.

Dinnen, S. (March 18, 2002). *Fraud from abroad: Pyramid schemes. Advance fee swindles. Religious-affinity-loan scams. Look what the Web dragged in.* Retrieved May 17, 2005, from http:/www.csmonitor.com/2002/0318/p15s02-wmpi.html

Dirks-Linhorst, A., & Laster, J. D. (1998). *Chemical castration: An alternative for sex offenders.* Paper presented at the meeting of the American Society of Criminology, Washington, DC.

Disaster Center, The (2005). *United States Crime Rates 1960–2004.* Retrieved March 20, 2006, from http://www.disastercenter.com/crime/uscrime.htm

DiscoverFrance. (2003). *Travel info for France.* Retrieved October 29, 2004, from http://www.discoverfrance.net/France/consulate_info.shtml

Dixon, N. (2001). *How the CIA created Osama bin Laden.* Retrieved May 21, 2004, from http://www.greenleft.org.au/back/2001/465/465p15.htm

Doctor's Guide Publishing Limited. (1995). *Brain dysfunction may explain murderer's crime.* Retrieved July 28, 2003, from http://www.pslgroup.com/dg/6B1E2.htm

Donahue, M. E., McLaughlin, C. V., & Damm, L. V. (1994). Accounting for carjackings: An analysis of police records in a southeastern city. *American Journal of Police, 13*(4), 91–111.

Dowd, M. G. (n. d.). *A woman is beaten every 15 seconds.* Retrieved October 10, 2003, from http://www.angelfire.com/biz4/females/every15sec.html

Downs, K., & Gold, S. (1997). The role of blame, distress, and anger in the hypermasculine man. *Violence and Victims, 12,* 19–36.

Doyke, K., & Kornbluh, P. (1997). *CIA and assassinations: The Guatemala 1954 documents.* Retrieved April 30, 2005, from http://www.gwu.edu/~nsarchiv/NSAEBB/NSAEBB4/

Drug Enforcement Administration. (2003). *Speaking out against drug legalization.* Retrieved May 10, 2006, from http://www.dea.gov/demand/speakout/speaking_out-may03.pdf

Drug Enforcement Administration. (2004). *DEA staffing & budget.* Retrieved December 9, 2004, from http://www.usdoj.gov/dea/agency/staffing.htm

Drug Policy Alliance. (2003). *Drug policy around the world: England.* Retrieved June 13, 2004, from http://www.lindesmith.org/global/drugpolicyby/westerneurop/england/

Dugan, L., & Apel, R. (2003). An exploratory study of the violent victimization of women: Race/ethnicity and situational context. *Criminology, 41*(3), 959–979.

Dugdale, R. L. (1877). *The Jukes: A study in crime, pauperism, disease and heredity.* New York: Putnam.

Duncan, F. (2003, August 20). *Women pleads for mercy in 12th shoplifting case.* Retrieved September 28, 2004, from http://www.journalism.com.za/moduls.php?op=modload&name=News&file=article&sid=670

Dunford, F. W., Huizinga, D., Elliott, D. S. (1990). The role of arrest in domestic assault: The Omaha police experiment. *Criminology, 28*(2), 183–206.

Dunham, H. W. (1944). The social personality of the catatonic schizophrenic. *American Journal of Sociology, 49,* 508–518.

Durkheim, E. (1938). *The rules of sociological method.* Chicago: University of Chicago Press. (Original work published 1895)

Durkheim, E. (1947). *The division of labor in society* (G. Simpson, Trans.). Glencoe, IL: Free Press. (Original work published 1893)

Durkheim, E. (1951). *Suicide* (J. A. Spaulding & G. Simpson, Trans.). Glencoe, IL: Free Press. (Original work published 1897)

Durkin, K. (1997). Misuse of the Internet by pedophiles: Implications for law enforcement and probation practice. *Federal Probation, 61*(3), 14–18.

Dutton, D. G. (1988). *The domestic assault of women.* Boston: Allyn and Bacon.

Dycus, J., & Dycus, B. (1988). *Not guilty! From convict to Christian: The Jim Dycus story.* San Francisco, CA: Harper and Row.

Easterlin, R. (1980). *Birth and fortune: The impact of numbers on personal welfare.* New York: Basic Books.

Ebbe, O. N. I. (1993a). *Kenya.* Retrieved May 16, 2004, from http://www.ojp.usdoj.gov/bjs/pub/ascii/wfbcjken.txt

Ebbe, O. N. I. (1993b). *Nigeria.* Retrieved May 16, 2004, from http://www.ojp.usdoj.gov/bjs/pub/ascii/wfbcjnig.txt

Eck, J. E., & Riccio, L. J. (1979). Relationship between reported crime rates and victimization survey results: An empirical and analytical study. *Journal of Criminal Justice, 7*(4), 293–308.

Edelhertz, H. (1970). *The nature, impact and prosecution of white-collar crime.* Washington, DC: National Institute of Law Enforcement and Criminal Justice, Law Enforcement Assistance Administration, U.S. Department of Justice.

Edelhertz, H., Cole, R. J., & Berk, B. (1983). *The containment of organized crime.* Lexington, MA: Lexington.

Edelman, B. (1980). Auto theft: For police, the joyride is over. *Police Magazine, 3*(5), 16–21.

Edwards, D. M. (1992). *Politics and pornography: Comparison of the findings of the President's Commission and the Meese Commission and the resulting response.* Retrieved December 31, 2004, from http://home.earthlink.net/~durangodave/html/writing/Censorship.htm

Eels, K. (1951). *Intelligence and cultural differences.* Chicago: University of Chicago Press.

Ehrhardt, M. E., & Tewksbury, R. (1998). Predicting risks of larceny theft victimization: A routine activity analysis using refined lifestyle measures. *Criminology, 36*(4), 829–857.

Ekirch, A. R. (1991). Bound for America: A profile of British convicts transported to the colonies, 1718–1775. In E. H. Monkkonen (Ed.), *Crime and justice in American History: Historical articles on the origins and evolution of American criminal justice.* (pp. 88–106). Westport, CT: Meckler.

Ekpenyong, S. (1989). Social inequalities, collusion, and armed robbery in Nigerian cities. *British Journal of Criminology, 29*(1), 21–34.

Elliott, D. S., & Ageton, S. S. (1980). Reconciling race and class differences in self-reported and official estimates of delinquency. *American Sociological Review, 45,* 95–110.

Elliott, D. S., Huizinga, D., & Ageton, S. S. (1985). *Explaining delinquency and drug use.* Beverly Hills, CA: Sage.

Ellis, L. (1982). Genetics and criminal behavior. *Criminology, 20,* 43–66.

Ellis, L. (1987). Neurohormonal bases of varying tendencies to learn delinquent and criminal behavior. In E. K. Morris & C. J. Braukman (Eds.), *Behavioral approaches to crime and delinquency: A handbook of application, research, and concepts* (pp. 499–518). New York: Plenum.

Ellis, L., & Walsh, A. (1997). Gene-based evolutionary theories in criminology. *Criminology, 35,* 229–276.

Elliston, J. (1996). *MKULTRA: CIA mind control.* Retrieved April 30, 2005, from http://peyote.com/jonstef/mkultra.htm

Ellwood, R. S. (2003). *Witchcraft.* Microsoft Online Encyclopedia 2003. Retrieved November 9, 2003, from http://encarta.msn.com

Empey, L. T. (1982). *American delinquency: Its meaning and construction.* Homewood, IL: Dorsey.

Encarta. (11 Oct. 2001). *Algeria.* Microsoft Encarta Online Encyclopedia 2001. Retrieved October 11, 2001, from http://encarta.msn.com

Encyclopedia Britannica. (1911). *William Henry Sleeman.* Retrieved May 2, 2004, from http://www.sciencedaily.com/encyclopedia/william_henry_sleeman

Ende, A. (1979). Battering and neglect: Children in Germany, 1860–1978. *The Journal of Psychohistory, 7*(1979), 260.

Engbersen, G., & Van der Leun, J. (2001). The social construction of illegality and criminality. *European Journal on Criminal Policy and Research, 9*(1), 51–70.

Environmental News Service. (2002). *Organized criminal gangs deal wildlife and drugs.* Retrieved November 28, 2004, from http://www.commondreams.org/headlines02/0619-07.htm

Erickson, R. J. (1996). *Armed robbers and their crimes.* Seattle, WA: Athena Research Corporation.

Erikson, K. T. (1966). *Wayward Puritans: A study in the sociology of deviance.* New York: Wiley.

Eronen, M. (1995). Mental disorders and homicidal behaviors in female subjects. *American Journal of Psychiatry, 152*(8), 1216–1218.

Esses, V. (1985). Field data on availability of pornography and incidence of sex crime in Denmark: Fuel for a heated debate. *Canadian Criminology Forum, 7*(2), 83–91.

Estrada, F. (2004). The transformation and politics of crime in high crime societies. *European Journal of Criminology, 1*(4), 419–443. Retrieved October 8, 2004, from http://euc.sagepub.com/cgi/reprint/1/4/419

Executive protection and international and transnational terrorism. (1981). *Security Letter, 11*(18), 1–4. New York.

EyeWorld. (2000, December). Vision-threatening paintball injuries on the rise. *Eyecare News.* Retrieved October 27, 2003, from http://www.stlukeseyc.com/news/Details.asp?ArticleID=181

Eyler, A. E., & Cohen, M. (1999). Case studies in partner violence. *American Family Physician, 60*(9). Retrieved June 16, 2005, from http://www.aafp.org/afp/991201ap/2569.html

Eysenick, H. J., & Gudjonsson, G. H. (1989). *The causes and cures of criminality.* New York: Plenum.

Faculty.ncwc.edu. (2004). *Organized crime: Characteristics, history, enforcement, genre, activities.* Retrieved November 4, 2004, from http://faculty.ncwc.edu/toconnor/427/427lect11.htm

Fairchild, E., & Dammer, H. R. (2001). *Comparative criminal justice systems.* Belmont, CA: Wadsworth/Thomson Learning.

Fajnzylber, P., Lederman, D., & Loayza, N. (2002). What causes violent crime? *European Economic Review, 46*(7), 1323–1357.

Falcone, D. N. (2005). *Dictionary of American criminal justice, criminology, & criminal law.* Upper Saddle River, NJ: Pearson/Prentice Hall.

Faley, J. (1998). *Fact sheet: Drug data summary.* Rockville, MD: Drug Policy Information Clearing House.

Faris, R. E. L. (1934). Cultural isolation and the schizophrenic personality. *American Journal of Sociology, 40,* 155–169.

Faris, R. E. L. (1944). Reflections of social disorganization in the behavior of a schizophrenic patient. *American Journal of Sociology, 50,* 134–141.

Faris, R. E. L., & Dunham, H. W. (1939). *Mental disorders in urban areas.* Chicago: University of Chicago Press.

Farrington, D. P. (1999). Measuring, explaining and preventing shoplifting: A review of British research. *Security Journal, 12*(1), 9–27.

Farrington, D. P., & Jolliffe, D. (2004). England and Wales. In D. P. Farrington, P.A. Langan, & M. Tonry (Eds.), *Cross-national studies in crime and justice.* Washington, DC: U.S. Department of Justice Office of Justice Programs. Retrieved October 15, 2004, from http://www.ojp.usdoj.gov/bjs/pub/ascii/cnscj.txt

Federal Bureau of Investigation. (1989). *Crime in the United States 1988: Uniform Crime Reports.* Washington, DC: U.S. Government Printing Office.

Federal Bureau of Investigation. (1992). *Health care fraud video text.* Retrieved May 21, 2005, from http://www.fbi.gov/hq/cid/fc/video_text/hcf_txt.htm

Federal Bureau of Investigation. (1995). *Crime in the United States 1995: Uniform crime reports.* Washington, D.C.: U.S. Government Printing Office.

Federal Bureau of Investigation. (1998). *Incidents of Family Violence: An Analysis of 1998 NIBRS Data*. Uniform Crime Reports, special report.Appendix: Section V. Retrieved May 21, 2005, from http://www.fbi.gov/ucr/Cius_98/98crime/98cius29.pdf

Federal Bureau of Investigation. (1999). *Terrorism in the United States 1999*. Washington, DC: U.S. Government Printing Office. Retrieved June 13, 2004, from http://www.fbi.gov/publications/terror/terror99.pdf

Federal Bureau of Investigation. (2000). *Crime in the United States 2001: Uniform Crime Reports*. Washington, DC: U.S. Government Printing Office. Retrieved September 1, 2001, from http://www.fbi.gov/ucr/ucr.htm

Federal Bureau of Investigation. (2001). *Crime in the United States 2001: Uniform Crime Reports*. Washington, DC: U.S. Government Printing Office. Retrieved September 1, 2001, from http://www.fbi.gov/ucr/ucr.htm

Federal Bureau of Investigation (2002). *National incident-based reporting system, 2002*. Retrieved March 29, 2005, from http://webapp.icpsr.umich.edu/cocoon/NACJD-PRINT-STUDY/04066.xml

Federal Bureau of Investigation. (2004). *Crime in the United States 2004: Uniform Crime Reports*. Washington, DC: U.S. Government Printing Office. Retrieved November 15, 2006, from http://www.fbi.gov/ucr/ucr.htm

Federal Deposit Insurance Corporation. (2002). *The S&L crisis: A chrono-bibliography*. Retrieved May 19, 2006, from http://www.fdic.gov/bank/historical/s&l/

Federal Trade Commission. (2003). *Facts for consumers—ID Theft: What it's all about*. Retrieved May 26, 2006, from http://www.ftc.gov/bcp/conline/pubs/credit/idtheftmini.htm

Federal Trade Commission. (2005). *Taking charge: Fighting back against identity theft*. Retrieved May 26, 2006, from http://www.ftc.gov/bcp/conline/pubs/credit/idtheft.htm

Feeney, F., Dill, F., & Weir, A. (1983). *Arrests without conviction: How often they occur and why*. Washington, DC: U.S. Government Printing Office.

Feeney, F., & Weir, A. (1974). *The prevention and control of robbery: A summary*. Davis, CA: University of California, Center on Administration of Criminal Justice.

Feldman, S. S. (1986). A comment on the Meese Commission report and the dangers of censorship. *Sexual Coercion and Assault Issues and Perspectives, 1*(6), 179–184.

Felson, M. (1998). *Crime and everyday life* (2nd ed.). Thousand Oaks, CA Pine Forge Press.

Felson, R. B., & Messner, S. F. (1996). To kill or not to kill? Lethal outcomes in injurious attacks. *Criminology, 34*(4), 519–545.

Field, L. H., & Williams, M. (1970). The hormonal treatment of sex offenders. *Medicine Science and the Law, 10*(1), 27–34.

Field, S., Clarke, R. V., & Harris, P. M. (1991). The Mexican vehicle market and auto theft in border areas of the United States. *Security Journal, 2*(4), 205–210.

Finckenauer, J. O., & Waring, E. J. (2001). *Russian Mafia in America: Immigration, culture, and crime*. Boston: Northeastern University Press.

Finkelhor, D., Hotaling, G. T., & Sedlak, A. J. (1992). The abduction of children by strangers and nonfamily members: Estimating the incidence using multiple methods. *Journal of Interpersonal Violence, 7*(2), 226–243.

Finkelhor, D., & Ormrod, R. (2000a). *Juvenile victims of property crime*. Washington, DC: U.S. Office of Juvenile Justice and Delinquency Prevention.

Finkelhor, D., & Ormrod, R. (2000b). *Kidnapping of juveniles: Patterns from NIBRS.* OJJDP's Crime Against Children Series. Washington, DC: Office of Juvenile Justice and Delinquency Prevention, U.S. Department of Justice.

Finkelhor, D., & Ormrod, R. (2001, May). *Child abuse reported to the police.* OJJDP Juvenile Justice Bulletin. Washington, DC: U.S. Department of Justice.

Finkelhor, D., & Yllo, K. (1985) *License to rape: Sexual abuse of wives.* New York: Holt, Rinehart and Winston.

Fishbein, D. H., (1990). Biological perspectives in criminology. *Criminology, 28,* 27–72.

Fleming, Z., Brantingham, P., & Brantingham, P. (1994). Exploring auto theft in British Columbia. In R. V. Clarke (Ed.), *Crime prevention studies, Vol. 3,* (pp. 47–90). Monsey, NY: Criminal Justice Press.

Fleshman, M. (2001). Targeting "conflict diamonds" in Africa. *Africa Recovery, 14*(4), 6. Retrieved November 4, 2003, from http://www.un.org/ecosocdev/geninfo/afrec/subjindx/144diam.htm

Follett, R. R. (2001). *Evangelicalism, penal theory and the politics of criminal law reform in England, 1808–30.* London: Palgrave.

Forston, R. C. (1976). Criminal victimization of the aged: The Houston Model Neighborhood Area. *Victomology Washington DC, 1*(2), 316–318.

Fox, J. A. (1996). *Trends in juvenile violence: A report to the United States Attorney General on current and future rates of juvenile offending.* Washington, DC: U.S. Bureau of Justice Statistics.

Fox, J. A., & Levin, J. (1999). *Serial murder: Myths and realities.* In M. D. Smith & M. A. Zahn (Eds.), Studying and preventing homicide: Issues and challenges (pp. 79–96). Thousand Oaks, CA: Sage.

FOX News/Opinion Dynamics Poll. (2003, March 11–12). *Do you favor or oppose . . . ?* Retrieved June 8, 2004, from http://www.foxnews.com/story/0,2933,81023,00.html

Fredrichs, D. O. (1996). *Trusted criminals: White-collar crime in contemporary society.* Belmont, CA: Wadworth.

Freedom House. (1999). *Survey methodology.* Retrieved 9/20/2003, from http://freedomhouse.org/survey99/method/

French, W. A. (1981). *National research report on shoplifting 1980.* Atlanta, GA: National Coalition to Prevent Shoplifting.

Freud, S. (1922). *Beyond the pleasure principle.* London: Inter-Psychoanalytic Press.

Friedlander, K. (1949). Latent delinquency and ego development. In K. R. Eissler (Ed.), *Searchlights on delinquency: New psychoanalytic studies* (pp. 205–215). New York: International University Press.

Friedman, I., & Peer, I. (1970). Drug addiction among pimps and prostitutes in Israel. In Shlomo Shoham (Ed.), *Israel studies in criminology, Vol. 1,* (pp. 141–176). Tel Aviv: Gomeh Publishing House.

Friedman, R. I. (2000, April 10). Another Ukrainian Jew makes good. *The New Yorker.* Retrieved November 27, 2004, from http://www.adlusa.com/adl/mafia2.htm

Friedman, R. I. (2000a). *Red Mafiya: How the Russian mob has invaded America.* Little, Brown and Company.

Friedman, R. I. (2000b). *Land of the stupid: When you need a used Russian submarine, call Tarzan.* Retrieved November 27, 2004, from http://www.libertypost .org/cgi-bin/readart.cgi?ArtNum=21729

Friedman, R. I. (2000c). *Red Mafiya: How the Russian mob has invaded America.* Retrieved November 26, 2004, from http://www.theunjustmedia.com/On%20 jewish%20organized%20crime.htm

Friends of Liberty. (2002). Retrieved May 9, 2006, from http://members.iimetro .com.au/~hubbca/cyclone.htm

Frisch, L. A. (1992). Research that succeeds, policies that fail. *The Journal of Criminal Law and Criminology, 83*(1), 209–216.

Fritz-reuter.com. (2005). *Commercial bribery.* Retrieved May 15, 2005, from http://fritz-reuter.com/data/gloss/c/commerci.htm

Frontline. (2001). *A biography of Osama bin Laden.* Retrieved June 5, 2004, from http://www.pbs.org/wgbh/pages/frontline/shows/binladen/who/bio.html

Fullerton, R. A., & Punj, G. N. (2004). Shoplifting as moral insanity: Historical perspectives on kleptomania. *Journal of Macromarketing, 24*(1), 8–16.

Gabor, T., & Normandeau, A. (1989). Armed robbery: Highlights of a Canadian study. *Canadian Police College Journal, 13*(4), 273–282.

Galiana C. (2000). *Trafficking in women: Working paper.* European Parliament Directorate-General for Research. Retrieved May 8, 2006, from http:// www.europarl.eu.int/workingpapers/libe/pdf/109_en.pdf

Galliher, J. F., Keys, D. P., & Eisner, M. (1998). *Journal of Criminal Law & Criminology.* Retrieved December 9, 2004, from http://www.druglibrary.org/ schaffer/History/anslingerlindesmith.htm

Gallup, G. H. (2003). *The Gallup Report.* Retrieved October 18, 2003, from http:// www.albany.edu/sourcebook/1995/pdf/t21.pdf

Galton, D. J., & Galton, C. J. (1998). Francis Galton and eugenics today. *Journal of Medical Ethics, 24*(2), 99–105.

Garden, T. (2001). *Refugees, immigration and xenophobia.* Retrieved October 15, 2004, from http://www.sourceuk.net/articles/a01882.html

Gardiner, S., Lowe, H., & Goode, J. B. (2002). *How drug dealers in Nigeria turned a 12-year old Nigerian-American kid into a courier who swallowed 87 condoms filled with heroin.* Retrieved November 28, 2004, from http://www.usafricaonline .com/drugs.umegbolu.html

Garner, J., Fagan, J., & Maxwell, C. (1995). Published findings from the spouse assault replication program: A critical review. *Journal of Quantitative Criminology, 11,* 3–28.

Garofalo, R. (1885). *Criminology.* Naples, Italy: n.p.

Gastil, R. (1971). Homicide and the regional culture of violence. *American Sociological Review, 36,* 12–27.

Gay, B. W., & Marquart, J. W. (1993). Jamaican posses: A new form of organized crime. *Journal of Crime and Justice, 16*(2), 139–170.

GayToday. (2003). *Three reggae stars accused of inciting the murders of gay citizens.* Retrieved November 11, 2003, from http://www.gaytoday.com/events/ 091903ev.asp

Geberth, V. J. (1998). *Anatomy of a lust murder.* Retrieved December 27, 2003, from http://www.practicalhomicide.com/articles/lustmurder.htm

Gebhard, P. H. (1971). Definitions. In D. S. Marshall & R. C. Suggs (Eds.), *Human sexual behavior.* New York: Basic Books.

Gebhard, P. H., Gagnon, J. H., Pomeroy, W. B., Christenson, C. V., & Hoeber, P. B. (1965). *Sex offenders.* New York: Harper and Row.

Geis, G. (1968). The heavy electrical equipment antitrust cases of 1961. In M. B. Clinard & R. Quinney (Eds.), *Criminal behavior systems* (pp. 137–150). New York: Holt, Rinehart and Winston.

Gelles, R. J. (1989). Child abuse and violence in single-parent families: parent absence and economic deprivation. *American Journal of Orthopsychiatry, 59*(4), 492–501.

Gelles, R. J. (1992). Poverty and violence toward children. *American Behavioral Scientist, 35*(3), 258–274.

Gelles, R. J. (1996). *The book of David: How preserving families can cost children's lives.* New York: Basic Books.

Gelles, R. J. (2004). *Domestic violence.* Microsoft Encarta Online Encyclopedia. Retrieved August 28, 2004, from http://encarca.msn.com

Gelles, R. J., & Straus, M. (1987). Is violence toward children increasing? A comparison of 1975 and 1985 national survey rates. *Journal of Interpersonal Violence, 2*(2), 212–222.

Gendreau, P., & Ross, R. R. (1983). Correctional treatment: Some recommendations for effective intervention. *Juvenile and Family Court Journal, 344,* 31–39.

Gentry, C. S. (1989). *Six models of rape: An empirical analysis.* Ann Arbor, MI: University Microfilms International.

Gentry, C. S. (1991). Pornography and rape: An empirical analysis. *Deviant Behavior, 12*(3), 277–288.

Gentzler, Richard H., Jr. (1999). *Elder abuse.* Retrieved June 16, 2005, from http://www.gbod.org/coa/elder_abuse/page1.html

Georges, A. D. E. (1981). Terrorism and the liberal state: A reasonable response. *Police Studies New York, 4*(3), 34–53.

Gerber, L. (October 2001). *Osama bin Laden.* No. 20. Retrieved June 4, 2004, from http://www.cosmopolis.ch/english/cosmo20/osama_bin_laden.htm

Gettings, J. (2005). *Milestones in federal gun control legislation: A timeline of gun legislation and organizations from 1791 to the present.* Retrieved June 11, 2005, from http://www.infoplease.com/spot/guntime1.html

Giacomazzi, A. L. (1995). *Community crime prevention, community policing, and public housing: An evaluation of a multi-level, collaborative drug-crime elimination program.* Ann Arbor, MI: University Microfilms International.

Giacopassi, D., & Stitt, B. G. (1994). Assessing the impact of casino gambling on crime in Mississippi. *American Journal of Criminal Justice, 18*(1), 117–131.

Gibbons, D. C. (1970). *Delinquent behavior.* Englewood Cliffs, NJ: Prentice Hall.

Gibbons, D. C. (1977). *Society, crime and criminal careers.* Englewood Cliffs, NJ: Prentice Hall.

Gibbens, T. C. N. (1958). Car thieves. *British Journal of Delinquency, 8*(4), 257–265.

Gibbens, T. C. N., & Prince, J. (1961). *Shoplifting.* London: Institute for the Study and Treatment of Delinquency, as cited in Fullerton & Punj, 2004, p. 13.

Ginat, J. (1984). Role of the mediator: With special reference to blood disputes. In S. G. Shoham (Ed.), *Israel studies in criminology, Vol. VII,* (pp. 98–131). New York: Sheridan House. Retrieved June 26, 2004, from the Criminal Justice Abstracts database at http://spweb.silverplatter.com/calstate

Gittler, J. (2004). *Prenatal substance abuse: An overview of the problem.* Retrieved June 10, 2005, from http://www.findarticles.com/p/articles/mi_m1053/is_n4_v19/ai_9153202/print

Global Survival Network. (1997). *Crime and servitude: An expose of the traffic in women for prostitution from the Newly Independent States.* Washington, DC: U.S. Government Printing Office.

Glueck, S., & Glueck, E. (1934). *One thousand juvenile delinquents: Their treatment by court and clinic.* Cambridge: Harvard University Press.

Glueck, S., & Glueck, E. (1950). *Unraveling juvenile delinquency.* Cambridge, MA: Harvard University Press.

Goddard, H. H. (1912) *The Kallikak family: A study in the heredity of feeblemindedness.* New York: Macmillan.

Goddard, H. H. (1914). *Feeblemindedness: Its causes and consequences.* New York: Macmillan.

Goddard, H. H. (1921). Feeblemindedness and delinquency. *Journal of Psycho-Asthenics, 25,* 168–176.

Goffman, E. (1961). *Asylums.* Garden City, NY: Anchor.

Gold M., & Reimer, D. J. (1975).Changing patterns of delinquent behavior among Americans 13 through 16 years old. *Crime and Delinquency Literature, 7,* 483–517.

Goldner, N. S. (1972). Rape as a heinous but understudied offense. *Journal of Criminal Law, Criminology and Police Science, 63,* 402–407.

Goldstein, P. J. (1978). *The relationship between prostitution and substance use.* Ann Arbor, MI: University Microfilms, Dissertation, Case Western Reserve University.

Goldstein, P. J. (1995). The drugs/violence nexus: A tripartite conceptual framework. In J. A. Inciardi & K. McElrath (Eds.), *The American Drug Scene.* Los Angeles: Roxbury.

Goldstein, P., Brownstein, H. H., Ryan, P. J., & Bellucci, P. A. (1989). Crack and homicide in New York City, 1988: A conceptually based event analysis. *Contemporary Drug Problems, 16,* 651–687.

Gondolf, E. W. (1988). Who are these guys? Toward a behavioral typology of batterers: Violence and victims. *Journal of Family Violence, 1*(4), 323–341.

Gonzalez, D. (2004, April15) *"Coyotes" Fuel car thefts.* Retrieved October 10, 2004, from http://www.azcentral.com/specials/special03/articles/0415stolencars.html

Goode, E. (1984). *Drugs in American society.* New York: Knopf.

Goodling, W. F. (1998). *Testimony U.S. House of Representatives Committee on Education and the Workforce: The American Worker at a Crossroads Project.* Retrieved April 28, 2006, from http://www.house.gov/ed_workforce/hearings/105th/oi/awp33198/goodling.htm

Goodwin, J. (1998, February). *Buried alive: Afghan women under the Taliban.* OTI Online. Retrieved October 27, 2003, from http://mosaic.echonyc.com/~onissues/su98goodwin.html

Gordon, D. (1997, July/August). INS aims at businesses, hits Mexicans. *The Chicago Reporter.* Retrieved May 15, 2005, from http://www.chicagoreporter.com/1997/07-97/0797INS%20Aims%20at%20Businesses,%20Hits%20Mexicans.htm

Gordon, M. T., & Riger, S. (1989). *The female fear.* New York: Free Press.

Gottfredson, M. R., & Hirschi, T. (1990). *A general theory of crime*. Palo Alto, CA, Stanford University Press.

Gould, L. C. (1969). The changing structure of property crime in an affluent society. *Social Forces, 48,* 50–59.

Gow, J., & Peggrem, A. (1991). *Car crime culture? A study of motor vehicle theft by juveniles*. Cardiff, Wales: Bernardo's Research & Development.

Grassi, A. (1990). Terrorism in Italy and response by the government. In B. Holst (Ed.), *EuroCriminolog* (Vol. 3, pp. 165–170). Warsaw: Polish Scientific Publishers.

Green, G. (1990). *Occupational crime*. Chicago: Nelson-Hall.

Grossman, D. (1995). *On killing: The psychological cost of learning to kill in war and society*. Boston: Little, Brown.

Groth, A. N., & Birnbaum, J. (1979). *Men who rape*. New York: Plenum. See The World Wide Web Virtual Library: The Men's Issues Page. Retrieved September 14, 2003, from http://www.menweb.org/throop/abuse/studies/causerape.html

Groups.google.com. (2006). *Difference between shoplifting and burglary*. Retrieved April 25, 2006, from http://groups.google.com/group/alt.lawenforcement/browse_thread/thread/ae6808eb3cbe760c/79169563d894b22f?lnk=st&q=shoplifter+in+store+after+hours+charged+with+burglary&rnum=3&hl=en

Gruver, D. (2005, Feb. 28). Congregation "still in shock". *The Wichita Eagle*. Retrieved February 28, 2005, from http://www.kansas.com/mld/kansas/news/special_packages/btk/11010878.htm

Gubash, C. (n. d.). *Egypt in turmoil-murder and rape on the rise?* Retrieved November 1, 2003, from http://www.kamilat.org/DV/Egypt.htm

Gulf Legal Services Ltd. (2001). *Background on the United Arab Emirates (UAE) Legal System*. Retrieved April 19, 2002, from http://gulf=law.com/uaecolaw_legalsystem.html

GunCite.com. (2003) *Gun control-international homicide comparisons: International homicide rate table*. Retrieved September 25, 2003, from http://www.guncite.com/gun_control_gcgvinco.html

Gunst, L. (1989, November). Johnny-too-bad and the sufferers. *The Nation, 13,* 549–553. Retrieved October 21, 2003, from http://debate.uvm.edu/dreadlibrary/thielen.html

Gup, B. E. (1995). *Targeting fraud: Uncovering and deterring fraud in financial institutions*. Chicago: Probus Publishing Company Securities Fraud link. Retrieved May 22, 2005, from http://www.trinity.edu/rjensen/fraud.htm

Guttmacher, M. (1951). *Sex offenses: The problem, causes, and prevention*. New York: Norton.

Hack, R. (2004). *Puppetmaster: The secret life of J. Edgar Hoover*. Beverly Hills, CA: New Millennium Press.

Hagan, J., Simpson, J. H., & Gillis, A. R. (1987). Class in the household: A power-control theory of gender and delinquency. *American Journal of Sociology, 92,* 788–816.

Haidar, L. (2006). *Anti-piracy actions boost business opportunities*. Retrieved May 23, 2006, from http://www.managingip.com/includes/magazine/PRINT.asp?SID=623671&ISS=21645&PUBID=34

Hakim, S., & Shachmurove, Y. (1996). Spatial and temporal patterns of commercial burglaries: The evidence examined. *American Journal of Economics and Sociology, 55*(4), 443–456.

Hall, K. A. (1994). *A primer on sexual harassment, and yes, some of my best friends are men.* Retrieved September 29, 2003, from http://mtprof.msun.edu/Win1994/Hall.html

Hamberger, K. L., & Hasting, J. E. (1986). Personality correlates of men who abuse their partners: A cross validation study. *Journal of Family Violence, 1*(4), 323–341.

Hamberger, K. L., & Hasting, J. E. (1988). Characteristics of male spouse abusers consistent with personality disorders. *Hospital and Community Psychiatry, 39,* 763–770.

Hammer, T. (2004). *Youth unemployment and social exclusion in Europe.* Retrieved October 8, 2004, from http://www.celpe.unisa.it/DP/Torild_Hammer.pdf

Hampton, R. L., Gelles, R. J., & Harrop, J. W. (1989). Is violence in black families increasing? A comparison of 1975 and 1985 national survey rates. *Journal of Marriage and the Family, 51,* 969–980.

Hanson, D. J. (2004). *Prohibition: The noble experiment.* Retrieved December 5, 2004, from http://www2.potsdam.edu/alcohol-info/FunFacts/Prohibition.html

Haran, J. F. (1982). *The losers' game: A sociological profile of 500 armed bank robbers* (Doctoral Dissertation, Fordham University). Ann Arbor, MI: University Microfilms International.

Haran, J. F., & Martin, J. M. (1984). The armed urban bank robber: A profile. *Federal Probation, 48*(4), 47–53.

Harmon, P. A., & Check, J. V. P. (1989). *The role of pornography in women abuse.* North York, Canada: LaMarsh Research Program, York University.

Harriott, A. (1998). Policing styles in the Commonwealth Carribean: The Jamaican case. *Caribbean Journal of Criminology and Social Psychology, 3*(1/2), 60–82.

Harrison, L. D. (Ed.). (1992). International perspectives on the interface of drug use and criminal behavior. *Contemporary Drug Problems, 19*(2), 181–385.

Hartwig, M. (2001). *Osama examined.* Retrieved June 4, 2004, from http://www.family.org/cforum/feature/a0017697.cfm

Hatzinger, S. (1998). *Machos and policewomen, battered women and anti-victims: Combating violence against women in Brazil* (Doctoral Dissertation, John Hopkins University). Ann Arbor, MI: University Microfilms International.

Hautzinger, S. (2002). Criminalising male violence in Brazil's women's police stations: From flawed essentialism to imaged communities. *Journal of Gender Studies, 11*(3), 243–251.

Hayes, R. (1997). Retail theft: An analysis of apprehended shoplifters. *Security Journal, 8*(3), 233–246.

Haynes, E. (1999). *Indian princely states.* Retrieved May 9, 2006, from http://faculty.winthrop.edu/haynese/india/pstates/pstates.html

Hazelip, A. C. (1980). *Twelve tenets of terrorism: An assessment of theory and practice* (Doctoral Dissertation, The Florida State University). Ann Arbor, MI: University Microfilms International.

Hazelwood, R. R., & Burgess, A. N. (Eds.). (1995). *Practical aspects of rape investigation: A multidisciplinary approach.* New York: CRC.

He, N., & Marshall, I. H. (1997). Social production of crime data: A critical examination of Chinese crime statistics. *International Criminal Justice Review, 7,* 46–63.

Head, J. (2002). *As an American, I believe . . .* Retrieved May 28, 2006, from http://www.angelfire.com/ny5/shenandoah/I_Believe.html

Healy, W., & Bronner, A. F. (1936). *New light on delinquency and its treatment.* New Haven, CT: Yale University Press.

Heiner, R. (1996). *Criminology: A cross-cultural perspective.* St. Paul, MN: West.

Helal, A. A., & Coston, C. T. M. (1991). Low crime rates in Bahrain: Islamic social control—testing the theory of synnomie. *International Journal of Comparative and Applied Criminal Justice, 15*(1), 125–144.

Helmer, J. (1975). *Drugs and minority oppression.* New York: Seabury.

Hempel, A. G., Levine, R. E., & Meloy, J. R. (2000). A cross-cultural review of sudden mass assault by a single individual in the Oriental and Occidental cultures. *Journal of Forensic Sciences, 45*(3), 582–588.

Henderson, E. A. (1995) The scholarship of white supremacy—Excerpted from the book *Afrocentrism and world politics: Towards a new paradigm.* Westport, CN: Praeger. Retrieved August 13, 2003, from http://www.nbufront.org/html/FRONTalView/BookExcerpts/EAH1.html

Henderson, L. (2006a). *Blind pool investment fraud offerings.* Retrieved December 23, 2004, from http://www.crimes-of-persuasion.com/Crimes/Telemarketing/Outbound/Major/Investments/blind_pools.htm

Henderson, L. (2006b). *Crimes of persuasion: Schemes, scams, frauds.* Retrieved May 21, 2006, from http://www.crimes-of-persuasion.com/index.htm

Henderson, L. (2006c). *Investment scams/Stock scam fraud/Boiler rooms.* Retrieved May 21, 2006, from http://www.crimes-of-persuasion.com/Crimes/ Telemarketing/Outbound/Major/Investments/investments.htm

Henderson, L. (2006d). *Viatical settlements investment fraud.* Retrieved May 21, 2006, from http://www.crimes-of-persuasion.com/Crimes/Telemarketing/Outbound/Major/Investments/viatical.htm

Henry, A. F., &. Short, J. F., Jr. (1954). *Suicide and homicide.* New York: Free Press.

Herer, J. (2003). *Chapter 5: Marijuana prohibition.* Retrieved December 11, 2004, from http://www.jackherer.com/chapter05.html

Herlihy, K. W. (1997). *Women on juries: The battles in Florida.* Retrieved December 8, 2003, from http://data.law.georgetown.edu/glh/herlihy.htm

Herrnstein, R. J., & Murray, C. (1996). *The bell curve.* New York: Free Press.

Hewitt, C. (1984). *The effectiveness of anti-terrorist policies.* Lanham, MD: University Press of America.

Higgins, K. (1997). *Exploring motor vehicle theft in Australia.* Canberra: Australian Institute of Criminology.

Hills, S. L., & Santiago, R. (1992). *Tragic magic: The life and crimes of a heroin addict.* Chicago: Nelson-Hall.

Hippchen, L. J. (1981). A social justice model for a world criminology. *International Journal of Comparative and Applied Criminal Justice, 5*(1), 107–117.

Hirschel, J. D, Hutchinson, I. W., & Dean, C. W. (1992). The failure of arrest to deter spouse abuse. *Journal of Research in Crime and Delinquency, 29*(1), 7–33.

Hirschi, T. (1969). *Causes of delinquency.* Berkeley: University of California Press.

Hirschi, T., & Hindelang, M. (1977). Intelligence and delinquency: A revisionist review. *American Sociological Review, 42,* 471–586.

Hobson, K. (n. d.). *The Indian caste system and the British.* Retrieved July 11, 2003, from http://www.britishempire.co.uk/article/castesystem.htm

Hochstetler, A., Kerley, K. R., & Mason, K. (2002). Structural predictors of embezzlement: A preliminary analysis. *Journal of Crime and Justice, 25*(1), 1–22.

Hoffman, B. (1999). Terrorism trends and prospects. In I. O. Lesser, B. Hoffman, J. Arquilla, D. F. Ronfeldt, M. Zanini, & B. M. Jenkins (Eds.), *Countering the new terrorism* (pp. 7–38). Santa Monica, CA: Rand Corporation. Retrieved June 3, 2004, from http://www.rand.org/publications/MR/MR989/MR989.chap2.pdf

Hollinger, R. C. (2003). *The National Retail Security Survey.* Data summarized in Ernst & Young Press Release, Retrieved May 20, 2006, from http://www.jrobertssecurity.com/security-news/security-crime-news0024.htm

Holmes, R., & DeBurger, J. (1985). Profiles in terror: The serial murderer. *Federal Probation, 49*(3) 29–34.

Holmstrom, L. L., & Burgess, A. W. (1978). *The victim of rape: Institutional reactions.* New York: Wiley.

Hology.com. (2006). School shootings. Retrieved August/20/06 from http://www.holology.com/shooting.html

Holzworth-Munroe, A., and Stuart, G. L. (1994). Social skills deficits in martially violent men: Interpreting the data using a social information processing model. *Clinical Psychology Review, 12,* 605–617.

Holtzworth-Munroe, A., & Stuart, G. L. (1994). Typologies of male batterers: Three subtypes and the differences among them. *Psychological Bulletin, 116*(3), 476–497.

Hooton, E. A. (1939a). *The American criminal.* Cambridge, MA: Harvard University Press.

Hooton, E. A. (1939b). *Crime and the man.* Cambridge, MA: Harvard University Press.

Hope, T., & Murphy, D. J. (1983). Problems of implementing crime prevention: The experience of a demonstration project. *Howard Journal of Penology and Crime Prevention, 22*(1), 38–50.

Hornberger, J. G. (2000). *Crack down in the war on drugs . . . or end it? Commentaries.* Retrieved November 18, 2003, from http://www.fff.org/comment/ed0200b.asp

Horwitz, C. B. (1986). *Factors influencing shoplifting activity among adult women.* Ann Arbor, MI: University Microfilms International.

Hotaling, G. T., Straus, M. A., & Lincoln, A. J. (1989). Intrafamily violence and crime and violence outside the family. In L. Ohlin & M. Tonry (Eds.), *Family violence* (pp. 315–375). Chicago: University of Chicago Press.

Hotaling, G. T., & Sugarman, D. B. (1986). An analysis of risk markers in husband to wife violence: The current state of knowledge. *Violence and Victims, 1,* 101–124.

Hotaling, G. T., & Sugarman, D. B. (1990). A risk marker analysis of assaulted wives. *Journal of Family Violence, 5*(1), 1–13.

Hotaling, G. T., & Finkelhor, D. (1990). Estimating the number of stranger-abduction homicides of children: A review of available evidence. *Journal of Criminal Justice, 18*(5), 385–399.

Houghton Mifflin. (2005). *The reader's companion to American history: The Jungle.* Retrieved May 15, 2005, from http://college.hmco.com/history/readerscomp/rcah/html/ah_049000_junglethe.htm

Howard, J. L., Liptzin, M. B., & Reifler, C. B. (1973). Is pornography a problem? *Journal of Social Issues, 29*(3), 133–143.

Howitt, D., & Cumberbatch, G. (1990). *Pornography, impacts and influences: A review of available research evidence on the effects of pornography.* London: Research and Planning Unit, UK Home Office.

Howlett, D. (2003, July 13). *Patriot Act battle is fought locally.* usa today.com. Retrieved June 8, 2004, from http://www.usatoday.com/news/nation/2003-07-13-patriot_x.htm

Hubbard, L. (1999). *The end of busing.* Retrieved November 30, 2004, from http://www.exodusnews.com/education/education020.htm

Hughes, D. R. (2001). *Recent statistics on Internet dangers.* Retrieved December 31, 2004, from http://www.protectkids.com/dangers/stats.htm

Huizinga, D., & Elliott, D. S. (1987). Juvenile offenders: Prevalence, offenders, and arrest rates by race. *Crime and Delinquency, 33,* 206–223.

Human Rights Watch. (1992). *Double jeopardy: Police abuse of women in Pakistan.* New York: Human Rights Watch Women's Rights Project, Asia-Watch.

Human Rights Watch. (1999). *Crime or custom? Violence against women in Pakistan.* New York: Human Rights Watch.

Human Rights Watch. (2001). *No escape: Male rape in U.S. Prisons: Summary and Recommendations.* Retrieved March 28, 2006, from http://www.hrw.org/reports/2001/prison/report1.html#_1_5

Human Rights Watch. (2002). *Presumption of guilt: Human rights abuses of post-September 11 detainees* (Vol. 14, No. 4). Retrieved January 4, 2004 from http://www.hrw.org/reports/2002/us911/USA0802.pdf

Human Rights Watch. (2003, October 22). United States: Mentally ill mistreated in prison—More mentally ill in prison than in hospitals. *Human Rights News.* Retrieved December 14, 2003, from http://www.hrw.org/press/2003/10/us102203.htm

Hummel, A. (2000). *Interview with a terrorist.* Retrieved August 13, 2004, from http://www.worldtrek.org/odyssey/mideast/020200/020200abejahamas.html

Hurley, J. T. (2003). *Violent crime hits home: Home invasion robbery.* Retrieved November 27, 2003, from http://www.flpd.org/hurley.html

Hutchings, B., & Mednick, S. A. (1977). Criminality in adoptees and their adoptive and biological parents: A pilot study. In S. A. Mednick & K. O. Christensen (Eds.), *Biological bases of criminal behavior* (pp. 127–142). New York: Gardner.

Hutchinson, A. (2002). *International drug trafficking and terrorism.* Testimony before the Senate Judiciary Committee Subcommittee on Technology, Terrorism, and Government Information. Retrieved May 4, 2006, from http://www.state.gov/p/inl/rls/rm/2002/9239.htm

Ianni, F. A. J. (1974). *Black Mafia.* New York: Simon and Schuster.

Idaho Credit Union League and Affiliates. (1999). *Check kiting 101: What it is and why its bad.* Retrieved December 23, 2004, from http://students.cup.edu/col4145/

Idea House. (2001). *College student cheating widespread.* Retrieved December 19, 2004, from http://www.ncpa.org/pi/edu/jan98o.html

Inciardi, J. A. (1984). Little girls and sex: A glimpse at the world of the "baby pro." *Deviant Behavior, 5,* 71–78.

Inciardi, J. A., Horowitz, R., & Pottieger, A. E. (1993). *Street kids, street drugs, street crime: An examination of drug use and serious delinquency in Miami.* Belmont, CA: Wadsworth.

Infocostarica Staff. (2003). *Safety for travelers.* Retrieved November 24, 2003, from the website http://www.infocostarica.com/travel/safety.html

Infoplease. (2004). *Uncovering African roots: DNA tests, new technology reveal African heritage.* Retrieved November 28, 2004, from http://www.infoplease.com/spot/slavery2.html

Infoplease. (2006). *United Arab Emirates.* Retrieved May 23, 2006, from http://www.infoplease.com/ipa/A0108074.html

Ingis, R. (1978). *Sins of the fathers: A study of the physical and emotional abuse of children.* New York: St. Martins.

Institute for Scientific Analysis. (1999). *Beyond deinstitutionalization, 1968–1998.* Retrieved July 20, 2003, from http://www.scientificanalysis.org/30yr3.html

Integrated Regional Information Networks (IRIN). (2002). *Swaziland: Focus on women and child abuse.* Retrieved October 10, 2003, from http://www.africahome.com/annews/categories/culture/EpFZFkkEuyKEUjbEgX.shtml

Internal Revenue Service. (2003). *Tax fraud in the restaurant industry fact sheet by criminal investigation.* Retrieved May 14, 2005, from http://www.irs.gov/compliance/enforcement/article/0,,id=112037,00.html

International Centre for Prison Studies. (2004a). *Prison brief for Sweden.* Retrieved October 10, 2004, from http://www.kcl.ac.uk/depsta/rel/icps/worldbrief/europe_records.php?code=165

International Centre for Prison Studies. (2004b). *Prison brief for United Kingdom: England and Wales.* Retrieved October 14, 2004, from http://www.kcl.ac.uk/depsta/rel/icps/worldbrief/europe_records.php?code=168

International Committee of the Red Cross (ICRC). (2004). *Report of the International Committee of the Red Cross (ICRC) on the Treatment by the Coalition Forces of Prisoners of War and Other Protected Persons by the Geneva Conventions in Iraq During Arrest, Internment and Interrogation.* Retrieved June 7, 2004, from http://www.cbsnews.com/htdocs/pdf/redcrossabuse.pdf

International Organization for Migration (IOM). (1999). *Migration in Central and Eastern Europe: 1999 Review.* New York: United Nations Publications.

Internet Encyclopedia of Philosophy. (2001). *Cesare Beccaria.* Retrieved July 18, 2003, from http://www.utm.edu/research/iep/b/beccaria.htm

Irfaifeh, A. A. (1990). *Causes of juvenile delinquency in Jordan* (Doctoral Dissertation, Western Michigan University). Ann Arbor, MI: University Microfilms International.

Irwin, J. (1970). *The felon.* Englewood Cliffs, NJ: Prentice Hall.

Isaac, R. J., & Armat, V. C. (1990) *Madness in the streets: How psychiatry and the law abandoned the mentally ill.* New York: Free Press.

Isenberg, D. (2003, July 29). World's trigger-happy population keeps growing. *Asia Times.* Retrieved September 25, 2003, from http://www.globalpolicy.org/security/smallarms/articles/2003/0729triggerhappy.htm

Islamic-world.net. (2000). *Islamic world countries.* Retrieved, March 11, 2006, from http://www.islamic-world.net/

Ivillage.com. (2004). *Car security devices.* Retrieved October 3, 2004, from http://magazines.ivillage.com/goodhousekeeping/consumer/cars/articles/0,,284541_2900 91-2,00.html?arrivalSA=1&cobrandRef=0&arrival_freqCap=1&pba=adid=10812930

Jacobs, B. A., Topalli, V., & Wright, R. (2000). Managing retaliation: Drug robbery and informal sanction threats. *Criminology, 38*(1), 171–197.

Jacobs, M. J. G., Essers, A. A. M., & Meijer, R. F. (2002) *A typology of car thieves: A preliminary investigation based on the WODC Criminal Justice Monitor and the Police Offenders Identification System.*

Jacobs, P. A., Brunton, M., & Melville, M. (1965). Aggressive behavior, mental subnormality, and the XYY male. *Nature, 208*(135), 1–22.

Jacobson, N., & Gottman, J. (1998). *When men batter women: New insights into ending abusive relationships.* New York: Simon and Schuster.

Jacoby, N. H., Nehemkis, P., & Eells, R. (1977). *Bribery and corruption.* New York: Macmillan.

Jason-Lloyd, L. (1998). *UK Drug and Alcohol Misuse White Papers—UK drugs legislation.* Retrieved October 15, 2004, from http://www.nadt.org.uk/suba/legislation.html

Jean, L. L. (1982). *The social world of the female prostitute in Los Angeles.* Ann Arbor, MI: University Microfilms International.

Jederlund, L. (1998). *From immigration policy to integration policy.* Retrieved October 10, 2004, from http://www.sweden.se/templates/Article____2283.asp

Jeffery, C. R. (1971). *Crime prevention through environmental design.* Beverly Hills, CA: Sage.

Jenkins, B. M. (1981). *International terrorism: Choosing the right target.* Santa Monica, CA: Rand Corporation.

Jesness, C. F. (1971). The Preston typology study: An experiment with differential treatment in an institution. *Journal of Research in Crime and Delinquency, 8*(1), 38–71.

Joan, S. (1999, December). *Hijab.* Retrieved December 17, 2003, from http://www.thetruereligion.org/hijabjoan.htm

Joe, K. A. (1994). The new criminal conspiracy? Asian gangs and organized crime in San Francisco. *Journal of Research in Crime and Delinquency, 31*(4), 390–415.

Johnson, A, G. (1980). On the prevalence of rape in the United States. *Signs, 6,* 136–145.

Johnston, L. D., Bachman, J. G., & O'Malley, P. M. (2003). *Monitoring the future.* Ann Arbor: Institute for Social Research, University of Michigan. Data downloaded from sourcebook of criminal justice statistics online. Retrieved April 2, 2005, from http://www.albany.edu/sourcebook/pdf/section3.pdf (Table 3.43, p. 222).

Jones, S. (2001). *Fundamentalism.* Retrieved June 2, 2005, from http://religious-movements.lib.virginia.edu/nrms/fund.html

Juergensmeyer, M. (2000). *Terror in the mind of God: The global rise of religious violence.* Berkeley: University of California Press.

Junger-Tas, J., & Klein, M. (1994). *International Self-Report Delinquency Survey.* Amsterdam, The Netherlands: Kluger.

Junger-Tas, J., Terlouw, G., & Klein, M. (Eds). (1994). *Delinquent behavior of young people in the western world—First results of the International Self-Report Delinquency Study.* Amsterdam, The Netherlands: Kluger.

Jura, J. (2005). *Drug war and peace.* Retrieved June 9, 2005, from http://www.orwelltoday.com/drugpeace.shtml

Kagner, K. (1999). *The rise of the Russian mafia.* Retrieved November 26, 2004, from http://www.policeman.ru/kiril_1.htm

Kamalakara, R. P., & Ramesh, B. M. (1984). Trends in homicide in India. *Indian Journal of Criminology, 12*(1), 61–64.

Kampf, H. A. (1980). On the appeals of extremism to the youth of affluent, democratic societies. *Terrorism: An International Journal, 4*(1–4), 161–193.

Kangas, S. (1999). *About me.* Retrieved May 1, 2005, from http://www.psnw .com/~bashford/aboutme.html

Kangas, S. (2002). *Timeline of CIA atrocities.* Retrieved April 30, 2005 from http://www.serendipity.li/cia/cia_time.htm

Kanin, E. J. (1957). Male aggression in dating-courtship relations. *American Journal of Sociology, 63,* 197–204.

Kantor, G. K., & Straus, M. A. (1989). *Substance abuse as a precipitant of wife abuse victimizations. American Journal of Drug and Alcohol Abuse, 15*(2), 173–189.

Kanwar, M. (1989). *Murder and homicide in Pakistan.* Lahore, Pakistan: Vanguard.

Kaplan, D. E. (2005, December 5). Paying for terror. *U.S. News and World Report.* Retrieved May 7, 2006, from http://www.usnews.com/usnews/news/articles/ 051205/5terror.htm

Kappeler, V. E., Blumberg, M., & Potter, G. W. (1996). *The mythology of crime and criminal justice.* Prospect Heights, IL: Waveland.

Katz, C. M., Webb, V. J., & Schaefer, D. R. (2000). The validity of police gang intelligence lists: Examining differences in delinquency between documented gang members and nondocumented delinquent. *Police Quarterly, 3*(4), 413–437.

Keel, R. O. (2004). *Drug law timeline: Significant events in the history of our drug laws.* Retrieved December 5, 2004, from http://www.druglibrary.org/schaffer/ History/drug_law_timeline.htm

Kefauver, E. (1951). *Crime in America.* Garden City, NY: Doubleday.

Kegel Exercise.com. (2003). *Child birth complication.* Retrieved June 10, 2005, from http://child.birth.complication.biolifedynamics.com/

Keily, J. F. (2001). *Making good citizens: The reformation of prisoners in China's first modern prisons, 1907–1937.* (Doctoral Dissertation). Berkeley: University of California.

Kelling, G. L., & Sousa, W. H. (2001). *Do police matter? An analysis of the impact of New York City's police reforms.* New York: Manhattan Institute for Policy Research.

Kennedy, L. W., & Silverman, R. A. (1988). *The elderly victim of homicide: limitations of the routine activity approach.* Discussion Paper 19. Edmonton, Canada: Center for Criminological Research, University of Alberta.

Kercher, L. C. (1981). *The Kenya penal system: Past, present and prospect.* Washington, DC: University Press of America.

Kesteren, J. N., Mayhew, P., & Nieuwbeerta, P. (2000) *Criminal victimization in seventeen industrialized countries: Key-findings from the 2000 international Crime Victims Survey.* The Hague, Ministry of Justice, WODC. Retrieved October 14, 2004, from http://www.unicri.it/icvs/publications/index_pub.htm

Kevin, M. (1995). *Women in prison with drug-related problems. Part I: Background characteristics.* Sydney, Australia: New South Wales Department of Corrective Services.

Khan, M. N. (1995). Biographical data: Agha Hasan Abedi. Retrieved May 24, 2006, from http://www.salaam.co.uk/knowledge/biography/vieentry.php?id=172

Kiernan, K. (2002). *Unmarried cohabitation and parenthood: Here to stay? European perspectives.* Conference on Public Policy and the Future of the Family. Retrieved October 7, 2004, from http://www-cpr.maxwell.syr.edu/moynihan-smeedingconference/kiernan.pdf

Kilchling, M. (2004). *Evaluating victim/offender mediation dealing with adult offenders in Austria and Germany.* Retrieved October 17, 2004, from http://www.iuscrim .mpg.de/forsch/krim/kilchling2_e.html

Killias, M. (1993). International correlations between gun ownership and rates of homicide and suicide. *Canadian Medical Association Journal, 148*(10), 1720–1776.

Killias, M., & Rabasa, J. (1998a). Does heroin prescription reduce crime? Results from the evaluation of the Swiss heroin prescription projects. *Studies on Crime and Prevention, 7*(1), 127–133. Retrieved June 26, 2004, from the Criminal Justice Abstracts database at http://spweb.silverplatter.com/calstate

Killias, M., & Rabasa, J. (1998b). Effects of the medical prescription of heroin on the delinquency of drug addicts. *Monatsschrift fuer Kriminologie und Strafrechtsreform, 81*(1), 1–16. Retrieved June 26, 2004, from the Criminal Justice Abstracts database at http://spweb.silverplatter.com/calstate

Kim, B. H. (1980). *The effects of urbanization on crime rates in Korea (1966–1975): A comparative analysis.* Retrieved June 26, 2004, from the Criminal Justice Abstracts database at http://spweb.silverplatter.com/calstate

Kinego, J. (2003). Domestic violence calls mean extra danger to police: Ambushed on the job, a West Virginia trooper is fighting for his life. *Eyewitness Local News.* Retrieved October 24, 2003, from http://www.wchstv.com/newsroom/eyewitness/0210/021011_1.shtml

King, R. (1972). *The drug hang up, America's fifty-year folly—Chapter Chairman Kefauver and the Mafia Myth.* Retrieved December 11, 2004 from http://www.druglibrary.org/special/king/dhu.dhu13.htm

Kivivuori, J., & Lehti, M. (2003). Homicide followed by suicide in Finland: Trend and social locus. *Journal of Scandinavian Studies in Criminology and Crime Prevention, 4*(2), 223–236.

Klaus, P. (1999). *Carjackings in the United States, 1992–96.* BJS Special Report Series. Washington, DC: U.S. Bureau of Justice Statistics.

Kleck, G., & DeLone, M. (1993). Victim resistance and offender weapon effects in robbery. *Journal of Quantitative Criminology, 9*(1), 55–81.

Klein, D. (1973). The etiology of female crime: A review of the literature. *Issues in Criminology, 8,* 3–30.

Klein, S. R., Bartholomew, G. S., & Bahr, S. J. (1999). Family education for adults in correctional settings: A conceptual framework. *International Journal of Offender Therapy and Comparative Criminology, 43*(3), 291–307.

Klemke, L. W. (1992). *The sociology of shoplifting: Boosters and snitches today.* Westport, CT: Praeger.

Kmet, M. A. (1981). Rx: security for pharmacists. *Security Management, 25*(4), 9–15.

Knight, J. (2000) *Appendix B: Pseudocommando mass murderers: 1913–99.* Retrieved July 16, 2003, from http://massmurder.zyns.com/julian_knight_doc_11.htm

Kohfeld, C. W., & Sprague, J. (1988). Urban unemployment drives urban crime. *Urban Affairs Quarterly, 24*(2), 215–241.

Korte, T., Pykalainen, J., & Seppala, T. (1998). Drug abuse of Finnish male prisoners in 1995. *Forensic Science International, 97*(2–3), 171–183.

Koss, M. P., Bachar, K. J., & Hopkins, C. Q. (2004). Expanding a community's justice response to sex crimes through advocacy, prosecutorial, and public health collaboration: Introducing the RESTORE program. *Journal of Interpersonal Violence, 19*(12), 1435–1463.

Koss, M. P., Gidycz, C. A., & Wisniewski, N. (1987). The scope of rape: Incidence and prevalence of sexual aggression and victimization in a national sample of students in higher education students. *Journal of Consulting and Clinical Psychology, 55*(2), 162–170.

Kovandzic, T. V., & Sloan, J. J. (2002). Police levels and crime rates revisited: A county-level analysis from Florida (1980–1998). *Journal of Criminal Justice, 30* (1), 65–76.

KPBS. (2004) *Methamphetamine: From the streets of San Diego.* Retrieved November 21, 2004, from http://www.kpbs.org/Other/DynPage.php?id=243

Krasnovsky, T., & Lane, R. C. (1998). Shoplifting: A review of the literature. *Aggression and Violent Behavior, 3*(3), 219–235.

Kreuzer, A., Romer, K. R., & Schneider, H. (1991). *Criminality of drug addicts.* Wiesbaden, Germany: Bundeskriminalamt.

Kroese, G. J., & Staring, R. H. J. M. (1993). *Prestige, professie en wanhoop: een Onderzoek onder Gedetineerde Overvallers* [Prestige, profession, and despair: A study among robbers in prison]. Amsterdam: Netherlands Ministry of Justice.

Kronfeld, M. (2002). *Readdressing the war on drugs.* Retrieved October 3, 2004, from http://www.gwhatchet.com/news/2002/09/26/UWireDcBureau/Column .Readdressing.The.War.On.Drugs-284318.shtml

Krug, E. G., Dahlberg, L. L., Mercy, J. A., Zwi, A. B., & Lozano, R. (Eds.). (2002). *World report on violence and health.* Geneva, Switzerland: World Health Organization.

Krug, E. G., Mercy, J. A., & Dahlberg, L. L. (1998). Firearm- and non-firearm-related homicide among children: an international comparison. *Homicide Studies, 2*(1), 83–95.

Krug, E. G., Powell, K. E., & Dahlberg, L. L. (1998). Firearm-related deaths in the United States and 35 other high- and upper-middle-income countries. *International Journal of Epidemiology, 27,* 214–221.

Kruise, P. (2001). *Choices of commercial robbers: A comparative study of commercial robbers in Denmark and the Netherlands.* Copenhagen, Denmark: DJOF.

Kube, E., & Kuckuck, W. (1992). Research and technological developments in the police: requirements from the Western European point of view. *Police Studies, 15*(1), 24–29.

Kushner, H. W. (1998). *Terrorism in America: A structured approach to understanding the terrorist threat.* Springfield, IL: Charles C. Thomas.

Kutchinsky, B. (1976). Deviance and criminology: The case of voyeur in a peeper's paradise. *Diseases of the Nervous System, 37*(3), 145–151.

Kwitny, J. (1987). *The crimes of patriots: A true tale of dope, dirty money, and the CIA.* New York: Norton.

Kykeon@lycaeum.org. (1991). *The duplicity of the War on Drugs.* Retrieved November 16, 2003, from http://www.lycaeum.org/drugwar/dupe.html

La Fave, W., & Scott, A. (1972). *Handbook on criminal law.* St. Paul, MN: West.

LaFree, G., & Drass, K. (2002). Counting crime booms among nations: Evidence for homicide victimization rates, 1956 to 1998. *Criminology, 40*(4), 769–800.

Laing, R. D. (1965). *The divided self.* Baltimore: Penguin.

Lancashire, M. J., Legg, P. K., Lowe, M., Davidson, S. M., & Ellis, B. W. (1988, April 9). International aspects of international drug smuggling. *British Medical Journal (Clinical Research Edition), 296*(6628), 1035–1037.

Lancaster, J. (2002). *Workplace violence: Monster career advice.* Retrieved July 27, 2003, from http://content.monster.co.nz/businesslife/7437/

Landau, S. F., & Fridman, D. (1993). The seasonality of violent crime: The case of robbery and homicide in Israel. *Journal of Research in Crime and Delinquency, 30,* 163–191.

Langan, P. A. (1978). *The measurement of robbery in Baltimore: A study of citizen discretion in the reporting of noncommercial predatory robbery to the Baltimore Police Department.* (Doctoral Dissertation, University of Michigan). Ann Arbor, MI: University Microfilms International.

Langevin, R. (1988). Pornography and sexual offenses. *Annals of Sex Research, 1*(3), 335–362.

Langley, J. T., Munger, M., Litteral, K., & Camper, S. (2001). *Colonial America, 1607–1783: Law.* Retrieved February 20, 2005, from http://www.uncp.edu/home/canada/work/allam/16071783/law.htm

Lanning, K. V., & Burgess, A. W. (Eds.). (1995). *Child molesters who abduct: Summary of the case in point series.* Alexandria, VA: National Center for Missing and Exploited Children.

Lasn, W. K. (1999). *The uncooling of America: The history of corporations in the United States.* Retrieved May 14, 2005, from http://www.thirdworldtraveler.com/Corporations/Hx_Corporations_US.html

Lawrence, F. (2004). *Not on the label: What really goes into the food on your plate.* London: Penguin.

Lawrence, J. S., & Shireman, C. H. (1980). *The findings of self-report studies of juvenile misbehavior: a summary.* Chicago: University of Chicago, National Center for the Assessment of Alternatives to Juvenile Justice Processing.

Laxley, W. (2001). Drug use, intoxication and offense type in two groups of alleged offenders in Perth: A pilot study. *Australian and New Zealand Journal of Criminology, 34*(1), 91–104.

Laycock, G., & Austin, C. (1992). Crime prevention in parking facilities. *Security Journal, 3*(3), 154–160.

Leape, L. L. (1989). Unnecessary surgery. *Health Services Research, 24*(3), 351–407.

Lee, L. J. (1982). *The social world of the female prostitute in Los Angeles.* Ann Arbor, MI: University Microfilms International.

Lee, R. E. (2004). *Sleeping with a virgin to cure AIDS.* Retrieved June 19, 2004, from: http://www.edifyingspectacle.org/sexuality/blog/archives/sexual_health/sleeping_with_a_virgin_to.php

Lemert, E. M. (1951). *Social pathology.* New York: McGraw-Hill.

Lester, B. Y. (1995). Property crime and unemployment: A new perspective. *Applied Economic Letters, 2,* 159–162.

Letters to the Editor. (2002, November). *A violent computer game produced by the U.S. Army to recruit new soldiers.* Menconi Ministries. Retrieved October 6, 2003, from http://www.almenconi.com/letters/nov02/112502b.html

Levene, S. (2005). *Civil law.* Microsoft Encarta Online Encyclopedia. Retrieved, May 28, 2005, from http://uk.encarta.msn.com/text_761565815__0/Civil_Law.html

Levin, J., & Fox, J. A. (1996). A psycho-social analysis of mass murder. In T. O'Reilly-Fleming, (Ed.), *Serial and mass murder: Theory, research, and policy.* Toronto: Canadian Scholars' Press.

LeVine, R. A. (1959). Gusii sex offense: A study in social control. *American Anthropologist, 61,* 1987.

Levine, S. (1999). Youth in terroristic groups, gangs, and cults: The allure, the animus, and the alienation. *Psychiatric Annals, 29*(6), 342–349.

Levitt, S. D. (1999). The changing relationship between income and crime victimization. *Economic Policy Review, 5*(3), 87–98.

Lewis, J. (2001). *18th Street Gang.* Retrieved November 23, 2004, from http://www.knowgangs.com/gang_resources/18th/18th_001.htm

Li, L. (1999). The ultimate loss: Rape and suicide in Qing China, 1744–1903. *International Journal of Comparative and Applied Criminal Justice, 23*(1), 91–101.

Li, X. (1998). *Crime and policing in China.* A paper presented at the Australian Institute of Criminology, September, 7. Retrieved March 3, 2006, from http://www.aic.gov.au/conferences/occasional/xiancui.html

Library of Congress. (1994a). Pakistan: Islam in India. Retrieved 4/2/06, from http://lcweb2.loc.gov/cgi-bin/query/r?frd/cstdy:@field(DOCID+pk0015)

Library of Congress. (1994b). Pakistan: Politicized Islam. Retrieved 4/2/06, from http://lcweb2.loc.gov/cgi-bin/query/r?frd/cstdy:@field(DOCID+pk0060)

Library of Congress. (1994c). Pakistan: Religious life. Retrieved 4/2/06, from http://lcweb2.loc.gov/cgi-bin/query/r?frd/cstdy:@field(DOCID+pk0058)

Light, R., Nee, C., & Ingham, H. (1993). *Car theft: The offender's perspective.* London: HMSO Books.

Lightfoot, E., & Umbreit, M. (2004). An analysis of state statutory provisions for victim-offender mediation. *Criminal Justice Policy Review, 15*(4), 418–436.

Lilly, J. R., Cullin, F. T. , & Ball, R. A. (1995). *Criminological theory: Context and consequences.* Thousand Oaks: CA: Sage.

Linder, D. (2000, July 10). *Speech on the occasion of the 75th Anniversary of the Scopes Trial.* Retrieved February 19, 2005, from http://www.law.umkc.edu/faculty/projects/ftrials/scopes/evolut.htm

Lindesmith, A. R. (1968). *Addiction and opiates.* Chicago: Aldine.

Lindesmith, A. R., & Strauss, A. L. (1949) *Social psychology.* New York: Dryden.

Link, B. G., Andrews, H., & Cullen, F. T. (1992). The violent and illegal behavior of mental patients reconsidered. *American Sociological Review, 57,* 275–292.

Lisaviolet. (2004). *Animal cruelty: Misdemeanor or felony.* Retrieved January 30, 2005, from http://www.lisaviolet.com/cathouse/cruelty.html

Lithner, K. (1986). Garofalo's Swedish source. *Crimcare Journal, 2*(1), 41–46.

Liu, J. (2005). Crime patterns during the market transition in China. *British Journal of Criminology, 45,* 613–633.

Loftin, C., & Hill, R. H. (1974). Regional subculture and homicide: A comparison of the Gastil-Hackney thesis. *American Sociological Review, 39,* 714–724.

Lombardo, R. M. (2002). The black mafia: African-American organized crime in Chicago 1890-1960. *Crime, Law & Social Change, 38,* 33–65.

Lombroso, C. (1876). *The criminal man.* Milan, Italy: Hoepli.

Lombroso, C. (1895). *The female offender.* New York: Appleton.

Lombroso, C. (1912). *Crime: Its causes and remedies.* Montclair, NJ: Patterson Smith.

Lorenz, K. (1966). *On aggression.* New York: Harcourt Brace Jovanovich.

Lott, J. R., Jr. (1998). *More guns; less crime: Understanding crime and gun control laws.* Chicago: University of Chicago Press.

Lott, J. R., & Landes, W. M. (1999). *Multiple victim public shootings, bombings, and right-to-carry concealed handgun laws: Contrasting private and public law enforcement.* Chicago: University of Chicago Law School.

Lottier, S. (1942). Tension theory and criminal behavior. *American Sociological Review, 7,* 843–844.

Lowney, J. (2001). *What were your parents doing back then?* New York: University Press of America.

Lowney, J., Winslow, R., & Winslow, V. (1981). *Deviant reality: Alternative world views.* Boston, Massachusetts: Allyn and Bacon, Inc.

Lu, H. (1999). Bang jaio and reintegrative shaming in China's urban neighborhoods. *International Journal of Comparative and Applied Criminal Justice, 23*(1), 115–125.

Luckenbill, D. F. (1981). Generating compliance: The case of robbery. *Urban Life, 10*(1), 25–46.

Ludwig, J., & Cook, P. J. (2000). Homicide and suicide rates associated with implementation of the Brady Handgun Violence Prevention Act. *Journal of the American Medical Association, 284*(5), 585–618.

Ludwig, J., & Cook, P. J. (2003). *Evaluating gun policy: Effects on crime and violence.* Washington, DC: Brookings Institution Press.

Lundberg, G. (1961) *Can science save us?* (2nd ed.). New York: Greenwood Press Reprint.

Lyengar, L. (1995). *The disproportionate representation of African-American youth at various decision points in the State of Maryland.* Baltimore: Maryland Department of Juvenile Justice.

Lynn, B. (1986). *Rushing to censorship: An interim report in the methods of evidence gathering and evaluation by the Attorney General's Commission on Pornography.* Washington, DC: American Civil Liberties Union.

MacKay, P. (1988). Crime prevention. *Criminologist,12*(2), 86–94.

Mackinnon, C. (1989). *Toward a feminist theory of the state.* Cambridge, MA: Harvard University Press.

Macko, S. (1996). Security problems in Latin America. *ENN Daily Report, 2*(237). Retrieved August 3, 2003, from http://www.emergency.com/ltn-scty.htm

Madge, J. (1962). *The origins of scientific sociology.* New York: Free Press.

Madriz, E. (1996). The perception of risk in the workplace: A test of routine activity theory. *Journal of Criminal Justice, 24*(5), 407–418.

Madsen, W. (2003, September 27). Respect rights of protest groups. *The Miami Herald.* Retrieved June 10, 2004, from http://www.commondreams.org/views03/0927-06.htm

Maguire, E. R., & Uchida, C. D. (2000). *Measurement and explanation in the comparative study of American police organizations.* Retrieved March 13, 2005, from http://www.ncjrs.org/criminal_justice2000/vol_4/04j.pdf

Maher, L., Dixon, D., & Hall, W. (2002). Property crime and income generation. *Australian and New Zealand Journal of Criminology, 35*(2), 187–202.

Malamuth, N. M., Addison, T., & Koss, M. (2000). Pornography and sexual aggression: Are there reliable effects and can we understand them? *Annual Review of Sex Research, 11,* 26–91.

Malcolm, J. L. (2002). *Guns and violence: The English experience.* Cambridge, MA: Harvard University Press.

Mannon, J. M. (1997). Domestic and intimate violence: An application of routine activities theory. *Aggression and violent behavior, 2*(1), 9–24.

Marc, C. C. H. (1840). *De la folie consideree dans ses rapports avec les questions medico-judicierres* [Madness considered in its relationship with medical-legal questions]. Paris: Balliere, as quoted in Fullerton & Punj, 2004, p. 14.

Marongiu, P., & Biddau, M. (1993). *Italy.* World Factbook of Criminal Justice Systems. Retrieved May 28, 2005, from http://www.ojp.usdoj.gov/bjs/pub/ascii/wfbcjita.txt

Marsh, P. (1978). *Aggro: The illusion of violence.* London: Dent.

Marsh, R. M. (1967). *Comparative sociology: A codification of cross-societal analysis.* New York: Harcourt, Brace and World.

Martell, D. A. (1991). Homeless mentally disordered offenders and violent crimes: Preliminary research findings. *Law and Human Behavior, 15*(4), 333–347.

Martell, D. A., & Dietz, P. E. (1992). Mentally disordered offenders who push or attempt to push victims onto subway tracks in New York City. *Archives of General Psychiatry, 49,* 472–475.

Martens, P. L. (1997). Immigrants, crime, and criminal justice in Sweden. In M. Tonry (Ed.), *Ethnicity, crime, and immigration: Comparative and cross-national perspectives* (pp. 183–255). Chicago: University of Chicago Press.

Martin, B. F. (1990). *Crime and criminal justice under the Third Republic: The shame of Marianne.* Baton Rouge and London: Louisiana State University Press.

Martin, D. (2002). Spatial patterns in residential burglary: Assessing the effect of neighborhood social capital. *Journal of Contemporary Criminal Justice, 18*(2), 132–146.

Martin, T. E., Jr., Esq. (2003). *Pennsylvania consolidated statutes.* Retrieved May 4, 2005, from http://members.aol.com/StatutesP4/18PA4108.html

Martinson, R. (1974). What works: Question and answers about prison reform. *Public Interest, 35,* 22–54.

Mathey, A. (1816). *Nouvelle recherches sur les maladies de l'esprit* [New research upon the diseases of the spirit]. Paris: Paschoud, as cited in Fullerton & Punj, 2004, p. 14.

Matza, D. (1964) *Delinquency and drift.* New York: Wiley.

Maxson, C. (1998). *Gang members on the move.* OJJDP Juvenile Justice Bulletin. Washington, DC: Office of Juvenile Justice and Delinquency Prevention, p. 5.

Maxson, C. L., Gordon, M. A., & Klein, M. W. (1985). Differences between gang and nongang homicides. *Criminology, 23*(2), 209–222.

Maxwell, C. (1996). *NCVS redesign information.* Retrieved March 20, 2005, from http:///www.icpsr.umich.edu/NACJD/NCVS/redesign.html

Mayhew, P. (1991). Displacement and vehicle theft: An attempt to reconcile some recent contradictory evidence. *Security Journal, 2*(4), 233–239.

Mayhew, P., & Van Dijk, J. J. M.(2000). *Criminal victimization in eleven industrialized countries: Key findings from the 1996 International Crime Victims Survey.* Retrieved July 5, 2004, from http://www.unicri.it/icvs/publications/pdf_files/summary162.PDF

McCabe, D. L., & Trevino, L. K. (1996). What we know about cheating in college: Longitudinal trends and recent developments. *Change, 28*(1), p. 31.

McCaghy, C., Giordano, P., & Henson, T. K. (1977). Auto theft. *Criminology, 15,* 367–81.

McClendon, J. G. (1990). *Puritan jurisprudence: Progress and inconsistency.* Retrieved March 3, 2005, from http://www.reformed.org/webfiles/antithesis/v1n1/ant_v1n1_juris.html

McCold, P. (2003). An experiment in police-based restorative justice: The Bethlehem (Pennsylvania) Project. *Police Practice & Research, 4*(4), 379–390.

McCord, J. (1988). Parental aggressiveness and physical punishment in long-term perspective. In G. T. Hotaling, D. Finkelhor, J. T. Kirkpatrick, & M. A. Straus. (Eds.), *Family abuse and its consequences.* Newbury Park, CA: Sage.

McCoy, A. W. (1972). *The politics of heroin in Southeast Asia.* New York: Harper & Row.

McCoy, A. W. (1991). *The politics of heroin: CIA complicity in the global drug trade.* Brooklyn, NY: Lawrence Hill, published online at: http://www.drugtext.org/library/books/McCoy/book See particularly "The GI heroin epidemic," at: http://www.drugtext.org/library/books/McCoy/book/38.htm

McCoy, A. W. (August 1997). Drug fallout. excerpted from *Progressive Magazine.* Retrieved 8/31/2006, from http://www.thirdworldtraveler.com/CIA/CIAdrug_fallout.html

McCulloch, J. (2000). *Black peril, white virtue: Sexual crime in Southern Rhodesia, 1902–1935.* Bloomington: Indiana University Press. Retrieved June 26, 2004, from the Criminal Justice Abstracts database at http://spweb.silverplatter.com/calstate

McCullough, D., Schmidt, T., & Lockhard, B. (1990). *Car theft in Northern Ireland: Recent Studies on a Persistent Problem.* Belfast, Ireland: Extern Organization.

McDonald, T. (2000, December 15). Report: Violent computer games sell guns. *NewsFactor Network.* Retrieved September 13, 2003, from http://www.newsfactor.com/perl/ story/6106.html

McElroy, J. E., Cosgrove, C. A., & Farrell, M. (1981). *Felony case preparation: Quality counts. Executive summary.* (Interim Report). New York: Vera Institute of Justice.

McGeorge, N. (2003). *Restorative justice in the EU.* Retrieved October 17, 2004, from http://www.quaker.org/qcea/AE252.htm

McGoey, C. E. (2004). *Shoplifting.* Retrieved October 3, 2004, from http://www.crimedoctor.com/shoplifting.htm

McGreal, C. (2003). *Killing of Hamas leader, Ismael Abu Shanab, ends truce.* Retrieved August 23, 2004, from http://www.fromoccupiedpalestine.org/node.php?id=690

McGuire, E. P. (1979). International terrorism and business security. *Information Bulletin Number, 65.* New York: The Conference Board.

McKenzie, J. (2002, June 12). Conflict of interest? Medical journal changes policy of finding independent doctors. *ABC News.*

McKim, W. A. (1991). *Drugs and alcohol behavior: An introduction to behavioral pharmacology.* Englewood Cliffs, NJ: Prentice Hall.

McShane, F. J., & Noonan, B. A. (1993). Classification of shoplifters by cluster analysis. *International Journal of Offender Therapy and Comparative Criminology, 37*(1), 29–40.

McWilliams, P. (1996). *Ain't nobody's business if you do.* Retrieved December 7, 2004, from http://www.mcwilliams.com/books/books/aint/

Mdluli-Sedibe, P. F. R. (1999). *The influence of transnational crime on national security.* Retrieved October 10, 2004, from http://www.mil.za/CSANDF/CJSupp/TrainingFormationDefenceCollege/ResearchPapers1999/mdluli-sedibe.htm

Mead, G. H. (1934) *Mind, self, and society.* Chicago: University of Chicago Press.

Meade, J. (1992). Cheating: Is academic dishonesty par for the course? *Prism, 1*(7), 30–32.

Mednick, S. A. (1977). A biosocial theory of the learning of law-abiding behavior. In S. A. Mednick & K. O. Christensen, (Eds.), *Biosocial bases of criminal behavior* (pp. 1–8). New York: Gardner.

Mednick, S. A., Gabrielli, W. F., Jr., & Hutchings, B. (1987). Genetic factors in the etiology of criminal behavior. In S. A. Mednick, T. E. Moffin, & S. A. Stack (Eds.), *The causes of crime: New behavioral approaches* (pp. 74–91). New York: Cambridge University Press.

Mehdi, R.(1990). The offence of rape in the Islamic law of Pakistan. *International Journal of the Sociology of Law, 18*(1), 19–29.

Mendoza, A. (2003) *Serial killer hit list.* Retrieved July 26, 2003, from http://www.mayhem.net/Crime/serial.html

Merriam-Webster Online (2006a). *Burg.* Retrieved August 30, 2006, from http://www.m-w.com/dictionary/burg

Merriam-Webster Online (2006b). *Curtilage.* Retrieved August 30, 2006, from http://www.m-w.com/dictionary/curtilage

Merriam-Webster Online. (2006c). *Diaspora.* Retrieved May 27, 2006, from http://www.mw.com/dictionary/diaspora+

Merton, R. K. (1938). Social structure and anomie. *American Sociological Review, 3,* 672–682.

Merton, R. K. (1968). *Social theory and social structure.* New York: Free Press.

Merton, R. K., & Montague, M. F. A. (1940). Crime and the anthropologist. *American Anthropologist, 42,* 384–408.

Messerschmidt, J. (1986). *Capitalism, patriarchy, and crime.* Totowa, NJ: Rowman & Littlefield.

Messerschmidt, J. (1987). Feminism, criminology, and the rise of the female sex "delinquent," 1880–1930. *Contemporary Crises, 11*(3), 243–63.

Messner, S. (1983). Regional and racial effects on the urban homicide rate: The subculture of violence revisited. *American Journal of Sociology, 88,* 997–1007.

Messner, S., & Rosenfeld, R. (1994). *Crime and the American Dream.* Belmont, CA: Wadsworth.

Michigan State University and Death Penalty Information Center. (2000). *History of the death penalty.* Retrieved February 27, 2005, from http://teacher.death penaltyinfo.msu.edu/c/about/history/history.PDF

Miller, B. A., Nochajski, T. H., Leonard, K. E., Blane, H. T., Gondoli, D. M., & Bowers, P. M. (1990). Spousal violence and alcohol/drug problems among parolees and their spouses. *Women and Criminal Justice, 1,* 55–72.

Miller, J. (1998). Up it up: Gender and the accomplishment of street robbery. *Criminology, 36*(1), 37–66.

Miller, L. L. (2001). Looking for postmodernism in all the wrong places: Implementing a new penology. *British Journal of Criminology, 41*(1), 168–184.

Miller, M. (2002, March 18). *Critics aim to bounce dodge ball off the schoolyard.* Retrieved October 17, 2003, from http://www.latimes.com/features/lifestyle/la-031802dodgeball.story

Miller v. California. (1973) 413 U.S. 15.

Miller, W. B. (1996). *The growth of youth gang problems in the United States: 1970–1995.* Tallahassee, FL: National Youth Gang Center, Institute for Intergovernmental Research.

Minnery, J. R. (1988). Crime perception, victimization and reporting in inner Brisbane. *Criminal Justice Abstracts, 1968–2003(13),* Abstract No. 45556.

Minnesota Department of Corrections. (2005). *Restorative justice: Peacemaking circle process.* Retrieved June 10, 2005, from http://www.doc.state.mn.us/aboutdoc/restorativejustice/rjpeacemakingcircleprocess.htm

Minuteman Civil Defense Corps., Inc. (2005). *Going national.* Retrieved May 15, 2005, from http://www.civilhomelanddefense.us/

Mishara, E. (1983, August). R. D. Laing's new home. *Omni,* p. 35.

Mizell, L. (1996). *Road rage.* Washington, DC: AAA Foundation for Traffic Safety. Retrieved October 17, 2003, from http://www.aaafoundation.org/resources/index.cfm?button=agdrtext#Road%20Rage

Mocan, H. N., & Rees, D. I. (1999). *Economic conditions, deterrence and juvenile crime: Evidence from micro data.* Cambridge, MA: National Bureau of Economic Research.

Modes, W. (2000). *Shoplifting 101.* Retrieved September 28, 2004, from http://www.thespoon.com/stories/shoplifting.html

Moffitt, T. E., & Caspi, A. (1999). *Findings about partner violence from the longitudinal Dunedin Multidisciplinary Health and Development Study.* Washington, DC: U.S. Department of Justice Office of Justice Programs National Institute of Justice. Retrieved October 20, 2003, from http://www.ncjrs.org/txtfiles1/170018.txt

Moffitt, T., & Silva, P. (1988). IQ and delinquency: A direct test of the differential detection hypothesis. *Journal of Abnormal Psychology, 97,* 1–4.

Moir, A., & Jessel, D. (1995). *A mind to crime: The controversial link between the mind and criminal behavior.* London, UK: Michael Joseph.

Mollaret, H. H. (2002). *The biological weapon: Bacteria, viruses, and terrorism.* Paris: Plon.

Moore, R. H. (1984). Shoplifting in Middle America: Patterns and motivational correlates. *International Journal of Offender Therapy and Comparative Criminology, 23*(1), 55–64.

Morris, N., & Hawkins, G. (1969). The honest politician's guide to crime control. Chicago: University of Chicago Press.

Morrissette, A. M., & Manitoba, B. (2004). *The experiences of women during the holocaust.* Retrieved May 12, 2006, from http://www.jhcwc.mb.ca/morrissette2004.pdf

Morrison, S., & O'Donnell, I. (1994). *Armed robbery: A study in London* (Occasional Paper #15). Oxford, UK: Centre for Criminological Research, University of Oxford.

Mrsevik, Z., & Hughes, D. M. (1997). Violence against women in Belgrade, Servia: SOS Hotline 1990–1993. *Violence Against Women, 3*(2), 101–128.

Muehnenhard, C. L., & Linton, M. A. (1987). Date rape and sexual aggression in dating situations: Incidence and risk factors. *Journal of Counseling Psychology, 34*(2), 186–196.

Mueller, G. O. W., & Adler, F. (1985). *Outlaws of the ocean: The complete book of contemporary crime on the high seas.* New York: Hearst Marine.

Mundt, R. (1990). Preventing crime: Current issues and debates. *Canadian Journal of Sociology, 32*(1), 1–22.

Murray, B. (2001, June). 81% of students undergo harassment, survey finds. *HustonChronicle.com.* Retrieved October 9, 2003, from http://www.chron.com/cs/CDA/story.hts/nation/935173

Muskie, Edwin S. School of Public Service. (2000). *The Snapshot Project.* Retrieved November 3, 2003, from http://muskie.usm.maine.edu/snapshot/profiles .html

Mustard Seed Communities. (2003). *Jamaica. Mustard Seed Communities.* Retrieved November 17, 2003, from http://www.mustardseed.com/locations/jamaica .html

Myers, A. L. (2004, October 10). Immigrant smugglers increasingly using stolen cars. Retrieved October 20, 2004, from http://www.nctimes.com/articles/ 2004/08/01/news/state/18_55_257_31_04.prt

Myrdal, G. (1944). *An American dilemma: The Negro problem and modern democracy.* New York: Harper & Row.

Naik, Z. (n. d.). *Women in Islam.* Retrieved October 24, 2003, from the Islamic Research Foundation Website http://www.sinc.sunysb.edu/Stu/hsyed/articles/ women.html

Nakhshab, S. (1979). *Juvenile delinquency in Tehran, Iran: An examination of Sutherland's theory of differential association* (Doctoral Dissertation, United States International University). Ann Arbor, MI: University Microfilms International. Retrieved June 26, 2004, from the Criminal Justice Abstracts database at http://spweb.silverplatter.com/calstate

Natalino, K. W. (1979). *Social correlates of rural and urban delinquency* (Doctoral Dissertation, Bowling Green State University). Ann Arbor, MI: University Microfilms International.

National Center for Education Statistics. (1998). *Violence and discipline problems in U.S. public schools: 1996–97.* Washington, DC: U.S. Department of Education National Center for Education Statistics.

National Center for Educational Statistics. (2005). *Digest of education statistics tables and figures.* Retrieved May 21, 2006, from http://nces.ed.gov/programs/digest/ d00/dt045.asp

National Child Abuse and Neglect Data System (NCANDS). (2002). *Summary findings 2002.* Washington, DC: Children's Bureau, Administration on Children, Youth, and Families, U.S. Department of Human Services.

National Conference of State Legislatures. (2001). *Computer crimes: Enacted legislation in 2000.* Retrieved May 21, 2006, from http://www.ncsl.org/programs/ lis/cip/compcrime2k.htm

National Criminal Intelligence Service (NCIS). (2004). *United Kingdom assessment of serious and organized crime 2003.* Retrieved October 10, 2004, from http://ncis.gov.uk/ukta/2003/threat01.asp

National Criminal Justice Reference Service (NCJRS). (2002, March). Belgium: The epicentre of terrorism in Europe. *Jane's Terrorism & Security Monitor* (pp. 4–6). Retrieved May 3, 2004, from http://abstractsdb.ncjrs.org/content/ AbstractsDB_Details.asp?index=10&perpage=25&ncjnum=194335&doc Index=25&chkBoxBitFlags=00000000000000000000000000

National Drug Intelligence Center. (2001). *United States-Canada Border Drug Threat Assessment.* Retrieved December 11, 2004, from http://www.usdoj.gov/ndic/ pubs07/794/

National Information Center. (2006). *Financial data and institution characteristics collected by the Federal Reserve System: Definitions of banking institutions on the NIC public Website.* Retrieved May 26, 2006, from http://www.ffiec.gov/nicpubweb/ content/help/HelpNICHomePage.htm

Nationmaster.com. (2004). Retrieved October 14, 2004, from http://www.nationmaster.com/country/uk/Immigration

Nedoroscik. J. A. (2002). Extremist groups in Egypt. *Terrorism and Political Violence, 14*(2), 47–76.

Neill, K. G. (2000, November). Duty, honor, rape: Sexual assault against women during war. *Journal of International Women's Studies.* Retrieved October 17, 2003, from http://www.bridgew.edu/depts/artscnce/jiws/nov00/duty.htm

Neilson, A. (2000). *Organized crime in Europe.* Retrieved October 14, 2004, from http://www.ex.ac.uk/politics/pol_data/undergrad/Neilson/index.html

Nelli, H. (1969). Italians and crime in Chicago: The formative years, 1890–1920. *American Journal of Sociology, 75,* 373–391.

Nettler, G. (1982). *Killing one another.* Cincinnati, OH: Anderson.

Network Reform Groups. (1999). *The effective national drug control strategy 1999.* Retrieved December 11, 2004 from http://www.csdp.org/edcs/theneed.htm

Neustrom, M. W., & Norton, W. N. (1995). Economic dislocation and property crime. *Journal of Criminal Justice, 23*(1), 29–39.

New Criminologist. (2002). *Marital Rape—A U.S. study: Violence against women.* U.S. Department of Justice. Retrieved August 21, 2004 from http://www.thecriminologist.com/new_criminologist/volume1/marital_rape/marital_rape.asp

New York State Department of Correctional Services. (1995). *Carjackers: A study of forcible minor vehicle thefts among new commitments 1985–1993.* Albany, NY: State Department of Correctional Services.

Newman, O. (1972). *Defensible space: Crime prevention through urban design.* New York: Macmillan.

Niehoff, D. (1999). *The biology of violence.* New York: Free Press.

Nkpa, N. K. U. (1976). Armed robbery in post-civil war Nigeria: The role of the victim. *Victimology, 1*(1), 71–83.

Nobile, P., & Nadler, E. (1986). *United States of America vs. sex: How the Meese Commission lied about pornography.* New York: Minotaur.

Npr.org. (2006, May 28). *Debating the PATRIOT ACT.* Retrieved May 28, 2006, from http://www.npr.org/templates/story/story.php?storyId=4759727&sourceCode=gaw

Null, G., Dean, C., Feldman, M., & Rasio, D. (2003). *Death by medicine.* Retrieved May 21, 2005, from http://garynull.com/documents/iatrogenic/deathbymedicine/DeathByMedicine1.htm

Nye, I. F. (1958). *Family relationships and delinquent behavior.* New York: Wiley.

Nye, J. S. (2002). *The paradox of American power.* New York: Oxford University Press.

Nytimes.com. (1985, June 26). 20-year term for Dominelli. *The New York Times Archives.* Retrieved May 21, 2006, from http://query.nytimes.com/gst/fullpage.html?res=9F03E3DA1139F936A15755C0A963948260

Oakland Museum of California. (2003). *Vietnam/Civil rights era: 1960–1970s.* Retrieved November 30, 2004, from http:/www.museumca.org/picturethis/5_4.html

O'Brien, R. M. (1989). Relative cohort size and age-specific crime rates: An age-period-relative-cohort-size model. *Criminology, 27*(1), 57–78.

O'Donnell, C. R. (1995). Firearm deaths among children and youth. *American Psychologist, 50*(9), 771–776.

Office for National Statistics. (2004). *Internal migration: Migrants entering or leaving the United Kingdom and England and Wales, 2002.* London: Office for National Statistics.

Office of National Drug Control Policy. (ONDCP). (1997). *The National Drug Control Strategy: 1997.* Washington, DC: U.S. Government Printing Office.

Office of Technology Assessment, U.S. Congress. (1978) *Assessing efficacy and safety of medical technology.* Washington, DC: Author.

Office of the Senior Coordinator for International Women's Issues. (2001). *Egypt: Report on female genital mutilation (FGM) or female genital cutting (FGC).* Retrieved June 14, 2005, from http://www.state.gov/g/wi/rls/rep/crfgm/10096.htm

Oldfield, M. (1996). *The Kent Reconviction Survey: A 5 year survey of reconvictions amongst offenders made subject to probation orders in Kent in 1991.* Maidstone, UK: Research and Information Department, Kent Probation Service.

Onlinepot.org. (2004). Retrieved December 7, 2004, from http://www.onlinepot.org/reefermadness/timeline.htm

Oran. (2004). *Defeating shoplifting security tags.* Retrieved October 3, 2004, from http://www.totse.com/en/bad_ideas/irresponsible_activities/165361.html

Orr, S. (1999, October). *Child protection at the crossroads: Child abuse, child protection, and recommendations for reform.* Reason Public Policy Institute Policy Study No. 262. Retrieved October 20, 2003, from http://www.rppi.org/socialservices/ps262.html

Ortega, S. T., & Burnett, C. (1987). Age variations in female crime: In search of the new female criminal. *Journal of Crime and Justice, 10*(1), 133–169.

Ortega, S. T., Corzine, J., & Burnett, C. (1992). Modernization, age structure, and regional context: a cross-national study of crime. *Sociological Spectrum, 12*(3), 257–277.

Osgood, D. W., O'Malley, P., Bachman, J., & Johnston, D. W. (1989). Time trends and age trends in arrests and self-reported behavior. *Criminology, 27,* 289–417.

Ousey, G. C. (1997). *The link between economic restructuring, economic deprivation, and serious crime in American cities, 1970–1990* (Doctoral Dissertation, Louisiana State University). Ann Arbor, MI: University Microfilms International.

Ove, T. (2005, March 9). *2 indicted in commercial bribery scheme: Charged with approving padded bills for Mercy Hospital, Allegheny Power.* Retrieved May 15, 2005, from http://www.post-gazette.com/pg/05068/468391.stm

Ozarin, L. (2001, May 18). Moral insanity: A brief history. *Psychiatric News, 36*(10), 21. Retrieved July 27, 2003, from http://pn.psychiatryonline.org/cgi/content/full/36/10/21

Painter, K. A., & Farrington, D. P. (2001). Evaluating situational crime prevention using a young people's survey. *British Journal of Criminology, 41*(2), 266–284.

Palacios, W. R. (1996). Side by side: An ethnographic study of a Miami gang. *Journal of Gang Research, 4*(1), 27–38.

Pallone, F., Jr. (1994). Pakistan's involvement in narco-terrorism (Extension of remarks—October 3, 1994). Retrieved May 7, 2006, from http://www.fas.org/irp/congress/1994_cr/h941003-terror-pak.htm

Pallone, N., & Hennessy, J. (1998). Brain dysfunction and criminal violence. *Society, 35,* 21–27.

ParaScope, Inc. (1999). *Marijuana timeline.* Retrieved December 11, 2004, from http://www.a1b2c3.com/drugs/mj004.htm

Park, R. E., Burgess, E. W., & McKenzie, R. D. (1967). *The city.* Chicago: University of Chicago Press.

Parker, H., & Bottomley, T. (1996). *Crack cocaine and drugs—criminal careers.* Manchester, UK: Department of Social Work, University of Manchester.

Parker, R. N. (1995). Bringing "booze" back in: The relationship between alcohol and homicide. *Journal of Research in Crime and Delinquency, 32*(1), 3–38.

Parker, R. N., & Rebhun, L. (1995). *Alcohol and homicide: a deadly combination of two American traditions.* Albany: State University of New York Press.

Parry, A. (1976). *Terrorism: from Robespierre to Arafat.* New York: Vanguard.

Patel, R. (2000). *A brief history of Tijuana.* Retrieved November 23, 2004, from http://icsdev.soe.umich.edu/confur/discuss/reader/fall/ody$d73c320d96898 108896e4cdba 023f7d6

Paton, D. (2001). Punishment, crime and the bodies of slaves in eighteenth-century Jamaica. *Journal of Social History, 34*(4), 923–954.

Patrignani, A. (1995). *Women's victimisation in developing countries. Issues & Reports, 5,* 3. Retrieved April 12, 2002, from http://www.unicri.it/documentation/ Issues&reports/I_R5.htm

Patsuris, P. (2002). The corporate scandal sheet. Retrieved May 22, 2005, from http://www.forbes.com/2002/07/25/accountingtracker.html

Patterns of Victimization among Small Retail Businesses. (2002). *Trends and issues in crime and criminal justice.* Criminal Justice Abstracts 1969–2003/12, Abstract No. 85177.

Payne, C. (2003). Understanding terrorism: Terrorist cells. *World Conflict Quarterly: News Analysis and Articles on Terrorists & Terrorism.* Retrieved May 29, 2006, from http://www.globalterrorism101.com/UTTerroristCells.html

Pearlstein, R. M. (1991). *The mind of the political terrorist.* Wilmington, DE: Scholarly Resources.

Peck, M. C. (2006). United Arab Emirates. *Microsoft®Online Encyclopedia 2006.* Retrieved May 23, 2006, from http://encarta.msn.com/encyclopedia_76156 0366_7/United_Arab_Emirates.html

Pelfey, W. (2000). *Final report of Utah crime assessment.* Nashville, TN: Community Research Associates.

Pepinsky, H., & Quinney, R. (Eds.). (1991). *Criminology as peacemaking.* Bloomington: Indiana University Press.

Petrosino, A. J., & Kass, M. (2000). The top ten types of robbers imprisoned in Massachusetts. *Journal of Security Administration, 23*(2), 29–36.

Petrovich, M., & Templer, D. I. (1984). Heterosexual molestation of children who later became rapists. *Psychological Records, 54,* 810.

Pflaum, J. (2002). Lasting benefits of the dot-com bubble. *E Commerce Times.* Retrieved May 23, 2006, from http://www.ecommercetimes.com/perl/board/ mboard.pl? board=ecttalkback&thread=5438&id=5450&display=1

Pfohl, S. J. (1985). *Images of deviance and social control: A sociological inquiry.* New York: McGraw-Hill.

Phillips, C., Cox, G., & Pease, K. (1996). *England and Wales.* Retrieved June 13, 2004, from http://www.ojp.usdoj.gov/bjs/pub/ascii/wfbcjeng.txt

Phoenix Police Department. (2005). *Historical crime data.* Retrieved March 13, 2005, from http://phoenix.gov/POLICE/partm1.html

Pike, J. (1996). *Central Intelligence Agency: History.* Retrieved April 30, 2005, from http://www.fas.org/irp/cia/ciahist.htm

Pitts. W. R. (2003). *PATRIOT Act finds trouble in Texas. Truthout.* Retrieved June 10, 2004, from http://truthout.org/docs_03/092203A.shtml

Pizzo, S., Fricker, M., & Muolo, P. (1989). *Insider job: The looting of America's savings and loans.* New York: McGraw-Hill.

Pluchinsky, D. A. (1998). Terrorism in the former Soviet Union: A primer, a puzzle, a prognosis. *Studies in Conflict and Terrorism, 21*(2), 119–147.

Polk, K., & Schafer, W. E. (Eds.). (1972). *Schools and delinquency.* Englewood Cliffs, NJ: Prentice Hall.

Pollak, O. (1950). *The criminality of women.* Philadelphia: University of Pennsylvania Press.

Polling Report, Inc., The. (2005). *Guns.* Retrieved June 11, 2005, from http://www.pollingreport.com/guns.htm

Pontell, H. N., Calavita, K., & Tillman, R. (1994). *Fraud in the savings and loan industry: White-collar crime and government response.* Irvine: Department of Criminology, Law and Society, University of California.

Porter, S., Fairweather, D., Drugge, J., Herve, H., Birt, A., & Boer, D. (2000) Profiles of psychopathy in incarcerated sexual offenders. *Criminal Justice and Behavior, 27,* 216–33.

Porterfield, A. L. (1943). Delinquency and its outcome in court and college. *American Journal of Sociology, 49*(3), 199–208.

Porterfield, A. L. (1946). *Youth in trouble.* Fort Worth, TX: Leo Potishman Foundation.

Potter, G. (1991, June 11). The single greatest case of fraud in the history of crime. *Seattle Times.*

Potter, G. (2005a). *State-organized crime: The OSS in Italy and Marselles.* Retrieved June 19, 2005, from http://www.jsnet.eku.edu/matt/ootter/crj401_15.htm

Potter, G. (2005b). *State-sponsored terrorism in U.S. foreign policy.* Retrieved February 12, 2005 from http://www.policestudies.eku.edu/POTTER/Module9.htm

Potter, M. (1999, September 30). Cover story: The Mr. San Diego follies. Retrieved May 20, 2006, from http://www.sdreader.com/php/cover.php?mode=article&showpg=2&id=19990930

Potter, M., & Phillips, R. (2002, March 13). *Six months after Sept. 11, hijackers' visa approval letters received.* Retrieved May 15, 2005, from http://archives.cnn.com/2002/US/03/12/inv.flight.school.visas/

Powers, R. G. (1987). *Secrecy and power: The life of J. Edgar Hoover.* New York: Free Press.

Poyner, B., & Woodall, R. (1987). *Preventing shoplifting: A study in Oxford Street.* London, UK: Police Foundation.

President's Commission on Law Enforcement and Administration of Justice. (1967). *Task Force Report: Organized crime.* Washington, DC: U. S. Government Printing Office.

President's Commission on Obscenity and Pornography. (1970). *Report of the Commission on Obscenity and Pornography.* Washington, DC: U.S. Government Printing Office.

President's Commission on Organized Crime. (1986). *The Impact: Organized crime today.* Washington, DC: U.S. Government Printing Office.

Pridemore, W. A. (2001). Using available homicide data to debunk two myths about violence in an international context: A research note. *Homicide Studies, 5*(3), 267–275. Retrieved June 26, 2004, from the Criminal Justice Abstracts database at http://spweb.silverplatter.com/calstate

Pridemore, W. A. (2002). Vodka and violence: Alcohol consumption and homicide rates in Russia. *American Journal of Public Health, 92* (12), 1921–1930. Retrieved June 26, 2004, from the Criminal Justice Abstracts database at http://spweb.silverplatter.com/calstate

Priestino, R. R., & Allen, H. E. (1975). *The Parole Office Aide Program in Ohio: An exemplary project.* Columbus: Ohio OH: State University.

Prime Minister (2003) Speech 8 given by Prime Minister of Swaziland to Parliament retrieved on October 25, 2003, from http://www.gov.sz/home.asp?pid=2540

Puerto Rico Criminal Justice Information System. (1983). *Recidivism among sentenced penal populations in penal institutions.* San Juan, Puerto Rico: Statistical Analysis Center.

Queensland Office of Economic and Statistical Research. (2001). *Queensland Crime Victimization Survey 2000.* Queensland, Australia: Author.

Quetelet, A. (1984). *Research on the propensity for crime at different ages.* (S. F. Sylvester, Trans.) Cincinnati, OH: Anderson.

Quinney, R. (1970). *The social reality of crime.* Boston: Little, Brown.

Quinney, R. (1974). *Critique of legal order: Crime control in capitalist society.* Boston: Little, Brown.

Quinney, R. (1977). *Class, state, and crime: On the theory and practice of criminal justice.* New York: Longman.

Raine, A. (1993). *The psychopathology of crime.* New York: Academic.

Raine, A., Venables, P. H., & Mednick, S. A. (1997). Low resting heart rate at age 3 years predisposes to aggression at age 11 years: Evidence from the Mauritius Child Health Project. *Journal of the American Academy of Child and Adolescent Psychiatry, 36,* 1457–1464.

Rana, M. A. (2003). *A to Z of Jehadi organizations in Pakistan.* Lahore, Pakistan: Mashal.

Rand Corporation. (2003). *Oklahoma City National Memorial Institute for the Prevention of Terrorism.* (Data updated on November 24, 2003). Retrieved June 3, 2004, from http://www.mipt.org

Rand, M. R. (1994). *Carjacking: BJS crime data brief.* Washington, DC: U.S. Bureau of Justice Statistics.

Rand, M. R. (1997). *Violence-related injuries treated in hospital emergency departments: U.S. Bureau of Justice Statistics special report.* Washington, DC: U.S. Department of Justice.

Raphael, S. (2000). *The deinstitutionalization of the mentally ill and growth in the U.S. prison populations: 1971–1996.* Berkeley: Goldman School of Public Policy, University of California.

Rasanen, P., Hakko, H., & Isohanni, M. (1999). Maternal smoking during pregnancy and risk of criminal behavior among adult male offspring in the northern Finland 1966 birth cohort. *American Journal of Psychiatry, 156*(6), 857–862.

Ratcliffe, D. T. (1999). *National Security Council.* Retrieved May 1, 2005, from http://www.ratical.org/ratville/JFK/USO/appC.html

Ray, O. (1983). *Drugs, society, and human behavior.* St. Louis, MO: Mosley.

Raymond, J. G., & Hughes, D. M. (2001). *Sex trafficking of women in the United States.* New York: Coalition Against Trafficking in Women. Retrieved December 14, 2004, from http://action.web.ca/home/catw/attach/sex_traff_us.pdf

Rayne, F. (1977). Doing business in a terrorist world. *Security World 14*(11), 22–23, 50, 53.

Rebovich, D. J., & Layne, J. (2000). *The national public survey on white-collar crime.* Morgantown, WV: National White Collar Crime Center.

Reckless, W. C. (1961). *The crime problem* (3rd ed.). New York: Appleton-Century-Crofts.

Reckless, W. C. (1967). *The crime problem* (4th ed.). New York: Appleton-Century-Crofts.

Reckless, W. C., Dinitz, S., & Murray, E. (1956). Self concept as insulator against delinquency. *American Sociological Review, 21,* 744–764.

ReclaimDemocracy.org. (2005). *Our hidden history: Corporations in America.* Retrieved May 14, 2005, from http://free.freespeech.org/americanstateterrorism/plutocracy/CorporateHidden.html

Rediff.com. (2003). India makes new peace proposals to Pakistan. Retrieved May 7, 2006, from http://www.rediff.com/news/2003/oct/22pak.htm

Reddy, B. M. (2001, September 11). *Dawood is king in Karachi.* Retrieved May 7, 2006, from http://www.hinduonnet.com/2001/09/11/stories/0311000b.htm

Reefer-Madness-Movie.com. (2004). Retrieved December 7, 2004, from Reefer-Madness-Movie.com, 2004.

Reich, R. B. (2004). *Reason: Why liberals will win the battle for America.* New York: Knopf.

Reichel, P. L. (2005). *Comparative criminal justice systems.* Upper Saddle River, NJ: Pearson/Prentice Hall.

Reiss, A. J. (1951). Delinquency as the failure of personal and social controls. *American Sociological Review, 16,* 196–207.

Reith, C. (1975). *The blind eye of history: A study of the origins of the present police era.* Montclair, NJ: Patterson Smith.

Rengert, G. F., Mattson, M. T., & Henderson, K. D. (2001). *Campus security: Situational crime prevention in high-density environments.* Monsey, NY: Criminal Justice Press.

Rennison, C., & Planty, M. (2003). Nonlethal intimate partner violence: Examining race, gender, and income patterns. *Violence and Victims, 18*(4), pp. 433–443.

Rhodes, R. (1999). *Why they kill: The discoveries of a maverick criminologist.* New York: Vintage.

Rhodes, W. M., & Conly, C. (1981). Crime and mobility: An empirical study. In P. J. Brantingham & P. Brantingham (Eds.), *Environmental criminology* (pp. 161–178). Beverly Hills, CA: Sage.

Richardb. (2003). *AngliaCampus: Car crime.* Retrieved October 14, 2004, from http://www.angliacampus.com/grwn/prnt/beyond/CarCrime/

Riemer, S. (1941). Embezzlement: Pathological basis. *Journal of Criminal Law and Criminology, 32,* 411–423.

Riese, W. (1969). *The legacy of Phillipe Pinel.* New York: Springer.

Risto, J. (1986). *Veli Verkko—A moral statistician and the first Finnish criminologist.* Helsinki, Finland: Oikeapoliittisen Tutkimuslaitoksen.

Rjohara.net. (2006). *Advance fee frauds and email scams.* Retrieved May 23, 2006, from http://rjohara.net/nigerian-419-fraud/2006-yousif-abdullah-fahad

Roberts, C. R. (January 24, 2006). *Unfathomed dangers in PATRIOT Act Reauthorization.* Retrieved May 28, 2006, from http://www.antiwar.com/roberts/?articleid=8434

Robinson, A. (2001). *Bin Laden: Behind the mask of the terrorist.* New York: Arcade.

Robinson, B. A. (1999). *Deism: The God that got away.* Retrieved February 19, 2005, from http://www.religioustolerance.org/deism.htm

Robison, S. M. (1936). *Can delinquency be measured?* New York: Columbia University Press.

Robison, S. M. (1960). *Juvenile delinquency: Its nature and control.* New York: Holt, Rinehart and Winston.

Roncek, D. W., & Lobosco, A. (1983). The effect of high schools in their neighborhoods. *Social Science Quarterly, 64*(3), 599–613.

Rosenfeld, R. (1997). Changing relationships between men and women: A note on the decline in intimate partner homicide. *Homicide Studies, 1*(1), 72–83.

Rosenhan, D. L. (1973, January 19). On being sane in insane places. *Science.*

Rosoff, S. M., Pontell, H. N., & Tillman, R. (1998). *Profit without honor: White-collar crime and the looting of America.* Upper Saddle River, NJ: Prentice Hall.

Rothman, D. J. (1980). *Conscience and convenience: The asylum and its alternatives in progressive America.* Boston: Little, Brown.

Rotton, J., & Cohn, E. G. (2003). Global warming and U.S. crime rates: An application of routine activities theory. *Environment and Behavior, 35*(6), 802–825.

Rowe, D. C. (1986). Genetic and environmental components of antisocial behavior: A study of 265 twin pairs. *Criminology, 24,* 513–532.

Roy, L., Claire, N., & Ingham, H. (1993). *Car theft: The offender's perspective.* London: HMSO Books.

Rubin, R. T. (1987). The neuroendocrinology and neurochemistry of antisocial behavior. In S. A. Mednick, T. E. Moffitt, & S. A. Stack (Eds.), *The causes of crime: New biological approaches* (pp. 230–262). New York: Cambridge University Press.

Rumm, P. D., Cummings, P., Krauss, M. R., Bell, M. A., & Rivara, F. P. (2000). Identified spouse abuse as a risk factor for child abuse. *Child abuse and neglect, 24*(11), 1375–1381.

Runblom, H. (1998). *Sweden as a multicultural society.* Retrieved October 10, 2004, from http://www.sweden.se/templates/PrinterFriendlyArticle.asp?id=2264

Russell, C. A., & Miller, B. H. (1977). Profile of a terrorist. *Terrorism New York, 1*(1), 17–34.

Russell, D. E. H. (1982). *Rape in marriage.* New York: Macmillan.

Russell, D. E. H. (1983). The prevalence of rape in the United States revisited. *Signs, 8,* 688–695.

Russell, D. E. H. (1988). Pornography and rape: A causal model. *Political Psychology, 9* (1), 41–73.

Sadat, M. H. (2001). *The CIA Operation Cyclone's blowback.* Retrieved May 9, 2006, from http://www.angelfire.com/ca/miroo/nest.html

Salter, S. (2004). *Double taxes paid on your single bourbon.* Retrieved December 5, 2004, from http://www.clarionledger.com/apps/pbcs.dll/article?AID=/20040418/OPINION03/404180328/1046/OPINION

Salzman, L., Mercy, J., O'Carroll, P., Rosenburg, M., & Rhodes, P. (1992). Weapon involvement and injury outcomes in family and intimate assaults. *Journal of the American Medical Association, 267,* 3043–3047.

Sampson, R. J. (1983). *The neighborhood context of criminal victimization* (Doctoral Dissertation, State University of New York at Albany). Ann Arbor, MI: University Microfilms International.

Sampson, R. J. (1985). Structural sources of variation in race-age-specific rates of offending across major U.S. cities. *Criminology, 23*(4), 647–673.

Sampson, R. J., & Cohen, J. (1988). Deterrent effects of the police on crime: A replication and theoretical extension. *Law and Society Review, 22*(1), 163–189.

Sanad, N. (1991). *The theory of crime and criminal responsibility in Islamic Law: Shari'a.* Chicago: University of Illinois at Chicago, The Office of International Criminal Justice.

Sanday, P. (1981). The socio-cultural context of rape: A cross-cultural study. *Journal of Social Issues 37,* 5–27.

Sanders, D. G. (1992). A typology of men who batter women: Three types derived from cluster analysis. *American Orthopsychiatry, 62,* 264–275.

Sanders, W. B. (1976). *Juvenile delinquency.* New York: Praeger.

Sands, J. (2002). *Europe in the age of globalization: A hotbed of transnational organized crime?* Retrieved October 10, 2004, from http://members.lycos.co.uk/ocnewsletter/SGOC0902/sands.html

Sanford Police Department. (1996). *Domestic violence FAQ's (frequently asked questions!).* Retrieved October 8, 2003, from http://home.gwi.net/~sanpd/domest3.html

Sanford, R. N. (1943). A psychoanalytic study of three Criminal types. *Journal of Criminal Psychopathology, 5,* 57–68.

Sarasalo, E., Bergman, B., & Toth, J. (1997). Theft behavior and its consequences among kleptomaniacs and shoplifters—a comparative study. *Forensic Science International, 86*(3), 109–205.

Satel, S. (2004, October 19). Doctors behind bars: Treating pain is now risky business. *New York Times.* Retrieved December 30, 2004, from http://opioids.com/legal/victims.html

Savolainen, J. (2000). Relative cohort size and age-specific arrest rates: a conditional interpretation of the Easterlin effect. *Criminology, 38*(1), 117–136.

Saytarley, T. A. (2004). *Fighting child pornography.* Retrieved December 31, 2004, from http://www.crime-research.org/library/Saytarly_nov.html

Schaffer Library of Drug Policy. (2004). *Statement of H. J. Anslinger in hearings (on prospective Marijuana Tax Act).* Retrieved December 9, 2004, from http://www.druglibrary.org/schaffer/hemp/taxact/anslng1.htm

Schatzberg, R., & Kelly, R. J. (1996). *African-American organized crime.* New York: Garland.

Scheck, R. (1987). Childhood in German autobiographical writings. *The Journal of Psychohistory, 15,* 402.

Scheff, T. J. (1966). *Being mentally ill.* Chicago: Aldine.

Schlossman, S., Zellman, G., & Shavelson, R., with Sedlak, M., & Cobb, J. (1984). *Delinquency prevention in south Chicago: A fifty-year assessment of the Chicago Area Project.* Santa Monica, CA: RAND.

Schmalleger, F. (1991). *Criminal justice today: An introductory text for the 21st century* Englewood Cliffs, NJ: Prentice Hall.

Schmalleger, F. (2002). *Criminology today: An integrative introduction* (3rd ed.). Upper Saddle River, NJ: Prentice Hall.

Schmalleger, F. (2003). *Criminal justice today: An introductory text for the 21st century* (7th ed.). Upper Saddle River, NJ: Prentice Hall.

Schmalleger, F. (2005). *Criminal justice today: An introductory text for the 21st century* (8th ed.). Upper Saddle River, NJ: Prentice Hall.

Schmalleger, F. (2006). *Criminal justice today: An integrative introduction* (4th ed.). Upper Saddle River, NJ: Prentice Hall.

Schmidt, P., & Witte, A. (1984). *An economic analysis of crime and justice.* New York: Academic.

Schneider, M. (1997). *California criminal law: Felonies & white collar crime.* Retrieved September 20, 2003, from http://www.weblocator.com/attorney/ca/law/c13.html#cac130600>

Schoenthaler, S. J. (1985). Diet and delinquency: Empirical testing of seven theories. *International Journal of Biosocial Research, 7*(2), 108–131.

Schoenthaler, S. J., & Doraz, W. E. (1983). Types of offenses which can be reduced in an institutional setting using nutritional intervention: a preliminary empirical evaluation. *International Journal of Biosocial Research, 4*(2), 74–84.

Schur, E. M. (1973). *Radical nonintervention: rethinking the delinquency problem.* Englewood Cliffs, NJ: Prentice Hall.

Schur, E. M. (1984). *Labeling women deviant: Gender, stigma, and social control.* New York: Random House.

Schwartz, S., Hennessey, M., & Levitas, L. (2003). Restorative justice and the transformation of jails: An urban sheriff's case study in reducing violence. *Police Practice & Research, 4*(4), 399–410.

Schwarz, J. (1998, March). When men batter women: New insights from UW professors. *News and Information.* Retrieved October 23, 2003, from http://depts.washington.edu/uweek/archives/1998.03.MAR_05/_article6.html)

Schwendinger, H. (1963). *An instrumental theory of delinquency: A tentative formulation.* Ann Arbor, MI: University Microfilms.

Schwendinger, J. R., & Schwendinger, H. (1983). *Rape and inequality.* Beverly Hills, CA: Sage.

Scot, W., Fischer, B., & Webster, C. (2002). Vice lessons: A survey of prostitution offenders enrolled in the Toronto "John School" diversion program. *Canadian Journal of Criminology, 44*(4), 369–402.

Scott, J. (2006). *BBS, the documentary.* Retrieved May 26, 2006, from http://www.bbsdocumentary.com/

Scott, J. E., & Schwalm, L. A. (1988). Pornography and rape: An examination of adult theater rates and rape rates by state. In J. E. Scott & T. Hirschi (Eds.), *Controversial issues in crime and justice* (pp. 40–53). Newbury Park, CA: Sage.

Seaberg, J. R. (1981). Operant conditioning and differential association: Toward application and verification. *Journal of Offender Counseling Services and Rehabilitation, 5*(3/4), 53–64.

Segue Esprit Inc. (2004). *Percentage of divorces in selected countries.* Retrieved October 7, 2004, from http://www.divorcemag.com/statistics/statsWorld.shtml

Sellen, B. C., & Young, P. A. (1987). *Feminists, pornography and the law: An annotated bibliography of conflict 1970–1986.* Hamden, CT: Library Professional Publications.

Sellin, T., & Wolfgang, M. E. (1964). *The measurement of delinquency.* New York: Wiley.

Serrill, M. S. (1977). Profile/Sweden. *Corrections Magazine New York, 3*(2), 26–34.

Sexatlas.com. (2006a). *Prostitution in Netherlands.* Retrieved April 29, 2006, from http://www.sexatlas.com/wsg/Netherlands.php

Sexatlas.com. (2006b). *The world sex guide.* Retrieved April 29, 2006, from http://www.sexatlas.com/wsg/index.php

Shalif, I. (1997) *Scotland Yardies Part 2.* Retrieved November 21, 2003, from http://www.ainfos.ca/A-Infos97/4/0610.html

Shanab, A. I., & Hilder, P. (2002, July). *The nail in the wood: An interview with Ismaeil Abu Shanab.* Retrieved August 13, 2004, from http://www.fromoccupied palestine.org/node.php?id=774

Sharon, A. M. (2001). Intimate partner violence in Jamaica: A descriptive study of women who access the services of the Women's Crisis Center in Kingston. *Violence Against Women, 7*(11), 1284–1302.

Sharp, I. (2004). The sexual unification of Germany. *Journal of the History of Sexuality, 13*(3), 348–365.

Shaw, C. R., & McKay, H. D. (1972). *Juvenile delinquency and urban areas.* Chicago: University of Chicago Press.

Shaw, J. A. (1999). Practice parameters for the assessment and treatment of children and adolescents who are sexually abusive of others. *Journal of the American Academy of Child and Adolescent Psychiatry.* Retrieved November 15, 2003, from http://www.findarticles.com/cf_0/m2250/12_38/58531555/print.jhtml

Sheldon, W. (1949). *Varieties of delinquent youth.* New York: Harper and Brothers.

Sherman, L. W. (1989). Violent stranger crime in a large hotel: A case study in risk assessment methods. *Security Journal, 1*(1), 40–46.

Sherman, L. W., & Berk, R. A. (1984). The Minneapolis domestic violence experiment. *Police Foundation Reports, 1,* 1–8.

Sherman, L. W., & Rogan, D. P. (1995). Effect of gun seizures on gun violence: "Hot spots" patrol in Kansas City. *Justice Quarterly, 12*(4), 673–693.

Sherman, L. W., Shaw, J. W., & Rogan, D. P. (1995). *The Kansas City Gun Experiment.* Washington, DC: U.S. National Institute of Justice.

Shichor, D. (1990). Crime patterns and socioeconomic development: a cross-national analysis. *Criminal Justice Review, 15*(1), 64–78.

Shikita, M., & Shinichi, T. (1990). *Crime and criminal policy in Japan from 1926 to 1988: Analysis and evaluation of the Showa Era.* Tokyo, Japan: Japan Criminal Policy Society.

Shoemaker, D. J. (2000). *Theories of delinquency* (4th ed.). New York: Oxford University Press.

Shore D., Filson, C. R., & Rae, D. S. (1990). Violent crime arrest rates of White House case subjects and matched control subjects. *American Journal of Psychiatry, 147,* 746–750.

Short, J. F., & Nye, F. I. (1957). Reported behavior as a criterion of deviant behavior. *Social Problems, 5,* 107–213.

Short, J. F., & Nye, F. I. (1958). Extent of unrecorded delinquency, tentative conclusions. *Journal of Criminal Law, Criminology, and Police Science, 49,* 296–302.

Short, J. F., & Strodtbeck, F. L. (1965). *Group process and gang delinquency.* Chicago: University of Chicago Press.

Shover, N. E. (1971). *Burglary as an occupation* (Doctoral Dissertation). Ann Arbor, MI: University Microfilms.

Shover, N. E. (1991). Burglary. In M. Tonry, (Ed.), *Crime and justice: A review of research* (pp. 73–113) Chicago: University of Chicago Press.

Shover, N., & Honaker, D. (1996). The socially bounded decision making of persistent property offenders. In P. Cromwell (Ed.), *In their own words: Criminals on crime* (pp. 10–21). Los Angeles, CA: Roxbury.

Shuster, B. (1998, August 23). Living in fear. *Los Angeles Times.* p. A1, 40 and 41. Retrieved October 18, 2003, from http://www.facts1.com/reasons/fear.htm# While

Siegel, L. J. (2000). *Criminology* (7th ed.). Belmont CA: Wadsworth/Thomson Learning.

Siegel, L. J. (2003). *Criminology* (8th ed.). Belmont, CA: Wadsworth/Thompson Learning.

Siegel, L. J. (2004). *Criminology: Theories, patterns, and typologies* (8th ed.). Belmont, CA: Wadsworth/Thompson Learning.

Siegel, L., & Senna, J. J. (2000). *Juvenile delinquency: Theory, practice, and law* (7th ed.). Belmont, CA: Wadsworth/Thomson Learning.

Sigler, R. T., & Koehlor, N. (1993). Victimization and crime on campus. *International Review of Victimology, 2*(4), 331–343.

Silverman, S. (*nd*). *Charles Ponzi: Double your money in 90 days.* Retrieved December 23, 2004, from http://home.nycap.rr.com/useless/ponzi/

Simon, D., & Eitzen, D S. (1993). *Elite deviance* (4th ed.). Boston: Allyn and Bacon.

Simon, R. J. (2004, June 24). *Immigration and crime across seven nations.* Talk given at Forschungsinstitut zur Zukunft der Arbeit GmbH (IZA) Annual Migration Meeting Retrieved October 15, 2004, from http://216.239.41.104/search?q= cache:XnW-1U5rcIQJ:www.iza.org/conference_files/amm_2004/simon_r1669 .pdf+immigration+and +crime+across+seven+nations&hl=en

Simon, R. J., & Landis, J. (1991). *The crimes women commit, the punishments they receive.* Lexington, MA: Lexington.

Simon. R. (1975). *Women and crime.* Lexington, MA: Lexington.

Singer, J. (2005). Statistics. *Microsoft® Encarta® Online Encyclopedia 2005.* Retrieved March 13, 2005, from http://encarta.msn.com/encyclopedia_761562521/ Statistics.html

Siren, R. (2002). Trends in assault: On the relationship between the assault rate and selected social indicators in post-war Finland. *Journal of Scandinavian Studies in Criminology and Crime Prevention, 3*(1), 22–49.

Skolnick, J. H. (1990). *Gang organization and migration.* Sacramento, CA: Office of the Attorney General of the State of California.

Skolnick, J. H., Correl, T., Navarro, T., & Rabb, R. (1990). The social structure of steet drug dealing. *American Journal of Police, 9*(1), 1–41.

Slawson, J. (1926). *The delinquent boys.* Boston: Budget.

Small, G. (1995). *Ruthless: the global rise of the yardies.* London: Warner.

Smartraveller.gov.au. (2004). *Travel advice: Mexico.* Retrieved May 17, 2004, from http://www.dfat.gov.au/zw-cgi/view/Advice/Mexico

Smith, J. (2003). *The nature of personal robbery* (Home Office Research Study, 254). London: Home Office, Development and Statistics Directorate.

Smith, M. D. (1987). Changes in the victimization of women: Is there a "new female victim"? *Journal of Research in Crime and Delinquency, 24*(4), 291–301.

Smith, M. D., & Bennett, N. (1985). Poverty, inequality, and theories of forcible rape. *Crime and Delinquency, 31*, 295–305.

Smith, M. D., & Hand, C. (1987). The pornography/aggression linkage: Results from a field study. *Deviant Behavior, 8*(4), 389–399.

Smith, M. J., & Clarke, R. V. (2000). Crime and public transport. In M. Tonry (Ed.), *Crime and justice: A review of research* (Vol. 27, pp. 169–233). Chicago, University of Chicago Press.

Smith, R. (1998). *From the Mtn. of gold to the Kam Wah Chung.* Retrieved December 7, 2004, from http://gesswhoto.com/chinese.html

Smith, T. W. (1987, Summer). The use of public opinion data by the Attorney General's Commission on Pornography. *Public Opinion Quarterly, 51*(2), 249–267.

Smith, W. R., Frazee, S. G., & Davison, E. L. (2000). Furthering the integration of routine activity and social disorganization theories: Small units of analysis and the study of street robbery. *Criminology, 38*(2), 489–523.

Smith, W. R., Torstensson, M., & Johansson, K. (2001). Perceived risk and fear of crime: Gender differences in contextual sensitivity. *International Review of Victimology, 8*(2), 159–181.

Sommers, E. K., & Check, J. V. P. (1987). An empirical investigation of the role of pornography in the verbal and physical abuse of women. *Violence and Victims, 2*(3), 189–209.

Souryal, S. S. (1987). The religionization of a society: The continuing application of Shariah law in Saudi Arabia. *Journal for the Scientific Study of Religion, 26*(4), 429–449.

South Dakota Chamber of Commerce and Industry (2001, May). *Newsletter: Business continuation series—embezzlement.* Retrieved May 20, 2006, from http://www.sdchamber.biz/pdf/embezzlement.pdf

Spartacus Educational. (2002). *Evangelical Protestantism.* Retrieved February 19, 2005, from http://www.spartacus.schoolnet.co.uk/REevangelical.htm

Spiegel Online. (2006, March 8). *Sex, violence and the World Cup: Blowing the whistle on forced prostitution.* Retrieved May 12, 2006, from http://service.spiegel.de/cache/international/0,1518,404955,00.html

St. James, M. (1987). The reclamation of whores. In L. Bell (Ed.), *In good girls/bad girls: Feminists and sex trade workers face to face* (pp. 81–87). Seattle, WA: Seal Press.

Stack, S. (1995). The effect of temporary residences on burglary: A test of criminal opportunity theory. *American Journal of Criminal Justice, 19*(2), 197–214.

Stalenkrantz, B. (2004). *The tragic outcome of Sweden's dream of a good drug free society.* Retrieved October 8, 2004, from http://www.senliscouncil.net/documents/Berne_paper

Stanley, L. A. (1989). The child porn myth. *Cardozo Arts and Entertainment Law Journal, 7*(2), 295–359.

Staten, C. (1996, January). "Roofies," the new "date rape" drug of choice. *Emergency Net News.* Retrieved October 27, 2003, from http://www.emergency.com/roofies.htm

Steffensmeier, D., Allan, E., & Streifel, C. (1989). Development of female crime: A cross-national test of alternative explanations. *Social Forces, 68*, 262–283.

Stein, J. (Ed.). (1970). *The Random House Dictionary of the English Language.* New York: Random House.

Steinwachs, D. M., Kasper, J. D., & Skinner, E. A. (1992). *Family perspectives on meeting the needs for care of severely mentally ill relatives: A national survey.* Arlington, VA: National Alliance for the Mentally Ill.

Stekel, W (1922/1924). *Peculiarities of behavior* (J. S. Van Teslaar, Trans.). New York: Liverrightm, as cited in Fullerton & Punj, 2004, p. 8.

Stekel, W. (1911). The sexual root of kleptomania. *Journal of the American Institute of Criminal Law and Criminology, 2*(2), 239–46.

Sterling, C. (1981, March 1). Terrorism: Tracing the international network. *New York Times Magazine New York*, 16–19, 54–60.

Stets, J. E. & Straus, M.A. (1990). Gender differences in reporting marital violence and its medical and psychological consequences. In M. A. Straus & R. J. Gelles (Eds.), *Physical violence in American families: Risk factors and adaptations to violence in 8,145 families* (pp. 227–244). New Brunswick, NJ: Transaction Publishing.

Stevens, D. J. (1999). *Inside the mind of a serial rapist.* San Francisco: Austin and Winfield.

Stevenson, R. J., & Forsythe, L. (1998). *The stolen goods market in New South Wales: An interview study with imprisoned burglars.* Sydney, Australia: New South Wales Bureau of Crime Statistics and Research.

Straus, M. A. (1985). Family training in crime and violence. In M. A. Straus & A. J. Lincoln (Eds.), *Crime and the family* (pp. 164–185). Springfield, IL: Thomas.

Straus, M. A., & Gelles, R. J. (1988). How violent are American families? Estimates from the National Family Violence Resurvey and other studies. In G. T. Hotaling, D. F. J. T. Kirkpatrick, & M. A. Straus (Eds.), *Family abuse and its consequence* (pp. 98–115). Newbury Park, CA: Sage.

Straus, M. A., & Gelles, R. J. (Eds.). (1990). *Physical violence in American families: Risk factors and adaptations to violence in 8,145 families.* New Brunswick and London: Transaction.

Straus, M. A., Gelles, R. J., & Steinmetz, S. K. (1980). *Behind closed doors: Violence in the American family.* New York: Anchor.

Straus, M. A., & Lincoln, A. J. (1985). The family as a criminal group. In M. A. Straus & A. J. Lincoln (Eds.), *Crime and the family* (pp. 153–163). Springfield, IL: Thomas.

Straus, M. A., & Sweet, S. (1992). Verbal/symbolic aggression in couples: Incidence rates and relationships to personal characteristics. *Journal of Marriage and the Family, 54*, 346–357.

Stubbs, P. M. (1998, September 25). Broken promises: The story of deinstitutionalization. *Perspectives.* Retrieved July 19, 2003, from http://www.mentalhelp.net/poc/view_doc.php/type/doc/id/368

Studyworld.com. (2004). *Facts about marijuana.* Retrieved December 7, 2004, from http://www.studyworld.com/newsite/ReportEssay/SocialIssues/Political%5CFacts_About_Marijuana-93.htm

Substance Abuse and Mental Health Services Administration. (2004). *Results from the 2003 National Survey on Drug Use and Health: National findings* (Office of Applied Studies, NSDUH Series H–25, DHHS Publication No. SMA 04–3964). Rockville, MD. Retrieved January 7, 2005, from: http://www.drugabusestatistics.samhsa.gov/NHSDA/2k3NSDUH/2k3results.htm#fig5.1

Suellentrop, C. (2001). *US: Which states have decriminalized marijuana possession?* Retrieved December 5, 2004, from http://www.mapinc.org/drugnews/v01.n276.a05.html

Sugarman, D. B., & Hotaling, G. T. (1989). Violent men in intimate relationships: An analysis of risk markers. *Journal of Applied Social Psychology, 19,* 1034–1048.

Sullivan, B. (2004). ID thief to the stars tells all. Excerpted from B. Sullivan (2004). *Your evil twin: Behind the identity theft epidemic.* New York: Wiley. Retrieved December 5, 2004, from http://www.msnbc.msn.com/id/5763781/

Sullivan, P. S. (1985). *Determinants of crime and clearance rates for seven index crimes.* (Dissertation, Vanderbilt University). Ann Arbor, MI: University Microfilms International.

Sutherland, E. H. (1937). *The professional thief.* Chicago: University of Chicago Press.

Sutherland, E. H. (1949). *White-Collar Crime.* New York: Dryden Press.

Sutherland, E. H. (1951). Critique of Sheldon's "Varieties of delinquent youth." *American Sociological Review, 18,* 11.

Sutherland, E. H. (1961). *White-Collar Crime.* New York: Holt, Rinehart and Winston.

Sutherland, E. H. (1973). Mental deficiency and crime. In K. Young (Ed.), *Social attitudes.* New York: Henry Holt.

Sutherland, E. H., & Cressey, D. R. (1947). *Criminology* (4th ed.). Philadelphia: J. B. Lippincott Company.

Sutherland, E. H., & Cressey, D. R. (1970). *Criminology* (8th ed.). Philadelphia: J. B. Lippincott Company.

Swami, P. (Oct 18, 2003). Terrorist Dawood, a symbolic label. *The Hindu.* Retrieved May 9, 2006, from http://www.hinduonnet.com/thehindu/2003/10/18/stories/2003101804761100.htm

Swann, R., & James, P. (1998). The effect of the prison environment upon inmate drug taking behavior. *Howard Journal of Criminal Justice, 37*(3), 252–265.

Swanson, J. W., Hozer, C. D., & Ganju, V. K. (1990). Violence and psychiatric disorder in the community: Evidence from the Epidemiologic Catchment Area surveys. *Hospital and Community Psychiatry, 41,* 761–770.

Swanson, J. W., Swartz, M. S., & Essock, S. M. (2002). The social-environmental context of violent behavior in persons treated for severe mental illness. *American Journal of Public Health, 92,* 1523–1531.

Sweden.se. (2004). *Equality between women and men.* Retrieved October 7, 2004, from http://www.sweden.se/templates/FactSheet_____4123.asp

Swiss, S., & Giller, J. E. (1993). Rape as a crime of war: A medical perspective. *Journal of American Medical Association, 270*(5), 612–615.

Sword of the Lord Publishers. (2002). William Jennings Bryan: 1860–1925. Retrieved February 19, 2005, from http://www.swordofthelord.com/biographies/bryan.htm

Sykes, G., & Matza, D. (1957). Techniques of neutralization: A theory of delinquency. *American Sociological Review, 22,* 664–673.

Sylvester, R. (2005, February 28). Report: BTK suspect confesses to killings. *The Wichita Eagle.* Retrieved February 28, 2005, from http://www.kansas.com/mld/kansas/news/special_packages/btk/11010878.htm

Symons, D. (1979). *The evolution of human sexuality.* Oxford, UK: Oxford University Press.

Szasz, T. S. (1970). *Ideology and insanity.* Garden City, NY: Anchor.

Taipei Times. (2003, October 30). *Child prostitution blooms on German-Czech border.* Retrieved May 13, 2006, from http://www.taipeitimes.com/News/world/archives/2003/10/30/2003073939

Talvi, S. J. A. (2003). *The truth about the Green River killer.* Retrieved December 14, 2004, from http://www.alternet.org/story/17171

Tannenbaum, F. (1938). *Crime and the community.* New York: Columbia University Press.

Tanner, R. E. S. (1970). *Crime in East Africa: Homicide in Uganda, 1964.* Uppsala, Sweden: Soderstrom and Finn. Retrieved June 26, 2004, from the Criminal Justice Abstracts database at http://spweb.silverplatter.com/calstate

Taylor, B. M., & Rand, M. R. (1995, August). *The National Crime Victimization Survey redesign: New understandings of victimization dynamics and measurements.* Paper prepared for presentation at the 1995 American Statistical Association Annual Meeting, Orlando, FL. Retrieved March 20, 2005, from http://www.ojp.usdoj.gov/bjs/ncvsrd96.txt

Taylor, D. L. (1978). *Terrorism and critical criminology: The application of a perspective.* West Lafayette, IN: Purdue University Institute for the Study of Social Change.

Taylor, E. R., Kelly, J., & Valescu, S. (2001). Is stealing a gateway crime? *Community Mental Health Journal, 37*(4), 347–358.

Taylor, L. (1984). *Born to crime: The genetic causes of human behavior.* Wesport, CT: Greenwood.

Telegraph, London. (2003, September 30). Culture clash led to "honour killing" of teen daughter. *Sydney Morning Herald.* Retrieved July 11, 2004 from http://www.smh.com.au/articles/2003/09/30/1064819905441.html? from=storys & oneclick=true

Telfer, J. (1998). *Howard Becker's labeling theory.* Retrieved December 8, 2003, from http://www.criminology.fsu.edu/crimtheory/becker.htm

Tenebril. (2006). *Spyware information: Credit card number finder.* Retrieved May 22, 2006, from http://www.tenebril.com/src/info.php?id=109859462

Terrorism Research Center, The. (2004). *Country Profiles: May 30, 2004.* Retrieved May 30, 2004, from http://www.terrorism.com/modules.php?op=modload& name=Countries&file=index

Terrorism Research Center, The. (2006). *Country Profiles: May 9, 2006.* Retrieved May 9, 2006, from http://www.terrorism.com/modules.php?op=modload& name=Countries&file=index

Theoharis, A. G. (2001). *American history: Hoover, J. Edgar.* Retrieved March 13, 2005, from http://www.answers.com/topic/j-edgar-hoover

Theoharis, A., & Cox, J. S. (1988). *The Boss.* Philadephia: Temple University Press.

Thio, A. (1988). *Deviant behavior* (3th ed.). New York: Harper & Row.

Thio, A. (1995). *Deviant behavior* (4th ed.). New York: HarperCollins.

Thomas, A. (1998). Ronald Reagan and the commitment of the mentally ill: Capital, interest groups, and the eclipse of social policy. *Electronic Journal of Sociology.* Retrieved July 19, 2003, from http://collection.nlc-nc.ca/100/201/300/ejofsociology/2002/v06n02/thomas2.html

Thomas, G. C., III. (1993). A critique of the anti-pornography syllogism. *Maryland Law Review, 52*(1), 122–161.

Thomas, J. B. (1990). *Conspicuous depredation: Automobile theft in Los Angeles, 1904 to 1987.* Sacramento, CA: California Attorney General.

Thomas (Library of Congress). (2006). *House Report 109–333–USA PATRIOT Improvement and Reauthorization Act of 2005.* Retrieved May 28, 2006, from http://thomas.loc.gov/cgi-bin/cpquery/?&dbname=cp109&sid=cp109lxkwK& refer=&r_n=hr333.109&item=&sel=TOC_2080728&

Thomas, W. I. (1907). *Sex and society.* Boston: Little, Brown.

Thomas, W. I. (1923). *The unadjusted girl.* Boston: Little, Brown.

Thompson, C. Y., & Fisher, B. (1996). Predicting household victimization utilizing a multi-level routine activity approach. *Journal of Crime and Justice, 19*(2), 49–66.

Thompson, M. (2004). *Porn profits go mainstream.* Retrieved December 31, 2004 from http://moneycentral.msn.com/content/CNBCTV/Articles/TVReports/P80813.asp

Thompson, R. B., & Erez, E. (1994). Wife abuse in Sierra Leone: Polygamous marriages in a dual legal system. *International Journal of Comparative and Applied Criminal Justice, 18*(1), 27–37. Retrieved June 26, 2004, from the Criminal Justice Abstracts database at http://spweb.silverplatter.com/calstate

Thompson, T. (2002, October). Look at Jamaica: Jamaica's poll bloodbath. *The Observer.* Retrieved November 20, 2003, from http://www.trinidadandtobagonews.com/forum/webbbs_config.pl/noframes/read/845)

Thornton, L., Clune, M., Maguire, R., Griffin, E., & O'Connor, J.O. (1990). *Irish Medical Journal, 83*(4), 139–142.

Thornton, S. P. (2001). Sigmund Freud (1856–1939). *The Internet Encyclopedia of Philosophy.* Retrieved July 20, 2003, from http://www.utm.edu/research/iep/f/freud.htm#Life

Thrasher, F. (1927). *The gang.* Chicago: University of Chicago Press.

Timmerman, G. (2003, March). Sexual harassment of adolescents perpetrated by teachers and by peers: An exploration of the dynamics of power, culture, and gender in secondary schools. *Sex Roles: A Journal of Research.* Retrieved October 15, 2003, from http://www.findarticles.com/cf_0/m2294/2003_March/100630995/print.jhtml

Timonen, M., Miettunen, J., & Hakko, H. (2000). Psychiatric admissions at different levels of the national health care services and male criminality: the Northern Finland 1966 Birth Cohort Study. *Social Psychiatry and Psychiatric Epidemiology, 35,* 198–201.

Tjaden, P., & Thoennes, N. (2000). *Full report of the prevalence, incidence and consequences of violence against women: Findings from the National Violence Against Women Survey.* Washington, DC: The National Institute of Justice and Centers for Disease Control and Prevention. Retrieved October 20, 2003, from http://www.ncjrs.org/pdffiles1/nij/183781.pdf

Tobolowsky, P. M. (1999). Victim participation in the criminal justice process: Fifteen years after the President's Task Force on Victims of Crime. *New England Journal on Criminal and Civil Confinement, 25*(1), 21–105.

Topalli, V., Wright, R., & Fornango, R. (2002). Drug dealers, robbery and retaliation: Vulnerability, deterrence and the contagion of violence. *The British Journal of Criminology, 42*(2), 337–351.

Torrey, E. F. (1988). *Nowhere to go: The tragic odyssey of the homeless mentally ill.* New York: Harper and Row.

Torrey, E. F. (1997, Summer) Let's stop being nutty about the mentally ill. *City Journal, 7*(3). Retrieved July 25, 2003, from http://www.city-journal.org/html/7_3_a2.html

Toy, C. (1992). Coming out to play: Reasons to join and participate in Asian gangs. *Gang Journal, 1*(1), 13–29.

Toy, C. (1993). A short history of Asian gangs in San Francisco. *Justice Quarterly, 9*(4), 647–665.

Transparency.org. (2004). *Corruption Perceptions Index 2004.* Retrieved May 16, 2005, from http://www.transparency.org/cpi/2004/cpi2004.en.html

Trasler, G. (1986). Situational crime control and rational choice theory: A critique. In K. Heal & G. Laycock (Eds.), *Situational crime prevention: From theory into practice* (pp. 17–24). London: HMSO Books.

Treatment Advocacy Center. (2003). *Briefing paper: Violence and untreated mental illness.* Retrieved July 20, 2003, from http://www.psychlaws.org/Briefing-Papers/BP8.htm

Tremblay, P., Clermont, Y., & Cusson, M. (1994). Jockeys and joyriders: Changing patterns in car theft opportunity structures. *British Journal of Criminology, 34*(3), 307–321.

Tripod. (2004). *Mafiosi dictionary.* Retrieved November 26, 2004, from http://da_wizeguy.tripod.com/omerta/id10.html

Trochim, M. K. (2002). *Nonprobability sampling.* Retrieved March 16, 2005, from http://www.socialresearchmethods.net/kb/sampnon.htm

Troppenhaur, H., & Seipel, C. (1994). Compensation inside and outside the criminal justice system; international dimensions . . . between Austrian and German criminal law systems. *Global Journal on Crime and Criminal Law, 2*(1), 41–92.

Truthorfiction.com. (2002, January 3). *Women and children in portions of Africa are being sexually violated by men who believe that sex with a virgin will cure their AIDS.* Retrieved June 19, 2004, from http://www.truthorfiction.com/rumors/a/aids-virgins.htm

Tseng, C-H., Duane, J., & Hadipriono, F. (2004). Performance of campus parking garages in preventing crime. *Journal of Performance of Constructed Facilities, 18*(1), 21–28.

Tunis, S. R., & Gelband, H. (1995). *Health care technology and its assessment in eight countries. Health care technology in the United States.* Washington, DC: OTA.

Tweed, J. (2004). *Heroin: Do you know. . .* Retrieved December 5, 2004, from http://www.jeantweed.com/heroin.htm

Twyman, T. R. (2001). *The Stepford whores: Project Monarch and mind-controlled sex slaves.* Retrieved May 13, 2006, from http://www.dragonkeypress.com/blog/?page_id=778

U.K. Home Office. (2002). *Entitlement cards and identity fraud: A consultative paper.* London: HMSO Books.

Umbreit, M. S. (2000). *National survey of victim-offender mediation programs in the United States.* St. Paul, MO: Center for Restorative Justice and Peacemaking.

Umbreit, M. S., Coates, R. B., & Vos, B. (2001). The impact of victim-offender mediation. Two decades of research. *Federal Probation, 65*(3), 29–35.

Umbreit, M. S., Coates, R. B., & Vos, B. (2002). The impact of restorative justice conferencing: A multi-national perspective. *British Journal of Community Justice, 1*(2), 21–48.

Umbreit, M. S., & Greenwood, J. (2000). *National survey of victim-offender mediation programs in the United States.* Washington, DC: U.S. Office for Victims of Crime.

Underwood, B. J., Duncan, C. P., Taylor, J. A., & Cotton, J. W. (1954). *Elementary statistics.* New York: Appleton-Century-Crofts.

United Nations Office on Drugs and Crime (UNODC). (2000). *United Nations surveys of crime trends and operations of criminal justice systems, covering the period 1990–2000.* Retrieved October 30, 2004, from http://www.unodc.org/pdf/crime/seventh_survey/567pvr.pdf

United Nations Office on Drugs and Crime. (2002). *Global program against transnational organized crime: Results of pilot survey of forty selected organized criminal groups in sixteen countries.* Retrieved November 2, 2004, from http://www.unodc.org/unodc/en/organized_crime.html

United Nations Office on Drugs and Crime. (2003a). Global illicit drug trends 2003. Retrieved November 16, 2003, from http://www.unodc.org/unodc/en/research.html?print=yes

United Nations Office on a Drugs and Crime. (2003b). *Pakistan: Country profile.* Retrieved May 7, 2006, from http://www.unodc.org/pakistan/country_profile.html

United Nations Office on Drugs and Crime. (2004). *Afghanistan Opium Survey 2004.* Retrieved May 7, 2004, from http://www.unodc.org/pdf/afg/afghanistan_opium_survey_2004.pdf

United Nations Office on Drugs and Crime. (2005). *World drug report.* Retrieved May 7, 2006 from http://www.unodc.org/unodc/de/world_drug_report.html

University of Ottawa. (2003). *Legal systems.* Retrieved March 5, 2005, from http://www.droitcivil.uottawa.ca/world-legal-systems/eng-presentation.html

Urwin, D. W. (2004). European Union. *Microsoft Encarta Online Encyclopedia 2004.* Retrieved October 12, 2004, from http://encarta.msn.com/text_761579567__0/European_Union.html

Usdoj.gov. (2003). *Computer crime and intellectual property section (CCIPS): Federal computer intrusion laws.* Retrieved May 21, 2006, from http://www.usdoj.gov/criminal/cybercrime/cclaws.html

Usdoj.gov. (2006). *Identity theft and fraud.* Retrieved May 26, 2006, from http://www.usdoj.gov/criminal/fraud/idtheft.html

Usnews.com. (2005, December 5). A godfather's lethal mix of business and politics. *U.S. News & World Report.* Retrieved May 7, 2006, from http://www.usnews.com/usnews/news/articles/051205/5terror.b.htm

U.S. Bureau of Democracy, Human Rights, and Labor. (2006). *Country Reports on Human Rights Practices—2005.* Retrieved May 13, 2006, from http://www.state.gov/g/drl/rls/hrrpt/2005/61650.htm

U.S. Census Bureau. (2006). *State and county quickFacts: Data derived from population estimates, 2000 census of population and housing.* Retrieved April 23, 2004, from http://quickfacts.census.gov/qfd/states/00000.html

U.S. Department of Justice. (1994). *President Clinton announces new crime bill grants to put police officers on the beat.* Retrieved March 29, 2005, from http://www.usdoj.gov/opa/pr/Pre_96/October94/590.txt.html

U.S. Department of Justice. (2000). *Crime and justice in America: An overview of recent trends and emerging challenges. Fiscal Years 2000–2005 Strategic Plan.* Washington, DC: US Government Printing Office. Retrieved March 28, 2005, from http://www.usdoj.gov/archive/mps/strategic2000_2005/chapter1.htm

U.S. Department of Justice. (2003, August 21). *The USA PATRIOT Act: Preserving Life and Liberty.* Retrieved June 8, 2004, from http://www.lifeandliberty.gov/

U.S. Department of Justice United States Attorney Southern District of New York. (2002). U.S. announces what is believed the largest identity theft case in history. Retrieved September 3, 2006, from http://www.usdoj.gov/criminal/cybercrime/cummingsIndict.htm

U.S. Department of State. (1994, January 31). *United Arab Emirates human rights practices, 1993.* Retrieved May 23, 2006, from http://dosfan.lib.uic.edu/erc/democracy/1993_hrp_report/93hrp_report_nea/UnitedArabEmirates.html

U.S. Department of State. (2002). Jamaica: *Country reports on human rights practices—2002: Jamaica.* Retrieved November 20, 2003, from http://www.state.gov/g/drl/rls/hrrpt/2002/18337pf.htm

U.S. Department of State's Bureau of International Information Programs. (2005). *Outline of the U.S. legal system.* Retrieved February 20, 2005 from http://usinfo.state.gov/products/pubs/legalotln/state.htm

U.S. Department of State. (2006). *Current background notes.* Retrieved May 6, 2006, from http://www.state.gov/r/pa/ei/bgn/

U.S. General Accounting Office. (1998). *Identity fraud: Information on prevalence, cost, and Internet impact is limited.* Washington, DC: U.S. General Accounting Office.

U.S. General Accounting Office. (2002a). *Identity theft: Prevalence and cost appear to be growing.* Washington, DC: U.S. General Accounting Office.

U.S. General Accounting Office. (2002b). *Immigration benefit fraud: Focused approach is needed to address problems.* Washington, DC: United States General Accounting Office.

U.S. House Committee Subcommittee on Civil and Constitutional Rights. (1981). *Report on domestic and international terrorism.* Washington, DC: U.S. Government Printing Office.

U.S. National Commission on Law Observance and Enforcement. (1931). *Report on criminal justice.* Washington, DC: U.S. Government Printing Office.

U.S. National Highway Traffic Safety Administration. (1998). *Auto theft and recovery: Effects of the Anti Car Theft Act of 1992 and the Motor Vehicle Theft Law Enforcement Act of 1984.* Washington, DC: US National Highway Traffic Safety Administration.

U.S. Postal Inspection Service. (2006). *Employment theft and embezzlement.* Retrieved May 26, 2006, from http://www.usps.com/postalinspectors/usc18/employ.htm

U.S. Secret Service. (2002). *Public awareness advisory regarding "419" or "advance fee fraud" schemes.* Retrieved May 17, 2005, from http://www.secretservice.gov/alert419.shtml

U.S. Securities and Exchange Commission. (2001). *"Ponzi" schemes.* Retrieved December 23, 2004, from http://www.sec.gov/answers/ponzi.htm

U.S. Securities and Exchange Commission. (2004). *Pyramid schemes.* Retrieved May 19, 2006, from http://www.sec.gov/answers/pyramid.htm

U.S. Senate Committee on Labor and Human Resources Subcommittee on Alcoholism and Drug Abuse. (1984). *Drugs and terrorism, 1984.* Hearing, August 2, 1984. Washington, DC: U.S. Government Printing Office.

U.S. Senate Judiciary Committee Criminal Law and Procedures Subcommittee. (1978). *West Germany's political response to terrorism.* Washington, DC: U.S. Government Printing Office.

Van-Eck, C. M. (2000). Honour killings in Turkey: Protest against "traditional killings." *Justitiele Verkenningen, 26*(8), 87–97. Retrieved June 26, 2004, from the Criminal Justice Abstracts database at http://spweb.silverplatter.com/calstate

Van Kesteren, J., Mayhew, P., & Nieuwbeerta, P. (2000). *Criminal victimisation in seventeen industrialized countries: Key findings from the 2000 International Crime.*

Verkenningen, 26(8), 87–97. Retrieved June 26, 2004, from the Criminal Justice Abstracts database at http://spweb.silverplatter.com/calstate

Van Winkle, E. (2000). The toxic mind: The biology of mental illness and violence. *Medical Hypotheses, 54*(1), 146–156.

Van Wyhe, J. (2002). *The history of phrenology on the Web.* Retrieved June 5, 2005, from http://pages.britishlibrary.net/phrenology/overview.htm

Vanknin, S. (2002). *Analysis: The Jackson-Vanik debate.* Retrieved November 27, 2004, from http://www.upi.com/view.cfm?StoryID=29052002-105921-5171r

Victim Surveys. The Hague, The Netherlands: Dutch Minister of Justice. Retrieved March 24, 2006. A summary of this report can be accessed at: http://www.minjust.nl:8080/b_organ/wodc/publications/06-icvs-summar.pdf

Victoria-Parliament. (2002). *Inquiry into motor vehicle theft: Final report.* Melbourne, Australia: Victoria Parliament.

Vinnie. (2003). *Asian categories—Where do you fit in?* Retrieved November 25, 2003, from http://vinniehp.virtualave.net/jkac.html

Vold, G. B. (1958). *Theoretical criminology.* New York: Oxford University Press.

Vold, G. B., Bernard, T. J., & Snipes, J. B. (1998). *Theoretical criminology* (4th ed.). New York: Oxford University Press.

Volkow, N. D., & Tancredi, L. (1987). Neutral substrates of violent behavior: A preliminary study with Positron Emission Tomography. *British Journal of Psychiatry, 151,* 673–688.

Von Hofer, H. (1999). Crime and punishment in Scandinavia: An overview. *Justitiele Verkenningen, 25*(8), 82–95.

Von Hofer, H., & Henrik, T. (2000). Theft in Sweden: 1831–1998. *Journal of Scandinavian Studies in Criminology and Crime Prevention, 1*(2), 195–210.

Von Lampe, K. (2003). *Definitions of organized crime.* Retrieved November 4, 2004, from http://people.freenet.de/kvlampe/OCDEF1.htm

Vreese, S. D. (2000). Hooliganism under the statistical magnifying glass: A Belgian case study. *European Journal on Criminal Policy and Research, 8*(2), 201–223.

Wacquant, L. (1999). *"Suitable enemies": Foreigners and immigrants in the prisons of Europe.* Retrieved October 15, 2004, from http://www.penalreform.org/english/article_wacquant2.htm

Waldorf, D. (1993). When the Crips invaded San Francisco: Gang migration. *The Gang Journal, 1*(4).

Walker, J. T., Golden, J. W., & VanHouten, A. C. (2001). The geographic link between sex offenders and potential victims: A routine activities approach. *Justice Research and Policy, 3*(2), 15–33.

Walker, J. (1994). *The first Australian national survey of crimes against businesses.* Canberra, Australia: Australian Institute of Criminology.

Walker, J. (n. d.). *Australia.* Retrieved December 23, 2003, from http://www.unicri.it/icvs/publications/pdf_files/understanding_files/35_AUSTRALIA.pdf

Wallerstein, J. S., & Wyle, C. J. (1947). Our law-abiding law breakers. *Probation, 25,* 107–112.

Walters, G. D. (1992). A meta-analysis of the gene-crime relationship. *Criminology, 30,* 595–613.

Walters, G. D., & White, T. W. (1989). Heredity and crime: Bad genes or bad research. *Criminology, 27,* 455–486.

WannaSurf.com. (2003). *Surf of the world.* Retrieved December 23, 2003, from http://www.wannasurf.com/site/FAQ_all_spots/faq_aus_pac.html

Warr, M. (1985). Fear of rape among urban women. *Social Problems, 32*(3), 238–50.

Wattenberg, W. W., & Balliestri, J. (1952). Automobile theft: A favored group delinquency. *American Journal of Sociology, 57,* 575.

Watts, M. (2005). United States Economy. *Microsoft Encarta Online Encyclopedia 2005.* Retrieved May 14, 2005, from http://encarta.msn.com

Webb, B., & Laycock, G. (1992) *Tackling car crime: The nature and extent of the problem: Car Prevention Unit Paper 32.* London: U.K. Home Office.

Weber, M. (1947). *The theory of social and economic organization* (T. Parsons, Ed., A. M. Henderson & T. Parsons, Trans.). New York: Oxford University Press.

Weber, M. (1958). *The Protestant ethic and the spirit of capitalism.* New York: Scribner's.

Webopedia. (2006). *Phishing.* Retrieved May 26, 2006, from http://www.webopedia.com/TERM/p/phishing.html

Webster, D. W., Freed, L. H., & Frattaroli, S. (2002). How delinquent youths acquire guns: Initial versus most recent gun acquisitions. *Journal of Urban Health Bulletin of the New York Academy of Medicine, 79*(1), 60–69.

Webster, N. (1984). *New concise Webster's dictionary.* New York: Modern.

Wedge, R. F, White, R. D, & Palmer, T. (1980). I-level and the treatment of delinquents. *California Youth Authority Quarterly, 33*(4), 26–37.

Weicker, L. P., Jr. (1985, November). Dangerous routine. *Psychology Today,* 60–62.

Weinberg, S. K. (1952). *Society and personality disorders.* Englewood Cliffs, NJ: Prentice Hall.

Weiner, J. (1996, January 1). Smoking and cancer: The cigarette papers—How the industry is trying to smoke us all. *The Nation,* pp. 11–18.

Welford, C. F., MacDonald, J. M., & Weiss, J. C. (1997). *Multistate study of convenience store robberies: Summary of findings.* Washington, DC: Justice Research and Statistics Association.

Wells, L. E., & Rankin, J. H. (1995). Juvenile victimization: Convergent validation of alternative measurements. *Journal of Research in Crime and Delinquency, 32*(3), 287–307.

White, G. (1999). Crime and the decline of manufacturing, 1970–1990. *Justice Quarterly, 16*(1), 81–97.

Whitebread, C. (1995). *The history of the non-medical use of drugs in the United States.* Retrieved December 7, 2004, from http://www.druglibrary.org/olsen/dpf/whitebread05.html

White Collar Crime FYI. (2006). *Embezzlement.* Retrieved May 20, 2006, from http://www.whitecollarcrimefyi.com/embezzlement.html

Who2. (2004). *J. Edgar Hoover.* Retrieved March 13, 2005, from http://www.answers.com/topic/j-edgar-hoover

Wikipedia. (2004a). *Black market.* Retrieved November 18, 2004, from http:/en.wikipedia.org/wiki/Black_market

Wikipedia. (2004b). *Charles Keating.* Retrieved January 1, 2004, from http://en.wikipedia.org/wiki/Charles_Keating

Wikipedia. (2004c). *Child sexual abuse.* Retrieved June 19, 2004, from http://en.wikipedia.org/wiki/Child_sexual_abuse

Wikipedia. (2004d). *Commonwealth of nations.* Retrieved October 16, 2004, from http://en.wikipedia.org/wiki/Commonwealth_of_Nations#Benefits_of_membership_and_Contemporary_Concerns

Wikipedia. (2004e). *Sicily.* Retrieved November 25, 2004, from http://en.wikipedia.org/wiki/Sicily

Wikipedia. (2005a). *Christian democracy.* Retrieved May 1, 2005, from http://www.answers.com/topic/christian-democracy-italy

Wikipedia (2005b). *Developed country.* Retrieved June 18, 2005, from http://en .wikipedia.org/wiki/Developed_country

Wikipedia. (2006a). *Civil law (legal system).* Retrieved March 23, 2006, from http://en .wikipedia.org/wiki/Civil_law_(legal_system)

Wikipedia. (2006b). *History of pedophile activisim.* Retrieved May 13, 2006, from http://en.wikipedia.org/wiki/History_of_pedophile_activism

Wikipedia. (2006c). *Pedophile activism.* Retrieved May 13, 2006, from http://en .wikipedia.org/wiki/Pedophile_activism

Wikstrom, P. H., & Dolmen, L. (1994). *Sweden.* From the World Factbook of Criminal Justice Systems. Retrieved March 25, 2003, from http://www.ojp .usdoj.gov/bjs/pub/ascii/wfbcjswe.txt

Wilbanks, W. (1995). Homicide in Singapore. *International Journal of Comparative and Applied Criminal Justice, 19*(1), 151–164. Retrieved June 26, 2004, from the Criminal Justice Abstracts database at http://spweb.silverplatter.com/ calstate

Wilcox, B. L. (1987). Pornography, social science, and politics: When research and ideology collide. *American Psychologist, 42,* 941–943.

Wille, R., & Beier, K. M. (1989). Castration in Germany. *Annals of Sex Research, 2*(2), 103–133. Retrieved July 27, 2004, from the Criminal Justice Abstracts database at http://80-md1.csa.com.libproxy.sdsu.edu/htbin/ids65/procskel.cgi

Williams, F. P., III, & McShane, M. D. (1998). *Criminological theory: Selected classic readings.* Cincinnati, OH: Anderson.

Williams, J. R., & Gold, M. (1972). From delinquent behavior to official delinquency. *Social Problems, 20,* 209–229.

Williams, P. (2001, November 26). By any means necessary. *The Nation.* Retrieved June 6, 2004, from http://www.commondreams.org/views01/1109-02.htm

Williams, R., Jr. (1960). *American society.* New York: Knopf.

Willis, C. L. (1983). *Division of labor, anomie, and crime rate: A test of a Durkheimian model.* Ann Arbor, MI: University Microfilms International.

Wilson, C. (1990). *Research on one- and two- person patrols: Distinguishing fact from fiction, Report Series No. 94.* Payneham SA: Australasian Centre for Policing Research.

Wilson, J. Q., & Boland, B. (1978). The effect of the police on crime. *Law and Society Review, 12*(3), 367–390.

Wilson, J. Q., & Herrnstein, R. J. (1985). *Crime and human nature.* New York: Simon & Schuster.

Wilson, J. Q., & Kelling, G. L. (1982). Broken windows. *Atlantic Monthly New York, 249*(3), 29–38.

Wilson, M., & Daly, M. (1996). Male sexual proprietariness and violence against wives. *Current Directions in Psychological Science, 5,* 2–7.

Winslow, R. W. (1966). *An organizational theory of delinquency and alienation.* Ann Arbor, MI: University Microfilms.

Winslow, R. W. (1969). *Crime in a free society: Selections from the President's Commission on Law Enforcement and Administration of Justice.* Belmont, CA: Dickenson.

Winslow, R. W. (1970). *Society in transition: A social approach to deviancy.* New York: Free Press.

Winslow, R. W. (1972). *The emergence of deviant minorities: Social problems and social change.* San Ramon, CA: Consensus.

Winslow, R. W. (1976). *Juvenile delinquency in a free society* (3rd ed.). Belmont, CA: Dickenson.

Winslow, R. W. (2003). *Crime and society: A comparative criminology tour of the world.* Retrieved December 13, 2003, from http://www-rohan.sdsu.edu/faculty/rwinslow/index.html

Winslow, R. W., & Winslow, V. (1974). *Deviant reality: Alternative world views.* Boston: Allyn and Bacon.

Wisotsky, S. (1983). Exposing the war on cocaine: The futility and destructiveness of prohibition. *Wisconsin Law Review, 6*, 1305–1426.

Wolf, J. B. (1981). Enforcement terrorism. *Police Studies, 3*(4), 45–54.

Wolf, J. B. (1989). *Antiterrorist initiatives.* New York: Plenum.

Wolf, J. B. (1999). *The Iran-Contra Affair.* Retrieved May 20, 2004 from http://www.pbs.org/wgbh/amex/reagan/peopleevents/pande08.html).

Wolf, P. (2004). *OSS and the development of psychological warfare.* Retrieved May 1, 2005, from http://www.icdc.com/~paulwolf/oss/foundations.htm

Wolfgang, M. (1958). *Patterns in criminal homicide.* Philadelphia: University of Pennsylvania Press.

Wolfgang, M. E. (1973). Cesare Lombroso. In Hermann Mannheim (Ed.). *Pioneers in criminology* (2nd ed.), (pp. 232–291). Montclair, NJ: Patterson Smith.

Wolfgang, M., & Ferracuti, F. (1967). *The subculture of violence.* London: Tavistock.

Wolfgang, M. E., Figlio, R. M., & Sellin, T. (1972). *Delinquency in a birth cohort.* Chicago: University of Chicago Press.

Woloch, N., Johnson, P. E., & Turque, B. (2003). United States History. *Microsoft Encarta Online Encyclopedia.* Retrieved April 3, 2003, from http://encarta.msn.com/encyclopedia_1741500823/United_States_(History).html

Wooley, A. (2002). *Homicide investigation tracking system: Child abduction murder research project.* Washington State Attorney General's Office, Criminal Justice Division. Retrieved July 4, 2004, from http://www.atg.wa.gov/hits/childmur.shtml

WordReference.com. (2005). *Fatwah.* Retrieved May 28, 2006, from http://www.wordreference.com/definition/fatwah

WordWeb Online. (2005). *Fraudster, fraudsters—WordWeb dictionary definition.* Retrieved May 26, 2006, from http://www.wordwebonline.com/en/FRAUDSTER

World Book, Inc. (2003). *The African American Journey: Segregation.* Retrieved November 30, 2004, from http://www2.worldbook.com/wc/features/aajourney_new/html/ aa_3_segregation.shtml

World Health Organization. (June, 2000). *Fact sheet No 242: Women and HIV/AIDS.* Retrieved June 19, 2004, from http://www.who.int/mediacentre/factsheets/fs242/en/

World's Vehicle Documents. (2001). *Vehicle crime in Europe.* Retrieved October 7, 2004, from http://www.vehicle-documents.it/articoli_veicoli/art_47.htm

Wright, R. A. (2003). *Encyclopedia of criminology: Sample entry: Sutherland, Edwin H.* Retrieved July 3, 2003, from http://www.fitzroydearborn.com/chicago/criminology/sample-sutherland-edwin.php3

Wright, R. T., & Decker, Scott H. (1994). *Burglars on the job: Streetlife and residential breakins.* Boston: Northeastern University Press.

Wright, R. T., & Decker, S. H. (1997). *Armed robbers in action: Stickups and street culture.* Boston: Northeastern University Press.

Xinhua. (2005). India, Pakistan begin talks on terrorism, drug trafficking. *People's Daily Online*. Retrieved May 4, 2006, from http://english.people.com.cn/200508/29/eng20050829_205124.html

Xiogang, D., & Zhang, L. (1998). Correlates of self-control: An empirical test of self-control theory. *Journal of Crime and Justice, 21*(2), 89–110.

Yablonsky, L. (1990). *Criminology: Crime and criminality* (4th ed.). New York: HarperCollins.

Yablonsky, L. (2002). Whatever happened to Synanon? The birth of the anticriminal therapeutic community methodology. *Criminal Justice Policy Review, 134,* 329–336.

Yamada, T., Yamada, T., & Kang, J. M. (1991). *Crime rate versus labor market conditions: Theory and times-series evidence.* Cambridge, MA: National Bureau of Economic Research, Inc.

YesPakistan.com Staff. (2002). *Chronology of India-Pakistan wars.* Retrieved May 10, 2006, from http://www.yespakistan.com/kashmir/war_chronology.asp

Yokihama, M. (1999). *Japan Quarterly, 46*(3), 76–82. Retrieved August 21, 2004, from the Criminal Justice Abstracts database at http://80-ca1.csa.com.libproxy.sdsu.edu/htbin/ids65/procskel.cgi?fn=f_advselect.html&cat=cja&ctx=/csa/ids/context/ctx48aa8Z

YourDictionary.com. (2000). *Feticide.* Retrieved June 6, 2005, from http://www.yourdictionary.com/ahd/f/f0092700.html

Yu, O., & Zhang, L. (1999). The under-recording of crime by police in China: A case study. *Policing: An International Journal of Police Strategies and Management, 22,* 252–263.

Yun, M. (2002). *Earnings inequality in USA, 1961–1999: Comparing inequality using earnings equations.* Retrieved September 17, 2003, from http://research.umbc.edu/~tgindlin/Yun2002.pdf

Zaczkiewicz, A. (1998). *The child abuse prevention and treatment act.* Retrieved November 3, 2003, from http://www.recordonline.com/1998/04/04-03-98/suazsi.htm

Zak, P. J. (2000). *Larceny. Economics of Governance, 1,* 158–179.

Zamora, J. (2000, January). Home invasion: High risk, high yield. *SFGate.com.* Retrieved November 15, 2003, from http://www.sfgate.com/cgi-bin/article.cgi?file=/examiner/archive/2000/01/06/NEWS423.dtl

Zander, S. (2001). *Young Sweden.* Stockholm: The Swedish National Board for Youth Affairs, p. 30. Retrieved October 8, 2004, from http:www.ungdomsstyrelsen.se/young_sweden.pdf

Zehr, H., & Toews, B. (2004). *Critical issues in restorative justice.* Monsey, NY: Criminal Justice Press.

Zhang, L. (2003). Official offense status and self-esteem among Chinese youths. *Journal of Criminal Justice, 31*(2), 99–105. Retrieved June 26, 2004, from the Criminal Justice Abstracts database at http://spweb.silverplatter.com/calstate

Zhang, L., & Messner, S. F. (1999). Bonds to the work unit and official offense status in urban China. *International Journal of Offender Therapy and Comparative Criminology, 43*(3), 375–390.

Zhang, L., Zhou, D. Z., & Messner, S. F. (1996). Crime prevention in a communitarian society: "bang-jiao" and "tiao-jie" in the People's Republic of China. *Justice Quarterly, 13*(2), 199–222.

Zhang, S. X., & Chin, K-L. (2003). The declining significance of Triad societies in transnational illegal activities: A structural deficiency perspective. *British Journal of Criminology, 43*(3), 469–488.

Zhang, S. X., & Gaylord, M. S. (1996). Bound for the Golden Mountain: The social organization of Chinese alien smuggling. *Crime Law and Social Change, 25*(1), 1–16.

Ziegenhagen, E. A. (1977). *Victims, crime and social control.* New York: Praeger.

Zimring, F. E. (1977). Determinants of the death rate from robbery: A Detroit time study. *Journal of Legal Studies Chicago, 6*(2), 317–332.

Zimring, F. E., & Zuehl, J. (1986). Victim injury and death in urban robbery: A Chicago study. *Journal of Legal Studies, 15*(1), 1–40.